# INTRODUCCIÓN

Estamos muy satisfechos de que ha[...]
esperamos que lo disfrutes y que te s[...]
en el trabajo, en tus vacaciones o en casa.

Esta introducción pretende darte algunas indicaciones para ayurdarte a sacar el mayor provecho de este diccionario; no solo de su extenso vocabulario, sino de toda la información que te proporciona cada entrada. Esta te ayudará a leer y comprender – y también a comunicarte y a expresarte – en inglés moderno. Este diccionario comienza con una lista de abreviaturas utilizadas en el texto y con una ilustración de los sonidos representados por los símbolos fonéticos.

### EL MANEJO DE TU DICCIONARIO

La amplia información que te ofrece este diccionario aparece presentada en distintas tipografías, con caracteres de diversos tamaños y con distintos símbolos, abreviaturas y paréntesis. Los apartados siguientes explican las reglas y símbolos utilizados.

### ENTRADAS

Las palabras que consultas en el diccionario – las entradas – aparecen ordenadas alfabéticamente y en **negrita** para una identificación más rápida. La palabra que aparece en la parte superior de cada página es la primera entrada (si aparece en la página izquierda) y la última entrada (si aparece en la página derecha) de la página en cuestión.La información sobre el uso o la forma de determinadas entradas aparece entre paréntesis, detrás de la transcripción fonética, y generalmente en forma abreviada y en cursiva (p. ej.: (*fam*), (*Com*)). En algunos casos se ha considerado oportuno agrupar palabras de una misma familia (**nación**, **nacionalismo**; **accept**, **acceptance**) bajo una misma entrada que aparece en **negrita**.

Las expresiones de uso corriente en las que aparece una entrada se dan en negrita (p. ej.: **hurry:** [...] **to be in a ~**).

### SÍMBOLOS FONÉTICOS

La transcripción fonética de cada entrada inglesa(que indica su pronunciación) aparece entre corchetes, inmediatamente después de la entrada (p. ej **knife** [naif]). En las páginas xii–xv encontrarás una lista de los símbolos fonéticos utilizados en este diccionario.

## TRADUCCIONES

Las traducciones de las entradas aparecen en caracteres normales, y en los casos en los que existen significados o usos diferentes, estos aparecen separados mediante un punto y coma. A menudo encontrarás también otras palabras en cursiva y entre paréntesis antes de las traducciones. Estas sugieren contextos en los que la entrada podría aparecer (p. ej.: **alto** (*persona*) o (*sonido*)) o proporcionan sinónimos (p. ej.: **mismo** (*semejante*)).

## PALABRAS CLAVE

Particular relevancia reciben ciertas palabras inglesas y españolas que han sido consideradas palabras 'clave' en cada lengua. Estas pueden, por ejemplo, ser de utilización muy corriente o tener distintos usos (**de**, **haber**; **get**, **that**). La combinación de triángulos y números te permitirá distinguir las diferentes categorías gramaticales y los diferentes significados. Las indicaciones en cursiva y entre paréntesis proporcionan además importante información adicional.

## FALSOS AMIGOS

Las palabras que se prestan a confusión al traducir han sido identificadas. En tales entradas existen unas notas que te ayudaran a evitar errores.

## INFORMACIÓN GRAMATICAL

Las categorías gramaticales aparecen en forma abreviada y en cursiva después de la transcripción fonética de cada entrada (*vt*, *adv*, *conj*). También se indican la forma femenina y los plurales irregulares de los sustantivos del inglés (**child, -ren**).

# INTRODUCTION

We are delighted that you have decided to buy this Spanish dictionary and hope you will enjoy and benefit from using it at school, at home, on holiday or at work.

This introduction gives you a few tips on how to get the most out of your dictionary – not simply from its comprehensive wordlist but also from the information provided in each entry. This will help you to read and understand modern Spanish, as well as communicate and express yourself in the language. This dictionary begins by listing the abbreviations used in the text and illustrating the sounds shown by the phonetic symbols.

## USING YOUR DICTIONARY
A wealth of information is presented in the dictionary, using various typefaces, sizes of type, symbols, abbreviations and brackets. The various conventions and symbols used are explained in the following sections.

## HEADWORDS
The words you look up in a dictionary – 'headwords' – are listed alphabetically. They are printed in **bold** for rapid identification. The headwords appearing at the top of each page indicate the first (if it appears on a left-hand page) and last word (if it appears on a right-hand page) dealt with on the page in question.

Information about the usage or form of certain headwords is given in brackets after the phonetic spelling. This usually appears in abbreviated form and in italics (e.g. (*fam*), (*Com*)).

Where appropriate, words related to headwords are grouped in the same entry (**nación**, **nacionalismo**; **accept**, **acceptance**) and are also in **bold**. Common expressions in which the headword appears are shown in a different bold roman type (e.g. **cola:** [...] **hacer ~**).

## PHONETIC SPELLINGS
The phonetic spelling of each headword (indicating its pronunciation) is given in square brackets immediately after the headword (e.g. **cohete** [ko'ete]). A list of these symbols is given on pages xii–xv.

## TRANSLATIONS

Headword translations are given in ordinary type and, where more than one meaning or usage exists, these are separated by a semi-colon. You will often find other words in italics in brackets before the translations. These offer suggested contexts in which the headword might appear (e.g. **fare** (*on trains, buses*) or provide synonyms (e.g. **litter** (*rubbish*) o (*young animals*)). The gender of the Spanish translation also appears in italics immediately following the key element of the translation, except where this is a regular masculine singular noun ending in 'o', or a regular feminine noun ending in 'a'.

## KEY WORDS

Special status is given to certain Spanish and English words which are considered as 'key' words in each language. They may, for example, occur very frequently or have several types of usage (e.g. **de**, **haber**; **get**, **that**). A combination of triangles and numbers helps you to distinguish different parts of speech and different meanings. Further helpful information is provided in brackets and italics.

## FALSE FRIENDS

Words which can be easily confused have been identified in the dictionary. Notes at such entries will help you to avoid these common translation pitfalls.

## GRAMMATICAL INFORMATION

Parts of speech are given in abbreviated form in italics after the phonetic spellings of headwords (e.g. *vt, adv, conj*). Genders of Spanish nouns are indicated as follows: *nm* for a masculine and *nf* for a feminine noun. Feminine and irregular plural forms of nouns are also shown (**irlandés**, **esa**; **luz** (*pl* **luces**)).

| ABREVIATURAS | | ABBREVIATIONS |
|---|---|---|
| abreviatura | *ab(b)r* | abbreviation |
| adjetivo, locución adjetiva | *adj* | adjective, adjectival phrase |
| administración | *Admin* | administration |
| adverbio, locución adverbial | *adv* | adverb, adverbial phrase |
| agricultura | *Agr* | agriculture |
| anatomía | *Anat* | anatomy |
| Argentina | *Arg* | Argentina |
| arquitectura | *Arq, Arch* | architecture |
| Australia | *Aust* | Australia |
| el automóvil | *Aut(o)* | the motor car and motoring |
| aviación, viajes aéreos | *Aviac, Aviat* | flying, air travel |
| biología | *Bio(l)* | biology |
| botánica, flores | *Bot* | botany |
| inglés británico | BRIT | British English |
| Centroamérica | CAM | Central America |
| química | *Chem* | chemistry |
| comercio, finanzas, banca | *Com(m)* | commerce, finance, banking |
| informática | *Comput* | computing |
| conjunción | *conj* | conjunction |
| construcción | *Constr* | building |
| compuesto | *cpd* | compound element |
| Cono Sur | CS | Southern Cone |
| cocina | *Culin* | cookery |
| economía | *Econ* | economics |
| eletricidad, electrónica | *Elec* | electricity, electronics |
| enseñanza, sistema escolar y universitario | *Escol* | schooling, schools and universities |
| España | ESP | Spain |
| especialmente | *esp* | especially |
| exclamación, interjección | *excl* | exclamation, interjection |
| femenino | *f* | feminine |
| lengua familiar (! vulgar) | *fam(!)* | colloquial usage (! particularly offensive) |

| ABREVIATURAS | | ABBREVIATIONS |
|---|---|---|
| ferrocarril | *Ferro* | railways |
| uso figurado | *fig* | figurative use |
| fotografía | *Foto* | photography |
| (verbo inglés) del cual la partícula es inseparable | *fus* | (phrasal verb) where the particle is inseparable |
| generalmente | *gen* | generally |
| geografía, geología | *Geo* | geography, geology |
| geometría | *Geom* | geometry |
| historia | *Hist* | history |
| uso familiar (! vulgar) | *inf(!)* | colloquial usage (! particularly offensive) |
| infinitivo | *infin* | infinitive |
| informática | *Inform* | computing |
| invariable | *inv* | invariable |
| irregular | *irreg* | irregular |
| lo jurídico | *Jur* | law |
| América Latina | *LAm* | Latin America |
| gramática, lingüística | *Ling* | grammar, linguistics |
| masculino | *m* | masculine |
| matemáticas | *Mat(h)* | mathematics |
| masculino/femenino | *m/f* | masculine/feminine |
| medicina | *Med* | medicine |
| México | *MÉX, MEX* | Mexico |
| lo militar, ejército | *Mil* | military matters |
| música | *Mús, Mus* | music |
| sustantivo, nombre | *n* | noun |
| navegación, náutica | *Náut, Naut* | sailing, navigation |
| sustantivo numérico | *num* | numeral noun |
| Nueva Zelanda | *NZ* | New Zealand |
| complemento | *obj* *o.s.* | (grammatical) object oneself |
| peyorativo | *pey, pej* | derogatory, pejorative |
| fotografía | *Phot* | photography |
| fisiología | *Physiol* | physiology |
| plural | *pl* | plural |

| ABREVIATURAS | | ABBREVIATIONS |
|---|---|---|
| política | *Pol* | politics |
| participio de pasado | *pp* | past participle |
| preposición | *prep* | preposition |
| pronombre | *pron* | pronoun |
| psicología, psiquiatría | *Psico, Psych* | psychology, psychiatry |
| tiempo pasado | *pt* | past tense |
| química | *Quím* | chemistry |
| ferrocarril | *Rail* | railways |
| religión | *Rel* | religion |
| Río de la Plata | RPL | River Plate |
| | *sb* | somebody |
| Cono Sur | sc | Southern Cone |
| enseñanza, sistema escolar y universitario | *Scol* | schooling, schools and universities |
| singular | *sg* | singular |
| España | SP | Spain |
| | *sth* | something |
| sujeto | *su(b)j* | (grammatical) subject |
| subjuntivo | *subjun* | subjunctive |
| tauromaquia | *Taur* | bullfighting |
| también | *tb* | also |
| técnica, tecnología | *Tec(h)* | technical term, technology |
| telecomunicaciones | *Telec, Tel* | telecommunications |
| imprenta, tipografía | *Tip, Typ* | typography, printing |
| televisión | *TV* | television |
| universidad | *Univ* | university |
| inglés norteamericano | us | American English |
| verbo | *vb* | verb |
| verbo intransitivo | *vi* | intransitive verb |
| verbo pronominal | *vr* | reflexive verb |
| verbo transitivo | *vt* | transitive verb |
| zoología | *Zool* | zoology |
| marca registrada | ® | registered trademark |
| indica un equivalente cultural | ≈ | introduces a cultural equivalent |

## SPANISH PRONUNCIATION

**VOWELS**

| | | | |
|---|---|---|---|
| a | [ a ] | p**a**ta | not as long as *a* in f*a*r. When followed by a consonant in the same syllable (i.e. in a closed syllable), as in *a*mante, the *a* is short, as in b*a*t |
| e | [ e ] | m**e** | like *e* in th*ey*. In a closed syllable, as in g*e*nte, the *e* is short as in p*e*t |
| i | [ i ] | p**i**no | as in m*ea*n or mach*i*ne |
| o | [ o ] | l**o** | as in l*o*cal. In a closed syllable, as in c*o*ntrol, the *o* is short as in c*o*t |
| u | [ u ] | l**u**nes | as in r*u*le. It is silent after q, and in g*ue*, g*ui*, unless marked g*üe*, g*üi* e.g. antig*üe*dad, when it is pronounced like *w* in *w*olf |

**SEMIVOWELS**

| | | | |
|---|---|---|---|
| i, y | [ j ] | b**i**en<br>h**i**elo<br>**y**unta | pronounced like *y* in *y*es |
| u | [ w ] | h**u**evo | unstressed *u* between consonant and f**u**ento vowel is pronounced like *w* in *w*ell. |
| | | antig**ü**edad | See notes on *u* above. |

**DIPHTHONGS**

| | | | |
|---|---|---|---|
| ai, ay | [ ai ] | b**ai**le | as *i* in r*i*de |
| au | [ au ] | **au**to | as *ou* in sh*ou*t |
| ei, ey | [ ei ] | bu**ey** | as *ey* in gr*ey* |
| eu | [ eu ] | d**eu**da | both elements pronounced independently [e] + [u] |
| oi, oy | [ oi ] | h**oy** | as *oy* in t*oy* |

**CONSONANTS**

| | | | |
|---|---|---|---|
| b | [b, β] | **b**oda<br>**b**omba<br>la**b**or | see notes on *v* below |
| c | [ k ] | **c**aja | *c* before *a, o, u* is pronounced as in *c*at |
| ce, ci | [θe, θi] | **c**ero<br>**c**ielo | *c* before *e* or *i* is pronounced as in *th*in |
| ch | [ tʃ ] | **ch**iste | *ch* is pronounced as *ch* in *ch*air |

| d | [d, ð] | **d**anés<br>ciu**dad** | at the beginning of a phrase or after *l* or *n*, *d* is pronounced as in English. In any other position it is pronounced like *th* in *the* |
|---|---|---|---|
| g | [g, ɣ] | **g**afas<br>pa**g**a | *g* before *a, o* or *u* is pronounced as in *gap*, if at the beginning of a phrase or after *n*. In other positions the sound is softened |
| ge, gi | [xe, xi] | **g**ente<br>**g**irar | *g* before *e* or *i* is pronounced similar to *ch* in Scottish lo*ch* |
| h | | **h**aber | *h* is always silent in Spanish |
| j | [ x ] | **j**ugar | *j* is pronounced similar to *ch* in Scottish lo*ch* |
| ll | [ ʎ ] | ta**ll**e | *ll* is pronounced like the *y* in *yet* or the *lli* in mi*lli*on |
| ñ | [ ʃ ] | ni**ñ**o | *ñ* is pronounced like the *ni* in o*ni*on |
| q | [ k ] | **q**ue | *q* is pronounced as *k* in *king* |
| r, rr | [r, rr] | quita**r**<br>ga**rr**a | *r* is always pronounced in Spanish, unlike the silent *r* in dance*r*. *rr* is trilled like a Scottish *r* |
| s | [ s ] | quizá**s**<br>i**s**la | *s* is usually pronounced as in pa*ss*, but before *b, d, g, l, m* or *n* it is pronounced as in ro*s*e |
| v | [b, β] | **v**ía | *v* is pronounced something like *b*. At the beginning of a phrase or after *m* or *n* it is pronounced as *b* in *boy*. In any other position the sound is softened |
| z | [ θ ] | tena**z** | *z* is pronounced as *th* in *th*in |

f, k, l, m, n, p, t and x are pronounced as in English.

## STRESS

The rules of stress in Spanish are as follows:

(a)    when a word ends in a vowel or in *n* or *s*, the second last syllable is stressed:<br>    pat*a*ta, pat*a*tas; c*o*me, c*o*men

(b)    when a word ends in a consonant other than *n* or *s*, the stress falls on the last syllable:<br>    par*ed*, habl*ar*

(c)    when the rules set out in (a) and (b) are not applied, an acute accent appears over the stressed vowel:<br>    com*ún*, geograf*ía*, ingl*és*

In the phonetic transcription, the symbol [ ' ] precedes the syllable on which the stress falls.

# LA PRONUNCIACIÓN INGLESA

## VOCALES

|  | Ejemplo inglés | Explicación |
|---|---|---|
| [ ɑː ] | father | Entre a de padre y o de noche |
| [ ʌ ] | but, come | a muy breve |
| [ æ ] | man, cat | Con los labios en la posición de e en pena y luego se pronuncia el sonido a parecido a la a de carro |
| [ ə ] | father, ago | Vocal neutra parecida a una e u o casi muda |
| [ əː ] | bird, heard | Entre e abierta y o cerrada, sonido alargado |
| [ ɛ ] | get, bed | Como en perro |
| [ ɪ ] | it, big | Más breve que en si |
| [ iː ] | tea, see | Como en fino |
| [ ɔ ] | hot, wash | Como en torre |
| [ ɔː ] | saw, all | Como en por |
| [ u ] | put, book | Sonido breve, más cerrado que burro |
| [ uː ] | too, you | Sonido largo, como en uno |

## DIPTONGOS

|  | Ejemplo inglés | Explicación |
|---|---|---|
| [ aɪ ] | fly, high | Como en fraile |
| [ au ] | how, house | Como en pausa |
| [ ɛə ] | there, bear | Casi como en vea, pero el sonido a se mezcla con el indistinto [ə] |
| [ eɪ ] | day, obey | e cerrada seguida por una i débil |
| [ ɪə ] | here, hear | Como en manía, mezclándose el sonido a con el indistinto [ə] |
| [ əu ] | go, note | [ə] seguido por una breve u |
| [ əɪ ] | boy, oil | Como en voy |
| [ uə ] | poor, sure | u bastante larga más el sonido indistinto [ə] |

**CONSONANTES**

| | Ejemplo inglés | Explicación |
|---|---|---|
| [ b ] | **b**ig, lo**bb**y | Como en tum**b**an |
| [ d ] | men**d**e**d** | Como en con**d**e, an**d**ar |
| [ g ] | **g**o, **g**et, bi**g** | Como en **g**rande, **g**ol |
| [ dʒ ] | **g**in, ju**dg**e | Como en la **ll** andaluza y en Generalitat (*catalán*) |
| [ ŋ ] | si**ng** | Como en ví**n**culo |
| [ h ] | **h**ouse, **h**e | Como la jota hispanoamericana |
| [ j ] | **y**oung, **y**es | Como en **y**a |
| [ k ] | **c**ome, mo**ck** | Como en **c**aña, Es**c**ocia |
| [ r ] | **r**ed, t**r**ead | Se pronuncia con la punta de la lengua hacia atrás y sin hacerla vibrar |
| [ s ] | **s**and, ye**s** | Como en ca**s**a, **s**esión |
| [ z ] | ro**s**e, **z**ebra | Como en de**s**de, mi**s**mo |
| [ ʃ ] | **sh**e, ma**ch**ine | Como en **ch**ambre (*francés*), ro**x**o (*portugués*) |
| [ tʃ ] | **ch**in, ri**ch** | Como en **ch**ocolate |
| [ v ] | **v**alley | Como *f*, pero se retiran los dientes superiores vibrándolos contra el labio inferior |
| [ w ] | **w**ater, **wh**ich | Como la *u* de h**u**evo, p**u**ede |
| [ ʒ ] | vi**s**ion | Como en journal (*francés*) |
| [ θ ] | **th**ink, my**th** | Como en re**c**eta, **z**apato |
| [ ð ] | **th**is, **th**e | Como en habla**d**o, verda**d** |

f, l, m, n, p, t y x iguales que en español.

El signo [ * ] indica que la r final escrita apenas se pronuncia en inglés británico cuando la palabra siguiente empieza con vocal. El signo [ ' ] indica la sílaba acentuada.

# SPANISH VERB TABLES

**1** Gerund **2** Imperative **3** Present **4** Preterite **5** Future **6** Present subjunctive
**7** Imperfect subjunctive **8** Past participle **9** Imperfect

*Etc* indicates that the irregular root is used for all persons of the tense, e.g. **oír:**
**6** oiga, oigas, oigamos, oigáis, oigan

**1a** **HABLAR** **1** hablando **2** habla, hablad **3** hablo, hablas, habla, hablamos, habláis, hablan **4** hablé, hablaste, habló, hablamos, hablasteis, hablaron **5** hablaré, hablarás, hablará, hablaremos, hablaréis, hablarán **6** hable, hables, hable, hablemos, habléis, hablen **7** hablara, hablaras, hablara, habláramos, hablarais, hablaran **8** hablado **9** hablaba, hablabas, hablaba, hablábamos, hablabais, hablaban

**1b** **cambiar** **2** cambia **3** cambio *etc* **6** cambie *etc*

**1c** **enviar** **2** envía **3** envío, envías, envía, envíen **6** envíe, envíes, envíe, envíen

**1d** **evacuar** **2** evacua **3** evacuo *etc* **6** evacue *etc*

**1e** **situar** **2** sitúa **3** sitúo, sitúas, sitúa, sitúen **6** sitúe, sitúes, sitúe, sitúen

**1f** **cruzar** **4** crucé **6** cruce *etc*

**1g** **picar** **4** piqué **6** pique *etc*

**1h** **pagar** **4** pagué **6** pague *etc*

**1i** **averiguar** **4** averigüé **6** averigüe *etc*

**1j** **cerrar** **2** cierra **3** cierro, cierras, cierra, cierran **6** cierre, cierres, cierre, cierren

**1k** **errar** **2** yerra **3** yerro, yerras, yerra, yerran **6** yerre, yerres, yerre, yerren

**1l** **contar** **2** cuenta **3** cuento, cuentas, cuenta, cuentan **6** cuente, cuentes, cuente, cuenten

**1m** **degollar** **2** degüella **3** degüello, degüellas, degüella, degüellan **6** degüelle, degüelles, degüelle, degüellen

**1n** **jugar** **2** juega **3** juego, juegas, juega, jueguen **6** juegue, juegues, juegue, jueguen

**1o** **ESTAR** **2** está **3** estoy, estás, está, están **4** estuve, estuviste, estuvo, estuvimos, estuvisteis, estuvieron **6** esté, estés, esté, estén **7** estuviera *etc*

**1p** **andar** **4** anduve *etc* **7** anduviera *etc*

**1q** **dar** **3** doy **4** di, diste, dio, dimos, disteis, dieron **7** diera *etc*

**2a** **COMER** **1** comiendo **2** come, comed **3** como, comes, come, comemos, coméis, comen **4** comí, comiste, comió, comimos, comisteis, comieron **5** comeré, comerás, comerá, comeremos, comeréis, comerán **6** coma, comas, coma, comamos, comáis, coman **7** comiera, comieras, comiera, comiéramos, comierais, comieran **8** comido **9** comía, comías, comía, comíamos, comíais, comían

**2b** **vencer** **3** venzo **6** venza *etc*

**2c**  **coger** 3 cojo 6 coja *etc*

**2d**  **parecer** 3 parezco 6 parezca *etc*

**2e**  **leer** 1 leyendo 4 leyó, leyeron 7 leyera *etc*

**2f**  **tañer** 1 tañendo 4 tañó, tañeron

**2g**  **perder** 2 pierde 3 pierdo, pierdes, pierde, pierden 6 pierda, pierdas, pierda, pierdan

**2h**  **mover** 2 mueve 3 muevo, mueves, mueve, mueven 6 mueva, muevas, mueva, muevan

**2i**  **oler** 2 huele 3 huelo, hueles, huele, huelen 6 huela, huelas, huela, huelan

**2j**  **HABER** 3 he, has, ha, hemos, han 4 hube, hubiste, hubo, hubimos, hubisteis, hubieron 5 habré *etc* 6 haya *etc* 7 hubiera *etc*

**2k**  **tener** 2 ten 3 tengo, tienes, tiene, tienen 4 tuve, tuviste, tuvo, tuvimos, tuvisteis, tuvieron 5 tendré *etc* 6 tenga *etc* 7 tuviera *etc*

**2l**  **caber** 3 quepo 4 cupe, cupiste, cupo, cupimos, cupisteis, cupieron 5 cabré *etc* 6 quepa *etc* 7 cupiera *etc*

**2m**  **saber** 3 sé 4 supe, supiste, supo, supimos, supisteis, supieron 5 sabré *etc* 6 sepa *etc* 7 supiera *etc*

**2n**  **caer** 1 cayendo 3 caigo 4 cayó, cayeron 6 caiga *etc* 7 cayera *etc*

**2o**  **traer** 1 trayendo 3 traigo 4 traje, trajiste, trajo, trajimos, trajisteis, trajeron 6 traiga *etc* 7 trajera *etc*

**2p**  **valer** 2 vale 3 valgo 5 valdré *etc* 6 valga *etc*

**2q**  **poner** 2 pon 3 pongo 4 puse, pusiste, puso, pusimos, pusisteis, pusieron 5 pondré *etc* 6 ponga *etc* 7 pusiera *etc* 8 puesto

**2r**  **hacer** 2 haz 3 hago 4 hice, hiciste, hizo, hicimos, hicisteis, hicieron 5 haré *etc* 6 haga *etc* 7 hiciera *etc* 8 hecho

**2s**  **poder** 1 pudiendo 2 puede 3 puedo, puedes, puede, pueden 4 pude, pudiste, pudo, pudimos, pudisteis, pudieron 5 podré *etc* 6 pueda, puedas, pueda, puedan 7 pudiera *etc*

**2t**  **querer** 2 quiere 3 quiero, quieres, quiere, quieren 4 quise, quisiste, quiso, quisimos, quisisteis, quisieron 5 querré *etc* 6 quiera, quieras, quiera, quieran 7 quisiera *etc*

**2u**  **ver** 3 veo 6 vea *etc* 8 visto 9 veía *etc*

**2v**  **SER** 2 sé 3 soy, eres, es, somos, sois, son 4 fui, fuiste, fue, fuimos, fuisteis, fueron 6 sea *etc* 7 fuera *etc* 9 era, eras, era, éramos, erais, eran

**2w**  **placer** 3 plazco 6 plazca *etc*

**2x**  **yacer** 2 yace or yaz 3 yazco or yazgo 6 yazca or yazga *etc*

**2y**  **roer** 1 royendo 3 roo or roigo 7 royó, royeron, 6 roa or roiga *etc* 7 royera *etc*

**3a VIVIR** 1 viviendo 2 vive, vivid 3 vivo, vives, vive, vivimos, vivís, viven 4 viví, viviste, vivió, vivimos, vivisteis, vivieron 5 viviré, vivirás, vivirá, viviremos, viviréis, vivirán 6 viva, vivas, viva, vivamos, viváis, vivan 7 viviera, vivieras, viviera, viviéramos, vivierais, vivieran 8 vivido 9 vivía, vivías, vivía, vivíamos, vivíais, vivían

**3b esparcir** 3 esparzo 6 esparza *etc*

**3c dirigir** 3 dirijo 6 dirija *etc*

**3d distinguir** 3 distingo 6 distinga *etc*

**3e delinquir** 3 delinco 6 delinca *etc*

**3f lucir** 3 luzco 6 luzca *etc*

**3g instruir** 1 instruyendo 2 instruye 3 instruyo, instruyes, instruye, instruyen 4 instruyó, instruyeron 6 instruya *etc* 7 instruyera *etc*

**3h gruñir** 1 gruñendo 4 gruñó, gruñeron

**3i sentir** 1 sintiendo 2 siente 3 siento, sientes, siente, sienten 4 sintió, sintieron 6 sienta, sientas, sienta, sintamos, sintáis, sientan 7 sintiera *etc*

**3j dormir** 1 durmiendo 2 duerme 3 duermo, duermes, duerme, duermen 4 durmió, durmieron 6 duerma, duermas, duerma, durmamos, durmáis, duerman 7 durmiera *etc*

**3k pedir** 1 pidiendo 2 pide 3 pido, pides, pide, piden 4 pidió, pidieron 6 pida *etc* 7 pidiera *etc*

**3l reír** 2 ríe 3 río, ríes, ríe, ríen 4 reí, rieron 6 ría, rías, ría, riamos, riáis, rían 7 riera *etc*

**3m erguir** 1 irguiendo 2 yergue 3 yergo, yergues, yergue, yerguen 4 irguió, irguieron 7 irguiera *etc*

**3n reducir** 3 reduzco 5 reduje *etc* 6 reduzca *etc* 7 redujera *etc*

**3o decir** 2 di 3 digo 4 dije, dijiste, dijo, dijimos, dijisteis, dijeron 5 diré *etc* 6 diga *etc* 7 dijera *etc* 8 dicho

**3p oír** 1 oyendo 2 oye 3 oigo, oyes, oye, oyen 4 oyó, oyeron 6 oiga *etc* 7 oyera *etc*

**3q salir** 2 sal 3 salgo 5 saldré *etc* 6 salga *etc*

**3r venir** 2 ven 3 vengo, vienes, viene, vienen 4 vine, viniste, vino, vinimos, vinisteis, vinieron 5 vendré *etc* 6 venga *etc* 7 viniera *etc*

**3s ir** 1 yendo 2 ve 3 voy, vas, va, vamos, vais, van 4 fui, fuiste, fue, fuimos, fuisteis, fueron 6 vaya, vayas, vaya, vayamos, vayáis, vayan 7 fuera *etc* 9 iba, ibas, iba, íbamos, ibais, iban

# VERBOS IRREGULARES EN INGLÉS

| PRESENTE | PASADO | PARTICIPIO |
|---|---|---|
| arise | arose | arisen |
| awake | awoke | awoken |
| be (am, is, are; being) | was, were | been |
| bear | bore | born(e) |
| beat | beat | beaten |
| become | became | become |
| begin | began | begun |
| bend | bent | bent |
| bet | bet, betted | bet, betted |
| bid (at auction, cards) | bid | bid |
| bid (say) | bade | bidden |
| bind | bound | bound |
| bite | bit | bitten |
| bleed | bled | bled |
| blow | blew | blown |
| break | broke | broken |
| breed | bred | bred |
| bring | brought | brought |
| build | built | built |
| burn | burnt, burned | burnt, burned |
| burst | burst | burst |
| buy | bought | bought |
| can | could | (been able) |
| cast | cast | cast |
| catch | caught | caught |
| choose | chose | chosen |
| cling | clung | clung |
| come | came | come |
| cost (be valued at) | cost | cost |
| cost (work out price of) | costed | costed |
| creep | crept | crept |
| cut | cut | cut |
| deal | dealt | dealt |
| dig | dug | dug |
| do (does) | did | done |

| PRESENTE | PASADO | PARTICIPIO |
|---|---|---|
| draw | drew | drawn |
| dream | dreamed, dreamt | dreamed, dreamt |
| drink | drank | drunk |
| drive | drove | driven |
| dwell | dwelt | dwelt |
| eat | ate | eaten |
| fall | fell | fallen |
| feed | fed | fed |
| feel | felt | felt |
| fight | fought | fought |
| find | found | found |
| flee | fled | fled |
| fling | flung | flung |
| fly | flew | flown |
| forbid | forbad(e) | forbidden |
| forecast | forecast | forecast |
| forget | forgot | forgotten |
| forgive | forgave | forgiven |
| forsake | forsook | forsaken |
| freeze | froze | frozen |
| get | got | got, (US) gotten |
| give | gave | given |
| go (goes) | went | gone |
| grind | ground | ground |
| grow | grew | grown |
| hang | hung | hung |
| hang (execute) | hanged | hanged |
| have | had | had |
| hear | heard | heard |
| hide | hid | hidden |
| hit | hit | hit |
| hold | held | held |
| hurt | hurt | hurt |
| keep | kept | kept |
| kneel | knelt, kneeled | knelt, kneeled |
| know | knew | known |
| lay | laid | laid |

| PRESENTE | PASADO | PARTICIPIO |
|---|---|---|
| lead | led | led |
| lean | leant, leaned | leant, leaned |
| leap | leapt, leaped | leapt, leaped |
| learn | learnt, learned | learnt, learned |
| leave | left | left |
| lend | lent | lent |
| let | let | let |
| lie (lying) | lay | lain |
| light | lit, lighted | lit, lighted |
| lose | lost | lost |
| make | made | made |
| may | might | – |
| mean | meant | meant |
| meet | met | met |
| mistake | mistook | mistaken |
| mow | mowed | mown, mowed |
| must | (had to) | (had to) |
| pay | paid | paid |
| put | put | put |
| quit | quit, quitted | quit, quitted |
| read | read | read |
| rid | rid | rid |
| ride | rode | ridden |
| ring | rang | rung |
| rise | rose | risen |
| run | ran | run |
| saw | sawed | sawed, sawn |
| say | said | said |
| see | saw | seen |
| seek | sought | sought |
| sell | sold | sold |
| send | sent | sent |
| set | set | set |
| sew | sewed | sewn |
| shake | shook | shaken |
| shear | sheared | shorn, sheared |
| shed | shed | shed |

| PRESENTE | PASADO | PARTICIPIO |
|---|---|---|
| shine | shone | shone |
| shoot | shot | shot |
| show | showed | shown |
| shrink | shrank | shrunk |
| shut | shut | shut |
| sing | sang | sung |
| sink | sank | sunk |
| sit | sat | sat |
| slay | slew | slain |
| sleep | slept | slept |
| slide | slid | slid |
| sling | slung | slung |
| slit | slit | slit |
| smell | smelt, smelled | smelt, smelled |
| sow | sowed | sown, sowed |
| speak | spoke | spoken |
| speed | sped, speeded | sped, speeded |
| spell | spelt, spelled | spelt, spelled |
| spend | spent | spent |
| spill | spilt, spilled | spilt, spilled |
| spin | spun | spun |
| spit | spat | spat |
| spoil | spoiled, spoilt | spoiled, spoilt |
| spread | spread | spread |
| spring | sprang | sprung |
| stand | stood | stood |
| steal | stole | stolen |
| stick | stuck | stuck |
| sting | stung | stung |
| stink | stank | stunk |
| stride | strode | stridden |
| strike | struck | struck |
| strive | strove | striven |
| swear | swore | sworn |
| sweep | swept | swept |
| swell | swelled | swollen, swelled |
| swim | swam | swum |

| PRESENTE | PASADO | PARTICIPIO |
| --- | --- | --- |
| swing | swung | swung |
| take | took | taken |
| teach | taught | taught |
| tear | tore | torn |
| tell | told | told |
| think | thought | thought |
| throw | threw | thrown |
| thrust | thrust | thrust |
| tread | trod | trodden |
| wake | woke, waked | woken, waked |
| wear | wore | worn |
| weave (on loom) | wove | woven |
| weave (wind) | weaved | weaved |
| wed | wedded, wed | wedded, wed |
| weep | wept | wept |
| win | won | won |
| wind | wound | wound |
| wring | wrung | wrung |
| write | wrote | written |

# Español – Inglés

# Spanish – English

# a

**PALABRA CLAVE**

**a** [a] prep **1** (dirección) to; **fueron a Madrid/ Grecia** they went to Madrid/Greece; **me voy a casa** I'm going home
**2** (distancia): **está a 15 km de aquí** it's 15 km from here
**3** (posición): **estar a la mesa** to be at table; **al lado de** next to, beside; V tb **puerta**
**4** (tiempo): **a las 10/a medianoche** at 10/midnight; **a la mañana siguiente** the following morning; **a los pocos días** after a few days; **estamos a 9 de julio** it's the 9th of July; **a los 24 años** at the age of 24; **al año/a la semana** a year/week later
**5** (manera): **a la francesa** the French way; **a caballo** on horseback; **a oscuras** in the dark
**6** (medio, instrumento): **a lápiz** in pencil; **a mano** by hand; **cocina a gas** gas stove
**7** (razón): **a dos euros el kilo** at two euros a kilo; **a más de 50 km por hora** at more than 50 km per hour
**8** (dativo): **se lo di a él** I gave it to him; **se lo compré a él** I bought it from him
**9** (complemento directo): **vi al policía** I saw the police officer
**10** (tras ciertos verbos): **voy a verle** I'm going to see him; **empezó a trabajar** he started working o to work
**11** (+ infin): **al verle, le reconocí inmediatamente** when I saw him I recognized him at once; **el camino a recorrer** the distance we etc have to travel; **¡a callar!** keep quiet!; **¡a comer!** let's eat!

**abad, esa** [a'βað, 'ðesa] nm/f abbot/ abbess; **abadía** nf abbey
**abajo** [a'βaxo] adv (situación) (down) below, underneath; (en edificio) downstairs; (dirección) down, downwards; **el piso de ~** the downstairs flat; **la parte de ~** the lower part; **¡~ el gobierno!** down with the government!; **cuesta/río ~** downhill/ downstream; **de arriba ~** from top to bottom; **el ~ firmante** the undersigned; **más ~** lower o further down
**abalanzarse** [aβalan'θarse] /1f/ vr: **~ sobre** o **contra** to throw o.s. at
**abanderado, -a** [aβande'raðo, a] nm/f (portaestandarte) standard bearer; (de un movimiento) champion, leader; (LAM: linier) linesman, assistant referee
**abandonado, -a** [aβando'naðo, a] adj derelict; (desatendido) abandoned; (desierto) deserted; (descuidado) neglected
**abandonar** [aβando'nar] /1a/ vt to leave; (persona) to abandon, desert; (cosa) to abandon, leave behind; (descuidar) to neglect; (renunciar a) to give up; (Inform) to quit; **abandonarse** vr: **~se a** to abandon o.s. to; **abandono** nm (acto) desertion, abandonment; (estado) abandon, neglect; (renuncia) withdrawal, retirement; **ganar por abandono** to win by default
**abanico** [aβa'niko] nm fan; (Naut) derrick
**abarcar** [aβar'kar] /1g/ vt to include, embrace; (LAM) to monopolize
**abarrotado, -a** [aβarro'taðo, a] adj packed
**abarrotar** [aβarro'tar] /1a/ vt (local, estadio, teatro) to fill, pack
**abarrote** [aβa'rrote] nm packing; **abarrotes** nmpl (LAM) groceries; **tienda de ~s** (LAM) grocery store
**abarrotero, -a** [aβarro'tero, a] nm/f (LAM) grocer
**abastecer** [aβaste'θer] /2d/ vt: **~ (de)** to supply (with); **abastecimiento** nm supply
**abasto** [a'βasto] nm supply; **no dar ~ a algo** not to be able to cope with sth
**abatible** [aβa'tiβle] adj: **asiento ~** tip-up seat; (Auto) reclining seat
**abatido, -a** [aβa'tiðo, a] adj dejected, downcast
**abatir** [aβa'tir] /3a/ vt (muro) to demolish; (pájaro) to shoot o bring down; (fig) to depress
**abdicar** [aβði'kar] /1g/ vi to abdicate
**abdomen** [aβ'ðomen] nm abdomen
**abdominal** [aβðomi'nal] nm: **~es** abdominals; (Deporte: tb: **ejercicios ~es**) sit-ups
**abecedario** [aβeθe'ðarjo] nm alphabet
**abedul** [aβe'ðul] nm birch
**abeja** [a'βexa] nf bee
**abejorro** [aβe'xorro] nm bumblebee
**abertura** [aβer'tura] nf = **apertura**
**abeto** [a'βeto] nm fir

**abierto, -a** [a'βjerto, a] pp de **abrir** ▷ adj open

**abismal** [aβis'mal] adj (fig) vast, enormous

**abismo** [a'βismo] nm abyss

**ablandar** [aβlan'dar] /1a/ vt to soften
▷ **ablandarse** vr to get softer

**abocado, -a** [aβo'kaðo, a] adj: **verse ~ al desastre** to be heading for disaster

**abochornar** [aβotʃor'nar] /1a/ vt to embarrass; **abochornarse** vr to get flustered; (Bot) to wilt; **~se de** to get embarrassed about

**abofetear** [aβofete'ar] /1a/ vt to slap (in the face)

**abogado, -a** [aβo'ɣaðo, a] nm/f lawyer; (notario) solicitor; (en tribunal) barrister, advocate, attorney (US); **~ defensor** defence lawyer (BRIT), defense attorney (US)

**abogar** [aβo'ɣar] /1h/ vi: **~ por** to plead for; (fig) to advocate

**abolir** [aβo'lir] vt to abolish; (cancelar) to cancel

**abolladura** [aβoʎa'ðura] nf dent

**abollar** [aβo'ʎar] /1a/ vt to dent

**abombarse** [aβom'barse] /1a/ (LAM) vr to go bad

**abominable** [aβomi'naβle] adj abominable

**abonado, -a** [aβo'naðo, a] adj (deuda) paid(-up) ▷ nm/f subscriber

**abonar** [aβo'nar] /1a/ vt (deuda) to settle; (terreno) to fertilize; (idea) to endorse; **abonarse** vr to subscribe; **abono** nm payment; fertilizer; subscription

**abordar** [aβor'ðar] /1a/ vt (barco) to board; (asunto) to broach

**aborigen** [aβo'rixen] nmf aborigine

**aborrecer** [aβorre'θer] /2d/ vt to hate, loathe

**abortar** [aβor'tar] /1a/ vi (malparir) to have a miscarriage; (deliberadamente) to have an abortion; **aborto** nm miscarriage; abortion

**abovedado, -a** [aβoβe'ðaðo, a] adj vaulted, domed

**abrasar** [aβra'sar] /1a/ vt to burn (up); (Agr) to dry up, parch

**abrazar** [aβra'θar] /1f/ vt to embrace, hug

**abrazo** [a'βraθo] nm embrace, hug; **un ~** (en carta) with best wishes

**abrebotellas** [aβreβo'teʎas] nm inv bottle opener

**abrecartas** [aβre'kartas] nm inv letter opener

**abrelatas** [aβre'latas] nm inv tin (BRIT) o can (US) opener

**abreviatura** [aβreβja'tura] nf abbreviation

**abridor** [aβri'ðor] nm bottle opener; (de latas) tin (BRIT) o can (US) opener

**abrigador, a** [aβriga'ðor, a] adj (LAM) warm

**abrigar** [aβri'ɣar] /1h/ vt (proteger) to shelter; (ropa) to keep warm; (fig) to cherish

**abrigo** [a'βriɣo] nm (prenda) coat, overcoat; (lugar protegido) shelter

**abril** [a'βril] nm April; V tb **julio**

**abrillantador** [aβriʎanta'ðor] nm polish

**abrillantar** [aβriʎan'tar] /1a/ vt (pulir) to polish

**abrir** [a'βrir] /3a/ vt to open (up) ▷ vi to open; **abrirse** vr to open (up); (extenderse) to open out; (cielo) to clear; **~se paso** to find o force a way through

**abrochar** [aβro'tʃar] /1a/ vt (con botones) to button (up); (zapato, con broche) to do up

**abrupto, -a** [a'βrupto, a] adj abrupt; (empinado) steep

**absoluto, -a** [aβso'luto, a] adj absolute; **en ~** adv not at all

**absolver** [aβsol'βer] /2h/ vt to absolve; (Jur) to pardon; (: acusado) to acquit

**absorbente** [aβsor'βente] adj absorbent; (interesante) absorbing

**absorber** [aβsor'βer] /2a/ vt to absorb; (embeber) to soak up

**absorción** [aβsor'θjon] nf absorption; (Com) takeover

**abstemio, -a** [aβs'temjo, a] adj teetotal

**abstención** [aβsten'θjon] nf abstention

**abstenerse** [aβste'nerse] /2k/ vr: **~ (de)** to abstain o refrain (from)

**abstinencia** [aβsti'nenθja] nf abstinence; (ayuno) fasting

**abstracto, -a** [aβs'trakto, a] adj abstract

**abstraer** [aβstra'er] /2o/ vt to abstract; **abstraerse** vr to be o become absorbed

**abstraído, -a** [aβstra'iðo, a] adj absent-minded

**absuelto** [aβ'swelto] pp de **absolver**

**absurdo, -a** [aβ'surðo, a] adj absurd

**abuchear** [aβutʃe'ar] /1a/ vt to boo

**abuela** [a'βwela] nf grandmother

**abuelo** [a'βwelo] nm grandfather; **abuelos** nmpl grandparents

**abultado, -a** [aβul'taðo, a] adj bulky

**abultar** [aβul'tar] /1a/ vi to be bulky

**abundancia** [aβun'danθja] nf: **una ~ de** plenty of; **abundante** adj abundant, plentiful

**abundar** [aβun'dar] /1a/ vi to abound, be plentiful

**aburrido, -a** [aβu'rriðo, a] adj (hastiado) bored; (que aburre) boring; **aburrimiento** nm boredom, tedium

**aburrir** [aβu'rrir] /3a/ vt to bore; **aburrirse** vr to be bored, get bored

**abusado, -a** [aβu'saðo, a] adj (LAM fam: astuto) sharp, cunning ▷ excl: **¡~!** (inv) look out!, careful!

**abusar** [aβu'sar] /1a/ vi to go too far; ~ **de** to abuse

**abusivo, -a** [aβu'siβo, a] adj (precio) exorbitant

**abuso** [a'βuso] nm abuse

**acá** [a'ka] adv (lugar) here

**acabado, -a** [aka'βaðo, a] adj finished, complete; (perfecto) perfect; (agotado) worn out; (fig) masterly ▷ nm finish

**acabar** [aka'βar] /1a/ vt (llevar a su fin) to finish, complete; (consumir) to use up; (rematar) to finish off ▷ vi to finish, end; **acabarse** vr to finish, stop; (terminarse) to be over; (agotarse) to run out; ~ **con** to put an end to; ~ **de llegar** to have just arrived; ~ **haciendo** o **por hacer algo** to end up (by) doing sth; **¡se acabó!** (¡basta!) that's enough!; (se terminó) it's all over!

**acabose** [aka'βose] nm: **esto es el** ~ this is the last straw

**academia** [aka'ðemja] nf academy; ~ **de idiomas** language school; V tb **colegio**; **académico, -a** adj academic

**acalorado, -a** [akalo'raðo, a] adj (discusión) heated

**acampar** [akam'par] /1a/ vi to camp

**acantilado** [akanti'laðo] nm cliff

**acaparar** [akapa'rar] /1a/ vt to monopolize; (acumular) to hoard

**acariciar** [akari'θjar] /1b/ vt to caress; (esperanza) to cherish

**acarrear** [akarre'ar] /1a/ vt to transport; (fig) to cause, result in

**acaso** [a'kaso] adv perhaps, maybe; **(por) si** ~ (just) in case

**acatar** [aka'tar] /1a/ vt to respect; (ley) to obey, observe

**acatarrarse** [akata'rrarse] /1a/ vr to catch a cold

**acceder** [akθe'ðer] /2a/ vi to accede, agree; ~ **a** (petición etc) to agree to; (tener acceso a) to have access to; (Inform) to access

**accesible** [akθe'siβle] adj accessible

**acceso** [ak'θeso] nm access, entry; (camino) access road; (Med) attack, fit

**accesorio, -a** [akθe'sorjo, a] adj accessory ▷ nm accessory

**accidentado, -a** [akθiðen'taðo, a] adj uneven; (montañoso) hilly; (azaroso) eventful ▷ nm/f accident victim

**accidental** [akθiðen'tal] adj accidental

**accidente** [akθi'ðente] nm accident; **accidentes** nmpl (de terreno) unevenness sg; ~ **laboral** o **de trabajo/de tráfico** industrial/road o traffic accident

**acción** [ak'θjon] nf action; (acto) action, act; (Com) share; (Jur) action, lawsuit; **accionar** /1a/ vt to work, operate; (ejecutar) to activate

**accionista** [akθjo'nista] nmf shareholder

**acebo** [a'θeβo] nm holly; (árbol) holly tree

**acechar** [aθe'tʃar] /1a/ vt to spy on; (aguardar) to lie in wait for; **acecho** nm: **estar al acecho (de)** to lie in wait (for)

**aceite** [a'θeite] nm oil; ~ **de girasol/oliva** olive/sunflower oil; **aceitera** nf oilcan; **aceitoso, -a** adj oily

**aceituna** [aθei'tuna] nf olive; ~ **rellena** stuffed olive

**acelerador** [aθelera'ðor] nm accelerator

**acelerar** [aθele'rar] /1a/ vt to accelerate

**acelga** [a'θelɣa] nf chard, beet

**acento** [a'θento] nm accent; (acentuación) stress

**acentuar** [aθen'twar] /1e/ vt to accent; to stress; (fig) to accentuate

**acepción** [aθep'θjon] nf meaning

**aceptable** [aθep'taβle] adj acceptable

**aceptación** [aθepta'θjon] nf acceptance; (aprobación) approval

**aceptar** [aθep'tar] /1a/ vt to accept; (aprobar) to approve; ~ **hacer algo** to agree to do sth

**acequia** [a'θekja] nf irrigation ditch

**acera** [a'θera] nf pavement (BRIT), sidewalk (US)

**acerca** [a'θerka]: ~ **de** prep about, concerning

**acercar** [aθer'kar] /1g/ vt to bring o move nearer; **acercarse** vr to approach, come near

**acero** [a'θero] nm steel

**acérrimo, -a** [a'θerrimo, a] adj (partidario) staunch; (enemigo) bitter

**acertado, -a** [aθer'taðo, a] adj correct; (apropiado) apt; (sensato) sensible

**acertar** [aθer'tar] /1j/ vt (blanco) to hit; (solución) to get right; (adivinar) to guess ▷ vi to get it right, be right; ~ **a** to manage to; ~ **con** o to happen o hit on

**acertijo** [aθer'tixo] nm riddle, puzzle

**achacar** [atʃa'kar] /1g/ vt to attribute

**achacoso, -a** [atʃa'koso, a] adj sickly

**achicar** [atʃi'kar] /1g/ vt to reduce; (Naut) to bale out

**achicharrar** [atʃitʃa'rrar] /1a/ vt to scorch, burn

**achichincle** [atʃi'tʃinkle] nmf (LAM fam) minion

**achicoria** [atʃi'korja] nf chicory

**achuras** [a'tʃuras] nf (LAM Culin) offal

**acicate** [aθi'kate] nm spur

**acidez** [aθi'ðeθ] nf acidity

**ácido, -a** ['aθiðo, a] adj sour, acid ▷ nm acid

**acierto** etc [a'θjerto] vb V **acertar** ▷ nm success; (buen paso) wise move; (solución) solution; (habilidad) skill, ability

**acitronar** [aθitro'nar] /1a/ (LAM) vt (fam) to brown

**aclamar** [akla'mar] /1a/ vt to acclaim; (aplaudir) to applaud

**aclaración** [aklara'θjon] nf clarification, explanation

**aclarar** [akla'rar] /1a/ vt to clarify, explain; (ropa) to rinse ▷ vi to clear up; **aclararse** vr (explicarse) to understand; **~se la garganta** to clear one's throat

**aclimatación** [aklimata'θjon] nf acclimatization

**aclimatar** [aklima'tar] /1a/ vt to acclimatize; **aclimatarse** vr to become o get acclimatized

**acné** [ak'ne] nm acne

**acobardar** [akoβar'ðar] /1a/ vt to daunt, intimidate

**acogedor, a** [akoxe'ðor, a] adj welcoming; (hospitalario) hospitable

**acoger** [ako'xer] /2c/ vt to welcome; (abrigar) to shelter

**acogida** [ako'xiða] nf reception; refuge

**acomedido, -a** [akome'ðiðo, a] (LAM) adj helpful, obliging

**acometer** [akome'ter] /2a/ vt to attack; (emprender) to undertake; **acometida** nf attack, assault

**acomodado, -a** [akomo'ðaðo, a] adj (persona) well-to-do

**acomodador, a** [akomoða'ðor, a] nm/f usher(ette)

**acomodar** [akomo'ðar] /1a/ vt to adjust; (alojar) to accommodate; **acomodarse** vi to conform; (instalarse) to install o.s.; (adaptarse) to adapt o.s.; **~se (a)** to adapt (to)

**acompañar** [akompa'nar] /1a/ vt to accompany; (documentos) to enclose

**acondicionar** [akondiθjo'nar] /1a/ vt to get ready, prepare; (pelo) to condition

**aconsejar** [akonse'xar] /1a/ vt to advise, counsel; **~ a algn hacer** o **que haga algo** to advise sb to do sth

**acontecer** [akonte'θer] /2d/ vi to happen, occur; **acontecimiento** nm event

**acopio** [a'kopjo] nm store, stock

**acoplar** [ako'plar] /1a/ vt to fit; (Elec) to connect; (vagones) to couple

**acorazado, -a** [akora'θaðo, a] adj armour-plated, armoured ▷ nm battleship

**acordar** [akor'ðar] /1l/ vt (resolver) to agree, resolve; (recordar) to remind; **acordarse** vr to agree; **~ hacer algo** to agree to do sth; **~se (de algo)** to remember (sth); **acorde** adj (Mus) harmonious ▷ nm chord; **acorde con** (medidas etc) in keeping with

**acordeón** [akorðe'on] nm accordion

**acordonado, -a** [akorðo'naðo, a] adj (calle) cordoned-off

**acorralar** [akorra'lar] /1a/ vt to round up, corral

**acortar** [akor'tar] /1a/ vt to shorten; (duración) to cut short; (cantidad) to reduce; **acortarse** vr to become shorter

**acosar** [ako'sar] /1a/ vt to pursue relentlessly; (fig) to hound, pester; **acoso** nm harassment; **acoso escolar** bullying; **acoso sexual** sexual harassment

**acostar** [akos'tar] /1l/ vt (en cama) to put to bed; (en suelo) to lay down; **acostarse** vr to go to bed; to lie down; **~se con algn** to sleep with sb

**acostumbrado, -a** [akostum'braðo, a] adj usual; **estar ~ a (hacer) algo** to be used to (doing) sth

**acostumbrar** [akostum'brar] /1a/ vt: **~ a algn a algo** to get sb used to sth ▷ vi: **~ (a hacer algo)** to be in the habit (of doing sth); **acostumbrarse** vr: **~se a** to get used to

**acotación** [akota'θjon] nf marginal note; (Geo) elevation mark; (de límite) boundary mark; (Teat) stage direction

**acotamiento** [akota'mjento] (LAM) nm hard shoulder (BRIT), berm (US)

**acre** ['akre] adj (olor) acrid; (fig) biting ▷ nm acre

**acreditar** [akreði'tar] /1a/ vt (garantizar) to vouch for, guarantee; (autorizar) to authorize; (dar prueba de) to prove; (Com: abonar) to credit; (embajador) to accredit

**acreedor, a** [akree'ðor, a] nm/f creditor

**acribillar** [akriβi'ʎar] /1a/ vt: **~ a balazos** to riddle with bullets

**acróbata** [a'kroβata] nmf acrobat

**acta** ['akta] nf certificate; (de comisión) minutes pl, record; **~ de nacimiento/de matrimonio** birth/marriage certificate; **~ notarial** affidavit

**actitud** [akti'tuð] nf attitude; (postura) posture

**activar** [akti'βar] /1a/ vt to activate; (acelerar) to speed up

**actividad** [aktiβi'ðað] nf activity

**activo, -a** [ak'tiβo, a] adj active; (vivo) lively ▷ nm (Com) assets pl

**acto** ['akto] nm act, action; (ceremonia) ceremony; (Teat) act; **en el ~** immediately

**actor** [ak'tor] nm actor; (Jur) plaintiff ▷ adj: **parte ~** prosecution

**actriz** [ak'triθ] nf actress

**actuación** [aktwa'θjon] nf action; (comportamiento) conduct, behaviour; (Jur) proceedings pl; (desempeño) performance

**actual** [ak'twal] adj present(-day), current; **actualidad** nf present; **en la actualidad** at present; (hoy día) nowadays; **actualizar** /1f/ vt to update, modernize; **actualmente** adv at present; (hoy día) nowadays

No confundir *actual* con la palabra inglesa *actual*.
No confundir *actualmente* con la palabra inglesa *actually*.

**actuar** [ak'twar] /1e/ vi (*obrar*) to work, operate; (*actor*) to act, perform ▷ vt to work, operate; **~ de** to act as

**acuarela** [akwa'rela] nf watercolour

**acuario** [a'kwarjo] nm aquarium; **A~** (*Astro*) Aquarius

**acuático, -a** [a'kwatiko, a] adj aquatic

**acudir** [aku'ðir] /3a/ vi to attend, turn up; (*ir*) to go; **~ a** to turn to; **~ en ayuda de** to go to the aid of; **~ a una cita** to keep an appointment

**acuerdo** [a'kwerðo] vb V **acordar** ▷ nm agreement; **¡de ~!** agreed!; **de ~ con** (*persona*) in agreement with; (*acción, documento*) in accordance with; **estar de ~** (*persona*) to agree

**acumular** [akumu'lar] /1a/ vt to accumulate, collect

**acuñar** [aku'ɲar] /1a/ vt (*moneda*) to mint; (*frase*) to coin

**acupuntura** [akupun'tura] nf acupuncture

**acurrucarse** [akurru'karse] /1g/ vr to crouch; (*ovillarse*) to curl up

**acusación** [akusa'θjon] nf accusation

**acusar** [aku'sar] /1a/ vt to accuse; (*revelar*) to reveal; (*denunciar*) to denounce

**acuse** [a'kuse] nm: **~ de recibo** acknowledgement of receipt

**acústico, -a** [a'kustiko, a] adj acoustic ▷ nf acoustics pl

**adaptación** [aðapta'θjon] nf adaptation

**adaptador** [aðapta'ðor] nm (*Elec*) adapter; **~ universal** universal adapter

**adaptar** [aðap'tar] /1a/ vt to adapt; (*acomodar*) to fit

**adecuado, -a** [aðe'kwaðo, a] adj (*apto*) suitable; (*oportuno*) appropriate

**a. de J.C.** abr (= antes de Jesucristo) B.C.

**adelantado, -a** [aðelan'taðo, a] adj advanced; (*reloj*) fast; **pagar por ~** to pay in advance

**adelantamiento** [aðelanta'mjento] nm (*Auto*) overtaking

**adelantar** [aðelan'tar] /1a/ vt to move forward; (*avanzar*) to advance; (*acelerar*) to speed up; (*Auto*) to overtake ▷ vi (*ir delante*) to go ahead; (*progresar*) to improve; **adelantarse** vr to move forward

**adelante** [aðe'lante] adv forward(s), ahead ▷ excl come in!; **de hoy en ~** from now on; **más ~** later on; (*más allá*) further on

**adelanto** [aðe'lanto] nm advance; (*mejora*) improvement; (*progreso*) progress

**adelgazar** [aðelɣa'θar] /1f/ vt to thin (down) ▷ vi to get thin; (*con régimen*) to slim down, lose weight

**ademán** [aðe'man] nm gesture; **ademanes** nmpl manners

**además** [aðe'mas] adv besides; (*por otra parte*) moreover; (*también*) also; **~ de** besides, in addition to

**adentrarse** [aðen'trarse] /1a/ vr: **~ en** to go into, get inside; (*penetrar*) to penetrate (into)

**adentro** [a'ðentro] adv inside, in; **mar ~** out at sea; **tierra ~** inland

**adepto, -a** [a'ðepto, a] nm/f supporter

**aderezar** [aðere'θar] /1f/ vt (*ensalada*) to dress; (*comida*) to season; **aderezo** nm dressing; seasoning

**adeudar** [aðeu'ðar] /1a/ vt to owe

**adherirse** [aðe'rirse] /3i/ vr: **~ a** to adhere to; (*partido*) to join

**adhesión** [aðe'sjon] nf adhesion; (*fig*) adherence

**adicción** [aðik'θjon] nf addiction

**adición** [aði'θjon] nf addition

**adicto, -a** [a'ðikto, a] adj: **~ a** addicted to; (*dedicado*) devoted to ▷ nm/f supporter, follower; (*toxicómano etc*) addict

**adiestrar** [aðjes'trar] /1a/ vt to train, teach; (*conducir*) to guide, lead

**adinerado, -a** [aðine'raðo, a] adj wealthy

**adiós** [a'ðjos] excl (*para despedirse*) goodbye!, cheerio!; (*al pasar*) hello!

**aditivo** [aði'tiβo] nm additive

**adivinanza** [aðiβi'nanθa] nf riddle

**adivinar** [aðiβi'nar] /1a/ vt to prophesy; (*conjeturar*) to guess; **adivino, -a** nm/f fortune-teller

**adj** abr (= adjunto) encl

**adjetivo** [aðxe'tiβo] nm adjective

**adjudicar** [aðxuði'kar] /1g/ vt to award; **adjudicarse** vr: **~se algo** to appropriate sth

**adjuntar** [aðxun'tar] /1a/ vt to attach, enclose; **adjunto, -a** adj attached, enclosed ▷ nm/f assistant

**administración** [aðministra'θjon] nf administration; (*dirección*) management; **administrador, a** nm/f administrator; manager(ess)

**administrar** [aðminis'trar] /1a/ vt to administer; **administrativo, -a** adj administrative

**admirable** [aðmi'raβle] adj admirable

**admiración** [aðmira'θjon] nf admiration; (*asombro*) wonder; (*Ling*) exclamation mark

**admirar** [aðmi'rar] /1a/ vt to admire; (*extrañar*) to surprise

**admisible** [aðmi'siβle] adj admissible

**admisión** [aðmi'sjon] nf admission; (*reconocimiento*) acceptance

**admitir** [aðmi'tir] /3a/ vt to admit; (aceptar) to accept
**adobar** [aðo'βar] /1a/ vt (cocinar) to season
**adobe** [a'ðoβe] nm adobe, sun-dried brick
**adolecer** [aðole'θer] /2d/ vi: ~ de to suffer from
**adolescente** [aðoles'θente] nmf adolescent, teenager
**adonde** conj (to) where
**adónde** [a'ðonde] adv = **dónde**
**adopción** [aðop'θjon] nf adoption
**adoptar** [aðop'tar] /1a/ vt to adopt
**adoptivo, -a** [aðop'tiβo, a] adj (padres) adoptive; (hijo) adopted
**adoquín** [aðo'kin] nm paving stone
**adorar** [aðo'rar] /1a/ vt to adore
**adornar** [aðor'nar] /1a/ vt to adorn
**adorno** [a'ðorno] nm (objeto) ornament; (decoración) decoration
**adosado, -a** [aðo'saðo, a] adj (casa) semidetached
**adosar** [aðo'sar] /1a/ (LAM) vt (adjuntar) to attach, enclose (with a letter)
**adquiera** etc vb V **adquirir**
**adquirir** [aðki'rir] /3i/ vt to acquire, obtain
**adquisición** [aðkisi'θjon] nf acquisition
**adrede** [a'ðreðe] adv on purpose
**ADSL** nm abr ADSL
**aduana** [a'ðwana] nf customs pl
**aduanero, -a** [aðwa'nero, a] adj customs cpd ▷ nm/f customs officer
**adueñarse** [aðwe'narse] /1a/ vr: ~ de to take possession of
**adular** [aðu'lar] /1a/ vt to flatter
**adulterar** [aðulte'rar] /1a/ vt to adulterate
**adulterio** [aðul'terjo] nm adultery
**adúltero, -a** [a'ðultero, a] adj adulterous ▷ nm/f adulterer/adulteress
**adulto, -a** [a'ðulto, a] adj, nm/f adult
**adverbio** [að'βerβjo] nm adverb
**adversario, -a** [að'βer'sarjo, a] nm/f adversary
**adversidad** [aðβersi'ðað] nf adversity; (contratiempo) setback
**adverso, -a** [að'βerso, a] adj adverse
**advertencia** [aðβer'tenθja] nf warning; (prefacio) preface, foreword
**advertir** [aðβer'tir] /3i/ vt to notice; (avisar): ~ a algn de to warn sb about o of
**Adviento** [að'βjento] nm Advent
**advierta** etc vb V **advertir**
**aéreo, -a** [a'ereo, a] adj aerial
**aerobic** [ae'roβik] nm, (LAM) **aerobics** [ae'roβiks] nmpl aerobics sg
**aerodeslizador** [aeroðesliθa'ðor] nm hovercraft
**aeromozo, -a** [aero'moθo, a] nm/f (LAM) air steward(ess)

**aeronáutica** [aero'nautika] nf aeronautics sg
**aeronave** [aero'naβe] nm spaceship
**aeroplano** [aero'plano] nm aeroplane
**aeropuerto** [aero'pwerto] nm airport
**aerosol** [aero'sol] nm aerosol
**afamado, -a** [afa'maðo, a] adj famous
**afán** [a'fan] nm hard work; (deseo) desire
**afanador, a** [afana'ðor, a] (LAM) nm/f (de limpieza) cleaner
**afanar** [afa'nar] /1a/ vt to harass; (fam) to pinch; **afanarse** vr: ~se por to strive to
**afear** [afe'ar] /1a/ vt to disfigure
**afección** [afek'θjon] nf (Med) disease
**afectado, -a** [afek'taðo, a] adj affected
**afectar** [afek'tar] /1a/ vt to affect
**afectísimo, -a** [afek'tisimo, a] adj affectionate; **suyo** ~ yours truly
**afectivo, -a** [afek'tiβo, a] adj (problema etc) emotional
**afecto** [a'fekto] nm affection; **tenerle** ~ a algn to be fond of sb
**afectuoso, -a** [afek'twoso, a] adj affectionate
**afeitar** [afei'tar] /1a/ vt to shave; **afeitarse** vr to shave
**afeminado, -a** [afemi'naðo, a] adj effeminate
**Afganistán** [afɣanis'tan] nm Afghanistan
**afianzar** [afjan'θar] /1f/ vt to strengthen, secure; **afianzarse** vr to become established
**afiche** [a'fitʃe] nm (LAM) poster
**afición** [afi'θjon] nf: ~ a fondness o liking for; **la** ~ the fans pl; **pinto por** ~ I paint as a hobby; **aficionado, -a** adj keen, enthusiastic; (no profesional) amateur ▷ nm/f enthusiast, fan; amateur; **ser aficionado a algo** to be very keen on o fond of sth
**aficionar** [afiθjo'nar] /1a/ vt: ~ a algn a algo to make sb like sth; **aficionarse** vr: ~se a algo to grow fond of sth
**afilado, -a** [afi'laðo, a] adj sharp
**afilar** [afi'lar] /1a/ vt to sharpen
**afiliarse** [afi'ljarse] /1b/ vr to affiliate
**afín** [a'fin] adj (parecido) similar; (conexo) related
**afinar** [afi'nar] /1a/ vt (Tec) to refine; (Mus) to tune ▷ vi (tocar) to play in tune; (cantar) to sing in tune
**afincarse** [afin'karse] /1g/ vr to settle
**afinidad** [afini'ðað] nf affinity; (parentesco) relationship; **por** ~ by marriage
**afirmación** [afirma'θjon] nf affirmation
**afirmar** [afir'mar] /1a/ vt to affirm, state; **afirmativo, -a** adj affirmative
**afligir** [afli'xir] /3c/ vt to afflict; (apenar) to distress

**aflojar** [aflo'xar] /1a/ vt to slacken;
(desatar) to loosen, undo; (relajar) to relax
▷ vi to drop; (bajar) to go down; **aflojarse**
vr to relax

**afluente** [aflu'ente] adj flowing ▷ nm (Geo)
tributary

**afmo., -a.** abr (= afectísimo/a suyo/a) Yours

**afónico, -a** [a'foniko, a] adj: **estar ~** to
have a sore throat; to have lost one's voice

**aforo** [a'foro] nm (de teatro etc) capacity

**afortunado, -a** [afortu'naðo, a] adj
fortunate, lucky

**África** ['afrika] nf Africa; **~ del Sur** South
Africa; **africano, -a** adj, nm/f African

**afrontar** [afron'tar] /1a/ vt to confront;
(poner cara a cara) to bring face to face

**afrutado, -a** [afru'taðo, a] adj fruity

**after** ['after] nm, **afterhours** ['afterauars]
nm inv after-hours club

**afuera** [a'fwera] adv out, outside; **afueras**
nfpl outskirts

**agachar** [aɣa'tʃar] /1a/ vt to bend, bow;
**agacharse** vr to stoop, bend

**agalla** [a'ɣaʎa] nf (Zool) gill; **tener ~s** (fam)
to have guts

**agarradera** [aɣarra'ðera] nf (LAM),
**agarradero** [aɣarra'ðero] nm handle

**agarrado, -a** [aɣa'rraðo, a] adj mean,
stingy

**agarrar** [aɣa'rrar] /1a/ vt to grasp, grab;
(LAM: tomar) to take, catch; (recoger) to pick
up ▷ vi (planta) to take root; **agarrarse** vr to
hold on (tightly)

**agencia** [a'xenθja] nf agency; **~ de
créditos/publicidad/viajes** credit/
advertising/travel agency; **~ inmobiliaria**
estate agent's (office) (BRIT), real estate
office (US)

**agenciar** [axen'θjar] /1b/ vt to bring about;
**agenciarse** vr to look after o.s.; **~se algo** to
get hold of sth

**agenda** [a'xenda] nf diary; **~ electrónica**
PDA

⬛ No confundir agenda con la palabra
inglesa agenda.

**agente** [a'xente] nmf agent; (tb: **~ de
policía**) police officer; **~ de seguros**
insurance broker; **~ de tránsito** (LAM) traffic
cop; **~ inmobiliario** estate agent (BRIT),
realtor (US)

**ágil** ['axil] adj agile, nimble; **agilidad** nf
agility, nimbleness

**agilizar** [axili'θar] /1f/ vt (trámites) to
speed up

**agiotista** [axjo'tista] (LAM) nmf (usurero)
usurer

**agitación** [axita'θjon] nf (de mano etc)
shaking, waving; (de líquido etc) stirring;
agitation

**agitado, -a** [axi'aðo, a] adj hectic; (viaje)
bumpy

**agitar** [axi'tar] /1a/ vt to wave, shake;
(líquido) to stir; (fig) to stir up, excite;
**agitarse** vr to get excited; (inquietarse) to
get worried o upset

**aglomeración** [aɣlomera'θjon] nf: **~ de
tráfico/gente** traffic jam/mass of people

**agnóstico, -a** [aɣ'nostiko, a] adj, nm/f
agnostic

**agobiar** [aɣo'βjar] /1b/ vt to weigh down;
(oprimir) to oppress; (cargar) to burden

**agolparse** [aɣol'parse] /1a/ vr to crowd
together

**agonía** [aɣo'nia] nf death throes pl; (fig)
agony, anguish

**agonizante** [aɣoni'θante] adj dying

**agonizar** [aɣoni'θar] /1f/ vi to be dying

**agosto** [a'ɣosto] nm August

**agotado, -a** [aɣo'taðo, a] adj (persona)
exhausted; (acabado) finished; (Com) sold
out; (: libros) out of print; **agotador, a** adj
exhausting

**agotamiento** [aɣota'mjento] nm
exhaustion

**agotar** [aɣo'tar] /1a/ vt to exhaust;
(consumir) to drain; (recursos) to use up,
deplete; **agotarse** vr to be exhausted;
(acabarse) to run out; (libro) to go out of
print

**agraciado, -a** [aɣra'θjaðo, a] adj (atractivo)
attractive; (en sorteo etc) lucky

**agradable** [aɣra'ðaβle] adj pleasant, nice

**agradar** [aɣra'ðar] /1a/ vt, vi to please; **él
me agrada** I like him

**agradecer** [aɣraðe'θer] /2d/ vt to thank;
(favor etc) to be grateful for; **agradecido, -a**
adj grateful; **¡muy agradecido!** thanks a lot!;
**agradecimiento** nm thanks pl; gratitude

**agradezca** etc [aɣra'ðeθka] vb V **agradecer**

**agrado** [a'ɣraðo] nm: **ser de tu** etc **~** to be to
your etc liking

**agrandar** [aɣran'dar] /1a/ vt to enlarge;
(fig) to exaggerate; **agrandarse** vr to get
bigger

**agrario, -a** [a'ɣrarjo, a] adj agrarian, land
cpd; (política) agricultural, farming cpd

**agravante** [aɣra'βante] adj aggravating
▷ nm o f: **con el** or **la ~ de que ...** with the
further difficulty that ...

**agravar** [aɣra'βar] /1a/ vt (pesar sobre)
to make heavier; (irritar) to aggravate;
**agravarse** vr to worsen, get worse

**agraviar** [aɣra'βjar] /1b/ vt to offend; (ser
injusto con) to wrong

**agredir** [aɣre'ðir] /3a/ vt to attack

**agregado** [aɣre'ɣaðo] nm aggregate;
(persona) attaché; **A~** ≈ teacher (who is not
head of department)

**agregar** [aɣre'ɣar] /1h/ vt to gather; (añadir) to add; (persona) to appoint

**agresión** [aɣre'sjon] nf aggression

**agresivo, -a** [aɣre'siβo, a] adj aggressive

**agriar** [a'ɣrjar] vt to (turn) sour

**agrícola** [a'ɣrikola] adj farming cpd, agricultural

**agricultor, a** [aɣrikul'tor, a] nm/f farmer

**agricultura** [aɣrikul'tura] nf agriculture, farming

**agridulce** [aɣri'ðulθe] adj bittersweet; (Culin) sweet and sour

**agrietarse** [aɣrje'tarse] /1a/ vr to crack; (la piel) to chap

**agrio, -a** ['aɣrjo, a] adj bitter

**agrupación** [aɣrupa'θjon] nf group; (acto) grouping

**agrupar** [aɣru'par] /1a/ vt to group

**agua** ['aɣwa] nf water; (Naut) wake; (Arq) slope of a roof; **aguas** nfpl (Med) water sg, urine sg; (Naut) waters; **~s abajo/arriba** downstream/upstream; **~ bendita/ destilada/potable** holy/distilled/drinking water; **~ caliente** hot water; **~ corriente** running water; **~ de colonia** eau de cologne; **~ mineral (con/sin gas)** (fizzy/ non-fizzy) mineral water; **~ oxigenada** hydrogen peroxide; **~s jurisdiccionales** territorial waters

**aguacate** [aɣwa'kate] nm avocado (pear)

**aguacero** [aɣwa'θero] nm (heavy) shower, downpour

**aguado, -a** [a'ɣwaðo, a] adj watery, watered down

**aguafiestas** [aɣwa'fjestas] nm inv, nf inv spoilsport

**aguamiel** [aɣwa'mjel] (LAM) nf fermented maguey o agave juice

**aguanieve** [aɣwa'njeβe] nf sleet

**aguantar** [aɣwan'tar] /1a/ vt to bear, put up with; (sostener) to hold up ▷ vi to last; **aguantarse** vr to restrain o.s.; **aguante** nm (paciencia) patience; (resistencia) endurance

**aguar** [a'ɣwar] /1i/ vt to water down

**aguardar** [aɣwar'ðar] /1a/ vt to wait for

**aguardiente** [aɣwar'ðjente] nm brandy, liquor

**aguarrás** [aɣwa'rras] nm turpentine

**aguaviva** [aɣwa'βiβa] (RPL) nf jellyfish

**agudeza** [aɣu'ðeθa] nf sharpness; (ingenio) wit

**agudo, -a** [a'ɣuðo, a] adj sharp; (voz) high-pitched, piercing; (dolor, enfermedad) acute

**agüero** [a'ɣwero] nm: **buen/mal ~** good/ bad omen

**aguijón** [aɣi'xon] nm sting; (fig) spur

**águila** ['aɣila] nf eagle; (fig) genius

**aguileño, -a** [aɣi'leɲo, a] adj (nariz) aquiline; (rostro) sharp-featured

**aguinaldo** [aɣi'naldo] nm Christmas box

**aguja** [a'ɣuxa] nf needle; (de reloj) hand; (Arq) spire; (Tec) firing-pin; **agujas** nfpl (Zool) ribs; (Ferro) points

**agujerear** [aɣuxere'ar] /1a/ vt to make holes in

**agujero** [aɣu'xero] nm hole

**agujetas** [aɣu'xetas] nfpl stitch sg; (rigidez) stiffness sg

**ahí** [a'i] adv there; (allá) over there; **de ~ que** so that, with the result that; **~ llega** here he comes; **por ~** that way; **200 o por ~** 200 or so

**ahijado, -a** [ai'xaðo, a] nm/f godson/ daughter

**ahogar** [ao'ɣar] /1h/ vt to drown; (asfixiar) to suffocate, smother; (fuego) to put out; **ahogarse** vr (en agua) to drown; (por asfixia) to suffocate

**ahogo** [a'oɣo] nm breathlessness; (económico) financial difficulty

**ahondar** [aon'dar] /1a/ vt to deepen, make deeper; (fig) to study thoroughly ▷ vi: **~ en** to study thoroughly

**ahora** [a'ora] adv now; (hace poco) a moment ago, just now; (dentro de poco) in a moment; **~ voy** I'm coming; **~ mismo** right now; **~ bien** now then; **por ~** for the present

**ahorcar** [aor'kar] /1g/ vt to hang

**ahorita** [ao'rita] adv (esp LAM fam: en este momento) right now; (hace poco) just now; (dentro de poco) in a minute

**ahorrar** [ao'rrar] /1a/ vt (dinero) to save; (esfuerzos) to save, avoid; **ahorro** nm (acto) saving; **ahorros** nmpl (dinero) savings

**ahuecar** [awe'kar] /1g/ vt to hollow (out); (voz) to deepen; **ahuecarse** vr to give o.s. airs

**ahumar** [au'mar] /1a/ vt to smoke, cure; (llenar de humo) to fill with smoke ▷ vi to smoke; **ahumarse** vr to fill with smoke

**ahuyentar** [aujen'tar] /1a/ vt to drive off, frighten off; (fig) to dispel

**aire** ['aire] nm air; (viento) wind; (corriente) draught; (Mus) tune; **al ~ libre** in the open air; **~ aclimatizado** o **acondicionado** air conditioning; **airear** /1a/ vt to air; **airearse** vr to get some fresh air; **airoso, -a** adj windy; draughty; (fig) graceful

**aislado, -a** [ais'laðo, a] adj isolated; (incomunicado) cut off; (Elec) insulated

**aislar** [ais'lar] /1a/ vt to isolate; (Elec) to insulate

**ajardinado, -a** [axarði'naðo, a] adj landscaped

**ajedrez** [axe'ðreθ] nm chess

**ajeno, -a** [a'xeno, a] adj (que pertenece a otro) somebody else's; **~ a** foreign to

**ajetreado, -a** [axetre'aðo, a] adj busy

**ajetreo** [axe'treo] nm bustle

**ají** [a'xi] nm chil(l)i, red pepper; (salsa) chil(l)i sauce

**ajillo** [a'xiʎo] nm: **gambas al ~** garlic prawns

**ajo** ['axo] nm garlic

**ajuar** [a'xwar] nm household furnishings pl; (de novia) trousseau; (de niño) layette

**ajustado, -a** [axus'taðo, a] adj (tornillo) tight; (cálculo) right; (ropa) tight(-fitting); (resultado) close

**ajustar** [axus'tar] /1a/ vt (adaptar) to adjust; (encajar) to fit; (Tec) to engage; (Tip) to make up; (apretar) to tighten; (concertar) to agree (on); (reconciliar) to reconcile; (cuenta, deudas) to settle ▷ vi to fit; **ajustarse** vr: **~se a** (precio etc) to be in keeping with, fit in with; **~ las cuentas a algn** to get even with sb

**ajuste** [a'xuste] nm adjustment; (Costura) fitting; (acuerdo) compromise; (de cuenta) settlement

**al** [al] = **a + el**; V **a**

**ala** ['ala] nf wing; (de sombrero) brim; (futbolista) winger; **~ delta** hang-glider

**alabanza** [ala'βanθa] nf praise

**alabar** [ala'βar] /1a/ vt to praise

**alacena** [ala'θena] nf cupboard (BRIT), closet (US)

**alacrán** [ala'kran] nm scorpion

**alambrada** [alam'braða] nm wire fence; (red) wire netting

**alambre** [a'lambre] nm wire; **~ de púas** barbed wire

**alameda** [ala'meða] nf (plantío) poplar grove; (lugar de paseo) avenue, boulevard

**álamo** ['alamo] nm poplar

**alarde** [a'larðe] nm show, display; **hacer ~ de** to boast of

**alargador** [alarɣa'ðor] nm extension cable o lead

**alargar** [alar'ɣar] /1h/ vt to lengthen, extend; (paso) to hasten; (brazo) to stretch out; (cuerda) to pay out; (conversación) to spin out; **alargarse** vr to get longer

**alarma** [a'larma] nf alarm; **~ de incendios** fire alarm; **alarmante** adj alarming; **alarmar** /1a/ vt to alarm; **alarmarse** vr to get alarmed

**alba** ['alβa] nf dawn

**albahaca** [al'βaka] nf (Bot) basil

**Albania** [al'βanja] nf Albania

**albañil** [alβa'ɲil] nm bricklayer; (cantero) mason

**albarán** [alβa'ran] nm (Com) delivery note, invoice

**albaricoque** [alβari'koke] nm apricot

**albedrío** [alβe'ðrio] nm: **libre ~** free will

**alberca** [al'βerka] nf reservoir; (LAM) swimming pool

**albergar** [alβer'ɣar] /1h/ vt to shelter

**albergue** [al'βerɣe] vb V **albergar** ▷ nm shelter, refuge; **~ juvenil** youth hostel

**albóndiga** [al'βondiɣa] nf meatball

**albornoz** [alβor'noθ] nm (de los árabes) burnous; (para el baño) bathrobe

**alborotar** [alβoro'tar] /1a/ vi to make a row ▷ vt to agitate, stir up; **alborotarse** vr to get excited; (mar) to get rough; **alboroto** nm row, uproar

**álbum** ['alβum] (pl **álbums** o **álbumes**) nm album; **~ de recortes** scrapbook

**albur** [al'βur] (LAM) nm (juego de palabras) pun; (doble sentido) double entendre

**alcachofa** [alka'tʃofa] nf (globe) artichoke

**alcalde, -esa** [al'kalde, alkal'desa] nm/f mayor(ess)

**alcaldía** [alkal'dia] nf mayoralty; (lugar) mayor's office

**alcance** [al'kanθe] vb V **alcanzar** ▷ nm (Mil, Radio) range; (fig) scope; (Com) adverse balance; **estar al/fuera del ~ de algn** to be within/beyond sb's reach

**alcancía** [alkan'θia] (LAM) nf (para ahorrar) money box; (para colectas) collection box

**alcantarilla** [alkanta'riʎa] nf (de aguas cloacales) sewer; (en la calle) gutter

**alcanzar** [alkan'θar] /1f/ vt (algo: con la mano, el pie) to reach; (alguien: en el camino etc) to catch up (with); (autobús) to catch; (bala) to hit, strike ▷ vi (ser suficiente) to be enough; **~ a hacer** to manage to do

**alcaparra** [alka'parra] nf (Bot) caper

**alcayata** [alka'jata] nf hook

**alcázar** [al'kaθar] nm fortress; (Naut) quarter-deck

**alcoba** [al'koβa] nf bedroom

**alcohol** [al'kol] nm alcohol; **~ metílico** methylated spirits pl (BRIT), wood alcohol (US); **alcohólico, -a** adj, nm/f alcoholic; **alcoholímetro** nm Breathalyser®, drunkometer (US); **alcoholismo** nm alcoholism

**alcornoque** [alkor'noke] nm cork tree; (fam) idiot

**aldea** [al'dea] nf village; **aldeano, -a** adj village cpd ▷ nm/f villager

**aleación** [alea'θjon] nf alloy

**aleatorio, -a** [alea'torjo, a] adj random

**aleccionar** [alekθjo'nar] /1a/ vt to instruct; (adiestrar) to train

**alegar** [ale'ɣar] /1h/ vt (dificultad etc) to plead; (Jur) to allege ▷ vi (LAM) to argue

**alegoría** [aleɣo'ria] nf allegory

**alegrar** [ale'ɣrar] /1a/ vt (causar alegría) to cheer (up); (fuego) to poke; (fiesta) to liven up; **alegrarse** vr (fam) to get merry o tight; **~se de** to be glad about

**alegre** [a'leɣre] adj happy, cheerful; (fam) merry, tight; (chiste) risqué, blue; **alegría** nf happiness; merriment

**alejar** [ale'xar] /1a/ vt to move away, remove; (fig) to estrange; **alejarse** vr to move away

**alemán, -ana** [ale'man, ana] adj, nm/f German ▷ nm (lengua) German

**Alemania** [ale'manja] nf Germany

**alentador, a** [alenta'ðor, a] adj encouraging

**alentar** [alen'tar] /1j/ vt to encourage

**alergia** [a'lerxja] nf allergy

**alero** [a'lero] nm (de tejado) eaves pl; (Auto) mudguard

**alerta** [a'lerta] adj inv, nm alert

**aleta** [a'leta] nf (de pez) fin; (de ave) wing; (de foca, Deporte) flipper; (de coche) mudguard

**aletear** [alete'ar] /1a/ vi to flutter

**alevín** [ale'βin] nm fry, young fish

**alevosía** [aleβo'sia] nf treachery

**alfabeto** [alfa'βeto] nm alphabet

**alfalfa** [al'falfa] nf alfalfa, lucerne

**alfarería** [alfare'ria] nf pottery; (tienda) pottery shop; **alfarero, -a** nm/f potter

**alféizar** [al'feiθar] nm window-sill

**alférez** [al'fereθ] nm (Mil) second lieutenant; (Naut) ensign

**alfil** [al'fil] nm (Ajedrez) bishop

**alfiler** [alfi'ler] nm pin; (broche) clip

**alfombra** [al'fombra] nf carpet; (más pequeña) rug; **alfombrilla** nf rug, mat; (Inform) mouse mat o pad

**alforja** [al'forxa] nf saddlebag

**algas** ['alɣas] nfpl seaweed sg

**álgebra** ['alxeβra] nf algebra

**algo** ['alɣo] pron something; (en frases interrogativas) anything ▷ adv somewhat, rather; **¿~ más?** anything else?; (en tienda) is that all?; **por ~ será** there must be some reason for it

**algodón** [alɣo'ðon] nm cotton; (planta) cotton plant; **~ de azúcar** candy floss (BRIT), cotton candy (US); **~ hidrófilo** cotton wool (BRIT), absorbent cotton (US)

**alguien** ['alɣjen] pron someone, somebody; (en frases interrogativas) anyone, anybody

**alguno, -a** [al'ɣuno, a] adj some; (después de n): **no tiene talento ~** he has no talent, he doesn't have any talent ▷ pron (alguien) someone, somebody; **algún que otro libro** some book or other; **algún día iré** I'll go one o some day; **sin interés ~** without the slightest interest; **~ que otro** an occasional one; **~s piensan** some (people) think

**alhaja** [a'laxa] nf jewel; (tesoro) precious object, treasure

**alhelí** [ale'li] nm wallflower, stock

**aliado, -a** [a'ljaðo, a] adj allied

**alianza** [a'ljanθa] nf alliance; (anillo) wedding ring

**aliar** [a'ljar] /1c/ vt to ally; **aliarse** vr to form an alliance

**alias** ['aljas] adv alias

**alicatado** [alika'taðo] (ESP) nm tiling

**alicate** [ali'kate] nm, **alicates** [ali'kates] nmpl pliers pl

**aliciente** [ali'θjente] nm incentive; (atracción) attraction

**alienación** [aljena'θjon] nf alienation

**aliento** [a'ljento] nm breath; (respiración) breathing; **sin ~** breathless

**aligerar** [alixe'rar] /1a/ vt to lighten; (reducir) to shorten; (aliviar) to alleviate; (mitigar) to ease; (paso) to quicken

**alijo** [a'lixo] nm (Naut: descarga) unloading

**alimaña** [ali'maɲa] nf pest

**alimentación** [alimenta'θjon] nf (comida) food; (acción) feeding; (tienda) grocer's (shop)

**alimentar** [alimen'tar] /1a/ vt to feed; (nutrir) to nourish; **alimentarse** vr: **~se (de)** to feed (on)

**alimenticio, -a** [alimen'tiθjo, a] adj food cpd; (nutritivo) nourishing, nutritious

**alimento** [ali'mento] nm food; (nutrición) nourishment

**alineación** [alinea'θjon] nf alignment; (Deporte) line-up

**alinear** [aline'ar] /1a/ vt to align; (Deporte) to select, pick; **alinearse**

**aliñar** [ali'ɲar] /1a/ vt (Culin) to dress; **aliño** nm (Culin) dressing

**alioli** [ali'oli] nm garlic mayonnaise

**alisar** [ali'sar] /1a/ vt to smooth

**alistar** [ali'star] /1a/ vt to recruit; **alistarse** vr to enlist; (inscribirse) to enrol

**aliviar** [ali'βjar] /1b/ vt (carga) to lighten; (persona) to relieve; (dolor) to relieve, alleviate

**alivio** [a'liβjo] nm alleviation, relief

**aljibe** [al'xiβe] nm cistern

**allá** [a'ʎa] adv (lugar) there; (por ahí) over there; (tiempo) then; **~ abajo** down there; **más ~** further on; **más ~ de** beyond; **¡~ tú!** that's your problem!

**allanamiento** [aʎana'mjento] nm (LAM Policía) raid, search; **~ de morada** breaking and entering

**allanar** [aʎa'nar] /1a/ vt to flatten, level (out); (igualar) to smooth (out); (fig) to subdue; (Jur) to burgle, break into

**allegado, -a** [aʎe'ɣaðo, a] adj near, close ▷ nm/f relation

**allí** [a'ʎi] adv there; **~ mismo** right there; **por ~** over there; (por ese camino) that way

**alma** ['alma] nf soul; (persona) person

**almacén** [alma'θen] nm (depósito) warehouse, store; (Mil) magazine; (LAM) grocer's shop, food store, grocery store (US); **(grandes) almacenes** nmpl department store sg; **almacenaje** nm storage

**almacenar** [almaθe'nar] /1a/ vt to store, put in storage; (proveerse) to stock up with

**almanaque** [alma'nake] nm almanac

**almeja** [al'mexa] nf clam

**almendra** [al'mendra] nf almond; **almendro** nm almond tree

**almíbar** [al'miβar] nm syrup

**almidón** [almi'ðon] nm starch

**almirante** [almi'rante] nm admiral

**almohada** [almo'aða] nf pillow; (funda) pillowcase; **almohadilla** nf cushion; (Tec) pad; (LAM) pincushion

**almohadón** [almoa'ðon] nm large pillow

**almorranas** [almo'rranas] nfpl piles, haemorrhoids (BRIT), hemorrhoids (US)

**almorzar** [almor'θar] /1f, 1l/ vt: ~ **una tortilla** to have an omelette for lunch ▷ vi to (have) lunch

**almuerzo** [al'mwerθo] vb V **almorzar** ▷ nm lunch

**alocado, -a** [alo'kaðo, a] adj crazy

**alojamiento** [aloxa'mjento] nm lodging(s) (pl); (viviendas) housing

**alojar** [alo'xar] /1a/ vt to lodge; **alojarse** vr: ~**se en** to stay at; (bala) to lodge in

**alondra** [a'londra] nf lark, skylark

**alpargata** [alpar'ɣata] nf rope-soled shoe, espadrille

**Alpes** ['alpes] nmpl: **los** ~ the Alps

**alpinismo** [alpi'nismo] nm mountaineering, climbing; **alpinista** nmf mountaineer, climber

**alpiste** [al'piste] nm birdseed

**alquilar** [alki'lar] /1a/ vt (propietario, inmuebles) to let, rent (out); (coche) to hire out; (TV) to rent (out); (alquilador, inmuebles, TV) to rent; (coche) to hire; **"se alquila casa"** "house to let (BRIT) o for rent (US)"

**alquiler** [alki'ler] nm renting; letting; hiring; (arriendo) rent; hire charge; **de** ~ for hire; ~ **de automóviles** car hire

**alquimia** [al'kimja] nf alchemy

**alquitrán** [alki'tran] nm tar

**alrededor** [alreðe'ðor] adv around, about; **alrededores** nmpl surroundings; ~ **de** around, about; **mirar a su** ~ to look (round) about one

**alta** ['alta] nf (certificate of) discharge

**altar** [al'tar] nm altar

**altavoz** [alta'βoθ] nm loudspeaker; (amplificador) amplifier

**alteración** [altera'θjon] nf alteration; (alboroto) disturbance

**alterar** [alte'rar] /1a/ vt to alter; to disturb; **alterarse** vr (persona) to get upset

**altercado** [alter'kaðo] nm argument

**alternar** [alter'nar] /1a/ vt to alternate ▷ vi to alternate; (turnar) to take turns; **alternarse** vr to alternate; (turnar) to take turns; ~ **con** to mix with; **alternativo, -a** adj alternative; (alterno) alternating ▷ nf alternative; (elección) choice; **alterno, -a** adj alternate; (Elec) alternating

**Alteza** [al'teθa] nf (tratamiento) Highness

**altibajos** [alti'βaxos] nmpl ups and downs

**altiplanicie** [altipla'niθje] nf, **altiplano** [alti'plano] nm high plateau

**altisonante** [altiso'nante] adj high-flown, high-sounding

**altitud** [alti'tuð] nf height; (Aviat, Geo) altitude

**altivo, -a** [al'tiβo, a] adj haughty, arrogant

**alto, -a** ['alto, a] adj high; (persona) tall; (sonido) high, sharp; (noble) high, lofty ▷ nm halt; (Mus) alto; (Geo) hill ▷ adv (estar) high; (hablar) loud, loudly ▷ excl halt!; **la pared tiene dos metros de** ~ the wall is two metres high; **en alta mar** on the high seas; **en voz alta** in a loud voice; **las altas horas de la noche** the small (BRIT) o wee (US) hours; **en lo** ~ **de** at the top of; **pasar por** ~ to overlook; **altoparlante** nm (LAM) loudspeaker

**altura** [al'tura] nf height; (Naut) depth; (Geo) latitude; **la pared tiene 1.80 de** ~ the wall is 1 metre 80 (cm) high; **a estas** ~**s** at this stage; **a esta** ~ **del año** at this time of the year

**alubia** [a'luβja] nf bean; (judía verde) French bean; (judía blanca) cannellini bean

**alucinación** [aluθina'θjon] nf hallucination

**alucinar** [aluθi'nar] /1a/ vi to hallucinate ▷ vt to deceive; (fascinar) to fascinate

**alud** [a'luð] nm avalanche; (fig) flood

**aludir** [alu'ðir] /3a/ vi: ~ **a** to allude to; **darse por aludido** to take the hint

**alumbrado** [alum'braðo] nm lighting

**alumbrar** [alum'brar] /1a/ vt to light (up) ▷ vi (Med) to give birth

**aluminio** [alu'minjo] nm aluminium (BRIT), aluminum (US)

**alumno, -a** [a'lumno, a] nm/f pupil, student

**alusión** [alu'sjon] nf allusion

**alusivo, -a** [alu'siβo, a] adj allusive

**aluvión** [alu'βjon] nm (Geo) alluvium; (fig) flood

**alverja** [al'βerxa] (LAM) nf pea

**alza** ['alθa] nf rise; (Mil) sight

**alzamiento** [alθa'mjento] nm (rebelión) rising

**alzar** [al'θar] /1f/ vt to lift (up); (precio, muro) to raise; (cuello de abrigo) to turn up; (Agr) to gather in; (Tip) to gather; **alzarse** vr to get up, rise; (rebelarse) to revolt; (Com) to go fraudulently bankrupt; (Jur) to appeal

**ama** ['ama] nf lady of the house; (dueña) owner; (institutriz) governess; (madre adoptiva) foster mother; **~ de casa** housewife; **~ de llaves** housekeeper

**amabilidad** [amaβili'ðað] nf kindness; (simpatía) niceness; **amable** adj kind; nice; **es usted muy amable** that's very kind of you

**amaestrado, -a** [amaes'traðo, a] adj (en circo etc) performing

**amaestrar** [amaes'trar] /1a/ vt to train

**amago** [a'maɣo] nm threat; (gesto) threatening gesture; (Med) symptom

**amainar** [amai'nar] /1a/ vi (viento) to die down

**amamantar** [amaman'tar] /1a/ vt to suckle, nurse

**amanecer** [amane'θer] /2d/ vi to dawn ▷ nm dawn; **~ afiebrado** to wake up with a fever

**amanerado, -a** [amane'raðo, a] adj affected

**amante** [a'mante] adj: **~ de** fond of ▷ nmf lover

**amapola** [ama'pola] nf poppy

**amar** [a'mar] /1a/ vt to love

**amargado, -a** [amar'ɣaðo, a] adj bitter

**amargar** [amar'ɣar] /1h/ vt to make bitter; (fig) to embitter; **amargarse** vr to become embittered

**amargo, -a** [a'marɣo, a] adj bitter

**amarillento, -a** [amari'ʎento, a] adj yellowish; (tez) sallow

**amarillo, -a** [ama'riʎo, a] adj, nm yellow

**amarra** [a'marra] nf (Naut) mooring line; **amarras** nfpl: **soltar ~s** (Naut) to set sail

**amarrado, -a** [ama'rraðo, a] adj (LAM) (fam) mean, stingy

**amarrar** [ama'rrar] /1a/ vt to moor; (sujetar) to tie up

**amasar** [ama'sar] /1a/ vt (masa) to knead; (mezclar) to mix, prepare; (confeccionar) to concoct

**amateur** ['amatur] nmf amateur

**amazona** [ama'θona] nf horsewoman; **Amazonas** nm: **el (río) Amazonas** the Amazon

**ámbar** ['ambar] nm amber

**ambición** [ambi'θjon] nf ambition; **ambicionar** /1a/ vt to aspire to; **ambicioso, -a** adj ambitious

**ambidextro, -a** [ambi'ðekstro, a] adj ambidextrous

**ambientación** [ambjenta'θjon] nf (Cine, Lit etc) setting; (Radio etc) sound effects pl

**ambiente** [am'bjente] nm atmosphere; (medio) environment

**ambigüedad** [ambiɣwe'ðað] nf ambiguity; **ambiguo, -a** adj ambiguous

**ámbito** ['ambito] nm (campo) field; (fig) scope

**ambos, -as** ['ambos, as] adj pl, pron pl both

**ambulancia** [ambu'lanθja] nf ambulance

**ambulante** [ambu'lante] adj travelling, itinerant

**ambulatorio** [ambula'torio] nm state health-service clinic

**amén** [a'men] excl amen; **~ de** besides

**amenaza** [ame'naθa] nf threat; **amenazar** /1f/ vt to threaten ▷ vi: **amenazar con hacer** to threaten to do

**ameno, -a** [a'meno, a] adj pleasant

**América** [a'merika] nf America; **~ del Norte/del Sur** North/South America; **~ Central/Latina** Central/Latin America; **americano, -a** adj, nm/f American; Latin o South American

**ametralladora** [ametraʎa'ðora] nf machine gun

**amigable** [ami'ɣaβle] adj friendly

**amígdala** [a'miɣðala] nf tonsil; **amigdalitis** nf tonsillitis

**amigo, -a** [a'miɣo, a] adj friendly ▷ nm/f friend; (amante) lover; **ser ~ de** to like, be fond of

**aminorar** [amino'rar] /1a/ vt to diminish; (reducir) to reduce; **~ la marcha** to slow down

**amistad** [amis'tað] nf friendship; **amistades** nfpl (amigos) friends; **amistoso, -a** adj friendly

**amnesia** [am'nesja] nf amnesia

**amnistía** [amnis'tia] nf amnesty

**amo** ['amo] nm owner; (jefe) boss

**amolar** [amo'lar] /1l/ vt to annoy; (MÉX fam) to ruin, damage

**amoldar** [amol'dar] /1a/ vt to mould; (adaptar) to adapt

**amonestación** [amonesta'θjon] nf warning; **amonestaciones** nfpl marriage banns

**amonestar** [amones'tar] /1a/ vt to warn; (Rel) to publish the banns of

**amontonar** [amonto'nar] /1a/ vt to collect, pile up; **amontonarse** vr to crowd together; (acumularse) to pile up

**amor** [a'mor] nm love; (amante) lover; **hacer el ~ to** make love; **~ propio** self-respect

**amoratado, -a** [amora'taðo, a] adj purple

**amordazar** [amorða'θar] /1f/ vt to muzzle; (fig) to gag

**amorfo, -a** [a'morfo, a] adj amorphous, shapeless

**amoroso, -a** [amoˈroso, a] *adj* affectionate, loving

**amortiguador** [amortiɣwaˈðor] *nm* shock absorber; (*parachoques*) bumper; **amortiguadores** *nmpl* (*Auto*) suspension *sg*

**amortiguar** [amortiˈɣwar] /1i/ *vt* to deaden; (*ruido*) to muffle; (*color*) to soften

**amotinar** [amotiˈnar] /1a/ *vt* to stir up, incite (to riot); **amotinarse** *vr* to mutiny

**amparar** [ampaˈrar] /1a/ *vt* to protect; **ampararse** *vr* to seek protection; (*de la lluvia etc*) to shelter; **amparo** *nm* help, protection; **al amparo de** under the protection of

**amperio** [amˈperjo] *nm* ampère, amp

**ampliación** [ampljaˈθjon] *nf* enlargement; (*extensión*) extension

**ampliar** [amˈpljar] /1c/ *vt* to enlarge; to extend

**amplificador** [amplifikaˈðor] *nm* amplifier

**amplificar** [amplifiˈkar] /1g/ *vt* to amplify

**amplio, -a** [ˈampljo, a] *adj* spacious; (*falda etc*) full; (*extenso*) extensive; (*ancho*) wide; **amplitud** *nf* spaciousness; extent; (*fig*) amplitude

**ampolla** [amˈpoʎa] *nf* blister; (*Med*) ampoule

**amputar** [ampuˈtar] /1a/ *vt* to cut off, amputate

**amueblar** [amweˈβlar] /1a/ *vt* to furnish

**anales** [aˈnales] *nmpl* annals

**analfabetismo** [analfaβeˈtismo] *nm* illiteracy; **analfabeto, -a** *adj*, *nm/f* illiterate

**analgésico** [analˈxesiko] *nm* painkiller, analgesic

**análisis** [aˈnalisis] *nm inv* analysis

**analista** [anaˈlista] *nmf* (*gen*) analyst

**analizar** [analiˈθar] /1f/ *vt* to analyse

**analógico, -a** [anaˈloxiko, a] *adj* (*Inform*) analog; (*reloj*) analogue (BRIT), analog (US)

**análogo, -a** [aˈnaloɣo, a] *adj* analogous, similar

**ananá** [anaˈna] *nm* pineapple

**anarquía** [anarˈkia] *nf* anarchy; **anarquista** *nmf* anarchist

**anatomía** [anatoˈmia] *nf* anatomy

**anca** [ˈanka] *nf* rump, haunch; **ancas** *nfpl* (*fam*) behind *sg*

**ancho, -a** [ˈantʃo, a] *adj* wide; (*falda*) full; (*fig*) liberal ▷ *nm* width; (*Ferro*) gauge; **le viene muy ~ el cargo** (*fig*) the job is too much for him; **ponerse ~** to get conceited; **quedarse tan ~** to go on as if nothing had happened; **estar a sus anchas** to be at one's ease

**anchoa** [anˈtʃoa] *nf* anchovy

**anchura** [anˈtʃura] *nf* width; (*amplitud*) wideness

**anciano, -a** [anˈθjano, a] *adj* old, aged ▷ *nm/f* old man/woman ▷ *nm* elder

**ancla** [ˈankla] *nf* anchor

**Andalucía** [andaluˈθia] *nf* Andalusia; **andaluz, a** *adj*, *nm/f* Andalusian

**andamiaje** [andaˈmjaxe], **andamio** [anˈdamjo] *nm* scaffold(ing)

**andar** [anˈdar] /1p/ *vt* to go, cover, travel ▷ *vi* to go, walk, travel; (*funcionar*) to go, work; (*estar*) to be ▷ *nm* walk, gait, pace; **andarse** *vr* (*irse*) to go away o off; **~ a pie/a caballo/en bicicleta** to go on foot/on horseback/by bicycle; **¡anda!** (*sorpresa*) go on!; **anda en** o **por los 40** he's about 40; **~ haciendo algo** to be doing sth

**andén** [anˈden] *nm* (*Ferro*) platform; (*Naut*) quayside; (*LAM: acera*) pavement (BRIT), sidewalk (US)

**Andes** [ˈandes] *nmpl*: **los ~** the Andes

**andinismo** [andinˈismo] *nm* (LAM) mountaineering, climbing

**Andorra** [anˈdorra] *nf* Andorra

**andrajoso, -a** [andraˈxoso, a] *adj* ragged

**anduve** [anˈduβe] *vb V* **andar**

**anécdota** [aˈnekðota] *nf* anecdote, story

**anegar** [aneˈɣar] /1h/ *vt* to flood; (*ahogar*) to drown

**anemia** [aˈnemja] *nf* anaemia

**anestesia** [anesˈtesja] *nf* anaesthetic; **~ general/local** general/local anaesthetic

**anexar** [anekˈsar] /1a/ *vt* to annex; (*documento*) to attach; **anexión** [anekˈsjon] *nm* annexation; **anexo, -a** *adj* attached ▷ *nm* annexe

**anfibio, -a** [anˈfiβjo, a] *adj* amphibious ▷ *nm* amphibian

**anfiteatro** [anfiteˈatro] *nm* amphitheatre; (*Teat*) dress circle

**anfitrión, -ona** [anfiˈtrjon, ona] *nm/f* host(ess)

**ánfora** [ˈanfora] *nf* (*cántaro*) amphora; (LAM Pol) ballot box

**ángel** [ˈanxel] *nm* angel; **~ de la guarda** guardian angel

**angina** [anˈxina] *nf* (*Med*) inflammation of the throat; **~ de pecho** angina; **tener ~s** to have tonsillitis, have a sore throat

**anglicano, -a** [angliˈkano, a] *adj*, *nm/f* Anglican

**anglosajón, -ona** [anglosaˈxon, ˈxona] *adj* Anglo-Saxon

**anguila** [anˈgila] *nf* eel

**angula** [anˈgula] *nf* elver, baby eel

**ángulo** [ˈangulo] *nm* angle; (*esquina*) corner; (*curva*) bend

**angustia** [anˈgustja] *nf* anguish

**anhelar** [aneˈlar] /1a/ *vt* to be eager for; (*desear*) to long for, desire ▷ *vi* to pant, gasp; **anhelo** *nm* eagerness; desire

**anidar** [ani'ðar] /1a/ *vi* to nest

**anillo** [a'niʎo] *nm* ring; **~ de boda** wedding ring; **~ de compromiso** engagement ring

**animación** [anima'θjon] *nf* liveliness; (*vitalidad*) life; (*actividad*) bustle

**animado, -a** [ani'maðo, a] *adj* lively; (*vivaz*) animated; **animador, a** *nm/f* (*TV*) host(ess), compère ▷ *nf* (*Deporte*) cheerleader

**animal** [ani'mal] *adj* animal; (*fig*) stupid ▷ *nm* animal; (*fig*) fool; (*bestia*) brute

**animar** [ani'mar] /1a/ *vt* (*Bio*) to animate, give life to; (*fig*) to liven up, brighten up, cheer up; (*estimular*) to stimulate; **animarse** *vr* to cheer up, feel encouraged; (*decidirse*) to make up one's mind

**ánimo** ['animo] *nm* (*alma*) soul; (*mente*) mind; (*valentía*) courage ▷ *excl* cheer up!

**animoso, -a** [ani'moso, a] *adj* brave; (*vivo*) lively

**aniquilar** [aniki'lar] /1a/ *vt* to annihilate, destroy

**anís** [a'nis] *nm* aniseed; (*licor*) anisette

**aniversario** [aniβer'sarjo] *nm* anniversary

**anoche** [a'notʃe] *adv* last night; **antes de ~** the night before last

**anochecer** [anotʃe'θer] /2d/ *vi* to get dark ▷ *nm* nightfall, dark; **al ~** at nightfall

**anodino, -a** [ano'ðino, a] *adj* dull, anodyne

**anomalía** [anoma'lia] *nf* anomaly

**anonadado, -a** [anona'ðaðo, a] *adj*: **estar ~** to be stunned

**anonimato** [anoni'mato] *nm* anonymity

**anónimo, -a** [a'nonimo, a] *adj* anonymous; (*Com*) limited ▷ *nm* (*carta*) anonymous letter; (: *maliciosa*) poison-pen letter

**anormal** [anor'mal] *adj* abnormal

**anotación** [anota'θjon] *nf* note; annotation

**anotar** [ano'tar] /1a/ *vt* to note down; (*comentar*) to annotate

**ansia** ['ansja] *nf* anxiety; (*añoranza*) yearning; **ansiar** /1b/ *vt* to long for

**ansiedad** [ansje'ðað] *nf* anxiety

**ansioso, -a** [an'sjoso, a] *adj* anxious; (*anhelante*) eager; **~ de** o **por algo** greedy for sth

**antaño** [an'taɲo] *adv* in years gone by, long ago

**Antártico** [an'tartiko] *nm*: **el (océano) ~** the Antarctic (Ocean)

**ante** ['ante] *prep* before, in the presence of; (*encarado con*) faced with ▷ *nm* (*piel*) suede; **~ todo** above all

**anteanoche** [antea'notʃe] *adv* the night before last

**anteayer** [antea'jer] *adv* the day before yesterday

**antebrazo** [ante'βraθo] *nm* forearm

**antecedente** [anteθe'ðente] *adj* previous ▷ *nm* antecedent; **antecedentes** *nmpl* (*profesionales*) background *sg*; **~s penales** criminal record

**anteceder** [anteθe'ðer] /2a/ *vt* to precede, go before

**antecesor, a** [anteθe'sor, a] *nm/f* predecessor

**antelación** [antela'θjon] *nf*: **con ~** in advance

**antemano** [ante'mano]: **de ~** *adv* beforehand, in advance

**antena** [an'tena] *nf* antenna; (*de televisión etc*) aerial; **~ parabólica** satellite dish

**antenoche** [ante'notʃe] (*LAM*) *adv* the night before last

**anteojo** [ante'oxo] *nm* eyeglass; **anteojos** *nmpl* (*esp LAM*) glasses, spectacles

**antepasados** [antepa'saðos] *nmpl* ancestors

**anteponer** [antepo'ner] /2q/ *vt* to place in front; (*fig*) to prefer

**anterior** [ante'rjor] *adj* preceding, previous; **anterioridad** *nf*: **con anterioridad a** prior to, before

**antes** ['antes] *adv* (*con anterioridad*) before ▷ *prep*: **~ de** before ▷ *conj*: **~ (de) que** before; **~ bien** (but) rather; **dos días ~** two days before o previously; **no quiso venir ~** she didn't want to come any earlier; **tomo el avión ~ que el barco** I take the plane rather than the boat; **~ de** o **que nada** (*en el tiempo*) first of all; (*indicando preferencia*) above all; **~ que yo** before me; **lo ~ posible** as soon as possible; **cuanto ~ mejor** the sooner the better

**antibalas** [anti'βalas] *adj inv*: **chaleco ~** bulletproof jacket

**antibiótico** [anti'βjotiko] *nm* antibiotic

**anticaspa** [anti'kaspa] *adj inv* anti-dandruff *cpd*

**anticipación** [antiθipa'θjon] *nf* anticipation; **con 10 minutos de ~** 10 minutes early

**anticipado, -a** [antiθi'paðo, a] *adj* (in) advance; **por ~** in advance

**anticipar** [antiθi'par] /1a/ *vt* to anticipate; (*adelantar*) to bring forward; (*Com*) to advance; **anticiparse** *vr*: **~se a su época** to be ahead of one's time

**anticipo** [anti'θipo] *nm* (*Com*) advance

**anticonceptivo, -a** [antikonθep'tiβo, a] *adj*, *nm* contraceptive

**anticongelante** [antikonxe'lante] *nm* antifreeze

**anticuado, -a** [anti'kwaðo, a] *adj* out-of-date, old-fashioned; (*desusado*) obsolete

**anticuario** [anti'kwarjo] *nm* antique dealer

**anticuerpo** [anti'kwerpo] *nm (Med)* antibody

**antidepresivo** [antiðepre'siβo] *nm* antidepressant

**antidoping** [anti'ðopin] *adj inv*: **control ~** drugs test

**antídoto** [an'tiðoto] *nm* antidote

**antiestético, -a** [anties'tetiko, a] *adj* unsightly

**antifaz** [anti'faθ] *nm* mask; (*velo*) veil

**antiglobalización** [antiglobaliθa'θjon] *nf* anti-globalization; **antiglobalizador, a** *adj* anti-globalization *cpd*

**antiguamente** [antiɣwa'mente] *adv* formerly; (*hace mucho tiempo*) long ago

**antigüedad** [antiɣwe'ðað] *nf* antiquity; (*artículo*) antique; (*rango*) seniority

**antiguo, -a** [an'tiɣwo, a] *adj* old, ancient; (*que fue*) former

**Antillas** [an'tiʎas] *nfpl*: **las ~** the West Indies

**antílope** [an'tilope] *nm* antelope

**antinatural** [antinatu'ral] *adj* unnatural

**antipatía** [antipa'tia] *nf* antipathy, dislike; **antipático, -a** *adj* disagreeable, unpleasant

**antirrobo** [anti'rroβo] *adj inv (alarma etc)* anti-theft

**antisemita** [antise'mita] *adj* anti-Semitic ▷ *nmf* anti-Semite

**antiséptico, -a** [anti'septiko, a] *adj* antiseptic ▷ *nm* antiseptic

**antisistema** [antisis'tema] *adj inv* anticapitalist

**antivirus** [anti'birus] *nm inv (Inform)* antivirus program

**antojarse** [anto'xarse] /1a/ *vr (desear)*: **se me antoja comprarlo** I have a mind to buy it; (*pensar*): **se me antoja que ...** I have a feeling that ...

**antojo** [an'toxo] *nm* caprice, whim; (*rosa*) birthmark; (*lunar*) mole

**antología** [antolo'xia] *nf* anthology

**antorcha** [an'tortʃa] *nf* torch

**antro** ['antro] *nm* cavern

**antropología** [antropolo'xia] *nf* anthropology

**anual** [a'nwal] *adj* annual

**anuario** [a'nwarjo] *nm* yearbook

**anublado, -a** *adj* overcast

**anulación** [anula'θjon] *nf (de un matrimonio)* annulment; (*cancelación*) cancellation

**anular** [anu'lar] /1a/ *vt (contrato)* to annul, cancel; (*suscripción*) to cancel; (*ley*) to repeal ▷ *nm* ring finger

**anunciar** [anun'θjar] /1b/ *vt* to announce; (*proclamar*) to proclaim; (*Com*) to advertise

**anuncio** [a'nunθjo] *nm* announcement; (*señal*) sign; (*Com*) advertisement; (*cartel*) poster

**anzuelo** [an'θwelo] *nm* hook; (*para pescar*) fish hook

**añadidura** [aɲaði'ðura] *nf* addition, extra; **por ~** besides, in addition

**añadir** [aɲa'ðir] /3a/ *vt* to add

**añejo, -a** [a'ɲexo, a] *adj* old; (*vino*) mature

**añicos** [a'ɲikos] *nmpl*: **hacer ~** to smash, shatter

**año** ['aɲo] *nm* year; **¡Feliz A~ Nuevo!** Happy New Year!; **tener 15 ~s** to be 15 (years old); **los ~s 80** the eighties; **~ bisiesto/escolar/fiscal/sabático** leap/school/tax/sabbatical year; **el ~ que viene** next year

**añoranza** [aɲo'ranθa] *nf* nostalgia; (*anhelo*) longing

**apa** ['apa] *excl (LAM)* goodness me!, good gracious!

**apabullar** [apaβu'ʎar] /1a/ *vt* to crush

**apacible** [apa'θiβle] *adj* gentle, mild

**apaciguar** [apaθi'ɣwar] /1i/ *vt* to pacify, calm (down)

**apadrinar** [apaðri'nar] /1a/ *vt* to sponsor, support; (*Rel: niño*) to be godfather to

**apagado, -a** [apa'ɣaðo, a] *adj (volcán)* extinct; (*color*) dull; (*voz*) quiet; (*sonido*) muted, muffled; (*persona: apático*) listless; **estar ~** (*fuego, luz*) to be out; (*radio, TV etc*) to be off

**apagar** [apa'ɣar] /1h/ *vt* to put out; (*sonido*) to silence, muffle; (*sed*) to quench; (*Elec, Radio, TV*) to turn off; (*Inform*) to toggle off

**apagón** [apa'ɣon] *nm* blackout, power cut

**apalabrar** [apala'βrar] /1a/ *vt* to agree to; (*obrero*) to engage

**apalear** [apale'ar] /1a/ *vt* to beat, thrash

**apantallar** [apanta'ʎar] /1a/ *vt (LAM)* to impress

**apañar** [apa'ɲar] /1a/ *vt* to pick up; (*asir*) to take hold of, grasp; (*reparar*) to mend, patch up; **apañarse** *vr* to manage, get along

**apapachar** [apapa'tʃar] /1a/ *vt (LAM fam)* to cuddle, hug

**aparador** [apara'ðor] *nm* sideboard; (*LAM: escaparate*) shop window

**aparato** [apa'rato] *nm* apparatus; (*máquina*) machine; (*doméstico*) appliance; (*boato*) ostentation; **al ~** (*Telec*) speaking; **~ digestivo** digestive system; **aparatoso, -a** *adj* showy, ostentatious

**aparcamiento** [aparka'mjento] *nm* car park (BRIT), parking lot (US)

**aparcar** [apar'kar] /1g/ *vt, vi* to park

**aparear** [apare'ar] /1a/ *vt (objetos)* to pair, match; (*animales*) to mate; **aparearse** *vr* to form a pair; to mate

**aparecer** [apare'θer] /2d/ *vi* to appear; **aparecerse** *vr* to appear

**aparejador, a** [aparexa'ðor, a] *nm/f (Arq)* quantity surveyor

**aparejo** [apa'rexo] nm harness; (Naut) rigging; (de poleas) block and tackle

**aparentar** [aparen'tar] /1a/ vt (edad) to look; (fingir): ~ **tristeza** to pretend to be sad

**aparente** [apa'rente] adj apparent; (adecuado) suitable

**aparezca** etc vb V **aparecer**

**aparición** [apari'θjon] nf appearance; (de libro) publication; (de fantasma) apparition

**apariencia** [apa'rjenθja] nf (outward) appearance; **en ~** outwardly, seemingly

**apartado, -a** [apar'taðo, a] adj separate; (lejano) remote ▷ nm (tipográfico) paragraph; **~ de correos** (ESP), **~ postal** (LAM) post office box

**apartamento** [aparta'mento] nm apartment, flat (BRIT)

**apartar** [apar'tar] /1a/ vt to separate; (quitar) to remove; **apartarse** vr to separate, part; (irse) to move away; (mantenerse aparte) to keep away

**aparte** [a'parte] adv (separadamente) separately; (además) besides ▷ nm aside; (tipográfico) new paragraph

**aparthotel** [aparto'tel] nm serviced apartments

**apasionado, -a** [apasjo'naðo, a] adj passionate

**apasionar** [apasjo'nar] /1a/ vt to excite; **apasionarse** vr to get excited; **le apasiona el fútbol** she's crazy about football

**apatía** [apa'tia] nf apathy

**apático, -a** [a'patiko, a] adj apathetic

**Apdo.** nm abr (= Apartado (de Correos)) P.O. Box

**apeadero** [apea'ðero] nm halt, stopping place

**apearse** [ape'arse] /1a/ vr (jinete) to dismount; (bajarse) to get down o out; (de coche) to get out

**apechugar** [apetʃu'ɣar] /1h/ vi: ~ **con algo** to face up to sth

**apegarse** [ape'ɣarse] /1h/ vr: ~ **a** to become attached to; **apego** nm attachment, devotion

**apelar** [ape'lar] /1a/ vi to appeal; ~ **a** (fig) to resort to

**apellidar** [apeʎi'ðar] /1a/ vt to call, name; **apellidarse** vr: **se apellida Pérez** her (sur) name's Pérez

**apellido** [ape'ʎiðo] nm surname

**apenar** [ape'nar] /1a/ vt to grieve, trouble; (LAM: avergonzar) to embarrass; **apenarse** vr to grieve; (LAM: avergonzarse) to be embarrassed

**apenas** [a'penas] adv scarcely, hardly ▷ conj as soon as, no sooner

**apéndice** [a'pendiθe] nm appendix; **apendicitis** nf appendicitis

**aperitivo** [aperi'tiβo] nm (bebida) aperitif; (comida) appetizer

**apertura** [aper'tura] nf opening; (Pol) liberalization

**apestar** [apes'tar] /1a/ vt to infect ▷ vi: ~ **(a)** to stink (of)

**apetecer** [apete'θer] /2d/ vt: **¿te apetece una tortilla?** do you fancy an omelette?; **apetecible** adj desirable; (comida) appetizing

**apetito** [ape'tito] nm appetite; **apetitoso, -a** adj appetizing; (fig) tempting

**apiadarse** [apja'ðarse] /1a/ vr: ~ **de** to take pity on

**ápice** ['apiθe] nm whit, iota

**apilar** [api'lar] /1a/ vt to pile o heap up

**apiñar** [api'nar] /1a/ vt to crowd; **apiñarse** vr to crowd o press together

**apio** ['apjo] nm celery

**apisonadora** [apisona'ðora] nf steamroller

**aplacar** [apla'kar] /1g/ vt to placate

**aplastante** [aplas'tante] adj overwhelming; (lógica) compelling

**aplastar** [aplas'tar] /1a/ vt to squash (flat); (fig) to crush

**aplaudir** [aplau'ðir] /3a/ vt to applaud

**aplauso** [a'plauso] nm applause; (fig) approval, acclaim

**aplazamiento** [aplaθa'mjento] nm postponement

**aplazar** [apla'θar] /1f/ vt to postpone, defer

**aplicación** [aplika'θjon] nf application; (para móvil, internet) app; (esfuerzo) effort

**aplicado, -a** [apli'kaðo, a] adj diligent, hard-working

**aplicar** [apli'kar] /1g/ vt (ejecutar) to apply; **aplicarse** vr to apply o.s.

**aplique** etc [a'plike] vb V **aplicar** ▷ nm wall light o lamp

**aplomo** [a'plomo] nm aplomb, self-assurance

**apodar** [apo'ðar] /1a/ vt to nickname

**apoderado** [apoðe'raðo] nm agent, representative

**apoderar** [apoðe'rar] /1a/ vt to authorize; **apoderarse** vr: ~**se de** to take possession of

**apodo** [a'poðo] nm nickname

**apogeo** [apo'xeo] nm peak, summit

**apoquinar** [apoki'nar] /1a/ vt (fam) to cough up, fork out

**aporrear** [aporre'ar] /1a/ vt to beat (up)

**aportar** [apor'tar] /1a/ vt to contribute ▷ vi to reach port; **aportarse** vr (LAM: llegar) to arrive, come

**aposta** [a'posta] adv deliberately, on purpose

**apostar** [apos'tar] /1a, 1l/ vt to bet, stake; (tropas etc) to station, post ▷ vi to bet

**apóstol** [a'postol] *nm* apostle

**apóstrofo** [a'postrofo] *nm* apostrophe

**apoyar** [apo'jar] /1a/ *vt* to lean, rest; *(fig)* to support, back; **apoyarse** *vr*: **~se en** to lean on; **apoyo** *nm* support, backing

**apreciable** [apre'θjaβle] *adj* considerable; *(fig)* esteemed

**apreciar** [apre'θjar] /1b/ *vt* to evaluate, assess; *(Com)* to appreciate, value; *(persona)* to respect; *(tamaño)* to gauge, assess; *(detalles)* to notice

**aprecio** [a'preθjo] *nm* valuation, estimate; *(fig)* appreciation

**aprehender** [apreen'der] /2a/ *vt* to apprehend, detain

**apremio** [a'premjo] *nm* urgency

**aprender** [apren'der] /2a/ *vt, vi* to learn; **aprenderse** *vr*: **~se algo de memoria** to learn sth (off) by heart

**aprendiz, a** [apren'diθ, a] *nm/f* apprentice; *(principiante)* learner; **aprendizaje** *nm* apprenticeship

**aprensión** [apren'sjon] *nf* apprehension, fear; **aprensivo, -a** *adj* apprehensive

**apresar** [apre'sar] /1a/ *vt* to seize; *(capturar)* to capture

**apresurado, -a** [apresu'raðo, a] *adj* hurried, hasty

**apresurar** [apresu'rar] /1a/ *vt* to hurry, accelerate; **apresurarse** *vr* to hurry, make haste

**apretado, -a** [apre'taðo, a] *adj* tight; *(escritura)* cramped

**apretar** [apre'tar] /1j/ *vt* to squeeze; *(Tec)* to tighten; *(presionar)* to press together, pack ▷ *vi* to be too tight

**apretón** [apre'ton] *nm* squeeze; **~ de manos** handshake

**aprieto** [a'prjeto] *nm* squeeze; *(dificultad)* difficulty; **estar en un ~** to be in a fix

**aprisa** [a'prisa] *adv* quickly, hurriedly

**aprisionar** [aprisjo'nar] /1a/ *vt* to imprison

**aprobación** [aproβa'θjon] *nf* approval

**aprobar** [apro'βar] /1l/ *vt* to approve (of); *(examen, materia)* to pass ▷ *vi* to pass

**apropiado, -a** [apro'pjaðo, a] *adj* appropriate, suitable

**apropiarse** [apro'pjarse] /1b/ *vr*: **~ de** to appropriate

**aprovechado, -a** [aproβe'tʃaðo, a] *adj* industrious, hardworking; *(económico)* thrifty; *(pey)* unscrupulous

**aprovechar** [aproβe'tʃar] /1a/ *vt* to use; *(explotar)* to exploit; *(experiencia)* to profit from; *(oferta, oportunidad)* to take advantage of ▷ *vi* to progress, improve; **aprovecharse** *vr*: **~se de** to make use of; *(pey)* to take advantage of; **¡que aproveche!** enjoy your meal!

**aproximación** [aproksima'θjon] *nf* approximation; *(de lotería)* consolation prize

**aproximadamente** [aproksimaða'mente] *adv* approximately

**aproximar** [aproksi'mar] /1a/ *vt* to bring nearer; **aproximarse** *vr* to come near, approach

**apruebe** *etc vb* V **aprobar**

**aptitud** [apti'tuð] *nf* aptitude

**apto, -a** ['apto, a] *adj*: **~ (para)** suitable (for)

**apuesto, -a** [a'pwesto, a] *adj* neat, elegant ▷ *nf* bet, wager

**apuntar** [apun'tar] /1a/ *vt* *(con arma)* to aim at; *(con dedo)* to point at *o* to; *(anotar)* to note (down); *(Teat)* to prompt; **apuntarse** *vr* *(Deporte: tanto, victoria)* to score; *(Escol)* to enrol

    No confundir *apuntar* con la palabra inglesa *appoint*.

**apunte** [a'punte] *nm* note

**apuñalar** [apuɲa'lar] /1a/ *vt* to stab

**apurado, -a** [apu'raðo, a] *adj* needy; *(difícil)* difficult; *(peligroso)* dangerous; *(LAM: con prisa)* hurried, rushed

**apurar** [apu'rar] /1a/ *vt* *(agotar)* to drain; *(recursos)* to use up; *(molestar)* to annoy; **apurarse** *vr* *(preocuparse)* to worry; *(esp LAM: darse prisa)* to hurry

**apuro** [a'puro] *nm* *(aprieto)* fix, jam; *(escasez)* want, hardship; *(vergüenza)* embarrassment; *(LAM: prisa)* haste, urgency

**aquejado, -a** [ake'xaðo, a] *adj*: **~ de** *(Med)* afflicted by

**aquel, aquella, aquellos, -as** [a'kel, a'keʎa, a'keʎos, -as] *adj* that, those *pl* ▷ *pron* that (one), those (ones) *pl*

**aquél, aquélla, aquéllos, -as** [a'kel, a'keʎa, a'keʎos, -as] *pron* that (one), those (ones) *pl*

**aquello** [a'keʎo] *pron* that, that business

**aquí** [a'ki] *adv* *(lugar)* here; *(tiempo)* now; **~ arriba** up here; **~ mismo** right here; **~ yace** here lies; **de ~ a siete días** a week from now

**ara** ['ara] *nf*: **en ~s de** for the sake of

**árabe** ['araβe] *adj* Arab ▷ *nmf* Arab ▷ *nm* *(Ling)* Arabic

**Arabia** [a'raβja] *nf* Arabia; **~ Saudí** *o* **Saudita** Saudi Arabia

**arado** [a'raðo] *nm* plough

**Aragón** [ara'ɣon] *nm* Aragon; **aragonés, -esa** *adj, nm/f* Aragonese

**arancel** [aran'θel] *nm* tariff, duty

**arandela** [aran'dela] *nf* *(Tec)* washer

**araña** [a'raɲa] *nf* *(Zool)* spider; *(lámpara)* chandelier

**arañar** [ara'ɲar] /1a/ *vt* to scratch

**arañazo** [ara'ɲaθo] *nm* scratch

**arbitrar** [arβi'trar] /1a/ *vt* to arbitrate in; *(Deporte)* to referee ▷ *vi* to arbitrate

**arbitrario, -a** [arβi'trarjo, a] *adj* arbitrary

**árbitro** ['arβitro] *nm* arbitrator; (*Deporte*) referee; (*Tenis*) umpire

**árbol** ['arβol] *nm* (*Bot*) tree; (*Naut*) mast; (*Tec*) axle, shaft; **~ de Navidad** Christmas tree

**arboleda** [arβo'leða] *nf* grove, plantation

**arbusto** [ar'βusto] *nm* bush, shrub

**arca** ['arka] *nf* chest, box

**arcada** [ar'kaða] *nf* arcade; (*de puente*) arch, span; **arcadas** *nfpl* (*náuseas*) retching *sg*

**arcaico, -a** [ar'kaiko, a] *adj* archaic

**arce** ['arθe] *nm* maple tree

**arcén** [ar'θen] *nm* (*de autopista*) hard shoulder; (*de carretera*) verge

**archipiélago** [artʃi'pjelaɣo] *nm* archipelago

**archivador** [artʃiβa'ðor] *nm* filing cabinet

**archivar** [artʃi'βar] /1a/ *vt* to file (away); **archivo** *nm* archive(s) (*pl*); (*Inform*) file; **archivo adjunto** (*Inform*) attachment; **archivo de seguridad** (*Inform*) backup file

**arcilla** [ar'θiʎa] *nf* clay

**arco** ['arko] *nm* arch; (*Mat*) arc; (*Mil, Mus*) bow; **~ iris** rainbow

**arder** [ar'ðer] /2a/ *vt, vi* to burn; **estar que arde** (*persona*) to fume

**ardid** [ar'ðið] *nm* ploy, trick

**ardiente** [ar'ðjente] *adj* ardent

**ardilla** [ar'ðiʎa] *nf* squirrel

**ardor** [ar'ðor] *nm* (*calor*) heat; (*fig*) ardour; **~ de estómago** heartburn

**arduo, -a** ['arðwo, a] *adj* arduous

**área** ['area] *nf* area; (*Deporte*) penalty area

**arena** [a'rena] *nf* sand; (*de una lucha*) arena; **arenal** *nm* (*terreno arenoso*) sandy area

**arenisca** [are'niska] *nf* sandstone; (*cascajo*) grit

**arenoso, -a** [are'noso, a] *adj* sandy

**arenque** [a'renke] *nm* herring

**arete** [a'rete] *nm* (*LAM*) earring

**Argel** [ar'xel] *n* Algiers

**Argelia** [ar'xelja] *nf* Algeria; **argelino, -a** *adj, nm/f* Algerian

**Argentina** [arxen'tina] *nf*: **(la) ~** Argentina

**argentino, -a** [arxen'tino, a] *adj* Argentinian; (*de plata*) silvery ▷ *nm/f* Argentinian

**argolla** [ar'ɣoʎa] *nf* (large) ring

**argot** [ar'ɣo] *nm* slang

**argucia** [ar'ɣuθja] *nf* subtlety, sophistry

**argumentar** [arɣumen'tar] /1a/ *vt, vi* to argue

**argumento** [arɣu'mento] *nm* argument; (*razonamiento*) reasoning; (*de novela etc*) plot; (*Cine, TV*) storyline

**aria** ['arja] *nf* aria

**aridez** [ari'ðeθ] *nf* aridity, dryness

**árido, -a** ['ariðo, a] *adj* arid, dry

**Aries** ['arjes] *nm* Aries

**arisco, -a** [a'risko, a] *adj* surly; (*insociable*) unsociable

**aristócrata** [aris'tokrata] *nmf* aristocrat

**arma** ['arma] *nf* arm; **armas** *nfpl* arms; **~ blanca** blade, knife; **~ de doble filo** double-edged sword; **~ de fuego** firearm; **~s de destrucción masiva** weapons of mass destruction

**armada** [ar'maða] *nf* armada; (*flota*) fleet

**armadillo** [arma'ðiʎo] *nm* armadillo

**armado, -a** [ar'maðo, a] *adj* armed; (*Tec*) reinforced

**armadura** [arma'ðura] *nf* (*Mil*) armour; (*Tec*) framework; (*Zool*) skeleton; (*Física*) armature

**armamento** [arma'mento] *nm* armament; (*Naut*) fitting-out

**armar** [ar'mar] /1a/ *vt* (*soldado*) to arm; (*máquina*) to assemble; (*navío*) to fit out; **~la, ~ un lío** to start a row, kick up a fuss

**armario** [ar'marjo] *nm* wardrobe; (*de cocina, baño*) cupboard; **~ empotrado** built-in cupboard

**armatoste** [arma'toste] *nm* (*mueble*) monstrosity; (*máquina*) contraption

**armazón** [arma'θon] *nm o f* body, chassis; (*de mueble etc*) frame; (*Arq*) skeleton

**armiño** [ar'miɲo] *nm* stoat; (*piel*) ermine

**armisticio** [armis'tiθjo] *nm* armistice

**armonía** [armo'nia] *nf* harmony

**armónica** [ar'monika] *nf* harmonica

**armonizar** [armoni'θar] /1f/ *vt* to harmonize; (*diferencias*) to reconcile

**aro** ['aro] *nm* ring; (*tejo*) quoit; (*LAM*: *pendiente*) earring

**aroma** [a'roma] *nm* aroma; **aromaterapia** *nf* aromatherapy; **aromático, -a** *adj* aromatic

**arpa** ['arpa] *nf* harp

**arpía** [ar'pia] *nf* shrew

**arpón** [ar'pon] *nm* harpoon

**arqueología** [arkeolo'xia] *nf* archaeology; **arqueólogo, -a** *nm/f* archaeologist

**arquetipo** [arke'tipo] *nm* archetype

**arquitecto, -a** *nm/f* architect; **arquitectura** *nf* architecture

**arrabal** [arra'βal] *nm* suburb; (*LAM*) slum; **arrabales** *nmpl* (*afueras*) outskirts

**arraigar** [arrai'ɣar] /1h/ *vi* to take root

**arrancar** [arran'kar] /1g/ *vt* (*sacar*) to extract, pull out; (*arrebatar*) to snatch (away); (*Inform*) to boot; (*fig*) to extract ▷ *vi* (*Auto, máquina*) to start; (*ponerse en marcha*) to get going; **~ de** to stem from

**arranque** *etc* [a'rranke] *vb V* **arrancar** ▷ *nm* sudden start; (*Auto*) start; (*fig*) fit, outburst

**arrasar** [arra'sar] /1a/ *vt* (*aplanar*) to level, flatten; (*destruir*) to demolish

**arrastrar** [arras'trar] /1a/ vt to drag (along); (fig) to drag down, degrade; (agua, viento) to carry away ▷ vi to drag, trail on the ground; **arrastrarse** vr to crawl; (fig) to grovel; **llevar algo arrastrado** to drag sth along

**arrear** [arre'ar] /1a/ vt to drive on, urge on ▷ vi to hurry along

**arrebatar** [arreβa'tar] /1a/ vt to snatch (away), seize; (fig) to captivate

**arrebato** [arre'βato] nm fit of rage, fury; (éxtasis) rapture

**arrecife** [arre'θife] nm reef

**arreglado, -a** [arre'ɣlaðo, a] adj (ordenado) neat, orderly; (moderado) moderate, reasonable

**arreglar** [arre'ɣlar] /1a/ vt (poner orden) to tidy up; (algo roto) to fix, repair; (problema) to solve; **arreglarse** vr to reach an understanding; **arreglárselas** (fam) to get by, manage

**arreglo** [a'rreɣlo] nm settlement; (orden) order; (acuerdo) agreement; (Mus) arrangement, setting

**arremangar** [arreman'gar] /1h/ vt to roll up, turn up; **arremangarse** vr to roll up one's sleeves

**arremeter** [arreme'ter] /2a/ vi: ~ **contra algn** to attack sb

**arrendamiento** [arrenda'mjento] nm letting; (el alquilar) hiring; (contrato) lease; (alquiler) rent; **arrendar** /1j/ vt to let; to lease; to rent; **arrendatario, -a** nm/f tenant

**arreos** [a'rreos] nmpl (de caballo) harness sg, trappings

**arrepentimiento** [arrepenti'mjento] nm regret, repentance

**arrepentirse** [arrepen'tirse] /3i/ vr to repent; ~ **de (haber hecho) algo** to regret (doing) sth

**arresto** [a'rresto] nm arrest; (Mil) detention; (audacia) boldness, daring; ~ **domiciliario** house arrest

**arriar** [a'rrjar] /1c/ vt (velas) to haul down; (bandera) to lower, strike; (un cable) to pay out

**PALABRA CLAVE**

**arriba** [a'rriβa] adv **1** (posición) above; **desde arriba** from above; **arriba del todo** at the very top, right on top; **Juan está arriba** Juan is upstairs; **lo arriba mencionado** the aforementioned
**2** (dirección): **calle arriba** up the street
**3**: **de arriba abajo** from top to bottom; **mirar a algn de arriba abajo** to look sb up and down

**4**: **para arriba: de 50 euros para arriba** from 50 euros up(wards)
▶ adj: **de arriba: el piso de arriba** the upstairs flat (BRIT) o apartment; **la parte de arriba** the top o upper part
▶ prep: **arriba de** (LAM: por encima de) above; **arriba de 200 dólares** more than 200 dollars
▶ excl: ¡**arriba**! up!; ¡**manos arriba**! hands up!; ¡**arriba España**! long live Spain!

**arribar** [arri'βar] /1a/ vi to put into port; (llegar) to arrive

**arriendo** etc [a'rrjendo] vb V **arrendar**
▷ nm = **arrendamiento**

**arriesgado, -a** [arrjes'ɣaðo, a] adj (peligroso) risky; (audaz) bold, daring

**arriesgar** [arrjes'ɣar] /1h/ vt to risk; (poner en peligro) to endanger; **arriesgarse** vr to take a risk

**arrimar** [arri'mar] /1a/ vt (acercar) to bring close; (poner de lado) to set aside; **arrimarse** vr to come close o closer; ~**se a** to lean on

**arrinconar** [arrinko'nar] /1a/ vt (colocar) to put in a corner; (enemigo) to corner; (fig) to put on one side; (abandonar) to push aside

**arroba** [a'rroβa] nf (en dirección electrónica) at sign, @

**arrodillarse** [arroði'ʎarse] /1a/ vr to kneel (down)

**arrogante** [arro'ɣante] adj arrogant

**arrojar** [arro'xar] /1a/ vt to throw, hurl; (humo) to emit, give out; (Com) to yield, produce; **arrojarse** vr to throw o hurl o.s.

**arrojo** [a'rroxo] nm daring

**arrollador, a** [arroʎa'ðor, a] adj overwhelming

**arrollar** [arro'ʎar] /1a/ vt (Auto) to run over; (Deporte) to crush

**arropar** [arro'par] /1a/ vt to cover (up), wrap up; **arroparse** vr to wrap o.s. up

**arroyo** [a'rrojo] nm stream; (de la calle) gutter

**arroz** [a'rroθ] nm rice; ~ **con leche** rice pudding

**arruga** [a'rruɣa] nf (de cara) wrinkle; (de vestido) crease; **arrugar** /1h/ vt to wrinkle; to crease; **arrugarse** vr to get creased

**arruinar** [arrwi'nar] /1a/ vt to ruin, wreck; **arruinarse** vr to be ruined

**arsenal** [arse'nal] nm naval dockyard; (Mil) arsenal

**arte** ['arte] nm (gen m en sg, f en pl) art; (maña) skill, guile; **artes** nfpl arts; **Bellas A~s** Fine Art sg

**artefacto** [arte'fakto] nm appliance

**arteria** [ar'terja] nf artery

**artesanía** [artesa'nia] nf craftsmanship; (artículos) handicrafts pl; **artesano, -a** nm/f artisan, craftsman/woman

**ártico, -a** ['artiko, a] adj Arctic
▷ nm: **el (océano) Á~** the Arctic (Ocean)
**articulación** [artikula'θjon] nf
articulation; (Med, Tec) joint
**artículo** [ar'tikulo] nm article; (cosa)
thing, article; **artículos** nmpl goods; **~s de
escritorio** stationery
**artífice** [ar'tifiθe] nmf (fig) architect
**artificial** [artifi'θjal] adj artificial
**artillería** [artiʎe'ria] nf artillery
**artilugio** [arti'luxjo] nm gadget
**artimaña** [arti'maɲa] nf trap, snare;
(astucia) cunning
**artista** [ar'tista] nmf (pintor) artist, painter;
(Teat) artist, artiste; **~ de cine** film actor/
actress; **artístico, -a** [ar'tistiko, a] adj artistic
**artritis** [ar'tritis] nf arthritis
**arveja** [ar'βexa] nf (LAM) pea
**arzobispo** [arθo'βispo] nm archbishop
**as** [as] nm ace
**asa** ['asa] nf handle; (fig) lever
**asado** [a'saðo] nm roast (meat); (LAM:
barbacoa) barbecue

● **ASADO**
●
● Traditional Latin American barbecues,
● especially in the River Plate area, are
● celebrated in the open air around a large
● grill which is used to grill mainly beef
● and various kinds of spicy pork sausage.
● They are usually very common during the
● summer and can go on for several days.

**asador** [asa'ðor] nm spit
**asadura, asaduras** [asa'ðura(s)] nf, nfpl
entrails pl, offal sg
**asalariado, -a** [asala'rjaðo, a] adj paid,
salaried ▷ nm/f wage earner
**asaltar** [asal'tar] /1a/ vt to attack, assault;
(fig) to assail; **asalto** nm attack, assault;
(Deporte) round
**asamblea** [asam'blea] nf assembly;
(reunión) meeting
**asar** [a'sar] /1a/ vt to roast
**ascendencia** [asθen'denθja] nf ancestry;
(LAM: influencia) ascendancy; **de ~ francesa**
of French origin
**ascender** [asθen'der] /2g/ vi (subir)
to ascend, rise; (ser promovido) to gain
promotion ▷ vt to promote; **~ a** to amount
to; **ascendiente** nm influence ▷ nmf
ancestor
**ascensión** [asθen'sjon] nf ascent; **la A~**
the Ascension
**ascenso** [as'θenso] nm ascent; (promoción)
promotion
**ascensor** [asθen'sor] nm lift (BRIT),
elevator (US)

**asco** ['asko] nm: **el ajo me da ~** I hate o
loathe garlic; **estar hecho un ~** to be filthy;
**¡qué ~!** how revolting o disgusting!
**ascua** ['askwa] nf ember
**aseado, -a** [ase'aðo, a] adj clean; (arreglado)
tidy; (pulcro) smart
**asear** [ase'ar] /1a/ vt (lavar) to wash;
(ordenar) to tidy (up)
**asediar** [ase'ðjar] /1b/ vt (Mil) to besiege,
lay siege to; (fig) to chase, pester; **asedio**
nm siege; (Com) run
**asegurado, a** [aseɣu'raðo, a] adj insured
**asegurador, -a** [aseɣura'ðor, a] nm/f
insurer
**asegurar** [aseɣu'rar] /1a/ vt (consolidar)
to secure, fasten; (dar garantía de) to
guarantee; (preservar) to safeguard;
(afirmar, dar por cierto) to assure, affirm;
(tranquilizar) to reassure; (hacer un seguro)
to insure; **asegurarse** vr to assure o.s.,
make sure
**asemejarse** [aseme'xarse] /1a/ vr to be
alike; **~ a** to be like, resemble
**asentado, -a** [asen'taðo, a] adj
established, settled
**asentar** [asen'tar] /1j/ vt (sentar) to seat, sit
down; (poner) to place, establish; (alisar) to
level, smooth down o out; (anotar) to note
down ▷ vi to be suitable, suit
**asentir** [asen'tir] /3i/ vi to assent, agree;
**~ con la cabeza** to nod (one's head)
**aseo** [a'seo] nm cleanliness; **aseos** nmpl
toilet sg (BRIT), cloakroom sg (BRIT),
restroom sg (US)
**aséptico, -a** [a'septiko, a] adj germ-free,
free from infection
**asequible** [ase'kiβle] adj (precio)
reasonable; (meta) attainable; (persona)
approachable
**asesinar** [asesi'nar] /1a/ vt to murder;
(Pol) to assassinate; **asesinato** nm murder;
assassination
**asesino, -a** [ase'sino, a] nm/f murderer,
killer; (Pol) assassin
**asesor, a** [ase'sor, a] nm/f adviser,
consultant; **asesorar** /1a/ vt (Jur) to
advise, give legal advice to; (Com) to act as
consultant to; **asesorarse** vr: **asesorarse
con** o **de** to take advice from, consult;
**asesoría** nf (cargo) consultancy; (oficina)
consultant's office
**asestar** [ases'tar] /1a/ vt (golpe) to deal
**asfalto** [as'falto] nm asphalt
**asfixia** [as'fiksja] nf asphyxia, suffocation;
**asfixiar** /1b/ vt to asphyxiate, suffocate;
**asfixiarse** vr to be asphyxiated, suffocate
**así** [a'si] adv (de esta manera) in this way, like
this, thus; (aunque) although; (tan pronto
como) as soon as; **~ que** so; **~ como** as well

as; **~ y todo** even so; **¿no es ~?** isn't it?, didn't you? etc; **~ de grande** this big

**Asia** ['asja] nf Asia; **asiático, -a** adj, nm/f Asian, Asiatic

**asiduo, -a** [a'siðwo, a] adj assiduous; (frecuente) frequent ▷ nm/f regular (customer)

**asiento** [a'sjento] nm (mueble) seat, chair; (de coche, en tribunal etc) seat; (localidad) seat, place; (fundamento) site; **~ delantero/ trasero** front/back seat

**asignación** [asiɣna'θjon] nf (atribución) assignment; (reparto) allocation; (sueldo) salary; (Com) allowance; **~ (semanal)** (weekly) pocket money

**asignar** [asiɣ'nar] /1a/ vt to assign, allocate

**asignatura** [asiɣna'tura] nf subject; (curso) course

**asilo** [a'silo] nm (refugio) asylum, refuge; (establecimiento) home, institution; **~ político** political asylum

**asimilar** [asimi'lar] /1a/ vt to assimilate

**asimismo** [asi'mismo] adv in the same way, likewise

**asistencia** [asis'tenθja] nf audience; (Med) attendance; (ayuda) assistance; **~ en carretera** roadside assistance; **asistente, -a** nm/f assistant; **los asistentes** those present; **asistente social** social worker

**asistido, -a** [asis'tiðo, a] adj: **~ por ordenador** computer-assisted

**asistir** [asis'tir] /3a/ vt to assist, help ▷ vi: **~ a** to attend, be present at

**asma** ['asma] nf asthma

**asno** ['asno] nm donkey; (fig) ass

**asociación** [asoθja'θjon] nf association; (Com) partnership; **asociado, -a** adj associate ▷ nm/f associate; (Com) partner

**asociar** [aso'θjar] /1b/ vt to associate

**asomar** [aso'mar] /1a/ vt to show, stick out ▷ vi to appear; **asomarse** vr to appear, show up; **~ la cabeza por la ventana** to put one's head out of the window

**asombrar** [asom'brar] /1a/ vt to amaze, astonish; **asombrarse** vr: **~se (de)** (sorprenderse) to be amazed (at); (asustarse) to be frightened (at); **asombro** nm amazement, astonishment; (susto) fright; **asombroso, -a** adj amazing

**asomo** [a'somo] nm hint, sign

**aspa** ['aspa] nf (cruz) cross; (de molino) sail; **en ~** X-shaped

**aspaviento** [aspa'βjento] nm exaggerated display of feeling; (fam) fuss

**aspecto** [as'pekto] nm (apariencia) look, appearance; (fig) aspect

**áspero, -a** ['aspero, a] adj (al tacto) rough; (al gusto) sharp, sour; (voz) harsh

**aspersión** [asper'sjon] nf sprinkling

**aspiración** [aspira'θjon] nf breath, inhalation; (Mus) short pause; **aspiraciones** nfpl (ambiciones) aspirations

**aspirador** [aspira'ðor] nm = **aspiradora**

**aspiradora** [aspira'ðora] nf vacuum cleaner, Hoover®

**aspirante** [aspi'rante] nmf (candidato) candidate; (Deporte) contender

**aspirar** [aspi'rar] /1a/ vt to breathe in ▷ vi: **~ a** to aspire to

**aspirina** [aspi'rina] nf aspirin

**asqueroso, -a** [aske'roso, a] adj disgusting, sickening

**asta** ['asta] nf lance; (arpón) spear; (mango) shaft, handle; (Zool) horn; **a media ~** at half mast

**asterisco** [aste'risko] nm asterisk

**astilla** [as'tiʎa] nf splinter; (pedacito) chip; **astillas** nfpl (leña) firewood sg

**astillero** [asti'ʎero] nm shipyard

**astro** ['astro] nm star

**astrología** [astrolo'xia] nf astrology; **astrólogo, -a** nm/f astrologer

**astronauta** [astro'nauta] nmf astronaut

**astronomía** [astrono'mia] nf astronomy

**astucia** [as'tuθja] nf astuteness; (destreza) clever trick

**asturiano, -a** [astu'rjano, a] adj, nm/f Asturian

**astuto, -a** [as'tuto, a] adj astute; (taimado) cunning

**asumir** [asu'mir] /3a/ vt to assume

**asunción** [asun'θjon] nf assumption; (Rel): **A~** Assumption

**asunto** [a'sunto] nm (tema) matter, subject; (negocio) business

**asustar** [asus'tar] /1a/ vt to frighten; **asustarse** vr to be/become frightened

**atacar** [ata'kar] /1g/ vt to attack

**atadura** [ata'ðura] nf bond, tie

**atajar** [ata'xar] /1a/ vt (enfermedad, mal) to stop ▷ vi (persona) to take a short cut

**atajo** [a'taxo] nm short cut

**atañer** [ata'ɲer] vi: **~ a** to concern

**ataque** etc [a'take] vb V **atacar** ▷ nm attack; **~ cardíaco** heart attack

**atar** [a'tar] /1a/ vt to tie, tie up

**atarantado, -a** [ataran'taðo, a] adj (LAM: aturdido) dazed

**atardecer** [atarðe'θer] /2d/ vi to get dark ▷ nm evening; (crepúsculo) dusk

**atareado, -a** [atare'aðo, a] adj busy

**atascar** [atas'kar] /1g/ vt (obstruir) to jam; (fig) to hinder; **atascarse** vr to stall; (cañería) to get blocked up; **atasco** nm obstruction; (Auto) traffic jam

**ataúd** [ata'uð] nm coffin

**ataviar** [ata'βjar] /1c/ vt to deck, array

**atemorizar** [atemori'θar] /1f/ vt to frighten, scare

**Atenas** [a'tenas] nf Athens

**atención** [aten'θjon] nf attention; (bondad) kindness ▷ excl (be) careful!, look out!; **en ~ a esto** in view of this

**atender** [aten'der] /2g/ vt to attend to, look after; (Telec) to answer ▷ vi to pay attention

**atenerse** [ate'nerse] /2k/ vr: **~ a** to abide by, adhere to

**atentado** [aten'taðo] nm crime, illegal act; (asalto) assault; (tb: **~ terrorista**) terrorist attack; **~ contra la vida de algn** attempt on sb's life; **~ suicida** suicide bombing

**atentamente** [atenta'mente] adv: **Le saluda ~** Yours faithfully

**atentar** [aten'tar] /1a/ vi: **~ a o contra** to commit an outrage against

**atento, -a** [a'tento, a] adj attentive, observant; (cortés) polite, thoughtful; **estar ~ a** (explicación) to pay attention to

**atenuar** [ate'nwar] /1e/ vt (disminuir) to lessen, minimize

**ateo, -a** [a'teo, a] adj atheistic ▷ nm/f atheist

**aterrador, a** [aterra'ðor, a] adj frightening

**aterrizaje** [aterri'θaxe] nm landing; **~ forzoso** emergency o forced landing

**aterrizar** [aterri'θar] /1f/ vi to land

**aterrorizar** [aterrori'θar] /1f/ vt to terrify

**atesorar** [ateso'rar] /1a/ vt to hoard

**atestar** [ates'tar] /1a, 1j/ vt to pack, stuff; (Jur) to attest, testify to

**atestiguar** [atesti'ɣwar] /1i/ vt to testify to, bear witness to

**atiborrar** [atiβo'rrar] /1a/ vt to fill, stuff; **atiborrarse** vr to stuff o.s.

**ático** ['atiko] nm (desván) attic; **~ de lujo** penthouse flat

**atinado, -a** [ati'naðo, a] adj correct; (sensato) wise, sensible

**atinar** [ati'nar] /1a/ vi (acertar) to be right; **~ al blanco** to hit the target; (fig) to be right

**atizar** [ati'θar] /1f/ vt to poke; (horno etc) to stoke; (fig) to stir up, rouse

**atlántico, -a** [at'lantiko, a] adj Atlantic ▷ nm: **el (océano) A~** the Atlantic (Ocean)

**atlas** ['atlas] nm inv atlas

**atleta** [at'leta] nmf athlete; **atlético, -a** adj athletic; **atletismo** nm athletics sg

**atmósfera** [at'mosfera] nf atmosphere

**atolladero** [atoʎa'ðero] nm: **estar en un ~** to be in a jam

**atómico, -a** [a'tomiko, a] adj atomic

**átomo** ['atomo] nm atom

**atónito, -a** [a'tonito, a] adj astonished, amazed

**atontado, -a** [aton'taðo, a] adj stunned; (bobo) silly, daft

**atormentar** [atormen'tar] /1a/ vt to torture; (molestar) to torment; (acosar) to plague, harass

**atornillar** [atorni'ʎar] /1a/ vt to screw on o down

**atosigar** [atosi'ɣar] /1h/ vt to harass, pester

**atracador, a** [atraka'ðor, a] nm/f robber

**atracar** [atra'kar] /1g/ vt (Naut) to moor; (robar) to hold up, rob ▷ vi to moor; **atracarse** vr: **~se (de)** to stuff o.s. (with)

**atracción** [atrak'θjon] nf attraction

**atraco** [a'trako] nm holdup, robbery

**atracón** [atra'kon] nm: **darse o pegarse un ~ (de)** (fam) to stuff o.s. (with)

**atractivo, -a** [atrak'tiβo, a] adj attractive ▷ nm appeal

**atraer** [atra'er] /2o/ vt to attract

**atragantarse** [atraɣan'tarse] /1a/ vr: **~ (con algo)** to choke (on sth); **se me ha atragantado el chico ese/el inglés** I can't stand that boy/English

**atrancar** [atran'kar] /1g/ vt (con tranca, barra) to bar, bolt

**atrapar** [atra'par] /1a/ vt to trap; (resfriado etc) to catch

**atrás** [a'tras] adv (movimiento) back(wards); (lugar) behind; (tiempo) previously; **ir hacia ~** to go back(wards); to go to the rear; **estar ~** to be behind o at the back

**atrasado, -a** [atra'saðo, a] adj slow; (pago) overdue, late; (país) backward

**atrasar** [atra'sar] /1a/ vi to be slow; **atrasarse** vr to stay behind; (tren) to be o run late; (llegar tarde) to be late; **atraso** nm slowness; lateness, delay; (de país) backwardness; **atrasos** nmpl (Com) arrears

**atravesar** [atraβe'sar] /1j/ vt (cruzar) to cross (over); (traspasar) to pierce; (período) to go through; (poner al través) to lay o put across; **atravesarse** vr to come in between; (intervenir) to interfere

**atraviese** etc [atra'βjese] vb V **atravesar**

**atreverse** [atre'βerse] /2a/ vr to dare; (insolentarse) to be insolent; **atrevido, -a** adj daring; insolent; **atrevimiento** nm daring; insolence

**atribución** [atriβu'θjon] nf attribution; **atribuciones** nfpl (Pol) powers, functions; (Admin) responsibilities

**atribuir** [atriβu'ir] /3g/ vt to attribute; (funciones) to confer

**atributo** [atri'βuto] nm attribute

**atril** [a'tril] nm (para libro) lectern; (Mus) music stand

**atropellar** [atrope'ʎar] /1a/ vt (derribar) to knock over o down; (empujar) to push (aside); (Auto) to run over o down; (agraviar) to insult; **atropello** nm (Auto) accident; (empujón) push; (agravio) wrong; (atrocidad) outrage

**atroz** [a'troθ] adj atrocious, awful

**A.T.S.** nm abr, nf abr (= Ayudante Técnico Sanitario) nurse

**atuendo** [a'twendo] nm attire

**atún** [a'tun] nm tuna, tunny

**aturdir** [atur'ðir] /3a/ vt to stun; (ruido) to deafen; (fig) to dumbfound, bewilder

**audacia** [au'ðaθja] nf boldness, audacity; **audaz** adj bold, audacious

**audición** [auði'θjon] nf hearing; (Teat) audition

**audiencia** [au'ðjenθja] nf audience; (Jur) high court

**audífono** [au'ðifono] nm (para sordos) hearing aid

**auditor** [auði'tor] nm (Jur) judge advocate; (Com) auditor

**auditorio** [auði'torjo] nm audience; (sala) auditorium

**auge** ['auxe] nm boom; (clímax) climax

**augurar** [auɣu'rar] /1a/ vt to predict; (presagiar) to portend

**augurio** [au'ɣurjo] nm omen

**aula** ['aula] nf classroom; (en universidad etc) lecture room

**aullar** [au'ʎar] /1a/ vi to howl, yell

**aullido** [au'ʎiðo] nm howl, yell

**aumentar** [aumen'tar] /1a/ vt to increase; (precios) to put up; (producción) to step up; (con microscopio, anteojos) to magnify ▷ vi to increase, be on the increase; **aumento** nm increase; rise

**aun** [a'un] adv even; ~ **así** even so; ~ **más** even o yet more

**aún** [a'un] adv still, yet; ~ **está aquí** he's still here; ~ **no lo sabemos** we don't know yet; ¿no ha venido ~? hasn't she come yet?

**aunque** [a'unke] conj though, although, even though

**aúpa** [a'upa] excl come on!

**auricular** [auriku'lar] nm (Telec) earpiece; **auriculares** nmpl (cascos) headphones

**aurora** [au'rora] nf dawn

**ausencia** [au'senθja] nf absence

**ausentarse** [ausen'tarse] /1a/ vr to go away; (por poco tiempo) to go out

**ausente** [au'sente] adj absent

**austero, -a** [aus'tero, a] adj austere

**austral** [aus'tral] adj southern ▷ nm monetary unit of Argentina (1985-1991)

**Australia** [aus'tralja] nf Australia; **australiano, -a** adj, nm/f Australian

**Austria** ['austrja] nf Austria

**austriaco, -a, austríaco, -a** [aus'triako, a] adj Austrian ▷ nm/f Austrian

**auténtico, -a** [au'tentiko, a] adj authentic

**auto** ['auto] nm (Jur) edict, decree; (: orden) writ; **autos** nmpl (Jur) proceedings; (: acta) court record sg

**autoadhesivo, -a** [autoaðe'siβo, a] adj self-adhesive; (sobre) self-sealing

**autobiografía** [autoβjoɣra'fia] nf autobiography

**autobomba** [auto'bomba] nm (RPL) fire engine

**autobronceador, a** [autoβronθea'ðor, a] adj (self-)tanning

**autobús** [auto'βus] nm bus; ~ **de línea** long-distance coach

**autocar** [auto'kar] nm coach (BRIT), (passenger) bus (US); ~ **de línea** intercity coach o bus

**autóctono, -a** [au'toktono, a] adj native, indigenous

**autodefensa** [autoðe'fensa] nf self-defence

**autodidacta** [autoði'ðakta] adj self-taught

**autoescuela** [autoes'kwela] nf (ESP) driving school

**autofoto** [auto'foto] nf selfie

**autógrafo** [au'toɣrafo] nm autograph

**autolesionarse** [auto'lesjonarsi] vt to self-harm

**autómata** [au'tomata] nm automaton

**automático, -a** [auto'matiko, a] adj automatic ▷ nm press stud

**automóvil** [auto'moβil] nm (motor) car (BRIT), automobile (US); **automovilismo** nm (actividad) motoring; (Deporte) motor racing; **automovilista** nmf motorist, driver

**autonomía** [autono'mia] nf autonomy; **autónomo, -a,** (ESP) **autonómico** adj autonomous

**autopista** [auto'pista] nf motorway (BRIT), freeway (US); ~ **de cuota** (LAM) o peaje (ESP) toll (BRIT) o turnpike (US) road

**autopsia** [au'topsja] nf post-mortem, autopsy

**autor, a** [au'tor, a] nm/f author

**autoridad** [autori'ðað] nf authority; **autoritario, -a** adj authoritarian

**autorización** [autoriθa'θjon] nf authorization; **autorizado, -a** adj authorized; (aprobado) approved

**autorizar** [autori'θar] /1f/ vt to authorize; to approve

**autoservicio** [autoser'βiθjo] nm (tienda) self-service shop o store; (restaurante) self-service restaurant

**autostop** [auto'stop] nm hitch-hiking; **hacer** ~ to hitch-hike; **autostopista** nmf hitch-hiker

**autovía** [auto'βia] nf ≈ dual carriageway (BRIT), ≈ divided highway (US)

**auxiliar** [auksi'ljar] /1b/ vt to help ▷ nmf assistant; **auxilio** nm assistance, help; **primeros auxilios** first aid sg

**Av** abr (= Avenida) Av(e)

**aval** [a'βal] nm guarantee; (persona) guarantor

**avalancha** [aβa'lantʃa] nf avalanche

**avance** [a'βanθe] nm advance; (pago) advance payment; (Cine) trailer

**avanzar** [aβan'θar] /1f/ vt, vi to advance

**avaricia** [aβa'riθja] nf avarice, greed; **avaricioso, -a** adj avaricious, greedy

**avaro, -a** [a'βaro, a] adj miserly, mean ▷ nm/f miser

**Avda** abr (= Avenida) Av(e)

**AVE** ['aβe] nm abr (= Alta Velocidad Española) ≈ bullet train

**ave** ['aβe] nf bird; **~ de rapiña** bird of prey

**avecinarse** [aβeθi'narse] /1a/ vr (tormenta, fig) be on the way

**avellana** [aβe'ʎana] nf hazelnut; **avellano** nm hazel tree

**avemaría** [aβema'ria] nm Hail Mary, Ave Maria

**avena** [a'βena] nf oats pl

**avenida** [aβe'niða] nf (calle) avenue

**aventajar** [aβenta'xar] /1a/ vt (sobrepasar) to surpass, outstrip

**aventón** [aβen'ton] nm (LAM) push; **pedir ~** to hitch a lift, hitch a ride (US)

**aventura** [aβen'tura] nf adventure; **aventurero, -a** adj adventurous

**avergonzar** [aβerɣon'θar] /1f, 1l/ vt to shame; (desconcertar) to embarrass; **avergonzarse** vr to be ashamed; to be embarrassed

**avería** [aβe'ria] nf (Tec) breakdown, fault

**averiado, -a** [aβe'rjaðo, a] adj broken-down; "**~**" "out of order"

**averiar** [aβe'rjar] /1c/ vt to break; **averiarse** vr to break down

**averiguar** [aβeri'ɣwar] /1i/ vt to investigate; (descubrir) to find out, ascertain

**avestruz** [aβes'truθ] nm ostrich

**aviación** [aβja'θjon] nf aviation; (fuerzas aéreas) air force

**aviador, a** [aβja'ðor, a] nm/f aviator, airman/woman

**ávido, -a** ['aβiðo, a] adj avid, eager

**avinagrado, -a** [aβina'ɣraðo, a] adj sour, acid

**avión** [a'βjon] nm aeroplane; (ave) martin; **~ de reacción** jet (plane)

**avioneta** [aβjo'neta] nf light aircraft

**avisar** [aβi'sar] /1a/ vt (advertir) to warn, notify; (informar) to tell; (aconsejar) to advise, counsel; **aviso** nm warning; (noticia) notice

**avispa** [a'βispa] nf wasp

**avispado, -a** [aβis'paðo, a] adj sharp, clever

**avivar** [aβi'βar] /1a/ vt to strengthen, intensify

**axila** [ak'sila] nf armpit

**ay** [ai] excl (dolor) ow!, ouch!; (aflicción) oh!, oh dear!; **¡ay de mí!** poor me!

**ayer** [a'jer] adv, nm yesterday; **antes de ~** the day before yesterday; **~ por la tarde** yesterday afternoon/evening; **~ mismo** only yesterday

**ayote** [a'jote] nm (LAM) pumpkin

**ayuda** [a'juða] nf help, assistance ▷ nm page; **ayudante, -a** nm/f assistant, helper; (Escol) assistant; (Mil) adjutant

**ayudar** [aju'ðar] /1a/ vt to help, assist

**ayunar** [aju'nar] /1a/ vi to fast; **ayunas** nfpl: **estar en ayunas** to be fasting; **ayuno** nm fast, fasting

**ayuntamiento** [ajunta'mjento] nm (consejo) town/city council; (edificio) town/city hall

**azafata** [aθa'fata] nf air hostess (BRIT) o stewardess

**azafrán** [aθa'fran] nm saffron

**azahar** [aθa'ar] nm orange/lemon blossom

**azar** [a'θar] nm (casualidad) chance, fate; (desgracia) misfortune, accident; **por ~** by chance; **al ~** at random

**Azores** [a'θores] nfpl: **las (Islas) ~** the Azores

**azotar** [aθo'tar] /1a/ vt to whip, beat; (pegar) to spank; **azote** nm (látigo) whip; (latigazo) lash, stroke; (en las nalgas) spank; (calamidad) calamity

**azotea** [aθo'tea] nf (flat) roof

**azteca** [aθ'teka] adj, nmf Aztec

**azúcar** [a'θukar] nm sugar; **azucarado, -a** adj sugary, sweet

**azucarero, -a** [aθuka'rero, a] adj sugar cpd ▷ nm sugar bowl

**azucena** [aθu'θena] nf white lily

**azufre** [a'θufre] nm sulphur

**azul** [a'θul] adj, nm blue; **~ celeste/marino** sky/navy blue

**azulejo** [aθu'lexo] nm tile

**azuzar** [aθu'θar] /1f/ vt to incite, egg on

**B.A.** *abr* (= *Buenos Aires*) B.A.

**baba** ['baβa] *nf* spittle, saliva; **babear** /1a/ *vi* to drool, slaver

**babero** [ba'βero] *nm* bib

**babor** [ba'βor] *nm* port (side)

**babosada** [baβo'saða] *nf*: **decir ~s** (*LAM fam*) to talk rubbish; **baboso, -a** *adj* (*LAM*) silly

**baca** ['baka] *nf* (*Auto*) luggage o roof rack

**bacalao** [baka'lao] *nm* cod(fish)

**bache** ['batʃe] *nm* pothole, rut; (*fig*) bad patch

**bachillerato** [batʃiʎe'rato] *nm* two-year *advanced secondary school course*

**bacinica** [baθi'nika] *nf* potty

**bacteria** [bak'terja] *nf* bacterium, germ

**Bahama** [ba'ama]: **las (Islas) ~, las ~s** *nfpl* the Bahamas

**bahía** [ba'ia] *nf* bay

**bailar** [bai'lar] /1a/ *vt, vi* to dance; **bailarín, -ina** *nm/f* dancer; (*de ballet*) ballet dancer; **baile** *nm* dance; (*formal*) ball

**baja** ['baxa] *nf* drop, fall; (*Mil*) casualty; **dar de ~** (*soldado*) to discharge; (*empleado*) to dismiss

**bajada** [ba'xaða] *nf* descent; (*camino*) slope; (*de aguas*) ebb

**bajar** [ba'xar] /1a/ *vi* to go o come down; (*temperatura, precios*) to drop, fall ▷ *vt* (*cabeza*) to bow; (*escalera*) to go o come down; (*precio, voz*) to lower; (*llevar abajo*) to take down; **bajarse** *vr* (*de vehículo*) to get out; (*de autobús*) to get off; **~ de** (*coche*) to get out of; (*autobús*) to get off; **~se algo de Internet** to download sth from the internet

**bajío** [ba'xio] *nm* (*LAM*) lowlands *pl*

**bajo, -a** ['baxo, a] *adj* (*mueble, número, precio*) low; (*piso*) ground *cpd*; (*de estatura*) small, short; (*color*) pale; (*sonido*) faint, soft, low; (*voz, tono*) deep; (*metal*) base; (*humilde*) low, humble ▷ *adv* (*hablar*) softly, quietly; (*volar*) low ▷ *prep* under, below, underneath ▷ *nm* (*Mus*) bass; **~ la lluvia** in the rain

**bajón** [ba'xon] *nm* fall, drop

**bakalao** [baka'lao] *nm* (*Mus*) rave music

**bala** ['bala] *nf* bullet

**balacear** [balaθe'ar] /1a/ *vt* (*LAM, CAM*) to shoot

**balance** [ba'lanθe] *nm* (*Com*) balance; (: *libro*) balance sheet; (: *cuenta general*) stocktaking

**balancear** [balanθe'ar] /1a/ *vt* to balance ▷ *vi* to swing (to and fro); (*vacilar*) to hesitate; **balancearse** *vr* to swing (to and fro); (*vacilar*) to hesitate

**balanza** [ba'lanθa] *nf* scales *pl*, balance; **~ comercial** balance of trade; **~ de pagos/ de poder(es)** balance of payments/of power

**balaustrada** [balaus'traða] *nf* balustrade; (*pasamanos*) banister

**balazo** [ba'laθo] *nm* (*tiro*) shot; (*herida*) bullet wound

**balbucear** [balβuθe'ar] /1a/ *vi, vt* to stammer, stutter

**balcón** [bal'kon] *nm* balcony

**balde** ['balde] *nm* bucket, pail; **de ~** (for) free, for nothing; **en ~** in vain

**baldosa** [bal'dosa] *nf* (*azulejo*) floor tile; (*grande*) flagstone; **baldosín** *nm* tile

**Baleares** [bale'ares] *nfpl*: **las (Islas) ~** the Balearic Islands

**balero** [ba'lero] *nm* (*LAM: juguete*) cup-and-ball toy

**baliza** [ba'liθa] *nf* (*Aviat*) beacon; (*Naut*) buoy

**ballena** [ba'ʎena] *nf* whale

**ballet** (*pl* **ballets**) [ba'le] *nm* ballet

**balneario, -a** [balne'arjo, a] *adj* ▷ *nm* spa; (*LAM: en la costa*) seaside resort

**balón** [ba'lon] *nm* ball

**baloncesto** [balon'θesto] *nm* basketball

**balonmano** [balon'mano] *nm* handball

**balonred** [balon'reð] *nm* netball

**balsa** ['balsa] *nf* raft; (*Bot*) balsa wood

**bálsamo** ['balsamo] *nm* balsam, balm

**baluarte** [ba'lwarte] *nm* bastion, bulwark

**bambú** [bam'bu] *nm* bamboo

**banana** [ba'nana] *nf* (*LAM*) banana; **banano** *nm* (*LAM*) banana tree; (*fruta*) banana

**banca** ['banka] *nf* (*Com*) banking

**bancario, -a** [ban'karjo, a] *adj* banking *cpd*, bank *cpd*

**bancarrota** [banka'rrota] *nf* bankruptcy; **declararse en** o **hacer ~** to go bankrupt

**banco** ['banko] *nm* bench; (*Escol*) desk; (*Com*) bank; (*Geo*) stratum; **~ de crédito/de ahorros** credit/savings bank; **~ de arena** sandbank; **~ de datos** (*Inform*) data bank

**banda** ['banda] *nf* band; (*pandilla*) gang; (*Naut*) side, edge; **la B~ Oriental** Uruguay; **~ sonora** soundtrack

**bandada** [ban'daða] nf (de pájaros) flock; (de peces) shoal

**bandazo** [ban'daθo] nm: **dar ~s** to veer from side to side

**bandeja** [ban'dexa] nf tray; **~ de entrada/ salida** in-tray/out-tray

**bandera** [ban'dera] nf flag

**banderilla** [bande'riʎa] nf banderilla

**bandido** [ban'diðo] nm bandit

**bando** ['bando] nm (edicto) edict, proclamation; (facción) faction; **los ~s** (Rel) the banns

**bandolera** [bando'lera] nf: **llevar en ~** to wear across one's chest

**banquero** [ban'kero] nm banker

**banqueta** [ban'keta] nf stool; (LAM: acera) pavement (BRIT), sidewalk (US)

**banquete** [ban'kete] nm banquet; (para convidados) formal dinner; **~ de boda** wedding reception

**banquillo** [ban'kiʎo] nm (Jur) dock, prisoner's bench; (banco) bench; (para los pies) footstool

**banquina** [ban'kina] nf (RPL) hard shoulder (BRIT), berm (US)

**bañadera** [baɲa'ðera] nf (LAM) bath (tub)

**bañador** [baɲa'ðor] nm swimming costume (BRIT), bathing suit (US)

**bañar** [ba'ɲar] /1a/ vt to bath, bathe; (objeto) to dip; (de barniz) to coat; **bañarse** vr (en el mar) to bathe, swim; (en la bañera) to have a bath

**bañera** [ba'ɲera] nf (ESP) bath (tub)

**bañero, -a** [ba'ɲero, a] nm/f lifeguard

**bañista** [ba'ɲista] nmf bather

**baño** ['baɲo] nm (en bañera) bath; (en río, mar) dip, swim; (cuarto) bathroom; (bañera) bath(tub); (capa) coating; **darse o tomar un ~** (en bañera) to have o take a bath; (en mar, piscina) to have a swim; **~ María** bain-marie

**bar** [bar] nm bar

**barahúnda** [bara'unda] nf uproar, hubbub

**baraja** [ba'raxa] nf pack (of cards); **barajar** /1a/ vt (naipes) to shuffle; (fig) to jumble up

**baranda** [ba'randa], **barandilla** [baran'diʎa] nf rail, railing

**barata** [ba'rata] nf (LAM) (bargain) sale

**baratillo** [bara'tiʎo] nm (tienda) junk shop; (subasta) bargain sale; (conjunto de cosas) second-hand goods pl

**barato, -a** [ba'rato, a] adj cheap ▷ adv cheap, cheaply

**barba** ['barβa] nf (mentón) chin; (pelo) beard

**barbacoa** [barβa'koa] nf (parrilla) barbecue; (carne) barbecued meat

**barbaridad** [barβari'ðað] nf barbarity; (acto) barbarism; (atrocidad) outrage; **una ~ de** (fam) loads of; **¡qué ~!** (fam) how awful!

**barbarie** [bar'βarje] nm barbarism; (crueldad) barbarity

**bárbaro, -a** ['barβaro, a] adj barbarous, cruel; (grosero) rough, uncouth ▷ nm/f barbarian ▷ adv: **lo pasamos ~** (fam) we had a great time; **¡qué ~!** (fam) how marvellous!; **un éxito ~** (fam) a terrific success; **es un tipo ~** (fam) he's a great bloke

**barbero** [bar'βero] nm barber, hairdresser

**barbilla** [bar'βiʎa] nf chin, tip of the chin

**barbudo, -a** [bar'βuðo, a] adj bearded

**barca** ['barka] nf (small) boat; **barcaza** nf barge

**Barcelona** [barθe'lona] nf Barcelona

**barco** ['barko] nm boat; (buque) ship; **~ de carga** cargo boat; **~ de vela** sailing ship

**barda** ['barða] nf (LAM: de madera) fence

**baremo** [ba'remo] nm scale

**barítono** [ba'ritono] nm baritone

**barman** ['barman] nm barman

**barniz** [bar'niθ] nm varnish; (en la loza) glaze; (fig) veneer; **barnizar** /1f/ vt to varnish; (loza) to glaze

**barómetro** [ba'rometro] nm barometer

**barquillo** [bar'kiʎo] nm cone, cornet

**barra** ['barra] nf bar, rod; (de un bar, café) bar; (de pan) French loaf; (palanca) lever; **~ de carmín** o **de labios** lipstick; **~ libre** free bar

**barraca** [ba'rraka] nf hut, cabin

**barranco** [ba'rranko] nm ravine; (fig) difficulty

**barrena** [ba'rrena] nf drill

**barrer** [ba'rrer] /2a/ vt to sweep; (quitar) to sweep away

**barrera** [ba'rrera] nf barrier

**barriada** [ba'rrjaða] nf quarter, district

**barricada** [barri'kaða] nf barricade

**barrida** [ba'rriða] nm sweep, sweeping

**barriga** [ba'rriɣa] nf belly; (panza) paunch; **barrigón, -ona, barrigudo, -a** adj potbellied

**barril** [ba'rril] nm barrel, cask

**barrio** ['barrjo] nm (vecindad) area, neighborhood (US); (en las afueras) suburb; **~ chino** red-light district

**barro** ['barro] nm (lodo) mud; (objetos) earthenware; (Med) pimple

**barroco, -a** [ba'rroko, a] adj, nm Baroque

**barrote** [ba'rrote] nm (de ventana etc) bar

**bartola** [bar'tola] nf: **tirarse a la ~** to take it easy, be lazy

**bártulos** ['bartulos] nmpl things, belongings

**barullo** [ba'ruʎo] nm row, uproar

**basar** [ba'sar] /1a/ vt to base; **basarse** vr: **~se en** to be based on

**báscula** [ba'skula] nf (platform) scales pl

**base** ['base] nf base; **a ~ de** on the basis of; (mediante) by means of; **~ de datos** database

**básico, -a** ['basiko, a] *adj* basic
**basílica** [ba'silika] *nf* basilica
**básquetbol** ['basketbol] *nm* (LAM) basketball

**PALABRA CLAVE**

**bastante** [bas'tante] *adj* **1** (*suficiente*) enough; **bastante dinero** enough o sufficient money; **bastantes libros** enough books **2** (*valor intensivo*): **bastante gente** quite a lot of people; **tener bastante calor** to be rather hot
▶ *adv*: **bastante bueno/malo** quite good/rather bad; **bastante rico** pretty rich; **(lo) bastante inteligente (como) para hacer algo** clever enough o sufficiently clever to do sth

**bastar** [bas'tar] /1a/ *vi* to be enough o sufficient; **bastarse** *vr* to be self-sufficient; **~ para** to be enough to; **¡basta!** (that's) enough!
**bastardo, -a** [bas'tarðo, a] *adj, nm/f* bastard
**bastidor** [basti'ðor] *nm* frame; (*de coche*) chassis; (*Teat*) wing; **entre ~es** behind the scenes
**basto, -a** ['basto, a] *adj* coarse, rough ▷ *nmpl*: **~s** (*Naipes*) one of the suits in the Spanish card deck
**bastón** [bas'ton] *nm* stick, staff; (*para pasear*) walking stick
**bastoncillo** [baston'θiʎo] *nm* cotton bud
**basura** [ba'sura] *nf* rubbish, refuse (BRIT), garbage (US) ▷ *adj*: **comida/televisión ~** junk food/TV
**basurero** [basu'rero] *nm* (*hombre*) dustman (BRIT), garbage collector o man (US); (*lugar*) rubbish dump; (*cubo*) (rubbish) bin (BRIT), trash can (US)
**bata** ['bata] *nf* (*gen*) dressing gown; (*cubretodo*) smock, overall; (*Med, Tec etc*) lab(oratory) coat
**batalla** [ba'taʎa] *nf* battle; **de ~** for everyday use; **~ campal** pitched battle
**batallón** [bata'ʎon] *nm* battalion
**batata** [ba'tata] *nf* sweet potato
**batería** [bate'ria] *nf* battery; (*Mus*) drums *pl*; **~ de cocina** kitchen utensils *pl*
**batido, -a** [ba'tiðo, a] *adj* (*camino*) beaten, well-trodden ▷ *nm* (*Culin*) batter; **~ (de leche)** milk shake
**batidora** [bati'ðora] *nf* beater, mixer; **~ eléctrica** food mixer, blender
**batir** [ba'tir] /3a/ *vt* to beat, strike; (*vencer*) to beat, defeat; (*revolver*) to beat, mix; **batirse** *vr* to fight; **~ palmas** to clap, applaud

**batuta** [ba'tuta] *nf* baton; **llevar la ~** (*fig*) to be the boss
**baúl** [ba'ul] *nm* trunk; (LAM Auto) boot (BRIT), trunk (US)
**bautismo** [bau'tismo] *nm* baptism, christening
**bautizar** [bauti'θar] /1f/ *vt* to baptize, christen; (*fam: diluir*) to water down; **bautizo** *nm* baptism, christening
**bayeta** [ba'jeta] *nf* floor cloth
**baza** ['baθa] *nf* trick; **meter ~** to butt in
**bazar** [ba'θar] *nm* bazaar
**bazofia** [ba'θofja] *nf* trash
**be** [be] *nf* name of the letter B; **be chica/grande** (LAM) V/B; **be larga** (LAM) B
**beato, -a** [be'ato, a] *adj* blessed; (*piadoso*) pious
**bebé** [be'βe] (*pl* **bebés**) *nm* baby
**bebedero** [beβe'ðero] *nm* (*para animales*) drinking trough
**bebedor, a** [beβe'ðor, a] *adj* hard-drinking
**beber** [be'βer] /2a/ *vt, vi* to drink
**bebido, -a** [be'βiðo, a] *adj* drunk ▷ *nf* drink
**beca** ['beka] *nf* grant, scholarship; **becario, -a** [be'karjo, a] *nm/f* scholarship holder, grant holder; (*en prácticas laborales*) intern
**bedel** [be'ðel] *nm* porter, janitor; (*Univ*) porter
**béisbol** ['beisβol] *nm* baseball
**Belén** [be'len] *nm* Bethlehem; **belén** (*de Navidad*) nativity scene, crib
**belga** ['belɣa] *adj, nmf* Belgian
**Bélgica** ['belxika] *nf* Belgium
**bélico, -a** ['beliko, a] *adj* (*actitud*) warlike
**belleza** [be'ʎeθa] *nf* beauty
**bello, -a** ['beʎo, a] *adj* beautiful, lovely; **Bellas Artes** Fine Art *sg*
**bellota** [be'ʎota] *nf* acorn
**bemol** [be'mol] *nm* (*Mus*) flat; **esto tiene ~es** (*fam*) this is a tough one
**bencina** [ben'sina] *nf* (LAM: *gasolina*) petrol (BRIT), gas (US)
**bendecir** [bende'θir] /3o/ *vt* to bless
**bendición** [bendi'θjon] *nf* blessing
**bendito, -a** [ben'dito, a] *pp de* **bendecir** ▷ *adj* holy; (*afortunado*) lucky; (*feliz*) happy; (*sencillo*) simple ▷ *nm/f* simple soul
**beneficencia** [benefi'θenθja] *nf* charity
**beneficiario, -a** [benefi'θjarjo, a] *nm/f* beneficiary
**beneficio** [bene'fiθjo] *nm* (*bien*) benefit, advantage; (*Com*) profit, gain; **a ~ de** for the benefit of; **beneficioso, -a** *adj* beneficial
**benéfico, -a** [be'nefiko, a] *adj* charitable
**beneplácito** [bene'plaθito] *nm* approval, consent
**benévolo, -a** [be'neβolo, a] *adj* benevolent, kind
**benigno, -a** [be'niɣno, a] *adj* kind; (*suave*) mild; (*Med: tumor*) benign, non-malignant

**berberecho** [berβe'retʃo] nm cockle
**berenjena** [beren'xena] nf aubergine
(BRIT), eggplant (US)
**Berlín** [ber'lin] nm Berlin
**berlinesa** [berli'nesa] nf (LAM) doughnut,
donut (US)
**bermudas** [ber'muðas] nfpl Bermuda shorts
**berrido** [be'rriðo] nm bellow(ing)
**berrinche** [be'rrintʃe] nm (fam) temper,
tantrum
**berro** ['berro] nm watercress
**berza** ['berθa] nf cabbage
**besamel** [besa'mel] nf (Culin) white sauce,
bechamel sauce
**besar** [be'sar] /1a/ vt to kiss; (fig: tocar) to
graze; **besarse** vr to kiss (one another);
**beso** nm kiss
**bestia** ['bestja] nf beast, animal; (fig)
idiot; ~ **de carga** beast of burden; **bestial**
adj bestial; (fam) terrific; **bestialidad** nf
bestiality; (fam) stupidity
**besugo** [be'suɣo] nm sea bream; (fam) idiot
**besuquear** [besuke'ar] /1a/ vt to cover
with kisses; **besuquearse** vr to kiss and
cuddle
**betabel** [beta'bel] nm (LAM) beetroot (BRIT),
beet (US)
**betún** [be'tun] nm shoe polish; (Química)
bitumen
**biberón** [biβe'ron] nm feeding bottle
**Biblia** ['biβlja] nf Bible
**bibliografía** [biβljoɣra'fia] nf bibliography
**biblioteca** [biβljo'teka] nf library; (estantes)
bookshelves pl; ~ **de consulta** reference
library; **bibliotecario, -a** nm/f librarian
**bicarbonato** [bikarβo'nato] nm
bicarbonate
**bicho** ['bitʃo] nm (animal) small animal;
(sabandija) bug, insect; (Taur) bull
**bici** ['biθi] nf (fam) bike
**bicicleta** [biθi'kleta] nf bicycle, cycle; **ir
en** ~ to cycle
**bidé** [bi'ðe] nm bidet
**bidón** [bi'ðon] nm (grande) drum; (pequeño)
can

**PALABRA CLAVE**

**bien** [bjen] nm **1** (bienestar) good; **te lo digo
por tu bien** I'm telling you for your own
good; **el bien y el mal** good and evil
**2** (posesión): **bienes** goods; **bienes de
consumo/equipo** consumer/capital goods;
**bienes inmuebles** o **raíces/bienes muebles**
real estate sg/personal property sg
▶ adv **1** (de manera satisfactoria, correcta etc)
well; **trabaja/come bien** she works/eats
well; **contestó bien** he answered correctly;
**me siento bien** I feel fine; **no me siento**

**bien** I don't feel very well; **se está bien aquí**
it's nice here
**2**: **hiciste bien en llamarme** you were right
to call me
**3** (valor intensivo) very; **un cuarto bien
caliente** a nice warm room; **bien se ve
que ...** it's quite clear that ...
**4**: **estar bien: estoy muy bien aquí** I feel
very happy here; **está bien que vengan** it's
all right for them to come; **¡está bien! lo
haré** oh all right, I'll do it
**5** (de buena gana): **yo bien que iría pero ...**
I'd gladly go but ...
▶ excl: **¡bien!** (aprobación) OK!; **¡muy bien!**
well done!
▶ adj inv: **gente bien** posh people
▶ conj **1**: **bien ... bien: bien en coche bien
en tren** either by car or by train
**2**: **no bien** (esp LAM): **no bien llegue
te llamaré** as soon as I arrive I'll call you
**3**: **si bien** even though; V tb **más**

**bienal** [bje'nal] adj biennial
**bienestar** [bjenes'tar] nm well-being
**bienvenido, -a** [bjembe'niðo, a] excl
welcome! ▶ nf welcome; **dar la bienvenida
a algn** to welcome sb
**bife** ['bife] nm (LAM) steak
**bifurcación** [bifurka'θjon] nf fork
**bígamo, -a** ['biɣamo, a] adj bigamous
▷ nm/f bigamist
**bigote** [bi'ɣote] nm moustache;
**bigotudo, -a** adj with a big moustache
**bikini** [bi'kini] nm bikini; (Culin) toasted
cheese and ham sandwich
**bilingüe** [bi'lingwe] adj bilingual
**billar** [bi'ʎar] nm billiards sg; **billares** nmpl
(lugar) billiard hall; (galería de atracciones)
amusement arcade; ~ **americano** pool
**billete** [bi'ʎete] nm ticket; (de banco)
banknote (BRIT), bill (US); (carta) note; ~ **de
ida** o **sencillo** single (BRIT) o one-way (US)
ticket; ~ **de ida y vuelta** return (BRIT) o
round-trip (US) ticket; ~ **electrónico**
e-ticket; **sacar (un)** ~ to get a ticket; **un** ~
**de cinco libras** a five-pound note
**billetera** [biʎe'tera] nf wallet
**billón** [bi'ʎon] nm billion
**bimensual** [bimen'swal] adj twice monthly
**bingo** ['bingo] nm bingo
**biocarburante** [biokarβu'rante],
**biocombustible** [biokomβus'tiβle] nm
biofuel
**biodegradable** [bioðeɣra'ðaβle] adj
biodegradable
**biografía** [bjoɣra'fia] nf biography
**biología** [biolo'xia] nf biology; **biológico, -a**
adj biological; (cultivo, producto) organic;
**biólogo, -a** nm/f biologist

**biombo** ['bjombo] nm (folding) screen
**bioterrorismo** [bioterro'rismo] nm bioterrorism
**bipolar** [bi'polar] adj (Med) bipolar
**biquini** [bi'kini] nm = **bikini**
**birlar** [bir'lar] /1a/ vt (fam) to pinch
**Birmania** [bir'manja] nf Burma
**birome** [bi'rome] nf (LAM) ballpoint (pen)
**birria** ['birrja] nf (fam): **ser una ~** (película, libro) to be rubbish
**bis** [bis] excl encore!
**bisabuelo, -a** [bisa'βwelo, a] nm/f great-grandfather/mother
**bisagra** [bi'saɣra] nf hinge
**bisiesto** [bi'sjesto] adj: **año ~** leap year
**bisnieto, -a** [bis'njeto, a] nm/f great-grandson/daughter
**bisonte** [bi'sonte] nm bison
**bistec** [bis'tek], **bisté** [bis'te] nm steak
**bisturí** [bistu'ri] nm scalpel
**bisutería** [bisute'ria] nf imitation o costume jewellery
**bit** [bit] nm (Inform) bit
**bizco, -a** ['biθko, a] adj cross-eyed
**bizcocho** [biθ'kotʃo] nm (Culin) sponge cake
**blanco, -a** ['blanko, a] adj white ▷ nm/f white man/woman, white ▷ nm (color) white; (en texto) blank; (Mil, fig) target; **en ~** blank; **noche en ~** sleepless night; **estar sin blanca** to be broke
**blandir** [blan'dir] vt to brandish
**blando, -a** ['blando, a] adj soft; (tierno) tender, gentle; (carácter) mild; (fam) cowardly
**blanqueador** [blankea'ðor] nm (LAM) bleach
**blanquear** [blanke'ar] /1a/ vt to whiten; (fachada) to whitewash; (paño) to bleach; (dinero) to launder ▷ vi to turn white
**blanquillo** [blan'kiʎo] nm (LAM, CAM) egg
**blasfemar** [blasfe'mar] /1a/ vi to blaspheme; (fig) to curse
**bledo** ['bleðo] nm: **(no) me importa un ~** I couldn't care less
**blindado, -a** [blin'daðo, a] adj (Mil) armour-plated; (antibalas) bulletproof; **coche** o (LAM) **carro ~** armoured car
**bloc** [blok] (pl **blocs**) nm writing pad
**blof** [blof] nm (LAM) bluff; **blofear** /1a/ vi (LAM) to bluff
**blog** [bloɣ] (pl **blogs**) nm blog
**blogosfera** [bloɣos'fera] nf blogosphere
**bloguero, -a** [blo'ɣero, a] nm/f blogger
**bloque** ['bloke] nm block; (Pol) bloc
**bloquear** [bloke'ar] /1a/ vt to blockade; **bloqueo** nm blockade; (Com) freezing, blocking; **bloqueo mental** mental block
**blusa** ['blusa] nf blouse
**bobada** [bo'βaða] nf foolish action (o statement); **decir ~s** to talk nonsense

**bobina** [bo'βina] nf (Tec) bobbin; (Foto) spool; (Elec) coil
**bobo, -a** ['boβo, a] adj (tonto) daft, silly; (cándido) naïve ▷ nm/f fool, idiot ▷ nm (Teat) clown, funny man
**boca** ['boka] nf mouth; (de crustáceo) pincer; (de cañón) muzzle; (entrada) mouth, entrance; **bocas** nfpl (de río) mouth sg; **~ abajo/arriba** face down/up; **se me hace la ~ agua** my mouth is watering; **~ de incendios** hydrant; **~ del estómago** pit of the stomach; **~ de metro** tube (BRIT) o subway (US) entrance
**bocacalle** [boka'kaʎe] nf side street; **la primera ~** the first turning o street
**bocadillo** [boka'ðiʎo] nm sandwich
**bocado** [bo'kaðo] nm mouthful, bite; (de caballo) bridle
**bocajarro** [boka'xarro]: **a ~** adv (Mil) at point-blank range
**bocanada** [boka'naða] nf (de vino) mouthful, swallow; (de aire) gust, puff
**bocata** [bo'kata] nm (fam) sandwich
**bocazas** [bo'kaθas] nm inv, nf inv (fam) bigmouth
**boceto** [bo'θeto] nm sketch, outline
**bochorno** [bo'tʃorno] nm (vergüenza) embarrassment; (calor): **hace ~** it's very muggy
**bocina** [bo'θina] nf (Mus) trumpet; (Auto) horn; (para hablar) megaphone
**boda** ['boða] nf (tb: **~s**) wedding, marriage; (fiesta) wedding reception; **~s de plata/de oro** silver/golden wedding sg
**bodega** [bo'ðeɣa] nf (de vino) (wine) cellar; (depósito) storeroom; (de barco) hold
**bodegón** [bode'ɣon] nm (Arte) still life
**bofetada** [bofe'taða] nf slap (in the face)
**boga** ['boɣa] nf: **en ~** in vogue
**Bogotá** [boɣo'ta] n Bogota
**bohemio, -a** [bo'emjo, a] adj, nm/f Bohemian
**bohío** [bo'io] nm (LAM) shack, hut
**boicot** [boi'ko(t)] (pl **boicots**) nm boycott; **boicotear** /1a/ vt to boycott
**bóiler** ['boiler] nm (LAM) boiler
**boina** ['boina] nf beret
**bola** ['bola] nf ball; (canica) marble; (Naipes) (grand) slam; (betún) shoe polish; (mentira) tale, story; **bolas** nfpl (LAM) bolas; **~ de billar** billiard ball; **~ de nieve** snowball
**boleadoras** [bolea'ðoras] nfpl bolas sg
**bolear** [bole'ar] /1a/ vt (LAM: zapatos) to polish, shine
**bolera** [bo'lera] nf skittle o bowling alley
**bolero, -a** [bo'lero, a] nm bolero ▷ nm/f (LAM: limpiabotas) shoeshine boy/girl
**boleta** [bo'leta] nf (LAM: permiso) pass, permit; (de rifa) ticket; (recibo) receipt;

(*para votar*) ballot; **~ de calificaciones** report card

**boletería** [bolete'ria] *nf* (LAM) ticket office

**boletín** [bole'tin] *nm* bulletin; (*periódico*) journal, review; **~ de noticias** news bulletin

**boleto** [bo'leto] *nm* (*esp* LAM) ticket; **~ de apuestas** betting slip; **~ de ida y vuelta** (LAM) round-trip ticket; **~ electrónico** (LAM) e-ticket; **~ redondo** (LAM) round-trip ticket

**boli** ['boli] *nm* Biro®

**bolígrafo** [bo'liɣrafo] *nm* ball-point pen, Biro®

**bolilla** [bo'liʎa] *nf* (LAM) topic

**bolillo** [bo'liʎo] *nm* (LAM) (bread) roll

**bolita** [bo'lita] *nf* (LAM) marble

**bolívar** [bo'liβar] *nm* monetary unit of Venezuela

**Bolivia** [bo'liβja] *nf* Bolivia; **boliviano, -a** *adj, nm/f* Bolivian

**bollería** [boʎe'ria] *nf* cakes *pl* and pastries *pl*

**bollo** ['boʎo] *nm* (*de pan*) roll; (*chichón*) bump, lump; (*abolladura*) dent

**bolo** ['bolo] *nm* skittle; (*píldora*) (large) pill; **(juego de) ~s** skittles *sg*

**bolsa** ['bolsa] *nf* (*saco*) bag; (LAM) pocket; (*de mujer*) handbag; (*Anat*) cavity, sac; (*Com*) stock exchange; (*Minería*) pocket; **~ de agua caliente** hot water bottle; **~ de aire** air pocket; **~ de dormir** (LAM) sleeping bag; **~ de papel** paper bag; **~ de plástico** plastic (*o* carrier) bag; **~ de la compra** shopping bag

**bolsillo** [bol'siʎo] *nm* pocket; (*cartera*) purse; **de ~** pocket

**bolso** ['bolso] *nm* (*bolsa*) bag; (*de mujer*) handbag

**bomba** ['bomba] *nf* (Mil) bomb; (Tec) pump ▷ *adj* (*fam*): **noticia ~** bombshell ▷ *adv* (*fam*): **pasarlo ~** to have a great time; **~ atómica/ de humo/de retardo** atomic/smoke/time bomb

**bombacha** [bom'batʃa] *nf* (LAM) panties *pl*

**bombardear** [bombarðe'ar] /1a/ *vt* to bombard; (Mil) to bomb; **bombardeo** *nm* bombardment; bombing

**bombazo** [bom'baθo] *nm* (LAM: *explosión*) explosion; (*fam: notición*) bombshell; (*éxito*) smash hit

**bombear** [bombe'ar] /1a/ *vt* (*agua*) to pump (out *o* up)

**bombero** [bom'bero] *nm* firefighter

**bombilla** [bom'biʎa] (ESP), **bombita** [bom'bita] (LAM) *nf* (light) bulb

**bombo** ['bombo] *nm* (Mus) bass drum; (Tec) drum

**bombón** [bom'bon] *nm* chocolate; (LAM: *de caramelo*) marshmallow

**bombona** [bom'bona] *nf*: **~ de butano** gas cylinder

**bonachón, -ona** [bona'tʃon, ona] *adj* good-natured

**bonanza** [bo'nanθa] *nf* (Naut) fair weather; (*fig*) bonanza; (*Minería*) rich pocket *o* vein

**bondad** [bon'dað] *nf* goodness, kindness; **tenga la ~ de** (please) be good enough to

**bonito, -a** [bo'nito, a] *adj* pretty; (*agradable*) nice ▷ *nm* (*atún*) tuna (fish)

**bono** ['bono] *nm* voucher; (*Finanzas*) bond

**bonobús** [bono'βus] *nm* (ESP) bus pass

**Bono Loto, bonoloto** [bono'loto] *nm o f* (ESP) state-run weekly lottery; V *tb* **lotería**

**boquerón** [boke'ron] *nm* (*pez*) (kind of) anchovy; (*agujero*) large hole

**boquete** [bo'kete] *nm* gap, hole

**boquiabierto, -a** [bokia'βjerto, a] *adj* open-mouthed (in astonishment); **quedarse ~** to be amazed *o* flabbergasted

**boquilla** [bo'kiʎa] *nf* (*de riego*) nozzle; (*de cigarro*) cigarette holder; (Mus) mouthpiece

**borbotón** [borβo'ton] *nm*: **salir a borbotones** to gush out

**borda** ['borða] *nf* (Naut) gunwale, rail; **echar** *o* **tirar algo por la ~** to throw sth overboard

**bordado** [bor'ðaðo] *nm* embroidery

**bordar** [bor'ðar] /1a/ *vt* to embroider

**borde** ['borðe] *nm* edge, border; (*de camino etc*) side; (*en la costura*) hem; **al ~ de** (*fig*) on the verge *o* brink of ▷ *adj*: **ser ~** (ESP *fam*) to be rude; **bordear** /1a/ *vt* to border

**bordillo** [bor'ðiʎo] *nm* kerb (BRIT), curb (US)

**bordo** ['borðo] *nm* (Naut) side; **a ~** on board

**borlote** [bor'lote] *nm* (LAM) row, uproar

**borrachera** [borra'tʃera] *nf* (*ebriedad*) drunkenness; (*orgía*) spree, binge

**borracho, -a** [bo'rratʃo, a] *adj* drunk ▷ *nm/f* (*que bebe mucho*) drunkard, drunk; (*temporalmente*) drunk, drunk man/woman

**borrador** [borra'ðor] *nm* (*escritura*) first draft, rough sketch; (*goma*) rubber (BRIT), eraser

**borrar** [bo'rrar] /1a/ *vt* to erase, rub out

**borrasca** [bo'rraska] *nf* storm

**borrego, -a** [bo'rreɣo, a] *nm/f* lamb; (*oveja*) sheep; (*fig*) simpleton ▷ *nm* (LAM *fam*) false rumour

**borrico, -a** [bo'rriko, a] *nm* donkey; (*fig*) stupid man ▷ *nf* she-donkey; (*fig*) stupid woman

**borrón** [bo'rron] *nm* (*mancha*) stain

**borroso, -a** [bo'rroso, a] *adj* vague, unclear; (*escritura*) illegible

**bosque** ['boske] *nm* wood; (*grande*) forest

**bostezar** [boste'θar] /1f/ *vi* to yawn; **bostezo** *nm* yawn

**bota** ['bota] *nf* (*calzado*) boot; (*de vino*) leather wine bottle; **~s de agua** *o* **goma** Wellingtons

**botánico, -a** [boˈtaniko, a] *adj* botanical
▷ *nm/f* botanist
**botar** [boˈtar] /1a/ *vt* to throw, hurl; (*Naut*)
to launch; (*esp* LAM *fam*) to throw out ▷ *vi*
to bounce
**bote** [ˈbote] *nm* (*salto*) bounce; (*golpe*)
thrust; (*vasija*) tin, can; (*embarcación*) boat;
(LAM *pey*: *cárcel*) jail; **de ~ en ~** packed,
jammed full; **~ salvavidas** lifeboat; **~ de la
basura** (LAM) dustbin (BRIT), trash can (US)
**botella** [boˈteʎa] *nf* bottle; **botellín** *nm*
small bottle; **botellón** *nm* (ESP *fam*) outdoor
drinking session (*involving groups of young
people*)
**botijo** [boˈtixo] *nm* (earthenware) jug
**botín** [boˈtin] *nm* (*calzado*) half boot;
(*polaina*) spat; (*Mil*) booty
**botiquín** [botiˈkin] *nm* (*armario*) medicine
chest; (*portátil*) first-aid kit
**botón** [boˈton] *nm* button; (*Bot*) bud
**botones** [boˈtones] *nm inv* bellboy,
bellhop (US)
**bóveda** [ˈboβeða] *nf* (*Arq*) vault
**boxeador** [bokseaˈðor] *nm* boxer
**boxeo** [bokˈseo] *nm* boxing
**boya** [ˈboja] *nf* (*Naut*) buoy; (*flotador*) float
**boyante** [boˈjante] *adj* prosperous
**bozal** [boˈθal] *nm* (*de caballo*) halter; (*de
perro*) muzzle
**braga** [ˈbraɣa] *nf* (*de bebé*) nappy, diaper
(US); **bragas** *nfpl* (*de mujer*) panties
**bragueta** [braˈɣeta] *nf* fly (BRIT), flies *pl*
(BRIT), zipper (US)
**braille** [breil] *nm* braille
**brasa** [ˈbrasa] *nf* live *o* hot coal
**brasero** [braˈsero] *nm* brazier
**brasier** [braˈsjer] *nm* (LAM) bra
**Brasil** [braˈsil] *nm*: **(el) ~** Brazil;
**brasileño, -a** *adj*, *nm/f* Brazilian
**brassier** [braˈsjer] *nm* (LAM) V **brasier**
**bravo, -a** [ˈbraβo, a] *adj* (*valiente*) brave;
(*feroz*) ferocious; (*salvaje*) wild; (*mar etc*)
rough, stormy ▷ *excl* bravo!; **bravura** *nf*
bravery; ferocity
**braza** [ˈbraθa] *nf* fathom; **nadar a la ~** to
swim (the) breast-stroke
**brazalete** [braθaˈlete] *nm* (*pulsera*)
bracelet; (*banda*) armband
**brazo** [ˈbraθo] *nm* arm; (*Zool*) foreleg; (*Bot*)
limb, branch; **cogidos** *etc* **del ~** arm in arm
**brebaje** [breˈβaxe] *nm* potion
**brecha** [ˈbretʃa] *nf* (*hoyo, vacío*) gap,
opening; (*Mil*, *fig*) breach
**brega** [ˈbreɣa] *nf* (*lucha*) struggle; (*trabajo*)
hard work
**breva** [ˈbreβa] *nf* (*Bot*) early fig
**breve** [ˈbreβe] *adj* short, brief; **en ~** (*pronto*)
shortly ▷ *nf* (*Mus*) breve; **brevedad** *nf*
brevity, shortness

**bribón, -ona** [briˈβon, ona] *adj* idle, lazy
▷ *nm/f* (*pícaro*) rascal, rogue
**bricolaje** [brikoˈlaxe] *nm* do-it-yourself,
DIY
**brida** [ˈbriða] *nf* bridle, rein; (*Tec*) clamp
**bridge** [britʃ] *nm* bridge
**brigada** [briˈɣaða] *nf* (*unidad*) brigade;
(*trabajadores*) squad, gang ▷ *nm* ≈ sergeant
major
**brillante** [briˈʎante] *adj* brilliant ▷ *nm*
diamond
**brillar** [briˈʎar] /1a/ *vi* to shine; (*joyas*) to
sparkle
**brillo** [ˈbriʎo] *nm* shine; (*brillantez*)
brilliance; (*fig*) splendour; **sacar ~ a** to
polish
**brincar** [brinˈkar] /1g/ *vi* to skip about, hop
about, jump about
**brinco** [ˈbrinko] *nm* jump, leap
**brindar** [brinˈdar] /1a/ *vi*: **~ a o por** to drink
(a toast) to ▷ *vt* to offer, present
**brindis** [ˈbrindis] *nm inv* toast
**brío** [ˈbrio] *nm* spirit, dash
**brisa** [ˈbrisa] *nf* breeze
**británico, -a** [briˈtaniko, a] *adj* British
▷ *nm/f* Briton, British person
**brizna** [ˈbriθna] *nf* (*de hierba*) blade; (*de
tabaco*) leaf
**broca** [ˈbroka] *nf* (*Tec*) drill bit
**brocha** [ˈbrotʃa] *nf* (*large*) paintbrush; **~ de
afeitar** shaving brush
**broche** [ˈbrotʃe] *nm* brooch
**broma** [ˈbroma] *nf* joke; **en ~** in fun, as a
joke; **~ pesada** practical joke; **bromear**
/1a/ *vi* to joke
**bromista** [broˈmista] *adj* fond of joking
▷ *nmf* joker, wag
**bronca** [ˈbronka] *nf* row; **echar una ~ a
algn** to tell sb off
**bronce** [ˈbronθe] *nm* bronze; **bronceado, -a**
*adj* bronze *cpd*; (*por el sol*) tanned ▷ *nm* (sun)
tan; (*Tec*) bronzing
**bronceador** [bronθeaˈðor] *nm* suntan
lotion
**broncearse** [bronθeˈarse] /1a/ *vr* to get a
suntan
**bronquios** [ˈbronkjos] *nmpl* bronchial
tubes
**bronquitis** [bronˈkitis] *nf inv* bronchitis
**brotar** [broˈtar] /1a/ *vi* (*Bot*) to sprout;
(*aguas*) to gush (forth); (*Med*) to break out
**brote** [ˈbrote] *nm* (*Bot*) shoot; (*Med*, *fig*)
outbreak
**bruces** [ˈbruθes]: **de ~** *adv*, **caer** *o* **dar de ~**
to fall headlong, fall flat
**bruja** [ˈbruxa] *nf* witch; **brujería** *nf*
witchcraft
**brujo** [ˈbruxo] *nm* wizard, magician
**brújula** [ˈbruxula] *nf* compass

**bruma** ['bruma] nf mist

**brusco, -a** ['brusko, a] adj (súbito) sudden; (áspero) brusque

**Bruselas** [bru'selas] nf Brussels

**brutal** [bru'tal] adj brutal; **brutalidad** nf brutality

**bruto, -a** ['bruto, a] adj (idiota) stupid; (bestial) brutish; (peso) gross; **en ~** raw, unworked

**Bs.As.** abr = **Buenos Aires**

**bucal** [bu'kal] adj oral; **por vía ~** orally

**bucear** [buθe'ar] /1a/ vi to dive ▷ vt to explore; **buceo** nm diving

**bucle** ['bukle] nm curl

**budismo** [bu'ðismo] nm Buddhism

**buen** [bwen] adj V **bueno**

**buenamente** [bwena'mente] adv (fácilmente) easily; (voluntariamente) willingly

**buenaventura** [bwenaβen'tura] nf (suerte) good luck; (adivinación) fortune

**buenmozo** [bwen'moθo] adj (LAM) handsome

 **PALABRA CLAVE**

**bueno, -a** antes de nmsg **buen** ['bweno, a] adj **1** (excelente etc) good; **es un libro bueno, es un buen libro** it's a good book; **hace bueno, hace buen tiempo** the weather is fine, it is fine; **el bueno de Paco** good old Paco; **fue muy bueno conmigo** he was very nice o kind to me
**2** (apropiado): **ser bueno para** to be good for; **creo que vamos por buen camino** I think we're on the right track
**3** (irónico): **le di un buen rapapolvo** I gave him a good o real ticking off; **¡buen conductor estás hecho!** some driver o a fine driver you are!; **¡estaría bueno que ...!** a fine thing it would be if ...!
**4** (atractivo, sabroso): **está bueno este bizcocho** this sponge is delicious; **Julio está muy bueno** (fam) Julio's gorgeous
**5** (saludos): **¡buen día!** (LAM), **¡buenos días!** (good) morning!; **¡buenas (tardes)!** good afternoon!; (más tarde) good evening!; **¡buenas noches!** good night!
**6** (otras locuciones): **estar de buenas** to be in a good mood; **por las buenas o por las malas** by hook or by crook; **de buenas a primeras** all of a sudden
▶ excl: **¡bueno!** all right!; **bueno, ¿y qué?** well, so what?

**Buenos Aires** [bweno'saires] nm Buenos Aires

**buey** [bwei] nm ox

**búfalo** ['bufalo] nm buffalo

**bufanda** [bu'fanda] nf scarf

**bufete** [bu'fete] nm (despacho de abogado) lawyer's office

**bufón** [bu'fon] nm clown

**buhardilla** [buar'ðiʎa] nf attic

**búho** ['buo] nm owl; (fig) hermit, recluse

**buitre** ['bwitre] nm vulture

**bujía** [bu'xia] nf (vela) candle; (Elec) candle (power); (Auto) spark plug

**bula** ['bula] nf (papal) bull

**bulbo** ['bulβo] nm (Bot) bulb

**bulevar** [bule'βar] nm boulevard

**Bulgaria** [bul'yarja] nf Bulgaria; **búlgaro, -a** adj, nm/f Bulgarian

**bulla** ['buʎa] nf (ruido) uproar; (de gente) crowd

**bullicio** [bu'ʎiθjo] nm (ruido) uproar; (movimiento) bustle

**bulto** ['bulto] nm (paquete) package; (fardo) bundle; (tamaño) size, bulkiness; (Med) swelling, lump; (silueta) vague shape

**buñuelo** [bu'ɲwelo] nm ≈ doughnut, ≈ donut (us); (fruta de sartén) fritter

**buque** ['buke] nm ship, vessel; **~ de guerra** warship

**burbuja** [bur'βuxa] nf bubble

**burdel** [bur'ðel] nm brothel

**burgués, -esa** [bur'yes, esa] adj middle-class, bourgeois; **burguesía** nf middle class, bourgeoisie

**burla** ['burla] nf (mofa) gibe; (broma) joke; (engaño) trick; **burlar** /1a/ vt (engañar) to deceive ▷ vi to joke; **burlarse** vr to joke; **burlarse de** to make fun of

**burlón, -ona** [bur'lon, ona] adj mocking

**buró** [bu'ro] nm bureau

**burocracia** [buro'kraθja] nf bureaucracy

**burrada** [bu'rraða] nf: **decir ~s** to talk nonsense; **hacer ~s** to act stupid; **una ~** (ESP: mucho) a (hell of a) lot

**burro, -a** ['burro, a] nm/f (Zool) donkey; (fig) ass, idiot

**bursátil** [bur'satil] adj stock-exchange cpd

**bus** [bus] nm bus

**busca** ['buska] nf search, hunt ▷ nm bleeper; **en ~ de** in search of

**buscador** [buska'ðor] nm (Internet) search engine

**buscar** [bus'kar] /1g/ vt to look for; (Inform) to search ▷ ví to look, search, seek; **se busca secretaria** secretary wanted

**busque etc** ['buske] vb V **buscar**

**búsqueda** ['buskeða] nf = **busca**

**busto** ['busto] nm (Anat, Arte) bust

**butaca** [bu'taka] nf armchair; (de cine, teatro) stall, seat

**butano** [bu'tano] nm butane (gas)

**buzo** ['buθo] nm diver

**buzón** [bu'θon] nm (gen) letter box; (en la calle) pillar box (BRIT)

# C

**C.** abr (= centígrado) C.; (= compañía) Co

**C/** abr (= calle) St

**cabal** [ka'βal] adj (exacto) exact; (correcto) right, proper; (acabado) finished, complete; **cabales** nmpl: **estar en sus ~es** to be in one's right mind

**cabalgar** [kaβal'ɣar] /1h/ vt, vi to ride

**cabalgata** [kaβal'ɣata] nf procession

**caballa** [ka'βaʎa] nf mackerel

**caballería** [kaβaʎe'ria] nf mount; (Mil) cavalry

**caballero** [kaβa'ʎero] nm gentleman; (de la orden de caballería) knight; (trato directo) sir

**caballete** [kaβa'ʎete] nm (Arte) easel; (Tec) trestle

**caballito** [kaβa'ʎito] nm (caballo pequeño) small horse, pony; **caballitos** nmpl merry-go-round sg

**caballo** [ka'βaʎo] nm horse; (Ajedrez) knight; (Naipes) ≈ queen; **ir en ~** to ride; **~ de carreras** racehorse; **~ de vapor** o **de fuerza** horsepower

**cabaña** [ka'βaɲa] nf (casita) hut, cabin

**cabecear** [kaβeθe'ar] /1a/ vt, vi to nod

**cabecera** [kaβe'θera] nf head; (Imprenta) headline

**cabecilla** [kaβe'θiʎa] nm ringleader

**cabellera** [kaβe'ʎera] nf (head of) hair; (de cometa) tail

**cabello** [ka'βeʎo] nm (tb: **~s**) hair sg; **~ de ángel** confectionery and pastry filling made of pumpkin and syrup

**caber** [ka'βer] /2l/ vi (entrar) to fit, go; **caben tres más** there's room for three more

**cabestrillo** [kaβes'triʎo] nm sling

**cabeza** [ka'βeθa] nf head; (Pol) chief, leader; **~ de ajo** bulb of garlic; **~ de familia** head of the household; **~ rapada** skinhead; **cabezada** nf (golpe) butt; **dar una cabezada** to nod off; **cabezón, -ona** adj

with a big head; (vino) heady; (obstinado) pig-headed

**cabida** [ka'βiða] nf space

**cabina** [ka'βina] nf cabin; (de avión) cockpit; (de camión) cab; **~ telefónica** (tele)phone box (BRIT) o booth

**cabizbajo, -a** [kaβiθ'βaxo, a] adj crestfallen, dejected

**cable** ['kaβle] nm cable

**cabo** ['kaβo] nm (de objeto) end, extremity; (Mil) corporal; (Naut) rope, cable; (Geo) cape; **al ~ de tres días** after three days; **llevar a ~** to carry out

**cabra** ['kaβra] nf goat

**cabré** etc [ka'βre] vb V **caber**

**cabrear** [kaβre'ar] /1a/ vt to annoy; **cabrearse** vr (enfadarse) to fly off the handle

**cabrito** [ka'βrito] nm kid

**cabrón** [ka'βron] nm cuckold; (fam!) bastard (!)

**caca** ['kaka] nf pooh

**cacahuete** [kaka'wete] nm (ESP) peanut

**cacao** [ka'kao] nm cocoa; (Bot) cacao

**cacarear** [kakare'ar] /1a/ vi (persona) to boast; (gallo) to crow

**cacarizo, -a** [kaka'riθo, a] adj (LAM) pockmarked

**cacería** [kaθe'ria] nf hunt

**cacerola** [kaθe'rola] nf pan, saucepan

**cachalote** [katʃa'lote] nm sperm whale

**cacharro** [ka'tʃarro] nm (cerámica) piece of pottery; **cacharros** nmpl pots and pans

**cachear** [katʃe'ar] /1a/ vt to search, frisk

**cachemir** [katʃe'mir] nm cashmere

**cachetada** [katʃe'taða] nf (LAM fam: bofetada) slap

**cachete** [ka'tʃete] nm (Anat) cheek; (bofetada) slap (in the face)

**cachivache** [katʃi'βatʃe] nm piece of junk; **cachivaches** nmpl junk sg

**cacho** ['katʃo] nm (small) bit; (LAM: cuerno) horn

**cachondeo** [katʃon'deo] nm (ESP fam) farce, joke

**cachondo, -a** [ka'tʃondo, a] adj (Zool) on heat; (caliente) randy, sexy; (gracioso) funny

**cachorro, -a** [ka'tʃorro, a] nm/f (de perro) pup, puppy; (de león) cub

**cachucha** [ka'tʃutʃa] (MÉX fam) nf cap

**cacique** [ka'θike] nm chief, local ruler; (Pol) local party boss

**cacto** ['kakto] nm, **cactus** ['kaktus] nm inv cactus

**cada** ['kaða] adj inv each; (antes de número) every; **~ día** each day, every day; **~ dos días** every other day; **~ uno/a** each one, every one; **~ vez más/menos** more and more/less and less; **~ vez que ...** whenever, every time (that) ...; **uno de ~ diez** one out of every ten

**cadáver** [ka'ðaβer] nm (dead) body, corpse

**cadena** [ka'ðena] nf chain; (TV) channel; **trabajo en ~** assembly line work; **~ montañosa** mountain range; **~ perpetua** (Jur) life imprisonment; **~ de caracteres** (Inform) character string

**cadera** [ka'ðera] nf hip

**cadete** [ka'ðete] nm cadet

**caducar** [kaðu'kar] /1g/ vi to expire; **caduco, -a** adj (idea etc) outdated, outmoded; **de hoja caduca** deciduous

**caer** [ka'er] /2n/ vi to fall; **caerse** vr to fall (down); **dejar ~** to drop; **su cumpleaños cae en viernes** her birthday falls on a Friday

**café** [ka'fe] (pl **cafés**) nm (bebida, planta) coffee; (lugar) café ▷ adj (color) brown; **~ con leche** white coffee; **~ solo, ~ negro** (LAM) (small) black coffee

**cafetera** [kafe'tera] nf V **cafetero**

**cafetería** [kafete'ria] nf cafe

**cafetero, -a** [kafe'tero, a] adj coffee cpd ▷ nf coffee pot; **ser muy ~** to be a coffee addict

**cagar** [ka'ɣar] /1h/ (fam!) vt to bungle, mess up ▷ vi to have a shit (!)

**caído, -a** [ka'iðo, a] adj fallen ▷ nf fall; (declive) slope; (disminución) fall, drop

**caiga** etc ['kaiɣa] vb V **caer**

**caimán** [kai'man] nm alligator

**caja** ['kaxa] nf box; (para reloj) case; (de ascensor) shaft; (Com) cash box; (donde se hacen los pagos) cashdesk; (en supermercado) checkout, till; **~ de ahorros** savings bank; **~ de cambios** gearbox; **~ de fusibles** fuse box; **~ fuerte** o **de caudales** safe, strongbox

**cajero, -a** [ka'xero, a] nm/f cashier ▷ nm: **~ automático** cash dispenser

**cajetilla** [kaxe'tiʎa] nf (de cigarrillos) packet

**cajón** [ka'xon] nm big box; (de mueble) drawer

**cajuela** [kax'wela] nf (MÉX: Auto) boot (BRIT), trunk (US)

**cal** [kal] nf lime

**cala** ['kala] nf (Geo) cove, inlet; (de barco) hold

**calabacín** [kalaβa'θin] nm (Bot) baby marrow; (: más pequeño) courgette (BRIT), zucchini (US)

**calabacita** [kalaβa'θita] (LAM) nf courgette (BRIT), zucchini (US)

**calabaza** [kala'βaθa] nf (Bot) pumpkin

**calabozo** [kala'βoθo] nm (cárcel) prison; (celda) cell

**calado, -a** [ka'laðo, a] adj (prenda) lace cpd ▷ nm (Naut) draught ▷ nf (de cigarrillos) puff; **estar ~ (hasta los huesos)** to be soaked (to the skin)

**calamar** [kala'mar] nm squid

**calambre** [ka'lambre] nm (Elec) shock

**calar** [ka'lar] /1a/ vt to soak, drench; (penetrar) to pierce, penetrate; (comprender) to see through; (vela, red) to lower; **calarse** vr (Auto) to stall; **~se las gafas** to stick one's glasses on

**calavera** [kala'βera] nf skull

**calcar** [kal'kar] /1g/ vt (reproducir) to trace; (imitar) to copy

**calcetín** [kalθe'tin] nm sock

**calcio** ['kalθjo] nm calcium

**calcomanía** [kalkoma'nia] nf transfer

**calculador, a** [kalkula'ðor, a] adj calculating ▷ nf calculator

**calcular** [kalku'lar] /1a/ vt (Mat) to calculate, compute; **~ que ...** to reckon that ...

**cálculo** ['kalkulo] nm calculation

**caldera** [kal'dera] nf boiler

**calderilla** [kalde'riʎa] nf (moneda) small change

**caldo** ['kaldo] nm stock; (consomé) consommé

**calefacción** [kalefak'θjon] nf heating; **~ central** central heating

**calefón** [kale'fon] nm (RPL) boiler

**calendario** [kalen'darjo] nm calendar

**calentador** [kalenta'ðor] nm heater

**calentamiento** [kalenta'mjento] nm (Deporte) warm-up; **~ global** global warming

**calentar** [kalen'tar] /1j/ vt to heat (up); **calentarse** vr to heat up, warm up; (fig: discusión etc) to get heated

**calentón, -ona** [kalen'ton, ona] (RPL fam) adj (sexualmente) horny, randy (BRIT)

**calentura** [kalen'tura] nf (Med) fever, (high) temperature

**calesita** [kale'sita] nf (LAM) merry-go-round, carousel

**calibre** [ka'liβre] nm (de cañón) calibre, bore; (diámetro) diameter; (fig) calibre

**calidad** [kali'ðað] nf quality; **de ~** quality cpd; **en ~ de** in the capacity of

**cálido, -a** ['kaliðo, a] adj hot; (fig) warm

**caliente** [ka'ljente] vb V **calentar** ▷ adj hot; (fig) fiery; (disputa) heated; (fam: cachondo) horny, randy (BRIT)

**calificación** [kalifika'θjon] nf qualification; (de alumno) grade, mark

**calificado, -a** [kalifi'kaðo, a] adj (LAM: competente) qualified; (obrero) skilled

**calificar** [kalifi'kar] /1g/ vt to qualify; (alumno) to grade, mark; **~ de** to describe as

**calima** [ka'lima] nf (cerca del mar) mist

**cáliz** ['kaliθ] nm chalice

**caliza** [ka'liθa] nf limestone

**callado, -a** [ka'ʎaðo, a] adj quiet

**callar** [ka'ʎar] /1a/ vt (asunto delicado) to keep quiet about, say nothing about;

(*persona, oposición*) to silence ▷ *vi* to keep
quiet, be silent; (*dejar de hablar*) to stop
talking; **callarse** *vr* to keep quiet, be silent;
¡**calla!** be quiet!

**calle** ['kaʎe] *nf* street; (*Deporte*) lane; **~ arriba/
abajo** up/down the street; **~ de sentido
único** one-way street; **~ mayor** (*ESP*) high
(*BRIT*) o main (*US*) street; **~ peatonal**
pedestrianized o pedestrian street;
**~ principal** (*LAM*) high (*BRIT*) o main (*US*)
street; **poner a algn (de patitas) en la ~**
to kick sb out; **callejear** /1a/ *vi* to wander
(about) the streets; **callejero, -a** *adj* street
*cpd* ▷ *nm* street map; **callejón** *nm* alley,
passage; **callejón sin salida** cul-de-sac;
**callejuela** *nf* side-street, alley

**callista** [ka'ʎista] *nmf* chiropodist

**callo** ['kaʎo] *nm* callus; (*en el pie*) corn; **callos**
*nmpl* (*Culin*) tripe *sg*

**calma** ['kalma] *nf* calm

**calmante** [kal'mante] *nm* sedative,
tranquillizer

**calmar** [kal'mar] /1a/ *vt* to calm, calm
down; **calmarse** *vr* (*tempestad*) to abate;
(*mente etc*) to become calm

**calor** [ka'lor] *nm* heat; (*color agradable*)
warmth; **tener ~** to be o feel hot

**caloría** [kalo'ria] *nf* calorie

**calumnia** [ka'lumnja] *nf* slander

**caluroso, -a** [kalu'roso, a] *adj* hot; (*sin
exceso*) warm; (*fig*) enthusiastic

**calva** ['kalβa] *nf* bald patch; (*en bosque*)
clearing

**calvario** [kal'βarjo] *nm* stations *pl* of the
cross

**calvicie** [kal'βiθje] *nf* baldness

**calvo, -a** ['kalβo, a] *adj* bald; (*terreno*) bare,
barren; (*tejido*) threadbare

**calza** ['kalθa] *nf* wedge, chock

**calzado, -a** [kal'θaðo, a] *adj* shod ▷ *nm*
footwear ▷ *nf* roadway, highway

**calzador** [kalθa'ðor] *nm* shoehorn

**calzar** [kal'θar] /1f/ *vt* (*zapatos etc*) to wear;
(*un mueble*) to put a wedge under; **calzarse**
*vr*: **~se los zapatos** to put on one's shoes;
¿**qué (número) calza?** what size do you
take?

**calzón** [kal'θon] *nm* (*tb*: **calzones**) shorts
*pl*; (*LAM*: *de hombre*) pants *pl*; (: *de mujer*)
panties *pl*

**calzoncillos** [kalθon'θiʎos] *nmpl*
underpants

**cama** ['kama] *nf* bed; **~ individual/de
matrimonio** single/double bed; **hacer la ~**
to make the bed

**camaleón** [kamale'on] *nm* chameleon

**cámara** ['kamara] *nf* chamber; (*habitación*)
room; (*sala*) hall; (*Cine*) cine camera;
(*fotográfica*) camera; **~ de aire** inner tube;

**~ de comercio** chamber of commerce;
**~ digital** digital camera; **~ de gas** gas
chamber; **~ frigorífica** cold-storage room

**camarada** [kama'raða] *nm* comrade,
companion

**camarero, -a** [kama'rero, a] *nm* waiter
▷ *nf* (*en restaurante*) waitress; (*en casa, hotel*)
maid

**camarógrafo, -a** [kama'rografo, a] *nm/f*
(*LAM*) cameraman/camerawoman

**camarón** [kama'ron] *nm* shrimp

**camarote** [kama'rote] *nm* cabin

**cambiable** [kam'bjaβle] *adj* (*variable*)
changeable, variable; (*intercambiable*)
interchangeable

**cambiante** [kam'bjante] *adj* variable

**cambiar** [kam'bjar] /1b/ *vt* to change;
(*trocar*) to exchange ▷ *vi* to change;
**cambiarse** *vr* (*mudarse*) to move; (*de ropa*)
to change; **~ de idea** u **opinión** to change
one's mind; **~se de ropa** to change (one's
clothes)

**cambio** ['kambjo] *nm* change; (*trueque*)
exchange; (*Com*) rate of exchange; (*oficina*)
bureau de change; (*dinero menudo*) small
change; **a ~ de** in return o exchange for;
**en ~** on the other hand; (*en lugar de eso*)
instead; **~ climático** climate change;
**~ de divisas** (*Com*) foreign exchange; **~ de
velocidades** gear lever

**camelar** [kame'lar] /1a/ *vt* (*persuadir*) to
sweet-talk

**camello** [ka'meʎo] *nm* camel; (*fam*:
*traficante*) pusher

**camerino** [kame'rino] *nm* dressing room

**camilla** [ka'miʎa] *nf* (*Med*) stretcher

**caminar** [kami'nar] /1a/ *vi* (*marchar*) to
walk, go ▷ *vt* (*recorrer*) to cover, travel

**caminata** [kami'nata] *nf* long walk; (*por el
campo*) hike

**camino** [ka'mino] *nm* way, road; (*sendero*)
track; **a medio ~** halfway (there); **en el ~**
on the way, en route; **~ de** on the way to;
**~ particular** private road; **C~ de Santiago**
Way of St James

**CAMINO DE SANTIAGO**

- The *Camino de Santiago* is a
- medieval pilgrim route stretching from
- the Pyrenees to Santiago de Compostela
- in north-west Spain, where tradition has
- it the body of the Apostle James is buried.
- Nowadays it is a popular tourist route as
- well as a religious one. The *concha*
- (cockleshell) is a symbol of the *Camino
- de Santiago*, because it is said that when
- St James' body was found it was covered
- in shells.

**camión** [ka'mjon] *nm* lorry, truck (*US*); (*LAM*: *autobús*) bus; ~ **cisterna** tanker; ~ **de la basura** dustcart, refuse lorry; ~ **de mudanzas** removal (*BRIT*) o moving (*US*) van; **camionero** *nm* lorry o truck (*US*) driver, trucker (*esp US*); **camioneta** [kamjo'neta] *nf* van, small truck; **camionista** *nmf* (*LAM*) lorry o truck driver

**camisa** [ka'misa] *nf* shirt; (*Bot*) skin; ~ **de fuerza** straitjacket

**camiseta** [kami'seta] *nf* tee-shirt; (*ropa interior*) vest; (*de deportista*) top

**camisón** [kami'son] *nm* nightdress, nightgown

**camorra** [ka'morra] *nf*: **buscar** ~ to look for trouble

**camote** [ka'mote] *nm* (*LAM*) sweet potato; (*bulbo*) tuber, bulb; (*fam: enamoramiento*) crush

**campamento** [kampa'mento] *nm* camp

**campana** [kam'pana] *nf* bell; **campanada** *nf* peal; **campanario** *nm* belfry

**campanilla** [kampa'niʎa] *nf* small bell

**campaña** [kam'paɲa] *nf* (*Mil*, *Pol*) campaign; ~ **electoral** election campaign

**campechano, -a** [kampe'tʃano, a] *adj* (*franco*) open

**campeón, -ona** [kampe'on, ona] *nm/f* champion; **campeonato** *nm* championship

**cámper** ['kamper] *nm* o *f* (*LAM*) caravan (*BRIT*), trailer (*US*)

**campera** [kam'pera] *nf* (*RPL*) anorak

**campesino, -a** [kampe'sino, a] *adj* country *cpd*, rural; (*gente*) peasant *cpd* ▷ *nm/f* countryman/woman; (*agricultor*) farmer

**campestre** [kam'pestre] *adj* country *cpd*, rural

**camping** ['kampin] *nm* camping; (*lugar*) campsite; **ir de** o **hacer** ~ to go camping

**campista** [kam'pista] *nmf* camper

**campo** ['kampo] *nm* (*fuera de la ciudad*) country, countryside; (*Agr*, *Elec*, *Inform*) field; (*de fútbol*) pitch; (*de golf*) course; (*Mil*) camp; ~ **de batalla** battlefield; ~ **de minas** minefield; ~ **petrolífero** oilfield; ~ **visual** field of vision; ~ **de concentración/de internación/de trabajo** concentration/ internment/labour camp; ~ **de deportes** sports ground, playing field

**camuflaje** [kamu'flaxe] *nm* camouflage

**cana** ['kana] *nf* V **cano**

**Canadá** [kana'ða] *nm* Canada; **canadiense** *adj*, *nmf* Canadian ▷ *nf* fur-lined jacket

**canal** [ka'nal] *nm* canal; (*Geo*) channel, strait; (*de televisión*) channel; (*de tejado*) gutter; **C~ de la Mancha** English Channel; **C~ de Panamá** Panama Canal

**canaleta** [kana'leta] *nf* (*LAM*: *de tejado*) gutter

**canalizar** [kanali'θar] /1f/ *vt* to channel

**canalla** [ka'naʎa] *nf* rabble, mob ▷ *nm* swine

**canapé** [kana'pe] (*pl* **canapés**) *nm* sofa, settee; (*Culin*) canapé

**Canarias** [ka'narjas] *nfpl*: **las (Islas)** ~ the Canaries

**canario, -a** [ka'narjo, a] *adj* of o from the Canary Isles ▷ *nm/f* native o inhabitant of the Canary Isles ▷ *nm* (*Zool*) canary

**canasta** [ka'nasta] *nf* (round) basket

**canasto** [ka'nasto] *nm* large basket

**cancela** [kan'θela] *nf* (wrought-iron) gate

**cancelación** [kanθela'θjon] *nf* cancellation

**cancelar** [kanθe'lar] /1a/ *vt* to cancel; (*una deuda*) to write off

**cáncer** ['kanθer] *nm* (*Med*) cancer; **C~** (*Astro*) Cancer

**cancha** ['kantʃa] *nf* (*de baloncesto, tenis etc*) court; (*LAM*: *de fútbol etc*) pitch; ~ **de tenis** (*LAM*) tennis court

**canciller** [kanθi'ʎer] *nm* chancellor

**canción** [kan'θjon] *nf* song; ~ **de cuna** lullaby

**candado** [kan'daðo] *nm* padlock

**candente** [kan'dente] *adj* red-hot; (*tema*) burning

**candidato, -a** [kandi'ðato, a] *nm/f* candidate

**cándido, -a** ['kandiðo, a] *adj* simple; naive
▌ No confundir *cándido* con la palabra inglesa *candid*.

**candil** [kan'dil] *nm* oil lamp; **candilejas** *nfpl* (*Teat*) footlights

**canela** [ka'nela] *nf* cinnamon

**canelones** [kane'lones] *nmpl* cannelloni

**cangrejo** [kan'grexo] *nm* crab

**canguro** [kan'guro] *nm* kangaroo; **hacer de** ~ to baby-sit

**caníbal** [ka'niβal] *adj*, *nmf* cannibal

**canica** [ka'nika] *nf* marble

**canijo, -a** [ka'nixo, a] *adj* frail, sickly

**canilla** [ka'niʎa] *nf* (*LAM*) tap (*BRIT*), faucet (*US*)

**canjear** [kanxe'ar] /1a/ *vt* to exchange

**cano, -a** ['kano, a] *adj* grey-haired, white-haired ▷ *nf* (*tb*: **canas**) white o grey hair; **tener canas** to be going grey

**canoa** [ka'noa] *nf* canoe

**canon** ['kanon] *nm* canon; (*pensión*) rent; (*Com*) tax

**canonizar** [kanoni'θar] /1f/ *vt* to canonize

**canoso, -a** [ka'noso, a] *adj* grey-haired

**cansado, -a** [kan'saðo, a] *adj* tired, weary; (*tedioso*) tedious, boring

**cansancio** [kan'sanθjo] nm tiredness, fatigue

**cansar** [kan'sar] /1a/ vt (fatigar) to tire, tire out; (aburrir) to bore; (fastidiar) to bother; **cansarse** vr to tire, get tired; (aburrirse) to get bored

**cantábrico, -a** [kan'taβriko, a] adj Cantabrian

**cantante** [kan'tante] adj singing ▷ nmf singer

**cantar** [kan'tar] /1a/ vt to sing ▷ vi to sing; (insecto) to chirp ▷ nm (acción) singing; (canción) song; (poema) poem

**cántaro** ['kantaro] nm pitcher, jug; **llover a ~s** to rain cats and dogs

**cante** ['kante] nm Andalusian folk song; **~ jondo** flamenco singing

**cantera** [kan'tera] nf quarry

**cantero** [kan'tero] nm (LAM: arriate) border

**cantidad** [kanti'ðað] nf quantity, amount; **~ de** lots of

**cantimplora** [kantim'plora] nf water bottle, canteen

**cantina** [kan'tina] nf canteen; (de estación) buffet; (esp LAM) bar

**cantinero, -a** [kanti'nero, a] nm/f (LAM) barman/barmaid, bartender (US)

**canto** ['kanto] nm singing; (canción) song; (borde) edge, rim; (de un cuchillo) back; **~ rodado** boulder

**cantor, a** [kan'tor, a] nm/f singer

**canturrear** [kanturre'ar] /1a/ vi to sing softly

**canuto** [ka'nuto] nm (tubo) small tube; (fam: porro) joint

**caña** ['kaɲa] nf (Bot: tallo) stem, stalk; (: carrizo) reed; (de cerveza) glass of beer; (Anat) shinbone; **~ de azúcar** sugar cane; **~ de pescar** fishing rod

**cañada** [ka'ɲaða] nf (entre dos montañas) gully, ravine; (camino) cattle track

**cáñamo** ['kaɲamo] nm hemp

**cañería** [kaɲe'ria] nf (tubo) pipe

**caño** ['kaɲo] nm (tubo) tube, pipe; (de aguas servidas) sewer; (Mus) pipe; (de fuente) jet

**cañón** [ka'ɲon] nm (Mil) cannon; (de fusil) barrel; (Geo) canyon, gorge

**caoba** [ka'oβa] nf mahogany

**caos** ['kaos] nm chaos

**capa** ['kapa] nf cloak, cape; (Geo) layer, stratum; **~ de ozono** ozone layer

**capacidad** [kapaθi'ðað] nf (medida) capacity; (aptitud) capacity, ability

**capacitar** [kapaθi'tar] /1a/ vt: **~ a algn para algo** to qualify sb for sth; **capacitarse** vr: **~se para algo** to qualify for sth

**caparazón** [kapara'θon] nm shell

**capataz** [kapa'taθ] nm foreman

**capaz** [ka'paθ] adj able, capable; (amplio) capacious, roomy

**capellán** [kape'ʎan] nm chaplain; (sacerdote) priest

**capicúa** [kapi'kua] adj inv (número, fecha) reversible

**capilla** [ka'piʎa] nf chapel

**capital** [kapi'tal] adj capital ▷ nm (Com) capital ▷ nf (de nación) capital (city); **~ social** equity o share capital

**capitalismo** [kapita'lismo] nm capitalism; **capitalista** adj, nmf capitalist

**capitán** [kapi'tan] nm captain

**capítulo** [ka'pitulo] nm chapter

**capó** [ka'po] nm (Auto) bonnet (BRIT), hood (US)

**capón** [ka'pon] nm (gallo) capon

**capota** [ka'pota] nf (de mujer) bonnet; (Auto) hood (BRIT), top (US)

**capote** [ka'pote] nm (abrigo: de militar) greatcoat; (: de torero) cloak

**capricho** [ka'pritʃo] nm whim, caprice; **caprichoso, -a** adj capricious

**Capricornio** [kapri'kornjo] nm Capricorn

**cápsula** ['kapsula] nf capsule

**captar** [kap'tar] /1a/ vt (comprender) to understand; (Radio) to pick up; (atención, apoyo) to attract

**captura** [kap'tura] nf capture; (Jur) arrest; **~ de pantalla** (Inform) screenshot; **capturar** /1a/ vt to capture; (Jur) to arrest

**capucha** [ka'putʃa] nf hood, cowl

**capuchón** [kapu'tʃon] nm (ESP: de bolígrafo) cap

**capullo** [ka'puʎo] nm (Zool) cocoon; (Bot) bud; (fam!) idiot

**caqui** ['kaki] nm khaki

**cara** ['kara] nf (Anat, de moneda) face; (de disco) side; (fig) boldness ▷ prep: **~ a** facing; **de ~ a** opposite, facing; **dar la ~** to face the consequences; **¿~ o cruz?** heads or tails?; **¡qué ~ más dura!** what a nerve!

**Caracas** [ka'rakas] nf Caracas

**caracol** [kara'kol] nm (Zool) snail; (concha) (sea)shell

**carácter** (pl **caracteres**) [ka'rakter, karak'teres] nm character; **tener buen/mal ~** to be good-natured/bad tempered

**característico, -a** [karakte'ristiko, a] adj characteristic ▷ nf characteristic

**caracterizar** [karakteri'θar] /1f/ vt to characterize, typify

**caradura** [kara'ðura] nmf: **es un ~** he's got a nerve

**carajillo** [kara'xiʎo] nm black coffee with brandy

**carajo** [ka'raxo] nm (fam!): **¡~!** shit! (!)

**caramba** [ka'ramba] excl good gracious!

**caramelo** [kara'melo] *nm* (*dulce*) sweet; (*azúcar fundido*) caramel

**caravana** [kara'βana] *nf* caravan; (*fig*) group; (*de autos*) tailback

**carbón** [kar'βon] *nm* coal; **papel ~** carbon paper

**carbono** [kar'βono] *nm* carbon

**carburador** [karβura'ðor] *nm* carburettor

**carburante** [karβu'rante] *nm* fuel

**carcajada** [karka'xaða] *nf* (loud) laugh, guffaw

**cárcel** ['karθel] *nf* prison, jail; (*Tec*) clamp

**carcoma** [kar'koma] *nf* woodworm

**cardar** [kar'ðar] /1a/ *vt* (*Tec*) to card, comb; (*pelo*) to backcomb

**cardenal** [karðe'nal] *nm* (*Rel*) cardinal; (*Med*) bruise

**cardiaco, -a** [kar'ðjako, a], **cardíaco, a** [kar'ðiako, a] *adj* cardiac; (*ataque*) heart *cpd*

**cardinal** [karði'nal] *adj* cardinal

**cardo** ['karðo] *nm* thistle

**carecer** [kare'θer] /2d/ *vi*: **~ de** to lack, be in need of

**carencia** [ka'renθja] *nf* lack; (*escasez*) shortage; (*Med*) deficiency

**careta** [ka'reta] *nf* mask

**carga** ['karγa] *nf* (*peso, Elec*) load; (*de barco*) cargo, freight; (*Mil*) charge; (*obligación, responsabilidad*) duty, obligation

**cargado, -a** [kar'γaðo, a] *adj* loaded; (*Elec*) live; (*café, té*) strong; (*cielo*) overcast

**cargamento** [karγa'mento] *nm* (*acción*) loading; (*mercancías*) load, cargo

**cargar** [kar'γar] /1h/ *vt* (*barco, arma*) to load; (*Elec*) to charge; (*Com: algo en cuenta*) to charge, debit; (*Mil*) to charge; (*Inform*) to load ▷ *vi* (*Auto*) to load (up); **~ con** to pick up, carry away; (*peso: fig*) to shoulder, bear; **cargarse** *vr* (*fam: estropear*) to break; (: *matar*) to bump off

**cargo** ['karγo] *nm* (*puesto*) post, office; (*responsabilidad*) duty, obligation; (*Jur*) charge; **hacerse ~ de** to take charge of *o* responsibility for

**carguero** [kar'γero] *nm* freighter, cargo boat; (*avión*) freight plane

**Caribe** [ka'riβe] *nm*: **el ~** the Caribbean; **del ~** Caribbean; **caribeño, -a** *adj* Caribbean

**caricatura** [karika'tura] *nf* caricature

**caricia** [ka'riθja] *nf* caress

**caridad** [kari'ðað] *nf* charity

**caries** ['karjes] *nf inv* tooth decay

**cariño** [ka'riɲo] *nm* affection, love; (*caricia*) caress; (*en carta*) love ...; **tener ~ a** to be fond of; **cariñoso, -a** *adj* affectionate

**carisma** [ka'risma] *nm* charisma

**caritativo, -a** [karita'tiβo, a] *adj* charitable

**cariz** [ka'riθ] *nm*: **tener** *o* **tomar buen/mal ~** to look good/bad

**carmín** [kar'min] *nm* (*tb*: **~ de labios**) lipstick

**carnal** [kar'nal] *adj* carnal; **primo ~** first cousin

**carnaval** [karna'βal] *nm* carnival

● **CARNAVAL**
●
● The 3 days before *miércoles de ceniza* (Ash
● Wednesday), when fasting traditionally
● starts, are the time for *carnaval*, an
● exuberant celebration which dates
● back to pre-Christian times. Although
● in decline during the Franco years,
● the *carnaval* has grown in popularity
● recently in Spain, Cádiz and Tenerife
● being particularly well-known for their
● celebrations. *El martes de carnaval* (Shrove
● Tuesday) is the biggest day, with colourful
● street parades, fancy dress, fireworks and
● a general party atmosphere.

**carne** ['karne] *nf* flesh; (*Culin*) meat; **se me pone la ~ de gallina sólo verlo** I get the creeps just seeing it; **~ de cerdo/de cordero/de ternera/de vaca** pork/lamb/veal/beef; **~ molida** (*LAM*), **~ picada** (*ESP*) mince (*BRIT*), ground meat (*US*); **~ de gallina** (*fig*) gooseflesh

**carné** [kar'ne] (*pl* **carnés**) (*ESP*) *nm*: **~ de conducir** driving licence (*BRIT*), driver's license (*US*); **~ de identidad** identity card; **~ de socio** membership card

**carnero** [kar'nero] *nm* sheep, ram; (*carne*) mutton

**carnet** [kar'ne] (*pl* **carnets**) *nm* (*ESP*) = **carné**

**carnicería** [karniθe'ria] *nf* butcher's (shop); (*fig: matanza*) carnage, slaughter

**carnicero, -a** [karni'θero, a] *adj* carnivorous ▷ *nm/f* (*tb fig*) butcher ▷ *nm* carnivore

**carnívoro, -a** [kar'niβoro, a] *adj* carnivorous

**caro, -a** ['karo, a] *adj* dear; (*Com*) dear, expensive ▷ *adv* dear, dearly

**carpa** ['karpa] *nf* (*pez*) carp; (*de circo*) big top; (*LAM: de camping*) tent

**carpeta** [kar'peta] *nf* folder, file

**carpintería** [karpinte'ria] *nf* carpentry, joinery; **carpintero** *nm* carpenter

**carraspear** [karraspe'ar] /1a/ *vi* to clear one's throat

**carraspera** [karras'pera] *nf* hoarseness

**carrera** [ka'rrera] *nf* (*acción*) run(ning); (*espacio recorrido*) run; (*certamen*) race; (*trayecto*) course; (*profesión*) career; **a la ~**

at (full) speed; **~ de obstáculos** (*Deporte*) steeplechase

**carrete** [ka'rrete] *nm* reel, spool; (*Tec*) coil

**carretera** [karre'tera] *nf* (main) road, highway; **~ nacional** ≈ A road (*BRIT*), ≈ state highway (*US*); **~ de circunvalación** ring road

**carretilla** [karre'tiʎa] *nf* trolley; (*Agr*) (wheel)barrow

**carril** [ka'rril] *nm* furrow; (*de autopista*) lane; (*Ferro*) rail

**carril bici** [karil'βiθi] *nm* cycle lane, bikeway (*US*)

**carrito** [ka'rrito] *nm* trolley

**carro** ['karro] *nm* cart, wagon; (*Mil*) tank; (*LAM: coche*) car; **~ patrulla** (*LAM*) patrol o panda (*BRIT*) car

**carrocería** [karroθe'ria] *nf* bodywork no pl (*BRIT*)

**carroña** [ka'rroɲa] *nf* carrion no pl

**carroza** [ka'rroθa] *nf* (*vehículo*) coach

**carrusel** [karru'sel] *nm* merry-go-round, roundabout (*BRIT*)

**carta** ['karta] *nf* letter; (*Culin*) menu; (*naipe*) card; (*mapa*) map; (*Jur*) document; **~ certificada/urgente** registered/special delivery letter

**cartabón** [karta'βon] *nm* set square

**cartearse** [karte'arse] /1a/ *vr* to correspond

**cartel** [kar'tel] *nm* (*anuncio*) poster, placard; (*Escol*) wall chart; (*Com*) cartel; **cartelera** *nf* hoarding, billboard; (*en periódico etc*) entertainments guide; **"en cartelera"** "showing"

**cartera** [kar'tera] *nf* (*de bolsillo*) wallet; (*de colegial, cobrador*) satchel; (*de señora*) handbag (*BRIT*), purse (*US*); (*para documentos*) briefcase; (*Com*) portfolio; **ocupa la ~ de Agricultura** he is Minister of Agriculture

**carterista** [karte'rista] *nmf* pickpocket

**cartero** [kar'tero] *nm* postman

**cartilla** [kar'tiʎa] *nf* primer, first reading book; **~ de ahorros** savings book

**cartón** [kar'ton] *nm* cardboard; **~ piedra** papier-mâché

**cartucho** [kar'tutʃo] *nm* (*Mil*) cartridge

**cartulina** [kartu'lina] *nf* card

**casa** ['kasa] *nf* house; (*hogar*) home; (*Com*) firm, company; **~ consistorial** town hall; **~ de huéspedes** boarding house; **~ de socorro** first aid post; **~ independiente** detached house; **~ rodante** (*cs*) caravan (*BRIT*), trailer (*US*); **en ~** at home

**casado, -a** [ka'saðo, a] *adj* married ▷ *nm/f* married man/woman

**casar** [ka'sar] /1a/ *vt* to marry; (*Jur*) to quash, annul; **casarse** *vr* to marry, get married

**cascabel** [kaska'βel] *nm* (small) bell

**cascada** [kas'kaða] *nf* waterfall

**cascanueces** [kaska'nweθes] *nm inv* (a pair of) nutcrackers, nutcracker *sg*

**cascar** [kas'kar] /1g/ *vt* to split; (*nuez*) to crack; **cascarse** *vr* to crack, split, break (open)

**cáscara** ['kaskara] *nf* (*de huevo, fruta seca*) shell; (*de fruta*) skin; (*de limón*) peel

**casco** ['kasko] *nm* (*de bombero, soldado*) helmet; (*Naut: de barco*) hull; (*Zool: de caballo*) hoof; (*botella*) empty bottle; (*de ciudad*): **el ~ antiguo** the old part; **el ~ urbano** the town centre; **los ~s azules** the UN peace-keeping force, the blue helmets

**cascote** [kas'kote] *nm* piece of rubble; **cascotes** *nmpl* rubble *sg*

**caserío** [kase'rio] *nm* hamlet, group of houses; (*casa*) farmhouse

**casero, -a** [ka'sero, a] *adj* (*pan etc*) home-made; (*persona*): **ser muy ~** to be home-loving ▷ *nm/f* (*propietario*) landlord/lady; **"comida casera"** "home cooking"

**caseta** [ka'seta] *nf* hut; (*para bañista*) cubicle; (*de feria*) stall

**casete** [ka'sete] *nm o f* cassette

**casi** ['kasi] *adv* almost; **~ nunca** hardly ever, almost never; **~ nada** next to nothing; **~ te caes** you almost o nearly fell

**casilla** [ka'siʎa] *nf* (*casita*) hut, cabin; (*para cartas*) pigeonhole; (*Ajedrez*) square; **C~ postal** o **de Correo(s)** (*LAM*) P.O. Box; **casillero** (*para cartas*) pigeonholes *pl*

**casino** [ka'sino] *nm* club; (*de juego*) casino

**caso** ['kaso] *nm* case; **en ~ de ...** in case of ...; **el ~ es que** the fact is that; **en ese ~** in that case; **en todo ~** in any case; **hacer ~ a** to pay attention to; **hacer** o **venir al ~** to be relevant

**caspa** ['kaspa] *nf* dandruff

**cassette** [ka'set] *nm o f* = **casete**

**castaña** [kas'taɲa] *nf* V **castaño**

**castaño, -a** [kas'taɲo, a] *adj* chestnut(-coloured), brown ▷ *nm* chestnut tree ▷ *nf* chestnut

**castañuelas** [kasta'ɲwelas] *nfpl* castanets

**castellano, -a** [kaste'ʎano, a] *adj* Castilian ▷ *nm/f* Castilian ▷ *nm* (*Ling*) Castilian, Spanish

**castigar** [kasti'ɣar] /1h/ *vt* to punish; (*Deporte*) to penalize; **castigo** *nm* punishment; (*Deporte*) penalty

**Castilla** [kas'tiʎa] *nf* Castile

**castillo** [kas'tiʎo] *nm* castle

**castizo, -a** [kas'tiθo, a] *adj* (*Ling*) pure

**casto, -a** ['kasto, a] *adj* chaste, pure

**castor** [kas'tor] *nm* beaver

**castrar** [kas'trar] /1a/ *vt* to castrate

**casual** [ka'swal] *adj* chance, accidental;
**casualidad** *nf* chance, accident;
(*combinación de circunstancias*) coincidence;
**da la casualidad de que …** it (just) so
happens that …; **¡qué casualidad!** what a
coincidence!

▌ No confundir *casual* con la palabra
inglesa *casual*.

**cataclismo** [kata'klismo] *nm* cataclysm
**catador** [kata'ðor] *nm* taster
**catalán, -ana** [kata'lan, ana] *adj, nm/f*
Catalan ▷ *nm* (*Ling*) Catalan
**catalizador** [kataliθa'ðor] *nm* catalyst;
(*Auto*) catalytic converter
**catalogar** [katalo'ɣar] /1h/ *vt* to
catalogue; **~ (de)** (*fig*) to classify as
**catálogo** [ka'taloɣo] *nm* catalogue
**Cataluña** [kata'luɲa] *nf* Catalonia
**catar** [ka'tar] /1a/ *vt* to taste, sample
**catarata** [kata'rata] *nf* (*Geo*) (water)fall;
(*Med*) cataract
**catarro** [ka'tarro] *nm* catarrh; (*constipado*)
cold
**catástrofe** [ka'tastrofe] *nf* catastrophe
**catear** [kate'ar] /1a/ *vt* (*fam: examen,
alumno*) to fail
**cátedra** ['kateðra] *nf* (*Univ*) chair,
professorship
**catedral** [kate'ðral] *nf* cathedral
**catedrático, -a** [kate'ðratiko, a] *nm/f*
professor
**categoría** [kateɣo'ria] *nf* category; (*rango*)
rank, standing; (*calidad*) quality; **de ~** (*hotel*)
top-class
**cateto, -a** [ka'teto, a] *nm/f* yokel
**catolicismo** [katoli'θismo] *nm*
Catholicism
**católico, -a** [ka'toliko, a] *adj, nm/f* Catholic
**catorce** [ka'torθe] *num* fourteen
**cauce** ['kauθe] *nm* (*de río*) riverbed; (*fig*)
channel
**caucho** ['kautʃo] *nm* rubber
**caudal** [kau'ðal] *nm* (*de río*) volume, flow;
(*fortuna*) wealth; (*abundancia*) abundance
**caudillo** [kau'ðiʎo] *nm* leader, chief
**causa** ['kausa] *nf* cause; (*razón*) reason;
(*Jur*) lawsuit, case; **a o por ~ de** because of;
**causar** /1a/ *vt* to cause
**cautela** [kau'tela] *nf* caution,
cautiousness; **cauteloso, -a** *adj* cautious,
wary
**cautivar** [kauti'βar] /1a/ *vt* to capture; (*fig*)
to captivate
**cautiverio** [kauti'βerjo] *nm*, **cautividad**
[kautiβi'ðað] *nf* captivity
**cautivo, -a** [kau'tiβo, a] *adj, nm/f* captive
**cauto, -a** ['kauto, a] *adj* cautious, careful
**cava** ['kaβa] *nm* champagne-type wine
**cavar** [ka'βar] /1a/ *vt* to dig

**caverna** [ka'βerna] *nf* cave, cavern
**cavidad** [kaβi'ðað] *nf* cavity
**cavilar** [kaβi'lar] /1a/ *vt* to ponder
**cayendo** *etc* [ka'jendo] *vb V* **caer**
**caza** ['kaθa] *nf* (*acción: gen*) hunting; (*: con
fusil*) shooting; (*una caza*) hunt, chase;
(*animales*) game ▷ *nm* (*Aviat*) fighter; **ir de ~**
to go hunting; **~ mayor** game hunting;
**cazador, a** *nm/f* hunter/huntress ▷ *nf*
jacket; **cazar** /1f/ *vt* to hunt; (*perseguir*) to
chase; (*prender*) to catch
**cazo** ['kaθo] *nm* saucepan
**cazuela** [ka'θwela] *nf* (*vasija*) pan; (*guisado*)
casserole
**CD** *nm abr* (= *compact disc*) CD
**CD-ROM** [θeðe'rom] *nm abr* CD-ROM
**CE** *nm abr* (= *Consejo de Europa*) Council of
Europe
**cebada** [θe'βaða] *nf* barley
**cebar** [θe'βar] /1a/ *vt* (*animal*) to fatten (up);
(*anzuelo*) to bait; (*Mil, Tec*) to prime
**cebo** ['θeβo] *nm* (*para animales*) feed, food;
(*para peces, fig*) bait; (*de arma*) charge
**cebolla** [θe'βoʎa] *nf* onion; **cebolleta** *nf*
spring onion
**cebra** ['θeβra] *nf* zebra
**cecear** [θeθe'ar] /1a/ *vi* to lisp
**ceder** [θe'ðer] /2a/ *vt* to hand over;
(*renunciar a*) to give up, part with ▷ *vi*
(*renunciar*) to give in, yield; (*disminuir*) to
diminish, decline; (*romperse*) to give way
**cederom** [θeðe'rom] *nm* CD-ROM
**cedro** ['θeðro] *nm* cedar
**cédula** ['θeðula] *nf* certificate, document;
**~ de identidad** (*LAM*) identity card; **~ electoral**
(*LAM*) ballot
**cegar** [θe'ɣar] /1h, 1j/ *vt* to blind; (*tubería
etc*) to block up, stop up ▷ *vi* to go blind;
**cegarse** *vr*: **~se (de)** to be blinded (by)
**ceguera** [θe'ɣera] *nf* blindness
**ceja** ['θexa] *nf* eyebrow
**cejar** [θe'xar] /1a/ *vi* (*fig*) to back down
**celador, a** [θela'ðor, a] *nm/f* (*de edificio*)
watchman; (*de museo etc*) attendant
**celda** ['θelda] *nf* cell
**celebración** [θeleβra'θjon] *nf* celebration
**celebrar** [θele'βrar] /1a/ *vt* to celebrate;
(*alabar*) to praise ▷ *vi* to be glad; **celebrarse**
*vr* to occur, take place
**célebre** ['θeleβre] *adj* famous
**celebridad** [θeleβri'ðað] *nf* fame; (*persona*)
celebrity
**celeste** [θe'leste] *adj* sky-blue
**celestial** [θeles'tjal] *adj* celestial, heavenly
**celo¹** ['θelo] *nm* zeal; (*Rel*) fervour; **celos**
*nmpl* jealousy *sg*; **dar ~s a algn** to make sb
jealous; **tener ~s de algn** to be jealous of
sb; **en ~** (*animales*) on heat
**celo²®** ['θelo] *nm* Sellotape®

**celofán** [θelo'fan] nm Cellophane®
**celoso, -a** [θe'loso, a] adj jealous;
(trabajador) zealous
**celta** ['θelta] adj Celtic ▷ nmf Celt
**célula** ['θelula] nf cell
**celulitis** [θelu'litis] nf cellulite
**cementerio** [θemen'terjo] nm cemetery,
graveyard
**cemento** [θe'mento] nm cement;
(hormigón) concrete; (LAM: cola) glue
**cena** ['θena] nf evening meal, dinner; **cenar**
/1a/ vt to have for dinner ▷ vi to have dinner
**cenicero** [θeni'θero] nm ashtray
**ceniza** [θe'niθa] nf ash, ashes pl
**censo** ['θenso] nm census; **~ electoral**
electoral roll
**censura** [θen'sura] nf (Pol) censorship;
**censurar** /1a/ vt (idea) to censure; (cortar:
película) to censor
**centella** [θen'teʎa] nf spark
**centenar** [θente'nar] nm hundred
**centenario, -a** [θente'narjo, a] adj
hundred-year-old ▷ nm centenary; **ser ~** to
be one hundred years old
**centeno** [θen'teno] nm rye
**centésimo, -a** [θen'tesimo, a] adj
hundredth
**centígrado** [θen'tiɣraðo] adj centigrade
**centímetro** [θen'timetro] nm centimetre
(BRIT), centimeter (US)
**céntimo** ['θentimo] nm cent
**centinela** [θenti'nela] nm sentry, guard
**centollo, -a** [θen'toʎo, a] nm/f large (o
spider) crab
**central** [θen'tral] adj central ▷ nf head
office; (Tec) plant; (Telec) exchange;
**~ eléctrica** power station; **~ nuclear**
nuclear power station; **~ telefónica**
telephone exchange
**centralita** [θentra'lita] nf switchboard
**centralizar** [θentrali'θar] /1f/ vt to
centralize
**centrar** [θen'trar] /1a/ vt to centre
**céntrico, -a** ['θentriko, a] adj central
**centrifugar** [θentrifu'ɣar] /1h/ vt to
spin-dry
**centro** ['θentro] nm centre; **~ comercial**
shopping centre; **~ de atención al cliente**
call centre; **~ de salud** health centre;
**~ escolar** school; **~ juvenil** youth club;
**~ social** community centre; **~ turístico**
(lugar muy visitado) tourist centre; **~ urbano**
urban area, city
**centroamericano, -a**
[θentroameri'kano, a] adj, nm/f Central
American
**ceñido, -a** [θe'ɲiðo, a] adj tight
**ceñir** [θe'ɲir] vt (rodear) to encircle,
surround; (ajustar) to fit (tightly)

**ceño** ['θeɲo] nm frown, scowl; **fruncir el ~**
to frown, knit one's brow
**cepillar** [θepi'ʎar] /1a/ vt to brush; (madera)
to plane (down)
**cepillo** [θe'piʎo] nm brush; (para madera)
plane; **~ de dientes** toothbrush
**cera** ['θera] nf wax
**cerámica** [θe'ramika] nf pottery; (arte)
ceramics sg
**cerca** ['θerka] nf fence ▷ adv near, nearby,
close ▷ prep: **~ de** near, close to
**cercanía** [θerka'nia] nf closeness;
**cercanías** nfpl outskirts, suburbs
**cercano, -a** [θer'kano, a] adj close, near
**cercar** [θer'kar] /1g/ vt to fence in; (rodear)
to surround
**cerco** ['θerko] nm (Agr) enclosure; (LAM)
fence; (Mil) siege
**cerdo** ['θerðo] nm pig; **carne de ~** pork
**cereal** [θere'al] nm cereal; **cereales** nmpl
cereals, grain sg
**cerebro** [θe'reβro] nm brain; (fig) brains pl
**ceremonia** [θere'monja] nf ceremony;
**ceremonioso, -a** adj ceremonious
**cereza** [θe'reθa] nf cherry
**cerilla** [θe'riʎa] nf, **cerillo** [se'riʎo] nm
(LAM) match
**cero** ['θero] nm nothing, zero
**cerquillo** [θer'kiʎo] nm (LAM) fringe (BRIT),
bangs pl (US)
**cerrado, -a** [θe'rraðo, a] adj closed, shut;
(con llave) locked; (tiempo) cloudy, overcast;
(curva) sharp; (acento) thick, broad
**cerradura** [θerra'ðura] nf (acción) closing;
(mecanismo) lock
**cerrajero, -a** [θerra'xero, a] nm/f
locksmith
**cerrar** [θe'rrar] /1j/ vt to close, shut; (paso,
carretera) to close; (grifo) to turn off; (trato,
cuenta, negocio) to close ▷ vi to close, shut;
(la noche) to come down; **cerrarse** vr to
close, shut; **~ con llave** to lock; **~ un trato**
to strike a bargain
**cerro** ['θerro] nm hill
**cerrojo** [θe'rroxo] nm (herramienta) bolt; (de
puerta) latch
**certamen** [θer'tamen] nm competition,
contest
**certero, -a** [θer'tero, a] adj accurate
**certeza** [θer'teθa] nf certainty
**certidumbre** [θerti'ðumβre] nf = **certeza**
**certificado, -a** [θertifi'kaðo, a] adj
certified; (Correos) registered ▷ nm
certificate; **~ médico** medical certificate
**certificar** [θertifi'kar] /1g/ vt (asegurar,
atestar) to certify
**cervatillo** [θerβa'tiʎo] nm fawn
**cervecería** [θerβeθe'ria] nf (fábrica)
brewery; (taberna) public house, pub

**cerveza** [θer'βeθa] nf beer
**cesar** [θe'sar] /1a/ vi to cease, stop ▷ vt to remove from office
**cesárea** [θe'sarea] nf Caesarean (section)
**cese** ['θese] nm (de trabajo) dismissal; (de pago) suspension
**césped** ['θespeð] nm grass, lawn
**cesta** ['θesta] nf basket
**cesto** ['θesto] nm (large) basket, hamper
**cfr** abr (= confróntese, compárese) cf
**chabacano, -a** [tʃaβa'kano, a] adj vulgar, coarse
**chabola** [tʃa'βola] nf shack; **barriada** or **barrio de ~s** shanty town
**chacal** [tʃa'kal] nm jackal
**chacha** ['tʃatʃa] nf (fam) maid
**cháchara** ['tʃatʃara] nf chatter; **estar de ~** to chatter away
**chacra** ['tʃakra] nf (LAM) smallholding
**chafa** ['tʃafa] adj (LAM fam) useless, dud
**chafar** [tʃa'far] /1a/ vt (aplastar) to crush; (arruinar) to ruin
**chal** [tʃal] nm shawl
**chalado, -a** [tʃa'laðo, a] adj (fam) crazy
**chalé** [tʃa'le] (pl **chalés**) nm = **chalet**
**chaleco** [tʃa'leko] nm waistcoat, vest (US); **~ salvavidas** life jacket; **~ de seguridad, ~ reflectante** (Auto) high-visibility vest
**chalet** (pl **chalets**) [tʃa'le, tʃa'les] nm villa, ≈ detached house
**chamaco, -a** [tʃa'mako, a] nm/f (LAM) kid
**champán** [tʃam'pan] nm champagne
**champiñón** [tʃampi'ɲon] nm mushroom
**champú** [tʃam'pu] (pl **champús** o **champúes**) nm shampoo
**chamuscar** [tʃamus'kar] /1g/ vt to scorch, singe
**chance** ['tʃanθe] nm o f (LAM) chance, opportunity
**chancho, -a** ['tʃantʃo, a] nm/f (LAM) pig
**chanchullo** [tʃan'tʃuʎo] nm (fam) fiddle
**chandal** [tʃan'dal] nm tracksuit
**chantaje** [tʃan'taxe] nm blackmail
**chapa** ['tʃapa] nf (de metal) plate, sheet; (de madera) board, panel; (LAM Auto) number (BRIT) o license (US) plate; **chapado, -a** adj: **chapado en oro** gold-plated
**chaparrón** [tʃapa'rron] nm downpour, cloudburst
**chaperón** [tʃape'ron] nm (LAM): **hacer de ~** to play gooseberry; **chaperona** nf (LAM): **hacer de chaperona** to play gooseberry
**chapulín** [tʃapu'lin] nm (LAM) grasshopper
**chapurrar** [tʃapurr'ar] /1a/, **chapurrear** [tʃapurre'ar] /1a/ vt (idioma) to speak badly
**chapuza** [tʃa'puθa] nf botched job
**chapuzón** [tʃapu'θon] nm: **darse un ~** to go for a dip
**chaqueta** [tʃa'keta] nf jacket

**chaquetón** nm (three-quarter-length) coat
**charca** ['tʃarka] nf pond, pool
**charco** ['tʃarko] nm pool, puddle
**charcutería** [tʃarkute'ria] nf (tienda) shop selling chiefly pork meat products; (productos) cooked pork meats pl
**charla** ['tʃarla] nf talk, chat; (conferencia) lecture; **charlar** /1a/ vi to talk, chat; **charlatán, -ana** nm/f chatterbox; (estafador) trickster
**charol¹** [tʃa'rol] nm varnish; (cuero) patent leather
**charol²** [tʃa'rol] nm, **charola** [tʃa'rola] nf (LAM) tray
**charro** ['tʃarro] nm (vaquero) typical Mexican
**chasco** ['tʃasko] nm (desengaño) disappointment
**chasis** ['tʃasis] nm inv chassis
**chasquido** [tʃas'kiðo] nm (de lengua) click; (de látigo) crack
**chat** [tʃat] nm (Internet) chat room
**chatarra** [tʃa'tarra] nf scrap (metal)
**chatear** [tʃate'ar] /1a/ vi (Internet) to chat
**chato, -a** ['tʃato, a] adj flat; (nariz) snub
**chaucha** ['tʃautʃa] (LAM) nf runner (BRIT) o pole (US) bean
**chaval, a** [tʃa'βal, a] nm/f kid (fam), lad/lass
**chavo, -a** ['tʃaβo, a] nm/f (LAM fam) guy/girl
**checar** [tʃe'kar] /1g/ vt (LAM): **~ tarjeta** (al entrar) to clock in o on; (al salir) to clock off o out
**checo, -a** ['tʃeko, a] adj, nm/f Czech ▷ nm (Ling) Czech
**checo(e)slovaco, -a** [tʃeko(e)slo'βako, a] adj, nm/f Czech, Czechoslovak
**Checo(e)slovaquia** [tʃeko(e)slo'βakja] nf Czechoslovakia
**cheque** ['tʃeke] nm cheque (BRIT), check (US); **cobrar un ~** to cash a cheque; **~ abierto/en blanco/cruzado** open/blank/crossed cheque; **~ al portador** cheque payable to bearer; **~ de viajero** traveller's cheque
**chequeo** [tʃe'keo] nm (Med) check-up; (Auto) service
**chequera** [tʃe'kera] nf (LAM) chequebook (BRIT), checkbook (US)
**chévere** ['tʃeβere] adj (LAM) great
**chícharo** ['tʃitʃaro] nm (LAM) pea
**chichón** [tʃi'tʃon] nm bump, lump
**chicle** ['tʃikle] nm chewing gum
**chico, -a** ['tʃiko, a] adj small, little ▷ nm/f child; (muchacho) boy; (muchacha) girl
**chiflado, -a** [tʃi'flaðo, a] adj crazy
**chiflar** [tʃi'flar] /1a/ vt to hiss, boo ▷ vi (esp LAM) to whistle
**chilango, -a** [tʃi'lango, a] adj (LAM) of o from Mexico City

**Chile** ['tʃile] nm Chile

**chile** ['tʃile] nm chilli pepper

**chileno, -a** adj, nm/f Chilean

**chillar** [tʃi'ʎar] /1a/ vi (persona) to yell, scream; (animal salvaje) to howl; (cerdo) to squeal

**chillido** [tʃi'ʎiðo] nm (de persona) yell, scream; (de animal) howl

**chimenea** [tʃime'nea] nf chimney; (hogar) fireplace

**China** ['tʃina] nf: (la) ~ China

**chinche** ['tʃintʃe] nf bug; (Tec) drawing pin (BRIT), thumbtack (US) ▷ nmf nuisance, pest

**chincheta** [tʃin'tʃeta] nf drawing pin (BRIT), thumbtack (US)

**chingado, -a** [tʃin'gaðo, a] adj (esp LAM fam!) lousy; **hijo de la chingada** bastard (!)

**chino, -a** [tʃino, a] adj, nm/f Chinese ▷ nm (Ling) Chinese

**chipirón** [tʃipi'ron] nm squid

**Chipre** ['tʃipre] nf Cyprus; **chipriota** adj Cypriot ▷ nmf Cypriot

**chiquillo, -a** [tʃi'kiʎo, a] nm/f kid (fam)

**chirimoya** [tʃiri'moja] nf custard apple

**chiringuito** [tʃirin'gito] nm small open-air bar

**chiripa** [tʃi'ripa] nf fluke

**chirriar** [tʃi'rrjar] /1b/ vi to creak, squeak

**chirrido** [tʃi'rriðo] nm creak(ing), squeak(ing)

**chisme** ['tʃisme] nm (habladurías) piece of gossip; (fam: objeto) thingummyjig

**chismoso, -a** [tʃis'moso, a] adj gossiping ▷ nm/f gossip

**chispa** ['tʃispa] nf spark; (fig) sparkle; (ingenio) wit; (fam) drunkenness

**chispear** [tʃispe'ar] /1a/ vi (lloviznar) to drizzle

**chiste** ['tʃiste] nm joke, funny story

**chistoso, -a** [tʃis'toso, a] adj funny, amusing

**chivo, -a** ['tʃiβo, a] nm/f (billy/nanny-)goat; ~ **expiatorio** scapegoat

**chocante** [tʃo'kante] adj startling; (extraño) odd; (ofensivo) shocking

**chocar** [tʃo'kar] /1g/ vi (coches etc) to collide, crash ▷ vt to shock; (sorprender) to startle; ~ **con** to collide with; (fig) to run into, run up against; **¡chócala!** (fam) put it there!

**chochear** [tʃotʃe'ar] /1a/ vi to dodder, be senile

**chocho, -a** ['tʃotʃo, a] adj doddering, senile; (fig) soft, doting

**choclo** ['tʃoklo] (LAM) nm (grano) sweetcorn; (mazorca) corn on the cob

**chocolate** [tʃoko'late] adj chocolate ▷ nm chocolate; **chocolatina** nf chocolate

**chófer** ['tʃofer] nm driver

**chollo** ['tʃoʎo] nm (fam) bargain, snip

**choque** ['tʃoke] vb V **chocar** ▷ nm (impacto) impact; (golpe) jolt; (Auto) crash; (fig) conflict; ~ **frontal** head-on collision

**chorizo** [tʃo'riθo] nm hard pork sausage (type of salami)

**chorrada** [tʃo'rraða] nf (fam): **¡es una ~!** that's crap! (!); **decir ~s** to talk crap (!)

**chorrear** [tʃorre'ar] /1a/ vi to gush (out), spout (out); (gotear) to drip, trickle

**chorro** ['tʃorro] nm jet; (fig) stream

**choza** ['tʃoθa] nf hut, shack

**chubasco** [tʃu'βasko] nm squall

**chubasquero** [tʃuβas'kero] nm cagoule, raincoat

**chuche** ['tʃutʃe] nf (fam) sweetie (BRIT fam), candy (US)

**chuchería** [tʃutʃe'ria] nf trinket

**chuleta** [tʃu'leta] nf chop, cutlet

**chulo, -a** ['tʃulo, a] adj (encantador) charming; (fam: estupendo) great, fantastic ▷ nm (tb: ~ **de putas**) pimp

**chupaleta** [tʃupa'leta] nf (LAM) lollipop

**chupar** [tʃu'par] /1a/ vt to suck; (absorber) to absorb; **chuparse** vr to grow thin

**chupete** [tʃu'pete] nm dummy (BRIT), pacifier (US)

**chupetín** [tʃupe'tin] nf (LAM) lollipop

**chupito** [tʃu'pito] nm (fam) shot

**chupón** [tʃu'pon] nm (piruleta) lollipop; (LAM: chupete) dummy (BRIT), pacifier (US)

**churrería** [tʃurre'ria] nf stall or shop which sells "churros"

**churro** ['tʃurro] nm (type of) fritter

**chusma** ['tʃusma] nf rabble, mob

**chutar** [tʃu'tar] /1a/ vi to shoot (at goal)

**Cía** abr (= compañía) Co.

**cianuro** [θja'nuro] nm cyanide

**ciberacoso** [θiβera'koso] nm cyberbullying

**ciberataque** [θiβera'take] nm cyber attack

**cibercafé** [θiβerka'fe] nm cybercafé

**cibernauta** [θiβer'nauta] nmf cybernaut

**ciberterrorista** [θiβerterro'rista] nmf cyberterrorist

**cicatriz** [θika'triθ] nf scar

**cicatrizar** [θikatri'θar] /1f/ vt to heal; **cicatrizarse** vr to heal (up), form a scar

**ciclismo** [θi'klismo] nm cycling

**ciclista** [θi'klista] adj cycle cpd ▷ nmf cyclist

**ciclo** ['θiklo] nm cycle

**ciclón** [θi'klon] nm cyclone

**cicloturismo** [θiklotu'rismo] nm touring by bicycle

**ciego, -a** ['θjeɣo, a] adj blind ▷ nm/f blind man/woman

**cielo** ['θjelo] nm sky; (Rel) heaven; **¡~s!** good heavens!

**ciempiés** [θjem'pjes] nm inv centipede

**cien** [θjen] num V **ciento**

**ciencia** ['θjenθja] nf science; **ciencias** nfpl
science sg; **ciencia-ficción** nf science fiction
**científico, -a** [θjen'tifiko, a] adj scientific
▷ nm/f scientist
**ciento** ['θjento] num hundred; **pagar al 10
por ~** to pay at 10 per cent
**cierre** ['θjerre] vb V cerrar ▷ nm closing,
shutting; (con llave) locking; **~ de
cremallera** zip (fastener)
**cierro** etc vb V cerrar
**cierto, -a** ['θjerto, a] adj sure, certain; (un tal)
a certain; (correcto) right, correct; **~ hombre**
a certain man; **ciertas personas** certain o
some people; **sí, es ~** yes, that's correct;
**por ~** by the way
**ciervo** ['θjerβo] nm deer; (macho) stag
**cifra** ['θifra] nf number; (secreta) code;
**cifrar** /1a/ vt to code, write in code
**cigala** [θi'yala] nf Norway lobster
**cigarra** [θi'yarra] nf cicada
**cigarrillo** [θiya'rriʎo] nm cigarette;
**~ electrónico** e-cigarette
**cigarro** [θi'yarro] nm cigarette; (puro) cigar
**cigüeña** [θi'ɣweɲa] nf stork
**cilíndrico, -a** [θi'lindriko, a] adj cylindrical
**cilindro** [θi'lindro] nm cylinder
**cima** ['θima] nf (de montaña) top, peak; (de
árbol) top; (fig) height
**cimentar** [θimen'tar] /1j/ vt to lay the
foundations of; (fig: fundar) to found
**cimiento** [θi'mjento] nm foundation
**cincel** [θin'θel] nm chisel
**cinco** ['θinko] num five
**cincuenta** [θin'kwenta] num fifty
**cine** ['θine] nm cinema; **cinematográfico,
-a** adj cine-, film cpd
**cínico, -a** ['θiniko, a] adj cynical ▷ nm/f
cynic
**cinismo** [θi'nismo] nm cynicism
**cinta** ['θinta] nf band, strip; (de tela) ribbon;
(película) reel; (de máquina de escribir) ribbon;
(magnetofónica) tape; **~ adhesiva** sticky
tape; **~ aislante** insulating tape; **~ de vídeo**
videotape; **~ métrica** tape measure
**cintura** [θin'tura] nf waist
**cinturón** [θintu'ron] nm belt; **~ de
seguridad** safety belt
**ciprés** [θi'pres] nm cypress (tree)
**circo** ['θirko] nm circus
**circuito** [θir'kwito] nm circuit
**circulación** [θirkula'θjon] nf circulation;
(Auto) traffic
**circular** [θirku'lar] /1a/ adj, nf circular ▷ vt
to circulate ▷ vi (Auto) to drive; **"circule por
la derecha"** "keep (to the) right"
**círculo** ['θirkulo] nm circle; **~ vicioso**
vicious circle
**circunferencia** [θirkunfe'renθja] nf
circumference

**circunstancia** [θirkuns'tanθja] nf
circumstance
**cirio** ['θirjo] nm (wax) candle
**ciruela** [θi'rwela] nf plum; **~ pasa** prune
**cirugía** [θiru'xia] nf surgery; **~ estética** o
**plástica** plastic surgery
**cirujano** [θiru'xano] nm surgeon
**cisne** ['θisne] nm swan
**cisterna** [θis'terna] nf cistern, tank
**cita** ['θita] nf appointment, meeting; (de
novios) date; (referencia) quotation
**citación** [θita'θjon] nf (Jur) summons sg
**citar** [θi'tar] /1a/ vt to make an
appointment with; (Jur) to summons; (un
autor, texto) to quote; **citarse** vr: **se ~on en
el cine** they arranged to meet at the cinema
**cítrico, -a** ['θitriko, a] adj citric ▷ nm: **~s**
citrus fruits
**ciudad** [θju'ðað] nf town; (capital de país etc)
city; **ciudadano, -a** nm/f citizen
**cívico, -a** ['θiβiko, a] adj civic
**civil** [θi'βil] adj civil ▷ nm (guardia) police
officer; **civilización** nf civilization; **civilizar**
/1f/ vt to civilize
**cizaña** [θi'θaɲa] nf (fig) discord
**cl** abr (= centilitro) cl.
**clamor** [kla'mor] nm clamour, protest
**clandestino, -a** [klandes'tino, a] adj
clandestine; (Pol) underground
**clara** ['klara] nf (de huevo) egg white
**claraboya** [klara'βoja] nf skylight
**clarear** [klare'ar] /1a/ vi (el día) to dawn; (el
cielo) to clear up, brighten up; **clarearse** vr
to be transparent
**claridad** [klari'ðað] nf (del día) brightness;
(de estilo) clarity
**clarificar** [klarifi'kar] /1g/ vt to clarify
**clarinete** [klari'nete] nm clarinet
**claro, -a** ['klaro, a] adj clear; (luminoso)
bright; (color) light; (evidente) clear, evident;
(poco espeso) thin ▷ nm (en bosque) clearing
▷ adv clearly ▷ excl: **¡~ que sí!** of course!;
**¡~ que no!** of course not!
**clase** ['klase] nf class; **~ alta/media/
obrera** upper/middle/working class; **dar
~s** to teach; **~s particulares** private lessons
o tuition sg
**clásico, -a** ['klasiko, a] adj classical
**clasificación** [klasifika'θjon] nf
classification; (Deporte) league (table)
**clasificar** [klasifi'kar] /1g/ vt to classify
**claustro** ['klaustro] nm cloister
**cláusula** ['klausula] nf clause
**clausura** [klau'sura] nf closing, closure
**clavar** [kla'βar] /1a/ vt (clavo) to hammer
in; (cuchillo) to stick, thrust
**clave** ['klaβe] nf key; (Mus) clef; **~ de acceso**
password; **~ lada** (LAM) dialling (BRIT) o area
(US) code

**clavel** [kla'βel] nm carnation
**clavícula** [kla'βikula] nf collar bone
**clavija** [kla'βixa] nf peg, pin; (Elec) plug
**clavo** ['klaβo] nm (de metal) nail; (Bot) clove
**claxon** ['klakson] (pl **claxons**) nm horn
**clérigo** ['kleriɣo] nm priest
**clero** ['klero] nm clergy
**clicar** [kli'kar] /1a/ vi (Inform) to click; **clica en el icono** click on the icon; **~ dos veces** to double-click
**cliché** [kli'tʃe] nm cliché; (Foto) negative
**cliente, -a** ['kljente, a] nm/f client, customer; **clientela** nf clientele, customers pl
**clima** ['klima] nm climate; **climatizado, -a** adj air-conditioned
**clímax** ['klimaks] nm inv climax
**clínico, -a** ['kliniko, a] adj clinical ▷ nf clinic; (particular) private hospital
**clip** [klip] (pl **clips**) nm paper clip
**clítoris** ['klitoris] nm inv clitoris
**cloaca** [klo'aka] nf sewer, drain
**clonar** [klo'nar] /1a/ vt to clone
**cloro** ['kloro] nm chlorine
**club** [klub] (pl **clubs** o **clubes**) nm club; **~ nocturno** night club
**cm** abr (= centímetro) cm
**coágulo** [ko'aɣulo] nm clot
**coalición** [koali'θjon] nf coalition
**coartada** [koar'taða] nf alibi
**coartar** [koar'tar] /1a/ vt to limit, restrict
**coba** ['koβa] nf: **dar ~ a algn** (adular) to suck up to sb
**cobarde** adj cowardly ▷ nmf coward; **cobardía** nf cowardice
**cobaya** [ko'βaja] nf guinea pig
**cobertizo** [koβer'tiθo] nm shelter
**cobertura** [koβer'tura] nf cover; (Com) coverage; **~ de dividendo** (Com) dividend cover; **no tengo ~** (Telec) I can't get a signal
**cobija** [ko'βixa] nf (LAM) blanket; **cobijar** /1a/ vt (cubrir) to cover; (abrigar) to shelter; **cobijo** nm shelter
**cobra** ['koβra] nf cobra
**cobrador, a** [koβra'ðor, a] nm/f (de autobús) conductor/conductress; (de impuestos, gas) collector
**cobrar** [ko'βrar] /1a/ vt (cheque) to cash; (sueldo) to collect, draw; (objeto) to recover; (precio) to charge; (deuda) to collect ▷ vi to be paid; **cóbrese al entregar** cash on delivery (COD) (BRIT), collect on delivery (COD) (US); **¿me cobra, por favor?** (en tienda) how much do I owe you?; (en restaurante) can I have the bill, please?
**cobre** ['koβre] nm copper; **cobres** nmpl (Mus) brass instruments
**cobro** ['koβro] nm (de cheque) cashing; **presentar al ~** to cash

**cocaína** [koka'ina] nf cocaine
**cocción** [kok'θjon] nf (Culin) cooking; (el hervir) boiling
**cocer** [ko'θer] /2b, 2h/ vt, vi to cook; (en agua) to boil; (en horno) to bake
**coche** ['kotʃe] nm (Auto) car, automobile (US); (de tren, de caballos) coach, carriage; (para niños) pram (BRIT), baby carriage (US); **ir en ~** to drive; **~ de bomberos** fire engine; **~ (comedor)** (Ferro) (dining) car; **~ de carreras** racing car; **~-escuela** learner car; **~ fúnebre** hearse; **coche-cama** nm (Ferro) sleeping car, sleeper
**cochera** [ko'tʃera] nf garage; (de autobuses, trenes) depot
**coche-restaurante** ['kotʃerestau'rante] (pl **coches-restaurante**) nm (Ferro) dining-car, diner
**cochinillo** [kotʃi'niʎo] nm suckling pig
**cochino, -a** [ko'tʃino, a] adj filthy, dirty ▷ nm/f pig
**cocido** [ko'θiðo] nm stew
**cocina** [ko'θina] nf kitchen; (aparato) cooker, stove; (actividad) cookery; **~ eléctrica** electric cooker; **~ de gas** gas cooker; **cocinar** /1a/ vt, vi to cook
**cocinero, -a** [koθi'nero, a] nm/f cook
**coco** ['koko] nm coconut
**cocodrilo** [koko'ðrilo] nm crocodile
**cocotero** [koko'tero] nm coconut palm
**cóctel** ['koktel] nm cocktail; **~ Molotov** Molotov cocktail, petrol bomb
**codazo** [ko'ðaθo] nm: **dar un ~ a algn** to nudge sb
**codicia** [ko'ðiθja] nf greed; **codiciar** /1b/ vt to covet
**código** ['koðiɣo] nm code; **~ de barras** bar code; **~ de (la) circulación** highway code; **~ de la zona** (LAM) dialling (BRIT) o area (US) code; **~ postal** postcode
**codillo** [ko'ðiʎo] nm (Zool) knee; (Tec) elbow (joint)
**codo** ['koðo] nm (Anat, de tubo) elbow; (Zool) knee
**codorniz** [koðor'niθ] nf quail
**coexistir** [koeksis'tir] /3a/ vi to coexist
**cofradía** [kofra'ðia] nf brotherhood, fraternity
**cofre** ['kofre] nm (de joyas) box; (de dinero) chest
**coger** [ko'xer] /2c/ vt (ESP) to take (hold of); (: objeto caído) to pick up; (: frutas) to pick, harvest; (: resfriado, ladrón, pelota) to catch ▷ vi: **~ por el buen camino** to take the right road; **cogerse** vr (el dedo) to catch; **~se a algo** to get hold of sth
**cogollo** [ko'ɣoʎo] nm (de lechuga) heart
**cogote** [ko'ɣote] nm back o nape of the neck
**cohabitar** [koaβi'tar] /1a/ vi to live together, cohabit

**coherente** [koe'rente] *adj* coherent
**cohesión** [koe'sjon] *nm* cohesion
**cohete** [ko'ete] *nm* rocket
**cohibido, -a** [koi'βiðo, a] *adj* (*Psico*) inhibited; (*tímido*) shy
**coincidencia** [koinθi'ðenθja] *nf* coincidence
**coincidir** [koinθi'ðir] /3a/ *vi* (*en idea*) to coincide, agree; (*en lugar*) to coincide
**coito** ['koito] *nm* intercourse, coitus
**coja** *etc vb V* **coger**
**cojear** [koxe'ar] /1a/ *vi* (*persona*) to limp, hobble; (*mueble*) to wobble, rock
**cojera** [ko'xera] *nf* limp
**cojín** [ko'xin] *nm* cushion
**cojo, -a** ['koxo, a] *vb V* **coger** ▷ *adj* (*que no puede andar*) lame, crippled; (*mueble*) wobbly ▷ *nm/f* lame person
**cojón** [ko'xon] *nm* (*fam!*): **¡cojones!** shit! (*!*); **cojonudo, -a** *adj* (*fam*) great, fantastic
**col** [kol] *nf* cabbage; **~es de Bruselas** Brussels sprouts
**cola** ['kola] *nf* tail; (*de gente*) queue; (*lugar*) end, last place; (*para pegar*) glue, gum; **hacer ~** to queue (up)
**colaborador, a** [kolaβora'ðor, a] *nm/f* collaborator
**colaborar** [kolaβo'rar] /1a/ *vi* to collaborate
**colado, -a** [ko'laðo, a] *adj* (*metal*) cast ▷ *nf*: **hacer la colada** to do the washing
**colador** [kola'ðor] *nm* (*de té*) strainer; (*para verduras etc*) colander
**colapso** [ko'lapso] *nm* collapse
**colar** [ko'lar] /1l/ *vt* (*líquido*) to strain off; (*metal*) to cast ▷ *vi* to ooze, seep (through); **colarse** *vr* to jump the queue; **~se en** to get into without paying; (*en una fiesta*) to gatecrash
**colcha** ['koltʃa] *nf* bedspread
**colchón** [kol'tʃon] *nm* mattress; **~ inflable** air bed, inflatable mattress
**colchoneta** [koltʃo'neta] *nf* (*en gimnasio*) mat; **~ hinchable** air bed, inflatable mattress
**colección** [kolek'θjon] *nf* collection; **coleccionar** /1a/ *vt* to collect; **coleccionista** *nmf* collector
**colecta** [ko'lekta] *nf* collection
**colectivo, -a** [kolek'tiβo, a] *adj* collective, joint ▷ *nm* (*LAM: autobús*) (small) bus
**colega** [ko'leɣa] *nmf* colleague; (*ESP: amigo*) mate
**colegial, a** [kole'xjal, a] *nm/f* schoolboy/girl
**colegio** [ko'lexjo] *nm* college; (*escuela*) school; (*de abogados etc*) association; **~ electoral** polling station; **~ mayor** (*ESP*) hall of residence

○ **COLEGIO**
○
○ A *colegio* is often a private primary or
○ secondary school. In the state system
○ it means a primary school although
○ these are also called *escuela*. State
○ secondary schools are called *institutos*.
○ Extracurricular subjects, such as
○ computing or foreign languages, are
○ offered in private schools called *academias*.

**cólera** ['kolera] *nf* (*ira*) anger ▷ *nm* (*Med*) cholera
**colesterol** [koleste'rol] *nm* cholesterol
**coleta** [ko'leta] *nf* pigtail
**colgante** [kol'ɣante] *adj* hanging ▷ *nm* (*joya*) pendant
**colgar** [kol'ɣar] /1h, 1l/ *vt* to hang (up); (*ropa*) to hang out ▷ *vi* to hang; (*teléfono*) to hang up
**cólico** ['koliko] *nm* colic
**coliflor** [koli'flor] *nf* cauliflower
**colilla** [ko'liʎa] *nf* cigarette end, butt
**colina** [ko'lina] *nf* hill
**colisión** [koli'sjon] *nf* collision; **~ frontal** head-on crash
**collar** [ko'ʎar] *nm* necklace; (*de perro*) collar
**colmar** [kol'mar] /1a/ *vt* to fill to the brim; (*fig*) to fulfil, realize
**colmena** [kol'mena] *nf* beehive
**colmillo** [kol'miʎo] *nm* (*diente*) eye tooth; (*de elefante*) tusk; (*de perro*) fang
**colmo** ['kolmo] *nm*: **¡eso es ya el ~!** that's beyond a joke!
**colocación** [koloka'θjon] *nf* (*acto*) placing; (*empleo*) job, position
**colocar** [kolo'kar] /1g/ *vt* to place, put, position; (*poner en empleo*) to find a job for; **~ dinero** to invest money; **colocarse** *vr* (*conseguir trabajo*) to find a job
**Colombia** [ko'lombja] *nf* Colombia; **colombiano, -a** *adj, nm/f* Colombian
**colonia** [ko'lonja] *nf* colony; (*de casas*) housing estate; (*agua de colonia*) cologne; **~ proletaria** (*LAM*) shantytown
**colonización** [koloniθa'θjon] *nf* colonization; **colonizador, a** *adj* colonizing ▷ *nm/f* colonist, settler
**colonizar** [koloni'θar] /1f/ *vt* to colonize
**coloquio** [ko'lokjo] *nm* conversation; (*congreso*) conference
**color** [ko'lor] *nm* colour
**colorado, -a** [kolo'raðo, a] *adj* (*rojo*) red; (*LAM: chiste*) rude
**colorante** [kolo'rante] *nm* colouring (matter)
**colorear** [kolore'ar] /1a/ *vt* to colour
**colorete** [kolo'rete] *nm* blusher
**colorido** [kolo'riðo] *nm* colour(ing)

**columna** [ko'lumna] nf column; (pilar)
pillar; (apoyo) support; **~ vertebral** spine,
spinal column; (fig) backbone

**columpiar** [kolum'pjar] /1b/ vt to swing;
**columpiarse** vr to swing; **columpio** nm
swing

**coma** ['koma] nf comma ▷ nm (Med) coma

**comadre** [ko'maðre] nf (madrina)
godmother; (chismosa) gossip; **comadrona**
nf midwife

**comal** [ko'mal] nm (LAM) griddle

**comandante** [koman'dante] nm
commandant

**comarca** [ko'marka] nf region

**comba** ['komba] nf (cuerda) skipping rope;
**saltar a la ~** to skip

**combate** [kom'bate] nm fight

**combatir** [komba'tir] /3a/ vt to fight,
combat

**combinación** [kombina'θjon] nf
combination; (Química) compound;
(prenda) slip

**combinar** [kombi'nar] /1a/ vt to combine

**combustible** [kombus'tiβle] nm fuel

**comedia** [ko'meðja] nf comedy; (Teat) play,
drama; **comediante** nmf (comic) actor/
actress

**comedido, -a** [kome'ðiðo, a] adj
moderate

**comedor** [kome'ðor] nm (habitación) dining
room; (cantina) canteen

**comensal** [komen'sal] nmf fellow guest/
diner

**comentar** [komen'tar] /1a/ vt to comment
on; **comentario** nm comment, remark; (Lit)
commentary; **comentarios** nmpl gossip sg;
**comentarista** nmf commentator

**comenzar** [komen'θar] /1f, 1j/ vt, vi to
begin, start; **~ a hacer algo** to begin o start
doing o to do sth

**comer** [ko'mer] /2a/ vt to eat; (Damas,
Ajedrez) to take, capture ▷ vi to eat;
(almorzar) to have lunch; **comerse** vr to
eat up

**comercial** [komer'θjal] adj commercial;
(relativo al negocio) business cpd;
**comercializar** /1f/ vt (producto) to market;
(pey) to commercialize

**comerciante** [komer'θjante] nmf trader,
merchant

**comerciar** [komer'θjar] /1b/ vi to trade,
do business

**comercio** [ko'merθjo] nm commerce,
trade; (tienda) shop, store; (negocio)
business; (grandes empresas) big business;
(fig) dealings pl; **~ electrónico** e-commerce;
**~ exterior** foreign trade

**comestible** [komes'tiβle] adj eatable,
edible ▷ nm: **~s** food sg, foodstuffs

**cometa** [ko'meta] nm comet ▷ nf kite

**cometer** [kome'ter] /2a/ vt to commit

**cometido** [kome'tiðo] nm task,
assignment

**cómic** ['komik] (pl **cómics**) nm comic

**comicios** [ko'miθjos] nmpl elections

**cómico, -a** ['komiko, a] adj comic(al)
▷ nm/f comedian

**comida** [ko'miða] nf (alimento) food;
(almuerzo, cena) meal; (de mediodía) lunch;
**~ basura** junk food; **~ chatarra** (LAM) junk
food

**comidilla** [komi'ðiʎa] nf: **ser la ~ del
barrio** o **pueblo** to be the talk of the town

**comienzo** [ko'mjenθo] vb V **comenzar**
▷ nm beginning, start

**comillas** [ko'miʎas] nfpl quotation marks

**comilón, -ona** [komi'lon, ona] adj greedy
▷ nf (fam) blow-out

**comino** [ko'mino] nm cumin (seed); **no me
importa un ~** I don't give a damn!

**comisaría** [komisa'ria] nf police station;
(Mil) commissariat

**comisario** [komi'sarjo] nm (Mil etc)
commissary; (Pol) commissar

**comisión** [komi'sjon] nf commission

**comité** [komi'te] (pl **comités**) nm
committee

**comitiva** [komi'tiβa] nf retinue

**como** ['komo] adv as; (tal como) like;
(aproximadamente) about, approximately
▷ conj (ya que, puesto que) as, since; **i~ no!** of
course!; **~ no lo haga hoy** unless he does it
today; **~ si** as if; **es tan alto ~ ancho** it is as
high as it is wide

**cómo** ['komo] adv how?, why? ▷ excl what?,
I beg your pardon? ▷ nm: **el ~ y el porqué**
the whys and wherefores

**cómoda** ['komoða] nf chest of drawers

**comodidad** [komoði'ðað] nf comfort

**comodín** [komo'ðin] nm joker

**cómodo, -a** ['komoðo, a] adj comfortable;
(práctico, de fácil uso) convenient

**compact** [kom'pakt] (pl **compacts**) nm (tb:
**~ disc**) compact disk

**compacto, -a** [kom'pakto, a] adj compact

**compadecer** [kompaðe'θer] /2d/ vt to
pity, be sorry for; **compadecerse** vr: **~se de**
to pity, be sorry for

**compadre** [kom'paðre] nm (padrino)
godfather; (amigo) friend, pal

**compañero, -a** [kompa'ɲero, a] nm/f
companion; (novio) boyfriend/girlfriend;
**~ de clase** classmate

**compañía** [kompa'ɲia] nf company;
**hacer ~ a algn** to keep sb company

**comparación** [kompara'θjon] nf
comparison; **en** o **con** in comparison with

**comparar** [kompa'rar] /1a/ vt to compare

**comparecer** [kompare'θer] /2d/ vi to appear (in court)

**comparsa** [kom'parsa] nmf extra

**compartim(i)ento** [komparti'm(i)ento] nm (Ferro) compartment

**compartir** [kompar'tir] /3a/ vt to share; (dinero, comida etc) to divide (up), share (out)

**compás** [kom'pas] nm (Mus) beat, rhythm; (Mat) compasses pl; (Naut etc) compass

**compasión** [kompa'sjon] nf compassion, pity

**compasivo, -a** [kompa'siβo, a] adj compassionate

**compatible** [kompa'tiβle] adj compatible

**compatriota** [kompa'trjota] nmf compatriot, fellow countryman/woman

**compenetrarse** [kompene'trarse] /1a/ vr to be in tune

**compensación** [kompensa'θjon] nf compensation

**compensar** [kompen'sar] /1a/ vt to compensate

**competencia** [kompe'tenθja] nf (incumbencia) domain, field; (Jur, habilidad) competence; (rivalidad) competition

**competente** [kompe'tente] adj competent

**competición** [kompeti'θjon] nf competition

**competir** [kompe'tir] /3k/ vi to compete

**compinche** [kom'pintʃe] nmf (LAM fam) mate, buddy (US)

**complacer** [kompla'θer] /2w/ vt to please; **complacerse** vr to be pleased

**complaciente** [kompla'θjente] adj kind, obliging, helpful

**complejo, -a** [kom'plexo, a] adj, nm complex

**complementario, -a** [komplemen'tarjo, a] adj complementary

**completar** [komple'tar] /1a/ vt to complete

**completo, -a** [kom'pleto, a] adj complete; (perfecto) perfect; (lleno) full ▷ nm full complement

**complicado, -a** [kompli'kaðo, a] adj complicated; **estar ~ en** to be mixed up in

**cómplice** ['kompliθe] nmf accomplice

**complot** [kom'plo(t)] (pl **complots**) nm plot

**componer** [kompo'ner] /2q/ vt (Mus, Lit, Imprenta) to compose; (algo roto) to mend, repair; (arreglar) to arrange; **componerse** vr: **~se de** to consist of

**comportamiento** [komporta'mjento] nm behaviour, conduct

**comportarse** [kompor'tarse] /1a/ vr to behave

**composición** [komposi'θjon] nf composition

**compositor, a** [komposi'tor, a] nm/f composer

**compostura** [kompos'tura] nf (actitud) composure

**compra** ['kompra] nf purchase; **hacer la ~/ir de ~s** to do the/go shopping; **comprador, a** nm/f buyer, purchaser; **comprar** /1a/ vt to buy, purchase

**comprender** [kompren'der] /2a/ vt to understand; (incluir) to comprise, include

**comprensión** [kompren'sjon] nf understanding; **comprensivo, -a** adj (actitud) understanding

**compresa** [kom'presa] nf (higiénica) sanitary towel (BRIT) o napkin (US)

**comprimido, -a** [kompri'miðo, a] adj compressed ▷ nm (Med) pill, tablet

**comprimir** /3a/ vt to compress; (Inform) to compress, zip

**comprobante** [kompro'βante] nm proof; (Com) voucher; **~ de compra** proof of purchase

**comprobar** [kompro'βar] /1l/ vt to check; (probar) to prove; (Tec) to check, test

**comprometer** [komprome'ter] /2a/ vt to compromise; (exponer) to endanger; **comprometerse** vr (involucrarse) to get involved

**compromiso** [kompro'miso] nm (obligación) obligation; (cometido) commitment; (convenio) agreement; (dificultad) awkward situation

**compuesto, -a** [kom'pwesto, a] adj: **~ de** composed of, made up of ▷ nm compound

**computador** [komputa'ðor] nm, **computadora** [komputa'ðora] nf computer; **~ central** mainframe computer; **~ de escritorio** desktop; **~ personal** personal computer

**cómputo** ['komputo] nm calculation

**comulgar** [komul'ɣar] /1h/ vi to receive communion

**común** [ko'mun] adj common ▷ nm: **el ~** the community

**comunicación** [komunika'θjon] nf communication; (informe) report

**comunicado** [komuni'kaðo] nm announcement; **~ de prensa** press release

**comunicar** [komuni'kar] /1g/ vt to communicate ▷ vi to communicate; **comunicarse** vr to communicate; **está comunicando** (Telec) the line's engaged (BRIT) o busy (US); **comunicativo, -a** adj communicative

**comunidad** [komuni'ðað] nf community; **~ autónoma** (ESP) autonomous region; **~ de vecinos** residents' association; **C~ Económica Europea (CEE)** European Economic Community (EEC)

**comunión** [komu'njon] *nf* communion
**comunismo** [komu'nismo] *nm* communism; **comunista** *adj*, *nmf* communist

⭕ **PALABRA CLAVE**

**con** [kon] *prep* **1** (*medio, compañía, modo*) with; **comer con cuchara** to eat with a spoon; **pasear con algn** to go for a walk with sb
**2** (*a pesar de*): **con todo, merece nuestros respetos** all the same *o* even so, he deserves our respect
**3** (*para con*): **es muy bueno para con los niños** he's very good with (the) children
**4** (*+ infin*): **con llegar tan tarde se quedó sin comer** by arriving *o* because he arrived so late he missed out on eating
▶ *conj*: **con que: será suficiente con que le escribas** it will be enough if you write to her

**concebir** [konθe'βir] /3k/ *vt* to conceive ▷ *vi* to conceive
**conceder** [konθe'ðer] /2a/ *vt* to concede
**concejal, a** [konθe'xal, a] *nm/f* town councillor
**concentración** [konθentra'θjon] *nf* concentration
**concentrar** [konθen'trar] /1a/ *vt* to concentrate; **concentrarse** *vr* to concentrate
**concepto** [kon'θepto] *nm* concept
**concernir** [konθer'nir] *vi* to concern; **en lo que concierne a ...** with regard to ...; **en lo que a mí concierne** as far as I'm concerned
**concertar** [konθer'tar] /1j/ *vt* (*entrevista*) to arrange; (*precio*) to agree ▷ *vi* to harmonize, be in tune
**concesión** [konθe'sjon] *nf* concession
**concesionario, -a** [konθesjo'narjo, a] *nm/f* (*Com*) (licensed) dealer, agent
**concha** ['kontʃa] *nf* shell
**conciencia** [konθjen'θja] *nf* conscience; **tener/tomar ~ de** to be/become aware of; **tener la ~ limpia** *o* **tranquila** to have a clear conscience
**concienciar** [konθjen'θjar] /1b/ *vt* to make aware; **concienciarse** *vr* to become aware
**concienzudo, -a** [konθjen'θuðo, a] *adj* conscientious
**concierto** [kon'θjerto] *vb* V **concertar** ▷ *nm* concert; (*obra*) concerto
**conciliar** [konθi'ljar] /1b/ *vt* to reconcile; **~ el sueño** to get to sleep
**concilio** [kon'θiljo] *nm* council
**conciso, -a** [kon'θiso, a] *adj* concise
**concluir** [konklu'ir] /3g/ *vt* to conclude ▷ **concluirse** *vr* to conclude

**conclusión** [konklu'sjon] *nf* conclusion
**concordar** [konkor'ðar] /1l/ *vt* to reconcile ▷ *vi* to agree, tally
**concordia** [kon'korðja] *nf* harmony
**concretar** [konkre'tar] /1a/ *vt* to make concrete, make more specific; **concretarse** *vr* to become more definite
**concreto, -a** [kon'kreto, a] *adj*, *nm* (*LAM*) concrete; **en ~** (*en resumen*) to sum up; (*específicamente*) specifically; **no hay nada en ~** there's nothing definite
**concurrido, -a** [konku'rriðo, a] *adj* (*calle*) busy; (*local, reunión*) crowded
**concursante** [konkur'sante] *nm* competitor
**concurso** [kon'kurso] *nm* (*de público*) crowd; (*Escol, Deporte, competición*) competition; (*ayuda*) help, cooperation
**condal** [kon'dal] *adj*: **la ciudad ~** Barcelona
**conde** ['konde] *nm* count
**condecoración** [kondekora'θjon] *nf* (*Mil*) medal
**condena** [kon'dena] *nf* sentence; **condenación** *nf* condemnation; (*Rel*) damnation; **condenar** /1a/ *vt* to condemn; (*Jur*) to convict; **condenarse** *vr* (*Rel*) to be damned
**condesa** [kon'desa] *nf* countess
**condición** [kondi'θjon] *nf* condition; **a ~ de que ...** on condition that ...; **condicional** *adj* conditional
**condimento** [kondi'mento] *nm* seasoning
**condominio** [kondo'minjo] *nm* condominium
**condón** [kon'don] *nm* condom
**conducir** [kondu'θir] /3n/ *vt* to take, convey; (*Auto*) to drive ▷ *vi* to drive; (*fig*) to lead; **conducirse** *vr* to behave
**conducta** [kon'dukta] *nf* conduct, behaviour
**conducto** [kon'dukto] *nm* pipe, tube; (*fig*) channel
**conductor, a** [konduk'tor, a] *adj* leading, guiding ▷ *nm* (*Física*) conductor; (*de vehículo*) driver
**conduje** *etc* [kon'duxe] *vb* V **conducir**
**conduzco** *etc* *vb* V **conducir**
**conectado, -a** [konek'taðo, a] *adj* (*Inform*) on-line
**conectar** [konek'tar] /1a/ *vt* to connect (up); (*enchufar*) plug in
**conejillo** [kone'xiʎo] *nm*: **~ de Indias** guinea pig
**conejo** [ko'nexo] *nm* rabbit
**conexión** [konek'sjon] *nf* connection
**confección** [konfek'θjon] *nf* preparation; (*industria*) clothing industry
**confeccionar** [konfekθjo'nar] /1a/ *vt* to make (up)

**conferencia** [konfe'renθja] nf conference; (lección) lecture; (Telec) call; **~ de prensa** press conference

**conferir** [konfe'rir] /3i/ vt to award

**confesar** [konfe'sar] /1j/ vt to confess, admit

**confesión** [konfe'sjon] nf confession

**confesionario** [konfesjo'narjo] nm confessional

**confeti** [kon'feti] nm confetti

**confiado, -a** [kon'fjaðo, a] adj (crédulo) trusting; (seguro) confident

**confianza** [kon'fjanθa] nf trust; (aliento, confidencia) confidence; (familiaridad) intimacy, familiarity

**confiar** [kon'fjar] /1c/ vt to entrust ▷ vi to trust; **~ en algn** to trust sb; **~ en que...** to hope that...

**confidencial** [konfiðen'θjal] adj confidential

**confidente** [konfi'ðente] nmf confidant/ confidante; (policial) informer

**configurar** [konfiɣu'rar] /1a/ vt to shape, form

**confín** [kon'fin] nm limit; **confines** nmpl confines, limits

**confirmar** [konfir'mar] /1a/ vt to confirm

**confiscar** [konfis'kar] /1g/ vt to confiscate

**confite** [kon'fite] nm sweet (BRIT), candy (US); **confitería** nf (tienda) confectioner's (shop)

**confitura** [konfi'tura] nf jam

**conflictivo, -a** [konflik'tiβo, a] adj (asunto, propuesta) controversial; (país, situación) troubled

**conflicto** [kon'flikto] nm conflict; (fig) clash

**confluir** [konflu'ir] /3g/ vi (ríos etc) to meet; (gente) to gather

**conformar** [konfor'mar] /1a/ vt to shape, fashion ▷ vi to agree; **conformarse** vr to conform; (resignarse) to resign o.s.; **~se con algo** to be happy with sth

**conforme** [kon'forme] adj (correspondiente): **~ con** in line with; (de acuerdo) agreed ▷ adv as ▷ excl agreed! ▷ prep: **~ a** in accordance with; **estar ~s (con algo)** to be in agreement (with sth); **quedarse ~ (con algo)** to be satisfied (with sth)

**confortable** [konfor'taβle] adj comfortable

**confortar** [konfor'tar] /1a/ vt to comfort

**confrontar** [konfron'tar] /1a/ vt to confront; (dos personas) to bring face to face; (cotejar) to compare

**confundir** [konfun'dir] /3a/ vt (equivocar) to mistake, confuse; (turbar) to confuse;

**confundirse** vr (turbarse) to get confused; (equivocarse) to make a mistake; (mezclarse) to mix

**confusión** [konfu'sjon] nf confusion

**confuso, -a** [kon'fuso, a] adj confused

**congelado, -a** [konxe'laðo, a] adj frozen ▷ nmpl: **~s** frozen food sg o foods; **congelador** nm freezer, deep freeze

**congelar** [konxe'lar] /1a/ vt to freeze; **congelarse** vr (sangre, grasa) to congeal

**congeniar** [konxe'njar] /1b/ vi to get on (BRIT) o along (US) (well)

**congestión** [konxes'tjon] nf congestion

**congestionar** [konxestjo'nar] /1a/ vt to congest

**congraciarse** [kongra'θjarse] /1b/ vr to ingratiate o.s.

**congratular** [kongratu'lar] /1a/ vt to congratulate

**congregar** [kongre'ɣar] /1h/ vt to gather together; **congregarse** vr to gather together

**congresista** [kongre'sista] nmf delegate, congressman/woman

**congreso** [kon'greso] nm congress

**conjetura** [konxe'tura] nf guess; **conjeturar** /1a/ vt to guess

**conjugar** [konxu'ɣar] /1h/ vt to combine, fit together; (Ling) to conjugate

**conjunción** [konxun'θjon] nf conjunction

**conjunto, -a** [kon'xunto, a] adj joint, united ▷ nm whole; (Mus) band; **en ~** as a whole

**conmemoración** [konmemora'θjon] nf commemoration

**conmemorar** [konmemo'rar] /1a/ vt to commemorate

**conmigo** [kon'miɣo] pron with me

**conmoción** [konmo'θjon] nf shock; (fig) upheaval; **~ cerebral** (Med) concussion

**conmovedor, a** [konmoβe'ðor, a] adj touching, moving; (emocionante) exciting

**conmover** [konmo'βer] /2h/ vt to shake, disturb; (fig) to move

**conmutador** [konmuta'ðor] nm switch; (LAM: Telec) switchboard; (: central) telephone exchange

**cono** ['kono] nm cone; **C~ Sur** Southern Cone

**conocedor, a** [konoθe'ðor, a] adj expert, knowledgeable ▷ nm/f expert

**conocer** [kono'θer] /2d/ vt to know; (por primera vez) to meet, get to know; (entender) to know about; (reconocer) to recognize; **conocerse** vr (una persona) to know o.s.; (dos personas) to (get to) know each other; **~ a algn de vista** to know sb by sight

**conocido, -a** [kono'θiðo, a] adj (well-) known ▷ nm/f acquaintance

**conocimiento** [konoθi'mjento] nm knowledge; (Med) consciousness; **conocimientos** nmpl (saber) knowledge sg

**conozco** etc [ko'noθko] vb V **conocer**

**conque** ['konke] conj and so, so then

**conquista** [kon'kista] nf conquest; **conquistador, a** adj conquering ▷ nm conqueror; **conquistar** /1a/ vt to conquer

**consagrar** [konsa'ɣrar] /1a/ vt (Rel) to consecrate; (fig) to devote

**consciente** [kons'θjente] adj conscious

**consecución** [konseku'θjon] nf acquisition; (de fin) attainment

**consecuencia** [konse'kwenθja] nf consequence, outcome; (firmeza) consistency

**consecuente** [konse'kwente] adj consistent

**consecutivo, -a** [konseku'tiβo, a] adj consecutive

**conseguir** [konse'ɣir] /3d, 3k/ vt to get, obtain; (sus fines) to attain

**consejero, -a** [konse'xero, a] nm/f adviser, consultant; (Pol) minister (in a regional government)

**consejo** [kon'sexo] nm advice; (Pol) council; (Com) board; **~ de administración** board of directors; **~ de guerra** court-martial; **~ de ministros** cabinet meeting

**consenso** [kon'senso] nm consensus

**consentimiento** [konsenti'mjento] nm consent

**consentir** [konsen'tir] /3i/ vt (permitir, tolerar) to consent to; (mimar) to pamper, spoil; (aguantar) to put up with ▷ vi to agree, consent; **~ que algn haga algo** to allow sb to do sth

**conserje** [kon'serxe] nm caretaker; (portero) porter

**conserva** [kon'serβa] nf: **en ~** (alimentos) tinned (BRIT), canned; **conservas** nfpl (tb: **~s alimenticias**) tinned (BRIT) o canned foods

**conservación** [konserβa'θjon] nf conservation; (de alimentos, vida) preservation

**conservador, a** [konserβa'ðor, a] adj (Pol) conservative ▷ nm/f conservative

**conservante** [konser'βante] nm preservative

**conservar** [konser'βar] /1a/ vt to conserve, keep; (alimentos, vida) to preserve; **conservarse** vr to survive

**conservatorio** [konserβa'torjo] nm (Mus) conservatoire, conservatory

**considerable** [konsiðe'raβle] adj considerable

**consideración** [konsiðera'θjon] nf consideration; (estimación) respect

**considerado, -a** [konsiðe'raðo, a] adj (atento) considerate; (respetado) respected

**considerar** [konsiðe'rar] /1a/ vt to consider

**consigna** [kon'siɣna] nf (orden) order, instruction; (para equipajes) left-luggage office (BRIT), checkroom (US)

**consigo** [kon'siɣo] vb V **conseguir** ▷ pron (m) with him; (f) with her; (usted) with you; (reflexivo) with o.s.

**consiguiendo** etc [konsi'ɣjendo] vb V **conseguir**

**consiguiente** [konsi'ɣjente] adj consequent; **por ~** and so, therefore, consequently

**consistente** [konsis'tente] adj consistent; (sólido) solid, firm; (válido) sound

**consistir** [konsis'tir] /3a/ vi: **~ en** (componerse de) to consist of

**consola** [kon'sola] nf (mueble) console table; **~ de juegos** games console

**consolación** [konsola'θjon] nf consolation

**consolar** [konso'lar] /1l/ vt to console

**consolidar** [konsoli'ðar] /1a/ vt to consolidate

**consomé** [konso'me] (pl **consomés**) nm consommé, clear soup

**consonante** [konso'nante] adj consonant, harmonious ▷ nf consonant

**consorcio** [kon'sorθjo] nm consortium

**conspiración** [konspira'θjon] nf conspiracy

**conspirar** [konspi'rar] /1a/ vi to conspire

**constancia** [kons'tanθja] nf constancy; **dejar ~ de algo** to put sth on record

**constante** [kons'tante] adj, nf constant

**constar** [kons'tar] /1a/ vi (evidenciarse) to be clear o evident; **~ de** to consist of

**constipado, -a** [konsti'paðo, a] adj: **estar ~** to have a cold ▷ nm cold

⚠ No confundir constipado con la palabra inglesa constipated.

**constitución** [konstitu'θjon] nf constitution

**constituir** [konstitu'ir] /3g/ vt (formar, componer) to constitute, make up; (fundar, erigir, ordenar) to constitute, establish

**construcción** [konstruk'θjon] nf construction, building

**constructor, a** [konstruk'tor, a] nm/f builder

**construir** [konstru'ir] /3g/ vt to build, construct

**construyendo** etc [konstru'jendo] vb V **construir**

**consuelo** [kon'swelo] nm consolation, solace

**cónsul** ['konsul] nm consul; **consulado** nm consulate

**consulta** [kon'sulta] *nf* consultation;
**horas de ~** (*Med*) surgery hours; **consultar**
/1a/ *vt* to consult; **consultar algo con algn**
to discuss sth with sb; **consultorio** *nm*
(*Med*) surgery

**consumición** [konsumi'θjon] *nf*
consumption; (*bebida*) drink; (*comida*) food;
**~ mínima** cover charge

**consumidor, a** [konsumi'ðor, a] *nm/f*
consumer

**consumir** [konsu'mir] /3a/ *vt* to consume;
**consumirse** *vr* to be consumed; (*persona*) to
waste away

**consumismo** [konsu'mismo] *nm*
consumerism

**consumo** [kon'sumo] *nm* consumption

**contabilidad** [kontaβili'ðað] *nf*
accounting, book-keeping; (*profesión*)
accountancy; **contable** *nmf* accountant

**contactar** [kontak'tar] /1a/ *vi*: **~ con algn**
to contact sb

**contacto** [kon'takto] *nm* contact; (*Auto*)
ignition; **estar en ~ con** to be in touch with

**contado, -a** [kon'taðo, a] *adj*: **~s** (*escasos*)
numbered, scarce, few ▷ *nm*: **pagar al ~ to**
pay (in) cash

**contador** [konta'ðor] *nm* (*aparato*) meter;
(*LAM*: *contable*) accountant

**contagiar** [konta'xjar] /1b/ *vt* (*enfermedad*)
to pass on, transmit; (*persona*) to infect;
**contagiarse** *vr* to become infected

**contagio** [kon'taxjo] *nm* infection;
**contagioso, -a** *adj* infectious; (*fig*)
catching

**contaminación** [kontamina'θjon] *nf*
contamination; (*del ambiente etc*) pollution

**contaminar** [kontami'nar] /1a/ *vt* to
contaminate; (*aire, agua*) to pollute

**contante** [kon'tante] *adj*: **dinero ~
(y sonante)** hard cash

**contar** [kon'tar] /1l/ *vt* (*páginas, dinero*) to
count; (*anécdota etc*) to tell ▷ *vi* to count;
**~ con** to rely on, count on

**contemplar** [kontem'plar] /1a/ *vt* to
contemplate; (*mirar*) to look at

**contemporáneo, -a** [kontempo'raneo, a]
*adj, nm/f* contemporary

**contenedor** [kontene'ðor] *nm* container

**contener** [konte'ner] /2k/ *vt* to contain,
hold; (*risa etc*) to hold back, contain;
**contenerse** *vr* to control o restrain o.s.

**contenido, -a** [konte'niðo, a] *adj*
(*moderado*) restrained; (*risa etc*) suppressed
▷ *nm* contents *pl*, content

**contentar** [konten'tar] /1a/ *vt* (*satisfacer*)
to satisfy; (*complacer*) to please;
**contentarse** *vr* to be satisfied

**contento, -a** [kon'tento, a] *adj* (*alegre*)
pleased; (*feliz*) happy

**contestación** [kontesta'θjon] *nf* answer,
reply

**contestador** [kontesta'ðor] *nm*:
**~ automático** answering machine

**contestar** [kontes'tar] /1a/ *vt* to answer
(back), reply; (*Jur*) to corroborate, confirm
No confundir *contestar* con la palabra
inglesa *contest*.

**contexto** [kon'teksto] *nm* context

**contigo** [kon'tiɣo] *pron* with you

**contiguo, -a** [kon'tiɣwo, a] *adj* adjacent,
adjoining

**continente** [konti'nente] *adj, nm*
continent

**continuación** [kontinwa'θjon] *nf*
continuation; **a ~** then, next

**continuar** [konti'nwar] /1e/ *vt* to
continue, go on with ▷ *vi* to continue, go
on; **~ hablando** to continue talking o to
talk

**continuidad** [kontinwi'ðað] *nf*
continuity

**continuo, -a** [kon'tinwo, a] *adj*
(*sin interrupción*) continuous; (*acción*
*perseverante*) continual

**contorno** [kon'torno] *nm* outline; (*Geo*)
contour; **contornos** *nmpl* neighbourhood
*sg*, surrounding area *sg*

**contra** ['kontra] *prep* against ▷ *adv* against
▷ *nm* con ▷ *nf*: **la C~ (nicaragüense)** the
Contras *pl*

**contraataque** [kontraa'take] *nm*
counterattack

**contrabajo** [kontra'βaxo] *nm* double bass

**contrabandista** [kontraβan'dista] *nmf*
smuggler

**contrabando** [kontra'βando] *nm* (*acción*)
smuggling; (*mercancías*) contraband

**contracción** [kontrak'θjon] *nf*
contraction

**contracorriente** [kontrako'rrjente] *nf*
cross-current

**contradecir** [kontraðe'θir] /3o/ *vt* to
contradict

**contradicción** [kontraðik'θjon] *nf*
contradiction

**contradictorio, -a** [kontraðik'torjo, a]
*adj* contradictory

**contraer** [kontra'er] /2o/ *vt* to contract;
(*limitar*) to restrict; **contraerse** *vr* to
contract; (*limitarse*) to limit o.s.

**contraluz** [kontra'luθ] *nm o f* view against
the light

**contrapartida** [kontrapar'tiða] *nf*: **como
~ (de)** in return (for)

**contrapelo** [kontra'pelo]: **a ~** *adv* the
wrong way

**contrapeso** [kontra'peso] *nm*
counterweight

**contraportada** [kontrapor'taða] nf (de revista) back cover

**contraproducente** [kontraproðu'θente] adj counterproductive

**contrario, -a** [kon'trarjo, a] adj contrary; (persona) opposed; (sentido, lado) opposite ▷ nm/f enemy, adversary; (Deporte) opponent; **al ~, por el ~** on the contrary; **de lo ~** otherwise

**contrarreloj** [kontrarre'lo(x)] nf (tb: **prueba ~**) time trial

**contrarrestar** [kontrarres'tar] /1a/ vt to counteract

**contrasentido** [kontrasen'tiðo] nm contradiction

**contraseña** [kontra'seɲa] nf (frase) password

**contrastar** [kontras'tar] /1a/ vt to verify ▷ vi to contrast

**contraste** [kon'traste] nm contrast

**contratar** [kontra'tar] /1a/ vt (firmar un acuerdo para) to contract for; (empleados, obreros) to hire, engage

**contratiempo** [kontra'tjempo] nm setback

**contratista** [kontra'tista] nmf contractor

**contrato** [kon'trato] nm contract

**contraventana** [kontraβen'tana] nf shutter

**contribución** [kontriβu'θjon] nf (municipal etc) tax; (ayuda) contribution

**contribuir** [kontriβu'ir] /3g/ vt, vi to contribute; (Com) to pay (in taxes)

**contribuyente** [kontriβu'jente] nmf (Com) taxpayer; (que ayuda) contributor

**contrincante** [kontrin'kante] nm opponent

**control** [kon'trol] nm control; (inspección) inspection, check; **~ de pasaportes** passport inspection; **controlador, a** nm/f controller; **controlador aéreo** air-traffic controller; **controlar** /1a/ vt to control; to inspect, check

**contundente** [kontun'dente] adj (argumento) convincing; **instrumento ~** blunt instrument

**contusión** [kontu'sjon] nf bruise

**convalecencia** [kombale'θenθja] nf convalescence

**convalecer** [kombale'θer] /2d/ vi to convalesce, get better

**convalidar** [kombali'ðar] /1a/ vt (título) to recognize

**convencer** [komben'θer] /2b/ vt to convince; (persuadir) to persuade

**convención** [komben'θjon] nf convention

**conveniente** [kombe'njente] adj suitable; (útil) useful

**convenio** [kom'benjo] nm agreement, treaty

**convenir** [kombe'nir] /3r/ vi (estar de acuerdo) to agree; (ser conveniente) to suit, be suitable

▌ No confundir convenir con la palabra inglesa convene.

**convento** [kom'bento] nm monastery; (de monjas) convent

**convenza** etc [kom'benθa] vb V **convencer**

**converger** [komber'xer] /2c/, **convergir** [komber'xir] /3c/ vi to converge

**conversación** [kombersa'θjon] nf conversation

**conversar** [komber'sar] /1a/ vi to talk, converse

**conversión** [komber'sjon] nf conversion

**convertir** [komber'tir] /3i/ vt to convert

**convidar** [kombi'ðar] /1a/ vt to invite; **~ a algn a una cerveza** to buy sb a beer

**convincente** [kombin'θente] adj convincing

**convite** [kom'bite] nm invitation; (banquete) banquet

**convivencia** [kombi'βenθja] nf coexistence, living together

**convivir** [kombi'βir] /3a/ vi to live together

**convocar** [kombo'kar] /1g/ vt to summon, call (together)

**convocatoria** [komboka'torja] nf summons sg; (anuncio) notice of meeting

**cónyuge** ['konyuxe] nmf spouse

**coñac** ['koɲa(k)] (pl **coñacs**) nm cognac, brandy

**coño** ['koɲo] (fam!) excl (enfado) shit (!); (sorpresa) bloody hell (!)

**cool** [kul] adj (fam) cool

**cooperación** [koopera'θjon] nf cooperation

**cooperar** [koope'rar] /1a/ vi to cooperate

**coordinar** [koorði'nar] /1a/ vt to coordinate

**copa** ['kopa] nf cup; (vaso) glass; (de árbol) top; (de sombrero) crown; **copas** nfpl (Naipes) one of the suits in the Spanish card deck; **(tomar una) ~** (to have a) drink

**copia** ['kopja] nf copy; (Inform): **~ de respaldo** o **de seguridad** backup copy; **copiar** /1b/ vt to copy

**copla** ['kopla] nf verse; (canción) (popular) song

**copo** ['kopo] nm: **~s de maíz** cornflakes; **~ de nieve** snowflake

**coqueta** [ko'keta] adj flirtatious, coquettish; **coquetear** /1a/ vi to flirt

**coraje** [ko'raxe] nm courage; (ánimo) spirit; (ira) anger

**coral** [ko'ral] adj choral ▷ nf choir ▷ nm (Zool) coral

**coraza** [ko'raθa] nf (armadura) armour; (blindaje) armour-plating

**corazón** [kora'θon] nm heart
**corazonada** [koraθo'naða] nf impulse; (*presentimiento*) hunch
**corbata** [kor'βata] nf tie
**corchete** [kor'tʃete] nm catch, clasp
**corcho** ['kortʃo] nm cork; (*Pesca*) float
**cordel** [kor'ðel] nm cord, line
**cordero** [kor'ðero] nm lamb
**cordial** [kor'ðjal] adj cordial
**cordillera** [korði'ʎera] nf range (of mountains)
**Córdoba** ['korðoβa] nf Cordova
**cordón** [kor'ðon] nm (*cuerda*) cord, string; (*de zapatos*) lace; (*Mil etc*) cordon; **~ umbilical** umbilical cord
**cordura** [kor'ðura] nf: **con ~** (*obrar, hablar*) sensibly
**corneta** [kor'neta] nf bugle
**cornisa** [kor'nisa] nf cornice
**coro** ['koro] nm chorus; (*conjunto de cantores*) choir
**corona** [ko'rona] nf crown; (*de flores*) garland
**coronel** [koro'nel] nm colonel
**coronilla** [koro'niʎa] nf (*Anat*) crown (of the head)
**corporal** [korpo'ral] adj corporal, bodily
**corpulento, -a** [korpu'lento, a] adj (*persona*) heavily-built
**corral** [ko'rral] nm farmyard
**correa** [ko'rrea] nf strap; (*cinturón*) belt; (*de perro*) lead, leash; **~ del ventilador** (*Auto*) fan belt
**corrección** [korrek'θjon] nf correction; (*reprensión*) rebuke; **correccional** nm reformatory
**correcto, -a** [ko'rrekto, a] adj correct; (*persona*) well-mannered
**corredizo, -a** [korre'ðiθo, a] adj (*puerta etc*) sliding
**corredor, a** [korre'ðor, a] nm/f (*Deporte*) runner ▷ nm (*pasillo*) corridor; (*balcón corrido*) gallery; (*Com*) agent, broker
**corregir** [korre'xir] /3c, 3k/ vt (*error*) to correct; **corregirse** vr to reform
**correo** [ko'rreo] nm post, mail; (*persona*) courier; **Correos** nmpl Post Office sg; **~ aéreo** airmail; **~ basura** (*por Internet*) spam; **~ electrónico** email, electronic mail; **~ web** webmail
**correr** [ko'rrer] /2a/ vt to run; (*cortinas*) to draw; (*cerrojo*) to shoot ▷ vi to run; (*líquido*) to run, flow; **correrse** vr to slide, move; (*colores*) to run
**correspondencia** [korrespon'denθja] nf correspondence; (*Ferro*) connection
**corresponder** [korrespon'der] /2a/ vi to correspond; (*convenir*) to be suitable; (*pertenecer*) to belong; (*tocar*) to concern;

**corresponderse** vr (*por escrito*) to correspond; (*amarse*) to love one another
**correspondiente** [korrespon'djente] adj corresponding
**corresponsal** [korrespon'sal] nmf (newspaper) correspondent
**corrido, -a** [ko'rriðo, a] adj (*avergonzado*) abashed ▷ nf (*de toros*) bullfight; **un kilo ~** a good kilo
**corriente** [ko'rrjente] adj (*agua*) running; (*dinero, cuenta etc*) current; (*común*) ordinary, normal ▷ nf current ▷ nm current month; **~ eléctrica** electric current; **estar al ~ de** to be informed about
**corrija** etc [ko'rrixa] vb V **corregir**
**corro** ['korro] nm ring, circle (of people)
**corromper** [korrom'per] /2a/ vt (*madera*) to rot; (*fig*) to corrupt
**corrosivo, -a** [korro'siβo, a] adj corrosive
**corrupción** [korrup'θjon] nf rot, decay; (*fig*) corruption
**corsé** [kor'se] nm corset
**cortacésped** [korta'θespeð] nm lawn mower
**cortado, -a** [kor'taðo, a] adj (*con cuchillo*) cut; (*leche*) sour; (*desconcertado*) embarrassed; (*tímido*) shy ▷ nm coffee with a little milk
**cortafuegos** [korta'fweɣos] nm inv (*en el bosque*) firebreak, fire lane (*US*); (*Internet*) firewall
**cortalápices** nm inv (pencil) sharpener
**cortar** [kor'tar] /1a/ vt to cut; (*suministro*) to cut off; (*un pasaje*) to cut out ▷ vi to cut; **cortarse** vr (*turbarse*) to become embarrassed; (*leche*) to turn, curdle; **~se el pelo** to have one's haircut
**cortauñas** [korta'uɲas] nm inv nail clippers pl
**corté** ['korte] nm cut, cutting; (*de tela*) piece, length ▷ nf (*real*) court; **~ y confección** dressmaking; **~ de corriente** o **luz** power cut; **las C~s** the Spanish Parliament sg
**cortejo** [kor'texo] nm entourage; **~ fúnebre** funeral procession
**cortés** [kor'tes] adj courteous, polite
**cortesía** [korte'sia] nf courtesy
**corteza** [kor'teθa] nf (*de árbol*) bark; (*de pan*) crust
**cortijo** [kor'tixo] nm (*ESP*) farm, farmhouse
**cortina** [kor'tina] nf curtain
**corto, -a** ['korto, a] adj (*breve*) short; (*tímido*) bashful; **~ de luces** not very bright; **~ de vista** short-sighted; **estar ~ de fondos** to be short of funds; **cortocircuito** nm short-circuit; **cortometraje** nm (*Cine*) short
**cosa** ['kosa] nf thing; **~ de** about; **eso es ~ mía** that's my business

**coscorrón** [kosko'rron] nm bump on the head

**cosecha** [ko'setʃa] nf (Agr) harvest; (de vino) vintage; **cosechar** /1a/ vt to harvest, gather (in)

**coser** [ko'ser] /2a/ vt to sew

**cosmético, -a** [kos'metiko, a] adj, nm cosmetic

**cosquillas** [kos'kiʎas] nfpl: **hacer ~** to tickle; **tener ~** to be ticklish

**costa** ['kosta] nf (Geo) coast; **C~ Brava** Costa Brava; **C~ Cantábrica** Cantabrian Coast; **C~ del Sol** Costa del Sol; **a toda ~** at any price

**costado** [kos'taðo] nm side

**costanera** [kosta'nera] nf (LAM) promenade, sea front

**costar** [kos'tar] /1l/ vt (valer) to cost; **me cuesta hablarle** I find it hard to talk to him

**Costa Rica** [kosta'rika] nf Costa Rica; **costarricense** adj, nmf Costa Rican

**coste** ['koste] nm V **costo**

**costear** [koste'ar] /1a/ vt to pay for

**costero, -a** [kos'tero, a] adj coastal

**costilla** [kos'tiʎa] nf rib; (Culin) cutlet

**costo** ['kosto] nm cost, price; **~ de la vida** cost of living; **costoso, -a** adj costly, expensive

**costra** ['kostra] nf (corteza) crust; (Med) scab

**costumbre** [kos'tumbre] nf custom, habit; **como de ~** as usual

**costura** [kos'tura] nf sewing, needlework; (zurcido) seam

**costurera** [kostu'rera] nf dressmaker

**costurero** [kostu'rero] nm sewing box o case

**cotidiano, -a** [koti'ðjano, a] adj daily, day to day

**cotilla** [ko'tiʎa] nf gossip; **cotillear** /1a/ vi to gossip; **cotilleo** nm gossip(ing)

**cotizar** [koti'θar] /1f/ vt (Com) to quote, price; **cotizarse** vr: **~se a** to sell at, fetch; (Bolsa) to stand at, be quoted at

**coto** ['koto] nm (terreno cercado) enclosure; (de caza) reserve

**cotorra** [ko'torra] nf parrot

**coyote** [ko'jote] nm coyote, prairie wolf

**coz** [koθ] nf kick

**crack** [krak] nm (droga) crack

**cráneo** ['kraneo] nm skull, cranium

**cráter** ['krater] nm crater

**crayón** [kra'jon] nm (LAM: lápiz) (coloured) pencil; (cera) crayon

**creación** [krea'θjon] nf creation

**creador, a** [krea'ðor, a] adj creative ⊳ nm/f creator

**crear** [kre'ar] /1a/ vt to create, make

**creativo, -a** [krea'tiβo, a] adj creative

**crecer** [kre'θer] /2d/ vi to grow; (precio) to rise

**creces** ['kreθes]: **con ~** adv amply, fully

**crecido, -a** [kre'θiðo, a] adj (persona, planta) full-grown; (cantidad) large

**crecimiento** [kreθi'mjento] nm growth; (aumento) increase

**credencial** [kreðen'θjal] nf (LAM: tarjeta) card; **credenciales** nfpl credentials; **~ de socio** (LAM) membership card

**crédito** ['kreðito] nm credit

**credo** ['kreðo] nm creed

**creencia** [kre'enθja] nf belief

**creer** [kre'er] /2e/ vt, vi to think, believe; **creerse** vr to believe o.s. (to be); **~ en** to believe in; **creo que sí/no** I think/don't think so; **¡ya lo creo!** I should think so!

**creído, -a** [kre'iðo, a] adj (engreído) conceited

**crema** ['krema] nf cream; **~ batida** (LAM) whipped cream; **~ pastelera** (confectioner's) custard

**cremallera** [krema'ʎera] nf zip (fastener) (BRIT), zipper (US)

**crepe** ['krepe] nf (ESP) pancake

**cresta** ['kresta] nf (Geo, Zool) crest

**creyendo** etc [kre'jendo] vb V **creer**

**creyente** [kre'jente] nmf believer

**creyó** etc [kre'jo] vb V **creer**

**crezco** etc vb V **crecer**

**cría** ['kria] vb V **criar** ⊳ nf (de animales) rearing, breeding; (animal) young; V tb **crío**

**criadero** [kria'ðero] nm (Zool) breeding place

**criado, -a** [kri'aðo, a] nm servant ⊳ nf servant, maid

**criador** [kria'ðor] nm breeder

**crianza** [kri'anθa] nf rearing, breeding; (fig) breeding

**criar** [kri'ar] /1c/ vt (educar) to bring up; (producir) to grow, produce; (animales) to breed

**criatura** [kria'tura] nf creature; (niño) baby, (small) child

**cribar** [kri'βar] /1a/ vt to sieve

**crimen** ['krimen] nm crime

**criminal** [krimi'nal] adj, nmf criminal

**crin** [krin] nf (tb: **~es**) mane

**crío, -a** ['krio, a] nm/f (fam: chico) kid

**crisis** ['krisis] nf inv crisis; **~ nerviosa** nervous breakdown

**crismas** ['krismas] nm inv (ESP) Christmas card

**cristal** [kris'tal] nm crystal; (de ventana) glass, pane; (lente) lens; **cristalino, -a** adj crystalline; (fig) clear ⊳ nm lens of the eye

**cristianismo** [kristja'nismo] nm Christianity

**cristiano, -a** [kris'tjano, a] adj, nm/f Christian

**Cristo** ['kristo] nm Christ; (crucifijo) crucifix
**criterio** [kri'terjo] nm criterion; (juicio) judgement
**criticar** [kriti'kar] /1g/ vt to criticize
**crítico, -a** ['kritiko, a] adj critical ▷ nm critic ▷ nf criticism
**Croacia** [kro'aθja] nf Croatia
**croissant, croissan** [krwa'san] nm croissant
**cromo** ['kromo] nm chrome
**crónico, -a** ['kroniko, a] adj chronic ▷ nf chronicle, account
**cronómetro** [kro'nometro] nm stopwatch
**croqueta** [kro'keta] nf croquette, rissole
**cruce** ['kruθe] vb V **cruzar** ▷ nm (para peatones) crossing; (de carreteras) crossroads
**crucero** [kru'θero] nm (viaje) cruise
**crucificar** [kruθifi'kar] /1g/ vt to crucify
**crucifijo** [kruθi'fixo] nm crucifix
**crucigrama** [kruθi'ɣrama] nm crossword (puzzle)
**cruda** ['kruða] nf (LAM fam) hangover
**crudo, -a** ['kruðo, a] adj raw; (no maduro) unripe; (petróleo) crude; (rudo, cruel) cruel ▷ nm crude (oil)
**cruel** [krwel] adj cruel; **crueldad** nf cruelty
**crujiente** [kru'xjente] adj (galleta etc) crunchy
**crujir** [kru'xir] /3a/ vi (madera etc) to creak; (dedos) to crack; (dientes) to grind; (nieve, arena) to crunch
**cruz** [kruθ] nf cross; (de moneda) tails sg; **~ gamada** swastika; **C~ Roja** Red Cross
**cruzado, -a** [kru'θaðo, a] adj crossed ▷ nm crusader ▷ nf crusade
**cruzar** [kru'θar] /1f/ vt to cross; **cruzarse** vr (líneas etc) to cross; (personas) to pass each other
**cuaderno** [kwa'ðerno] nm notebook; (de escuela) exercise book; (Naut) logbook
**cuadra** ['kwaðra] nf (caballeriza) stable; (LAM) (city) block
**cuadrado, -a** [kwa'ðraðo, a] adj square ▷ nm (Mat) square
**cuadrar** [kwa'ðrar] /1a/ vt to square ▷ vi: **~ con** to square with, tally with; **cuadrarse** vr (soldado) to stand to attention
**cuadrilátero** [kwaðri'latero] nm (Deporte) boxing ring; (Mat) quadrilateral
**cuadrilla** [kwa'ðriʎa] nf party, group
**cuadro** ['kwaðro] nm square; (Arte) painting; (Teat) scene; (diagrama) chart; (Deporte, Med) team; **tela a ~s** checked (BRIT) o chequered (US) material
**cuajar** [kwa'xar] /1a/ vt (leche) to curdle; (sangre) to congeal; (Culin) to set; **cuajarse** vr to curdle; to congeal; (llenarse) to fill up
**cuajo** ['kwaxo] nm: **de ~** (arrancar) by the roots; (cortar) completely

**cual** [kwal] adv like, as ▷ pron: **el ~** etc which; (persona, sujeto) who; (persona, objeto) whom ▷ adj such as; **cada ~** each one; **tal ~** just as it is
**cuál** [kwal] pron interrogativo which (one)
**cualesquier** [kwales'kjer], **cualesquiera** [kwales'kjera] adj pl, pron pl de **cualquier**
**cualidad** [kwali'ðað] nf quality
**cualquier** [kwal'kjer], **cualquiera** [kwal'kjera] adj any ▷ pron anybody; **~ día/libro** any day/book; **un coche ~ servirá** any car will do; **no es un hombre ~** he isn't just anybody; **eso ~ lo sabe hacer** anybody can do that; **es un ~** he's a nobody
**cuando** ['kwando] adv when; (aún si) if, even if ▷ conj (puesto que) since ▷ prep: **yo, ~ niño ...** when I was a child o as a child I ...; **~ no sea así** even if it is not so; **~ más** at (the) most; **~ menos** at least; **~ no** if not, otherwise; **de ~ en ~** from time to time
**cuándo** ['kwando] adv when; **¿desde ~?** since when?
**cuantía** [kwan'tia] nf (importe: de pérdidas, deuda, daños) extent

⭕ **PALABRA CLAVE**

**cuanto, -a** ['kwanto, a] adj **1** (todo): **tiene todo cuanto desea** he's got everything he wants; **le daremos cuantos ejemplares necesite** we'll give him as many copies as o all the copies he needs; **cuantos hombres la ven** all the men who see her
**2**: **unos cuantos: había unos cuantos periodistas** there were (quite) a few journalists
**3** (+ más): **cuanto más vino bebas peor te sentirás** the more wine you drink the worse you'll feel
▶ pron: **tiene cuanto desea** he has everything he wants; **tome cuanto/cuantos quiera** take as much/many as you want
▶ adv: **en cuanto: en cuanto profesor** as a teacher; **en cuanto a mí** as for me; V tb **antes**
▶ conj **1**: **cuanto más gana menos gasta** the more he earns the less he spends; **cuanto más joven se es más se es confiado** the younger you are the more trusting you are
**2**: **en cuanto: en cuanto llegue/llegué** as soon as I arrive/arrived

**cuánto, -a** ['kwanto, a] adj (exclamación) what a lot of; (interrogativo: sg) how much?; (: pl) how many? ▷ pron, adv how;

(*interrogativo: sg*) how much?; (: *pl*) how many?; **¡cuánta gente!** what a lot of people!; **¿~ cuesta?** how much does it cost?; **¿a ~s estamos?** what's the date?

**cuarenta** [kwa'renta] *num* forty

**cuarentena** [kwaren'tena] *nf* quarantine

**cuaresma** [kwa'resma] *nf* Lent

**cuarta** ['kwarta] *nf* V **cuarto**

**cuartel** [kwar'tel] *nm* (*Mil*) barracks *pl*; **~ de bomberos** (*LAM*) fire station; **~ general** headquarters *pl*

**cuarteto** [kwar'teto] *nm* quartet

**cuarto, -a** ['kwarto, a] *adj* fourth ▷ *nm* (*Mat*) quarter, fourth; (*habitación*) room ▷ *nf* (*Mat*) quarter, fourth; (*palmo*) span; **~ de baño** bathroom; **~ de estar** living room; **~ de hora** quarter (of an) hour; **~ de kilo** quarter kilo; **~s de final** quarter finals

**cuatro** ['kwatro] *num* four

**Cuba** ['kuβa] *nf* Cuba

**cuba** ['kuβa] *nf* cask, barrel

**cubalibre** [kuβa'liβre] *nm* (white) rum and coke®

**cubano, -a** [ku'βano, a] *adj, nm/f* Cuban

**cubata** [ku'βata] *nm* = **cubalibre**

**cubeta** [ku'βeta] *nf* (*balde*) bucket, tub

**cúbico, -a** ['kuβiko, a] *adj* cubic

**cubierto, -a** [ku'βjerto, a] *pp de* **cubrir** ▷ *adj* covered ▷ *nm* cover; (*en la mesa*) place ▷ *nf* cover, covering; (*neumático*) tyre; (*Naut*) deck; **cubiertos** *nmpl* cutlery *sg*; **a ~** under cover

**cubilete** [kuβi'lete] *nm* (*en juegos*) cup

**cubito** [ku'βito] *nm*: **~ de hielo** ice cube

**cubo** ['kuβo] *nm* cube; (*balde*) bucket, tub; (*Tec*) drum; **~ de (la) basura** dustbin (*BRIT*), trash can (*US*)

**cubrir** [ku'βrir] /3a/ *vt* to cover; **cubrirse** *vr* (*cielo*) to become overcast

**cucaracha** [kuka'ratʃa] *nf* cockroach

**cuchara** [ku'tʃara] *nf* spoon; (*Tec*) scoop; **cucharada** *nf* spoonful; **cucharadita** *nf* teaspoonful

**cucharilla** [kutʃa'riʎa] *nf* teaspoon

**cucharón** [kutʃa'ron] *nm* ladle

**cuchilla** [ku'tʃiʎa] *nf* (large) knife; (*de arma blanca*) blade; **~ de afeitar** razor blade

**cuchillo** [ku'tʃiʎo] *nm* knife

**cuchitril** [kutʃi'tril] *nm* hovel

**cuclillas** [ku'kliʎas] *nfpl*: **en ~** squatting

**cuco, -a** ['kuko, a] *adj* pretty; (*astuto*) sharp ▷ *nm* cuckoo

**cucurucho** [kuku'rutʃo] *nm* cornet

**cueca** ['kweka] *nf* Chilean national dance

**cuello** ['kweʎo] *nm* (*Anat*) neck; (*de vestido, camisa*) collar

**cuenca** ['kwenka] *nf* (*Anat*) eye socket; (*Geo*) bowl, deep valley

**cuenco** ['kwenko] *nm* (earthenware) bowl

**cuenta** ['kwenta] *vb* V **contar** ▷ *nf* (*cálculo*) count, counting; (*en café, restaurante*) bill (*BRIT*), check (*US*); (*Com*) account; (*de collar*) bead; **a fin de ~s** in the end; **caer en la ~** to catch on; **darse ~ de** to realize; **tener en ~** to bear in mind; **echar ~s** to take stock; **~ atrás** countdown; **~ corriente/de ahorros/a plazo (fijo)** current/savings/deposit account; **~ de correo** (*Internet*) email account; **cuentakilómetros** *nm inv* ≈ milometer, clock; (*velocímetro*) speedometer

**cuento** ['kwento] *vb* V **contar** ▷ *nm* story; **~ chino** tall story; **~ de hadas** fairy tale *o* story

**cuerda** ['kwerða] *nf* rope; (*hilo*) string; (*de reloj*) spring; **~ floja** tightrope; **~s vocales** vocal cords; **dar ~ a un reloj** to wind up a clock

**cuerdo, -a** ['kwerðo, a] *adj* sane; (*prudente*) wise, sensible

**cuerno** ['kwerno] *nm* horn

**cuero** ['kwero] *nm* leather; **en ~s** stark naked; **~ cabelludo** scalp

**cuerpo** ['kwerpo] *nm* body

**cuervo** ['kwerβo] *nm* crow

**cuesta** ['kwesta] *vb* V **costar** ▷ *nf* slope; (*en camino etc*) hill; **~ arriba/abajo** uphill/downhill; **a ~s** on one's back

**cueste** *etc vb* V **costar**

**cuestión** [kwes'tjon] *nf* matter, question, issue

**cuete** ['kwete] *adj* (*LAM fam*) drunk ▷ *nm* (*cohete*) rocket; (*fam: embriaguez*) drunkenness; (*Culin*) steak

**cueva** ['kweβa] *nf* cave

**cuidado** [kwi'ðaðo] *nm* care, carefulness; (*preocupación*) care, worry ▷ *excl* careful!, look out!; **eso me tiene sin ~** I'm not worried about that

**cuidadoso, -a** [kwiða'ðoso, a] *adj* careful; (*preocupado*) anxious

**cuidar** [kwi'ðar] /1a/ *vt* (*Med*) to care for; (*ocuparse de*) to take care of, look after ▷ *vi*: **~ de** to take care of, look after; **cuidarse** *vr* to look after o.s.; **~se de hacer algo** to take care to do sth

**culata** [ku'lata] *nf* (*de fusil*) butt

**culebra** [ku'leβra] *nf* snake

**culebrón** [kule'βron] *nm* (*fam*) soap (opera)

**culo** ['kulo] *nm* bottom, backside; (*de vaso*) bottom

**culpa** ['kulpa] *nf* fault; (*Jur*) guilt; **por ~ de** because of; **echar la ~ a algn** to blame sb for sth; **tener la ~ (de)** to be to blame (for); **culpable** *adj* guilty ▷ *nmf* culprit; **culpar** /1a/ *vt* to blame; (*acusar*) to accuse

**cultivar** [kulti'βar] /1a/ *vt* to cultivate

**cultivo** [kul'tiβo] *nm* (*acto*) cultivation; (*plantas*) crop; **~ transgénico** GM crop

**culto, -a** ['kulto, a] *adj* (*que tiene cultura*) cultured, educated ▷ *nm* (*homenaje*) worship; (*religión*) cult

**cultura** [kul'tura] *nf* culture

**culturismo** [kultu'rismo] *nm* body-building

**cumbia** ['kumbja] *nf* popular Colombian dance

**cumbre** ['kumbre] *nf* summit, top

**cumpleaños** [kumple'aɲos] *nm inv* birthday

**cumplido, -a** [kum'pliðo, a] *adj* (*abundante*) plentiful; (*cortés*) courteous ▷ *nm* compliment; **visita de ~** courtesy call

**cumplidor, a** [kumpli'ðor, a] *adj* reliable

**cumplimiento** [kumpli'mjento] *nm* (*de un deber*) fulfilment; (*acabamiento*) completion

**cumplir** [kum'plir] /3a/ *vt* (*orden*) to carry out, obey; (*promesa*) to carry out, fulfil; (*condena*) to serve; **cumplirse** *vr* (*plazo*) to expire; **hoy cumple dieciocho años** he is eighteen today; **~ con** (*deber*) to carry out, fulfil

**cuna** ['kuna] *nf* cradle, cot

**cundir** [kun'dir] /3a/ *vi* (*noticia, rumor, pánico*) to spread; (*rendir*) to go a long way

**cuneta** [ku'neta] *nf* ditch

**cuña** ['kuɲa] *nf* wedge

**cuñado, -a** [ku'ɲaðo, a] *nm/f* brother-/sister-in-law

**cuota** ['kwota] *nf* (*parte proporcional*) share; (*cotización*) fee, dues *pl*

**cupe** *etc* ['kupe] *vb* V **caber**

**cupiera** *etc* [ku'pjera] *vb* V **caber**

**cupo** *etc* ['kupo] *vb* V **caber** ▷ *nm* quota

**cupón** [ku'pon] *nm* coupon

**cúpula** ['kupula] *nf* dome

**cura** ['kura] *nf* (*curación*) cure; (*método curativo*) treatment ▷ *nm* priest

**curación** [kura'θjon] *nf* cure; (*acción*) curing

**curandero, -a** [kuran'dero, a] *nm/f* healer; (*pey*) quack

**curar** [ku'rar] /1a/ *vt* (*Med: herida*) to treat, dress; (: *enfermo*) to cure; (*Culin*) to cure, salt; (*cuero*) to tan ▷ **curarse** *vr* to get well, recover

**curiosear** [kurjose'ar] /1a/ *vt* to glance at, look over ▷ *vi* to look round, wander round; (*explorar*) to poke about

**curiosidad** [kurjosi'ðað] *nf* curiosity

**curioso, -a** [ku'rjoso, a] *adj* curious ▷ *nm/f* bystander, onlooker

**curita** [ku'rita] *nf* (*LAM*) sticking plaster

**currante** [ku'rrante] *nmf* (*fam*) worker

**currar** [ku'rrar] /1a/ *vi* to work

**currículo** [ku'rrikulo], **currículum** [ku'rrikulum] *nm* curriculum vitae

**cursi** ['kursi] *adj* (*fam*) affected

**cursillo** [kur'siʎo] *nm* short course

**cursiva** [kur'siβa] *nf* italics *pl*

**curso** ['kurso] *nm* course; **en ~** (*año*) current; (*proceso*) going on, under way

**cursor** [kur'sor] *nm* (*Inform*) cursor

**curul** [ku'rul] *nm* (*LAM: escaño*) seat

**custodia** [kus'toðja] *nf* (*cuidado*) safekeeping; (*Jur*) custody

**cutis** ['kutis] *nm inv* skin, complexion

**cutre** ['kutre] *adj* (*fam: lugar*) grotty

**cuyo, -a** ['kujo, a] *pron* (*de quien*) whose; (*de que*) whose, of which; **en ~ caso** in which case

**C.V.** *abr* (= *caballos de vapor*) H.P.

# d

**D.** abr (= Don) Esq

**dado, -a** ['daðo, a] pp de **dar** ▷ nm die;
**dados** nmpl dice; **~ que** given that

**daltónico, -a** [dal'toniko, a] adj colour-
blind

**dama** ['dama] nf (gen) lady; (Ajedrez)
queen; **damas** nfpl draughts; **~ de honor**
bridesmaid

**damasco** [da'masko] nm (LAM) apricot

**danés, -esa** [da'nes, esa] adj Danish ▷ nm/f
Dane

**dañar** [da'ɲar] /1a/ vt (objeto) to damage;
(persona) to hurt; **dañarse** vr (objeto) to get
damaged

**dañino, -a** [da'ɲino, a] adj harmful

**daño** ['daɲo] nm (a un objeto) damage; (a una
persona) harm, injury; **~s y perjuicios** (Jur)
damages; **hacer ~ a** to damage; (persona)
to hurt, injure; **hacerse ~** to hurt o.s.

**dañoso, -a** [da'ɲoso, a] adj harmful

## ○ PALABRA CLAVE

**dar** [dar] /1q/ vt **1** (gen) to give; (obra de
teatro) to put on; (film) to show; (fiesta) to
have; **dar algo a algn** to give sb sth o sth to
sb; **dar de beber a algn** to give sb a drink;
**dar de comer** to feed

**2** (producir: intereses) to yield; (: fruta) to
produce

**3** (locuciones + n): **da gusto escucharle** it's a
pleasure to listen to him; V tb **paseo**

**4** (+ n: perífrasis de verbo): **me da asco** it
sickens me

**5** (considerar): **dar algo por descontado/
entendido** to take sth for granted/as read;
**dar algo por concluido** to consider sth
finished

**6** (hora): **el reloj dio las seis** the clock struck
six (o'clock)

**7**: **me da lo mismo** it's all the same to me;
V tb **igual; más**

▶ vi **1**: **dar a** (habitación) to overlook, look on
to; (accionar: botón etc) to press, hit

**2**: **dar con: dimos con él dos horas más
tarde** we came across him two hours later;
**al final di con la solución** I eventually came
up with the answer

**3**: **dar en** (blanco, suelo) to hit; **el sol me
da en la cara** the sun is shining (right) in
my face

**4**: **dar de sí** (zapatos etc) to stretch, give

▶ **darse** vr **1**: **darse un baño** to have a bath;
**darse un golpe** to hit o.s.

**2**: **darse por vencido** to give up

**3** (ocurrir): **se han dado muchos casos**
there have been a lot of cases

**4**: **darse a: se ha dado a la bebida** he's
taken to drinking

**5**: **se me dan bien/mal las ciencias** I'm
good/bad at science

**6**: **dárselas de: se las da de experto** he
fancies himself o poses as an expert

**dardo** ['darðo] nm dart

**dátil** ['datil] nm date

**dato** ['dato] nm fact, piece of information;
**~s personales** personal details

**dcha.** abr (= derecha) r

**d. de C.** abr (= después de Cristo) A.D. = **Anno
Domini**

## ○ PALABRA CLAVE

**de** [de] prep (**de + el = del**) **1** (posesión,
pertenencia) of; **la casa de Isabel/mis
padres** Isabel's/my parents' house; **es de
ellos/ella** it's theirs/hers

**2** (origen, distancia, con números) from; **soy
de Gijón** I'm from Gijón; **de 8 a 20** from
8 to 20; **salir del cine** to go out of o leave
the cinema; **de 2 en 2** 2 by 2, at a time

**3** (valor descriptivo): **una copa de vino** a
glass of wine; **la mesa de la cocina** the
kitchen table; **un billete de 50 euros** a
50-euro note; **un niño de tres años** a
three-year-old (child); **una máquina de
coser** a sewing machine; **ir vestido de gris**
to be dressed in grey; **la niña del vestido
azul** the girl in the blue dress; **trabaja de
profesora** she works as a teacher; **de lado**
sideways; **de atrás/delante** rear/front

**4** (hora, tiempo): **a las 8 de la mañana** at
8 o'clock in the morning; **de día/noche** by
day/night; **de hoy en ocho días** a week
from now; **de niño era gordo** as a child he
was fat

**5** (comparaciones): **más/menos de cien
personas** more/less than a hundred

people; **el más caro de la tienda** the most expensive in the shop; **menos/más de lo pensado** less/more than expected
**6** (causa): **del calor** from the heat
**7** (tema) about; **clases de inglés** English classes; **¿sabes algo de él?** do you know anything about him?; **un libro de física** a physics book
**8** (adj + de + infin): **fácil de entender** easy to understand
**9** (oraciones pasivas): **fue respetado de todos** he was loved by all
**10** (condicional + infin) if; **de ser posible** if possible; **de no terminarlo hoy** if I etc don't finish it today

**dé** [de] vb V **dar**
**debajo** [de'βaxo] adv underneath; **~ de** below, under; **por ~ de** beneath
**debate** [de'βate] nm debate; **debatir** /3a/ vt to debate
**deber** [de'βer] /2a/ nm duty ▷ vt to owe ▷ vi: **debe (de)** it must, it should; **deberse** vr: **~se a** to be owing o due to; **deberes** nmpl (Escol) homework sg; **debo hacerlo** I must do it; **debe de ir** he should go
**debido, -a** [de'βiðo, a] adj proper, due; **~ a** due to, because of
**débil** ['deβil] adj weak; (luz) dim; **debilidad** nf weakness; dimness
**debilitar** [deβili'tar] /1a/ vt to weaken; **debilitarse** vr to grow weak
**débito** ['deβito] nm debit; **~ bancario** (LAM) direct debit (BRIT) o billing (US)
**debutar** [deβu'tar] /1a/ vi to make one's debut
**década** ['dekaða] nf decade
**decadencia** [deka'ðenθja] nf (estado) decadence; (proceso) decline, decay
**decaído, -a** [deka'iðo, a] adj: **estar ~** (persona) to be down
**decano, -a** [de'kano, a] nm/f (Univ etc) dean
**decena** [de'θena] nf: **una ~** ten (or so)
**decente** [de'θente] adj decent
**decepción** [deθep'θjon] nf disappointment

No confundir decepción con la palabra inglesa deception.

**decepcionar** [deθepθjo'nar] /1a/ vt to disappoint
**decidir** [deθi'ðir] /3a/ vt to decide ▷ vi to decide; **decidirse** vr: **~se a** to make up one's mind to
**décimo, -a** ['deθimo, a] num tenth ▷ nf tenth
**decir** [de'θir] /3o/ vt to say; (contar) to tell; (hablar) to speak ▷ nm saying; **decirse** vr: **se dice** it is said; **~ para** o **entre sí** to say to o.s.; **querer ~** to mean; **es ~** that is to

say; **¡dígame!** (en tienda etc) can I help you?; (Telec) hello?
**decisión** [deθi'sjon] nf decision; (firmeza) decisiveness
**decisivo, -a** [deθi'siβo, a] adj decisive
**declaración** [deklara'θjon] nf (manifestación) statement; (de amor) declaration; **~ de ingresos** o **de la renta** income tax return
**declarar** [dekla'rar] /1a/ vt to declare ▷ vi to declare; (Jur) to testify; **declararse** vr to propose
**decoración** [dekora'θjon] nf decoration
**decorado** [deko'raðo] nm (Cine, Teat) scenery, set
**decorar** [deko'rar] /1a/ vt to decorate; **decorativo, -a** adj ornamental, decorative
**decreto** [de'kreto] nm decree
**dedal** [de'ðal] nm thimble
**dedicación** [deðika'θjon] nf dedication
**dedicar** [deði'kar] /1g/ vt (libro) to dedicate; (tiempo, dinero) to devote; (palabras: decir, consagrar) to dedicate, devote; **dedicatoria** nf (de libro) dedication
**dedo** ['deðo] nm finger; **~ (del pie)** toe; **~ pulgar** thumb; **~ índice** index finger; **~ mayor** o **cordial** middle finger; **~ anular** ring finger; **~ meñique** little finger
**deducción** [deðuk'θjon] nf deduction
**deducir** [deðu'θir] /3n/ vt (concluir) to deduce, infer; (Com) to deduct
**defecto** [de'fekto] nm defect, flaw; **defectuoso, -a** adj defective, faulty
**defender** [defen'der] /2g/ vt to defend; **defenderse** vr: **me defiendo en inglés** (fig) I can get by in English
**defensa** [de'fensa] nf defence ▷ nm (Deporte) defender, back; **defensivo, -a** adj defensive ▷ nf: **a la defensiva** on the defensive
**defensor, -a** [defen'sor, a] adj defending ▷ nm/f (abogado defensor) defending counsel; (protector) protector
**deficiencia** [defi'θjenθja] nf deficiency
**deficiente** [defi'θjente] adj (defectuoso) defective; **~ en** lacking o deficient in ▷ nmf: **ser un ~ mental** to have learning difficulties
**déficit** ['defiθit] (pl **déficits**) nm deficit
**definición** [defini'θjon] nf definition
**definir** [defi'nir] /3a/ vt (determinar) to determine, establish; (decidir) to define; (aclarar) to clarify; **definitivo, -a** adj definitive; **en definitiva** definitively; (en resumen) in short
**deformación** [deforma'θjon] nf (alteración) deformation; (Radio etc) distortion
**deformar** [defor'mar] /1a/ vt (gen) to deform; **deformarse** vr to become

deformed; **deforme** adj (informe) deformed; (feo) ugly; (mal hecho) misshapen

**defraudar** [defrau'ðar] /1a/ vt (decepcionar) to disappoint; (estafar) to defraud

**defunción** [defun'θjon] nf death, demise

**degenerar** [dexene'rar] /1a/ vi to degenerate

**degollar** /1m/ vt to slaughter

**degradar** [deɣra'ðar] /1a/ vt to debase, degrade; **degradarse** vr to demean o.s.

**degustación** [deɣusta'θjon] nf sampling, tasting

**dejar** [de'xar] /1a/ vt to leave; (permitir) to allow, let; (abandonar) to abandon, forsake; (beneficios) to produce, yield ▷ vi: ~ **de** (parar) to stop; (no hacer) to fail to; **dejarse**: ~ **a un lado** to leave o set aside; ~ **entrar/salir** to let in/out; ~ **pasar** to let through

**del** [del] = **de + el**; V **de**

**delantal** [delan'tal] nm apron

**delante** [de'lante] adv in front; (enfrente) opposite; (adelante) ahead ▷ prep: ~ **de** in front of, before

**delantero, -a** [delan'tero, a] adj front; (patas de animal) fore ▷ nm (Deporte) forward, striker

**delatar** [dela'tar] /1a/ vt to inform on o against, betray; **delator, -a** nm/f informer

**delegación** [deleɣa'θjon] nf (acción: delegados) delegation; (Com: oficina) district office, branch; ~ **de policía** (LAM) police station

**delegado, -a** [dele'ɣaðo, a] nm/f delegate; (Com) agent

**delegar** [dele'ɣar] /1h/ vt to delegate

**deletrear** [deletre'ar] /1a/ vt to spell (out)

**delfín** [del'fin] nm dolphin

**delgado, -a** [del'ɣaðo, a] adj thin; (persona) slim, thin; (tela etc) light, delicate

**deliberar** [deliβe'rar] /1a/ vt to debate, discuss

**delicadeza** [delika'ðeθa] nf delicacy; (refinamiento, sutileza) refinement

**delicado, -a** [deli'kaðo, a] adj delicate; (sensible) sensitive; (sensible) touchy

**delicia** [de'liθja] nf delight

**delicioso, -a** [deli'θjoso, a] adj (gracioso) delightful; (exquisito) delicious

**delimitar** [delimi'tar] /1a/ vt (función, responsabilidades) to define

**delincuencia** [delin'kwenθja] nf: ~ **juvenil** juvenile delinquency; **delincuente** nmf delinquent; (criminal) criminal

**delineante** [deline'ante] nmf draughtsman/draughtswoman; (US) draftsman/draftswoman

**delirante** [deli'rante] adj delirious

**delirar** [deli'rar] /1a/ vi to be delirious, rave

**delirio** [de'lirjo] nm (Med) delirium; (palabras insensatas) ravings pl

**delito** [de'lito] nm (gen) crime; (infracción) offence

**delta** ['delta] nm delta

**demacrado, -a** [dema'kraðo, a] adj: **estar ~** to look pale and drawn, be wasted away

**demanda** [de'manda] nf (pedido, Com) demand; (petición) request; (Jur) action, lawsuit; **demandar** /1a/ vt (gen) to demand; (Jur) to sue, file a lawsuit against

**demás** [de'mas] adj: **los ~ niños** the other children, the remaining children ▷ pron: **los/las ~** the others, the rest (of them); **lo ~** the rest (of it)

**demasía** [dema'sia] nf (exceso) excess, surplus; **comer en ~** to eat to excess

**demasiado, -a** [dema'sjaðo, a] adj: ~ **vino** too much wine ▷ adv (antes de adj, adv) too; ~**s libros** too many books; **¡es ~!** it's too much!; ~ **despacio** too slowly; ~**s** too many

**demencia** [de'menθja] nf (locura) madness

**democracia** [demo'kraθja] nf democracy

**demócrata** [de'mokrata] nmf democrat; **democrático, -a** adj democratic

**demoler** [demo'ler] /2h/ vt to demolish; **demolición** nf demolition

**demonio** [de'monjo] nm devil, demon; **¡~!** hell!, damn!; **¿cómo ~s?** how the hell?

**demora** [de'mora] nf delay

**demos** ['demos] vb V **dar**

**demostración** [demostra'θjon] nf demonstration; (de cariño, fuerza) show; (de cólera, gimnasia) display

**demostrar** [demos'trar] /1l/ vt (probar) to prove; (mostrar) to show; (manifestar) to demonstrate

**den** [den] vb V **dar**

**denegar** [dene'ɣar] /1h, 1j/ vt (rechazar) to refuse; (Jur) to reject

**denominación** [denomina'θjon] nf (acto) naming

○ **DENOMINACIÓN**
○
○ The denominación de origen, often
○ abbreviated to D.O., is a prestigious
○ product classification given to designated
○ regions by the awarding body, the Consejo
○ Regulador de la Denominación de Origen,
○ when their produce meets the required
○ quality and production standards. It is
○ often associated with manchego cheeses
○ and many of the wines from the Rioja and
○ Ribera de Duero regions.

**densidad** [densi'ðað] nf density; (fig) thickness

**denso, -a** ['denso, a] adj (apretado) solid; (espeso, pastoso) thick, dense; (fig) heavy

**dentadura** [denta'ðura] nf (set of) teeth
pl; ~ **postiza** false teeth pl

**dentera** [den'tera] nf (grima): **dar ~ a** algn
to set sb's teeth on edge

**dentífrico, -a** [den'tifriko, a] adj dental
▷ nm toothpaste

**dentista** [den'tista] nmf dentist

**dentro** ['dentro] adv inside ▷ prep: ~ **de** in,
inside, within; **por ~** (on the) inside; **mirar
por ~** to look inside; ~ **de tres meses** within
three months

**denuncia** [de'nunθja] nf (delación)
denunciation; (acusación) accusation; (de
accidente) report; **denunciar** /1b/ vt to
report; (delatar) to inform on o against

**departamento** [departa'mento] nm
(sección) department, section; (LAM: piso)
flat (BRIT), apartment (US)

**depender** [depen'der] /2a/ vi: ~ **de** to
depend on; **depende** it (all) depends

**dependienta** [depen'djenta] nf
saleswoman, shop assistant

**dependiente** [depen'djente] adj
dependent ▷ nm salesman, shop assistant

**depilar** [depi'lar] /1a/ vt (con cera) to wax;
(cejas) to pluck

**deportar** [depor'tar] /1a/ vt to deport

**deporte** [de'porte] nm sport; **hacer ~** to
play sports; **deportista** adj sports cpd
▷ nmf sportsman/woman; **deportivo, -a**
adj (club, periódico) sports cpd ▷ nm sports
car

**depositar** [deposi'tar] /1a/ vt (dinero) to
deposit; (mercaderías) to put away, store;
**depositarse** vr to settle

**depósito** [de'posito] nm (gen) deposit; (de
mercaderías) warehouse, store; (de agua,
gasolina etc) tank; ~ **de cadáveres** mortuary

**depredador, a** [depreða'ðor, a] adj
predatory ▷ nm predator

**depresión** [depre'sjon] nf depression;
~ **nerviosa** nervous breakdown

**deprimido, -a** [depri'miðo, a] adj
depressed

**deprimir** [depri'mir] /3a/ vt to depress;
**deprimirse** vr (persona) to become
depressed

**deprisa** [de'prisa] adv quickly, hurriedly

**depurar** [depu'rar] /1a/ vt to purify;
(purgar) to purge

**derecha** [de'retʃa] nf V **derecho**

**derecho, -a** [de'retʃo, a] adj right,
right-hand ▷ nm (privilegio) right;
(lado) right(-hand) side; (leyes) law ▷ nf
right(-hand) side; (Pol) right ▷ adv straight,
directly; **derechos** nmpl (impuestos) taxes;
(de autor) royalties; **la(s) derecha(s)** (Pol)
the Right; **tener ~ a** to have a right to; **a la
derecha** on the right; (dirección) to the right

**deriva** [de'riβa] nf: **ir** o **estar a la ~** to drift,
be adrift

**derivado** [deri'βaðo] nm (Industria,
Química) by-product

**derivar** [deri'βar] /1a/ vt to derive; (desviar)
to direct ▷ vi to derive, be derived; (Naut) to
drift; **derivarse** vr to derive, be derived

**derramamiento** [derrama'mjento] nm
(dispersión) spilling; ~ **de sangre** bloodshed

**derramar** [derra'mar] /1a/ vt to spill;
(verter) to pour out; (esparcir) to scatter;
**derramarse** vr to pour out

**derrame** [de'rrame] nm (de líquido) spilling;
(de sangre) shedding; (de tubo etc) overflow;
(pérdida) leakage; ~ **cerebral** brain
haemorrhage

**derredor** [derre'ðor] adv: **al** o **en ~ de**
around, about

**derretir** [derre'tir] /3k/ vt (gen) to melt;
(nieve) to thaw; **derretirse** vr to melt

**derribar** [derri'βar] /1a/ vt to knock
down; (construcción) to demolish; (persona,
gobierno, político) to bring down

**derrocar** [derro'kar] /1g/ vt (gobierno) to
bring down, overthrow

**derrochar** [derro'tʃar] /1a/ vt to squander;
**derroche** nm (despilfarro) waste,
squandering

**derrota** [de'rrota] nf (Naut) course; (Mil)
defeat, rout; **derrotar** /1a/ vt (gen) to
defeat; **derrotero** nm (rumbo) course

**derrumbar** [derrum'bar] /1a/ vt (edificio)
to knock down; **derrumbarse** vr to collapse

**des** [des] vb V **dar**

**desabrochar** [desaβro'tʃar] /1a/ vt (botones,
broches) to undo, unfasten; **desabrocharse**
vr (ropa etc) to come undone

**desacato** [desa'kato] nm (falta de respeto)
disrespect; (Jur) contempt

**desacertado, -a** [desaθer'taðo, a] adj
(equivocado) mistaken; (inoportuno) unwise

**desacierto** [desa'θjerto] nm mistake, error

**desaconsejar** [desakonse'xar] /1a/ vt:
~ **algo a** algn to advise sb against sth

**desacreditar** [desakreði'tar] /1a/ vt
(desprestigiar) to discredit, bring into
disrepute; (denigrar) to run down

**desacuerdo** [desa'kwerðo] nm
disagreement, discord

**desafiar** [desa'fjar] /1c/ vt (retar) to
challenge; (enfrentarse a) to defy

**desafilado, -a** [desafi'laðo, a] adj blunt

**desafinado, -a** [desafi'naðo, a] adj:
**estar ~** to be out of tune

**desafinar** [desafi'nar] /1a/ vi to be out of
tune; **desafinarse** vr to go out of tune

**desafío** [desa'fio] nm (reto)
challenge; (combate) duel; (resistencia)
defiance

**desafortunado, -a** [desafortuˈnaðo, a]
adj (desgraciado) unfortunate, unlucky
**desagradable** [desaɣraˈðaβle] adj
(fastidioso, enojoso) unpleasant; (irritante)
disagreeable
**desagradar** [desaɣraˈðar] /1a/ vi
(disgustar) to displease; (molestar) to bother
**desagradecido, -a** [desaɣraðeˈθiðo, a] adj
ungrateful
**desagrado** [desaˈɣraðo] nm (disgusto)
displeasure; (contrariedad) dissatisfaction
**desagüe** [deˈsaɣwe] nm (de un líquido)
drainage; (cañería) drainpipe; (salida) outlet,
drain
**desahogar** [desaoˈɣar] /1h/ vt (aliviar) to
ease, relieve; (ira) to vent; **desahogarse** vr
(distenderse) to relax; (desfogarse) to let off
steam (fam)
**desahogo** [desaˈoɣo] nm (alivio) relief;
(comodidad) comfort, ease
**desahuciar** [desauˈθjar] /1b/ vt (enfermo)
to give up hope for; (inquilino) to evict
**desairar** [desaiˈrar] /1a/ vt (menospreciar)
to slight, snub
**desalentador, -a** [desalentaˈðor, a] adj
discouraging
**desaliño** [desaˈliɲo] nm slovenliness
**desalmado, -a** [desalˈmaðo, a] adj (cruel)
cruel, heartless
**desalojar** [desaloˈxar] /1a/ vt (expulsar,
echar) to eject; (abandonar) to move out of
▷ vi to move out
**desamor** [desaˈmor] nm (frialdad)
indifference; (odio) dislike
**desamparado, -a** [desampaˈraðo, a] adj
(persona) helpless; (lugar: expuesto) exposed;
(: desierto) deserted
**desangrar** [desanˈɡrar] /1a/ vt to bleed;
(fig: persona) to bleed dry; **desangrarse** vr to
lose a lot of blood
**desanimado, -a** [desaniˈmaðo, a] adj
(persona) downhearted; (espectáculo, fiesta)
dull
**desanimar** [desaniˈmar] /1a/ vt
(desalentar) to discourage; (deprimir) to
depress; **desanimarse** vr to lose heart
**desapacible** [desapaˈθiβle] adj unpleasant
**desaparecer** [desapareˈθer] /2d/ vi to
disappear; (el sol, la luz) to vanish;
**desaparecido, -a** adj missing; **desaparición**
nf disappearance; (de especie etc) extinction
**desapercibido, -a** [desaperθiˈβiðo, a] adj
(desprevenido) unprepared; **pasar ~** to go
unnoticed
**desaprensivo, -a** [desaprenˈsiβo, a] adj
unscrupulous
**desaprobar** [desaproˈβar] /1l/ vt (reprobar)
to disapprove of; (condenar) to condemn; (no
consentir) to reject

**desaprovechado, -a** [desaproβeˈtʃaðo, a]
adj (oportunidad, tiempo) wasted; (estudiante)
slack
**desaprovechar** [desaproβeˈtʃar] /1a/ vt
to waste
**desarmador** [desarmaˈðor] nm (LAM)
screwdriver
**desarmar** [desarˈmar] /1a/ vt (Mil, fig)
to disarm; (Tec) to take apart, dismantle;
**desarme** nm disarmament
**desarraigar** [desarraiˈɣar] /1h/ vt to
uproot; **desarraigo** nm uprooting
**desarreglar** [desarreˈɣlar] /1a/ vt (desordenar)
to disarrange; (trastocar) to upset, disturb
**desarrollar** [desarroˈʎar] /1a/ vt (gen)
to develop; **desarrollarse** vr to develop;
(ocurrir) to take place; (film) to develop;
**desarrollo** nm development
**desarticular** [desartikuˈlar] /1a/ vt
(huesos) to dislocate; (objeto) to take apart;
(grupo terrorista etc) to break up
**desasosegar** [desasoseˈɣar] /1h, 1j/ vt
(inquietar) to disturb, make uneasy
**desasosiego** etc [desasoˈsjeɣo] vb
V **desasosegar** ▷ nm (intranquilidad)
uneasiness, restlessness; (ansiedad) anxiety
**desastre** [deˈsastre] nm disaster;
**desastroso, -a** adj disastrous
**desatar** [desaˈtar] /1a/ vt (nudo) to untie;
(paquete) to undo; (separar) to detach;
**desatarse** vr (zapatos) to come untied;
(tormenta) to break
**desatascar** [desatasˈkar] /1g/ vt (cañería)
to unblock, clear
**desatender** [desatenˈder] /2g/ vt (no
prestar atención a) to disregard; (abandonar)
to neglect
**desatino** [desaˈtino] nm (idiotez)
foolishness, folly; (error) blunder
**desatornillar** [desatorniˈʎar] /1a/ vt to
unscrew
**desatrancar** [desatranˈkar] /1g/ vt
(puerta) to unbolt; (cañería) to unblock
**desautorizado, -a** [desautoriˈθaðo, a] adj
unauthorized
**desautorizar** [desautoriˈθar] /1f/ vt
(oficial) to deprive of authority; (informe)
to deny
**desayunar** [desajuˈnar] /1a/ vi to have
breakfast ▷ vt to have for breakfast;
**desayuno** nm breakfast
**desazón** [desaˈθon] nf anxiety
**desbarajuste** [desβaraˈxuste] nm
confusion, disorder
**desbaratar** [desβaraˈtar] /1a/ vt (deshacer,
destruir) to ruin
**desbloquear** [desβlokeˈar] /1a/ vt
(negociaciones, tráfico) to get going again;
(Com: cuenta) to unfreeze

**desbordar** [desβor'ðar] /1a/ vt (*sobrepasar*) to go beyond; (*exceder*) to exceed
▷ **desbordarse** vr (*líquido, río*) to overflow; (*entusiasmo*) to erupt

**descabellado, -a** [deskaβe'ʎaðo, a] adj (*disparatado*) wild, crazy

**descafeinado, -a** [deskafei'naðo, a] adj decaffeinated ▷ nm decaffeinated coffee

**descalabro** [deska'laβro] nm blow; (*desgracia*) misfortune

**descalificar** [deskalifi'kar] /1g/ vt to disqualify; (*desacreditar*) to discredit

**descalzar** [deskal'θar] /1f/ vt (*zapato*) to take off; **descalzo, -a** adj barefoot(ed)

**descambiar** [deskam'bjar] /1b/ vt to exchange

**descaminado, -a** [deskami'naðo, a] adj (*equivocado*) on the wrong road; (*fig*) misguided

**descampado** [deskam'paðo] nm open space

**descansado, -a** [deskan'saðo, a] adj (*gen*) rested; (*que tranquiliza*) restful

**descansar** [deskan'sar] /1a/ vt (*gen*) to rest ▷ vi to rest, have a rest; (*echarse*) to lie down

**descansillo** [deskan'siʎo] nm (*de escalera*) landing

**descanso** [des'kanso] nm (*reposo*) rest; (*alivio*) relief; (*pausa*) break; (*Deporte*) interval, half time

**descapotable** [deskapo'taβle] nm (tb: **coche ~**) convertible

**descarado, -a** [deska'raðo, a] adj shameless; (*insolente*) cheeky

**descarga** [des'karɣa] nf (*Arq, Elec, Mil*) discharge; (*Naut*) unloading; (*Inform*) download; **descargable** adj downloadable; **descargar** /1h/ vt to unload; (*golpe*) to let fly; **descargarse** vr to unburden o.s.; **descargarse algo de Internet** to download sth from the internet

**descaro** [des'karo] nm nerve

**descarriar** [deska'rrjar] /1c/ vt (*descaminar*) to misdirect; (*fig*) to lead astray; **descarriarse** vr (*perderse*) to lose one's way; (*separarse*) to stray; (*pervertirse*) to err, go astray

**descarrilamiento** [deskarrila'mjento] nm (*de tren*) derailment

**descarrilar** [deskarri'lar] /1a/ vi to be derailed

**descartar** [deskar'tar] /1a/ vt (*rechazar*) to reject; (*eliminar*) to rule out; **descartarse** vr (*Naipes*) to discard; **~se de** to shirk

**descendencia** [desθen'denθja] nf (*origen*) origin, descent; (*hijos*) offspring

**descender** [desθen'der] /2g/ vt (*bajar: escalera*) to go down ▷ vi to descend; (*temperatura, nivel*) to fall, drop; **~ de** to be descended from

**descendiente** [desθen'djente] nmf descendant

**descenso** [des'θenso] nm descent; (*de temperatura*) drop

**descifrar** [desθi'frar] /1a/ vt to decipher; (*mensaje*) to decode

**descolgar** [deskol'ɣar] /1h, 1l/ vt (*bajar*) to take down; (*teléfono*) to pick up; **descolgarse** vr to let o.s. down

**descolorido, -a** [deskolo'riðo, a] adj faded; (*pálido*) pale

**descompasado, -a** [deskompa'saðo, a] adj (*sin proporción*) out of all proportion; (*excesivo*) excessive

**descomponer** [deskompo'ner] /2q/ vt (*desordenar*) to disarrange, disturb; (*Tec*) to put out of order; **descomponerse** vr (*corromperse*) to rot, decompose; (*Tec*) to break down

**descomposición** [deskomposi'θjon] nf (*de un objeto*) breakdown; (*de fruta etc*) decomposition; **~ de vientre** (*Med*) stomach upset, diarrhoea, diarrhea (us)

**descompostura** [deskompos'tura] nf breakdown, fault; (*LAM: diarrea*) diarrhoea, diarrhea (us)

**descompuesto, -a** [deskom'pwesto, a] adj (*corrompido*) decomposed; (*roto*) broken (down)

**desconcertado, -a** [deskonθer'taðo, a] adj disconcerted, bewildered

**desconcertar** [deskonθer'tar] /1j/ vt (*confundir*) to baffle; (*incomodar*) to upset, put out; **desconcertarse** vr (*turbarse*) to be upset

**desconchado, -a** [deskon'tʃaðo, a] adj (*pintura*) peeling

**desconcierto** etc [deskon'θjerto] vb V **desconcertar** ▷ nm (*gen*) disorder; (*desorientación*) uncertainty; (*inquietud*) uneasiness

**desconectar** [deskonek'tar] /1a/ vt to disconnect

**desconfianza** [deskon'fjanθa] nf distrust

**desconfiar** [deskon'fjar] /1c/ vi to be distrustful; **~ de** to mistrust, suspect

**descongelar** [deskonxe'lar] /1a/ vt to defrost; (*Com, Pol*) to unfreeze

**descongestionar** [desconxestjo'nar] /1a/ vt (*cabeza, tráfico*) to clear

**desconocer** [deskono'θer] /2d/ vt (*ignorar*) not to know, be ignorant of

**desconocido, -a** [deskono'θiðo, a] adj unknown ▷ nm/f stranger

**desconocimiento** [deskonoθi'mjento] nm (*falta de conocimientos*) ignorance

**desconsiderado, -a** [deskonsiðe'raðo, a] adj inconsiderate; (*insensible*) thoughtless

**desconsuelo** [deskon'swelo] nm (tristeza) distress; (desesperación) despair

**descontado, -a** [deskon'taðo, a] adj: **dar por ~ (que)** to take it for granted (that)

**descontar** [deskon'tar] /1l/ vt (deducir) to take away, deduct; (rebajar) to discount

**descontento, -a** [deskon'tento, a] adj dissatisfied ▷ nm dissatisfaction, discontent

**descorchar** [deskor'tʃar] /1a/ vt to uncork

**descorrer** [desko'rrer] /2a/ vt (cortina, cerrojo) to draw back

**descortés** [deskor'tes] adj (mal educado) discourteous; (grosero) rude

**descoser** [desko'ser] /2a/ vt to unstitch; **descoserse** vr to come apart (at the seams)

**descosido, -a** [desko'siðo, a] adj (costura) unstitched

**descreído, -a** [deskre'iðo, a] adj (incrédulo) incredulous; (falto de fe) unbelieving

**descremado, -a** [deskre'maðo, a] adj skimmed

**describir** [deskri'βir] /3a/ vt to describe; **descripción** nf description

**descrito** [des'krito] pp de **describir**

**descuartizar** [deskwarti'θar] /1f/ vt (animal) to carve up, cut up

**descubierto, -a** [desku'βjerto, a] pp de **descubrir** ▷ adj uncovered, bare; (persona) bare-headed ▷ nm (bancario) overdraft; **al ~** in the open

**descubrimiento** [deskuβri'mjento] nm (hallazgo) discovery; (revelación) revelation

**descubrir** [desku'βrir] /3a/ vt to discover, find; (inaugurar) to unveil; (vislumbrar) to detect; (revelar) to reveal, show; (quitar la tapa de) to uncover; **descubrirse** vr to reveal o.s.; (quitarse sombrero) to take off one's hat; (confesar) to confess

**descuento** [des'kwento] vb V **descontar** ▷ nm discount

**descuidado, -a** [deskwi'ðaðo, a] adj (sin cuidado) careless; (desordenado) untidy; (olvidadizo) forgetful; (dejado) neglected; (desprevenido) unprepared

**descuidar** [deskwi'ðar] /1a/ vt (dejar) to neglect; (olvidar) to overlook ▷ **descuidarse** vr (distraerse) to be careless; (estar desaliñado) to let o.s. go; (desprevenirse) to drop one's guard; **¡descuida!** don't worry!; **descuido** nm (dejadez) carelessness; (olvido) negligence

⭕ **PALABRA CLAVE**

**desde** ['desðe] prep **1** (lugar) from; **desde Burgos hasta mi casa hay 30 km** it's 30 km from Burgos to my house
**2** (posición): **hablaba desde el balcón** she was speaking from the balcony
**3** (tiempo, + adv, n): **desde ahora** from now on; **desde entonces/la boda** since then/the wedding; **desde niño** since I etc was a child; **desde tres años atrás** since three years ago
**4** (tiempo, + vb) since; for; **nos conocemos desde 1988/desde hace 20 años** we've known each other since 1988/for 20 years; **no le veo desde 2005/desde hace 5 años** I haven't seen him since 2005/for 5 years
**5** (gama): **desde los más lujosos hasta los más económicos** from the most luxurious to the most reasonably priced
**6**: **desde luego (que no)** of course (not)
▶ conj: **desde que: desde que recuerdo** for as long as I can remember; **desde que llegó no ha salido** he hasn't been out since he arrived

**desdén** [des'ðen] nm scorn

**desdeñar** [desðe'ɲar] /1a/ vt (despreciar) to scorn

**desdicha** [des'ðitʃa] nf (desgracia) misfortune; (infelicidad) unhappiness; **desdichado, -a** adj (sin suerte) unlucky; (infeliz) unhappy

**desear** [dese'ar] /1a/ vt to want, desire, wish for

**desechar** [dese'tʃar] /1a/ vt (basura) to throw out o away; (ideas) to reject, discard

**desecho** [de'setʃo] nm (desprecio) contempt; **desechos** nmpl rubbish sg, waste sg

**desembalar** [desemba'lar] /1a/ vt to unpack

**desembarazar** [desembara'θar] /1f/ vt (desocupar) to clear; (desenredar) to free; **desembarazarse** vr: **~se de** to free o.s. of, get rid of

**desembarcar** [desembar'kar] /1g/ vt (mercancías etc) to unload ▷ vi to disembark

**desembocadura** [desemboka'ðura] nf (de río) mouth; (de calle) opening

**desembocar** [desembo'kar] /1g/ vi: **~ en** to flow into; (fig) to result in

**desembolso** [desem'bolso] nm payment

**desembrollar** [desembro'ʎar] /1a/ vt (madeja) to unravel; (asunto, malentendido) to sort out

**desemejanza** [deseme'xanθa] nf dissimilarity

**desempaquetar** [desempake'tar] /1a/ vt (regalo) to unwrap; (mercancía) to unpack

**desempate** [desem'pate] nm (Fútbol) replay, play-off; (Tenis) tie-break(er)

**desempeñar** [desempe'ɲar] /1a/ vt (cargo) to hold; (deber, función) to perform; (lo empeñado) to redeem; **~ un papel** (fig) to play (a role)

**desempleado, -a** [desemple'aðo, a] *nm/f* unemployed person; **desempleo** *nm* unemployment

**desencadenar** [desenkaðe'nar] /1a/ *vt* to unchain; (*ira*) to unleash; **desencadenarse** *vr* to break loose; (*tormenta*) to burst; (*guerra*) to break out

**desencajar** [desenka'xar] /1a/ *vt* (*mandíbula*) to dislocate; (*mecanismo, pieza*) to disconnect, disengage

**desencanto** [desen'kanto] *nm* disillusionment

**desenchufar** [desentʃu'far] /1a/ *vt* to unplug

**desenfadado, -a** [desenfa'ðaðo, a] *adj* (*desenvuelto*) uninhibited; (*descarado*) forward; **desenfado** *nm* (*libertad*) freedom; (*comportamiento*) free and easy manner; (*descaro*) forwardness

**desenfocado, -a** [desenfo'kaðo, a] *adj* (*Foto*) out of focus

**desenfreno** [desen'freno] *nm* wildness; (*falta de control*) lack of self-control

**desenganchar** [desengan'tʃar] /1a/ *vt* (*gen*) to unhook; (*Ferro*) to uncouple

**desengañar** [desenga'nar] /1a/ *vt* to disillusion; **desengañarse** *vr* to become disillusioned; **desengaño** *nm* disillusionment; (*decepción*) disappointment

**desenlace** *etc* [desen'laθe] *nm* outcome

**desenmascarar** [desenmaska'rar] /1a/ *vt* to unmask

**desenredar** [desenre'ðar] /1a/ *vt* (*pelo*) to untangle; (*problema*) to sort out

**desenroscar** [desenros'kar] /1g/ *vt* to unscrew

**desentenderse** [desenten'derse] /2g/ *vr*: ~ **de** to pretend not to know about; (*apartarse*) to have nothing to do with

**desenterrar** [desente'rrar] /1j/ *vt* to exhume; (*tesoro, fig*) to unearth, dig up

**desentonar** [desento'nar] /1a/ *vi* (*Mus*) to sing (*o play*) out of tune; (*color*) to clash

**desentrañar** [desentra'nar] /1a/ *vt* (*misterio*) to unravel

**desenvoltura** [desembol'tura] *nf* ease

**desenvolver** [desembol'ßer] /2h/ *vt* (*paquete*) to unwrap; (*fig*) to develop; **desenvolverse** *vr* (*desarrollarse*) to unfold, develop; (*arreglárselas*) to cope

**deseo** [de'seo] *nm* desire, wish; **deseoso, -a** *adj*: **estar deseoso de hacer** to be anxious to do

**desequilibrado, -a** [desekili'ßraðo, a] *adj* unbalanced

**desertar** [deser'tar] /1a/ *vi* to desert

**desértico, -a** [de'sertiko, a] *adj* desert *cpd*

**desesperación** [desespera'θjon] *nf* desperation, despair; (*irritación*) fury

**desesperar** [desespe'rar] /1a/ *vt* to drive to despair; (*exasperar*) to drive to distraction ▷ *vi*: ~ **de** to despair of; **desesperarse** *vr* to despair, lose hope

**desestabilizar** [desestaßili'θar] /1f/ *vt* to destabilize

**desestimar** [desesti'mar] /1a/ *vt* (*menospreciar*) to have a low opinion of; (*rechazar*) to reject

**desfachatez** [desfatʃa'teθ] *nf* (*insolencia*) impudence; (*descaro*) rudeness

**desfalco** [des'falko] *nm* embezzlement

**desfallecer** [desfaʎe'θer] /2d/ *vi* (*perder las fuerzas*) to become weak; (*desvanecerse*) to faint

**desfasado, -a** [desfa'saðo, a] *adj* (*anticuado*) old-fashioned; **desfase** *nm* (*diferencia*) gap

**desfavorable** [desfaßo'raßle] *adj* unfavourable

**desfigurar** [desfiɣu'rar] /1a/ *vt* (*cara*) to disfigure; (*cuerpo*) to deform

**desfiladero** [desfila'ðero] *nm* gorge

**desfilar** [desfi'lar] /1a/ *vi* to parade; **desfile** *nm* procession; **desfile de modelos** fashion show

**desgana** [des'ɣana] *nf* (*falta de apetito*) loss of appetite; (*renuencia*) unwillingness; **desganado, -a** *adj*: **estar desganado** (*sin apetito*) to have no appetite; (*sin entusiasmo*) to have lost interest

**desgarrar** [desɣa'rrar] /1a/ *vt* to tear (up); (*fig*) to shatter; **desgarro** *nm* (*en tela*) tear; (*aflicción*) grief

**desgastar** [desɣas'tar] /1a/ *vt* (*deteriorar*) to wear away *o* down; (*estropear*) to spoil; **desgastarse** *vr* to get worn out; **desgaste** *nm* wear (and tear)

**desglosar** [desɣlo'sar] /1a/ *vt* to detach; (*factura*) to break down

**desgracia** [des'ɣraθja] *nf* misfortune; (*accidente*) accident; (*vergüenza*) disgrace; (*contratiempo*) setback; **por ~** unfortunately; **desgraciado, -a** *adj* (*sin suerte*) unlucky, unfortunate; (*infeliz*) miserable; (*miserable*) wretched; (*infeliz*) miserable

**desgravar** [desɣra'ßar] /1a/ *vt* (*producto*) to reduce the tax *o* duty on

**desguace** [des'ɣwaθe] *nm* (*lugar*) scrapyard

**deshabitado, -a** [desaßi'taðo, a] *adj* uninhabited

**deshacer** [desa'θer] /2r/ *vt* (*casa*) to break up; (*Tec*) to take apart; (*enemigo*) to defeat; (*diluir*) to melt; (*contrato*) to break; (*intriga*) to solve; **deshacerse** *vr* (*disolverse*) to melt; (*despedazarse*) to come apart *o* undone; **~se de** to get rid of; **~se en lágrimas** to burst into tears

**deshecho, -a** [de'setʃo, a] *adj* undone;
(*roto*) smashed; (*persona*) weak; **estoy ~** I'm
shattered

**desheredar** [desere'ðar] /1a/ *vt* to
disinherit

**deshidratar** [desiðra'tar] /1a/ *vt* to
dehydrate

**deshielo** [des'jelo] *nm* thaw

**deshonesto, -a** [deso'nesto, a] *adj*
indecent

**deshonra** [de'sonra] *nf* (*deshonor*)
dishonour; (*vergüenza*) shame

**deshora** [de'sora]: **a ~** *adv* at the wrong
time

**deshuesadero** [deswesa'ðero] *nm* (LAM)
junkyard

**deshuesar** [deswe'sar] /1a/ *vt* (*carne*) to
bone; (*fruta*) to stone

**desierto, -a** [de'sjerto, a] *adj* (*casa, calle,
negocio*) deserted ▷ *nm* desert

**designar** [desiɣ'nar] /1a/ *vt* (*nombrar*) to
designate; (*indicar*) to fix

**desigual** [desi'ɣwal] *adj* (*lucha*) unequal;
(*terreno*) uneven

**desilusión** [desilu'sjon] *nf* disillusionment;
(*decepción*) disappointment; **desilusionar**
/1a/ *vt* to disillusion; (*decepcionar*) to
disappoint; **desilusionarse** *vr* to become
disillusioned

**desinfectar** [desinfek'tar] /1a/ *vt* to
disinfect

**desinflar** [desin'flar] /1a/ *vt* to deflate

**desintegración** [desinteɣra'θjon] *nf*
disintegration

**desinterés** [desinte'res] *nm* (*desgana*) lack
of interest; (*altruismo*) unselfishness

**desintoxicar** [desintoksi'kar] /1g/ *vt*
to detoxify; **desintoxicación** *n* detox;
**desintoxicarse** *vr* (*drogadicto*) to undergo
detoxification

**desistir** [desis'tir] /3a/ *vi* (*renunciar*) to
stop, desist

**desleal** [desle'al] *adj* (*infiel*) disloyal;
(*Com: competencia*) unfair; **deslealtad** *nf*
disloyalty

**desligar** [desli'ɣar] /1h/ *vt* (*desatar*)
to untie, undo; (*separar*) to separate;
**desligarse** *vr* (*de un compromiso*) to
extricate o.s.

**desliz** [des'liθ] *nm* (*fig*) lapse; **deslizar** /1f/
*vt* to slip, slide

**deslumbrar** [deslum'brar] /1a/ *vt* to
dazzle

**desmadrarse** [desma'ðrarse] /1a/ *vr* (*fam:
descontrolarse*) to run wild; (: *divertirse*) to
let one's hair down; **desmadre** *nm* (*fam:
desorganización*) chaos; (: *jaleo*) commotion

**desmán** [des'man] *nm* (*exceso*) outrage;
(*abuso de poder*) abuse

**desmantelar** [desmante'lar] /1a/ *vt*
(*deshacer*) to dismantle; (*casa*) to strip

**desmaquillador** [desmakiʎa'ðor] *nm*
make-up remover

**desmayar** [desma'jar] /1a/ *vi* to lose
heart; **desmayarse** *vr* (*Med*) to faint;
**desmayo** *nm* (*Med: acto*) faint; (: *estado*)
unconsciousness

**desmemoriado, -a** [desmemo'rjaðo, a]
*adj* forgetful

**desmentir** [desmen'tir] /3i/ *vt* (*contradecir*)
to contradict; (*refutar*) to deny

**desmenuzar** [desmenu'θar] /1f/ *vt*
(*deshacer*) to crumble; (*carne*) to chop;
(*examinar*) to examine closely

**desmesurado, -a** [desmesu'raðo, a] *adj*
disproportionate

**desmontable** [desmon'taβle] *adj* (*que se
quita*) detachable; (*que se puede plegar etc*)
collapsible, folding

**desmontar** [desmon'tar] /1a/ *vt* (*deshacer*)
to dismantle; (*tierra*) to level ▷ *vi* to
dismount

**desmoralizar** [desmorali'θar] /1f/ *vt* to
demoralize

**desmoronar** [desmoro'nar] /1a/ *vt* to
wear away, erode; **desmoronarse** *vr*
(*edificio, dique*) to collapse; (*economía*) to
decline

**desnatado, -a** [desna'taðo, a] *adj*
skimmed

**desnivel** [desni'βel] *nm* (*de terreno*)
unevenness

**desnudar** [desnu'ðar] /1a/ *vt* (*desvestir*) to
undress; (*despojar*) to strip; **desnudarse** *vr*
(*desvestirse*) to get undressed; **desnudo, -a**
*adj* naked ▷ *nm* nude; **desnudo de** devoid
o bereft of

**desnutrición** [desnutri'θjon] *nf*
malnutrition; **desnutrido, -a** *adj*
undernourished

**desobedecer** [desoβeðe'θer] /2d/ *vt, vi* to
disobey; **desobediencia** *nf* disobedience

**desocupado, -a** [desoku'paðo, a] *adj*
at leisure; (*desempleado*) unemployed;
(*deshabitado*) empty, vacant

**desodorante** [desoðo'rante] *nm*
deodorant

**desolación** [desola'θjon] *nf* (*de lugar*)
desolation; (*fig*) grief

**desolar** [deso'lar] /1a/ *vt* to ruin, lay waste

**desorbitado, -a** [desorβi'taðo, a] *adj*
(*excesivo: ambición*) boundless; (: *deseos*)
excessive; (: *precio*) exorbitant

**desorden** [de'sorðen] *nm* confusion;
(*político*) disorder

**desorganización** [desorɣaniθa'θjon] *nf*
(*de persona*) disorganization; (*en empresa,
oficina*) disorder, chaos

**desorientar** [desorjen'tar] /1a/ vt (extraviar) to mislead; (confundir, desconcertar) to confuse; **desorientarse** vr (perderse) to lose one's way

**despabilado, -a** [despaβi'laðo, a] adj (despierto) wide-awake; (fig) alert, sharp

**despachar** [despa'tʃar] /1a/ vt (negocio) to do, complete; (enviar) to send, dispatch; (vender) to sell, deal in; (billete) to issue; (mandar ir) to send away

**despacho** [des'patʃo] nm (oficina) office; (de paquetes) dispatch; (venta) sale (of goods); (comunicación) message; **~ de billetes** o (LAM) **boletos** booking office

**despacio** [des'paθjo] adv slowly

**desparpajo** [despar'paxo] nm self-confidence; (pey) nerve

**desparramar** [desparra'mar] /1a/ vt (esparcir) to scatter; (líquido) to spill

**despecho** [des'petʃo] nm spite

**despectivo, -a** [despek'tiβo, a] adj (despreciativo) derogatory; (Ling) pejorative

**despedida** [despe'ðiða] nf (adiós) farewell; (de obrero) sacking

**despedir** [despe'ðir] /3k/ vt (visita) to see off, show out; (empleado) to dismiss; (inquilino) to evict; (objeto) to hurl; (olor etc) to give out o off; **despedirse** vr: **~se de** to say goodbye to

**despegar** [despe'ɣar] /1h/ vt to unstick ▷ vi (avión) to take off; **despegarse** vr to come loose, come unstuck; **despego** nm detachment

**despegue** etc [des'peɣe] vb V **despegar** ▷ nm takeoff

**despeinado, -a** [despei'naðo, a] adj dishevelled, unkempt

**despejado, -a** [despe'xaðo, a] adj (lugar) clear, free; (cielo) clear; (persona) wide-awake, bright

**despejar** [despe'xar] /1a/ vt (gen) to clear; (misterio) to clarify, clear up ▷ vi (el tiempo) to clear; **despejarse** vr (tiempo, cielo) to clear (up); (misterio) to become clearer; (cabeza) to clear

**despensa** [des'pensa] nf larder

**despeñar** [despe'ɲar] /1a/ vt (arrojar) to fling down; **despeñarse** vr to fling o.s. down; (coche) to tumble over

**desperdicio** [desper'ðiθjo] nm (despilfarro) squandering; **desperdicios** nmpl (basura) rubbish sg, garbage sg (us); (residuos) waste sg

**desperezarse** [despere'θarse] /1f/ vr to stretch

**desperfecto** [desper'fekto] nm (deterioro) slight damage; (defecto) flaw, imperfection

**despertador** [desperta'ðor] nm alarm clock

**despertar** [desper'tar] /1j/ vt (persona) to wake up; (recuerdos) to revive; (sentimiento) to arouse ▷ vi to awaken, wake up; **despertarse** vr to awaken, wake up

**despido** etc [des'piðo] vb V **despedir** ▷ nm dismissal, sacking

**despierto, -a** [des'pjerto, a] pp de **despertar** ▷ adj awake; (fig) sharp, alert

**despilfarro** [despil'farro] nm (derroche) squandering; (lujo desmedido) extravagance

**despistar** [despis'tar] /1a/ vt to throw off the track o scent; (fig) to mislead, confuse; **despistarse** vr to take the wrong road; (fig) to become confused

**despiste** [des'piste] nm absent-mindedness; **un ~** a mistake o a slip

**desplazamiento** [desplaθa'mjento] nm displacement

**desplazar** [despla'θar] /1f/ vt to move; (Física, Naut, Tec) to displace; (fig) to oust; (Inform) to scroll; **desplazarse** vr (persona, vehículo) to travel

**desplegar** [desple'ɣar] /1h, 1j/ vt (tela, papel) to unfold, open out; (bandera) to unfurl

**despliegue** etc [des'pljeɣe] vb V **desplegar** ▷ nm display

**desplomarse** [desplo'marse] /1a/ vr (edificio, gobierno, persona) to collapse

**desplumar** [desplu'mar] /1a/ vt (ave) to pluck; (fam: estafar) to fleece

**despoblado, -a** [despo'βlaðo, a] adj (sin habitantes) uninhabited

**despojar** [despo'xar] /1a/ vt (a alguien: de sus bienes) to divest of, deprive of; (casa) to strip, leave bare; (de su cargo) to strip of

**despojo** [des'poxo] nm (acto) plundering; (objetos) plunder, loot; **despojos** nmpl (de ave, res) offal sg

**desposado, -a** [despo'saðo, a] adj, nm/f newly-wed

**despreciar** [despre'θjar] /1b/ vt (desdeñar) to despise, scorn; (afrentar) to slight; **desprecio** nm scorn, contempt; slight

**desprender** [despren'der] /2a/ vt (desatar) to unfasten; (olor) to give off; **desprenderse** vr (botón: caerse) to fall off; (broche) to come unfastened; (olor, perfume) to be given off; **~se de algo que ...** to draw from sth that ...

**desprendimiento** [desprendi'mjento] nm (gen) loosening; (generosidad) disinterestedness; (de tierra, rocas) landslide; **~ de retina** detachment of the retina

**despreocupado, -a** [despreoku'paðo, a] adj (sin preocupación) unworried; nonchalant; (negligente) careless

**despreocuparse** [despreoku'parse] /1a/ vr to be carefree, not to worry; **~ de** to have no interest in

**desprestigiar** [despresti'xjar] /1b/ vt (criticar) to run down; (desacreditar) to discredit

**desprevenido, -a** [despreβe'niðo, a] adj (no preparado) unprepared, unready

**desproporcionado, -a** [desproporθjo'naðo, a] adj disproportionate, out of proportion

**desprovisto, -a** [despro'βisto, a] adj: ~ de devoid of

**después** [des'pwes] adv afterwards, later; (próximo paso) next; **poco ~** soon after; **un año ~** a year later; **~ se debatió el tema** next the matter was discussed; **~ de comer** after lunch; **~ de corregido el texto** after the text had been corrected; **~ de todo** after all

**desquiciado, -a** [deski'θjaðo, a] adj deranged

**destacar** [desta'kar] /1g/ vt to emphasize, point up; (Mil) to detach, detail ▷ vi (resaltarse) to stand out; (persona) to be outstanding o exceptional; **destacarse** vr to stand out; (persona) to be outstanding o exceptional

**destajo** [des'taxo] nm: **trabajar a ~** to do piecework

**destapar** [desta'par] /1a/ vt (botella) to open; (cacerola) to take the lid off; (descubrir) to uncover; **destaparse** vr (revelarse) to reveal one's true character

**destartalado, -a** [destarta'laðo, a] adj (desordenado) untidy; (ruinoso) tumbledown

**destello** [des'teʎo] nm (de estrella) twinkle; (de faro) signal light

**destemplado, -a** [destem'plaðo, a] adj (Mus) out of tune; (voz) harsh; (Med) out of sorts; (Meteorología) unpleasant, nasty

**desteñir** [deste'ɲir] vt, vi to fade; **desteñirse** vr to fade; **esta tela no destiñe** this fabric will not run

**desternillarse** [desterni'ʎarse] /1a/ vr: **~ de risa** to split one's sides laughing

**desterrar** [deste'rrar] /1j/ vt (exilar) to exile; (fig) to banish, dismiss

**destiempo** [des'tjempo]: **a ~** adv at the wrong time

**destierro** etc [des'tjerro] vb V **desterrar** ▷ nm exile

**destilar** [desti'lar] /1a/ vt to distil; **destilería** nf distillery

**destinar** [desti'nar] /1a/ vt (funcionario) to appoint, assign; (fondos) to set aside

**destinatario, -a** [destina'tarjo, a] nm/f addressee

**destino** [des'tino] nm (suerte) destiny; (de viajero) destination; **con ~ a Londres** (avión, barco) (bound) for London; (carta) to London

**destituir** [destitu'ir] /3g/ vt to dismiss

**destornillador** [destorniʎa'ðor] nm screwdriver

**destornillar** [destorni'ʎar] /1a/ vt (tornillo) to unscrew; **destornillarse** vr to unscrew

**destreza** [des'treθa] nf (habilidad) skill; (maña) dexterity

**destrozar** [destro'θar] /1f/ vt (romper) to smash, break (up); (estropear) to ruin; (nervios) to shatter

**destrozo** [des'troθo] nm (acción) destruction; (desastre) smashing; **destrozos** nmpl (pedazos) pieces; (daños) havoc sg

**destrucción** [destruk'θjon] nf destruction

**destruir** [destru'ir] /3g/ vt to destroy

**desuso** [de'suso] nm disuse; **caer en ~** to fall into disuse, become obsolete

**desvalijar** [desβali'xar] /1a/ vt (persona) to rob; (casa, tienda) to burgle; (coche) to break into

**desván** [des'βan] nm attic

**desvanecer** [desβane'θer] /2d/ vt (disipar) to dispel; (borrar) to blur; **desvanecerse** vr (humo etc) to vanish, disappear; (duda) to be dispelled; (color) to fade; (recuerdo, sonido) to fade away; (Med) to pass out

**desvariar** [desβa'rjar] /1c/ vi (enfermo) to be delirious

**desvelar** [desβe'lar] /1a/ vt to keep awake; **desvelarse** vr (no poder dormir) to stay awake; (vigilar) to be vigilant o watchful

**desventaja** [desβen'taxa] nf disadvantage

**desvergonzado, -a** [desβerɣon'θaðo, a] adj shameless

**desvestir** [desβes'tir] /3k/ vt to undress; **desvestirse** vr to undress

**desviación** [desβja'θjon] nf deviation; (Auto) diversion, detour

**desviar** [des'βjar] /1c/ vt to turn aside; (río) to alter the course of; (navío) to divert, re-route; (conversación) to sidetrack; **desviarse** vr (apartarse del camino) to turn aside; (: barco) to go off course

**desvío** [des'βio] vb V **desviar** ▷ nm (desviación) detour, diversion; (fig) indifference

**desvivirse** [desβi'βirse] /3a/ vr: **~ por** to long for, crave for; **~ por los amigos** to do anything for one's friends

**detallar** [deta'ʎar] /1a/ vt to detail

**detalle** [de'taʎe] nm detail; (fig) gesture, token; **al ~** in detail; (Com) retail cpd

**detallista** [deta'ʎista] nmf retailer

**detective** [detek'tiβe] nmf detective; **~ privado** private detective

**detención** [deten'θjon] nf (arresto) arrest; (prisión) detention

**detener** [dete'ner] /2k/ vt (gen) to stop; (Jur) to arrest; (objeto) to keep; **detenerse** vr to stop; **~se en** (*demorarse*) to delay over, linger over

**detenidamente** [deteniða'mente] *adv* (*minuciosamente*) carefully; (*extensamente*) at great length

**detenido, -a** [dete'niðo, a] *adj* (*arrestado*) under arrest ▷ *nm/f* person under arrest, prisoner

**detenimiento** [deteni'mjento] *nm:* **con ~** thoroughly; (*observar, considerar*) carefully

**detergente** [deter'xente] *nm* detergent

**deteriorar** [deterjo'rar] /1a/ *vt* to spoil, damage; **deteriorarse** *vr* to deteriorate; **deterioro** *nm* deterioration

**determinación** [determina'θjon] *nf* (*empeño*) determination; (*decisión*) decision; **determinado, -a** *adj* (*preciso*) certain

**determinar** [determi'nar] /1a/ *vt* (*plazo*) to fix; (*precio*) to settle; **determinarse** *vr* to decide

**detestar** [detes'tar] /1a/ *vt* to detest

**detractor, a** [detrak'tor, a] *nm/f* detractor

**detrás** [de'tras] *adv* (*tb:* **por ~**) behind; (*atrás*) at the back ▷ *prep:* **~ de** behind

**detrimento** [detri'mento] *nm:* **en ~ de** to the detriment of

**deuda** [de'uða] *nf* debt; **~ exterior/pública** foreign/national debt

**devaluación** [deβalwa'θjon] *nf* devaluation

**devastar** [deβas'tar] /1a/ *vt* (*destruir*) to devastate

**deveras** [de'βeras] *adv* (LAM): **un amigo ~** a true *o* real friend

**devoción** [deβo'θjon] *nf* devotion

**devolución** [deβolu'θjon] *nf* (*reenvío*) return, sending back; (*reembolso*) repayment; (*Jur*) devolution

**devolver** [deβol'βer] /2h/ *vt* to return; (*lo extraviado, prestado*) to give back; (*carta al correo*) to send back; (*Com*) to repay, refund; (*fam: vomitar*) to throw up ▷ *vi* (*fam*) to be sick

**devorar** [deβo'rar] /1a/ *vt* to devour

**devoto, -a** [de'βoto, a] *adj* devout ▷ *nm/f* admirer

**devuelto** [de'βwelto], **devuelva** *etc* [de'βwelβa] *vb V* **devolver**

**di** [di] *vb V* **dar; decir**

**día** ['dia] *nm* day; **~ libre** day off; **D~ de Reyes** Epiphany (6 January); **D~ de la Independencia** Independence Day; **¿qué ~ es?** what's the date?; **estar/poner al ~** to be/keep up to date; **el ~ de hoy/de mañana** today/tomorrow; **al ~ siguiente** on the following day; **vivir al ~** to live from hand to mouth; **de ~** by day; **en pleno ~** in full daylight

**diabetes** [dja'betes] *nf* diabetes *sg*

**diablo** ['djaβlo] *nm* devil; **diablura** *nf* prank

**diadema** [dja'ðema] *nf* tiara

**diafragma** [dja'fraɣma] *nm* diaphragm

**diagonal** [djaɣo'nal] *adj* diagonal

**diagrama** [dja'ɣrama] *nm* diagram

**dial** [di'al] *nm* dial

**dialecto** [dja'lekto] *nm* dialect

**dialogar** [djalo'ɣar] /1h/ *vi:* **~ con** (*Pol*) to hold talks with

**diálogo** ['djaloɣo] *nm* dialogue

**diamante** [dja'mante] *nm* diamond

**diana** ['djana] *nf* (*Mil*) reveille; (*de blanco*) centre, bull's-eye

**diapositiva** [djaposi'tiβa] *nf* (*Foto*) slide, transparency

**diario, -a** ['djarjo, a] *adj* daily ▷ *nm* newspaper; **a ~** daily; **de** *o* **para ~** everyday

**diarrea** [dja'rrea] *nf* diarrhoea

**dibujar** [diβu'xar] /1a/ *vt* to draw, sketch; **dibujo** *nm* drawing; **dibujos animados** cartoons

**diccionario** [dikθjo'narjo] *nm* dictionary

**dice** *etc vb V* **decir**

**dicho, -a** ['ditʃo, a] *pp de* **decir** ▷ *adj* (*susodicho*) aforementioned ▷ *nm* saying

**dichoso, -a** [di'tʃoso, a] *adj* happy

**diciembre** [di'θjembre] *nm* December

**dictado** [dik'taðo] *nm* dictation

**dictador** [dikta'ðor] *nm* dictator; **dictadura** *nf* dictatorship

**dictar** [dik'tar] /1a/ *vt* (*carta*) to dictate; (*Jur: sentencia*) to pass; (*decreto*) to issue;(LAM: *clase*) to give

**didáctico, -a** [di'ðaktiko, a] *adj* educational

**diecinueve** [djeθinu'eβe] *num* nineteen

**dieciocho** [djeθi'otʃo] *num* eighteen

**dieciséis** [djeθi'seis] *num* sixteen

**diecisiete** [djeθi'sjete] *num* seventeen

**diente** ['djente] *nm* (*Anat, Tec*) tooth; (*Zool*) fang; (: *de elefante*) tusk; (*de ajo*) clove

**diera** *etc* ['djera] *vb V* **dar**

**diesel** ['disel] *adj:* **motor ~** diesel engine

**diestro, -a** ['djestro, a] *adj* (*derecho*) right; (*hábil*) skilful

**dieta** ['djeta] *nf* diet; **estar a ~** to be on a diet

**diez** [djeθ] *num* ten

**diferencia** [dife'renθja] *nf* difference; **a ~ de** unlike; **diferenciar** /1b/ *vt* to differentiate between ▷ *vi* to differ; **diferenciarse** *vr* to differ, be different; (*distinguirse*) to distinguish o.s.

**diferente** [dife'rente] *adj* different

**diferido** [dife'riðo] *nm:* **en ~** (*TV etc*) recorded

**difícil** [di'fiθil] *adj* difficult

**dificultad** [difikul'taθ] *nf* difficulty; (*problema*) trouble

**dificultar** [difikul'tar] /1a/ vt (complicar) to complicate, make difficult; (estorbar) to obstruct

**difundir** [difun'dir] /3a/ vt (calor, luz) to diffuse; (Radio) to broadcast; **difundirse** vr to spread (out); ~ **una noticia** to spread a piece of news

**difunto, -a** [di'funto, a] adj dead, deceased ▷ nm/f deceased (person)

**difusión** [difu'sjon] nf (de programa) broadcasting

**diga** etc ['diɣa] vb V **decir**

**digerir** [dixe'rir] /3i/ vt to digest; (fig) to absorb; **digestión** nf digestion; **digestivo, -a** adj digestive

**digital** [dixi'tal] adj digital

**dignarse** [diɣ'narse] /1a/ vr to deign to

**dignidad** [diɣni'ðað] nf dignity

**digno, -a** ['diɣno, a] adj worthy

**digo** etc vb V **decir**

**dije** etc vb V **decir**

**dilatar** [dila'tar] /1a/ vt to dilate; (prolongar) to prolong

**dilema** [di'lema] nm dilemma

**diluir** [dilu'ir] /3g/ vt to dilute

**diluvio** [di'luβjo] nm deluge, flood

**dimensión** [dimen'sjon] nf dimension

**diminuto, -a** [dimi'nuto, a] adj tiny, diminutive

**dimitir** [dimi'tir] /3a/ vi to resign

**dimos** ['dimos] vb V **dar**

**Dinamarca** [dina'marka] nf Denmark

**dinámico, -a** [di'namiko, a] adj dynamic

**dinamita** [dina'mita] nf dynamite

**dinamo** [di'namo], (LAM) **dínamo** ['dinamo] nf dynamo

**dineral** [dine'ral] nm fortune

**dinero** [di'nero] nm money; ~ **efectivo** o **metálico** cash; ~ **suelto** (loose) change

**dio** [djo] vb V **dar**

**dios** [djos] nm god; D~ God; **¡D~ mío!** (oh) my God!; **¡por D~!** for God's sake!; **diosa** nf goddess

**diploma** [di'ploma] nm diploma

**diplomacia** [diplo'maθja] nf diplomacy; (fig) tact

**diplomado, -a** [diplo'maðo, a] adj qualified

**diplomático, -a** [diplo'matiko, a] adj diplomatic ▷ nm/f diplomat

**diputación** [diputa'θjon] nf (tb: ~ **provincial**) ≈ county council

**diputado, -a** [dipu'taðo, a] nm/f delegate; (Pol) ≈ member of parliament (BRIT) ≈ representative (US)

**dique** ['dike] nm dyke

**diré** etc [di're] vb V **decir**

**dirección** [direk'θjon] nf direction; (señas) address; (Auto) steering; (gerencia) management; (Pol) leadership; "~ **única**" "one-way street"; "~ **prohibida**" "no entry"

**direccional** [direkθjo'nal] nf (LAM Auto) indicator

**directa** [di'rekta] nf (Auto) top gear

**directivo, -a** [direk'tiβo, a] adj (junta) managing ▷ nf (tb: **junta directiva**) board of directors

**directo, -a** [di'rekto, a] adj direct; (TV) live; **transmitir en** ~ to broadcast live

**director, a** [direk'tor, a] adj leading ▷ nm/f director; (Escol) head (teacher) (BRIT), principal (US); (gerente) manager/ manageress; (Prensa) editor; ~ **de cine** film director; ~ **general** general manager

**directorio** [direk'torjo] nm (LAM: telefónico) phone book

**dirigente** [diri'xente] nmf (Pol) leader

**dirigir** [diri'xir] /3c/ vt to direct; (carta) to address; (obra de teatro, film) to direct; (Mus) to conduct; (comercio) to manage; **dirigirse** vr: ~**se a** to go towards, make one's way towards; (hablar con) to speak to

**dirija** etc [di'rixa] vb V **dirigir**

**disciplina** [disθi'plina] nf discipline

**discípulo, -a** [dis'θipulo, a] nm/f disciple

**Discman®** ['diskman] nm Discman®

**disco** ['disko] nm disc (BRIT), disk (US); (Deporte) discus; (Telec) dial; (Auto: semáforo) light; (Mus) record; ~ **compacto** compact disc; ~ **de larga duración** long-playing record (LP); ~ **flexible** o **floppy** floppy disk; ~ **de freno** brake disc; ~ **rígido** hard disk

**disconforme** [diskon'forme] adj differing; **estar** ~ (**con**) to be in disagreement (with)

**discordia** [dis'korðja] nf discord

**discoteca** [disko'teka] nf disco(theque)

**discreción** [diskre'θjon] nf discretion; (reserva) prudence; **comer a** ~ to eat as much as one wishes

**discreto, -a** [dis'kreto, a] adj discreet

**discriminación** [diskrimina'θjon] nf discrimination

**disculpa** [dis'kulpa] nf excuse; (pedir perdón) apology; **pedir ~s a/por** to apologize to/for; **disculpar** /1a/ vt to excuse, pardon; **disculparse** vr to excuse o.s.; to apologize

**discurso** [dis'kurso] nm speech

**discusión** [disku'sjon] nf (diálogo) discussion; (riña) argument

**discutir** [disku'tir] /3a/ vt (debatir) to discuss; (pelear) to argue about; (contradecir) to argue against ▷ vi to discuss; (disputar) to argue

**disecar** [dise'kar] /1g/ vt (para conservar: animal) to stuff; (: planta) to dry

**diseñar** [dise'nar] /1a/ vt, vi to design

**diseño** [di'seno] nm design

**disfraz** [dis'fraθ] nm (máscara) disguise;
(excusa) pretext; **disfrazar** /1f/ vt to
disguise; **disfrazarse** vr: **disfrazarse de** to
disguise o.s. as
**disfrutar** [disfru'tar] /1a/ vt to enjoy ⊳ vi to
enjoy o.s.; ~ **de** to enjoy, possess
**disgustar** [disɣus'tar] /1a/ vt (no gustar)
to displease; (contrariar, enojar) to annoy;
to upset; **disgustarse** vr to get upset; (dos
personas) to fall out

▮ No confundir disgustar con la palabra
inglesa disgust.

**disgusto** [dis'ɣusto] nm (contrariedad)
annoyance; (tristeza) grief; (riña) quarrel
**disimular** [disimu'lar] /1a/ vt (ocultar) to
hide, conceal ⊳ vi to dissemble
**diskette** [dis'ket] nm (Inform) diskette,
floppy disk
**dislocar** [dislo'kar] /1g/ vt to dislocate;
**dislocarse** vr (articulación) to sprain,
dislocate
**disminución** [disminu'θjon] nf decrease,
reduction
**disminuido, -a** [disminu'iðo, a] nm/f:
~ **mental/físico** person with a mental/
physical disability
**disminuir** [disminu'ir] /3g/ vt to decrease,
diminish
**disolver** [disol'βer] /2h/ vt (gen) to dissolve;
**disolverse** vr to dissolve; (Com) to go into
liquidation
**dispar** [dis'par] adj different
**disparar** [dispa'rar] /1a/ vt, vi to shoot,
fire
**disparate** [dispa'rate] nm (tontería) foolish
remark; (error) blunder; **decir ~s** to talk
nonsense
**disparo** [dis'paro] nm shot
**dispersar** [disper'sar] /1a/ vt to disperse;
**dispersarse** vr to scatter
**disponer** [dispo'ner] /2q/ vt (arreglar) to
arrange; (ordenar) to put in order; (preparar)
to prepare, get ready ⊳ vi: ~ **de** to have,
own; **disponerse** vr: ~**se para** to prepare
to, prepare for
**disponible** [dispo'niβle] adj available
**disposición** [disposi'θjon] nf
arrangement, disposition; (voluntad)
willingness; (Inform) layout; **a su** ~ at your
service
**dispositivo** [disposi'tiβo] nm device,
mechanism
**dispuesto, -a** [dis'pwesto, a] pp de
**disponer** ⊳ adj (arreglado) arranged;
(preparado) disposed
**disputar** [dispu'tar] /1a/ vt (carrera) to
compete in
**disquete** [dis'kete] nm (Inform) diskette,
floppy disk

**distancia** [dis'tanθja] nf distance;
**distanciar** /1b/ vt to space out;
**distanciarse** vr to become estranged;
**distante** adj distant
**diste** ['diste], **disteis** ['disteis] vb V **dar**
**distinción** [distin'θjon] nf distinction;
(elegancia) elegance; (honor) honour
**distinguido, -a** [distin'ɡiðo, a] adj
distinguished
**distinguir** [distin'ɡir] /3d/ vt to
distinguish; (escoger) to single out;
**distinguirse** vr to be distinguished
**distintivo** [distin'tiβo] nm badge; (fig)
characteristic
**distinto, -a** [dis'tinto, a] adj different;
(claro) clear
**distracción** [distrak'θjon] nf distraction;
(pasatiempo) hobby, pastime; (olvido)
absent-mindedness, distraction
**distraer** [distra'er] /2o/ vt (atención) to
distract; (divertir) to amuse; (fondos) to
embezzle; **distraerse** vr (entretenerse) to
amuse o.s.; (perder la concentración) to allow
one's attention to wander
**distraído, -a** [distra'iðo, a] adj (gen)
absent-minded; (entretenido) amusing
**distribuidor, a** [distriβui'ðor, a] nm/f
distributor; (Com) dealer, agent
**distribuir** [distriβu'ir] /3g/ vt to distribute
**distrito** [dis'trito] nm (sector, territorio)
region; (barrio) district; ~ **postal** postal
district; **D~ Federal** (LAM) Federal District
**disturbio** [dis'turβjo] nm disturbance;
(desorden) riot
**disuadir** [diswa'ðir] /3a/ vt to dissuade
**disuelto** [di'swelto] pp de **disolver**
**DIU** nm abr (= dispositivo intrauterino) IUD
**diurno, -a** ['djurno, a] adj day cpd
**divagar** [diβa'ɣar] /1h/ vi (desviarse) to
digress
**diván** [di'βan] nm divan
**diversidad** [diβersi'ðað] nf diversity,
variety
**diversión** [diβer'sjon] nf (gen)
entertainment; (actividad) hobby, pastime
**diverso, -a** [di'βerso, a] adj diverse ⊳ nm:
~**s** (Com) sundries; ~**s libros** several books
**divertido, -a** [diβer'tiðo, a] adj (chiste)
amusing; (fiesta etc) enjoyable
**divertir** [diβer'tir] /3i/ vt (entretener, recrear)
to amuse; **divertirse** vr (pasarlo bien) to
have a good time; (distraerse) to amuse o.s.
**dividendo** [diβi'ðendo] nm (Com: often pl)
dividend, dividends
**dividir** [diβi'ðir] /3a/ vt (gen) to divide;
(distribuir) to distribute, share out
**divierta** etc [di'βjerta] vb V **divertir**
**divino, -a** [di'βino, a] adj divine
**divirtiendo** etc [diβir'tjendo] vb V **divertir**

**divisa** [di'βisa] *nf* (*emblema*) emblem, badge; **divisas** *nfpl* foreign exchange *sg*

**divisar** [diβi'sar] /1a/ *vt* to make out, distinguish

**división** [diβi'sjon] *nf* division; (*de partido*) split; (*de país*) partition

**divorciar** [diβor'θjar] /1b/ *vt* to divorce; **divorciarse** *vr* to get divorced; **divorcio** *nm* divorce

**divulgar** [diβul'ɣar] /1h/ *vt* (*desparramar*) to spread; (*hacer circular*) to divulge

**DNI** *nm abr* (*ESP*) = **Documento Nacional de Identidad**

● **DNI**
●
● The *Documento Nacional de Identidad* is a
● Spanish ID card which must be carried
● at all times and produced on request for
● the police. It contains the holder's photo,
● fingerprints and personal details. It is also
● known as the *DNI* or *carnet de identidad*.

**Dña.** *abr* (= **Doña**) Mrs

**do** [do] *nm* (*Mus*) C

**dobladillo** [doβla'ðiʎo] *nm* (*de vestido*) hem; (*de pantalón: vuelta*) turn-up (*BRIT*), cuff (*US*)

**doblar** [do'βlar] /1a/ *vt* to double; (*papel*) to fold; (*caño*) to bend; (*la esquina*) to turn, go round; (*film*) to dub ▷ *vi* to turn; (*campana*) to toll; **doblarse** *vr* (*plegarse*) to fold (up), crease; (*encorvarse*) to bend; **~ a la derecha/izquierda** to turn right/left

**doble** ['doβle] *adj* double; (*de dos aspectos*) dual; (*fig*) two-faced ▷ *nm* double ▷ *nmf* (*Teat*) double, stand-in; **dobles** *nmpl* (*Deporte*) doubles *sg*; **con ~ sentido** with a double meaning

**doce** ['doθe] *num* twelve; **docena** *nf* dozen

**docente** [do'θente] *adj*: **personal ~** teaching staff; **centro ~** educational institution

**dócil** ['doθil] *adj* (*pasivo*) docile; (*obediente*) obedient

**doctor, a** [dok'tor, a] *nm/f* doctor

**doctorado** [dokto'raðo] *nm* doctorate

**doctrina** [dok'trina] *nf* doctrine, teaching

**documentación** [dokumenta'θjon] *nf* documentation; (*de identidad etc*) papers *pl*

**documental** [dokumen'tal] *adj, nm* documentary

**documento** [doku'mento] *nm* (*certificado*) document; **~ adjunto** (*Inform*) attachment; **D~ Nacional de Identidad** national identity card; V **DNI**

**dólar** ['dolar] *nm* dollar

**doler** [do'ler] /2h/ *vt, vi* to hurt; (*fig*) to grieve; **dolerse** *vr* (*de su situación*) to grieve,

feel sorry; (*de las desgracias ajenas*) to sympathize; **me duele el brazo** my arm hurts

**dolor** [do'lor] *nm* pain; (*fig*) grief, sorrow; **~ de cabeza** headache; **~ de estómago** stomach ache

**domar** [do'mar] /1a/ *vt* to tame

**domesticar** [domesti'kar] /1g/ *vt* to tame

**doméstico, -a** [do'mestiko, a] *adj* (*vida, servicio*) home; (*tareas*) household; (*animal*) tame, pet

**domicilio** [domi'θiljo] *nm* home; **~ particular** private residence; **servicio a ~** delivery service; **sin ~ fijo** of no fixed abode

**dominante** [domi'nante] *adj* dominant; (*persona*) domineering

**dominar** [domi'nar] /1a/ *vt* to dominate; (*idiomas*) to be fluent in ▷ *vi* to dominate, prevail

**domingo** [do'mingo] *nm* Sunday; **D~ de Ramos** Palm Sunday; **D~ de Resurrección** Easter Sunday

**dominio** [do'minjo] *nm* (*tierras*) domain; (*autoridad*) power, authority; (*de las pasiones*) grip, hold; (*de idioma*) command

**don** [don] *nm* (*talento*) gift; **D~ Juan Gómez** Mr Juan Gómez, Juan Gómez Esq. (*BRIT*)

● **DON**
●
● *Don* or *doña* is a term used before
● someone's first name – eg Don Diego,
● Doña Inés – when showing respect or
● being polite to someone of a superior
● social standing or to an older person.
● It is becoming somewhat rare, but it does
● however continue to be used with names
● and surnames in official documents
● and in correspondence: eg Sr. D. Pedro
● Rodríguez Hernández, Sra. Dña Inés
● Rodríguez Hernández.

**dona** ['dona] *nf* (*LAM*) doughnut, donut (*US*)

**donar** [do'nar] /1a/ *vt* to donate

**donativo** [dona'tiβo] *nm* donation

**donde** ['donde] *adv* where ▷ *prep*: **el coche está allí ~ el farol** the car is over there by the lamppost *o* where the lamppost is; **en ~** where, in which

**dónde** ['donde] *adv interrogativo* where?; **¿a ~ vas?** where are you going (to)?; **¿de ~ vienes?** where have you been?; **¿por ~?** where?, whereabouts?

**dondequiera** [donde'kjera] *adv* anywhere ▷ *conj*: **~ que** wherever; **por ~** everywhere, all over the place

**donut®** [do'nut] *nm* (*ESP*) doughnut, donut (*US*)

**doña** ['dona] *nf*: **~ Alicia** Alicia; **D~ Carmen Gómez** Mrs Carmen Gómez; *V tb* **don**

**dorado, -a** [do'raðo, a] *adj (color)* golden; *(Tec)* gilt

**dormir** [dor'mir] /3j/ *vt*: **~ la siesta** to have an afternoon nap ▷ *vi* to sleep; **dormirse** *vr* to fall asleep

**dormitorio** [dormi'torjo] *nm* bedroom

**dorsal** [dor'sal] *nm (Deporte)* number

**dorso** ['dorso] *nm (de mano)* back; *(de hoja)* other side

**dos** [dos] *num* two

**dosis** ['dosis] *nf inv* dose, dosage

**dotado, -a** [do'taðo, a] *adj* gifted; **~ de** endowed with

**dotar** [do'tar] /1a/ *vt* to endow; **dote** *nf* dowry; **dotes** *nfpl (talentos)* gifts

**doy** [doj] *vb V* **dar**

**drama** ['drama] *nm* drama; **dramaturgo, -a** *nm/f* dramatist, playwright

**drástico, -a** ['drastiko, a] *adj* drastic

**drenaje** [dre'naxe] *nm* drainage

**droga** ['droɣa] *nf* drug; **drogadicto, -a** *nm/f* drug addict

**drogar** [dro'ɣar] /1h/ *vt* to drug; **drogarse** *vr* to take drugs

**droguería** [droɣe'ria] *nf* ≈ hardware shop *(BRIT) o* store *(US)*

**ducha** ['dutʃa] *nf (baño)* shower; *(Med)* douche

**ducharse** [du'tʃarse] /1a/ *vr* to take a shower

**duda** ['duða] *nf* doubt; **no cabe ~** there is no doubt about it; **dudar** /1a/ *vt* to doubt ▷ *vi* to doubt; **dudoso, -a** *adj (incierto)* hesitant; *(sospechoso)* doubtful

**duela** *etc vb V* **doler**

**duelo** ['dwelo] *vb V* **doler** ▷ *nm (combate)* duel; *(luto)* mourning

**duende** ['dwende] *nm* imp, goblin

**dueño, -a** ['dweno, a] *nm/f (propietario)* owner; *(de pensión, taberna)* landlord/lady; *(empresario)* employer

**duerma** *etc* ['dwerma] *vb V* **dormir**

**dulce** ['dulθe] *adj* sweet ▷ *adv* gently, softly ▷ *nm* sweet

**dulcería** [dulθe'ria] *nf (LAM)* confectioner's (shop)

**dulzura** [dul'θura] *nf* sweetness; *(ternura)* gentleness

**dúo** ['duo] *nm* duet

**duplicar** [dupli'kar] /1g/ *vt (hacer el doble de)* to duplicate

**duque** ['duke] *nm* duke; **duquesa** *nf* duchess

**durable** [du'raβle] *adj* durable

**duración** [dura'θjon] *nf (de película, disco etc)* length; *(de pila etc)* life; *(curso: de acontecimientos etc)* duration

**duradero, -a** [dura'ðero, a] *adj (tela)* hard-wearing; *(fe, paz)* lasting

**durante** [du'rante] *adv* during

**durar** [du'rar] /1a/ *vi* to last; *(recuerdo)* to remain

**durazno** [du'rasno] *nm (LAM: fruta)* peach; *(: árbol)* peach tree

**durex** ['dureks] *nm (LAM: tira adhesiva)* Sellotape® *(BRIT)*, Scotch tape® *(US)*

**dureza** [du'reθa] *nf (cualidad)* hardness

**duro, -a** ['duro, a] *adj* hard; *(carácter)* tough ▷ *adv* hard ▷ *nm (moneda)* five peseta coin

**DVD** *nm abr (= disco de vídeo digital)* DVD

# e

**E** *abr* (= *este*) E

**e** [e] *conj* and

**ébano** ['eβano] *nm* ebony

**ebrio, -a** ['eβrjo, a] *adj* drunk

**ebullición** [eβuʎi'θjon] *nf* boiling

**echar** [e'tʃar] /1a/ *vt* to throw; (*agua, vino*) to pour (out); (*empleado: despedir*) to fire, sack; (*hojas*) to sprout; (*cartas*) to post; (*humo*) to emit, give out ▷ *vi*: ~ **a correr** to start running *o* to run, break into a run; ~ **a llorar** to burst into tears; **echarse** *vr* to lie down; ~ **llave a** to lock (up); ~ **abajo** (*gobierno*) to overthrow; (*edificio*) to demolish; ~ **mano a** to lay hands on; ~ **una mano a algn** (*ayudar*) to give sb a hand; ~ **de menos** to miss; ~ **una mirada** to give a look; ~ **sangre** to bleed; **~se atrás** to back out

**eclesiástico, -a** [ekle'sjastiko, a] *adj* ecclesiastical

**eco** ['eko] *nm* echo; **tener ~** to catch on

**ecología** [ekolo'xia] *nf* ecology; **ecológico, -a** *adj* (*producto, método*) environmentally-friendly; (*agricultura*) organic; **ecologista** *adj* environmental, conservation *cpd* ▷ *nmf* environmentalist

**economía** [ekono'mia] *nf* (*sistema*) economy; (*carrera*) economics

**económico, -a** [eko'nomiko, a] *adj* (*barato*) cheap, economical; (*persona*) thrifty; (*Com: año etc*) financial; (*: situación*) economic

**economista** [ekono'mista] *nmf* economist

**ecotasa** [eko'tasa] *nf* green tax

**Ecuador** [ekwa'ðor] *nm* Ecuador

**ecuador** [ekwa'ðor] *nm* equator

**ecuatoriano, -a** [ekwato'rjano, a] *adj, nm/f* Ecuador(i)an

**ecuestre** [e'kwestre] *adj* equestrian

**edad** [e'ðað] *nf* age; **¿qué ~ tienes?** how old are you?; **tiene ocho años de ~** he is eight (years old); **ser de ~ mediana/avanzada** to be middle-aged/getting on; **la E~ Media** the Middle Ages

**edición** [eði'θjon] *nf* (*acto*) publication; (*ejemplar*) edition

**edificar** [eðifi'kar] /1g/ *vt, vi* to build

**edificio** [eði'fiθjo] *nm* building; (*fig*) edifice, structure

**Edimburgo** [eðim'burɣo] *nm* Edinburgh

**editar** [eði'tar] /1a/ *vt* (*publicar*) to publish; (*preparar textos*) to edit

**editor, a** [eði'tor, a] *nm/f* (*que publica*) publisher; (*redactor*) editor ▷ *adj*: **casa ~a** publishing company; **editorial** *adj* editorial ▷ *nm* leading article, editorial; (*tb*: **casa editorial**) publisher

**edredón** [eðre'ðon] *nm*; duvet

**educación** [eðuka'θjon] *nf* education; (*crianza*) upbringing; (*modales*) (good) manners *pl*

**educado, -a** [eðu'kaðo, a] *adj* well-mannered; **mal ~** ill-mannered

**educar** [eðu'kar] /1g/ *vt* to educate; (*criar*) to bring up; (*voz*) to train

**efectivamente** [efektiβa'mente] *adv* (*como respuesta*) exactly, precisely; (*verdaderamente*) really; (*de hecho*) in fact

**efectivo, -a** [efek'tiβo, a] *adj* effective; (*real*) actual, real ▷ *nm*: **pagar en ~** to pay (in) cash; **hacer ~ un cheque** to cash a cheque

**efecto** [e'fekto] *nm* effect, result; **efectos** *nmpl* (*personales*) effects; (*bienes*) goods; (*Com*) assets; **~ invernadero** greenhouse effect; **~s especiales** special effects; **~s secundarios** side effects; **~s sonoros** sound effects; **en ~** in fact; (*respuesta*) exactly, indeed

**efectuar** [efek'twar] /1e/ *vt* to carry out; (*viaje*) to make

**eficacia** [efi'kaθja] *nf* (*de persona*) efficiency; (*de medicamento etc*) effectiveness

**eficaz** [efi'kaθ] *adj* (*persona*) efficient; (*acción*) effective

**eficiente** [efi'θjente] *adj* efficient

**egipcio, -a** [e'xipθjo, a] *adj, nm/f* Egyptian

**Egipto** [e'xipto] *nm* Egypt

**egoísmo** [eɣo'ismo] *nm* egoism

**egoísta** [eɣo'ista] *adj* egoistical, selfish ▷ *nmf* egoist

**Eire** ['eire] *nm* Eire

**ej.** *abr* (= *ejemplo*) e.g.

**eje** ['exe] *nm* (*Geo, Mat*) axis; (*de rueda*) axle; (*de máquina*) shaft, spindle

**ejecución** [exeku'θjon] *nf* execution; (*cumplimiento*) fulfilment; (*actuación*) performance; (*Jur: embargo de deudor*) attachment

**ejecutar** [exeku'tar] /1a/ vt to execute, carry out; (*matar*) to execute; (*cumplir*) to fulfil; (*Mus*) to perform; (*Jur: embargar*) to attach, distrain

**ejecutivo, -a** [exeku'tiβo, a] adj executive; **el (poder)** ~ the executive (power)

**ejemplar** [exem'plar] adj exemplary ▷ nm example; (*Zool*) specimen; (*de libro*) copy; (*de periódico*) number, issue

**ejemplo** [e'xemplo] nm example; **por** ~ for example

**ejercer** [exer'θer] /2b/ vt to exercise; (*influencia*) to exert; (*un oficio*) to practise ▷ vi: ~ **de** to practise as

**ejercicio** [exer'θiθjo] nm exercise; (*período*) tenure; ~ **comercial** business year; **hacer** ~ to take exercise

**ejército** [e'xerθito] nm army; **E~ del Aire/ de Tierra** Air Force/Army; **entrar en el** ~ to join the army, join up

**ejote** [e'xote] nm (LAM) green bean

**PALABRA CLAVE**

**el** [el] (*fem* **la**, *neutro* **lo**, *pl* **los, las**) *artículo definido* **1** the; **el libro/la mesa/los estudiantes/las flores** the book/table/students/flowers
**2** (*con n abstracto o propio, no se traduce*): **el amor/la juventud** love/youth
**3** (*posesión, se traduce a menudo por adj posesivo*): **romperse el brazo** to break one's arm; **levantó la mano** he put his hand up; **se puso el sombrero** she put her hat on
**4** (*valor descriptivo*): **tener la boca grande/ los ojos azules** to have a big mouth/blue eyes
**5** (*con días*) on; **me iré el viernes** I'll leave on Friday; **los domingos suelo ir a nadar** on Sundays I generally go swimming
**6** (*lo + adj*): **lo difícil/caro** what is difficult/expensive; (*cuán*): **no se da cuenta de lo pesado que es** he doesn't realize how boring he is
▶ *pron demostrativo* **1**: **mi libro y el de usted** my book and yours; **las de Pepe son mejores** Pepe's are better; **no la(s) blanca(s) sino la(s) gris(es)** not the white one(s) but the grey one(s)
**2**: **lo de: lo de ayer** what happened yesterday; **lo de las facturas** that business about the invoices
▶ *pron relativo* **1**: **el que** etc (*indef*): **el (los) que quiera(n) que se vaya(n)** anyone who wants to can leave; **llévese el/la que más le guste** take the one you like best; (*def*): **el que compré ayer** the one I bought yesterday; **los que se van** those who leave
**2**: **lo que: lo que pienso yo/más me gusta** what I think/like most
▶ *conj*: **el que: el que lo diga** the fact that he says so; **el que sea tan vago me molesta** his being so lazy bothers me
▶ *excl*: **¡el susto que me diste!** what a fright you gave me!
▶ *pron personal* **1** (*persona: m*) him; (*: f*) her; (*: pl*) them; **lo/las veo** I can see him/them
**2** (*animal, cosa: sg*) it; (*: pl*) them; **lo (o la) veo** I can see it; **los (o las) veo** I can see them
**3**: **lo** (*como sustituto de frase*): **no lo sabía** I didn't know; **ya lo entiendo** I understand now

**él** [el] pron (*persona*) he; (*cosa*) it; (*después de prep: persona*) him; (*: cosa*) it; **mis libros y los de él** my books and his

**elaborar** [elaβo'rar] /1a/ vt (*producto*) to make, manufacture; (*preparar*) to prepare; (*madera, metal etc*) to work; (*proyecto etc*) to work on o out

**elástico, -a** [e'lastiko, a] adj elastic; (*flexible*) flexible ▷ nm elastic; (*gomita*) elastic band

**elección** [elek'θjon] nf election; (*selección*) choice, selection; **elecciones generales** general election sg

**electorado** [elekto'raðo] nm electorate, voters pl

**electricidad** [elektriθi'ðað] nf electricity

**electricista** [elektri'θista] nmf electrician

**eléctrico, -a** [e'lektriko, a] adj electric

**electro...** [elektro] pref electro...;
**electrocardiograma** nm electrocardiogram; **electrocutar** /1a/ vt to electrocute; **electrodo** nm electrode; **electrodomésticos** nmpl (electrical) household appliances

**electrónico, -a** [elek'troniko, a] adj electronic ▷ nf electronics sg

**electrotren** [elektro'tren] nm express electric train

**elefante** [ele'fante] nm elephant

**elegancia** [ele'γanθja] nf elegance, grace; (*estilo*) stylishness

**elegante** [ele'γante] adj elegant, graceful; (*estiloso*) stylish, fashionable

**elegir** [ele'xir] /3c, 3k/ vt (*escoger*) to choose, select; (*optar*) to opt for; (*presidente*) to elect

**elemental** [elemen'tal] adj (*claro, obvio*) elementary; (*fundamental*) elemental, fundamental

**elemento** [ele'mento] nm element; (*fig*) ingredient; **elementos** nmpl elements, rudiments

**elepé** [ele'pe] nm LP

**elevación** [eleβa'θjon] nf elevation; (*acto*) raising, lifting; (*de precios*) rise; (*Geo etc*) height, altitude

**elevado, -a** [ele'βaðo, a] *pp de* **elevar** ▷ *adj* high

**elevar** [ele'βar] /1a/ *vt* to raise, lift (up); *(precio)* to put up; **elevarse** *vr (edificio)* to rise; *(precios)* to go up

**eligiendo** *etc* [eli'xjenðo], **elija** *etc* [e'lixa] *vb V* **elegir**

**eliminar** [elimi'nar] /1a/ *vt* to eliminate, remove

**eliminatoria** [elimina'torja] *nf* heat, preliminary (round)

**elite** [e'lite], **élite** ['elite] *nf* elite

**ella** ['eʎa] *pron (persona)* she; *(cosa)* it; *(después de prep: persona)* her; (: *cosa*) it; **de ~** hers

**ellas** ['eʎas] *pron V* **ellos**

**ello** ['eʎo] *pron neutro* it; **es por ~ que ...** that's why ...

**ellos, -as** ['eʎos, as] *pron personal pl* they; *(después de prep)* them; **de ~** theirs

**elogiar** [elo'xjar] /1b/ *vt* to praise; **elogio** *nm* praise

**elote** [e'lote] *nm (LAM)* corn on the cob

**eludir** [elu'ðir] /3a/ *vt* to avoid

**email** ['imeil] *nm* email *m; (dirección)* email address; **mandar un ~ a algn** to email sb, send sb an email

**embajada** [emba'xaða] *nf* embassy

**embajador, a** [embaxa'ðor, a] *nm/f* ambassador/ambassadress

**embalar** [emba'lar] /1a/ *vt* to parcel, wrap (up); **embalarse** *vr* to go fast

**embalse** [em'balse] *nm (presa)* dam; *(lago)* reservoir

**embarazada** [embara'θaða] *adj f* pregnant ▷ *nf* pregnant woman

> ⬛ No confundir *embarazada* con la palabra inglesa *embarrassed*.

**embarazo** [emba'raθo] *nm (de mujer)* pregnancy; *(impedimento)* obstacle, obstruction; *(timidez)* embarrassment; **embarazoso, -a** *adj* awkward; *(violento)* embarrassing

**embarcación** [embarka'θjon] *nf (barco)* boat, craft; *(acto)* embarkation

**embarcadero** [embarka'ðero] *nm* pier, landing stage

**embarcar** [embar'kar] /1g/ *vt (cargamento)* to ship, stow; *(persona)* to embark, put on board; **embarcarse** *vr* to embark, go on board

**embargar** [embar'ɣar] /1h/ *vt (Jur)* to seize, impound

**embargo** [em'barɣo] *nm (Jur)* seizure; *(Com etc)* embargo

**embargue** *etc* [em'barɣe] *vb V* **embargar**

**embarque** *etc* [em'barke] *vb V* **embarcar** ▷ *nm* shipment, loading

**embellecer** [embeʎe'θer] /2d/ *vt* to embellish, beautify

**embestida** [embes'tiða] *nf* attack, onslaught; *(carga)* charge

**embestir** [embes'tir] /3k/ *vt* to attack, assault; to charge, attack ▷ *vi* to attack

**emblema** [em'blema] *nm* emblem

**embobado, -a** [embo'βaðo, a] *adj (atontado)* stunned, bewildered

**embolia** [em'bolja] *nf (Med)* clot, embolism

**émbolo** ['embolo] *nm (Auto)* piston

**emborrachar** [emborra'tʃar] /1a/ *vt* to make drunk, intoxicate; **emborracharse** *vr* to get drunk

**emboscada** [embos'kaða] *nf* ambush

**embotar** [embo'tar] /1a/ *vt* to blunt, dull

**embotellamiento** [emboteʎa'mjento] *nm (Auto)* traffic jam

**embotellar** [embote'ʎar] /1a/ *vt* to bottle

**embrague** [em'braɣe] *nm (tb: **pedal de ~**)* clutch

**embrión** [em'brjon] *nm* embryo

**embrollo** [em'broʎo] *nm (enredo)* muddle, confusion; *(aprieto)* fix, jam

**embrujado, -a** [embru'xaðo, a] *adj* bewitched; **casa embrujada** haunted house

**embrutecer** [embrute'θer] /2d/ *vt (atontar)* to stupefy

**embudo** [em'buðo] *nm* funnel

**embuste** [em'buste] *nm (mentira)* lie; **embustero, -a** *adj* lying, deceitful ▷ *nm/f (mentiroso)* liar

**embutido** [embu'tiðo] *nm (Culin)* sausage; *(Tec)* inlay

**emergencia** [emer'xenθja] *nf* emergency; *(surgimiento)* emergence

**emerger** [emer'xer] /2c/ *vi* to emerge, appear

**emigración** [emiɣra'θjon] *nf* emigration; *(de pájaros)* migration

**emigrar** [emi'ɣrar] /1a/ *vi (personas)* to emigrate; *(pájaros)* to migrate

**eminente** [emi'nente] *adj* eminent, distinguished; *(elevado)* high

**emisión** [emi'sjon] *nf (acto)* emission; *(Com etc)* issue; *(Radio, TV: acto)* broadcasting; (: *programa*) broadcast, programme, program *(us)*

**emisor, a** [emi'sor, a] *nm* transmitter ▷ *nf* radio o broadcasting station

**emitir** [emi'tir] /3a/ *vt (olor etc)* to emit, give off; *(moneda etc)* to issue; *(opinión)* to express; *(Radio)* to broadcast

**emoción** [emo'θjon] *nf* emotion; *(excitación)* excitement; *(sentimiento)* feeling

**emocionante** [emoθjo'nante] *adj (excitante)* exciting, thrilling

**emocionar** [emoθjo'nar] /1a/ *vt (excitar)* to excite, thrill; *(conmover)* to move, touch; *(impresionar)* to impress

**emoticón** [emoti'kon], **emoticono**
[emoti'kono] nm smiley
**emotivo, -a** [emo'tiβo, a] adj emotional
**empacho** [em'patʃo] nm (Med) indigestion;
(fig) embarrassment
**empalagoso, -a** [empala'ɣoso, a] adj
cloying; (fig) tiresome
**empalmar** [empal'mar] /1a/ vt to join,
connect ▷ vi (dos caminos) to meet, join;
**empalme** nm joint, connection; (de vías)
junction; (de trenes) connection
**empanada** [empa'naða] nf pie, pasty
**empañarse** [empa'narse] /1a/ vr (nublarse)
to get misty, steam up
**empapar** [empa'par] /1a/ vt (mojar) to
soak, saturate; (absorber) to soak up,
absorb; **empaparse** vr: **~se de** to soak up
**empapelar** [empape'lar] /1a/ vt (paredes)
to paper
**empaquetar** [empake'tar] /1a/ vt to pack,
parcel up
**empastar** [empas'tar] /1a/ vt (embadurnar)
to paste; (diente) to fill
**empaste** [em'paste] nm (de diente) filling
**empatar** [empa'tar] /1a/ vi to draw, tie;
**~on a dos** they drew two-all; **empate** nm
draw, tie
**empecé** [empe'θe] vb V **empezar**
**empedernido, -a** [empeðer'niðo, a] adj
hard, heartless; (fijado) inveterate; **un
fumador ~** a heavy smoker
**empeine** [em'peine] nm (de pie, zapato)
instep
**empeñado, -a** [empe'naðo, a] adj (persona)
determined; (objeto) pawned
**empeñar** [empe'nar] /1a/ vt (objeto)
to pawn, pledge; (persona) to compel;
**empeñarse** vr (endeudarse) to get into
debt; **~se en hacer** to be set on doing, be
determined to do
**empeño** [em'peno] nm (determinación)
determination; **casa de ~s** pawnshop
**empeorar** [empeo'rar] /1a/ vt to
make worse, worsen ▷ vi to get worse,
deteriorate
**empezar** [empe'θar] /1f, 1j/ vt, vi to begin,
start
**empiece** etc [em'pjeθe] vb V **empezar**
**empiezo** etc [em'pjeθo] vb V **empezar**
**emplasto** [em'plasto] nm (Med) plaster
**emplazar** [empla'θar] /1f/ vt (ubicar)
to site, place, locate; (Jur) to summons;
(convocar) to summon
**empleado, -a** [emple'aðo, a] nm/f (gen)
employee; (de banco etc) clerk
**emplear** [emple'ar] /1a/ vt (usar) to
use, employ; (dar trabajo a) to employ;
**emplearse** vr (conseguir trabajo) to be
employed; (ocuparse) to occupy o.s.

**empleo** [em'pleo] nm (puesto) job; (puestos:
colectivamente) employment; (uso) use,
employment
**empollar** [empo'ʎar] /1a/ vt (fam) to swot
(up); **empollón, -ona** nm/f (fam) swot
**emporio** [em'porjo] nm (LAM: gran almacén)
department store
**empotrado, -a** [empo'traðo, a] adj
(armario etc) built-in
**emprender** [empren'der] /2a/ vt (empezar)
to begin, embark on; (acometer) to tackle,
take on
**empresa** [em'presa] nf enterprise; (Com)
firm, company; **empresariales** nfpl
business studies; **empresario, -a** nm/f
(Com) businessman/woman
**empujar** [empu'xar] /1a/ vt to push, shove
**empujón** [empu'xon] nm push, shove
**empuñar** [empu'nar] /1a/ vt (asir) to grasp,
take (firm) hold of

🔵 **PALABRA CLAVE**

**en** [en] prep **1** (posición) in; (: sobre) on;
**está en el cajón** it's in the drawer; **en
Argentina/La Paz** in Argentina/La Paz; **en
el colegio/la oficina** at school/the office;
**está en el suelo/quinto piso** it's on the
floor/the fifth floor
**2** (dirección) into; **entró en el aula** she went
into the classroom; **meter algo en el bolso**
to put sth into one's bag
**3** (tiempo) in; on; **en 1605/3 semanas/
invierno** in 1605/3 weeks/winter; **en (el
mes de) enero** in (the month of) January;
**en aquella ocasión/época** on that
occasion/at that time
**4** (precio) for; **lo vendió en 20 dólares** he
sold it for 20 dollars
**5** (diferencia) by; **reducir/aumentar en una
tercera parte/un 20 por ciento** to reduce/
increase by a third/20 per cent
**6** (manera, forma): **en avión/autobús** by
plane/bus; **escrito en inglés** written in
English
**7** (después de vb que indica gastar etc) on; **han
cobrado demasiado en dietas** they've
charged too much to expenses; **se le va la
mitad del sueldo en comida** half his salary
goes on food
**8** (tema, ocupación): **experto en la materia**
expert on the subject; **trabaja en la
construcción** he works in the building
industry
**9** (adj + en + infin): **lento en reaccionar** slow
to react

**enagua(s)** [ena'ɣwa(s)] nf (pl) (esp LAM)
petticoat sg, underskirt sg

**enajenación** [enaxena'θjon] *nf*: ~**mental**
mental derangement

**enamorado, -a** [enamo'raðo, a] *adj* in love
▷ *nm/f* lover; **estar ~ (de)** to be in love (with)

**enamorar** [enamo'rar] /1a/ *vt* to win the
love of; **enamorarse** *vr*: ~**se (de)** to fall in
love (with)

**enano, -a** [e'nano, a] *adj* tiny ▷ *nm/f* person
of small stature

**encabezamiento** [enkaβeθa'mjento] *nm*
(*de carta*) heading; (*de periódico*) headline

**encabezar** [enkaβe'θar] /1f/ *vt*
(*movimiento, revolución*) to lead, head; (*lista*)
to head; (*carta*) to put a heading to

**encadenar** [enkaðe'nar] /1a/ *vt* to chain
(together); (*poner grilletes a*) to shackle

**encajar** [enka'xar] /1a/ *vt* (*ajustar*): ~ **en**
to fit (into) ▷ *vi* to fit (well); (*fig: corresponder a*)
to match

**encaje** [en'kaxe] *nm* (*labor*) lace

**encallar** [enka'ʎar] /1a/ *vi* (*Naut*) to run
aground

**encaminar** [enkami'nar] /1a/ *vt* to direct,
send

**encantado, -a** [enkan'taðo, a] *adj* (*hechizado*)
bewitched; (*muy contento*) delighted; **¡~!**
how do you do!, pleased to meet you

**encantador, a** [enkanta'ðor, a] *adj*
charming, lovely ▷ *nm/f* magician,
enchanter/enchantress

**encantar** [enkan'tar] /1a/ *vt* to charm,
delight; (*hechizar*) to bewitch, cast a spell
on; **me encanta eso** I love that; **encanto**
*nm* (*magia*) spell, charm; (*fig*) charm, delight

**encarcelar** [enkarθe'lar] /1a/ *vt* to
imprison, jail

**encarecer** [enkare'θer] /2d/ *vt* to put up
the price of ▷ **encarecerse** *vr* to get dearer

**encargado, -a** [enkar'ɣaðo, a] *adj* in
charge ▷ *nm/f* agent, representative;
(*responsable*) person in charge

**encargar** [enkar'ɣar] /1h/ *vt* to entrust;
(*recomendar*) to urge, recommend;
**encargarse** *vr*: ~**se de** to look after, take
charge of; ~ **algo a algn** to put sb in charge
of sth

**encargo** [en'karɣo] *nm* (*pedido*)
assignment, job; (*responsabilidad*)
responsibility; (*Com*) order

**encariñarse** [enkari'narse] /1a/ *vr*: ~ **con**
to grow fond of, get attached to

**encarnación** [enkarna'θjon] *nf*
incarnation, embodiment

**encarrilar** [enkarri'lar] /1a/ *vt* (*tren*) to put
back on the rails; (*fig*) to correct, put on the
right track

**encasillar** [enkasi'ʎar] /1a/ *vt* (*Teat*) to
typecast; (*pey*) to pigeonhole

**encendedor** [enθende'ðor] *nm* lighter

**encender** [enθen'der] /2g/ *vt* (*con fuego*)
to light; (*luz, radio*) to put on, switch on;
(*avivar: pasiones etc*) to inflame; **encenderse**
*vr* to catch fire; (*excitarse*) to get excited; (*de
cólera*) to flare up; (*el rostro*) to blush

**encendido, -a** [enθen'diðo, a] *adj* alight;
(*aparato*) (switched) on ▷ *nm* (*Auto*) ignition

**encerado, -a** [enθe'raðo, a] *adj* (*suelo*)
waxed ▷ *nm* (*Escol*) blackboard

**encerrar** [enθe'rrar] /1j/ *vt* (*confinar*) to
shut in o up; (*comprender, incluir*) to include,
contain; **encerrarse** *vr* to shut o lock o.s.
up o in

**encharcado, -a** [entʃar'kaðo, a] *adj*
(*terreno*) flooded

**encharcar** [entʃar'kar] /1g/ *vt* to swamp,
flood; **encharcarse** *vr* to become flooded

**enchufado, -a** [entʃu'faðo, a] *nm/f* (*fam*)
well-connected person

**enchufar** [entʃu'far] /1a/ *vt* (*Elec*) to plug
in; (*Tec*) to connect, fit together; **enchufe**
*nm* (*Elec: clavija*) plug; (*: toma*) socket; (*de
dos tubos*) joint, connection; (*fam: influencia*)
contact, connection; (*: puesto*) cushy job

**encía** [en'θia] *nf* gum

**encienda** *etc* [en'θjenda] *vb* V **encender**

**encierro** *etc* [en'θjerro] *vb* V **encerrar** ▷ *nm*
shutting in o up; (*calabozo*) prison

**encima** [en'θima] *adv* (*sobre*) above, over;
(*además*) besides; ~ **de** (*en*) on, on top of;
(*sobre*) above, over; (*además de*) besides, on
top of; **por ~ de** over; **¿llevas dinero ~?** have
you (got) any money on you?; **se me vino ~**
it took me by surprise

**encina** [en'θina] *nf* (*holm*) oak

**encinta** [en'θinta] *adj f* pregnant

**enclenque** [en'klenke] *adj* weak, sickly

**encoger** [enko'xer] /2c/ *vt* (*gen*) to shrink,
contract; **encogerse** *vr* to shrink, contract;
(*fig*) to cringe; ~**se de hombros** to shrug
one's shoulders

**encomendar** [enkomen'dar] /1j/ *vt* to
entrust, commend; **encomendarse** *vr*: ~**se
a** to put one's trust in

**encomienda** *etc* [enko'mjenda] *vb* V
**encomendar** ▷ *nf* (*encargo*) charge,
commission; (*elogio*) tribute; (LAM) parcel,
package; ~ **postal** (LAM: *servicio*) parcel post

**encontrar** [enkon'trar] /1l/ *vt* (*hallar*) to
find; (*inesperadamente*) to meet, run into;
**encontrarse** *vr* to meet (each other);
(*situarse*) to be (situated); ~**se con** to meet;
~**se bien (de salud)** to feel well

**encrucijada** [enkruθi'xaða] *nf* crossroads *sg*

**encuadernación** [enkwaðerna'θjon] *nf*
binding

**encuadrar** [enkwa'ðrar] /1a/ *vt* (*retrato*)
to frame; (*ajustar*) to fit, insert; (*encerrar*)
to contain

**encubrir** [enku'βrir] /3a/ vt (ocultar) to hide, conceal; (criminal) to harbour, shelter

**encuentro** [en'kwentro] vb V **encontrar** ▷ nm (de personas) meeting; (Auto etc) collision, crash; (Deporte) match, game; (Mil) encounter

**encuerado, -a** [enkwe'raðo, a] adj (LAM) nude, naked

**encuesta** [en'kwesta] nf inquiry, investigation; (sondeo) public opinion poll

**encumbrar** [enkum'brar] /1a/ vt (persona) to exalt

**endeble** [en'deβle] adj (argumento, excusa, persona) weak

**endemoniado, -a** [endemo'njaðo, a] adj possessed (of the devil); (travieso) devilish

**enderezar** [endere'θar] /1f/ vt (poner derecho) to straighten (out); (: verticalmente) to set upright; (fig) to straighten o sort out; (dirigir) to direct; **enderezarse** vr (persona sentada) to sit up straight

**endeudarse** [endeu'ðarse] /1a/ vr to get into debt

**endiablado, -a** [endja'βlaðo, a] adj devilish, diabolical; (humorístico) mischievous

**endilgar** [endil'ɣar] /1h/ vt (fam): ~ algo a algn to lumber sb with sth

**endiñar** [endi'nar] /1a/ vt: ~ algo a algn to land sth on sb

**endosar** [endo'sar] /1a/ vt (cheque etc) to endorse

**endulzar** [endul'θar] /1f/ vt to sweeten; (suavizar) to soften

**endurecer** [endure'θer] /2d/ vt to harden; **endurecerse** vr to harden, grow hard

**enema** [e'nema] nm (Med) enema

**enemigo, -a** [ene'miɣo, a] adj enemy, hostile ▷ nm/f enemy

**enemistad** [enemis'tað] nf enmity

**enemistar** [enemis'tar] /1a/ vt to make enemies of, cause a rift between; **enemistarse** vr to become enemies; (amigos) to fall out

**energía** [ener'xia] nf (vigor) energy, drive; (empuje) push; (Tec, Elec) energy, power; ~ atómica/eléctrica/eólica atomic/electric/wind power; ~ solar solar energy o power

**enérgico, -a** [e'nerxiko, a] adj (gen) energetic; (voz, modales) forceful

**energúmeno, -a** [ener'ɣumeno, a] nm/f madman/woman

**enero** [e'nero] nm January

**enfadado, -a** [enfa'ðaðo, a] adj angry, annoyed

**enfadar** [enfa'ðar] /1a/ vt to anger, annoy; **enfadarse** vr to get angry o annoyed

**enfado** [en'faðo] nm (enojo) anger, annoyance; (disgusto) trouble, bother

**énfasis** ['enfasis] nm emphasis, stress

**enfático, -a** [en'fatiko, a] adj emphatic

**enfermar** [enfer'mar] /1a/ vt to make ill ▷ vi to fall ill, be taken ill

**enfermedad** [enferme'ðað] nf illness; ~ venérea venereal disease

**enfermera** [enfer'mera] nf V **enfermero**

**enfermería** [enferme'ria] nf infirmary; (de colegio etc) sick bay

**enfermero, -a** [enfer'mero, a] nm (male) nurse ▷ nf nurse

**enfermizo, -a** [enfer'miθo, a] adj (persona) sickly, unhealthy; (fig) unhealthy

**enfermo, -a** [en'fermo, a] adj ill, sick ▷ nm/f invalid, sick person; (en hospital) patient; **caer** o **ponerse ~** to fall ill

**enfocar** [enfo'kar] /1g/ vt (foto etc) to focus; (problema etc) to consider, look at

**enfoque** etc [en'foke] vb V **enfocar** ▷ nm focus

**enfrentar** [enfren'tar] /1a/ vt (peligro) to face (up to), confront; (oponer) to bring face to face; **enfrentarse** vr (dos personas) to face o confront each other; (Deporte: dos equipos) to meet; ~**se** a o **con** to face up to, confront

**enfrente** [en'frente] adv opposite; ~ **de** opposite, facing; **la casa de ~** the house opposite, the house across the street

**enfriamiento** [enfria'mjento] nm chilling, refrigeration; (Med) cold, chill

**enfriar** [enfri'ar] /1c/ vt (alimentos) to cool, chill; (algo caliente) to cool down; **enfriarse** vr to cool down; (Med) to catch a chill; (amistad) to cool

**enfurecer** [enfure'θer] /2d/ vt to enrage, madden; **enfurecerse** vr to become furious, fly into a rage; (mar) to get rough

**enganchar** [engan'tʃar] /1a/ vt to hook; (dos vagones) to hitch up; (Tec) to couple, connect; (Mil) to recruit; **engancharse** vr (Mil) to enlist, join up

**enganche** [en'gantʃe] nm hook; (Tec) coupling, connection; (acto) hooking (up); (Mil) recruitment, enlistment; (LAM: depósito) deposit

**engañar** [enga'nar] /1a/ vt to deceive; (estafar) to cheat, swindle; **engañarse** vr (equivocarse) to be wrong; (asimismo) to deceive o kid o.s.

**engaño** [en'gano] nm deceit; (estafa) trick, swindle; (error) mistake, misunderstanding; (ilusión) delusion; **engañoso, -a** adj (tramposo) crooked; (mentiroso) dishonest, deceitful; (aspecto) deceptive; (consejo) misleading

**engatusar** [engatu'sar] /1a/ vt (fam) to coax

**engendro** [en'xendro] nm (Bio) foetus; (fig) monstrosity

**englobar** [englo'βar] /1a/ vt to include, comprise

**engordar** [engor'ðar] /1a/ vt to fatten ▷ vi to get fat, put on weight

**engorroso, -a** [engo'rroso, a] adj bothersome, trying

**engranaje** [engra'naxe] nm (Auto) gear

**engrasar** [engra'sar] /1a/ vt (Tec: poner grasa) to grease; (: lubricar) to lubricate, oil; (manchar) to make greasy

**engreído, -a** [engre'iðo, a] adj vain, conceited

**enhebrar** [ene'βrar] /1a/ vt to thread

**enhorabuena** [enora'βwena] excl: ¡~! congratulations! ▷ nf: **dar la ~ a** to congratulate

**enigma** [e'niɣma] nm enigma; (problema) puzzle; (misterio) mystery

**enjambre** [en'xambre] nm swarm

**enjaular** [enxau'lar] /1a/ vt to (put in a) cage; (fam) to jail, lock up

**enjuagar** [enxwa'ɣar] /1h/ vt (ropa) to rinse (out)

**enjuague** etc [en'xwaɣe] vb V **enjuagar** ▷ nm (Med) mouthwash; (de ropa) rinse, rinsing

**enjugar** [enxu'ɣar] /1h/ vt to wipe (off); (lágrimas) to dry; (déficit) to wipe out

**enlace** [en'laθe] nm link, connection; (relación) relationship; (tb: ~ **matrimonial**) marriage; (de trenes) connection; ~ **sindical** shop steward

**enlatado, -a** [enla'taðo, a] adj (alimentos, productos) tinned, canned

**enlazar** [enla'θar] /1f/ vt (unir con lazos) to bind together; (atar) to tie; (conectar) to link, connect; (LAM) to lasso

**enloquecer** [enloke'θer] /2d/ vt to drive mad ▷ vi to go mad

**enmarañar** [enmara'ɲar] /1a/ vt (enredar) to tangle up, entangle; (complicar) to complicate; (confundir) to confuse

**enmarcar** [enmar'kar] /1g/ vt (cuadro) to frame

**enmascarar** [enmaska'rar] /1a/ vt to mask; **enmascararse** vr to put on a mask

**enmendar** [enmen'dar] /1j/ vt to emend, correct; (constitución etc) to amend; (comportamiento) to reform; **enmendarse** vr to reform, mend one's ways; **enmienda** nf correction; amendment; reform

**enmudecer** [enmuðe'θer] /2d/ vi (perder el habla) to fall silent; (guardar silencio) to remain silent

**ennoblecer** [ennoβle'θer] /2d/ vt to ennoble

**enojado, -a** [eno'xaðo, a] adj (LAM) angry

**enojar** [eno'xar] /1a/ vt (encolerizar) to anger; (disgustar) to annoy, upset; **enojarse** vr to get angry; to get annoyed

**enojo** [e'noxo] nm (cólera) anger; (irritación) annoyance

**enorme** [e'norme] adj enormous, huge; (fig) monstrous

**enredadera** [enreða'ðera] nf (Bot) creeper, climbing plant

**enredar** [enre'ðar] /1a/ vt (cables, hilos etc) to tangle (up), entangle; (situación) to complicate, confuse; (meter cizaña) to sow discord among o between; (implicar) to embroil, implicate; **enredarse** vr to get entangled, get tangled (up); (situación) to get complicated; (persona) to get embroiled; (LAM fam) to meddle

**enredo** [en'reðo] nm (maraña) tangle; (confusión) mix-up, confusion; (intriga) intrigue

**enriquecer** [enrike'θer] /2d/ vt to make rich; (fig) to enrich; **enriquecerse** vr to get rich

**enrojecer** [enroxe'θer] /2d/ vt to redden ▷ vi (persona) to blush; **enrojecerse** vr to blush

**enrollar** [enro'ʎar] /1a/ vt to roll (up), wind (up)

**ensalada** [ensa'laða] nf salad

**ensaladilla** [ensala'ðiʎa] nf (tb: ~ **rusa**) ≈ Russian salad

**ensanchar** [ensan'tʃar] /1a/ vt (hacer más ancho) to widen; (agrandar) to enlarge, expand; (Costura) to let out; **ensancharse** vr to get wider, expand

**ensayar** [ensa'jar] /1a/ vt to test, try (out); (Teat) to rehearse

**ensayo** [en'sajo] nm test, trial; (Química) experiment; (Teat) rehearsal; (Deporte) try; (Escol, Lit) essay

**enseguida** [ense'ɣwiða] adv at once, right away

**ensenada** [ense'naða] nf inlet, cove

**enseñanza** [ense'ɲanθa] nf (educación) education; (acción) teaching; (doctrina) teaching, doctrine; ~ **primaria/ secundaria/superior** primary/secondary/ higher education

**enseñar** [ense'ɲar] /1a/ vt (educar) to teach; (mostrar, señalar) to show

**enseres** [en'seres] nmpl belongings

**ensuciar** [ensu'θjar] /1b/ vt (manchar) to dirty, soil; (fig) to defile; **ensuciarse** vr to get dirty; (niño) to dirty one's nappy

**entablar** [enta'βlar] /1a/ vt (recubrir) to board (up); (Ajedrez, Damas) to set up; (conversación) to strike up; (Jur) to file ▷ vi to draw

**ente** ['ente] nm (organización) body, organization; (fam: persona) odd character

**entender** [enten'der] /2g/ vt (comprender) to understand; (darse cuenta) to realize ▷ vi to understand; (creer) to think, believe ▷ nm: **a mí** ~ in my opinion; **entenderse** vr (comprenderse) to be understood; (ponerse de acuerdo) to agree, reach an agreement; ~ **de** to know all about; ~ **algo de** to know a little about; ~ **en** to deal with, have to do with; **~se mal** to get on badly

**entendido, -a** [enten'diðo, a] adj (comprendido) understood; (hábil) skilled; (inteligente) knowledgeable ▷ nm/f (experto) expert ▷ excl agreed!; **entendimiento** nm (comprensión) understanding; (inteligencia) mind, intellect; (juicio) judgement

**enterado, -a** [ente'raðo, a] adj well-informed; **estar ~ de** to know about, be aware of

**enteramente** [entera'mente] adv entirely, completely

**enterar** [ente'rar] /1a/ vt (informar) to inform, tell; **enterarse** vr to find out, get to know

**enterito** [ente'rito] nm (LAM) boiler suit (BRIT), overalls (US)

**entero, -a** [en'tero, a] adj (total) whole, entire; (fig: recto) honest; (: firme) firm, resolute ▷ nm (Com: punto) point

**enterrar** [ente'rrar] /1j/ vt to bury

**entidad** [enti'ðað] nf (empresa) firm, company; (organismo) body; (sociedad) society; (Filosofía) entity

**entienda** etc [en'tjenda] vb V **entender**

**entierro** [en'tjerro] nm (acción) burial; (funeral) funeral

**entonación** [entona'θjon] nf (Ling) intonation

**entonar** [ento'nar] /1a/ vt (canción) to intone; (colores) to tone; (Med) to tone up ▷ vi to be in tune

**entonces** [en'tonθes] adv then, at that time; **desde ~** since then; **en aquel ~** at that time; **(pues) ~** and so

**entornar** [entor'nar] /1a/ vt (puerta, ventana) to half close, leave ajar; (los ojos) to screw up

**entorno** [en'torno] nm setting, environment; ~ **de redes** (Inform) network environment

**entorpecer** [entorpe'θer] /2d/ vt (entendimiento) to dull; (impedir) to obstruct, hinder; (: tránsito) to slow down, delay

**entrado, -a** [en'traðo, a] adj: ~ **en años** elderly; **(una vez) ~ el verano** in the summer(time), when summer comes ▷ nf (acción) entry, access; (sitio) entrance, way in; (Com) receipts pl, takings pl; (Culin) entrée; (Deporte) innings sg; (Teat) house, audience; (para el cine etc) ticket; (Inform) input; **entradas y salidas** (Com) income and expenditure; **entrada de aire** (Tec) air intake o inlet; **de entrada** from the outset

**entramparse** [entram'parse] /1a/ vr to get into debt

**entrante** [en'trante] adj next, coming; **entrantes** nmpl starters; **mes/año ~** next month/year

**entraña** [en'traɲa] nf (fig: centro) heart, core; (raíz) root; **entrañas** nfpl (Anat) entrails; (fig) heart sg; **entrañable** adj (amigo) dear; (recuerdo) fond; **entrañar** /1a/ vt to entail

**entrar** [en'trar] /1a/ vt (introducir) to bring in; (Inform) to input ▷ vi (meterse) to go o come in, enter; (comenzar): ~ **diciendo** to begin by saying; **me entró sed/sueño** I started to feel thirsty/sleepy; **no me entra** I can't get the hang of it

**entre** ['entre] prep (dos) between; (en medio de) among(st)

**entreabrir** [entrea'βrir] /3a/ vt to half-open, open halfway

**entrecejo** [entre'θexo] nm: **fruncir el ~** to frown

**entredicho** [entre'ðitʃo] nm (Jur) injunction; **poner en ~** to cast doubt on; **estar en ~** to be in doubt

**entrega** [en'treɣa] nf (de mercancías) delivery; (de novela etc) instalment; **entregar** /1h/ vt (dar) to hand (over), deliver; **entregarse** vr (rendirse) to surrender, give in, submit; **entregarse a** (dedicarse) to devote o.s. to

**entremeses** [entre'meses] nmpl hors d'œuvres

**entremeter** [entreme'ter] /2a/ vt to insert, put in; **entremeterse** vr to meddle, interfere; **entremetido, -a** adj meddling, interfering

**entremezclar** [entremeθ'klar] /1a/ vt to intermingle; **entremezclarse** vr to intermingle

**entrenador, a** [entrena'ðor, a] nm/f trainer, coach

**entrenar** [entre'nar] /1a/ vt (Deporte) to train ▷ **entrenarse** vr to train

**entrepierna** [entre'pjerna] nf crotch

**entresuelo** [entre'swelo] nm mezzanine

**entretanto** [entre'tanto] adv meanwhile, meantime

**entretecho** [entre'tetʃo] nm (LAM) attic

**entretejer** [entrete'xer] /2a/ vt to interweave

**entretener** [entrete'ner] /2k/ vt (divertir) to entertain, amuse; (detener) to hold up, delay; **entretenerse** vr (divertirse) to amuse o.s.; (retrasarse) to delay, linger; **entretenido, -a** adj entertaining, amusing;

**entretenimiento** nm entertainment, amusement

**entrever** [entre'βer] /2u/ vt to glimpse, catch a glimpse of

**entrevista** [entre'βista] nf interview; **entrevistar** /1a/ vt to interview; **entrevistarse** vr: **entrevistarse con** to have an interview with

**entristecer** [entriste'θer] /2d/ vt to sadden, grieve; **entristecerse** vr to grow sad

**entrometerse** [entrome'terse] /2a/ vr: **~ (en)** to interfere (in o with)

**entumecer** [entume'θer] /2d/ vt to numb, benumb; **entumecerse** vr (por el frío) to go o become numb

**enturbiar** [entur'βjar] /1b/ vt (el agua) to make cloudy; (fig) to confuse; **enturbiarse** vr (oscurecerse) to become cloudy; (fig) to get confused, become obscure

**entusiasmar** [entusjas'mar] /1a/ vt to excite, fill with enthusiasm; (gustar mucho) to delight; **entusiasmarse** vr: **~se con** o **por** to get enthusiastic o excited about

**entusiasmo** [entu'sjasmo] nm enthusiasm; (excitación) excitement

**entusiasta** [entu'sjasta] adj enthusiastic ▷ nmf enthusiast

**enumerar** [enume'rar] /1a/ vt to enumerate

**envainar** [embai'nar] /1a/ vt to sheathe

**envalentonar** [embalento'nar] /1a/ vt to give courage to; **envalentonarse** vr (pey: jactarse) to boast, brag

**envasar** [emba'sar] /1a/ vt (empaquetar) to pack, wrap; (enfrascar) to bottle; (enlatar) to can; (embolsar) to pocket

**envase** [em'base] nm packing, wrapping; bottling; canning; (recipiente) container; (paquete) package; (botella) bottle; (lata) tin (BRIT), can

**envejecer** [embexe'θer] /2d/ vt to make old, age ▷ vi (volverse viejo) to grow old; (parecer viejo) to age

**envenenar** [embene'nar] /1a/ vt to poison; (fig) to embitter

**envergadura** [emberγa'ðura] nf (fig) scope

**enviar** [em'bjar] /1c/ vt to send; **~ un mensaje a algn** (por móvil) to text sb, send sb a text message

**enviciar** [embi'θjar] /1b/ vi (trabajo etc) to be addictive; **enviciarse** vr: **~se (con** o **en)** to get addicted (to)

**envidia** [em'biðja] nf envy; **tener ~ a** to envy, be jealous of; **envidiar** /1b/ vt to envy

**envío** [em'bio] nm (acción) sending; (de mercancías) consignment; (de dinero) remittance

**enviudar** [embju'ðar] /1d/ vi to be widowed

**envoltorio** [embol'torjo] nm package

**envoltura** [embol'tura] nf (cobertura) cover; (embalaje) wrapper, wrapping

**envolver** [embol'βer] /2h/ vt to wrap (up); (cubrir) to cover; (enemigo) to surround; (implicar) to involve, implicate

**envuelto** [em'bwelto] vb V **envolver**

**enyesar** [enje'sar] /1a/ vt (pared) to plaster; (Med) to put in plaster

**enzarzarse** [enθar'θarse] /1f/ vr. **~ en algo** to get mixed up in sth; (disputa) to get involved in sth

**épico, -a** ['epiko, a] adj epic ▷ nf epic (poetry)

**epidemia** [epi'ðemja] nf epidemic

**epilepsia** [epi'lepsja] nf epilepsy

**episodio** [epi'soðjo] nm episode

**época** ['epoka] nf period, time; (Historia) age, epoch; **hacer ~** to be epoch-making

**equilibrar** [ekili'βrar] /1a/ vt to balance; **equilibrio** nm balance, equilibrium; **mantener/perder el equilibrio** to keep/ lose one's balance; **equilibrista** nmf (funámbulo) tightrope walker; (acróbata) acrobat

**equipaje** [eki'paxe] nm (conjunto de cosas) equipment; (Deporte) team; (de obreros) shift; **~ de música** music centre

**equipar** [eki'par] /1a/ vt (proveer) to equip

**equiparar** [ekipa'rar] /1a/ vt (comparar): **~ con** to compare with; **equipararse** vr: **~se con** to be on a level with

**equipo** [e'kipo] nm (conjunto de cosas) equipment; (Deporte) team; (de obreros) shift; **~ de música** music centre

**equis** ['ekis] nf (the letter) X

**equitación** [ekita'θjon] nf (acto) riding

**equivalente** [ekiβa'lente] adj, nm equivalent

**equivaler** [ekiβa'ler] /2p/ vi: **~ a** to be equivalent o equal to

**equivocación** [ekiβoka'θjon] nf mistake, error

**equivocado, -a** [ekiβo'kaðo, a] adj wrong, mistaken

**equivocarse** [ekiβo'karse] /1g/ vr to be wrong, make a mistake; **~ de camino** to take the wrong road

**era** ['era] vb V **ser** ▷ nf era, age

**erais** ['erais], **éramos** ['eramos], **eran** ['eran] vb V **ser**

**eras** ['eras], **eres** ['eres] vb V **ser**

**erección** [erek'θjon] nf erection lift; (poner derecho) to straighten

**erigir** [eri'xir] /3c/ vt to erect, build; **erigirse** vr: **~se en** to set o.s. up as

**erizo** [e'riθo] nm hedgehog; **~ de mar** sea urchin

**ermita** [er'mita] nf hermitage;
  **ermitaño, -a** nm/f hermit
**erosión** [ero'sjon] nf erosion
**erosionar** [erosjo'nar] /1a/ vt to erode
**erótico, -a** [e'rotiko, a] adj erotic;
  **erotismo** nm eroticism
**errante** [e'rrante] adj wandering, errant
**errar** vt: ~ **el camino** to take the wrong
  road; ~ **el tiro** to miss
**erróneo, -a** [e'rroneo, a] adj (equivocado)
  wrong, mistaken
**error** [e'rror] nm error, mistake; (Inform)
  bug; ~ **de imprenta** misprint
**eructar** [eruk'tar] /1a/ vt to belch, burp
**erudito, -a** [eru'ðito, a] adj erudite, learned
**erupción** [erup'θjon] nf eruption; (Med)
  rash
**es** [es] vb V **ser**
**esa** ['esa], **esas** ['esas] adj demostrativo,
  pron V **ese**
**ésa** ['esa], **ésas** pron V **ése**
**esbelto, -a** [es'βelto, a] adj slim, slender
**esbozo** [es'βoθo] nm sketch, outline
**escabeche** [eska'βetʃe] nm brine; (de
  aceitunas etc) pickle; **en** ~ pickled
**escabullirse** [eskaβu'ʎirse] /3a/ vr to slip
  away; (largarse) to clear out
**escafandra** [eska'fandra] nf (buzo) diving
  suit; (escafandra espacial) spacesuit
**escala** [es'kala] nf (proporción, Mus) scale;
  (de mano) ladder; (Aviat) stopover; **hacer** ~
  **en** (gen) to stop off at o call in at; (Aviat) to
  stop over in
**escalafón** [eskala'fon] nm (escala de
  salarios) salary scale, wage scale
**escalar** [eska'lar] /1a/ vt to climb, scale
**escalera** [eska'lera] nf stairs pl, staircase;
  (escala) ladder; (Naipes) run; ~ **mecánica**
  escalator; ~ **de caracol** spiral staircase;
  ~ **de incendios** fire escape
**escalfar** [eskal'far] /1a/ vt (huevos) to
  poach
**escalinata** [eskali'nata] nf staircase
**escalofriante** [eskalo'frjante] adj chilling
**escalofrío** [eskalo'frio] nm (Med) chill;
  **escalofríos** nmpl (fig) shivers
**escalón** [eska'lon] nm step, stair; (de
  escalera) rung
**escalope** [eska'lope] nm (Culin) escalope
**escama** [es'kama] nf (de pez, serpiente)
  scale; (de jabón) flake; (fig) resentment
**escampar** [eskam'par] /1a/ vb impersonal
  to stop raining
**escandalizar** [eskandali'θar] /1f/ vt to
  scandalize, shock; **escandalizarse** vr to be
  shocked; (ofenderse) to be offended
**escándalo** [es'kandalo] nm scandal;
  (alboroto, tumulto) row, uproar;
  **escandaloso, -a** adj scandalous, shocking

**escandinavo, -a** [eskandi'naβo, a] adj,
  nm/f Scandinavian
**escanear** [eskane'ar] /1a/ vt to scan
**escaño** [es'kaɲo] nm bench; (Pol) seat
**escapar** [eska'par] /1a/ vi (gen) to escape,
  run away; (Deporte) to break away;
  **escaparse** vr to escape, get away; (agua,
  gas, noticias) to leak (out)
**escaparate** [eskapa'rate] nm shop
  window; **ir de ~s** to go window shopping
**escape** [es'kape] nm (de agua, gas) leak; (de
  motor) exhaust
**escarabajo** [eskara'βaxo] nm beetle
**escaramuza** [eskara'muθa] nf skirmish
**escarbar** [eskar'βar] /1a/ vt (gallina) to
  scratch
**escarceos** [eskar'θeos] nmpl: **en sus ~
  con la política** in his occasional forays into
  politics; ~ **amorosos** love affairs
**escarcha** [es'kartʃa] nf frost; **escarchado, -a**
  adj (Culin: fruta) crystallized
**escarlatina** [eskarla'tina] nf scarlet
  fever
**escarmentar** [eskarmen'tar] /1j/ vt to
  punish severely ▷ vi to learn one's lesson
**escarmiento** etc [eskar'mjento] vb V
  **escarmentar** ▷ nm (ejemplo) lesson;
  (castigo) punishment
**escarola** [eska'rola] nf endive
**escarpado, -a** [eskar'paðo, a] adj
  (pendiente) sheer, steep; (rocas) craggy
**escasear** [eskase'ar] /1a/ vi to be scarce
**escasez** [eska'seθ] nf (falta) shortage,
  scarcity; (pobreza) poverty
**escaso, -a** [es'kaso, a] adj (poco) scarce;
  (raro) rare; (ralo) thin, sparse; (limitado)
  limited
**escatimar** [eskati'mar] /1a/ vt to skimp
  (on), be sparing with
**escayola** [eska'jola] nf plaster
**escena** [es'θena] nf scene; **escenario**
  nm (Teat) stage; (Cine) set; (fig) scene;
  **escenografía** nf set o stage design
  ▮ No confundir escenario con la palabra
  inglesa scenery.
**escéptico, -a** [es'θeptiko, a] adj sceptical
  ▷ nm/f sceptic
**esclarecer** [esklare'θer] /2d/ vt (misterio,
  problema) to shed light on
**esclavitud** [esklaβi'tuð] nf slavery
**esclavizar** [esklaβi'θar] /1f/ vt to enslave
**esclavo, -a** [es'klaβo, a] nm/f slave
**escoba** [es'koβa] nf broom; **escobilla** nf
  brush
**escocer** [esko'θer] /2b, 2h/ vi to burn, sting;
  **escocerse** vr to chafe, get chafed
**escocés, -esa** [esko'θes, esa] adj Scottish
  ▷ nm/f Scotsman/woman, Scot
**Escocia** [es'koθja] nf Scotland

**escoger** [esko'xer] /2c/ vt to choose, pick, select; **escogido, -a** adj chosen, selected
**escolar** [esko'lar] adj school cpd ▷ nmf schoolboy/girl, pupil
**escollo** [es'koʎo] nm (fig) pitfall
**escolta** [es'kolta] nf escort; **escoltar** /1a/ vt to escort
**escombros** [es'kombros] nmpl (basura) rubbish sg; (restos) debris sg
**esconder** [eskon'der] /2a/ vt to hide, conceal; **esconderse** vr to hide; **escondidas** nfpl: **a escondidas** secretly; **escondite** nm hiding place; (juego) hide-and-seek; **escondrijo** nm hiding place, hideout
**escopeta** [esko'peta] nf shotgun
**escoria** [es'korja] nf (desecho mineral) slag; (fig) scum, dregs pl
**Escorpio** [es'korpjo] nm Scorpio
**escorpión** [eskor'pjon] nm scorpion
**escotado, -a** [esko'taðo, a] adj low-cut
**escote** [es'kote] nm (de vestido) low neck; **pagar a ~** to share the expenses
**escotilla** [esko'tiʎa] nf (Naut) hatchway
**escozor** [esko'θor] nm (dolor) sting(ing)
**escribible** [eskri'βiβle] adj writable
**escribir** [eskri'βir] /3a/ vt, vi to write; **~ a máquina** to type; **¿cómo se escribe?** how do you spell it?
**escrito, -a** [es'krito, a] pp de **escribir** ▷ nm (documento) document; (manuscrito) text, manuscript; **por ~** in writing
**escritor, a** [eskri'tor, a] nm/f writer
**escritorio** [eskri'torjo] nm desk
**escritura** [eskri'tura] nf (acción) writing; (caligrafía) (hand)writing; (Jur: documento) deed
**escrúpulo** [es'krupulo] nm scruple; (minuciosidad) scrupulousness; **escrupuloso, -a** adj scrupulous
**escrutinio** [eskru'tinjo] nm (examen atento) scrutiny; (Pol: recuento de votos) count(ing)
**escuadra** [es'kwaðra] nf (Mil etc) squad; (Naut) squadron; (de coches etc) fleet; **escuadrilla** nf (de aviones) squadron; (LAM: de obreros) gang
**escuadrón** [eskwa'ðron] nm squadron
**escuálido, -a** [es'kwaliðo, a] adj skinny, scraggy; (sucio) squalid
**escuchar** [esku'tʃar] /1a/ vt to listen to ▷ vi to listen
**escudo** [es'kuðo] nm shield
**escuela** [es'kwela] nf school; **~ de artes y oficios** (ESP) ≈ technical college; **~ de choferes** (LAM) driving school; **~ de manejo** (LAM) driving school
**escueto, -a** [es'kweto, a] adj plain; (estilo) simple
**escuincle** [es'kwinkle] nm (LAM fam) kid

**esculpir** [eskul'pir] /3a/ vt to sculpt; (grabar) to engrave; (tallar) to carve; **escultor, a** nm/f sculptor; **escultura** nf sculpture
**escupidera** [eskupi'ðera] nf spittoon
**escupir** [esku'pir] /3a/ vt to spit (out) ▷ vi to spit
**escurreplatos** [eskurre'platos] nm inv plate rack
**escurridero** [eskurri'ðero] nm (LAM) draining board (BRIT), drainboard (US)
**escurridizo, -a** [eskurri'ðiθo, a] adj slippery
**escurridor** [eskurri'ðor] nm colander
**escurrir** [esku'rrir] /3a/ vt (ropa) to wring out; (verduras, platos) to drain ▷ vi (los líquidos) to drip; **escurrirse** vr (secarse) to drain; (resbalarse) to slip, slide; (escaparse) to slip away
**ese** ['ese], **esa** ['esa], **esos** ['esos], **esas** ['esas] adj demostrativo that sg, those pl ▷ pron that (one) sg, those (ones) pl
**ése** ['ese], **ésa** ['esa], **ésos** ['esos], **ésas** ['esas] pron that (one) sg, those (ones) pl; **~ ... éste ...** the former ... the latter ...; **¡no me vengas con ésas!** don't give me any more of that nonsense!
**esencia** [e'senθja] nf essence; **esencial** adj essential
**esfera** [es'fera] nf sphere; (de reloj) face; **esférico, -a** adj spherical
**esforzarse** [esfor'θarse] /1f, 1l/ vr to exert o.s., make an effort
**esfuerzo** [es'fwerθo] vb V **esforzarse** ▷ nm effort
**esfumarse** [esfu'marse] /1a/ vr (apoyo, esperanzas) to fade away
**esgrima** [es'xrima] nf fencing
**esguince** [es'xinθe] nm (Med) sprain
**eslabón** [esla'βon] nm link
**eslip** [ez'lip] nm pants pl (BRIT), briefs pl
**eslovaco, -a** [eslo'βako, a] adj, nm/f Slovak, Slovakian ▷ nm (Ling) Slovak, Slovakian
**Eslovaquia** [eslo'βakja] nf Slovakia
**esmalte** [es'malte] nm enamel; **~ de uñas** nail varnish o polish
**esmeralda** [esme'ralda] nf emerald
**esmerarse** [esme'rarse] /1a/ vr (aplicarse) to take great pains, exercise great care; (afanarse) to work hard
**esmero** [es'mero] nm (great) care
**esnob** [es'nob] adj inv (persona) snobbish ▷ nmf snob
**eso** ['eso] pron that, that thing o matter; **~ de su coche** that business about his car; **~ de ir al cine** all that about going to the cinema; **a ~ de las cinco** at about five o'clock; **en ~** thereupon, at that point;

**~ es** that's it; **¡~ sí que es vida!** now this is really living!; **por ~ te lo dije** that's why I told you; **y ~ que llovía** in spite of the fact it was raining

**esos** ['esos] adj demostrativo V **ese**

**ésos** ['esos] pron V **ése**

**espacial** [espa'θjal] adj (del espacio) space cpd

**espaciar** [espa'θjar] /1b/ vt to space (out)

**espacio** [es'paθjo] nm space; (Mus) interval; (Radio, TV) programme, program (us); **el ~** space; **~ aéreo/exterior** air/outer space; **espacioso, -a** adj spacious, roomy

**espada** [es'paða] nf sword; **espadas** nfpl (Naipes) one of the suits in the Spanish card deck

**espaguetis** [espa'ɣetis] nmpl spaghetti sg

**espalda** [es'palda] nf (gen) back; **~s** nf pl (hombros) shoulders; **a ~s de algn** behind sb's back; **estar de ~s** to have one's back turned; **tenderse de ~s** to lie (down) on one's back; **volver la ~ a algn** to cold-shoulder sb

**espantajo** [espan'taxo] nm, **espantapájaros** [espanta'paxaros] nm inv scarecrow

**espantar** [espan'tar] /1a/ vt (asustar) to frighten, scare; (ahuyentar) to frighten off; (asombrar) to horrify, appal; **espantarse** vr to get frightened o scared; to be appalled

**espanto** [es'panto] nm (susto) fright; (terror) terror; (asombro) astonishment; **espantoso, -a** adj frightening, terrifying; (ruido) dreadful

**España** [es'paɲa] nf Spain; **español, a** adj Spanish ▷ nm/f Spaniard ▷ nm (Ling) Spanish

**esparadrapo** [espara'ðrapo] nm surgical tape

**esparcir** [espar'θir] /3b/ vt to spread; (derramar) to scatter; **esparcirse** vr to spread (out); to scatter; (divertirse) to enjoy o.s.

**espárrago** [es'parraɣo] nm asparagus

**esparto** [es'parto] nm esparto (grass)

**espasmo** [es'pasmo] nm spasm

**espátula** [es'patula] nf spatula

**especia** [es'peθja] nf spice

**especial** [espe'θjal] adj special; **especialidad** nf speciality, specialty (us)

**especie** [es'peθje] nf (Bio) species; (clase) kind, sort; **pagar en ~** to pay in kind

**especificar** [espeθifi'kar] /1g/ vt to specify; **específico, -a** adj specific

**espécimen** [es'peθimen] (pl **especímenes**) nm specimen

**espectáculo** [espek'takulo] nm (gen) spectacle; (Teat etc) show

**espectador, a** [espekta'ðor, a] nm/f spectator

**especular** [espeku'lar] /1a/ vt, vi to speculate

**espejismo** [espe'xismo] nm mirage

**espejo** [es'pexo] nm mirror; **~ retrovisor** rear-view mirror

**espeluznante** [espeluθ'nante] adj horrifying, hair-raising

**espera** [es'pera] nf (pausa, intervalo) wait; (Jur: plazo) respite; **en ~ de** waiting for; (con expectativa) expecting

**esperanza** [espe'ranθa] nf (confianza) hope; (expectativa) expectation; **hay pocas ~s de que venga** there is little prospect of his coming; **~ de vida** life expectancy

**esperar** [espe'rar] /1a/ vt (aguardar) to wait for; (tener expectativa de) to expect; (desear) to hope for ▷ vi to wait; to expect; to hope; **hacer ~ a algn** to keep sb waiting; **~ un bebé** to be expecting (a baby)

**esperma** [es'perma] nf sperm

**espía** [es'pia] nmf spy; **espiar** /1c/ vt (observar) to spy on

**espiga** [es'piɣa] nf (Bot: de trigo etc) ear

**espigón** [espi'ɣon] nm (Bot) ear; (Naut) breakwater

**espina** [es'pina] nf thorn; (de pez) bone; **~ dorsal** (Anat) spine

**espinaca** [espi'naka] nf spinach

**espinazo** [espi'naθo] nm spine, backbone

**espinilla** [espi'niʎa] nf (Anat: tibia) shin(bone); (: en la piel) blackhead

**espinoso, -a** [espi'noso, a] adj (planta) thorny, prickly; (asunto) difficult

**espionaje** [espjo'naxe] nm spying, espionage

**espiral** [espi'ral] adj, nf spiral

**espirar** [espi'rar] /1a/ vt to breathe out, exhale

**espiritista** [espiri'tista] adj, nmf spiritualist

**espíritu** [es'piritu] nm spirit; **E~ Santo** Holy Ghost; **espiritual** adj spiritual

**espléndido, -a** [es'plendiðo, a] adj (magnífico) magnificent, splendid; (generoso) generous

**esplendor** [esplen'dor] nm splendour

**espolvorear** [espolβore'ar] /1a/ vt to dust, sprinkle

**esponja** [es'ponxa] nf sponge; (fig) sponger; **esponjoso, -a** adj spongy

**espontaneidad** [espontanei'ðað] nf spontaneity; **espontáneo, -a** adj spontaneous

**esposa** [es'posa] nf V **esposo**; **esposar** /1a/ vt to handcuff

**esposo, -a** [es'poso, a] nm husband ▷ nf wife; **esposas** nfpl handcuffs

**espray** [es'prai] nm spray

**espuela** [es'pwela] nf spur
**espuma** [es'puma] nf foam; (de cerveza) froth, head; (de jabón) lather; **~ de afeitar** shaving foam; **espumadera** nf skimmer; **espumoso, -a** adj frothy, foamy; (vino) sparkling
**esqueleto** [eske'leto] nm skeleton
**esquema** [es'kema] nm (diagrama) diagram; (dibujo) plan; (Filosofía) schema
**esquí** [es'ki] (pl **esquís**) nm (objeto) ski; (deporte) skiing; **~ acuático** water-skiing; **esquiar** /1c/ vi to ski
**esquilar** [eski'lar] /1a/ vt to shear
**esquina** [es'kina] nf corner; **esquinazo** nm: **dar esquinazo a algn** to give sb the slip
**esquirol** [eski'rol] nm (ESP) strikebreaker, blackleg
**esquivar** [eski'βar] /1a/ vt to avoid
**esta** ['esta] adj demostrativo, pron V **este¹**
**está** [es'ta] vb V **estar**
**ésta** ['esta] pron V **éste**
**estabilidad** [estaβili'ðað] nf stability; **estable** adj stable
**establecer** [estaβle'θer] /2d/ vt to establish; **establecerse** vr to establish o.s.; (echar raíces) to settle (down); **establecimiento** nm establishment
**establo** [es'taβlo] nm (Agr) stall; (para vacas) cowshed; (para caballos) stable; (esp LAM) barn
**estaca** [es'taka] nf stake, post; (de tienda de campaña) peg
**estacada** [esta'kaða] nf (cerca) fence, fencing; (palenque) stockade
**estación** [esta'θjon] nf station; (del año) season; **~ de autobuses/ferrocarril** bus/ railway station; **~ balnearia (de turistas)** seaside resort; **~ de servicio** service station
**estacionamiento** [estaθjona'mjento] nm (Auto) parking; (Mil) stationing
**estacionar** [estaθjo'nar] /1a/ vt (Auto) to park; (Mil) to station
**estada** [es'taða], **estadía** [esta'ðia] nf (LAM) stay
**estadio** [es'taðjo] nm (fase) stage, phase; (Deporte) stadium
**estadista** [esta'ðista] nm (Pol) statesman; (Estadística) statistician
**estadística** [esta'ðistika] nf figure, statistic; (ciencia) statistics sg
**estado** [es'taðo] nm (Pol: condición) state; **~ civil** marital status; **~ de ánimo** state of mind; **~ de cuenta(s)** bank statement; **~ mayor** staff; **E~s Unidos (EE.UU.)** United States (of America) (USA); **estar en ~ (de buena esperanza)** to be pregnant
**estadounidense** [estaðouni'ðense] adj United States cpd, American ▷ nmf American

**estafa** [es'tafa] nf swindle, trick; **estafar** /1a/ vt to swindle, defraud
**estáis** vb V **estar**
**estallar** [esta'ʎar] /1a/ vi to burst; (bomba) to explode, go off; (epidemia, guerra, rebelión) to break out; **~ en llanto** to burst into tears; **estallido** nm explosion; (fig) outbreak
**estampa** [es'tampa] nf print, engraving; **estampado, -a** adj printed ▷ nm (dibujo) print; (impresión) printing; **estampar** /1a/ vt (imprimir) to print; (marcar) to stamp; (metal) to engrave; (poner sello en) to stamp; (fig) to stamp, imprint
**estampida** [estam'piða] nf stampede
**estampido** [estam'piðo] nm bang, report
**estampilla** [estam'piʎa] nf (LAM) (postage) stamp
**están** [es'tan] vb V **estar**
**estancado, -a** [estan'kaðo, a] adj stagnant
**estancar** [estan'kar] /1g/ vt (aguas) to hold up, hold back; (Com) to monopolize; (fig) to block, hold up; **estancarse** vr to stagnate
**estancia** [es'tanθja] nf (permanencia) stay; (sala) room; (LAM) farm, ranch; **estanciero** nm (LAM) farmer, rancher
**estanco, -a** [es'tanko, a] adj watertight ▷ nm tobacconist's (shop)

- **ESTANCO**
-
- Cigarettes, tobacco, postage stamps
- and official forms are all sold under state
- monopoly and usually through a shop
- called an *estanco*. Tobacco products are
- also sold in *quioscos* and bars but are
- generally more expensive. The number of
- *estanco* licences is regulated by the state.

**estándar** [es'tandar] adj, nm standard
**estandarte** [estan'darte] nm banner, standard
**estanque** [es'tanke] nm (lago) pool, pond; (Agr) reservoir
**estanquero, -a** [estan'kero, a] nm/f tobacconist
**estante** [es'tante] nm (armario) rack, stand; (biblioteca) bookcase; (anaquel) shelf; **estantería** nf shelving, shelves pl

🅞 **PALABRA CLAVE**

**estar** [es'tar] /1o/ vi **1** (posición) to be; **está en la plaza** it's in the square; **¿está Juan?** is Juan in?; **estamos a 30 km de Junín** we're 30 km from Junín
**2** (+ adj o adv: estado) to be; **estar enfermo** to be ill; **está muy elegante** he's looking very smart; **¿cómo estás?** how are you keeping?

**3** (+ *gerundio*) to be; **estoy leyendo** I'm reading

**4** (*uso pasivo*): **está condenado a muerte** he's been condemned to death; **está envasado en ...** it's packed in ...

**5**: **estar a**: **¿a cuántos estamos?** what's the date today?; **estamos a 9 de mayo** it's the 9th of May

**6** (*locuciones*): **¿estamos?** (*¿de acuerdo?*) okay?; (*¿listo?*) ready?

**7**: **estar con**: **está con gripe** he's got (the) flu

**8**: **estar de**: **estar de vacaciones/viaje** to be on holiday/away o on a trip; **está de camarero** he's working as a waiter

**9**: **estar para**: **está para salir** he's about to leave; **no estoy para bromas** I'm not in the mood for jokes

**10**: **estar por** (*propuesta etc*) to be in favour of; (*persona etc*) to support, side with; **está por limpiar** it still has to be cleaned

**11**: **estar sin**: **estar sin dinero** to have no money; **está sin terminar** it isn't finished yet

▶ **estarse** *vr*: **se estuvo en la cama toda la tarde** he stayed in bed all afternoon

**estas** ['estas] *adj demostrativo*, *pron* V **este**[1]
**éstas** ['estas] *pron* V **éste**
**estatal** [esta'tal] *adj state cpd*
**estático, -a** [es'tatiko, a] *adj static*
**estatua** [es'tatwa] *nf statue*
**estatura** [esta'tura] *nf stature, height*
**este**[1] ['este] *nm east*
**este**[2] ['este], **esta** ['esta], **estos** ['estos], **estas** ['estas] *adj demostrativo* V **este**[1] this *sg*, these *pl* ▷ *pron* this (one) *sg*, these (ones) *pl*
**esté** [es'te] *vb* V **estar**
**éste** ['este], **ésta** ['esta], **éstos** ['estos], **éstas** ['estas] *pron* this (one) *sg*, these (ones) *pl*; **ése ... ~ ...** the former ... the latter ...
**estén** [es'ten] *vb* V **estar**
**estepa** [es'tepa] *nf* (*Geo*) steppe
**estera** [es'tera] *nf matting*
**estéreo** [es'tereo] *adj inv, nm* stereo; **estereotipo** *nm* stereotype
**estéril** [es'teril] *adj* sterile, barren; (*fig*) vain, futile; **esterilizar** /1f/ *vt* to sterilize
**esterlina** [ester'lina] *adj*: **libra ~** pound sterling
**estés** [es'tes] *vb* V **estar**
**estético, -a** [es'tetiko, a] *adj* aesthetic ▷ *nf* aesthetics *sg*
**estiércol** [es'tjerkol] *nm* dung, manure
**estigma** [es'tiɣma] *nm* stigma
**estilo** [es'tilo] *nm* style; (*Tec*) stylus; (*Natación*) stroke; **algo por el ~** something along those lines

**estima** [es'tima] *nf* esteem, respect
**estimación** [estima'θjon] *nf* (*evaluación*) estimation; (*aprecio, afecto*) esteem, regard
**estimar** [esti'mar] /1a/ *vt* (*evaluar*) to estimate; (*valorar*) to value; (*apreciar*) to esteem, respect; (*pensar, considerar*) to think, reckon
**estimulante** [estimu'lante] *adj* stimulating ▷ *nm* stimulant
**estimular** [estimu'lar] /1a/ *vt* to stimulate; (*excitar*) to excite
**estímulo** [es'timulo] *nm* stimulus; (*ánimo*) encouragement
**estirar** [esti'rar] /1a/ *vt* to stretch; (*dinero, suma etc*) to stretch out; **estirarse** *vr* to stretch
**estirón** [esti'ron] *nm* pull, tug; (*crecimiento*) spurt, sudden growth; **dar un ~** (*niño*) to shoot up
**estirpe** [es'tirpe] *nf* stock, lineage
**estival** [esti'βal] *adj* summer *cpd*
**esto** ['esto] *pron* this, this thing o matter; **~ de la boda** this business about the wedding
**Estocolmo** [esto'kolmo] *nm* Stockholm
**estofado** [esto'faðo] *nm* stew
**estómago** [es'tomaɣo] *nm* stomach; **tener ~ to be** thick-skinned
**estorbar** [estor'βar] /1a/ *vt* to hinder, obstruct; (*fig*) to bother, disturb ▷ *vi* to be in the way; **estorbo** *nm* (*molestia*) bother, nuisance; (*obstáculo*) hindrance, obstacle
**estornudar** [estornu'ðar] /1a/ *vi* to sneeze
**estos** ['estos] *adj demostrativo* V **este**[1]
**éstos** ['estos] *pron* V **éste**
**estoy** [es'toi] *vb* V **estar**
**estrado** [es'traðo] *nm* platform
**estrafalario, -a** [estrafa'larjo, a] *adj* odd, eccentric
**estrago** [es'traɣo] *nm* ruin, destruction; **hacer ~s en** to wreak havoc among
**estragón** [estra'ɣon] *nm* tarragon
**estrambótico, -a** [estram'botiko, a] *adj* odd, eccentric; (*peinado, ropa*) outlandish
**estrangular** [estrangu'lar] /1a/ *vt* (*persona*) to strangle; (*Med*) to strangulate
**estratagema** [estrata'xema] *nf* (*Mil*) stratagem; (*astucia*) cunning
**estrategia** [estra'texja] *nf* strategy; **estratégico, -a** *adj* strategic
**estrato** [es'trato] *nm* stratum, layer
**estrechar** [estre'tʃar] /1a/ *vt* (*reducir*) to narrow; (*vestido*) to take in; (*persona*) to hug, embrace; **estrecharse** *vr* (*reducirse*) to narrow, grow narrow; (*2 personas*) to embrace; **~ la mano** to shake hands
**estrechez** [estre'tʃeθ] *nf* narrowness; (*de ropa*) tightness; **estrecheces** *nfpl* financial difficulties

**estrecho, -a** [es'tretʃo, a] *adj* narrow; (*apretado*) tight; (*íntimo*) close, intimate; (*miserable*) mean ▷ *nm* strait; **~ de miras** narrow-minded

**estrella** [es'treʎa] *nf* star; **~ fugaz** shooting star; **~ de mar** starfish

**estrellar** [estre'ʎar] /1a/ *vt* (*hacer añicos*) to smash (to pieces); (*huevos*) to fry; **estrellarse** *vr* to smash; (*chocarse*) to crash; (*fracasar*) to fail

**estremecer** [estreme'θer] /2d/ *vt* to shake; **estremecerse** *vr* to shake, tremble

**estrenar** [estre'nar] /1a/ *vt* (*vestido*) to wear for the first time; (*casa*) to move into; (*película, obra de teatro*) to première; **estrenarse** *vr* (*persona*) to make one's début; **estreno** *nm* (*Cine etc*) première

**estreñido, -a** [estre'niðo, a] *adj* constipated

**estreñimiento** [estreni'mjento] *nm* constipation

**estrepitoso, -a** [estrepi'toso, a] *adj* noisy; (*fiesta*) rowdy

**estrés** [es'tres] *nm* stress

**estría** [es'tria] *nf* groove

**estribar** [estri'βar] /1a/ *vi*: **~ en** to rest on

**estribillo** [estri'βiʎo] *nm* (*Lit*) refrain; (*Mus*) chorus

**estribo** [es'triβo] *nm* (*de jinete*) stirrup; (*de coche, tren*) step; (*de puente*) support; (*Geo*) spur; **perder los ~s** to fly off the handle

**estribor** [estri'βor] *nm* (*Naut*) starboard

**estricto, -a** [es'trikto, a] *adj* (*riguroso*) strict; (*severo*) severe

**estridente** [estri'ðente] *adj* (*color*) loud; (*voz*) raucous

**estropajo** [estro'paxo] *nm* scourer

**estropear** [estrope'ar] /1a/ *vt* to spoil; (*dañar*) to damage; **estropearse** *vr* (*objeto*) to get damaged; (*la piel etc*) to be ruined

**estructura** [estruk'tura] *nf* structure

**estrujar** [estru'xar] /1a/ *vt* (*apretar*) to squeeze; (*aplastar*) to crush; (*fig*) to drain, bleed

**estuario** [es'twarjo] *nm* estuary

**estuche** [es'tutʃe] *nm* box, case

**estudiante** [estu'ðjante] *nmf* student; **estudiantil** *adj inv* student *cpd*

**estudiar** [estu'ðjar] /1b/ *vt* to study

**estudio** [es'tuðjo] *nm* study; (*Cine, Arte, Radio*) studio; **estudios** *nmpl* studies; (*erudición*) learning *sg*; **estudioso, -a** *adj* studious

**estufa** [es'tufa] *nf* heater, fire

**estupefaciente** [estupefa'θjente] *nm* narcotic

**estupefacto, -a** [estupe'fakto, a] *adj* speechless, thunderstruck

**estupendo, -a** [estu'pendo, a] *adj* wonderful, terrific; (*fam*) great; **¡~!** that's great!, fantastic!

**estupidez** [estupi'ðeθ] *nf* (*torpeza*) stupidity; (*acto*) stupid thing (to do)

**estúpido, -a** [es'tupiðo, a] *adj* stupid, silly

**estuve** *etc* [es'tuβe] *vb* V **estar**

**ETA** ['eta] *nf abr* (*Pol*: = *Euskadi Ta Askatasuna*) ETA

**etapa** [e'tapa] *nf* (*de viaje*) stage; (*Deporte*) leg; (*parada*) stopping place; (*fig*) stage, phase

**etarra** [e'tarra] *nmf* member of ETA

**etc.** *abr* (= *etcétera*) etc

**etcétera** [et'θetera] *adv* etcetera

**eternidad** [eterni'ðað] *nf* eternity; **eterno, -a** *adj* eternal, everlasting; (*despectivo*) never-ending

**ético, -a** ['etiko, a] *adj* ethical ▷ *nf* ethics

**etiqueta** [eti'keta] *nf* (*modales*) etiquette; (*rótulo*) label, tag

**Eucaristía** [eukaris'tia] *nf* Eucharist

**euforia** [eu'forja] *nf* euphoria

**euro** ['euro] *nm* (*moneda*) euro

**eurodiputado, -a** [euroðipu'taðo, a] *nm/f* Euro MP, MEP

**Europa** [eu'ropa] *nf* Europe; **europeo, -a** *adj, nm/f* European

**Euskadi** [eus'kaði] *nm* the Basque Provinces *pl*

**euskera** [eus'kera] *nm* (*Ling*) Basque

**evacuación** [eβakwa'θjon] *nf* evacuation

**evacuar** [eβa'kwar] /1d/ *vt* to evacuate

**evadir** [eβa'ðir] /3a/ *vt* to evade, avoid; **evadirse** *vr* to escape

**evaluar** [eβa'lwar] /1e/ *vt* to evaluate

**evangelio** [eβan'xeljo] *nm* gospel

**evaporar** [eβapo'rar] /1a/ *vt* to evaporate; **evaporarse** *vr* to vanish

**evasión** [eβa'sjon] *nf* escape, flight; (*fig*) evasion; **~ de capitales** flight of capital

**evasivo, -a** [eβa'siβo, a] *adj* evasive ▷ *nf* (*pretexto*) excuse; **contestar con evasivas** to avoid giving a straight answer

**evento** [e'βento] *nm* event

**eventual** [eβen'twal] *adj* possible, conditional (upon circumstances); (*trabajador*) casual, temporary

> No confundir *eventual* con la palabra inglesa *eventual*.

**evidencia** [eβi'ðenθja] *nf* evidence, proof

**evidente** [eβi'ðente] *adj* obvious, clear, evident

**evitar** [eβi'tar] /1a/ *vt* (*evadir*) to avoid; (*impedir*) to prevent; **~ hacer algo** to avoid doing sth

**evocar** [eβo'kar] /1g/ *vt* to evoke, call forth

**evolución** [eβolu'θjon] *nf* (*desarrollo*) evolution, development; (*cambio*) change; (*Mil*) manoeuvre; **evolucionar** /1a/ *vi* to evolve; (*Mil, Aviat*) to manoeuvre

**ex** [eks] *adj* ex-; **el ex ministro** the former minister, the ex-minister

**exactitud** [eksakti'tuð] nf exactness; (precisión) accuracy; (puntualidad) punctuality; **exacto, -a** adj exact; accurate; punctual; **¡exacto!** exactly!

**exageración** [eksaxera'θjon] nf exaggeration

**exagerar** [eksaxe'rar] /1a/ vt to exaggerate

**exaltar** [eksal'tar] /1a/ vt to exalt, glorify; **exaltarse** vr (excitarse) to get excited o worked up

**examen** [ek'samen] nm examination; **~ de conducir** driving test; **~ de ingreso** entrance examination

**examinar** [eksami'nar] /1a/ vt to examine; **examinarse** vr to be examined, take an examination

**excavadora** [ekskaβa'ðora] nf digger

**excavar** [ekska'βar] /1a/ vt to excavate

**excedencia** [eksθe'ðenθja] nf (Mil) leave; **estar en ~** to be on leave; **pedir** o **solicitar la ~** to ask for leave

**excedente** [eksθe'ðente] adj, nm excess, surplus

**exceder** [eksθe'ðer] /2a/ vt to exceed, surpass; **excederse** vr (extralimitarse) to go too far

**excelencia** [eksθe'lenθja] nf excellence; **E~** Excellency; **excelente** adj excellent

**excéntrico, -a** [eks'θentriko, a] adj, nm/f eccentric

**excepción** [eksθep'θjon] nf exception; **a ~ de** with the exception of, except for; **excepcional** adj exceptional

**excepto** [eks'θepto] adv excepting, except (for)

**exceptuar** [eksθep'twar] /1e/ vt to except, exclude

**excesivo, -a** [eksθe'siβo, a] adj excessive

**exceso** [eks'θeso] nm excess; (Com) surplus; **~ de equipaje/peso** excess luggage/weight; **~ de velocidad** speeding

**excitado, -a** [eksθi'taðo, a] adj excited; (emociones) aroused

**excitar** [eksθi'tar] /1a/ vt to excite; (incitar) to urge; **excitarse** vr to get excited

**exclamación** [eksklama'θjon] nf exclamation

**exclamar** [ekskla'mar] /1a/ vi to exclaim

**excluir** [eksklu'ir] /3g/ vt to exclude; (dejar fuera) to shut out; (solución) to reject

**exclusiva** [eksklu'siβa] nf V **exclusivo**

**exclusivo, -a** [eksklu'siβo, a] adj exclusive ▷ nf (Prensa) exclusive, scoop; (Com) sole right o agency; **derecho ~** sole o exclusive right

**Excmo.** abr (= Excelentísimo) courtesy title

**excomulgar** [ekskomul'ɣar] /1h/ vt (Rel) to excommunicate

**excomunión** [ekskomu'njon] nf excommunication

**excursión** [ekskur'sjon] nf excursion, outing; **excursionista** nmf (turista) sightseer

**excusa** [eks'kusa] nf excuse; (disculpa) apology; **excusar** /1a/ vt to excuse

**exhaustivo, -a** [eksaus'tiβo, a] adj (análisis) thorough; (estudio) exhaustive

**exhausto, -a** [ek'sausto, a] adj exhausted

**exhibición** [eksiβi'θjon] nf exhibition; (demostración) display, show

**exhibir** [eksi'βir] /3a/ vt to exhibit; to display, show

**exigencia** [eksi'xenθja] nf demand, requirement; **exigente** adj demanding

**exigir** [eksi'xir] /3c/ vt (gen) to demand, require; **~ el pago** to demand payment

**exiliado, -a** [eksi'ljaðo, a] adj exiled ▷ nm/f exile

**exilio** [ek'siljo] nm exile

**eximir** [eksi'mir] /3a/ vt to exempt

**existencia** [eksis'tenθja] nf existence; **existencias** nfpl stock sg

**existir** [eksis'tir] /3a/ vi to exist, be

**éxito** ['eksito] nm (triunfo) success; (Mus, Teat) hit; **tener ~** to be successful

> No confundir éxito con la palabra inglesa exit.

**exorbitante** [eksorβi'tante] adj (precio) exorbitant; (cantidad) excessive

**exótico, -a** [ek'sotiko, a] adj exotic

**expandir** [ekspan'dir] /3a/ vt to expand

**expansión** [ekspan'sjon] nf expansion

**expansivo, -a** [ekspan'siβo, a] adj: **onda expansiva** shock wave

**expatriarse** [ekspa'trjarse] /1b/ vr to emigrate; (Pol) to go into exile

**expectativa** [ekspekta'tiβa] nf (espera) expectation; (perspectiva) prospect

**expedición** [ekspeði'θjon] nf (excursión) expedition

**expediente** [ekspe'ðjente] nm expedient; (Jur: procedimiento) action, proceedings pl; (: papeles) dossier, file, record

**expedir** [ekspe'ðir] /3k/ vt (despachar) to send, forward; (pasaporte) to issue

**expensas** [eks'pensas] nfpl: **a ~ de** at the expense of

**experiencia** [ekspe'rjenθja] nf experience

**experimentado, -a** [eksperimen'taðo, a] adj experienced

**experimentar** [eksperimen'tar] /1a/ vt (en laboratorio) to experiment with; (probar) to test, try out; (notar, observar) to experience; (deterioro, pérdida) to suffer; **experimento** nm experiment

**experto, -a** [eks'perto, a] adj expert ▷ nm/f expert

**expirar** [ekspi'rar] /1a/ vi to expire

**explanada** [ekspla'naða] nf (paseo) esplanade

**explayarse** [ekspla'jarse] /1a/ vr (en discurso) to speak at length; ~ **con algn** to confide in sb

**explicación** [eksplika'θjon] nf explanation

**explicar** [ekspli'kar] /1g/ vt to explain; **explicarse** vr to explain (o.s.)

**explícito, -a** [eks'pliθito, a] adj explicit

**explique** etc [eks'plike] vb V **explicar**

**explorador, a** [eksplora'ðor, a] nm/f (pionero) explorer; (Mil) scout ▷ nm (Med) probe; (radar) scanner

**explorar** [eksplo'rar] /1a/ vt to explore; (Med) to probe; (radar) to scan

**explosión** [eksplo'sjon] nf explosion; **explosivo, -a** adj explosive

**explotación** [eksplota'θjon] nf exploitation; (de planta etc) running

**explotar** [eksplo'tar] /1a/ vt to exploit; (planta) to run, operate ▷ vi to explode

**exponer** [ekspo'ner] /2q/ vt to expose; (cuadro) to display; (vida) to risk; (idea) to explain; **exponerse** vr: ~se a (hacer) algo to run the risk of (doing) sth

**exportación** [eksporta'θjon] nf (acción) export; (mercancías) exports pl

**exportar** [ekspor'tar] /1a/ vt to export

**exposición** [eksposi'θjon] nf (gen) exposure; (de arte) show, exhibition; (explicación) explanation; (narración) account, statement

**expresamente** [ekspresa'mente] adv (decir) clearly; (concretamente) expressly

**expresar** [ekspre'sar] /1a/ vt to express; **expresión** nf expression

**expresivo, -a** [ekspre'siβo, a] adj expressive; (cariñoso) affectionate

**expreso, -a** [eks'preso, a] adj (explícito) express; (claro) specific, clear; (tren) fast

**express** [eks'pres] adv (LAM): **enviar algo ~** to send sth special delivery

**exprimidor** [eksprimi'ðor] nm (lemon) squeezer

**exprimir** [ekspri'mir] /3a/ vt (fruta) to squeeze; (zumo) to squeeze out

**expuesto, -a** [eks'pwesto, a] pp de **exponer** ▷ adj exposed; (cuadro etc) on show, on display

**expulsar** [ekspul'sar] /1a/ vt (echar) to eject, throw out; (alumno) to expel; (despedir) to sack, fire; (Deporte) to send off; **expulsión** nf expulsion; sending-off

**exquisito, -a** [ekski'sito, a] adj exquisite; (comida) delicious

**éxtasis** ['ekstasis] nm ecstasy

**extender** [eksten'der] /2g/ vt to extend; (los brazos) to stretch out, hold out; (mapa, tela) to spread (out), open (out); (mantequilla) to spread; (certificado) to issue; (cheque, recibo) to make out; (documento) to draw up; **extenderse** vr to extend; (persona: en el suelo) to stretch out; (costumbre, epidemia) to spread; **extendido, -a** adj (abierto) spread out, open; (brazos) outstretched; (costumbre etc) widespread

**extensión** [eksten'sjon] nf (de terreno, mar) expanse, stretch; (de tiempo) length, duration; (Telec) extension; **en toda la ~ de la palabra** in every sense of the word

**extenso, -a** [eks'tenso, a] adj extensive

**exterior** [ekste'rjor] adj (de fuera) external; (afuera) outside, exterior; (apariencia) outward; (deuda, relaciones) foreign ▷ nm exterior, outside; (aspecto) outward appearance; (Deporte) wing(er); (países extranjeros) abroad; **al ~** outwardly, on the outside

**exterminar** [makestermi'nar] /1a/ vt to exterminate

**externo, -a** [eks'terno, a] adj (exterior) external, outside; (superficial) outward ▷ nm/f day pupil

**extinguir** [ekstin'gir] /3d/ vt (fuego) to extinguish, put out; (raza, población) to wipe out; **extinguirse** vr (fuego) to go out; (Bio) to die out, become extinct

**extintor** [ekstin'tor] nm (fire) extinguisher

**extirpar** [ekstir'par] /1a/ vt (Med) to remove (surgically)

**extra** ['ekstra] adj inv (tiempo) extra; (vino) vintage; (chocolate) good-quality ▷ nmf extra ▷ nm extra; (bono) bonus

**extracción** [ekstrak'θjon] nf extraction; (en lotería) draw

**extracto** [eks'trakto] nm extract

**extradición** [ekstraði'θjon] nf extradition

**extraer** [ekstra'er] /2o/ vt to extract, take out

**extraescolar** [ekstraesko'lar] adj: **actividad ~** extracurricular activity

**extranjero, -a** [ekstran'xero, a] adj foreign ▷ nm/f foreigner ▷ nm foreign countries pl; **en el ~** abroad

No confundir extranjero con la palabra inglesa stranger.

**extrañar** [ekstra'ɲar] /1a/ vt (sorprender) to find strange o odd; (echar de menos) to miss; **extrañarse** vr (sorprenderse) to be amazed, be surprised; **me extraña** I'm surprised

**extraño, -a** [eks'traɲo, a] adj (extranjero) foreign; (raro, sorprendente) strange, odd

**extraordinario, -a** [ekstraorði'narjo, a] adj extraordinary; (edición, número) special ▷ nm (de periódico) special edition; **horas extraordinarias** overtime sg

**extrarradio** [ekstra'rraðjo] nm suburbs pl

**extravagante** [ekstraβa'ɣante] *adj* (*excéntrico*) eccentric; (*estrafalario*) outlandish

**extraviado, -a** [ekstra'βjaðo, a] *adj* lost, missing

**extraviar** [ekstra'βjar] /1c/ *vt* to mislead, misdirect; (*perder*) to lose, misplace; **extraviarse** *vr* to lose one's way, get lost

**extremar** [ekstre'mar] /1a/ *vt* to carry to extremes

**extremaunción** [ekstremaun'θjon] *nf* extreme unction

**extremidad** [ekstremi'ðað] *nf* (*punta*) extremity; **extremidades** *nfpl* (*Anat*) extremities

**extremo, -a** [eks'tremo, a] *adj* extreme; (*último*) last ▷ *nm* end; (*situación*) extreme; **en último ~** as a last resort

**extrovertido, -a** [ekstroβer'tiðo, a] *adj* ▷ *nm/f* extrovert

**exuberante** [eksuβe'rante] *adj* exuberant; (*fig*) luxuriant, lush

**eyacular** [ejaku'lar] /1a/ *vt, vi* to ejaculate

**fa** [fa] *nm* (*Mus*) F

**fabada** [fa'βaða] *nf* bean and sausage stew

**fábrica** ['faβrika] *nf* factory; **marca de ~** trademark; **precio de ~** factory price

  No confundir *fábrica* con la palabra inglesa *fabric*.

**fabricación** [faβrika'θjon] *nf* (*manufactura*) manufacture; (*producción*) production; **de ~ casera** home-made; **~ en serie** mass production

**fabricante** [faβri'kante] *nmf* manufacturer

**fabricar** [faβri'kar] /1g/ *vt* (*manufacturar*) to manufacture, make; (*construir*) to build; (*cuento*) to fabricate, devise

**fábula** ['faβula] *nf* (*cuento*) fable; (*chisme*) rumour; (*mentira*) fib

**fabuloso, -a** [faβu'loso, a] *adj* fabulous, fantastic

**facción** [fak'θjon] *nf* (*Pol*) faction; **facciones** *nfpl* (*del rostro*) features

**faceta** [fa'θeta] *nf* facet

**facha** ['fatʃa] (*fam*) *nf* (*aspecto*) look; (*cara*) face

**fachada** [fa'tʃaða] *nf* (*Arq*) façade, front

**fácil** ['faθil] *adj* (*simple*) easy; (*probable*) likely

**facilidad** [faθili'ðað] *nf* (*capacidad*) ease; (*sencillez*) simplicity; (*de palabra*) fluency; **facilidades** *nfpl* facilities; **"~es de pago"** "credit facilities"

**facilitar** [faθili'tar] /1a/ *vt* (*hacer fácil*) to make easy; (*proporcionar*) to provide

**factor** [fak'tor] *nm* factor

**factura** [fak'tura] *nf* (*cuenta*) bill; **facturación** *nf*: **facturación de equipajes** luggage check-in; **facturar** /1a/ *vt* (*Com*) to invoice, charge for; (*Aviat*) to check in

**facultad** [fakul'tað] *nf* (*aptitud, Escol etc*) faculty; (*poder*) power

**faena** [fa'ena] nf (trabajo) work; (quehacer) task, job

**faisán** [fai'san] nm pheasant

**faja** ['faxa] nf (para la cintura) sash; (de mujer) corset; (de tierra) strip

**fajo** ['faxo] nm (de papeles) bundle; (de billetes) wad

**falda** ['falda] nf (prenda de vestir) skirt; **~ pantalón** culottes pl, split skirt

**falla** ['faʎa] nf (defecto) fault, flaw; **~ humana** (LAM) human error

**fallar** [fa'ʎar] /1a/ vt (Jur) to pronounce sentence on; (Naipes) to trump ▷ vi (memoria) to fail; (plan) to go wrong; (motor) to miss; **~ a algn** to let sb down

**Fallas** ['faʎas] nfpl see note

● **FALLAS**

● In the week of the 19th of March (the feast
● of St Joseph, San José), Valencia honours
● its patron saint with a spectacular fiesta
● called las Fallas. The Fallas are huge
● sculptures, made of wood, cardboard,
● paper and cloth, depicting famous
● politicians and other targets for ridicule,
● which are set alight and burned by the
● falleros, members of the competing local
● groups who have just spent months
● preparing them.

**fallecer** [faʎe'θer] /2d/ vi to pass away, die; **fallecimiento** nm decease, demise

**fallido, -a** [fa'ʎiðo, a] adj frustrated, unsuccessful

**fallo** ['faʎo] nm (Jur) verdict, ruling; (fracaso) failure; **~ cardíaco** heart failure; **~ humano** (ESP) human error

**falsificar** [falsifi'kar] /1g/ vt (firma etc) to forge; (moneda) to counterfeit

**falso, -a** ['falso, a] adj false; (moneda etc) fake; **en ~** falsely

**falta** ['falta] nf (defecto) fault, flaw; (privación) lack, want; (ausencia) absence; (carencia) shortage; (equivocación) mistake; (Deporte) foul; **echar en ~** to miss; **hacer ~ algo** to be necessary to do sth; **me hace ~ una pluma** I need a pen; **~ de educación** bad manners pl; **~ de ortografía** spelling mistake

**faltar** [fal'tar] /1a/ vi (escasear) to be lacking, be wanting; (ausentarse) to be absent, be missing; **faltan dos horas para llegar** there are two hours to go till arrival; **~ (al respeto) a algn** to be disrespectful to sb; **¡no faltaba más!** (no hay de qué) don't mention it!

**fama** ['fama] nf (renombre) fame; (reputación) reputation

**familia** [fa'milja] nf family; **~ numerosa** large family; **~ política** in-laws pl

**familiar** [fami'ljar] adj (relativo a la familia) family cpd; (conocido, informal) familiar ▷ nmf relative, relation

**famoso, -a** [fa'moso, a] adj famous ▷ nm/f celebrity

**fan** [fan] (pl fans) nm fan

**fanático, -a** [fa'natiko, a] adj fanatical ▷ nm/f fanatic; (Cine, Deporte etc) fan

**fanfarrón, -ona** [fanfa'rron, ona] adj boastful

**fango** ['fango] nm mud

**fantasía** [fanta'sia] nf fantasy, imagination; **joyas de ~** imitation jewellery sg

**fantasma** [fan'tasma] nm (espectro) ghost, apparition; (presumido) show-off

**fantástico, -a** [fan'tastiko, a] adj fantastic

**farmacéutico, -a** [farma'θeutiko, a] adj pharmaceutical ▷ nm/f chemist (BRIT), pharmacist

**farmacia** [far'maθja] nf chemist's (shop) (BRIT), pharmacy; **~ de guardia** all-night chemist

**fármaco** ['farmako] nm drug

**faro** ['faro] nm (Naut: torre) lighthouse; (Auto) headlamp; **~s antiniebla** fog lamps; **~s delanteros/traseros** headlights/rear lights

**farol** [fa'rol] nm lantern, lamp

**farola** [fa'rola] nf street lamp (BRIT) o light (US)

**farra** ['farra] nf (LAM fam) party; **ir de ~** to go on a binge

**farsa** ['farsa] nf farce

**farsante** [far'sante] nmf fraud, fake

**fascículo** [fas'θikulo] nm part, instalment (BRIT), installment (US)

**fascinar** [fasθi'nar] /1a/ vt to fascinate

**fascismo** [fas'θismo] nm fascism; **fascista** adj, nmf fascist

**fase** ['fase] nf phase

**fashion** ['faʃon] adj (fam) trendy

**fastidiar** [fasti'ðjar] /1b/ vt (disgustar) to annoy, bother; (estropear) to spoil; **fastidiarse** vr: **¡que se fastidie!** (fam) he'll just have to put up with it!

**fastidio** [fas'tiðjo] nm (disgusto) annoyance; **fastidioso, -a** adj (molesto) annoying

**fatal** [fa'tal] adj (gen) fatal; (desgraciado) ill-fated; (fam: malo, pésimo) awful; **fatalidad** nf (destino) fate; (mala suerte) misfortune

**fatiga** [fa'tiɣa] nf (cansancio) fatigue, weariness

**fatigar** [fati'ɣar] /1h/ vt to tire, weary

**fatigoso, -a** [fati'ɣoso, a] adj (que cansa) tiring

**fauna** ['fauna] *nf* fauna
**favor** [fa'βor] *nm* favour (BRIT), favor (US);
**haga el ~ de ...** would you be so good as
to ..., kindly ...; **por ~** please; **a ~ de** in
favo(u)r of; **favorable** *adj* favourable (BRIT),
favorable (US)
**favorecer** [faβore'θer] /2d/ *vt* to favour
(BRIT), favor (US); (*vestido etc*) to become,
flatter; **este peinado le favorece** this
hairstyle suits him
**favorito, -a** [faβo'rito, a] *adj, nm/f*
favourite (BRIT), favorite (US)
**fax** [faks] *nm inv* fax; **mandar por ~** to fax
**fe** [fe] *nf* (*Rel*) faith; (*documento*) certificate;
**actuar con buena/mala fe** to act in good/
bad faith
**febrero** [fe'βrero] *nm* February
**fecha** ['fetʃa] *nf* date; **~ límite** o **tope** closing
o last date; **~ de caducidad** (*de alimentos*)
sell-by date; (*de contrato*) expiry date; **con
~ adelantada** postdated; **en ~ próxima**
soon; **hasta la ~** to date, so far
**fecundo, -a** [fe'kundo, a] *adj* (*fértil*) fertile;
(*fig*) prolific; (*productivo*) productive
**federación** [feðera'θjon] *nf* federation
**felicidad** [feliθi'ðað] *nf* happiness;
**felicidades** *nfpl* best wishes,
congratulations; (*en cumpleaños*) happy
birthday
**felicitación** [feliθita'θjon] *nf* (*tarjeta*)
greetings card
**felicitar** [feliθi'tar] /1a/ *vt* to congratulate
**feliz** [fe'liθ] *adj* happy
**felpudo** [fel'puðo] *nm* doormat
**femenino, -a** [feme'nino, a] *adj* ▷ *nm*
feminine
**feminista** [femi'nista] *adj, nmf* feminist
**fenomenal** [fenome'nal] *adj* phenomenal
**fenómeno** [fe'nomeno] *nm* phenomenon;
(*fig*) freak, accident ▷ *excl* great!,
marvellous!
**feo, -a** ['feo, a] *adj* (*gen*) ugly; (*desagradable*)
bad, nasty
**féretro** ['feretro] *nm* (*ataúd*) coffin;
(*sarcófago*) bier
**feria** ['ferja] *nf* (*gen*) fair; (*descanso*) holiday,
rest day; (LAM: *cambio*) small change; (LAM:
*mercado*) village market
**feriado, -a** [fe'rjaðo, a] (LAM) *nm* (public)
holiday
**fermentar** [fermen'tar] /1a/ *vi* to
ferment
**feroz** [fe'roθ] *adj* (*cruel*) cruel; (*salvaje*)
fierce
**férreo, -a** ['ferreo, a] *adj* iron *cpd*
**ferretería** [ferrete'ria] *nf* (*tienda*)
ironmonger's (shop) (BRIT), hardware store;
**ferretero** *nm* ironmonger
**ferrocarril** [ferroka'rril] *nm* railway

**ferroviario, -a** [ferrovja'rjo, a] *adj* rail *cpd*
**ferry** ['ferri] (*pl* **ferrys** o **ferries**) *nm* ferry
**fértil** ['fertil] *adj* (*productivo*) fertile;
(*rico*) rich; **fertilidad** *nf* (*gen*) fertility;
(*productividad*) fruitfulness
**fervor** [fer'βor] *nm* fervour (BRIT), fervor
(US)
**festejar** [feste'xar] /1a/ *vt* (*celebrar*) to
celebrate
**festejo** [fes'texo] *nm* celebration; **festejos**
*nmpl* (*fiestas*) festivals
**festín** [fes'tin] *nm* feast, banquet
**festival** [festi'βal] *nm* festival
**festividad** [festiβi'ðað] *nf* festivity
**festivo, -a** [fes'tiβo, a] *adj* (*de fiesta*) festive;
(*Cine, Lit*) humorous; **día ~** holiday
**feto** ['feto] *nm* foetus
**fiable** [fi'aβle] *adj* (*persona*) trustworthy;
(*máquina*) reliable
**fiambre** ['fjambre] *nm* (*Culin*) cold meat
(BRIT), cold cut (US)
**fiambrera** [fjam'brera] *nf* ≈ lunch box
**fianza** [fjanθa] *nf* surety; (*Jur*): **libertad
bajo ~** release on bail
**fiar** [fi'ar] /1c/ *vt* (*salir garante de*) to
guarantee; (*vender a crédito*) to sell on credit;
(*secreto*) to confide ▷ *vi*: **~ (de)** to trust (in);
**fiarse** *vr*: **~se de** to trust (in), rely on; **~se de
algn** to rely on sb
**fibra** ['fiβra] *nf* fibre (BRIT), fiber (US);
**~ óptica** (*Inform*) optical fibre (BRIT) o fiber
(US)
**ficción** [fik'θjon] *nf* fiction
**ficha** ['fitʃa] *nf* (*Telec*) token; (*en juegos*)
counter, marker; (*tarjeta*) (index) card;
**fichaje** *nm* signing(-up); **fichar** /1a/ *vt*
(*archivar*) to file, index; (*Deporte*) to sign (up);
**estar fichado** to have a record; **fichero** *nm*
box file; (*Inform*) file
**ficticio, -a** [fik'tiθjo, a] *adj* (*imaginario*)
fictitious; (*falso*) fabricated
**fidelidad** [fiðeli'ðað] *nf* (*lealtad*) fidelity,
loyalty; **alta ~** high fidelity, hi-fi
**fideos** [fi'ðeos] *nmpl* noodles
**fiebre** ['fjeβre] *nf* (*Med*) fever; (*fig*) fever,
excitement; **tener ~** to have a temperature;
**~ aftosa** foot-and-mouth disease
**fiel** [fjel] *adj* (*leal*) faithful, loyal; (*fiable*)
reliable; (*exacto*) accurate; **los fieles** *nmpl*
the faithful
**fieltro** ['fjeltro] *nm* felt
**fiera** ['fjera] *nf* V **fiero**
**fiero, -a** ['fjero, a] *adj* (*cruel*) cruel; (*feroz*)
fierce; (*duro*) harsh ▷ *nf* (*animal feroz*) wild
animal o beast; (*fig*) dragon
**fierro** ['fjerro] *nm* (LAM) iron
**fiesta** ['fjesta] *nf* party; (*de pueblo*) festival;
(**día de) ~** (public) holiday; **~ mayor** annual
festival; **~ patria** (LAM) independence day

**figura** [fi'ɣura] *nf* (*gen*) figure; (*forma, imagen*) shape, form; (*Naipes*) face card

**figurar** [fiɣu'rar] /1a/ *vt* (*representar*) to represent; (*fingir*) to feign ▷ *vi* to figure; **figurarse** *vr* (*imaginarse*) to imagine; (*suponer*) to suppose

**fijador** [fixa'ðor] *nm* (*Foto etc*) fixative; (*de pelo*) gel

**fijar** [fi'xar] /1a/ *vt* (*gen*) to fix; (*estampilla*) to affix, stick (on); **fijarse** *vr*: ~**se en** to notice

**fijo, -a** ['fixo, a] *adj* (*gen*) fixed; (*firme*) firm; (*permanente*) permanent ▷ *adv*: **mirar ~** to stare; **teléfono ~** landline

**fila** ['fila] *nf* row; (*Mil*) rank; ~ **india** single file; **ponerse en ~** to line up, get into line

**filatelia** [fila'telja] *nf* philately, stamp collecting

**filete** [fi'lete] *nm* (*de carne*) fillet steak; (*pescado*) fillet

**filiación** [filja'θjon] *nf* (*Pol etc*) affiliation

**filial** [fi'ljal] *adj* filial ▷ *nf* subsidiary

**Filipinas** [fili'pinas] *nfpl*: **las (Islas) ~** the Philippines; **filipino, -a** *adj, nm/f* Philippine

**filmar** [fil'mar] /1a/ *vt* to film, shoot

**filo** ['filo] *nm* (*gen*) edge; **sacar ~ a** to sharpen; **al ~ del medio día** at about midday; **de doble ~** double-edged

**filología** [filolo'xia] *nf* philology; ~ **inglesa** (*Univ*) English Studies

**filón** [fi'lon] *nm* (*Minería*) vein, lode; (*fig*) gold mine

**filosofía** [filoso'fia] *nf* philosophy; **filósofo, -a** *nm/f* philosopher

**filtrar** [fil'trar] /1a/ *vt, vi* to filter, strain; **filtrarse** *vr* to filter; **filtro** *nm* (*Tec, utensilio*) filter

**fin** [fin] *nm* end; (*objetivo*) aim, purpose; **al ~ y al cabo** when all's said and done; **a ~ de** in order to; **por ~** finally; **en ~** in short; ~ **de semana** weekend

**final** [fi'nal] *adj* final ▷ *nm* end, conclusion ▷ *nf* final; **al ~** in the end; **a ~es de** at the end of; **finalidad** *nf* (*propósito*) purpose,

aim; **finalista** *nmf* finalist; **finalizar** /1f/ *vt* to end, finish ▷ *vi* to end, come to an end; (*Inform*) to log out o off

**financiar** [finan'θjar] /1b/ *vt* to finance; **financiero, -a** *adj* financial ▷ *nm/f* financier

**finca** ['finka] *nf* (*casa de recreo*) house in the country; (*ESP: bien inmueble*) property, land; (*LAM: granja*) farm

**finde** ['finde] *nm abr* (*fam*: = *fin de semana*) weekend

**fingir** [fin'xir] /3c/ *vt* (*simular*) to simulate, feign ▷ *vi* (*aparentar*) to pretend

**finlandés, -esa** [finlan'des, esa] *adj* Finnish ▷ *nm/f* Finn ▷ *nm* (*Ling*) Finnish

**Finlandia** [fin'landja] *nf* Finland

**fino, -a** ['fino, a] *adj* fine; (*delgado*) slender; (*de buenas maneras*) polite, refined; (*jerez*) fino, dry

**firma** ['firma] *nf* signature; (*Com*) firm, company

**firmamento** [firma'mento] *nm* firmament

**firmar** [fir'mar] /1a/ *vt* to sign

**firme** ['firme] *adj* firm; (*estable*) stable; (*sólido*) solid; (*constante*) steady; (*decidido*) resolute ▷ *nm* road (surface); **firmeza** *nf* firmness; (*constancia*) steadiness; (*solidez*) solidity

**fiscal** [fis'kal] *adj* fiscal ▷ *nm* (*Jur*) public prosecutor; **año ~** tax o fiscal year

**fisgonear** [fisɣone'ar] /1a/ *vt* to poke one's nose into ▷ *vi* to pry, spy

**físico, -a** ['fisiko, a] *adj* physical ▷ *nm* physique ▷ *nm/f* physicist ▷ *nf* physics *sg*

**fisura** [fi'sura] *nf* crack; (*Med*) fracture

**flác(c)ido, -a** ['flakθiðo, a] *adj* flabby

**flaco, -a** ['flako, a] *adj* (*muy delgado*) skinny, thin; (*débil*) weak, feeble

**flagrante** [fla'ɣrante] *adj* flagrant

**flama** ['flama] *nf* (*LAM*) flame; **flamable** *adj* (*LAM*) flammable

**flamante** [fla'mante] *adj* (*fam*) brilliant; (: *nuevo*) brand-new

**flamenco, -a** [fla'menko, a] *adj* (*de Flandes*) Flemish; (*baile, música*) flamenco ▷ *nm* (*baile, música*) flamenco; (*Zool*) flamingo

**flamingo** [fla'mingo] *nm* (*LAM*) flamingo

**flan** [flan] *nm* creme caramel

🔖 No confundir *flan* con la palabra inglesa *flan*.

**flash** [flaʃ o flas] (*pl* **flashes**) *nm* (*Foto*) flash

**flauta** ['flauta] *nf* (*Mus*) flute

**flecha** ['fletʃa] *nf* arrow

**flechazo** [fle'tʃaθo] *nm*: **fue un ~** it was love at first sight

**fleco** ['fleko] *nm* fringe

**flema** ['flema] *nm* phlegm

**flequillo** [fle'kiʎo] *nm* (*de pelo*) fringe

**flexible** [flek'siβle] *adj* flexible

**flexión** [flek'sjon] *nf* press-up
**flexo** ['flekso] *nm* adjustable table lamp
**flirtear** [flirte'ar] /1a/ *vi* to flirt
**flojera** [flo'xera] *nf (LAM)*: **me da ~** I can't be bothered
**flojo, -a** ['floxo, a] *adj (gen)* loose; *(sin fuerzas)* limp; *(débil)* weak
**flor** [flor] *nf* flower; **a ~ de** on the surface of; **flora** *nf* flora; **florecer** /2d/ *vi (Bot)* to flower, bloom; *(fig)* to flourish; **florería** *nf (LAM)* florist's (shop); **florero** *nm* vase; **floristería** *nf* florist's (shop)
**flota** ['flota] *nf* fleet
**flotador** [flota'ðor] *nm (gen)* float; *(para nadar)* rubber ring
**flotar** [flo'tar] /1a/ *vi* to float; **flote** *nm*: **a flote** afloat; **salir a flote** *(fig)* to get back on one's feet
**fluidez** [flui'ðeθ] *nf* fluidity; *(fig)* fluency
**fluido, -a** ['flwiðo, a] *adj* ▷ *nm* fluid
**fluir** [flu'ir] /3g/ *vi* to flow
**flujo** ['fluxo] *nm* flow; **~ y re~** ebb and flow
**flúor** ['fluor] *nm* fluoride
**fluorescente** [flwores'θente] *adj* fluorescent ▷ *nm (tb: **tubo ~**)* fluorescent tube
**fluvial** [fluβi'al] *adj (navegación, cuenca)* fluvial, river *cpd*
**fobia** ['fobja] *nf* phobia; **~ a las alturas** fear of heights
**foca** ['foka] *nf* seal
**foco** ['foko] *nm* focus; *(Elec)* floodlight; *(Teat)* spotlight; *(LAM)* (light) bulb
**fofo, -a** ['fofo, a] *adj (gen)* soft, spongy; *(músculo)* flabby
**fogata** [fo'ɣata] *nf* bonfire
**fogón** [fo'ɣon] *nm (de cocina)* ring, burner
**folio** [fo'ljo] *nm (hoja)* sheet (of paper), page
**follaje** [fo'ʎaxe] *nm* foliage
**folleto** [fo'ʎeto] *nm* pamphlet
**follón** [fo'ʎon] *nm (fam: lío)* mess; *(: conmoción)* fuss; **armar un ~** to kick up a fuss
**fomentar** [fomen'tar] /1a/ *vt (Med)* to foment
**fonda** ['fonda] *nf* ≈ boarding house
**fondo** ['fondo] *nm (de caja etc)* bottom; *(de coche, sala)* back; *(Arte etc)* background; *(reserva)* fund; **fondos** *nmpl (Com)* funds, resources; **una investigación a ~** a thorough investigation; **en el ~** at bottom, deep down
**fonobuzón** [fonoβu'θon] *nm* voice mail
**fontanería** [fontane'ria] *nf* plumbing; **fontanero** *nm* plumber
**footing** ['futin] *nm* jogging; **hacer ~** to jog
**forastero, -a** [foras'tero, a] *nm/f* stranger
**forcejear** [forθexe'ar] /1a/ *vi (luchar)* to struggle

**forense** [fo'rense] *nmf* pathologist
**forma** ['forma] *nf (figura)* form, shape; *(Med)* fitness; *(método)* way, means; **estar en ~** to be fit; **las ~s** the conventions; **de ~ que ...** so that ...; **de todas ~s** in any case
**formación** [forma'θjon] *nf (gen)* formation; *(enseñanza)* training; **~ profesional** vocational training
**formal** [for'mal] *adj (gen)* formal; *(fig: persona)* serious; *(: de fiar)* reliable; **formalidad** *nf* formality; seriousness; **formalizar** /1f/ *vt (Jur)* to formalize; *(situación)* to put in order, regularize; **formalizarse** *vr (situación)* to be put in order, be regularized
**formar** [for'mar] /1a/ *vt (componer)* to form, shape; *(constituir)* to make up, constitute; *(Escol)* to train, educate; **formarse** *vr (Escol)* to be trained *(o educated)*; *(cobrar forma)* to form, take form; *(desarrollarse)* to develop
**formatear** [formate'ar] /1a/ *vt* to format
**formato** [for'mato] *nm* format; **sin ~**
**formidable** [formi'ðaβle] *adj (temible)* formidable; *(asombroso)* tremendous
**fórmula** ['formula] *nf* formula
**formulario** [formu'larjo] *nm* form
**fornido, -a** [for'niðo, a] *adj* well-built
**foro** ['foro] *nm* forum
**forrar** [fo'rrar] /1a/ *vt (abrigo)* to line; *(libro)* to cover; **forro** *nm (de cuaderno)* cover; *(costura)* lining; *(de sillón)* upholstery; **forro polar** fleece
**fortalecer** [fortale'θer] /2d/ *vt* to strengthen
**fortaleza** [forta'leθa] *nf (Mil)* fortress, stronghold; *(fuerza)* strength; *(determinación)* resolution
**fortuito, -a** [for'twito, a] *adj* accidental
**fortuna** [for'tuna] *nf (suerte)* fortune, (good) luck; *(riqueza)* fortune, wealth
**forzar** [for'θar] /1f, 1l/ *vt (puerta)* to force (open); *(compeler)* to compel
**forzoso, -a** [for'θoso, a] *adj* necessary
**fosa** ['fosa] *nf (sepultura)* grave; *(en tierra)* pit; **~s nasales** nostrils
**fósforo** ['fosforo] *nm (Química)* phosphorus; *(cerilla)* match
**fósil** ['fosil] *nm* fossil
**foso** ['foso] *nm* ditch; *(Teat)* pit
**foto** ['foto] *nf* photo, snap(shot); **sacar una ~** to take a photo *o* picture; **~ (de) carné** passport(-size) photo
**fotocopia** [foto'kopja] *nf* photocopy; **fotocopiadora** *nf* photocopier; **fotocopiar** /1b/ *vt* to photocopy
**fotografía** [fotoɣra'fia] *nf (arte)* photography; *(una fotografía)* photograph; **fotografiar** /1c/ *vt* to photograph
**fotógrafo, -a** [fo'toɣrafo, a] *nm/f* photographer

**fotomatón** [fotoma'ton] *nm* photo booth

**FP** *nf abr* (ESP) = **Formación Profesional**

**fracasar** [fraka'sar] /1a/ *vi* (gen) to fail

**fracaso** [fra'kaso] *nm* failure

**fracción** [frak'θjon] *nf* fraction

**fractura** [frak'tura] *nf* fracture, break;
  ~ **hidráulica** fracking

**fragancia** [fra'ɣanθja] *nf* (olor) fragrance,
  perfume

**frágil** ['fraxil] *adj* (débil) fragile; (Com)
  breakable

**fragmento** [fraɣ'mento] *nm* fragment

**fraile** ['fraile] *nm* (Rel) friar; (: monje) monk

**frambuesa** [fram'bwesa] *nf* raspberry

**francés, -esa** [fran'θes, esa] *adj* French
  ▷ *nm/f* Frenchman/woman ▷ *nm* (Ling)
  French

**Francia** ['franθja] *nf* France

**franco, -a** ['franko, a] *adj* (cándido) frank,
  open; (Com: exento) free ▷ *nm* (moneda)
  franc

**francotirador, a** [frankotira'ðor, a] *nm/f*
  sniper

**franela** [fra'nela] *nf* flannel

**franja** ['franxa] *nf* fringe

**franquear** [franke'ar] /1a/ *vt* (camino)
  to clear; (carta, paquete) to frank, stamp;
  (obstáculo) to overcome

**franqueo** [fran'keo] *nm* postage

**franqueza** [fran'keθa] *nf* frankness

**frasco** ['frasko] *nm* bottle, flask

**frase** ['frase] *nf* sentence; ~ **hecha** set
  phrase; (pey) stock phrase

**fraterno, -a** [fra'terno, a] *adj* brotherly,
  fraternal

**fraude** ['frauðe] *nm* (cualidad) dishonesty;
  (acto) fraud

**frazada** [fra'saða] *nf* (LAM) blanket

**frecuencia** [fre'kwenθja] *nf* frequency;
  **con** ~ frequently, often

**frecuentar** [frekwen'tar] /1a/ *vt* to
  frequent

**frecuente** [fre'kwente] *adj* frequent

**fregadero** [freɣa'ðero] *nm* (kitchen) sink

**fregar** [fre'ɣar] /1h, 1j/ *vt* (frotar) to scrub;
  (platos) to wash (up); (LAM fam: fastidiar) to
  annoy; (: malograr) to screw up

**freír** [fre'ir] /3l/ *vt* to fry

**frenar** [fre'nar] /1a/ *vt* to brake; (fig) to
  check

**frenazo** [fre'naθo] *nm*: **dar un** ~ to brake
  sharply

**frenesí** [frene'si] *nm* frenzy

**freno** ['freno] *nm* (Tec, Auto) brake; (de
  cabalgadura) bit; (fig) check; ~ **de mano**
  handbrake

**frente** ['frente] *nm* (Arq, Mil, Pol) front; (de
  objeto) front part ▷ *nf* forehead, brow; ~ **a**
  in front of; (en situación opuesta a) opposite;

**chocar de** ~ to crash head-on; **hacer** ~ **a** to
  face up to

**fresa** ['fresa] *nf* (ESP) strawberry

**fresco, -a** ['fresko, a] *adj* (nuevo) fresh; (frío)
  cool; (fam: descarado) cheeky ▷ *nm* (aire)
  fresh air; (Arte) fresco; (LAM: bebida) fruit
  juice o drink ▷ *nm/f* (fam): **ser un(a)** ~/**a** to
  have a nerve; **tomar el** ~ to get some fresh
  air; **frescura** *nf* freshness; (descaro) cheek,
  nerve

**frialdad** [frjal'dað] *nf* (gen) coldness;
  (indiferencia) indifference

**frigidez** [frixi'ðeθ] *nf* frigidity

**frigo** ['friɣo] *nm* fridge

**frigorífico** [friɣo'rifiko] *nm* refrigerator

**frijol** [fri'xol] *nm* kidney bean

**frío, -a** ['frio, a] *vb V* **freír** ▷ *adj* cold;
  (indiferente) indifferent ▷ *nm* cold(ness);
  indifference; **hace** ~ it's cold; **tener** ~ to
  be cold

**frito, -a** ['frito, a] *adj* fried; **fritos** *nmpl* fried
  food; **me trae** ~ **ese hombre** I'm sick and
  tired of that man

**frívolo, -a** ['friβolo, a] *adj* frivolous

**frontal** [fron'tal] *adj* frontal ▷ *nm*:
  **choque** ~ head-on collision

**frontera** [fron'tera] *nf* frontier; **fronterizo,
  -a** *adj* frontier *cpd*; (contiguo) bordering

**frontón** [fron'ton] *nm* (Deporte: cancha)
  pelota court; (: juego) pelota

**frotar** [fro'tar] /1a/ *vt* to rub; **frotarse** *vr*:
  ~**se las manos** to rub one's hands

**fructífero, -a** [fruk'tifero, a] *adj* fruitful

**fruncir** [frun'θir] /3b/ *vt* to pucker;
  (Costura) to gather; ~ **el ceño** to knit one's
  brow

**frustrar** [frus'trar] /1a/ *vt* to frustrate

**fruta** ['fruta] *nf* fruit; **frutería** *nf* fruit shop;
  **frutero, -a** *adj* fruit *cpd* ▷ *nm/f* fruiterer
  ▷ *nm* fruit dish o bowl

**frutilla** [fru'tiʎa] *nf* (LAM) strawberry

**fruto** ['fruto] *nm* fruit; (fig: resultado) result;
  (: beneficio) benefit; ~**s secos** nuts and dried
  fruit

**fucsia** ['fuksja] *nf* fuchsia

**fue** [fwe] *vb V* **ser**; **ir**

**fuego** ['fweɣo] *nm* (gen) fire; ~ **amigo**
  friendly fire; ~**s artificiales** o **de artificio**
  fireworks; **a** ~ **lento** on a low flame o gas;
  **¿tienes** ~? have you (got) a light?

**fuente** ['fwente] *nf* fountain; (manantial,
  fig) spring; (origen) source; (plato) large
  dish

**fuera** ['fwera] *vb V* **ser**; **ir** ▷ *adv* out(side);
  (en otra parte) away; (excepto, salvo) except,
  save ▷ *prep*: ~ **de** outside; (fig) besides; ~ **de
  sí** beside o.s.; **por** ~ (on the) outside

**fuera-borda** [fwera'βorða] *nm inv* (barco)
  speedboat

**fuerte** ['fwerte] *adj* strong; (*golpe*) hard; (*ruido*) loud; (*comida*) rich; (*lluvia*) heavy; (*dolor*) intense ▷ *adv* strongly; hard; loud(ly); **ser ~ en** to be good at

**fuerza** ['fwerθa] *vb* V **forzar** ▷ *nf* (*fortaleza*) strength; (*Tec, Elec*) power; (*coacción*) force; (*Mil: tb*: **~s**) forces *pl*; **~s armadas (FF.AA.)** armed forces; **~s aéreas** air force *sg*; **a ~ de** by (dint of); **cobrar ~s** to recover one's strength; **tener ~s para** to have the strength to; **a la ~** forcibly, by force; **por ~** of necessity; **~ de voluntad** willpower

**fuga** ['fuɣa] *nf* (*huida*) flight, escape; (*de gas etc*) leak

**fugarse** [fu'ɣarse] /1h/ *vr* to flee, escape

**fugaz** [fu'ɣaθ] *adj* fleeting

**fugitivo, -a** [fuxi'tiβo, a] *adj* fugitive ▷ *nm/f* fugitive

**fui** *etc* [fwi] *vb* V **ser**; **ir**

**fulano, -a** [fu'lano, a] *nm/f* so-and-so, what's-his-name

**fulminante** [fulmi'nante] *adj* (*fig: mirada*) withering; (*Med*) sudden, serious; (*fam*) terrific, tremendous; (*éxito, golpe*) sudden; **ataque ~** stroke

**fumador, a** [fuma'ðor, a] *nm/f* smoker

**fumar** [fu'mar] /1a/ *vt, vi* to smoke; **~ en pipa** to smoke a pipe

**función** [fun'θjon] *nf* function; (*de puesto*) duties *pl*; (*Teat etc*) show; **entrar en funciones** to take up one's duties

**funcionar** [funθjo'nar] /1a/ *vi* (*gen*) to function; (*máquina*) to work; **"no funciona"** "out of order"

**funcionario, -a** [funθjo'narjo, a] *nm/f* civil servant

**funda** ['funda] *nf* (*gen*) cover; (*de almohada*) pillowcase

**fundación** [funda'θjon] *nf* foundation

**fundamental** [fundamen'tal] *adj* fundamental, basic

**fundamento** [funda'mento] *nm* (*base*) foundation

**fundar** [fun'dar] /1a/ *vt* to found; **fundarse** *vr*: **~se en** to be founded on

**fundición** [fundi'θjon] *nf* (*acción*) smelting; (*fábrica*) foundry

**fundir** [fun'dir] /3a/ *vt* (*gen*) to fuse; (*metal*) to smelt, melt down; (*nieve etc*) to melt; (*Com*) to merge; (*estatua*) to cast; **fundirse** *vr* (*colores etc*) to merge, blend; (*unirse*) to fuse together; (*Elec: fusible, lámpara etc*) to blow; (*nieve etc*) to melt

**fúnebre** ['funeβre] *adj* funeral *cpd*, funereal

**funeral** [fune'ral] *nm* funeral; **funeraria** *nf* undertaker's (BRIT), mortician's (US)

**funicular** [funiku'lar] *nm* (*tren*) funicular; (*teleférico*) cable car

**furgón** [fur'ɣon] *nm* wagon; **furgoneta** *nf* (*Auto, Com*) (transit) van (BRIT), pickup (truck) (US)

**furia** ['furja] *nf* (*ira*) fury; (*violencia*) violence; **furioso, -a** *adj* (*iracundo*) furious; (*violento*) violent

**furtivo, -a** [fur'tiβo, a] *adj* furtive ▷ *nm* poacher

**fusible** [fu'siβle] *nm* fuse

**fusil** [fu'sil] *nm* rifle; **fusilar** /1a/ *vt* to shoot

**fusión** [fu'sjon] *nf* (*gen*) melting; (*unión*) fusion; (*Com*) merger, amalgamation

**fútbol** ['futβol] *nm* football (BRIT), soccer (US); **~ americano** American football (BRIT), football (US); **~ sala** indoor football (BRIT) *o* soccer (US); **futbolín** *nm* table football; **futbolista** *nmf* footballer

**futuro, -a** [fu'turo, a] *adj* future ▷ *nm* future

# g

**gabardina** [gaβar'ðina] nf gabardine; (prenda) raincoat

**gabinete** [gaβi'nete] nm (Pol) cabinet; (estudio) study; (de abogados etc) office

**gachas** ['gatʃas] nfpl porridge sg

**gafas** ['gafas] nfpl glasses; ~ **de sol** sunglasses

**gafe** ['gafe] nm (fam) jinx

**gaita** ['gaita] nf bagpipes pl

**gajes** ['gaxes] nmpl: **los ~ del oficio** occupational hazards

**gajo** ['gaxo] nm (de naranja) segment

**gala** ['gala] nf full dress; **galas** nfpl finery sg; **estar de ~** to be in one's best clothes; **hacer ~ de** to display

**galápago** [ga'lapaɣo] nm (Zool) turtle, sea/ freshwater turtle (US)

**galardón** [galar'ðon] nm award, prize

**galaxia** [ga'laksja] nf galaxy

**galera** [ga'lera] nf (nave) galley; (carro) wagon; (Tip) galley

**galería** [gale'ria] nf (gen) gallery; (balcón) veranda(h); (de casa) corridor; ~ **comercial** shopping mall

**Gales** ['gales] nm: **(el País de) ~** Wales; **galés, -esa** adj Welsh ▷ nm/f Welshman/ woman ▷ nm (Ling) Welsh

**galgo, -a** ['galɣo, a] nm/f greyhound

**gallego, -a** [ga'ʎeɣo, a] adj ▷ nm/f Galician

**galleta** [ga'ʎeta] nf biscuit (BRIT), cookie (US)

**gallina** [ga'ʎina] nf hen ▷ nm (fam) chicken; **gallinero** nm henhouse; (Teat) top gallery

**gallo** ['gaʎo] nm cock, rooster

**galopar** [galo'par] /1a/ vi to gallop

**gama** ['gama] nf (fig) range

**gamba** ['gamba] nf prawn (BRIT), shrimp (US)

**gamberro, -a** [gam'berro, a] nm/f hooligan, lout

**gamuza** [ga'muθa] nf chamois

**gana** ['gana] nf (deseo) desire, wish; (apetito) appetite; (voluntad) will; (añoranza) longing; **de buena ~** willingly; **de mala ~** reluctantly; **me da ~s de** I feel like, I want to; **tener ~s de** to feel like; **no me da la (real) ~** I (really) don't feel like it

**ganadería** [ganaðe'ria] nf (ganado) livestock; (ganado vacuno) cattle pl; (cría, comercio) cattle raising

**ganadero, -a** [gana'ðero, a] nm/f (hacendado) rancher

**ganado** [ga'naðo] nm livestock; ~ **caballar/ cabrío** horses pl/goats pl; ~ **porcino/ vacuno** pigs pl/cattle pl

**ganador, -a** [gana'ðor, a] adj winning ▷ nm/f winner

**ganancia** [ga'nanθja] nf (lo ganado) gain; (aumento) increase; (beneficio) profit; **ganancias** nfpl (ingresos) earnings; (beneficios) profit sg, winnings

**ganar** [ga'nar] /1a/ vt (obtener) to get, obtain; (sacar ventaja) to gain; (Com) to earn; (Deporte, premio) to win; (derrotar) to beat; (alcanzar) to reach ▷ vi (Deporte) to win; **ganarse** vr: ~**se la vida** to earn one's living

**ganchillo** [gan'tʃiʎo] nm crochet

**gancho** ['gantʃo] nm (gen) hook; (colgador) hanger

**gandul, -a** [gan'dul, a] adj, nm/f good-for- nothing, layabout

**ganga** ['ganga] nf bargain

**gangrena** [gan'grena] nf gangrene

**ganso, -a** ['ganso, a] nm/f (Zool) gander/ goose; (fam) idiot

**ganzúa** [gan'θua] nf skeleton key

**garabato** [gara'βato] nm (escritura) scrawl, scribble

**garaje** [ga'raxe] nm garage; **garajista** nmf mechanic

**garantía** [garan'tia] nf guarantee

**garantizar** [garanti'θar] /1f/ vt to guarantee

**garbanzo** [gar'βanθo] nm chickpea

**garfio** ['garfjo] nm grappling iron

**garganta** [gar'ɣanta] nf (interna) throat; (externa, de botella) neck; **gargantilla** nf necklace

**gárgara** ['garɣara] nf gargling; **hacer ~s** to gargle

**gargarear** [garɣare'ar] /1a/ vi (LAM) to gargle

**garita** [ga'rita] nf cabin, hut; (Mil) sentry box

**garra** ['garra] nf (de gato, Tec) claw; (de ave) talon; (fam) hand, paw

**garrafa** [ga'rrafa] nf carafe, decanter

**garrapata** [garra'pata] nf tick

**gas** [gas] nm gas; ~**es lacrimógenos** tear gas sg

**gasa** ['gasa] nf gauze

**gaseoso, -a** [gase'oso, a] adj gassy, fizzy ▷ nf lemonade, pop (fam)

**gasoil** [ga'soil], **gasóleo** [ga'soleo] nm diesel (oil)

**gasolina** [gaso'lina] nf petrol, gas(oline) (US); **gasolinera** nf petrol (BRIT) o gas (US) station

**gastado, -a** [gas'taðo, a] adj (dinero) spent; (ropa) worn out; (usado: frase etc) trite

**gastar** [gas'tar] /1a/ vt (dinero, tiempo) to spend; (consumir) to use (up); (desperdiciar) to waste; (llevar) to wear; **gastarse** vr to wear out; (estropearse) to waste; **~ en** to spend on; **~ bromas** to crack jokes; **¿qué número gastas?** what size (shoe) do you take?

**gasto** ['gasto] nm (desembolso) expenditure, spending; (consumo, uso) use; **gastos** nmpl (desembolsos) expenses; (cargos) charges, costs

**gastronomía** [gastrono'mia] nf gastronomy

**gatear** [gate'ar] /1a/ vi (andar a gatas) to go on all fours

**gatillo** [ga'tiʎo] nm (de arma de fuego) trigger; (de dentista) forceps

**gato** ['gato] nm cat; (Tec) jack; **andar a gatas** to go on all fours

**gaucho, -a** ['gautʃo, a] nm/f gaucho

**gaviota** [ga'βjota] nf seagull

**gay** [ge] adj gay, homosexual

**gazpacho** [gaθ'patʃo] nm gazpacho

**gel** [xel] nm gel; **~ de baño/ducha** bath/ shower gel

**gelatina** [xela'tina] nf jelly; (polvos etc) gelatine

**gema** ['xema] nf gem

**gemelo, -a** [xe'melo, a] adj, nm/f twin; **gemelos** nmpl (de camisa) cufflinks; **~s de campo** field glasses, binoculars

**gemido** [xe'miðo] nm (quejido) moan, groan; (lamento) howl

**Géminis** ['xeminis] nm Gemini

**gemir** [xe'mir] /3k/ vi (quejarse) to moan, groan; (viento) to howl

**generación** [xenera'θjon] nf generation

**general** [xene'ral] adj general ▷ nm general; **por lo** o **en ~** in general; **Generalitat** nf regional government of Catalonia; **generalizar** /1f/ vt to generalize; **generalizarse** vr to become generalized, spread

**generar** [xene'rar] /1a/ vt to generate

**género** ['xenero] nm (clase) kind, sort; (tipo) type; (Bio) genus; (Ling) gender; (Com) material; **~ humano** human race

**generosidad** [xenerosi'ðað] nf generosity; **generoso, -a** adj generous

**genial** [xe'njal] adj inspired; (idea) brilliant; (estupendo) wonderful

**genio** ['xenjo] nm (carácter) nature, disposition; (humor) temper; (facultad creadora) genius; **de mal ~** bad-tempered

**genital** [xeni'tal] adj genital ▷ nm: **~es** genitals

**genoma** [xe'noma] nm genome

**gente** ['xente] nf (personas) people pl; (parientes) relatives pl

**gentil** [xen'til] adj (elegante) graceful; (encantador) charming

⬛ No confundir gentil con la palabra inglesa gentle.

**genuino, -a** [xe'nwino, a] adj genuine

**geografía** [xeoɣra'fia] nf geography

**geología** [xeolo'xia] nf geology

**geometría** [xeome'tria] nf geometry

**gerente** [xe'rente] nm/f (supervisor) manager; (jefe) director

**geriatría** [xerja'tria] nf (Med) geriatrics sg

**germen** ['xermen] nm germ

**gesticulación** [xestikula'θjon] nf (ademán) gesticulation; (mueca) grimace

**gesticular** [xestiku'lar] /1a/ vi (con ademanes) to gesticulate; (con muecas) to make faces

**gestión** [xes'tjon] nf management; (diligencia, acción) negotiation

**gesto** ['xesto] nm (mueca) grimace; (ademán) gesture

**Gibraltar** [xiβral'tar] nm Gibraltar; **gibraltareño, -a** adj of o from Gibraltar, Gibraltarian ▷ nm/f Gibraltarian

**gigante** [xi'ɣante] adj, nm/f giant; **gigantesco, -a** adj gigantic

**gilipollas** [xili'poʎas] (fam) adj inv daft ▷ nm/f berk (BRIT), jerk (esp US)

**gimnasia** [xim'nasja] nf gymnastics pl; **gimnasio** nm gym(nasium); **gimnasta** nm/f gymnast; **gimnástica** nf gymnastics sg

**ginebra** [xi'neβra] nf gin

**ginecólogo, -a** [xine'koloɣo, a] nm/f gyn(a)ecologist

**gira** ['xira] nf tour, trip

**girar** [xi'rar] /1a/ vt (dar la vuelta) to turn (around); (: rápidamente) to spin; (Com: giro postal) to draw; (comerciar: letra de cambio) to issue ▷ vi to turn (round); (rápido) to spin

**girasol** [xira'sol] nm sunflower

**giratorio, -a** [xira'torjo, a] adj revolving

**giro** ['xiro] nm (movimiento) turn, revolution; (Ling) expression; (Com) draft; **~ bancario** bank draft; **~ postal** money order

**gis** [xis] nm (LAM) chalk

**gitano, -a** [xi'tano, a] adj, nm/f gypsy

**glacial** [gla'θjal] adj icy, freezing

**glaciar** [gla'θjar] nm glacier

**glándula** ['glandula] nf gland

**global** [glo'βal] *adj* global; **globalización** *nf* globalization

**globo** ['gloβo] *nm* (*esfera*) globe, sphere; (*aeróstato, juguete*) balloon

**glóbulo** ['gloβulo] *nm* globule; (*Anat*) corpuscle

**gloria** ['glorja] *nf* glory

**glorieta** [glo'rjeta] *nf* (*de jardín*) bower, arbour, arbor (*us*); (*Auto*) roundabout (*BRIT*), traffic circle (*us*)

**glorioso, -a** [glo'rjoso, a] *adj* glorious

**glotón, -ona** [glo'ton, ona] *adj* gluttonous, greedy ▷ *nm/f* glutton

**glucosa** [glu'kosa] *nf* glucose

**gobernador, -a** [goβerna'ðor, a] *adj* governing ▷ *nm/f* governor; **gobernante** *adj* governing

**gobernar** [goβer'nar] /1j/ *vt* (*dirigir*) to guide, direct; (*Pol*) to rule, govern ▷ *vi* to govern; (*Naut*) to steer

**gobierno** [go'βjerno] *vb V* **gobernar** ▷ *nm* (*Pol*) government; (*dirección*) guidance, direction; (*Naut*) steering

**goce** *etc* ['goθe] *vb V* **gozar** ▷ *nm* enjoyment

**gol** [gol] *nm* goal

**golf** [golf] *nm* golf

**golfo, -a** ['golfo, a] *nm/f* (*pilluelo*) street urchin; (*vagabundo*) tramp; (*gorrón*) loafer; (*gamberro*) lout ▷ *nm* (*Geo*) gulf ▷ *nf* (*fam!*: *prostituta*) slut

**golondrina** [golon'drina] *nf* swallow

**golosina** [golo'sina] *nf* (*dulce*) sweet; **goloso, -a** *adj* sweet-toothed

**golpe** ['golpe] *nm* blow; (*de puño*) punch; (*de mano*) smack; (*de remo*) stroke; (*fig*: *choque*) clash; **no dar ~** to be bone idle; **de un ~** with one blow; **de ~** suddenly; **~ (de estado)** coup (d'état); **golpear** /1a/ *vt, vi* to strike, knock; (*asestar*) to beat; (*de puño*) to punch; (*golpetear*) to tap

**goma** ['goma] *nf* (*caucho*) rubber; (*elástico*) elastic; (*tira*) rubber o elastic (*BRIT*) band; **~ (de borrar)** eraser, rubber (*BRIT*); **~ espuma** foam rubber

**gomina** [go'mina] *nf* hair gel

**gomita** [go'mita] *nf* rubber o elastic (*BRIT*) band

**gordo, -a** ['gorðo, a] *adj* (*gen*) fat; (*fam*) enormous; **el (premio) ~** (*en lotería*) first prize

**gorila** [go'rila] *nm* gorilla

**gorra** ['gorra] *nf* cap; (*de niño*) bonnet; (*militar*) bearskin; **andar** o **ir** o **vivir de ~** to sponge; **entrar de ~** (*fam*) to gatecrash

**gorrión** [go'rrjon] *nm* sparrow

**gorro** ['gorro] *nm* cap; (*de niño, mujer*) bonnet

**gorrón, -ona** [go'rron, ona] *nm/f* scrounger; **gorronear** /1a/ *vi* (*fam*) to sponge, scrounge

**gota** ['gota] *nf* (*gen*) drop; (*de sudor*) bead; (*Med*) gout; **gotear** /1a/ *vi* to drip; (*lloviznar*) to drizzle; **gotera** *nf* leak

**gozar** [go'θar] /1f/ *vi* to enjoy o.s.; **~ de** (*disfrutar*) to enjoy; (*poseer*) to possess

**GPS** *nm abr* (= *global positioning system*) GPS

**gr** *abr* (= *gramo(s)*) g

**grabación** [graβa'θjon] *nf* recording

**grabado** [gra'βaðo] *nm* print, engraving

**grabador, -a** [graβa'ðor, a] *nm/f* engraver ▷ *nf* tape-recorder; **~a de CD/DVD** CD/DVD writer

**grabar** [gra'βar] /1a/ *vt* to engrave; (*discos, cintas*) to record

**gracia** ['graθja] *nf* (*encanto*) grace, gracefulness; (*humor*) humour, wit; **¡muchas ~s!** thanks very much!; **~s a** thanks to; **tener ~** (*chiste etc*) to be funny; **no me hace ~** I am not too keen; **dar las ~s a algn por algo** to thank sb for sth; **gracioso, -a** *adj* (*garboso*) graceful; (*chistoso*) funny; (*cómico*) comical ▷ *nm/f* (*Teat*) comic character

**grada** ['graða] *nf* (*de escalera*) step; (*de anfiteatro*) tier, row; **gradas** *nfpl* (*de estadio*) terraces

**grado** ['graðo] *nm* degree; (*de aceite, vino*) grade; (*grada*) step; (*Mil*) rank; **de buen ~** willingly; **~ centígrado/Fahrenheit** degree centigrade/Fahrenheit

**graduación** [graðwa'θjon] *nf* (*del alcohol*) proof, strength; (*Escol*) graduation; (*Mil*) rank

**gradual** [gra'ðwal] *adj* gradual

**graduar** [gra'ðwar] /1e/ *vt* (*gen*) to graduate; (*Mil*) to commission; **graduarse** *vr* to graduate; **~se la vista** to have one's eyes tested

**gráfico, -a** ['grafiko, a] *adj* graphic ▷ *nm* diagram ▷ *nf* graph; **gráficos** *nmpl* (*tb Inform*) graphics

**grajo** ['graxo] *nm* rook

**gramático, -a** [gra'matiko, a] *nm/f* (*persona*) grammarian ▷ *nf* grammar

**gramo** ['gramo] *nm* gramme (*BRIT*), gram (*us*)

**gran** [gran] *adj V* **grande**

**grana** ['grana] *nf* (*color*) scarlet

**granada** [gra'naða] *nf* pomegranate; (*Mil*) grenade

**granate** [gra'nate] *adj inv* maroon

**Gran Bretaña** [grambre'tana] *nf* Great Britain

**grande** ['grande], **gran** (*antes de nmsg*) *adj* (*de tamaño*) big, large; (*alto*) tall; (*distinguido*) great; (*impresionante*) grand ▷ *nm* grandee

**granel** [gra'nel] *nm*: **a ~** (*Com*) in bulk

**granero** [gra'nero] *nm* granary, barn

**granito** [gra'nito] *nm* (*Agr*) small grain; (*roca*) granite

**granizado** [graniˈθaðo] *nm* iced drink
**granizar** [graniˈθar] /1f/ *vi* to hail; **granizo** *nm* hail
**granja** [ˈgranxa] *nf (gen)* farm; **granjero, -a** *nm/f* farmer
**grano** [ˈgrano] *nm* grain; *(semilla)* seed; *(Med)* pimple, spot; ~ **de café** coffee bean
**granuja** [graˈnuxa] *nm* rogue; *(golfillo)* urchin
**grapa** [ˈgrapa] *nf* staple; *(Tec)* clamp; **grapadora** *nf* stapler
**grasa** [ˈgrasa] *nf* V **graso**; **grasiento, -a** *adj* greasy; *(de aceite)* oily; **graso, -a** *adj* fatty; *(aceitoso)* greasy ▷ *nf* grease; *(de cocina)* fat, lard; *(sebo)* suet; *(mugre)* filth
**gratinar** [gratiˈnar] /1a/ *vt* to cook au gratin
**gratis** [ˈgratis] *adv* free
**grato, -a** [ˈgrato, a] *adj (agradable)* pleasant, agreeable
**gratuito, -a** [graˈtwito, a] *adj (gratis)* free; *(sin razón)* gratuitous
**grave** [ˈgraβe] *adj* heavy; *(fig, Med)* grave, serious; **gravedad** *nf* gravity
**Grecia** [ˈgreθja] *nf* Greece
**gremio** [ˈgremjo] *nm* trade, industry
**griego, -a** [ˈgrjeɣo, a] *adj* ▷ *nm/f* Greek
**grieta** [ˈgrjeta] *nf* crack
**grifo** [ˈgrifo] *nm* tap *(BRIT)*, faucet *(US)*
**grillo** [ˈgriʎo] *nm (Zool)* cricket
**gripa** [ˈgripa] *nf (LAM)* flu, influenza
**gripe** [ˈgripe] *nf* flu, influenza; ~ **A** swine flu; ~ **aviar** bird flu
**gris** [gris] *adj* grey
**gritar** [griˈtar] /1a/ *vt, vi* to shout, yell; **grito** *nm* shout, yell; *(de horror)* scream
**grosella** [groˈseʎa] *nf (red)*currant
**grosero, -a** [groˈsero, a] *adj (poco cortés)* rude, bad-mannered; *(ordinario)* vulgar, crude
**grosor** [groˈsor] *nm* thickness
**grúa** [ˈgrua] *nf (Tec)* crane; *(de petróleo)* derrick
**grueso, -a** [ˈgrweso, a] *adj* thick; *(persona)* stout ▷ *nm* bulk; **el** ~ **de** the bulk of
**grulla** [ˈgruʎa] *nf* crane
**grumo** [ˈgrumo] *nm* clot, lump
**gruñido** [gruˈɲiðo] *nm* grunt; *(fig)* grumble
**gruñir** [gruˈɲir] /3h/ *vi (animal)* to grunt, growl; *(fam)* to grumble
**grupo** [ˈgrupo] *nm* group; *(Tec)* unit, set; ~ **de presión** pressure group
**gruta** [ˈgruta] *nf* grotto
**guacho, -a** [ˈgwatʃo, a] *nm/f (LAM)* homeless child
**guajolote** [gwaxoˈlote] *nm (LAM)* turkey
**guante** [ˈgwante] *nm* glove; ~**s de goma** rubber gloves; **guantera** *nf* glove compartment

**guapo, -a** [ˈgwapo, a] *adj* good-looking; attractive; *(elegante)* smart
**guarda** [ˈgwarða] *nmf (persona)* warden, keeper ▷ *nf (acto)* guarding; *(custodia)* custody; ~ **jurado** (armed) security guard; **guardabarros** *nm inv* mudguard *(BRIT)*, fender *(US)*; **guardabosques** *nm inv* gamekeeper; **guardacostas** *nm inv* coastguard vessel ▷ *nmf* guardian, protector; **guardaespaldas** *nm inv, nf inv* bodyguard; **guardameta** *nm* goalkeeper; **guardar** /1a/ *vt (gen)* to keep; *(vigilar)* to guard, watch over; *(dinero: ahorrar)* to save; **guardarse** *vr (preservarse)* to protect o.s.; **guardarse de algo** *(evitar)* to avoid sth; **guardar cama** to stay in bed; **guardarropa** *nm (armario)* wardrobe; *(en establecimiento público)* cloakroom
**guardería** [gwarðeˈria] *nf* nursery
**guardia** [ˈgwarðja] *nf (Mil)* guard; *(cuidado)* care, custody ▷ *nmf* guard; *(policía)* police officer; **estar de** ~ to be on guard; **montar** ~ to mount guard; **la G- Civil** the Civil Guard
**guardián, -ana** [gwarˈðjan, ana] *nm/f (gen)* guardian, keeper
**guarida** [gwaˈriða] *nf (de animal)* den, lair; *(refugio)* refuge
**guarnición** [gwarniˈθjon] *nf (de vestimenta)* trimming; *(de piedra)* mount; *(Culin)* garnish; *(arneses)* harness; *(Mil)* garrison
**guarro, -a** [ˈgwarro, a] *nm/f* pig
**guasa** [ˈgwasa] *nf* joke; **guasón, -ona** *adj (bromista)* joking ▷ *nm/f* wit; joker
**Guatemala** [gwateˈmala] *nf* Guatemala
**guay** [gwai] *adj (fam)* super, great
**güero, -a** [ˈgwero, a] *adj (LAM)* blond(e)
**guerra** [ˈgerra] *nf* war; ~ **civil/fría** civil/cold war; **dar** ~ to be a nuisance; **guerrero, -a** *adj* fighting; *(carácter)* warlike ▷ *nm/f* warrior
**guerrilla** [geˈrriʎa] *nf* guerrilla warfare; *(tropas)* guerrilla band o group
**guía** [ˈgia] *vb* V **guiar** ▷ *nmf (persona)* guide ▷ *nf (libro)* guidebook; ~ **telefónica** telephone directory; ~ **del turista/del viajero** tourist/traveller's guide
**guiar** [giˈar] /1c/ *vt* to guide, direct; *(Auto)* to steer; **guiarse** *vr*: ~**se por** to be guided by
**guinda** [ˈginda] *nf* morello cherry
**guindilla** [ginˈdiʎa] *nf* chil(l)i pepper
**guiñar** [giˈɲar] /1a/ *vi* to wink
**guión** [giˈon] *nm (Ling)* hyphen, dash; *(Cine)* script; **guionista** *nmf* scriptwriter
**guiri** [ˈgiri] *nmf (fam, pey)* foreigner
**guirnalda** [girˈnalda] *nf* garland
**guisado** [giˈsaðo] *nm* stew
**guisante** [giˈsante] *nm* pea
**guisar** [giˈsar] /1a/ *vt, vi* to cook; **guiso** *nm* cooked dish

**guitarra** [gi'tarra] *nf* guitar
**gula** ['gula] *nf* gluttony, greed
**gusano** [gu'sano] *nm* worm; (*lombriz*) earthworm
**gustar** [gus'tar] /1a/ *vt* to taste, sample ▷ *vi* to please, be pleasing; **~ de algo** to like *o* enjoy sth; **me gustan las uvas** I like grapes; **le gusta nadar** she likes *o* enjoys swimming
**gusto** ['gusto] *nm* (*sentido, sabor*) taste; (*placer*) pleasure; **tiene un ~ amargo** it has a bitter taste; **tener buen ~** to have good taste; **sentirse a ~** to feel at ease; **¡mucho** *o* **tanto ~ (en conocerle)!** how do you do?, pleased to meet you; **el ~ es mío** the pleasure is mine; **tomar ~ a** to take a liking to; **con ~** willingly, gladly

**ha** [a] *vb* V **haber**
**haba** ['aβa] *nf* bean
**Habana** [a'βana] *nf*: **la ~** Havana
**habano** [a'βano] *nm* Havana cigar
**habéis** *vb* V **haber**

 **PALABRA CLAVE**

**haber** [a'βer] /2j/ *vb auxiliar* **1** (*tiempos compuestos*) to have; **había comido** I have/ had eaten; **antes/después de haberlo visto** before seeing/after seeing *o* having seen it
**2**: **¡haberlo dicho antes!** you should have said so before!
**3**: **haber de: he de hacerlo** I must do it; **ha de llegar mañana** it should arrive tomorrow
▶ *vb impersonal* **1** (*existencia: sg*) there is; (*: pl*) there are; **hay un hermano/dos hermanos** there is one brother/there are two brothers; **¿cuánto hay de aquí a Sucre?** how far is it from here to Sucre?
**2** (*obligación*): **hay que hacer algo** something must be done; **hay que apuntarlo para acordarse** you have to write it down to remember
**3**: **¡hay que ver!** well I never!
**4**: **¡no hay de qué!**, (*LAM*) **¡no hay por qué!** don't mention it!, not at all!
**5**: **¿qué hay?** (*¿qué pasa?*) what's up?, what's the matter?; (*¿qué tal?*) how's it going?
▶ **haberse** *vb impersonal*: **habérselas con algn** to have it out with sb
▶ *vt*: **he aquí unas sugerencias** here are some suggestions
▶ *nm* (*en cuenta*) credit side
▶ **haberes** *nmpl* assets; **¿cuánto tengo en el haber?** how much do I have in my account?; **tiene varias novelas en su haber** he has several novels to his credit

**habichuela** [aβiˈtʃwela] nf kidney bean

**hábil** [ˈaβil] adj (listo) clever, smart; (capaz) fit, capable; (experto) expert; **día ~** working day; **habilidad** nf skill, ability

**habitación** [aβitaˈθjon] nf (cuarto) room; (Bio: morada) habitat; **~ sencilla** o **individual** single room; **~ doble** o **de matrimonio** double room

**habitante** [aβiˈtante] nmf inhabitant

**habitar** [aβiˈtar] /1a/ vt (residir en) to inhabit; (ocupar) to occupy ▷ vi to live

**hábito** [ˈaβito] nm habit

**habitual** [aβiˈtwal] adj habitual

**habituar** [aβiˈtwar] /1e/ vt to accustom; **habituarse** vr: **~se a** to get used to

**habla** [ˈaβla] nf (capacidad de hablar) speech; (idioma) language; (dialecto) dialect; **perder el ~** to become speechless; **de ~ francesa** French-speaking; **estar al ~** to be in contact; (Telec) to be on the line; **¡González al ~!** (Telec) Gonzalez speaking!

**hablador, a** [aβlaˈðor, a] adj talkative ▷ nm/f chatterbox

**habladuría** [aβlaðuˈria] nf rumour; **habladurías** nfpl gossip sg

**hablante** [aˈβlante] adj speaking ▷ nmf speaker

**hablar** [aˈβlar] /1a/ vt to speak, talk ▷ vi to speak; **hablarse** vr to speak to each other; **~ con** to speak to; **de eso ni ~** no way, that's out of the question; **~ de** to speak of o about; **"se habla inglés"** "English spoken here"

**habré** etc [aˈβre] vb V **haber**

**hacendado, -a** [aθenˈdaðo, a] nm/f (LAM) rancher, farmer

**hacendoso, -a** [aθenˈdoso, a] adj industrious

## ⬤ PALABRA CLAVE

**hacer** [aˈθer] /2r/ vt 1 (fabricar, producir, conseguir) to make; **hacer una película/un ruido** to make a film/noise; **el guisado lo hice yo** I made o cooked the stew

2 (ejecutar: trabajo etc) to do; **hacer la colada** to do the washing; **hacer la comida** to do the cooking; **¿qué haces?** what are you doing?; **hacer el malo** o **el papel del malo** (Teat) to play the villain

3 (estudios, algunos deportes) to do; **hacer español/económicas** to do o study Spanish/economics; **hacer yoga/ gimnasia** to do yoga/go to the gym

4 (transformar, incidir en): **esto lo hará más difícil** this will make it more difficult; **salir te hará sentir mejor** going out will make you feel better

5 (cálculo): **2 y 2 hacen 4** 2 and 2 make 4; **éste hace 100** this one makes 100

6 (+ sub): **esto hará que ganemos** this will make us win; **harás que no quiera venir** you'll stop him wanting to come

7 (como sustituto de vb) to do; **él bebió y yo hice lo mismo** he drank and I did likewise

8: **no hace más que criticar** all he does is criticize

▷ vb semi-auxiliar (+ infin: directo): **les hice venir** I made o had them come; **hacer trabajar a los demás** to get others to work

▷ vi 1: **haz como que no lo sabes** act as if you don't know

2 (ser apropiado): **si os hace** if it's alright with you

3: **hacer de: hacer de Otelo** to play Othello

▷ vb impersonal 1: **hace calor/frío** it's hot/ cold; V tb **bueno; sol; tiempo**

2 (tiempo): **hace tres años** three years ago; **hace un mes que voy/no voy** I've been going/I haven't been for a month

3: **¿cómo has hecho para llegar tan rápido?** how did you manage to get here so quickly?

▷ **hacerse** vr 1 (volverse) to become; **se hicieron amigos** they became friends

2 (acostumbrarse): **hacerse a** to get used to

3: **se hace con huevos y leche** it's made out of eggs and milk; **eso no se hace** that's not done

4 (obtener): **hacerse de** o **con algo** to get hold of sth

5 (fingirse): **hacerse el sordo/sueco** to turn a deaf ear/pretend not to notice

**hacha** [ˈatʃa] nf axe; (antorcha) torch

**hachís** [aˈtʃis] nm hashish

**hacia** [ˈaθja] prep (en dirección de) towards; (cerca de) near; (actitud) towards; **~ adelante/ atrás** forwards/backwards; **~ arriba/ abajo** up(wards)/down(wards); **~ mediodía** about noon

**hacienda** [aˈθjenda] nf (propiedad) property; (finca) farm; (LAM) ranch; **~ pública** public finance; **(Ministerio de) H~** Exchequer (BRIT), Treasury Department (US)

**hada** [ˈaða] nf fairy

**haga** etc [ˈaɣa] vb V **hacer**

**Haití** [aiˈti] nm Haiti

**halagar** [alaˈɣar] /1h/ vt to flatter

**halago** [aˈlaɣo] nm flattery

**halcón** [alˈkon] nm falcon, hawk

**hallar** [aˈʎar] /1a/ vt (gen) to find; (descubrir) to discover; (toparse con) to run into; **hallarse** vr to be (situated)

**halterofilia** [alteroˈfilja] nf weightlifting

**hamaca** [aˈmaka] nf hammock

**hambre** [ˈambre] nf hunger; (carencia) famine; (fig) longing; **tener ~** to be

hungry; **¡me muero de ~!** I'm starving!;
**hambriento, -a** adj hungry, starving

**hamburguesa** [ambur'ɣesa] nf
hamburger; **hamburguesería** nf burger bar

**hámster** ['xamster] nm hamster

**han** [an] vb V **haber**

**harapo** [a'rapo] nm rag

**haré** etc [a're] vb V **hacer**

**harina** [a'rina] nf flour; **~ de maíz** cornflour
(BRIT), cornstarch (US); **~ de trigo** wheat
flour

**hartar** [ar'tar] /1a/ vt to satiate, glut; (fig)
to tire, sicken; **hartarse** vr (de comida) to fill
o.s., gorge o.s.; (cansarse): **~se de** to get fed
up with; **harto, -a** adj (lleno) full; (cansado)
fed up ▷ adv (bastante) enough; (muy) very;
**estar harto de** to be fed up with

**has** [as] vb V **haber**

**hashtag** [xas'taɣ] nm (en Twitter) hashtag

**hasta** ['asta] adv even ▷ prep (alcanzando a)
as far as, up/down to; (de tiempo: a tal hora)
till, until; (: antes de) before ▷ conj : **~ que**
until; **~ luego** o **ahora/el sábado** see you
soon/on Saturday; **~ pronto** see you soon

**hay** [ai] vb V **haber**

**Haya** ['aja] nf : **la ~** The Hague

**haya** etc ['aja] vb V **haber** ▷ nf beech tree

**haz** [aθ] vb V **hacer** ▷ nm (de luz) beam

**hazaña** [a'θaɲa] nf feat, exploit

**hazmerreír** [aθmerre'ir] nm inv laughing
stock

**he** [e] vb V **haber**

**hebilla** [e'βiʎa] nf buckle, clasp

**hebra** ['eβra] nf thread; (Bot: fibra) fibre,
grain

**hebreo, -a** [e'βreo, a] adj, nm/f Hebrew
▷ nm (Ling) Hebrew

**hechizar** [etʃi'θar] /1f/ vt to cast a spell on,
bewitch

**hechizo** [e'tʃiθo] nm witchcraft, magic;
(acto de magia) spell, charm

**hecho, -a** ['etʃo, a] pp de **hacer** ▷ adj (carne)
done; (Costura) ready-to-wear ▷ nm deed,
act; (dato) fact; (cuestión) matter; (suceso)
event ▷ excl agreed!, done!; **¡bien ~!** well
done!; **de ~** in fact, as a matter of fact; **el ~
es que ...** the fact is that ...

**hechura** [e'tʃura] nf (forma) form, shape;
(de persona) build

**hectárea** [ek'tarea] nf hectare

**helada** [e'laða] nf frost

**heladera** [ela'ðera] nf (LAM: refrigerador)
refrigerator

**helado, -a** [e'laðo, a] adj frozen; (glacial) icy;
(fig) chilly, cold ▷ nm ice-cream

**helar** [e'lar] /1j/ vt to freeze, ice (up); (dejar
atónito) to amaze ▷ vi to freeze; **helarse** vr
to freeze

**helecho** [e'letʃo] nm fern

**hélice** ['eliθe] nf (Tec) propeller

**helicóptero** [eli'koptero] nm helicopter

**hembra** ['embra] nf (Bot, Zool) female;
(mujer) woman; (Tec) nut

**hemorragia** [emo'rraxja] nf haemorrhage
(BRIT), hemorrhage (US)

**hemorroides** [emo'rroiðes] nfpl
haemorrhoids (BRIT), hemorrhoids (US)

**hemos** ['emos] vb V **haber**

**heno** ['eno] nm hay

**heredar** [ere'ðar] /1a/ vt to inherit;
**heredero, -a** nm/f heir(ess)

**hereje** [e'rexe] nmf heretic

**herencia** [e'renθja] nf inheritance

**herido, -a** [e'riðo, a] adj injured, wounded
▷ nm/f casualty ▷ nf wound, injury

**herir** [e'rir] /3i/ vt to wound, injure; (fig) to
offend

**hermanación** [ermana'θjon] nf (de
ciudades) twinning

**hermanado, -a** [erma'naðo, a] adj (ciudad)
twinned

**hermanastro, -a** [erma'nastro, a] nm/f
stepbrother/sister

**hermandad** [erman'dað] nf brotherhood

**hermano, -a** [er'mano, a] nm brother ▷ nf
sister; **~ gemelo** twin brother; **~ político**
brother-in-law; **hermana política** sister-
in-law

**hermético, -a** [er'metiko, a] adj hermetic;
(fig) watertight

**hermoso, -a** [er'moso, a] adj beautiful,
lovely; (estupendo) splendid; (guapo)
handsome; **hermosura** nf beauty

**hernia** ['ernja] nf hernia; **~ discal** slipped
disc

**héroe** ['eroe] nm hero

**heroína** [ero'ina] nf (mujer) heroine; (droga)
heroin

**herradura** [erra'ðura] nf horseshoe

**herramienta** [erra'mjenta] nf tool

**herrero** [e'rrero] nm blacksmith

**hervidero** [erβi'ðero] nm (fig) swarm; (Pol
etc) hotbed

**hervir** [er'βir] /3i/ vi to boil; (burbujear) to
bubble; **~ a fuego lento** to simmer; **hervor**
nm boiling; (fig) ardour, fervour

**heterosexual** [eterosek'swal] adj
heterosexual

**hice** etc ['iθe] vb V **hacer**

**hidratante** [iðra'tante] adj : **crema ~**
moisturizing cream, moisturizer; **hidratar**
/1a/ vt to moisturize; **hidrato** nm hydrate;
**hidrato de carbono** carbohydrate

**hidráulico, -a** [i'ðrauliko, a] adj hydraulic

**hidro...** [iðro] pref hydro..., water-...;
**hidrodeslizador** nm hovercraft;
**hidroeléctrico, -a** adj hydroelectric;
**hidrógeno** nm hydrogen

**hiedra** ['jeðra] nf ivy

**hiel** [jel] nf gall, bile; (fig) bitterness

**hielo** ['jelo] vb V **helar** ▷ nm (gen) ice; (escarcha) frost; (fig) coldness, reserve

**hiena** ['jena] nf hyena

**hierba** ['jerβa] nf (pasto) grass; (Culin, Med: planta) herb; **mala ~** weed; (fig) evil influence; **hierbabuena** nf mint

**hierro** ['jerro] nm (metal) iron; (objeto) iron object

**hígado** ['iɣaðo] nm liver

**higiene** [i'xjene] nf hygiene; **higiénico, -a** adj hygienic

**higo** ['iɣo] nm fig; **~ seco** dried fig; **higuera** nf fig tree

**hijastro, -a** [i'xastro, a] nm/f stepson/daughter

**hijo, -a** ['ixo, a] nm/f son/daughter, child; (uso vocativo) dear; **hijos** nmpl children, sons and daughters; **~/hija político/a** son-/daughter-in-law; **~ adoptivo** adopted child; **~ de papá/mamá** daddy's/mummy's boy; **~ de puta** (fam!) bastard (!), son of a bitch (!); **~ único** only child

**hilera** [i'lera] nf row, file

**hilo** ['ilo] nm thread; (Bot) fibre; (de metal) wire; (de agua) trickle, thin stream

**hilvanar** [ilβa'nar] /1a/ vt (Costura) to tack (BRIT), baste (US); (fig) to do hurriedly

**himno** ['imno] nm hymn; **~ nacional** national anthem

**hincapié** [inka'pje] nm: **hacer ~ en** to emphasize

**hincar** [in'kar] /1g/ vt to drive (in), thrust (in)

**hincha** ['intʃa] nmf (fam) fan

**hinchado, -a** [in'tʃaðo, a] adj (gen) swollen; (persona) pompous

**hinchar** [in'tʃar] /1a/ vt (gen) to swell; (inflar) to blow up, inflate; (fig) to exaggerate; **hincharse** vr (inflarse) to swell up; (fam: llenarse) to stuff o.s.; **hinchazón** nf (Med) swelling; (altivez) arrogance

**hinojo** [i'noxo] nm fennel

**hipermercado** [ipermer'kaðo] nm hypermarket, superstore

**hípico, -a** ['ipiko, a] adj horse cpd

**hipnotismo** [ipno'tismo] nm hypnotism; **hipnotizar** /1f/ vt to hypnotize

**hipo** ['ipo] nm hiccups pl

**hipocresía** [ipokre'sia] nf hypocrisy; **hipócrita** adj hypocritical ▷ nmf hypocrite

**hipódromo** [i'poðromo] nm racetrack

**hipopótamo** [ipo'potamo] nm hippopotamus

**hipoteca** [ipo'teka] nf mortgage

**hipótesis** [i'potesis] nf inv hypothesis

**hispánico, -a** [is'paniko, a] adj Hispanic

**hispano, -a** [is'pano, a] adj Hispanic, Spanish, Hispano- ▷ nm/f Spaniard;

**Hispanoamérica** nf Spanish o Latin America; **hispanoamericano, -a** adj, nm/f Spanish o Latin American

**histeria** [is'terja] nf hysteria

**historia** [is'torja] nf history; (cuento) story, tale; **historias** nfpl (chismes) gossip sg; **dejarse de ~s** to come to the point; **pasar a la ~** to go down in history; **historiador, a** nm/f historian; **historial** nm (profesional) curriculum vitae, C.V.; (Med) case history; **histórico, -a** adj historical; (fig) historic

**historieta** [isto'rjeta] nf tale, anecdote; (de dibujos) comic strip

**hito** ['ito] nm (fig) landmark

**hizo** ['iθo] vb V **hacer**

**hocico** [o'θiko] nm snout

**hockey** ['xoki] nm hockey; **~ sobre hielo** ice hockey

**hogar** [o'ɣar] nm fireplace, hearth; (casa) home; (vida familiar) home life; **hogareño, -a** adj home cpd; (persona) home-loving

**hoguera** [o'ɣera] nf (gen) bonfire

**hoja** ['oxa] nf (gen) leaf; (de flor) petal; (de papel) sheet; (página) page; **~ de afeitar** razor blade; **~ de cálculo electrónica** spreadsheet; **~ informativa** leaflet, handout; **~ de solicitud** application form

**hojalata** [oxa'lata] nf tin(plate)

**hojaldre** [o'xaldre] nm (Culin) puff pastry

**hojear** [oxe'ar] /1a/ vt to leaf through, turn the pages of

**hojuela** [o'xwela] nf (LAM) flake

**hola** ['ola] excl hello!

**Holanda** [o'landa] nf Holland; **holandés, -esa** adj Dutch ▷ nm/f Dutchman/woman ▷ nm (Ling) Dutch

**holgado, -a** [ol'ɣaðo, a] adj loose, baggy; (rico) well-to-do

**holgar** [ol'ɣar] /1h, 1l/ vi (descansar) to rest; (sobrar) to be superfluous

**holgazán, -ana** [olɣa'θan, ana] adj idle, lazy ▷ nm/f loafer

**hollín** [o'ʎin] nm soot

**hombre** ['ombre] nm man; (raza humana) **el ~** man(kind) ▷ excl (para énfasis) man, old chap; ¡sí **~!** (claro) of course!; **~ de negocios** businessman; **~-rana** frogman; **~ de bien** o **pro** honest man

**hombrera** [om'brera] nf shoulder strap

**hombro** ['ombro] nm shoulder

**homenaje** [ome'naxe] nm (gen) homage; (tributo) tribute

**homicida** [omi'θiða] adj homicidal ▷ nmf murderer; **homicidio** nm murder, homicide

**homologar** [omolo'ɣar] /1h/ vt (Com) to standardize

**homólogo, -a** [o'moloɣo, a] nm/f counterpart, opposite number

**homosexual** [omosek'swal] *adj, nmf* homosexual

**honda** ['onda] *nf* (cs) catapult

**hondo, -a** ['ondo, a] *adj* deep; **lo ~** the depth(s) (pl), the bottom; **hondonada** *nf* hollow, depression; (*cañón*) ravine

**Honduras** [on'duras] *nf* Honduras

**hondureño, -a** [ondu'reno, a] *adj, nm/f* Honduran

**honestidad** [onesti'ðað] *nf* purity, chastity; (*decencia*) decency; **honesto, -a** *adj* chaste; decent, honest; (*justo*) just

**hongo** ['ongo] *nm* (*Bot: gen*) fungus; (: *comestible*) mushroom; (: *venenoso*) toadstool

**honor** [o'nor] *nm* (*gen*) honour (BRIT), honor (US); **en ~ a la verdad** to be fair; **honorable** *adj* honourable (BRIT), honorable (US)

**honorario, -a** [ono'rarjo, a] *adj* honorary ▷ *nm:* **~s fees**

**honra** ['onra] *nf* (*gen*) honour (BRIT), honor (US); (*renombre*) good name; **honradez** *nf* honesty; (*de persona*) integrity; **honrado, -a** *adj* honest, upright; **honrar** /1a/ *vt* to honour (BRIT) o honor (US)

**hora** ['ora] *nf* hour; (*tiempo*) time; **¿qué ~ es?** what time is it?; **¿a qué ~?** at what time?; **media ~** half an hour; **a la ~ de comer/de recreo** at lunchtime/at playtime; **a primera ~** first thing (in the morning); **a última ~** at the last moment; **a altas ~s** in the small hours; **¡a buena ~!** about time, too!; **pedir ~** to make an appointment; **dar la ~** to strike the hour; **~s de oficina/de trabajo** office/working hours; **~s de visita** visiting times; **~s extras** o **extraordinarias** overtime *sg*; **~s pico** (LAM) rush o peak hours; **~s punta** rush hours

**horario, -a** [o'rarjo, a] *adj* hourly, hour *cpd* ▷ *nm* timetable; **~ comercial** business hours

**horca** ['orka] *nf* gallows *sg*

**horcajadas** [orka'xaðas]: **a ~** *adv* astride

**horchata** [or'tʃata] *nf* cold drink made from tiger nuts and water, tiger nut milk

**horizontal** [oriθon'tal] *adj* horizontal

**horizonte** [ori'θonte] *nm* horizon

**horma** ['orma] *nf* mould

**hormiga** [or'miɣa] *nf* ant; **hormigas** *nfpl* (*Med*) pins and needles

**hormigón** [ormi'ɣon] *nm* concrete; **~ armado/pretensado** reinforced/ prestressed concrete; **hormigonera** *nf* cement mixer

**hormigueo** [ormi'ɣeo] *nm* (*comezón*) itch

**hormona** [or'mona] *nf* hormone

**hornillo** [or'niʎo] *nm* (*cocina*) portable stove; **~ de gas** gas ring

**horno** ['orno] *nm* (*Culin*) oven; (*Tec*) furnace; **alto ~** blast furnace

**horóscopo** [o'roskopo] *nm* horoscope

**horquilla** [or'kiʎa] *nf* hairpin; (*Agr*) pitchfork

**horrendo, -a** [o'rrendo, a] *adj* horrendous, frightful

**horrible** [o'rriβle] *adj* horrible, dreadful

**horripilante** [orripi'lante] *adj* hair-raising, horrifying

**horror** [o'rror] *nm* horror, dread; (*atrocidad*) atrocity; **¡qué ~!** (*fam*) how awful!; **horrorizar** /1f/ *vt* to horrify, frighten; **horrorizarse** *vr* to be horrified; **horroroso, -a** *adj* horrifying, ghastly

**hortaliza** [orta'liθa] *nf* vegetable

**hortelano, -a** [orte'lano, a] *nm/f* (market) gardener

**hortera** [or'tera] *adj* (*fam*) tacky

**hospedar** [ospe'ðar] /1a/ *vt* to put up; **hospedarse** *vr:* **~se (con/en)** to stay o lodge (with/at)

**hospital** [ospi'tal] *nm* hospital

**hospitalario, -a** [ospita'larjo, a] *adj* (*acogedor*) hospitable; **hospitalidad** *nf* hospitality

**hostal** [os'tal] *nm* small hotel

**hostelería** [ostele'ria] *nf* hotel business o trade

**hostia** ['ostja] *nf* (*Rel*) host, consecrated wafer; (*fam: golpe*) whack, punch ▷ *excl:* **¡~(s)!** (*fam!*) damn!

**hostil** [os'til] *adj* hostile

**hotdog** [ot'dog] *nm* (LAM) hot dog

**hotel** [o'tel] *nm* hotel; *see note* **"hotel"**; **hotelero, -a** *adj* hotel *cpd* ▷ *nm/f* hotelier

**HOTEL**

- In Spain you can choose from the
- following categories of accommodation,
- in descending order of quality and price:
- hotel (from 5 stars to 1), *hostal*, *pensión*,
- *casa de huéspedes*, *fonda*. Quality can vary
- widely even within these categories.
- The State also runs luxury hotels called
- *paradores*, which are usually sited in places
- of particular historical interest and are
- often historic buildings themselves.

**hoy** [oi] *adv* (*este día*) today; (*en la actualidad*) now(adays) ▷ *nm* present time; **~ (en) día** now(adays)

**hoyo** ['ojo] *nm* hole, pit

**hoz** [oθ] *nf* sickle

**hube** *etc* ['uβe] *vb* V **haber**

**hucha** ['utʃa] *nf* money box

**hueco, -a** ['weko, a] *adj* (*vacío*) hollow, empty; (*resonante*) booming ▷ *nm* hollow, cavity

**huelga** ['welɣa] *vb* V **holgar** ▷ *nf* strike; **declararse en ~** to go on strike, come out on strike; **~ general** general strike; **~ de hambre** hunger strike

**huelguista** [wel'ɣista] *nmf* striker

**huella** ['weʎa] *nf* (*acto de pisar, pisada*) tread(ing); (*marca del paso*) footprint, footstep; (: *de animal, máquina*) track; **~ de carbono** carbon footprint; **~ dactilar** o **digital** fingerprint

**huelo** *etc vb* V **oler**

**huérfano, -a** ['werfano, a] *adj* orphan(ed) ▷ *nm/f* orphan

**huerta** ['werta] *nf* market garden (BRIT), truck farm (US); (*de Murcia, Valencia*) irrigated region

**huerto** ['werto] *nm* kitchen garden; (*de árboles frutales*) orchard

**hueso** ['weso] *nm* (Anat) bone; (*de fruta*) stone

**huésped, a** ['wespeð, a] *nm/f* guest

**huevas** ['weβas] *nfpl* roe *sg*

**huevera** [we'βera] *nf* eggcup

**huevo** ['weβo] *nm* egg; **~ duro/escalfado/ estrellado** o **frito/pasado por agua** hard-boiled/poached/fried/soft-boiled egg; **~s revueltos** scrambled eggs; **~ tibio** (LAM) soft-boiled egg

**huida** [u'iða] *nf* escape, flight

**huir** [u'ir] /3g/ *vt* (*escapar*) to flee, escape; (*evadir*) to avoid

**hule** ['ule] *nm* oilskin; (*esp* LAM) rubber

**hulera** [u'lera] *nf* (LAM) catapult

**humanidad** [umani'ðað] *nf* (*género humano*) man(kind); (*cualidad*) humanity

**humanitario, -a** [umani'tarjo, a] *adj* humanitarian

**humano, -a** [u'mano, a] *adj* (*gen*) human; (*humanitario*) humane ▷ *nm* human; **ser ~** human being

**humareda** [uma'reða] *nf* cloud of smoke

**humedad** [ume'ðað] *nf* (*del clima*) humidity; (*de pared etc*) dampness; **a prueba de ~** damp-proof; **humedecer** /2d/ *vt* to moisten, wet; **humedecerse** *vr* to get wet

**húmedo, -a** ['umeðo, a] *adj* (*mojado*) damp, wet; (*tiempo etc*) humid

**humilde** [u'milde] *adj* humble, modest

**humillación** [umiʎa'θjon] *nf* humiliation; **humillante** *adj* humiliating

**humillar** [umi'ʎar] /1a/ *vt* to humiliate

**humo** ['umo] *nm* (*de fuego*) smoke; (*gas nocivo*) fumes *pl*; (*vapor*) steam, vapour; **humos** *nmpl* (*fig*) conceit *sg*

**humor** [u'mor] *nm* (*disposición*) mood, temper; (*lo que divierte*) humour; **de buen/ mal ~** in a good/bad mood; **humorista** *nmf* comic; **humorístico, -a** *adj* funny, humorous

**hundimiento** [undi'mjento] *nm* (*gen*) sinking; (*colapso*) collapse

**hundir** [un'dir] /3a/ *vt* to sink; (*edificio, plan*) to ruin, destroy; **hundirse** *vr* to sink, collapse

**húngaro, -a** ['ungaro, a] *adj, nm/f* Hungarian

**Hungría** [un'gria] *nf* Hungary

**huracán** [ura'kan] *nm* hurricane

**huraño, -a** [u'raɲo, a] *adj* (*antisocial*) unsociable

**hurgar** [ur'ɣar] /1h/ *vt* to poke, jab; (*remover*) to stir (up); **hurgarse** *vr*: **~se (las narices)** to pick one's nose

**hurón** [u'ron] *nm* (Zool) ferret

**hurtadillas** [urta'ðiʎas]: **a ~** *adv* stealthily, on the sly

**hurtar** [ur'tar] /1a/ *vt* to steal; **hurto** *nm* theft, stealing

**husmear** [usme'ar] /1a/ *vt* (*oler*) to sniff out, scent; (*fam*) to pry into

**huyo** *etc vb* V **huir**

**I**

**iba** etc ['iβa] vb V **ir**
**ibérico, -a** [i'βeriko, a] adj Iberian
**iberoamericano, -a** [iβeroameri'kano, a] adj, nm/f Latin American
**Ibiza** [i'βiθa] nf Ibiza
**iceberg** [iθe'βer] nm iceberg
**icono** [i'kono] nm icon
**ida** ['iða] nf going, departure; **~ y vuelta** round trip, return
**idea** [i'ðea] nf idea; **no tengo la menor ~** I haven't a clue
**ideal** [iðe'al] adj, nm ideal; **idealista** nmf idealist; **idealizar** /1f/ vt to idealize
**ídem** ['iðem] pron ditto
**idéntico, -a** [i'ðentiko, a] adj identical
**identidad** [iðenti'ðað] nf identity
**identificación** [iðentifika'θjon] nf identification
**identificar** [iðentifi'kar] /1g/ vt to identify; **identificarse** vr: **~se con** to identify with
**ideología** [iðeolo'xia] nf ideology
**idilio** [i'ðiljo] nm love affair
**idioma** [i'ðjoma] nm language
⬛ No confundir *idioma* con la palabra inglesa *idiom*.
**idiota** [i'ðjota] adj idiotic ▷ nmf idiot
**ídolo** ['iðolo] nm (tb fig) idol
**idóneo, -a** [i'ðoneo, a] adj suitable
**iglesia** [i'ɣlesja] nf church
**ignorante** [iɣno'rante] adj ignorant, uninformed ▷ nmf ignoramus
**ignorar** [iɣno'rar] /1a/ vt not to know, be ignorant of; (no hacer caso a) to ignore
**igual** [i'ɣwal] adj equal; (similar) like, similar; (mismo) (the) same; (constante) constant; (temperatura) even ▷ nmf, conj equal; **al ~ que** prep like, just like; **~ que** the same as; **me da o es ~** I don't care; **son ~es** they're the same

**igualar** [iɣwa'lar] /1a/ vt (gen) to equalize, make equal; (terreno) to make even; (allanar, nivelar) to level (off); **igualarse** vr (platos de balanza) to balance out
**igualdad** [iɣwal'dað] nf equality; (similaridad) sameness; (uniformidad) uniformity
**igualmente** [iɣwal'mente] adv equally; (también) also, likewise ▷ excl the same to you!
**ilegal** [ile'ɣal] adj illegal
**ilegítimo, -a** [ile'xitimo, a] adj illegitimate
**ileso, -a** [i'leso, a] adj unhurt
**ilimitado, -a** [ilimi'taðo, a] adj unlimited
**iluminación** [ilumina'θjon] nf illumination; (alumbrado) lighting
**iluminar** [ilumi'nar] /1a/ vt to illuminate, light (up); (fig) to enlighten
**ilusión** [ilu'sjon] nf illusion; (quimera) delusion; (esperanza) hope; **hacerse ilusiones** to build up one's hopes; **ilusionado, -a** adj excited; **ilusionar** /1a/ vi: **le ilusiona ir de vacaciones** he's looking forward to going on holiday; **ilusionarse** vr (entusiasmarse) to get excited
**iluso, -a** [i'luso, a] adj easily deceived ▷ nm/f dreamer
**ilustración** [ilustra'θjon] nf illustration; (saber) learning, erudition; **la I~** the Enlightenment; **ilustrado, -a** adj illustrated; learned
**ilustrar** [ilus'trar] /1a/ vt to illustrate; (instruir) to instruct; (explicar) to explain, make clear
**ilustre** [i'lustre] adj famous, illustrious
**imagen** [i'maxen] nf (gen) image; (dibujo) picture
**imaginación** [imaxina'θjon] nf imagination
**imaginar** [imaxi'nar] /1a/ vt (gen) to imagine; (idear) to think up; (suponer) to suppose; **imaginarse** vr to imagine; **imaginario, -a** adj imaginary; **imaginativo, -a** adj imaginative
**imán** [i'man] nm magnet; (Rel) imam
**imbécil** [im'beθil] nmf imbecile, idiot
**imitación** [imita'θjon] nf imitation; **a ~ de** in imitation of
**imitar** [imi'tar] /1a/ vt to imitate; (parodiar, remedar) to mimic, ape
**impaciente** [impa'θjente] adj impatient; (nervioso) anxious
**impacto** [im'pakto] nm impact
**impar** [im'par] adj odd
**imparcial** [impar'θjal] adj impartial, fair
**impecable** [impe'kaβle] adj impeccable
**impedimento** [impeði'mento] nm impediment, obstacle

**impedir** [impe'ðir] /3k/ vt (obstruir) to impede, obstruct; (estorbar) to prevent; **~ a algn hacer** o **que algn haga algo** to prevent sb (from) doing sth

**imperativo, -a** [impera'tiβo, a] adj (urgente, Ling) imperative

**imperdible** [imper'ðiβle] nm safety pin

**imperdonable** [imperðo'naβle] adj unforgivable, inexcusable

**imperfecto, -a** [imper'fekto, a] adj imperfect

**imperio** [im'perjo] nm empire; (autoridad) rule, authority; (fig) pride, haughtiness

**impermeable** [imperme'aβle] adj waterproof ▷ nm raincoat, mac (BRIT)

**impersonal** [imperso'nal] adj impersonal

**impertinente** [imperti'nente] adj impertinent

**ímpetu** ['impetu] nm (impulso) impetus, impulse; (impetuosidad) impetuosity; (violencia) violence

**implantar** [implan'tar] /1a/ vt (costumbre) to introduce

**implemento** [imple'mento] nm (LAM) tool, implement

**implicar** [impli'kar] /1g/ vt to involve; (entrañar) to imply

**implícito, -a** [im'pliθito, a] adj (tácito) implicit; (sobreentendido) implied

**imponente** [impo'nente] adj (impresionante) impressive, imposing; (solemne) grand

**imponer** [impo'ner] /2q/ vt (gen) to impose; (exigir) to exact; **imponerse** vr to assert o.s.; (prevalecer) to prevail; **imponible** adj (Com) taxable

**impopular** [impopu'lar] adj unpopular

**importación** [importa'θjon] nf (acto) importing; (mercancías) imports pl

**importancia** [impor'tanθja] nf importance; (valor) value, significance; (extensión) size, magnitude; **no tiene ~** it's nothing; **importante** adj important; valuable, significant

**importar** [impor'tar] /1a/ vt (del extranjero) to import; (costar) to amount to ▷ vi to be important, matter; **me importa un rábano** o **un bledo** I couldn't care less; **¿le importa que fume?** do you mind if I smoke?; **no importa** it doesn't matter

**importe** [im'porte] nm (cantidad) amount; (valor) value

**imposible** [impo'siβle] adj impossible; (insoportable) unbearable, intolerable

**imposición** [imposi'θjon] nf imposition; (Com) tax; (inversión) deposit

**impostor, a** [impos'tor, a] nm/f impostor

**impotencia** [impo'tenθja] nf impotence; **impotente** adj impotent

**impreciso, -a** [impre'θiso, a] adj imprecise, vague

**impregnar** [impreɣ'nar] /1a/ vt to impregnate; **impregnarse** vr to become impregnated

**imprenta** [im'prenta] nf (acto) printing; (aparato) press; (casa) printer's; (letra) print

**imprescindible** [impresθin'diβle] adj essential, vital

**impresión** [impre'sjon] nf impression; (Imprenta) printing; (edición) edition; (Foto) print; (marca) imprint; **~ digital** fingerprint

**impresionante** [impresjo'nante] adj impressive; (tremendo) tremendous; (maravilloso) great, marvellous

**impresionar** [impresjo'nar] /1a/ vt (conmover) to move; (afectar) to impress, strike; (película fotográfica) to expose; **impresionarse** vr to be impressed; (conmoverse) to be moved

**impreso, -a** [im'preso, a] pp de **imprimir** ▷ adj printed; **impresos** nmpl printed matter sg; **impresora** nf printer

**imprevisto, -a** [impre'βisto, a] adj unforeseen; (inesperado) unexpected

**imprimir** [impri'mir] /3a/ vt to stamp; (textos) to print; (Inform) to output, print out

**improbable** [impro'βaβle] adj improbable; (inverosímil) unlikely

**impropio, -a** [im'propjo, a] adj improper

**improvisado, -a** [improβi'saðo, a] adj improvised

**improvisar** [improβi'sar] /1a/ vt to improvise

**improviso** [impro'βiso] adv: **de ~** unexpectedly, suddenly

**imprudencia** [impru'ðenθja] nf imprudence; (indiscreción) indiscretion; (descuido) carelessness; **imprudente** adj unwise, imprudent; (indiscreto) indiscreet

**impuesto, -a** [im'pwesto, a] adj imposed ▷ nm tax; **~ de venta** sales tax; **~ ecológico** green tax; **~ sobre el valor añadido (IVA)** value added tax (VAT)

**impulsar** [impul'sar] /1a/ vt to drive; (promover) to promote, stimulate

**impulsivo, -a** [impul'siβo, a] adj impulsive; **impulso** nm impulse; (fuerza, empuje) thrust, drive; (fig: sentimiento) urge, impulse

**impureza** [impu're θa] nf impurity; **impuro, -a** adj impure

**inaccesible** [inakθe'siβle] adj inaccessible

**inaceptable** [inaθep'taβle] adj unacceptable

**inactivo, -a** [inak'tiβo, a] adj inactive

**inadecuado, -a** [inaðe'kwaðo, a] adj (insuficiente) inadequate; (inapto) unsuitable

**inadvertido, -a** [inað̞ßer'tiðo, a] *adj* (*no visto*) unnoticed

**inaguantable** [inaɣwan'taβle] *adj* unbearable

**inalámbrico, -a** [ina'lambriko, a] *adj* cordless, wireless

**inanimado, -a** [inani'maðo, a] *adj* inanimate

**inaudito, -a** [inau'ðito, a] *adj* unheard-of

**inauguración** [inauɣura'θjon] *nf* inauguration; (*de exposición*) opening

**inaugurar** [inauɣu'rar] /1a/ *vt* to inaugurate; (*exposición*) to open

**inca** ['inka] *nmf* Inca

**incalculable** [inkalku'laβle] *adj* incalculable

**incandescente** [inkandes'θente] *adj* incandescent

**incansable** [inkan'saβle] *adj* tireless, untiring

**incapacidad** [inkapaθi'ðað] *nf* incapacity; (*incompetencia*) incompetence; **~ física/mental** physical/mental disability

**incapacitar** [inkapaθi'tar] /1a/ *vt* (*inhabilitar*) to incapacitate, handicap; (*descalificar*) to disqualify

**incapaz** [inka'paθ] *adj* incapable

**incautarse** [inkau'tarse] /1a/ *vr*: **~ de** to seize, confiscate

**incauto, -a** [in'kauto, a] *adj* (*imprudente*) incautious, unwary

**incendiar** [inθen'djar] /1b/ *vt* to set fire to; (*fig*) to inflame; **incendiarse** *vr* to catch fire; **incendiario, -a** *adj* incendiary

**incendio** [in'θendjo] *nm* fire

**incentivo** [inθen'tiβo] *nm* incentive

**incertidumbre** [inθerti'ðumbre] *nf* (*inseguridad*) uncertainty; (*duda*) doubt

**incesante** [inθe'sante] *adj* incessant

**incesto** [in'θesto] *nm* incest

**incidencia** [inθi'ðenθja] *nf* (*Mat*) incidence

**incidente** [inθi'ðente] *nm* incident

**incidir** [inθi'ðir] /3a/ *vi*: **~ en** (*influir*) to influence; (*afectar*) to affect

**incienso** [in'θjenso] *nm* incense

**incierto, -a** [in'θjerto, a] *adj* uncertain

**incineración** [inθinera'θjon] *nf* incineration; (*de cadáveres*) cremation

**incinerar** [inθine'rar] /1a/ *vt* to burn; (*cadáveres*) to cremate

**incisión** [inθi'sjon] *nf* incision

**incisivo, -a** [inθi'siβo, a] *adj* sharp, cutting; (*fig*) incisive

**incitar** [inθi'tar] /1a/ *vt* to incite, rouse

**inclemencia** [inkle'menθja] *nf* (*severidad*) harshness, severity; (*del tiempo*) inclemency

**inclinación** [inklina'θjon] *nf* (*gen*) inclination; (*de tierras*) slope, incline; (*de cabeza*) nod, bow; (*fig*) leaning, bent

**inclinar** [inkli'nar] /1a/ *vt* to incline; (*cabeza*) to nod, bow; **inclinarse** *vr* to lean, slope; to bow; (*encorvarse*) to stoop; **~se a** (*parecerse*) to take after, resemble; **~se ante** to bow down to; **me inclino a pensar que ...** I'm inclined to think that ...

**incluir** [inklu'ir] /3g/ *vt* to include; (*incorporar*) to incorporate; (*meter*) to enclose

**inclusive** [inklu'siβe] *adv* inclusive ▷ *prep* including

**incluso, -a** [in'kluso, a] *adv* even

**incógnita** [in'koɣnita] *nf* (*Mat*) unknown quantity

**incógnito** [in'koɣnito] *nm*: **de ~** incognito

**incoherente** [inkoe'rente] *adj* incoherent

**incoloro, -a** [inko'loro, a] *adj* colourless

**incomodar** [inkomo'ðar] /1a/ *vt* to inconvenience; (*molestar*) to bother, trouble; (*fastidiar*) to annoy

**incomodidad** [inkomoði'ðað] *nf* inconvenience; (*fastidio, enojo*) annoyance; (*de vivienda*) discomfort

**incómodo, -a** [in'komoðo, a] *adj* (*inconfortable*) uncomfortable; (*molesto*) annoying; (*inconveniente*) inconvenient

**incomparable** [inkompa'raβle] *adj* incomparable

**incompatible** [inkompa'tiβle] *adj* incompatible

**incompetente** [inkompe'tente] *adj* incompetent

**incompleto, -a** [inkom'pleto, a] *adj* incomplete, unfinished

**incomprensible** [inkompren'siβle] *adj* incomprehensible

**incomunicado, -a** [inkomuni'kaðo, a] *adj* (*aislado*) cut off, isolated; (*confinado*) in solitary confinement

**incondicional** [inkondiθjo'nal] *adj* unconditional; (*apoyo*) wholehearted; (*partidario*) staunch

**inconfundible** [inkonfun'diβle] *adj* unmistakable

**incongruente** [inkon'grwente] *adj* incongruous

**inconsciente** [inkons'θjente] *adj* unconscious; thoughtless

**inconsecuente** [inkonse'kwente] *adj* inconsistent

**inconstante** [inkons'tante] *adj* inconstant

**incontable** [inkon'taβle] *adj* countless, innumerable

**inconveniencia** [inkombe'njenθja] *nf* unsuitability, inappropriateness; (*falta de cortesía*) impoliteness; **inconveniente** *adj*

unsuitable; impolite ▷ *nm* obstacle;
(*desventaja*) disadvantage; **el inconveniente
es que ...** the trouble is that ...
**incordiar** [inkor'ðjar] /1b/ *vt* (*fam*) to
hassle
**incorporar** [inkorpo'rar] /1a/ *vt* to
incorporate; **incorporarse** *vr* to sit up;
**~se a** to join
**incorrecto, -a** [inko'rrekto, a] *adj* incorrect,
wrong; (*comportamiento*) bad-mannered
**incorregible** [inkorre'xiβle] *adj*
incorrigible
**incrédulo, -a** [in'kreðulo, a] *adj*
incredulous, unbelieving; sceptical
**increíble** [inkre'iβle] *adj* incredible
**incremento** [inkre'mento] *nm* increment;
(*aumento*) rise, increase
**increpar** [inkre'par] /1a/ *vt* to reprimand
**incruento, -a** [in'krwento, a] *adj* bloodless
**incrustar** [inkrus'tar] /1a/ *vt* to incrust;
(*piedras: en joya*) to inlay
**incubar** [inku'βar] /1a/ *vt* to incubate
**inculcar** [inkul'kar] /1g/ *vt* to inculcate
**inculto, -a** [in'kulto, a] *adj* (*persona*)
uneducated; (*grosero*) uncouth ▷ *nm/f*
ignoramus
**incumplimiento** [inkumpli'mjento] *nm*
non-fulfilment; **~ de contrato** breach of
contract
**incurrir** [inku'rrir] /3a/ *vi*: **~ en** to incur;
(*crimen*) to commit
**indagar** [inda'ɣar] /1h/ *vt* to investigate; to
search; (*averiguar*) to ascertain
**indecente** [inde'θente] *adj* indecent,
improper; (*lascivo*) obscene
**indeciso, -a** [inde'θiso, a] *adj* (*por decidir*)
undecided; (*vacilante*) hesitant
**indefenso, -a** [inde'fenso, a] *adj*
defenceless
**indefinido, -a** [indefi'niðo, a] *adj*
indefinite; (*vago*) vague, undefined
**indemne** [in'demne] *adj* (*objeto*)
undamaged; (*persona*) unharmed, unhurt
**indemnizar** [indemni'θar] /1f/ *vt* to
indemnify; (*compensar*) to compensate
**independencia** [indepen'denθja] *nf*
independence
**independiente** [indepen'djente] *adj* (*libre*)
independent; (*autónomo*) self-sufficient
**indeterminado, -a** [indetermi'naðo, a]
*adj* indefinite; (*desconocido*) indeterminate
**India** ['indja] *nf*: **la ~** India
**indicación** [indika'θjon] *nf* indication;
(*señal*) sign; (*sugerencia*) suggestion, hint
**indicado, -a** [indi'kaðo, a] *adj* (*momento,
método*) right; (*tratamiento*) appropriate;
(*solución*) likely
**indicador** [indika'ðor] *nm* indicator; (*Tec*)
gauge, meter

**indicar** [indi'kar] /1g/ *vt* (*mostrar*) to
indicate, show; (*termómetro etc*) to read,
register; (*señalar*) to point to
**índice** ['indiθe] *nm* index; (*catálogo*)
catalogue; (*Anat*) index finger, forefinger;
**~ de materias** table of contents
**indicio** [in'diθjo] *nm* indication, sign; (*en
pesquisa etc*) clue
**indiferencia** [indife'renθja] *nf*
indifference; (*apatía*) apathy; **indiferente**
*adj* indifferent
**indígena** [in'dixena] *adj* indigenous,
native ▷ *nmf* native
**indigestión** [indixes'tjon] *nf* indigestion
**indigesto, -a** [indi'xesto, a] *adj*
indigestible; (*fig*) turgid
**indignación** [indiɣna'θjon] *nf*
indignation
**indignar** [indiɣ'nar] /1a/ *vt* to anger, make
indignant; **indignarse** *vr*: **~se por** to get
indignant about
**indigno, -a** [in'diɣno, a] *adj* (*despreciable*)
low, contemptible; (*inmerecido*)
unworthy
**indio, -a** ['indjo, a] *adj*, *nm/f* Indian
**indirecto, -a** [indi'rekto, a] *adj* indirect
▷ *nf* insinuation, innuendo; (*sugerencia*)
hint
**indiscreción** [indiskre'θjon] *nf*
(*imprudencia*) indiscretion; (*irreflexión*)
tactlessness; (*acto*) gaffe, faux pas
**indiscreto, -a** [indis'kreto, a] *adj*
indiscreet
**indiscutible** [indisku'tiβle] *adj*
indisputable, unquestionable
**indispensable** [indispen'saβle] *adj*
indispensable, essential
**indispuesto, -a** [indis'pwesto, a] *adj*
(*enfermo*) unwell, indisposed
**indistinto, -a** [indis'tinto, a] *adj*
indistinct; (*vago*) vague
**individual** [indiβi'ðwal] *adj* individual;
(*habitación*) single ▷ *nm* (*Deporte*) singles *sg*
**individuo, -a** [indi'βiðwo, a] *adj* ▷ *nm*
individual
**índole** ['indole] *nf* (*naturaleza*) nature;
(*clase*) sort, kind
**inducir** [indu'θir] /3n/ *vt* to induce; (*inferir*)
to infer; (*persuadir*) to persuade
**indudable** [indu'ðaβle] *adj* undoubted;
(*incuestionable*) unquestionable
**indultar** [indul'tar] /1a/ *vt* (*perdonar*) to
pardon, reprieve; (*librar de pago*) to exempt;
**indulto** *nm* pardon; exemption
**industria** [in'dustrja] *nf* industry;
(*habilidad*) skill; **industrial** *adj* industrial
▷ *nm* industrialist
**inédito, -a** [i'neðito, a] *adj* (*libro*)
unpublished; (*nuevo*) new

**ineficaz** [inefi'kaθ] *adj* (*inútil*) ineffective; (*ineficiente*) inefficient

**ineludible** [inelu'ðiβle] *adj* inescapable, unavoidable

**ineptitud** [inepti'tuð] *nf* ineptitude, incompetence; **inepto, -a** *adj* inept, incompetent

**inequívoco, -a** [ine'kiβoko, a] *adj* unequivocal; (*inconfundible*) unmistakable

**inercia** [i'nerθja] *nf* inertia; (*pasividad*) passivity

**inerte** [i'nerte] *adj* inert; (*inmóvil*) motionless

**inesperado, -a** [inespe'raðo, a] *adj* unexpected, unforeseen

**inestable** [ines'taβle] *adj* unstable

**inevitable** [ineβi'taβle] *adj* inevitable

**inexacto, -a** [inek'sakto, a] *adj* inaccurate; (*falso*) untrue

**inexperto, -a** [ineks'perto, a] *adj* (*novato*) inexperienced

**infalible** [infa'liβle] *adj* infallible; (*plan*) foolproof

**infame** [in'fame] *adj* infamous; **infamia** *nf* infamy; (*deshonra*) disgrace

**infancia** [in'fanθja] *nf* infancy, childhood

**infantería** [infante'ria] *nf* infantry

**infantil** [infan'til] *adj* child's, children's; (*pueril, aniñado*) infantile; (*cándido*) childlike

**infarto** [in'farto] *nm* (*tb*: **~ de miocardio**) heart attack; **~ cerebral** stroke

**infatigable** [infati'γaβle] *adj* tireless, untiring

**infección** [infek'θjon] *nf* infection; **infeccioso, -a** *adj* infectious

**infectar** [infek'tar] /1a/ *vt* to infect; **infectarse** *vr*

**infeliz** [infe'liθ] *adj* unhappy, wretched ▷ *nmf* wretch

**inferior** [infe'rjor] *adj* inferior; (*situación*) lower ▷ *nmf* inferior, subordinate

**inferir** [infe'rir] /3i/ *vt* (*deducir*) to infer, deduce; (*causar*) to cause

**infidelidad** [infiðeli'ðað] *nf* infidelity, unfaithfulness

**infiel** [in'fjel] *adj* unfaithful, disloyal; (*falso*) inaccurate ▷ *nmf* infidel, unbeliever

**infierno** [in'fjerno] *nm* hell

**ínfimo, -a** ['infimo, a] *adj* (*vil*) vile, mean; (*más bajo*) lowest

**infinidad** [infini'ðað] *nf* infinity; (*abundancia*) great quantity

**infinito, -a** [infi'nito, a] *adj* ▷ *nm* infinite

**inflación** [infla'θjon] *nf* (*hinchazón*) swelling; (*monetaria*) inflation; (*fig*) conceit

**inflamable** [infla'maβle] *adj* flammable

**inflamar** [infla'mar] /1a/ *vt* (*Med, fig*) to inflame; **inflamarse** *vr* to catch fire; to become inflamed

**inflar** [in'flar] /1a/ *vt* (*hinchar*) to inflate, blow up; (*fig*) to exaggerate; **inflarse** *vr* to swell (up); (*fig*) to get conceited

**inflexible** [inflek'siβle] *adj* inflexible; (*fig*) unbending

**influencia** [in'flwenθja] *nf* influence

**influir** [influ'ir] /3g/ *vt* to influence

**influjo** [in'fluxo] *nm* influence

**influya** *etc vb* V **influir**

**influyente** [influ'jente] *adj* influential

**información** [informa'θjon] *nf* information; (*noticias*) news *sg*; (*Jur*) inquiry; **I~** (*oficina*) information desk; (*Telec*) Directory Enquiries (BRIT), Directory Assistance (US); (*mostrador*) Information Desk

**informal** [infor'mal] *adj* informal

**informar** [infor'mar] /1a/ *vt* (*gen*) to inform; (*revelar*) to reveal, make known ▷ *vi* (*Jur*) to plead; (*denunciar*) to inform; (*dar cuenta de*) to report on; **informarse** *vr* to find out; **~se de** to inquire into

**informática** [infor'matika] *nf* V **informático**

**informático, -a** [infor'matiko, a] *adj* computer *cpd* ▷ *nf* (*Tec*) information technology; computing; (*Escol*) computer science *o* studies

**informe** [in'forme] *adj* shapeless ▷ *nm* report

**infracción** [infrak'θjon] *nf* infraction, infringement

**infravalorar** [infraβalo'rar] /1a/ *vt* to undervalue; (*Finanzas*) to underestimate

**infringir** [infrin'xir] /3c/ *vt* to infringe, contravene

**infundado, -a** [infun'daðo, a] *adj* groundless, unfounded

**infundir** [infun'dir] /3a/ *vt* to infuse, instil

**infusión** [infu'sjon] *nf* infusion; **~ de manzanilla** camomile tea

**ingeniería** [inxenje'ria] *nf* engineering; **~ genética** genetic engineering; **ingeniero, -a** *nm/f* engineer; **ingeniero de caminos** civil engineer

**ingenio** [in'xenjo] *nm* (*talento*) talent; (*agudeza*) wit; (*habilidad*) ingenuity, inventiveness; **~ azucarero** sugar refinery; **ingenioso, -a** *adj* ingenious, clever; (*divertido*) witty

**ingenuo, -a** [in'xenwo, a] *adj* ingenuous

**ingerir** [inxe'rir] /3i/ *vt* to ingest; (*tragar*) to swallow; (*consumir*) to consume

**Inglaterra** [ingla'terra] *nf* England

**ingle** ['ingle] *nf* groin

**inglés, -esa** [in'gles, esa] *adj* English ▷ *nm/f* Englishman/woman ▷ *nm* (*Ling*) English

**ingrato, -a** [in'grato, a] *adj* ungrateful
**ingrediente** [ingre'ðjente] *nm* ingredient
**ingresar** [ingre'sar] /1a/ *vt* (*dinero*) to deposit ▷ *vi* to come o go in; ~ **en el hospital** to go into hospital
**ingreso** [in'greso] *nm* (*entrada*) entry; (: *en hospital etc*) admission; **ingresos** *nmpl* (*dinero*) income *sg*; (: *Com*) takings *pl*
**inhabitable** [inaβi'taβle] *adj* uninhabitable
**inhalar** [ina'lar] /1a/ *vt* to inhale
**inhibir** [ini'βir] /3a/ *vt* to inhibit
**inhóspito, -a** [i'nospito, a] *adj* (*región, paisaje*) inhospitable
**inhumano, -a** [inu'mano, a] *adj* inhuman
**inicial** [ini'θjal] *adj*, *nf* initial
**iniciar** [ini'θjar] /1b/ *vt* (*persona*) to initiate; (*empezar*) to begin, commence; (*conversación*) to start up
**iniciativa** [iniθja'tiβa] *nf* initiative; ~ **privada** private enterprise
**ininterrumpido, -a** [ininterrum'piðo, a] *adj* uninterrupted
**injertar** [inxer'tar] /1a/ *vt* to graft; **injerto** *nm* graft
**injuria** [in'xurja] *nf* (*agravio, ofensa*) offence; (*insulto*) insult

> No confundir *injuria* con la palabra inglesa *injury*.

**injusticia** [inxus'tiθja] *nf* injustice
**injusto, -a** [in'xusto, a] *adj* unjust, unfair
**inmadurez** [inmaðu'reθ] *nf* immaturity
**inmediaciones** [inmeðja'θjones] *nfpl* neighbourhood *sg*, environs
**inmediato, -a** [inme'ðjato, a] *adj* immediate; (*contiguo*) adjoining; (*rápido*) prompt; (*próximo*) neighbouring, next; **de ~** immediately
**inmejorable** [inmexo'raβle] *adj* unsurpassable; (*precio*) unbeatable
**inmenso, -a** [in'menso, a] *adj* immense, huge
**inmigración** [inmiɣra'θjon] *nf* immigration
**inmolar** [inmo'lar] /1a/ *vt* to immolate, sacrifice
**inmoral** [inmo'ral] *adj* immoral
**inmortal** [inmor'tal] *adj* immortal; **inmortalizar** /1f/ *vt* to immortalize
**inmóvil** [in'moβil] *adj* immobile
**inmueble** [in'mweβle] *adj*: **bienes ~s** real estate *sg*, landed property *sg* ▷ *nm* property
**inmundo, -a** [in'mundo, a] *adj* filthy
**inmune** [in'mune] *adj*: ~ **(a)** (*Med*) immune (to)
**inmunidad** [inmuni'ðað] *nf* immunity
**inmutarse** [inmu'tarse] /1a/ *vr* to turn pale; **no se inmutó** he didn't turn a hair; **siguió sin ~** he carried on unperturbed

**innato, -a** [in'nato, a] *adj* innate
**innecesario, -a** [inneθe'sarjo, a] *adj* unnecessary
**innovación** [innoβa'θjon] *nf* innovation
**innovar** [inno'βar] /1a/ *vt* to introduce
**inocencia** [ino'θenθja] *nf* innocence
**inocentada** [inoθen'taða] *nf* practical joke
**inocente** [ino'θente] *adj* (*ingenuo*) naive, innocent; (*no culpable*) innocent; (*sin malicia*) harmless ▷ *nmf* simpleton; **día de los (Santos) I~s** ≈ April Fools' Day

○ **DÍA DE LOS INOCENTES**
○
○ The 28th December, *el día de los*
○ *(Santos) Inocentes*, is when the Church
○ commemorates the story of Herod's
○ slaughter of the innocent children of
○ Judea in the time of Christ. On this day
○ Spaniards play *inocentadas* (practical
○ jokes) on each other, much like our April
○ Fools' Day pranks, eg typically sticking
○ a *monigote* (cut-out paper figure) on
○ someone's back, or broadcasting unlikely
○ news stories.

**inodoro** [ino'ðoro] *nm* toilet (BRIT), lavatory (BRIT), washroom (US)
**inofensivo, -a** [inofen'siβo, a] *adj* inoffensive
**inolvidable** [inolβi'ðaβle] *adj* unforgettable
**inoportuno, -a** [inopor'tuno, a] *adj* untimely; (*molesto*) inconvenient
**inoxidable** [inoksi'ðaβle] *adj*: **acero ~** stainless steel
**inquietar** [inkje'tar] /1a/ *vt* to worry, trouble; **inquietarse** *vr* to worry, get upset; **inquieto, -a** *adj* anxious, worried; **inquietud** *nf* anxiety, worry
**inquilino, -a** [inki'lino, a] *nm/f* tenant
**insaciable** [insa'θjaβle] *adj* insatiable
**inscribir** [inskri'βir] /3a/ *vt* to inscribe; (*en lista*) to put; (*en censo*) to register
**inscripción** [inskrip'θjon] *nf* inscription; (*Escol etc*) enrolment; (*en censo*) registration
**insecticida** [insekti'θiða] *nm* insecticide
**insecto** [in'sekto] *nm* insect
**inseguridad** [inseɣuri'ðað] *nf* insecurity; ~ **ciudadana** lack of safety in the streets
**inseguro, -a** [inse'ɣuro, a] *adj* insecure; (*inconstante*) unsteady; (*incierto*) uncertain
**insensato, -a** [insen'sato, a] *adj* foolish, stupid
**insensible** [insen'siβle] *adj* (*gen*) insensitive; (*movimiento*) imperceptible; (*sin sensación*) numb
**insertar** [inser'tar] /1a/ *vt* to insert
**inservible** [inser'βiβle] *adj* useless

**insignia** [in'siɣnja] *nf (señal distintiva)* badge; *(estandarte)* flag

**insignificante** [insiɣnifi'kante] *adj* insignificant

**insinuar** [insi'nwar] /1e/ *vt* to insinuate, imply

**insípido, -a** [in'sipiðo, a] *adj* insipid

**insistir** [insis'tir] /3a/ *vi* to insist; **~ en algo** to insist on sth; *(enfatizar)* to stress sth

**insolación** [insola'θjon] *nf (Med)* sunstroke

**insolente** [inso'lente] *adj* insolent

**insólito, -a** [in'solito, a] *adj* unusual

**insoluble** [inso'luβle] *adj* insoluble

**insomnio** [in'somnjo] *nm* insomnia

**insonorizado, -a** [insonori'θaðo, a] *adj (cuarto etc)* soundproof

**insoportable** [insopor'taβle] *adj* unbearable

**inspección** [inspek'θjon] *nf* inspection, check; **inspeccionar** /1a/ *vt (examinar)* to inspect, examine; *(controlar)* to check

**inspector, a** [inspek'tor, a] *nm/f* inspector

**inspiración** [inspira'θjon] *nf* inspiration

**inspirar** [inspi'rar] /1a/ *vt* to inspire; *(Med)* to inhale; **inspirarse** *vr:* **~se en** to be inspired by

**instalación** [instala'θjon] *nf (equipo)* fittings *pl*, equipment; **~ eléctrica** wiring

**instalar** [insta'lar] /1a/ *vt (establecer)* to instal; *(erguir)* to set up, erect; **instalarse** *vr* to establish o.s.; *(en una vivienda)* to move into

**instancia** [ins'tanθja] *nf (ruego)* request; *(Jur)* petition; **en última ~** as a last resort

**instantáneo, -a** [instan'taneo, a] *adj* instantaneous; **café ~** instant coffee

**instante** [ins'tante] *nm* instant, moment; **al ~** right now

**instar** [ins'tar] /1a/ *vt* to press, urge

**instaurar** [instau'rar] /1a/ *vt (costumbre)* to establish; *(normas, sistema)* to bring in, introduce; *(gobierno)* to install

**instigar** [insti'ɣar] /1h/ *vt* to instigate

**instinto** [ins'tinto] *nm* instinct; **por ~** instinctively

**institución** [institu'θjon] *nf* institution, establishment

**instituir** [institu'ir] /3g/ *vt* to establish; *(fundar)* to found; **instituto** *nm (gen)* institute; **Instituto Nacional de Enseñanza** *(esp)* ≈ (state) secondary *(BRIT)* o high *(US)* school

**institutriz** [institu'triθ] *nf* governess

**instrucción** [instruk'θjon] *nf* instruction

**instructor** [instruk'tor] *nm* instructor

**instruir** [instru'ir] /3g/ *vt (gen)* to instruct; *(enseñar)* to teach, educate

**instrumento** [instru'mento] *nm* instrument; *(herramienta)* tool, implement

**insubordinarse** [insuβorði'narse] /1a/ *vr* to rebel

**insuficiente** [insufi'θjente] *adj (gen)* insufficient; *(Escol: nota)* unsatisfactory

**insular** [insu'lar] *adj* insular

**insultar** [insul'tar] /1a/ *vt* to insult; **insulto** *nm* insult

**insuperable** [insupe'raβle] *adj (excelente)* unsurpassable; *(problema etc)* insurmountable

**insurrección** [insurrek'θjon] *nf* insurrection, rebellion

**intachable** [inta'tʃaβle] *adj* irreproachable

**intacto, -a** [in'takto, a] *adj* intact

**integral** [inte'ɣral] *adj* integral; *(completo)* complete; **pan ~** wholemeal bread

**integrar** [inte'ɣrar] /1a/ *vt* to make up, compose; *(Mat, fig)* to integrate

**integridad** [inteɣri'ðað] *nf* wholeness; *(carácter)* integrity; **íntegro, -a** *adj* whole, entire; *(honrado)* honest

**intelectual** [intelek'twal] *adj, nmf* intellectual

**inteligencia** [inteli'xenθja] *nf* intelligence; *(ingenio)* ability; **inteligente** *adj* intelligent

**intemperie** [intem'perje] *nf:* **a la ~** outdoors, out in the open, exposed to the elements

**intención** [inten'θjon] *nf* intention, purpose; **con segundas intenciones** maliciously; **con ~** deliberately

**intencionado, -a** [intenθjo'naðo, a] *adj* deliberate; **mal ~** ill-disposed, hostile

**intensidad** [intensi'ðað] *nf (gen)* intensity; *(Elec, Tec)* strength; **llover con ~** to rain hard

**intenso, -a** [in'tenso, a] *adj* intense; *(sentimiento)* profound, deep

**intentar** [inten'tar] /1a/ *vt (tratar)* to try, attempt; **intento** *nm* attempt

**interactivo, -a** [interak'tiβo, a] *adj* interactive

**intercalar** [interka'lar] /1a/ *vt* to insert

**intercambio** [inter'kambjo] *nm* exchange; swap

**interceder** [interθe'ðer] /2a/ *vi* to intercede

**interceptar** [interθep'tar] /1a/ *vt* to intercept

**interés** [inte'res] *nm* interest; *(parte)* share, part; *(pey)* self-interest; **intereses creados** vested interests

**interesado, -a** [intere'saðo, a] *adj* interested; *(prejuiciado)* prejudiced; *(pey)* mercenary, self-seeking

**interesante** [intere'sante] *adj* interesting

**interesar** [intere'sar] /1a/ *vt* to interest, be of interest to ▷ *vi* to interest, be of interest; **interesarse** *vr:* **~se en** o **por** to take an interest in

**interferir** [interfe'rir] /3i/ vt to interfere with; (Telec) to jam ▷ vi to interfere

**interfono** [inter'fono] nm intercom, entry phone

**interino, -a** [inte'rino, a] adj temporary ▷ nm/f temporary holder of a post; (Med) locum; (Escol) supply teacher

**interior** [inte'rjor] adj inner, inside; (Com) domestic, internal ▷ nm interior, inside; (fig) soul, mind; **Ministerio del I~** ≈ Home Office (BRIT), ≈ Department of the Interior (US)

**interjección** [interxek'θjon] nf interjection

**interlocutor, a** [interloku'tor, a] nm/f speaker

**intermedio, -a** [inter'meðjo, a] adj intermediate ▷ nm interval

**interminable** [intermi'naβle] adj endless

**intermitente** [intermi'tente] adj intermittent ▷ nm (Auto) indicator

**internacional** [internaθjo'nal] adj international

**internado** [inter'naðo] nm boarding school

**internar** [inter'nar] /1a/ vt to intern; (en un manicomio) to commit; **internarse** vr (penetrar) to penetrate

**internauta** [inter'nauta] nmf web surfer, internet user

**Internet** [inter'net] nm o f internet, Internet

**interno, -a** [in'terno, a] adj internal, interior; (Pol etc) domestic ▷ nm/f (alumno) boarder

**interponer** [interpo'ner] /2q/ vt to interpose, put in; **interponerse** vr to intervene

**interpretación** [interpreta'θjon] nf interpretation

**interpretar** [interpre'tar] /1a/ vt to interpret; (Teat, Mus) to perform, play; **intérprete** nmf (Ling) interpreter, translator; (Mus, Teat) performer, artist(e)

**interrogación** [interroɣa'θjon] nf interrogation; (Ling: tb: **signo de ~**) question mark

**interrogar** [interro'ɣar] /1h/ vt to interrogate, question

**interrumpir** [interrum'pir] /3a/ vt to interrupt

**interrupción** [interrup'θjon] nf interruption

**interruptor** [interrup'tor] nm (Elec) switch

**intersección** [intersek'θjon] nf intersection

**interurbano, -a** [interur'βano, a] adj (Telec) long-distance

**intervalo** [inter'βalo] nm interval; (descanso) break

**intervenir** [interβe'nir] /3r/ vt (controlar) to control, supervise; (Med) to operate on ▷ vi (participar) to take part, participate; (mediar) to intervene

**interventor, a** [interβen'tor, a] nm/f inspector; (Com) auditor

**intestino** [intes'tino] nm intestine

**intimar** [inti'mar] /1a/ vi to become friendly

**intimidad** [intimi'ðað] nf intimacy; (familiaridad) familiarity; (vida privada) private life; (Jur) privacy

**íntimo, -a** ['intimo, a] adj intimate

**intolerable** [intole'raβle] adj intolerable, unbearable

**intoxicación** [intoksika'θjon] nf poisoning; **~ alimenticia** food poisoning

**intranet** [intra'net] nf intranet

**intranquilo, -a** [intran'kilo, a] adj worried

**intransitable** [intransi'taβle] adj impassable

**intrépido, -a** [in'trepiðo, a] adj intrepid

**intriga** [in'triɣa] nf intrigue; (plan) plot; **intrigar** /1h/ vt, vi to intrigue

**intrínseco, -a** [in'trinseko, a] adj intrinsic

**introducción** [introðuk'θjon] nf introduction

**introducir** [introðu'θir] /3n/ vt (gen) to introduce; (moneda) to insert; (Inform) to input, enter

**intromisión** [intromi'sjon] nf interference, meddling

**introvertido, -a** [introβer'tiðo, a] adj, nm/f introvert

**intruso, -a** [in'truso, a] adj intrusive ▷ nm/f intruder

**intuición** [intwi'θjon] nf intuition

**inundación** [inunda'θjon] nf flood(ing); **inundar** /1a/ vt to flood; (fig) to swamp, inundate

**inusitado, -a** [inusi'taðo, a] adj unusual

**inútil** [i'nutil] adj useless; (esfuerzo) vain, fruitless

**inutilizar** [inutili'θar] /1f/ vt to make unusable

**invadir** [imba'ðir] /3a/ vt to invade

**inválido, -a** [im'baliðo, a] adj invalid ▷ nm/f invalid

**invasión** [imba'sjon] nf invasion

**invasor, a** [imba'sor, a] adj invading ▷ nm/f invader

**invención** [imben'θjon] nf invention

**inventar** [imben'tar] /1a/ vt to invent

**inventario** [imben'tarjo] nm inventory

**invento** [im'bento] nm invention

**inventor, a** [imben'tor, a] nm/f inventor

**invernadero** [imberna'ðero] nm greenhouse

**inverosímil** [imbero'simil] adj implausible

**inversión** [imber'sjon] nf (Com)
investment

**inverso, a** [im'berso, a] adj inverse,
opposite; **en el orden ~** in reverse order;
**a la inversa** inversely, the other way round

**inversor, -a** [imber'sor, a] nm/f (Com)
investor

**invertir** [imber'tir] /3i/ vt (Com) to invest;
(volcar) to turn upside down; (tiempo etc)
to spend

**investigación** [imbestiɣa'θjon] nf
investigation; (Univ) research; **~
y desarrollo** (Com) research and
development (R & D)

**investigar** [imbesti'ɣar] /1h/ vt to
investigate; (estudiar) to do research into

**invierno** [im'bjerno] nm winter

**invisible** [imbi'siβle] adj invisible

**invitación** [imbita'θjon] nf invitation

**invitado, -a** [imbi'taðo, a] nm/f guest

**invitar** [imbi'tar] /1a/ vt to invite; (incitar)
to entice; **~ a algo** to pay for sth

**invocar** [imbo'kar] /1g/ vt to invoke,
call on

**involucrar** [imbolu'krar] /1a/ vt: **~ a algn
en algo** to involve sb in sth; **involucrarse** vr
to get involved

**involuntario, -a** [imbolun'tarjo, a] adj
involuntary; (ofensa etc) unintentional

**inyección** [injek'θjon] nf injection

**inyectar** [injek'tar] /1a/ vt to inject

**iPod®** ['ipoð] (pl **iPods**) nm iPod®

**PALABRA CLAVE**

**ir** [ir] /3s/ vi **1** to go; **ir caminando** to walk;
**fui en tren** I went o travelled by train;
**¡(ahora) voy!** (I'm just) coming!

**2**: **ir (a) por**: **ir (a) por el médico** to fetch
the doctor

**3** (progresar: persona, cosa) to go; **el trabajo
va muy bien** work is going very well;
**¿cómo te va?** how are things going?; **me
va muy bien** I'm getting on very well; **le fue
fatal** it went awfully badly for him

**4** (funcionar): **el coche no va muy bien** the
car isn't running very well

**5**: **te va estupendamente ese color** that
colour suits you fantastically well

**6** (aspecto): **iba muy bien vestido** he was
very well dressed

**7** (locuciones): **¿vino? — ¡que va!** did he
come? — of course not!; **vamos, no
llores** come on, don't cry; **¡vaya coche!**
(admiración) what a car!, that's some car!

**8**: **no vaya a ser: tienes que correr, no
vaya a ser que pierdas el tren** you'll have to
run so as not to miss the train

**9**: **no me** etc **va ni me viene** I etc don't care

▸ vb auxiliar **1**: **ir a**: **voy/iba a hacerlo hoy**
I am/was going to do it today

**2** (+ gerundio): **iba anocheciendo** it was
getting dark; **todo se me iba aclarando**
everything was gradually becoming clearer
to me

**3** (+ pp = pasivo): **van vendidos 300
ejemplares** 300 copies have been sold so
far

▸ **irse** vr **1**: **¿por dónde se va al zoológico?**
which is the way to the zoo?

**2** (marcharse) to leave; **ya se habrán ido**
they must already have left o gone

**ira** ['ira] nf anger, rage

**Irak** [i'rak] nm Iraq; **irakí** adj, nmf Iraqui

**Irán** [i'ran] nm Iran; **iraní** adj, nmf Iranian

**Iraq** [i'rak] nm = **Irak**

**iris** ['iris] nm inv (arco iris) rainbow; (Anat) iris

**Irlanda** [ir'landa] nf Ireland; **~ del Norte**
Northern Ireland; **irlandés, -esa** adj Irish
▷ nm/f Irishman/woman; **los irlandeses**
the Irish

**ironía** [iro'nia] nf irony; **irónico, -a** adj
ironic(al)

**IRPF** nm abr (ESP) = **impuesto sobre la
renta de las personas físicas**

**irreal** [irre'al] adj unreal

**irregular** [irreɣu'lar] adj irregular;
(situación) abnormal

**irremediable** [irreme'ðjaβle] adj
irremediable; (vicio) incurable

**irreparable** [irrepa'raβle] adj (daños)
irreparable; (pérdida) irrecoverable

**irrespetuoso, -a** [irrespe'twoso, a] adj
disrespectful

**irresponsable** [irrespon'saβle] adj
irresponsible

**irreversible** [irreβer'siβle] adj irreversible

**irrigar** [irri'ɣar] /1h/ vt to irrigate

**irrisorio, -a** [irri'sorjo, a] adj derisory,
ridiculous

**irritar** [irri'tar] /1a/ vt to irritate, annoy

**irrupción** [irrup'θjon] nf irruption;
(invasión) invasion

**isla** ['isla] nf island

**Islam** [is'lam] nm Islam; **islámico, -a** adj
Islamic

**islandés, -esa** [islan'des, esa] adj Icelandic
▷ nm/f Icelander

**Islandia** [is'landja] nf Iceland

**isleño, -a** [is'leɲo, a] adj island cpd ▷ nm/f
islander

**Israel** [isra'el] nm Israel; **israelí** adj, nmf
Israeli

**istmo** ['istmo] nm isthmus

**Italia** [i'talja] nf Italy; **italiano, -a** adj, nm/f
Italian

**itinerario** [itine'rarjo] nm itinerary, route

**ITV** *nf abr* (= *Inspección Técnica de Vehículos*) ≈ MOT (test)

**IVA** ['iβa] *nm abr* (= *Impuesto sobre el Valor Añadido*) VAT

**izar** [i'θar] /1f/ *vt* to hoist

**izdo, izq.°** *abr* (= *izquierdo*) L, l

**izquierda** [iθ'kjerða] *nf V* **izquierdo**

**izquierdo, -a** [iθ'kjerðo, a] *adj* left ▷ *nf* left; (*Pol*) left (wing); **a la izquierda** on the left; (*torcer etc*) (to the) left

**jabalí** [xaβa'li] *nm* wild boar

**jabalina** [xaβa'lina] *nf* javelin

**jabón** [xa'βon] *nm* soap

**jaca** ['xaka] *nf* pony

**jacal** [xa'kal] *nm* (*LAM*) shack

**jacinto** [xa'θinto] *nm* hyacinth

**jactarse** [xak'tarse] /1a/ *vr*: **~ (de)** to boast *o* brag (about *o* of)

**jadear** [xaðe'ar] /1a/ *vi* to pant, gasp for breath

**jaguar** [xa'ɣwar] *nm* jaguar

**jaiba** ['xaiβa] *nf* (*LAM*) crab

**jalar** [xa'lar] /1a/ *vt* (*LAM*) to pull

**jalea** [xa'lea] *nf* jelly

**jaleo** [xa'leo] *nm* racket, uproar; **armar un ~** to kick up a racket

**jalón** [xa'lon] *nm* (*LAM*) tug

**jamás** [xa'mas] *adv* never

**jamón** [xa'mon] *nm* ham; **~ (de) York** boiled ham; **~ dulce/serrano** boiled/cured ham

**Japón** [xa'pon] *nm*: Japan; **japonés, -esa** *adj, nm/f* Japanese ▷ *nm* (*Ling*) Japanese

**jaque** ['xake] *nm*: **~ mate** checkmate

**jaqueca** [xa'keka] *nf* (very bad) headache, migraine

**jarabe** [xa'raβe] *nm* syrup

**jardín** [xar'ðin] *nm* garden; **~ de (la) infancia** (*ESP*) *o* **de niños** (*LAM*) *o* **infantil** nursery school; **jardinaje** *nm* gardening; **jardinería** *nf* gardening; **jardinero, -a** *nm/f* gardener

**jarra** ['xarra] *nf* jar; (*jarro*) jug

**jarro** ['xarro] *nm* jug

**jarrón** [xa'rron] *nm* vase

**jaula** ['xaula] *nf* cage

**jauría** [xau'ria] *nf* pack of hounds

**jazmín** [xaθ'min] *nm* jasmine

**J. C.** *abr* = **Jesucristo**

**jeans** [jins, dʒins] *nmpl* (*LAM*) jeans, denims; **unos ~** a pair of jeans

**jefatura** [xefa'tura] *nf*: ~ **de policía** police headquarters *sg*

**jefe, -a** ['xefe, a] *nm/f* (*gen*) chief, head; (*patrón*) boss; ~ **de cocina** chef; ~ **de estación** stationmaster; ~ **de estado** head of state; ~ **de estudios** (*Escol*) director of studies; ~ **de gobierno** head of government

**jengibre** [xen'xiβre] *nm* ginger

**jeque** ['xeke] *nm* sheik(h)

**jerárquico, -a** [xe'rarkiko, a] *adj* hierarchic(al)

**jerez** [xe'reθ] *nm* sherry

**jerga** ['xerɣa] *nf* jargon

**jeringa** [xe'ringa] *nf* syringe; (*LAM*) annoyance, bother; **jeringuilla** *nf* syringe

**jeroglífico** [xero'ɣlifiko] *nm* hieroglyphic

**jersey** [xer'sei] (*pl* **jerseys**) *nm* jersey, pullover, jumper

**Jerusalén** [xerusa'len] *n* Jerusalem

**Jesucristo** [xesu'kristo] *nm* Jesus Christ

**jesuita** [xe'swita] *adj, nm* Jesuit

**Jesús** [xe'sus] *nm* Jesus; ¡~! good heavens!; (*al estornudar*) bless you!

**jinete, -a** [xi'nete, a] *nm/f* horseman/woman

**jipijapa** [xipi'xapa] *nm* (*LAM*) straw hat

**jirafa** [xi'rafa] *nf* giraffe

**jirón** [xi'ron] *nm* rag, shred

**jitomate** [xito'mate] *nm* (*LAM*) tomato

**joder** [xo'ðer] /2a/ (*fam!*) *vt* to fuck (!)

**jogging** ['joɣin] *nm* (*LAM*) tracksuit (*BRIT*), sweat suit (*US*)

**jornada** [xor'naða] *nf* (*viaje de un día*) day's journey; (*camino o viaje entero*) journey; (*día de trabajo*) working day

**jornal** [xor'nal] *nm* (day's) wage; **jornalero, -a** *nm/f* (day) labourer

**joroba** [xo'roβa] *nf* hump; **jorobado, -a** *adj* hunchbacked ▷ *nm/f* hunchback

**jota** ['xota] *nf* letter J; (*danza*) Aragonese dance; **no saber ni** ~ to have no idea

**joven** ['xoβen] *adj* young ▷ *nm* young man, youth ▷ *nf* young woman, girl

**joya** ['xoja] *nf* jewel, gem; (*fig: persona*) gem; ~**s de fantasía** imitation jewellery *sg*; **joyería** *nf* (*joyas*) jewellery; (*tienda*) jeweller's (shop); **joyero** *nm* (*persona*) jeweller; (*caja*) jewel case

**Juan** [xwan] *nm*: **Noche de San ~** V **noche**

**juanete** [xwa'nete] *nm* (*del pie*) bunion

**jubilación** [xuβila'θjon] *nf* (*retiro*) retirement

**jubilado, -a** [xuβi'laðo, a] *adj* retired ▷ *nm/f* pensioner (*BRIT*), senior citizen

**jubilar** [xuβi'lar] /1a/ *vt* to pension off, retire; (*fam*) to discard; **jubilarse** *vr* to retire

**júbilo** ['xuβilo] *nm* joy, rejoicing; **jubiloso, -a** *adj* jubilant

**judía** [xu'ðia] *nf* V **judío**

**judicial** [xuði'θjal] *adj* judicial

**judío, -a** [xu'ðio, a] *adj* Jewish ▷ *nm* Jew ▷ *nf* Jewish woman; (*Culin*) bean; **judía blanca** haricot bean; **judía verde** French o string bean

**judo** ['juðo] *nm* judo

**juego** ['xweɣo] *vb* V **jugar** ▷ *nm* (*gen*) play; (*pasatiempo, partido*) game; (*en casino*) gambling; (*conjunto*) set; ~ **de mesa** board game; ~ **de palabras** pun, play on words; **J~s Olímpicos** Olympic Games®; **fuera de** ~ (*Deporte: persona*) offside; (*: pelota*) out of play

**juerga** ['xwerɣa] *nf* binge; (*fiesta*) party; **ir de** ~ to go out on a binge

**jueves** ['xweβes] *nm inv* Thursday

**juez** [xweθ] *nmf* judge; ~ **de instrucción** examining magistrate; ~ **de línea** linesman; ~ **de salida** starter

**jugada** [xu'ɣaða] *nf* play; **buena** ~ good move (*o shot o stroke*) *etc*

**jugador, a** [xuɣa'ðor, a] *nm/f* player; (*en casino*) gambler

**jugar** [xu'ɣar] /1h, 1n/ *vt* to play; (*en casino*) to gamble; (*apostar*) to bet; ~ **al fútbol** to play football

**juglar** [xu'ɣlar] *nm* minstrel

**jugo** ['xuɣo] *nm* (*Bot*) juice; (*fig*) essence, substance; ~ **de naranja** (*esp LAM*) orange juice; **jugoso, -a** *adj* juicy; (*fig*) substantial, important

**juguete** [xu'ɣete] *nm* toy; **juguetear** /1a/ *vi* to play; **juguetería** *nf* toyshop

**juguetón, -ona** [xuɣe'ton, ona] *adj* playful

**juicio** ['xwiθjo] *nm* judgement; (*sana razón*) sanity, reason; (*opinión*) opinion

**julio** ['xuljo] *nm* July

**jumper** ['dʒumper] *nm* (*LAM*) pinafore dress (*BRIT*), jumper (*US*)

**junco** ['xunko] *nm* rush, reed

**jungla** ['xungla] *nf* jungle

**junio** ['xunjo] *nm* June

**junta** ['xunta] *nf* V **junto**

**juntar** [xun'tar] /1a/ *vt* to join, unite; (*maquinaria*) to assemble, put together; (*dinero*) to collect; **juntarse** *vr* to join, meet; (*reunirse: personas*) to meet, assemble; (*arrimarse*) to approach, draw closer; ~**se con algn** to join sb

**junto, -a** ['xunto, a] *adj* joined; (*unido*) united; (*anexo*) near, close; (*contiguo, próximo*) next, adjacent ▷ *nf* (*asamblea*) meeting, assembly; (*comité, consejo*) board, council, committee; (*articulación*) joint ▷ *adv*: **todo** ~ all at once ▷ *prep*: ~ **a** near (to), next to; ~**s** together; ~ **con** (together) with

**jurado** [xu'raðo] *nm* (*Jur: individuo*) juror; (*: grupo*) jury; (*de concurso: grupo*) panel (of judges); (*: individuo*) member of a panel

**juramento** [xura'mento] *nm* oath;
(*maldición*) oath, curse; **prestar ~** to take
the oath; **tomar ~ a** to swear in, administer
the oath to
**jurar** [xu'rar] /1a/ *vt, vi* to swear; **~ en falso**
to commit perjury; **jurárselas a algn** to
have it in for sb
**jurídico, -a** [xu'riðiko, a] *adj* legal
**jurisdicción** [xurisðik'θjon] *nf* (*poder,*
*autoridad*) jurisdiction; (*territorio*) district
**justamente** [xusta'mente] *adv* justly,
fairly; (*precisamente*) just, exactly
**justicia** [xus'tiθja] *nf* justice; (*equidad*)
fairness, justice
**justificación** [xustifika'θjon] *nf*
justification; **justificar** /1g/ *vt* to justify
**justo, -a** ['xusto, a] *adj* (*equitativo*) just,
fair, right; (*preciso*) exact, correct; (*ajustado*)
tight ▷ *adv* (*precisamente*) exactly, precisely;
(*apenas a tiempo*) just in time
**juvenil** [xuβe'nil] *adj* youthful
**juventud** [xuβen'tuð] *nf* (*adolescencia*)
youth; (*jóvenes*) young people *pl*
**juzgado** [xuθ'γaðo] *nm* tribunal; (*Jur*) court
**juzgar** [xuθ'γar] /1h/ *vt* to judge; **a ~ por ...**
to judge by ..., judging by ...

# k

**kárate** ['karate], **karate** [ka'rate] *nm*
karate
**Kg, kg** *abr* (= *kilogramo(s)*) K, kg
**kilo** ['kilo] *nm* kilo; **kilogramo** *nm*
kilogramme (*BRIT*), kilogram (*US*);
**kilometraje** *nm* distance in kilometres,
≈ mileage; **kilómetro** *nm* kilometre (*BRIT*),
kilometer (*US*); **kilovatio** *nm* kilowatt
**kiosco** ['kjosko] *nm* = **quiosco**
**kleenex®** [kli'neks] *nm* paper
handkerchief, tissue
**km** *abr* (= *kilómetro(s)*) km
**Kosovo** [koso'βo] *nm* Kosovo
**kv** *abr* (= *kilovatio*) kw

**l** abr (= litro(s)) l

**la** [la] artículo definido f sg the ▷ pron her; (en relación a usted) you; (en relación a una cosa) it ▷ nm (Mus) A; **está en la cárcel** he's in jail; **la del sombrero rojo** the woman/girl/one in the red hat

**laberinto** [laβe'rinto] nm labyrinth

**labio** ['laβjo] nm lip

**labor** [la'βor] nf labour; (Agr) farm work; (tarea) job, task; (Costura) needlework; **~es domésticas** o **del hogar** household chores; **laborable** adj (Agr) workable; **día laborable** working day; **laboral** adj (accidente, conflictividad) industrial; (jornada) working

**laboratorio** [laβora'torjo] nm laboratory

**laborista** [laβo'rista] adj: **Partido L~** Labour Party

**labrador, a** [laβra'ðor, a] adj farming cpd ▷ nm/f farmer

**labranza** [la'βranθa] nf (Agr) cultivation

**labrar** [la'βrar] /1a/ vt (gen) to work; (madera etc) to carve; (fig) to cause, bring about

**laca** ['laka] nf lacquer

**lacio, -a** ['laθjo, a] adj (pelo) straight

**lacón** [la'kon] nm shoulder of pork

**lactancia** [lak'tanθja] nf lactation, breast-feeding

**lácteo, -a** ['lakteo, a] adj: **productos ~s** dairy products

**ladear** [laðe'ar] /1a/ vt to tip, tilt ▷ vi to tilt; **ladearse** vr to lean

**ladera** [la'ðera] nf slope

**lado** ['laðo] nm (gen) side; (fig) protection; (Mil) flank; **al ~ de** beside; **poner de ~** to put on its side; **poner a un ~** to put aside; **por todos ~s** on all sides, all round (BRIT)

**ladrar** [la'ðrar] /1a/ vi to bark; **ladrido** nm bark, barking

**ladrillo** [la'ðriʎo] nm (gen) brick; (azulejo) tile

**ladrón, -ona** [la'ðron, ona] nm/f thief

**lagartija** [laɣar'tixa] nf (small) lizard

**lagarto** [la'ɣarto] nm (Zool) lizard

**lago** ['laɣo] nm lake

**lágrima** ['laɣrima] nf tear

**laguna** [la'ɣuna] nf lagoon; (en escrito, conocimientos) gap

**lamentable** [lamen'taβle] adj lamentable, regrettable; (miserable) pitiful

**lamentar** [lamen'tar] /1a/ vt (sentir) to regret; (deplorar) to lament; **lamentarse** vr to lament; **lo lamento mucho** I'm very sorry

**lamer** [la'mer] /2a/ vt to lick

**lámina** ['lamina] nf (plancha delgada) sheet; (para estampar, estampa) plate

**lámpara** ['lampara] nf lamp; **~ de alcohol/gas** spirit/gas lamp; **~ de pie** standard lamp

**lana** ['lana] nf wool

**lancha** ['lantʃa] nf launch; **~ motora** motorboat

**langosta** [lan'gosta] nf (crustáceo) lobster; (: de río) crayfish; **langostino** nm prawn

**lanza** ['lanθa] nf (arma) lance, spear

**lanzamiento** [lanθa'mjento] nm (gen) throwing; (Naut, Com) launch, launching; **~ de pesos** putting the shot

**lanzar** [lan'θar] /1f/ vt (gen) to throw; (Deporte: pelota) to bowl; to launch; (Jur) to evict; **lanzarse** vr to throw o.s.

**lapa** ['lapa] nf limpet

**lapicero** [lapi'θero] nm pencil; (LAM) propelling (BRIT) o mechanical (US) pencil; (: bolígrafo) ballpoint pen, Biro®

**lápida** ['lapiða] nf stone; **~ mortuoria** headstone

**lápiz** ['lapiθ] nm pencil; **~ de color** coloured pencil; **~ de labios** lipstick; **~ de ojos** eyebrow pencil

**largar** [lar'ɣar] /1h/ vt (soltar) to release; (aflojar) to loosen; (lanzar) to launch; (fam) to let fly; (velas) to unfurl; (LAM) to throw; **largarse** vr (fam) to beat it; **~se a** (LAM) to start to

**largo, -a** ['larɣo, a] adj (longitud) long; (tiempo) lengthy; (fig) generous ▷ nm length; (Mus) largo; **dos años ~s** two long years; **a lo ~ de** along; (tiempo) all through, throughout; **a la larga** in the long run; **largometraje** nm full-length o feature film

No confundir largo con la palabra inglesa large.

**laringe** [la'rinxe] nf larynx; **laringitis** nf laryngitis

**las** [las] artículo definido f pl the ▷ pron them; **~ que cantan** the ones/women/girls who sing

**lasaña** [la'saɲa] *nf* lasagne, lasagna

**láser** ['laser] *nm* laser

**lástima** ['lastima] *nf* (*pena*) pity; **dar ~** to be pitiful; **es una ~ que** it's a pity that; **¡qué ~!** what a pity!; **estar hecho una ~** to be a sorry sight

**lastimar** [lasti'mar] /1a/ *vt* (*herir*) to wound; (*ofender*) to offend; **lastimarse** *vr* to hurt o.s.

**lata** ['lata] *nf* (*metal*) tin; (*envase*) tin, can; (*fam*) nuisance; **en ~** tinned; **dar (la) ~** to be a nuisance

**latente** [la'tente] *adj* latent

**lateral** [late'ral] *adj* side, lateral ▷ *nm* (*Teat*) wings *pl*

**latido** [la'tiðo] *nm* (*del corazón*) beat

**latifundio** [lati'fundjo] *nm* large estate

**latigazo** [lati'ɣaθo] *nm* (*golpe*) lash; (*sonido*) crack

**látigo** ['latiɣo] *nm* whip

**latín** [la'tin] *nm* Latin

**latino, -a** [la'tino, a] *adj* Latin; **latinoamericano, -a** *adj, nm/f* Latin American

**latir** [la'tir] /3a/ *vi* (*corazón, pulso*) to beat

**latitud** [lati'tuð] *nf* (*Geo*) latitude

**latón** [la'ton] *nm* brass

**laurel** [lau'rel] *nm* (*Bot*) laurel; (*Culin*) bay

**lava** ['laβa] *nf* lava

**lavabo** [la'βaβo] *nm* (*jofaina*) washbasin; (*retrete*) toilet (*BRIT*), washroom (*US*)

**lavado** [la'βaðo] *nm* washing; (*de ropa*) laundry; (*Arte*) wash; **~ de cerebro** brainwashing; **~ en seco** dry-cleaning

**lavadora** [laβa'ðora] *nf* washing machine

**lavanda** [la'βanda] *nf* lavender

**lavandería** [laβande'ria] *nf* laundry; **~ automática** launderette

**lavaplatos** [laβa'platos] *nm inv* dishwasher

**lavar** [la'βar] /1a/ *vt* to wash; (*borrar*) to wipe away; **lavarse** *vr* to wash o.s.; **~se las manos** to wash one's hands; **~se los dientes** to brush one's teeth; **~ y marcar** (*pelo*) to shampoo and set; **~ en seco** to dry-clean; **~ los platos** to wash the dishes

**lavarropas** [laβa'rropas] *nm inv* (*RPL*) washing machine

**lavavajillas** [laβaβa'xiʎas] *nm inv* dishwasher

**laxante** [lak'sante] *nm* laxative

**lazarillo** [laθa'riʎo] *nm*: **perro de ~** guide dog

**lazo** ['laθo] *nm* knot; (*lazada*) bow; (*para animales*) lasso; (*trampa*) snare; (*vínculo*) tie

**le** [le] *pron* (*directo*) him (*o* her); (: *en relación a usted*) you; (*indirecto*) to him (*o* her *o* it); (: *a usted*) to you

**leal** [le'al] *adj* loyal; **lealtad** *nf* loyalty

**lección** [lek'θjon] *nf* lesson

**leche** ['letʃe] *nf* milk; **tener mala ~** (*fam*) to be a nasty piece of work; **~ condensada/en polvo** condensed/powdered milk; **~ desnatada** skimmed milk

**lechería** [letʃe'ria] *nf* dairy

**lecho** ['letʃo] *nm* (*cama, de río*) bed; (*Geo*) layer

**lechón** [le'tʃon] *nm* sucking (*BRIT*) *o* suckling (*US*) pig

**lechoso, -a** [le'tʃoso, a] *adj* milky

**lechuga** [le'tʃuɣa] *nf* lettuce

**lechuza** [le'tʃuθa] *nf* (barn) owl

**lector, a** [lek'tor, a] *nm/f* reader ▷ *nm*: **~ de discos compactos** CD player

**lectura** [lek'tura] *nf* reading

**leer** [le'er] /2e/ *vt* to read

**legado** [le'ɣaðo] *nm* (*don*) bequest; (*herencia*) legacy; (*enviado*) legate

**legajo** [le'ɣaxo] *nm* file

**legal** [le'ɣal] *adj* legal; (*persona*) trustworthy; **legalizar** /1f/ *vt* to legalize; (*documento*) to authenticate

**legaña** [le'ɣaɲa] *nf* sleep (*in eyes*)

**legión** [le'xjon] *nf* legion; **legionario, -a** *adj* legionary ▷ *nm* legionnaire

**legislación** [lexisla'θjon] *nf* legislation

**legislar** [lexis'lar] /1a/ *vt* to legislate

**legislatura** [lexisla'tura] *nf* (*Pol*) period of office

**legítimo, -a** [le'xitimo, a] *adj* (*genuino*) authentic; (*legal*) legitimate

**legua** ['leɣwa] *nf* league

**legumbres** [le'ɣumbres] *nfpl* pulses

**leído, -a** [le'iðo, a] *adj* well-read

**lejanía** [lexa'nia] *nf* distance; **lejano, -a** *adj* far-off; (*en el tiempo*) distant; (*fig*) remote

**lejía** [le'xia] *nf* bleach

**lejos** ['lexos] *adv* far, far away; **a lo ~** in the distance; **de** *o* **desde ~** from a distance; **~ de** far from

**lema** ['lema] *nm* motto; (*Pol*) slogan

**lencería** [lenθe'ria] *nf* linen, drapery

**lengua** ['lengwa] *nf* tongue; (*Ling*) language; **morderse la ~** to hold one's tongue

**lenguado** [len'gwaðo] *nm* sole

**lenguaje** [len'gwaxe] *nm* language; **~ de programación** programming language

**lengüeta** [len'gweta] *nf* (*Anat*) epiglottis; (*de zapatos*) tongue; (*Mus*) reed

**lente** ['lente] *nm o* f *lens*; (*lupa*) magnifying glass; **lentes** *nmpl* glasses; **~s bifocales/ de sol** (*LAM*) bifocals/sunglasses; **~s de contacto** contact lenses

**lenteja** [len'texa] *nf* lentil; **lentejuela** *nf* sequin

**lentilla** [len'tiʎa] *nf* contact lens

**lentitud** [lenti'tuð] *nf* slowness; **con ~** slowly

**lento, -a** ['lento, a] *adj* slow

**leña** ['leɲa] *nf* firewood; **leñador, a** *nm/f* woodcutter

**leño** ['leɲo] *nm* (*trozo de árbol*) log; (*madera*) timber; (*fig*) blockhead

**Leo** ['leo] *nm* Leo

**león** [le'on] *nm* lion; **~ marino** sea lion

**leopardo** [leo'parðo] *nm* leopard

**leotardos** [leo'tarðos] *nmpl* tights

**lepra** ['lepra] *nf* leprosy; **leproso, -a** *nm/f* leper

**les** [les] *pron* (*directo*) them; (: *en relación a ustedes*) you; (*indirecto*) to them; (: *a ustedes*) to you

**lesbiana** [les'βjana] *adj*, *nf* lesbian

**lesión** [le'sjon] *nf* wound, lesion; (*Deporte*) injury; **lesionado, -a** *adj* injured ▷ *nm/f* injured person

**letal** [le'tal] *adj* lethal

**letanía** [leta'nia] *nf* litany

**letra** ['letra] *nf* letter; (*escritura*) handwriting; (*Mus*) lyrics *pl*; **~ de cambio** bill of exchange; **~ de imprenta** print; **letrado, -a** *adj* learned ▷ *nm/f* lawyer; **letrero** *nm* (*cartel*) sign; (*etiqueta*) label

**letrina** [le'trina] *nf* latrine

**leucemia** [leu'θemja] *nf* leukaemia

**levadura** [leβa'ðura] *nf* yeast; **~ de cerveza** brewer's yeast

**levantar** [leβan'tar] /1a/ *vt* (*gen*) to raise; (*del suelo*) to pick up; (*hacia arriba*) to lift (up); (*plan*) to make, draw up; (*mesa*) to clear; (*campamento*) to strike; (*fig*) to cheer up, hearten; **levantarse** *vr* to get up; (*enderezarse*) to straighten up; (*rebelarse*) to rebel; **~ el ánimo** to cheer up

**levante** [le'βante] *nm* east; **el L~** *region of Spain extending from Castellón to Murcia*

**levar** [le'βar] /1a/ *vt*, *vi*: **~ (anclas)** to weigh anchor

**leve** ['leβe] *adj* light; (*fig*) trivial

**levita** [le'βita] *nf* frock coat

**léxico** ['leksiko] *nm* vocabulary

**ley** [lei] *nf* (*gen*) law; (*metal*) standard

**leyenda** [le'jenda] *nf* legend

**leyó** *etc* *vb V* **leer**

**liar** [li'ar] /1c/ *vt* to tie (up); (*unir*) to bind; (*envolver*) to wrap (up); (*enredar*) to confuse; (*cigarrillo*) to roll; **liarse** *vr* (*fam*) to get involved; **~se a palos** to get involved in a fight

**Líbano** ['liβano] *nm*: **el ~** the Lebanon

**libélula** [li'βelula] *nf* dragonfly

**liberación** [liβera'θjon] *nf* liberation; (*de la cárcel*) release

**liberal** [liβe'ral] *adj*, *nmf* liberal

**liberar** [liβe'rar] /1a/ *vt* to liberate

**libertad** [liβer'tað] *nf* liberty, freedom; **~ de asociación/de culto/de prensa/de comercio/de palabra** freedom of association/of worship/of the press/of trade/of speech; **~ condicional** probation; **~ bajo palabra** parole; **~ bajo fianza** bail

**libertar** [liβer'tar] /1a/ *vt* (*preso*) to set free; (*de una obligación*) to release; (*eximir*) to exempt

**libertino, -a** [liβer'tino, a] *adj* permissive ▷ *nm/f* permissive person

**libra** ['liβra] *nf* pound; **L~** (*Astro*) Libra; **~ esterlina** pound sterling

**libramiento** [liβra'mjento] (*LAM*) *nm* ring road (*BRIT*), beltway (*US*)

**librar** [li'βrar] /1a/ *vt* (*de peligro*) to save; (*batalla*) to wage, fight; (*de impuestos*) to exempt; (*cheque*) to make out; (*Jur*) to exempt; **librarse** *vr*: **~se de** to escape from, free o.s. from

**libre** ['liβre] *adj* free; (*lugar*) unoccupied; (*asiento*) vacant; (*de deudas*) free of debts; **~ de impuestos** free of tax; **tiro ~** free kick; **los 100 metros ~** the 100 metres freestyle (race); **al aire ~** in the open air

**librería** [liβre'ria] *nf* (*tienda*) bookshop; **librero, -a** *nm/f* bookseller

> No confundir *librería* con la palabra inglesa *library*.

**libreta** [li'βreta] *nf* notebook

**libro** ['liβro] *nm* book; **~ de bolsillo** paperback; **~ electrónico** e-book; (*aparato*) e-reader; **~ de texto** textbook

**Lic.** *abr* = **Licenciado, a**

**licencia** [li'θenθja] *nf* (*gen*) licence; (*permiso*) permission; **~ por enfermedad/con goce de sueldo** sick/paid leave; **~ de armas/de caza** gun/game licence; **licenciado, -a** *adj* licensed ▷ *nm/f* graduate; **licenciar** /1b/ *vt* (*empleado*) to dismiss; (*permitir*) to permit, allow; (*soldado*) to discharge; (*estudiante*) to confer a degree upon; **licenciarse** *vr*: **licenciarse en derecho** to graduate in law

**licenciatura** [liθenθja'tura] *nf* (*título*) degree; (*estudios*) degree course

**lícito, -a** ['liθito, a] *adj* (*legal*) lawful; (*justo*) fair, just; (*permisible*) permissible

**licor** [li'kor] *nm* spirits *pl* (*BRIT*), liquor (*US*); (*con hierbas etc*) liqueur

**licuadora** [likwa'ðora] *nf* blender

**líder** ['liðer] *nmf* leader; **liderazgo, liderato** *nm* leadership

**lidia** ['liðja] *nf* bullfighting; (*una lidia*) bullfight; **toros de ~** fighting bulls; **lidiar** /1b/ *vt*, *vi* to fight

**liebre** ['ljeβre] *nf* hare

**lienzo** ['ljenθo] *nm* linen; (*Arte*) canvas; (*Arq*) wall

**liga** ['liɣa] *nf* (*de medias*) garter, suspender; (*confederación*) league; (*LAM: gomita*) rubber band

**ligadura** [liɣa'ðura] nf bond, tie; (Med, Mus) ligature

**ligamento** [liɣa'mento] nm ligament

**ligar** [li'ɣar] /1h/ vt (atar) to tie; (unir) to join; (Med) to bind up; (Mus) to slur ▷ vi to mix, blend; **ligarse** vr to commit o.s.; **(él) liga mucho** (fam) he pulls a lot of women

**ligero, -a** [li'xero, a] adj (de peso) light; (tela) thin; (rápido) swift, quick; (ágil) agile, nimble; (de importancia) slight; (de carácter) flippant, superficial ▷ adv: **a la ligera** superficially

**liguero** [li'ɣero] nm suspender (BRIT) o garter (US) belt

**lija** ['lixa] nf (Zool) dogfish; **(papel de) ~** sandpaper

**lila** ['lila] nf lilac

**lima** ['lima] nf file; (Bot) lime; **~ de uñas** nail file; **limar** /1a/ vt to file

**limitación** [limita'θjon] nf limitation, limit

**limitar** [limi'tar] /1a/ vt to limit; (reducir) to reduce, cut down ▷ vi: **~ con** to border on; **limitarse** vr: **~se a** to limit o confine o.s. to

**límite** ['limite] nm (gen) limit; (fin) end; (frontera) border; **~ de velocidad** speed limit

**limítrofe** [li'mitrofe] adj neighbouring

**limón** [li'mon] nm lemon ▷ adj: **amarillo ~** lemon-yellow; **limonada** nf lemonade

**limosna** nf alms pl; **pedir ~** to beg; **vivir de ~** to live on charity

**limpiador, a** [limpja'ðor, a] adj cleaning, cleansing ▷ nm/f cleaner ▷ nm (LAM) = **limpiaparabrisas**

**limpiaparabrisas** [limpjapara'βrisas] nm inv windscreen (BRIT) o windshield (US) wiper

**limpiar** [lim'pjar] /1b/ vt to clean; (con trapo) to wipe; (quitar) to wipe away; (zapatos) to shine, polish; (Inform) to debug; (fig) to clean up

**limpieza** [lim'pjeθa] nf (estado) cleanliness; (acto) cleaning; (: de las calles) cleansing; (: de zapatos) polishing; (habilidad) skill; (fig: Policía) clean-up; (pureza) purity; (Mil): **operación de ~** mopping-up operation; **~ en seco** dry cleaning

**limpio, -a** ['limpjo, a] adj clean; (moralmente) pure; (Com) clear, net; (fam) honest ▷ adv: **jugar ~** to play fair; **pasar a ~** to make a fair copy

**lince** ['linθe] nm lynx

**linchar** [lin'tʃar] /1a/ vt to lynch

**lindar** [lin'dar] /1a/ vi to adjoin; **~ con** to border on

**lindo, -a** ['lindo, a] adj pretty, lovely ▷ adv: **canta muy ~** (LAM) he sings beautifully; **se divertían de lo ~** they enjoyed themselves enormously

**línea** ['linea] nf line; (Inform): **en ~** on line; **~ aérea** airline; **~ de meta** goal line; (de carrera) finishing line; **~ discontinua** (Auto) broken line; **~ recta** straight line

**lingote** [lin'gote] nm ingot

**lingüista** [lin'gwista] nmf linguist; **lingüística** nf linguistics sg

**lino** ['lino] nm linen; (Bot) flax

**linterna** [lin'terna] nf: torch (BRIT), flashlight (US)

**lío** ['lio] nm bundle; (desorden) muddle, mess; (fam: follón) fuss; **armar un ~** to make a fuss

**liquen** ['liken] nm lichen

**liquidación** [likiða'θjon] nf liquidation; **venta de ~** clearance sale

**liquidar** [liki'ðar] /1a/ vt (Com) to liquidate; (deudas) to pay off; (empresa) to wind up

**líquido, -a** ['likiðo, a] adj liquid; (ganancia) net ▷ nm liquid; **~ imponible** net taxable income

**lira** ['lira] nf (Mus) lyre; (moneda) lira

**lírico, -a** ['liriko, a] adj lyrical

**lirio** ['lirjo] nm (Bot) iris

**lirón** [li'ron] nm (Zool) dormouse; (fig) sleepyhead

**Lisboa** [lis'βoa] nf Lisbon

**lisiar** [li'sjar] /1b/ vt to maim

**liso, -a** ['liso, a] adj (terreno) flat; (cabello) straight; (superficie) even; (tela) plain

**lista** ['lista] nf list; (en escuela) school register; (de libros) catalogue; (tb: **~ de platos**) menu; (tb: **~ de precios**) price list; **pasar ~** to call the roll; **~ de espera** waiting list; **tela a ~s** striped material

**listo, -a** ['listo, a] adj (perspicaz) smart, clever; (preparado) ready

**listón** [lis'ton] nm (de madera, metal) strip

**litera** [li'tera] nf (en barco, tren) berth; (en dormitorio) bunk, bunk bed

**literal** [lite'ral] adj literal

**literario, -a** [lite'rarjo, a] adj literary

**literato, -a** [lite'rato, a] adj literary ▷ nm/f writer

**literatura** [litera'tura] nf literature

**litigio** [li'tixjo] nm (Jur) lawsuit; (fig): **en ~ con** in dispute with

**litografía** [litoɣra'fia] nf lithography; (una litografía) lithograph

**litoral** [lito'ral] adj coastal ▷ nm coast, seaboard

**litro** ['litro] nm litre, liter (US)

**lívido, -a** ['liβiðo, a] adj livid

**llaga** ['ʎaɣa] nf wound

**llama** ['ʎama] nf flame; (Zool) llama

**llamada** [ʎa'maða] nf call; **~ a cobro revertido** reverse-charge call; **~ al orden** call to order; **~ de atención** warning; **~ metropolitana, ~ local** local call; **~ por cobrar** (LAM) reverse-charge call

**llamamiento** [ʎama'mjento] nm call

**llamar** [ʎa'mar] /1a/ vt to call; (atención) to attract ▷ vi (por teléfono) to phone; (a la puerta) to knock (o ring); (por señas) to beckon; **llamarse** vr to be called, be named; **¿cómo se llama usted?** what's your name?

**llamativo, -a** [ʎama'tiβo, a] adj showy; (color) loud

**llano, -a** ['ʎano, a] adj (superficie) flat; (persona) straightforward; (estilo) clear ▷ nm plain, flat ground

**llanta** ['ʎanta] nf (wheel) rim; (LAM: neumático) tyre; (: cámara) (inner) tube; **~ de repuesto** (LAM) spare tyre

**llanto** ['ʎanto] nm weeping

**llanura** [ʎa'nura] nf plain

**llave** ['ʎaβe] nf key; (de gas, agua) tap (BRIT), faucet (US); (Mecánica) spanner; (de la luz) switch; (Mus) key; **~ inglesa** monkey wrench; **~ maestra** master key; **~ de contacto, ~ de encendido** (LAM Auto) ignition key; **~ de paso** stopcock; **echar ~ a** to lock up; **llavero** nm keyring

**llegada** [ʎe'ɣaða] nf arrival

**llegar** [ʎe'ɣar] /1h/ vi to arrive; (bastar) to be enough; **llegarse** vr: **~se a** to approach; **~ a** (alcanzar) to reach; to manage to, succeed in; **~ a saber** to find out; **~ a las manos de** to come into the hands of

**llenar** [ʎe'nar] /1a/ vt to fill; (superficie) to cover; (formulario) to fill in o out; (fig) to heap

**lleno, -a** ['ʎeno, a] adj full, filled; (repleto) full up ▷ nm (Teat) full house; **dar de ~ contra un muro** to hit a wall head-on

**llevadero, -a** [ʎeβa'ðero, a] adj bearable, tolerable

**llevar** [ʎe'βar] /1a/ vt to take; (ropa) to wear; (cargar) to carry; (quitar) to take away; (en coche) to drive; (transportar) to transport; (traer: dinero) to carry; (conducir) to lead; (Mat) to carry ▷ vi (suj: camino etc): **~ a** to lead to; **llevarse** vr to carry off, take away; **llevamos dos días aquí** we have been here for two days; **él me lleva dos años** he's two years older than me; **~ los libros** (Com) to keep the books; **~se bien** to get on well (together)

**llorar** [ʎo'rar] /1a/ vt to cry ▷ vi to cry, weep; **~ de risa** to cry with laughter

**llorón, -ona** [ʎo'ron, ona] adj tearful ▷ nm/f cry-baby

**lloroso, -a** [ʎo'roso, a] adj (gen) weeping, tearful; (triste) sad, sorrowful

**llover** [ʎo'βer] /2h/ vi to rain

**llovizna** [ʎo'βiθna] nf drizzle; **lloviznar** /1a/ vi to drizzle

**llueve** etc ['ʎweβe] vb V **llover**

**lluvia** ['ʎuβja] nf rain; **~ radioactiva** radioactive fallout; **lluvioso, -a** adj rainy

**lo** [lo] artículo definido neutro: **lo bueno** the good ▷ pron (en relación a una persona) him; (en relación a una cosa) it; **lo que** what, that which; **lo que sea** whatever; V tb **el**

**loable** [lo'aβle] adj praiseworthy

**lobo** ['loβo] nm wolf; **~ de mar** (fig) sea dog

**lóbulo** ['loβulo] nm lobe

**local** [lo'kal] adj local ▷ nm place, site; (oficinas) premises pl; **localidad** nf (barrio) locality; (lugar) location; (Teat) seat, ticket; **localizar** /1f/ vt (ubicar) to locate, find; (restringir) to localize; (situar) to place

**loción** [lo'θjon] nf lotion

**loco, -a** ['loko, a] adj mad ▷ nm/f madman/woman; **estar ~ con** o **por algo/por algn** to be mad about sth/sb

**locomotora** [lokomo'tora] nf engine, locomotive

**locuaz** [lo'kwaθ] adj loquacious

**locución** [loku'θjon] nf expression

**locura** [lo'kura] nf madness; (acto) crazy act

**locutor, a** [loku'tor, a] nm/f (Radio) announcer; (comentarista) commentator; (TV) newsreader

**locutorio** [loku'torjo] nm (Telec) telephone box o booth

**lodo** ['loðo] nm mud

**lógico, -a** ['loxiko, a] adj logical ▷ nf logic

**login** ['loxin] nm login

**logotipo** [loɣo'tipo] nm logo

**logrado, -a** [lo'ɣraðo, a] adj (interpretación, reproducción) polished, excellent

**lograr** [lo'ɣrar] /1a/ vt (obtener) to get, obtain; (conseguir) to achieve; **~ hacer** to manage to do; **~ que algn venga** to manage to get sb to come

**logro** ['loɣro] nm achievement, success

**lóker** ['loker] nm (LAM) locker

**loma** ['loma] nf hillock, low ridge

**lombriz** [lom'briθ] nf (earth)worm

**lomo** ['lomo] nm (de animal) back; (Culin: de cerdo) pork loin; (: de vaca) rib steak; (de libro) spine

**lona** ['lona] nf canvas

**loncha** ['lontʃa] nf = **lonja**

**lonchería** [lontʃe'ria] nf (LAM) snack bar, diner (US)

**Londres** ['londres] nm London

**longaniza** [longa'niθa] nf pork sausage

**longitud** [lonxi'tuð] nf length; (Geo) longitude; **tener tres metros de ~** to be three metres long; **~ de onda** wavelength

**lonja** ['lonxa] nf slice; (de tocino) rasher; **~ de pescado** fish market

**loro** ['loro] nm parrot

**los** [los] artículo definido mpl the ▷ pron them; (en relación a ustedes) you; **mis libros y ~ tuyos** my books and yours

**losa** ['losa] nf stone

**lote** ['lote] nm portion; (Com) lot
**lotería** [lote'ria] nf lottery; (juego) lotto

**loza** ['loθa] nf crockery
**lubina** [lu'βina] nf sea bass
**lubricante** [luβri'kante] nm lubricant
**lubricar** [luβri'kar] /1g/ vt to lubricate
**lucha** ['lutʃa] nf fight, struggle; ~ **de clases**
class struggle; ~ **libre** wrestling; **luchar**
/1a/ vi to fight
**lúcido, -a** ['luθiðo, a] adj (persona) lucid;
(mente) logical; (idea) crystal-clear
**luciérnaga** [lu'θjernaɣa] nf glow-worm
**lucir** [lu'θir] /3f/ vt to illuminate, light (up);
(ostentar) to show off ▷ vi (brillar) to shine;
**lucirse** vr (irónico) to make a fool of o.s.
**lucro** ['lukro] nm profit, gain
**lúdico, -a** ['luðiko, a] adj playful; (actividad)
recreational
**luego** ['lweɣo] adv (después) next; (más
tarde) later, afterwards
**lugar** [lu'ɣar] nm place; (sitio) spot; **en ~ de**
instead of; **en primer ~** in the first place,
firstly; **dar ~ a** to give rise to; **hacer ~** to
make room; **fuera de ~** out of place; **sin ~ a**
**dudas** without doubt, undoubtedly;
**tener ~** to take place; **~ común**
commonplace; **yo en su ~** if I were him
**lúgubre** ['luɣuβre] adj mournful
**lujo** ['luxo] nm luxury; (fig) profusion,
abundance; **de ~** luxury cpd, de luxe;
**lujoso, -a** adj luxurious
**lujuria** [lu'xurja] nf lust
**lumbre** ['lumbre] nf (luz) light; (fuego) fire;
¿**tienes ~?** (para cigarro) have you got a light?
**luminoso, -a** [lumi'noso, a] adj luminous,
shining
**luna** ['luna] nf moon; (de un espejo) glass;
(de gafas) lens; (fig) crescent; ~ **creciente/**
**llena/menguante/nueva** crescent/full/
waning/new moon; ~ **de miel** honeymoon;
**estar en la ~** to have one's head in the
clouds
**lunar** [lu'nar] adj lunar ▷ nm (Anat) mole;
**tela a ~es** spotted material
**lunes** ['lunes] nm inv Monday

**lupa** ['lupa] nf magnifying glass
**lustre** ['lustre] nm polish; (fig) lustre; **dar ~**
**a** to polish
**luto** ['luto] nm mourning; **llevar el o**
**vestirse de ~** to be in mourning
**Luxemburgo** [luksem'burɣo] nm
Luxembourg
**luz** [luθ] (pl **luces**) nf light; **dar a ~ un niño**
to give birth to a child; **sacar a la ~** to bring
to light; **dar la ~** to switch on the light;
**encender** (ESP) o **prender** (LAM)/**apagar**
**la ~** to switch the light on/off; **tener pocas**
**luces** to be dim o stupid; ~ **roja/verde** red/
green light; ~ **de freno** brake light; **luces**
**de tráfico** traffic lights; **traje de luces**
bullfighter's costume

# m

**m** abr (= metro(s)) m; (= minuto(s)) min., m

**macana** [ma'kana] nf (LAM: porra) club

**macarrones** [maka'rrones] nmpl macaroni sg

**macedonia** [maθe'ðonja] nf: **~ de frutas** fruit salad

**maceta** [ma'θeta] nf (de flores) pot of flowers; (para plantas) flowerpot

**machacar** [matʃa'kar] /1g/ vt to crush, pound ▷ vi (insistir) to go on, keep on

**machete** [ma'tʃete] nm machete, (large) knife

**machetear** [matʃete'ar] /1a/ vt (LAM) to swot (BRIT), grind away (US)

**machismo** [ma'tʃismo] nm male chauvinism; **machista** adj, nm sexist

**macho** ['matʃo] adj male; (fig) virile ▷ nm male; (fig) he-man

**macizo, -a** [ma'θiθo, a] adj (grande) massive; (fuerte, sólido) solid ▷ nm mass, chunk

**madeja** [ma'ðexa] nf (de lana) skein, hank; (de pelo) mass, mop

**madera** [ma'ðera] nf wood; (fig) nature, character; **una ~** a piece of wood

**madrastra** [ma'ðrastra] nf stepmother

**madre** ['maðre] adj mother cpd ▷ nf mother; (de vino etc) dregs pl; **~ adoptiva/política/soltera** foster mother/mother-in-law/unmarried mother

**Madrid** [ma'ðrið] n Madrid

**madriguera** [maðri'ɣera] nf burrow

**madrileño, -a** [maðri'leɲo, a] adj of o from Madrid ▷ nm/f native o inhabitant of Madrid

**madrina** [ma'ðrina] nf godmother; (Arq) prop, shore; (Tec) brace; **~ de boda** bridesmaid

**madrugada** [maðru'ɣaða] nf early morning; (alba) dawn, daybreak

**madrugador, a** [maðruɣa'ðor, a] adj early-rising

**madrugar** [maðru'ɣar] /1h/ vi to get up early; (fig) to get ahead

**madurar** [maðu'rar] /1a/ vt, vi (fruta) to ripen; (fig) to mature; **madurez** nf ripeness; (fig) maturity; **maduro, -a** adj ripe; (fig) mature

**maestra** [ma'estra] nf V **maestro**

**maestría** [maes'tria] nf mastery; (habilidad) skill, expertise

**maestro, -a** [ma'estro, a] adj masterly; (principal) main ▷ nm/f master/mistress; (profesor) teacher ▷ nm (autoridad) authority; (Mus) maestro; (experto) master; **~ albañil** master mason

**magdalena** [maɣða'lena] nf fairy cake

**magia** ['maxja] nf magic; **mágico, -a** adj magic(al) ▷ nm/f magician

**magisterio** [maxis'terjo] nm (enseñanza) teaching; (profesión) teaching profession; (maestros) teachers pl

**magistrado** [maxis'traðo] nm magistrate

**magistral** [maxis'tral] adj magisterial; (fig) masterly

**magnate** [maɣ'nate] nm magnate, tycoon

**magnético, -a** [maɣ'netiko, a] adj magnetic

**magnetofón** [maɣneto'fon], **magnetófono** [maɣne'tofono] nm tape recorder

**magnífico, -a** [maɣ'nifiko, a] adj splendid, magnificent

**magnitud** [maɣni'tuð] nf magnitude

**mago, -a** ['maɣo, a] nm/f magician; **los Reyes M~s** the Three Wise Men

**magro, -a** ['maɣro, a] adj (carne) lean

**mahonesa** [mao'nesa] nf mayonnaise

**maître** ['metre] nm head waiter

**maíz** [ma'iθ] nm maize (BRIT), corn (US); sweet corn

**majestad** [maxes'tað] nf majesty

**majo, -a** ['maxo, a] adj nice; (guapo) attractive, good-looking; (elegante) smart

**mal** [mal] adv badly; (equivocadamente) wrongly ▷ adj = **malo** ▷ nm evil; (desgracia) misfortune; (daño) harm, damage; (Med) illness; **ir de ~ en peor** to go from bad to worse; **~ que bien** rightly or wrongly

**malabarista** [malaβa'rista] nmf juggler

**malaria** [ma'larja] nf malaria

**malcriado, -a** [mal'krjaðo, a] adj spoiled

**maldad** [mal'dað] nf evil, wickedness

**maldecir** [malde'θir] /3o/ vt to curse

**maldición** [maldi'θjon] nf curse

**maldito, -a** [mal'dito, a] adj (condenado) damned; (perverso) wicked; **¡~ sea!** damn it!

**malecón** [male'kon] *nm* pier, jetty; (*LAM: paseo*) sea front, promenade

**maleducado, -a** [maleðu'kaðo, a] *adj* bad-mannered, rude

**malentendido** [malenten'diðo] *nm* misunderstanding

**malestar** [males'tar] *nm* (*gen*) discomfort; (*fig: inquietud*) uneasiness; (*Pol*) unrest

**maleta** [ma'leta] *nf* case, suitcase; (*Auto*) boot (*BRIT*), trunk (*US*); **hacer la ~** to pack; **maletero** *nm* (*Auto*) boot (*BRIT*), trunk (*US*); **maletín** *nm* small case, bag

**maleza** [ma'leθa] *nf* (*malas hierbas*) weeds *pl*; (*arbustos*) thicket

**malgastar** [malɣas'tar] /1a/ *vt* (*tiempo, dinero*) to waste; (*salud*) to ruin

**malhechor, a** [male'tʃor, a] *nm/f* delinquent

**malhumorado, -a** [malumo'raðo, a] *adj* bad-tempered

**malicia** [ma'liθja] *nf* (*maldad*) wickedness; (*astucia*) slyness, guile; (*mala intención*) malice, spite; (*carácter travieso*) mischievousness

**maligno, -a** [ma'liɣno, a] *adj* evil; (*malévolo*) malicious; (*Med*) malignant

**malla** ['maʎa] *nf* mesh; (*de baño*) swimsuit; (*de ballet, gimnasia*) leotard; **mallas** *nfpl* tights; **~ de alambre** wire mesh

**Mallorca** [ma'ʎorka] *nf* Majorca

**malo, -a** ['malo, a] *adj* bad; false ▷ *nm/f* villain; **estar ~** to be ill

**malograr** [malo'ɣrar] /1a/ *vt* to spoil; (*plan*) to upset; (*ocasión*) to waste

**malparado, -a** [malpa'raðo, a] *adj*: **salir ~** to come off badly

**malpensado, -a** [malpen'saðo, a] *adj* nasty

**malteada** [malte'aða] *nf* (*LAM*) milk shake

**maltratar** [maltra'tar] /1a/ *vt* to ill-treat, mistreat

**malvado, -a** [mal'βaðo, a] *adj* evil, villainous

**Malvinas** [mal'βinas] *nfpl*: **Islas ~** Falkland Islands

**mama** ['mama] *nf* (*de animal*) teat; (*de mujer*) breast

**mamá** [ma'ma] *nf* (*fam*) mum, mummy

**mamar** [ma'mar] /1a/ *vt* to suck ▷ *vi* to suck

**mamarracho** [mama'rratʃo] *nm* sight, mess

**mameluco** [mameluko] (*LAM*) *nm* dungarees *pl* (*BRIT*), overalls *pl* (*US*)

**mamífero** [ma'mifero] *nm* mammal

**mampara** [mam'para] *nf* (*entre habitaciones*) partition; (*biombo*) screen

**mampostería** [mamposte'ria] *nf* masonry

**manada** [ma'naða] *nf* (*Zool*) herd; (*: de leones*) pride; (*: de lobos*) pack

**manantial** [manan'tjal] *nm* spring

**mancha** ['mantʃa] *nf* stain, mark; (*de vegetación*) patch; **manchar** /1a/ *vt* to stain, mark; (*ensuciar*) to soil, dirty

**manchego, -a** [man'tʃeɣo, a] *adj* of o from La Mancha

**manco, -a** ['manko, a] *adj* (*de un brazo*) one-armed; (*de una mano*) one-handed; (*fig*) defective, faulty

**mandado** [man'daðo] *nm* errand

**mandamiento** [manda'mjento] *nm* (*orden*) order, command; (*Rel*) commandment

**mandar** [man'dar] /1a/ *vt* (*ordenar*) to order; (*dirigir*) to lead, command; (*enviar*) to send; (*pedir*) to order, ask for ▷ *vi* to be in charge; (*pey*) to be bossy; **¿mande?** pardon?, excuse me? (*US*); **~ hacer un traje** to have a suit made

**mandarina** [manda'rina] *nf* (*fruta*) tangerine, mandarin (orange)

**mandato** [man'dato] *nm* (*orden*) order; (*Pol: período*) term of office; (*: territorio*) mandate

**mandíbula** [man'diβula] *nf* jaw

**mandil** [man'dil] *nm* apron

**mando** ['mando] *nm* (*Mil*) command; (*de país*) rule; (*el primer lugar*) lead; (*Pol*) term of office; (*Tec*) control; **~ a la izquierda** left-hand drive; **~ a distancia** remote control

**mandón, -ona** [man'don, ona] *adj* bossy, domineering

**manejar** [mane'xar] /1a/ *vt* to manage; (*máquina*) to work, operate; (*caballo etc*) to handle; (*casa*) to run, manage; (*LAM Auto*) to drive; **manejarse** *vr* (*comportarse*) to act, behave; (*arreglárselas*) to manage; **manejo** *nm* (*de bicicleta*) handling; (*de negocio*) management, running; (*Auto*) driving; (*facilidad de trato*) ease, confidence; **manejos** *nmpl* intrigues

**manera** [ma'nera] *nf* way, manner, fashion; **maneras** *nfpl* (*modales*) manners; **su ~ de ser** the way he is; (*aire*) his manner; **de ninguna ~** no way, by no means; **de otra ~** otherwise; **de todas ~s** at any rate; **no hay ~ de persuadirle** there's no way of convincing him

**manga** ['manga] *nf* (*de camisa*) sleeve; (*de riego*) hose

**mango** ['mango] *nm* handle; (*Bot*) mango

**manguera** [man'gera] *nf* hose

**maní** [ma'ni] *nm* peanut

**manía** [ma'nia] *nf* (*Med*) mania; (*fig: moda*) rage, craze; (*disgusto*) dislike; (*malicia*) spite; **coger ~ a algn** to take a dislike to sb;

tener ~ a algn to dislike sb; **maníaco, -a** adj maniac(al) ▷ nm/f maniac

**maniático, -a** [ma'njatiko, a] adj maniac(al) ▷ nm/f maniac

**manicomio** [mani'komjo] nm psychiatric hospital

**manifestación** [manifesta'θjon] nf (declaración) statement, declaration; (demostración) show, display; (Pol) demonstration; (concentración) mass meeting

**manifestar** [manifes'tar] /1j/ vt to show, manifest; (declarar) to state, declare; **manifiesto, -a** adj clear, manifest ▷ nm manifesto

**manillar** [mani'ʎar] nm handlebars pl

**maniobra** [ma'njoβra] nf manœuvre; **maniobras** nfpl manœuvres; **maniobrar** /1a/ vt to manœuvre

**manipulación** [manipula'θjon] nf manipulation

**manipular** [manipu'lar] /1a/ vt to manipulate; (manejar) to handle

**maniquí** [mani'ki] nmf model ▷ nm dummy

**manivela** [mani'βela] nf crank

**manjar** [man'xar] nm (tasty) dish

**mano** ['mano] nf hand; (Zool) foot, paw; (de pintura) coat; (serie) lot, series; **a ~** by hand; **a ~ derecha/izquierda** on (o to) the right(-hand side)/left(-hand side); **robo a ~ armada** armed robbery; **de primera ~** (at) first hand; **de segunda ~** (at) second hand; **estrechar la ~ a algn** to shake sb's hand; **~ de obra** labour, manpower

**manojo** [ma'noxo] nm handful, bunch; **~ de llaves** bunch of keys

**manopla** [ma'nopla] nf (paño) flannel; **manoplas** nfpl mittens

**manosear** [manose'ar] /1a/ vt (tocar) to handle, touch; (desordenar) to mess up, rumple; (insistir en) to overwork; (acariciar) to caress, fondle

**manos libres** adj inv (teléfono, dispositivo) hands-free ▷ nm inv hands-free kit

**manotazo** [mano'taθo] nm slap, smack

**mansalva** [man'salβa]: **a ~** adv indiscriminately

**mansión** [man'sjon] nf mansion

**manso, -a** ['manso, a] adj gentle, mild; (animal) tame

**manta** ['manta] nf blanket

**manteca** [man'teka] nf fat; (LAM) butter; **~ de cerdo** lard

**mantecado** [mante'kaðo] nm (ESP: dulce navideño) Christmas sweet made from flour, almonds and lard; (helado) ice cream

**mantel** [man'tel] nm tablecloth

**mantendré** etc [manten'dre] vb V **mantener**

**mantener** [mante'ner] /2k/ vt to support, maintain; (alimentar) to sustain; (conservar) to keep; (Tec) to maintain, service; **mantenerse** vr (seguir de pie) to be still standing; (no ceder) to hold one's ground; (subsistir) to sustain o.s., keep going; **mantenimiento** nm maintenance; sustenance; (sustento) support

**mantequilla** [mante'kiʎa] nf butter

**mantilla** [man'tiʎa] nf mantilla; **mantillas** nfpl baby clothes

**manto** ['manto] nm (capa) cloak; (de ceremonia) robe, gown

**mantuve** etc [man'tuβe] vb V **mantener**

**manual** [ma'nwal] adj manual ▷ nm manual, handbook

**manuscrito, -a** [manus'krito, a] adj handwritten ▷ nm manuscript

**manutención** [manuten'θjon] nf maintenance; (sustento) support

**manzana** [man'θana] nf apple; (Arq) block

**manzanilla** [manθa'niʎa] nf (planta) camomile; (infusión) camomile tea

**manzano** [man'θano] nm apple tree

**maña** ['maɲa] nf (destreza) skill; (pey) guile; (ardid) trick

**mañana** [ma'ɲana] adv tomorrow ▷ nm future ▷ nf morning; **de o por la ~** in the morning; **¡hasta ~!** see you tomorrow!; **~ por la ~** tomorrow morning

**mapa** ['mapa] nm map

**maple** ['maple] nm (LAM) maple

**maqueta** [ma'keta] nf (scale) model

**maquillador, a** [makiʎa'ðor, a] nm/f (Teat etc) make-up artist ▷ nf (LAM Com) bonded assembly plant

**maquillaje** [maki'ʎaxe] nm make-up; (acto) making up

**maquillar** [maki'ʎar] /1a/ vt to make up; **maquillarse** vr to put on (some) make-up

**máquina** ['makina] nf machine; (de tren) locomotive, engine; (Foto) camera; (fig) machinery; **escrito a ~** typewritten; **~ de afeitar** electric razor; **~ de coser** sewing machine; **~ de escribir** typewriter; **~ fotográfica** camera

**maquinaria** [maki'narja] nf (máquinas) machinery; (mecanismo) mechanism, works pl

**maquinilla** [maki'niʎa] nf: **~ de afeitar** razor

**maquinista** [maki'nista] nmf (Ferro) engine driver (BRIT), engineer (US); (Tec) operator; (Naut) engineer

**mar** [mar] nm sea; **~ adentro** o **afuera** out at sea; **en alta ~** on the high seas; **un ~ de** lots of; **el M~ Negro/Báltico** the Black/ Baltic Sea

**maraña** [ma'raɲa] nf (*maleza*) thicket; (*confusión*) tangle

**maravilla** [mara'βiʎa] nf marvel, wonder; (*Bot*) marigold; **maravillar** /1a/ vt to astonish, amaze; **maravillarse** vr to be astonished, be amazed; **maravilloso, -a** adj wonderful, marvellous

**marca** ['marka] nf mark; (*sello*) stamp; (*Com*) make, brand; **de ~** excellent, outstanding; **~ de fábrica** trademark; **~ registrada** registered trademark

**marcado, -a** [mar'kaðo, a] adj marked, strong

**marcador** [marka'ðor] nm (*Deporte*) scoreboard; (: *persona*) scorer

**marcapasos** [marka'pasos] nm inv pacemaker

**marcar** [mar'kar] /1g/ vt to mark; (*número de teléfono*) to dial; (*gol*) to score; (*números*) to record, keep a tally of; (*el pelo*) to set ▷ vi (*Deporte*) to score; (*Telec*) to dial

**marcha** ['martʃa] nf march; (*Tec*) running, working; (*Auto*) gear; (*velocidad*) speed; (*fig*) progress; (*curso*) course; **dar ~ atrás** to reverse, put into reverse; **estar en ~** to be under way, be in motion; **poner en ~** to put into gear; **ponerse en ~** to start, get going; **marchar** /1a/ vi (*ir*) to go; (*funcionar*) to work, go; **marcharse** vr to go (away), leave

**marchitar** [martʃi'tar] /1a/ vt to wither, dry up; **marchitarse** vr (*Bot*) to wither; (*fig*) to fade away; **marchito, -a** adj withered, faded; (*fig*) in decline

**marciano, -a** [mar'θjano, a] adj Martian

**marco** ['marko] nm frame; (*moneda*) mark; (*fig*) framework

**marea** [ma'rea] nf tide; **~ negra** oil slick

**marear** [mare'ar] /1a/ vt (*fig*) to annoy, upset; (*Med*): **~ a algn** to make sb feel sick; **marearse** vr (*tener náuseas*) to feel sick; (*desvanecerse*) to feel faint; (*aturdirse*) to feel dizzy; (*fam: emborracharse*) to get tipsy

**maremoto** [mare'moto] nm tidal wave

**mareo** [ma'reo] nm (*náusea*) sick feeling; (*en viaje*) travel sickness; (*aturdimiento*) dizziness; (*fam: lata*) nuisance

**marfil** [mar'fil] nm ivory

**margarina** [marɣa'rina] nf margarine

**margarita** [marɣa'rita] nf (*Bot*) daisy; (*en máquina impresora*) daisy wheel

**margen** ['marxen] nm (*borde*) edge, border; (*fig*) margin, space ▷ nf (*de río etc*) bank; **dar ~ para** to give an opportunity for; **mantenerse al ~** to keep out (of things)

**marginar** [marxi'nar] /1a/ vt to exclude; (*socialmente*) to marginalize, ostracize

**mariachi** [ma'rjatʃi] nm (*música*) mariachi music; (*grupo*) mariachi band; (*persona*) mariachi musician

**MARIACHI**

Mariachi music is the musical style most characteristic of Mexico. From the state of Jalisco in the 19th century, this music spread rapidly throughout the country, until each region had its own particular style of the mariachi "sound". A mariachi band can be made up of several singers, up to eight violins, two trumpets, guitars, a *vihuela* (an old form of guitar), and a harp. The dance associated with this music is called the *zapateado*.

**marica** [ma'rika] nm (*fam!*) sissy

**maricón** [mari'kon] nm (*fam!*) queer (!)

**marido** [ma'riðo] nm husband

**marihuana** [mari'wana] nf marijuana, cannabis

**marina** [ma'rina] nf navy; **~ mercante** merchant navy

**marinero, -a** [mari'nero, a] adj sea cpd ▷ nm sailor, seaman

**marino, -a** [ma'rino, a] adj sea cpd, marine ▷ nm sailor

**marioneta** [marjo'neta] nf puppet

**mariposa** [mari'posa] nf butterfly

**mariquita** [mari'kita] nf ladybird (BRIT), ladybug (US)

**marisco** [ma'risko] nm (tb: **~s**) shellfish, seafood

**marítimo, -a** [ma'ritimo, a] adj sea cpd, maritime

**mármol** ['marmol] nm marble

**marqués, -esa** [mar'kes, esa] nm/f marquis/marchioness

**marrón** [ma'rron] adj brown

**marroquí** [marro'ki] adj, nmf Moroccan ▷ nm Morocco (leather)

**Marruecos** [ma'rrwekos] nm Morocco

**martes** ['martes] nm inv Tuesday; **~ y trece** ≈ Friday 13th

**MARTES Y TRECE**

According to Spanish superstition Tuesday is an unlucky day, even more so if it falls on the 13th day of the month.

**martillo** [mar'tiʎo] nm hammer

**mártir** ['martir] nmf martyr; **martirio** nm martyrdom; (*fig*) torture, torment

**marxismo** [mark'sismo] nm Marxism

**marzo** ['marθo] nm March

**mas** [mas] conj but

○ **PALABRA CLAVE**

**más** [mas] *adj, adv* **1**: **más (que, de)**
(*compar*) more (than), …+ er (than);
**más grande/inteligente** bigger/more
intelligent; **trabaja más (que yo)** he works
more (than me); *V tb* **cada**
**2** (*superl*): **el más** the most, …+ est; **el más
grande/inteligente (de)** the biggest/most
intelligent (in)
**3** (*negativo*): **no tengo más dinero** I haven't
got any more money; **no viene más por
aquí** he doesn't come round here any
more
**4** (*adicional*): **no le veo más solución
que …** I see no other solution than to …;
**¿quién más?** anybody else?
**5** (+ *adj, valor intensivo*): **¡qué perro más
sucio!** what a filthy dog!; **¡es más tonto!**
he's so stupid!
**6** (*locuciones*): **más o menos** more or less;
**los más** most people; **es más** furthermore;
**más bien** rather; **¡qué más da!** what does
it matter!; *V tb* **no**
**7**: **por más**: **por más que lo intento** no
matter how much o hard I try; **por más
que quisiera ayudar** much as I should like
to help
**8**: **de más**: **veo que aquí estoy de más**
I can see I'm not needed here; **tenemos
uno de más** we've got one extra
▶ *prep*: **2 más 2 son 2** 2 and o plus 2 are 4
▶ *nm inv*: **este trabajo tiene sus más y sus
menos** this job's got its good points and its
bad points

**masa** ['masa] *nf* (*mezcla*) dough; (*volumen*)
volume, mass; (*Física*) mass; **en ~** en masse;
**las ~s** (*Pol*) the masses
**masacre** [ma'sakre] *nf* massacre
**masaje** [ma'saxe] *nm* massage
**máscara** ['maskara] *nf* mask; **~ antigás**
gas mask; **mascarilla** *nf* mask
**masculino, -a** [masku'lino, a] *adj*
masculine; (*Bio*) male
**masía** [ma'sia] *nf* farmhouse
**masivo, -a** [ma'siβo, a] *adj* (*en masa*) mass
**masoquista** [maso'kista] *nmf* masochist
**máster** ['master] *nm* master's degree
**masticar** [masti'kar] /1g/ *vt* to chew
**mástil** ['mastil] *nm* (*de navío*) mast; (*de
guitarra*) neck
**mastín** [mas'tin] *nm* mastiff
**masturbarse** [mastur'βarse] /1a/ *vr* to
masturbate
**mata** ['mata] *nf* (*arbusto*) bush, shrub; (*de
hierbas*) tuft
**matadero** [mata'ðero] *nm*
slaughterhouse, abattoir

**matador, a** [mata'ðor, a] *adj* killing ▷ *nm*
(*Taur*) matador, bullfighter
**matamoscas** [mata'moskas] *nm inv* (*palo*)
fly swat
**matanza** [ma'tanθa] *nf* slaughter
**matar** [ma'tar] /1a/ *vt, vi* to kill; **matarse**
*vr* (*suicidarse*) to kill o.s., commit suicide;
(*morir*) to be o get killed; **~ el hambre** to
stave off hunger
**matasellos** [mata'seʎos] *nm inv* postmark
**mate** ['mate] *adj* matt ▷ *nm* (*en ajedrez*)
(check)mate; (*LAM: hierba*) maté; (: *vasija*)
gourd
**matemáticas** [mate'matikas] *nfpl*
mathematics; **matemático, -a** *adj*
mathematical ▷ *nm/f* mathematician
**materia** [ma'terja] *nf* (*gen*) matter;
(*Tec*) material; (*Escol*) subject; **en ~ de**
on the subject of; **~ prima** raw material;
**material** *adj* material ▷ *nm* material;
(*Tec*) equipment; **materialista** *adj*
materialist(ic); **materialmente** *adv*
materially; (*fig*) absolutely
**maternal** [mater'nal] *adj* motherly,
maternal
**maternidad** [materni'ðað] *nf*
motherhood, maternity; **materno, -a** *adj*
maternal; (*lengua*) mother *cpd*
**matinal** [mati'nal] *adj* morning *cpd*
**matiz** [ma'tiθ] *nm* shade; **matizar** /1f/ *vt*
(*variar*) to vary; (*Arte*) to blend; **matizar de**
to tinge with
**matón** [ma'ton] *nm* bully
**matorral** [mato'rral] *nm* thicket
**matrícula** [ma'trikula] *nf* (*registro*)
register; (*Auto*) registration number;
(: *placa*) number plate; **~ de honor** (*Univ*)
top marks in a subject at university with the
right to free registration the following year;
**matricular** /1a/ *vt* to register, enrol
**matrimonio** [matri'monjo] *nm* (*pareja*)
(married) couple; (*acto*) marriage
**matriz** [ma'triθ] *nf* (*Anat*) womb; (*Tec*)
mould
**matrona** [ma'trona] *nf* (*mujer de edad*)
matron; (*comadrona*) midwife
**matufia** [ma'tufja] *nf* (*LAM fam*) put-up job
**maullar** [mau'ʎar] /1a/ *vi* to mew, miaow
**maxilar** [maksi'lar] *nm* jaw(bone)
**máxima** ['maksima] *nf V* **máximo**
**máximo, -a** ['maksimo, a] *adj* maximum;
(*más alto*) highest; (*más grande*) greatest
▷ *nm* maximum ▷ *nf* maxim; **como ~** at
most
**mayo** ['majo] *nm* May
**mayonesa** [majo'nesa] *nf* mayonnaise
**mayor** [ma'jor] *adj* main, chief; (*adulto*)
adult; elderly; (*Mus*) major; (*comparativo: de
tamaño*) bigger; (: *de edad*) older; (*superlativo*:

de tamaño) biggest; (: de edad) oldest ▷ nm adult; **mayores** nmpl (antepasados) ancestors; **al por ~** wholesale; **~ de edad** adult

**mayoral** [majo'ral] nm foreman

**mayordomo** [major'ðomo] nm butler

**mayoría** [majo'ria] nf majority, greater part

**mayorista** [majo'rista] nmf wholesaler

**mayoritario, -a** [majori'tarjo, a] adj majority cpd

**mayúsculo, -a** [ma'juskulo, a] adj (fig) big, tremendous ▷ nf capital (letter)

**mazapán** [maθa'pan] nm marzipan

**mazo** ['maθo] nm (martillo) mallet; (de flores) bunch; (Deporte) bat

**me** [me] pron (directo) me; (indirecto) (to) me; (reflexivo) (to) myself; **¡dámelo!** give it to me!

**mear** [me'ar] /1a/ (fam) vi to pee, piss (!)

**mecánica** [me'kanika] nf V **mecánico**

**mecánico, -a** [me'kaniko, a] adj mechanical ▷ nm/f mechanic ▷ nf (estudio) mechanics sg; (mecanismo) mechanism

**mecanismo** [meka'nismo] nm mechanism; (engranaje) gear

**mecanografía** [mekanoɣra'fia] nf typewriting; **mecanógrafo, -a** nm/f (copy) typist

**mecate** [me'kate] nm (LAM) rope

**mecedor** [mese'ðor] nm (LAM), **mecedora** [meθe'ðora] nf rocking chair

**mecer** [me'θer] /2b/ vt (cuna) to rock; **mecerse** vr to rock; (rama) to sway

**mecha** ['metʃa] nf (de vela) wick; (de bomba) fuse

**mechero** [me'tʃero] nm (cigarette) lighter

**mechón** [me'tʃon] nm (gen) tuft; (de pelo) lock

**medalla** [me'ðaʎa] nf medal

**media** ['meðja] nf V **medio**

**mediado, -a** [me'ðjaðo, a] adj half-full; (trabajo) half-completed; **a ~s de** in the middle of, halfway through

**mediano, -a** [me'ðjano, a] adj (regular) medium, average; (mediocre) mediocre

**medianoche** [meðja'notʃe] nf midnight

**mediante** [me'ðjante] adv by (means of), through

**mediar** [me'ðjar] /1b/ vi (interceder) to mediate, intervene

**medicamento** [meðika'mento] nm medicine, drug

**medicina** [meði'θina] nf medicine

**médico, -a** ['meðiko, a] adj medical ▷ nm/f doctor

**medida** [me'ðiða] nf measure; (medición) measurement; (moderación) moderation, prudence; **en cierta/gran ~** up to a point/

to a great extent; **un traje a la ~** a made-to-measure suit; **~ de cuello** collar size; **a ~ de** in proportion to; (de acuerdo con) in keeping with; **a ~ que ...** (at the same time) as ...; **medidor** nm (LAM) meter

**medio, -a** ['meðjo, a] adj half (a); (punto) mid, middle; (promedio) average ▷ adv half- ▷ nm (centro) middle, centre; (método) means, way; (ambiente) environment ▷ nf stocking; (LAM) sock; (promedio) average; **medias** nfpl tights; **~ litro** half a litre; **las tres y media** half past three; **M~ Oriente** Middle East; **~ de transporte** means of transport; **a ~ terminar** half finished; **~ ambiente** environment; **V tb medios**; **medioambiental** adj environmental

**mediocre** [me'ðjokre] adj mediocre

**mediodía** [meðjo'ðia] nm midday, noon

**medios** ['meðjos] nmpl means, resources; **los ~ de comunicación** the media; **los ~ sociales** social media

**medir** [me'ðir] /3k/ vt to measure

**meditar** [meði'tar] /1a/ vt to ponder, think over, meditate on; (planear) to think out

**mediterráneo, -a** [meðite'rraneo, a] adj Mediterranean ▷ nm: **el (mar) M~** the Mediterranean (Sea)

**médula** ['meðula] nf (Anat) marrow; **~ espinal** spinal cord

**medusa** [me'ðusa] nf (ESP) jellyfish

**megáfono** [me'ɣafono] nm megaphone

**megapíxel** [meɣa'piksel] (pl **megapixels** o **megapíxeles**) nm megapixel

**mejicano, -a** [mexi'kano, a] adj, nm/f Mexican

**Méjico** ['mexiko] nm Mexico

**mejilla** [me'xiʎa] nf cheek

**mejillón** [mexi'ʎon] nm mussel

**mejor** [me'xor] adj, adv (comparativo) better; (superlativo) best; **a lo ~** probably; (quizá) maybe; **~ dicho** rather; **tanto ~** so much the better; **mejora** [me'xora] nm improvement; **mejorar** /1a/ vt to improve, make better ▷ vi to improve, get better; **mejorarse** vr to improve, get better

**melancólico, -a** [melan'koliko, a] adj (triste) sad, melancholy; (soñador) dreamy

**melena** [me'lena] nf (de persona) long hair; (Zool) mane

**mellizo, -a** [me'ʎiθo, a] adj, nm/f twin

**melocotón** [meloko'ton] nm (ESP) peach

**melodía** [melo'ðia] nf melody; tune

**melodrama** [melo'ðrama] nm melodrama; **melodramático, -a** adj melodramatic

**melón** [me'lon] nm melon

**membrete** [mem'brete] nm letterhead

**membrillo** [mem'briʎo] nm quince; **carne de ~** quince jelly

**memoria** [me'morja] nf (gen) memory;
  **memorias** nfpl (de autor) memoirs;
  **memorizar** /1f/ vt to memorize
**menaje** [me'naxe] nm (tb: **artículos de ~**)
  household items pl
**mencionar** [menθjo'nar] /1a/ vt to
  mention
**mendigo, -a** [men'diɣo, a] nm/f beggar
**menear** [mene'ar] /1a/ vt to move;
  **menearse** vr to shake; (balancearse) to sway;
  (moverse) to move; (fig) to get a move on
**menestra** [me'nestra] nf: **~ de verduras**
  vegetable stew
**menopausia** [meno'pausja] nf
  menopause
**menor** [me'nor] adj (más pequeño:
  comparativo) smaller; (: superlativo)
  smallest; (más joven: comparativo) younger;
  (: superlativo) youngest; (Mus) minor ▷ nmf
  (joven) young person, juvenile; **no tengo la
  ~ idea** I haven't the faintest idea; **al por ~**
  retail; **~ de edad** minor
**Menorca** [me'norka] nf Minorca

○ **PALABRA CLAVE**

**menos** [menos] adj **1** (compar): **menos
  (que, de)** (cantidad) less (than); (número)
  fewer (than); **con menos entusiasmo**
  with less enthusiasm; **menos gente** fewer
  people; V tb **cada**
  **2** (superl): **es el que menos culpa tiene** he is
  the least to blame
  ▶ adv **1** (compar): **menos (que, de)** less
  (than); **me gusta menos que el otro** I like it
  less than the other one
  **2** (superl): **es el menos listo (de su clase)**
  he's the least bright (in his class); **de todas
  ellas es la que menos me agrada** out of all
  of them she's the one I like least
  **3** (locuciones): **no quiero verle y menos
  visitarle** I don't want to see him let alone
  visit him; **tenemos siete (de) menos** we're
  seven short; **al/por lo menos** at (the very)
  least; **¡menos mal!** thank goodness!
  ▶ prep except; (cifras) minus; **todos menos
  él** everyone except (for) him; **5 menos 2** 5
  minus 2; **las 7 menos 20** (hora) 20 to 7
  ▶ conj: **a menos que: a menos que venga
  mañana** unless he comes tomorrow

**menospreciar** [menospre'θjar] /1b/ vt to
  underrate, undervalue; (despreciar) to scorn,
  despise
**mensaje** [men'saxe] nm message; **enviar
  un ~ a algn** (por móvil) to text sb, send sb a
  text message; **~ de texto** text message;
  **~ electrónico** email; **mensajero, -a** nm/f
  messenger

**menso, -a** ['menso, a] adj (LAM fam) stupid
**menstruación** [menstrwa'θjon] nf
  menstruation
**mensual** [men'swal] adj monthly; **10
  euros ~es** 10 euros a month; **mensualidad**
  nf (salario) monthly salary; (Com) monthly
  payment o instalment
**menta** ['menta] nf mint
**mental** [men'tal] adj mental; **mentalidad**
  nf mentality; **mentalizar** /1f/ vt
  (sensibilizar) to make aware; (convencer) to
  convince; (preparar) to prepare
  mentally; **mentalizarse** vr (concienciarse)
  to become aware; **mentalizarse (de)** to
  get used to the idea (of); **mentalizarse de
  que ...** (convencerse) to get it into one's head
  that ...
**mente** ['mente] nf mind
**mentir** [men'tir] /3i/ vi to lie; **mentira** nf
  (una mentira) lie; (acto) lying; (invención)
  fiction; **parece mentira que ...** it seems
  incredible that ..., I can't believe that ...;
  **mentiroso, -a** adj lying ▷ nm/f liar
**menú** [me'nu] nm menu; (tb: **~ del día**) set
  meal; **~ turístico** tourist menu
**menudo, -a** [me'nuðo, a] adj (pequeño)
  small, tiny; (sin importancia) petty,
  insignificant; **¡~ negocio!** (fam) some deal!;
  **a ~** often, frequently
**meñique** [me'ɲike] nm little finger
**mercadillo** [merka'ðiʎo] nm (ESP) flea
  market
**mercado** [mer'kaðo] nm market; **~ de
  pulgas** (LAM) flea market
**mercancía** [merkan'θia] nf commodity;
  **mercancías** nfpl goods, merchandise sg
**mercenario, -a** [merθe'narjo, a] adj, nm
  mercenary
**mercería** [merθe'ria] nf haberdashery
  (BRIT), notions pl (US); (tienda)
  haberdasher's shop (BRIT), drapery (BRIT),
  notions store (US)
**mercurio** [mer'kurjo] nm mercury
**merecer** [mere'θer] /2d/ vt to deserve,
  merit ▷ vi to be deserving, be worthy;
  **merece la pena** it's worthwhile;
  **merecido, -a** adj (well) deserved; **llevarse
  su merecido** to get one's deserts
**merendar** [meren'dar] /1j/ vt to have for
  tea ▷ vi to have tea; (en el campo) to have a
  picnic; **merendero** nm (open-air) café
**merengue** [me'renge] nm meringue
**meridiano** [meri'ðjano] nm (Astro, Geo)
  meridian
**merienda** [me'rjenda] nf (light) tea,
  afternoon snack; (de campo) picnic
**mérito** ['merito] nm merit; (valor) worth,
  value
**merluza** [mer'luθa] nf hake

**mermelada** [merme'laða] nf jam

**mero, -a** ['mero, a] adj mere; (LAM fam) very

**merodear** [meroðe'ar] /1a/ vi (de noche) to prowl (about)

**mes** [mes] nm month

**mesa** ['mesa] nf table; (de trabajo) desk; (Geo) plateau; **~ electoral** officials in charge of a polling station; **~ redonda** (reunión) round table; **poner/quitar la ~** to lay/clear the table; **mesero, -a** nm/f (LAM) waiter/ waitress

**meseta** [me'seta] nf (Geo) tableland

**mesilla** [me'siʎa] nf: **~ de noche** bedside table

**mesón** [me'son] nm inn

**mestizo, -a** [mes'tiθo, a] adj mixed-race ▷ nm/f person of mixed race

**meta** ['meta] nf goal; (de carrera) finish

**metabolismo** [metaβo'lismo] nm metabolism

**metáfora** [me'tafora] nf metaphor

**metal** [me'tal] nm (materia) metal; (Mus) brass; **metálico, -a** adj metallic; (de metal) metal ▷ nm (dinero contante) cash

**meteorología** [meteorolo'xia] nf meteorology

**meter** [me'ter] /2a/ vt (colocar) to put, place; (introducir) to put in, insert; (involucrar) to involve; (causar) to make, cause; **meterse** vr: **~se en** to go into, enter; (fig) to interfere in, meddle in; **~se a** to start; **~se a escritor** to become a writer; **~se con algn** to provoke sb, pick a quarrel with sb

**meticuloso, -a** [metiku'loso, a] adj meticulous, thorough

**metódico, -a** [me'toðiko, a] adj methodical

**método** ['metoðo] nm method

**metralleta** [metra'ʎeta] nf sub-machine-gun

**métrico, -a** ['metriko, a] adj metric

**metro** ['metro] nm metre; (tren) underground (BRIT), subway (US)

**metrosexual** [metrosexu'al] adj, nm metrosexual

**mexicano, -a** [mexi'kano, a] adj, nm/f Mexican

**México** ['mexiko] nm Mexico; **Ciudad de ~** Mexico City

**mezcla** ['meθkla] nf mixture; **mezclar** /1a/ vt to mix (up); **mezclarse** vr to mix, mingle; **mezclar en** to get mixed up in, get involved in

**mezquino, -a** [meθ'kino, a] adj mean

**mezquita** [meθ'kita] nf mosque

**mg** abr (= miligramo(s)) mg

**mi** [mi] adj posesivo my ▷ nm (Mus) E

**mí** [mi] pron me, myself

**mía** ['mia] pron V **mío**

**michelín** [mitʃe'lin] nm (fam) spare tyre

**microbio** [mi'kroβjo] nm microbe

**micrófono** [mi'krofono] nm microphone

**microonda** [mikro'onda] nf, **microondas** [mikro'ondas] nm inv microwave; **(horno) ~s** microwave (oven)

**microscopio** [mikros'kopjo] nm microscope

**miedo** ['mjeðo] nm fear; (nerviosismo) apprehension, nervousness; **tener ~** to be afraid; **de ~** wonderful, marvellous; **hace un frío de ~** (fam) it's terribly cold; **miedoso, -a** adj fearful, timid

**miel** [mjel] nf honey

**miembro** ['mjembro] nm limb; (socio) member; **~ viril** penis

**mientras** ['mjentras] conj while; (duración) as long as ▷ adv meanwhile; **~ tanto** meanwhile

**miércoles** ['mjerkoles] nm inv Wednesday

**mierda** ['mjerða] nf (fam!) shit (!)

**miga** ['miɣa] nf crumb; (fig: meollo) essence; **hacer buenas ~s** (fam) to get on well

**mil** [mil] num thousand; **dos ~ libras** two thousand pounds

**milagro** [mi'laɣro] nm miracle; **milagroso, -a** adj miraculous

**milésima** [mi'lesima] nf (de segundo) thousandth

**mili** ['mili] nf: **hacer la ~** (fam) to do one's military service

**milímetro** [mi'limetro] nm millimetre (BRIT), millimeter (US)

**militante** [mili'tante] adj militant

**militar** [mili'tar] /1a/ adj military ▷ nmf soldier ▷ vi to serve in the army

**milla** ['miʎa] nf mile

**millar** [mi'ʎar] num thousand

**millón** [mi'ʎon] num million; **millonario, -a** nm/f millionaire

**milusos** [mi'lusos] nm inv (LAM) odd-job man

**mimar** [mi'mar] /1a/ vt to spoil, pamper

**mimbre** ['mimbre] nm wicker

**mímica** ['mimika] nf (para comunicarse) sign language; (imitación) mimicry

**mimo** ['mimo] nm (caricia) caress; (de niño) spoiling; (Teat) mime; (: actor) mime artist

**mina** ['mina] nf mine

**mineral** [mine'ral] adj mineral ▷ nm (Geo) mineral; (mena) ore

**minero, -a** [mi'nero, a] adj mining cpd ▷ nm/f miner

**miniatura** [minja'tura] adj inv, nf miniature

**minidisco** [mini'ðisko] nm diskette

**minifalda** [mini'falda] nf miniskirt

**mínimo, -a** ['minimo, a] adj ▷ nm minimum

**minino, -a** [mi'nino, a] nm/f (fam) puss,
pussy
**ministerio** [minis'terjo] nm ministry
(BRIT), department (US); **M~ de Asuntos
Exteriores** Foreign Office (BRIT), State
Department (US); **M~ de Hacienda**
Treasury (BRIT), Treasury Department (US)
**ministro, -a** [mi'nistro, a] nm/f minister
**minoría** [mino'ria] nf minority
**minúsculo, -a** [mi'nuskulo, a] adj tiny,
minute ▷ nf small letter
**minusválido, -a** [minus'βaliðo, a] adj
with a physical disability ▷ nm/f person
with a disability
**minuta** [mi'nuta] nf (de comida) menu
**minutero** [minu'tero] nm minute hand
**minuto** [mi'nuto] nm minute
**mío, -a** ['mio, a] pron: **el ~** mine; **un amigo ~**
a friend of mine; **lo ~** what is mine
**miope** ['mjope] adj short-sighted
**mira** ['mira] nf (de arma) sight(s) pl; (fig) aim,
intention
**mirada** [mi'raða] nf look, glance; (expresión)
look, expression; **clavar la ~ en** to stare at;
**echar una ~ a** to glance at
**mirado, -a** [mi'raðo, a] adj (sensato)
sensible; (considerado) considerate; **bien/
mal ~** well/not well thought of; **bien ~ ...** all
things considered ...
**mirador** [mira'ðor] nm viewpoint, vantage
point
**mirar** [mi'rar] /1a/ vt to look at; (observar)
to watch; (considerar) to consider, think
over; (vigilar, cuidar) to watch, look after
▷ vi to look; (Arq) to face; **mirarse** vr (dos
personas) to look at each other; **~ bien/mal**
to think highly of/have a poor opinion of;
**~se al espejo** to look at o.s. in the mirror
**mirilla** [mi'riʎa] nf spyhole, peephole
**mirlo** ['mirlo] nm blackbird
**misa** ['misa] nf mass
**miserable** [mise'raβle] adj (avaro) mean,
stingy; (nimio) miserable, paltry; (lugar)
squalid; (fam) vile, despicable ▷ nmf
(malvado) rogue
**miseria** [mi'serja] nf (pobreza) poverty;
(tacañería) meanness, stinginess;
(condiciones) squalor; **una ~** a pittance
**misericordia** [miseri'korðja] nf
(compasión) compassion, pity; (perdón)
mercy
**misil** [mi'sil] nm missile
**misión** [mi'sjon] nf mission; **misionero, -a**
nm/f missionary
**mismo, -a** ['mismo, a] adj (semejante)
same; (después de pronombre) -self; (para
énfasis) very ▷ adv: **aquí/ayer/hoy ~** right
here/only yesterday/this very day; **ahora ~**
right now ▷ conj: **lo ~ que** just like, just as;

**por lo ~** for the same reason; **el ~ traje** the
same suit; **en ese ~ momento** at that very
moment; **vino el ~ Ministro** the Minister
himself came; **yo ~ lo vi** I saw it myself; **lo ~**
the same (thing); **da lo ~** it's all the same;
**quedamos en las mismas** we're no further
forward
**misterio** [mis'terjo] nm mystery;
**misterioso, -a** adj mysterious
**mitad** [mi'tað] nf (medio) half; (centro)
middle; **a ~ de precio** (at) half-price; **en
o a ~ del camino** halfway along the road;
**cortar por la ~** to cut through the middle
**mitin** ['mitin] nm meeting
**mito** ['mito] nm myth
**mixto, -a** ['miksto, a] adj mixed
**ml** abr (= mililitro(s)) ml
**mm** abr (= milímetro(s)) mm
**mobiliario** [moβi'ljarjo] nm furniture
**mochila** [mo'tʃila] nf rucksack (BRIT),
backpack
**moco** ['moko] nm mucus; **mocos** nmpl (fam)
snot; **limpiarse los ~s** to blow one's nose
**moda** ['moða] nf fashion; (estilo) style; **de o
a la ~** in fashion, fashionable; **pasado de ~**
out of fashion
**modal** [mo'ðal] adj modal; **modales** nmpl
manners
**modelar** [moðe'lar] /1a/ vt to model
**modelo** [mo'ðelo] adj inv ▷ nmf model
**módem** ['moðem] nm (Inform) modem
**moderado, -a** [moðe'raðo, a] adj
moderate
**moderar** [moðe'rar] /1a/ vt to moderate;
(violencia) to restrain, control; (velocidad)
to reduce; **moderarse** vr to restrain o.s.,
control o.s.
**modernizar** [moðerni'θar] /1f/ vt to
modernize
**moderno, -a** [mo'ðerno, a] adj modern;
(actual) present-day
**modestia** [mo'ðestja] nf modesty;
**modesto, -a** adj modest
**modificar** [moðifi'kar] /1g/ vt to modify
**modisto, -a** [mo'ðisto, a] nm/f (diseñador)
couturier, designer; (que confecciona)
dressmaker
**modo** ['moðo] nm way, manner; (Inform,
Mus) mode; **modos** nmpl manners; **"~ de
empleo"** "instructions for use"; **de ningún ~**
in no way; **de todos ~s** at any rate
**mofarse** [mo'farse] /1a/ vr: **~ de** to mock,
scoff at
**mofle** ['mofle] nm (LAM) silencer (BRIT),
muffler (US)
**mogollón** [moɣo'ʎon] (fam) adv: **un ~** a
hell of a lot
**moho** ['moo] nm mould, mildew; (en metal)
rust

**mojar** [mo'xar] /1a/ vt to wet; (humedecer) to damp(en), moisten; (calar) to soak; **mojarse** vr to get wet

**molcajete** [molka'xete] (LAM) nm mortar

**molde** ['molde] nm mould; (de costura) pattern; (fig) model; **moldeado** nm soft perm; **moldear** /1a/ vt to mould

**mole** ['mole] nf mass, bulk; (edificio) pile

**moler** [mo'ler] /2h/ vt to grind, crush

**molestar** [moles'tar] /1a/ vt to bother; (fastidiar) to annoy; (incomodar) to inconvenience, put out ▷ vi to be a nuisance; **molestarse** vr to bother; (incomodarse) to go to a lot of trouble; (ofenderse) to take offence; **¿le molesta el ruido?** do you mind the noise?

No confundir molestar con la palabra inglesa molest.

**molestia** [mo'lestja] nf bother, trouble; (incomodidad) inconvenience; (Med) discomfort; **es una ~** it's a nuisance; **molesto, -a** adj (que fastidia) annoying; (incómodo) inconvenient; (inquieto) uncomfortable, ill at ease; (enfadado) annoyed

**molido, -a** [mo'liðo, a] adj: **estar ~** (fig) to be exhausted o dead beat

**molinillo** [moli'niʎo] nm hand mill; **~ de carne/café** mincer/coffee grinder

**molino** [mo'lino] nm (edificio) mill; (máquina) grinder

**momentáneo, -a** [momen'taneo, a] adj momentary

**momento** [mo'mento] nm moment; **de ~** at the moment, for the moment

**momia** ['momja] nf mummy

**monarca** [mo'narka] nmf monarch, ruler; **monarquía** nf monarchy

**monasterio** [monas'terjo] nm monastery

**mondar** [mon'dar] /1a/ vt to peel; **mondarse** vr: **~se de risa** (fam) to split one's sides laughing

**mondongo** [mon'dongo] nm (LAM) tripe

**moneda** [mo'neða] nf (tipo de dinero) currency, money; (pieza) coin; **una ~ de 50 céntimos** a 50-cent coin; **monedero** nm purse

**monitor, a** [moni'tor, a] nm/f instructor, coach ▷ nm (TV) set; (Inform) monitor

**monja** ['monxa] nf nun

**monje** ['monxe] nm monk

**mono, -a** ['mono, a] adj (bonito) lovely, pretty; (gracioso) nice, charming ▷ nm/f monkey, ape ▷ nm dungarees pl; (traje de faena) overalls pl

**monopatín** [monopa'tin] nm skateboard

**monopolio** [mono'poljo] nm monopoly; **monopolizar** /1f/ vt to monopolize

**monótono, -a** [mo'notono, a] adj monotonous

**monstruo** ['monstrwo] nm monster ▷ adj inv fantastic; **monstruoso, -a** adj monstrous

**montaje** [mon'taxe] nm assembly; (Teat) décor; (Cine) montage

**montaña** [mon'taɲa] nf (monte) mountain; (sierra) mountains pl, mountainous area; **~ rusa** roller coaster; **montañero, -a** nm/f mountaineer; **montañismo** nm mountaineering

**montar** [mon'tar] /1a/ vt (subir a) to mount, get on; (Tec) to assemble, put together; (negocio) to set up; (colocar) to lift on to; (Culin) to whip, beat ▷ vi to mount, get on; (sobresalir) to overlap; **~ en bicicleta** to ride a bicycle; **~ en cólera** to get angry; **~ a caballo** to ride, go horseriding

**monte** ['monte] nm (montaña) mountain; (bosque) woodland; (área sin cultivar) wild area, wild country; **~ de piedad** pawnshop

**montón** [mon'ton] nm heap, pile; **un ~ de** (fig) heaps of, lots of

**monumento** [monu'mento] nm monument

**moño** ['moɲo] nm bun

**moqueta** [mo'keta] nf fitted carpet

**mora** ['mora] nf blackberry

**morado, -a** [mo'raðo, a] adj purple, violet ▷ nm bruise

**moral** [mo'ral] adj moral ▷ nf (ética) ethics pl; (moralidad) morals pl, morality; (ánimo) morale

**moraleja** [mora'lexa] nf moral

**morboso, -a** [mor'βoso, a] adj morbid

**morcilla** [mor'θiʎa] nf blood sausage, ≈ black pudding (BRIT)

**mordaza** [mor'ðaθa] nf (para la boca) gag; (Tec) clamp

**morder** [mor'ðer] /2h/ vt to bite; (fig: consumir) to eat away, eat into; **mordisco** nm bite

**moreno, -a** [mo'reno, a] adj (color) (dark) brown; (de tez) dark; (de pelo moreno) dark-haired; (negro) black

**morfina** [mor'fina] nf morphine

**moribundo, -a** [mori'βundo, a] adj dying

**morir** [mo'rir] /3j/ vi to die; (fuego) to die down; (luz) to go out; **morirse** vr to die; (fig) to be dying; **fue muerto a tiros/en un accidente** he was shot (dead)/was killed in an accident; **~se por algo** to be dying for sth

**moro, -a** ['moro, a] adj Moorish ▷ nm/f Moor

**moroso, -a** [mo'roso, a] nm/f (Com) bad debtor, defaulter

**morro** ['morro] nm (Zool) snout, nose; (Auto, Aviat) nose

**morsa** ['morsa] nf walrus

**mortadela** [morta'ðela] nf mortadella

**mortal** [mor'tal] adj mortal; (golpe) deadly; **mortalidad** nf mortality

**mortero** [mor'tero] nm mortar

**mosca** ['moska] nf fly

**Moscú** [mos'ku] nm Moscow

**mosquear** [moske'ar] /1a/ (fam) vt (fastidiar) to annoy; **mosquearse** vr (enfadarse) to get annoyed; (ofenderse) to take offence

**mosquitero** [moski'tero] nm mosquito net

**mosquito** [mos'kito] nm mosquito

**mostaza** [mos'taθa] nf mustard

**mosto** ['mosto] nm unfermented grape juice

**mostrador** [mostra'ðor] nm (de tienda) counter; (de café) bar

**mostrar** [mos'trar] /1l/ vt to show; (exhibir) to display, exhibit; (explicar) to explain; **mostrarse** vr: ~se amable to be kind; to prove to be kind; **no se muestra muy inteligente** he doesn't seem (to be) very intelligent

**mota** ['mota] nf speck, tiny piece; (en diseño) dot

**mote** ['mote] nm nickname

**motín** [mo'tin] nm (del pueblo) revolt, rising; (del ejército) mutiny

**motivar** [moti'βar] /1a/ vt (causar) to cause, motivate; (explicar) to explain, justify; **motivo** nm motive, reason

**moto** ['moto] nf, **motocicleta** [motoθi'kleta] nf motorbike (BRIT), motorcycle

**motociclista** [motoθi'klista] nmf motorcyclist, biker

**motoneta** [moto'neta] nf (LAM) (motor) scooter

**motor, a** [mo'tor, a] nm motor, engine ▷ nf motorboat; ~ **a chorro** o **de reacción/de explosión** jet engine/internal combustion engine

**movedizo, -a** [moβe'ðiθo, a] adj (inseguro) unsteady; (fig) unsettled

**mover** [mo'βer] /2h/ vt to move; (cabeza) to shake; (accionar) to drive; (fig) to cause, provoke; **moverse** vr to move; (fig) to get a move on

**móvil** ['moβil] adj mobile; (pieza de máquina) moving; (mueble) movable ▷ nm (motivo) motive; (teléfono) mobile, cellphone (US)

**movimiento** [moβi'mjento] nm movement; (Tec) motion; (actividad) activity

**mozo, -a** ['moθo, a] adj (joven) young ▷ nm/f youth, young man/girl; (camarero) waiter; (camarera) waitress

**MP3** nm MP3; **reproductor (de)** ~ MP3 player

**mucama** [mu'kama] nf (LAM) maid

**muchacho, -a** [mu'tʃatʃo, a] nm/f (niño) boy/girl; (criado) servant/servant o maid

**muchedumbre** [mutʃe'ðumbre] nf crowd

 **PALABRA CLAVE**

**mucho, -a** ['mutʃo, a] adj **1** (cantidad) a lot of, much; (número) lots of, a lot of, many; **mucho dinero** a lot of money; **hace mucho calor** it's very hot; **muchas amigas** lots o a lot of o many friends

**2** (sg: fam): **ésta es mucha casa para él** this house is much too big for him

▶ pron **1**: **tengo mucho que hacer** I've got a lot to do; **muchos dicen que …** a lot of people say that …; V tb **tener**

▶ adv **1**: **me gusta mucho** I like it a lot o very much; **lo siento mucho** I'm very sorry; **come mucho** he eats a lot; **¿te vas a quedar mucho?** are you going to be staying long?

**2** (respuesta) very; **¿estás cansado?** — **¡mucho!** are you tired? — very!

**3** (locuciones): **como mucho** at (the) most; **el mejor con mucho** by far the best; **no es rico ni mucho menos** he's far from being rich

**4**: **por mucho que: por mucho que le creas** however much o no matter how much you believe him

**muda** ['muða] nf change of clothing

**mudanza** [mu'ðanθa] nf (de casa) move

**mudar** [mu'ðar] /1a/ vt to change; (Zool) to shed ▷ vi to change; **mudarse** vr (la ropa) to change; ~**se de casa** to move house

**mudo, -a** ['muðo, a] adj with a speech impairment; (callado) silent

**mueble** ['mweβle] nm piece of furniture; **muebles** nmpl furniture sg

**mueca** ['mweka] nf face, grimace; **hacer** ~**s a** to make faces at

**muela** ['mwela] nf tooth; ~ **del juicio** wisdom tooth

**muelle** ['mweʎe] nm spring; (Naut) wharf; (malecón) pier

**muerte** ['mwerte] nf death; (homicidio) murder; **dar** ~ **a** to kill

**muerto, -a** ['mwerto, a] pp de **morir** ▷ adj dead ▷ nm/f dead man/woman; (difunto) deceased; (cadáver) corpse; **estar** ~ **de cansancio** to be dead tired; **Día de los M~s** (LAM) All Souls' Day

● **DÍA DE LOS MUERTOS**

● All Souls' Day (or "Day of the Dead") in
● Mexico coincides with All Saints' Day,
● which is celebrated in the Catholic

- countries of Latin America on November
- 1st and 2nd. All Souls' Day is actually a
- celebration which begins in the evening
- of October 31st and continues until
- November 2nd. It is a combination of
- the Catholic tradition of honouring the
- Christian saints and martyrs, and the
- ancient Mexican or Aztec traditions, in
- which death was not something sinister.
- For this reason all the dead are honoured
- by bringing offerings of food, flowers and
- candles to the cemetery.

**muestra** ['mwestra] *nf (señal)* indication,
sign; *(demostración)* demonstration;
*(prueba)* proof; *(estadística)* sample; *(modelo)*
model, pattern; *(testimonio)* token
**muestro** *etc vb V* **mostrar**
**muevo** *etc vb V* **mover**
**mugir** [mu'xir] /3c/ *vi (vaca)* to moo
**mugre** ['muɣre] *nf* dirt, filth
**mujer** [mu'xer] *nf* woman; *(esposa)* wife;
 **mujeriego** *nm* womaniser
**mula** ['mula] *nf* mule
**muleta** [mu'leta] *nf (para andar)* crutch;
 *(Taur)* stick with red cape attached
**multa** ['multa] *nf* fine; **echar** *o* **poner
 una ~ a** to fine; **multar** /1a/ *vt* to fine
**multicines** [multi'θine] *nmpl* multiscreen
 cinema
**multinacional** [multinaθjo'nal] *nf*
 multinational
**múltiple** ['multiple] *adj* multiple, many *pl*,
 numerous
**multiplicar** [multipli'kar] /1g/ *vt (Mat)* to
 multiply; *(fig)* to increase; **multiplicarse**
 *vr (Bio)* to multiply; *(fig)* to be everywhere
 at once
**multitud** [multi'tuð] *nf (muchedumbre)*
 crowd; **~ de** lots of
**mundial** [mun'djal] *adj* world-wide,
 universal; *(guerra, récord)* world *cpd*
**mundo** ['mundo] *nm* world; **todo el ~**
 everybody; **tener ~** to be experienced,
 know one's way around
**munición** [muni'θjon] *nf* ammunition
**municipal** [muniθi'pal] *adj* municipal;
 local
**municipio** [muni'θipjo] *nm (ayuntamiento)*
 town council, corporation; *(territorio
 administrativo)* town, municipality
**muñeca** [mu'ɲeka] *nf (Anat)* wrist; *(juguete)*
 doll
**muñeco** [mu'ɲeko] *nm (figura)* figure;
 *(marioneta)* puppet; *(fig)* puppet, pawn
**mural** [mu'ral] *adj* mural, wall *cpd* ▷ *nm*
 mural
**muralla** [mu'raʎa] *nf (city)* walls *pl*
**murciélago** [mur'θjelaɣo] *nm* bat

**murmullo** [mur'muʎo] *nm* murmur(ing);
 *(cuchicheo)* whispering
**murmurar** [murmu'rar] /1a/ *vi* to
 murmur, whisper; *(cotillear)* to gossip
**muro** ['muro] *nm* wall
**muscular** [musku'lar] *adj* muscular
**músculo** ['muskulo] *nm* muscle
**museo** [mu'seo] *nm* museum; **~ de arte** *o*
 **de pintura** art gallery
**musgo** ['musɣo] *nm* moss
**músico, -a** ['musiko, a] *adj* musical ▷ *nm/f*
 musician ▷ *nf* music
**muslo** ['muslo] *nm* thigh
**musulmán, -ana** [musul'man, ana] *nm/f*
 Moslem
**mutación** [muta'θjon] *nf (Bio)* mutation;
 *(cambio)* (sudden) change
**mutilar** [muti'lar] /1a/ *vt* to mutilate;
 *(a una persona)* to maim
**mutuo, -a** ['mutwo, a] *adj* mutual
**muy** [mwi] *adv* very; *(demasiado)* too;
 **M~ Señor mío** Dear Sir; **~ de noche** very
 late at night; **eso es ~ de él** that's just like
 him

**n**

**N** *abr* (= *norte*) N

**nabo** ['naβo] *nm* turnip

**nacer** [na'θer] /2d/ *vi* to be born; (*huevo*) to hatch; (*vegetal*) to sprout; (*río*) to rise; **nací en Barcelona** I was born in Barcelona; **nacido, -a** *adj* born; **recién nacido** newborn; **nacimiento** *nm* birth; (*de Navidad*) Nativity; (*de río*) source

**nación** [na'θjon] *nf* nation; **nacional** *adj* national; **nacionalidad** *nf* nationality; **nacionalismo** *nm* nationalism

**nada** ['naða] *pron* nothing ▷ *adv* not at all, in no way; **no decir ~ (más)** to say nothing (else), not to say anything (else); **¡~ más!** that's all; **de ~** don't mention it

**nadador, a** [naða'ðor, a] *nm/f* swimmer

**nadar** [na'ðar] /1a/ *vi* to swim

**nadie** ['naðje] *pron* nobody, no-one; **~ habló** nobody spoke; **no había ~** there was nobody there, there wasn't anybody there

**nado** ['naðo]: **a ~** *adv*: **pasar a ~** to swim across

**nafta** ['nafta] *nf* (LAM) petrol (BRIT), gas(oline) (US)

**naipe** ['naipe] *nm* (playing) card; **naipes** *nmpl* cards

**nalgas** ['nalɣas] *nfpl* buttocks

**nalguear** [nalɣe'ar] /1a/ *vt* (LAM, CAM) to spank

**nana** ['nana] *nf* lullaby

**naranja** [na'ranxa] *adj inv, nf* orange; **media ~** (*fam*) better half; **naranjada** *nf* orangeade; **naranjo** *nm* orange tree

**narciso** [nar'θiso] *nm* narcissus

**narcótico, -a** [nar'kotiko, a] *adj, nm* narcotic; **narcotizar** /1f/ *vt* to drug; **narcotráfico** *nm* narcotics o drug trafficking

**nariz** [na'riθ] *nf* nose; **~ chata/respingona** snub/turned-up nose

**narración** [narra'θjon] *nf* narration

**narrar** [na'rrar] /1a/ *vt* to narrate, recount

**narrativo, -a** [narra'tiβo, a] *adj, nf* narrative

**nata** ['nata] *nf* cream (*tb fig*); (*en leche cocida etc*) skin; **~ batida** whipped cream

**natación** [nata'θjon] *nf* swimming

**natal** [na'tal] *adj*: **ciudad ~** home town; **natalidad** *nf* birth rate

**natillas** [na'tiʎas] *nfpl* (egg) custard *sg*

**nativo, -a** [na'tiβo, a] *adj, nm/f* native

**natural** [natu'ral] *adj* natural; (*fruta etc*) fresh ▷ *nmf* native ▷ *nm* disposition, temperament; **buen ~** good nature

**naturaleza** [natura'leθa] *nf* nature; (*género*) nature, kind; **~ muerta** still life

**naturalmente** [natural'mente] *adv* (*de modo natural*) in a natural way; **¡~!** of course!

**naufragar** [naufra'ɣar] /1h/ *vi* to sink; **naufragio** *nm* shipwreck

**náusea** ['nausea] *nf* nausea; **me da ~s** it makes me feel sick

**nauseabundo, -a** [nausea'βundo, a] *adj* nauseating, sickening

**náutico, -a** ['nautiko, a] *adj* nautical

**navaja** [na'βaxa] *nf* penknife; **~ (de afeitar)** razor

**naval** [na'βal] *adj* naval

**Navarra** [na'βarra] *nf* Navarre

**nave** ['naβe] *nf* (*barco*) ship, vessel; (*Arq*) nave; **~ espacial** spaceship; **~ industrial** factory premises *pl*

**navegador** [naβeɣa'ðor] *nm* (*Inform*) browser

**navegante** [naβe'ɣante] *nmf* navigator

**navegar** [naβe'ɣar] /1h/ *vi* (*barco*) to sail; (*avión*) to fly; **~ por Internet** to surf the Net

**Navidad** [naβi'ðað] *nf* Christmas; **Navidades** *nfpl* Christmas time *sg*; **¡Feliz ~!** Merry Christmas!; **navideño, -a** *adj* Christmas *cpd*

**nazca** *etc vb* V **nacer**

**nazi** ['naθi] *adj, nmf* Nazi

**NE** *abr* (= *nor(d)este*) NE

**neblina** [ne'βlina] *nf* mist

**necesario, -a** [neθe'sarjo, a] *adj* necessary

**neceser** [neθe'ser] *nm* toilet bag; (*bolsa grande*) holdall

**necesidad** [neθesi'ðað] *nf* need; (*lo inevitable*) necessity; (*miseria*) poverty; **en caso de ~** in case of need o emergency; **hacer sus ~es** to relieve o.s.

**necesitado, -a** [neθesi'taðo, a] *adj* needy, poor; **~ de** in need of

**necesitar** [neθesi'tar] /1a/ *vt* to need, require

**necio, -a** ['neθjo, a] *adj* foolish

**nectarina** [nekta'rina] *nf* nectarine

**nefasto, -a** [ne'fasto, a] *adj* ill-fated, unlucky

**negación** [neɣa'θjon] *nf* negation; (*rechazo*) refusal, denial

**negar** [ne'ɣar] /1h, 1j/ *vt* (*renegar, rechazar*) to refuse; (*prohibir*) to refuse, deny; (*desmentir*) to deny; **negarse** *vr*: **~se a hacer algo** to refuse to do sth

**negativo, -a** [neɣa'tiβo, a] *adj, nm* negative ▷ *nf* negative; (*rechazo*) refusal, denial

**negligente** [neɣli'xente] *adj* negligent

**negociación** [neɣoθja'θjon] *nf* negotiation

**negociante** [neɣo'θjante] *nmf* businessman/woman

**negociar** [neɣo'θjar] /1b/ *vt, vi* to negotiate; **~ en** to deal in, trade in

**negocio** [ne'ɣoθjo] *nm* (*Com*) business; (*asunto*) affair, business; (*operación comercial*) deal, transaction; (*lugar*) place of business; **los ~s** business *sg*; **hacer ~** to do business

**negra** ['neɣra] *nf* (*Mus*) crotchet; V *tb* **negro**

**negro, -a** ['neɣro, a] *adj* black; (*suerte*) awful ▷ *nm/f* black person

**nene, -a** ['nene, a] *nm/f* baby, small child

**neón** [ne'on] *nm*: **luces/lámpara de ~** neon lights/lamp

**neoyorquino, -a** [neojor'kino, a] *adj* New York *cpd*

**nervio** ['nerβjo] *nm* nerve; **nerviosismo** *nm* nervousness, nerves *pl*; **nervioso, -a** *adj* nervous

**neto, -a** ['neto, a] *adj* net

**neumático, -a** [neu'matiko, a] *adj* pneumatic ▷ *nm* (*ESP*) tyre (*BRIT*), tire (*US*); **~ de recambio** spare tyre

**neurólogo, -a** [neu'roloɣo, a] *nm/f* neurologist

**neurona** [neu'rona] *nf* neuron

**neutral** [neu'tral] *adj* neutral; **neutralizar** /1f/ *vt* to neutralize; (*contrarrestar*) to counteract

**neutro, -a** [ˈneutro, a] *adj* (*Bio, Ling*) neuter; **~ en carbono** carbon-neutral

**neutrón** [neu'tron] *nm* neutron

**nevado, -a** [ne'βaðo, a] *adj* snow-covered ▷ *nf* snowstorm; (*caída de nieve*) snowfall

**nevar** [ne'βar] /1j/ *vi* to snow

**nevera** [ne'βera] *nf* (*ESP*) refrigerator (*BRIT*), icebox (*US*)

**nevería** [neβe'ria] *nf* (*LAM*) ice-cream parlour

**nexo** ['nekso] *nm* link, connection

**ni** [ni] *conj* nor, neither; (*tb*: **ni siquiera**) not even; **ni que** not even if; **ni blanco ni negro** neither white nor black

**Nicaragua** [nika'raɣwa] *nf* Nicaragua; **nicaragüense** *adj, nmf* Nicaraguan

**nicho** ['nitʃo] *nm* niche

**nicotina** [niko'tina] *nf* nicotine

**nido** ['niðo] *nm* nest

**niebla** ['njeβla] *nf* fog; (*neblina*) mist

**niego** *etc* ['njeɣo] *vb* V **negar**

**nieto, -a** ['njeto, a] *nm/f* grandson/granddaughter; **nietos** *nmpl* grandchildren

**nieve** ['njeβe] *vb* V **nevar** ▷ *nf* snow; (*LAM*) ice cream

**ninfa** ['ninfa] *nf* nymph

**ningún** [nin'gun] *adj* V **ninguno**

**ninguno, -a** [nin'guno, a] *adj* no ▷ *pron* (*nadie*) nobody; (*ni uno*) none, not one; (*ni uno ni otro*) neither; **de ninguna manera** by no means, not at all

**niña** ['niɲa] *nf* V **niño**

**niñera** [ni'ɲera] *nf* nursemaid, nanny

**niñez** [ni'ɲeθ] *nf* childhood; (*infancia*) infancy

**niño, -a** ['niɲo, a] *adj* (*joven*) young; (*inmaduro*) immature ▷ *nm* boy, child ▷ *nf* girl, child; (*Anat*) pupil

**nipón, -ona** [ni'pon, ona] *adj, nm/f* Japanese

**níquel** ['nikel] *nm* nickel

**níspero** ['nispero] *nm* medlar

**nítido, -a** [ˈnitiðo, a] *adj* clear, sharp

**nitrato** [ni'trato] *nm* nitrate

**nitrógeno** [ni'troxeno] *nm* nitrogen

**nivel** [ni'βel] *nm* (*Geo*) level; (*norma*) level, standard; (*altura*) height; **~ de aceite** oil level; **~ de aire** spirit level; **~ de vida** standard of living; **nivelar** /1a/ *vt* to level out; (*fig*) to even up; (*Com*) to balance

**no** [no] *adv* no; (*con verbo*) not ▷ *excl* no!; **no tengo nada** I don't have anything, I have nothing; **no es el mío** it's not mine; **ahora no** not now; **¿no lo sabes?** don't you know?; **no mucho** not much; **no bien termine, lo entregaré** as soon as I finish I'll hand it over; **ayer no más** just yesterday; **¡pase no más!** come in!; **¡a que no lo sabes!** I bet you don't know!; **¡cómo no!** of course!; **la no intervención** non-intervention

**noble** ['noβle] *adj, nmf* noble; **nobleza** *nf* nobility

**noche** ['notʃe] *nf* night, night-time; (*la tarde*) evening; **de ~, por la ~** at night; **ayer por la ~** last night; **esta ~** tonight; **(en) toda la ~** all night; **hacer ~ en un sitio** to spend the night in a place; **se hace de ~** it's getting dark; **es de ~** it's dark; **N~ de San Juan** *see note*

● **NOCHE DE SAN JUAN**

● The *Noche de San Juan* on the 24th June is a
● *fiesta* coinciding with the summer solstice
● and which has taken the place of other
● ancient pagan festivals. Traditionally fire
● plays a major part in these festivities with
● celebrations and dancing taking place
● around bonfires in towns and villages
● across the country.

**nocivo, -a** [no'θiβo, a] *adj* harmful
**noctámbulo, -a** [nok'tambulo, a] *nm/f*
sleepwalker
**nocturno, -a** [nok'turno, a] *adj (de la noche)*
nocturnal, night *cpd; (de la tarde)* evening
*cpd* ▷ *nm* nocturne
**nogal** [no'ɣal] *nm* walnut tree
**nómada** ['nomaða] *adj* nomadic ▷ *nmf*
nomad
**nombrar** [nom'brar] /1a/ *vt* to name;
*(mencionar)* to mention; *(designar)* to
appoint
**nombre** ['nombre] *nm* name; *(sustantivo)*
noun; **~ y apellidos** name in full; **poner ~ a**
to call, name; **~ común/propio** common/
proper noun; **~ de pila/de soltera**
Christian/maiden name; **~ de usuario**
*(Inform)* username
**nómina** ['nomina] *nf (Com)* payroll; *(hoja)*
payslip
**nominal** [nomi'nal] *adj* nominal
**nominar** [nomi'nar] /1a/ *vt* = **nominate**
**nominativo, -a** [nomina'tiβo, a] *adj*
*(Com)*: **un cheque ~ a X** a cheque made
out to X
**nordeste** [nor'ðeste] *adj* north-east, northeastern, north-easterly ▷ *nm* north-east
**nórdico, -a** ['norðiko, a] *adj* Nordic
**noreste** [no'reste] *adj, nm* = **nordeste**
**noria** ['norja] *nf (Agr)* waterwheel; *(de
carnaval)* big *(BRIT)* o Ferris *(US)* wheel
**norma** ['norma] *nf* rule
**normal** [nor'mal] *adj (corriente)* normal;
*(habitual)* usual, natural; **normalizar** /1f/
*vt* to normalize; *(Com, Tec)* to standardize;
**normalizarse** *vr* to return to normal;
**normalmente** *adv* normally
**normativo, -a** [norma'tiβo, a] *adj*: **es ~ en
todos los coches nuevos** it is standard in all
new cars ▷ *nf* rules *pl*, regulations *pl*
**noroeste** [noro'este] *adj* north-west,
north-western, north-westerly ▷ *nm*
north-west
**norte** ['norte] *adj* north, northern,
northerly ▷ *nm* north; *(fig)* guide
**norteamericano, -a** [norteameri'kano, a]
*adj, nm/f* (North) American
**Noruega** [no'rweɣa] *nf* Norway

**noruego, -a** [no'rweɣo, a] *adj, nm/f*
Norwegian
**nos** [nos] *pron (directo)* us; *(indirecto)* (to) us;
*(reflexivo)* (to) ourselves; *(recíproco)* (to) each
other; **~ levantamos a las siete** we get up
at seven
**nosotros, -as** [no'sotros, as] *pron (sujeto)*
we; *(después de prep)* us
**nostalgia** [nos'talxja] *nf* nostalgia
**nota** ['nota] *nf* note; *(Escol)* mark
**notable** [no'taβle] *adj* notable; *(Escol etc)*
outstanding
**notar** [no'tar] /1a/ *vt* to notice, note;
**notarse** *vr* to be obvious; **se nota que ...**
you can tell that ...
**notario** [no'tarjo] *nm* notary
**noticia** [no'tiθja] *nf (información)* piece of
news; **las ~s** the news *sg*; **tener ~s de algn**
to hear from sb

▌ No confundir *noticia* con la palabra
inglesa *notice*.

**noticiero** [noti'θjero] *nm (LAM)* news
bulletin
**notificar** [notifi'kar] /1g/ *vt* to notify,
inform
**notorio, -a** [no'torjo, a] *adj (público)* well-
known; *(evidente)* obvious
**novato, -a** [no'βato, a] *adj* inexperienced
▷ *nm/f* beginner, novice
**novecientos, -as** [noβe'θjentos, as] *num*
nine hundred
**novedad** [noβe'ðað] *nf (calidad de nuevo)*
newness; *(noticia)* piece of news; *(cambio)*
change, (new) development
**novel** [no'βel] *adj* new; *(inexperto)*
inexperienced ▷ *nmf* beginner
**novela** [no'βela] *nf* novel
**noveno, -a** [no'βeno, a] *num* ninth
**noventa** [no'βenta] *num* ninety
**novia** ['noβja] *nf* V **novio**
**noviazgo** [no'βjaθɣo] *nm* engagement
**novicio, -a** [no'βiθjo, a] *nm/f* novice
**noviembre** [no'βjembre] *nm* November
**novillada** [noβi'ʎaða] *nf (Taur)* bullfight
with young bulls; **novillero** *nm* novice
bullfighter; **novillo** *nm* young bull, bullock;
**hacer novillos** *(fam)* to play truant *(BRIT)* o
hooky *(US)*
**novio, -a** ['noβjo, a] *nm/f* boyfriend/
girlfriend; *(prometido)* fiancé/fiancée;
*(recién casado)* bridegroom/bride; **los ~s** the
newly-weds
**nube** ['nuβe] *nf* cloud
**nublado, -a** [nu'βlaðo, a] *adj* cloudy
**nublar** [nu'βlar] /1a/ *vt (oscurecer)* to
darken; *(confundir)* to cloud; **nublarse** *vr* to
cloud over
**nuboso, -a** [nu'βoso, a] *adj* cloudy
**nuca** ['nuka] *nf* nape of the neck

**nuclear** [nukle'ar] *adj* nuclear
**núcleo** ['nukleo] *nm* (*centro*) core; (*Física*) nucleus; **~ urbano** city centre
**nudillo** [nu'ðiʎo] *nm* knuckle
**nudista** [nu'dista] *adj* nudist
**nudo** ['nuðo] *nm* knot; (*Ferro*) junction
**nuera** ['nwera] *nf* daughter-in-law
**nuestro, -a** ['nwestro, a] *adj posesivo* our
  ▷ *pron* ours; **~ padre** our father; **un amigo ~** a friend of ours; **es el ~** it's ours
**Nueva York** [-'jork] *nf* New York
**Nueva Zelanda** [-θe'landa] *nf* New Zealand
**nueve** ['nweβe] *num* nine
**nuevo, -a** ['nweβo, a] *adj* (*gen*) new; **de ~** again
**nuez** [nweθ] *nf* walnut; **~ de Adán** Adam's apple; **~ moscada** nutmeg
**nulo, -a** ['nulo, a] *adj* (*inepto, torpe*) useless; (*inválido*) (null and) void; (*Deporte*) drawn, tied
**núm.** *abr* (= *número*) no.
**numerar** [nume'rar] /1a/ *vt* to number
**número** ['numero] *nm* (*gen*) number; (*tamaño: de zapato*) size; (*ejemplar: de diario*) number, issue; **sin ~** numberless, unnumbered; **~ de matrícula/de teléfono** registration/telephone number; **~ impar/par** odd/even number; **~ romano** Roman numeral; **~ atrasado** back number
**numeroso, -a** [nume'roso, a] *adj* numerous
**nunca** ['nunka] *adv* (*jamás*) never; **~ lo pensé** I never thought it; **no viene ~** he never comes; **~ más** never again; **más que ~** more than ever
**nupcias** ['nupθjas] *nfpl* wedding *sg*, nuptials
**nutria** ['nutrja] *nf* otter
**nutrición** [nutri'θjon] *nf* nutrition
**nutrir** [nu'trir] /3a/ *vt* (*alimentar*) to nourish; (*dar de comer*) to feed; (*fig*) to strengthen; **nutritivo, -a** *adj* nourishing, nutritious
**nylon** [ni'lon] *nm* nylon
**ñango, -a** ['nango, a] *adj* (*LAM*) puny
**ñapa** ['napa] *nf* (*LAM*) extra
**ñata** ['nata] *nf* (*LAM fam*) nose; *V tb* **ñato**
**ñato, -a** ['nato, a] *adj* (*LAM*) snub-nosed
**ñoñería** [none'ria] *nf* insipidness
**ñoño, -a** ['nono, a] *adj* (*fam: tonto*) silly, stupid; (*soso*) insipid; (*débil: persona*) spineless; (*ESP: película, novela*) sentimental

# O

**O** *abr* (= *oeste*) W
**o** [o] *conj* or; **o ... o** either ... or
**oasis** [o'asis] *nm inv* oasis
**obcecarse** [oβθe'karse] /1g/ *vr* to become obsessed
**obedecer** [oβeðe'θer] /2d/ *vt* to obey; **obediente** *adj* obedient
**obertura** [oβer'tura] *nf* overture
**obeso, -a** [o'βeso, a] *adj* obese
**obispo** [o'βispo] *nm* bishop
**obituario** [oβi'twarjo] *nm* (*LAM*) obituary
**objetar** [oβxe'tar] /1a/ *vt, vi* to object
**objetivo, -a** [oβxe'tiβo, a] *adj* ▷ *nm* objective
**objeto** [oβ'xeto] *nm* (*cosa*) object; (*fin*) aim
**objetor, a** [oβxe'tor, a] *nm/f* objector
**obligación** [oβliɣa'θjon] *nf* obligation; (*Com*) bond
**obligar** [oβli'ɣar] /1h/ *vt* to force; **obligarse** *vr*: **~se a** to commit o.s. to; **obligatorio, -a** *adj* compulsory, obligatory
**oboe** [o'βoe] *nm* oboe
**obra** ['oβra] *nf* work; (*Arq*) construction, building; (*Teat*) play; **~ maestra** masterpiece; **~s públicas** public works; **por ~ de** thanks to (the efforts of); **obrar** /1a/ *vt* to work; (*tener efecto*) to have an effect on ▷ *vi* to act, behave; (*tener efecto*) to have an effect; **la carta obra en su poder** the letter is in his/her possession
**obrero, -a** [o'βrero, a] *adj* working; (*movimiento*) labour *cpd* ▷ *nm/f* (*gen*) worker; (*sin oficio*) labourer
**obsceno, -a** [oβs'θeno, a] *adj* obscene
**obscu...** *pref* = **oscu...**
**obsequiar** [oβse'kjar] /1b/ *vt* (*ofrecer*) to present; (*agasajar*) to make a fuss of, lavish attention on; **obsequio** *nm* (*regalo*) gift; (*cortesía*) courtesy, attention
**observación** [oβserβa'θjon] *nf* observation; (*reflexión*) remark

**observador, a** [oβserβa'ðor, a] nm/f
observer

**observar** [oβser'βar] /1a/ vt to observe;
(notar) to notice; **observarse** vr to keep to,
observe

**obsesión** [oβse'sjon] nf obsession;
**obsesivo, -a** adj obsessive

**obstáculo** [oβs'takulo] nm obstacle;
(impedimento) hindrance, drawback

**obstante** [oβs'tante]: **no ~** adv
nevertheless

**obstinado, -a** [oβsti'naðo, a] adj
obstinate; stubborn

**obstinarse** [oβsti'narse] /1a/ vr to be
obstinate; **~ en** to persist in

**obstruir** [oβstru'ir] /3g/ vt to obstruct

**obtener** [oβte'ner] /2k/ vt to obtain;
(ganar) to gain; (premio) to win

**obturador** [oβtura'ðor] nm (Foto) shutter

**obvio, -a** ['oββjo, a] adj obvious

**oca** ['oka] nf goose; (tb: **juego de la ~**)
≈ snakes and ladders

**ocasión** [oka'sjon] nf (oportunidad)
opportunity, chance; (momento) occasion,
time; (causa) cause; **de ~** secondhand;
**ocasionar** /1a/ vt to cause

**ocaso** nm (fig) decline

**occidente** [okθi'ðente] nm west

**O.C.D.E.** nf abr (= Organización de
Cooperación y Desarrollo Económicos) OECD

**océano** [o'θeano] nm ocean; **el ~ Índico** the
Indian Ocean

**ochenta** [o'tʃenta] num eighty

**ocho** ['otʃo] num eight; **dentro de ~ días**
within a week

**ocio** ['oθjo] nm (tiempo) leisure; (pey)
idleness

**octavilla** [okta'βiʎa] nf leaflet, pamphlet

**octavo, -a** [ok'taβo, a] num eighth

**octubre** [ok'tuβre] nm October

**oculista** [oku'lista] nmf oculist

**ocultar** [okul'tar] /1a/ vt (esconder) to hide;
(callar) to conceal; **oculto, -a** adj hidden;
(fig) secret

**ocupación** [okupa'θjon] nf occupation

**ocupado, -a** [oku'paðo, a] adj (persona)
busy; (plaza) occupied, taken; (teléfono)
engaged

**ocupar** /1a/ vt (gen) to occupy; **ocuparse**
vr: **~se de o en** to concern o.s. with; (cuidar)
to look after

**ocurrencia** [oku'rrenθja] nf (idea) bright
idea

**ocurrir** [oku'rrir] /3a/ vi to happen;
**ocurrirse** vr: **se me ocurrió que ...** it
occurred to me that ...

**odiar** [o'ðjar] /1b/ vt to hate; **odio** nm hate,
hatred; **odioso, -a** adj (gen) hateful; (malo)
nasty

**odontólogo, -a** [oðon'toloɣo, a] nm/f
dentist, dental surgeon

**oeste** [o'este] nm west; **una película del ~**
a western

**ofender** [ofen'der] /2a/ vt (agraviar) to
offend; (insultar) to insult; **ofenderse** vr to
take offence; **ofensa** nf offence;
**ofensivo, -a** adj offensive ▷ nf offensive

**oferta** [o'ferta] nf offer; (propuesta)
proposal; **la ~ y la demanda** supply and
demand; **artículos en ~** goods on offer

**oficial** [ofi'θjal] adj official ▷ nm (Mil) officer

**oficina** [ofi'θina] nf office; **~ de correos**
post office; **~ de información** information
bureau; **~ de turismo** tourist office;
**oficinista** nmf clerk

**oficio** [o'fiθjo] nm (profesión) profession;
(puesto) post; (Rel) service; **ser del ~** to be
an old hand; **tener mucho ~** to have a lot of
experience; **~ de difuntos** funeral service

**ofimática** [ofi'matika] nf office
automation

**ofrecer** [ofre'θer] /2d/ vt (dar) to offer;
(proponer) to propose; **ofrecerse** vr (persona)
to offer o.s., volunteer; (situación) to
present itself; **¿qué se le ofrece?, ¿se le
ofrece algo?** what can I do for you?, can I
get you anything?

**ofrecimiento** [ofreθi'mjento] nm offer

**oftalmólogo, -a** [oftal'moloɣo, a] nm/f
ophthalmologist

**oída** [o'iða] nf: **de ~s** by hearsay

**oído** [o'iðo] nm (Anat, Mus) ear; (sentido)
hearing

**oigo** etc vb V **oír**

**oír** [o'ir] /3p/ vt (gen) to hear; (escuchar) to
listen to; **¡oiga!** excuse me!; (Telec) hullo?;
**~ misa** to attend mass; **como quien oye
llover** without paying (the slightest)
attention

**ojal** [o'xal] nm buttonhole

**ojalá** [oxa'la] excl if only (it were so)!, some
hope! ▷ conj if only...!, would that...!; **~ que
venga hoy** I hope he comes today

**ojeada** [oxe'aða] nf glance

**ojera** [o'xera] nf: **tener ~s** to have bags
under one's eyes

**ojo** ['oxo] nm eye; (de puente) span; (de
cerradura) keyhole ▷ excl careful!; **tener ~
para** to have an eye for; **~ de buey** porthole

**okey** ['okei] excl (LAM) O.K.

**okupa** [o'kupa] nmf (fam) squatter

**ola** ['ola] nf wave

**olé** [o'le] excl bravo!, olé!

**oleada** [ole'aða] nf big wave, swell; (fig)
wave

**oleaje** [ole'axe] nm swell

**óleo** ['oleo] nm oil; **oleoducto** nm (oil)
pipeline

**oler** [o'ler] /2i/ vt (gen) to smell; (inquirir) to pry into; (fig: sospechar) to sniff out ▷ vi to smell; ~ **a** to smell of

**olfatear** [olfate'ar] /1a/ vt to smell; (inquirir) to pry into; **olfato** nm sense of smell

**olimpiada** [olim'piaða] nf: **la ~ o las ~s** the Olympics®; **olímpico, -a** adj Olympic®

**oliva** [o'liβa] nf (aceituna) olive; **aceite de ~** olive oil; **olivo** nm olive tree

**olla** ['oλa] nf pan; (comida) stew; ~ **a presión** pressure cooker; ~ **podrida** type of Spanish stew

**olmo** ['olmo] nm elm (tree)

**olor** [o'lor] nm smell; **oloroso, -a** adj scented

**olvidar** [olβi'ðar] /1a/ vt to forget; (omitir) to omit; **olvidarse** vr (fig) to forget o.s.; **se me olvidó** I forgot

**olvido** [ol'βiðo] nm oblivion; (despiste) forgetfulness

**ombligo** [om'bliɣo] nm navel

**omelette** [ome'lete] nf (LAM) omelet(te)

**omisión** [omi'sjon] nf (abstención) omission; (descuido) neglect

**omiso, -a** [o'miso, a] adj: **hacer caso ~ de** to ignore, pass over

**omitir** [omi'tir] /3a/ vt to leave o miss out, omit

**omnipotente** [omnipo'tente] adj omnipotent

**omoplato** [omo'plato], **omóplato** [o'moplato] nm shoulder-blade

**OMS** nf abr (= Organización Mundial de la Salud) WHO

**once** ['onθe] num eleven; **onces** nfpl tea break sg

**onda** ['onda] nf wave; ~ **corta/larga/media** short/long/medium wave; **ondear** /1a/ vi to wave; (tener ondas) to be wavy; (agua) to ripple

**ondulación** [ondula'θjon] nf undulation; **ondulado, -a** adj wavy

**ONG** nf abr (= organización no gubernamental) NGO

**ONU** ['onu] nf abr (= Organización de las Naciones Unidas) UN

**opaco, -a** [o'pako, a] adj opaque

**opción** [op'θjon] nf (gen) option; (derecho) right, option

**O.P.E.P.** [o'pep] nf abr (= Organización de Países Exportadores de Petróleo) OPEC

**ópera** ['opera] nf opera; ~ **bufa o cómica** comic opera

**operación** [opera'θjon] nf (gen) operation; (Com) transaction, deal

**operador, a** [opera'ðor, a] nm/f operator; (Cine: proyección) projectionist; (: rodaje) cameraman

**operar** [ope'rar] /1a/ vt (producir) to produce, bring about; (Med) to operate on ▷ vi (Com) to operate, deal; **operarse** vr to occur; (Med) to have an operation

**opereta** [ope'reta] nf operetta

**opinar** [opi'nar] /1a/ vt to think ▷ vi to give one's opinion; **opinión** nf (creencia) belief; (criterio) opinion

**opio** ['opjo] nm opium

**oponer** [opo'ner] /2q/ vt (resistencia) to put up, offer; **oponerse** vr (objetar) to object; (estar frente a frente) to be opposed; (dos personas) to oppose each other; ~ **A a B** to set A against B; **me opongo a pensar que ...** I refuse to believe o think that ...

**oportunidad** [oportuni'ðað] nf (ocasión) opportunity; (posibilidad) chance

**oportuno, -a** [opor'tuno, a] adj (en su tiempo) opportune, timely; (respuesta) suitable; **en el momento ~** at the right moment

**oposición** [oposi'θjon] nf opposition; **oposiciones** nfpl (Escol) public examinations

**opositor, -a** [oposi'tor, a] nm/f (Admin) candidate to a public examination; (adversario) opponent; ~ **(a)** candidate (for)

**opresión** [opre'sjon] nf oppression; **opresor, a** [o'presor, a] adj oppressor

**oprimir** [opri'mir] /3a/ vt to squeeze; (fig) to oppress

**optar** [op'tar] /1a/ vi (elegir) to choose; ~ **a o por** to opt for; **optativo, -a** adj optional

**óptico, -a** ['optiko, a] adj optic(al) ▷ nm/f optician ▷ nf (ciencia) optics sg; (tienda) optician's; (fig) viewpoint; **desde esta óptica** from this point of view

**optimismo** [opti'mismo] nm optimism; **optimista** nmf optimist

**opuesto, -a** [o'pwesto, a] adj (contrario) opposite; (antagónico) opposing

**oración** [ora'θjon] nf (Rel) prayer; (Ling) sentence

**orador, a** [ora'ðor, a] nm/f orator; (conferenciante) speaker

**oral** [o'ral] adj oral

**orangután** [oranɡu'tan] nm orang-utan

**orar** [o'rar] /1a/ vi to pray

**oratoria** [ora'torja] nf oratory

**órbita** ['orβita] nf orbit

**orden** ['orðen] nm (colocación) order ▷ nf (mandato) order; (Inform) command; **en ~ de prioridad** in order of priority; **el ~ del día** the agenda

**ordenado, -a** [orðe'naðo, a] adj (metódico) methodical; (arreglado) orderly

**ordenador** [orðena'ðor] nm computer; ~ **central** mainframe computer; ~ **de sobremesa** desktop

**ordenar** [orðe'nar] /1a/ vt (mandar) to order; (poner orden) to put in order, arrange; **ordenarse** vr (Rel) to be ordained

**ordeñar** [orðe'ɲar] /1a/ vt to milk

**ordinario, -a** [orði'narjo, a] adj (común) ordinary, usual; (vulgar) vulgar, common

**orégano** [o'reɣano] nm oregano

**oreja** [o'rexa] nf ear; (Mecánica) lug, flange

**orfanato** [orfa'nato] nm orphanage

**orfebrería** [orfeβre'ria] nf gold/silver work

**orgánico, -a** [or'ɣaniko, a] adj organic

**organismo** [orɣa'nismo] nm (Bio) organism; (Pol) organization

**organización** [orɣaniθa'θjon] nf organization; **O~ de las Naciones Unidas (ONU)** United Nations Organization; **O~ del Tratado del Atlántico Norte (OTAN)** North Atlantic Treaty Organization (NATO); **organizar** /1f/ vt to organize

**órgano** ['orɣano] nm organ

**orgasmo** [or'ɣasmo] nm orgasm

**orgía** [or'xia] nf orgy

**orgullo** [or'ɣuʎo] nm pride; **orgulloso, -a** adj (gen) proud; (altanero) haughty

**orientación** [orjenta'θjon] nf (posición) position; (dirección) direction

**oriental** [orjen'tal] adj oriental; (región etc) eastern

**orientar** [orjen'tar] /1a/ vt (situar) to orientate; (señalar) to point; (dirigir) to direct; (guiar) to guide; **orientarse** vr to get one's bearings

**oriente** [o'rjente] nm east; **Cercano/ Medio/Lejano O~** Near/Middle/Far East

**origen** [o'rixen] nm origin

**original** [orixi'nal] adj (nuevo) original; (extraño) odd, strange; **originalidad** nf originality

**originar** [orixi'nar] /1a/ vt to start, cause; **originarse** vr to originate; **originario, -a** adj original; **ser originario de** to originate from

**orilla** [o'riʎa] nf (borde) border; (de río) bank; (de bosque, tela) edge; (de mar) shore

**orina** [o'rina] nf urine; **orinal** nm (chamber) pot; **orinar** /1a/ vi to urinate; **orinarse** vr to wet o.s.

**oro** ['oro] nm gold; V tb **oros**

**oros** ['oros] nmpl (Naipes) one of the suits in the Spanish card deck

**orquesta** [or'kesta] nf orchestra; **~ de cámara/sinfónica** chamber/symphony orchestra

**orquídea** [or'kiðea] nf orchid

**ortiga** [or'tiɣa] nf nettle

**ortodoxo, -a** [orto'ðokso, a] adj orthodox

**ortografía** [ortoɣra'fia] nf spelling

**ortopedia** [orto'peðja] nf orthop(a)edics sg; **ortopédico, -a** adj orthop(a)edic

**oruga** [o'ruɣa] nf caterpillar

**orzuelo** [or'θwelo] nm stye

**os** [os] pron you; (a vosotros) (to) you

**osa** ['osa] nf (she-)bear; **O~ Mayor/Menor** Great/Little Bear

**osadía** [osa'ðia] nf daring

**osar** [o'sar] /1a/ vi to dare

**oscilación** [osθila'θjon] nf (movimiento) oscillation; (fluctuación) fluctuation

**oscilar** [osθi'lar] /1a/ vi to oscillate; to fluctuate

**oscurecer** [oskure'θer] /2d/ vt to darken ▷ vi to grow dark; **oscurecerse** vr to grow o get dark

**oscuridad** [oskuri'ðað] nf obscurity; (tinieblas) darkness

**oscuro, -a** [os'kuro, a] adj dark; (fig) obscure; **a oscuras** in the dark

**óseo, -a** ['oseo, a] adj bone cpd

**oso** ['oso] nm bear; **~ de peluche** teddy bear; **~ hormiguero** anteater

**ostentar** [osten'tar] /1a/ vt (gen) to show; (pey) to flaunt, show off; (poseer) to have, possess

**ostión** [os'tjon] nm (LAM) = **ostra**

**ostra** ['ostra] nf oyster

**OTAN** ['otan] nf abr (= Organización del Tratado del Atlántico Norte) NATO

**otitis** [o'titis] nf earache

**otoñal** [oto'ɲal] adj autumnal

**otoño** [o'toɲo] nm autumn, fall (US)

**otorgar** [otor'ɣar] /1h/ vt (conceder) to concede; (dar) to grant

**otorrinolaringólogo, -a** [otorrinolarin'goloɣo, a] nm/f (Med: tb: **otorrino**) ear, nose and throat specialist

**PALABRA CLAVE**

**otro, -a** ['otro, a] adj **1** (distinto: sg) another; (: pl) other; **con otros amigos** with other o different friends
**2** (adicional): **tráigame otro café (más), por favor** can I have another coffee please; **otros 10 días más** another 10 days
▶ pron **1**: **el otro** the other one; **de otro** somebody o someone else's; **que lo haga otro** let somebody o someone else do it
**2** (pl): **(los) otros** (the) others
**3** (recíproco): **se odian (la) una a (la) otra** they hate one another o each other
**4**: **otro tanto: comer otro tanto** to eat the same o as much again; **recibió una decena de telegramas y otras tantas llamadas** he got about ten telegrams and as many calls

**ovación** [oβa'θjon] nf ovation

**oval** [o'βal], **ovalado, -a** [oβa'laðo, a] adj oval; **óvalo** nm oval

**ovario** [o'βarjo] nm ovary
**oveja** [o'βexa] nf sheep
**overol** [oβe'rol] nm (LAM) overalls pl
**ovillo** [o'βiʎo] nm (de lana) ball
**OVNI** ['oβni] nm abr (= objeto volante (o volador) no identificado) UFO
**ovulación** [oβula'θjon] nf ovulation; **óvulo** nm ovum
**oxidación** [oksiδa'θjon] nf rusting
**oxidar** [oksi'δar] /1a/ vt to rust; **oxidarse** vr to go rusty
**óxido** ['oksiδo] nm oxide
**oxigenado, -a** [oksixe'naδo, a] adj (Química) oxygenated; (pelo) bleached
**oxígeno** [ok'sixeno] nm oxygen
**oyente** [o'jente] nmf listener
**oyes** etc vb V **oír**
**ozono** [o'θono] nm ozone

# P

**pabellón** [paβe'ʎon] nm bell tent; (Arq) pavilion; (de hospital etc) block, section; (bandera) flag
**pacer** [pa'θer] /2d/ vi to graze
**paciencia** [pa'θjenθja] nf patience
**paciente** [pa'θjente] adj, nmf patient
**pacificación** [paθifika'θjon] nf pacification
**pacífico, -a** [pa'θifiko, a] adj (persona) peaceable; (existencia) peaceful; **el (océano) P~** the Pacific (Ocean)
**pacifista** [paθi'fista] nmf pacifist
**pacotilla** [pako'tiʎa] nf: **de ~** shoddy
**pactar** [pak'tar] /1a/ vt to agree to, agree on ▷ vi to come to an agreement
**pacto** ['pakto] nm (tratado) pact; (acuerdo) agreement
**padecer** [paδe'θer] /2d/ vt (sufrir) to suffer; (soportar) to endure, put up with; **padecimiento** nm suffering
**padrastro** [pa'δrastro] nm stepfather
**padre** ['paδre] nm father ▷ adj (fam): **un éxito ~** a tremendous success; **padres** nmpl parents; **~ político** father-in-law
**padrino** [pa'δrino] nm godfather; (fig) sponsor, patron; **padrinos** nmpl godparents; **~ de boda** best man
**padrón** [pa'δron] nm (censo) census, roll
**padrote** [pa'δrote] nm (LAM fam) pimp
**paella** [pa'eʎa] nf paella dish of rice with meat, shellfish etc
**paga** ['paɣa] nf (dinero pagado) payment; (sueldo) pay, wages pl
**pagano, -a** [pa'ɣano, a] adj, nm/f pagan, heathen
**pagar** [pa'ɣar] /1h/ vt to pay; (las compras, crimen) to pay for; (fig: favor) to repay ▷ vi to pay; **~ al contado/a plazos** to pay (in) cash/in instalments
**pagaré** [paɣa're] nm IOU

**página** ['paxina] nf page; **~ de inicio** (Inform) home page; **~ web** (Internet) web page

**pago** ['paɣo] nm (dinero) payment; (fig) return; **~ anticipado/a cuenta/a la entrega/en especie/inicial** advance payment/payment on account/cash on delivery/payment in kind/down payment; **en ~ de** in return for

**pág(s).** abr (= página(s)) p(p)

**pague** etc ['paɣe] vb V **pagar**

**país** [pa'is] nm (gen) country; (región) land; **los P~es Bajos** the Low Countries; **el P~ Vasco** the Basque Country

**paisaje** [pai'saxe] nm landscape; (vista) scenery

**paisano, -a** [pai'sano, a] adj of the same country ▷ nm/f (compatriota) fellow countryman/woman; **vestir de ~** (soldado) to be in civilian clothes; (guardia) to be in plain clothes

**paja** ['paxa] nf straw; (fig) trash, rubbish

**pajarita** [paxa'rita] nf bow tie

**pájaro** ['paxaro] nm bird; **~ carpintero** woodpecker

**pajita** [pa'xita] nf (drinking) straw

**pala** ['pala] nf spade; shovel; (raqueta etc) bat; (: de tenis) racquet; (Culin) slice; **~ mecánica** power shovel

**palabra** [pa'laβra] nf word; (facultad) (power of) speech; (derecho de hablar) right to speak; **tomar la ~** to speak, take the floor

**palabrota** [pala'βrota] nf swearword

**palacio** [pa'laθjo] nm palace; (mansión) mansion, large house; **~ de justicia** courthouse; **~ municipal** town/city hall

**paladar** [pala'ðar] nm palate; **paladear** /1a/ vt to taste

**palanca** [pa'lanka] nf lever; (fig) pull, influence

**palangana** [palaŋ'gana] nf washbasin

**palco** ['palko] nm box

**Palestina** [pales'tina] nf Palestine; **palestino, -a** nm/f Palestinian

**paleto, -a** [pa'leto, a] nm/f yokel, hick (US) ▷ nf (pala) small shovel; (Arte) palette; (Deporte: de ping-pong) bat; (LAM: helado) ice lolly (BRIT), Popsicle® (US)

**palidecer** [paliðe'θer] /2d/ vi to turn pale; **palidez** nf paleness; **pálido, -a** adj pale

**palillo** [pa'liʎo] nm (para dientes) toothpick; **~s (chinos)** chopsticks

**paliza** [pa'liθa] nf beating, thrashing

**palma** ['palma] nf (Anat) palm; (árbol) palm tree; **batir** o **dar ~s** to clap, applaud; **palmada** nf slap; **palmadas** nfpl clapping sg, applause sg

**palmar** [pal'mar] /1a/ vi (tb: **~la**) to die, kick the bucket

**palmear** [palme'ar] /1a/ vi to clap

**palmera** [pal'mera] nf (Bot) palm tree

**palmo** ['palmo] nm (medida) span; (fig) small amount; **~ a ~** inch by inch

**palo** ['palo] nm stick; (poste) post, pole; (mango) handle, shaft; (golpe) blow, hit; (de golf) club; (de béisbol) bat; (Naut) mast; (Naipes) suit

**paloma** [pa'loma] nf dove, pigeon

**palomitas** [palo'mitas] nfpl popcorn sg

**palpar** [pal'par] /1a/ vt to touch, feel

**palpitar** [palpi'tar] /1a/ vi to palpitate; (latir) to beat

**palta** ['palta] nf (LAM) avocado

**paludismo** [palu'ðismo] nm malaria

**pamela** [pa'mela] nf sun hat

**pampa** ['pampa] nf (LAM) pampa(s), prairie

**pan** [pan] nm bread; (una barra) loaf; **~ integral** wholemeal bread; **~ rallado** breadcrumbs pl; **~ tostado** toast

**pana** ['pana] nf corduroy

**panadería** [panaðe'ria] nf baker's (shop); **panadero, -a** nm/f baker

**Panamá** [pana'ma] nm Panama; **panameño, -a** adj Panamanian

**pancarta** [paŋ'karta] nf placard, banner

**panceta** [pan'θeta] nf bacon

**pancho, -a** ['pantʃo, a] adj: **estar tan ~** to remain perfectly calm ▷ nm (LAM) hot dog

**pancito** [pan'sito] nm (LAM) (bread) roll

**panda** ['panda] nm panda

**pandemia** [pan'demja] nf pandemic

**pandereta** [pande'reta] nf tambourine

**pandilla** [pan'diʎa] nf set, group; (de criminales) gang; (pey) clique

**panecillo** [pane'θiʎo] nm (bread) roll

**panel** [pa'nel] nm panel; **~ solar** solar panel

**panfleto** [pan'fleto] nm pamphlet

**pánico** ['paniko] nm panic

**panorama** [pano'rama] nm panorama; (vista) view

**panqué** [pan'ke], **panqueque** [pan'keke] nm (LAM) pancake

**pantalla** [pan'taʎa] nf (de cine) screen; (cubreluz) lampshade

**pantallazo** [panta'ʎaθo] nm (Inform) screenshot

**pantalón, pantalones** [panta'lon(es)] nm(pl) trousers pl, pants pl (US); **pantalones cortos** shorts pl

**pantano** [pan'tano] nm (ciénaga) marsh, swamp; (depósito: de agua) reservoir; (fig) jam, difficulty

**panteón** [pante'on] nm (monumento) pantheon

**pantera** [pan'tera] nf panther

**pantimedias** [panti'meðjas] nfpl (LAM) = **pantis**

**pantis** ['pantis] nm(pl) tights (BRIT), pantyhose (US)

# pantomima | 148

**pantomima** [panto'mima] nf pantomime
**pantorrilla** [panto'rriʎa] nf calf (of the leg)
**pants** [pants] nmpl (LAM) tracksuit (BRIT), sweat suit (US)
**pantufla** [pan'tufla] nf slipper
**panty(s)** ['panti(s)] nm(pl) tights (BRIT), pantyhose (US)
**panza** ['panθa] nf belly, paunch
**pañal** [pa'ɲal] nm nappy, diaper (US); (fig) early stages, infancy sg
**paño** ['paɲo] nm (tela) cloth; (pedazo de tela) (piece of) cloth; (trapo) duster, rag; **~s menores** underclothes
**pañuelo** [pa'ɲwelo] nm handkerchief, hanky (fam); (para la cabeza) (head)scarf
**papa** ['papa] nf (LAM: patata) potato ⊳ nm: **el P~** the Pope; **~s fritas** (LAM) French fries, chips (BRIT), (de bolsa) crisps (BRIT), potato chips (US)
**papá** [pa'pa] nm (fam) dad, daddy, pop (US)
**papada** [pa'paða] nf double chin
**papagayo** [papa'ɣajo] nm parrot
**papalote** [papa'lote] nm (LAM) kite
**papanatas** [papa'natas] nm inv (fam) simpleton
**papaya** [pa'paja] nf papaya
**papear** [pape'ar] /1a/ vt, vi (fam) to eat
**papel** [pa'pel] nm paper; (hoja de papel) sheet of paper; (Teat) role; **~ de arroz/envolver/fumar** rice/wrapping/cigarette paper; **~ de aluminio/lija** tinfoil/sandpaper; **~ higiénico** toilet paper; **~ moneda** paper money; **~ pintado** wallpaper; **~ secante** blotting paper
**papeleo** [pape'leo] nm red tape
**papelera** [pape'lera] nf wastepaper basket; **~ de reciclaje** (Inform) wastebasket
**papelería** [papele'ria] nf stationer's (shop)
**papeleta** [pape'leta] nf (Pol) ballot paper
**paperas** [pa'peras] nfpl mumps sg
**papilla** [pa'piʎa] nf (de bebé) baby food
**paquete** [pa'kete] nm (caja) packet; (bulto) parcel
**par** [par] adj (igual) like, equal, equal; (Mat) even ⊳ nm equal; (de guantes) pair; (de veces) couple; (título) peer; (Golf, Com) par; **abrir de ~ en ~** to open wide
**para** ['para] prep for; **no es ~ comer** it's not for eating; **decir ~ sí** to say to o.s.; **¿~ qué lo quieres?** what do you want it for?; **se casaron ~ separarse otra vez** they married only to separate again; **lo tendré ~ mañana** I'll have it for tomorrow; **ir ~ casa** to go home, head for home; **~ profesor es muy estúpido** he's very stupid for a teacher; **¿quién es usted ~ gritar así?** who are you to shout like that?; **tengo bastante ~ vivir** I have enough to live on
**parabién** [para'βjen] nm congratulations pl

**parábola** [pa'raβola] nf parable; (Mat) parabola; **parabólica** nf (tb: **antena parabólica**) satellite dish
**parabrisas** [para'βrisas] nm inv windscreen, windshield (US)
**paracaídas** [paraka'iðas] nm inv parachute; **paracaidista** nmf parachutist; (Mil) paratrooper
**parachoques** [para'tʃokes] nm inv bumper; shock absorber
**parada** [pa'raða] nf V **parado**
**paradero** [para'ðero] nm stopping-place; (situación) whereabouts
**parado, -a** [pa'raðo, a] adj (persona) motionless, standing still; (fábrica) closed, at a standstill; (coche) stopped; (LAM: de pie) standing (up); (sin empleo) unemployed, idle ⊳ nf stop; (acto) stopping; (de industria) shutdown, stoppage; (lugar) stopping-place; **parada de autobús** bus stop; **parada de taxis** taxi rank
**paradoja** [para'ðoxa] nf paradox
**parador** [para'ðor] nm (ESP) (luxury) hotel (owned by the state)
**paragolpes** [para'golpes] nm inv (LAM Auto) bumper, fender (US)
**paraguas** [pa'raɣwas] nm inv umbrella
**Paraguay** [para'ɣwai] nm: Paraguay; **paraguayo, -a** adj, nm/f Paraguayan
**paraíso** [para'iso] nm paradise, heaven
**paraje** [pa'raxe] nm place, spot
**paralelo, -a** [para'lelo, a] adj parallel
**parálisis** [pa'ralisis] nf inv paralysis; **paralítico, -a** adj, nm/f paralytic
**paralizar** [parali'θar] /1f/ vt to paralyse; **paralizarse** vr to become paralysed; (fig) to come to a standstill
**páramo** ['paramo] nm bleak plateau
**paranoico, -a** [para'noiko, a] nm/f paranoid
**parapente** [para'pente] nm (deporte) paragliding; (aparato) paraglider
**parapléjico, -a** [para'plexiko, a] adj, nm/f paraplegic
**parar** [pa'rar] /1a/ vt to stop; (golpe) to ward off ⊳ vi to stop; **pararse** vr to stop; (LAM) to stand up; **ha parado de llover** it has stopped raining; **van a ~ en la comisaría** they're going to end up in the police station; **~se en** to pay attention to
**pararrayos** [para'rrajos] nm inv lightning conductor
**parásito, -a** [pa'rasito, a] nm/f parasite
**parasol** [para'sol] nm parasol, sunshade
**parcela** [par'θela] nf plot, piece of ground
**parche** ['partʃe] nm patch
**parchís** [par'tʃis] nm ludo
**parcial** [par'θjal] adj (pago) part-; (eclipse) partial; (juez) prejudiced, biased; (Pol) partisan

**parecer** [pare'θer] /2d/ nm (opinión) opinion, view; (aspecto) looks pl ▷ vi (tener apariencia) to seem, look; (asemejarse) to look like, seem like; (aparecer, llegar) to appear; **parecerse** vr to look alike, resemble each other; **según parece** evidently, apparently; **~se a** to look like, resemble; **al ~** apparently; **me parece que** I think (that), it seems to me that

**parecido, -a** [pare'θiðo, a] adj similar ▷ nm similarity, likeness, resemblance; **bien ~** good-looking, nice-looking

**pared** [pa'reð] nf wall

**parejo, -a** [pa'rexo, a] adj equal ▷ nf pair; (de personas) couple; (el otro: de un par) other one (of a pair); (: persona) partner

**parentesco** [paren'tesko] nm relationship

**paréntesis** [pa'rentesis] nm inv parenthesis; (en escrito) bracket

**parezco** etc vb V **parecer**

**pariente, -a** [pa'rjente, a] nm/f relative, relation

> No confundir *pariente* con la palabra inglesa *parent*.

**parir** [pa'rir] /3a/ vt to give birth to ▷ vi (mujer) to give birth, have a baby

**París** [pa'ris] nm Paris

**parka** ['parka] nf (LAM) anorak

**parking** ['parkin] nm car park, parking lot (US)

**parlamentar** [parlamen'tar] /1a/ vi to parley

**parlamentario, -a** [parlamen'tarjo, a] adj parliamentary ▷ nm/f member of parliament

**parlamento** [parla'mento] nm parliament

**parlanchín, -ina** [parlan'tʃin, ina] adj indiscreet ▷ nm/f chatterbox

**parlar** [par'lar] /1a/ vi to chatter (away)

**paro** ['paro] nm (huelga) stoppage (of work), strike; (desempleo) unemployment; **~ cardíaco** cardiac arrest; **estar en ~** (ESP) to be unemployed; **subsidio de ~** unemployment benefit

**parodia** [pa'roðja] nf parody; **parodiar** /1b/ vt to parody

**parpadear** [parpaðe'ar] /1a/ vi (los ojos) to blink; (luz) to flicker

**párpado** ['parpaðo] nm eyelid

**parque** ['parke] nm (lugar verde) park; (LAM: munición) ammunition; **~ de atracciones/ de bomberos** fairground/fire station; **~ infantil/temático/zoológico** playground/theme park/zoo

**parqué** [par'ke] nm parquet

**parquímetro** [par'kimetro] nm parking meter

**parra** ['parra] nf grapevine

**párrafo** ['parrafo] nm paragraph; **echar un ~** (fam) to have a chat

**parranda** [pa'rranda] nf (fam) spree, binge

**parrilla** [pa'rriʎa] nf (Culin) grill; **(carne a la) ~** grilled meat, barbecue; **parrillada** nf barbecue

**párroco** ['parroko] nm parish priest

**parroquia** [pa'rrokja] nf parish; (iglesia) parish church; (Com) clientele, customers pl; **parroquiano, -a** nm/f parishioner; client, customer

**parte** ['parte] nm message; (informe) report ▷ nf part; (lado, cara) side; (de reparto) share; (Jur) party; **en alguna ~ de Europa** somewhere in Europe; **en o por todas ~s** everywhere; **en gran ~** to a large extent; **la mayor ~ de los españoles** most Spaniards; **de algún tiempo a esta ~** for some time past; **de ~ de algn** on sb's behalf; **¿de ~ de quién?** (Telec) who is speaking?; **por ~ de** on the part of; **yo por mi ~** I for my part; **por una ... por otra ~** on the one hand, ... on the other (hand); **dar ~ a algn** to report to sb; **tomar ~** to take part; **~ meteorológico** weather forecast o report

**participación** [partiθipa'θjon] nf (acto) participation, taking part; (parte) share; (Com) share, stock (US); (de lotería) shared prize; (aviso) notice, notification

**participante** [partiθi'pante] nmf participant

**participar** [partiθi'par] /1a/ vt to notify, inform ▷ vi to take part, participate

**partícipe** [par'tiθipe] nmf participant

**particular** [partiku'lar] adj (especial) particular, special; (individual, personal) private, personal ▷ nm (punto, asunto) particular, point; (individuo) individual; **tiene coche ~** he has a car of his own

**partida** [par'tiða] nf (salida) departure; (Com) entry, item; (juego) game; (grupo, bando) band, group; **mala ~** dirty trick; **~ de nacimiento/matrimonio/defunción** birth/marriage/death certificate

**partidario, -a** [parti'ðarjo, a] adj partisan ▷ nm/f supporter

**partido** [par'tiðo] nm (Pol) party; (encuentro) game, match; **sacar ~ de** to profit from, benefit from; **tomar ~** to take sides

**partir** [par'tir] /3a/ vt (dividir) to split, divide; (compartir, distribuir) to share (out), distribute; (romper) to break open, split open; (rebanada) to cut (off) ▷ vi (ponerse en camino) to set off, set out; **partirse** vr to crack o split o break (in two etc); **a ~ de** (starting) from

**partitura** [parti'tura] nf score

**parto** ['parto] nm birth, delivery; (fig) product, creation; **estar de ~** to be in labour

**parvulario** [parβu'larjo] nm nursery school, kindergarten

**pasa** ['pasa] nf V **paso**

**pasacintas** [pasa'θintas] nm (LAM) cassette player

**pasada** [pa'saða] nf V **pasado**

**pasadizo** [pasa'ðiθo] nm (pasillo) passage, corridor; (callejuela) alley

**pasado, -a** [pa'saðo, a] adj past; (malo: comida, fruta) bad; (muy cocido) overdone; (anticuado) out of date ▷ nm past; ~ **mañana** the day after tomorrow; **el mes** ~ last month; **de pasada** in passing, incidentally; **una mala pasada** a dirty trick

**pasador** [pasa'ðor] nm (gen) bolt; (de pelo) slide; (horquilla) grip

**pasaje** [pa'saxe] nm passage; (pago de viaje) fare; (los pasajeros) passengers pl; (pasillo) passageway

**pasajero, -a** [pasa'xero, a] adj passing; (situación, estado) temporary; (amor, enfermedad) brief ▷ nm/f passenger

**pasamontañas** [pasamon'taɲas] nm inv balaclava (helmet)

**pasaporte** [pasa'porte] nm passport

**pasar** [pa'sar] /1a/ vt (gen) to pass; (tiempo) to spend; (durezas) to suffer, endure; (noticia) to give, pass on; (película) to show; (río) to cross; (barrera) to pass through; (falta) to overlook, tolerate; (contrincante) to surpass, do better than; (coche) to overtake; (enfermedad) to give, infect with ▷ vi (gen) to pass; (terminarse) to be over; (ocurrir) to happen; **pasarse** vr (flores) to fade; (comida) to go bad, go off; (fig) to overdo it, go too far o over the top, ~ **de** to go beyond, exceed; ¡**pase!** come in!; ~ **por** to fetch; ~**lo bien/ bomba** o **de maravilla** to have a great/good time; ~**se al enemigo** to go over to the enemy; **se me pasó** I forgot; **no se le pasa nada** he misses nothing; **ya se te** ~**á** you'll get over it; ¿**qué pasa?** what's going on?, what's up?; ¿**qué te pasa?** what's wrong?

**pasarela** [pasa'rela] nf footbridge; (en barco) gangway

**pasatiempo** [pasa'tjempo] nm pastime, hobby

**Pascua** ['paskwa] nf: ~ **(de Resurrección)** Easter; **Pascuas** nfpl Christmas time sg; ¡**felices** ~**s!** Merry Christmas!

**pase** ['pase] nm pass; (Cine) performance, showing

**pasear** [pase'ar] /1a/ vt to take for a walk; (exhibir) to parade, show off ▷ vi to walk, go for a walk; **pasearse** vr to walk, go for a walk; ~ **en coche** to go for a drive; **paseo** nm (distancia corta) (short) walk, stroll; (avenida) avenue; **paseo marítimo** promenade; **dar un paseo** to go for a walk

**pasillo** [pa'siʎo] nm passage, corridor

**pasión** [pa'sjon] nf passion

**pasivo, -a** [pa'siβo, a] adj passive; (inactivo) inactive ▷ nm (Com) liabilities pl, debts pl

**pasmoso, -a** [pas'moso, a] adj amazing, astonishing

**paso, -a** ['paso, a] adj dried ▷ nm step; (modo de andar) walk; (huella) footprint; (rapidez) speed, pace, rate; (camino accesible) way through, passage; (cruce) crossing; (pasaje) passing, passage; (Geo) pass; (estrecho) strait ▷ nf raisin; **pasa de Corinto/de Esmirna** currant/sultana; **a ese** ~ (fig) at that rate; **estar de** ~ to be passing through; **prohibido el** ~ no entry; **ceda el** ~ give way; ~ **a nivel** (Ferro) level-crossing; ~ **(de) cebra** (ESP) zebra crossing; ~ **de peatones** pedestrian crossing; ~ **elevado** flyover

**pasota** [pa'sota] adj, nmf (fam) ≈ dropout; **ser un (tipo)** ~ to be a bit of a dropout; (ser indiferente) not to care about anything

**pasta** ['pasta] nf paste; (Culin: masa) dough; (: de bizcochos etc) pastry; (fam) dough; **pastas** nfpl (bizcochos) pastries, small cakes; (espaguetis etc) pasta sg; ~ **de dientes** o **dentífrica** toothpaste

**pastar** [pas'tar] /1a/ vt, vi to graze

**pastel** [pas'tel] nm (dulce) cake; (Arte) pastel; ~ **de carne** meat pie; **pastelería** nf cake shop

**pastilla** [pas'tiʎa] nf (de jabón, chocolate) bar; (píldora) tablet, pill

**pasto** ['pasto] nm (hierba) grass; (lugar) pasture, field; **pastor, a** nm/f shepherd(ess) ▷ nm clergyman, pastor; **pastor alemán** Alsatian

**pata** ['pata] nf (pierna) leg; (pie) foot; (de muebles) leg; ~**s arriba** upside down; **meter la** ~ to put one's foot in it; ~ **de cabra** (Tec) crowbar; **metedura de** ~ (fam) gaffe; **tener buena/mala** ~ to be lucky/unlucky; **patada** nf stamp; (puntapié) kick

**patata** [pa'tata] nf potato; ~**s fritas** o **a la española** chips, French fries; (de bolsa) crisps

**paté** [pa'te] nm pâté

**patente** [pa'tente] adj obvious, evident; (Com) patent ▷ nf patent

**paternal** [pater'nal] adj fatherly, paternal; **paterno, -a** adj paternal

**patético, -a** [pa'tetiko, a] adj pathetic, moving

**patilla** [pa'tiʎa] nf (de gafas) sidepiece; **patillas** nfpl sideburns

**patín** [pa'tin] nm skate; (de tobogán) runner; **patines de ruedas** rollerskates; **patinaje** nm skating; **patinar** /1a/ vi to skate; (resbalarse) to skid, slip; (fam) to slip up, blunder

**patineta** [pati'neta] nf (patinete) scooter; (LAM: monopatín) skateboard

**patinete** [pati'nete] nm scooter

**patio** ['patjo] nm (de casa) patio, courtyard; **~ de recreo** playground

**pato** ['pato] nm duck; **pagar el ~** (fam) to take the blame, carry the can

**patoso, -a** [pa'toso, a] adj clumsy

**patotero** [pato'tero] nm (LAM) hooligan, lout

**patraña** [pa'traɲa] nf story, fib

**patria** ['patrja] nf native land, mother country

**patrimonio** [patri'monjo] nm inheritance; (fig) heritage

**patriota** [pa'trjota] nmf patriot

**patrocinar** [patroθi'nar] /1a/ vt to sponsor

**patrón, -ona** [pa'tron, ona] nm/f (jefe) boss, chief, master/mistress; (propietario) landlord/lady; (Rel) patron saint ▷ nm (Costura) pattern

**patronato** [patro'nato] nm sponsorship; (acto) patronage; (fundación) trust

**patrulla** [pa'truʎa] nf patrol

**pausa** ['pausa] nf pause; break

**pauta** ['pauta] nf line, guide line

**pava** ['paβa] nf (LAM) kettle

**pavimento** [paβi'mento] nm (de losa) pavement, paving

**pavo** ['paβo] nm turkey; **~ real** peacock

**payaso, -a** [pa'jaso, a] nm/f clown

**payo, -a** ['pajo, a] nm/f non-gipsy

**paz** [paθ] nf peace; (tranquilidad) peacefulness, tranquillity; **hacer las paces** to make peace; (fig) to make up; **¡déjame en ~!** leave me alone!

**PC** nm PC, personal computer

**P.D.** abr (= posdata) P.S.

**peaje** [pe'axe] nm toll

**peatón** [pea'ton] nm pedestrian; **peatonal** adj pedestrian

**peca** ['peka] nf freckle

**pecado** [pe'kaðo] nm sin; **pecador, a** adj sinful ▷ nm/f sinner

**pecaminoso, -a** [pekami'noso, a] adj sinful

**pecar** [pe'kar] /1g/ vi (Rel) to sin; (fig): **~ de generoso** to be too generous

**pecera** [pe'θera] nf fish tank; (redonda) goldfish bowl

**pecho** ['petʃo] nm (Anat) chest; (de mujer) breast(s pl); **dar el ~ a** to breast-feed; **tomar algo a ~** to take sth to heart

**pechuga** [pe'tʃuɣa] nf breast

**peculiar** [peku'ljar] adj special, peculiar; (característico) typical, characteristic

**pedal** [pe'ðal] nm pedal; **pedalear** /1a/ vi to pedal

**pédalo** ['peðalo] nm pedalo, pedal boat

**pedante** [pe'ðante] adj pedantic ▷ nmf pedant

**pedazo** [pe'ðaθo] nm piece, bit; **hacerse ~s** to smash, shatter

**pediatra** [pe'ðjatra] nmf paediatrician (BRIT), pediatrician (US)

**pedido** [pe'ðiðo] nm (Com) order; (petición) request

**pedir** [pe'ðir] /3k/ vt to ask for, request; (comida, Com: mandar) to order; (necesitar) to need, demand, require ▷ vi to ask; **me pidió que cerrara la puerta** he asked me to shut the door; **¿cuánto piden por el coche?** how much are they asking for the car?

**pedo** ['peðo] (fam) nm fart (!)

**pega** ['peɣa] nf snag; **poner ~s** to raise objections

**pegadizo, -a** [peɣa'ðiθo, a] adj (canción etc) catchy

**pegajoso, -a** [peɣa'xoso, a] adj sticky, adhesive

**pegamento** [peɣa'mento] nm gum, glue

**pegar** [pe'ɣar] /1h/ vt (papel, sellos) to stick (on); (cartel) to post, stick up; (coser) to sew (on); (unir: partes) to join, fix together; (Inform) to paste; (Med) to give, infect with; (dar: golpe) to give, deal ▷ vi (adherirse) to stick, adhere; (ir juntos: colores) to match, go together; (golpear) to hit; (quemar: el sol) to strike hot, burn; **pegarse** vr (gen) to stick; (dos personas) to hit each other, fight; **~ un grito** to let out a yell; **~ un salto** to jump (with fright); **~ fuego** to set fire; **~ en** to touch; **~se un tiro** to shoot o.s.

**pegatina** [peɣa'tina] nf sticker

**pegote** [pe'ɣote] nm (fam) eyesore, sight

**peinado** [pei'naðo] nm hairstyle

**peinar** [pei'nar] /1a/ vt to comb sb's hair; (con un cierto estilo) to style; **peinarse** vr to comb one's hair

**peine** ['peine] nm comb; **peineta** nf ornamental comb

**p.ej.** abr (= por ejemplo) e.g.

**Pekín** [pe'kin] n Peking, Beijing

**pelado, -a** [pe'laðo, a] adj (cabeza) shorn; (fruta) peeled; (campo, fig) bare; (fam: sin dinero) broke

**pelar** [pe'lar] /1a/ vt (fruta, patatas) to peel; (cortar el pelo a) to cut the hair of; (quitar la piel: animal) to skin; **pelarse** vr (la piel) to peel off; **voy a ~me** I'm going to get my hair cut

**peldaño** [pel'daɲo] nm step

**pelea** [pe'lea] nf (lucha) fight; (discusión) quarrel, row; **peleado, -a** adj: **estar peleado (con algn)** to have fallen out (with sb); **pelear** /1a/ vi to fight; **pelearse** vr to fight; (reñir) to fall out, quarrel

**pelela** [pe'lela] nf (LAM) potty

**peletería** [pele'tria] nf furrier's, fur shop
**pelícano** [pe'likano] nm pelican
**película** [pe'likula] nf film; (cobertura ligera) thin covering; (Foto: rollo) roll o reel of film; **~ de dibujos (animados)** cartoon film
**peligro** [pe'liɣro] nm danger; (riesgo) risk; **correr ~ de** to be in danger of, run the risk of; **peligroso, -a** adj dangerous; risky
**pelirrojo, -a** [peli'rroxo, a] adj red-haired, red-headed ▷ nm/f redhead
**pellejo** [pe'ʎexo] nm (de animal) skin, hide
**pellizcar** [peʎiθ'kar] /1g/ vt to pinch, nip
**pelma** ['pelma] nmf, **pelmazo, -a** [pel'maθo, a] nm/f (fam) pain (in the neck)
**pelo** ['pelo] nm (cabellos) hair; (de barba, bigote) whisker; (de animal: piel) fur, coat; (de perro etc) hair, coat; **venir al ~** to be exactly what one needs; **un hombre de ~ en pecho** a brave man; **por los ~s** by the skin of one's teeth; **no tener ~s en la lengua** to be outspoken, not mince words; **con ~s y señales** in minute detail; **tomar el ~ a algn** to pull sb's leg
**pelota** [pe'lota] nf ball; **en ~(s)** stark naked; **~ vasca** pelota; **hacer la ~ (a algn)** to creep (to sb)
**pelotón** [pelo'ton] nm (Mil) squad, detachment
**peluca** [pe'luka] nf wig
**peluche** [pe'lutʃe] nm: **muñeco de ~** soft toy
**peludo, -a** [pe'luðo, a] adj hairy, shaggy
**peluquería** [peluke'ria] nf hairdresser's; **peluquero, -a** nm/f hairdresser
**pelusa** [pe'lusa] nf (Bot) down; (Costura) fluff
**pena** ['pena] nf (congoja) grief, sadness; (remordimiento) regret; (dificultad) trouble; (dolor) pain; (Jur) sentence; **~ capital** capital punishment; **~ de muerte** death penalty; **merecer** o **valer la ~** to be worthwhile; **a duras ~s** with great difficulty; **¡qué ~!** what a shame o pity!
**penal** [pe'nal] adj penal ▷ nm (cárcel) prison
**penalidad** [penali'ðað] nf (problema, dificultad) trouble, hardship; (Jur) penalty, punishment; **penalidades** nfpl trouble sg, hardship sg
**penalti, penalty** [pe'nalti] (pl **penalties** o **penaltys**) nm (Deporte) penalty (kick)
**pendiente** [pen'djente] adj pending, unsettled ▷ nm earring ▷ nf hill, slope
**pene** ['pene] nm penis
**penetrante** [pene'trante] adj (herida) deep; (persona, arma) sharp; (sonido) penetrating, piercing; (mirada) searching; (viento, ironía) biting
**penetrar** [pene'trar] /1a/ vt to penetrate, pierce; (entender) to grasp ▷ vi to penetrate,

go in; (entrar) to enter; (líquido) to soak in; (emoción) to pierce
**penicilina** [peniθi'lina] nf penicillin
**península** [pe'ninsula] nf peninsula; **peninsular** adj peninsular
**penique** [pe'nike] nm penny
**penitencia** [peni'tenθja] nf penance
**penoso, -a** [pe'noso, a] adj laborious, difficult; (lamentable) distressing
**pensador, a** [pensa'ðor, a] nm/f thinker
**pensamiento** [pensa'mjento] nm thought; (mente) mind; (idea) idea
**pensar** [pen'sar] /1j/ vt to think; (considerar) to think over, think out; (proponerse) to intend, plan; (imaginarse) to think up, invent ▷ vi to think; **~ en** to aim at, aspire to; **pensativo, -a** adj thoughtful, pensive
**pensión** [pen'sjon] nf (casa) ≈ guest house; (dinero) pension; (cama y comida) board and lodging; **~ completa** full board; **media ~** half board; **pensionista** nmf (jubilado) (old-age) pensioner; (el que vive en una pensión) lodger
**penúltimo, -a** [pe'nultimo, a] adj penultimate, second last
**penumbra** [pe'numbra] nf half-light
**peña** ['peɲa] nf (roca) rock; (acantilado) cliff, crag; (grupo) group, circle; (LAM: club) folk club
**peñasco** [pe'ɲasko] nm large rock, boulder
**peñón** [pe'ɲon] nm crag; **el P~** the Rock (of Gibraltar)
**peón** [pe'on] nm labourer; (LAM) farm labourer, farmhand; (Ajedrez) pawn
**peonza** [pe'onθa] nf spinning top
**peor** [pe'or] adj (comparativo) worse; (superlativo) worse ▷ adv worse; worst; **de mal en ~** from bad to worse
**pepinillo** [pepi'niʎo] nm gherkin
**pepino** [pe'pino] nm cucumber; **(no) me importa un ~** I don't care one bit
**pepita** [pe'pita] nf (Bot) pip; (Minería) nugget
**pepito** [pe'pito] nm (ESP: tb: **~ de ternera**) steak sandwich
**pequeño, -a** [pe'keɲo, a] adj small, little
**pera** ['pera] nf pear; **peral** nm pear tree
**percance** [per'kanθe] nm setback, misfortune
**percatarse** [perka'tarse] /1a/ vr: **~ de** to notice, take note of
**percebe** [per'θeβe] nm barnacle
**percepción** [perθep'θjon] nf (vista) perception; (idea) notion, idea
**percha** ['pertʃa] nf coat hanger; (ganchos) coat hooks pl; (de ave) perch
**percibir** [perθi'βir] /3a/ vt to perceive, notice; (Com) to earn, get
**percusión** [perku'sjon] nf percussion

**perdedor, a** [perðe'ðor, a] *adj* losing ▷ *nm/f* loser

**perder** [per'ðer] /2g/ *vt* to lose; (*tiempo, palabras*) to waste; (*oportunidad*) to lose, miss; (*tren*) to miss ▷ *vi* to lose; **perderse** *vr* (*extraviarse*) to get lost; (*desaparecer*) to disappear, be lost to view; (*arruinarse*) to be ruined; **echar a ~** (*comida*) to spoil, ruin; (*oportunidad*) to waste

**pérdida** ['perðiða] *nf* loss; (*de tiempo*) waste; **pérdidas** *nfpl* (Com) losses

**perdido, -a** [per'ðiðo, a] *adj* lost

**perdiz** [per'ðiθ] *nf* partridge

**perdón** [per'ðon] *nm* (*disculpa*) pardon, forgiveness; (*clemencia*) mercy; **¡~!** sorry!, I beg your pardon!; **perdonar** /1a/ *vt* to pardon, forgive; (*la vida*) to spare; (*excusar*) to exempt, excuse; **¡perdone (usted)!** sorry!, I beg your pardon!

**perecedero, -a** [pereθe'ðero, a] *adj* perishable

**perecer** [pere'θer] /2d/ *vi* to perish, die

**peregrinación** [pereɣrina'θjon] *nf* (Rel) pilgrimage

**peregrino, -a** [pere'ɣrino, a] *adj* (*extraño*) strange ▷ *nm/f* pilgrim

**perejil** [pere'xil] *nm* parsley

**perenne** [pe'renne] *adj* perennial

**pereza** [pe'reθa] *nf* laziness; **perezoso, -a** *adj* lazy

**perfección** [perfek'θjon] *nf* perfection; **perfeccionar** /1a/ *vt* to perfect; (*mejorar*) to improve; (*acabar*) to complete, finish

**perfecto, -a** [per'fekto, a] *adj* perfect ▷ *nm* (Ling) perfect (tense)

**perfil** [per'fil] *nm* profile; (*silueta*) silhouette, outline; (Tec) (cross) section; **perfiles** *nmpl* features

**perforación** [perfora'θjon] *nf* perforation; (*con taladro*) drilling

**perforadora** [perfora'ðora] *nf* card-punch

**perforar** [perfo'rar] /1a/ *vt* to perforate; (*agujero*) to drill, bore; (*papel*) to punch a hole in ▷ *vi* to drill, bore

**perfume** [per'fume] *nm* perfume, scent

**periferia** [peri'ferja] *nf* periphery; (*de ciudad*) outskirts *pl*

**periférico, -a** [peri'feriko, a] *adj* peripheral ▷ *nm* (LAM Auto) ring road (BRIT), beltway (US)

**perilla** [pe'riʎa] *nf* (*barba*) goatee; (LAM: *de puerta*) doorknob, door handle

**perímetro** [pe'rimetro] *nm* perimeter

**periódico, -a** [pe'rjoðiko, a] *adj* periodic(al) ▷ *nm* (news)paper

**periodismo** [perjo'ðismo] *nm* journalism; **periodista** *nmf* journalist

**periodo** [pe'rjoðo], **período** [pe'rioðo] *nm* period

**periquito** [peri'kito] *nm* budgerigar, budgie (*fam*)

**perito, -a** [pe'rito, a] *adj* (*experto*) expert; (*diestro*) skilled, skilful ▷ *nm/f* expert; skilled worker; (*técnico*) technician

**perjudicar** [perxuði'kar] /1g/ *vt* (*gen*) to damage, harm; **perjudicial** *adj* damaging, harmful; (*en detrimento*) detrimental; **perjuicio** *nm* damage, harm

**perjurar** [perxu'rar] /1a/ *vi* to commit perjury

**perla** ['perla] *nf* pearl; **me viene de ~s** it suits me fine

**permanecer** [permane'θer] /2d/ *vi* (*quedarse*) to stay, remain; (*seguir*) to continue to be

**permanente** [perma'nente] *adj* permanent; (*constante*) constant ▷ *nf* perm

**permiso** [per'miso] *nm* permission; (*licencia*) permit, licence (BRIT), license (US); **con ~** excuse me; **estar de ~** (Mil) to be on leave; **~ de conducir** *o* **conductor** driving licence (BRIT), driver's license (US); **~ por enfermedad** (LAM) sick leave

**permitir** [permi'tir] /3a/ *vt* to permit, allow

**pernera** [per'nera] *nf* trouser leg

**pero** ['pero] *conj* but; (*aún*) yet ▷ *nm* (*defecto*) flaw, defect; (*reparo*) objection

**perpendicular** [perpendiku'lar] *adj* perpendicular

**perpetuo, -a** [per'petwo, a] *adj* perpetual

**perplejo, -a** [per'plexo, a] *adj* perplexed, bewildered

**perra** ['perra] *nf* (Zool) bitch; (fam: *dinero*) money; **estar sin una ~** to be flat broke

**perrera** [pe'rrera] *nf* kennel

**perrito** [pe'rrito] *nm* (tb: **~ caliente**) hot dog

**perro** ['perro] *nm* dog

**persa** ['persa] *adj, nmf* Persian

**persecución** [perseku'θjon] *nf* pursuit, chase; (Rel, Pol) persecution

**perseguir** [perse'ɣir] /3d, 3k/ *vt* to pursue, hunt; (*cortejar*) to chase after; (*molestar*) to pester, annoy; (Rel, Pol) to persecute

**persiana** [per'sjana] *nf* (Venetian) blind

**persistente** [persis'tente] *adj* persistent

**persistir** [persis'tir] /3a/ *vi* to persist

**persona** [per'sona] *nf* person; **~ mayor** elderly person

**personaje** [perso'naxe] *nm* important person, celebrity; (Teat) character

**personal** [perso'nal] *adj* (*particular*) personal; (*para una persona*) single, for one person ▷ *nm* personnel, staff; **personalidad** *nf* personality

**personarse** [perso'narse] /1a/ *vr* to appear in person

**personificar** [personifi'kar] /1g/ *vt* to personify

**perspectiva** [perspek'tiβa] nf perspective; (vista, panorama) view, panorama; (posibilidad futura) outlook, prospect

**persuadir** [perswa'ðir] /3a/ vt (gen) to persuade; (convencer) to convince; **persuadirse** vr to become convinced; **persuasión** nf persuasion

**pertenecer** [pertene'θer] /2d/ vi: ~ a to belong to; (fig) to concern; **perteneciente** adj: **perteneciente a** belonging to; **pertenencia** nf ownership; **pertenencias** nfpl possessions, property sg

**pertenezca** etc [perte'neθka] vb V **pertenecer**

**pértiga** ['pertiɣa] nf: **salto de ~** pole vault

**pertinente** [perti'nente] adj relevant, pertinent; (apropiado) appropriate; ~ **a** concerning, relevant to

**perturbación** [perturβa'θjon] nf (Pol) disturbance; (Med) upset, disturbance

**Perú** [pe'ru] nm Peru; **peruano, -a** adj, nm/f Peruvian

**perversión** [perβer'sjon] nf perversion; **perverso, -a** adj perverse; (depravado) depraved

**pervertido, -a** [perβer'tiðo, a] adj perverted ⊳ nm/f pervert

**pervertir** [perβer'tir] /3i/ vt to pervert, corrupt

**pesa** ['pesa] nf weight; (Deporte) shot

**pesadez** [pesa'ðeθ] nf (calidad de pesado) heaviness; (lentitud) slowness; (aburrimiento) tediousness

**pesadilla** [pesa'ðiʎa] nf nightmare, bad dream

**pesado, -a** [pe'saðo, a] adj heavy; (lento) slow; (difícil, duro) hard, tough; (aburrido) tedious, boring; (bochornoso) sultry

**pésame** ['pesame] nm expression of condolence, message of sympathy; **dar el ~** to express one's condolences

**pesar** [pe'sar] /1a/ vt to weigh ⊳ vi to weigh; (ser pesado) to weigh a lot, be heavy; (fig: opinión) to carry weight ⊳ nm (sentimiento) regret; (pena) grief, sorrow; **no pesa mucho** it's not very heavy; **a ~ de (que)** in spite of, despite

**pesca** ['peska] nf (acto) fishing; (cantidad de pescado) catch; **ir de ~** to go fishing

**pescadería** [peskaðe'ria] nf fish shop, fishmonger's

**pescadilla** [peska'ðiʎa] nf whiting

**pescado** [pes'kaðo] nm fish

**pescador, a** [peska'ðor, a] nm/f fisherman/woman

**pescar** [pes'kar] /1g/ vt (coger) to catch; (tratar de coger) to fish for; (conseguir: trabajo) to manage to get ⊳ vi to fish, go fishing

**pesebre** [pe'seβre] nm manger

**peseta** [pe'seta] nf peseta

**pesimista** [pesi'mista] adj pessimistic ⊳ nmf pessimist

**pésimo, -a** ['pesimo, a] adj awful, dreadful

**peso** ['peso] nm weight; (balanza) scales pl; (moneda) peso; ~ **bruto/neto** gross/net weight; ~ **mosca/pesado** fly-/heavyweight; **vender a ~** to sell by weight

**pesquero, -a** [pes'kero, a] adj fishing cpd

**pestaña** [pes'taɲa] nf (Anat) eyelash; (borde) rim

**peste** ['peste] nf plague; (mal olor) stink, stench

**pesticida** [pesti'θiða] nm pesticide

**pestillo** [pes'tiʎo] nm bolt; (picaporte) (door) handle

**petaca** [pe'taka] nf (de cigarrillos) cigarette case; (de pipa) tobacco pouch; (LAM: maleta) suitcase

**pétalo** ['petalo] nm petal

**petardo** [pe'tarðo] nm firework, firecracker

**petición** [peti'θjon] nf (pedido) request, plea; (memorial) petition; (Jur) plea

**peto** ['peto] nm dungarees pl, overalls pl (US)

**petróleo** [pe'troleo] nm oil, petroleum; **petrolero, -a** adj petroleum cpd ⊳ nm (oil) tanker

**peyorativo, -a** [pejora'tiβo, a] adj pejorative

**pez** [peθ] nm fish; ~ **de colores** goldfish; ~ **espada** swordfish

**pezón** [pe'θon] nm teat, nipple

**pezuña** [pe'θuɲa] nf hoof

**pianista** [pja'nista] nmf pianist

**piano** ['pjano] nm piano

**piar** [pjar] /1c/ vi to cheep

**pibe, -a** ['piβe, a] nm/f (LAM) boy/girl

**picadero** [pika'ðero] nm riding school

**picadillo** [pika'ðiʎo] nm mince, minced meat

**picado, -a** [pi'kaðo, a] adj pricked, punctured; (Culin) minced, chopped; (mar) choppy; (diente) bad; (tabaco) cut; (enfadado) cross

**picador** [pika'ðor] nm (Taur) picador; (minero) faceworker

**picadura** [pika'ðura] nf (pinchazo) puncture; (de abeja) sting; (de mosquito) bite; (tabaco picado) cut tobacco

**picante** [pi'kante] adj hot; (comentario) racy, spicy

**picaporte** [pika'porte] nm (tirador) handle; (pestillo) latch

**picar** [pi'kar] /1g/ vt (agujerear, perforar) to prick, puncture; (abeja) to sting; (mosquito, serpiente) to bite; (Culin) to mince, chop; (incitar) to incite, goad; (dañar, irritar) to annoy, bother; (quemar: lengua) to burn, sting ⊳ vi (pez) to bite, take the bait; (el sol) to burn, scorch; (*abeja, Med*) to sting; (*mosquito*) to bite; **picarse** *vr* (*agriarse*) to turn sour, go off; (*ofenderse*) to take offence

**picardía** [pikar'ðia] *nf* villainy; (*astucia*) slyness, craftiness; (*una picardía*) dirty trick; (*palabra*) rude/bad word o expression

**pícaro, -a** ['pikaro, a] *adj* (*malicioso*) villainous; (*travieso*) mischievous ▷ *nm* (*astuto*) sly sort; (*sinvergüenza*) rascal, scoundrel

**pichi** ['pitʃi] *nm* (*ESP*) pinafore dress (*BRIT*), jumper (*US*)

**pichón** [pi'tʃon] *nm* young pigeon

**pico** ['piko] *nm* (*de ave*) beak; (*punta agudo*) sharp point; (*Tec*) pick, pickaxe; (*Geo*) peak, summit; **y ~** and a bit; **las seis y ~** six and a bit

**picor** [pi'kor] *nm* itch

**picoso, -a** [pi'koso, a] (*LAM*) *adj* (*comida*) hot

**picudo, -a** [pi'kuðo, a] *adj* pointed, with a point

**pidió** *etc vb V* **pedir**

**pido** *etc vb V* **pedir**

**pie** [pje] (*pl* **pies**) *nm* foot; (*fig: motivo*) motive, basis; (: *fundamento*) foothold; **ir a ~** to go on foot, walk; **estar de ~** to be standing (up); **ponerse de ~** to stand up; **al ~ de la letra** (*citar*) literally, verbatim; (*copiar*) exactly, word for word; **de ~s a cabeza** from head to foot; **en ~ de guerra** on a war footing; **dar ~ a** to give cause for; **hacer ~** (*en el agua*) to touch (the) bottom

**piedad** [pje'ðað] *nf* (*lástima*) pity, compassion; (*clemencia*) mercy; (*devoción*) piety, devotion

**piedra** ['pjeðra] *nf* stone; (*roca*) rock; (*de mechero*) flint; (*Meteorología*) hailstone; **~ preciosa** precious stone

**piel** [pjel] *nf* (*Anat*) skin; (*Zool*) skin, hide; fur; (*cuero*) leather; (*Bot*) skin, peel

**pienso** *etc* ['pjenso] *vb V* **pensar**

**pierdo** *etc* ['pjerðo] *vb V* **perder**

**pierna** ['pjerna] *nf* leg

**pieza** ['pjeθa] *nf* piece; (*habitación*) room; **~ de recambio** o **repuesto** spare (part)

**pigmeo, -a** [piɣ'meo, a] *adj, nm/f* pigmy

**pijama** [pi'xama] *nm* pyjamas *pl*

**pila** ['pila] *nf* (*Elec*) battery; (*montón*) heap, pile; (*de fuente*) sink

**píldora** ['pildora] *nf* pill; **la ~ (anticonceptiva)** the pill

**pileta** [pi'leta] *nf* (*LAM: de cocina*) sink; (: *piscina*) swimming pool

**pillar** [pi'ʎar] /1a/ *vt* (*saquear*) to pillage, plunder; (*fam: coger*) to catch; (: *agarrar*) to grasp, seize; (: *entender*) to grasp, catch on to; **pillarse** *vr*: **~se un dedo con la puerta** to catch one's finger in the door

**pillo, -a** ['piʎo, a] *adj* villainous; (*astuto*) sly, crafty ▷ *nm/f* rascal, rogue, scoundrel

**piloto** [pi'loto] *nm* pilot; (*de aparato*) (pilot) light; (*Auto*) rear light, tail light; (*conductor*) driver; **~ automático** automatic pilot

**pimentón** [pimen'ton] *nm* paprika

**pimienta** [pi'mjenta] *nf* pepper

**pimiento** [pi'mjento] *nm* pepper, pimiento

**pin** [pin] (*pl* **pins**) *nm* badge

**pinacoteca** [pinako'teka] *nf* art gallery

**pinar** [pi'nar] *nm* pinewood

**pincel** [pin'θel] *nm* paintbrush

**pinchadiscos** [pintʃa'diskos] *nm/f inv* disc jockey, DJ

**pinchar** [pin'tʃar] /1a/ *vt* (*perforar*) to prick, pierce; (*neumático*) to puncture; (*incitar*) to prod; (*Inform*) to click

**pinchazo** [pin'tʃaθo] *nm* (*perforación*) prick; (*de llanta*) puncture; (*fig*) prod

**pincho** ['pintʃo] *nm* savoury (snack); **~ moruno** shish kebab; **~ de tortilla** small slice of omelette

**ping-pong** ['pimpon] *nm* table tennis

**pingüino** [pin'gwino] *nm* penguin

**pino** ['pino] *nm* pine (tree)

**pinta** ['pinta] *nf* spot, drop; (*aspecto*) appearance, look(s) *pl*; **pintado, -a** *adj* spotted; (*de muchos colores*) colourful; **pintadas** *nfpl* political graffiti *sg*

**pintalabios** [pinta'laβjos] *nm inv* (*ESP*) lipstick

**pintar** [pin'tar] /1a/ *vt* to paint ▷ *vi* to paint; (*fam*) to count, be important; **pintarse** *vr* to put on make-up

**pintor, a** [pin'tor, a] *nm/f* painter

**pintoresco, -a** [pinto'resko, a] *adj* picturesque

**pintura** [pin'tura] *nf* painting; **~ al óleo** oil painting

**pinza** ['pinθa] *nf* (*Zool*) claw; (*para colgar ropa*) clothes peg; (*Tec*) pincers *pl*; **pinzas** *nfpl* (*para depilar*) tweezers

**piña** ['piɲa] *nf* (*fruto del pino*) pine cone; (*fruta*) pineapple; (*fig*) group

**piñata** [pi'ɲata] *nf* piñata (*figurine hung up at parties to be beaten with sticks until sweets or presents fall out*)

**piñón** [pi'ɲon] *nm* (*Bot*) pine nut; (*Tec*) pinion

**pío, -a** ['pio, a] *adj* (*devoto*) pious, devout; (*misericordioso*) merciful

**piojo** ['pjoxo] *nm* louse

**pipa** ['pipa] *nf* pipe; (*Bot*) seed, pip; (*de girasol*) sunflower seed

**pipí** [pi'pi] *nm* (*fam*): **hacer ~** to have a wee(-wee)

**pique** ['pike] *nm* (*resentimiento*) pique, resentment; (*rivalidad*) rivalry, competition; **irse a ~** to sink; (*familia*) to be ruined

**piqueta** [pi'keta] nf pick(axe)
**piquete** [pi'kete] nm (Mil) squad, party; (de obreros) picket; (LAM: de insecto) bite
**pirado, -a** [pi'raðo, a] adj (fam) round the bend ▷ nm/f nutter
**piragua** [pi'raɣwa] nf canoe; **piragüismo** nm canoeing
**pirámide** [pi'ramiðe] nf pyramid
**pirata** [pi'rata] adj, nm pirate; (tb: **~ informático**) hacker
**Pirineo(s)** [piri'neo(s)] nm(pl) Pyrenees pl
**pirómano, -a** [pi'romano, a] nm/f (Jur) arsonist
**piropo** [pi'ropo] nm compliment, (piece of) flattery
**pirueta** [pi'rweta] nf pirouette
**piruleta** [piru'leta] nf lollipop
**pis** [pis] nm (fam) pee; **hacer ~** to have a pee; (para niños) to wee-wee
**pisada** [pi'saða] nf (paso) footstep; (huella) footprint
**pisar** [pi'sar] /1a/ vt (caminar sobre) to walk on, tread on; (apretar con el pie) to press; (fig) to trample on, walk all over ▷ vi to tread, step, walk
**piscina** [pis'θina] nf swimming pool
**Piscis** [pis'θis] nm Pisces
**piso** [piso] nm (suelo) floor; (LAM) ground; (apartamento) flat, apartment; **primer ~** (ESP) first o second (US) floor; (LAM) ground o first (US) floor
**pisotear** [pisote'ar] /1a/ vt to trample (on o underfoot)
**pista** [pista] nf track, trail; (indicio) clue; **~ aterrizaje** runway; **~ de baile** dance floor; **~ de tenis** tennis court; **~ de hielo** ice rink
**pistola** [pis'tola] nf pistol; (Tec) spray-gun
**pistón** [pis'ton] nm (Tec) piston; (Mus) key
**pitar** [pi'tar] /1a/ vt (hacer sonar) to blow; (rechiflar) to whistle at, boo ▷ vi to whistle; (Auto) to sound o toot one's horn; (LAM) to smoke
**pitillo** [pi'tiʎo] nm cigarette
**pito** [pito] nm whistle; (de coche) horn
**pitón** [pi'ton] nm (Zool) python
**pitonisa** [pito'nisa] nf fortune-teller
**pitorreo** [pito'rreo] nm joke, laugh; **estar de ~** to be in a joking mood
**píxel** [piksel] nm (Inform) pixel
**piyama** [pi'jama] nm (LAM) pyjamas pl, pajamas pl (US)
**pizarra** [pi'θarra] nf (piedra) slate; (encerado) blackboard; **~ blanca** whiteboard; **~ interactiva** interactive whiteboard
**pizarrón** [piθa'rron] nm (LAM) blackboard
**pizca** [piθka] nf pinch, spot; (fig) spot, speck; **ni ~** not a bit
**placa** [plaka] nf plate; (distintivo) badge; **~ de matrícula** number plate

**placard** [pla'kar] nm (LAM) built-in cupboard
**placer** [pla'θer] /2w/ nm pleasure ▷ vt to please; **a ~** at one's pleasure
**plaga** [plaɣa] nf (Zool) pest; (Med) plague; (fig) swarm; (: abundancia) abundance
**plagio** [plaxjo] nm plagiarism
**plan** [plan] nm (esquema, proyecto) plan; (idea, intento) idea, intention; **tener ~** (fam) to have a date; **tener un ~** (fam) to have an affair; **en ~ económico** (fam) on the cheap; **vamos en ~ de turismo** we're going as tourists; **si te pones en ese ~ ...** if that's your attitude ...
**plana** [plana] nf V **plano**
**plancha** [plantʃa] nf (para planchar) iron; (rótulo) plate, sheet; (Naut) gangway; **a la ~** (Culin) grilled; **planchar** /1a/ vt to iron ▷ vi to do the ironing
**planeta** [plane'ar] /1a/ vt to plan ▷ vi to glide
**planeta** [pla'neta] nm planet
**plano, -a** [plano, a] adj flat, level, even ▷ nm (Mat, Tec, Aviat) plane; (Foto) shot; (Arq) plan; (Geo) map; (de ciudad) map, street plan ▷ nf sheet of paper, page; (Tec) trowel; **primer ~** close-up; **en primera plana** on the front page
**planta** [planta] nf (Bot, Tec) plant; (Anat) sole of the foot, foot; (piso) floor; (LAM: personal) staff; **~ baja** ground floor
**plantar** [plan'tar] /1a/ vt (Bot) to plant; (levantar) to erect, set up; **plantarse** vr to stand firm; **~ a algn en la calle** to chuck sb out; **dejar plantado a algn** (fam) to stand sb up
**plantear** [plante'ar] /1a/ vt (problema) to pose; (dificultad) to raise
**plantilla** [plan'tiʎa] nf (de zapato) insole; (personal) personnel; **ser de ~** to be on the staff
**plantón** [plan'ton] nm (Mil) guard, sentry; (fam) long wait; **dar (un) ~ a algn** to stand sb up
**plasta** [plasta] nf soft mass, lump ▷ nmf (ESP fam) bore ▷ adj (ESP fam) boring
**plástico, -a** [plastiko, a] adj plastic ▷ nm plastic
**Plastilina®** [plasti'lina] nf Plasticine®
**plata** [plata] nf (metal) silver; (cosas hechas de plata) silverware; (LAM) cash
**plataforma** [plata'forma] nf platform; **~ de lanzamiento/perforación** launch(ing) pad/drilling rig
**plátano** [platano] nm (fruta) banana; (árbol) plane tree; banana tree
**platea** [pla'tea] nf (Teat) pit
**plática** [platika] nf talk, chat; **platicar** /1g/ vi to talk, chat

**platillo** [pla'tiʎo] *nm* saucer; **platillos** *nmpl* cymbals; **~ volador** *o* **volante** flying saucer

**platino** [pla'tino] *nm* platinum; **platinos** *nmpl* (*Auto*) (contact) points

**plato** ['plato] *nm* plate, dish; (*parte de comida*) course; (*guiso*) dish; **primer ~** first course; **~ combinado** set main course (*served on one plate*); **~ fuerte** main course

**playa** ['plaja] *nf* beach; (*costa*) seaside; **~ de estacionamiento** (*LAM*) car park

**playero, -a** [pla'jero, a] *adj* beach *cpd* ▷ *nf* (*LAM: camiseta*) T-shirt; **playeras** *nfpl* canvas shoes

**plaza** ['plaθa] *nf* square; (*mercado*) market(place); (*sitio*) room, space; (*en vehículo*) seat, place; (*colocación*) post, job; **~ de toros** bullring

**plazo** ['plaθo] *nm* (*lapso de tiempo*) time, period; (*fecha de vencimiento*) expiry date; (*pago parcial*) instalment; **a corto/largo ~** short-/long-term; **comprar a ~s** to buy on hire purchase, pay for in instalments

**plazoleta** [plaθo'leta] *nf* small square

**plebeyo, -a** [ple'βejo, a] *adj* plebeian; (*pey*) coarse, common

**plegable** [ple'ɣaβle] *adj* pliable; (*silla*) folding

**pleito** ['pleito] *nm* (*Jur*) lawsuit, case; (*fig*) dispute, feud

**plenitud** [pleni'tuð] *nf* plenitude, fullness; (*abundancia*) abundance

**pleno, -a** ['pleno, a] *adj* full; (*completo*) complete ▷ *nm* plenum; **en ~ día** in broad daylight; **en ~ verano** at the height of summer; **en plena cara** full in the face

**pliego** ['pljeɣo] *nm* (*hoja*) sheet (of paper); (*carta*) sealed letter/document; **~ de condiciones** details *pl*, specifications *pl*

**pliegue** ['pljeɣe] *nm* fold, crease; (*de vestido*) pleat

**plomería** [plome'ria] *nf* (*LAM*) plumbing; **plomero** *nm* (*LAM*) plumber

**plomo** ['plomo] *nm* (*metal*) lead; (*Elec*) fuse; **sin ~** unleaded

**pluma** ['pluma] *nf* feather; (*para escribir*): **~ (estilográfica)** ink pen; **~ fuente** (*LAM*) fountain pen

**plumero** [plu'mero] *nm* (*quitapolvos*) feather duster

**plumón** [plu'mon] *nm* (*de ave*) down

**plural** [plu'ral] *adj* plural

**pluriempleo** [pluriem'pleo] *nm* having more than one job

**plus** [plus] *nm* bonus

**población** [poβla'θjon] *nf* population; (*pueblo, ciudad*) town, city

**poblado, -a** [po'βlaðo, a] *adj* inhabited ▷ *nm* (*aldea*) village; (*pueblo*) (small) town; **densamente ~** densely populated

**poblador, a** [poβla'ðor, a] *nm/f* settler, colonist

**pobre** ['poβre] *adj* poor ▷ *nmf* poor person; **pobreza** *nf* poverty

**pocilga** [po'θilɣa] *nf* pigsty

 **PALABRA CLAVE**

**poco, -a** ['poko, a] *adj* **1** (*sg*) little, not much; **poco tiempo** little *o* not much time; **de poco interés** of little interest, not very interesting; **poca cosa** not much
**2** (*pl*) few, not many; **unos pocos** a few, some; **pocos niños comen lo que les conviene** few children eat what they should
▶ *adv* **1** little, not much; **cuesta poco** it doesn't cost much
**2** (+ *adj: negativo, antónimo*): **poco amable/inteligente** not very nice/intelligent
**3**: **por poco me caigo** I almost fell
**4**: **a poco de haberse casado** shortly after getting married
**5**: **poco a poco** little by little
▶ *nm* a little, a bit; **un poco triste/de dinero** a little sad/money

**podar** [po'ðar] /1a/ *vt* to prune

**podcast** ['poðkast] *nm* podcast; **podcastear** /1a/ *vi* to podcast

**PALABRA CLAVE**

**poder** [po'ðer] /2s/ *vi* **1** (*capacidad*) can, be able to; **no puedo hacerlo** I can't do it, I'm unable to do it
**2** (*permiso*) can, may, be allowed to; **¿se puede?** may I (*o* we)?; **puedes irte ahora** you may go now; **no se puede fumar en este hospital** smoking is not allowed in this hospital
**3** (*posibilidad*) may, might, could; **puede llegar mañana** he may *o* might arrive tomorrow; **pudiste haberte hecho daño** you might *o* could have hurt yourself; **¡podías habérmelo dicho antes!** you might have told me before!
**4**: **puede (ser)** perhaps; **puede que lo sepa Tomás** Tomás may *o* might know
**5**: **¡no puedo más!** I've had enough!; **es tonto a más no poder** he's as stupid as they come
**6**: **poder con: no puedo con este crío** this kid's too much for me
▶ *nm* power; **el poder** the Government; **poder adquisitivo** purchasing power; **detentar** *u* **ocupar** *o* **estar en el poder** to be in power *o* office; **poder judicial** judiciary

**poderoso, -a** [poðe'roso, a] *adj* powerful
**podio** ['poðjo] *nm* podium
**podium** ['poðjum] = **podio**
**podrido, -a** [po'ðriðo, a] *adj* rotten, bad; (*fig*) rotten, corrupt
**podrir** [po'ðrir] = **pudrir**
**poema** [po'ema] *nm* poem
**poesía** [poe'sia] *nf* poetry
**poeta** [po'eta] *nm* poet; **poético, -a** *adj* poetic(al); **poetisa** *nf* (woman) poet
**póker** ['poker] *nm* poker
**polaco, -a** [po'lako, a] *adj* Polish ⊳ *nm/f* Pole
**polar** [po'lar] *adj* polar
**polea** [po'lea] *nf* pulley
**polémica** [po'lemika] *nf* polemics *sg*; (*una polémica*) controversy
**polen** ['polen] *nm* pollen
**policía** [poli'θia] *nmf* police officer ⊳ *nf* police; **policíaco, -a** *adj* police *cpd*; **novela policíaca** detective story; **policial** *adj* police *cpd*
**polideportivo** [poliðepor'tiβo] *nm* sports centre
**polígono** [po'liɣono] *nm* (*Mat*) polygon; **~ industrial** industrial estate
**polilla** [po'liʎa] *nf* moth
**polio** ['poljo] *nf* polio
**político, -a** [po'litiko, a] *adj* political; (*discreto*) tactful; (*pariente*) in-law ⊳ *nm/f* politician ⊳ *nf* politics *sg*; (*económica, agraria*) policy; **padre ~** father-in-law; **política exterior/de ingresos y precios** foreign/prices and incomes policy
**póliza** ['poliθa] *nf* certificate, voucher; (*impuesto*) tax o fiscal stamp; **~ de seguro(s)** insurance policy
**polizón** [poli'θon] *nm* stowaway
**pollera** [po'ʎera] *nf* (*LAM*) skirt
**pollo** ['poʎo] *nm* chicken
**polo** ['polo] *nm* (*Geo, Elec*) pole; (*helado*) ice lolly (*BRIT*), Popsicle® (*US*); (*Deporte*) polo; (*suéter*) polo-neck; **P~ Norte/Sur** North/South Pole
**Polonia** [po'lonja] *nf* Poland
**poltrona** [pol'trona] *nf* easy chair
**polución** [polu'θjon] *nf* pollution
**polvera** [pol'βera] *nf* powder compact
**polvo** ['polβo] *nm* dust; (*Química, Culin, Med*) powder; **polvos** *nmpl* (*maquillaje*) powder *sg*; **en ~** powdered; **~ de talco** talcum powder; **estar hecho ~** to be worn out o exhausted
**pólvora** ['polβora] *nf* gunpowder
**polvoriento, -a** [polβo'rjento, a] *adj* (*superficie*) dusty; (*sustancia*) powdery
**pomada** [po'maða] *nf* cream
**pomelo** [po'melo] *nm* grapefruit
**pómez** ['pomeθ] *nf*: **piedra ~** pumice stone
**pomo** ['pomo] *nm* knob, handle
**pompa** ['pompa] *nf* (*burbuja*) bubble; (*bomba*) pump; (*esplendor*) pomp, splendour
**pómulo** ['pomulo] *nm* cheekbone
**pon** [pon] *vb V* **poner**
**ponchadura** [pontʃa'dura] *nf* (*LAM*) puncture (*BRIT*), flat (*US*); **ponchar** /1a/ *vt* (*LAM*: *llanta*) to puncture
**ponche** ['pontʃe] *nm* punch
**poncho** ['pontʃo] *nm* poncho
**pondré** *etc* [pon'dre] *vb V* **poner**

○ **PALABRA CLAVE**

**poner** [po'ner] /2q/ *vt* **1** to put; (*colocar*) to place; (*telegrama*) to send; (*obra de teatro*) to put on; (*película*) to show; **ponlo más alto** turn it up; **¿qué ponen en el Excelsior?** what's on at the Excelsior?
**2** (*tienda*) to open; (*instalar: gas etc*) to put in; (*radio, TV*) to switch o turn on
**3** (*suponer*): **pongamos que ...** let's suppose that ...
**4** (*contribuir*): **el gobierno ha puesto otro millón** the government has contributed another million
**5** (*Telec*): **póngame con el Sr. López** can you put me through to Mr. López?
**6**: **poner de**: **le han puesto de director general** they've appointed him general manager
**7** (*+ adj*) to make; **me estás poniendo nerviosa** you're making me nervous
**8** (*dar nombre*): **al hijo le pusieron Diego** they called their son Diego
▶ *vi* (*gallina*) to lay
▶ **ponerse** *vr* (*colocarse*): **se puso a mi lado** he came and stood beside me; **tú ponte en esa silla** you go and sit on that chair; **ponerse en camino** to set off
**2** (*vestido, cosméticos*) to put on; **¿por qué no te pones el vestido nuevo?** why don't you put on o wear your new dress?
**3** (*sol*) to set
**4** (*+ adj*) to get, become; to turn; **se puso muy serio** he got very serious; **después de lavarla la tela se puso azul** after washing it the material turned blue
**5**: **ponerse a**: **se puso a llorar** he started to cry; **tienes que ponerte a estudiar** you must get down to studying

**pongo** *etc* ['pongo] *vb V* **poner**
**poniente** [po'njente] *nm* west; (*viento*) west wind
**pontífice** [pon'tifiθe] *nm* pope, pontiff
**pop** [pop] *adj inv, nm* (*Mus*) pop
**popa** ['popa] *nf* stern; **a ~** astern, abaft; **de ~ a proa** fore and aft
**popote** [po'pote] *nm* (*LAM*) straw

**popular** [popu'lar] *adj* popular; *(del pueblo)* of the people; **popularidad** *nf* popularity

⬤ **PALABRA CLAVE**

**por** [por] *prep* **1** *(objetivo)* for; **luchar por la patria** to fight for one's country
**2** (+ *infin*): **por no llegar tarde** so as not to arrive late; **por citar unos ejemplos** to give a few examples
**3** *(causa)* out of, because of; **por escasez de fondos** through o for lack of funds
**4** *(tiempo)*: **por la mañana/noche** in the morning/at night; **se queda por una semana** she's staying (for) a week
**5** *(lugar)*: **pasar por Madrid** to pass through Madrid; **ir a Guayaquil por Quito** to go to Guayaquil via Quito; **caminar por la calle** to walk along the street; **¿hay un banco por aquí?** is there a bank near here?
**6** *(cambio, precio)*: **te doy uno nuevo por el que tienes** I'll give you a new one (in return) for the one you've got
**7** *(valor distributivo)*: **30 euros por hora/cabeza** 30 euros an o per hour/a o per head
**8** *(modo, medio)* by; **por correo/avión** by post/air; **entrar por la entrada principal** to go in through the main entrance
**9** *(agente)* by; **hecho por él** done by him
**10**: **10 por 10 son 100** 10 times 10 is 100
**11** *(en lugar de)*: **vino él por su jefe** he came instead of his boss
**12**: **por mí que revienten** as far as I'm concerned they can drop dead
**13**: **por qué** why; **¿por qué?** why?; **¿por qué no?** why not?

**porcelana** [porθe'lana] *nf* porcelain; *(china)* china
**porcentaje** [porθen'taxe] *nm* percentage
**porción** [por'θjon] *nf (parte)* portion, share; *(cantidad)* quantity, amount
**porfiar** [por'fjar] /1c/ *vi* to persist, insist; *(disputar)* to argue stubbornly
**pormenor** [porme'nor] *nm* detail, particular
**pornografía** [pornoɣra'fia] *nf* pornography
**poro** ['poro] *nm* pore
**pororó** [poro'ro] *nm* (LAM) popcorn
**poroso, -a** [po'roso, a] *adj* porous
**poroto** [po'roto] *nm* (LAM) kidney bean
**porque** ['porke] *conj (a causa de)* because; *(ya que)* since; *(con el fin de)* so that, in order that
**porqué** [por'ke] *nm* reason, cause
**porquería** [porke'ria] *nf (suciedad)* filth, dirt; *(acción)* dirty trick; *(objeto)* small thing, trifle; *(fig)* rubbish

**porra** ['porra] *nf (arma)* stick, club
**porrazo** [po'rraθo] *nm (golpe)* blow; *(caída)* bump
**porro** ['porro] *nm (fam: droga)* joint
**porrón** [po'rron] *nm glass wine jar with a long spout*
**portaaviones** [port(a)a'βjones] *nm inv* aircraft carrier
**portada** [por'taða] *nf (de revista)* cover
**portador, a** [porta'ðor, a] *nm/f* carrier, bearer; *(Com)* bearer, payee
**portaequipajes** [portaeki'paxes] *nm inv* boot (BRIT), trunk (US); *(baca)* luggage rack
**portafolio** [porta'foljo] *nm* briefcase
**portal** [por'tal] *nm (entrada)* vestibule, hall; *(pórtico)* porch, doorway; *(puerta de entrada)* main door; *(Internet)* portal; **portales** *nmpl* arcade *sg*
**portamaletas** [portama'letas] *nm inv* (Auto: maletero) boot; (: baca) roof rack
**portamonedas** [portamo'neðas] *nm inv* (LAM) purse
**portar** [por'tar] /1a/ *vt* to carry; **portarse** *vr* to behave, conduct o.s.
**portátil** [por'tatil] *adj* portable; **(ordenador) ~** laptop (computer)
**portavoz** [porta'βoθ] *nmf* spokesman/woman
**portazo** [por'taθo] *nm*: **dar un ~** to slam the door
**porte** ['porte] *nm (Com)* transport; *(precio)* transport charges *pl*
**portentoso, -a** [porten'toso, a] *adj* marvellous, extraordinary
**porteño, -a** [por'teɲo, a] *adj* of o from Buenos Aires
**portería** [porte'ria] *nf (oficina)* porter's office; *(gol)* goal
**portero, -a** [por'tero, a] *nm/f* porter; *(conserje)* caretaker; *(ujier)* doorman; *(Deporte)* goalkeeper; **~ automático** (ESP) entry phone
**pórtico** ['portiko] *nm (porche)* portico, porch; *(fig)* gateway; *(arcada)* arcade
**portorriqueño, -a** [portorri'keɲo, a] *adj* Puerto Rican
**Portugal** [portu'ɣal] *nm* Portugal; **portugués, -esa** *adj, nm/f* Portuguese ▷ *nm (Ling)* Portuguese
**porvenir** [porβe'nir] *nm* future
**pos** [pos]: **en ~ de** *prep* after, in pursuit of
**posaderas** [posa'ðeras] *nfpl* backside *sg*, buttocks
**posar** [po'sar] /1a/ *vt (en el suelo)* to lay down, put down; *(la mano)* to place, put gently ▷ *vi* to sit, pose; **posarse** *vr* to settle; *(pájaro)* to perch; *(avión)* to land, come down

**posavasos** [posa'basos] *nm inv* coaster; (*para cerveza*) beermat

**posdata** [pos'ðata] *nf* postscript

**pose** ['pose] *nf* pose

**poseedor, a** [posee'ðor, a] *nm/f* owner, possessor; (*de récord, puesto*) holder

**poseer** [pose'er] /2e/ *vt* to have, possess, own; (*ventaja*) to enjoy; (*récord, puesto*) to hold

**posesivo, -a** [pose'siβo, a] *adj* possessive

**posgrado** [pos'ɣraðo] *nm* = **postgrado**

**posibilidad** [posiβili'ðað] *nf* possibility; (*oportunidad*) chance; **posibilitar** /1a/ *vt* to make possible; (*hacer factible*) to make feasible

**posible** [po'siβle] *adj* possible; (*factible*) feasible; **de ser ~** if possible; **en** o **dentro de lo ~** as far as possible

**posición** [posi'θjon] *nf* position; (*rango social*) status

**positivo, -a** [posi'tiβo, a] *adj* positive

**poso** ['poso] *nm* sediment; (*heces*) dregs *pl*

**posponer** [pospo'ner] /2q/ *vt* (*relegar*) to put behind o below; (*aplazar*) to postpone

**post** [post] (*pl* **posts**) *nm* (*en sitio web*) post

**posta** ['posta] *nf*: **a ~** on purpose, deliberately

**postal** [pos'tal] *adj* postal ▷ *nf* postcard

**poste** ['poste] *nm* (*de telégrafos*) post, pole; (*columna*) pillar

**póster** ['poster] (*pl* **posters**) *nm* poster

**posterior** [poste'rjor] *adj* back, rear; (*siguiente*) following, subsequent; (*más tarde*) later

**postgrado** [post'ɣraðo] *nm*: **curso de ~** postgraduate course

**postizo, -a** [pos'tiθo, a] *adj* false, artificial ▷ *nm* hairpiece

**postre** ['postre] *nm* sweet, dessert

**póstumo, -a** ['postumo, a] *adj* posthumous

**postura** [pos'tura] *nf* (*del cuerpo*) posture, position; (*fig*) attitude, position

**potable** [po'taβle] *adj* drinkable; **agua ~** drinking water

**potaje** [po'taxe] *nm* thick vegetable soup

**potencia** [po'tenθja] *nf* power; **potencial** *adj, nm* potential

**potente** [po'tente] *adj* powerful

**potro** ['potro] *nm* (*Zool*) colt; (*Deporte*) vaulting horse

**pozo** ['poθo] *nm* well; (*de río*) deep pool; (*de mina*) shaft

**PP** *nm abr* = **Partido Popular**

**práctica** ['praktika] *nf* V **práctico**

**practicable** [prakti'kaβle] *adj* practicable; (*camino*) passable

**practicante** [prakti'kante] *nmf* (*Med: ayudante de doctor*) medical assistant; (: *enfermero*) nurse; (*el que practica algo*) practitioner ▷ *adj* practising

**practicar** [prakti'kar] /1g/ *vt* to practise; (*deporte*) to go in for, play; (*ejecutar*) to carry out, perform

**práctico, -a** ['praktiko, a] *adj* practical; (*instruido: persona*) skilled, expert ▷ *nf* practice; (*método*) method; (*arte, capacidad*) skill; **en la práctica** in practice

**practique** *etc* [prak'tike] *vb* V **practicar**

**pradera** [pra'ðera] *nf* meadow; (*de Canadá*) prairie

**prado** ['praðo] *nm* (*campo*) meadow, field; (*pastizal*) pasture

**Praga** ['praɣa] *nf* Prague

**pragmático, -a** [praɣ'matiko, a] *adj* pragmatic

**precario, -a** [pre'karjo, a] *adj* precarious

**precaución** [prekau'θjon] *nf* (*medida preventiva*) preventive measure, precaution; (*prudencia*) caution, wariness

**precedente** [preθe'ðente] *adj* preceding; (*anterior*) former ▷ *nm* precedent

**preceder** [preθe'ðer] /2a/ *vt, vi* to precede, go/come before

**precepto** [pre'θepto] *nm* precept

**precinto** [pre'θinto] *nm* (*tb*: **~ de garantía**) seal

**precio** ['preθjo] *nm* price; (*costo*) cost; (*valor*) value, worth; (*de viaje*) fare; **~ de coste** o **de cobertura** cost price; **~ al contado** cash price; **~ al detalle** o **al por menor** retail price; **~ de salida** upset price; **~ tope** top price

**preciosidad** [preθjosi'ðað] *nf* (*valor*) (high) value, (great) worth; (*encanto*) charm; (*cosa bonita*) beautiful thing; **es una ~** it's lovely, it's really beautiful

**precioso, -a** [pre'θjoso, a] *adj* precious; (*de mucho valor*) valuable; (*fam*) lovely, beautiful

**precipicio** [preθi'pjeθjo] *nm* cliff, precipice; (*fig*) abyss

**precipitación** [preθipita'θjon] *nf* haste; (*lluvia*) rainfall

**precipitado, -a** [preθipi'taðo, a] *adj* hasty, rash; (*salida*) hasty, sudden

**precipitar** [preθipi'tar] /1a/ *vt* (*arrojar*) to hurl, throw; (*apresurar*) to hasten; (*acelerar*) to speed up, accelerate; **precipitarse** *vr* to throw o.s.; (*apresurarse*) to rush; (*actuar sin pensar*) to act rashly

**precisamente** [preθisa'mente] *adv* precisely; (*justo*) precisely, exactly

**precisar** [preθi'sar] /1a/ *vt* (*necesitar*) to need, require; (*fijar*) to determine exactly, fix; (*especificar*) to specify

**precisión** [preθi'sjon] *nf* (*exactitud*) precision

**preciso, -a** [pre'θiso, a] adj (exacto) precise; (necesario) necessary, essential

**preconcebido, -a** [prekonθe'βiðo, a] adj preconceived

**precoz** [pre'koθ] adj (persona) precocious; (calvicie) premature

**predecir** [preðe'θir] /3o/ vt to predict, forecast

**predestinado, -a** [preðesti'naðo, a] adj predestined

**predicar** [preði'kar] /1g/ vt, vi to preach

**predicción** [preðik'θjon] nf prediction

**predilecto, -a** [preði'lekto, a] adj favourite

**predisposición** [preðisposi'θjon] nf inclination; prejudice, bias

**predominar** [preðomi'nar] /1a/ vt to dominate ▷ vi to predominate; (prevalecer) to prevail; **predominio** nm predominance; prevalence

**preescolar** [preesko'lar] adj preschool

**prefabricado, -a** [prefaβri'kaðo, a] adj prefabricated

**prefacio** [pre'faθjo] nm preface

**preferencia** [prefe'renθja] nf preference; **de ~** preferably, for preference

**preferible** [prefe'riβle] adj preferable

**preferido, -a** [prefe'riðo, a] adj, nm/f favourite, favorite (us)

**preferir** [prefe'rir] /3i/ vt to prefer

**prefiero** etc [pre'fjero] vb V **preferir**

**prefijo** [pre'fixo] nm (Telec) (dialling) code

**pregunta** [pre'γunta] nf question; **hacer una ~** to ask a question; **~s frecuentes** FAQs, frequently asked questions; **preguntar** /1a/ vt to ask; (cuestionar) to question ▷ vi to ask; **preguntarse** vr to wonder; **preguntar por algn** to ask for sb; **preguntón, -ona** adj inquisitive

**prehistórico, -a** [preis'toriko, a] adj prehistoric

**prejuicio** [pre'xwiθjo] nm prejudgement; (preconcepción) preconception; (pey) prejudice, bias

**preludio** [pre'luðjo] nm prelude

**prematuro, -a** [prema'turo, a] adj premature

**premeditar** [premeði'tar] /1a/ vt to premeditate

**premiar** [pre'mjar] /1b/ vt to reward; (en un concurso) to give a prize to

**premio** ['premjo] nm reward; prize; (Com) premium

**prenatal** [prena'tal] adj antenatal, prenatal

**prenda** ['prenda] nf (de ropa) garment, article of clothing; (garantía) pledge; **prendas** nfpl talents, gifts

**prender** [pren'der] /2a/ vt (captar) to catch, capture; (detener) to arrest; (coser) to pin, attach; (sujetar) to fasten ▷ vi to catch; (arraigar) to take root; **prenderse** vr (encenderse) to catch fire

**prendido, -a** [pren'diðo, a] adj (LAM: luz) on

**prensa** ['prensa] nf press; **la P~** the press

**preñado, -a** [pre'naðo, a] adj pregnant; **~ de** pregnant with, full of

**preocupación** [preokupa'θjon] nf worry, concern; (ansiedad) anxiety

**preocupado, -a** [preoku'paðo, a] adj worried, concerned; anxious

**preocupar** [preoku'par] /1a/ vt to worry; **preocuparse** vr to worry; **~se de algo** (hacerse cargo de algo) to take care of sth

**preparación** [prepara'θjon] nf (acto) preparation; (estado) readiness; (entrenamiento) training

**preparado, -a** [prepa'raðo, a] adj (dispuesto) prepared; (Culin) ready (to serve) ▷ nm preparation

**preparar** [prepa'rar] /1a/ vt (disponer) to prepare, get ready; (Tec: tratar) to prepare, process; (entrenar) to teach, train; **prepararse** vr: **~se a o para hacer algo** to prepare o get ready to do sth; **preparativo, -a** adj preparatory, preliminary; **preparativos** nmpl preparations; **preparatoria** nf (LAM) sixth form college (BRIT), senior high school (us)

**presa** ['presa] nf (cosa apresada) catch; (víctima) victim; (de animal) prey; (de agua) dam

**presagiar** [presa'xjar] /1b/ vt to presage; **presagio** nm omen

**prescindir** [presθin'dir] /3a/ vi: **~ de** (privarse de) to do without, go without; (descartar) to dispense with

**prescribir** [preskri'βir] /3a/ vt to prescribe

**presencia** [pre'senθja] nf presence; **presenciar** /1b/ vt to be present at; (asistir a) to attend; (ver) to see, witness

**presentación** [presenta'θjon] nf presentation; (introducción) introduction

**presentador, a** [presenta'ðor, a] nm/f compère

**presentar** [presen'tar] /1a/ vt to present; (ofrecer) to offer; (mostrar) to show, display; (a una persona) to introduce; **presentarse** vr (llegar inesperadamente) to appear, turn up; (ofrecerse: como candidato) to run, stand; (aparecer) to show, appear; (solicitar empleo) to apply

**presente** [pre'sente] adj present ▷ nm present; **hacer ~** to state, declare; **tener ~** to remember, bear in mind

**presentimiento** [presenti'mjento] nm premonition, presentiment

**presentir** [presen'tir] /3i/ vt to have a premonition of

**preservación** [preserβa'θjon] nf
protection, preservation
**preservar** [preser'βar] /1a/ vt to protect,
preserve; **preservativo** nm sheath,
condom
**presidencia** [presi'ðeneja] nf presidency;
(de comité) chairmanship
**presidente** [presi'ðente] nmf president; (de
comité) chairman/woman
**presidir** [presi'ðir] /3a/ vt (dirigir) to preside
at, preside over; (: comité) to take the chair
at; (dominar) to dominate, rule ▷ vi to
preside; to take the chair
**presión** [pre'sjon] nf pressure; ~ **atmosférica**
atmospheric o air pressure; **presionar** /1a/
vt to press; (fig) to press, put pressure on
▷ vi: **presionar para** o **por** to press for
**preso, -a** ['preso, a] nm/f prisoner; **tomar** o
**llevar ~ a algn** to arrest sb, take sb prisoner
**prestación** [presta'θjon] nf service;
(subsidio) benefit; **prestaciones** nfpl (Auto)
performance features
**prestado, -a** [pres'taðo, a] adj on loan;
**pedir ~** to borrow
**prestamista** [presta'mista] nmf
moneylender
**préstamo** ['prestamo] nm loan;
**~ hipotecario** mortgage
**prestar** [pres'tar] /1a/ vt to lend, loan;
(atención) to pay; (ayuda) to give; (servicio)
to do, render; (juramento) to take, swear;
**prestarse** vr (ofrecerse) to offer o volunteer
**prestigio** [pres'tixjo] nm prestige;
**prestigioso, -a** adj (honorable) prestigious;
(famoso, renombrado) renowned, famous
**presumido, -a** [presu'miðo, a] adj
conceited
**presumir** [presu'mir] /3a/ vt to presume
▷ vi (darse aires) to be conceited; **presunto,
-a** adj (supuesto) supposed, presumed; (así
llamado) so-called; **presuntuoso, -a** adj
conceited, presumptuous
**presupuesto** [presu'pwesto] nm (Finanzas)
budget; (estimación: de costo) estimate
**pretencioso, -a** [preten'θjoso, a] adj
pretentious
**pretender** [preten'der] /2a/ vt (intentar)
to try to, seek to; (reivindicar) to claim;
(buscar) to seek, try for; (cortejar) to woo,
court; **~ que** to expect that; **pretendiente**
nmf (amante) suitor; (al trono) pretender;
**pretensión** nf (aspiración) aspiration;
(reivindicación) claim; (orgullo) pretension
    No confundir pretender con la palabra
inglesa pretend.
**pretexto** [pre'teksto] nm pretext; (excusa)
excuse
**prevención** [preβen'θjon] nf prevention;
(precaución) precaution

**prevenido, -a** [preβe'niðo, a] adj prepared,
ready; (cauteloso) cautious
**prevenir** [preβe'nir] /3r/ vt (impedir) to
prevent; (predisponer) to prejudice, bias;
(avisar) to warn; (preparar) to prepare,
get ready; **prevenirse** vr to get ready,
prepare; **~se contra** to take precautions
against; **preventivo, -a** adj preventive,
precautionary
**prever** [pre'βer] /2u/ vt to foresee
**previo, -a** ['preβjo, a] adj (anterior)
previous; (preliminar) preliminary ▷ prep:
**~ acuerdo de los otros** subject to the
agreement of the others
**previsión** [preβi'sjon] nf (perspicacia)
foresight; (predicción) forecast; **previsto, -a**
adj anticipated, forecast
**prima** ['prima] nf V **primo**
**primario, -a** [pri'marjo, a] adj primary
**primavera** [prima'βera] nf (temporada)
spring; (período) springtime
**Primer Ministro** [pri'mer-] nm Prime
Minister
**primero, -a** [pri'mero, a] adj first; (fig)
prime ▷ adv first; (más bien) sooner, rather
▷ nf (Auto) first gear; (Ferro) first class;
**de primera** (fam) first-class, first-rate;
**primera plana** front page
**primitivo, -a** [primi'tiβo, a] adj primitive;
(original) original
**primo, -a** ['primo, a] adj (Mat) prime ▷ nm/f
cousin; (fam) fool, idiot ▷ nf (Com) bonus; (de
seguro) premium; **~ hermano** first cousin;
**hacer el ~** to be taken for a ride
**primogénito, -a** [primo'xenito, a] adj
first-born
**primoroso, -a** [primo'roso, a] adj
exquisite, fine
**princesa** [prin'θesa] nf princess
**principal** [prinθi'pal] adj principal, main
▷ nm (jefe) chief, principal
**príncipe** ['prinθipe] nm prince
**principiante** [prinθi'pjante] nmf beginner
**principio** [prin'θipjo] nm (comienzo)
beginning, start; (origen) origin; (base)
rudiment, basic idea; (moral) principle; **a ~s
de** at the beginning of; **desde el ~** from the
first; **en un ~** at first
**pringue** ['pringe] nm (grasa) grease, fat,
dripping
**prioridad** [priori'ðað] nf priority
**prisa** ['prisa] nf (apresuramiento) hurry,
haste; (rapidez) speed; (urgencia) (sense
of) urgency; **a** o **de ~** quickly; **correr ~** to
be urgent; **darse ~** to hurry up; **estar de** o
**tener ~** to be in a hurry
**prisión** [pri'sjon] nf (cárcel) prison; (período
de cárcel) imprisonment; **prisionero, -a**
nm/f prisoner

**prismáticos** [pris'matikos] *nmpl* binoculars

**privado, -a** [pri'βaðo, a] *adj* private

**privar** [pri'βar] /1a/ *vt* to deprive;
**privativo, -a** *adj* exclusive

**privilegiar** [priβile'xjar] /1b/ *vt* to grant a
privilege to; (*favorecer*) to favour

**privilegio** [priβi'lexjo] *nm* privilege;
(*concesión*) concession

**pro** [pro] *nm o f* profit, advantage ▷ *prep*:
**asociación ~ ciegos** association for the
blind ▷ *pref*: **~ soviético/americano** pro-
Soviet/-American; **en ~ de** on behalf of, for;
**los ~s y los contras** the pros and cons

**proa** ['proa] *nf* (*Naut*) bow, prow; **de ~** bow
*cpd*, fore; *V tb* **popa**

**probabilidad** [proβaβili'ðað] *nf*
probability, likelihood; (*oportunidad,
posibilidad*) chance, prospect; **probable** *adj*
probable, likely

**probador** [proβa'ðor] *nm* (*en una tienda*)
fitting room

**probar** [pro'βar] /1l/ *vt* (*demostrar*) to
prove; (*someter a prueba*) to test, try out;
(*ropa*) to try on; (*comida*) to taste ▷ *vi* to try;
**probarse** *vr*: **~se un traje** to try on a suit

**probeta** [pro'βeta] *nf* test tube

**problema** [pro'βlema] *nm* problem

**procedente** [proθe'ðente] *adj* (*razonable*)
reasonable; (*conforme a derecho*) proper,
fitting; **~ de** coming from, originating in

**proceder** [proθe'ðer] /2a/ *vi* (*avanzar*)
to proceed; (*actuar*) to act; (*ser correcto*)
to be right (and proper), be fitting ▷ *nm*
(*comportamiento*) behaviour, conduct; **~ de**
to come from, originate in; **procedimiento**
*nm* procedure; (*proceso*) process; (*método*)
means, method

**procesador** [proθesa'ðor] *nm*: **~ de textos**
word processor

**procesar** [proθe'sar] /1a/ *vt* to try, put on
trial; (*Inform*) to process

**procesión** [proθe'sjon] *nf* procession

**proceso** [pro'θeso] *nm* process; (*Jur*) trial

**proclamar** [prokla'mar] /1a/ *vt* to
proclaim

**procrear** [prokre'ar] /1a/ *vt*, *vi* to procreate

**procurador, a** [prokura'ðor, a] *nm/f*
attorney

**procurar** [proku'rar] /1a/ *vt* (*intentar*) to
try, endeavour; (*conseguir*) to get, obtain;
(*asegurar*) to secure; (*producir*) to produce

**prodigio** [pro'ðixjo] *nm* prodigy; (*milagro*)
wonder, marvel; **prodigioso, -a** *adj*
prodigious, marvellous

**pródigo, -a** ['proðiɣo, a] *adj*: **hijo ~** prodigal
son

**producción** [proðuk'θjon] *nf* production;
(*suma de productos*) output; **~ en serie** mass
production

**producir** [proðu'θir] /3n/ *vt* to produce;
(*generar*) to cause, bring about; **producirse**
*vr* (*cambio*) to come about; (*hacerse*) to be
produced, be made; (*estallar*) to break out;
(*accidente*) to take place; (*problema etc*) to arise

**productividad** [proðuktiβi'ðað] *nf*
productivity; **productivo, -a** *adj*
productive; (*provechoso*) profitable

**producto** [pro'ðukto] *nm* product

**productor, a** [proðuk'tor, a] *adj*
productive, producing ▷ *nm/f* producer

**proeza** [pro'eθa] *nf* exploit, feat

**profano, -a** [pro'fano, a] *adj* profane
▷ *nm/f* layman/woman

**profecía** [profe'θia] *nf* prophecy

**profesión** [profe'sjon] *nf* profession; (*en
formulario*) occupation; **profesional** *adj*
professional

**profesor, a** [profe'sor, a] *nm/f* teacher;
**profesorado** *nm* teaching profession

**profeta** [pro'feta] *nmf* prophet

**prófugo, -a** ['profuɣo, a] *nm/f* fugitive;
(*desertor*) deserter

**profundidad** [profundi'ðað] *nf* depth;
**profundizar** /1f/ (*fig*) *vt* to go into deeply
▷ *vi*: **profundizar en** to go into deeply;
**profundo, -a** *adj* deep; (*misterio, pensador*)
profound

**progenitor** [proxeni'tor] *nm* ancestor;
**progenitores** *nmpl* parents

**programa** [pro'ɣrama] *nm* programme;
(*Inform*) program; **~ de estudios**
curriculum, syllabus; **programación** *nf*
(*Inform*) programming; **programador, a**
*nm/f* (*computer*) programmer; **programar**
/1a/ *vt* (*Inform*) to program

**progresar** [proɣre'sar] /1a/ *vi* to
progress, make progress; **progresista**
*adj*, *nmf* progressive; **progresivo, -a** *adj*
progressive; (*gradual*) gradual; (*continuo*)
continuous; **progreso** *nm* progress

**prohibición** [proiβi'θjon] *nf* prohibition,
ban; **levantar la ~ de** to remove the ban on

**prohibir** [proi'βir] /3a/ *vt* to prohibit, ban,
forbid; **se prohíbe fumar** no smoking;
**"prohibido el paso"** "no entry"

**prójimo** ['proximo] *nm* fellow man

**prólogo** ['proloɣo] *nm* prologue

**prolongar** [prolon'gar] /1h/ *vt* to extend;
(*en el tiempo*) to prolong; (*calle, tubo*) to
make longer, extend

**promedio** [pro'meðjo] *nm* average; (*de
distancia*) middle, mid-point

**promesa** [pro'mesa] *nf* promise

**prometer** [prome'ter] /2a/ *vt* to promise
▷ *vi* to show promise; **prometerse** *vr* (*dos
personas*) to get engaged; **prometido, -a**
*adj* promised; engaged ▷ *nm/f* fiancé/
fiancée

**prominente** [promi'nente] *adj* prominent

**promoción** [promo'θjon] *nf* promotion

**promotor** [promo'tor] *nm* promoter; *(instigador)* instigator

**promover** [promo'βer] /2h/ *vt* to promote; *(causar)* to cause; *(motín)* to instigate, stir up

**promulgar** [promul'ɣar] /1h/ *vt* to promulgate; *(fig)* to proclaim

**pronombre** [pro'nombre] *nm* pronoun

**pronosticar** [pronosti'kar] /1g/ *vt* to predict, foretell, forecast; **pronóstico** *nm* prediction, forecast; **pronóstico del tiempo** weather forecast

**pronto, -a** ['pronto, a] *adj (rápido)* prompt, quick; *(preparado)* ready ▷ *adv* quickly, promptly; *(en seguida)* at once, right away; *(dentro de poco)* soon; *(temprano)* early ▷ *nm*: **de ~** suddenly; **tiene unos ~s muy malos** he gets ratty all of a sudden *(fam)*; **por lo ~** meanwhile, for the present

**pronunciación** [pronunθja'θjon] *nf* pronunciation

**pronunciar** [pronun'θjar] /1b/ *vt* to pronounce; *(discurso)* to make, deliver; **pronunciarse** *vr* to revolt, rebel; *(declararse)* to declare o.s.

**propagación** [propaɣa'θjon] *nf* propagation

**propaganda** [propa'ɣanda] *nf (política)* propaganda; *(comercial)* advertising

**propenso, -a** [pro'penso, a] *adj*: **~ a** prone o inclined to; **ser ~ a hacer algo** to be inclined o have a tendency to do sth

**propicio, -a** [pro'piθjo, a] *adj* favourable, propitious

**propiedad** [propje'ðað] *nf* property; *(posesión)* possession, ownership; **~ particular** private property

**propietario, -a** [propje'tarjo, a] *nm/f* owner, proprietor

**propina** [pro'pina] *nf* tip

**propio, -a** ['propjo, a] *adj* own, of one's own; *(característico)* characteristic, typical; *(conveniente)* proper; *(mismo)* selfsame, very; **el ~ ministro** the minister himself; **¿tienes casa propia?** have you a house of your own?

**proponer** [propo'ner] /2q/ *vt* to propose, put forward; *(problema)* to pose; **proponerse** *vr* to propose, intend

**proporción** [propor'θjon] *nf* proportion; *(Mat)* ratio; **proporciones** *nfpl (fig)* dimensions; size *sg*; **proporcionado, -a** *adj* proportionate; *(regular)* medium, middling; *(justo)* just right; **proporcionar** /1a/ *vt (dar)* to give, supply, provide

**proposición** [proposi'θjon] *nf* proposition; *(propuesta)* proposal

**propósito** [pro'posito] *nm* purpose; *(intento)* aim, intention ▷ *adv*: **a ~** by the way, incidentally; *(a posta)* on purpose, deliberately; **a ~ de** about, with regard to

**propuesto, -a** [pro'pwesto, a] *pp de* **proponer** ▷ *nf* proposal

**propulsar** [propul'sar] /1a/ *vt* to drive, propel; *(fig)* to promote, encourage; **propulsión** *nf* propulsion; **propulsión a chorro** *o* **por reacción** jet propulsion

**prórroga** ['prorroɣa] *nf* extension; *(Jur)* stay; *(Com)* deferment; *(Deporte)* extra time; **prorrogar** /1h/ *vt (período)* to extend; *(decisión)* to defer, postpone

**prosa** ['prosa] *nf* prose

**proseguir** [prose'ɣir] /3d, 3k/ *vt* to continue, carry on ▷ *vi* to continue, go on

**prospecto** [pros'pekto] *nm* prospectus

**prosperar** [prospe'rar] /1a/ *vi* to prosper, thrive, flourish; **prosperidad** *nf* prosperity; *(éxito)* success; **próspero, -a** *adj* prosperous, thriving; *(que tiene éxito)* successful

**prostíbulo** [pros'tiβulo] *nm* brothel

**prostitución** [prostitu'θjon] *nf* prostitution

**prostituir** [prosti'twir] /3g/ *vt* to prostitute; **prostituirse** *vr* to prostitute o.s., become a prostitute

**prostituta** [prosti'tuta] *nf* prostitute

**protagonista** [protaɣo'nista] *nmf* protagonist

**protección** [protek'θjon] *nf* protection

**protector, a** [protek'tor, a] *adj* protective, protecting ▷ *nm/f* protector

**proteger** [prote'xer] /2c/ *vt* to protect; **protegido, -a** *nm/f* protégé/protégée

**proteína** [prote'ina] *nf* protein

**protesta** [pro'testa] *nf* protest; *(declaración)* protestation

**protestante** [protes'tante] *adj* Protestant

**protestar** [protes'tar] /1a/ *vt* to protest, declare ▷ *vi* to protest

**protocolo** [proto'kolo] *nm* protocol

**prototipo** [proto'tipo] *nm* prototype

**provecho** [pro'βetʃo] *nm* advantage, benefit; *(Finanzas)* profit; **¡buen ~!** bon appétit!; **en ~ de** to the benefit of; **sacar ~ de** to benefit from, profit by

**provenir** [proβe'nir] /3r/ *vi*: **~ de** to come from

**proverbio** [pro'βerβjo] *nm* proverb

**providencia** [proβi'ðenθja] *nf* providence

**provincia** [pro'βinθja] *nf* province

**provisión** [proβi'sjon] *nf* provision; *(abastecimiento)* provision, supply; *(medida)* measure, step

**provisional** [proβisjo'nal] *adj* provisional

**provocar** [proβo'kar] /1g/ *vt* to provoke; *(alentar)* to tempt, invite; *(causar)* to bring about, lead to; *(promover)* to promote;

(*estimular*) to rouse, stimulate; (LAM): **¿te provoca un café?** would you like a coffee?; **provocativo, -a** *adj* provocative

**proxeneta** [prokse'neta] *nmf* (*de prostitutas*) pimp/procuress

**próximamente** [proksima'mente] *adv* shortly, soon

**proximidad** [proksimi'ðað] *nf* closeness, proximity; **próximo, -a** *adj* near, close; (*vecino*) neighbouring; (*el que viene*) next

**proyectar** [projek'tar] /1a/ *vt* (*objeto*) to hurl, throw; (*luz*) to cast, shed; (*Cine*) to screen, show; (*planear*) to plan

**proyectil** [projek'til] *nm* projectile, missile

**proyecto** [pro'jekto] *nm* plan; (*estimación de costo*) detailed estimate

**proyector** [projek'tor] *nm* (*Cine*) projector

**prudencia** [pru'ðenθja] *nf* (*sabiduría*) wisdom; (*cautela*) care; **prudente** *adj* sensible, wise; (*cauteloso*) careful

**prueba** ['prweβa] *vb* V **probar** ▷ *nf* proof; (*ensayo*) test, trial; (*saboreo*) testing, sampling; (*de ropa*) fitting; **a ~** on trial; **a ~ de** proof against; **a ~ de agua/fuego** waterproof/fireproof; **someter a ~** to put to the test

**psico...** [siko] *pref* psycho...; **psicología** *nf* psychology; **psicológico, -a** *adj* psychological; **psicólogo, -a** *nm/f* psychologist; **psicópata** *nmf* psychopath; **psicosis** *nf inv* psychosis

**psiquiatra** [si'kjatra] *nmf* psychiatrist; **psiquiátrico, -a** *adj* psychiatric

**PSOE** [pe'soe] *nm abr* = **Partido Socialista Obrero Español**

**púa** *nf* (*Bot, Zool*) prickle, spine; (*para guitarra*) plectrum; **alambre de ~s** barbed wire

**pubertad** [puβer'tað] *nf* puberty

**publicación** [puβlika'θjon] *nf* publication

**publicar** [puβli'kar] /1g/ *vt* (*editar*) to publish; (*hacer público*) to publicize; (*divulgar*) to make public, divulge

**publicidad** [puβliθi'ðað] *nf* publicity; (*Com*) advertising; **publicitario, -a** *adj* publicity *cpd*; advertising *cpd*

**público, -a** ['puβliko, a] *adj* public ▷ *nm* public; (*Teat etc*) audience

**puchero** [pu'tʃero] *nm* (*Culin: olla*) cooking pot; (: *guiso*) stew; **hacer ~s** to pout

**pucho** ['putʃo] (LAM *fam*) *nm* cigarette, fag (BRIT)

**pude** *etc vb* V **poder**

**pudiente** [pu'ðjente] *adj* (*opulento*) wealthy

**pudiera** *etc vb* V **poder**

**pudor** [pu'ðor] *nm* modesty

**pudrir** [pu'ðrir] /3a/ *vt* to rot; **pudrirse** *vr* to rot, decay

**pueblo** ['pweβlo] *nm* people; (*nación*) nation; (*aldea*) village

**puedo** *etc* ['pweðo] *vb* V **poder**

**puente** ['pwente] *nm* bridge; **~ aéreo** shuttle service; **~ colgante** suspension bridge; **~ levadizo** drawbridge; **hacer ~** (*fam*) to take a long weekend

- **HACER PUENTE**
-
- When a public holiday in Spain falls on
- a Tuesday or Thursday it is common
- practice for employers to make the
- Monday or Friday a holiday as well and
- to give everyone a four-day weekend.
- This is known as *hacer puente*. When a
- named public holiday such as the *Día de la
- Constitución* falls on a Tuesday or Thursday,
- people refer to the whole holiday period
- as e.g. the *puente de la Constitución*.

**puerco, -a** ['pwerko, a] *adj* (*sucio*) dirty, filthy; (*obsceno*) disgusting ▷ *nm/f* pig/sow; **~ espín** porcupine

**pueril** [pwe'ril] *adj* childish

**puerro** ['pwerro] *nm* leek

**puerta** ['pwerta] *nf* door; (*de jardín*) gate; (*portal*) doorway; (*fig*) gateway; (*gol*) goal; **a la ~** at the door; **a ~ cerrada** behind closed doors; **~ corredera/giratoria** sliding/swing o revolving door

**puerto** ['pwerto] *nm* port; (*paso*) pass; (*fig*) haven, refuge

**Puerto Rico** [pwerto'riko] *nm* Puerto Rico; **puertorriqueño, -a** *adj, nm/f* Puerto Rican

**pues** [pwes] *adv* (*entonces*) then; (*¡entonces!*) well, well then; (*así que*) so ▷ *conj* (*porque*) since; **¡~ sí!** yes!, certainly!

**puesto, -a** ['pwesto, a] *pp de* **poner** ▷ *adj* dressed ▷ *nm* (*lugar, posición*) place; (*trabajo*) post, job; (*Com*) stall ▷ *conj*: **~ que** since, as ▷ *nf* (*apuesta*) bet, stake; **tener algo ~** to have sth on, be wearing sth; **~ de mercado** market stall; **~ de policía** police station; **~ de socorro** first aid post; **puesta al día** updating; **puesta en marcha** starting; **puesta a punto** fine tuning; **puesta del sol** sunset

**púgil** ['puxil] *nm* boxer

**pulga** ['pulɣa] *nf* flea

**pulgada** [pul'ɣaða] *nf* inch

**pulgar** [pul'ɣar] *nm* thumb

**pulir** [pu'lir] /3a/ *vt* to polish; (*alisar*) to smooth; (*fig*) to polish up, touch up

**pulmón** [pul'mon] *nm* lung; **pulmonía** *nf* pneumonia

**pulpa** ['pulpa] *nf* pulp; (*de fruta*) flesh, soft part

**pulpería** [pulpe'ria] *nf* (LAM) small grocery store

**púlpito** ['pulpito] *nm* pulpit

**pulpo** ['pulpo] nm octopus
**pulque** ['pulke] nm pulque

● **PULQUE**
●
● *Pulque* is a thick, white, alcoholic drink
● which is very popular in Mexico. In ancient
● times it was considered sacred by the
● Aztecs. It is produced by fermenting the
● juice of the *maguey*, a Mexican cactus
● similar to the agave. It can be drunk by
● itself or mixed with fruit or vegetable
● juice.

**pulsación** [pulsa'θjon] nf beat;
**pulsaciones** nfpl pulse rate
**pulsar** [pul'sar] /1a/ vt (tecla) to touch, tap;
(Mus) to play; (botón) to press, push ▷ vi to
pulsate; (latir) to beat, throb
**pulsera** [pul'sera] nf bracelet
**pulso** ['pulso] nm (Med) pulse; (fuerza)
strength; (firmeza) steadiness, steady hand
**pulverizador** [pulβeriθa'ðor] nm spray,
spray gun
**pulverizar** [pulβeri'θar] /1f/ vt to
pulverize; (líquido) to spray
**puna** ['puna] nf (LAM) mountain sickness
**punta** ['punta] nf point, tip; (extremidad)
end; (fig) touch, trace; **horas ~s** peak hours,
rush hours; **sacar ~ a** to sharpen
**puntada** [pun'taða] nf (Costura) stitch
**puntal** [pun'tal] nm prop, support
**puntapié** [punta'pje] nm kick
**puntería** [punte'ria] nf (de arma) aim,
aiming; (destreza) marksmanship
**puntero, -a** [pun'tero, a] adj leading ▷ nm
(señal, Inform) pointer
**puntiagudo, -a** [puntja'ɣuðo, a] adj
sharp, pointed
**puntilla** [pun'tiʎa] nf (Costura) lace edging;
**(andar) de ~s** (to walk) on tiptoe
**punto** ['punto] nm (gen) point; (señal
diminuta) spot, dot; (lugar) spot, place;
(momento) point, moment; (Costura) stitch;
**a ~** ready; **estar a ~ de** to be on the point of
o about to; **en ~** on the dot; **hasta cierto ~**
to some extent; **hacer ~** to knit; **~ de vista**
point of view, viewpoint; **~ muerto** dead
centre; (Auto) neutral (gear); **~ final** full
stop; **dos ~s** colon; **~ y coma** semicolon;
**~ acápite** (LAM) full stop, new paragraph;
**~ de interrogación** question mark
**puntocom** [punto'kom] nf inv, adj inv dotcom
**puntuación** [puntwa'θjon] nf
punctuation; (puntos: en examen) mark(s) pl;
(: Deporte) score
**puntual** [pun'twal] adj (a tiempo) punctual;
(cálculo) exact, accurate; **puntualidad** nf
punctuality; exactness, accuracy

**puntuar** [pun'twar] /1e/ vi (Deporte) to
score, count
**punzante** [pun'θante] adj (dolor) shooting,
sharp; (herramienta) sharp
**puñado** [pu'ɲaðo] nm handful (tb fig)
**puñal** [pu'ɲal] nm dagger; **puñalada** nf
stab
**puñetazo** [puɲe'taθo] nm punch
**puño** ['puɲo] nm (Anat) fist; (cantidad)
fistful, handful; (Costura) cuff; (de
herramienta) handle
**pupila** [pu'pila] nf pupil
**pupitre** [pu'pitre] nm desk
**puré** [pu're] nm purée; (sopa) (thick) soup;
**~ de patatas** (ESP), **~ de papas** (LAM)
mashed potatoes
**purga** ['purɣa] nf purge; **purgante** adj, nm
purgative
**purgatorio** [purɣa'torjo] nm purgatory
**purificar** [purifi'kar] /1g/ vt to purify;
(refinar) to refine
**puritano, -a** [puri'tano, a] adj (actitud)
puritanical; (iglesia, tradición) puritan
▷ nm/f puritan
**puro, -a** ['puro, a] adj pure; (verdad) simple,
plain ▷ nm cigar
**púrpura** ['purpura] nf purple
**pus** [pus] nm pus
**puse** etc ['puse] vb V **poner**
**pusiera** etc vb V **poder**
**puta** ['puta] nf whore, prostitute
**putrefacción** [putrefak'θjon] nf rotting,
putrefaction
**PVP** abr (ESP: = Precio Venta al Público) ≈ RRP
**PYME** ['pime] nf abr (= Pequeña y Mediana
Empresa) SME

# q

▷ nm/f bankrupt ▷ nm (Mat) fraction

**quebrantar** [keβran'tar] /1a/ vt (*infringir*) to violate, transgress

**quebrar** [ke'βrar] /1j/ vt to break, smash ▷ vi to go bankrupt

**quedar** [ke'ðar] /1a/ vi to stay, remain; (*encontrarse*) to be; (*restar*) to remain, be left; **quedarse** vr to remain, stay (behind); ~ **en** (*acordar*) to agree on/to; ~ **por hacer** to be still to be done; ~ **ciego** to be left blind; **no te queda bien ese vestido** that dress doesn't suit you; **quedamos a las seis** we agreed to meet at six; ~**se (con) algo** to keep sth; ~**se con algn** (*fam*) to swindle sb; ~**se en nada** to come to nothing o nought

**quedo, -a** ['keðo, a] adj still ▷ adv softly, gently

**quehacer** [kea'θer] nm task, job; ~**es (domésticos)** household chores

**queja** ['kexa] nf complaint; **quejarse** /1a/ vr (*enfermo*) to moan, groan; (*protestar*) to complain; **quejarse de que ...** to complain (about the fact) that ...; **quejido** nm moan

**quemado, -a** [ke'maðo, a] adj burnt

**quemadura** [kema'ðura] nf burn, scald

**quemar** [ke'mar] /1a/ vt to burn; (*fig*: *malgastar*) to burn up, squander ▷ vi to be burning hot; **quemarse** vr (*consumirse*) to burn (up); (*del sol*) to get sunburnt

**quemarropa** [kema'rropa]: **a** ~ adv point-blank

**quepo** etc ['kepo] vb V **caber**

**querella** [ke'reʎa] nf (*Jur*) charge; (*disputa*) dispute

---

○ **PALABRA CLAVE**

**que** [ke] conj **1** (*con oración subordinada*: *muchas veces no se traduce*) that; **dijo que vendría** he said (that) he would come; **espero que lo encuentres** I hope (that) you find it; V tb **el**

**2** (*en oración independiente*): **¡que entre!** send him in; **¡que aproveche!** enjoy your meal!; **¡que se mejore tu padre!** I hope your father gets better

**3** (*enfático*): **¿me quieres? — ¡que sí!** do you love me? — of course!

**4** (*consecutivo: muchas veces no se traduce*) that; **es tan grande que no lo puedo levantar** it's so big (that) I can't lift it

**5** (*comparaciones*) than; **yo que tú/él** if I were you/him; V tb **más**; **menos**

**6** (*valor disyuntivo*): **que le guste o no** whether he likes it or not; **que venga o que no venga** whether he comes or not

**7** (*porque*): **no puedo, que tengo que quedarme en casa** I can't, I've got to stay in

▶ pron **1** (*cosa*) that, which; (: + *prep*) which; **el sombrero que te compraste** the hat (that o which) you bought; **la cama en que dormí** the bed (that o which) I slept in

**2** (*persona*: *suj*) that, who; (: *objeto*) that, whom; **el amigo que me acompañó al museo** the friend that o who went to the museum with me; **la chica que invité** the girl (that o whom) I invited

---

**qué** [ke] adj what?, which? ▷ pron what?; **¡~ divertido/asco!** how funny/revolting!; **¿~ edad tienes?** how old are you?; **¿de ~ me hablas?** what are you saying to me?; **¿~ tal?** how are you?, how are things?; **¿~ hay (de nuevo)?** what's new?

**quebrado, -a** [ke'βraðo, a] adj (*roto*) broken

---

○ **PALABRA CLAVE**

**querer** [ke'rer] /2t/ vt **1** (*desear*) to want; **quiero más dinero** I want more money; **quisiera** o **querría un té** I'd like a tea; **sin querer** unintentionally; **quiero ayudar/que vayas** I want to help/you to go

**2** (*preguntas: para pedir u ofrecer algo*): **¿quiere abrir la ventana?** could you open the window?; **¿quieres echarme una mano?** can you give me a hand?

**3** (*amar*) to love; **te quiero** I love you; **no estoy enamorado, pero la quiero mucho** I'm not in love, but I'm very fond of her

---

**querido, -a** [ke'riðo, a] adj dear ▷ nm/f darling; (*amante*) lover

**queso** ['keso] nm cheese; ~ **rallado** grated cheese; ~ **crema** (*LAM*), ~ **de untar** (*ESP*) cream cheese; ~ **manchego** sheep's milk cheese made in La Mancha; **dárselas con ~ a algn** (*fam*) to take sb in

**quicio** ['kiθjo] nm hinge; **sacar a algn de ~** to drive sb up the wall

**quiebra** ['kjeβra] *nf* break, split; (*Com*) bankruptcy; (*Econ*) slump

**quiebro** *etc* ['kjeβro] *nm* (*del cuerpo*) swerve

**quien** [kjen] *pron relativo* (*suj*) who; **hay ~ piensa que** there are those who think that; **no hay ~ lo haga** no-one will do it

**quién** [kjen] *pron interrogativo* who; (*complemento*) whom; **¿~ es?** who's there?

**quienquiera** [kjen'kjera] (*pl* **quienesquiera**) *pron* whoever

**quiero** *etc vb* V **querer**

**quieto, -a** ['kjeto, a] *adj* still; (*carácter*) placid; **quietud** *nf* stillness

  No confundir *quieto* con la palabra inglesa *quiet*.

**quilate** [ki'late] *nm* carat

**químico, -a** ['kimiko, a] *adj* chemical ▷ *nm/f* chemist ▷ *nf* chemistry

**quincalla** [kin'kaʎa] *nf* hardware, ironmongery (*BRIT*)

**quince** ['kinθe] *num* fifteen; **~ días** a fortnight; **quinceañero, -a** *nm/f* teenager; **quincena** *nf* fortnight; (*pago*) fortnightly pay; **quincenal** *adj* fortnightly

**quiniela** [ki'njela] *nf* football pools *pl*; **quinielas** *nfpl* pools coupon *sg*

**quinientos, -as** [ki'njentos, as] *num* five hundred

**quinto, -a** ['kinto, a] *adj* fifth ▷ *nf* country house; (*Mil*) call-up, draft

**quiosco** ['kjosko] *nm* (*de música*) bandstand; (*de periódicos*) news stand (*also selling sweets, cigarettes etc*)

**quirófano** [ki'rofano] *nm* operating theatre

**quirúrgico, -a** [ki'rurxiko, a] *adj* surgical

**quise** *etc* ['kise] *vb* V **querer**

**quisiera** *etc vb* V **querer**

**quisquilloso** [kiski'ʎoso, a] *adj* (*susceptible*) touchy; (*meticuloso*) pernickety

**quiste** ['kiste] *nm* cyst

**quitaesmalte** [kitaes'malte] *nm* nail polish remover

**quitamanchas** [kita'mantʃas] *nm inv* stain remover

**quitanieves** [kita'njeβes] *nm inv* snowplough (*BRIT*), snowplow (*US*)

**quitar** [ki'tar] /1a/ *vt* to remove, take away; (*ropa*) to take off; (*dolor*) to relieve ▷ *vi*: **¡quita de ahí!** get away!; **quitarse** *vr* to withdraw; (*ropa*) to take off; **se quitó el sombrero** he took off his hat

**Quito** ['kito] *n* Quito

**quizá(s)** [ki'θa(s)] *adv* perhaps, maybe

# r

**rábano** ['raβano] *nm* radish; **me importa un ~** I don't give a damn

**rabia** ['raβja] *nf* (*Med*) rabies *sg*; (*ira*) fury, rage; **rabiar** /1b/ *vi* to have rabies; to rage, be furious; **rabiar por algo** to long for sth

**rabieta** [ra'βjeta] *nf* tantrum, fit of temper

**rabino** [ra'βino] *nm* rabbi

**rabioso, -a** [ra'βjoso, a] *adj* rabid; (*fig*) furious

**rabo** ['raβo] *nm* tail

**racha** ['ratʃa] *nf* gust of wind; **buena/ mala ~** spell of good/bad luck

**racial** [ra'θjal] *adj* racial, race *cpd*

**racimo** [ra'θimo] *nm* bunch

**ración** [ra'θjon] *nf* portion; **raciones** *nfpl* rations

**racional** [raθjo'nal] *adj* (*razonable*) reasonable; (*lógico*) rational

**racionar** [raθjo'nar] /1a/ *vt* to ration (out)

**racismo** [ra'θismo] *nm* racism; **racista** *adj*, *nmf* racist

**radar** [ra'ðar] *nm* radar

**radiador** [raðja'ðor] *nm* radiator

**radiante** [ra'ðjante] *adj* radiant

**radical** [raði'kal] *adj*, *nmf* radical

**radicar** [raði'kar] /1g/ *vi*: **~ en** (*dificultad, problema*) to lie in; (*solución*) to consist in

**radio** ['raðjo] *nf* radio; (*aparato*) radio (set) ▷ *nm* (*Mat*) radius; (*Química*) radium; **radioactividad** *nf* radioactivity; **radioactivo, -a** *adj* radioactive; **radiografía** *nf* X-ray; **radioterapia** *nf* radiotherapy; **radioyente** *nmf* listener

**ráfaga** ['rafaɣa] *nf* gust; (*de luz*) flash; (*de tiros*) burst

**raíz** [ra'iθ] *nf* root; **~ cuadrada** square root; **a ~ de** as a result of

**raja** ['raxa] *nf* (*de melón etc*) slice; (*grieta*) crack; **rajar** /1a/ *vt* to split; (*fam*) to slash;

**rajarse** vr to split, crack; **rajarse de** to back out of

**rajatabla** [raxa'taβla]: **a ~** adv (estrictamente) strictly, to the letter

**rallador** [raʎa'ðor] nm grater

**rallar** [ra'ʎar] /1a/ vt to grate

**rama** ['rama] nf branch; **ramaje** nm branches pl, foliage; **ramal** nm (de cuerda) strand; (Ferro) branch line; (Auto) branch (road)

**rambla** ['rambla] nf (avenida) avenue

**ramo** ['ramo] nm branch; (sección) department, section

**rampa** ['rampa] nf ramp; **~ de acceso** entrance ramp

**rana** ['rana] nf frog; **salto de ~** leapfrog

**ranchero** [ran'tʃero] nm (LAM) rancher; (pequeño propietario) smallholder

**rancho** ['rantʃo] nm (grande) ranch; (pequeño) small farm

**rancio, -a** ['ranθjo, a] adj (comestibles) rancid; (vino) aged, mellow; (fig) ancient

**rango** ['rango] nm rank; (prestigio) standing

**ranura** [ra'nura] nf groove; (de teléfono etc) slot

**rapar** [ra'par] /1a/ vt to shave; (los cabellos) to crop

**rapaz** [ra'paθ] adj (Zool) predatory ⊳ nm young boy

**rape** ['rape] nm (pez) monkfish; **al ~** cropped

**rapé** [ra'pe] nm snuff

**rapidez** [rapi'ðeθ] nf speed, rapidity; **rápido, -a** adj fast, quick ⊳ adv quickly ⊳ nm (Ferro) express; **rápidos** nmpl rapids

**rapiña** [ra'piɲa] nf robbery; **ave de ~** bird of prey

**raptar** [rap'tar] /1a/ vt to kidnap; **rapto** nm kidnapping; (impulso) sudden impulse; (éxtasis) ecstasy, rapture

**raqueta** [ra'keta] nf racket

**raquítico, -a** [ra'kitiko, a] adj stunted; (fig) poor, inadequate

**rareza** [ra'reθa] nf rarity; (fig) eccentricity

**raro, -a** ['raro, a] adj (poco común) rare; (extraño) odd, strange; (excepcional) remarkable

**ras** [ras] nm: **a ~ de** level with; **a ~ de tierra** at ground level

**rasar** [ra'sar] /1a/ vt to level

**rascacielos** [raska'θjelos] nm inv skyscraper

**rascar** [ras'kar] /1g/ vt (con las uñas etc) to scratch; (raspar) to scrape; **rascarse** vr to scratch (o.s.)

**rasgar** [ras'yar] /1h/ vt to tear, rip (up)

**rasgo** ['rasyo] nm (con pluma) stroke; **rasgos** nmpl features, characteristics; **a grandes ~s** in outline, broadly

**rasguño** [ras'yuɲo] nm scratch

**raso, -a** ['raso, a] adj (liso) flat, level; (a baja altura) very low ⊳ nm satin; **cielo ~** clear sky

**raspadura** [raspa'ðura] nf (acto) scrape, scraping; (marca) scratch; **raspaduras** nfpl (de papel etc) scrapings

**raspar** [ras'par] /1a/ vt to scrape; (arañar) to scratch; (limar) to file

**rastra** ['rastra] nf (Agr) rake; **a ~s** by dragging; (fig) unwillingly

**rastrear** [rastre'ar] /1a/ vt (seguir) to track

**rastrero, -a** [ras'trero, a] adj (Bot, Zool) creeping; (fig) despicable, mean

**rastrillo** [ras'triʎo] nm rake

**rastro** ['rastro] nm (Agr) rake; (pista) track, trail; (vestigio) trace; **el R~** the Madrid flea market

**rasurado** [rasu'raðo] nm (LAM) shaving; **rasurador** nm, (LAM) **rasuradora** [rasura'ðora] nf electric shaver o razor; **rasurar** /1a/ vt (LAM) to shave; **rasurarse** vr to shave

**rata** ['rata] nf rat

**ratear** [rate'ar] /1a/ vt (robar) to steal

**ratero, -a** [ra'tero, a] adj light-fingered ⊳ nm/f (carterista) pickpocket; (ladrón) petty thief

**rato** ['rato] nm while, short time; **a ~s** from time to time; **al poco ~** shortly after, soon afterwards; **~s libres** o **de ocio** free o leisure time sg; **hay para ~** there's still a long way to go

**ratón** [ra'ton] nm mouse; **ratonera** nf mousetrap

**raudal** [rau'ðal] nm torrent; **a ~es** in abundance

**raya** ['raja] nf line; (marca) scratch; (en tela) stripe; (puntuación) dash; (de pelo) parting; (límite) boundary; (pez) ray; **a ~s** striped; **pasarse de la ~** to overstep the mark; **tener a ~** to keep in check; **rayar** /1a/ vt to line; to scratch; (subrayar) to underline ⊳ vi: **rayar en** o **con** to border on

**rayo** ['rajo] nm (del sol) ray, beam; (de luz) shaft; (en una tormenta) (flash of) lightning; **~s X** X-rays

**raza** ['raθa] nf race; **~ humana** human race

**razón** [ra'θon] nf reason; (justicia) right, justice; (razonamiento) reasoning; (motivo) reason, motive; (Mat) ratio; **a ~ de 10 cada día** at the rate of 10 a day; **en ~ de** with regard to; **dar ~ a algn** to agree that sb is right; **tener/no tener ~** to be right/wrong; **~ directa/inversa** direct/inverse proportion; **~ de ser** raison d'être; **razonable** adj reasonable; (justo, moderado) fair; **razonamiento** nm (juicio) judgement; (argumento) reasoning; **razonar** /1a/ vt, vi to reason, argue

**re** [re] nm (Mus) D

**reacción** [reak'θjon] nf reaction; **avión a ~** jet plane; **~ en cadena** chain reaction; **reaccionar** /1a/ vi to react

**reacio, -a** [re'aθjo, a] adj stubborn

**reactivar** [reakti'βar] /1a/ vt to reactivate

**reactor** [reak'tor] nm reactor

**real** [re'al] adj real; (del rey, fig) royal

**realidad** [reali'ðað] nf reality; (verdad) truth

**realista** [rea'lista] nmf realist

**realización** [realiθa'θjon] nf fulfilment

**realizador, a** [realiθa'ðor, a] nm/f film-maker; (TV etc) producer

**realizar** [reali'θar] /1f/ vt (objetivo) to achieve; (plan) to carry out; (viaje) to make, undertake; **realizarse** vr to come about, come true

**realmente** [real'mente] adv really, actually

**realzar** [real'θar] /1f/ vt to enhance; (acentuar) to highlight

**reanimar** [reani'mar] /1a/ vt to revive; (alentar) to encourage; **reanimarse** vr to revive

**reanudar** [reanu'ðar] /1a/ vt (renovar) to renew; (historia, viaje) to resume

**reaparición** [reapari'θjon] nf reappearance

**rearme** [re'arme] nm rearmament

**rebaja** [re'βaxa] nf reduction, lowering; (Com) discount; **rebajas** nfpl (Com) sale; **"grandes ~s"** "big reductions", "sale"; **rebajar** /1a/ vt (bajar) to lower; (reducir) to reduce; (disminuir) to lessen; (humillar) to humble

**rebanada** [reβa'naða] nf slice

**rebañar** [reβa'ɲar] /1a/ vt (comida) to scrape up; (plato) to scrape clean

**rebaño** [re'βaɲo] nm herd; (de ovejas) flock

**rebatir** [reβa'tir] /3a/ vt to refute

**rebeca** [re'βeka] nf cardigan

**rebelarse** [reβe'larse] /1a/ vr to rebel, revolt

**rebelde** [re'βelde] adj rebellious; (niño) unruly ▷ nmf rebel; **rebeldía** nf rebelliousness; (desobediencia) disobedience

**rebelión** [reβe'ljon] nf rebellion

**reblandecer** [reβlande'θer] /2d/ vt to soften

**rebobinar** [reβoβi'nar] /1a/ vt to rewind

**rebosante** [reβo'sante] adj: **~ de** (fig) brimming o overflowing with

**rebosar** [reβo'sar] /1a/ vi to overflow; (abundar) to abound, be plentiful

**rebotar** [reβo'tar] /1a/ vt to bounce; (rechazar) to repel ▷ vi (pelota) to bounce; (bala) to ricochet; **rebote** nm rebound; **de rebote** on the rebound

**rebozado, -a** [reβo'θaðo, a] adj fried in batter o breadcrumbs o flour

**rebozar** [reβo'θar] /1f/ vt to wrap up; (Culin) to fry in batter etc

**rebuscado, -a** [reβus'kaðo, a] adj (amanerado) affected; (palabra) recherché; (idea) far-fetched

**rebuscar** [reβus'kar] /1g/ vi (en habitación) to search high and low

**recado** [re'kaðo] nm message; (encargo) errand; **dejar/tomar un ~** (Telec) to leave/take a message

**recaer** [reka'er] /2n/ vi to relapse; **~ en** to fall to o on; (criminal etc) to fall back into, relapse into; **recaída** nf relapse

**recalcar** [rekal'kar] /1g/ vt (fig) to stress, emphasize

**recalentar** [rekalen'tar] /1j/ vt (comida) to warm up, reheat; (demasiado) to overheat

**recámara** [re'kamara] nf (LAM) bedroom

**recambio** [re'kambjo] nm spare; (de pluma) refill

**recapacitar** [rekapaθi'tar] /1a/ vi to reflect

**recargado, -a** [rekar'ɣaðo, a] adj overloaded; (exagerado) over-elaborate

**recargar** [rekar'ɣar] /1h/ vt to overload; (batería) to recharge; (tarjeta de móvil) to top up; **recargo** nm surcharge; (aumento) increase

**recatado, -a** [reka'taðo, a] adj (modesto) modest, demure; (prudente) cautious

**recaudación** [rekauða'θjon] nf (acción) collection; (cantidad) takings pl; (en deporte) gate; **recaudador, a** nmf tax collector

**recelar** [reθe'lar] /1a/ vt: **~ que** (sospechar) to suspect that; (temer) to fear that ▷ vi: **~(se) de** to distrust; **recelo** nm distrust, suspicion

**recepción** [reθep'θjon] nf reception; **recepcionista** nmf receptionist

**receptor, a** [reθep'tor, a] nm/f recipient ▷ nm (Telec) receiver

**recesión** [reθe'sjon] nf (Com) recession

**receta** [re'θeta] nf (Culin) recipe; (Med) prescription

> No confundir *receta* con la palabra inglesa *receipt*.

**rechazar** [retʃa'θar] /1f/ vt to repel; (idea) to reject; (oferta) to turn down

**rechazo** [re'tʃaθo] nm (de propuesta, tb Med: de un órgano) rejection

**rechinar** [retʃi'nar] /1a/ vi to creak; (dientes) to grind

**rechistar** [retʃis'tar] /1a/ vi: **sin ~** without complaint

**rechoncho, -a** [re'tʃontʃo, a] adj (fam) thickset (BRIT), heavy-set (US)

**rechupete** [retʃu'pete]: **de ~** adj (comida) delicious

**recibidor** [reθiβi'ðor] nm entrance hall

**recibimiento** [reθiβi'mjento] nm
reception, welcome
**recibir** [reθi'βir] /3a/ vt to receive; (dar la
bienvenida) to welcome ▷ vi to entertain;
**recibo** nm receipt
**reciclable** [reθi'klaβle] adj recyclable
**reciclar** [reθi'klar] /1a/ vt to recycle
**recién** [re'θjen] adv recently, newly;
**~ casado** newly-wed; **el ~ llegado** the
newcomer; **el ~ nacido** the newborn child
**reciente** [re'θjente] adj recent; (fresco) fresh
**recinto** [re'θinto] nm enclosure; (área)
area, place
**recio, -a** ['reθjo, a] adj strong, tough; (voz)
loud ▷ adv hard; loud(ly)
**recipiente** [reθi'pjente] nm receptacle
**recíproco, -a** [re'θiproco, a] adj reciprocal
**recital** [reθi'tal] nm (Mus) recital; (Lit)
reading
**recitar** [reθi'tar] /1a/ vt to recite
**reclamación** [reklama'θjon] nf claim,
demand; (queja) complaint; **libro de
reclamaciones** complaints book
**reclamar** [rekla'mar] /1a/ vt to claim,
demand ▷ vi: **~ contra** to complain about;
**reclamo** nm (anuncio) advertisement;
(tentación) attraction
**reclinar** [rekli'nar] /1a/ vt to recline, lean;
**reclinarse** vr to lean back
**reclusión** [reklu'sjon] nf (prisión) prison;
(refugio) seclusion
**recluta** [re'kluta] nmf recruit ▷ nf
recruitment; **reclutamiento** nm
recruitment; **reclutar** /1a/ vt (datos) to
collect; (dinero) to collect up
**recobrar** [reko'βrar] /1a/ vt (recuperar) to
recover; (rescatar) to get back; **recobrarse**
vr to recover
**recodo** [re'koðo] nm (de río, camino) bend
**recogedor, a** [rekoxe'ðor, a] nm dustpan
▷ nm/f picker, harvester
**recoger** [reko'xer] /2c/ vt to collect; (Agr)
to harvest; (levantar) to pick up; (juntar) to
gather; (pasar a buscar) to come for, get; (dar
asilo) to give shelter to; (faldas) to gather
up; (pelo) to put up; **recogerse** vr (retirarse)
to retire; **recogido, -a** adj (lugar) quiet,
secluded; (pequeño) small ▷ nf (Correos)
collection; (Agr) harvest
**recolección** [rekolek'θjon] nf (Agr)
harvesting; (colecta) collection
**recomendación** [rekomenda'θjon] nf
(sugerencia) suggestion, recommendation;
(referencia) reference
**recomendar** [rekomen'dar] /1j/ vt to
suggest, recommend; (confiar) to entrust
**recompensa** [rekom'pensa] nf reward,
recompense; **recompensar** /1a/ vt to
reward, recompense

**reconciliación** [rekonθilja'θjon] nf
reconciliation
**reconciliar** [rekonθi'ljar] /1b/ vt to
reconcile; **reconciliarse** vr to become
reconciled
**recóndito, -a** [re'kondito, a] adj (lugar)
hidden, secret
**reconocer** [rekono'θer] /2d/ vt to
recognize; (registrar) to search; (Med) to
examine; **reconocido, -a** adj recognized;
(agradecido) grateful; **reconocimiento** nm
recognition; (registro) search; (inspección)
examination; (gratitud) gratitude;
(confesión) admission
**reconquista** [rekon'kista] nf reconquest;
**la R~** the Reconquest (of Spain)
**reconstituyente** [rekonstitu'jente] nm
tonic
**reconstruir** [rekonstru'ir] /3g/ vt to
reconstruct
**reconversión** [recomber'sjon] nf
restructuring, reorganization; (tb:
**~ industrial**) rationalization
**recopilación** [rekopila'θjon] nf (resumen)
summary; (compilación) compilation;
**recopilar** /1a/ vt to compile
**récord** ['rekorð] nm record
**recordar** [rekor'ðar] /1l/ vt (acordarse de) to
remember; (recordar a otro) to remind ▷ vi
to remember

> No confundir recordar con la palabra
> inglesa record.

**recorrer** [reko'rrer] /2a/ vt (país) to
cross, travel through; (distancia) to cover;
(registrar) to search; (repasar) to look over;
**recorrido** nm run, journey; **tren de
largo recorrido** main-line o inter-city
(BRIT) train
**recortar** [rekor'tar] /1a/ vt to cut out;
**recorte** nm (acción, de prensa) cutting;
(de telas, chapas) trimming; **recorte
presupuestario** budget cut
**recostar** [rekos'tar] /1l/ vt to lean;
**recostarse** vr to lie down
**recoveco** [reko'βeko] nm (de camino, río etc)
bend; (en casa) cubbyhole
**recreación** [rekrea'θjon] nf recreation
**recrear** [rekre'ar] /1a/ vt (entretener) to
entertain; (volver a crear) to recreate;
**recreativo, -a** adj recreational; **recreo** nm
recreation; (Escol) break, playtime
**recriminar** [rekrimi'nar] /1a/ vt to
reproach ▷ vi to recriminate; **recriminarse**
vr to reproach each other
**recrudecer** [rekruðe'θer] /2d/ vt, vi to
worsen; **recrudecerse** vr to worsen
**recta** ['rekta] nf V **recto**
**rectángulo, -a** [rek'tangulo, a] adj
rectangular ▷ nm rectangle

**rectificar** [rektifi'kar] /1g/ vt to rectify; (*volverse recto*) to straighten ▷ vi to correct o.s.

**rectitud** [rekti'tuð] nf straightness

**recto, -a** ['rekto, a] adj straight; (*persona*) honest, upright ▷ nm rectum ▷ nf straight line; **siga todo ~** go straight on

**rector, a** [rek'tor, a] adj governing

**recuadro** [re'kwaðro] nm box; (*Tip*) inset

**recubrir** [reku'βir] /3a/ vt: **~ (con)** (*pintura, crema*) to cover (with)

**recuento** [re'kwento] nm inventory; **hacer el ~ de** to count o reckon up

**recuerdo** [re'kwerðo] nm souvenir; **recuerdos** nmpl memories; **¡~s a tu madre!** give my regards to your mother!

**recular** [reku'lar] /1a/ vi to back down

**recuperación** [rekupera'θjon] nf recovery

**recuperar** [rekupe'rar] /1a/ vt to recover; (*tiempo*) to make up; **recuperarse** vr to recuperate

**recurrir** [reku'rrir] /3a/ vi (*Jur*) to appeal; **~ a** to resort to; (*persona*) to turn to; **recurso** nm resort; (*medio*) means pl, resource; (*Jur*) appeal; **recursos naturales** natural resources

**red** [reð] nf net, mesh; (*Ferro, Inform*) network; (*trampa*) trap; **la R~** (*Internet*) the Net; **~es sociales** social networks; (*páginas web*) social networking sites

**redacción** [reðak'θjon] nf (*acción*) writing; (*Escol*) essay, composition; (*limpieza de texto*) editing; (*personal*) editorial staff

**redactar** [reðak'tar] /1a/ vt to draw up, draft; (*periódico*) to edit

**redactor, a** [reðak'tor, a] nm/f editor

**redada** [re'ðaða] nf: **~ policial** police raid, round-up

**rededor** [reðe'ðor] nm: **al o en ~** around, round about

**redoblar** [reðo'βlar] /1a/ vt to redouble ▷ vi (*tambor*) to roll

**redonda** [re'ðonda] nf V **redondo**

**redondear** [reðonde'ar] /1a/ vt to round, round off

**redondel** [reðon'del] nm (*círculo*) circle; (*Taur*) bullring, arena

**redondo, -a** [re'ðondo, a] adj (*circular*) round; (*completo*) complete ▷ nf: **a la redonda** around, round about

**reducción** [reðuk'θjon] nf reduction

**reducido, -a** [reðu'θiðo, a] adj reduced; (*limitado*) limited; (*pequeño*) small

**reducir** [reðu'θir] /3n/ vt to reduce, limit; **reducirse** vr to diminish

**redundancia** [reðun'danθja] nf redundancy

**reembolsar** [re(e)mbol'sar] /1a/ vt (*persona*) to reimburse; (*dinero*) to repay, pay back; (*depósito*) to refund; **reembolso** nm reimbursement; refund

**reemplazar** [re(e)mpla'θar] /1f/ vt to replace; **reemplazo** nm replacement; **de reemplazo** (*Mil*) reserve

**reencuentro** [re(e)n'kwentro] nm reunion

**reescribible** [reeskri'βiβle] adj rewritable

**refacción** [refak'θjon] nf (*LAM*) repair(s); **refacciones** nfpl (*piezas de repuesto*) spare parts

**referencia** [refe'renθja] nf reference; **con ~ a** with reference to

**referéndum** [refe'rendum] (*pl* **referéndums**) nm referendum

**referente** [refe'rente] adj: **~ a** concerning, relating to

**réferi** ['referi] nmf (*LAM*) referee

**referir** [refe'rir] /3i/ vt (*contar*) to tell, recount; (*relacionar*) to refer, relate; **referirse** vr: **~se a** to refer to

**refilón** [refi'lon]: **de ~** adv obliquely

**refinado, -a** [refi'naðo, a] adj refined

**refinar** [refi'nar] /1a/ vt to refine; **refinería** nf refinery

**reflejar** [refle'xar] /1a/ vt to reflect; **reflejo, -a** adj reflected; (*movimiento*) reflex ▷ nm reflection; (*Anat*) reflex

**reflexión** [reflek'sjon] nf reflection; **reflexionar** /1a/ vt to reflect on ▷ vi to reflect; (*detenerse*) to pause (to think)

**reflexivo, -a** [reflek'siβo, a] adj thoughtful; (*Ling*) reflexive

**reforma** [re'forma] nf reform; (*Arq etc*) repair; **~ agraria** agrarian reform

**reformar** [refor'mar] /1a/ vt to reform; (*modificar*) to change, alter; (*Arq*) to repair; **reformarse** vr to mend one's ways

**reformatorio** [reforma'torjo] nm reformatory

**reforzar** [refor'θar] /1f, 1l/ vt to strengthen; (*Arq*) to reinforce; (*fig*) to encourage

**refractario, -a** [refrak'tarjo, a] adj (*Tec*) heat-resistant

**refrán** [re'fran] nm proverb, saying

**refregar** [refre'ɣar] /1h, 1j/ vt to scrub

**refrescante** [refres'kante] adj refreshing, cooling

**refrescar** [refres'kar] /1g/ vt to refresh ▷ vi to cool down; **refrescarse** vr to get cooler; (*tomar aire fresco*) to go out for a breath of fresh air; (*beber*) to have a drink

**refresco** [re'fresko] nm soft drink, cool drink; **"~s"** "refreshments"

**refriega** etc [re'frjeɣa] nf scuffle, brawl

**refrigeración** [refrixera'θjon] nf refrigeration; (*de casa*) air-conditioning

**refrigerador** [refrixera'ðor] nm refrigerator, icebox (*US*)

**refrigerar** [refrixe'rar] /1a/ vt to refrigerate; (*sala*) to air-condition

**refuerzo** *etc* [re'fwerθo] *nm* reinforcement; (*Tec*) support

**refugiado, -a** [refu'xjaðo, a] *nm/f* refugee

**refugiarse** [refu'xjarse] /1b/ vr to take refuge, shelter

**refugio** [re'fuxjo] *nm* refuge; (*protección*) shelter

**refunfuñar** [refunfu'ɲar] /1a/ vi to grunt, growl; (*quejarse*) to grumble

**regadera** [reɣa'ðera] *nf* watering can

**regadío** [reɣa'ðio] *nm* irrigated land

**regalado, -a** [reɣa'laðo, a] *adj* comfortable, luxurious; (*gratis*) free, for nothing

**regalar** [reɣa'lar] /1a/ vt (*dar*) to give (as a present); (*entregar*) to give away; (*mimar*) to pamper, make a fuss of

**regaliz** [reɣa'liθ] *nm* liquorice

**regalo** [re'ɣalo] *nm* (*obsequio*) gift, present; (*gusto*) pleasure

**regañadientes** [reɣaɲa'ðjentes]: **a ~** *adv* reluctantly

**regañar** [reɣa'ɲar] /1a/ vt to scold ▷ vi to grumble; **regañón, -ona** *adj* nagging

**regar** [re'ɣar] /1h, 1j/ vt to water, irrigate; (*fig*) to scatter, sprinkle

**regatear** [reɣate'ar] /1a/ vt (*Com*) to bargain over; (*escatimar*) to be mean with ▷ vi to bargain, haggle; (*Deporte*) to dribble; **regateo** *nm* bargaining; (*Deporte*) dribbling; (*con el cuerpo*) swerve, dodge

**regazo** [re'ɣaθo] *nm* lap

**regenerar** [rexene'rar] /1a/ vt to regenerate

**régimen** ['reximen] (*pl* **regímenes**) *nm* regime; (*Med*) diet

**regimiento** [rexi'mjento] *nm* regiment

**regio, -a** ['rexjo, a] *adj* royal, regal; (*fig: suntuoso*) splendid; (*LAm fam*) great, terrific

**región** [re'xjon] *nf* region

**regir** [re'xir] /3c, 3k/ vt to govern, rule; (*dirigir*) to manage, run ▷ vi to apply, be in force

**registrar** [rexis'trar] /1a/ vt (*buscar*) to search; (*en cajón*) to look through; (*inspeccionar*) to inspect; (*anotar*) to register, record; (*Inform*) to log; **registrarse** vr to register; (*ocurrir*) to happen

**registro** [re'xistro] *nm* (*acto*) registration; (*Mus, libro*) register; (*inspección*) inspection, search; ~ **civil** registry office

**regla** ['reɣla] *nf* (*ley*) rule, regulation; (*de medir*) ruler, rule; (*Med: período*) period; **en ~** in order

**reglamentación** [reɣlamenta'θjon] *nf* (*acto*) regulation; (*lista*) rules *pl*

**reglamentar** [reɣlamen'tar] /1a/ vt to regulate; **reglamentario, -a** *adj* statutory; **reglamento** *nm* rules *pl*, regulations *pl*

**regocijarse** [reɣoθi'xarse] /1a/ vr: **~ de** *o* **por** to rejoice at; **regocijo** *nm* joy, happiness

**regrabadora** [reɣraβa'ðora] *nf* rewriter; **~ de DVD** DVD rewriter

**regresar** [reɣre'sar] /1a/ vi to come/go back, return; **regreso** *nm* return

**reguero** [re'ɣero] *nm* (*de sangre*) trickle; (*de humo*) trail

**regulador** [reɣula'ðor] *nm* regulator; (*de radio etc*) knob, control

**regular** [reɣu'lar] /1a/ adj regular; (*normal*) normal, usual; (*común*) ordinary; (*organizado*) regular, orderly; (*mediano*) average; (*fam*) not bad, so-so ▷ *adv*: **estar ~** to be so-so *o* all right ▷ vt (*controlar*) to control, regulate; (*Tec*) to adjust; **por lo ~** as a rule; **regularidad** *nf* regularity; **regularizar** /1f/ vt to regularize

**rehabilitación** [reaβilita'θjon] *nf* rehabilitation; (*Arq*) restoration

**rehabilitar** [reaβili'tar] /1a/ vt to rehabilitate; (*Arq*) to restore; (*reintegrar*) to reinstate

**rehacer** [rea'θer] /2r/ vt (*reparar*) to mend, repair; (*volver a hacer*) to redo, repeat; **rehacerse** vr (*Med*) to recover

**rehén** [re'en] *nmf* hostage

**rehuir** [reu'ir] /3g/ vt to avoid, shun

**rehusar** [reu'sar] /1a/ vt, vi to refuse

**reina** ['reina] *nf* queen; **reinado** *nm* reign

**reinar** [rei'nar] /1a/ vi to reign

**reincidir** [reinθi'ðir] /3a/ vi to relapse

**reincorporarse** [reinkorpo'rarse] /1a/ vr: **~ a** to rejoin

**reino** ['reino] *nm* kingdom; **~ animal/ vegetal** animal/plant kingdom; **el R~ Unido** the United Kingdom

**reintegrar** [reinte'ɣrar] /1a/ vt (*reconstituir*) to reconstruct; (*persona*) to reinstate; (*dinero*) to refund, pay back; **reintegrarse** vr: **~se a** to return to

**reír** [re'ir] vi to laugh; **reírse** vr to laugh; **~se de** to laugh at

**reiterar** [reite'rar] /1a/ vt to reiterate

**reivindicación** [reiβindika'θjon] *nf* (*demanda*) claim, demand; (*justificación*) vindication

**reivindicar** [reiβindi'kar] /1g/ vt to claim

**reja** ['rexa] *nf* (*de ventana*) grille, bars *pl*; (*en la calle*) grating

**rejilla** [re'xiʎa] *nf* grating, grille; (*muebles*) wickerwork; (*de ventilación*) vent; (*de coche etc*) luggage rack

**rejoneador** [rexonea'ðor] *nm* mounted bullfighter

**rejuvenecer** [rexuβene'θer] /2d/ *vt, vi* to rejuvenate

**relación** [rela'θjon] *nf* relation, relationship; (*Mat*) ratio; (*narración*) report; **relaciones laborales/públicas** labour/public relations; **con ~ a, en ~ con** in relation to; **relacionar** /1a/ *vt* to relate, connect; **relacionarse** *vr* to be connected *o* linked

**relajación** [relaxa'θjon] *nf* relaxation

**relajar** [rela'xar] /1a/ *vt* to relax; **relajarse** *vr* to relax

**relamerse** [rela'merse] /2a/ *vr* to lick one's lips

**relámpago** [re'lampaγo] *nm* flash of lightning; **visita/huelga ~** lightning visit/strike

**relatar** [rela'tar] /1a/ *vt* to tell, relate

**relativo, -a** [rela'tiβo, a] *adj* relative; **en lo ~ a** concerning

**relato** [re'lato] *nm* (*narración*) story, tale

**relegar** [rele'γar] /1h/ *vt* to relegate

**relevante** [rele'βante] *adj* eminent, outstanding

**relevar** [rele'βar] /1a/ *vt* (*sustituir*) to relieve; **relevarse** *vr* to relay; **~ a algn de un cargo** to relieve sb of his post

**relevo** [re'leβo] *nm* relief; **carrera de ~s** relay race

**relieve** [re'ljeβe] *nm* (*Arte, Tec*) relief; (*fig*) prominence, importance; **bajo ~** bas-relief

**religión** [reli'xjon] *nf* religion; **religioso, -a** *adj* religious ▷ *nm/f* monk/nun

**relinchar** [relin'tʃar] /1a/ *vi* to neigh

**reliquia** [re'likja] *nf* relic; **~ de familia** heirloom

**rellano** [re'ʎano] *nm* (*Arq*) landing

**rellenar** [reʎe'nar] /1a/ *vt* (*llenar*) to fill up; (*Culin*) to stuff; (*Costura*) to pad; **relleno, -a** *adj* full up; (*Culin*) stuffed ▷ *nm* stuffing; (*de tapicería*) padding

**reloj** [re'lo(x)] *nm* clock; **poner el ~ (en hora)** to set one's watch *o* the clock; **~ (de pulsera)** (wrist)watch; **~ despertador** alarm (clock); **~ digital** digital watch; **relojero, -a** *nm/f* clockmaker; watchmaker

**reluciente** [relu'θjente] *adj* brilliant, shining

**relucir** [relu'θir] /3f/ *vi* to shine; (*fig*) to excel

**remachar** [rema'tʃar] /1a/ *vt* to rivet; (*fig*) to hammer home, drive home; **remache** *nm* rivet

**remangar** [reman'gar] /1h/ *vt* to roll up; **remangarse** *vr* to roll one's sleeves up

**remanso** [re'manso] *nm* pool

**remar** [re'mar] /1a/ *vi* to row

**rematado, -a** [rema'taðo, a] *adj* complete, utter

**rematar** [rema'tar] /1a/ *vt* to finish off; (*Com*) to sell off cheap ▷ *vi* to end, finish off; (*Deporte*) to shoot

**remate** [re'mate] *nm* end, finish; (*punta*) tip; (*Deporte*) shot; (*Arq*) top; **de *o* para ~** to crown it all (*BRIT*), to top it off

**remedar** [reme'ðar] /1a/ *vt* to imitate

**remediar** [reme'ðjar] /1b/ *vt* to remedy; (*subsanar*) to make good, repair; (*evitar*) to avoid

**remedio** [re'meðjo] *nm* remedy; (*alivio*) relief, help; (*Jur*) recourse, remedy; **poner ~ a** to correct, stop; **no tener más ~** to have no alternative; **¡qué ~!** there's no choice!; **sin ~** hopeless

**remendar** [remen'dar] /1j/ *vt* to repair; (*con parche*) to patch

**remiendo** [re'mjendo] *nm* mend; (*con parche*) patch; (*cosido*) darn

**remilgado, -a** [remil'γaðo, a] *adj* prim; (*afectado*) affected

**remiso, -a** [re'miso, a] *adj* slack, slow

**remite** [re'mite] *nm* (*en sobre*) name and address of sender; **remitente** *nmf* (*Correos*) sender; **remitir** /3a/ *vt* to remit, send ▷ *vi* to slacken; (*en carta*): **~ : X** sender: X

**remo** ['remo] *nm* (*de barco*) oar; (*Deporte*) rowing

**remojar** [remo'xar] /1a/ *vt* to steep, soak; (*galleta etc*) to dip, dunk

**remojo** [re'moxo] *nm*: **dejar la ropa en ~** to leave clothes to soak

**remolacha** [remo'latʃa] *nf* beet, beetroot (*BRIT*)

**remolcador** [remolka'ðor] *nm* (*Naut*) tug; (*Auto*) breakdown lorry

**remolcar** [remol'kar] /1g/ *vt* to tow

**remolino** [remo'lino] *nm* eddy; (*de agua*) whirlpool; (*de viento*) whirlwind; (*de gente*) crowd

**remolque** [re'molke] *nm* tow, towing; (*cuerda*) towrope; **llevar a ~** to tow

**remontar** [remon'tar] /1a/ *vt* to mend; **remontarse** *vr* to soar; **~se a** (*Com*) to amount to; **~ el vuelo** to soar

**remorder** [remor'ðer] /2h/ *vt* to distress, disturb; **~le la conciencia a algn** to have a guilty conscience; **remordimiento** *nm* remorse

**remoto, -a** [re'moto, a] *adj* remote

**remover** [remo'βer] /2h/ *vt* to stir; (*tierra*) to turn over; (*objetos*) to move round

**remuneración** [remunera'θjon] *nf* remuneration

**remunerar** [remune'rar] /1a/ *vt* to remunerate; (*premiar*) to reward

**renacer** [rena'θer] /2d/ *vi* to be reborn; (*fig*) to revive; **renacimiento** *nm* rebirth; **el Renacimiento** the Renaissance

**renacuajo** [rena'kwaxo] *nm* (*Zool*) tadpole

**renal** [re'nal] *adj* renal, kidney *cpd*

**rencilla** [ren'θiʎa] *nf* quarrel

**rencor** [ren'kor] *nm* rancour, bitterness; **rencoroso, -a** *adj* spiteful

**rendición** [rendi'θjon] *nf* surrender

**rendido, -a** [ren'diðo, a] *adj* (*sumiso*) submissive; (*agotado*) worn-out, exhausted

**rendija** [ren'dixa] *nf* (*hendidura*) crack

**rendimiento** [rendi'mjento] *nm* (*producción*) output; (*Tec, Com*) efficiency

**rendir** [ren'dir] /3k/ *vt* (*vencer*) to defeat; (*producir*) to produce; (*dar beneficio*) to yield; (*agotar*) to exhaust ▷ *vi* to pay; **rendirse** *vr* (*someterse*) to surrender; (*cansarse*) to wear o.s. out; **~ homenaje** o **culto a** to pay homage to

**renegar** [rene'ɣar] /1h, 1j/ *vi* (*blasfemar*) to blaspheme; **~ de** (*renunciar*) to renounce; (*quejarse*) to complain about

**RENFE** ['renfe] *nf abr* = **Red Nacional de Ferrocarriles Españoles**

**renglón** [ren'glon] *nm* (*línea*) line; (*Com*) item, article; **a ~ seguido** immediately after

**renombre** [re'nombre] *nm* renown

**renovación** [renoβa'θjon] *nf* (*de contrato*) renewal; (*Arq*) renovation

**renovar** [reno'βar] /1l/ *vt* to renew; (*Arq*) to renovate

**renta** ['renta] *nf* (*ingresos*) income; (*beneficio*) profit; (*alquiler*) rent; **~ vitalicia** annuity; **rentable** *adj* profitable

**renuncia** [re'nunθja] *nf* resignation; **renunciar** /1b/ *vt* to renounce, give up ▷ *vi* to resign; **renunciar a** (*tabaco, alcohol etc*) to give up; (*oferta, oportunidad*) to turn down; (*puesto*) to resign

**reñido, -a** [re'niðo, a] *adj* (*batalla*) bitter, hard-fought; **estar ~ con algn** to be on bad terms with sb

**reñir** [re'nir] /3h, 3k/ *vt* (*regañar*) to scold ▷ *vi* (*estar peleado*) to quarrel, fall out; (*combatir*) to fight

**reo** ['reo] *nmf* culprit, offender; (*Jur*) accused

**reojo** [re'oxo] : **de ~** *adv* out of the corner of one's eye

**reparación** [repara'θjon] *nf* (*acto*) mending, repairing; (*Tec*) repair; (*fig*) amends, reparation

**reparador, -a** [repara'ðor, a] *adj* refreshing; (*comida*) fortifying ▷ *nm* repairer

**reparar** [repa'rar] /1a/ *vt* to repair; (*fig*) to make amends for; (*observar*) to observe ▷ *vi*: **~ en** (*darse cuenta de*) to notice; (*poner atención en*) to pay attention to

**reparo** [re'paro] *nm* (*advertencia*) observation; (*duda*) doubt; (*dificultad*) difficulty; **poner ~s (a)** to raise objections (to)

**repartidor, a** [reparti'ðor, a] *nm/f* distributor

**repartir** [repar'tir] /3a/ *vt* to distribute, share out; (*Com, Correos*) to deliver; **reparto** *nm* distribution; (*Com, Correos*) delivery; (*Teat, Cine*) cast; (*LAM: urbanización*) housing estate (*BRIT*), real estate development (*US*)

**repasar** [repa'sar] /1a/ *vt* (*Escol*) to revise; (*Mecánica*) to check, overhaul; (*Costura*) to mend; **repaso** *nm* revision; (*Mecánica*) overhaul, checkup; (*Costura*) mending

**repecho** [re'petʃo] *nm* steep incline

**repelente** [repe'lente] *adj* repellent, repulsive

**repeler** [repe'ler] /2a/ *vt* to repel

**repente** [re'pente] *nm*: **de ~** suddenly

**repentino, -a** [repen'tino, a] *adj* sudden

**repercusión** [reperku'sjon] *nf* repercussion

**repercutir** [reperku'tir] /3a/ *vi* (*objeto*) to rebound; (*sonido*) to echo; **~ en** (*fig*) to have repercussions o effects on

**repertorio** [reper'torjo] *nm* list; (*Teat*) repertoire

**repetición** [repeti'θjon] *nf* repetition

**repetir** [repe'tir] /3k/ *vt* to repeat; (*plato*) to have a second helping of ▷ *vi* to repeat; (*sabor*) to come back; **repetirse** *vr* to repeat o.s.

**repetitivo, -a** [repeti'tiβo, a] *adj* repetitive, repetitious

**repique** [re'pike] *nm* pealing, ringing; **repiqueteo** *nm* pealing; (*de tambor*) drumming

**repisa** [re'pisa] *nf* ledge, shelf; **~ de chimenea** mantelpiece; **~ de ventana** windowsill

**repito** *etc vb V* **repetir**

**replantear** [replante'ar] /1a/ *vt* (*cuestión pública*) to readdress; **replantearse** *vr*: **~se algo** to reconsider sth

**repleto, -a** [re'pleto, a] *adj* replete, full up

**réplica** ['replika] *nf* answer; (*Arte*) replica

**replicar** [repli'kar] /1g/ *vi* to answer; (*objetar*) to argue, answer back

**repliegue** [re'pljeɣe] *nm* (*Mil*) withdrawal

**repoblación** [repoβla'θjon] *nf* repopulation; (*de río*) restocking; **~ forestal** reafforestation

**repoblar** [repo'βlar] /1l/ *vt* to repopulate; (*con árboles*) to reafforest

**repollito** [repo'ʎito] *nm* (*LAM*): **~s de Bruselas** (Brussels) sprouts

**repollo** [re'poʎo] *nm* cabbage

**reponer** [repo'ner] /2q/ *vt* to replace, put back; (*Teat*) to revive; **reponerse** *vr* to recover; **~ que** to reply that

**reportaje** [repor'taxe] *nm* report, article

**reportero, -a** [repor'tero, a] *nm/f* reporter

**reposacabezas** [reposaka'βeθas] *nm inv* headrest

**reposar** [repo'sar] /1a/ *vi* to rest, repose

**reposición** [reposi'θjon] *nf* replacement; (*Cine*) second showing

**reposo** [re'poso] *nm* rest

**repostar** [repos'tar] /1a/ *vt* to replenish; (*Auto*) to fill up (with petrol *o* gasoline)

**repostería** [reposte'ria] *nf* confectioner's (shop)

**represa** [re'presa] *nf* dam; (*lago artificial*) lake, pool

**represalia** [repre'salja] *nf* reprisal

**representación** [representa'θjon] *nf* representation; (*Teat*) performance; **representante** *nmf* representative; (*Teat*) performer

**representar** [represen'tar] /1a/ *vt* to represent; (*Teat*) to perform; (*edad*) to look; **representarse** *vr* to imagine; **representativo, -a** *adj* representative

**represión** [repre'sjon] *nf* repression

**reprimenda** [repri'menda] *nf* reprimand, rebuke

**reprimir** [repri'mir] /3a/ *vt* to repress

**reprobar** [repro'βar] /1l/ *vt* to censure, reprove

**reprochar** [repro'tʃar] /1a/ *vt* to reproach; **reproche** *nm* reproach

**reproducción** [reproðuk'θjon] *nf* reproduction

**reproducir** [reproðu'θir] /3n/ *vt* to reproduce; **reproducirse** *vr* to breed; (*situación*) to recur

**reproductor, a** [reproðuk'tor, a] *adj* reproductive ▷ *nm*: **~ de CD** CD player

**reptil** [rep'til] *nm* reptile

**república** [re'puβlika] *nf* republic; **R~ Dominicana** Dominican Republic; **republicano, -a** *adj*, *nm/f* republican

**repudiar** [repu'ðjar] /1b/ *vt* to repudiate; (*fe*) to renounce

**repuesto** [re'pwesto] *nm* (*pieza de recambio*) spare (part); (*abastecimiento*) supply; **rueda de ~** spare wheel

**repugnancia** [repuɣ'nanθja] *nf* repugnance; **repugnante** *adj* repugnant, repulsive

**repugnar** [repuɣ'nar] /1a/ *vt* to disgust

**repulsa** [re'pulsa] *nf* rebuff

**repulsión** [repul'sjon] *nf* repulsion, aversion; **repulsivo, -a** *adj* repulsive

**reputación** [reputa'θjon] *nf* reputation

**requerir** [reke'rir] /3i/ *vt* (*pedir*) to ask, request; (*exigir*) to require; (*llamar*) to send for, summon

**requesón** [reke'son] *nm* cottage cheese

**requete...** [rekete] *pref* (*fam*) extremely

**réquiem** ['rekjem] *nm* requiem

**requisito** [reki'sito] *nm* requirement, requisite

**res** [res] *nf* beast, animal

**resaca** [re'saka] *nf* (*en el mar*) undertow, undercurrent; (*fam*) hangover

**resaltar** [resal'tar] /1a/ *vi* to project, stick out; (*fig*) to stand out

**resarcir** [resar'θir] /3b/ *vt* to compensate; **resarcirse** *vr* to make up for

**resbaladero** [resβala'ðero] *nm* (*LAM*) slide

**resbaladizo, -a** [resβala'ðiθo, a] *adj* slippery

**resbalar** [resβa'lar] /1a/ *vi* to slip, slide; (*fig*) to slip (up); **resbalarse** *vr* to slip, slide; (*fig*) to slip (up); **resbalón** *nm* (*acción*) slip

**rescatar** [reska'tar] /1a/ *vt* (*salvar*) to save, rescue; (*objeto*) to get back, recover; (*cautivos*) to ransom

**rescate** [res'kate] *nm* rescue; (*de objeto*) recovery; **pagar un ~** to pay a ransom

**rescindir** [resθin'dir] /3a/ *vt* rescind

**rescisión** [resθi'sjon] *nf* cancellation

**resecar** [rese'kar] /1g/ *vt* to dry off, dry thoroughly; (*Med*) to cut out, remove; **resecarse** *vr* to dry up

**reseco, -a** [re'seko, a] *adj* very dry; (*fig*) skinny

**resentido, -a** [resen'tiðo, a] *adj* resentful

**resentimiento** [resenti'mjento] *nm* resentment, bitterness

**resentirse** [resen'tirse] /3i/ *vr* (*debilitarse: persona*) to suffer; **~ de** (*sufrir las consecuencias de*) to feel the effects of; **~ de** *o* **por algo** to resent sth, be bitter about sth

**reseña** [re'seɲa] *nf* (*cuenta*) account; (*informe*) report; (*Lit*) review; **reseñar** /1a/ *vt* to describe; (*Lit*) to review

**reserva** [re'serβa] *nf* reserve; (*reservación*) reservation

**reservación** [reserβa'θjon] *nf* (*LAM*) reservation

**reservado, -a** [reser'βaðo, a] *adj* reserved; (*retraído*) cold, distant ▷ *nm* private room

**reservar** [reser'βar] /1a/ *vt* (*guardar*) to keep; (*Ferro, Teat etc*) to reserve, book; **reservarse** *vr* to save o.s.; (*callar*) to keep to o.s.

**resfriado** [res'friaðo] *nm* cold; **resfriarse** /1c/ *vr* to cool off; (*Med*) to catch (a) cold

**resguardar** [resɣwar'ðar] /1a/ *vt* to protect, shield; **resguardarse** *vr*: **~se de** to guard against; **resguardo** *nm* defence; (*vale*) voucher; (*recibo*) receipt, slip

**residencia** [resi'ðenθja] *nf* residence; (*Univ*) hall of residence; **~ para ancianos** *o* **jubilados** residential home, old people's home; **residencial** *adj* residential

**residente** [resi'ðente] *adj*, *nmf* resident

**residir** [resi'ðir] /3a/ vi to reside, live; **~ en** to reside o lie in

**residuo** [re'siðwo] nm residue

**resignación** [resiɣna'θjon] nf resignation; **resignarse** /1a/ vr: **resignarse a** o **con** to resign o.s. to, be resigned to

**resina** [re'sina] nf resin

**resistencia** [resis'tenθja] nf (dureza) endurance, strength; (oposición, Elec) resistance; **resistente** adj strong, hardy; (Tec) resistant

**resistir** [resis'tir] /3a/ vt (soportar) to bear; (oponerse a) to resist, oppose; (aguantar) to put up with ▷ vi to resist; (aguantar) to last, endure; **resistirse** vr: **~se a** to refuse to, resist

**resoluto, -a** [reso'luto, a] adj resolute

**resolver** [resol'βer] /2h/ vt to resolve; (solucionar) to solve, resolve; (decidir) to decide, settle; **resolverse** vr to make up one's mind

**resonar** [reso'nar] /1l/ vi to ring, echo

**resoplar** [reso'plar] /1a/ vi to snort; **resoplido** nm heavy breathing

**resorte** [re'sorte] nm spring; (fig) lever

**resortera** [resor'tera] nf (LAM) catapult

**respaldar** [respal'dar] /1a/ vt to back (up), support; **respaldarse** vr to lean back; **~se con** o **en** (fig) to take one's stand on; **respaldo** nm (de sillón) back; (fig) support, backing

**respectivo, -a** [respek'tiβo, a] adj respective; **en lo ~ a** with regard to

**respecto** [res'pekto] nm: **al ~** on this matter; **con ~ a, ~ de** with regard to, in relation to

**respetable** [respe'taβle] adj respectable

**respetar** [respe'tar] /1a/ vt to respect; **respeto** nm respect; (acatamiento) deference; **respetos** nmpl respects; **respetuoso, -a** adj respectful

**respingo** [res'pingo] nm start, jump

**respiración** [respira'θjon] nf breathing; (Med) respiration; (ventilación) ventilation; **~ asistida** artificial respiration (by machine)

**respirar** [respi'rar] /1a/ vi to breathe; **respiratorio, -a** adj respiratory; **respiro** nm breathing; (fig: descanso) respite

**resplandecer** [resplande'θer] /2d/ vi to shine; **resplandeciente** adj resplendent, shining; **resplandor** nm brilliance, brightness; (del fuego) blaze

**responder** [respon'der] /2a/ vt to answer ▷ vi to answer; (fig) to respond; (pey) to answer back; **~ de** o **por** to answer for; **respondón, -ona** adj cheeky

**responsabilidad** [responsaβili'ðað] nf responsibility

**responsabilizarse** [responsaβili'θarse] /1f/ vr to make o.s. responsible, take charge

**responsable** [respon'saβle] adj responsible

**respuesta** [res'pwesta] nf answer, reply

**resquebrajar** [reskeβra'xar] /1a/ vt to crack, split; **resquebrajarse** vr to crack, split

**resquicio** [res'kiθjo] nm chink; (hendidura) crack

**resta** ['resta] nf (Mat) remainder

**restablecer** [restaβle'θer] /2d/ vt to re-establish, restore; **restablecerse** vr to recover

**restante** [res'tante] adj remaining; **lo ~** the remainder

**restar** [res'tar] /1a/ vt (Mat) to subtract; (fig) to take away ▷ vi to remain, be left

**restauración** [restaura'θjon] nf restoration

**restaurante** [restau'rante] nm restaurant

**restaurar** [restau'rar] /1a/ vt to restore

**restituir** [restitu'ir] /3g/ vt (devolver) to return, give back; (rehabilitar) to restore

**resto** ['resto] nm (residuo) rest, remainder; (apuesta) stake; **restos** nmpl remains

**restorán** [resto'ran] nm (LAM) restaurant

**restregar** [restre'ɣar] /1h, 1j/ vt to scrub, rub

**restricción** [restrik'θjon] nf restriction

**restringir** [restrin'xir] /3c/ vt to restrict, limit

**resucitar** [resuθi'tar] /1a/ vt, vi to resuscitate, revive

**resuelto, -a** [re'swelto, a] pp de **resolver** ▷ adj resolute, determined

**resultado** [resul'taðo] nm result; (conclusión) outcome; **resultante** adj resulting, resultant

**resultar** [resul'tar] /1a/ vi (ser) to be; (llegar a ser) to turn out to be; (salir bien) to turn out well; (Com) to amount to; **~ de** to stem from; **me resulta difícil hacerlo** it's difficult for me to do it

**resumen** [re'sumen] nm summary, résumé; **en ~** in short

**resumir** [resu'mir] /3a/ vt to sum up; (cortar) to abridge, cut down

▪ No confundir resumir con la palabra inglesa resume.

**resurgir** [resur'xir] /3c/ vi (reaparecer) to reappear

**resurrección** [resurrek'θjon] nf resurrection

**retablo** [re'taβlo] nm altarpiece

**retaguardia** [reta'ɣwarðja] nf rearguard

**retahíla** [reta'ila] nf series, string

**retal** [re'tal] nm remnant

**retar** [re'tar] /1a/ vt to challenge; (desafiar) to defy, dare

**retazo** [re'taθo] nm snippet (BRIT), fragment

**retención** [reten'θjon] nf (tráfico) hold-up; **~ fiscal** deduction for tax purposes

**retener** [rete'ner] /2k/ vt (intereses) to withhold

**reticente** [reti'θente] adj (insinuador) insinuating; (postura) reluctant; **ser ~ a hacer algo** to be reluctant o unwilling to do sth

**retina** [re'tina] nf retina

**retintín** [retin'tin] nm jangle, jingle; **decir algo con ~** to say sth sarcastically

**retirado, -a** adj (lugar) remote; (vida) quiet; (jubilado) retired ▷ nf (Mil) retreat; (de dinero) withdrawal; (de embajador) recall; **batirse en retirada** to retreat

**retirar** [reti'rar] /1a/ vt to withdraw; (quitar) to remove; (jubilar) to retire, pension off; **retirarse** vr to retreat, withdraw; (jubilarse) to retire; (acostarse) to retire, go to bed; **retiro** nm retreat; (jubilación) retirement; (pago) pension

**reto** ['reto] nm dare, challenge

**retocar** [reto'kar] /1g/ vt (fotografía) to touch up, retouch

**retoño** [re'toɲo] nm sprout, shoot; (fig) offspring, child

**retoque** [re'toke] nm retouching

**retorcer** [retor'θer] /2b, 2h/ vt to twist; (manos, lavado) to wring; **retorcerse** vr to become twisted; (persona) to writhe

**retorcido, -a** [retor'θiðo, a] adj (tb fig) twisted

**retorcijón** [retorθi'xon] nm (LAM: tb: **~ de tripas**) stomach cramp

**retorno** [re'torno] nm return

**retortijón** [retorti'xon] nm: **~ de tripas** stomach cramp

**retozar** [reto'θar] /1f/ vi (juguetear) to frolic, romp; (saltar) to gambol

**retracción** [retrak'θjon] nf retraction

**retraerse** [retra'erse] /2o/ vr to retreat, withdraw; **retraído, -a** adj shy, retiring; **retraimiento** nm retirement; (timidez) shyness

**retransmisión** [retransmi'sjon] nf repeat (broadcast)

**retransmitir** [retransmi'tir] /3a/ vt (mensaje) to relay; (TV etc) to repeat, retransmit; (: en vivo) to broadcast live

**retrasado, -a** [retra'saðo, a] adj late; (fam!) backward (!); (país etc) underdeveloped

**retrasar** [retra'sar] /1a/ vt (demorar) to postpone, put off; (retardar) to slow down ▷ vi (atrasarse) to be late; (reloj) to be slow; (producción) to fall (off); (quedarse atrás) to lag behind; **retrasarse** vr to be late; to be slow; to fall (off); to lag behind

**retraso** [re'traso] nm (demora) delay; (lentitud) slowness; (tardanza) lateness; (atraso) backwardness; **retrasos** nmpl (Com) arrears; **llegar con ~** to arrive late

**retratar** [retra'tar] /1a/ vt (Arte) to paint the portrait of; (fotografiar) to photograph; (fig) to depict, describe; **retrato** nm portrait; (fig) likeness; **retrato-robot** nm Identikit® picture

**retrete** [re'trete] nm toilet

**retribuir** [retriβu'ir] /3g/ vt (recompensar) to reward; (pagar) to pay

**retro...** [retro] pref retro...

**retroceder** [retroθe'ðer] /2a/ vi (echarse atrás) to move back(wards); (fig) to back down

**retroceso** [retro'θeso] nm backward movement; (Med) relapse; (fig) backing down

**retrospectivo, -a** [retrospek'tiβo, a] adj retrospective

**retrovisor** [retroβi'sor] nm rear-view mirror

**retuitear** [retwite'ar] vt (en Twitter) to retweet

**retumbar** [retum'bar] /1a/ vi to echo, resound

**reuma** ['reuma] nm rheumatism

**reunión** [reu'njon] nf (asamblea) meeting; (fiesta) party

**reunir** [reu'nir] /3a/ vt (juntar) to reunite, join (together); (recoger) to gather (together); (personas) to bring o get together; (cualidades) to combine; **reunirse** vr (personas: en asamblea) to meet, gather

**revalidar** [reβali'ðar] /1a/ vt (ratificar) to confirm, ratify

**revalorizar** [reβalori'θar] /1f/ vt to revalue, reassess

**revancha** [re'βantʃa] nf revenge

**revelación** [reβela'θjon] nf revelation

**revelado** [reβe'laðo] nm developing

**revelar** [reβe'lar] /1a/ vt to reveal; (Foto) to develop

**reventa** [re'βenta] nf (de entradas) touting

**reventar** [reβen'tar] /1j/ vt to burst, explode

**reventón** [reβen'ton] nm (Auto) blow-out (BRIT), flat (US)

**reverencia** [reβe'renθja] nf reverence; **reverenciar** /1b/ vt to revere

**reverendo, -a** [reβe'rendo, a] adj reverend

**reverente** [reβe'rente] adj reverent

**reversa** [re'βersa] nf (LAM) (reverse) gear

**reversible** [reβer'siβle] adj reversible

**reverso** [re'βerso] nm back, other side; (de moneda) reverse

**revertir** [reβer'tir] /3i/ vi to revert

**revés** [re'βes] nm back, wrong side; (fig) reverse, setback; (Deporte) backhand; **al ~** the wrong way round; (de arriba abajo) upside down; (ropa) inside out; **volver algo del ~** to turn sth round; (ropa) to turn sth inside out

**revisar** [reβi'sar] /1a/ vt (examinar) to check; (texto etc) to revise; **revisión** nf revision; **revisión salarial** wage review

**revisor, a** [reβi'sor, a] nm/f inspector; (Ferro) ticket collector

**revista** [re'βista] nf magazine, review; (Teat) revue; (inspección) inspection; **~ del corazón** magazine featuring celebrity gossip and real-life romance stories; **pasar ~ a** to review, inspect

**revivir** [reβi'βir] /3a/ vi to revive

**revolcar** [reβol'kar] /1g, 1l/ vt to knock down; **revolcarse** vr to roll about

**revoltijo** [reβol'tixo] nm mess, jumble

**revoltoso, -a** [reβol'toso, a] adj (travieso) naughty, unruly

**revolución** [reβolu'θjon] nf revolution; **revolucionario, -a** adj, nm/f revolutionary

**revolver** [reβol'βer] /2h/ vt (desordenar) to disturb, mess up; (mover) to move about ▷ vi: **~ en** to go through, rummage (about) in; **revolverse** vr: **~se contra** to turn on o against

**revólver** [re'βolβer] nm revolver

**revuelo** [re'βwelo] nm fluttering; (fig) commotion

**revuelto, -a** [re'βwelto, a] pp de **revolver** ▷ adj (mezclado) mixed-up, in disorder ▷ nf (motín) revolt; (agitación) commotion

**rey** [rei] nm king; **Día de R~es** Twelfth Night; **los R~es Magos** the Three Wise Men, the Magi

○ **REYES MAGOS**

○
○ The night before the 6th of January (the
○ Epiphany), which is a holiday in Spain,
○ children go to bed expecting los Reyes
○ Magos, the Three Wise Men who visited
○ the baby Jesus, to bring them presents.
○ Twelfth night processions, known as
○ cabalgatas, take place that evening, when
○ 3 people dressed as los Reyes Magos arrive
○ in the town by land or sea to the delight of
○ the children.

**reyerta** [re'jerta] nf quarrel, brawl

**rezagado, -a** [reθa'ɣaðo, a] nm/f straggler

**rezar** [re'θar] /1f/ vi to pray; **~ con** (fam) to concern, have to do with; **rezo** nm prayer

**rezumar** [reθu'mar] /1a/ vt to ooze

**ría** ['ria] nf estuary

**riada** [ri'aða] nf flood

**ribera** [ri'βera] nf (de río) bank; (: área) riverside

**ribete** [ri'βete] nm (de vestido) border; (fig) addition

**ricino** [ri'θino] nm: **aceite de ~** castor oil

**rico, -a** ['riko, a] adj (adinerado) rich; (lujoso) luxurious; (comida) delicious; (niño) lovely, cute ▷ nm/f rich person

**ridiculez** [riðiku'leθ] nf absurdity

**ridiculizar** [riðikuli'θar] /1f/ vt to ridicule

**ridículo, -a** [ri'ðikulo, a] adj ridiculous; **hacer el ~** to make a fool of o.s.; **poner a algn en ~** to make a fool of sb

**riego** ['rjeɣo] nm (aspersión) watering; (irrigación) irrigation; **~ sanguíneo** blood flow o circulation

**riel** [rjel] nm rail

**rienda** ['rjenda] nf rein; **dar ~ suelta a** to give free rein to

**riesgo** ['rjesɣo] nm risk; **correr el ~ de** to run the risk of

**rifa** ['rifa] nf (lotería) raffle; **rifar** /1a/ vt to raffle

**rifle** ['rifle] nm rifle

**rigidez** [rixi'ðeθ] nf rigidity, stiffness; (fig) strictness; **rígido, -a** adj rigid, stiff; (moralmente) strict, inflexible

**rigor** [ri'ɣor] nm strictness, rigour; (inclemencia) harshness; **de ~** de rigueur, essential; **riguroso, -a** adj rigorous; (Meteorología) harsh; (severo) severe

**rimar** [ri'mar] /1a/ vi to rhyme

**rimbombante** [rimbom'bante] adj pompous

**rímel, rímmel** ['rimel] nm mascara

**rímmel** ['rimel] nm = **rímel**

**rin** [rin] nm (LAM) (wheel) rim

**rincón** [rin'kon] nm corner (inside)

**rinoceronte** [rinoθe'ronte] nm rhinoceros

**riña** ['riɲa] nf (disputa) argument; (pelea) brawl

**riñón** [ri'ɲon] nm kidney

**río** ['rio] vb V **reír** ▷ nm river; (fig) torrent, stream; **~ abajo/arriba** downstream/ upstream; **R~ de la Plata** River Plate

**rioja** [ri'oxa] nm rioja wine ▷ nf: **La R~** La Rioja

**rioplatense** [riopla'tense] adj of o from the River Plate region

**riqueza** [ri'keθa] nf wealth, riches pl; (cualidad) richness

**risa** ['risa] nf laughter; (una risa) laugh; **¡qué ~!** what a laugh!

**risco** ['risko] nm crag, cliff

**ristra** ['ristra] nf string

**risueño, -a** [ri'sweɲo, a] adj (sonriente) smiling; (contento) cheerful

**ritmo** ['ritmo] nm rhythm; **a ~ lento** slowly; **trabajar a ~ lento** to go slow; **~ cardíaco** heart rate

**rito** ['rito] *nm* rite
**ritual** [ri'twal] *adj, nm* ritual
**rival** [ri'βal] *adj, nmf* rival; **rivalidad** *nf* rivalry; **rivalizar** /1f/ *vi*: **rivalizar con** to rival, vie with
**rizado, -a** [ri'θaðo, a] *adj* curly ▷ *nm* curls *pl*
**rizar** [ri'θar] /1f/ *vt* to curl; **rizarse** *vr* (*el pelo*) to curl; (*agua*) to ripple; **rizo** *nm* curl; (*en agua*) ripple
**RNE** *nf abr* = **Radio Nacional de España**
**robar** [ro'βar] /1a/ *vt* to rob; (*objeto*) to steal; (*casa etc*) to break into; (*Naipes*) to draw
**roble** ['roβle] *nm* oak; **robledal** *nm* oakwood
**robo** ['roβo] *nm* robbery, theft
**robot** *adj, nm* robot ▷ *nm* (*tb*: **~ de cocina**) food processor
**robustecer** [roβuste'θer] /2d/ *vt* to strengthen
**robusto, -a** [ro'βusto, a] *adj* robust, strong
**roca** ['roka] *nf* rock
**roce** [ro'θe] *nm* (*caricia*) brush; (*Tec*) friction; (*en la piel*) graze; **tener ~ con** to have a brush with
**rociar** [ro'θjar] /1c/ *vt* to sprinkle, spray
**rocín** [ro'θin] *nm* nag, hack
**rocío** [ro'θio] *nm* dew
**rocola** [ro'kola] *nf* (*LAM*) jukebox
**rocoso, -a** [ro'koso, a] *adj* rocky
**rodaballo** [roða'βaʎo] *nm* turbot
**rodaja** [ro'ðaxa] *nf* slice
**rodaje** [ro'ðaxe] *nm* (*Cine*) shooting, filming; (*Auto*) running in; **en ~** running in
**rodar** [ro'ðar] /1l/ *vt* (*vehículo*) to wheel (along); (*escalera*) to roll down; (*viajar por*) to travel (over) ▷ *vi* to roll; (*coche*) to go, run; (*Cine*) to shoot, film
**rodear** [roðe'ar] /1a/ *vt* to surround ▷ *vi* to go round; **rodearse** *vr*: **~se de amigos** to surround o.s. with friends
**rodeo** [ro'ðeo] *nm* (*desvío*) detour; (*evasión*) evasion; (*LAM*) rodeo; **hablar sin ~s** to come to the point, speak plainly
**rodilla** [ro'ðiʎa] *nf* knee; **de ~s** kneeling; **ponerse de ~s** to kneel (down)
**rodillo** [ro'ðiʎo] *nm* roller; (*Culin*) rolling-pin
**roedor, a** [roe'ðor, a] *adj* gnawing ▷ *nm* rodent
**roer** [ro'er] /2y/ *vt* (*masticar*) to gnaw; (*corroer, fig*) to corrode
**rogar** [ro'ɣar] /1h, 1l/ *vt* (*pedir*) to beg, ask for ▷ *vi* (*suplicar*) to beg, plead; **rogarse** *vr*: **se ruega no fumar** please do not smoke
**rojizo, -a** [ro'xiθo, a] *adj* reddish
**rojo, -a** [ˈroxo, a] *adj* red ▷ *nm* red; **al ~ vivo** red-hot
**rol** [rol] *nm* list, roll; (*papel*) role
**rollito** [ro'ʎito] *nm* (*tb*: **~ de primavera**) spring roll

**rollizo, -a** [ro'ʎiθo] *adj* (*objeto*) cylindrical; (*persona*) plump
**rollo** ['roʎo] *nm* roll; (*de cuerda*) coil; (*de madera*) log; (*fam*) bore; **¡qué ~!** what a carry-on!
**Roma** ['roma] *nf* Rome
**romance** [ro'manθe] *nm* (*amoroso*) romance; (*Lit*) ballad
**romano, -a** [ro'mano, a] *adj* Roman ▷ *nm/f* Roman; **a la romana** in batter
**romanticismo** [romanti'θismo] *nm* romanticism
**romántico, -a** [ro'mantiko, a] *adj* romantic
**rombo** ['rombo] *nm* (*Mat*) rhombus
**romería** [rome'ria] *nf* (*Rel*) pilgrimage; (*excursión*) trip, outing

- **ROMERÍA**
- 
- Originally a pilgrimage to a shrine or
- church to express devotion to Our Lady or
- a local Saint, the *romería* has also become
- a rural *fiesta* which accompanies the
- pilgrimage. People come from all over to
- attend, bringing their own food and drink,
- and spend the day in celebration.

**romero, -a** [ro'mero, a] *nm/f* pilgrim ▷ *nm* rosemary
**romo, -a** ['romo, a] *adj* blunt; (*fig*) dull
**rompecabezas** [rompeka'βeθas] *nm inv* riddle, puzzle; (*juego*) jigsaw (puzzle)
**rompehuelgas** [rompe'welɣas] *nm inv* (*LAM*) strikebreaker, scab
**rompeolas** [rompe'olas] *nm inv* breakwater
**romper** [rom'per] /2a/ *vt* to break; (*hacer pedazos*) to smash; (*papel, tela etc*) to tear, rip ▷ *vi* (*olas*) to break; (*sol, diente*) to break through; **~ un contrato** to break a contract; **~ a** to start (suddenly) to; **~ a llorar** to burst into tears; **~ con algn** to fall out with sb
**ron** [ron] *nm* rum
**roncar** [ron'kar] /1g/ *vi* to snore
**ronco, -a** ['ronko, a] *adj* (*afónico*) hoarse; (*áspero*) raucous
**ronda** ['ronda] *nf* (*de bebidas etc*) round; (*patrulla*) patrol; **rondar** /1a/ *vt* to patrol ▷ *vi* to patrol; (*fig*) to prowl round
**ronquido** [ron'kiðo] *nm* snore, snoring
**ronronear** [ronrone'ar] /1a/ *vi* to purr
**roña** ['roɲa] *nf* (*en veterinaria*) mange; (*mugre*) dirt, grime; (*óxido*) rust
**roñoso, -a** [ro'ɲoso, a] *adj* (*mugriento*) filthy; (*tacaño*) mean
**ropa** ['ropa] *nf* clothes *pl*, clothing; **~ blanca** linen; **~ de cama** bed linen; **~ de color** coloureds *pl*; **~ interior** underwear; **~ sucia**

dirty clothes *pl*, dirty washing; **ropaje** *nm* gown, robes *pl*

**ropero** [ro'pero] *nm* linen cupboard; (*guardarropa*) wardrobe

**rosa** ['rosa] *adj inv* pink ▷ *nf* rose

**rosado, -a** [ro'saðo, a] *adj* pink ▷ *nm* rosé

**rosal** [ro'sal] *nm* rosebush

**rosario** [ro'sarjo] *nm* (*Rel*) rosary; **rezar el ~** to say the rosary

**rosca** ['roska] *nf* (*de tornillo*) thread; (*de humo*) coil, spiral; (*pan, postre*) ring-shaped roll/pastry

**rosetón** [rose'ton] *nm* rosette; (*Arq*) rose window

**rosquilla** [ros'kiʎa] *nf* ring-shaped cake

**rostro** ['rostro] *nm* (*cara*) face

**rotativo, -a** [rota'tiβo, a] *adj* rotary

**roto, -a** ['roto, a] *pp de* **romper** ▷ *adj* broken

**rotonda** [ro'tonda] *nf* roundabout

**rótula** ['rotula] *nf* kneecap; (*Tec*) ball-and-socket joint

**rotulador** [rotula'ðor] *nm* felt-tip pen

**rótulo** ['rotulo] *nm* heading, title; (*etiqueta*) label; (*letrero*) sign

**rotundamente** [rotunda'mente] *adv* (*negar*) flatly; (*responder, afirmar*) emphatically; **rotundo, -a** *adj* round; (*enfático*) emphatic

**rotura** [ro'tura] *nf* (*rompimiento*) breaking; (*Med*) fracture

**rozadura** [roθa'ðura] *nf* abrasion, graze

**rozar** [ro'θar] /1f/ *vt* (*frotar*) to rub; (*arañar*) to scratch; (*tocar ligeramente*) to shave; **rozarse** *vr* to rub (together); **~ con** (*fam*) to rub shoulders with

**Rte.** *abr* = **remite; remitente**

**RTVE** *nf abr* = **Radiotelevisión Española**

**rubí** [ru'βi] *nm* ruby; (*de reloj*) jewel

**rubio, -a** ['ruβjo, a] *adj* fair-haired, blond(e) ▷ *nm/f* blond/blonde; **tabaco ~** Virginia tobacco

**rubor** [ru'βor] *nm* (*sonrojo*) blush; (*timidez*) bashfulness; **ruborizarse** /1f/ *vr* to blush

**rúbrica** ['ruβrika] *nf* (*de la firma*) flourish; **rubricar** /1g/ *vt* (*firmar*) to sign with a flourish; (*concluir*) to sign and seal

**rudimentario, -a** [ruðimen'tarjo, a] *adj* rudimentary

**rudo, -a** ['ruðo, a] *adj* (*sin pulir*) unpolished; (*grosero*) coarse; (*violento*) violent; (*sencillo*) simple

**rueda** ['rweða] *nf* wheel; (*círculo*) ring, circle; (*rodaja*) slice, round; **~ de auxilio** (*LAM*) spare tyre; **~ delantera/trasera/de repuesto** front/back/spare wheel; **~ de prensa** press conference; **~ gigante** (*LAM*) big (*BRIT*) o Ferris (*US*) wheel

**ruedo** ['rweðo] *nm* (*círculo*) circle; (*Taur*) arena, bullring

**ruego** *etc* ['rweɣo] *vb V* **rogar** ▷ *nm* request

**rugby** ['ruɣβi] *nm* rugby

**rugido** [ru'xiðo] *nm* roar

**rugir** [ru'xir] /3c/ *vi* to roar

**rugoso, -a** [ru'ɣoso, a] *adj* (*arrugado*) wrinkled; (*áspero*) rough; (*desigual*) ridged

**ruido** ['rwiðo] *nm* noise; (*sonido*) sound; (*alboroto*) racket, row; (*escándalo*) commotion, rumpus; **ruidoso, -a** *adj* noisy, loud; (*fig*) sensational

**ruin** [rwin] *adj* contemptible, mean

**ruina** ['rwina] *nf* ruin; (*hundimiento*) collapse; (*de persona*) ruin, downfall

**ruinoso, -a** [rwi'noso, a] *adj* ruinous; (*destartalado*) dilapidated, tumbledown; (*Com*) disastrous

**ruiseñor** [rwise'ɲor] *nm* nightingale

**rulero** [ru'lero] *nm* (*LAM*) roller

**ruleta** [ru'leta] *nf* roulette

**rulo** ['rulo] *nm* (*para el pelo*) curler

**Rumania** [ru'manja] *nf* Rumania

**rumba** ['rumba] *nf* rumba

**rumbo** ['rumbo] *nm* (*ruta*) route, direction; (*ángulo de dirección*) course, bearing; (*fig*) course of events; **ir con ~ a** to be heading for

**rumiante** [ru'mjante] *nm* ruminant

**rumiar** [ru'mjar] /1b/ *vt* to chew; (*fig*) to chew over ▷ *vi* to chew the cud

**rumor** [ru'mor] *nm* (*ruido sordo*) low sound; (*murmuración*) murmur, buzz; **rumorearse** /1a/ *vr*: **se rumorea que** it is rumoured that

**rupestre** [ru'pestre] *adj* rock *cpd*

**ruptura** [rup'tura] *nf* rupture

**rural** [ru'ral] *adj* rural

**Rusia** ['rusja] *nf* Russia; **ruso, -a** *adj, nm/f* Russian

**rústico, -a** ['rustiko, a] *adj* rustic; (*ordinario*) coarse, uncouth ▷ *nm/f* yokel

**ruta** ['ruta] *nf* route

**rutina** [ru'tina] *nf* routine

# S

**s.** abr (= siglo) c.; (= siguiente) foll.
**S.A.** abr (= Sociedad Anónima) Ltd., Inc. (US)
**sábado** ['saβaðo] nm Saturday
**sábana** ['saβana] nf sheet
**sabañón** [saβa'ɲon] nm chilblain
**saber** [sa'βer] /2m/ vt to know; (llegar a conocer) to find out, learn; (tener capacidad de) to know how to ▷ vi: **~ a** to taste of, taste like ▷ nm knowledge, learning; **a ~** namely; **¿sabes conducir/nadar?** can you drive/swim?; **¿sabes francés?** do you o can you speak French?; **~ de memoria** to know by heart; **hacer ~** to inform, let know
**sabiduría** [saβiðu'ria] nf (conocimientos) wisdom; (instrucción) learning
**sabiendas** [sa'βjendas]: **a ~** adv knowingly
**sabio, -a** ['saβjo, a] adj (docto) learned; (prudente) wise, sensible
**sabor** [sa'βor] nm taste, flavour; **saborear** /1a/ vt to taste, savour; (fig) to relish
**sabotaje** [saβo'taxe] nm sabotage
**sabré** etc [sa'βre] vb V **saber**
**sabroso, -a** [sa'βroso, a] adj tasty; (fig: fam) racy, salty
**sacacorchos** [saka'kortʃos] nm inv corkscrew
**sacapuntas** [saka'puntas] nm inv pencil sharpener
**sacar** [sa'kar] /1g/ vt to take out; (fig: extraer) to get (out); (quitar) to remove, get out; (hacer salir) to bring out; (conclusión) to draw; (novela etc) to publish, bring out; (ropa) to take off; (obra) to make; (premio) to receive; (entradas) to get; (Tenis) to serve; **~ adelante** (niño) to bring up; (negocio) to carry on, go on with; **~ a algn a bailar** to get sb up to dance; **~ una foto** to take a photo; **~ la lengua** to stick out one's tongue; **~ buenas/malas notas** to get good/bad marks

**sacarina** [saka'rina] nf saccharin(e)
**sacerdote** [saθer'ðote] nm priest
**saciar** [sa'θjar] /1b/ vt to satisfy; **saciarse** vr (de comida) to get full up
**saco** ['sako] nm bag; (grande) sack; (contenido) bagful; (LAM: chaqueta) jacket; **~ de dormir** sleeping bag
**sacramento** [sakra'mento] nm sacrament
**sacrificar** [sakrifi'kar] /1g/ vt to sacrifice; **sacrificio** nm sacrifice
**sacristía** [sakris'tia] nf sacristy
**sacudida** [saku'ðiða] nf (agitación) shake, shaking; (sacudimiento) jolt, bump; **~ eléctrica** electric shock
**sacudir** [saku'ðir] /3a/ vt to shake; (golpear) to hit
**Sagitario** [saxi'tarjo] nm Sagittarius
**sagrado, -a** [sa'ɣraðo, a] adj sacred, holy
**Sáhara** ['saara] nm: **el ~** the Sahara (desert)
**sal** [sal] vb V **salir** ▷ nf salt; **~es de baño** bath salts
**sala** ['sala] nf large room; (tb: **~ de estar**) living room; (Teat) house, auditorium; (de hospital) ward; **~ de espera** waiting room; **~ de estar** living room
**salado, -a** [sa'laðo, a] adj salty; (fig) witty, amusing; **agua salada** salt water
**salar** [sa'lar] /1a/ vt to salt, add salt to
**salariado, -a** [sala'rjaðo, a] adj (empleado) salaried
**salario** [sa'larjo] nm wage, pay
**salchicha** [sal'tʃitʃa] nf (pork) sausage; **salchichón** nm (salami-type) sausage
**saldo** ['saldo] nm (pago) settlement; (de una cuenta) balance; (lo restante) remnant(s) (pl), remainder; (de móvil) credit; **saldos** nmpl (en tienda) sale
**saldré** etc [sal'dre] vb V **salir**
**salero** [sa'lero] nm salt cellar
**salgo** etc vb V **salir**
**salida** [sa'liða] nf (puerta etc) exit, way out; (acto) leaving, going out; (de tren, Aviat) departure; (Com, Tec) output, production; (fig) way out; (Com) opening; (Geo, válvula) outlet; (de gas) leak; **calle sin ~** cul-de-sac; **~ de baño** (LAM) bathrobe; **~ de incendios** fire escape

🔘 **PALABRA CLAVE**

**salir** [sa'lir] /3q/ vi **1** to leave; **Juan ha salido** Juan has gone out; **salió de la cocina** he came out of the kitchen
**2** (disco, libro) to come out; **anoche salió en la tele** she appeared o was on TV last night; **salió en todos los periódicos** it was in all the papers
**3** (resultar): **la muchacha nos salió muy trabajadora** the girl turned out to be a very hard worker; **la comida te ha salido**

exquisita the food was delicious; **sale muy caro** it's very expensive

**4**: **salir adelante: no sé como haré para salir adelante** I don't know how I'll get by
▶ **salirse** vr (líquido) to spill; (animal) to escape

**saliva** [sa'liβa] nf saliva
**salmo** ['salmo] nm psalm
**salmón** [sal'mon] nm salmon
**salmonete** [salmo'nete] nm red mullet
**salón** [sa'lon] nm (de casa) living-room, lounge; (muebles) lounge suite; **~ de belleza** beauty parlour; **~ de baile** dance hall; **~ de actos/sesiones** assembly hall
**salpicadera** [salpika'ðera] nf (LAM) mudguard (BRIT), fender (US)
**salpicadero** [salpika'ðero] nm (Auto) dashboard
**salpicar** [salpi'kar] /1g/ vt (rociar) to sprinkle, spatter; (esparcir) to scatter
**salpicón** [salpi'kon] nm (tb: **~ de marisco**) seafood salad
**salsa** ['salsa] nf sauce; (con carne asada) gravy; (fig) spice
**saltamontes** [salta'montes] nm inv grasshopper
**saltar** [sal'tar] /1a/ vt to jump (over), leap (over); (dejar de lado) to skip, miss out ▷ vi to jump, leap; (pelota) to bounce; (al aire) to fly up; (quebrarse) to break; (al agua) to dive; (fig) to explode, blow up
**salto** ['salto] nm jump, leap; (al agua) dive; **~ de agua** waterfall; **~ de altura** high jump
**salud** [sa'luð] nf health; **¡(a su) ~!** cheers!, good health!; **saludable** adj (de buena salud) healthy; (provechoso) good, beneficial
**saludar** [salu'ðar] /1a/ vt to greet; (Mil) to salute; **saludo** nm greeting; **saludos** (en carta) best wishes, regards
**salvación** [salβa'θjon] nf salvation; (rescate) rescue
**salvado** [sal'βaðo] nm bran
**salvaje** [sal'βaxe] adj wild; (tribu) savage
**salvamanteles** [salβaman'teles] nm inv table mat
**salvamento** [salβa'mento] nm rescue
**salvapantallas** [salβapan'taʎas] nm inv screensaver
**salvar** [sal'βar] /1a/ vt (rescatar) to save, rescue; (resolver) to overcome, resolve; (cubrir distancias) to cover, travel; (hacer excepción) to except, exclude; (un barco) to salvage
**salvavidas** [salβa'βiðas] adj inv: **bote/chaleco/cinturón ~** lifeboat/lifejacket/lifebelt
**salvo, -a** ['salβo, a] adj safe ▷ prep except (for), save; **a ~** out of danger; **~ que** unless
**san** [san] n saint; **~ Juan** St. John

**sanar** [sa'nar] /1a/ vt (herida) to heal; (persona) to cure ▷ vi (persona) to get well, recover; (herida) to heal
**sanatorio** [sana'torjo] nm sanatorium
**sanción** [san'θjon] nf sanction
**sancochado, -a** [sanko'tʃaðo, a] adj (LAM Culin) underdone, rare
**sandalia** [san'dalja] nf sandal
**sandía** [san'dia] nf watermelon
**sándwich** ['sandwitʃ] (pl **sándwichs** o **sandwiches**) nm sandwich
**Sanfermines** [sanfer'mines] nmpl festivities in celebration of San Fermín

◦ **SANFERMINES**
◦
◦ The Sanfermines are a week of fiestas in
◦ Pamplona, the capital of Navarre, made
◦ famous by Ernest Hemingway. From the
◦ 7th of July, the feast of San Fermín, crowds
◦ of mainly young people take to the streets
◦ drinking, singing and dancing. Early in
◦ the morning bulls are released along the
◦ narrow streets leading to the bullring, and
◦ people risk serious injury by running out
◦ in front of them, a custom which is also
◦ typical of many Spanish villages.

**sangrar** [san'grar] /1a/ vt, vi to bleed; **sangre** nf blood
**sangría** [san'gria] nf sangria (sweetened drink of red wine with fruit)
**sangriento, -a** [san'grjento, a] adj bloody
**sanguíneo, -a** [san'gineo, a] adj blood cpd
**sanidad** [sani'ðað] nf: **~ pública** public health (department)
**San Isidro** [sani'sidro] nm patron saint of Madrid

◦ **SAN ISIDRO**
◦
◦ San Isidro is the patron saint of Madrid,
◦ and gives his name to the week-long
◦ festivities which take place around the
◦ 15th May. Originally an 18th-century trade
◦ fair, the San Isidro celebrations now
◦ include music, dance, a famous romería,
◦ theatre and bullfighting.

**sanitario, -a** [sani'tarjo, a] adj health cpd; **sanitarios** nmpl toilets (BRIT), restroom sg (US)
**sano, -a** ['sano, a] adj healthy; (sin daños) sound; (comida) wholesome; (entero) whole, intact; **~ y salvo** safe and sound

▮ No confundir sano con la palabra inglesa sane.

**Santiago** [san'tjaɣo] nm: **~ (de Chile)** Santiago

**santiamén** [santja'men] *nm*: **en un ~** in no time at all

**santidad** [santi'ðað] *nf* holiness, sanctity

**santiguarse** [santi'ɣwarse] /1i/ *vr* to make the sign of the cross

**santo, -a** ['santo, a] *adj* holy; *(fig)* wonderful, miraculous ▷ *nm/f* saint ▷ *nm* saint's day; **~ y seña** password

**santuario** [san'twarjo] *nm* sanctuary, shrine

**sapo** ['sapo] *nm* toad

**saque** ['sake] *nm* (*Tenis*) service, serve; (*Fútbol*) throw-in; **~ de esquina** corner (kick)

**saquear** [sake'ar] /1a/ *vt* (*Mil*) to sack; (*robar*) to loot, plunder; *(fig)* to ransack

**sarampión** [saram'pjon] *nm* measles *sg*

**sarcástico, -a** [sar'kastiko, a] *adj* sarcastic

**sardina** [sar'ðina] *nf* sardine

**sargento** [sar'xento] *nm* sergeant

**sarmiento** [sar'mjento] *nm* vine shoot

**sarna** ['sarna] *nf* itch; (*Med*) scabies

**sarpullido** [sarpu'ʎiðo] *nm* (*Med*) rash

**sarro** ['sarro] *nm* (*en dientes*) tartar, plaque

**sartén** [sar'ten] *nf* frying pan

**sastre** ['sastre] *nm* tailor; **sastrería** *nf* (*arte*) tailoring; (*tienda*) tailor's (shop)

**Satanás** [sata'nas] *nm* Satan

**satélite** [sa'telite] *nm* satellite

**sátira** ['satira] *nf* satire

**satisfacción** [satisfak'θjon] *nf* satisfaction

**satisfacer** [satisfa'θer] /2r/ *vt* to satisfy; (*gastos*) to meet; (*pérdida*) to make good; **satisfacerse** *vr* to satisfy o.s., be satisfied; (*vengarse*) to take revenge; **satisfecho, -a** *adj* satisfied; (*contento*) content(ed), happy; (*tb*: **satisfecho de sí mismo**) self-satisfied, smug

**saturar** [satu'rar] /1a/ *vt* to saturate; **saturarse** *vr* (*mercado, aeropuerto*) to reach saturation point

**sauce** ['sauθe] *nm* willow; **~ llorón** weeping willow

**sauna** ['sauna] *nf* sauna

**savia** ['saβja] *nf* sap

**saxofón** [sakso'fon] *nm* saxophone

**sazonar** [saθo'nar] /1a/ *vt* to ripen; (*Culin*) to flavour, season

**scooter** [e'skuter] *nf* (*ESP*) scooter

**Scotch®** [skotʃ] *nm* (*LAM*) Sellotape® (*BRIT*), Scotch tape® (*US*)

**SE** *abr* (= *sudeste*) SE

**PALABRA CLAVE**

**se** [se] *pron* **1** (*reflexivo: sg: m*) himself; (: *f*) herself; (: *pl*) themselves; (: *cosa*) itself; (: *de Vd*) yourself; (: *deVds*) yourselves; **se está**
preparando she's getting (herself) ready
**2** (*como complemento indirecto*) to him; to her; to them; to it; to you; **se lo dije ayer** (*a Vd*) I told you yesterday; **se compró un sombrero** he bought himself a hat; **se rompió la pierna** he broke his leg
**3** (*uso recíproco*) each other, one another; **se miraron (el uno al otro)** they looked at each other *o* one another
**4** (*en oraciones pasivas*): **se han vendido muchos libros** a lot of books have been sold
**5** (*impers*): **se dice que** people say that, it is said that; **allí se come muy bien** the food there is very good, you can eat very well there

**sé** [se] *vb V* **saber; ser**

**sea** *etc* ['sea] *vb V* **ser**

**sebo** ['seβo] *nm* fat, grease

**secador** [seka'ðor] *nm*: **~ para el pelo** hairdryer

**secadora** [seka'ðora] *nf* tumble dryer

**secar** [se'kar] /1g/ *vt* to dry; **secarse** *vr* to dry (off); (*río, planta*) to dry up

**sección** [sek'θjon] *nf* section

**seco, -a** ['seko, a] *adj* dry; (*carácter*) cold; (*respuesta*) sharp, curt; **decir algo a secas** to say sth curtly; **parar en ~** to stop dead

**secretaría** [sekreta'ria] *nf* secretariat

**secretario, -a** [sekre'tarjo, a] *nm/f* secretary

**secreto, -a** [se'kreto, a] *adj* secret; (*persona*) secretive ▷ *nm* secret; (*calidad*) secrecy

**secta** ['sekta] *nf* sect

**sector** [sek'tor] *nm* sector (*tb Inform*)

**secuela** [se'kwela] *nf* consequence

**secuencia** [se'kwenθja] *nf* sequence

**secuestrar** [sekwes'trar] /1a/ *vt* to kidnap; (*bienes*) to seize, confiscate; **secuestro** *nm* kidnapping; seizure, confiscation

**secundario, -a** [sekun'darjo, a] *adj* secondary

**sed** [seð] *nf* thirst; **tener ~** to be thirsty

**seda** ['seða] *nf* silk

**sedal** [se'ðal] *nm* fishing line

**sedán** [se'ðan] *nm* (*LAM*) saloon (*BRIT*), sedan (*US*)

**sedante** [se'ðante] *nm* sedative

**sede** ['seðe] *nf* (*de gobierno*) seat; (*de compañía*) headquarters *pl*; **Santa S~** Holy See

**sedentario, -a** [seðen'tarjo, a] *adj* sedentary

**sediento, -a** [se'ðjento, a] *adj* thirsty

**sedimento** [seði'mento] *nm* sediment

**seducción** [seðuk'θjon] *nf* seduction

**seducir** [seðu'θir] /3n/ *vt* to seduce; (*cautivar*) to charm, fascinate; (*atraer*) to attract; **seductor, a** *adj* seductive;

charming, fascinating; attractive ▷ nm/f seducer

**segar** [se'ɣar] /1h, 1j/ vt (mies) to reap, cut; (hierba) to mow, cut

**seglar** [se'ɣlar] adj secular, lay

**seguido, -a** [se'ɣiðo, a] adj (continuo) continuous, unbroken; (recto) straight ▷ adv (directo) straight (on); (después) after; (LAM: a menudo) often ▷ nf: **en seguida** at once, right away; **cinco días ~s** five days running, five days in a row

**seguidor, a** [seɣi'[dd]or, a] nm/f follower

**seguir** [se'ɣir] /3d, 3k/ vt to follow; (venir después) to follow on, come after; (proseguir) to continue; (perseguir) to chase, pursue ▷ vi (gen) to follow; (continuar) to continue, carry o go on; **seguirse** vr to follow; **sigo sin comprender** I still don't understand; **sigue lloviendo** it's still raining

**según** [se'ɣun] prep according to ▷ adv: **~ (y conforme)** it all depends ▷ conj as

**segundo, -a** [se'ɣundo, a] adj second ▷ nm second ▷ nf second meaning; **segunda (clase)** second class; **segunda (marcha)** (Auto) second (gear); **de segunda mano** second hand

**seguramente** [seɣura'mente] adv surely; (con certeza) for sure, with certainty

**seguridad** [seɣuri'ðað] nf safety; (del estado, de casa etc) security; (certidumbre) certainty; (confianza) confidence; (estabilidad) stability; **~ social** social security

**seguro, -a** [se'ɣuro, a] adj (cierto) sure, certain; (fiel) trustworthy; (libre de peligro) safe; (bien defendido, firme) secure ▷ adv for sure, certainly ▷ nm (Com) insurance; **~ contra terceros/a todo riesgo** third party/ comprehensive insurance; **~s sociales** social security sg

**seis** [seis] num six

**seísmo** [se'ismo] nm tremor, earthquake

**selección** [selek'θjon] nf selection; **seleccionar** /1a/ vt to pick, choose, select

**selectividad** [selektiβi'ðað] nf (Univ) entrance examination

**selecto, -a** [se'lekto, a] adj select, choice; (escogido) selected

**sellar** [se'ʎar] /1a/ vt (documento oficial) to seal; (pasaporte, visado) to stamp

**sello** ['seʎo] nm stamp; (precinto) seal

**selva** ['selβa] nf (bosque) forest, woods pl; (jungla) jungle

**semáforo** [se'maforo] nm (Auto) traffic lights pl; (Ferro) signal

**semana** [se'mana] nf week; **S~ Santa** Holy Week; **entre ~** during the week; see note **"Semana Santa"**; **semanal** adj weekly; **semanario** nm weekly (magazine)

● **SEMANA SANTA**

Semana Santa is a holiday in Spain. All regions take Viernes Santo, Good Friday, Sábado Santo, Holy Saturday, and Domingo de Resurrección, Easter Sunday. Other holidays at this time vary according to each region. There are spectacular procesiones all over the country, with members of cofradías (brotherhoods) dressing in hooded robes and parading their pasos (religious floats or sculptures) through the streets. Seville has the most renowned celebrations, on account of the religious fervour shown by the locals.

**sembrar** [sem'brar] /1j/ vt to sow; (objetos) to sprinkle, scatter about; (noticias etc) to spread

**semejante** [seme'xante] adj (parecido) similar; **~s** alike, similar ▷ nm fellow man, fellow creature; **nunca hizo cosa ~** he never did such a thing; **semejanza** nf similarity, resemblance

**semejar** [seme'xar] /1a/ vi to seem like, resemble; **semejarse** vr to look alike, be similar

**semen** ['semen] nm semen

**semestral** [semes'tral] adj half-yearly, bi-annual

**semicírculo** [semi'θirkulo] nm semicircle

**semidesnatado, -a** [semiðesna'taðo, a] adj semi-skimmed

**semifinal** [semifi'nal] nf semifinal

**semilla** [se'miʎa] nf seed

**seminario** [semi'narjo] nm (Rel) seminary; (Escol) seminar

**sémola** ['semola] nf semolina

**senado** [se'naðo] nm senate; **senador, a** nm/f senator

**sencillez** [senθi'ʎeθ] nf simplicity; (de persona) naturalness; **sencillo, -a** adj simple; (carácter) natural, unaffected

**senda** ['senda] nm path, track

**senderismo** [sende'rismo] nm hiking

**sendero** [sen'dero] nm path, track

**sendos, -as** ['sendos, as] adj pl: **les dio ~ golpes** he hit both of them

**senil** [se'nil] adj senile

**seno** ['seno] nm (Anat) bosom, bust; (fig) bosom; **senos** nmpl breasts

**sensación** [sensa'θjon] nf sensation; (sentido) sense; (sentimiento) feeling; **sensacional** adj sensational

**sensato, -a** [sen'sato, a] adj sensible

**sensible** [sen'sible] adj sensitive; (apreciable) perceptible, appreciable; (pérdida) considerable; **sensiblero, -a** adj sentimental
▌ No confundir sensible con la palabra inglesa sensible.

**sensitivo, -a** [sensi'tiβo, a] *adj* sense *cpd*
**sensorial** [senso'rjal] *adj* sensory
**sensual** [sen'swal] *adj* sensual
**sentado, -a** [sen'taðo, a] *adj* (*establecido*)
settled ▷ *nf* sitting; (*Pol*) sit-in; **dar por ~** to
take for granted, assume; **estar ~** to sit, be
sitting (down)
**sentar** [sen'tar] /1j/ *vt* to sit, seat; (*fig*) to
establish ▷ *vi* (*vestido*) to suit; (*alimento*):
**~ bien/mal a** to agree/disagree with;
**sentarse** *vr* (*persona*) to sit, sit down; (*los
depósitos*) to settle
**sentencia** [sen'tenθja] *nf* (*máxima*) maxim,
saying; (*Jur*) sentence; **sentenciar** /1b/ *vt*
to sentence
**sentido, -a** [sen'tiðo, a] *adj* (*pérdida*)
regrettable; (*carácter*) sensitive ▷ *nm* sense;
(*sentimiento*) feeling; (*significado*) sense,
meaning; (*dirección*) direction; **mi más ~
pésame** my deepest sympathy; **~ del
humor** sense of humour; **~ común**
common sense; **tener ~** to make sense;
**~ único** one-way (street)
**sentimental** [sentimen'tal] *adj*
sentimental; **vida ~** love life
**sentimiento** [senti'mjento] *nm* feeling
**sentir** [sen'tir] /3i/ *vt* to feel; (*percibir*) to
perceive, sense; (*lamentar*) to regret, be
sorry for ▷ *vi* to feel; (*lamentarse*) to feel
sorry ▷ *nm* opinion, judgement; **sentirse**
*vr*: **lo siento** I'm sorry; **~se mejor/mal** to
feel better/ill
**seña** ['sena] *nf* sign; (*Mil*) password; **señas**
*nfpl* address *sg*; **~s personales** personal
description *sg*
**señal** [se'nal] *nf* sign; (*síntoma*) symptom;
(*Ferro, Telec*) signal; (*marca*) mark; (*Com*)
deposit; **en ~ de** as a token of, as a sign of;
**señalar** /1a/ *vt* to mark; (*indicar*) to point
out, indicate
**señor, a** [se'nor, a] *nm* (*hombre*) man;
(*caballero*) gentleman; (*dueño*) owner, master;
(*trato: antes de nombre propio*) Mr; (: *hablando
directamente*) sir ▷ *nf* (*dama*) lady; (*trato:
antes de nombre propio*) Mrs; (: *hablando
directamente*) madam; (*esposa*) wife; **Muy ~
mío** Dear Sir; **Nuestra S~a** Our Lady
**señorita** [seno'rita] *nf* Miss; (*mujer joven*)
young lady
**señorito** [seno'rito] *nm* young gentleman;
(*pey*) toff
**sepa** *etc* ['sepa] *vb* V **saber**
**separación** [separa'θjon] *nf* separation;
(*división*) division; (*distancia*) gap
**separar** [sepa'rar] /1a/ *vt* to separate;
(*dividir*) to divide; **separarse** *vr* (*parte*)
to come away; (*partes*) to come apart;
(*persona*) to leave, go away; (*matrimonio*) to
separate; **separatismo** *nm* separatism

**sepia** ['sepja] *nf* cuttlefish
**septentrional** [septentrjo'nal] *adj*
northern
**septiembre** [sep'tjembre] *nm* September
**séptimo, -a** ['septimo, a] *adj*, *nm* seventh
**sepulcral** [sepul'kral] *adj* (*fig*) gloomy,
dismal; (*silencio, atmósfera*) deadly;
**sepulcro** *nm* tomb, grave
**sepultar** [sepul'tar] /1a/ *vt* to bury;
**sepultura** *nf* (*acto*) burial; (*tumba*) grave,
tomb
**sequía** [se'kia] *nf* drought
**séquito** ['sekito] *nm* (*de rey etc*) retinue; (*Pol*)
followers *pl*

🔵 **PALABRA CLAVE**

**ser** [ser] /2v/ *vi* **1** (*descripción, identidad*) to
be; **es médica/muy alta** she's a doctor/
very tall; **su familia es de Cuzco** his family
is from Cuzco; **soy Ana** I'm Ana; (*por
teléfono*) it's Ana
**2** (*propiedad*): **es de Joaquín** it's Joaquín's, it
belongs to Joaquín
**3** (*horas, fechas, números*): **es la una** it's one
o'clock; **son las seis y media** it's half-past
six; **es el 1 de junio** it's the first of June;
**somos/son seis** there are six of us/them
**4** (*suceso*): **¿qué ha sido eso?** what was
that?; **la fiesta es en mi casa** the party's at
my house
**5** (*en oraciones pasivas*): **ha sido descubierto
ya** it's already been discovered
**6**: **es de esperar que ...** it is to be hoped *o*
I *etc* hope that ...
**7** (*locuciones con subjun*): **o sea** that is to
say; **sea él sea su hermana** either him or
his sister
**8**: **a** *o* **de no ser por él ...** but for him ...
**9**: **a no ser que: a no ser que tenga uno ya**
unless he's got one already
▷ *nm* being; **ser humano** human being

**sereno, -a** [se'reno, a] *adj* (*persona*) calm,
unruffled; (*tiempo*) fine, settled; (*ambiente*)
calm, peaceful ▷ *nm* night watchman
**serial** [se'rjal] *nm* serial
**serie** ['serje] *nf* series; (*cadena*) sequence,
succession; **fuera de ~** out of order; (*fig*)
special, out of the ordinary; **fabricación
en ~** mass production
**seriedad** [serje'ðað] *nf* seriousness;
(*formalidad*) reliability
**serigrafía** [seriɣra'fia] *nf* silk screen
printing
**serio, -a** ['serjo, a] *adj* serious; reliable,
dependable; grave, serious; **en ~**
seriously
**sermón** [ser'mon] *nm* (*Rel*) sermon

**seropositivo, -a** [seroposi'tiβo, a] *adj* HIV-positive

**serpentear** [serpente'ar] /1a/ *vi* to wriggle; (*camino, río*) to wind, snake

**serpentina** [serpen'tina] *nf* streamer

**serpiente** [ser'pjente] *nf* snake; **~ de cascabel** rattlesnake

**serranía** [serra'nia] *nf* mountainous area

**serrar** [se'rrar] /1j/ *vt* to saw

**serrín** [se'rrin] *nm* sawdust

**serrucho** [se'rrutʃo] *nm* handsaw

**service** [ser'βis] *nm* (LAM Auto) service

**servicio** [ser'βiθjo] *nm* service; (LAM Auto) service; **servicios** *nmpl* toilet(s); **~ incluido** service charge included; **~ militar** military service

**servidumbre** [serβi'ðumbre] *nf* (*sujeción*) servitude; (*criados*) servants *pl*, staff

**servil** [ser'βil] *adj* servile

**servilleta** [serβi'ʎeta] *nf* serviette, napkin

**servir** [ser'βir] /3k/ *vt* to serve ▷ *vi* to serve; (*tener utilidad*) to be of use, be useful; **servirse** *vr* to serve o help o.s.; **~se de algo** to make use of sth, use sth; **sírvase pasar** please come in

**sesenta** [se'senta] *num* sixty

**sesión** [se'sjon] *nf* (Pol) session, sitting; (*Cine*) showing

**seso** ['seso] *nm* brain; **sesudo, -a** *adj* sensible, wise

**seta** ['seta] *nf* mushroom; **~ venenosa** toadstool

**setecientos, -as** [sete'θjentos, as] *num* seven hundred

**setenta** [se'tenta] *num* seventy

**severo, -a** [se'βero, a] *adj* severe

**Sevilla** [se'βiʎa] *nf* Seville; **sevillano, -a** *adj* of o from Seville ▷ *nm/f* native o inhabitant of Seville

**sexo** ['sekso] *nm* sex

**sexto, -a** [s] a] *num* sixth

**sexual** [sek'swal] *adj* sexual; **vida ~** sex life

**si** [si] *conj* if; whether ▷ *nm* (*Mus*) B; **me pregunto si ...** I wonder if o whether ...

**sí** [si] *adv* yes ▷ *nm* consent ▷ *pron* (*uso impersonal*) oneself; (*sg: m*) himself; (: *f*) herself; (: *de cosa*) itself; (: *de usted*) yourself; (*pl*) themselves; (: *de ustedes*) yourselves; (: *recíproco*) each other; **él no quiere pero yo sí** he doesn't want to but I do; **ella sí vendrá** she will certainly come, she is sure to come; **claro que sí** of course; **creo que sí** I think so

**siamés, -esa** [sja'mes, esa] *adj, nm/f* Siamese

**SIDA** ['siða] *nm abr* (= *síndrome de inmunodeficiencia adquirida*) AIDS

**siderúrgico, -a** [siðe'rurxico, a] *adj* iron and steel *cpd*

**sidra** ['siðra] *nf* cider

**siembra** ['sjembra] *nf* sowing

**siempre** ['sjempre] *adv* always; (*todo el tiempo*) all the time ▷ *conj*: **~ que ...** (+ *indic*) whenever ...; (+ *subjun*) provided that ...; **como ~** as usual; **para ~** forever

**sien** [sjen] *nf* temple

**siento** *etc* ['sjento] *vb V* **sentar; sentir**

**sierra** ['sjerra] *nf* (Tec) saw; (Geo) mountain range

**siervo, -a** ['sjerβo, a] *nm/f* slave

**siesta** ['sjesta] *nf* siesta, nap; **dormir la** o **echarse una** o **tomar una ~** to have an afternoon nap o a doze

**siete** ['sjete] *num* seven

**sifón** [si'fon] *nm* syphon

**sigla** ['siɣla] *nf* abbreviation

**siglo** ['siɣlo] *nm* century; (*fig*) age

**significado** [siɣnifi'kaðo] *nm* (*de palabra etc*) meaning

**significar** [siɣnifi'kar] /1g/ *vt* to mean, signify; (*notificar*) to make known, express

**significativo, -a** [siɣnifika'tiβo, a] *adj* significant

**signo** ['siɣno] *nm* sign; **~ de admiración** o **exclamación** exclamation mark; **~ de interrogación** question mark

**sigo** *etc vb V* **seguir**

**siguiente** [si'ɣjente] *adj* following; (*próximo*) next

**siguió** *etc vb V* **seguir**

**sílaba** ['silaβa] *nf* syllable

**silbar** [sil'βar] /1a/ *vt*, *vi* to whistle; **silbato** *nm* whistle; **silbido** *nm* whistle, whistling

**silenciador** [silenθja'ðor] *nm* silencer

**silenciar** [silen'θjar] /1b/ *vt* (*persona*) to silence; (*escándalo*) to hush up; **silencio** *nm* silence, quiet; **silencioso, -a** *adj* silent, quiet

**silla** ['siʎa] *nf* (*asiento*) chair; (*tb:* **~ de montar**) saddle; **~ de ruedas** wheelchair

**sillón** [si'ʎon] *nm* armchair, easy chair

**silueta** [si'lweta] *nf* silhouette; (*de edificio*) outline; (*figura*) figure

**silvestre** [sil'βestre] *adj* wild

**simbólico, -a** [sim'boliko, a] *adj* symbolic(al)

**simbolizar** [simboli'θar] /1f/ *vt* to symbolize

**símbolo** ['simbolo] *nm* symbol

**similar** [simi'lar] *adj* similar

**simio** ['simjo] *nm* ape

**simpatía** [simpa'tia] *nf* liking; (*afecto*) affection; (*amabilidad*) kindness; **simpático, -a** *adj* nice, pleasant; (*bondadoso*) kind

▎No confundir *simpático* con la palabra inglesa *sympathetic*.

**simpatizante** [simpati'θante] *nmf*
 sympathizer
**simpatizar** [simpati'θar] /1f/ *vi*: ~ **con** to
 get on well with
**simple** ['simple] *adj* simple; (*elemental*)
 simple, easy; (*mero*) mere; (*puro*) pure, sheer
 ▷ *nmf* simpleton; **simpleza** *nf* simpleness;
 (*necedad*) silly thing; **simplificar** /1g/ *vt* to
 simplify
**simposio** [sim'posjo] *nm* symposium
**simular** [simu'lar] /1a/ *vt* to simulate
**simultáneo, -a** [simul'taneo, a] *adj*
 simultaneous
**sin** [sin] *prep* without ▷ *conj*: ~ **que**
 (+ *subjun*) without; **la ropa está ~ lavar**
 the clothes are unwashed; ~ **embargo**
 however
**sinagoga** [sina'ɣoɣa] *nf* synagogue
**sinceridad** [sinθeri'ðað] *nf* sincerity;
 **sincero, -a** *adj* sincere
**sincronizar** [sinkroni'θar] /1f/ *vt* to
 synchronize
**sindical** [sindi'kal] *adj* union *cpd*, trade-
 union *cpd*; **sindicalista** *adj* ▷ *nmf* trade
 unionist
**sindicato** [sindi'kato] *nm* (*de trabajadores*)
 trade(s) *o* labor (*US*) union; (*de negociantes*)
 syndicate
**síndrome** ['sindrome] *nm* syndrome; ~ **de**
 **abstinencia** withdrawal symptoms; ~ **de la**
 **clase turista** economy-class syndrome
**sinfín** [sin'fin] *nm*: **un ~ de** a great many,
 no end of
**sinfonía** [sinfo'nia] *nf* symphony
**singular** [singu'lar] *adj* singular; (*fig*)
 outstanding, exceptional; (*pey*) peculiar,
 odd
**siniestro, -a** [si'njestro, a] *adj* sinister ▷ *nm*
 (*accidente*) accident
**sinnúmero** [sin'numero] *nm* = **sinfín**
**sino** ['sino] *nm* fate, destiny ▷ *conj* (*pero*)
 but; (*salvo*) except, save
**sinónimo, -a** [si'nonimo, a] *adj*
 synonymous ▷ *nm* synonym
**síntesis** ['sintesis] *nf inv* synthesis;
 **sintético, -a** *adj* synthetic
**sintió** *vb* V **sentir**
**síntoma** ['sintoma] *nm* symptom
**sintonía** [sinto'nia] *nf* (*Radio*) tuning;
 **sintonizar** /1f/ *vt* (*Radio*) to tune (in) to
**sinvergüenza** [simber'ɣwenθa] *nmf*
 rogue, scoundrel; **¡es un ~!** he's got a nerve!
**siquiera** [si'kjera] *conj* even if, even though
 ▷ *adv* at least; **ni ~** not even
**Siria** ['sirja] *nf* Syria
**sirviente, -a** [sir'βjente, a] *nm/f* servant
**sirvo** *etc vb* V **servir**
**sistema** [sis'tema] *nm* system; (*método*)
 method; **sistemático, -a** *adj* systematic

**sitiar** [si'tjar] /1b/ *vt* to besiege, lay siege to
**sitio** ['sitjo] *nm* (*lugar*) place; (*espacio*) room,
 space; (*Mil*) siege; (*LAM*: *parada*)
 taxi stand *o* rank (*BRIT*); ~ **web** website
**situación** [sitwa'θjon] *nf* situation,
 position; (*estatus*) position, standing
**situado, -a** [si'twaðo, a] *adj* situated,
 placed
**situar** [si'twar] /1e/ *vt* to place, put;
 (*edificio*) to locate, situate
**slip** [es'lip] *nm* pants *pl*, briefs *pl*
**smartphone** [(e)'smarfon] *nm*
 smartphone
**smoking** [(e)'smokin] (*pl* **smokings**) *nm*
 dinner jacket (*BRIT*), tuxedo (*US*)
 ▌ No confundir *smoking* con la palabra
 ▌ inglesa *smoking*.
**SMS** *nm* (*mensaje*) text (message), SMS
 (message)
**snob** [es'nob] = **esnob**
**SO** *abr* (= *suroeste*) SW
**sobaco** [so'βako] *nm* armpit
**sobar** [so'βar] /1a/ *vt* (*ropa*) to rumple;
 (*comida*) to play around with
**soberanía** [soβera'nia] *nf* sovereignty;
 **soberano, -a** *adj* sovereign; (*fig*) supreme
 ▷ *nm/f* sovereign
**soberbio, -a** [so'βerβjo, a] *adj* (*orgulloso*)
 proud; (*altivo*) arrogant; (*fig*) magnificent,
 superb ▷ *nf* pride; haughtiness, arrogance;
 magnificence
**sobornar** [soβor'nar] /1a/ *vt* to bribe;
 **soborno** *nm* bribe
**sobra** ['soβra] *nf* excess, surplus; **sobras**
 *nfpl* left-overs, scraps; **de ~** surplus,
 extra; **tengo de ~** I've more than enough;
 **sobrado, -a** *adj* (*más que suficiente*) more
 than enough; (*superfluo*) excessive;
 **sobrante** *adj* remaining, extra ▷ *nm*
 surplus, remainder; **sobrar** /1a/ *vt* to
 exceed, surpass ▷ *vi* (*tener de más*) to be
 more than enough; (*quedar*) to remain, be
 left (over)
**sobrasada** [soβra'saða] *nf* ≈ sausage
 spread
**sobre** ['soβre] *prep* (*gen*) on; (*encima*) on (top
 of); (*por encima de, arriba de*) over, above;

*(más que)* more than; *(además)* in addition to, besides; *(alrededor de)* about ▷ *nm* envelope; **~ todo** above all

**sobrecama** [soβɾe'kama] *nf* bedspread

**sobrecargar** [soβɾekaɾ'ɣaɾ] /1h/ *vt* *(camión)* to overload; *(Com)* to surcharge

**sobredosis** [soβɾe'ðosis] *nf inv* overdose

**sobreentender** [soβɾeenten'deɾ] /2g/ *vt* to deduce, infer; **sobreentenderse** *vr*: **se sobreentiende que …** it is implied that …

**sobrehumano, -a** [soβɾeu'mano, a] *adj* superhuman

**sobrellevar** [soβɾeʎe'βaɾ] /1a/ *vt* to bear, endure

**sobremesa** [soβɾe'mesa] *nf*: **durante la ~** after dinner

**sobrenatural** [soβɾenatu'ɾal] *adj* supernatural

**sobrenombre** [soβɾe'nombɾe] *nm* nickname

**sobrepasar** [soβɾepa'saɾ] /1a/ *vt* to exceed, surpass

**sobreponer** [soβɾepo'neɾ] /2q/ *vt* *(poner encima)* to put on top; *(añadir)* to add; **sobreponerse** *vr*: **~se a** to overcome

**sobresaliente** [soβɾesa'ljente] *adj* outstanding, excellent

**sobresalir** [soβɾesa'liɾ] /3q/ *vi* to project, jut out; *(fig)* to stand out, excel

**sobresaltar** [soβɾesal'taɾ] /1a/ *vt* *(asustar)* to scare, frighten; *(sobrecoger)* to startle; **sobresalto** *nm (movimiento)* start; *(susto)* scare; *(turbación)* sudden shock

**sobretodo** [soβɾe'toðo] *nm* overcoat

**sobrevenir** [soβɾeβe'niɾ] /3r/ *vi (ocurrir)* to happen (unexpectedly); *(resultar)* to follow, ensue

**sobrevivir** [soβɾeβi'βiɾ] /3a/ *vi* to survive

**sobrevolar** [soβɾeβo'laɾ] /1l/ *vt* to fly over

**sobriedad** [soβɾje'ðað] *nf* sobriety, soberness; *(moderación)* moderation, restraint

**sobrino, -a** [so'βɾino, a] *nm/f* nephew/niece

**sobrio, -a** [so'βɾjo, a] *adj* sober; *(moderado)* moderate, restrained

**socarrón, -ona** [soka'rron, ona] *adj (sarcástico)* sarcastic, ironic(al)

**socavón** [soka'βon] *nm (en la calle)* hole

**sociable** [so'θjaβle] *adj (persona)* sociable, friendly; *(animal)* social

**social** [so'θjal] *adj* social; *(Com)* company *cpd*

**socialdemócrata** [soθjalde'mokɾata] *nmf* social democrat

**socialista** [soθja'lista] *adj, nmf* socialist

**socializar** [soθjali'θaɾ] /1f/ *vt* to socialize

**sociedad** [soθje'ðað] *nf* society; *(Com)* company; **~ anónima (S.A.)** limited company (Ltd) (BRIT), incorporated company (Inc) (US); **~ de consumo** consumer society

**socio, -a** ['soθjo, a] *nm/f (miembro)* member; *(Com)* partner

**sociología** [soθjolo'xia] *nf* sociology; **sociólogo, -a** *nm/f* sociologist

**socorrer** [soko'rreɾ] /2a/ *vt* to help; **socorrista** *nmf* first aider; *(en piscina, playa)* lifeguard; **socorro** *nm (ayuda)* help, aid; *(Mil)* relief; **¡socorro!** help!

**soda** ['soða] *nf (sosa)* soda; *(bebida)* soda (water)

**sofá** [so'fa] *nm* sofa, settee; **sofá-cama** *nm* studio couch, sofa bed

**sofocar** [sofo'kaɾ] /1g/ *vt* to suffocate; *(apagar)* to smother, put out; **sofocarse** *vr* to suffocate; *(fig)* to blush, feel embarrassed; **sofoco** *nm* suffocation; *(azoro)* embarrassment

**sofreír** [sofɾe'iɾ] /3l/ *vt* to fry lightly

**soft** ['sof], **software** ['sofweɾ] *nm (Inform)* software

**soga** ['soɣa] *nf* rope

**sois** [sois] *vb V* **ser**

**soja** ['soxa] *nf* soya

**sol** [sol] *nm* sun; *(luz)* sunshine, sunlight; *(Mus)* G; **hace ~** it is sunny

**solamente** [sola'mente] *adv* only, just

**solapa** [so'lapa] *nf (de chaqueta)* lapel; *(de libro)* jacket

**solapado, -a** [sola'paðo, a] *adj (intenciones)* underhand; *(gestos, movimiento)* sly

**solar** [so'laɾ] *adj* solar, sun *cpd* ▷ *nm (terreno)* plot (of ground)

**soldado** [sol'daðo] *nm* soldier; **~ raso** private

**soldador** [solda'ðoɾ] *nm* soldering iron; *(persona)* welder

**soldar** [sol'daɾ] /1l/ *vt* to solder, weld

**soleado, -a** [sole'aðo, a] *adj* sunny

**soledad** [sole'ðað] *nf* solitude; *(estado infeliz)* loneliness

**solemne** [so'lemne] *adj* solemn

**soler** [so'leɾ] *vi* to be in the habit of, be accustomed to; **suele salir a las ocho** she usually goes out at 8 o'clock

**solfeo** [sol'feo] *nm* sol-fa, singing of scales

**solicitar** [soliθi'taɾ] /1a/ *vt (permiso)* to ask for, seek; *(puesto)* to apply for; *(votos)* to canvass for; *(atención)* to attract

**solícito, -a** [so'liθito, a] *adj (diligente)* diligent; *(cuidadoso)* careful; **solicitud** *nf (calidad)* great care; *(petición)* request; *(a un puesto)* application

**solidaridad** [soliðaɾi'ðað] *nf* solidarity; **solidario, -a** *adj (participación)* joint, common; *(compromiso)* mutually binding

**sólido, -a** ['soliðo, a] *adj* solid

**soliloquio** [soli'lokjo] *nm* soliloquy

**solista** [so'lista] *nmf* soloist

**solitario, -a** [soli'tarjo, a] *adj (persona)* lonely, solitary; *(lugar)* lonely, desolate ▷ *nm/f (recluso)* recluse; *(en la sociedad)* loner ▷ *nm* solitaire

**sollozar** [soʎo'θar] /1f/ *vi* to sob; **sollozo** *nm* sob

**solo¹, -a** ['solo, a] *adj (único)* single, sole; *(sin compañía)* alone; *(solitario)* lonely; **hay una sola dificultad** there is just one difficulty; **a solas** alone, by o.s.

**solo², sólo** ['solo] *adv* only, just

**solomillo** [solo'miʎo] *nm* sirloin

**soltar** [sol'tar] /1l/ *vt (dejar ir)* to let go of; *(desprender)* to unfasten, loosen; *(librar)* to release, set free; *(risa etc)* to let out

**soltero, -a** [sol'tero, a] *adj* single, unmarried ▷ *nm* bachelor ▷ *nf* single woman; **solterón** *nm* confirmed bachelor

**solterona** [solte'rona] *nf* spinster

**soltura** [sol'tura] *nf* looseness, slackness; *(de los miembros)* agility, ease of movement; *(en el hablar)* fluency, ease

**soluble** [so'luβle] *adj (Química)* soluble; *(problema)* solvable; **~ en agua** soluble in water

**solución** [solu'θjon] *nf* solution; **solucionar** /1a/ *vt (problema)* to solve; *(asunto)* to settle, resolve

**solventar** [solβen'tar] /1a/ *vt (pagar)* to settle, pay; *(resolver)* to resolve; **solvente** *adj* solvent

**sombra** ['sombra] *nf* shadow; *(como protección)* shade; **sombras** *nfpl* darkness *sg*, shadows; **tener buena/mala ~** to be lucky/unlucky

**sombrero** [som'brero] *nm* hat

**sombrilla** [som'briʎa] *nf* parasol, sunshade

**sombrío, -a** [som'brio, a] *adj (oscuro)* dark; *(fig)* sombre, sad; *(persona)* gloomy

**someter** [some'ter] /2a/ *vt (país)* to conquer; *(persona)* to subject to one's will; *(informe)* to present, submit; **someterse** *vr* to give in, yield, submit; **~ a** to subject to

**somier** [so'mjer] *(pl* **somiers)** *nm* spring mattress

**somnífero** [som'nifero] *nm* sleeping pill *o* tablet

**somos** ['somos] *vb V* **ser**

**son** [son] *vb V* **ser** ▷ *nm* sound

**sonaja** [so'naxa] *nf* (LAM) = **sonajero**

**sonajero** [sona'xero] *nm* (baby's) rattle

**sonambulismo** [sonambu'lismo] *nm* sleepwalking; **sonámbulo, -a** *nm/f* sleepwalker

**sonar** [so'nar] /1l/ *vt* to ring ▷ *vi* to sound; *(hacer ruido)* to make a noise; *(Ling)* to be sounded, be pronounced; *(ser conocido)* to sound familiar; *(campana)* to ring; *(reloj)* to strike, chime; **sonarse** *vr*: **~se (la nariz)** to blow one's nose; **me suena ese nombre** that name rings a bell

**sonda** ['sonda] *nf (Naut)* sounding; *(Tec)* bore, drill; *(Med)* probe

**sondear** [sonde'ar] /1a/ *vt* to sound; to bore (into), drill; to probe, sound; *(fig)* to sound out; **sondeo** *nm* sounding; boring, drilling; *(encuesta)* poll, enquiry

**sonido** [so'niðo] *nm* sound

**sonoro, -a** [so'noro, a] *adj* sonorous; *(resonante)* loud, resonant

**sonreír** [sonre'ir] /3l/ *vi* to smile; **sonriente** *adj* smiling; **sonrisa** *nf* smile

**sonrojar** [sonro'xar] /1a/ *vt*: **~ a algn** to make sb blush; **sonrojarse** *vr*: **~se (de)** to blush (at)

**sonrojo** *nm* blush

**soñador, a** [soɲa'ðor, a] *nm/f* dreamer

**soñar** [so'ɲar] /1l/ *vt, vi* to dream; **~ con** to dream about *o* of

**soñoliento, -a** [soɲo'ljento, a] *adj* sleepy, drowsy

**sopa** ['sopa] *nf* soup

**soplar** [so'plar] /1a/ *vt (polvo)* to blow away, blow off; *(inflar)* to blow up; *(vela)* to blow out ▷ *vi* to blow; **soplo** *nm* blow, puff; *(de viento)* puff, gust

**soplón, -ona** [so'plon, ona] *nm/f (fam: chismoso)* telltale; (: *de policía)* informer, grass

**soporífero, -a** [sopo'rifero, a] *adj* sleep-inducing ▷ *nm* sleeping pill

**soportable** [sopor'taβle] *adj* bearable

**soportar** [sopor'tar] /1a/ *vt* to bear, carry; *(fig)* to bear, put up with; **soporte** *nm* support; *(fig)* pillar, support

No confundir *soportar* con la palabra inglesa *support*.

**soprano** [so'prano] *nf* soprano

**sorber** [sor'βer] /2a/ *vt (chupar)* to sip; *(inhalar)* to sniff, inhale; *(absorber)* to soak up, absorb

**sorbete** [sor'βete] *nm* iced fruit drink

**sorbo** ['sorβo] *nm (trago)* gulp, swallow; *(chupada)* sip

**sordera** [sor'ðera] *nf* deafness

**sórdido, -a** ['sorðiðo, a] *adj* dirty, squalid

**sordo, -a** ['sorðo, a] *adj (persona)* deaf ▷ *nm/f* deaf person; **sordomudo, -a** *adj* speech-and-hearing impaired

**sorna** ['sorna] *nf* sarcastic tone

**soroche** [so'rotʃe] *nm* (LAM) mountain sickness

**sorprendente** [sorpren'dente] *adj* surprising

**sorprender** [sorpren'der] /2a/ *vt* to surprise; **sorpresa** *nf* surprise

**sortear** [sorte'ar] /1a/ vt to draw lots for; (*rifar*) to raffle; (*dificultad*) to dodge, avoid; **sorteo** nm (*en lotería*) draw; (*rifa*) raffle

**sortija** [sor'tixa] nf ring; (*rizo*) ringlet, curl

**sosegado, -a** [sose'ɣaðo, a] adj quiet, calm

**sosiego** [so'sjeɣo] nm quiet(ness), calm(ness)

**soso, -a** ['soso, a] adj (*Culin*) tasteless; (*fig*) dull, uninteresting

**sospecha** [sos'petʃa] nf suspicion; **sospechar** /1a/ vt to suspect; **sospechoso, -a** adj suspicious; (*testimonio, opinión*) suspect ▷ nm/f suspect

**sostén** [sos'ten] nm (*apoyo*) support; (*sujetador*) bra; (*alimentación*) sustenance, food

**sostener** [soste'ner] /2k/ vt to support; (*mantener*) to keep up, maintain; (*alimentar*) to sustain, keep going; **sostenerse** vr to support o.s.; (*seguir*) to continue, remain; **sostenido, -a** adj continuous, sustained; (*prolongado*) prolonged

**sotana** [so'tana] nf (*Rel*) cassock

**sótano** ['sotano] nm basement

**soy** [soi] vb V **ser**

**soya** ['soja] nf (LAM) soya (bean)

**Sr.** abr (= Señor) Mr

**Sra.** abr (= Señora) Mrs

**Sras.** abr (= Señoras) Mrs

**Sres.** abr (= Señores) Messrs

**Srta.** abr (= Señorita) Miss, Ms

**Sta.** abr (= Santa) St

**Sto.** abr (= Santo) St

**su** [su] pron (*de él*) his; (*de ella*) her; (*de una cosa*) its; (*de ellos, ellas*) their; (*de usted, ustedes*) your

**suave** ['swaβe] adj gentle; (*superficie*) smooth; (*trabajo*) easy; (*música, voz*) soft, sweet; **suavidad** nf gentleness; (*de superficie*) smoothness; (*de música*) softness, sweetness; **suavizante** nm (*de ropa*) softener; (*del pelo*) conditioner; **suavizar** /1f/ vt to soften; (*quitar la aspereza*) to smooth (out)

**subasta** [su'βasta] nf auction; **subastar** /1a/ vt to auction (off)

**subcampeón, -ona** [suβkampe'on, ona] nm/f runner-up

**subconsciente** [suβkons'θjente] adj subconscious

**subdesarrollado, -a** [suβðesarro'ʎaðo, a] adj underdeveloped

**subdesarrollo** [suβðesa'rroʎo] nm underdevelopment

**subdirector, a** [suβðirek'tor, a] nm/f assistant o deputy manager

**súbdito, -a** ['suβðito, a] nm/f subject

**subestimar** [suβesti'mar] /1a/ vt to underestimate, underrate

**subir** [su'βir] /3a/ vt (*objeto*) to raise, lift up; (*cuesta, calle*) to go up; (*colina, montaña*) to climb; (*precio*) to raise, put up ▷ vi to go/come up; (*a un coche*) to get in; (*a un autobús, tren*) to get on; (*precio*) to rise, go up; (*río, marea*) to rise; **subirse** vr to get up, climb

**súbito, -a** ['suβito, a] adj (*repentino*) sudden; (*imprevisto*) unexpected

**subjetivo, -a** [suβxe'tiβo, a] adj subjective

**sublevar** [suβle'βar] /1a/ vt to rouse to revolt; **sublevarse** vr to revolt, rise

**sublime** [su'βlime] adj sublime

**submarinismo** [suβmari'nismo] nm scuba diving

**submarino, -a** [suβma'rino, a] adj underwater ▷ nm submarine

**subnormal** [suβnor'mal] adj subnormal ▷ nmf subnormal person

**subordinado, -a** [suβorði'naðo, a] adj, nm/f subordinate

**subrayar** [suβra'jar] /1a/ vt to underline

**subsanar** [suβsa'nar] /1a/ vt (*reparar*) to rectify

**subsidio** [suβ'siðjo] nm (*ayuda*) aid, financial help; (*subvención*) subsidy, grant; (*de enfermedad, paro etc*) benefit, allowance

**subsistencia** [suβsis'tenθja] nf subsistence

**subsistir** [suβsis'tir] /3a/ vi to subsist; (*sobrevivir*) to survive, endure

**subte** ['suβte] nm (RPL) underground (BRIT), subway (US)

**subterráneo, -a** [suβte'rraneo, a] adj underground, subterranean ▷ nm underpass, underground passage

**subtitulado, -a** [suβtitu'laðo, a] adj subtitled

**subtítulo** [suβ'titulo] nm subtitle

**suburbio** [su'βurβjo] nm (*barrio*) slum quarter

**subvención** [suββen'θjon] nf subsidy, grant; **subvencionar** /1a/ vt to subsidize

**sucedáneo, -a** [suθe'ðaneo, a] adj substitute ▷ nm substitute (food)

**suceder** [suθe'ðer] /2a/ vi to happen; (*seguir*) to succeed, follow; **lo que sucede es que ...** the fact is that ...; **sucesión** nf succession; (*serie*) sequence, series

**sucesivamente** [suθesiβa'mente] adv: **y así ~** and so on

**sucesivo, -a** [suθe'siβo, a] adj successive, following; **en lo ~** in future, from now on

**suceso** [su'θeso] nm (*hecho*) event, happening; (*incidente*) incident

▌ No confundir *suceso* con la palabra inglesa *success*.

**suciedad** [suθje'ðað] nf (*estado*) dirtiness; (*mugre*) dirt, filth

**sucio, -a** ['suθjo, a] adj dirty

**suculento, -a** [suku'lento, a] *adj* succulent

**sucumbir** [sukum'bir] /3a/ *vi* to succumb

**sucursal** [sukur'sal] *nf* branch (office)

**sudadera** [suða'ðera] *nf* sweatshirt

**Sudáfrica** [su'ðafrika] *nf* South Africa

**Sudamérica** [suða'merika] *nf* South America; **sudamericano, -a** *adj, nm/f* South American

**sudar** [su'ðar] /1a/ *vt, vi* to sweat

**sudeste** [su'ðeste] *nm* south-east

**sudoeste** [suðo'este] *nm* south-west

**sudoku** [su'ðoku] *nm* sudoku

**sudor** [su'ðor] *nm* sweat; **sudoroso, -a** *adj* sweaty, sweating

**Suecia** ['sweθja] *nf* Sweden; **sueco, -a** *adj* Swedish ▷ *nm/f* Swede

**suegro, -a** ['sweɣro, a] *nm/f* father-/mother-in-law

**suela** ['swela] *nf* sole

**sueldo** ['sweldo] *nm* pay, wage(s) (*pl*)

**suelo** ['swelo] *vb* V **soler** ▷ *nm* (*tierra*) ground; (*de casa*) floor

**suelto, -a** ['swelto, a] *adj* loose; (*libre*) free; (*separado*) detached; (*ágil*) quick, agile ▷ *nm* (*loose*) change, small change

**sueñito** [swe'ɲito] *nm* (LAM) nap

**sueño** ['sweɲo] *vb* V **soñar** ▷ *nm* sleep; (*somnolencia*) sleepiness, drowsiness; (*lo soñado, fig*) dream; **tener ~** to be sleepy

**suero** ['swero] *nm* (*Med*) serum; (*de leche*) whey

**suerte** ['swerte] *nf* (*fortuna*) luck; (*azar*) chance; (*destino*) fate, destiny; (*género*) sort, kind; **tener ~** to be lucky

**suéter** ['sweter] *nm* sweater

**suficiente** [sufi'θjente] *adj* enough, sufficient ▷ *nm* (*Escol*) pass

**sufragio** [su'fraxjo] *nm* (*voto*) vote; (*derecho de voto*) suffrage

**sufrido, -a** [su'friðo, a] *adj* (*de carácter fuerte*) tough; (*paciente*) long-suffering, patient

**sufrimiento** [sufri'mjento] *nm* suffering

**sufrir** [su'frir] /3a/ *vt* (*padecer*) to suffer; (*soportar*) to bear, put up with; (*apoyar*) to hold up, support ▷ *vi* to suffer

**sugerencia** [suxe'renθja] *nf* suggestion

**sugerir** [suxe'rir] /3i/ *vt* to suggest; (*sutilmente*) to hint

**sugestión** [suxes'tjon] *nf* suggestion; (*sutil*) hint; **sugestionar** /1a/ *vt* to influence

**sugestivo, -a** [suxes'tiβo, a] *adj* stimulating; (*fascinante*) fascinating

**suicida** [sui'θiða] *adj* suicidal ▷ *nmf* suicidal person; (*muerto*) suicide, person who has committed suicide; **suicidarse** /1a/ *vr* to commit suicide, kill o.s.; **suicidio** *nm* suicide

**Suiza** ['swiθa] *nf* Switzerland; **suizo, -a** *adj, nm/f* Swiss

**sujeción** [suxe'θjon] *nf* subjection

**sujetador** [suxeta'ðor] *nm* (*prenda femenina*) bra

**sujetar** [suxe'tar] /1a/ *vt* (*fijar*) to fasten; (*detener*) to hold down; **sujetarse** *vr* to subject o.s.; **sujeto, -a** *adj* fastened, secure ▷ *nm* subject; (*individuo*) individual; **sujeto a** subject to

**suma** ['suma] *nf* (*cantidad*) total, sum; (*de dinero*) sum; (*acto*) adding (up), addition; **en ~** in short

**sumamente** [suma'mente] *adv* extremely, exceedingly

**sumar** [su'mar] /1a/ *vt* to add (up) ▷ *vi* to add up

**sumergir** [sumer'xir] /3c/ *vt* to submerge; (*hundir*) to sink

**suministrar** [suminis'trar] /1a/ *vt* to supply, provide; **suministro** *nm* supply; (*acto*) supplying, providing

**sumir** [su'mir] /3a/ *vt* to sink, submerge; (*fig*) to plunge

**sumiso, -a** [su'miso, a] *adj* submissive, docile

**sumo, -a** ['sumo, a] *adj* great, extreme; (*mayor*) highest, supreme

**suntuoso, -a** [sun'twoso, a] *adj* sumptuous, magnificent

**supe** *etc* ['supe] *vb* V **saber**

**súper** ['super] *adj* (*fam*) super, great ▷ *nf* (*gasolina*) four-star (petrol)

**super...** [super] *pref* super..., over...

**superar** [supe'rar] /1a/ *vt* (*sobreponerse a*) to overcome; (*rebasar*) to surpass, do better than; (*pasar*) to go beyond; **superarse** *vr* to excel o.s.

**superbueno, a** [super'bweno, a] *adj* great, fantastic

**superficial** [superfi'θjal] *adj* superficial; (*medida*) surface *cpd*

**superficie** [super'fiθje] *nf* surface; (*área*) area

**superfluo, -a** [su'perflwo, a] *adj* superfluous

**superior** [supe'rjor] *adj* (*piso, clase*) upper; (*temperatura, número, nivel*) higher; (*mejor: calidad, producto*) superior, better ▷ *nmf* superior; **superioridad** *nf* superiority

**supermercado** [supermer'kaðo] *nm* supermarket

**superponer** [superpo'ner] /2q/ *vt* to superimpose

**superstición** [supersti'θjon] *nf* superstition; **supersticioso, -a** *adj* superstitious

**supervisar** [superβi'sar] /1a/ *vt* to supervise

**supervivencia** [superβi'βenθja] nf survival

**superviviente** [superβi'βjente] adj surviving

**supiera** etc vb V **saber**

**suplantar** [suplan'tar] /1a/ vt to supplant

**suplementario, -a** [suplemen'tarjo, a] adj supplementary

**suplemento** [suple'mento] nm supplement

**suplente** [su'plente] adj substitute ▷ nmf substitute

**supletorio, -a** [suple'torjo, a] adj supplementary ▷ nm supplement; **teléfono ~** extension

**súplica** ['suplika] nf request; (Jur) petition

**suplicar** [supli'kar] /1g/ vt (cosa) to beg (for), plead for; (persona) to beg, plead with

**suplicio** [su'pliθjo] nm torture

**suplir** [su'plir] /3a/ vt (compensar) to make good, make up for; (reemplazar) to replace, substitute ▷ vi: **~ a** to take the place of, substitute for

**supo** etc ['supo] vb V **saber**

**suponer** [supo'ner] /2q/ vt to suppose; **suposición** nf supposition

**suprimir** [supri'mir] /3a/ vt to suppress; (derecho, costumbre) to abolish; (palabra etc) to delete; (restricción) to cancel, lift

**supuesto, -a** [su'pwesto, a] pp de **suponer** ▷ adj (hipotético) supposed ▷ nm assumption, hypothesis ▷ conj: **~ que** since; **por ~** of course

**sur** [sur] nm south

**suramericano, -a** [surameri'kano, a] adj South American ▷ nm/f South American

**surcar** [sur'kar] /1g/ vt to plough; **surco** nm (en metal, disco) groove; (Agr) furrow

**surfear** [surfe'ar] /1a/ vt: **~ el Internet** to surf the internet

**surgir** [sur'xir] /3c/ vi to arise, emerge; (dificultad) to come up, crop up

**suroeste** [suro'este] nm south-west

**surtido, -a** [sur'tiðo, a] adj mixed, assorted ▷ nm (selección) selection, assortment; (abastecimiento) supply, stock; **surtidor** nm: **surtidor de gasolina** petrol (BRIT) o gas (US) pump

**surtir** [sur'tir] /3a/ vt to supply, provide ▷ vi to spout, spurt

**susceptible** [susθep'tiβle] adj susceptible; (sensible) sensitive; **~ de** capable of

**suscitar** [susθi'tar] /1a/ vt to cause, provoke; (interés, sospechas) to arouse

**suscribir** [suskri'βir] /3a/ vt (firmar) to sign; (respaldar) to subscribe to, endorse; **suscribirse** vr to subscribe; **suscripción** nf subscription

**susodicho, -a** [suso'ditʃo, a] adj above-mentioned

**suspender** [suspen'der] /2a/ vt (objeto) to hang (up), suspend; (trabajo) to stop, suspend; (Escol) to fail; (interrumpir) to adjourn; (atrasar) to postpone

**suspense** [sus'pense] nm suspense; **película/novela de ~** thriller

**suspensión** [suspen'sjon] nf suspension; (fig) stoppage, suspension

**suspenso, -a** [sus'penso, a] adj hanging, suspended; (Escol) failed ▷ nm (Escol) fail(ure); **quedar** o **estar en ~** to be pending; **película** o **novela de ~** (LAM) thriller

**suspicaz** [suspi'kaθ] adj suspicious, distrustful

**suspirar** [suspi'rar] /1a/ vi to sigh; **suspiro** nm sigh

**sustancia** [sus'tanθja] nf substance

**sustento** [sus'tento] nm support; (alimento) sustenance, food

**sustituir** [sustitu'ir] /3g/ vt to substitute, replace; **sustituto, -a** nm/f substitute, replacement

**susto** ['susto] nm fright, scare

**sustraer** [sustra'er] /2p/ vt to remove, take away; (Mat) to subtract

**susurrar** [susu'rrar] /1a/ vi to whisper; **susurro** nm whisper

**sutil** [su'til] adj (aroma) subtle; (tenue) thin; (inteligencia) sharp

**suyo, -a** ['sujo, a] adj (con artículo o después del verbo ser: de él) his; (: de ella) hers; (: de ellos, ellas) theirs; (: de usted, ustedes) yours; **un amigo ~** a friend of his (o hers o theirs o yours)

# t

**Tabacalera** [taβaka'lera] nf former Spanish state tobacco monopoly

**tabaco** [ta'βako] nm tobacco; (fam) cigarettes pl

**tabaquería** [tabake'ria] nf tobacconist's (BRIT), cigar store (US)

**taberna** [ta'βerna] nf bar

**tabique** [ta'βike] nm partition

**tabla** ['taβla] nf (de madera) plank; (estante) shelf; (de vestido) pleat; (Arte) panel; **tablas** nfpl: **estar o quedar en ~s** to draw; **tablado** nm (plataforma) platform; (Teat) stage

**tablao** [ta'βlao] nm (tb: **~ flamenco**) flamenco show

**tablero** [ta'βlero] nm (de madera) plank, board; (de ajedrez, damas) board; (Auto) dashboard; **~ de mandos** (LAM Auto) dashboard

**tableta** [ta'βleta] nf (Med) tablet; (de chocolate) bar; (Inform) tablet

**tablón** [ta'βlon] nm (de suelo) plank; (de techo) beam; (de anuncios) notice board

**tabú** [ta'βu] nm taboo

**taburete** [taβu'rete] nm stool

**tacaño, -a** [ta'kaɲo, a] adj mean

**tacha** ['tatʃa] nf flaw; (Tec) stud; **tachar** /1a/ vt (borrar) to cross out; **tachar de** to accuse of

**tacho** ['tatʃo] nm (LAM) bucket; **~ de la basura** rubbish bin (BRIT), trash can (US)

**taco** ['tako] nm (Billar) cue; (libro de billetes) book; (LAM) heel; (tarugo) peg; (palabrota) swear word

**tacón** [ta'kon] nm heel; **de ~ alto** high-heeled

**táctico, -a** ['taktiko, a] adj tactical ▷ nf tactics pl

**tacto** ['takto] nm touch; (fig) tact

**tajada** [ta'xaða] nf slice

**tajante** [ta'xante] adj sharp

**tajo** ['taxo] nm (corte) cut; (Geo) cleft

**tal** [tal] adj such ▷ pron (persona) someone, such a one; (cosa) something, such a thing; **~ como** such as; **~ para cual** two of a kind ▷ adv: **~ como** (igual) just as; **~ cual** (como es) just as it is; **¿qué ~?** how are things?; **¿qué ~ te gusta?** how do you like it? ▷ conj: **con ~ (de) que** provided that

**taladrar** [tala'ðrar] /1a/ vt to drill; **taladro** nm drill

**talante** [ta'lante] nm (humor) mood; (voluntad) will, willingness

**talar** [ta'lar] /1a/ vt to fell, cut down; (fig) to devastate

**talco** ['talko] nm (polvos) talcum powder

**talento** [ta'lento] nm talent; (capacidad) ability

**Talgo** ['talgo] nm abr (= tren articulado ligero Goicoechea Oriol) high-speed train

**talismán** [talis'man] nm talisman

**talla** ['taʎa] nf (estatura, fig, Med) height, stature; (de ropa) size; (palo) measuring rod; (Arte) carving

**tallar** [ta'ʎar] /1a/ vt (grabar) to engrave; (medir) to measure

**tallarín** [taʎa'rin] nm noodle

**talle** ['taʎe] nm (Anat) waist; (fig) appearance

**taller** [ta'ʎer] nm (Tec) workshop; (de artista) studio

**tallo** ['taʎo] nm (de planta) stem; (de hierba) blade; (brote) shoot

**talón** [ta'lon] nm heel; (Com) counterfoil; (cheque) cheque (BRIT), check (US)

**talonario** [talo'narjo] nm (de cheques) chequebook (BRIT), checkbook (US); (de recibos) receipt book

**tamaño, -a** [ta'maɲo, a] adj (tan grande) such a big; (tan pequeño) such a small ▷ nm size; **de ~ natural** full-size

**tamarindo** [tama'rindo] nm tamarind

**tambalearse** [tambale'arse] /1a/ vr (persona) to stagger; (vehículo) to sway

**también** [tam'bjen] adv (igualmente) also, too, as well; (además) besides

**tambor** [tam'bor] nm drum; (Anat) eardrum; **~ del freno** brake drum

**Támesis** ['tamesis] nm Thames

**tamizar** [tami'θar] /1f/ vt to sieve

**tampoco** [tam'poko] adv nor, neither; **yo ~ lo compré** I didn't buy it either

**tampón** [tam'pon] nm tampon

**tan** [tan] adv so; **~ es así que** so much so that

**tanda** ['tanda] nf (gen) series; (turno) shift

**tangente** [tan'xente] nf tangent

**tangerina** [tanxe'rina] nf (LAM) tangerine

**tangible** [tan'xiβle] adj tangible

**tanque** ['tanke] nm tank; (Auto, Naut) tanker

**tantear** [tante'ar] /1a/ vt (calcular) to reckon (up); (medir) to take the measure of; (probar) to test, try out; (tomar la medida: persona) to take the measurements of; (considerar) to weigh up; (persona: opinión) to sound out ▷ vi (Deporte) to score; **tanteo** nm (cálculo aproximado) (rough) calculation; (prueba) test, trial; (Deporte) scoring

 **PALABRA CLAVE**

**tanto, -a** ['tanto, a] adj (cantidad) so much, as much; **tantos** so many, as many; **20 y tantos** 20-odd
▶ adv (cantidad) so much, as much; (tiempo) so long, as long; **tanto tú como yo** both you and I; **tanto como eso** as much as that; **tanto más ... cuanto que** it's all the more ... because; **tanto mejor/peor** so much the better/the worse; **tanto si viene como si va** whether he comes or whether he goes; **tanto es así que** so much so that; **por tanto, por lo tanto** therefore
▶ conj: **en tanto que** while; **hasta tanto (que)** until such time as
▶ nm 1 (suma) certain amount; (proporción) so much; **un tanto perezoso** somewhat lazy
2 (punto) point; (: gol) goal
3 (locuciones): **al tanto** up to date; **al tanto de que** because of the fact that
▶ pron: **cada uno paga tanto** each one pays so much; **a tantos de agosto** on such and such a day in August; **entre tanto** meanwhile

**tapa** ['tapa] nf (de caja, olla) lid; (de botella) top; (de libro) cover; (de comida) snack
**tapadera** [tapa'ðera] nf lid, cover
**tapar** [ta'par] /1a/ vt (cubrir) to cover; (envolver) to wrap o cover up; (la vista) to obstruct; (persona, falta) to conceal; (LAM) to fill; **taparse** vr to wrap o.s. up
**taparrabo** [tapa'rraβo] nm loincloth
**tapete** [ta'pete] nm table cover
**tapia** ['tapja] nf (garden) wall
**tapicería** [tapiθe'ria] nf tapestry; (para muebles) upholstery; (tienda) upholsterer's (shop)
**tapiz** [ta'piθ] nm (alfombra) carpet; (tela tejida) tapestry; **tapizar** /1f/ vt (muebles) to upholster
**tapón** [ta'pon] nm (de botella) top; (Tec) plug; **~ de rosca** o **de tuerca** screw-top
**taquigrafía** [takiɣra'fia] nf shorthand; **taquígrafo, -a** nm/f shorthand writer, stenographer (us)
**taquilla** [ta'kiλa] nf (de estación etc) booking office; (suma recogida) takings pl

**tarántula** [ta'rantula] nf tarantula
**tararear** [tarare'ar] /1a/ vi to hum
**tardar** [tar'ðar] /1a/ vi (tomar tiempo) to take a long time; (llegar tarde) to be late; (demorar) to delay; **¿tarda mucho el tren?** does the train take long?; **a más ~** at the (very) latest; **no tardes en venir** come soon
**tarde** ['tarðe] adv late ▷ nf (de día) afternoon; (de noche) evening; **de ~ en ~** from time to time; **¡buenas ~s!** good afternoon!; **a** o **por la ~** in the afternoon; in the evening
**tardío, -a** [tar'ðio, a] adj (retrasado) late; (lento) slow (to arrive)
**tarea** [ta'rea] nf task; **tareas** nfpl (Escol) homework sg; **~ de ocasión** chore
**tarifa** [ta'rifa] nf (lista de precios) price list; (Com) tariff
**tarima** [ta'rima] nf (plataforma) platform
**tarjeta** [tar'xeta] nf card; **~ postal/de crédito/de Navidad** postcard/credit card/Christmas card; **~ de embarque** boarding pass; **~ de memoria** memory card; **~ prepago** top-up card; **~ SIM** SIM card
**tarro** ['tarro] nm jar, pot
**tarta** ['tarta] nf (pastel) cake; (torta) tart
**tartamudear** [tartamuðe'ar] /1a/ vi to stutter, stammer; **tartamudo, -a** adj stammering ▷ nm/f stammerer
**tártaro, -a** ['tartaro, a] adj: **salsa tártara** tartar(e) sauce
**tasa** ['tasa] nf (precio) (fixed) price, rate; (valoración) valuation; (medida, norma) measure, standard; **~ de cambio** exchange rate; **~s de aeropuerto** airport tax; **~s universitarias** university fees; **tasar** /1a/ vt (arreglar el precio) to fix a price for; (valorar) to value, assess
**tasca** ['taska] nf (fam) pub
**tatarabuelo, -a** [tatara'βwelo, a] nm/f great-great-grandfather/mother
**tatuaje** [ta'twaxe] nm (dibujo) tattoo; (acto) tattooing
**tatuar** [ta'twar] /1d/ vt to tattoo
**taurino, -a** [tau'rino, a] adj bullfighting cpd
**Tauro** ['tauro] nm Taurus
**tauromaquia** [tauro'makja] nf (art of) bullfighting
**taxi** ['taksi] nm taxi; **taxista** nmf taxi driver
**taza** ['taθa] nf cup; (de retrete) bowl; **~ para café** coffee cup; **~ de café** cup of coffee; **tazón** nm mug, large cup; (escudilla) basin
**te** [te] pron (complemento de objeto) you; (complemento indirecto) (to) you; (reflexivo) (to) yourself; **¿te duele mucho el brazo?** does your arm hurt a lot?; **te equivocas** you're wrong; **¡cálmate!** calm yourself!
**té** [te] nm tea
**teatral** [tea'tral] adj theatre cpd; (fig) theatrical

**teatro** [te'atro] *nm* theatre; (*Lit*) plays *pl*, drama

**tebeo** [te'βeo] *nm* children's comic

**techo** ['tetʃo] *nm* (*externo*) roof; (*interno*) ceiling

**tecla** ['tekla] *nf* (*Inform, Mus, Tip*) key; **teclado** *nm* keyboard (*tb Inform*); **teclear** /1a/ *vi* to strum; (*fam*) to drum ▷ *vt* (*Inform*) to key (in)

**técnico, -a** ['tekniko, a] *adj* technical ▷ *nm/f* technician; (*experto*) expert ▷ *nf* (*procedimientos*) technique; (*tecnología*) technology

**tecnología** [teknolo'xia] *nf* technology; **tecnológico, -a** *adj* technological

**tecolote** [teko'lote] *nm* (*LAM*) owl

**tedioso, -a** [te'ðjoso, a] *adj* boring; tedious

**teja** ['texa] *nf* tile; (*Bot*) lime (tree); **tejado** *nm* (tiled) roof

**tejano, -a** [te'xano, a] *adj, nm/f* Texan ▷ *nmpl*: **~s** (*vaqueros*) jeans

**tejemaneje** [texema'nexe] *nm* (*lío*) fuss; (*intriga*) intrigue

**tejer** [te'xer] /2a/ *vt* to weave; (*LAM*) to knit; (*fig*) to fabricate; **tejido** *nm* fabric; (*estofa, tela*) (knitted) material; (*telaraña*) web; (*Anat*) tissue

**tel.** *abr* (= *teléfono*) tel.

**tela** ['tela] *nf* (*material*) material; (*de fruta, en líquido*) skin; **~ de araña** cobweb, spider's web; **telar** *nm* (*máquina*) loom

**telaraña** [tela'raɲa] *nf* cobweb

**tele** ['tele] *nf* (*fam*) TV

**tele...** *pref* tele...; **telebasura** *nf* trash TV; **telecomunicación** *nf* telecommunication; **telediario** *nm* television news; **teledirigido, -a** *adj* remote-controlled

**teleférico** [tele'feriko] *nm* (*de esquí*) ski-lift

**telefonear** [telefone'ar] /1a/ *vi* to telephone

**telefónico, -a** [tele'foniko, a] *adj* telephone *cpd*

**telefonillo** [telefo'niʎo] *nm* (*de puerta*) intercom

**telefonista** [telefo'nista] *nmf* telephonist

**teléfono** [te'lefono] *nm* (tele)phone; **~ móvil** mobile phone; **está hablando por ~** he's on the phone; **llamar a algn por ~** to ring sb (up) o phone sb (up); **~ celular** (*LAM*) mobile phone; **~ con cámara** camera phone; **~ inalámbrico** cordless phone

**telégrafo** [te'leɣrafo] *nm* telegraph

**telegrama** [tele'ɣrama] *nm* telegram

**tele...**: **telenovela** *nf* soap (opera); **teleobjetivo** *nm* telephoto lens; **telepatía** *nf* telepathy; **telepático, -a** *adj* telepathic; **telerrealidad** *nf* reality TV; **telescopio** *nm* telescope; **telesilla** *nm* chairlift;

**telespectador, a** *nm/f* viewer; **telesquí** *nm* ski-lift; **teletarjeta** *nf* phonecard; **teletipo** *nm* teletype(writer); **teletrabajador, a** *nm/f* teleworker; **teletrabajo** *nm* teleworking; **televentas** *nfpl* telesales

**televidente** [teleβi'ðente] *nmf* viewer

**televisar** [teleβi'sar] /1a/ *vt* to televise

**televisión** [teleβi'sjon] *nf* television; **~ digital** digital television

**televisor** [teleβi'sor] *nm* television set

**télex** ['teleks] *nm* telex

**telón** [te'lon] *nm* curtain; **~ de acero** (*Pol*) iron curtain; **~ de fondo** backcloth, background

**tema** ['tema] *nm* (*asunto*) subject, topic; (*Mus*) theme; **temático, -a** *adj* thematic

**temblar** [tem'blar] /1j/ *vi* to shake, tremble; (*de frío*) to shiver; **temblor** *nm* trembling; (*de tierra*) earthquake; **tembloroso, -a** *adj* trembling

**temer** [te'mer] /2a/ *vt* to fear ▷ *vi* to be afraid; **temo que Juan llegue tarde** I am afraid Juan may be late

**temible** [te'miβle] *adj* fearsome

**temor** [te'mor] *nm* (*miedo*) fear; (*duda*) suspicion

**témpano** ['tempano] *nm*: **~ de hielo** ice floe

**temperamento** [tempera'mento] *nm* temperament

**temperatura** [tempera'tura] *nf* temperature

**tempestad** [tempes'tað] *nf* storm

**templado, -a** [tem'plaðo, a] *adj* (*agua*) lukewarm; (*clima*) mild; (*Mus*) well-tuned; **templanza** *nf* moderation

**templar** [tem'plar] /1a/ *vt* (*moderar*) to moderate; (*furia*) to restrain; (*calor*) to reduce; (*afinar*) to tune (up); (*acero*) to temper; (*tuerca*) to tighten up; **temple** *nm* (*ajuste*) tempering; (*afinación*) tuning; (*pintura*) tempera

**templo** ['templo] *nm* (*iglesia*) church; (*pagano etc*) temple

**temporada** [tempo'raða] *nf* time, period; (*estación, social*) season

**temporal** [tempo'ral] *adj* (*no permanente*) temporary ▷ *nm* storm

**temprano, -a** [tem'prano, a] *adj* early ▷ *adv* early; (*demasiado pronto*) too soon, too early

**ten** [ten] *vb V* **tener**

**tenaces** [te'naθes] *adj pl V* **tenaz**

**tenaz** [te'naθ] *adj* (*material*) tough; (*persona*) tenacious; (*terco*) stubborn

**tenaza(s)** [te'naθ(as)] *nf, nfpl* (*Med*) forceps; (*Tec*) pliers; (*Zool*) pincers

**tendedero** [tende'ðero] *nm* (*para ropa*) drying-place; (*cuerda*) clothes line

**tendencia** [ten'denθja] nf tendency;
  **tener ~ a** to tend o have a tendency to
**tender** [ten'der] /2g/ vt (extender) to spread
  out; (ropa) to hang out; (vía férrea, cable)
  to lay; (cuerda) to stretch ▷ vi to tend;
  **tenderse** vr to lie down; **~ la cama/la
  mesa** (LAM) to make the bed/lay the table
**tenderete** [tende'rete] nm (puesto) stall;
  (exposición) display of goods
**tendero, -a** [ten'dero, a] nm/f shopkeeper
**tendón** [ten'don] nm tendon
**tendré** etc [ten'dre] vb V **tener**
**tenebroso, -a** [tene'βroso, a] adj (oscuro)
  dark; (fig) gloomy
**tenedor** [tene'ðor] nm (Culin) fork
**tenencia** [te'nenθja] nf (de casa) tenancy;
  (de oficio) tenure; (de propiedad) possession

 **PALABRA CLAVE**

**tener** [te'ner] /2k/ vt **1** (poseer, gen) to have;
  (: en la mano) to hold; **¿tienes un boli?** have
  you got a pen?; **va a tener un niño** she's
  going to have a baby; **¡ten o tenga!, ¡aquí
  tienes o tiene!** here you are!
  **2** (edad, medidas) to be; **tiene siete años**
  she's seven (years old); **tiene 15 cm de largo**
  it's 15 cm long
  **3** (sentimientos, sensaciones): **tener sed/
  hambre/frío/calor** to be thirsty/hungry/
  cold/hot; **tener razón** to be right
  **4** (considerar): **lo tengo por brillante** I
  consider him to be brilliant; **tener en
  mucho a algn** to think very highly of sb
  **5** (+ pp): **tengo terminada ya la mitad del
  trabajo** I've done half the work already
  **6**: **tener que hacer algo** to have to do sth;
  **tengo que acabar este trabajo hoy** I have
  to finish this job today
  **7**: **¿qué tienes, estás enfermo?** what's the
  matter with you, are you ill?
  ▶ **tenerse** vr **1**: **tenerse en pie** to stand up
  **2**: **tenerse por** to think o.s.

**tengo** etc ['tengo] vb V **tener**
**tenia** ['tenja] nf tapeworm
**teniente** [te'njente] nm lieutenant;
  (ayudante) deputy
**tenis** ['tenis] nm tennis; **~ de mesa** table
  tennis; **tenista** nmf tennis player
**tenor** [te'nor] nm (sentido) meaning; (Mus)
  tenor; **a ~ de** on the lines of
**tensar** [ten'sar] /1a/ vt to tauten; (arco)
  to draw
**tensión** [ten'sjon] nf tension; (Tec) stress;
  **~ arterial** blood pressure; **tener la ~ alta** to
  have high blood pressure
**tenso, -a** ['tenso, a] adj tense
**tentación** [tenta'θjon] nf temptation

**tentáculo** [ten'takulo] nm tentacle
**tentador, a** [tenta'ðor, a] adj tempting
**tentar** [ten'tar] /1j/ vt (seducir) to tempt;
  (atraer) to attract
**tentempié** [tentem'pje] nm snack
**tenue** ['tenwe] adj (delgado) thin, slender;
  (neblina) light; (lazo, vínculo) slight
**teñir** [te'ɲir] vt to dye; (fig) to tinge; **teñirse**
  vr to dye; **~se el pelo** to dye one's hair
**teología** [teolo'xia] nf theology
**teoría** [teo'ria] nf theory; **en ~** in theory;
  **teórico, -a** adj theoretic(al) ▷ nm/f
  theoretician, theorist; **teorizar** /1f/ vi to
  theorize
**terapéutico, -a** [tera'peutiko, a] adj
  therapeutic(al)
**terapia** [te'rapja] nf therapy
**tercer** [ter'θer] adj V **tercero**
**tercermundista** [terθermun'dista] adj
  Third World cpd
**tercero, -a** [ter'θero, a] adj third ▷ nm (Jur)
  third party
**terceto** [ter'θeto] nm trio
**terciar** [ter'θjar] /1b/ vi (participar) to take
  part; (hacer de árbitro) to mediate;
  **terciario, -a** adj tertiary
**tercio** ['terθjo] nm third
**terciopelo** [terθjo'pelo] nm velvet
**terco, -a** ['terko, a] adj obstinate
**tergal®** [ter'yal] nm Terylene®, Dacron® (US)
**tergiversar** [terxiβer'sar] /1a/ vt to distort
**termal** [ter'mal] adj thermal
**termas** ['termas] nfpl hot springs
**térmico, -a** ['termiko, a] adj thermal
**terminal** [termi'nal] adj terminal ▷ nm, nf
  terminal
**terminante** [termi'nante] adj
  (final) final, definitive; (tajante)
  categorical; **terminantemente** adv:
  **terminantemente prohibido** strictly
  forbidden
**terminar** [termi'nar] /1a/ vt (completar) to
  complete, finish; (concluir) to end ▷ vi (llegar
  a su fin) to end; (parar) to stop; (acabar) to
  finish; **terminarse** vr to come to an end;
  **~ por hacer algo** to end up (by) doing sth
**término** ['termino] nm end, conclusion;
  (parada) terminus; (límite) boundary; **en
  último ~** (a fin de cuentas) in the last analysis;
  (como último recurso) as a last resort;
  **~ medio** average; (fig) middle way
**termo®** ['termo] nm Thermos® (flask)
**termómetro** [ter'mometro] nm
  thermometer
**termostato** [termos'tato] nm thermostat
**ternero, -a** [ter'nero, a] nm/f (animal) calf
  ▷ nf (carne) veal, beef
**ternura** [ter'nura] nf (trato) tenderness;
  (palabra) endearment; (cariño) fondness

**terrado** [te'rraðo] nm terrace

**terraplén** [terra'plen] nm embankment

**terrateniente** [terrate'njente] nm landowner

**terraza** [te'rraθa] nf (balcón) balcony; (techo) flat roof; (Agr) terrace

**terremoto** [terre'moto] nm earthquake

**terrenal** [terre'nal] adj earthly

**terreno** [te'rreno] nm (tierra) land; (parcela) plot; (suelo) soil; (fig) field; **un ~** a piece of land

**terrestre** [te'rrestre] adj terrestrial; (ruta) land cpd

**terrible** [te'rriβle] adj terrible; awful

**territorio** [terri'torjo] nm territory

**terrón** [te'rron] nm (de azúcar) lump; (de tierra) clod, lump

**terror** [te'rror] nm terror; **terrorífico, -a** adj terrifying; **terrorista** adj, nmf terrorist; **terrorista suicida** suicide bomber

**terso, -a** ['terso, a] adj (liso) smooth; (pulido) polished

**tertulia** [ter'tulja] nf (reunión informal) social gathering; (grupo) group, circle

**tesis** ['tesis] nf inv thesis

**tesón** [te'son] nm (firmeza) firmness; (tenacidad) tenacity

**tesorero, -a** [teso'rero, a] nm/f treasurer

**tesoro** [te'soro] nm treasure; (Com, Pol) treasury

**testamento** [testa'mento] nm will

**testarudo, -a** [testa'ruðo, a] adj stubborn

**testículo** [tes'tikulo] nm testicle

**testificar** [testifi'kar] /1g/ vt to testify; (fig) to attest ▷ vi to give evidence

**testigo** [tes'tiɣo] nmf witness; **~ de cargo/ descargo** witness for the prosecution/ defence; **~ ocular** eye witness

**testimonio** [testi'monjo] nm testimony

**teta** ['teta] nf (de biberón) teat; (Anat: fam) breast

**tétanos** ['tetanos] nm tetanus

**tetera** [te'tera] nf teapot

**tétrico, -a** ['tetriko, a] adj gloomy, dismal

**textear** [tekste'ar] /1a/ vt (LAM) to text

**textil** [teks'til] adj textile

**texto** ['teksto] nm text; **textual** adj textual

**textura** [teks'tura] nf (de tejido) texture

**tez** [teθ] nf (cutis) complexion

**ti** [ti] pron you; (reflexivo) yourself

**tía** ['tia] nf (pariente) aunt; (fam: mujer) girl

**tibio, -a** ['tiβjo, a] adj lukewarm

**tiburón** [tiβu'ron] nm shark

**tic** [tik] nm (ruido) click; (de reloj) tick; **~ nervioso** nervous tic

**tictac** [tik'tak] nm (de reloj) tick tock

**tiempo** ['tjempo] nm time; (época, período) age, period; (Meteorología) weather; (Ling) tense; (de juego) half; **a ~** in time; **a un o**

**al mismo ~** at the same time; **al poco ~** very soon (after); **se quedó poco ~** he didn't stay very long; **hace poco ~** not long ago; **mucho ~** a long time; **de ~ en ~** from time to time; **hace buen/mal ~** the weather is fine/bad; **estar a ~** to be in time; **hace ~** some time ago; **hacer ~** to while away the time; **motor de 2 ~s** two-stroke engine; **primer ~** first half

**tienda** ['tjenda] nf shop; store; **~ de campaña** tent; **~ de comestibles** grocer's (shop) (BRIT), grocery (store) (US)

**tiene** etc ['tjene] vb V **tener**

**tienta** ['tjenta] nf: **andar a ~s** to grope one's way along

**tiento** etc ['tjento] vb V **tentar** ▷ nm (tacto) touch; (precaución) wariness

**tierno, -a** ['tjerno, a] adj (blando, dulce) tender; (fresco) fresh

**tierra** ['tjerra] nf earth; (suelo) soil; (mundo) world; (país) country, land; **~ adentro** inland

**tieso, -a** ['tjeso, a] adj (rígido) rigid; (duro) stiff; (fam: orgulloso) conceited

**tiesto** ['tjesto] nm flowerpot

**tifón** [ti'fon] nm typhoon

**tifus** ['tifus] nm typhus

**tigre** ['tiɣre] nm tiger

**tijera** [ti'xera] nf (una tijera) (pair of) scissors pl; (Zool) claw; **tijeras** nfpl scissors; (para plantas) shears

**tila** ['tila] nf lime flower tea

**tildar** [til'dar] /1a/ vt: **~ de** to brand as

**tilde** ['tilde] nf (Tip) tilde

**tilín** [ti'lin] nm tinkle

**timar** [ti'mar] /1a/ vt (estafar) to swindle

**timbal** [tim'bal] nm small drum

**timbre** ['timbre] nm (sello) stamp; (campanilla) bell; (tono) timbre; (Com) stamp duty

**timidez** [timi'ðeθ] nf shyness; **tímido, -a** adj shy

**timo** ['timo] nm swindle

**timón** [ti'mon] nm helm, rudder; **timonel** nm helmsman

**tímpano** ['timpano] nm (Anat) eardrum; (Mus) small drum

**tina** ['tina] nf tub; (baño) bath(tub); **tinaja** nf large earthen jar

**tinieblas** [ti'njeβlas] nfpl darkness sg; (sombras) shadows

**tino** ['tino] nm (habilidad) skill; (juicio) insight

**tinta** ['tinta] nf ink; (Tec) dye; (Arte) colour

**tinte** ['tinte] nm dye

**tintero** [tin'tero] nm inkwell

**tinto** ['tinto] nm red wine

**tintorería** [tintore'ria] nf dry cleaner's

**tío** ['tio] nm (pariente) uncle; (fam: hombre) bloke, guy (US)

**tiovivo** [tio'βiβo] nm merry-go-round

**típico, -a** ['tipiko, a] adj typical

**tipo** ['tipo] nm (clase) type, kind; (hombre) fellow; (Anat) build; (: de mujer) figure; (Imprenta) type; **~ bancario/de descuento** bank/discount rate; **~ de interés** interest rate; **~ de cambio** exchange rate

**tipografía** [tipoɣra'fia] nf printing

**tíquet** ['tiket] (pl **tíquets**) nm ticket; (en tienda) cash slip

**tiquismiquis** [tikis'mikis] nm fussy person ⊳ nmpl (querellas) squabbling sg; (escrúpulos) silly scruples

**tira** ['tira] nf strip; (fig) abundance ⊳ nm: **~ y afloja** give and take

**tirabuzón** [tiraβu'θon] nm (rizo) curl

**tirachinas** [tira'tʃinas] nm inv catapult

**tirado, -a** [ti'raðo, a] adj (barato) dirt-cheap; (fam: fácil) very easy ⊳ nf (acto) cast, throw; (serie) series; (Tip) printing, edition; **de una tirada** at one go; **está ~** (fam) it's a cinch

**tirador** [tira'ðor] nm (mango) handle

**tirano, -a** [ti'rano, a] adj tyrannical ⊳ nm/f tyrant

**tirante** [ti'rante] adj (cuerda) tight, taut; (relaciones) strained ⊳ nm (Arq) brace; (Tec) stay; **tirantes** nmpl braces, suspenders (us); **tirantez** nf tightness; (fig) tension

**tirar** [ti'rar] /1a/ vt to throw; (volcar) to upset; (derribar) to knock down o over; (bomba) to drop; (desechar) to throw out o away; (disipar) to squander; (imprimir) to print ⊳ vi (disparar) to shoot; (dar un tirón) to pull; (fam: andar) to go; (tender a) to tend to; (Deporte) to shoot; **tirarse** vr to throw o.s.; **~ abajo** to bring down, destroy; **tira más a su padre** he takes more after his father; **ir tirando** to manage

**tirita** [ti'rita] nf (sticking) plaster, Band-Aid® (us)

**tiritar** [tiri'tar] /1a/ vi to shiver

**tiro** ['tiro] nm (lanzamiento) throw; (disparo) shot; (Deporte) shot; (Tenis, Golf) drive; (alcance) range; **~ al blanco** target practice; **caballo de ~** cart-horse

**tirón** [ti'ron] nm (sacudida) pull, tug; **de un ~** in one go

**tiroteo** [tiro'teo] nm exchange of shots, shooting

**tisis** ['tisis] nf consumption, tuberculosis

**títere** ['titere] nm puppet

**titubear** [tituβe'ar] /1a/ vi to stagger; (tartamudear) to stammer; (vacilar) to hesitate; **titubeo** nm staggering; stammering; hesitation

**titulado, -a** [titu'laðo, a] adj (libro) entitled; (persona) titled

**titular** [titu'lar] /1a/ adj titular ⊳ nmf holder ⊳ nm headline ⊳ vt to title;

**titularse** vr to be entitled; **título** nm title; (de diario) headline; (certificado) professional qualification; (universitario) university degree; **a título de** in the capacity of

**tiza** ['tiθa] nf chalk

**toalla** [to'aʎa] nf towel

**tobillo** [to'βiʎo] nm ankle

**tobogán** [toβo'ɣan] nm (montaña rusa) roller-coaster; (resbaladilla) chute, slide

**tocadiscos** [toka'ðiskos] nm inv record player

**tocado, -a** [to'kaðo, a] adj (fam) touched ⊳ nm headdress

**tocador** [toka'ðor] nm (mueble) dressing table; (cuarto) boudoir; (fam) ladies' room

**tocar** [to'kar] /1g/ vt to touch; (Mus) to play; (campana) to ring; (referirse a) to allude to ⊳ vi (a la puerta) to knock (on o at the door); (ser el turno) to fall to, be the turn of; (ser hora) to be due; **tocarse** vr (cubrirse la cabeza) to cover one's head; (tener contacto) to touch (each other); **por lo que a mí me toca** as far as I am concerned; **te toca a ti** it's your turn

**tocayo, -a** [to'kajo, a] nm/f namesake

**tocino** [to'θino] nm bacon

**todavía** [toða'βia] adv (aun) even; (aún) still, yet; **~ más** yet o still more; **~ no** not yet

**PALABRA CLAVE**

**todo, -a** ['toðo, a] adj **1** (sg) all; **toda la carne** all the meat; **toda la noche** all night, the whole night; **todo el libro** the whole book; **toda una botella** a whole bottle; **todo lo contrario** quite the opposite; **está toda sucia** she's all dirty; **por todo el país** throughout the whole country

**2** (pl) all; every; **todos los libros** all the books; **todas las noches** every night; **todos los que quieran salir** all those who want to leave

▶ pron **1** everything, all; **todos** everyone, everybody; **lo sabemos todo** we know everything; **todos querían más tiempo** everybody o everyone wanted more time; **nos marchamos todos** all of us left

**2** (con preposición): **con todo él me sigue gustando** even so I still like him; **no me agrada del todo** I don't entirely like it

▶ adv all; **vaya todo seguido** keep straight on o ahead

▶ nm: **como un todo** as a whole

**todopoderoso, -a** [toðopoðe'roso, a] adj all-powerful; (Rel) almighty

**todoterreno** [toðote'rreno] nm four-wheel drive, SUV (esp us)

**toga** ['toɣa] nf toga; (Escol) gown

**Tokio** ['tokjo] n Tokyo

**toldo** ['toldo] nm (para el sol) sunshade; (en tienda) marquee

**tolerancia** [tole'ranθja] nf tolerance; **tolerante** adj tolerant; (sociedad) liberal; (fig) open-minded

**tolerar** [tole'rar] /1a/ vt to tolerate; (resistir) to endure

**toma** ['toma] nf (gen) taking; (Med) dose; (Elec: tb: **~ de corriente**) socket; **~ de tierra** (Aviat) landing; **tomacorriente** nm (LAM) socket

**tomar** [to'mar] /1a/ vt to take; (aspecto) to take on; (beber) to drink ▷ vi to take; (LAM) to drink; **tomarse** vr to take; **~se por** to consider o.s. to be; **¡toma!** here you are!; **~ a bien/a mal** to take well/badly; **~ en serio** to take seriously; **~ el pelo a algn** to pull sb's leg; **~la con algn** to pick a quarrel with sb; **~ el sol** to sunbathe

**tomate** [to'mate] nm tomato

**tomillo** [to'miʎo] nm thyme

**tomo** ['tomo] nm (libro) volume

**ton** [ton] abr = **tonelada** ▷ nm: **sin ~ ni son** without rhyme or reason

**tonalidad** [tonali'ðað] nf tone

**tonel** [to'nel] nm barrel

**tonelada** [tone'laða] nf ton; **tonelaje** nm tonnage

**tónico, -a** ['toniko, a] adj tonic ▷ nm (Med) tonic ▷ nf (Mus) tonic; (fig) keynote

**tono** ['tono] nm tone; **fuera de ~** inappropriate; **~ de llamada** ringtone

**tontería** [tonte'ria] nf (estupidez) foolishness; (una tontería) silly thing; **tonterías** nfpl rubbish sg, nonsense sg

**tonto, -a** ['tonto, a] adj stupid; (ridículo) silly ▷ nm/f fool

**topar** [to'par] /1a/ vi: **~ contra** o **en** to run into; **~ con** to run up against

**tope** ['tope] adj maximum ▷ nm (fin) end; (límite) limit; (Ferro) buffer; (Auto) bumper; **al ~** end to end

**tópico, -a** ['topiko, a] adj topical ▷ nm platitude

**topo** ['topo] nm (Zool) mole; (fig) blunderer

**toque** etc ['toke] vb V **tocar** ▷ nm touch; (Mus) beat; (de campana) chime, ring; **dar un ~ a** to test; **~ de queda** curfew

**toqué** etc vb V **tocar**

**toquetear** [tokete'ar] /1a/ vt to finger

**toquilla** [to'kiʎa] nf (pañuelo) headscarf; (chal) shawl

**tórax** ['toraks] nm inv thorax

**torbellino** [torbe'ʎino] nm whirlwind; (fig) whirl

**torcedura** [torθe'ðura] nf twist; (Med) sprain

**torcer** [tor'θer] /2b, 2h/ vt to twist; (la esquina) to turn; (Med) to sprain ▷ vi (desviar)

to turn off; **torcerse** vr (doblar) to bend; (desviarse) to go astray; (fracasar) to go wrong; **torcido, -a** adj twisted; (fig) crooked ▷ nm curl

**tordo, -a** ['torðo, a] adj dappled ▷ nm thrush

**torear** [tore'ar] /1a/ vt (fig: evadir) to dodge; (jugar con) to tease ▷ vi to fight bulls; **toreo** nm bullfighting; **torero, -a** nm/f bullfighter

**tormenta** [tor'menta] nf storm; (fig: confusión) turmoil

**tormento** [tor'mento] nm torture; (fig) anguish

**tornar** [tor'nar] /1a/ vt (devolver) to return, give back; (transformar) to transform ▷ vi to go back

**tornasolado, -a** [tornaso'laðo, a] adj (brillante) iridescent; (reluciente) shimmering

**torneo** [tor'neo] nm tournament

**tornillo** [tor'niʎo] nm screw

**torniquete** [torni'kete] nm (Med) tourniquet

**torno** ['torno] nm (Tec) winch; (tambor) drum; **en ~ (a)** round, about

**toro** ['toro] nm bull; (fam) he-man; **los ~s** bullfighting sg

**toronja** [to'ronxa] nf grapefruit

**torpe** ['torpe] adj (poco hábil) clumsy, awkward; (necio) dim; (lento) slow

**torpedo** [tor'peðo] nm torpedo

**torpeza** [tor'peθa] nf (falta de agilidad) clumsiness; (lentitud) slowness; (error) mistake

**torre** ['torre] nf tower; (de petróleo) derrick

**torrefacto, -a** [torre'fakto, a] adj roasted

**torrente** [to'rrente] nm torrent

**torrija** [to'rrixa] nf fried bread; **~s** French toast sg

**torsión** [tor'sjon] nf twisting

**torso** ['torso] nm torso

**torta** ['torta] nf cake; (fam) slap

**tortícolis** [tor'tikolis] nm inv stiff neck

**tortilla** [tor'tiʎa] nf omelette; (LAM) maize pancake; **~ francesa/española** plain/ potato omelette

**tórtola** ['tortola] nf turtledove

**tortuga** [tor'tuɣa] nf tortoise

**tortuoso, -a** [tor'twoso, a] adj winding

**tortura** [tor'tura] nf torture; **torturar** /1a/ vt to torture

**tos** [tos] nf inv cough; **~ ferina** whooping cough

**toser** [to'ser] /2a/ vi to cough

**tostado, -a** [tos'taðo, a] adj toasted; (por el sol) dark brown; (piel) tanned ▷ nf piece of toast; **tostadas** nfpl toast sg

**tostador** [tosta'ðor] nm, **tostadora** [tosta'ðora] nf toaster

**tostar** [tos'tar] /1l/ vt to toast; (café) to roast; (al sol) to tan; **tostarse** vr to get brown

**total** [to'tal] adj total ▷ adv in short; (al fin y al cabo) when all is said and done ▷ nm total; en ~ in all; ~ que to cut a long story short

**totalidad** [totali'ðað] nf whole

**totalitario, -a** [totali'tarjo, a] adj totalitarian

**tóxico, -a** ['toksiko, a] adj toxic ▷ nm poison; **toxicómano, -a** nm/f drug addict

**toxina** [to'ksina] nf toxin

**tozudo, -a** [to'θuðo, a] adj obstinate

**trabajador, a** [traβaxa'ðor, a] nm/f worker ▷ adj hard-working; ~ **autónomo o por cuenta propia** self-employed person

**trabajar** [traβa'xar] /1a/ vt to work; (arar) to till; (empeñarse en) to work at; (convencer) to persuade ▷ vi to work; (esforzarse) to strive; **trabajo** nm work; (tarea) task; (Pol) labour; (fig) effort; **tomarse el trabajo de** to take the trouble to; **trabajo por turno/a destajo** shift work/piecework; **trabajo en equipo** teamwork; **trabajos forzados** hard labour sg

**trabalenguas** [traβa'lengwas] nm inv tongue twister

**tracción** [trak'θjon] nf traction; ~ **delantera/trasera** front-wheel/rear-wheel drive

**tractor** [trak'tor] nm tractor

**tradición** [traði'θjon] nf tradition; **tradicional** adj traditional

**traducción** [traðuk'θjon] nf translation

**traducir** [traðu'θir] /3n/ vt to translate; **traductor, a** nm/f translator

**traer** [tra'er] /2o/ vt to bring; (llevar) to carry; (ropa) to wear; (incluir) to carry; (fig) to cause; **traerse** vr: ~se algo to be up to sth

**traficar** [trafi'kar] /1g/ vi to trade

**tráfico** ['trafiko] nm (Com) trade; (Auto) traffic

**tragaluz** [traɣa'luθ] nm skylight

**tragamonedas** [traɣamo'neðas] nm inv, **tragaperras** [traɣa'perras] nm inv slot machine

**tragar** [tra'ɣar] /1h/ vt to swallow; (devorar) to devour, bolt down; **tragarse** vr to swallow

**tragedia** [tra'xeðja] nf tragedy; **trágico, -a** adj tragic

**trago** ['traɣo] nm (de líquido) drink; (comido de golpe) gulp; (fam: de bebida) swig; (desgracia) blow; **echar un** ~ to have a drink

**traición** [trai'θjon] nf treachery; (Jur) treason; (una traición) act of treachery; **traicionar** /1a/ vt to betray

**traidor, a** [trai'ðor, a] adj treacherous ▷ nm/f traitor

**traigo** etc ['traiɣo] vb V **traer**

**traje** ['traxe] vb V **traer** ▷ nm dress; (de hombre) suit; (traje típico) costume; ~ **de baño** swimsuit; ~ **de luces** bullfighter's costume

**trajera** etc [tra'xera] vb V **traer**

**trajín** [tra'xin] nm (fam: movimiento) bustle; **trajinar** /1a/ vi (moverse) to bustle about

**trama** ['trama] nf (intriga) plot; (de tejido) weft; **tramar** /1a/ vt to plot; (Tec) to weave

**tramitar** [trami'tar] /1a/ vt (asunto) to transact; (negociar) to negotiate

**trámite** ['tramite] nm (paso) step; (Jur) transaction; **trámites** nmpl (burocracia) procedures; (Jur) proceedings

**tramo** ['tramo] nm (de tierra) plot; (de escalera) flight; (de vía) section

**trampa** ['trampa] nf trap; (en el suelo) trapdoor; (engaño) trick; (fam) fiddle; **trampear** /1a/ vt, vi to cheat

**trampolín** nm trampoline; (de piscina etc) diving board

**tramposo, -a** [tram'poso, a] adj crooked, cheating ▷ nm/f crook, cheat

**tranca** ['tranka] nf (palo) stick; (de puerta, ventana) bar; **trancar** /1g/ vt to bar

**trance** ['tranθe] nm (momento difícil) difficult moment; (estado de hipnosis) trance

**tranquilidad** [trankili'ðað] nf (calma) calmness, stillness; (paz) peacefulness

**tranquilizar** [trankili'θar] /1f/ vt (calmar) to calm (down); (asegurar) to reassure; **tranquilizarse** vr to calm down; **tranquilo, -a** adj (calmado) calm; (apacible) peaceful; (mar) calm; (mente) untroubled

**transacción** [transak'θjon] nf transaction

**transbordador** [transβorða'ðor] nm ferry

**transbordo** [trans'βorðo] nm transfer; **hacer** ~ to change (trains)

**transcurrir** [transku'rrir] /3a/ vi (tiempo) to pass; (hecho) to turn out

**transcurso** [trans'kurso] nm: ~ **del tiempo** lapse (of time)

**transeúnte** [transe'unte] nmf passer-by

**transferencia** [transfe'renθja] nf transference; (Com) transfer

**transferir** [transfe'rir] /3i/ vt to transfer

**transformación** [transforma'θjon] nf transformation

**transformador** [transforma'ðor] nm transformer

**transformar** [transfor'mar] /1a/ vt to transform; (convertir) to convert

**transfusión** [transfu'sjon] nf (tb: ~ **de sangre**) (blood) transfusion

**transgénico, -a** [trans'xeniko, a] adj genetically modified

**transición** [transi'θjon] *nf* transition
**transigir** [transi'xir] /3c/ *vi* to compromise; (*ceder*) to make concessions
**transitar** [transi'tar] /1a/ *vi* to go (from place to place); **tránsito** *nm* transit; (*Auto*) traffic; **transitorio, -a** *adj* transitory
**transmisión** [transmi'sjon] *nf* (*Radio, TV*) transmission; (*transferencia*) transfer; **~ en directo/exterior** live/outside broadcast
**transmitir** [transmi'tir] /3a/ *vt* to transmit; (*Radio, TV*) to broadcast
**transparencia** [transpa'renθja] *nf* transparency; (*claridad*) clearness, clarity; (*foto*) slide
**transparentar** [transparen'tar] /1a/ *vt* to reveal ▷ *vi* to be transparent; **transparente** *adj* transparent; (*aire*) clear
**transpirar** [transpi'rar] /1a/ *vi* to perspire
**transportar** [transpor'tar] /1a/ *vt* to transport; (*llevar*) to carry; **transporte** *nm* transport; (*Com*) haulage
**transversal** [transβer'sal] *adj* transverse, cross
**tranvía** [tram'bia] *nm* tram
**trapeador** [trapea'ðor] *nm* (*LAM*) mop; **trapear** /1a/ *vt* (*LAM*) to mop
**trapecio** [tra'peθjo] *nm* trapeze; **trapecista** *nmf* trapeze artist
**trapero, -a** [tra'pero, a] *nm/f* ragman
**trapicheos** [trapi'tʃeos] *nmpl* (*fam*) schemes, fiddles
**trapo** ['trapo] *nm* (*tela*) rag; (*de cocina*) cloth
**tráquea** ['trakea] *nf* windpipe
**traqueteo** [trake'teo] *nm* rattling
**tras** [tras] *prep* (*detrás*) behind; (*después*) after
**trasatlántico** [trasat'lantiko] *nm* (*barco*) (cabin) cruiser
**trascendencia** [trasθen'denθja] *nf* (*importancia*) importance; (*en filosofía*) transcendence
**trascendental** [trasθenden'tal] *adj* important; transcendental
**trasero, -a** [tra'sero, a] *adj* back, rear ▷ *nm* (*Anat*) bottom
**trasfondo** [tras'fondo] *nm* background
**trasgredir** [trasɣre'ðir] /3a/ *vt* to contravene
**trashumante** [trasu'mante] *adj* migrating
**trasladar** [trasla'ðar] /1a/ *vt* to move; (*persona*) to transfer; (*postergar*) to postpone; (*copiar*) to copy; **trasladarse** *vr* (*mudarse*) to move; **traslado** *nm* move; (*mudanza*) move, removal
**traslucir** [traslu'θir] /3f/ *vt* to show
**trasluz** [tras'luθ] *nm* reflected light; **al ~** against o up to the light
**trasnochador, a** *nm/f* (*fig*) night owl

**trasnochar** [trasno'tʃar] /1a/ *vi* (*acostarse tarde*) to stay up late
**traspapelar** [traspape'lar] /1a/ *vt* (*documento, carta*) to mislay, misplace
**traspasar** [traspa'sar] /1a/ *vt* (*bala*) to pierce, go through; (*propiedad*) to sell, transfer; (*calle*) to cross over; (*límites*) to go beyond; (*ley*) to break; **traspaso** *nm* (*venta*) transfer, sale
**traspié** [tras'pje] *nm* (*tropezón*) trip; (*fig*) blunder
**trasplantar** [trasplan'tar] /1a/ *vt* to transplant
**traste** ['traste] *nm* (*Mus*) fret; **dar al ~ con algo** to ruin sth
**trastero** [tras'tero] *nm* lumber room
**trastienda** [tras'tjenda] *nf* back room (*of shop*)
**trasto** ['trasto] *nm* (*pey: cosa*) piece of junk; (*: persona*) dead loss
**trastornado, -a** [trastor'naðo, a] *adj* (*loco*) mad; crazy
**trastornar** [trastor'nar] /1a/ *vt* (*fig: ideas*) to confuse; (*: nervios*) to shatter; (*: persona*) to drive crazy; **trastornarse** *vr* (*volverse loco*) to go mad o crazy; **trastorno** *nm* (*acto*) overturning; (*confusión*) confusion
**tratable** [tra'taβle] *adj* friendly
**tratado** [tra'taðo] *nm* (*Pol*) treaty; (*Com*) agreement
**tratamiento** [trata'mjento] *nm* treatment; **~ de textos** (*Inform*) word processing
**tratar** [tra'tar] /1a/ *vt* (*ocuparse de*) to treat; (*manejar, Tec*) to handle; (*Med*) to treat; (*dirigirse a: persona*) to address ▷ *vi*: **~ de** (*hablar sobre*) to deal with, be about; (*intentar*) to try to; **tratarse** *vr* to treat each other; **~ con** (*Com*) to trade in; (*negociar con*) to negotiate with; (*tener tratos con*) to have dealings with; **¿de qué se trata?** what's it about?; **trato** *nm* dealings *pl*; (*relaciones*) relationship; (*comportamiento*) manner; (*Com, Jur*) agreement
**trauma** ['trauma] *nm* trauma
**través** [tra'βes] *nm* (*contratiempo*) reverse; **al ~** across, crossways; **a ~ de** across; (*sobre*) over; (*por*) through
**travesaño** [traβe'saɲo] *nm* (*Arq*) crossbeam; (*Deporte*) crossbar
**travesía** [traβe'sia] *nf* (*calle*) cross-street; (*Naut*) crossing
**travesura** [traβe'sura] *nf* (*broma*) prank; (*ingenio*) wit
**travieso, -a** [tra'βjeso, a] *adj* (*niño*) naughty
**trayecto** [tra'jekto] *nm* (*ruta*) road, way; (*viaje*) journey; (*tramo*) stretch; **trayectoria** *nf* trajectory; (*fig*) path

**traza** ['traθa] nf (aspecto) looks pl; (señal) sign; **trazado, -a** adj: **bien trazado** shapely, well-formed ▷ nm (Arq) plan, design; (fig) outline

**trazar** [tra'θar] /1f/ vt (Arq) to plan; (Arte) to sketch; (fig) to trace; (plan) to draw up; **trazo** nm (línea) line; (bosquejo) sketch

**trébol** ['treβol] nm (Bot) clover

**trece** ['treθe] num thirteen

**trecho** ['tretʃo] nm (distancia) distance; (de tiempo) while

**tregua** ['treɣwa] nf (Mil) truce; (fig) lull, respite

**treinta** ['treinta] num thirty

**tremendo, -a** [tre'mendo, a] adj (terrible) terrible; (imponente: cosa) imposing; (fam: fabuloso) tremendous

**tren** [tren] nm train; **~ de aterrizaje** undercarriage; **~ de cercanías** suburban train

**trenca** ['trenka] nf duffel coat

**trenza** ['trenθa] nf (de pelo) plait

**trepar** [tre'par] /1a/ vt, vi to climb

**tres** [tres] num three

**tresillo** [tre'siʎo] nm three-piece suite; (Mus) triplet

**treta** ['treta] nf trick

**triángulo** [tri'angulo] nm triangle

**tribu** ['triβu] nf tribe

**tribuna** [tri'βuna] nf (plataforma) platform; (Deporte) stand

**tribunal** [triβu'nal] nm (en juicio) court; (comisión, fig) tribunal; **~ popular** jury

**tributo** [tri'βuto] nm (Com) tax

**trigal** [tri'ɣal] nm wheat field

**trigo** ['triɣo] nm wheat

**trigueño, -a** [tri'ɣeɲo, a] adj (pelo) corn-coloured

**trillar** [tri'ʎar] /1a/ vt (Agr) to thresh

**trimestral** [trimes'tral] adj quarterly; (Escol) termly

**trimestre** [tri'mestre] nm (Escol) term

**trinar** [tri'nar] /1a/ vi (ave) to sing; (rabiar) to fume, be angry

**trinchar** [trin'tʃar] /1a/ vt to carve

**trinchera** [trin'tʃera] nf (fosa) trench

**trineo** [tri'neo] nm sledge

**trinidad** [trini'ðað] nf trio; (Rel): **la T~** the Trinity

**tripa** ['tripa] nf (Anat) intestine; (fam) belly; **tripas** nfpl insides

**triple** ['triple] adj triple

**triplicado, -a** [tripli'kaðo, a] adj: **por ~** in triplicate

**tripulación** [tripula'θjon] nf crew

**tripulante** [tripu'lante] nmf crewman/woman

**tripular** [tripu'lar] /1a/ vt (barco) to man; (Auto) to drive

**triquiñuela** [triki'ɲwela] nf trick

**tris** [tris] nm crack

**triste** ['triste] adj sad; (lamentable) sorry, miserable; **tristeza** nf (aflicción) sadness; (melancolía) melancholy

**triturar** [tritu'rar] /1a/ vt (moler) to grind; (mascar) to chew

**triunfar** [triun'far] /1a/ vi (tener éxito) to triumph; (ganar) to win; **triunfo** nm triumph

**trivial** [tri'βjal] adj trivial

**triza** ['triθa] nf: **hacer algo ~s** to smash sth to bits; (papel) to tear sth to shreds

**trocear** [troθe'ar] /1a/ vt to cut up

**trocha** ['trotʃa] nf short cut

**trofeo** [tro'feo] nm (premio) trophy

**tromba** ['tromba] nf: downpour

**trombón** [trom'bon] nm trombone

**trombosis** [trom'bosis] nf inv thrombosis

**trompa** ['trompa] nf horn; (trompo) humming top; (hocico) snout; **cogerse una ~** (fam) to get tight

**trompazo** [trom'paθo] nm (choque) bump, bang; (puñetazo) punch

**trompeta** [trom'peta] nf trumpet; (clarín) bugle

**trompicón** [trompi'kon] nm: **a trompicones** adv in fits and starts

**trompo** ['trompo] nm spinning top

**trompón** [trom'pon] nm bump

**tronar** [tro'nar] /1l/ vt (LAM) to shoot; (: examen) to flunk ▷ vi to thunder; (fig) to rage

**tronchar** [tron'tʃar] /1a/ vt (árbol) to chop down; (fig: vida) to cut short; (esperanza) to shatter; (persona) to tire out; **troncharse** vr to fall down

**tronco** ['tronko] nm (de árbol, Anat) trunk

**trono** ['trono] nm throne

**tropa** ['tropa] nf (Mil) troop; (soldados) soldiers pl

**tropezar** [trope'θar] /1f, 1j/ vi to trip, stumble; (fig) to slip up; **~ con** to run into; (topar con) to bump into; **tropezón** nm trip; (fig) blunder

**tropical** [tropi'kal] adj tropical

**trópico** ['tropiko] nm tropic

**tropiezo** etc [tro'pjeθo] vb V **tropezar** ▷ nm (error) slip, blunder; (desgracia) misfortune; (obstáculo) snag

**trotamundos** [trota'mundos] nm inv globetrotter

**trotar** [tro'tar] /1a/ vi to trot; **trote** nm trot; (fam) travelling; **de mucho trote** hard-wearing

**trozar** [tro'θar] /1f/ vt (LAM) to cut up, cut into pieces

**trozo** ['troθo] nm bit, piece

**trucha** ['trutʃa] nf trout

**truco** ['truko] nm (habilidad) knack; (engaño) trick

**trueno** ['trweno] nm thunder; (estampido) bang

**trueque** ['trweke] nm exchange; (Com) barter

**trufa** ['trufa] nf (Bot) truffle

**truhán, -ana** [tru'an, ana] nm/f rogue

**truncar** [trun'kar] /1g/ vt (cortar) to truncate; (la vida etc) to cut short; (el desarrollo) to stunt

**tu** [tu] adj your

**tú** [tu] pron you

**tubérculo** [tu'βerkulo] nm (Bot) tuber

**tuberculosis** [tuβerku'losis] nf inv tuberculosis

**tubería** [tuβe'ria] nf pipes pl; (conducto) pipeline

**tubo** ['tuβo] nm tube, pipe; ~ de ensayo test-tube; ~ de escape exhaust (pipe)

**tuerca** ['twerka] nf nut

**tuerto, -a** ['twerto, a] adj blind in one eye ⊳ nm/f one-eyed person

**tuerza** etc ['twerθa] vb V **torcer**

**tuétano** ['twetano] nm marrow; (Bot) pith

**tufo** ['tufo] nm (pey) stench

**tuitear** [tuite'ar] vt, vi to tweet

**tul** [tul] nm tulle

**tulipán** [tuli'pan] nm tulip

**tullido, -a** [tu'ʎiðo, a] adj crippled

**tumba** ['tumba] nf (sepultura) tomb

**tumbar** [tum'bar] /1a/ vt to knock down; **tumbarse** vr (echarse) to lie down; (extenderse) to stretch out

**tumbo** ['tumbo] nm: **dar ~s** to stagger

**tumbona** [tum'bona] nf (butaca) easy chair; (de playa) deckchair (BRIT), beach chair (US)

**tumor** [tu'mor] nm tumour

**tumulto** [tu'multo] nm turmoil

**tuna** ['tuna] nf (Mus) student music group; V tb **tuno**

⚬ **TUNA**

⚬ A tuna is made up of university students,
⚬ or quite often former students, who dress
⚬ up in costumes from the Edad de Oro,
⚬ the Spanish Golden Age. These musical
⚬ troupes go through the town playing
⚬ their guitars, lutes and tambourines
⚬ and serenade the young ladies in the
⚬ halls of residence, or make impromptu
⚬ appearances at weddings or parties
⚬ singing traditional Spanish songs for a
⚬ few coins.

**tunante** [tu'nante] nm rogue

**túnel** ['tunel] nm tunnel

**Túnez** ['tuneθ] nm Tunis

**tuning** ['tunin] nm (Auto) car styling, modding (fam)

**tuno, -a** ['tuno, a] nm/f (fam) rogue ⊳ nm (Mus) member of a "tuna"; V **tuna**

**tupido, -a** [tu'piðo, a] adj (denso) dense; (tela) close-woven

**turbante** [tur'βante] nm turban

**turbar** [tur'βar] /1a/ vt (molestar) to disturb; (incomodar) to upset

**turbina** [tur'βina] nf turbine

**turbio, -a** ['turβjo, a] adj cloudy; (tema) confused

**turbulencia** [turβu'lenθja] nf turbulence; (fig) restlessness; **turbulento, -a** adj turbulent; (fig: intranquilo) restless; (ruidoso) noisy

**turco, -a** ['turko, a] adj Turkish ⊳ nm/f Turk

**turismo** [tu'rismo] nm tourism; (coche) saloon car; **turista** nmf tourist; **turístico, -a** adj tourist cpd

**turnarse** [tur'narse] /1a/ vr to take (it in) turns; **turno** nm (de trabajo) shift; (Deporte etc) turn

**turquesa** [tur'kesa] nf turquoise

**Turquía** [tur'kia] nf Turkey

**turrón** [tu'rron] nm (dulce) nougat

**tutear** [tute'ar] /1a/ vt to address as familiar "tú"; **tutearse** vr to be on familiar terms

**tutela** [tu'tela] nf (legal) guardianship; **tutelar** /1a/ adj tutelary ⊳ vt to protect

**tutor, a** [tu'tor, a] nm/f (legal) guardian; (Escol) tutor

**tuve** etc ['tuβe] vb V **tener**

**tuviera** etc vb V **tener**

**tuyo, -a** ['tujo, a] adj yours, of yours ⊳ pron yours; **un amigo ~** a friend of yours; **los ~s** (fam) your relations, your family

**TV** nf abr (= televisión) TV

**TVE** nf abr = **Televisión Española**

**tweet** [twit] (pl **tweets**) nm (en Twitter) tweet

# u

**u** [u] *conj* or
**ubicar** [uβi'kar] /1g/ *vt* to place, situate; (*encontrar*) to find; **ubicarse** *vr* to be situated, be located
**ubre** ['uβre] *nf* udder
**UCI** *sigla f* (= *Unidad de Cuidados Intensivos*) ICU
**Ud(s)** *abr* = **usted**
**UE** *nf abr* (= *Unión Europea*) EU
**ufanarse** [ufa'narse] /1a/ *vr* to boast; **ufano, -a** *adj* (*arrogante*) arrogant; (*presumido*) conceited
**UGT** *nf abr* = **Unión General de Trabajadores (UGT)**
**úlcera** ['ulθera] *nf* ulcer
**ulterior** [ulte'rjor] *adj* (*más allá*) farther, further; (*subsecuente, siguiente*) subsequent
**últimamente** ['ultimamente] *adv* (*recientemente*) lately, recently
**ultimar** [ulti'mar] /1a/ *vt* to finish; (*finalizar*) to finalize; (LAM: *matar*) to kill
**ultimátum** [ulti'matum] *nm* ultimatum
**último, -a** ['ultimo, a] *adj* last; (*más reciente*) latest, most recent; (*más bajo*) bottom; (*más alto*) top; **en las últimas** on one's last legs; **por ~** finally
**ultra** ['ultra] *adj* ultra ⊳ *nmf* extreme right-winger
**ultraje** [ul'traxe] *nm* outrage; insult
**ultramar** [ultra'mar] *nm*: **de** *o* **en ~** abroad, overseas
**ultranza** [ul'tranθa]: **a ~** *adv* (*a toda costa*) at all costs; (*completo*) outright
**umbral** [um'bral] *nm* (*gen*) threshold

**PALABRA CLAVE**

**un, -una** [un, 'una] *artículo indefinido* **1** a; (*antes de vocal*) an; **una mujer/naranja** a woman/an orange
**2**: **unos/unas: hay unos regalos para ti** there are some presents for you; **hay unas cervezas en la nevera** there are some beers in the fridge; V tb **uno**

**unánime** [u'nanime] *adj* unanimous; **unanimidad** *nf* unanimity
**undécimo, -a** [un'deθimo, a] *adj* eleventh
**ungir** [un'xir] /3c/ *vt* to anoint
**ungüento** [un'gwento] *nm* ointment
**único, -a** ['uniko, a] *adj* only; sole; (*sin par*) unique
**unidad** [uni'ðað] *nf* unity; (*Tec*) unit
**unido, -a** [u'niðo, a] *adj* joined, linked; (*fig*) united
**unificar** [unifi'kar] /1g/ *vt* to unite, unify
**uniformar** [unifor'mar] /1a/ *vt* to make uniform; (*persona*) to put into uniform
**uniforme** [uni'forme] *adj* uniform, equal; (*superficie*) even ⊳ *nm* uniform
**unilateral** [unilate'ral] *adj* unilateral
**unión** [u'njon] *nf* union; (*acto*) uniting, joining; (*calidad*) unity; (*Tec*) joint; **U~ General de Trabajadores (UGT)** (ESP) Socialist Union Confederation; **U~ Europea** European Union
**unir** [u'nir] /3a/ *vt* (*juntar*) to join, unite; (*atar*) to tie, fasten; (*combinar*) to combine; **unirse** *vr* to join together, unite; (*empresas*) to merge
**unísono** [u'nisono] *nm*: **al ~** in unison
**universal** [uniβer'sal] *adj* universal; (*mundial*) world *cpd*
**universidad** [uniβersi'ðað] *nf* university
**universitario, -a** [uniβersi'tarjo, a] *adj* university *cpd* ⊳ *nm/f* (*profesor*) lecturer; (*estudiante*) (university) student; (*graduado*) graduate
**universo** [uni'βerso] *nm* universe

**PALABRA CLAVE**

**uno, -a** ['uno, a] *adj* one; **unos pocos** a few; **unos cien** about a hundred
▶ *pron* **1** one; **quiero uno solo** I only want one; **uno de ellos** one of them
**2** (*alguien*) somebody, someone; **conozco a uno que se te parece** I know somebody *o* someone who looks like you; **unos querían quedarse** some (people) wanted to stay
**3** (*impersonal*) one; **uno mismo** oneself
**4**: **unos ... otros ...** some ... others
▶ *nf* one; **es la una** it's one o'clock
▶ *num* (*number*) one; V tb **un**

**untar** [un'tar] /1a/ *vt* (*mantequilla*) to spread; (*engrasar*) to grease, oil
**uña** ['uɲa] *nf* (*Anat*) nail; (*garra*) claw; (*casco*) hoof; (*arrancaclavos*) claw
**uranio** [u'ranjo] *nm* uranium

**urbanización** [urβaniθa'θjon] nf (colonia, barrio) estate, housing scheme

**urbanizar** [urβani'θar] /1f/ vt (zona) to develop, urbanize

**urbano, -a** [ur'βano, a] adj (de ciudad) urban; (cortés) courteous, polite

**urbe** ['urβe] nf large city

**urdir** [ur'ðir] /3a/ vt to warp; (fig) to plot, contrive

**urgencia** [ur'xenθja] nf urgency; (prisa) haste, rush; (emergencia) emergency; **servicios de ~** emergency services; **"U~s"** "Casualty"; **urgente** adj urgent

**urgir** [ur'xir] /3c/ vi to be urgent; **me urge** I'm in a hurry for it

**urinario, -a** [uri'narjo, a] adj urinary ▷ nm urinal

**urna** ['urna] nf urn; (Pol) ballot box

**urraca** [u'rraka] nf magpie

**URSS** nf abr (Historia: = Unión de Repúblicas Socialistas Soviéticas) USSR

**Uruguay** [uru'ɣwai] nm: **El ~** Uruguay; **uruguayo, -a** adj, nm/f Uruguayan

**usado, -a** [u'saðo, a] adj used; (de segunda mano) secondhand

**usar** [u'sar] /1a/ vt to use; (ropa) to wear; (tener costumbre) to be in the habit of; **usarse** vr to be used; **uso** nm use; (Mecánica etc) wear; (costumbre) usage, custom; (moda) fashion; **al uso** in keeping with custom; **al uso de** in the style of; **de uso externo** (Med) for external use

**usted** [us'teð] pron you sg; **~es** you pl

**usual** [u'swal] adj usual

**usuario, -a** [usw'arjo, a] nm/f user

**usura** [u'sura] nf usury; **usurero, -a** nm/f usurer

**usurpar** [usur'par] /1a/ vt to usurp

**utensilio** [uten'siljo] nm tool; (Culin) utensil

**útero** ['utero] nm uterus, womb

**útil** ['util] adj useful ▷ nm tool; **utilidad** nf usefulness; (Com) profit; **utilizar** /1f/ vt to use, utilize

**utopía** [uto'pia] nf Utopia; **utópico, -a** adj Utopian

**uva** ['uβa] nf grape

* **UVA**
*
* In Spain las uvas play a big part on New
* Year's Eve (Nochevieja), when on the stroke
* of midnight people from every part of
* Spain, at home, in restaurants or in the
* plaza mayor eat a grape for each stroke of
* the clock – especially the one at Puerta del
* Sol in Madrid. It is said to bring luck for the
* following year.

**va** [ba] vb V **ir**

**vaca** ['baka] nf (animal) cow; (carne) beef

**vacaciones** [baka'θjones] nfpl holiday(s)

**vacante** [ba'kante] adj vacant, empty ▷ nf vacancy

**vaciar** [ba'θjar] /1c/ vt to empty (out); (ahuecar) to hollow out; (moldear) to cast; **vaciarse** vr to empty

**vacilar** [baθi'lar] /1a/ vi to be unsteady; to falter; to hesitate, waver; (memoria) to fail

**vacío, -a** [ba'θio, a] adj empty; (puesto) vacant; (desocupado) idle; (vano) vain ▷ nm emptiness; (Física) vacuum; (un vacío) (empty) space

**vacuna** [ba'kuna] nf vaccine; **vacunar** /1a/ vt to vaccinate

**vacuno, -a** [ba'kuno, a] adj bovine; **ganado ~** cattle

**vadear** [baðe'ar] /1a/ vt (río) to ford; **vado** nm ford; **"vado permanente"** "keep clear"

**vagabundo, -a** [baɣa'βundo, a] adj wandering ▷ nm/f tramp

**vagancia** [ba'ɣanθja] nf (pereza) idleness, laziness; (vagabundeo) vagrancy

**vagar** [ba'ɣar] /1h/ vi to wander; (no hacer nada) to idle

**vagina** [ba'xina] nf vagina

**vago, -a** ['baɣo, a] adj vague; (perezoso) lazy ▷ nm/f (vagabundo) tramp; (perezoso) lazybones sg, idler

**vagón** [ba'ɣon] nm (de pasajeros) carriage; (de mercancías) wagon

**vaho** ['bao] nm (vapor) vapour, steam; (respiración) breath

**vaina** ['baina] nf sheath

**vainilla** [bai'niʎa] nf vanilla

**vais** [bais] vb V **ir**

**vaivén** [bai'βen] nm to-and-fro movement; (de tránsito) coming and going; **vaivenes** nmpl (fig) ups and downs

**vajilla** [ba'xiʎa] nf crockery, dishes pl; (una vajilla) service

**valdré** etc vb V **valer**

**vale** ['bale] nm voucher; (recibo) receipt; (pagaré) IOU

**valedero, -a** [bale'ðero, a] adj valid

**valenciano, -a** [balen'θjano, a] adj Valencian

**valentía** [balen'tia] nf courage, bravery

**valer** [ba'ler] /2p/ vt to be worth; (Mat) to equal; (costar) to cost ⊳ vi (ser útil) to be useful; (ser válido) to be valid; **valerse** vr to take care of o.s.; **~ la pena** to be worthwhile; **¿vale?** O.K.?; **más vale que nos vayamos** we'd better go; **~se de** to make use of, take advantage of; **¡eso a mí no me vale!** (LAM fam: no importar) I couldn't care less about that

**valeroso, -a** [bale'roso, a] adj brave, valiant

**valgo** etc ['balɣo] vb V **valer**

**valía** [ba'lia] nf worth

**validar** [bali'ðar] /1a/ vt to validate; **validez** nf validity; **válido, -a** adj valid

**valiente** [ba'ljente] adj brave, valiant ⊳ nmf brave man/woman

**valija** [ba'lixa] nf (LAM) case, suitcase; **~ diplomática** diplomatic bag

**valioso, -a** [ba'ljoso, a] adj valuable

**valla** ['baʎa] nf fence; (Deporte) hurdle; **~ publicitaria** hoarding (esp BRIT), billboard (esp US); **vallar** /1a/ vt to fence in

**valle** ['baʎe] nm valley

**valor** [ba'lor] nm value, worth; (precio) price; (valentía) valour, courage; (importancia) importance; **valorar** /1a/ vt to value; **valores** nmpl (Com) securities

**vals** [bals] nm waltz

**válvula** ['balβula] nf valve

**vamos** ['bamos] vb V **ir**

**vampiro, -iresa** [bam'piro, i'resa] nm/f vampire

**van** [ban] vb V **ir**

**vanguardia** [ban'gwarðja] nf vanguard; (Arte) avant-garde

**vanidad** [bani'ðað] nf vanity; **vanidoso, -a** adj vain, conceited

**vano, -a** ['bano, a] adj vain

**vapor** [ba'por] nm vapour; (vaho) steam; **al ~** (Culin) steamed; **~ de agua** water vapour; **vaporizador** nm spray; **vaporizar** /1f/ vt to vaporize; **vaporoso, -a** adj vaporous

**vaquero, -a** [ba'kero, a] adj cattle cpd ⊳ nm cowboy; **vaqueros** nmpl jeans

**vaquilla** [ba'kiʎa] nf heifer

**vara** ['bara] nf stick; (Tec) rod

**variable** [ba'rjaβle] adj, nf variable (tb Inform)

**variación** [barja'θjon] nf variation

**variar** [ba'rjar] /1c/ vt to vary; (modificar) to modify; (cambiar de posición) to switch around ⊳ vi to vary

**varicela** [bari'θela] nf chicken pox

**varices** [ba'riθes] nfpl varicose veins

**variedad** [barje'ðað] nf variety

**varilla** [ba'riʎa] nf stick; (Bot) twig; (Tec) rod; (de rueda) spoke

**vario, -a** ['barjo, a] adj varied; **~s** various, several

**varita** [ba'rita] nf: **~ mágica** magic wand

**varón** [ba'ron] nm male, man; **varonil** adj manly

**Varsovia** [bar'soβja] nf Warsaw

**vas** [bas] vb V **ir**

**vasco, -a** ['basko, a], **vascongado, -a** [baskon'gaðo, a] adj, nm/f Basque

**vaselina** [base'lina] nf Vaseline®

**vasija** [ba'sixa] nf (earthenware) vessel

**vaso** ['baso] nm glass, tumbler; (Anat) vessel

⬛ No confundir vaso con la palabra inglesa vase.

**vástago** ['bastaɣo] nm (Bot) shoot; (Tec) rod; (fig) offspring

**vasto, -a** ['basto, a] adj vast, huge

**Vaticano** [bati'kano] nm: **el ~** the Vatican

**vatio** ['batjo] nm (Elec) watt

**vaya** etc ['baja] vb V **ir**

**Vd** abr = **usted**

**Vds** abr = **ustedes**; V **usted**

**ve** [be] vb V **ir; ver**

**vecindad** [beθin'dað] nf, **vecindario** [beθin'darjo] nm neighbourhood; (habitantes) residents pl

**vecino, -a** [be'θino, a] adj neighbouring ⊳ nm/f neighbour; (residente) resident

**veda** ['beða] nf prohibition; **vedar** /1a/ vt (prohibir) to ban, prohibit; (impedir) to stop, prevent

**vegetación** [bexeta'θjon] nf vegetation

**vegetal** [bexe'tal] adj, nm vegetable

**vegetariano, -a** [bexeta'rjano, a] adj, nm/f vegetarian

**vehículo** [be'ikulo] nm vehicle; (Med) carrier

**veía** etc vb V **ver**

**veinte** ['beinte] num twenty

**vejar** [be'xar] /1a/ vt (irritar) to annoy, vex; (humillar) to humiliate

**vejez** [be'xeθ] nf old age

**vejiga** [be'xiɣa] nf (Anat) bladder

**vela** ['bela] nf (de cera) candle; (Naut) sail; (insomnio) sleeplessness; (vigilia) vigil; (Mil) sentry duty; **estar a dos ~s** (fam) to be skint

**velado, -a** [be'laðo, a] adj veiled; (sonido) muffled; (Foto) blurred ⊳ nf soirée

**velar** [be'lar] /1a/ vt (vigilar) to keep watch over ⊳ vi to stay awake; **~ por** to watch over, look after

**velatorio** [bela'torjo] *nm* (funeral) wake
**velero** [be'lero] *nm* (*Naut*) sailing ship;
(*Aviat*) glider
**veleta** [be'leta] *nf* weather vane
**veliz** [be'lis] *nm* (ʟᴀᴍ) suitcase
**vello** ['beʎo] *nm* down, fuzz
**velo** ['belo] *nm* veil
**velocidad** [beloθi'ðað] *nf* speed; (*Tec*) rate;
(*Mecánica, Auto*) gear
**velocímetro** [belo'θimetro] *nm* speedometer
**velorio** [be'lorjo] *nm* (ʟᴀᴍ) (funeral) wake
**veloz** [be'loθ] *adj* fast
**ven** [ben] *vb* V **venir**
**vena** ['bena] *nf* vein
**venado** [be'naðo] *nm* deer
**vencedor, a** [benθe'ðor, a] *adj* victorious
▷ *nm/f* victor, winner
**vencer** [ben'θer] /2b/ *vt* (*dominar*) to
defeat, beat; (*derrotar*) to vanquish; (*superar,
controlar*) to overcome, master ▷ *vi* (*triunfar*)
to win (through), triumph; (*plazo*) to expire;
**vencido, -a** *adj* (*derrotado*) defeated,
beaten; (*Com*) due ▷ *adv*: **pagar vencido** to
pay in arrears
**venda** ['benda] *nf* bandage; **vendaje** *nm*
bandage, dressing; **vendar** /1a/ *vt* to
bandage; **vendar los ojos** to blindfold
**vendaval** [benda'βal] *nm* (*viento*) gale
**vendedor, a** [bende'ðor, a] *nm/f* seller
**vender** [ben'der] /2a/ *vt* to sell; **venderse**
*vr* (*estar a la venta*) to be on sale; **~ al
contado/al por mayor/al por menor/a
plazos** to sell for cash/wholesale/retail/on
credit; **"se vende"** "for sale"
**vendimia** [ben'dimja] *nf* grape harvest
**vendré** *etc* [ben'dre] *vb* V **venir**
**veneno** [be'neno] *nm* poison; (*de serpiente*)
venom; **venenoso, -a** *adj* poisonous;
venomous
**venerable** [bene'raβle] *adj* venerable;
**venerar** /1a/ *vt* (*respetar*) to revere;
(*reconocer*) to venerate; (*adorar*) to worship
**venéreo, -a** [be'nereo, a] *adj*: **enfermedad
venérea** venereal disease
**venezolano, -a** [beneθo'lano, a] *adj*
Venezuelan
**Venezuela** [bene'θwela] *nf* Venezuela
**venganza** [ben'ganθa] *nf* vengeance,
revenge; **vengar** /1h/ *vt* to avenge;
**vengarse** *vr* to take revenge; **vengativo, -a**
*adj* (*persona*) vindictive
**vengo** *etc vb* V **venir**
**venia** ['benja] *nf* (*perdón*) pardon; (*permiso*)
consent
**venial** [be'njal] *adj* venial
**venida** [be'niða] *nf* (*llegada*) arrival; (*regreso*)
return
**venidero, -a** [beni'ðero, a] *adj* coming,
future

**venir** [be'nir] /3r/ *vi* to come; (*llegar*) to
arrive; (*ocurrir*) to happen; **venirse** *vr*: **~se
abajo** to collapse; **~ bien** to be suitable;
**~ mal** to be unsuitable *o* inconvenient; **el
año que viene** next year
**venta** ['benta] *nf* (*Com*) sale; **~ a plazos** hire
purchase; **"en ~"** "for sale"; **~ al contado/al
por mayor/al por menor** *o* **al detalle** cash
sale/wholesale/retail; **~ a domicilio** door-
to-door selling; **estar de** *o* **en ~** to be (up)
for sale *o* on the market
**ventaja** [ben'taxa] *nf* advantage;
**ventajoso, -a** *adj* advantageous
**ventana** [ben'tana] *nf* window; **ventanilla**
*nf* (*de taquilla*) window
**ventilación** [bentila'θjon] *nf* ventilation;
(*corriente*) draught
**ventilador** [bentila'ðor] *nm* fan
**ventilar** [benti'lar] /1a/ *vt* to ventilate;
(*poner a secar*) to put out to dry; (*fig*) to air,
discuss
**ventisca** [ben'tiska] *nf* blizzard
**ventrílocuo, -a** [ben'trilokwo, a] *nm/f*
ventriloquist
**ventura** [ben'tura] *nf* (*felicidad*) happiness;
(*buena suerte*) luck; (*destino*) fortune; **a la
(buena) ~** at random; **venturoso, -a** *adj*
happy; (*afortunado*) lucky, fortunate
**veo** *etc vb* V **ver**
**ver** [ber] /2u/ *vt, vi* to see; (*mirar*) to look at,
watch; (*investigar*) to look into; (*entender*) to
see, understand; **verse** *vr* (*encontrarse*) to
meet; (*dejarse ver*) to be seen; (*hallarse: en un
apuro*) to find o.s., be; **a ~** let's see; **no tener
nada que ~ con** to have nothing to do with;
**a mi modo de ~** as I see it; **ya veremos**
we'll see
**vera** ['bera] *nf* edge, verge; (*de río*) bank
**veraneante** [berane'ante] *nmf*
holidaymaker, (summer) vacationer (*us*)
**veranear** [berane'ar] /1a/ *vi* to spend the
summer; **veraneo** *nm* summer holiday;
**veraniego, -a** *adj* summer *cpd*
**verano** [be'rano] *nm* summer
**veras** ['beras] **de ~** *adv* really, truly
**verbal** [ber'βal] *adj* verbal
**verbena** [ber'βena] *nf* street party; (*baile*)
open-air dance
**verbo** ['berβo] *nm* verb
**verdad** [ber'ðað] *nf* truth; (*fiabilidad*)
reliability; **de ~** real, proper; **a decir ~, no
quiero** to tell (you) the truth, I don't want
to; **verdadero, -a** *adj* (*veraz*) true, truthful;
(*fiable*) reliable; (*fig*) real
**verde** ['berðe] *adj* green; (*chiste etc*) blue,
dirty ▷ *nm* green; **viejo ~** dirty old man;
**verdear** /1a/ *vi* to turn green; **verdor** *nm*
greenness
**verdugo** [ber'ðuɣo] *nm* executioner

**verdulero, -a** [berðu'lero, a] *nm/f*
greengrocer

**verdura** [ber'ðura] *nf* greenness; **verduras**
*nfpl* (*Culin*) greens

**vereda** [be'reða] *nf* path; (*LAM*) pavement,
sidewalk (*US*)

**veredicto** [bere'ðikto] *nm* verdict

**vergonzoso, -a** [berɣon'θoso, a] *adj*
shameful; (*tímido*) timid, bashful

**vergüenza** [ber'ɣwenθa] *nf* shame, sense
of shame; (*timidez*) bashfulness; (*pudor*)
modesty; **me da ~ decírselo** I feel too shy *o*
it embarrasses me to tell him

**verídico, -a** [be'riðiko, a] *adj* true, truthful

**verificar** [berifi'kar] /1a/ *vt* to check;
(*corroborar*) to verify (*to* Inform); (*llevar a
cabo*) to carry out; **verificarse** *vr* (*profecía
etc*) to come *o* prove true

**verja** ['berxa] *nf* (*cancela*) iron gate; (*cerca*)
railing(s); (*rejado*) grating

**vermut** [ber'mu] (*pl* **vermuts**) *nm*
vermouth

**verosímil** [bero'simil] *adj* likely, probable;
(*relato*) credible

**verruga** [be'rruɣa] *nf* wart

**versátil** [ber'satil] *adj* versatile

**versión** [ber'sjon] *nf* version

**verso** ['berso] *nm* verse; **un ~ a** line of
poetry

**vértebra** ['berteβra] *nf* vertebra

**verter** [ber'ter] /2g/ *vt* (*vaciar*) to empty,
pour (out); (*sin querer*) to spill; (*basura*) to
dump ▷ *vi* to flow

**vertical** [berti'kal] *adj* vertical

**vértice** ['bertiθe] *nm* vertex, apex

**vertidos** [ber'tiðos] *nmpl* waste *sg*

**vertiente** [ber'tjente] *nf* slope; (*fig*) aspect

**vértigo** ['bertiɣo] *nm* vertigo; (*mareo*)
dizziness

**vesícula** [be'sikula] *nf* blister

**vespino®** [bes'pino] *nm o f ≈* moped

**vestíbulo** [bes'tiβulo] *nm* hall; (*de teatro*)
foyer

**vestido** [bes'tiðo] *nm* (*ropa*) clothes *pl*,
clothing; (*de mujer*) dress, frock

**vestidor** [besti'ðor] *nm* (*LAM Deporte*)
changing (*BRIT*) *o* locker (*US*) room

**vestimenta** [besti'menta] *nf* clothing

**vestir** [bes'tir] /3k/ *vt* (*poner: ropa*) to put
on; (*llevar: ropa*) to wear; (*pagar: la ropa*) to
clothe; (*sastre*) to make clothes for ▷ *vi* to
dress; (*verse bien*) to look good; **vestirse** *vr*
to get dressed, dress o.s.; **estar vestido de**
to be dressed *o* clad in; (*como disfraz*) to be
dressed as

**vestuario** [bes'twarjo] *nm* clothes *pl*,
wardrobe; (*Teat: para actores*) dressing
room; (*Deporte*) changing room

**vetar** [be'tar] /1a/ *vt* to veto

**veterano, -a** [bete'rano, a] *adj*, *nm/f*
veteran

**veterinario, -a** [beteri'narjo, a] *nm/f*
vet(erinary surgeon) ▷ *nf* veterinary science

**veto** ['beto] *nm* veto

**vez** [beθ] *nf* time; (*turno*) turn; **a la ~ que**
at the same time as; **a su ~** in its turn;
**una ~** once; **dos veces** twice; **de una ~**
in one go; **de una ~ para siempre** once
and for all; **en ~ de** instead of; **a veces**
sometimes; **otra ~** again; **una y otra ~**
repeatedly; **de ~ en cuando** from time to
time; **7 veces 9** 7 times 9; **hacer las veces
de** to stand in for; **tal ~** perhaps

**vía** ['bia] *nf* track, route; (*Ferro*) line; (*fig*)
way; (*Anat*) passage, tube ▷ *prep* via, by
way of; **por ~ judicial** by legal means; **en
~s de** in the process of; **~ aérea** airway;
**V~ Láctea** Milky Way; **~ pública** public
highway *o* thoroughfare

**viable** ['bjaβle] *adj* (*plan etc*) feasible

**viaducto** [bja'ðukto] *nm* viaduct

**viajante** [bja'xante] *nm* commercial
traveller

**viajar** [bja'xar] /1a/ *vi* to travel; **viaje** *nm*
journey; (*gira*) tour; (*Naut*) voyage; **estar
de viaje** to be on a journey; **viaje de ida
y vuelta** round trip; **viaje de novios**
honeymoon; **viajero, -a** *adj* travelling
(*BRIT*), traveling (*US*); (*Zool*) migratory
▷ *nm/f* (*quien viaja*) traveller; (*pasajero*)
passenger

**víbora** ['biβora] *nf* viper; (*LAM: venenoso*)
poisonous snake

**vibración** [biβra'θjon] *nf* vibration

**vibrar** [bi'βrar] /1a/ *vt* to vibrate ▷ *vi* to
vibrate

**vicepresidente** [biθepresi'ðente] *nmf* vice
president

**viceversa** [biθe'βersa] *adv* vice versa

**vicio** ['biθjo] *nm* vice; (*mala costumbre*) bad
habit; **vicioso, -a** *adj* (*muy malo*) vicious;
(*corrompido*) depraved ▷ *nm/f* depraved
person

**víctima** ['biktima] *nf* victim

**victoria** [bik'torja] *nf* victory; **victorioso,
-a** *adj* victorious

**vid** [bið] *nf* vine

**vida** ['biða] *nf* life; (*duración*) lifetime; **de
por ~** for life; **en la/mi ~** never; **estar con ~**
to be still alive; **ganarse la ~** to earn one's
living

**vídeo** ['biðeo] *nm* video; **película de ~**
videofilm; **videocámara** *nf* camcorder;
**videoclub** *nm* video club; **videojuego** *nm*
video game; **videollamada** *nf* video call;
**videoteléfono** *nf* videophone

**vidrio** ['biðrjo] *nm* glass

**vieira** ['bjeira] *nf* scallop

**viejo, -a** ['bjexo, a] *adj* old ▷ *nm/f* old man/ woman; **hacerse** o **ponerse ~** to grow o get old

**Viena** ['bjena] *nf* Vienna

**viene** *etc* ['bjene] *vb* V **venir**

**vienés, -esa** [bje'nes, esa] *adj* Viennese

**viento** ['bjento] *nm* wind; **hacer ~** to be windy

**vientre** ['bjentre] *nm* belly; (*matriz*) womb

**viernes** ['bjernes] *nm inv* Friday; **V~ Santo** Good Friday

**Vietnam** [bjet'nam] *nm*: Vietnam; **vietnamita** *adj* Vietnamese

**viga** ['biɣa] *nf* beam, rafter; (*de metal*) girder

**vigencia** [bi'xenθja] *nf* validity; **estar/ entrar en ~** to be in/come into effect o force; **vigente** *adj* valid, in force; (*imperante*) prevailing

**vigésimo, -a** [bi'xesimo, a] *num* twentieth

**vigía** [bi'xia] *nm* look-out

**vigilancia** [bixi'lanθja] *nf*: **tener a algn bajo ~** to keep watch on sb

**vigilar** [bixi'lar] /1a/ *vt* to watch over ▷ *vi* to be vigilant; (*hacer guardia*) to keep watch; **~ por** to take care of

**vigilia** [vi'xilja] *nf* wakefulness; (*Rel*) vigil; (: *ayuno*) fast

**vigor** [bi'ɣor] *nm* vigour, vitality; **en ~** in force; **entrar/poner en ~** to come/put into effect; **vigoroso, -a** *adj* vigorous

**VIH** *nm abr* (= *virus de inmunodeficiencia humana*) HIV; **~ negativo/positivo** HIV-negative/-positive

**vil** [bil] *adj* vile, low

**villa** ['biʎa] *nf* (*casa*) villa; (*pueblo*) small town; (*municipalidad*) municipality

**villancico** [biʎan'θiko] *nm* (Christmas) carol

**vilo** ['bilo]: **en ~** *adv* in the air, suspended; (*fig*) on tenterhooks, in suspense

**vinagre** [bi'naɣre] *nm* vinegar

**vinagreta** [bina'ɣreta] *nf* vinaigrette, French dressing

**vinculación** [binkula'θjon] *nf* (*lazo*) link, bond; (*acción*) linking

**vincular** [binku'lar] /1a/ *vt* to link, bind; **vínculo** *nm* link, bond

**vine** *etc* *vb* V **venir**

**vinicultor, -a** [binikul'tor, a] *nm/f* wine grower

**vinicultura** [binikul'tura] *nf* wine growing

**viniera** *etc* *vb* V **venir**

**vino** ['bino] *vb* V **venir** ▷ *nm* wine; **~ de solera/seco/tinto** vintage/dry/red wine

**viña** ['bina] *nf*, **viñedo** [bi'neðo] *nm* vineyard

**viola** ['bjola] *nf* viola

**violación** [bjola'θjon] *nf* violation; **~ (sexual)** rape

**violar** [bjo'lar] /1a/ *vt* to violate; (*cometer estupro*) to rape

**violencia** [bjo'lenθja] *nf* (*fuerza*) violence, force; (*embarazo*) embarrassment; (*acto injusto*) unjust act; **violentar** /1a/ *vt* to force; (*casa*) to break into; (*agredir*) to assault; (*violar*) to violate; **violento, -a** *adj* violent; (*furioso*) furious; (*situación*) embarrassing; (*acto*) forced, unnatural

**violeta** [bjo'leta] *nf* violet

**violín** [bjo'lin] *nm* violin

**violón** [bjo'lon] *nm* double bass

**viral** [bi'ral] *adj* (*tb Inform*) viral

**virar** [bi'rar] /1a/ *vi* to change direction

**virgen** ['birxen] *adj* virgin ▷ *nmf* virgin

**Virgo** ['birɣo] *nm* Virgo

**viril** [bi'ril] *adj* virile; **virilidad** *nf* virility

**virtud** [bir'tuð] *nf* virtue; **en ~ de** by virtue of; **virtuoso, -a** *adj* virtuous ▷ *nm/f* virtuoso

**viruela** [bi'rwela] *nf* smallpox

**virulento, -a** [biru'lento, a] *adj* virulent

**virus** ['birus] *nm inv* virus

**visa** ['bisa] *nf* (LAM), **visado** [bi'saðo] *nm* (ESP) visa

**víscera** ['bisθera] *nf* internal organ; **vísceras** *nfpl* entrails

**visceral** [bisθe'ral] *adj* (*odio*) deep-rooted; **reacción ~** gut reaction

**visera** [bi'sera] *nf* visor

**visibilidad** [bisiβili'ðað] *nf* visibility; **visible** *adj* visible; (*fig*) obvious

**visillo** [bi'siʎo] *nm* lace curtain

**visión** [bi'sjon] *nf* (*Anat*) vision, (eye)sight; (*fantasía*) vision, fantasy

**visita** [bi'sita] *nf* call, visit; (*persona*) visitor; **visitante** *adj* visiting ▷ *nmf* visitor; **visitar** /1a/ *vt* to visit, call on

**visón** [bi'son] *nm* mink

**visor** [bi'sor] *nm* (*Foto*) viewfinder

**víspera** ['bispera] *nf* day before; **la ~ o en ~s de** on the eve of

**vista** ['bista] *nf* sight, vision; (*capacidad de ver*) (eye)sight; (*mirada*) look(s); **a primera ~** at first glance; **hacer la ~ gorda** to turn a blind eye; **volver la ~** to look back; **está a la ~ que** it's obvious that; **en ~ de** in view of; **en ~ de que** in view of the fact that; **¡hasta la ~!** so long!, see you!; **con ~s a** with a view to; **vistazo** *nm* glance; **dar** o **echar un vistazo a** to glance at

**visto, -a** ['bisto, a] *vb* V **vestir** ▷ *pp de* **ver** ▷ *adj* seen; (*considerado*) considered ▷ *nm*: **~ bueno** approval; **por lo ~** apparently; **está ~ que** it's clear that; **está bien/mal ~** it's acceptable/unacceptable; **~ que** since, considering that

**vistoso, -a** [bis'toso, a] *adj* colourful

**visual** [bi'swal] *adj* visual

**vital** [bi'tal] *adj* life *cpd*, living *cpd*; (*fig*) vital; (*persona*) lively, vivacious; **vitalicio, -a** *adj* for life; **vitalidad** *nf* vitality; (*de persona, negocio*) energy; (*de ciudad*) liveliness

**vitamina** [bita'mina] *nf* vitamin

**vitorear** [bitore'ar] /1a/ *vt* to cheer, acclaim

**vitrina** [bi'trina] *nf* glass case; (*en casa*) display cabinet; (LAM) shop window

**viudo, -a** ['bjuðo, a] *adj* widowed ▷ *nm* widower ▷ *nf* widow

**viva** ['biβa] *excl* hurrah!; **¡~ el rey!** long live the King!

**vivaracho, -a** [biβa'ratʃo, a] *adj* jaunty, lively; (*ojos*) bright, twinkling

**vivaz** [bi'βaθ] *adj* lively

**víveres** ['biβeres] *nmpl* provisions

**vivero** [bi'βero] *nm* (*Horticultura*) nursery; (*para peces*) fish farm; (*fig*) hotbed

**viveza** [bi'βeθa] *nf* liveliness; (*agudeza: mental*) sharpness

**vivienda** [bi'βjenda] *nf* housing; (*casa*) house; (*piso*) flat (BRIT), apartment (US)

**viviente** [bi'βjente] *adj* living

**vivir** [bi'βir] /3a/ *vt* to live o go through ▷ *vi*: **~ (de)** to live (by, off, on) ▷ *nm* life, living

**vivo, -a** ['biβo, a] *adj* living, alive; (*fig*) vivid; (*persona: astuto*) smart, clever; **en ~** (TV *etc*) live

**vocablo** [bo'kaβlo] *nm* (*palabra*) word; (*término*) term

**vocabulario** [bokaβu'larjo] *nm* vocabulary

**vocación** [boka'θjon] *nf* vocation; **vocacional** *nf* (LAM) ≈ technical college

**vocal** [bo'kal] *adj* vocal ▷ *nf* vowel; **vocalizar** /1f/ *vt* to vocalize

**vocero, -a** [bo'θero, a] *nm/f* (LAM) spokesman/woman

**voces** ['boθes] *nfpl de* **voz**

**vodka** ['boðka] *nm* vodka

**vol** *abr* = **volumen**

**volado, -a** [bo'laðo, a] *adv* (LAM) in a rush, hastily

**volador, a** [bola'ðor, a] *adj* flying

**volandas** [bo'landas]: **en ~** *adv* in o through the air

**volante** [bo'lante] *adj* flying ▷ *nm* (*de máquina, coche*) steering wheel; (*de reloj*) balance

**volar** [bo'lar] /1l/ *vt* to blow up ▷ *vi* to fly

**volátil** [bo'latil] *adj* volatile

**volcán** [bol'kan] *nm* volcano; **volcánico, -a** *adj* volcanic

**volcar** [bol'kar] /1g, 1l/ *vt* to upset, overturn; (*tumbar, derribar*) to knock over; (*vaciar*) to empty out ▷ *vi* to overturn; **volcarse** *vr* to tip over

**voleibol** [bolei'βol] *nm* volleyball

**volqué** [bol'ke] *vb V* **volcar**

**voltaje** [bol'taxe] *nm* voltage

**voltear** [bolte'ar] /1a/ *vt* to turn over; (*volcar*) to knock over

**voltereta** [bolte'reta] *nf* somersault

**voltio** ['boltjo] *nm* volt

**voluble** [bo'luβle] *adj* fickle

**volumen** [bo'lumen] *nm* volume; **voluminoso, -a** *adj* voluminous; (*enorme*) massive

**voluntad** [bolun'tað] *nf* will, willpower; (*deseo*) desire, wish

**voluntario, -a** [bolun'tarjo, a] *adj* voluntary ▷ *nm/f* volunteer

**volver** [bol'βer] /2h/ *vt* to turn; (*boca abajo*) to turn (over); (*voltear*) to turn round, turn upside down; (*poner del revés*) to turn inside out; (*devolver*) to return ▷ *vi* to return, go/come back; **volverse** *vr* to turn round; **~ la espalda** to turn one's back; **~ a hacer** to do again; **~ en sí** to come to o round; **~ triste** *etc* **a algn** to make sb sad *etc*; **~se loco** to go mad

**vomitar** [bomi'tar] /1a/ *vt*, *vi* to vomit; **vómito** *nm* vomit

**voraz** [bo'raθ] *adj* voracious

**vos** [bos] *pron* (LAM) you

**vosotros, -as** [bo'sotros, as] *pron* you *pl*; (*reflexivo*): **entre ~** among yourselves

**votación** [bota'θjon] *nf* (*acto*) voting; (*voto*) vote

**votar** [bo'tar] /1a/ *vi* to vote; **voto** *nm* vote; (*promesa*) vow; **votos** *nmpl* (good) wishes

**voy** [boi] *vb V* **ir**

**voz** [boθ] *nf* voice; (*grito*) shout; (*chisme*) rumour; (*Ling*) word; **dar voces** to shout, yell; **en ~ baja** in a low voice; **de viva ~** verbally; **en ~ alta** aloud; **~ de mando** command

**vuelco** *etc* ['bwelko] *vb V* **volcar** ▷ *nm* spill, overturning

**vuelo** ['bwelo] *vb V* **volar** ▷ *nm* flight; (*encaje*) lace, frill; **coger al ~** to catch in flight; **~ libre** hang-gliding; **~ regular** scheduled flight

**vuelque** *etc* ['bwelke] *vb V* **volcar**

**vuelta** ['bwelta] *nf* turn; (*curva*) bend, curve; (*regreso*) return; (*revolución*) revolution; (*circuito*) lap; (*de papel, tela*) reverse; (*cambio*) change; **~ ciclista** (*Deporte*) (cycle) tour; **a la ~** (ESP) on one's return; **a la ~ de la esquina** round the corner; **a ~ de correo** by return of post; **dar ~s** to turn, revolve; (*cabeza*) to spin; **dar(se) la ~** (*volverse*) to turn round; **dar ~s a una idea** to turn over an idea (in one's mind); **dar una ~** to go for a walk; (*en coche*) to go for a drive

**vuelto** ['bwelto] *pp de* **volver**

**vuelvo** *etc* ['bwelβo] *vb V* **volver**

**vuestro, -a** ['bwestro, a] *adj* your ▷ *pron*: el ~/la vuestra/los ~s/las vuestras yours; un amigo ~ a friend of yours

**vulgar** [bul'ɣar] *adj (ordinario)* vulgar; *(común)* common; **vulgaridad** *nf* commonness; *(acto)* vulgarity; *(expresión)* coarse expression

**vulnerable** [bulne'raβle] *adj* vulnerable

**vulnerar** [bulne'rar] /1a/ *vt (Jur, Com)* to violate; *(derechos)* to violate, to interfere with; *(reputación)* to harm, damage

**walkie-talkie** [walki'talki] *nm* walkie-talkie

**walkman®** ['wal(k)man] *nm* Walkman®

**wáter** ['bater] *nm (taza)* toilet; *(LAM: lugar)* toilet *(BRIT)*, rest room *(US)*

**web** [web] *nm o f (página)* website; *(red)* (World Wide) Web; **webcam** *nf* webcam; **webmaster** *nmf* webmaster; **website** *nm* website

**western** ['western] *(pl* westerns*) nm* western

**whisky** ['wiski] *nm* whisky

**wifi** ['waifai] *nm* Wi-Fi

**windsurf** ['winsurf] *nm* windsurfing; **hacer ~** to go windsurfing

# X  y

**xenofobia** [seno'foβja] *nf* xenophobia
**xilófono** [si'lofono] *nm* xylophone
**xocoyote, -a** [ksoko'jote, a] *nm/f* (LAM)
baby of the family, youngest child

**y** [i] *conj* and; (*hora*): **la una y cinco** five past
one
**ya** [ja] *adv* (*gen*) already; (*ahora*) now; (*en
seguida*) at once; (*pronto*) soon ▷ *excl* all
right! ▷ *conj* (*ahora que*) now that; **ya lo sé**
I know; **¡ya está bien!** that's (quite)
enough!; **¡ya voy!** coming!; **ya que** since
**yacer** [ja'θer] /2x/ *vi* to lie
**yacimiento** [jaθi'mjento] *nm* deposit;
(*arqueológico*) site
**yanqui** ['janki] *adj* ▷ *nmf* Yankee
**yate** ['jate] *nm* yacht
**yazco** *etc* ['jaθko] *vb* V **yacer**
**yedra** ['jeðra] *nf* ivy
**yegua** ['jeɣwa] *nf* mare
**yema** ['jema] *nf* (*del huevo*) yolk; (*Bot*) leaf
bud; (*fig*) best part; ~ **del dedo** fingertip
**yerno** ['jerno] *nm* son-in-law
**yeso** ['jeso] *nm* plaster
**yo** [jo] *pron personal* I; **soy yo** it's me
**yodo** ['joðo] *nm* iodine
**yoga** ['joɣa] *nm* yoga
**yogur(t)** [jo'ɣur(t)] *nm* yogurt
**yuca** ['juka] *nf* (*Bot*) yucca; (*alimento*)
cassava, manioc root
**Yugoslavia** [juɣos'laβja] *nf* (*Historia*)
Yugoslavia
**yugular** [juɣu'lar] *adj* jugular
**yunque** ['junke] *nm* anvil
**yuyo** ['jujo] *nm* (LAM: *mala hierba*) weed

# Z

**zafar** [θa'far] /1a/ vt (soltar) to untie; (superficie) to clear; **zafarse** vr (escaparse) to escape; (Tec) to slip off

**zafiro** [θa'firo] nm sapphire

**zaga** ['θaɣa] nf: **a la ~** behind, in the rear

**zaguán** [θa'ɣwan] nm hallway

**zalamero, -a** [θala'mero, a] adj flattering; (relamido) suave

**zamarra** [θa'marra] nf (chaqueta) sheepskin jacket

**zambullirse** [θambuλ'λirse] /3h/ vr to dive

**zampar** [θam'par] /1a/ vt to gobble

**zanahoria** [θana'orja] nf carrot

**zancadilla** [θanka'ðiλa] nf trip

**zanco** ['θanko] nm stilt

**zángano** ['θangano] nm drone

**zanja** ['θanxa] nf ditch; **zanjar** /1a/ vt (conflicto) to resolve

**zapata** [θa'pata] nf (Mecánica) shoe

**zapatería** [θapate'ria] nf (oficio) shoemaking; (tienda) shoe-shop; (fábrica) shoe factory; **zapatero, -a** nm/f shoemaker

**zapatilla** [θapa'tiλa] nf slipper; (de deporte) training shoe

**zapato** [θa'pato] nm shoe

**zapping** ['θapin] nm channel-hopping; **hacer ~** to channel-hop, flick through the channels

**zar** [θar] nm tsar, czar

**zarandear** [θarande'ar] /1a/ vt (fam) to shake vigorously

**zarpa** ['θarpa] nf (garra) claw

**zarpar** [θar'par] /1a/ vi to weigh anchor

**zarza** ['θarθa] nf (Bot) bramble

**zarzamora** [θarθa'mora] nf blackberry

**zarzuela** [θar'θwela] nf Spanish light opera

**zigzag** [θiɣ'θaɣ] adj zigzag

**zinc** [θink] nm zinc

**zíper** ['siper] nm (LAM) zip, zipper (US)

**zócalo** ['θokalo] nm (Arq) plinth, base; (de pared) skirting board

**zoclo** ['θoklo] nm (LAM) skirting board (BRIT), baseboard (US)

**zodíaco** [θo'ðiako] nm zodiac

**zona** ['θona] nf area, zone; **~ fronteriza** border area; **~ roja** (LAM) red-light district

**zonzo, -a** ['θonθo, a] (LAM) adj silly ▷ nm/f fool

**zoo** ['θoo] nm zoo

**zoología** [θoolo'xia] nf zoology; **zoológico, -a** adj zoological ▷ nm (tb: **parque zoológico**) zoo; **zoólogo, -a** nm/f zoologist

**zoom** [θum] nm zoom lens

**zopilote** [θopi'lote] nm (LAM) buzzard

**zoquete** [θo'kete] nm (fam) blockhead

**zorro, -a** ['θorro, a] adj crafty ▷ nm/f fox/vixen

**zozobrar** [θoθo'βrar] /1a/ vi (hundirse) to capsize; (fig) to fail

**zueco** ['θweko] nm clog

**zumbar** [θum'bar] /1a/ vt (golpear) to hit ▷ vi to buzz; **zumbido** nm buzzing

**zumo** ['θumo] nm juice

**zurcir** [θur'θir] /3b/ vt (coser) to darn

**zurdo, -a** ['θurðo, a] adj (persona) left-handed

**zurrar** [θu'rrar] /1a/ vt (fam) to wallop

# Spanish Grammar

# 1 Nouns

## 1.2 The Gender of Nouns

Nouns denoting male people and animals are usually – but not always – masculine:

| | |
|---|---|
| **un hombre** | *a man* |
| **un toro** | *a bull* |

Nouns denoting female people and animals are usually – but not always – feminine:

| | |
|---|---|
| **una niña** | *a girl* |
| **una vaca** | *a cow* |

Some nouns are masculine or feminine depending on the sex of the person to whom they refer:

| | |
|---|---|
| **un marroquí** | *a Moroccan* (man) |
| **una marroquí** | *a Moroccan* (woman) |

Other nouns referring to either men or women have only one gender which applies to both:

| | |
|---|---|
| **una persona** | *a person* |
| **una visita** | *a visitor* |

Often the ending of a noun indicates its gender:

| Masculine endings | | |
|---|---|---|
| -o | **un clavo** | a nail |
| -l | **un tonel** | a barrel |
| -r | **un tractor** | a tractor |
| -y | **el rey** | the king |

| Feminine endings | | |
|---|---|---|
| -a | **una casa** | a house |
| -ión | **una canción** | a song |
| -dad | **una ciudad** | a town |
| -tad | **la libertad** | freedom |
| -ed | **una pared** | a wall |
| -sis | **una tesis** | a thesis |

Some nouns change meaning according to gender. The most common are set out below:

|  | Masculine | Feminine |
|---|---|---|
| **capital** | capital (*money*) | capital (*city*) |
| **corte** | cut | court (*royal*) |
| **cura** | priest | cure |
| **orden** | order (*arrangement*) | order (*command*) |
| **pendiente** | earring | slope |

## 1.2 The Formation of Feminines

As in English, male and female are sometimes differentiated by the use of two quite separate words:

| **mi marido** | *my husband* |
|---|---|
| **mi mujer** | *my wife* |

However, some words in Spanish show this distinction by the form of their ending:

• Nouns ending in **-o** change to **-a** to form the feminine:

| **un amigo** | a (male) *friend* |
|---|---|
| **una amiga** | a (female) *friend* |

• If the masculine singular form already ends in **-a**, no further **-a** is added to the feminine:

| **un deportista** | *a sportsman* |
|---|---|
| **una deportista** | *a sportswoman* |

• If the last letter of the masculine singular form is a consonant, an **-a** is normally added in the feminine:

| **un español** | *a Spaniard, a Spanish man* |
|---|---|
| **una española** | *a Spanish woman* |

• If the last syllable has an accent, it disappears in the feminine:

| **un león** | *a lion* |
|---|---|
| **una leona** | *a lioness* |

## 1.3 The Formation of Plurals

Nouns ending in an unstressed vowel add **-s** to the singular form:

**la casa** *the house* → **las casas** *the houses*

Most nouns ending in a consonant or a stressed vowel add **-es** to the singular form:

**un rumor** *a rumour* → **unos rumores** (*some*) *rumours*

Nouns ending in **-n** or **-s** with an accent on the last syllable drop this accent in the plural:

**la canción** *the song*   →   **las canciones** *the songs*

Nouns ending in **-n** with the stress on the last syllable but one in the singular add an accent to that syllable in the plural in order to show the correct position for stress:

**un examen** *an exam*   →   **unos exámenes** *(some) exams*

Nouns ending in **-z** change this to **c** in the plural:

**la luz** *the light*   →   **las luces** *the lights*

Nouns with an unstressed final syllable ending in **-s** do not change in the plural:

**el lunes** *Monday*   →   **los lunes** *Mondays*

# 2 Articles

## 2.1 The Definite Article

The article used depends on both the gender of the noun and whether it is singular or plural.

|  | with masculine noun | with feminine noun |  |
|---|---|---|---|
| singular | **el** | **la** | the |
| plural | **los** | **las** | the |

| | |
|---|---|
| **el tren** | *the train* |
| **la estación** | *the station* |
| **los hoteles** | *the hotels* |
| **las escuelas** | *the schools* |

## 2.2 The Indefinite Article

The indefinite article is used in Spanish largely as it is in English.

|  | with masculine noun | with feminine noun |  |
|---|---|---|---|
| singular | **un** | **una** | a |
| plural | **unos** | **unas** | some |

| | |
|---|---|
| **una revista** | *a magazine* |
| **unos periódicos** | *some newspapers* |

## 3 Adjectives

Most adjectives agree in number and gender with the noun or pronoun.
Spanish adjectives usually follow the noun.

Note that if the adjective refers to two or more singular nouns of different
genders, a masculine plural ending is required:

> **Nunca había visto árboles y flores tan raros.**
> *I had never seen such strange trees and flowers.*

### 3.1 The Formation of Feminines

Adjectives ending in **-o** change to **-a**:

| | |
|---|---|
| **mi hermano pequeño** | *my little brother* |
| **mi hermana pequeña** | *my little sister* |

Some adjectives add **-a**:

| | |
|---|---|
| **un niño encantador** | *a charming little boy* |
| **una niña encantadora** | *a charming little girl* |

Other adjectives do not change:

| | |
|---|---|
| **un final feliz** | *a happy ending* |
| **una infancia feliz** | *a happy childhood* |

### 3.2 The Formation of Plurals

Adjectives ending in an unstressed vowel add **-s**:

| | |
|---|---|
| **el último tren** | *the last train* |
| **los últimos trenes** | *the last trains* |

Adjectives ending in a stressed vowel or a consonant add **-es**:

| | |
|---|---|
| **un examen fácil** | *an easy exam* |
| **unos exámenes fáciles** | *(some) easy exams* |

Some adjectives and other parts of speech used adjectivally do not change in
the feminine or plural:

| | |
|---|---|
| **los vestidos naranja** | *the orange dresses* |

The following adjectives drop the final **-o** before a masculine singular noun:

| | |
|---|---|
| **bueno** | *good* |
| **un buen libro** | *a good book* |
| **alguno** | *some* |
| **algún libro** | *some book* |
| **uno** | *one* |
| **cuarenta y un años** | *forty-one years* |
| **primero** | *first* |
| **el primer hijo** | *the first child* |

Note that **grande** (*big*, *great*) is shortened to **gran** before a masculine or feminine singular noun, and **ciento** (*a hundred*) is shortened to **cien** before a masculine or feminine plural noun.

## 3.3 Demonstrative Adjectives

The forms **ese/a/os/as** are used to indicate distance from the speaker but proximity to the person addressed.

The forms **aquel/la/los/las** are used to indicate distance, in space or time.

|          | Masculine | Feminine |       |
|----------|-----------|----------|-------|
| singular | este      | esta     | this  |
|          | ese       | esa      |       |
|          | aquel     | aquella  | that  |
| plural   | estos     | estas    | these |
|          | esos      | esas     |       |
|          | aquellos  | aquellas | those |

## 3.4 Interrogative Adjectives

Interrogative adjectives, when not invariable, agree in number and gender with the noun. These forms shown are also used in indirect questions.

|          | Masculine | Feminine  |                |
|----------|-----------|-----------|----------------|
| singular | ¿qué?     | ¿qué?     | what?, which?  |
|          | ¿cuánto?  | ¿cuánta?  | how much?      |
| plural   | ¿qué?     | ¿qué?     | what?, which?  |
|          | ¿cuántos? | ¿cuántas? | how many?      |

## 3.5 Possessive Adjectives

### Weak forms

All possessive adjectives agree in number and (when applicable) in gender with the noun.

| with singular noun | | with plural noun | |  |
|-----------|----------|-----------|----------|-------------------------|
| Masculine | Feminine | Masculine | Feminine |  |
| mi        | mi       | mis       | mis      | my                      |
| tu        | tu       | tus       | tus      | your                    |
| su        | su       | sus       | sus      | his; her; its; your (of **Vd**) |
| nuestro   | nuestra  | nuestros  | nuestras | our                     |
| vuestro   | vuestra  | vuestros  | vuestras | your                    |
| su        | su       | sus       | sus      | their; your (of **Vds**) |

**Strong forms**

| with singular noun | | with plural noun | | |
|---|---|---|---|---|
| Masculine | Feminine | Masculine | Feminine | |
| **mío** | **mía** | **míos** | **mías** | my |
| **tuyo** | **tuya** | **tuyos** | **tuyas** | your |
| **suyo** | **suya** | **suyos** | **suyas** | his; her; its; your (*of* **Vd**) |
| **nuestro** | **nuestra** | **nuestros** | **nuestras** | our |
| **vuestro** | **vuestra** | **vuestros** | **vuestras** | your |
| **suyo** | **suya** | **suyos** | **suyas** | their; your (*of* **Vds**) |

Strong forms follow the noun, or the verb **ser**:

**un amigo nuestro**                    *a friend of ours*

# 4 Pronouns

## 4.1 Personal Pronouns

| | Subject pronouns | | | |
|---|---|---|---|---|
| | Singular | | Plural | |
| 1st person | **yo** | I | **nosotros** | we (*masc./masc.+ fem.*) |
| | | | **nosotras** | we (*all fem.*) |
| 2nd person | **tú** | you | **vosotros** | you (*masc./masc.+ fem.*) |
| | | | **vosotras** | you (*all fem.*) |
| 3rd person | **él** | he; it | **ellos** | they (*masc./masc.+ fem.*) |
| | **ella** | she; it | **ellas** | they (*all fem.*) |
| | **usted (Vd)** | you | **ustedes (Vds)** | you |

In Spanish, subject pronouns are only used with verbs for emphasis or for clarity:

**Tengo un hermano.**                    *I've got a brother.*
**Él lo hizo pero ella no.**                    *He did it but she didn't.*

| | Direct object pronouns | | | |
|---|---|---|---|---|
| | Singular | | Plural | |
| 1st person | **me** | me | **nos** | us |
| 2nd person | **te** | you | **os** | you |
| 3rd person (*masc.*) | **lo** | him; it; you (*of* **Vd**) | **los** | them; you (*of* **Vds**) |
| (*fem.*) | **la** | her; it; you (*of* **Vd**) | **las** | them; you (*of* **Vds**) |

| | Indirect object pronouns | | | |
|---|---|---|---|---|
| | Singular | | Plural | |
| 1st person | **me** | me | **nos** | us |
| 2nd person | **te** | you | **os** | you |
| 3rd person | **le** | him; her; it | **les** | them |

In constructions other than the affirmative imperative, the infinitive and the gerund, the pronoun comes before the verb:

| | |
|---|---|
| **Te quiero.** | *I love you.* |
| **Quiero decirte algo.** | *I want to tell you something.* |

When two object pronouns are combined, the order is: indirect before direct:

| me | | lo |
|---|---|---|
| te | | la |
| nos | before | los |
| os | | las |

| | |
|---|---|
| **No me lo digas.** | *Don't tell me (that).* |

Note that when two 3rd person object pronouns are combined, the indirect object pronoun **le** or **les** becomes **se**:

| | |
|---|---|
| **Se lo di ayer.** | *I gave it to him/her/them yesterday.* |

### 4.2 Possessive Pronouns

Possessive pronouns in Spanish are formed in exactly the same way as the strong forms of possessive adjectives (see page 6).

**Mi perro es más joven que el tuyo.**
*My dog is younger than yours.*

## 5 Verbs

### 5.1 Formation of Simple Tenses

In Spanish the simple tenses are:

• Present, Imperfect, Preterite

• Present Subjunctive, Imperfect Subjunctive

• Future, Conditional

They are formed by adding endings to a verb stem. The endings show the number and person of the subject of the verb.

The stem and endings of regular verbs are totally predictable. The following sections show all the patterns for regular verbs.

## 5.2 Regular Verbs

There are three regular verb patterns (called conjugations), each identifiable by the ending of the infinitive:

- First conjugation verbs end in **-ar** e.g. **hablar** *to speak*.
- Second conjugation verbs end in **-er** e.g. **comer** *to eat*.
- Third conjugation verbs end in **-ir** e.g. **vivir** *to live*.

To form the stem of all simple tenses apart from the future and the conditional, take the endings **-ar**, **-er** and **-ir** off the infinitive form of the verb, for example:

| hablar | → | habl- |
| comer | → | com- |
| vivir | → | viv- |

The future and conditional use the infinitive form of the verb as the stem.

### First conjugation

Add the following endings to the appropriate stem to form the first conjugation:

|  |  | Present | Imperfect | Preterite |
|---|---|---|---|---|
| singular | 1st person | -o | -aba | -é |
|  | 2nd person | -as | -abas | -aste |
|  | 3rd person | -a | -aba | -ó |
| plural | 1st person | -amos | -ábamos | -amos |
|  | 2nd person | -áis | -abais | -asteis |
|  | 3rd person | -an | -aban | -aron |

|  |  | Present subjunctive | Imperfect subjunctive |
|---|---|---|---|
| singular | 1st person | -e | -ara *or* -ase |
|  | 2nd person | -es | -aras *or* -ases |
|  | 3rd person | -e | -ara *or* -ase |
| plural | 1st person | -emos | -áramos *or* -ásemos |
|  | 2nd person | -éis | -arais *or* -aseis |
|  | 3rd person | -en | -aran *or* -asen |

|  |  | Future | Conditional |
|---|---|---|---|
| singular | 1st person | -é | -ía |
|  | 2nd person | -ás | -ías |
|  | 3rd person | -á | -ía |
| plural | 1st person | -emos | -íamos |
|  | 2nd person | -éis | -íais |
|  | 3rd person | -án | -ían |

## Second conjugation

Add the following endings to the appropriate stem to form the second conjugation:

|          |            | Present | Imperfect | Preterite |
|----------|------------|---------|-----------|-----------|
|          | 1st person | -o      | -ía       | -í        |
| singular | 2nd person | -es     | -ías      | -iste     |
|          | 3rd person | -e      | -ía       | -ió       |
|          | 1st person | -emos   | -íamos    | -imos     |
| plural   | 2nd person | -éis    | -íais     | -isteis   |
|          | 3rd person | -en     | -ían      | -ieron    |

|          |            | Present subjunctive | Imperfect subjunctive |
|----------|------------|---------------------|-----------------------|
|          | 1st person | -a                  | -iera or -iese        |
| singular | 2nd person | -as                 | -ieras or -ieses      |
|          | 3rd person | -a                  | -iera or -iese        |
|          | 1st person | -amos               | -iéramos or -iésemos  |
| plural   | 2nd person | -áis                | -ierais or -ieseis    |
|          | 3rd person | -an                 | -ieran or -iesen      |

|          |            | Future | Conditional |
|----------|------------|--------|-------------|
|          | 1st person | -é     | -ía         |
| singular | 2nd person | -ás    | -ías        |
|          | 3rd person | -á     | -ía         |
|          | 1st person | -emos  | -íamos      |
| plural   | 2nd person | -éis   | -íais       |
|          | 3rd person | -án    | -ían        |

## Third conjugation

Add the following endings to the appropriate stem to form the third conjugation:

|          |            | Present | Imperfect | Preterite |
|----------|------------|---------|-----------|-----------|
|          | 1st person | -o      | -ía       | -í        |
| singular | 2nd person | -es     | -ías      | -iste     |
|          | 3rd person | -e      | -ía       | -ió       |
|          | 1st person | -imos   | -íamos    | -imos     |
| plural   | 2nd person | -ís     | -íais     | -isteis   |
|          | 3rd person | -en     | -ían      | -ieron    |

|  |  | Present subjunctive | Imperfect subjunctive |
|---|---|---|---|
| singular | 1st person | -a | -iera or -iese |
|  | 2nd person | -as | -ieras or -ieses |
|  | 3rd person | -a | -iera or -iese |
| plural | 1st person | -amos | -iéramos or -iésemos |
|  | 2nd person | -áis | -ierais or -ieseis |
|  | 3rd person | -an | -ieran or -iesen |

|  |  | Future | Conditional |
|---|---|---|---|
| singular | 1st person | -é | -ía |
|  | 2nd person | -ás | -ías |
|  | 3rd person | -á | -ía |
| plural | 1st person | -emos | -íamos |
|  | 2nd person | -éis | -íais |
|  | 3rd person | -án | -ían |

## 5.3 Reflexive Verbs

A reflexive verb is one that is accompanied by a reflexive pronoun. The infinitive of a reflexive verb ends with the pronoun **se**:

| | |
|---|---|
| **levantarse** | *to get up* |
| **lavarse** | *to wash (oneself)* |

The reflexive pronouns are:

|  | Singular |  | Plural |  |
|---|---|---|---|---|
| 1st person | **me** | myself | **nos** | ourselves |
| 2nd person | **te** | yourself | **os** | yourselves |
| 3rd person | **se** | himself; herself; itself | **se** | themselves |

The forms of a reflexive verb work in the same way as an ordinary verb, but the reflexive pronoun goes before the verb. The reflexive pronoun 'reflects back' to the subject, but it is not always translated in English:

| | |
|---|---|
| **Me visto.** | *I'm dressing (myself).* |
| **Nos lavamos.** | *We're washing (ourselves).* |
| **¿Cómo se llama Vd?** | *What is your name?* |

## 5.4 Formation of Compound Tenses

In Spanish the compound tenses are:

Perfect

| **(yo) he hablado** | *I have spoken* |

Pluperfect

| **(yo) había hablado** | *I had spoken* |

Future Perfect

| **(yo) habré hablado** | *I shall have spoken* |

Conditional Perfect

| **(yo) habría hablado** | *I should/would have spoken* |

Past Anterior

| **(yo) hube hablado** | *I had spoken* |

Perfect Subjunctive

| **(que) (yo) haya hablado** | *(that) I spoke, have spoken* |

Pluperfect Subjunctive

| **(que) (yo) hubiera/<br>hubiese hablado** | *(that) I had spoken* |

They consist of the past participle of the verb together with the auxiliary verb **haber**. Compound tenses are formed in the same way for both regular and irregular verbs.

For all compound tenses you need to know how to form the past participle of the verb. For regular verbs this is as follows:

First conjugation: replace the **-ar** of the infinitive by **-ado**

| **cantar** *to sing* | → | **cantado** *sung* |

Second conjugation: replace the **-er** of the infinitive by **-ido**

| **comer** *to eat* | → | **comido** *eaten* |

Third conjugation: replace the **-ir** of the infinitive by **-ido**

| **vivir** *to live* | → | **vivido** *lived* |

## 5.5 The Subjunctive: when to use it

The subjunctive is used in Spanish after verbs of 'wishing' e.g. **querer que** (*to want*); 'emotion' **sentir que** (*to be sorry that*); 'asking' and 'advising' **pedir que** (*to ask that*), and after verbs expressing doubt or uncertainty e.g. **dudar que** (*to doubt that*).

**Queremos que esté contenta.** *We want her to be happy.*

## 5.6 *ser* and *estar*

In Spanish there are two irregular verbs, **ser** and **estar**, that both mean *to be*, although they are used very differently. In the present simple tense, they follow the patterns shown below.

| Pronoun | ser | estar | Meaning: *to be* |
|---|---|---|---|
| (yo) | soy | estoy | I am |
| (tú) | eres | estás | you are |
| (él/ella/usted) | es | está | he/she/it is, you are |
| (nosotros/nosotras) | somos | estamos | we are |
| (vosotros/vosotras) | sois | estáis | you are |
| (ellos/ellas/ustedes) | son | están | they/you are |

**ser** is used:

• with an adjective when talking about a characteristic or fairly permanent quality

    **Mi hermano es alto.**        *My brother is tall.*

• with a following noun or pronoun that tells you what someone or something is

    **Miguel es camarero.**        *Miguel is a waiter.*

• to say that something belongs to someone

    **La casa es de Javier.**        *The house belongs to Javier.*

• to talk about where someone or something comes from

    **Yo soy de Escocia.**        *I'm from Scotland.*

• to say what time it is or what the date is

    **Son las tres y media.**        *It's half past three.*

• in calculations

    **¿Cuánto es? – Son dos euros.**    *How much is it? – It's two euros.*

**estar** is used:

• to talk about where something or someone is

    **Estoy en Madrid.**        *I'm in Madrid.*

• with an adjective when there has been a change in the condition of someone or something

    **El café está frío.**        *The coffee's cold.*

• with a past participle used as an adjective, to describe the state that something is in

    **Las tiendas están cerradas.**    *The shops are closed.*

• when talking about someone's health

    **¿Cómo están ustedes?**        *How are you?*

• to form continuous tenses such as the present continuous tense

    **Está comiendo.**        *He's eating.*

## 5.7 The Gerund

To form the gerund, replace the **-ar** of the infinitive by **-ando** , or the **-er** or **-ir** of the infinitive by **-iendo**

The gerund is mainly used:

- after the verb **estar**, to form the continuous tenses

    **Estoy escribiendo una carta.**     *I am writing a letter.*

- after the verbs **seguir** and **continuar** *to continue*, and **ir** when meaning *to happen gradually*

    **Continuarán subiendo los precios.**
    *Prices will continue to go up.*

- in time constructions, after **llevar**

    **Lleva dos años estudiando inglés.**
    *He/She has been studying English for two years.*

# 6    Sentence Structure

## 6.1  Word Order

Word order in Spanish is much more flexible than in English. You can often find the subject placed after the verb or the object before the verb, either for emphasis or for stylistic reasons.

There are some cases, however, where the order is always different from English:

- object pronouns nearly always come before the verb

    | | |
    |---|---|
    | **Ya los veo.** | *I can see them now.* |
    | **Me lo dieron ayer.** | *They gave it to me yesterday.* |

- qualifying adjectives nearly always come after the noun

    | | |
    |---|---|
    | **una ciudad española** | *a Spanish town* |
    | **vino tinto** | *red wine* |

- following direct speech the subject always follows the verb

    | | |
    |---|---|
    | **– Pienso que sí – dijo Ana.** | *'I think so,' said Ana.* |
    | **– No importa –  replicó Daniel.** | *'It doesn't matter,' Daniel replied.* |

## 6.2  Negatives

A sentence is made negative by adding **no** between the subject (if stated explicitly) and the verb (and any preceding object pronouns):

| **El coche es suyo.** | → | **El coche no es suyo.** |
|---|---|---|
| *The car is his.* | | *The car is not his.* |

There are, however, some points to note:

• in phrases like *not her, not now* etc, the Spanish **no** usually comes after the word it qualifies

> **¿Quién lo ha hecho? — Ella no.**  *Who did it? — Not her.*
>
> **¿Quieres un cigarrillo? — Ahora no.**
> *Do you want a cigarette? — Not now.*

• with verbs of saying, hoping, thinking etc, *not* is translated by **que no**

> **Opino que no.**          *I think not.*
> **Dijeron que no.**         *They said not.*

The following are some of the most common negative pairs:

> **no ... nada**                    *nothing* (not ... anything)
> **no ... nadie**                   *nobody* (not ... anybody)
> **no ... nunca**                  *never* (not ... ever)
> **no ... ningún/ninguno/a**    *no* (not any)
> **no ... tampoco**               *not ... either*

## 6.3  Question Forms

There are two ways of forming direct questions in Spanish:

• by inverting the normal word order so that *subject + verb* → *verb + subject*:

> **¿Es posible eso?**             *Is it possible?*
> **¿Cuándo volverán Vds?**    *When will you come back?*

• by maintaining the word order *subject + verb*, but by using a rising intonation at the end of the sentence

> **El gato, ¿se bebió toda la leche?**  *Did the cat drink up all his milk?*
> **Andrés, ¿va a venir?**         *Is Andrés coming?*

There are inverted question marks and exclamation marks at the beginning of a question or exclamation, as well as upright ones at the end:

> **¿Cómo estás?**               *How are you?*
> **¡Qué asco!**                   *How revolting!*

# 7  Stress

## 7.1  Which syllable to stress

There are some very simple rules to help you remember which part of the word to stress in Spanish, and when to use an accent.

Words don't have a written acute accent if they follow the normal stress rules for Spanish. If they do not follow the normal stress rules, they do need an accent.

Words ending in a vowel (*a*, *e*, *i*, *o* or *u*) or **-n** or **-s** are normally stressed on the last syllable but one. If this is the case, they do not have any written accents:

**ca|sa** *house*                    **ca|sas** *houses*
**pa|la|bra** *word*                 **pa|la|bras** *words*

Whenever words ending in a vowel or **-n** or **-s** are not stressed on the last syllable but one, they have a written accent on the vowel that is stressed:

**úl|ti|mo**                          *last*
**jó|ve|nes**                         *young people*

Words ending in a consonant (a letter that isn't a vowel) other than **-n** or **-s** are normally stressed on the last syllable. If this is the case, they do not have an accent:

**re|loj**                            *clock, watch*
**ver|dad**                           *truth*

Whenever words ending in a consonant other than **-n** or **-s** are not stressed on the last syllable, they have an accent:

**ca|rác|ter**                        *character*
**di|fí|cil**                         *difficult*

If a word is stressed on the last but two syllables, the vowel to be stressed always has an accent:

**má|qui|na**                         *machine*
**ór|de|nes**                         *orders*

## 7.2 Which vowel to stress in vowel combinations

The vowels **i** and **u** are considered to be weak. The vowels **a**, **e** and **o** are considered to be strong.

When a weak vowel (**i** or **u**) combines with a strong one (**a**, **e** or **o**), they form one sound that is part of the same syllable. Technically speaking, this is called a diphthong. The strong vowel is emphasized more:

**bai|le**                            *dance*

When **i** combines with **u** or **u** with **i** (the two weak vowels), they form one sound within the same syllable; there is more emphasis on the second vowel:

**ciudad**                            *city, town*

When you combine two strong vowels (**a**, **e** or **o**), they form two separate sounds and are part of different syllables:

**ca|er**                             *to fall*

# Gramática inglesa

# 1 Los nombres

## 1.1 Los nombres contables e incontables

Hay cosas que se consideran como elementos individuales y pueden ser contadas una a una. Los nombres que se refieren a ellas son **nombres contables** y tienen forma de singular y de **plural**, normalmente la terminación **-s**.

... one **table**, ... two **cats**, ... three hundred **pounds**

A los nombres que acaban en **-s**, **-ch**, **-sh**, **-x** se les añade **-es**:

**class** → **classes**          **watch** → **watches**

Las palabras que acaban en **-y**, si van precedidas de consonante, cambian la **-y** por **-ies**:

**country** → **countries**          **party** → **parties**

La **-y** precedida de vocal no cambia:

**boy** → **boys**          **day** → **days**

Algunos nombres de uso frecuente tienen **plurales irregulares**, que no se forman con la terminación **-s**:

**child** → **children**          **foot** → **feet**

Por otra parte, hay cosas que no se pueden contar una a una y a las que se hace referencia con **nombres incontables**:

The donkey needed **food** and **water**.

All prices include **travel** to and from London.

Estos suelen hacer referencia a:

*sustancias:* **coal, food, ice, iron, rice, steel, water**
*cualidades humanas:* **courage, cruelty, honesty, patience**
*sentimientos:* **anger, happiness, joy, pride, relief, respect**
*ideas abstractas:* **beauty, death, freedom, fun, life, luck**

Hay casos en los que en inglés se usa un nombre no contable para algo que en español es contable; por ejemplo, *furniture* significa «mobiliario, muebles», pero para decir «un mueble» hay que usar la expresión *a piece of furniture*.

Los nombres incontables no tienen plural y se usan sin el artículo *a*. A menudo se usan con expresiones como *some* o *a loaf of*, *a piece of*:

Let me give you **some advice**.
*Déjame darte un consejo.*

## 4    Los adjetivos

En inglés los adjetivos van por regla general delante del nombre:

> She bought a loaf of **white bread.**
> *Compró un pan blanco.*

Algunos adjetivos se usan exclusivamente delante del nombre. Por ejemplo, se dice *an atomic bomb* pero no *The bomb was atomic*. Entre ellos:

> **eastern, northern, southern, western, atomic, countless, digital, existing, indoor, introductory, maximum, neighbouring, occasional, outdoor**
>
> He sent **countless** letters to the newspapers.
> *Envió un sinfín de cartas a los periódicos.*

Otros solo se usan detrás de un verbo copulativo. Por ejemplo, se puede decir *She was glad* pero no *a glad woman*:

> **afraid, alive, alone, asleep, aware, content, due, glad, ill, ready, sorry, sure, unable, well**
>
> I wanted to be **alone.**
> *Quería estar solo.*

## 5    Los verbos

### 5.1    Verbos regulares e irregulares

En inglés los verbos tienen menos terminaciones que en español. La información sobre la persona nos la da el sujeto del verbo y la información sobre el tiempo verbal a menudo viene indicada por verbos auxiliares o modales:

> **We wanted** to know what happened.
> **Did she phone** you?
> **We will see** how simple a language can be.
> **I might** not **go.**

Los verbos a los que se les puede añadir la terminación *-ed*, que son la mayoría, se llaman **verbos regulares**. Hay ciertos verbos que en vez de esta terminación tienen una o dos formas distintas. A estos se les llama **verbos irregulares**.

Los verbos regulares tienen cuatro formas:

a) la forma base, que se usa para casi todas las personas en el presente y con los verbos modales.

b) la forma en *-s*, que solo se usa en el presente para la tercera persona del singular.

c) la forma de gerundio *-ing*

d) la forma de participio *-ed*

Hay que tener en cuenta que los cambios ortográficos que se producen al añadir una terminación no significan que los verbos sean irregulares:

**ask → asks → asking → asked**

**try → tries → trying → tried**

**reach → reaches → reaching → reached**

**dance → dances → dancing → danced**

**dip → dips → dipping → dipped**

Los verbos **irregulares** pueden tener tres, cuatro o cinco formas distintas, a veces tienen una forma para el pasado y otra para el participio:

**cost → costs → costing → cost → cost**

**think → thinks → thinking → thought → thought**

**swim → swims → swimming → swam → swum**

El verbo principal puede ir precedido de verbos auxiliares y modales:

I **had met** him in Zermatt.
*Lo había conocido en Zermatt.*

You **can go** now.
*Puedes irte ya.*

She **would have been delighted** to see you.
*Le habría encantado verte.*

## 5.2 Los verbos auxiliares: *be, have, do*

|  | be | have | do |
|---|---|---|---|
| *presente* | am/is/are | have/has | do/does |
| *-ing* | being | having | doing |
| *pasado* | was/were | had | did |
| *participio* | been | had | done |

*Be* como verbo auxiliar puede ir acompañado de:

• un verbo en forma *-ing* para formar los tiempos continuos:

He **is** living in Germany.
*Vive en Alemania.*

• un participio, para formar la voz pasiva:

These cars **are** made in Japan.
*Estos coches se fabrican en Japón.*

*Have* se usa como verbo auxiliar con un participio para formar los tiempos de perfecto:

I **have** changed my mind.
*He cambiado de idea.*

*Do* se emplea como auxiliar para la forma negativa o interrogativa de los verbos en presente simple y pasado simple:

> **Do** you like her new haircut?
> *¿Te gusta su nuevo corte de pelo?*

> She **didn't** buy the house.
> *No compró la casa.*

### 5.3 Los tiempos continuos

Los tiempos continuos son los siguientes:

• presente continuo = presente del verbo *be* + *-ing*:

> **I'm looking** at the photographs my brother sent me.
> *Estoy viendo las fotografías que me mandó mi hermano.*

• futuro continuo = *will* + *be* + *-ing*:

> **They'll be staying** with us for a couple of weeks.
> *Se van a quedar con nosotros un par de semanas.*

• pasado continuo = pasado de *be* + *-ing*:

> He **was watching** television when the doorbell rang.
> *Estaba viendo la televisión cuando sonó el timbre.*

• presente perfecto continuo = presente de *have* + *been* + *-ing*:

> **She's been spending** the summer in Europe.
> *Ha pasado el verano en Europa.*

• pasado perfecto continuo = pasado de *have* + *been* + *-ing*:

> We **had been living** in Athens for five years.
> *Llevábamos cinco años viviendo en Atenas.*

### 5.4 Los tiempos simples

Los **tiempos simples** se usan sin verbo auxiliar cuando van en forma afirmativa. El verbo va justo detrás del sujeto:

> I **live** in London.
> George **came** every Tuesday.

Los tiempos simples son los siguientes:

• presente simple = la forma base del verbo (+ *-s* para *he/she/it*)

> I **live** just outside London.
> He **likes** Spain.

• pasado simple (o pretérito perfecto simple) = la forma base + *-ed* para los verbos regulares

> I **liked** her a lot.

• y el pasado simple para los verbos irregulares

> I **bought** six CDs.

## 5.5 Los tiempos de presente

- presente simple:

  George **lives** in Birmingham.
  *George vive en Birmingham.*

  **Do** you **eat** meat?
  *¿Comes carne?*

- presente continuo:

  I'm **cooking** the dinner.
  *Estoy haciendo la cena.*

  The Browns **are having** a party next week.
  *Los Brown hacen una fiesta la semana que viene.*

- presente perfecto:

  **Have** you **heard** from Jill recently?
  *¿Has sabido algo de Jill últimamente?*

  Karen **has** just **phoned** you.
  *Karen acaba de llamarte por teléfono.*

  He **has worked** here since 2015.
  *Trabaja aquí desde 2015.*

## 5.6 Los tiempos de pasado

- pasado simple:

  I **woke** up early and **got** out of bed.
  *Me desperté temprano y me levanté.*

  We usually **spent** the winter at Aunt Meg's house.
  *Solíamos pasar el invierno (o Pasábamos el invierno) en casa de tía Meg.*

- pasado continuo:

  They **were sitting** in the kitchen when they heard the explosion.
  *Estaban sentados en la cocina cuando oyeron la explosión.*

- pasado perfecto:

  I apologized because I **had forgotten** my book.
  *Pedí disculpas porque se me había olvidado el libro.*

## 5.7 El uso de los tiempos con *for, since, ago*

Con *ago*, el verbo de la frase principal está siempre en **pasado simple**:

  We **moved** into this house five years **ago**.
  *Nos mudamos a esta casa hace cinco años.*

Con *for*, el verbo de la oración principal puede estar en pasado, presente perfecto, pasado perfecto y futuro:

  We **lived** in China **for** two years.
  *Estuvimos dos años viviendo en China.*

We **have been living** here **for** five years.
*Llevamos cinco años viviendo aquí.*

We **had been working** o We **had worked** there **for** nine months when the company closed.
*Llevábamos trabajando allí nueve meses cuando cerró la empresa.*

I'll **be staying** with you for a month.
*Voy a quedarme en tu casa un mes.*

Con *since*, el verbo de la oración principal puede estar en presente perfecto y pasado perfecto:

We **have been living** here **since** 1990.
*Llevamos viviendo aquí desde 1990.*

He **hadn't cried since** he was a boy of ten.
*No había llorado desde que tenía diez años.*

## 5.8 Los verbos modales

**will, shall, would, can, could, may, might, must, should, ought to**

Estos verbos tienen una sola forma y, a excepción de *ought*, se usan con el infinitivo sin *to*.

Nunca se pueden usar dos modales juntos ni van precedidos por un verbo auxiliar. Por ejemplo, no se puede decir *He will can come*. En su lugar hay que decir *He will be able to come*, usando una expresión con significado idéntico al del modal.

*Will* es un verbo modal que se usa la mayoría de las veces para hablar del futuro:

The weather tomorrow **will be** warm and sunny.
*Mañana el tiempo será cálido y soleado.*

I'm tired. I think I'll **go** to bed.
*Estoy cansado. Creo que me voy a ir a la cama.*

Don't be late. I'll **be waiting** for you.
*No tardes. Te estaré esperando.*

También puede usarse para solicitar algo o hacer una invitación:

**Will you** do me a favour?
*¿Quieres hacerme un favor?*

**Will you** come to my party on Saturday?
*¿Vienes a mi fiesta el sábado?*

*Shall* se usa sólo con *I* y *we*, principalmente en forma interrogativa para hacer una sugerencia:

**Shall** we go and see a film?
*¿Vamos a ver una película?*

**Shall** I shut the door?
*¿Cierro la puerta?*

**Would** se usa para hacer una invitación o una petición:

**Would you tell** her Adrian phoned?
*¿Podrías decirle que llamó Adrian?*

**Would you like** a drink?
*¿Te apetece beber algo?*

**Can** y **could** se usan para indicar posibilidad o la capacidad de hacer algo:

Cooking **can** be a real pleasure.
*Cocinar puede ser un verdadero placer.*

You **could** have gone to Paris.
*Podrías haber ido a París.*

He **could** run faster than anybody else.
*Podía correr más que nadie.*

Para expresar estos significados en formas verbales que **can** no tiene, se usan formas de la expresión equivalente **be able to**:

Nobody else **will be able to** read it.
*Nadie más podrá leerlo.*

... the satisfaction of **being able to** do the job.
*... la satisfacción de poder hacer el trabajo.*

**Can** y **could** se usan en conversación para pedir algo o para ofrecerse a hacer algo:

**Can I** help you with the dishes?
*¿Te ayudo con los platos?*

**Could you** do me a favour?
*¿Podrías hacerme un favor?*

**Can**, **could** y **may** se usan para pedir permiso. La construcción con **may** es la más formal:

**Can I** ask a question?
*¿Puedo hacer una pregunta?*

**Could I** just interrupt a minute?
*¿Podría interrumpir un momento?*

**May I** have a cigarette?
*¿Me puede dar un cigarro?*

Solo **can** y **may** se usan para dar permiso:

You **can** borrow that pen if you want to.
*Te puedo dejar ese bolígrafo si quieres.*

You **may** leave as soon as you have finished.
*Se podrá ir tan pronto como haya acabado.*

*May* y *might* se usan para decir que existe la posibilidad de que suceda o haya sucedido algo:

> He **might** come.
> *Puede que venga.*

> You **may** have noticed this advertisement.
> *Puede ser que se haya fijado en este anuncio.*

*Must* se usa para decir que se debe hacer algo, que algo debe pasar o que algo debe ser como es:

> The plants **must** have plenty of sunshine.
> *Las plantas deben recibir sol en abundancia.*

> You **must** come to the meeting.
> *Tienes que venir a la reunión.*

*Should* y *ought to* son sinónimos y tienen los mismos significados que «debería» o «tendría que»:

> We **should** send her a postcard.
> *Deberíamos enviarle una postal.*

> You **ought not to** see him again.
> *No deberías volver a verlo.*

> We **ought to** have stayed in tonight.
> *Tendríamos que habernos quedado en casa esta noche.*

## 5.9 El imperativo

La forma **afirmativa** del **imperativo** es la misma que la forma base de un verbo y no va precedida de pronombre:

> **Come** to my place.
> **Start** when you hear the bell.

La forma negativa se construye con el auxiliar *do*:

> **Do not write** in this book.
> **Don't go** so fast.
> **Never open** the front door to strangers.

## 5.10 *Phrasal verbs*

Estos verbos van acompañados de un adverbio o preposición. El significado del verbo puede cambiar radicalmente:

> **Turn** right at the next corner.
> *Gire a la derecha en la próxima esquina.*

> She **turned off** the radio.
> *Apagó la radio.*

> She **broke** her arm in the accident.
> *Se rompió el brazo en el accidente.*

They **broke out** of prison on Thursday night.
*Se escaparon de la cárcel el jueves por la noche.*

Algunos verbos no tienen objeto:

**break out, catch on, check up, come in, get by, give in, go away, grow up, ring off, start up, stay up, stop off, watch out, wear off**

War **broke out** in September.
*La guerra estalló en septiembre.*

You'll have to **stay up** late tonight.
*Tendrás que quedarte levantado hasta tarde esta noche.*

Otros llevan el objeto detrás de la preposición o adverbio, que se considera parte del verbo porque le da un significado distinto:

**fall for, bargain for, deal with, look after, part with, pick on, set about, take after**

She **looked after** her invalid mother.
*Cuidó a su madre inválida.*

Peter **takes after** his father but John is more like me.
*Peter sale a su padre pero John se parece más a mí.*

Algunos llevan el objeto justo detrás del verbo:

**bring round, keep up, knock out**

They tried to **bring her round**.
*Intentaron reanimarla.*

Y con otros el objeto puede ir bien detrás de la preposición o adverbio o bien justo detrás del verbo:

**fold up, hand over, knock over, point out, pull down, put away, put up, rub out, sort out, take up, tear up, throw away, try out**

It took ages to **clean up** the mess.
It took ages to **clean** the mess **up**.
*Llevó un montón de tiempo limpiarlo todo.*

Sin embargo, si el objeto es un pronombre va siempre justo detrás del verbo:

There was such a mess. It took ages to **clean it up**.
*Había tal desorden. Llevó un montón de tiempo limpiarlo.*

## 5.11 La voz pasiva

Cuando se quiere centrar la atención sobre la persona o cosa que se ve afectada por la acción, más que en quien lleva a cabo la acción, se usa la **voz pasiva**. Solo los verbos que suelen llevar objeto admiten estas construcciones:

Mr Smith **locks** the gate at six o'clock every night.
The gate **is locked** at six o'clock every night.

The storm **destroyed** dozens of trees.
Dozens of trees **were destroyed**.

Cuando se usa la voz pasiva es habitual no mencionar el agente de la acción, bien porque no se sepa o no se quiera decir o bien porque dé igual. En caso de que sí se quiera mencionar, va detrás del verbo tras la preposición *by*:

Her boyfriend **was shot** in the chest.
He was brought up **by an aunt**.

En el caso de verbos con objeto directo e indirecto, cualquiera de ellos puede ser el sujeto de la oración pasiva:

The secretary **was given** the key. *o* The key **was given** to the secretary.
The books **will be sent** to you. *o* You **will be sent** the books.

## 5.12 *There is/there are*

Para decir «hay» o «había», usa una forma verbal en singular con **there** (*is...*, *has...*) si el grupo nominal que sigue al verbo (o el primer nombre, si hay más de uno) está en singular o es incontable:

**There is one point** we must add here.
**There was a sofa** and two chairs.

Se usa una forma verbal en plural si el grupo nominal está en plural y delante de frases como *a number (of)*, *a lot (of)*, y *a few (of)*:

**There were two men** in the room.
**There were a lot of shoppers** in the streets.

## 5.13 La forma verbal de gerundio en *-ing*

El gerundio se puede usar para formar un adjetivo a partir de un verbo. Si acompaña al nombre va normalmente delante él:

His novels are always **interesting** and **surprising**.
*Sus novelas son siempre interesantes y sorpendentes.*

He lives in a **charming** house just outside the town.
*Vive en una casa encantadora en las afueras de la ciudad.*

También se usa detrás del verbo principal para hablar de una acción cuando el sujeto es el mismo que el del verbo principal:

I don't mind **telling** you.
*No me importa decírtelo.*

I've just finished **reading** that book.
*Acabo de terminar ese libro.*

### 5.14 La forma verbal del infinitivo con *to*…

Se usa detrás de algunos verbos para referirse a una acción cuando el sujeto es el mismo que el del verbo principal. Suele equivaler al infinitivo en español:

> **She had agreed to let** us use her flat.
> *Había accedido a dejarnos su piso.*

> **I decided not to go** out for the evening.
> *Decidí no salir esa noche.*

En otras ocasiones se usa detrás del objeto del verbo, en cuyo caso equivale en español a «que» + subjuntivo:

> **I asked her to explain.**
> *Le pedí que diera una explicación.*

> **I want you to help** me.
> *Quiero que me ayudes.*

### 5.15 El participio

La forma verbal de participio se puede usar de la misma manera que un adjetivo:

> A **bored** student complained to his teacher.
> *Un estudiante aburrido se quejó a su profesor.*

> The bird had a **broken** wing.
> *El pájaro tenía un ala rota.*

## 6 Las preguntas

### 6.1 El orden de las palabras

En inglés, el orden de las palabras cambia al hacer una pregunta directa, pero no cuando se hace de manera indirecta. En este segundo caso se usan formas verbales simples, y no el auxiliar *do*:

> **What will you** talk about?
> I'd like to know **what you will talk about**.
> **Did you have** a good flight?
> I asked him **if he had a good flight**.

Para hacer una pregunta cuya respuesta es sí o no, el verbo auxiliar va seguido del sujeto.

Para responder a una de estas preguntas se usa, tras **yes** o **no**, el auxiliar, modal o forma de **be** correspondiente:

> **Is he** coming? —Yes, **he is**./No, **he isn't**.
> **Have you** finished yet? —Yes, **I have**./No, **I haven't**.

Los tiempos simples llevan *do* como verbo auxiliar en preguntas de este tipo:

**Do you** like wine? —Yes, I **do**/No, I **don't**.
**Did he** go to the theatre? —Yes, **he did**./No, **he didn't**.

## 6.2 *Question tags*

En inglés hablado es muy frecuente preguntar algo con una frase y una «pregunta coletilla» o *question tag* al final para pedir confirmación de lo que se acaba de decir. Esta pregunta repite la forma verbal de la oración pero usando únicamente el verbo auxiliar correspondiente seguido del sujeto:

It **is** quite warm, **isn't it**?
It **doesn't** work, **does it**?

También se puede hacer una pregunta de este tipo para expresar sorpresa, enfado u otros sentimientos. En ese caso tanto la frase como la pregunta van en forma afirmativa:

You **fell** on your back, **did you**?
You**'re** working late again, **are you**?

## 6.3 **Las partículas interrogativas**

Las **partículas interrogativas** en inglés son:

**what, which, when, where, who, whom, whose, why, how, how much, how many, how long**

*Whom* solo se usa en inglés culto.

Las partículas interrogativas van siempre al principio de la pregunta y se invierte el orden del verbo auxiliar y el sujeto como en cualquier pregunta:

**When** would you be coming down?
*¿Cuándo vas a bajar?*

**Why** did you do it?
*¿Por qué lo hiciste?*

**Where** did you get that from?
*¿De dónde sacaste eso?*

**Whose** idea was it?
*¿De quién fue esa idea?*

La única excepción se da cuando se está preguntando por el sujeto del verbo. En este caso se sigue el orden habitual de la oración y no se usa el verbo auxiliar *do*:

**Who** could have done it?
*¿Quién pudo haber hecho eso?*

**What** happened?
*¿Qué pasó?*

**Which** is the best restaurant?
*¿Cuál es el mejor restaurante?*

Si hay una preposición, va al final. Sin embargo, con **whom** siempre va delante del pronombre:

> **What's this for?**
> *¿Para qué es esto?*

> **What's the book about?**
> *¿De qué trata el libro?*

> **With whom** were you talking?
> *¿Con quién hablabas?*

Además de ir solo con el significado de «cómo», **how** también puede ir con adjetivos y adverbios, o con **many** y **much**:

> **How old** are your children?
> *¿Qué edad tienen tus hijos?*

> **How long** have you lived here?
> *¿Cuánto tiempo llevas viviendo aquí?*

> **How many** were there?
> *¿Cuántos había?*

# 7 La negación

La negación se forma con la palabra **not** (contraída o no) detrás del primer verbo. Las formas verbales simples necesitan un auxiliar en forma negativa:

> They **do not need** to talk.
> I **was not** smiling.
> I **haven't** been playing football.

Estas son las contracciones más frecuentes:

| isn't | haven't | can't | mustn't |
|-------|---------|-------|---------|
| aren't | hasn't | couldn't | mightn't |
| wasn't | hadn't | shan't | oughtn't |
| weren't | don't | shouldn't | daren't |
| | doesn't | won't | needn't |
| | didn't | wouldn't | |

Con **no one**, **nobody**, **nothing**, **nowhere**, **none**, **never** y **neither** (... **nor**...) no se usa **not**. En caso de que sí se use, o de que haya alguna otra negación, se emplean los equivalentes correspondientes:

> **anyone, anybody, anything, anywhere, any, ever, either**

> There is **nothing** you can do./There **isn't anything** you can do.
> *No hay nada que puedas hacer.*

# Inglés – Español

# English – Spanish

# a

**A** [eɪ] n (Mus) la m; **A road** n (BRIT Aut) ≈ carretera nacional

**a** [ə] indef art (before vowel and silent h **an**)
**1** un(a); **a book** un libro; **an apple** una manzana; **she's a nurse** (ella) es enfermera
**2** (instead of the number "one") un(a); **a year ago** hace un año; **a hundred/thousand pounds** cien/mil libras
**3** (in expressing ratios, prices etc): **three a day/week** tres al día/a la semana; **10 km an hour** 10 km por hora; **£5 a person** £5 por persona; **30p a kilo** 30p el kilo

**A2** n (BRIT Scol) segunda parte de los "A levels" (módulos 4–6)
**AA** n abbr (BRIT: = Automobile Association) ≈ RACE m (SP); (= Alcoholics Anonymous) A.A.
**AAA** n abbr (= American Automobile Association) ≈ RACE m (SP)
**aback** [ə'bæk] adv: **to be taken ~** quedar(se) desconcertado
**abandon** [ə'bændən] vt abandonar; (renounce) renunciar a
**abattoir** ['æbətwɑː'] n (BRIT) matadero
**abbey** ['æbɪ] n abadía
**abbreviation** [əbriːvɪ'eɪʃən] n (short form) abreviatura
**abdomen** ['æbdəmən] n abdomen m
**abduct** [æb'dʌkt] vt raptar, secuestrar
**abide** [ə'baɪd] vt: **I can't ~ it/him** no lo/ le puedo ver or aguantar; **abide by** vt fus atenerse a
**ability** [ə'bɪlɪtɪ] n habilidad f, capacidad f; (talent) talento
**able** ['eɪbl] adj capaz; (skilled) hábil; **to be ~ to do sth** poder hacer algo
**abnormal** [æb'nɔːməl] adj anormal

**aboard** [ə'bɔːd] adv a bordo ▷ prep a bordo de
**abolish** [ə'bɔlɪʃ] vt suprimir, abolir
**abolition** [æbəu'lɪʃən] n supresión f, abolición f
**abort** [ə'bɔːt] vt abortar; (Comput) interrumpir ▷ vi (Comput) interrumpir el programa; **abortion** n aborto; **to have an abortion** abortar

**about** [ə'baut] adv **1** (approximately) más o menos, aproximadamente; **about a hundred/thousand** etc unos/as or como cien/mil etc; **it takes about 10 hours** se tarda unas or más o menos 10 horas; **at about two o'clock** sobre las dos; **I've just about finished** casi he terminado
**2** (referring to place) por todas partes; **to leave things lying about** dejar las cosas (tiradas) por ahí; **to run about** correr por todas partes; **to walk about** pasearse, ir y venir
**3**: **to be about to do sth** estar a punto de hacer algo
▷ prep **1** (relating to) de, sobre, acerca de; **a book about London** un libro sobre or acerca de Londres; **what is it about?** ¿de qué se trata?; **we talked about it** hablamos de eso or ello; **what or how about doing this?** ¿qué tal si hacemos esto?
**2** (referring to place) por; **to walk about the town** caminar por la ciudad

**above** [ə'bʌv] adv encima, por encima, arriba ▷ prep encima de; (greater than: in number) más de; (: in rank) superior a; **mentioned ~** susodicho; **~ all** sobre todo
**abroad** [ə'brɔːd] adv (be) en el extranjero; (go) al extranjero
**abrupt** [ə'brʌpt] adj (sudden) brusco
**abscess** ['æbsɪs] n absceso
**absence** ['æbsəns] n ausencia
**absent** ['æbsənt] adj ausente; **absent-minded** adj distraído
**absolute** ['æbsəluːt] adj absoluto; **absolutely** adv totalmente; **oh yes, absolutely!** ¡claro or por supuesto que sí!
**absorb** [əb'zɔːb] vt absorber; **to be ~ed in a book** estar absorto en un libro; **absorbent** adj absorbente; **absorbent cotton** n (US) algodón m hidrófilo; **absorbing** adj absorbente
**abstain** [əb'steɪn] vi: **to ~ (from)** abstenerse (de)
**abstract** ['æbstrækt] adj abstracto
**absurd** [əb'səːd] adj absurdo
**abundance** [ə'bʌndəns] n abundancia

**abundant** [əˈbʌndənt] *adj* abundante
**abuse** [əˈbjuːs] *n* (*insults*) insultos *mpl*; (*misuse*) abuso ▷ *vt* [əˈbjuːz] (*ill-treat*) maltratar; (*take advantage of*) abusar de; **abusive** *adj* ofensivo
**abysmal** [əˈbɪzməl] *adj* pésimo; (*failure*) garrafal; (*ignorance*) supino
**academic** [ækəˈdɛmɪk] *adj* académico, universitario; (*pej: issue*) puramente teórico ▷ *n* estudioso/a; (*lecturer*) profesor(a) *m/f* universitario/a; **academic year** *n* (*Univ*) año académico
**academy** [əˈkædəmɪ] *n* (*learned body*) academia; (*school*) instituto, colegio
**accelerate** [ækˈsɛləreɪt] *vi* acelerar; **acceleration** *n* aceleración *f*; **accelerator** *n* (*BRIT*) acelerador *m*
**accent** [ˈæksɛnt] *n* acento; (*fig*) énfasis *m*
**accept** [əkˈsɛpt] *vt* aceptar; (*concede*) admitir; **acceptable** *adj* aceptable; **acceptance** *n* aceptación *f*
**access** [ˈæksɛs] *n* acceso ▷ *vt*: **to have ~ to** tener acceso a; **accessible** *adj* (*place, person*) accesible; (*knowledge etc*) asequible
**accessory** [ækˈsɛsərɪ] *n* accesorio, (*Law*): **~ to** cómplice de
**accident** [ˈæksɪdənt] *n* accidente *m*; (*chance*) casualidad *f*; **by ~** (*unintentionally*) sin querer; (*by coincidence*) por casualidad; **accidental** *adj* accidental, fortuito; **accidentally** *adv* sin querer; por casualidad; **Accident and Emergency Department** *n* (*BRIT*) Urgencias *fpl*; **accident insurance** *n* seguro contra accidentes
**acclaim** [əˈkleɪm] *vt* aclamar, aplaudir ▷ *n* aclamación *f*, aplausos *mpl*
**accommodate** [əˈkɔmədeɪt] *vt* alojar, hospedar; (*car, hotel etc*) tener cabida para; (*oblige, help*) complacer; **this car ~s four people comfortably** en este coche caben cuatro personas cómodamente
**accommodation** *n*, (*US*) **accommodations** *npl* [əkɔməˈdeɪʃən(z)] alojamiento
**accompaniment** [əˈkʌmpənɪmənt] *n* acompañamiento
**accompany** [əˈkʌmpənɪ] *vt* acompañar
**accomplice** [əˈkʌmplɪs] *n* cómplice *mf*
**accomplish** [əˈkʌmplɪʃ] *vt* (*finish*) concluir; **accomplishment** *n* (*bringing about*) realización *f*; (*skill*) talento
**accord** [əˈkɔːd] *n* acuerdo ▷ *vt* conceder; **of his own ~** espontáneamente; **accordance** *n*: **in accordance with** de acuerdo con; **according: according to** *prep* según; (*in accordance with*) conforme a; **accordingly** *adv* (*thus*) por consiguiente; (*appropriately*) de acuerdo con esto

**account** [əˈkaunt] *n* (*Comm*) cuenta; (*report*) informe *m*; **accounts** *npl* (*Comm*) cuentas *fpl*; **of little ~** de poca importancia; **on ~** a crédito; **to buy sth on ~** comprar algo a crédito; **on no ~** bajo ningún concepto; **on ~ of** a causa de, por motivo de; **to take into ~, take ~ of** tener en cuenta; **account for** *vt fus* (*explain*) explicar; **accountable** *adj*: **accountable (for)** responsable (de); **accountant** *n* contable *mf*, contador(a) *m/f* (*LAM*); **account number** *n* (*at bank etc*) número de cuenta
**accumulate** [əˈkjuːmjuleɪt] *vt* acumular ▷ *vi* acumularse
**accuracy** [ˈækjurəsɪ] *n* (*of total*) exactitud *f*; (*of description etc*) precisión *f*
**accurate** [ˈækjurɪt] *adj* (*number*) exacto; (*answer*) acertado; (*shot*) certero; **accurately** *adv* con precisión
**accusation** [ækjuˈzeɪʃən] *n* acusación *f*
**accuse** [əˈkjuːz] *vt* acusar; (*blame*) echar la culpa a; **to ~ sb (of sth)** acusar a algn (de algo); **accused** *n* acusado/a
**accustomed** [əˈkʌstəmd] *adj*: **~ to** acostumbrado a
**ace** [eɪs] *n* as *m*
**ache** [eɪk] *n* dolor *m* ▷ *vi* doler; **my head ~s** me duele la cabeza
**achieve** [əˈtʃiːv] *vt* (*reach*) alcanzar; (*victory, success*) lograr, conseguir; **achievement** *n* (*completion*) realización *f*; (*success*) éxito
**acid** [ˈæsɪd] *adj* ácido; (*bitter*) agrio ▷ *n* (*Chem, inf: LSD*) ácido
**acknowledge** [əkˈnɔlɪdʒ] *vt* (*letter: also*: **~ receipt of**) acusar recibo de; (*fact*) reconocer; **acknowledgement** *n* acuse *m* de recibo
**acne** [ˈæknɪ] *n* acné *m*
**acorn** [ˈeɪkɔːn] *n* bellota
**acoustic** [əˈkuːstɪk] *adj* acústico
**acquaintance** [əˈkweɪntəns] *n* conocimiento; (*person*) conocido/a; **to make sb's ~** conocer a algn
**acquire** [əˈkwaɪəʳ] *vt* adquirir
**acquisition** [ækwɪˈzɪʃən] *n* adquisición *f*
**acquit** [əˈkwɪt] *vt* absolver, exculpar; **to ~ o.s. well** salir con éxito
**acre** [ˈeɪkəʳ] *n* acre *m*
**acronym** [ˈækrənɪm] *n* siglas *fpl*
**across** [əˈkrɔs] *prep* (*on the other side of*) al otro lado de; (*crosswise*) a través de ▷ *adv* de un lado a otro, de una parte a otra a través, al través; **to run/swim ~** atravesar corriendo/nadando; **~ from** enfrente de; **the lake is 12 km ~** el lago tiene 12 km de ancho
**acrylic** [əˈkrɪlɪk] *adj* acrílico
**act** [ækt] *n* acto, acción *f*; (*Theat*) acto; (*in music-hall etc*) número; (*Law*) decreto, ley *f*

▷ vi (behave) comportarse; (Theat) actuar; (pretend) fingir; (take action) tomar medidas ▷ vt (part) hacer; **to catch sb in the ~** coger a algn in fraganti or con las manos en la masa; **to ~ Hamlet** hacer el papel de Hamlet; **to ~ as** actuar or hacer de; **act up** vi (inf: person) portarse mal; **acting** adj suplente ▷ n: **to do some acting** hacer algo de teatro

**action** ['ækʃən] n acción f, acto; (Mil) acción f; (Law) proceso, demanda; **out of ~** (person) fuera de combate; (thing) averiado, estropeado; **to take ~** tomar medidas; **action replay** n (TV) repetición f

**activate** ['æktɪveɪt] vt activar

**active** ['æktɪv] adj activo, enérgico; (volcano) en actividad; **actively** adv (participate) activamente; (discourage, dislike) enérgicamente

**activist** ['æktɪvɪst] n activista mf

**activity** [æk'tɪvɪtɪ] n actividad f; **activity holiday** n vacaciones con actividades organizadas

**actor** ['æktər] n actor m

**actress** ['æktrɪs] n actriz f

**actual** ['æktjuəl] adj verdadero, real

⬛ Be careful not to translate actual by the Spanish word actual.

**actually** ['æktjuəlɪ] adv realmente, en realidad

⬛ Be careful not to translate actually by the Spanish word actualmente.

**acupuncture** ['ækjupʌŋktʃər] n acupuntura

**acute** [ə'kju:t] adj agudo

**ad** [æd] n abbr = **advertisement**

**adamant** ['ædəmənt] adj firme, inflexible

**adapt** [ə'dæpt] vt adaptar ▷ vi: **to ~ (to)** adaptarse (a), ajustarse (a); **adapter, adaptor** n (Elec) adaptador m; (for several plugs) ladrón m

**add** [æd] vt añadir, agregar (esp LAM); **add up** vt (figures) sumar ▷ vi (fig): **it doesn't ~ up** no tiene sentido; **it doesn't ~ up to much** es poca cosa, no tiene gran or mucha importancia

**addict** ['ædɪkt] n adicto/a; (enthusiast) entusiasta mf; **addicted** [ə'dɪktɪd] adj: **to be addicted to** ser adicto a; ser aficionado a; **addiction** [ə'dɪkʃən] n (to drugs etc) adicción f; **addictive** [ə'dɪktɪv] adj que causa adicción

**addition** [ə'dɪʃən] n (adding up) adición f; (thing added) añadidura, añadido; **in ~** además, por añadidura; **in ~ to** además de; **additional** adj adicional

**additive** ['ædɪtɪv] n aditivo

**address** [ə'drɛs] n dirección f, señas fpl; (speech) discurso ▷ vt (letter) dirigir; (speak to)

dirigirse a, dirigir la palabra a; **to ~ o.s. to sth** (issue, problem) abordar; **address book** n agenda (de direcciones)

**adequate** ['ædɪkwɪt] adj (satisfactory) adecuado; (enough) suficiente

**adhere** [əd'hɪər] vi: **to ~ to** adherirse a; (fig: abide by) observar

**adhesive** [əd'hi:zɪv] n adhesivo; **adhesive tape** n (BRIT) cinta adhesiva; (US Med) esparadrapo

**adjacent** [ə'dʒeɪsənt] adj: **~ to** contiguo a, inmediato a

**adjective** ['ædʒɛktɪv] n adjetivo

**adjoining** [ə'dʒɔɪnɪŋ] adj contiguo, vecino

**adjourn** [ə'dʒɜ:n] vt aplazar ▷ vi suspenderse

**adjust** [ə'dʒʌst] vt (change) modificar; (arrange) arreglar; (machine) ajustar ▷ vi: **to ~ (to)** adaptarse (a); **adjustable** adj ajustable; **adjustment** n adaptación f; (of prices, wages) ajuste m

**administer** [əd'mɪnɪstər] vt administrar

**administration** [ædmɪnɪ'streɪʃən] n administración f; (government) gobierno

**administrative** [əd'mɪnɪstrətɪv] adj administrativo

**administrator** [əd'mɪnɪstreɪtər] n administrador(a) m/f

**admiral** ['ædmərəl] n almirante m

**admiration** [ædmə'reɪʃən] n admiración f

**admire** [əd'maɪər] vt admirar; **admirer** n admirador(a) m/f

**admission** [əd'mɪʃən] n (to exhibition, nightclub) entrada; (enrolment) ingreso; (confession) confesión f

**admit** [əd'mɪt] vt dejar entrar, dar entrada a; (permit) admitir; (acknowledge) reconocer; **to be ~ted to hospital** ingresar en el hospital; **admit to** vt fus confesarse culpable de; **admittance** n entrada; **admittedly** adv es cierto que

**adolescent** [ædəu'lɛsnt] adj, n adolescente mf

**adopt** [ə'dɔpt] vt adoptar; **adopted** adj adoptivo; **adoption** n adopción f

**adore** [ə'dɔ:r] vt adorar

**adorn** [ə'dɔ:n] vt adornar

**Adriatic** [eɪdrɪ'ætɪk] n: **the ~ (Sea)** el (Mar) Adriático

**adrift** [ə'drɪft] adv a la deriva

**ADSL** n abbr (= asymmetrical digital subscriber line) ADSL m

**adult** ['ædʌlt] n adulto/a ▷ adj: **~ education** educación f para adultos

**adultery** [ə'dʌltərɪ] n adulterio

**advance** [əd'vɑ:ns] n adelanto, progreso; (money) anticipo; (Mil) avance m ▷ vt avanzar, adelantar; (money) anticipar ▷ vi avanzar, adelantarse; **in ~** por adelantado;

to make ~s to sb hacer una proposición
a algn; (amorously) insinuarse a algn;
**advanced** adj avanzado; (Scol: studies)
adelantado
**advantage** [əd'vɑːntɪdʒ] n (also Tennis)
ventaja; to take ~ of aprovecharse de
**advent** ['ædvənt] n advenimiento; A~
Adviento
**adventure** [əd'vɛntʃəʳ] n aventura;
**adventurous** adj aventurero
**adverb** ['ædvəːb] n adverbio
**adversary** ['ædvəsərɪ] n adversario,
contrario
**adverse** ['ædvəːs] adj adverso, contrario
**advert** ['ædvəːt] n abbr (BRIT)
= advertisement
**advertise** ['ædvətaɪz] vi (in newspaper
etc) poner un anuncio, anunciarse; to ~
for buscar por medio de anuncios ▷ vt
anunciar; **advertisement** [əd'vəːtɪsmənt]
n anuncio; **advertiser** n anunciante
mf; **advertising** n publicidad f; anuncios
mpl; (industry) industria publicitaria
**advice** [əd'vaɪs] n consejo, consejos mpl;
(notification) aviso; **a piece of ~** un consejo;
to take legal ~ consultar a un abogado
**advisable** [əd'vaɪzəbl] adj aconsejable,
conveniente
**advise** [əd'vaɪz] vt aconsejar; to ~ sb of sth
informar a algn de algo; to ~ sb against
sth/doing sth desaconsejar algo a algn/
aconsejar a algn que no haga algo; **adviser**
n consejero/a; (business adviser) asesor(a)
m/f; **advisory** adj consultivo
**advocate** ['ædvəkeɪt] vt abogar por ▷ n
['ædvəkɪt] abogado/a; (supporter): ~ of
defensor(a) m/f de
**Aegean** [iː'dʒiːən] n: the ~ (Sea) el (Mar)
Egeo
**aerial** ['ɛərɪəl] n antena ▷ adj aéreo
**aerobics** [ɛə'rəubɪks] nsg aerobic m
**aeroplane** ['ɛərəpleɪn] n (BRIT) avión m
**aerosol** ['ɛərəsɔl] n aerosol m
**affair** [ə'fɛəʳ] n asunto; (also: love ~)
aventura f amorosa
**affect** [ə'fɛkt] vt afectar, influir en; (move)
conmover; **affected** adj afectado
**affection** n afecto, cariño; **affectionate** adj
afectuoso, cariñoso
**afflict** [ə'flɪkt] vt afligir
**affluent** ['æfluənt] adj acomodado; the ~
society la sociedad opulenta
**afford** [ə'fɔːd] vt (provide) proporcionar;
can we ~ a car? ¿podemos permitirnos el
gasto de comprar un coche?; **affordable**
adj asequible
**Afghanistan** [æf'gænɪstæn] n Afganistán m
**afraid** [ə'freɪd] adj: to be ~ of (person) tener
miedo a; (thing) tener miedo de; to be ~

to tener miedo de, temer; I am ~ that me
temo que; I'm ~ so me temo que sí; I'm ~
not lo siento, pero no
**Africa** ['æfrɪkə] n África; **African** adj, n
africano/a; **African-American** adj, n
afroamericano/a
**after** ['ɑːftəʳ] prep (time) después de; (place,
order) detrás de, tras ▷ adv después ▷ conj
después (de) que; what/who are you ~?
¿qué/a quién buscas?; ~ having done/
he left después de haber hecho/después
de que se marchó; to ask ~ sb preguntar
por algn; ~ all después de todo, al fin y al
cabo; ~ you! ¡pase usted!; **after-effects**
npl secuelas fpl, efectos mpl; **aftermath**
n consecuencias fpl, resultados mpl;
**afternoon** n tarde f; **after-shave (lotion)**
n aftershave m; **aftersun (lotion)** n
aftersun m inv; **afterwards** adv después,
más tarde
**again** [ə'gɛn] adv otra vez, de nuevo; to
do sth ~ volver a hacer algo; ~ and ~ una y
otra vez
**against** [ə'gɛnst] prep (opposed) en contra
de; (close to) contra, junto a
**age** [eɪdʒ] n edad f; (period) época ▷ vi
envejecer(se) ▷ vt envejecer; he is 20 years
of ~ tiene 20 años; under ~ menor de edad;
to come of ~ llegar a la mayoría de edad;
it's been ~s since I saw you hace siglos que
no te veo; **age group** n: to be in the same
age group tener la misma edad; **age limit**
n límite m de edad, edad f tope
**agency** ['eɪdʒənsɪ] n agencia
**agenda** [ə'dʒɛndə] n orden m del día
> Be careful not to translate agenda by the
Spanish word agenda.
**agent** ['eɪdʒənt] n agente mf;
(representative) representante mf
delegado/a
**aggravate** ['ægrəveɪt] vt agravar; (annoy)
irritar
**aggression** [ə'grɛʃən] n agresión f
**aggressive** [ə'grɛsɪv] adj agresivo;
(vigorous) enérgico
**agile** ['ædʒaɪl] adj ágil
**agitated** ['ædʒɪteɪtɪd] adj agitado
**AGM** n abbr (= annual general meeting) junta
f general
**ago** [ə'gəu] adv: two days ~ hace dos días;
not long ~ hace poco; how long ~? ¿hace
cuánto tiempo?
**agony** ['ægənɪ] n (pain) dolor m atroz;
(distress) angustia; to be in ~ retorcerse
de dolor
**agree** [ə'griː] vt (price) acordar, quedar en
▷ vi (statements etc) coincidir, concordar;
to ~ (with) (person) estar de acuerdo (con),
ponerse de acuerdo (con); to ~ to do

aceptar hacer; **to ~ to** sth consentir en algo; **to ~ that** (admit) estar de acuerdo en que; **garlic doesn't ~ with me** el ajo no me sienta bien; **agreeable** adj agradable; (person) simpático; (willing) de acuerdo, conforme; **agreed** adj (time, place) convenido; **agreement** n acuerdo; (Comm) contrato; **in agreement** de acuerdo, conforme

**agricultural** [ægrɪ'kʌltʃərəl] adj agrícola
**agriculture** ['ægrɪkʌltʃəʳ] n agricultura
**ahead** [ə'hɛd] adv delante; **~ of** delante de; (fig: schedule etc) antes de; **~ of time** antes de la hora; **go right** or **straight ~** siga adelante

**aid** [eɪd] n ayuda, auxilio ▷ vt ayudar, auxiliar; **in ~ of** a beneficio de
**aide** [eɪd] n ayudante mf
**AIDS** [eɪdz] n abbr (= acquired immune (or immuno-)deficiency syndrome) SIDA m
**ailing** ['eɪlɪŋ] adj enfermizo
**ailment** ['eɪlmənt] n enfermedad f, achaque m
**aim** [eɪm] vt (gun) apuntar; (missile, remark) dirigir; (blow) asestar ▷ vi (also: **take ~**) apuntar ▷ n puntería; (objective) propósito, meta; **to ~ at** (objective) aspirar a, pretender; **to ~ to do** tener la intención de hacer, aspirar a hacer
**ain't** [eɪnt] (inf) = **are not; aren't; isn't**
**air** [ɛəʳ] n aire m; (appearance) aspecto ▷ vt (room) ventilar; (clothes, bed, grievances, ideas) airear ▷ cpd aéreo; **to throw sth into the ~** (ball etc) lanzar algo al aire; **by ~** (travel) en avión; **to be on the ~** (Radio, TV: programme) estarse emitiendo; (: station) estar en antena; **airbag** n airbag m inv; **air bed** n (BRIT) colchoneta inflable or neumática; **airborne** adj (in the air) en el aire; **as soon as the plane was airborne** tan pronto como el avión estuvo en el aire; **air-conditioned** adj climatizado; **air conditioning** n aire m acondicionado; **aircraft** n (pl inv) avión m; **airfield** n campo de aviación; **Air Force** n fuerzas aéreas fpl, aviación f; **air hostess** (BRIT) n azafata; **airing cupboard** n (BRIT) armario m para oreo; **airlift** n puente m aéreo; **airline** n línea aérea; **airliner** n avión m de pasajeros; **airmail** n: **by airmail** por avión; **airplane** n (US) avión m; **airport** n aeropuerto; **air raid** n ataque m aéreo; **airsick** adj: **to be airsick** marearse (en avión); **airspace** n espacio aéreo; **airstrip** n pista de aterrizaje; **air terminal** n terminal f; **airtight** adj hermético; **air traffic controller** n controlador(a) m/f aéreo/a; **airy** adj (room) bien ventilado; (manners) desenfadado

**aisle** [aɪl] n (of church) nave f lateral; (of theatre, plane) pasillo; **aisle seat** n (on plane) asiento de pasillo
**ajar** [ə'dʒɑːʳ] adj entreabierto
**à la carte** [ælæ'kɑːt] adv a la carta
**alarm** [ə'lɑːm] n alarma; (anxiety) inquietud f ▷ vt asustar, alarmar; **alarm call** n (in hotel etc) alarma; **alarm clock** n despertador m; **alarmed** adj (person) alarmado, asustado; (house, car etc) con alarma; **alarming** adj alarmante
**Albania** [æl'beɪnɪə] n Albania
**album** ['ælbəm] n álbum m; (L.P.) elepé m
**alcohol** ['ælkəhɔl] n alcohol m; **alcohol-free** adj sin alcohol; **alcoholic** adj, n alcohólico/a
**alcove** ['ælkəuv] n nicho, hueco
**ale** [eɪl] n cerveza
**alert** [ə'lɜːt] adj alerta inv; (sharp) despierto, atento ▷ n alerta m, alarma ▷ vt poner sobre aviso; **to be on the ~** estar alerta or sobre aviso
**A levels** npl (BRIT) ≈ exámenes mpl de bachillerato superior
**algebra** ['ældʒɪbrə] n álgebra
**Algeria** [æl'dʒɪərɪə] n Argelia
**alias** ['eɪlɪəs] adv alias, conocido por ▷ n alias m; (of criminal) apodo; (of writer) seudónimo
**alibi** ['ælɪbaɪ] n coartada
**alien** ['eɪlɪən] n (foreigner) extranjero/a; (extraterrestrial) extraterrestre mf ▷ adj: **~ to** ajeno a; **alienate** vt enajenar, alejar
**alight** [ə'laɪt] adj ardiendo ▷ vi apearse, bajar
**align** [ə'laɪn] vt alinear
**alike** [ə'laɪk] adj semejantes, iguales ▷ adv igualmente, del mismo modo; **to look ~** parecerse
**alive** [ə'laɪv] adj vivo; (lively) alegre

 **KEYWORD**

**all** [ɔːl] adj todo/a sg, todos/as pl; **all day** todo el día; **all night** toda la noche; **all men** todos los hombres; **all five came** vinieron los cinco; **all the books** todos los libros; **all the time/his life** todo el tiempo/toda su vida
▶ pron **1** todo; **I ate it all, I ate all of it** me lo comí todo; **all of us went** fuimos todos; **all the boys went** fueron todos los chicos; **is that all?** ¿eso es todo?, ¿algo más?; (in shop) ¿algo más?, ¿alguna cosa más?
**2** (in phrases): **above all** sobre todo; por encima de todo; **after all** después de todo; **at all: anything at all** lo que sea; **not at all** (in answer to question) en absoluto; (in answer to thanks) ¡de nada!, ¡no hay de qué!; **I'm not at all tired** no estoy nada cansado/a;

**anything at all will do** cualquier cosa viene bien; **all in all** a fin de cuentas
▶ adv: **all alone** completamente solo/a; **it's not as hard as all that** no es tan difícil como lo pintas; **all the more/the better** tanto más/mejor; **all but** casi; **the score is two** all están empatados a dos

**Allah** ['ælə] n Alá m
**allegation** [ælɪ'ɡeɪʃən] n alegato
**alleged** [ə'lɛdʒd] adj supuesto, presunto; **allegedly** [ə'lɛdʒɪdlɪ] adv supuestamente, según se afirma
**allegiance** [ə'li:dʒəns] n lealtad f
**allergic** [ə'lə:dʒɪk] adj: **~ to** alérgico a
**allergy** ['ælədʒɪ] n alergia
**alleviate** [ə'li:vɪeɪt] vt aliviar
**alley** ['ælɪ] n callejuela
**alliance** [ə'laɪəns] n alianza
**allied** ['ælaɪd] adj aliado
**alligator** ['ælɪɡeɪtər] n caimán m
**all-in** ['ɔ:lɪn] adj, adv (BRIT: charge) todo incluido
**allocate** ['æləkeɪt] vt (share out) repartir; (devote) asignar
**allot** [ə'lɔt] vt asignar
**all-out** ['ɔ:laut] adj (effort etc) supremo
**allow** [ə'lau] vt permitir, dejar; (a claim) admitir; (sum to spend, time estimated) dar, conceder; (concede): **to ~ that** reconocer que; **to ~ sb to do** permitir a algn hacer; **he is ~ed to ...** se le permite ...; **allow for** vt fus tener en cuenta; **allowance** n subvención f, pensión f; (tax allowance) desgravación f; **to make allowances for** (person) disculpar a; (thing) tener en cuenta
**all right** adv bien; (as answer) ¡de acuerdo!, ¡está bien!
**ally** n ['ælaɪ] aliado/a ▷ vt [ə'laɪ]: **to ~ o.s. with** aliarse con
**almighty** [ɔ:l'maɪtɪ] adj todopoderoso; (row etc) imponente
**almond** ['ɑ:mənd] n almendra
**almost** ['ɔ:lməust] adv casi; **he ~ fell** casi or por poco se cae
**alone** [ə'ləun] adj solo ▷ adv solo; **to leave sb ~** dejar a algn en paz; **to leave sth ~** no tocar algo; **let ~ ...** y mucho menos ...
**along** [ə'lɔŋ] prep a lo largo de, por ▷ adv: **is he coming ~ with us?** ¿viene con nosotros?; **he was limping ~** iba cojeando; **~ with** junto con; **all ~** (all the time) desde el principio; **alongside** prep al lado de ▷ adv (Naut) de costado
**aloof** [ə'lu:f] adj distante ▷ adv: **to stand ~** mantenerse a distancia
**aloud** [ə'laud] adv en voz alta
**alphabet** ['ælfəbɛt] n alfabeto
**Alps** [ælps] npl: **the ~** los Alpes

**already** [ɔ:l'rɛdɪ] adv ya
**alright** ['ɔ:l'raɪt] adv (BRIT) = **all right**
**also** ['ɔ:lsəu] adv también, además
**altar** ['ɔltə] n altar m
**alter** ['ɔltər] vt cambiar, modificar ▷ vi cambiar, modificarse; **alteration** n cambio, modificación f; **alterations** npl (Sewing) arreglos mpl
**alternate** [ɔl'tə:nɪt] adj alterno ▷ vi ['ɔltəneɪt]: **to ~ (with)** alternar (con); **on ~ days** en días alternos
**alternative** [ɔl'tə:nətɪv] adj alternativo ▷ n alternativa; **~ medicine** medicina alternativa; **alternatively** adv: **alternatively one could ...** por otra parte se podría ...
**although** [ɔ:l'ðəu] conj aunque
**altitude** ['æltɪtju:d] n altura
**altogether** [ɔ:ltə'ɡɛðər] adv completamente, del todo; (on the whole, in all) en total, en conjunto
**aluminium** [ælju'mɪnɪəm], (US) **aluminum** [ə'lu:mɪnəm] n aluminio
**always** ['ɔ:lweɪz] adv siempre
**Alzheimer's** ['æltshaɪməz] n (also: **~ disease**) (enfermedad f de) m Alzheimer
**am** [æm] vb see **be**
**a.m.** adv abbr (= ante meridiem) de la mañana
**amalgamate** [ə'mælɡəmeɪt] vi amalgamarse ▷ vt amalgamar
**amass** [ə'mæs] vt amontonar, acumular
**amateur** ['æmətər] n aficionado/a, amateur mf
**amaze** [ə'meɪz] vt asombrar, pasmar; **to be ~d (at)** asombrarse (de); **amazed** adj asombrado; **amazement** n asombro, sorpresa; **amazing** adj extraordinario; (bargain, offer) increíble
**Amazon** ['æməzən] n (Geo) Amazonas m
**ambassador** [æm'bæsədər] n embajador(a) m/f
**amber** ['æmbər] n ámbar m; **at ~** (BRIT Aut) en amarillo
**ambiguous** [æm'bɪɡjuəs] adj ambiguo
**ambition** [æm'bɪʃən] n ambición f; **ambitious** adj ambicioso
**ambulance** ['æmbjuləns] n ambulancia
**ambush** ['æmbuʃ] n emboscada ▷ vt tender una emboscada a
**amen** [ɑː'mɛn] excl amén
**amend** [ə'mɛnd] vt enmendar; **to make ~s** dar cumplida satisfacción; **amendment** n enmienda
**amenities** [ə'mi:nɪtɪz] npl comodidades fpl
**America** [ə'mɛrɪkə] n América (del Norte); (USA) Estados mpl Unidos; **American** adj, n (norte)americano/a, estadounidense mf; **American football** n (BRIT) fútbol m americano

**amicable** ['æmɪkəbl] adj amistoso, amigable

**amid(st)** [ə'mɪd(st)] prep entre, en medio de

**ammunition** [æmju'nɪʃən] n municiones fpl

**amnesty** ['æmnɪstɪ] n amnistía

**among(st)** [ə'mʌŋ(st)] prep entre, en medio de

**amount** [ə'maunt] n cantidad f; (of bill etc) suma, importe m ▷ vi: **to ~ to** sumar; (be same as) equivaler a, significar

**amp(ère)** ['æmp(ɛəʳ)] n amperio

**ample** ['æmpl] adj (spacious) amplio; (abundant) abundante; **to have ~ time** tener tiempo de sobra

**amplifier** ['æmplɪfaɪəʳ] n amplificador m

**amputate** ['æmpjuteɪt] vt amputar

**Amtrak** ['æmtræk] n (US) empresa nacional de ferrocarriles de los EE.UU.

**amuse** [ə'mjuːz] vt divertir; (distract) distraer, entretener; **amusement** n diversión f; (pastime) pasatiempo; (laughter) risa; **amusement arcade** n salón m de juegos; **amusement park** n parque m de atracciones

**amusing** [ə'mjuːzɪŋ] adj divertido

**an** [æn, ən, n] indef art see **a**

**anaemia** [ə'niːmɪə] n anemia

**anaemic** [ə'niːmɪk] adj anémico; (fig) flojo

**anaesthetic** [ænɪs'θɛtɪk] n anestesia

**analog(ue)** ['ænələg] adj analógico

**analogy** [ə'nælədʒɪ] n analogía

**analyse** ['ænəlaɪz] vt (BRIT) analizar; **analysis** (pl **analyses**) [ə'næləsɪs] n análisis m inv; **analyst** ['ænəlɪst] n (political analyst, psychoanalyst) analista mf

**analyze** ['ænəlaɪz] vt (US) = **analyse**

**anarchy** ['ænəkɪ] n anarquía, desorden m

**anatomy** [ə'nætəmɪ] n anatomía

**ancestor** ['ænsɪstəʳ] n antepasado

**anchor** ['æŋkəʳ] n ancla, áncora ▷ vi (also: **to drop ~**) anclar; **to weigh ~** levar anclas

**anchovy** ['æntʃəvɪ] n anchoa

**ancient** ['eɪnʃənt] adj antiguo

**and** [ænd] conj y; (before i, hi) e; **~ so on** etcétera; **try ~ come** procura venir; **better ~ better** cada vez mejor

**Andes** ['ændiːz] npl: **the ~** los Andes

**Andorra** [æn'dɔːrə] n Andorra

**anemia** [ə'niːmɪə] n (US) = **anaemia**

**anemic** [ə'niːmɪk] adj (US) = **anaemic**

**anesthetic** [ænɪs'θɛtɪk] n (US) = **anaesthetic**

**angel** ['eɪndʒəl] n ángel m

**anger** ['æŋgəʳ] n cólera

**angina** [æn'dʒaɪnə] n angina (del pecho)

**angle** ['æŋgl] n ángulo; **from their ~** desde su punto de vista

**angler** ['æŋgləʳ] n pescador(a) m/f (de caña)

**Anglican** ['æŋglɪkən] adj, n anglicano/a

**angling** ['æŋglɪŋ] n pesca con caña

**angrily** ['æŋgrɪlɪ] adv enojado, enfadado

**angry** ['æŋgrɪ] adj enfadado, enojado (esp LAM); **to be ~ with sb/at sth** estar enfadado con algn/por algo; **to get ~** enfadarse, enojarse (esp LAM)

**anguish** ['æŋgwɪʃ] n (physical) tormentos mpl; (mental) angustia

**animal** ['ænɪməl] n animal m; (pej: person) bestia

**animated** ['ænɪmeɪtɪd] adj animado

**animation** [ænɪ'meɪʃən] n animación f

**aniseed** ['ænɪsiːd] n anís m

**ankle** ['æŋkl] n tobillo m

**annex** n ['ænɛks] (BRIT: also: **annexe**: building) edificio anexo ▷ vt [æ'nɛks] (territory) anexionar

**anniversary** [ænɪ'vəːsərɪ] n aniversario

**announce** [ə'nauns] vt anunciar; **announcement** n anuncio; (declaration) declaración f; **announcer** n (Radio) locutor(a) m/f; (TV) presentador(a) m/f

**annoy** [ə'nɔɪ] vt molestar, fastidiar; **don't get ~ed!** ¡no se enfade!; **annoying** adj molesto, fastidioso; (person) pesado

**annual** ['ænjuəl] adj anual ▷ n (Bot) anual m; (book) anuario; **annually** adv anualmente, cada año

**annum** ['ænəm] n see **per annum**

**anonymous** [ə'nɔnɪməs] adj anónimo

**anorak** ['ænəræk] n anorak m

**anorexia** [ænə'rɛksɪə] n (Med) anorexia

**anorexic** [ænə'rɛksɪk] n, a anoréxico/a

**another** [ə'nʌðəʳ] adj: **~ book** otro libro ▷ pron otro; see also **one**

**answer** ['ɑːnsəʳ] n respuesta, contestación f; (to problem) solución f ▷ vi contestar, responder ▷ vt (reply to) contestar a, responder a; (problem) resolver; **in ~ to your letter** contestando en o en contestación a su carta; **to ~ the phone** contestar el teléfono; **to ~ the bell** or **the door** abrir la puerta; **answer back** vi replicar, ser respondón/ona; **answer for** vt fus responder de or por; **answer to** vt fus (description) corresponder a; **answerphone** n (esp BRIT) contestador m (automático)

**ant** [ænt] n hormiga

**Antarctic** [ænt'ɑːktɪk] n: **the ~** el Antártico

**antelope** ['æntɪləup] n antílope m

**antenatal** [æntɪ'neɪtl] adj prenatal

**antenna** (pl **antennae**) [æn'tɛnə, -niː] n antena

**anthem** ['ænθəm] n: **national ~** himno nacional

**anthology** [æn'θɔlədʒɪ] n antología

**anthrax** ['ænθræks] n ántrax m

**anthropology** [ænθrə'pɔlədʒɪ] n antropología

**anti...** [ænti] pref anti...; **antibiotic**
[æntibaɪˈɒtɪk] adj, n antibiótico; **antibody**
[ˈæntɪbɒdɪ] n anticuerpo
**anticipate** [ænˈtɪsɪpeɪt] vt prever;
(expect) esperar, contar con; (forestall)
anticiparse a, adelantarse a; **anticipation**
[æntɪsɪˈpeɪʃən] n previsión f; esperanza;
anticipación f
**anticlimax** [æntɪˈklaɪmæks] n decepción f
**anticlockwise** [æntɪˈklɒkwaɪz] adv en
dirección contraria a la de las agujas del
reloj
**antics** [ˈæntɪks] npl gracias fpl
**anti: antidote** [ˈæntɪdəʊt] n antídoto;
**antifreeze** [ˈæntɪfriːz] n anticongelante
m; **antihistamine** [æntɪˈhɪstəmiːn]
n antihistamínico; **antiperspirant**
[ˈæntɪpəˈspɪrənt] n antitranspirante m
**antique** [ænˈtiːk] n antigüedad f ▷ adj
antiguo; **antique shop** n tienda de
antigüedades
**antiseptic** [æntɪˈsɛptɪk] adj, n antiséptico
**antisocial** [æntɪˈsəʊʃəl] adj antisocial
**antivirus** [æntɪˈvaɪərəs] adj antivirus;
**~ software** antivirus m
**antlers** [ˈæntləz] npl cornamenta
**anxiety** [æŋˈzaɪətɪ] n (worry) inquietud f;
(eagerness) ansia, anhelo
**anxious** [ˈæŋkʃəs] adj (worried) inquieto,
(keen) deseoso; **to be ~ to do** tener muchas
ganas de hacer

**KEYWORD**

**any** [ˈɛnɪ] adj 1 (in questions etc) algún/
alguna; **have you any butter/children?**
¿tienes mantequilla/hijos?; **if there are
any tickets left** si quedan billetes, si queda
algún billete
2 (with negative): **I haven't any money/
books** no tengo dinero/libros
3 (no matter which) cualquier; **any excuse
will do** valdrá or servirá cualquier excusa;
**choose any book you like** escoge el libro
que quieras
4 (in phrases): **in any case** de todas formas,
en cualquier caso; **any day now** cualquier
día (de estos); **at any moment** en cualquier
momento, de un momento a otro; **at any
rate** en todo caso; **any time: come (at)
any time** ven cuando quieras; **he might
come (at) any time** podría llegar de un
momento a otro
▶ pron 1 (in questions etc): **have you got
any?** ¿tienes alguno/a?; **can any of you
sing?** ¿sabe cantar alguno de vosotros/
ustedes?
2 (with negative): **I haven't any (of them)** no
tengo ninguno

3 (no matter which one(s)): **take any of those
books (you like)** toma el libro que quieras
de ésos
▶ adv 1 (in questions etc): **do you want any
more soup/sandwiches?** ¿quieres más
sopa/bocadillos?; **are you feeling any
better?** ¿te sientes algo mejor?
2 (with negative): **I can't hear him any more**
ya no le oigo; **don't wait any longer** no
esperes más

**anybody** [ˈɛnɪbɒdɪ] pron cualquiera; (in
interrogative sentences) alguien; (in negative
sentences): **I don't see ~** no veo a nadie
**anyhow** [ˈɛnɪhaʊ] adv de todos modos,
de todas maneras; (carelessly) de cualquier
manera; (haphazardly) de cualquier modo;
**I shall go ~** iré de todas maneras
**anyone** [ˈɛnɪwʌn] pron = **anybody**
**anything** [ˈɛnɪθɪŋ] pron cualquier cosa;
(in interrogative sentences) algo; (in negative
sentences) nada; (everything) todo; **~ else?**
¿algo más?; **can you see ~?** ¿ves algo?;
**he'll eat ~** come de todo or lo que sea
**anytime** [ˈɛnɪtaɪm] adv (at any moment)
en cualquier momento, de un momento
a otro; (whenever) no importa cuándo,
cuando quiera
**anyway** [ˈɛnɪweɪ] adv (at any rate) de todos
modos, de todas formas; (besides) además;
**~, I couldn't come even if I wanted to**
además, no podría venir aunque quisiera;
**I shall go ~** iré de todos modos; **why are
you phoning, ~?** ¿entonces, por qué
llamas?, ¿por qué llamas, pues?
**anywhere** [ˈɛnɪwɛə] adv dondequiera;
(interrogative) en algún sitio; (negative
sense) en ningún sitio; (everywhere) en o por
todas partes; **I don't see him ~** no le veo en
ningún sitio; **are you going ~?** ¿vas a algún
sitio?; **~ in the world** en cualquier parte
del mundo
**apart** [əˈpɑːt] adv aparte, separadamente;
**10 miles ~** separados por 10 millas; **to take ~**
desmontar; **~ from** prep aparte de
**apartment** [əˈpɑːtmənt] n (US) piso,
departamento (LAM), apartamento;
(room) cuarto; **apartment block,** (US)
**apartment building** n bloque m de
apartamentos
**apathy** [ˈæpəθɪ] n apatía, indiferencia
**ape** [eɪp] n mono ▷ vt imitar, remedar
**aperitif** [əˈpɛrɪtiːf] n aperitivo
**aperture** [ˈæpətʃjuə] n rendija, resquicio;
(Phot) abertura
**APEX** [ˈeɪpɛks] n abbr (Aviat: = advance
purchase excursion) tarifa f APEX
**apologize** [əˈpɒlədʒaɪz] vi: **to ~ (for sth to
sb)** disculparse (con algn por algo)

**apology** [ə'pɒlədʒɪ] n disculpa, excusa
▌ Be careful not to translate *apology* by the Spanish word *apología*.

**apostrophe** [ə'pɒstrəfɪ] n apóstrofo m

**app** n abbr (inf: Comput: = application) aplicación f

**appal** [ə'pɔ:l] vt horrorizar, espantar; **appalling** adj espantoso; (awful) pésimo

**apparatus** [æpə'reɪtəs] n (equipment) equipo; (organization) aparato; (in gymnasium) aparatos mpl

**apparent** [ə'pærənt] adj aparente; (obvious) evidente; **apparently** adv por lo visto, al parecer

**appeal** [ə'pi:l] vi (Law) apelar ▷ n (Law) apelación f; (request) llamamiento; (plea) petición f; (charm) atractivo; **to ~ for** solicitar; **to ~ to** (thing) atraer; **it doesn't ~ to me** no me atrae, no me llama la atención; **appealing** adj (nice) atractivo

**appear** [ə'pɪə'] vi aparecer, presentarse; (Law) comparecer; (publication) salir (a luz), publicarse; (seem) parecer; **to ~ on TV/in "Hamlet"** salir por la tele/hacer un papel en "Hamlet"; **it would ~ that** parecería que; **appearance** n aparición f; (look, aspect) apariencia, aspecto; **to keep up appearances** salvar las apariencias; **to all appearances** al parecer

**appendices** [ə'pendɪsi:z] npl of **appendix**

**appendicitis** [əpendɪ'saɪtɪs] n apendicitis f

**appendix** (pl **appendices**) [ə'pendɪks, -dɪsi:z] n apéndice m

**appetite** ['æpɪtaɪt] n apetito; (fig) deseo, anhelo

**appetizer** ['æpɪtaɪzə'] n (drink) aperitivo; (food) tapas fpl (SP)

**applaud** [ə'plɔ:d] vt, vi aplaudir

**applause** [ə'plɔ:z] n aplausos mpl

**apple** ['æpl] n manzana; **apple pie** n pastel m de manzana, pay m de manzana (LAM)

**appliance** [ə'plaɪəns] n aparato

**applicable** [ə'plɪkəbl] adj aplicable; **to be ~ to** referirse a

**applicant** ['æplɪkənt] n candidato/a; solicitante mf

**application** [æplɪ'keɪʃən] n (also Comput) aplicación f; (for a job, a grant etc) solicitud f; **application form** n solicitud f

**apply** [ə'plaɪ] vt: **to ~ (to)** aplicar (a); (fig) emplear (para) ▷ vi: **to ~ to** (ask) dirigirse a; (be suitable for) ser aplicable a; **to ~ for** (permit, grant, job) solicitar; **to ~ o.s. to** aplicarse a, dedicarse a

**appoint** [ə'pɔɪnt] vt (to post) nombrar
▌ Be careful not to translate *appoint* by the Spanish word *apuntar*.

**appointment** n (engagement) cita; (act) nombramiento; (post) puesto; **to make an ~ (with)** (doctor) pedir hora (con); (friend) citarse (con)

**appraisal** [ə'preɪzl] n evaluación f

**appreciate** [ə'pri:ʃɪeɪt] vt apreciar, tener en mucho; (be grateful for) agradecer; (be aware of) comprender ▷ vi (Comm) aumentar en valor; **appreciation** n apreciación f; (gratitude) reconocimiento, agradecimiento; (Comm) aumento en valor

**apprehension** [æprɪ'hɛnʃən] n (fear) aprensión f

**apprehensive** [æprɪ'hɛnsɪv] adj aprensivo

**apprentice** [ə'prɛntɪs] n aprendiz(a) m/f

**approach** [ə'prəʊtʃ] vi acercarse ▷ vt acercarse a; (ask, apply to) dirigirse a; (problem) abordar ▷ n acercamiento; (access) acceso; (to problem etc) enfoque m

**appropriate** [ə'prəʊpriɪt] adj apropiado, conveniente ▷ vt [-rieɪt] (take) apropiarse de

**approval** [ə'pru:vəl] n aprobación f, visto bueno; **on ~** (Comm) a prueba

**approve** [ə'pru:v] vt aprobar; **approve of** vt fus aprobar; **they don't ~ of her** (ella) no les parece bien

**approximate** [ə'prɒksɪmɪt] adj aproximado; **approximately** adv aproximadamente, más o menos

**Apr.** abbr (= April) abr

**apricot** ['eɪprɪkɒt] n albaricoque m (SP), damasco (LAM)

**April** ['eɪprəl] n abril m; **April Fools' Day** n ≈ día m de los (Santos) Inocentes

**apron** ['eɪprən] n delantal m

**apt** [æpt] adj acertado, oportuno; **~ to do** (likely) propenso a hacer

**aquarium** [ə'kwɛərɪəm] n acuario

**Aquarius** [ə'kwɛərɪəs] n Acuario

**Arab** ['ærəb] adj, n árabe mf

**Arabia** [ə'reɪbɪə] n Arabia; **Arabian** adj árabe; **Arabic** ['ærəbɪk] adj árabe, arábigo ▷ n árabe m; **Arabic numerals** numeración f arábiga

**arbitrary** ['ɑ:bɪtrərɪ] adj arbitrario

**arbitration** [ɑ:bɪ'treɪʃən] n arbitraje m

**arc** [ɑ:k] n arco

**arcade** [ɑ:'keɪd] n (round a square) soportales mpl; (shopping arcade) galería comercial

**arch** [ɑ:tʃ] n arco; (of foot) puente m ▷ vt arquear

**archaeology** [ɑ:kɪ'ɒlədʒɪ] n arqueología

**archbishop** [ɑ:tʃ'bɪʃəp] n arzobispo

**archeology** [ɑ:kɪ'ɒlədʒɪ] (US) = **archaeology**

**architect** ['ɑ:kɪtɛkt] n arquitecto/a; **architectural** adj arquitectónico; **architecture** n arquitectura

**archive** ['ɑ:kaɪv] n (often pl: also Comput) archivo

**Arctic** ['ɑːktɪk] *adj* ártico ▷ *n*: **the ~** el Ártico
**are** [ɑː<sup>r</sup>] *vb see* **be**
**area** ['ɛərɪə] *n* área; (*Math etc*) superficie *f*; (*zone*) región *f*, zona; (*of knowledge, experience*) campo; **area code** *n* (*us Tel*) prefijo
**arena** [ə'riːnə] *n* arena; (*of circus*) pista
**aren't** [ɑːnt] = **are not**
**Argentina** [ɑːdʒən'tiːnə] *n* Argentina; **Argentinian** [ɑːdʒən'tɪnɪən] *adj*, *n* argentino/a
**arguably** ['ɑːgjuəblɪ] *adv*: **it is ~** ... es discutiblemente ...
**argue** ['ɑːgjuː] *vi* (*quarrel*) discutir; (*reason*) razonar, argumentar; **to ~ that** sostener que
**argument** ['ɑːgjumənt] *n* (*reasons*) argumento; (*quarrel*) discusión *f*
**Aries** ['ɛərɪz] *n* Aries *m*
**arise** [ə'raɪz] (*pt* **arose**, *pp* **arisen** [ə'rɪzn]) *vi* surgir, presentarse
**arithmetic** [ə'rɪθmətɪk] *n* aritmética
**arm** [ɑːm] *n* brazo ▷ *vt* armar; **~ in ~** cogidos del brazo; **armchair** *n* sillón *m*, butaca
**armed** [ɑːmd] *adj* armado; **armed robbery** *n* robo a mano armada
**armour**, (*us*) **armor** ['ɑːmə<sup>r</sup>] *n* armadura
**armpit** ['ɑːmpɪt] *n* sobaco, axila
**armrest** ['ɑːmrɛst] *n* reposabrazos *m inv*
**army** ['ɑːmɪ] *n* ejército; (*fig*) multitud *f*
**A road** *n* (*BRIT*) ≈ carretera *f* nacional
**aroma** [ə'rəumə] *n* aroma *m*, fragancia; **aromatherapy** *n* aromaterapia
**arose** [ə'rəuz] *pt of* **arise**
**around** [ə'raund] *adv* alrededor; (*in the area*) a la redonda ▷ *prep* alrededor de
**arouse** [ə'rauz] *vt* despertar; (*anger*) provocar
**arrange** [ə'reɪndʒ] *vt* arreglar, ordenar; (*programme*) organizar; **to ~ to do sth** quedar en hacer algo; **arrangement** *n* arreglo; (*agreement*) acuerdo; **arrangements** *npl* (*preparations*) preparativos *mpl*
**array** [ə'reɪ] *n*: **~ of** (*things*) serie *f* or colección *f* de; (*people*) conjunto de
**arrears** [ə'rɪəz] *npl* atrasos *mpl*; **to be in ~ with one's rent** estar retrasado en el pago del alquiler
**arrest** [ə'rɛst] *vt* detener; (*sb's attention*) llamar ▷ *n* detención *f*; **under ~** detenido
**arrival** [ə'raɪvəl] *n* llegada; **new ~** recién llegado/a
**arrive** [ə'raɪv] *vi* llegar; **arrive at** *vt fus* (*decision, solution*) llegar a
**arrogance** ['ærəgəns] *n* arrogancia, prepotencia (*LAM*)
**arrogant** ['ærəgənt] *adj* arrogante
**arrow** ['ærəu] *n* flecha

**arse** [ɑːs] *n* (*BRIT inf!*) culo, trasero
**arson** ['ɑːsn] *n* incendio provocado
**art** [ɑːt] *n* arte *m*; (*skill*) destreza; **art college** *n* escuela *f* de Bellas Artes
**artery** ['ɑːtərɪ] *n* arteria
**art gallery** *n* pinacoteca; (*Comm*) galería de arte
**arthritis** [ɑː'θraɪtɪs] *n* artritis *f*
**artichoke** ['ɑːtɪtʃəuk] *n* alcachofa; **Jerusalem ~** aguaturma
**article** ['ɑːtɪkl] *n* artículo
**articulate** *adj* [ɑː'tɪkjulɪt] (*speech*) claro ▷ *vt* [ɑː'tɪkjuleɪt] expresar
**artificial** [ɑːtɪ'fɪʃəl] *adj* artificial
**artist** ['ɑːtɪst] *n* artista *mf*; (*Mus*) intérprete *mf*; **artistic** *adj* artístico
**art school** *n* escuela de bellas artes

**KEYWORD**

**as** [æz] *conj* **1** (*referring to time: while*) mientras; **as the years go by** con el paso de los años; **he came in as I was leaving** entró cuando me marchaba; **as from tomorrow** a partir de or desde mañana
**2** (*in comparisons*): **as big as** tan grande como; **twice as big as** el doble de grande que; **as much money/many books as** tanto dinero/tantos libros como; **as soon as** en cuanto
**3** (*since, because*) como, ya que; **as I don't speak German I can't understand him** no le entiendo ya que no hablo alemán
**4** (*referring to manner, way*): **do as you wish** haz lo que quieras; **as she said** como dijo
**5** (*concerning*): **as for** or **to that** por or en lo que respecta a eso
**6**: **as if** or **though** como si; **he looked as if he was ill** parecía como si estuviera enfermo, tenía aspecto de enfermo; *see also* **long**; **such**; **well**
▷ *prep* (*in the capacity of*): **he works as a barman** trabaja de barman; **as chairman of the company, he ...** como presidente de la compañía, ...; **he gave it to me as a present** me lo dio de regalo

**a.s.a.p.** *abbr* (= *as soon as possible*) cuanto antes
**asbestos** [æz'bɛstəs] *n* asbesto, amianto
**ascent** [ə'sɛnt] *n* subida; (*slope*) cuesta, pendiente *f*
**ash** [æʃ] *n* ceniza; (*tree*) fresno
**ashamed** [ə'ʃeɪmd] *adj* avergonzado; **to be ~ of** avergonzarse de
**ashore** [ə'ʃɔː<sup>r</sup>] *adv* en tierra; (*swim etc*) a tierra
**ashtray** ['æʃtreɪ] *n* cenicero
**Ash Wednesday** *n* miércoles *m* de Ceniza

**Asia** ['eɪʃə] n Asia; **Asian** adj, n asiático/a
**aside** [ə'saɪd] adv a un lado ▷ n aparte m
**ask** [ɑːsk] vt (question) preguntar; (invite)
invitar; **to ~ sb sth/to do sth** preguntar
algo a algn/pedir a algn que haga algo;
**to ~ sb about sth** preguntar algo a algn;
**to ~ (sb) a question** hacer una pregunta (a
algn); **to ~ sb out to dinner** invitar a cenar
a algn; **ask for** vt fus pedir; **it's just ~ing for
trouble** or **for it** es buscarse problemas
**asleep** [ə'sliːp] adj dormido; **to fall ~**
dormirse, quedarse dormido
**asparagus** [əs'pærəgəs] n espárragos mpl
**aspect** ['æspɛkt] n aspecto, apariencia;
(direction in which a building etc faces)
orientación f
**aspirations** [æspə'reɪʃənz] npl
aspiraciones fpl; (ambition) ambición f
**aspire** [əs'paɪər] vi: **to ~ to** aspirar a,
ambicionar
**aspirin** ['æsprɪn] n aspirina
**ass** [æs] n asno, burro; (inf) imbécil mf; (us
inf!) culo, trasero
**assassin** [ə'sæsɪn] n asesino/a;
**assassinate** vt asesinar
**assault** [ə'sɔːlt] n asalto; (Law) agresión f
▷ vt asaltar; (sexually) violar
**assemble** [ə'sɛmbl] vt reunir, juntar; (Tech)
montar ▷ vi reunirse, juntarse
**assembly** [ə'sɛmblɪ] n reunión f, asamblea;
(parliament) parlamento; (construction)
montaje m
**assert** [ə'səːt] vt afirmar; (insist on) hacer
valer; **assertion** n afirmación f
**assess** [ə'sɛs] vt valorar, calcular; (tax,
damages) fijar; (for tax) gravar; **assessment**
n valoración f; gravamen m
**asset** ['æsɛt] n ventaja; **assets** npl (funds)
activo sg, fondos mpl
**assign** [ə'saɪn] vt (date) fijar; (task) asignar;
(resources) destinar; **assignment** n tarea
**assist** [ə'sɪst] vt ayudar; **assistance** n
ayuda, auxilio; **assistant** n ayudante mf;
(BRIT: also: **shop assistant**) dependiente/a
m/f
**associate** [ adj, n ə'səʊʃɪɪt, vt, vi ə'səʊʃɪeɪt]
adj asociado ▷ n colega mf ▷ vt asociar;
(ideas) relacionar ▷ vi: **to ~ with sb** tratar
con algn
**association** [əsəʊsɪ'eɪʃən] n asociación f
**assorted** [ə'sɔːtɪd] adj surtido, variado
**assortment** [ə'sɔːtmənt] n (of shapes,
colours) surtido; (of books) colección f; (of
people) mezcla
**assume** [ə'sjuːm] vt suponer;
(responsibilities etc) asumir; (attitude, name)
adoptar, tomar
**assumption** [ə'sʌmpʃən] n suposición f,
presunción f; (act) asunción f

**assurance** [ə'ʃuərəns] n garantía,
promesa; (confidence) confianza, aplomo;
(insurance) seguro
**assure** [ə'ʃuər] vt asegurar
**asterisk** ['æstərɪsk] n asterisco
**asthma** ['æsmə] n asma
**astonish** [ə'stɒnɪʃ] vt asombrar, pasmar;
**astonished** adj estupefacto, pasmado;
**to be astonished (at)** asombrarse (de);
**astonishing** adj asombroso, pasmoso;
**I find it astonishing that ...** me asombra or
pasma que ...; **astonishment** n asombro,
sorpresa
**astound** [ə'staʊnd] vt asombrar, pasmar
**astray** [ə'streɪ] adv: **to go ~** extraviarse; **to
lead ~** llevar por mal camino
**astrology** [əs'trɒlədʒɪ] n astrología
**astronaut** ['æstrənɔːt] n astronauta mf
**astronomer** [əs'trɒnəmər] n astrónomo/a
**astronomical** [æstrə'nɒmɪkəl] adj
astronómico
**astronomy** [æs'trɒnəmɪ] n astronomía
**astute** [əs'tjuːt] adj astuto
**asylum** [ə'saɪləm] n (refuge) asilo; (hospital)
manicomio

○ **KEYWORD**

**at** [æt] prep **1** (referring to position) en;
(direction) a; **at the top** en lo alto; **at
home/school** en casa/la escuela; **to look
at sth/sb** mirar algo/a algn
**2** (referring to time): **at four o'clock** a
las cuatro; **at night** por la noche; **at
Christmas** en Navidad; **at times** a veces
**3** (referring to rates, speed etc): **at £1 a kilo** a
una libra el kilo; **two at a time** de dos en
dos; **at 50 km/h** a 50 km/h
**4** (referring to manner): **at a stroke** de un
golpe; **at peace** en paz
**5** (referring to activity): **to be at work** estar
trabajando; (in office) estar en el trabajo;
**to play at cowboys** jugar a los vaqueros;
**to be good at sth** ser bueno en algo
**6** (referring to cause): **shocked/surprised/
annoyed at sth** asombrado/sorprendido/
fastidiado por algo; **I went at his
suggestion** fui a instancias suyas
▶ n (symbol @) arroba

**ate** [ɛt, eɪt] pt of **eat**
**atheist** ['eɪθɪɪst] n ateo/a
**Athens** ['æθɪnz] n Atenas f
**athlete** ['æθliːt] n atleta mf
**athletic** [æθ'lɛtɪk] adj atlético; **athletics** n
atletismo
**Atlantic** [ət'læntɪk] adj atlántico ▷ n: **the ~
(Ocean)** el (Océano) Atlántico
**atlas** ['ætləs] n atlas m inv

**A.T.M.** n abbr (= Automated Telling Machine) cajero automático

**atmosphere** ['ætməsfɪəʳ] n atmósfera; (fig) ambiente m

**atom** ['ætəm] n átomo; **atomic** [ə'tɒmɪk] adj atómico; **atom(ic) bomb** n bomba atómica

**A to Z®** n (map) callejero

**atrocity** [ə'trɒsɪtɪ] n atrocidad f

**attach** [ə'tætʃ] vt sujetar; (document, email, letter) adjuntar; **to be ~ed to sb/sth** (like) tener cariño a algn/algo; **attachment** n (tool) accesorio; (Comput) archivo o documento adjunto; (love): **attachment (to)** apego (a)

**attack** [ə'tæk] vt (Mil) atacar; (criminal) agredir, asaltar; (criticize) criticar; (task etc) emprender ▷ n ataque m, asalto; (on sb's life) atentado; (fig: criticism) crítica; **heart ~** infarto (de miocardio); **attacker** n agresor(a) m/f, asaltante mf

**attain** [ə'teɪn] vt (also: **~ to**) alcanzar; (achieve) lograr, conseguir

**attempt** [ə'tɛmpt] n tentativa, intento; (attack) atentado ▷ vt intentar

**attend** vt asistir a; (patient) atender; **attend to** vt fus (needs, affairs etc) ocuparse de; (speech etc) prestar atención a; (customer) atender a; **attendance** n asistencia, presencia; (people present) concurrencia; **attendant** n sirviente/a m/f, ayudante mf ▷ adj concomitante

**attention** [ə'tɛnʃən] n atención f ▷ excl (Mil) ¡firme(s)!; **for the ~ of ...** (Admin) a la atención de ...

**attic** ['ætɪk] n desván m

**attitude** ['ætɪtjuːd] n actitud f; (disposition) disposición f

**attorney** [ə'tɜːnɪ] n (lawyer) abogado/a; **Attorney General** n (BRIT) ≈ fiscal mf general del Estado; (US) ≈ ministro/a de Justicia

**attract** [ə'trækt] vt atraer; (attention) llamar; **attraction** n encanto; (Physics) atracción f; (towards sth) atracción f; **attractive** adj atractivo

**attribute** ['ætrɪbjuːt] n atributo ▷ vt [ə'trɪbjuːt]: **to ~ sth to** atribuir algo a

**aubergine** ['əubəʒiːn] n (BRIT) berenjena; (colour) morado

**auburn** ['ɔːbən] adj color castaño rojizo

**auction** ['ɔːkʃən] n (also: **sale by ~**) subasta ▷ vt subastar

**audible** ['ɔːdɪbl] adj audible, que se puede oír

**audience** ['ɔːdɪəns] n público; (Radio) radioescuchas mpl; (TV) telespectadores mpl; (interview) audiencia

**audit** ['ɔːdɪt] vt revisar, intervenir

**audition** [ɔː'dɪʃən] n audición f

**auditor** ['ɔːdɪtəʳ] n interventor(a) m/f, censor(a) m/f de cuentas

**auditorium** [ɔːdɪ'tɔːrɪəm] n auditorio

**Aug.** abbr (= August) ag

**August** ['ɔːgəst] n agosto

**aunt** [ɑːnt] n tía; **auntie, aunty** ['ɑːntɪ] diminutive of **aunt**

**au pair** ['əu'pɛəʳ] n (also: **~ girl**) chica f au pair

**aura** ['ɔːrə] n aura; (atmosphere) ambiente m

**austerity** [ɔ'stɛrɪtɪ] n austeridad f

**Australia** [ɔs'treɪlɪə] n Australia; **Australian** adj, n australiano/a

**Austria** ['ɔstrɪə] n Austria; **Austrian** adj, n austríaco/a

**authentic** [ɔ'θɛntɪk] adj auténtico

**author** ['ɔːθəʳ] n autor(a) m/f

**authority** [ɔː'θɒrɪtɪ] n autoridad f; **the authorities** npl las autoridades

**authorize** ['ɔːθəraɪz] vt autorizar

**auto** ['ɔːtəu] n (US) coche m, carro (LAM), automóvil m; **autobiography** [ɔːtəbaɪ'ɒgrəfɪ] n autobiografía; **autograph** ['ɔːtəgrɑːf] n autógrafo ▷ vt (photo etc) dedicar; **automatic** [ɔːtə'mætɪk] adj automático ▷ n (gun) pistola automática; **automatically** adv automáticamente; **automobile** ['ɔːtəməbiːl] n (US) coche m, carro (LAM), automóvil m; **autonomous** [ɔː'tɒnəməs] adj autónomo; **autonomy** [ɔː'tɒnəmɪ] n autonomía

**autumn** ['ɔːtəm] n otoño

**auxiliary** [ɔːg'zɪlɪərɪ] adj auxiliar

**avail** [ə'veɪl] vt: **to ~ o.s. of** aprovechar(se) de ▷ n: **to no ~** en vano, sin resultado

**availability** [əveɪlə'bɪlɪtɪ] n disponibilidad f

**available** [ə'veɪləbl] adj disponible

**avalanche** ['ævəlɑːnʃ] n alud m, avalancha

**Ave.** abbr (= avenue) Av., Avda

**avenue** ['ævənjuː] n avenida; (fig) camino

**average** ['ævərɪdʒ] n promedio, media ▷ adj (mean) medio; (ordinary) regular, corriente ▷ vt alcanzar un promedio de; **on ~** por término medio

**avert** [ə'vɜːt] vt prevenir; (blow) desviar; (one's eyes) apartar

**avid** ['ævɪd] adj ávido

**avocado** [ævə'kɑːdəu] n (BRIT: also: **~ pear**) aguacate m, palta (LAM)

**avoid** [ə'vɔɪd] vt evitar, eludir

**await** [ə'weɪt] vt esperar, aguardar

**awake** [ə'weɪk] (pt **awoke**, pp **awoken** or **awaked**) adj despierto ▷ vt despertar ▷ vi despertarse; **to be ~** estar despierto

**award** [ə'wɔːd] n premio; (Law) fallo, sentencia ▷ vt otorgar, conceder; (Law: damages) adjudicar

**aware** [əˈwɛəʳ] *adj* consciente; **to become ~ of** darse cuenta de, enterarse de; **awareness** *n* conciencia, conocimiento

**away** [əˈweɪ] *adv* fuera; (*far away*) lejos; **two kilometres ~** a dos kilómetros (de distancia); **two hours ~ by car** a dos horas en coche; **the holiday was two weeks ~** faltaban dos semanas para las vacaciones; **he's ~ for a week** estará ausente una semana; **to work/pedal ~** seguir trabajando/pedaleando; **to fade ~** desvanecerse; (*sound*) apagarse

**awe** [ɔː] *n* respeto, admiración *f* respetuosa; **awesome** [ˈɔːsəm] *adj* (*esp us: excellent*) formidable

**awful** [ˈɔːfəl] *adj* terrible; **an ~ lot of** (*people, cars, dogs*) la mar de, muchísimos; **awfully** *adv* (*very*) terriblemente

**awkward** [ˈɔːkwəd] *adj* desmañado, torpe; (*shape, situation*) incómodo; (*question*) difícil

**awoke** [əˈwəuk] *pt of* **awake**

**awoken** [əˈwəukən] *pp of* **awake**

**axe**, (*us*) **ax** [æks] *n* hacha ▷ *vt* (*project etc*) cortar; (*jobs*) reducir

**axle** [ˈæksl] *n* eje *m*, árbol *m*

**ay(e)** [aɪ] *excl* (*yes*) sí

**azalea** [əˈzeɪlɪə] *n* azalea

**B** [biː] *n* (*Mus*) si *m*

**baby** [ˈbeɪbɪ] *n* bebé *mf*; (*us inf: darling*) mi amor; **baby carriage** *n* (*us*) cochecito; **baby-sit** *vi* hacer de canguro; **baby-sitter** *n* canguro *mf*; **baby wipe** *n* toallita húmeda (*para bebés*)

**bachelor** [ˈbætʃələʳ] *n* soltero; **B~ of Arts/ Science (BA/BSc)** licenciado/a en Filosofía y Letras/Ciencias

**back** [bæk] *n* (*of person*) espalda; (*of animal*) lomo; (*of hand, page*) dorso; (*as opposed to front*) parte *f* de atrás; (*of chair*) respaldo; (*of page*) reverso; (*Football*) defensa *m* ▷ *vt* (*candidate: also: ~ up*) respaldar, apoyar; (*horse: at races*) apostar a; (*car*) dar marcha atrás a or con ▷ *vi* (*car etc*) dar marcha atrás ▷ *adj* (*garden, room*) de atrás ▷ *adv* (*not forward*) (hacia) atrás; **he's ~** (*returned*) ha vuelto; **~ seats/wheels** (*Aut*) asientos *mpl* traseros, ruedas *fpl* traseras; **~ payments** pagos *mpl* con efecto retroactivo; **~ rent** renta atrasada; **he ran ~** volvió corriendo; **throw the ball ~** (*restitution*) devuelve la pelota; **can I have it ~?** ¿me lo devuelve?; **he called ~** (*again*) volvió a llamar; **back down** *vi* echarse atrás; **back out** *vi* (*of promise*) volverse atrás; **back up** *vt* (*person*) apoyar, respaldar; (*theory*) defender; (*Comput*) hacer una copia de reserva de; **backache** *n* dolor *m* de espalda; **backbencher** *n* (*BRIT*) diputado sin cargo oficial en el gobierno o la oposición; **backbone** *n* columna vertebral; **back door** *n* puerta *f* trasera; **backfire** *vi* (*Aut*) petardear; (*plans*) fallar, salir mal; **backgammon** *n* backgammon *m*; **background** *n* fondo; (*of events*) antecedentes *mpl*; (*basic knowledge*) bases *fpl*; (*experience*) conocimientos *mpl*, educación *f*; **family background** origen *m*, antecedentes *mpl* familiares; **backing** *n* (*fig*)

# bacon | 228

apoyo, respaldo; (*Comm*) respaldo financiero; (*Mus*) acompañamiento; **backlog** n: backlog of work trabajo atrasado; **backpack** n mochila; **backpacker** n mochilero/a; **backslash** n pleca, barra inversa; **backstage** adv entre bastidores; **backstroke** n espalda; **backup** adj suplementario; (*Comput: disk, file*) de reserva ▷ n (*support*) apoyo; (*also:* **backup file**) copia de reserva; **backward** adj (*person, country*) atrasado; **backwards** adv hacia atrás; (*read a list*) al revés; (*fall*) de espaldas; **backyard** n patio trasero

**bacon** ['beɪkən] n tocino, beicon m

**bacteria** [bæk'tɪərɪə] npl bacterias fpl

**bad** [bæd] adj malo; (*serious*) grave; (*meat, food*) podrido, pasado; **to go ~** pasarse

**badge** [bædʒ] n insignia; (*metal badge*) chapa; (*of police officer*) placa

**badger** ['bædʒər] n tejón m

**badly** ['bædlɪ] adv (*work, dress etc*) mal; **to reflect ~ on sb** influir negativamente en la reputación de algn; **~ wounded** gravemente herido; **he needs it ~** le hace mucha falta; **to be ~ off (for money)** andar mal de dinero

**bad-mannered** ['bæd'mænəd] adj mal educado

**badminton** ['bædmɪntən] n bádminton m

**bad-tempered** ['bæd'tempəd] adj de mal genio or carácter; (*temporarily*) de mal humor

**bag** [bæg] n bolsa; (*handbag*) bolso; (*satchel*) mochila; (*case*) maleta; **~s of** (*inf*) un montón de

**baggage** ['bægɪdʒ] n equipaje m; **baggage allowance** n límite m de equipaje; **baggage (re)claim** n recogida de equipajes

**baggy** ['bægɪ] adj (*trousers*) ancho, holgado

**bagpipes** ['bægpaɪps] npl gaita sg

**bail** [beɪl] n fianza ▷ vt (*prisoner: also:* **grant ~ to**) poner en libertad bajo fianza; (*boat: also:* **~ out**) achicar; **on ~** (*prisoner*) bajo fianza; **to ~ sb out** pagar la fianza de algn

**bait** [beɪt] n cebo ▷ vt poner el cebo en

**bake** [beɪk] vt cocer (al horno) ▷ vi cocerse; **baked beans** npl judías fpl en salsa de tomate; **baked potato** n patata al horno; **baker** n panadero/a; **bakery** n panadería; (*for cakes*) pastelería; **baking** n (*act*) cocción f; (*batch*) hornada; **baking powder** n levadura (en polvo)

**balance** ['bæləns] n equilibrio; (*Comm: sum*) balance m; (*remainder*) resto; (*scales*) balanza ▷ vt (*budget*) nivelar; (*account*) saldar; (*compensate*) compensar; **~ of trade/payments** balanza de comercio/pagos; **balanced** adj (*personality, diet*) equilibrado; (*report*) objetivo; **balance sheet** n balance m

**balcony** ['bælkənɪ] n (*open*) balcón m; (*closed*) galería; (*in theatre*) anfiteatro

**bald** [bɔːld] adj calvo; (*tyre*) liso

**ball** [bɔːl] n (*football*) balón m; (*for tennis, golf etc*) pelota; (*of wool, string*) ovillo; (*dance*) baile m; **to play ~ (with sb)** jugar a la pelota (con algn); (*fig*) cooperar

**ballerina** [bælə'riːnə] n bailarina

**ballet** ['bæleɪ] n ballet m; **ballet dancer** n bailarín/ina m/f (de ballet)

**balloon** [bə'luːn] n globo

**ballot** ['bælət] n votación f

**ballroom** ['bɔːlrum] n salón m de baile

**Baltic** ['bɔːltɪk] n: **the ~ (Sea)** el (Mar) Báltico

**bamboo** [bæm'buː] n bambú m

**ban** [bæn] n prohibición f ▷ vt prohibir; (*exclude*) excluir

**banana** [bə'nɑːnə] n plátano, banana (*LAM*)

**band** [bænd] n (*group*) banda; (*strip*) faja, tira; (*at a dance*) orquesta; (*Mil*) banda; (*rock band*) grupo

**bandage** ['bændɪdʒ] n venda, vendaje m ▷ vt vendar

**Band-Aid®** ['bændeɪd] n (*US*) tirita

**bandit** ['bændɪt] n bandido

**bang** [bæŋ] n (*of gun, exhaust*) estallido; (*of door*) portazo; (*blow*) golpe m ▷ vt (*door*) cerrar de golpe; (*one's head*) golpear ▷ vi estallar; *see also* **bangs**

**Bangladesh** [bæŋglə'deʃ] n Bangladesh f

**bangle** ['bæŋgl] n brazalete m, ajorca

**bangs** [bæŋz] npl (*US*) flequillo sg

**banish** ['bænɪʃ] vt desterrar

**banister(s)** ['bænɪstə(z)] n(pl) barandilla f, pasamanos m inv

**banjo** ['bændʒəu] n (pl **banjoes** or **banjos**) n banjo

**bank** [bæŋk] n (*Comm*) banco; (*of river, lake*) ribera, orilla; (*of earth*) terraplén m ▷ vi (*Aviat*) ladearse; **bank on** vt fus contar con; **bank account** n cuenta bancaria; **bank balance** n saldo; **bank card** n tarjeta bancaria; **bank charges** npl comisión fsg; **banker** n banquero; **bank holiday** n (*BRIT*) día m festivo or de fiesta; *ver nota* **"bank holiday"**; **banking** n banca; **bank manager** n director(a) m/f (de sucursal) de banco; **banknote** n billete m de banco

● **BANK HOLIDAY**

● El término *bank holiday* se aplica en el
● Reino Unido a todo día festivo oficial en
● el que cierran bancos y comercios. Los
● más destacados coinciden con Navidad,
● Semana Santa, finales de mayo y finales
● de agosto. Al contrario que en los países
● de tradición católica, no se celebran las
● festividades dedicadas a los santos.

**bankrupt** ['bæŋkrʌpt] adj quebrado, insolvente; **to go ~** hacer bancarrota; **to be ~** estar en quiebra; **bankruptcy** n quiebra

**bank statement** n extracto de cuenta

**banner** ['bænər] n pancarta

**bannister(s)** ['bænɪstə(z)] n(pl) = **banister(s)**

**banquet** ['bæŋkwɪt] n banquete m

**baptism** ['bæptɪzəm] n bautismo; (act) bautizo

**baptize** [bæp'taɪz] vt bautizar

**bar** [bɑːr] n barra; (on door) tranca; (of window, cage) reja; (of soap) pastilla; (of chocolate) tableta; (fig: hindrance) obstáculo; (prohibition) prohibición f; (pub) bar m; (counter) barra, mostrador m; (Mus) barra ▷ vt (road) obstruir; (person) excluir; (activity) prohibir; **behind ~s** entre rejas; **the B~** (Law) la abogacía; **~ none** sin excepción

**barbaric** [bɑːˈbærɪk] adj bárbaro

**barbecue** ['bɑːbɪkjuː] n barbacoa

**barbed wire** ['bɑːbd-] n alambre m de espino

**barber** ['bɑːbər] n peluquero, barbero; **barber's (shop)**, (US) **barber (shop)** n peluquería

**bar code** n código de barras

**bare** [bɛər] adj desnudo; (trees) sin hojas ▷ vt desnudar; **to ~ one's teeth** enseñar los dientes; **barefoot** adj, adv descalzo; **barely** adv apenas

**bargain** ['bɑːgɪn] n pacto; (transaction) negocio; (good buy) ganga ▷ vi negociar; (haggle) regatear; **into the ~** además, por añadidura; **bargain for** vt fus (inf): **he got more than he ~ed for** le resultó peor de lo que esperaba

**barge** [bɑːdʒ] n barcaza; **barge in** vi irrumpir; (in conversation) entrometerse

**bark** [bɑːk] n (of tree) corteza; (of dog) ladrido ▷ vi ladrar

**barley** ['bɑːlɪ] n cebada

**barmaid** ['bɑːmeɪd] n camarera

**barman** ['bɑːmən] n camarero, barman m

**barn** [bɑːn] n granero

**barometer** [bəˈrɔmɪtər] n barómetro

**baron** ['bærən] n barón m; (fig) magnate m; **baroness** n baronesa

**barracks** ['bærəks] npl cuartel msg

**barrage** ['bærɑːʒ] n (Mil) cortina de fuego; (dam) presa; (of criticism etc) lluvia, aluvión m

**barrel** ['bærəl] n barril m; (of gun) cañón m

**barren** ['bærən] adj estéril

**barrette** [bəˈrɛt] n (US) pasador m (LAM, SP), broche m (MEX)

**barricade** [bærɪˈkeɪd] n barricada

**barrier** ['bærɪər] n barrera

**barring** ['bɑːrɪŋ] prep excepto, salvo

**barrister** ['bærɪstər] n (BRIT) abogado/a

**barrow** ['bærəu] n (cart) carretilla

**bartender** ['bɑːtɛndər] n (US) camarero, barman m

**base** [beɪs] n base f ▷ vt: **to ~ sth on** basar or fundar algo en ▷ adj bajo, infame

**baseball** ['beɪsbɔːl] n béisbol m; **baseball cap** n gorra f de béisbol

**basement** ['beɪsmənt] n sótano

**bases** ['beɪsiːz] npl of **basis**

**bash** [bæʃ] vt (inf) golpear

**basic** ['beɪsɪk] adj básico; **basically** adv fundamentalmente, en el fondo; **basics** npl: **the basics** los fundamentos

**basil** ['bæzl] n albahaca

**basin** ['beɪsn] n cuenco, tazón m; (Geo) cuenca; (also: **wash~**) lavabo

**basis** ['beɪsɪs] (pl **bases**) n base f; **on a part-time/trial ~** a tiempo parcial/a prueba

**basket** ['bɑːskɪt] n cesta, cesto; **basketball** n baloncesto

**bass** [beɪs] n (Mus) bajo

**bastard** ['bɑːstəd] n bastardo/a; (inf!) hijo de puta (!)

**bat** [bæt] n (Zool) murciélago; (for ball games) palo; (BRIT: for table tennis) pala ▷ vt: **he didn't ~ an eyelid** ni pestañeó

**batch** [bætʃ] n lote m; (of bread) hornada

**bath** [bɑːθ] n (act) baño; (bathtub) bañera, tina (esp LAM) ▷ vt bañar; **to have a ~** bañarse, darse un baño; see also **baths**

**bathe** [beɪð] vi bañarse ▷ vt (wound etc) lavar

**bathing** ['beɪðɪŋ] n baño; **bathing costume**, (US) **bathing suit** n traje m de baño

**bath: bathrobe** n albornoz m; **bathroom** n (cuarto de) baño; **baths** [bɑːðz] npl piscina sg; **bath towel** n toalla de baño; **bathtub** n bañera

**baton** ['bætən] n (Mus) batuta; (weapon) porra

**batter** ['bætər] vt maltratar; (wind, rain) azotar ▷ n batido; **battered** adj (hat, pan) estropeado

**battery** ['bætərɪ] n batería; (of torch) pila; **battery farming** n cría intensiva

**battle** ['bætl] n batalla; (fig) lucha ▷ vi luchar; **battlefield** n campo m de batalla

**bay** [beɪ] n (Geo) bahía; **to hold sb at ~** mantener a alguien a raya

**bazaar** [bəˈzɑːr] n bazar m

**BBC** n abbr (= British Broadcasting Corporation) BBC f

 **KEYWORD**

**be** [biː] (pt **was**, **were**, pp **been**) aux vb
**1** (with present participle, forming continuous tenses): **what are you doing?** ¿qué estás haciendo?, ¿qué haces?; **they're coming**

tomorrow vienen mañana; **I've been
waiting for you for hours** llevo horas
esperándote

**2** (with pp: forming passives) ser (but often
replaced by active or reflexive constructions);
**to be murdered** ser asesinado; **the box
had been opened** habían abierto la caja;
**the thief was nowhere to be seen** no se
veía al ladrón por ninguna parte

**3** (in tag questions): **it was fun, wasn't it?**
fue divertido, ¿no? or ¿verdad?; **he's good-
looking, isn't he?** es guapo, ¿no te parece?;
**she's back again, is she?** entonces, ¿ha
vuelto?

**4** (+ to + infin): **the house is to be sold**
(necessity) hay que vender la casa; (future)
van a vender la casa; **he's not to open it** no
tiene que abrirlo

▶ vb +complement **1** (with n or num
complement) ser; **he's a doctor** es médico;
**2 and 2 are 4** 2 y 2 son 4

**2** (with adj complement, expressing permanent
or inherent quality) ser; (: expressing state seen
as temporary or reversible) estar; **I'm English**
soy inglés/esa; **she's tall/pretty** es alta/
bonita; **he's young** es joven; **be careful/
good/quiet** ten cuidado/pórtate bien/
cállate; **I'm tired** estoy cansado/a; **it's
dirty** está sucio/a

**3** (of health) estar; **how are you?** ¿cómo
estás?; **he's very ill** está muy enfermo; **I'm
better now** ya estoy mejor

**4** (of age) tener; **how old are you?** ¿cuántos
años tienes?; **I'm sixteen (years old)** tengo
dieciséis años

**5** (cost) costar; ser; **how much was the
meal?** ¿cuánto fue or costó la comida?;
**that'll be £5.75, please** son £5.75, por favor;
**this shirt is £17** esta camisa cuesta £17

▶ vi **1** (exist, occur etc) existir, haber; **the best
singer that ever was** el mejor cantante
que existió jamás; **is there a God?** ¿hay un
Dios?, ¿existe Dios?; **be that as it may** sea
como sea; **so be it** así sea

**2** (referring to place) estar; **I won't be here
tomorrow** no estaré aquí mañana

**3** (referring to movement): **where have you
been?** ¿dónde has estado?

▶ impers vb **1** (referring to time): **it's 5 o'clock**
son las 5; **it's the 28th of April** estamos a
28 de abril

**2** (referring to distance): **it's 10 km to the
village** el pueblo está a 10 km

**3** (referring to the weather): **it's too hot/
cold** hace demasiado calor/frío; **it's windy
today** hace viento hoy

**4** (emphatic): **it's me** soy yo; **it was Maria
who paid the bill** fue María la que pagó la
cuenta

**beach** [biːtʃ] n playa ▷ vt varar
**beacon** ['biːkən] n (lighthouse) faro; (marker)
guía
**bead** [biːd] n cuenta; (of dew, sweat) gota;
**beads** npl (necklace) collar m
**beak** [biːk] n pico
**beam** [biːm] n (Arch) viga; (of light) rayo, haz
m de luz ▷ vi brillar; (smile) sonreír
**bean** [biːn] n judía; **runner/broad ~**
habichuela/haba; **coffee ~** grano de café;
**bean sprouts** npl brotes mpl de soja
**bear** [bɛəʳ] (pt bore, pp borne) n oso
▷ vt (weight etc) llevar; (cost) pagar;
(responsibility) tener; (endure) soportar,
aguantar; (children) tener; (fruit) dar ▷ vi:
**to ~ right/left** torcer a la derecha/
izquierda
**beard** [bɪəd] n barba
**bearer** ['bɛərəʳ] n portador(a) m/f
**bearing** ['bɛərɪŋ] n porte m; (connection)
relación f
**beast** [biːst] n bestia; (inf) bruto, salvaje m
**beat** [biːt] (pt beat, pp beaten ['biːtn]) n
(of heart) latido; (Mus) ritmo, compás m; (of
police officer) ronda ▷ vt (hit) golpear, pegar;
(eggs) batir; (defeat) vencer, derrotar; (better)
sobrepasar; (drum) redoblar ▷ vi (heart) latir;
**off the ~ en track** aislado; **to ~ it** largarse;
**beat up** vt (inf: person) dar una paliza a;
**beating** n paliza
**beautiful** ['bjuːtɪful] adj hermoso, bello;
**beautifully** adv de maravilla
**beauty** ['bjuːtɪ] n belleza; **beauty parlour**,
(us) **beauty parlor** n salón m de belleza;
**beauty salon** n salón m de belleza; **beauty
spot** n (Tourism) lugar m pintoresco
**beaver** ['biːvəʳ] n castor m
**became** [bɪ'keɪm] pt of **become**
**because** [bɪ'kɔz] conj porque; **~ of** prep
debido a, a causa de
**beckon** ['bɛkən] vt (also: **~ to**) llamar con
señas
**become** [bɪ'kʌm] (irreg: like **come**) vi
(+ noun) hacerse, llegar a ser; (+ adj)
ponerse, volverse ▷ vt (suit) favorecer,
sentar bien a; **to ~ fat** engordar
**bed** [bɛd] n cama; (of flowers) macizo; (of
sea, lake) fondo; (of river) lecho; (of coal,
clay) capa; **to go to ~** acostarse; **bed and
breakfast** n ≈ pensión f; ver nota **"bed and
breakfast"**; **bedclothes** npl ropa de cama;
**bedding** n ropa de cama; **bed linen** n (BRIT)
ropa f de cama; **bedroom** n dormitorio;
**bedside** n: **at sb's bedside** a la cabecera
de alguien; **bedside lamp** n lámpara de
noche; **bedside table** n mesilla de noche;
**bedsit(ter)** n (BRIT) estudio; **bedspread** n
cubrecama m, colcha; **bedtime** n hora de
acostarse

**• BED AND BREAKFAST**

Se llama *Bed and Breakfast* a la casa de hospedaje particular, o granja si es en el campo, que ofrece cama y desayuno a tarifas inferiores a las de un hotel. El servicio se suele anunciar con carteles colocados en las ventanas del establecimiento, en el jardín o en la carretera y en ellos aparece a menudo únicamente el símbolo "*B & B*".

**bee** [biː] *n* abeja

**beech** [biːtʃ] *n* haya

**beef** [biːf] *n* carne *f* de vaca; **roast ~** rosbif *m*; **beefburger** *n* hamburguesa

**been** [biːn] *pp of* **be**

**beer** [bɪəʳ] *n* cerveza; **beer garden** *n* (BRIT) terraza *f* de verano, jardín *m* (de un bar)

**beet** [biːt] *n* (US) remolacha

**beetle** ['biːtl] *n* escarabajo

**beetroot** ['biːtruːt] *n* (BRIT) remolacha

**before** [bɪ'fɔːʳ] *prep* (*of time*) antes de; (*of space*) delante de ▷ *conj* antes (de) que ▷ *adv* (*time*) antes; (*space*) delante, adelante; **~ going** antes de marcharse; **she goes ~** she goes antes de que se vaya; **the week ~** la semana anterior; **I've never seen it ~** no lo he visto nunca; **beforehand** *adv* de antemano, con anticipación

**beg** [bɛg] *vi* pedir limosna ▷ *vt* pedir, rogar; (*entreat*) suplicar; **to ~ sb to do sth** rogar a algn que haga algo; *see also* **pardon**

**began** [bɪ'gæn] *pt of* **begin**

**beggar** ['bɛgəʳ] *n* mendigo/a

**begin** [bɪ'gɪn] (*pt* **began**, *pp* **begun**) *vt, vi* empezar, comenzar; **to ~ doing** *or* **to do sth** empezar a hacer algo; **beginner** *n* principiante *mf*; **beginning** *n* principio, comienzo

**begun** [bɪ'gʌn] *pp of* **begin**

**behalf** [bɪ'hɑːf] *n*: **on ~ of** en nombre de, por; (*for benefit of*) en beneficio de; **on my/his ~** por mí/él

**behave** [bɪ'heɪv] *vi* (*person*) portarse, comportarse; (*well: also*: **~ o.s.**) portarse bien; **behaviour**, (US) **behavior** *n* comportamiento, conducta

**behind** [bɪ'haɪnd] *prep* detrás de ▷ *adv* detrás, por detrás, atrás ▷ *n* trasero; **to be ~ (schedule)** ir retrasado; **~ the scenes** (*fig*) entre bastidores

**beige** [beɪʒ] *adj* (*color*) beige

**Beijing** ['beɪ'dʒɪŋ] *n* Pekín *m*

**being** ['biːɪŋ] *n* ser *m*; **to come into ~** nacer, aparecer

**belated** [bɪ'leɪtɪd] *adj* atrasado, tardío

**belch** [bɛltʃ] *vi* eructar ▷ *vt* (*also*: **~ out**: *smoke etc*) arrojar

**Belgian** ['bɛldʒən] *adj, n* belga *mf*

**Belgium** ['bɛldʒəm] *n* Bélgica

**belief** [bɪ'liːf] *n* opinión *f*; (*trust, faith*) fe *f*

**believe** [bɪ'liːv] *vt, vi* creer; **to ~ in** creer en; **believer** *n* partidario/a; (*Rel*) creyente *mf*, fiel *mf*

**bell** [bɛl] *n* campana; (*small*) campanilla; (*on door*) timbre *m*

**bellboy** ['bɛlbɔɪ], (US) **bellhop** ['bɛlhɔp] *n* botones *m inv*

**bellow** ['bɛləʊ] *vi* bramar; (*person*) rugir

**bell pepper** *n* (*esp* US) pimiento, pimentón *m* (LAM)

**belly** ['bɛlɪ] *n* barriga, panza; **belly button** (*inf*) *n* ombligo

**belong** [bɪ'lɔŋ] *vi*: **to ~ to** pertenecer a; (*club etc*) ser socio de; **this book ~s here** este libro va aquí; **belongings** *npl* pertenencias *fpl*

**beloved** [bɪ'lʌvɪd] *adj, n* querido/a

**below** [bɪ'ləʊ] *prep* bajo, debajo de; (*less than*) inferior a ▷ *adv* abajo, (por) debajo; **see ~** véase más abajo

**belt** [bɛlt] *n* cinturón *m*; (*Tech*) correa, cinta ▷ *vt* (*thrash*) pegar con correa; **beltway** *n* (US Aut) carretera de circunvalación

**bemused** [bɪ'mjuːzd] *adj* perplejo

**bench** [bɛntʃ] *n* banco; (BRIT Pol): **the Government/Opposition ~es** (los asientos de) los miembros del Gobierno/de la Oposición; **the B~** (*Law*) la magistratura

**bend** [bɛnd] (*pt, pp* **bent**) *vt* doblar ▷ *vi* inclinarse ▷ *n* (*in road, river*) recodo; (*in pipe*) codo; **bend down** *vi* inclinarse, doblarse; **bend over** *vi* inclinarse

**beneath** [bɪ'niːθ] *prep* bajo, debajo de; (*unworthy of*) indigno de ▷ *adv* abajo, (por) debajo

**beneficial** [bɛnɪ'fɪʃəl] *adj*: **~ to** beneficioso para

**benefit** ['bɛnɪfɪt] *n* beneficio; (*allowance of money*) subsidio ▷ *vt* beneficiar ▷ *vi*: **he'll ~ from it** le sacará provecho

**benign** [bɪ'naɪn] *adj* benigno; (*smile*) afable

**bent** [bɛnt] *pt, pp of* **bend** ▷ *n* inclinación *f* ▷ *adj*: **to be ~ on** estar empeñado en

**bereaved** [bɪ'riːvd] *n*: **the ~** los allegados *mpl* del difunto

**beret** ['bɛreɪ] *n* boina

**Berlin** [bəː'lɪn] *n* Berlín *m*

**Bermuda** [bəː'mjuːdə] *n* las (Islas) Bermudas

**berry** ['bɛrɪ] *n* baya

**berth** [bəːθ] *n* (*bed*) litera; (*cabin*) camarote *m*; (*for ship*) amarradero ▷ *vi* atracar, amarrar

**beside** [bɪ'saɪd] *prep* junto a, al lado de; **to be ~ o.s. with anger** estar fuera de sí; **that's ~ the point** eso no tiene nada que ver; **besides** *adv* además ▷ *prep* además de

**best** [bɛst] adj (el/la) mejor ▷ adv (lo) mejor;
**the ~ part of** (most) la mayor parte de; **at ~**
en el mejor de los casos; **to make the ~ of**
**sth** sacar el mejor partido de algo; **to do**
**one's ~** hacer todo lo posible; **to the ~ of**
**my knowledge** que yo sepa; **to the ~ of my**
**ability** como mejor puedo; **best-before**
**date** n fecha de consumo preferente; **best**
**man** n padrino de boda; **bestseller** n éxito
de ventas, bestseller m

**bet** [bɛt] n apuesta ▷ vt, vi (pt, pp **bet** or
**betted**): **to ~ (on)** apostar (a)

**betray** [bɪ'treɪ] vt traicionar; (trust) faltar a

**better** ['bɛtəʳ] adj mejor ▷ adv mejor ▷ vt
superar ▷ n: **to get the ~ of sb** quedar por
encima de algn; **you had ~ do it** más vale
que lo hagas; **he thought ~ of it** cambió de
parecer; **to get ~** mejorar(se)

**betting** ['bɛtɪŋ] n juego, apuestas fpl;
**betting shop** n (BRIT) casa de apuestas

**between** [bɪ'twiːn] prep entre ▷ adv (time)
mientras tanto; (place) en medio

**beverage** ['bɛvərɪdʒ] n bebida

**beware** [bɪ'wɛəʳ] vi: **to ~ (of)** tener cuidado
(con); **"~ of the dog"** "perro peligroso"

**bewildered** [bɪ'wɪldəd] adj aturdido,
perplejo

**beyond** [bɪ'jɔnd] prep más allá de; (past:
understanding) fuera de; (after: date) después
de, más allá de; (above) superior a ▷ adv (in
space) más allá; (in time) posteriormente;
**~ doubt** fuera de toda duda; **~ repair**
irreparable

**bias** ['baɪəs] n (prejudice) prejuicio;
(preference) predisposición f

**bias(s)ed** ['baɪəst] adj parcial

**bib** [bɪb] n babero

**Bible** ['baɪbl] n Biblia

**bicarbonate of soda** [baɪ'kɑːbənɪt-] n
bicarbonato sódico

**biceps** ['baɪsɛps] n bíceps m

**bicycle** ['baɪsɪkl] n bicicleta; **bicycle pump**
n bomba de bicicleta

**bid** [bɪd] n oferta, postura; (attempt)
tentativa, conato ▷ vi hacer una oferta ▷ vt
(offer) ofrecer; **to ~ sb good day** dar a algn
los buenos días; **bidder** n: **the highest**
**bidder** el mejor postor

**bidet** ['biːdeɪ] n bidet m

**big** [bɪg] adj grande; (brother, sister) mayor;
**bigheaded** adj engreído; **big toe** n dedo
gordo (del pie)

**bike** [baɪk] n bici f; **bike lane** n carril m bici

**bikini** [bɪ'kiːnɪ] n bikini m

**bilateral** [baɪ'lætərəl] adj (agreement)
bilateral

**bilingual** [baɪ'lɪŋgwəl] adj bilingüe

**bill** [bɪl] n cuenta; (invoice) factura; (Pol)
proyecto de ley; (us: banknote) billete m; (of

bird) pico; (Theat) programa m; **"post no ~s"**
"prohibido fijar carteles"; **to fit** or **fill the ~**
(fig) cumplir con los requisitos; **billboard** n
valla publicitaria; **billfold** n (us) cartera

**billiards** ['bɪljədz] n billar m

**billion** ['bɪljən] n (BRIT) billón m; (us) mil
millones mpl

**bin** [bɪn] n cubo or bote m (LAM) de la basura;
(litterbin) papelera

**bind** (pt, pp **bound**) [baɪnd, baund] vt atar;
(book) encuadernar; (oblige) obligar ▷ n (inf:
nuisance) lata

**binge** [bɪndʒ] n: **to go on a ~** ir de juerga

**bingo** ['bɪŋgəu] n bingo m

**binoculars** [bɪ'nɔkjuləz] npl prismáticos
mpl

**bio…: biochemistry** [baɪə'kɛmɪstrɪ]
n bioquímica; **biodegradable**
['baɪəudɪ'greɪdəbl] adj biodegradable;
**biofuel** ['baɪəufjuəl] n biocombustible m,
biocarburante m; **biography** [baɪ'ɔgrəfɪ]
n biografía; **biological** [baɪə'lɔdʒɪkəl] adj
biológico; **biology** [baɪ'ɔlədʒɪ] n biología;
**biometric** [baɪə'mɛtrɪk] adj biométrico

**bipolar** [baɪ'pəulə'] adj bipolar

**birch** [bəːtʃ] n abedul m

**bird** [bəːd] n ave f, pájaro; (BRIT inf: girl)
chica; **bird flu** n gripe aviar; **bird of prey**
n ave f de presa; **bird-watching** n: he
likes to go bird-watching on Sundays los
domingos le gusta ir a ver pájaros

**Biro®** ['baɪrəu] n bolígrafo

**birth** [bəːθ] n nacimiento; (Med) parto; **to**
**give ~ to** parir, dar a luz a; (fig) dar origen a;
**birth certificate** n partida de nacimiento;
**birth control** n control m de natalidad;
(methods) métodos mpl anticonceptivos;
**birthday** n cumpleaños m inv; **birthmark**
n antojo, marca de nacimiento; **birthplace**
n lugar m de nacimiento

**biscuit** ['bɪskɪt] n (BRIT) galleta

**bishop** ['bɪʃəp] n obispo; (Chess) alfil m

**bistro** ['biːstrəu] n café-bar m

**bit** [bɪt] pt of **bite** ▷ n trozo, pedazo,
pedacito; (Comput) bit m; (for horse) freno,
bocado; **a ~ of** un poco de; **a ~ mad** un poco
loco; **~ by ~** poco a poco

**bitch** [bɪtʃ] n (dog) perra; (inf!: woman)
zorra (!)

**bite** [baɪt] vt, vi (pt **bit**, pp **bitten**) morder;
(insect etc) picar ▷ n (of insect) picadura;
(mouthful) bocado; **to ~ one's nails**
morderse las uñas; **let's have a ~ (to eat)**
vamos a comer algo

**bitten** ['bɪtn] pp of **bite**

**bitter** ['bɪtəʳ] adj amargo; (wind, criticism)
cortante, penetrante; (battle) encarnizado
▷ n (BRIT: beer) cerveza típica británica a base
de lúpulos

**bizarre** [bɪ'zɑː'] adj raro, extraño
**black** [blæk] adj negro ▷ n color m negro
▷ vt (BRIT Industry) boicotear; **to give sb a ~
eye** ponerle a algn el ojo morado; **~ coffee**
café m solo; **~ and blue** adj amoratado;
**black out** vi (faint) desmayarse;
**blackberry** n zarzamora; **blackbird** n
mirlo; **blackboard** n pizarra; **blackcurrant**
n grosella negra; **black ice** n hielo invisible
en la carretera; **blackmail** n chantaje m
▷ vt chantajear; **black market** n mercado
negro; **blackout** n (Elec) apagón m; (TV)
bloqueo informativo; (fainting) desmayo,
pérdida de conocimiento; **black pepper**
n pimienta f negra; **black pudding** n
morcilla; **Black Sea** n: the Black Sea el
Mar Negro
**bladder** ['blædə'] n vejiga
**blade** [bleɪd] n hoja; **a ~ of grass** una brizna
de hierba
**blame** [bleɪm] n culpa ▷ vt: **to ~ sb for sth**
echar la culpa a algn de algo; **to be to ~
(for)** tener la culpa (de)
**bland** [blænd] adj (taste) soso
**blank** [blæŋk] adj en blanco; (look) sin
expresión ▷ n blanco, espacio en blanco;
(cartridge) cartucho sin bala or de fogueo;
**my mind is a ~** no puedo recordar nada
**blanket** ['blæŋkɪt] n manta, cobija (LAM);
(of snow) capa; (of fog) manto
**blast** [blɑːst] n (of wind) ráfaga, soplo; (of
explosive) explosión f ▷ vt (blow up) volar
**blatant** ['bleɪtənt] adj descarado
**blaze** [bleɪz] n (fire) fuego; (fig) arranque m
▷ vi (fire) arder en llamas; (fig) brillar ▷ vt:
**to ~ a trail** (fig) abrir (un) camino; **in a ~ of
publicity** bajo los focos de la publicidad
**blazer** ['bleɪzə'] n chaqueta de uniforme de
colegial o de socio de club
**bleach** [bliːtʃ] n (also: **household ~**) lejía
▷ vt blanquear; **bleachers** npl (US Sport)
gradas fpl
**bleak** [bliːk] adj (countryside) desierto;
(weather) desapacible; (smile) triste;
(prospect, future) poco prometedor(a)
**bled** [bled] pt, pp of **bleed**
**bleed** [bliːd] (pt, pp **bled**) vt sangrar
▷ vi sangrar; **my nose is ~ing** me está
sangrando la nariz
**blemish** ['blemɪʃ] n marca, mancha; (on
reputation) tacha
**blend** [blend] n mezcla ▷ vt mezclar ▷ vi
(colours etc) combinarse, mezclarse;
**blender** n (Culin) batidora
**bless** (pt, pp **blessed** or **blest**) [bles, blest]
vt bendecir; **~ you!** (after sneeze) ¡Jesús!;
**blessing** n bendición f; (advantage)
beneficio, ventaja; **it was a blessing in
disguise** no hay mal que por bien no venga

**blew** [bluː] pt of **blow**
**blight** [blaɪt] vt (hopes etc) frustrar, arruinar
**blind** [blaɪnd] adj ciego ▷ n (for window)
persiana ▷ vt cegar; (dazzle) deslumbrar;
**to ~ sb to ...** (deceive) cegar a algn a ...;
**~ people** los ciegos; **blind alley** n callejón m
sin salida; **blindfold** n venda ▷ adv con los
ojos vendados ▷ vt vendar los ojos a
**blink** [blɪŋk] vi parpadear, pestañear; (light)
oscilar
**bliss** [blɪs] n felicidad f
**blister** ['blɪstə'] n ampolla ▷ vi ampollarse
**blizzard** ['blɪzəd] n ventisca
**bloated** ['bləʊtɪd] adj hinchado
**blob** [blɔb] n (drop) gota; (stain, spot)
mancha
**block** [blɔk] n (also Comput) bloque m; (in
pipes) obstáculo; (of buildings) manzana,
cuadra (LAM) ▷ vt obstruir, cerrar; (progress)
estorbar; **~ of flats** (BRIT) bloque m de
pisos; **mental ~** bloqueo mental; **block
up** vt tapar, obstruir; (pipe) atascar;
**blockade** [blɔ'keɪd] n bloqueo ▷ vt
bloquear; **blockage** n estorbo, obstrucción
f; **blockbuster** n (book) best-seller m;
(film) éxito de público; **block capitals**
npl mayúsculas fpl; **block letters** npl
mayúsculas fpl
**blog** [blɔg] n blog m ▷ vi bloguear; **he ~s
about politics** tiene un blog sobre política
**blogger** ['blɔgə'] n (inf: person) blogero/a
**blogosphere** ['blɔgəsfɪə'] n blogosfera
**bloke** [bləʊk] n (BRIT inf) tipo, tío
**blond, blonde** [blɔnd] adj, n rubio/a
**blood** [blʌd] n sangre f; **blood donor** n
donante mf de sangre; **blood group** n
grupo sanguíneo; **blood poisoning** n
septicemia, envenenamiento de la sangre;
**blood pressure** n tensión f, presión f
sanguínea; **bloodshed** n baño de sangre;
**bloodshot** adj inyectado en sangre;
**bloodstream** n corriente f sanguínea;
**blood test** n análisis m de sangre; **blood
transfusion** n transfusión f de sangre;
**blood type** n grupo sanguíneo; **blood
vessel** n vaso sanguíneo; **bloody** adj
sangriento; (BRIT inf!): **this bloody ...** este
condenado or puñetero or fregado ... (LAM!)
▷ adv (BRIT inf!): **bloody strong/good**
terriblemente fuerte/bueno
**bloom** [bluːm] n floración f ▷ vi florecer
**blossom** ['blɔsəm] n flor f ▷ vi florecer
**blot** [blɔt] n borrón m ▷ vt (stain) manchar
**blouse** [blauz] n blusa
**blow** [bləʊ] (pt **blew**, pp **blown**) n golpe m
▷ vi soplar; (fuse) fundirse ▷ vt (fuse)
quemar; (instrument) tocar; **to ~ one's nose**
sonarse; **blow away** vt llevarse, arrancar;
**blow out** vt apagar ▷ vi apagarse; **blow up**

*vi* estallar ▷ *vt* volar; (*tyre*) inflar; (*Phot*) ampliar; **blow-dry** *n* secado con secador de mano

**blown** [bləun] *pp* of **blow**

**blue** [blu:] *adj* azul; **~ film** película porno; **~ joke** chiste verde; **to come out of the ~** (*fig*) ser completamente inesperado; **bluebell** *n* campanilla, campánula azul; **blueberry** *n* arándano; **blue cheese** *n* queso azul; **blues** *npl*: **the blues** (*Mus*) el blues; **to have the blues** estar triste; **bluetit** *n* herrerillo *m* (común)

**bluff** [blʌf] *vi* tirarse un farol, farolear ▷ *n* farol *m*; **to call sb's ~** coger a algn en un renuncio

**blunder** ['blʌndəʳ] *n* patinazo, metedura de pata ▷ *vi* cometer un error, meter la pata

**blunt** [blʌnt] *adj* (*knife*) desafilado; (*person*) franco, directo

**blur** [bləːʳ] *n* aspecto borroso; **to become a ~** hacerse borroso ▷ *vt* (*vision*) enturbiar; **blurred** *adj* borroso

**blush** [blʌʃ] *vi* ruborizarse, ponerse colorado ▷ *n* rubor *m*; **blusher** *n* colorete *m*

**board** [bɔːd] *n* tabla, tablero; (*on wall*) tablón *m*; (*for chess etc*) tablero; (*committee*) junta, consejo; (*in firm*) mesa or junta directiva; (*Naut, Aviat*): **on ~** a bordo ▷ *vt* (*ship*) embarcarse en; (*train*) subir a; **full ~** (*BRIT*) pensión *f* completa; **half ~** (*BRIT*) media pensión; **to go by the ~** (*fig*) irse por la borda; **board game** *n* juego de tablero; **boarding card** *n* (*BRIT Aviat, Naut*) tarjeta de embarque; **boarding pass** *n* (*US*) = **boarding card**; **boarding school** *n* internado; **board room** *n* sala de juntas

**boast** [bəust] *vi*: **to ~ (about or of)** alardear (de)

**boat** [bəut] *n* barco, buque *m*; (*small*) barca, bote *m*

**bob** [bɔb] *vi* (*also*: **~ up and down**) menearse, balancearse

**body** ['bɔdɪ] *n* cuerpo; (*corpse*) cadáver *m*; (*of car*) caja, carrocería; (*fig: public body*) organismo; **body-building** *n* culturismo; **bodyguard** *n* guardaespaldas *m inv*; **bodywork** *n* carrocería

**bog** [bɔg] *n* pantano, ciénaga ▷ *vt*: **to get ~ged down** (*fig*) empantanarse, atascarse

**bogus** ['bəugəs] *adj* falso, fraudulento

**boil** [bɔɪl] *vt* hervir; (*eggs*) pasar por agua ▷ *vi* hervir; (*fig: with anger*) estar furioso ▷ *n* (*Med*) furúnculo, divieso; **to come to the** (*BRIT*) **or a** (*US*) **~** comenzar a hervir; **~ed egg** huevo pasado por agua; **~ed potatoes** patatas *fpl* or papas *fpl* (*LAM*) cocidas; **boil over** *vi* (*liquid*) salirse; (*anger, resentment*) llegar al colmo; **boiler** *n* caldera; **boiling**

*adj*: **I'm boiling (hot)** (*inf*) estoy asado; **boiling point** *n* punto de ebullición *f*

**bold** [bəuld] *adj* valiente, audaz; (*pej*) descarado; (*colour*) llamativo

**Bolivia** [bə'lɪvɪə] *n* Bolivia; **Bolivian** *adj*, *n* boliviano/a

**bollard** ['bɔləd] *n* (*BRIT Aut*) poste *m*

**bolt** [bəult] *n* (*lock*) cerrojo; (*with nut*) perno, tornillo ▷ *adv*: **~ upright** rígido, erguido ▷ *vt* (*door*) echar el cerrojo a; (*food*) engullir ▷ *vi* fugarse; (*horse*) desbocarse

**bomb** [bɔm] *n* bomba ▷ *vt* bombardear

**bombard** [bɔm'baːd] *vt* bombardear; (*fig*) asediar

**bomb: bomber** *n* (*Aviat*) bombardero; **bomb scare** *n* amenaza de bomba

**bond** [bɔnd] *n* (*binding promise*) fianza; (*Finance*) bono; (*link*) vínculo, lazo; **in ~** (*Comm*) en depósito bajo fianza

**bone** [bəun] *n* hueso; (*of fish*) espina ▷ *vt* deshuesar; quitar las espinas a

**bonfire** ['bɔnfaɪəʳ] *n* hoguera, fogata

**bonnet** ['bɔnɪt] *n* gorra; (*BRIT: of car*) capó *m*

**bonus** ['bəunəs] *n* (*payment*) paga extraordinaria, plus *m*; (*fig*) bendición *f*

**boo** [bu:] *excl* ¡uh! ▷ *vt* abuchear

**book** [buk] *n* libro; (*of stamps etc*) librillo; **~s** (*Comm*) cuentas *fpl*, contabilidad *f* ▷ *vt* (*ticket, seat, room*) reservar; **book in** *vi* (*at hotel*) registrarse; **book up** *vt*: **the hotel is ~ed up** el hotel está completo; **bookcase** *n* librería, estante *m* para libros; **booking** *n* reserva; **booking office** *n* (*BRIT: Rail*) despacho de billetes or boletos (*LAM*); (: *Theat*) taquilla, boletería (*LAM*); **book-keeping** *n* contabilidad *f*; **booklet** *n* folleto; **bookmaker** *n* corredor *m* de apuestas; **bookmark** *n* (*Comput*) favorito, marcador *m*; **bookseller** *n* librero/a; **bookshelf** *n* estante *m*; **bookshop** *n* librería

**book store** *n* = **bookshop**

**boom** [bu:m] *n* (*noise*) trueno, estampido; (*in prices etc*) alza rápida; (*Econ*) boom *m* ▷ *vi* (*cannon*) hacer gran estruendo, retumbar; (*Econ*) estar en alza

**boost** [bu:st] *n* estímulo, empuje *m* ▷ *vt* estimular, empujar

**boot** [bu:t] *n* bota; (*BRIT: of car*) maleta, maletero *m* (*Comput*) arrancar; **to ~** (*in addition*) además, por añadidura

**booth** [bu:ð] *n* (*telephone booth, voting booth*) cabina

**booze** [bu:z] (*inf*) *n* bebida

**border** ['bɔːdəʳ] *n* borde *m*, margen *m*; (*of a country*) frontera; (*for flowers*) arriate *m* ▷ *adj* fronterizo; **the B~s** *región fronteriza entre Escocia e Inglaterra*; **border on** *vt fus* lindar con; **borderline** *n* (*fig*) frontera; **on the borderline** en el límite

**bore** [bɔːʳ] *pt of* **bear** ▷ *vt* (*hole*) hacer; (*person*) aburrir ▷ *n* (*person*) pelmazo, pesado; (*of gun*) calibre *m*; **bored** *adj* aburrido; **he's bored to tears** *or* **to death** *or* **stiff** está aburrido como una ostra, está muerto de aburrimiento; **boredom** *n* aburrimiento

**boring** [ˈbɔːrɪŋ] *adj* aburrido

**born** [bɔːn] *adj*: **to be ~** nacer; **I was ~ in 1960** nací en 1960

**borne** [bɔːn] *pp of* **bear**

**borough** [ˈbʌrə] *n* municipio

**borrow** [ˈbɔrəu] *vt*: **to ~ sth (from sb)** tomar algo prestado (a alguien)

**Bosnia** [ˈbɔznɪə] *n* Bosnia; **Bosnia-Herzegovina, Bosnia-Hercegovina** [ˈbɔːsnɪəhɜːzəˈɡəuviːnə] *n* Bosnia-Herzegovina; **Bosnian** *adj, n* bosnio/a

**bosom** [ˈbuzəm] *n* pecho

**boss** [bɔs] *n* jefe/a *m/f* ▷ *vt* (*also*: **~ about** *or* **around**) mangonear; **bossy** *adj* mandón/ona

**both** [bəuθ] *adj, pron* ambos/as, los/las dos; **~ of us went, we ~ went** fuimos los dos, ambos fuimos ▷ *adv*: **~ A and B** tanto A como B

**bother** [ˈbɔðəʳ] *vt* (*worry*) preocupar; (*disturb*) molestar, fastidiar ▷ *vi*: **to ~ o.s.** molestarse ▷ *n* (*trouble*) dificultad *f*; (*nuisance*) molestia, lata; **to ~ doing** tomarse la molestia de hacer

**bottle** [ˈbɔtl] *n* botella; (*small*) frasco; (*baby's*) biberón *m* ▷ *vt* embotellar; **bottle bank** *n* contenedor *m* de vidrio; **bottle-opener** *n* abrebotellas *m inv*

**bottom** [ˈbɔtəm] *n* (*of box, sea*) fondo; (*buttocks*) trasero, culo; (*of page, mountain, tree*) pie *m*; (*of list*) final *m* ▷ *adj* (*lowest*) más bajo; (*last*) último

**bought** [bɔːt] *pt, pp of* **buy**

**boulder** [ˈbəuldəʳ] *n* canto rodado

**bounce** [bauns] *vi* (*ball*) (re)botar; (*cheque*) ser rechazado ▷ *vt* hacer (re)botar ▷ *n* (*rebound*) (re)bote *m*; **bouncer** *n* (*inf*) gorila *m*

**bound** [baund] *pt, pp of* **bind** ▷ *n* (*leap*) salto; (*gen pl*: *limit*) límite *m* ▷ *vi* (*leap*) saltar ▷ *adj*: **~ by** rodeado de; **to be ~ to do sth** (*obliged*) tener el deber de hacer algo; **he's ~ to come** es seguro que vendrá; **"out of ~s to the public"** "prohibido el paso"; **~ for** con destino a

**boundary** [ˈbaundrɪ] *n* límite *m*

**bouquet** [ˈbukeɪ] *n* (*of flowers*) ramo

**bourbon** [ˈbuəbən] *n* (*US*: *also*: **~ whiskey**) whisky americano, bourbon *m*

**bout** [baut] *n* (*of malaria etc*) ataque *m*; (*Boxing etc*) combate *m*, encuentro

**boutique** [buːˈtiːk] *n* boutique *f*, tienda de ropa

**bow¹** [bəu] *n* (*knot*) lazo; (*weapon, Mus*) arco

**bow²** [bau] *n* (*of the head*) reverencia; (*Naut*: *also*: **~s**) proa ▷ *vi* inclinarse, hacer una reverencia

**bowels** [ˈbauəlz] *npl* intestinos *mpl*, vientre *m*; (*fig*) entrañas *fpl*

**bowl** [bəul] *n* tazón *m*, cuenco; (*ball*) bola ▷ *vi* (*Cricket*) arrojar la pelota; **see also bowls; bowler** *n* (*Cricket*) lanzador *m* (de la pelota); (*BRIT*: *also*: **bowler hat**) hongo, bombín *m*; **bowling** *n* (*game*) bolos *mpl*; **bowling alley** *n* bolera; **bowling green** *n* pista para bochas; **bowls** *n* juego de los bolos, bochas *fpl*

**bow tie** [ˈbəu-] *n* corbata de lazo, pajarita

**box** [bɔks] *n* (*also*: **cardboard ~**) caja, cajón *m*; (*Theat*) palco ▷ *vt* encajonar ▷ *vi* (*Sport*) boxear; **boxer** *n* (*person*) boxeador *m*; (*dog*) bóxer *m*; **boxer shorts** *npl* bóxers; **a pair of boxer shorts** unos bóxers; **boxing** *n* (*Sport*) boxeo; **Boxing Day** *n* (*BRIT*) día *m* de San Esteban; **boxing gloves** *npl* guantes *mpl* de boxeo; **boxing ring** *n* ring *m*, cuadrilátero; **box office** *n* taquilla, boletería (*LAM*)

**boy** [bɔɪ] *n* (*young*) niño; (*older*) muchacho, chico; (*son*) hijo; **boy band** *n* boy band *m* (*grupo musical de chicos*)

**boycott** [ˈbɔɪkɔt] *n* boicot *m* ▷ *vt* boicotear

**boyfriend** [ˈbɔɪfrend] *n* novio

**bra** [brɑː] *n* sostén *m*, sujetador *m*

**brace** [breɪs] *n* (*BRIT*: *on teeth*) corrector *m*, aparato; (*tool*) berbiquí *m* ▷ *vt* asegurar, reforzar; **to ~ o.s. (for)** (*fig*) prepararse (para); *see also* **braces**

**bracelet** [ˈbreɪslɪt] *n* pulsera, brazalete *m*

**braces** [ˈbreɪsɪz] *npl* (*on teeth*) corrector *m*; (*BRIT*: *for trousers*) tirantes *mpl*

**bracket** [ˈbrækɪt] *n* (*Tech*) soporte *m*, puntal *m*; (*group*) clase *f*, categoría; (*also*: **brace ~**) soporte *m*, abrazadera; (*also*: **round ~**) paréntesis *m inv*; **in ~s** entre paréntesis

**brag** [bræg] *vi* jactarse

**braid** [breɪd] *n* (*trimming*) galón *m*; (*of hair*) trenza

**brain** [breɪn] *n* cerebro; **brains** *npl* sesos *mpl*; **she's got ~s** es muy lista

**braise** [breɪz] *vt* cocer a fuego lento

**brake** [breɪk] *n* (*on vehicle*) freno ▷ *vi* frenar; **brake light** *n* luz *f* de frenado

**bran** [bræn] *n* salvado

**branch** [brɑːntʃ] *n* rama; (*Comm*) sucursal *f* ▷ *vi* ramificarse; (*fig*) extenderse; **branch off** *vi*: **a small road ~es off to the right** hay una carretera pequeña que sale hacia la derecha; **branch out** *vi* (*fig*) extenderse

**brand** [brænd] *n* marca; (*fig*: *type*) tipo ▷ *vt* (*cattle*) marcar con hierro candente; **brand name** *n* marca; **brand-new** *adj* flamante, completamente nuevo

**brandy** ['brændɪ] n coñac m

**brash** [bræʃ] adj (cheeky) descarado

**brass** [brɑːs] n latón m; **the ~** (Mus) los cobres; **brass band** n banda de metal

**brat** [bræt] n (pej) mocoso/a

**brave** [breɪv] adj valiente, valeroso ▷ vt (challenge) desafiar; (resist) aguantar; **bravery** n valor m, valentía

**brawl** [brɔːl] n pelea, reyerta

**Brazil** [brə'zɪl] n (el) Brasil; **Brazilian** adj, n brasileño/a

**breach** [briːtʃ] vt abrir brecha en ▷ n (gap) brecha; (breaking): **~ of contract** infracción f de contrato; **~ of the peace** perturbación f del orden público

**bread** [brɛd] n pan m; **breadbin** n panera; **breadbox** n (us) panera; **breadcrumbs** npl migajas fpl; (Culin) pan msg rallado

**breadth** [brɛtθ] n anchura; (fig) amplitud f

**break** [breɪk] (pt broke, pp broken) vt romper; (promise) faltar a; (law) violar, infringir; (record) batir ▷ vi romperse, quebrarse; (storm) estallar; (weather) cambiar; (news etc) darse a conocer ▷ n (gap) abertura; (fracture) fractura; (time) intervalo; (: at school) (período de) recreo; (chance) oportunidad f; **break down** vt (figures, data) analizar, descomponer ▷ vi estropearse; (Aut) averiarse; (person) romper a llorar; (talks) fracasar; **break in** vt (horse etc) domar ▷ vi (burglar) forzar una entrada; **break off** vi (speaker) pararse, detenerse; (branch) partir; **break out** vi estallar; (prisoner) escaparse; **to ~ out in spots** salir a algn granos; **break up** vi (marriage) deshacerse; (ship) hacerse pedazos; (crowd, meeting) disolverse; (Scol) terminar (el curso); (line) cortarse ▷ vt (rocks etc) partir; (journey) partir; (fight etc) acabar con; **the line's** or **you're ~ing up** se corta; **breakdown** n (Aut) avería; (in communications) interrupción f; (Med: also: **nervous breakdown**) colapso, crisis f nerviosa; (of marriage, talks) fracaso; (of figures) desglose m; **breakdown truck, breakdown van** n (camión m) grúa

**breakfast** ['brɛkfəst] n desayuno

**break: break-in** n robo con allanamiento de morada; **breakthrough** n (fig) avance m

**breast** [brɛst] n (of woman) pecho, seno; (chest) pecho; (of bird) pechuga; **breast-feed** vt, vi (irreg: like **feed**) amamantar, dar el pecho

**breaststroke** ['brɛststrəʊk] n braza de pecho

**breath** [brɛθ] n aliento, respiración f; **to take a deep ~** respirar hondo; **out of ~** sin aliento, sofocado

**Breathalyser®** ['brɛθəlaɪzə'] n (BRIT) alcoholímetro m

**breathe** [briːð] vt, vi respirar; **breathe in** vt, vi aspirar; **breathe out** vt, vi espirar; **breathing** n respiración f

**breath: breathless** adj sin aliento, jadeante; **breathtaking** adj imponente, pasmoso; **breath test** n prueba de la alcoholemia

**bred** [brɛd] pt, pp of **breed**

**breed** [briːd] (pt, pp **bred**) vt criar ▷ vi reproducirse, procrear ▷ n raza, casta

**breeze** [briːz] n brisa

**breezy** ['briːzɪ] adj de mucho viento, ventoso; (person) despreocupado

**brew** [bruː] vt (tea) hacer; (beer) elaborar ▷ vi (fig: trouble) prepararse; (storm) amenazar; **brewery** n fábrica de cerveza

**bribe** [braɪb] n soborno ▷ vt sobornar, cohechar; **bribery** n soborno, cohecho

**bric-a-brac** ['brɪkəbræk] n inv baratijas fpl

**brick** [brɪk] n ladrillo; **bricklayer** n albañil m

**bride** [braɪd] n novia; **bridegroom** n novio; **bridesmaid** n dama de honor

**bridge** [brɪdʒ] n puente m; (Naut) puente m de mando; (of nose) caballete m; (Cards) bridge m ▷ vt (fig): **to ~ a gap** llenar un vacío

**bridle** ['braɪdl] n brida, freno

**brief** [briːf] adj breve, corto ▷ n (Law) escrito ▷ vt informar; **briefcase** n cartera, portafolio(s) m inv (LAM); **briefing** n (Press) informe m; **briefly** adv (smile, glance) brevemente; (explain, say) en pocas palabras

**briefs** npl (for men) calzoncillos mpl; (for women) bragas fpl

**brigadier** [brɪgə'dɪə'] n general m de brigada

**bright** [braɪt] adj brillante; (room) luminoso; (day) de sol; (person: clever) listo, inteligente; (: lively) alegre; (colour) vivo; (future) prometedor(a)

**brilliant** ['brɪljənt] adj brillante; (clever) genial

**brim** [brɪm] n borde m; (of hat) ala

**brine** [braɪn] n (Culin) salmuera

**bring** [brɪŋ] (pt, pp **brought**) vt (thing) traer; (person) conducir; **bring about** vt ocasionar, producir; **bring back** vt volver a traer; (return) devolver; **bring down** vt (government, plane) derribar; (price) rebajar; **bring in** vt (harvest) recoger; (person) hacer entrar or pasar; (object) traer; (Pol: bill, law) presentar; (produce: income) producir, rendir; **bring on** vt (illness, attack) producir, causar; (player, substitute) sacar (de la reserva), hacer salir; **bring out** vt (object) sacar; (book) publicar; **bring round** vt (unconscious person) hacer volver en sí; (convince) convencer; **bring up** vt (person) educar, criar; (*question*) sacar a colación; (*food: vomit*) devolver, vomitar

**brink** [brɪŋk] *n* borde *m*

**brisk** [brɪsk] *adj* (*walk*) enérgico, vigoroso; (*speedy*) rápido; (*wind*) fresco; (*trade*) activo; (*abrupt*) brusco

**bristle** [ˈbrɪsl] *n* cerda ▷ *vi* (*fur*) erizarse; **to ~ in anger** temblar de rabia

**Brit** [brɪt] *n abbr* (*inf*: = *British person*) británico/a

**Britain** [ˈbrɪtən] *n* (*also*: **Great ~**) Gran Bretaña

**British** [ˈbrɪtɪʃ] *adj* británico; **the British** *npl* los británicos; **the British Isles** *npl* las Islas Británicas

**Briton** [ˈbrɪtən] *n* británico/a

**brittle** [ˈbrɪtl] *adj* quebradizo, frágil

**broad** [brɔːd] *adj* ancho; (*range*) amplio; (*accent*) cerrado; **in ~ daylight** en pleno día; **broadband** *n* banda ancha; **broad bean** *n* haba; **broadcast** (*pt, pp* **broadcast**) *n* emisión *f* ▷ *vt* (*Radio*) emitir; (*TV*) transmitir ▷ *vi* emitir; transmitir; **broaden** *vt* ampliar ▷ *vi* ensancharse; **to broaden one's mind** hacer más tolerante a algn; **broadly** *adv* en general; **broad-minded** *adj* tolerante, liberal

**broccoli** [ˈbrɔkəlɪ] *n* brécol *m*

**brochure** [ˈbrəʊʃjuəʳ] *n* folleto

**broil** [brɔɪl] *vt* (*US*) asar a la parrilla

**broiler** [ˈbrɔɪləʳ] *n* (*grill*) parrilla

**broke** [brəʊk] *pt of* **break** ▷ *adj* (*inf*) pelado, sin blanca

**broken** [ˈbrəʊkən] *pp of* **break** ▷ *adj* roto; **~ leg** pierna rota; **in ~ English** en un inglés chapurreado

**broken-down** [ˈbrəʊkn'daun] *adj* (*car*) averiado; (*machine*) estropeado

**broker** [ˈbrəʊkəʳ] *n* corredor(a) *m/f* de bolsa

**bronchitis** [brɔŋˈkaɪtɪs] *n* bronquitis *f*

**bronze** [brɔnz] *n* bronce *m*

**brooch** [brəʊtʃ] *n* broche *m*

**brood** [bruːd] *n* camada, cría ▷ *vi* (*hen*) empollar; **to ~ over** dar vueltas a

**broom** [brum] *n* escoba; (*Bot*) retama

**Bros.** *abbr* (*Comm*: = *Brothers*) Hnos

**broth** [brɔθ] *n* caldo

**brothel** [ˈbrɔθl] *n* burdel *m*

**brother** [ˈbrʌðəʳ] *n* hermano; **brother-in-law** *n* cuñado

**brought** [brɔːt] *pt, pp of* **bring**

**brow** [brau] *n* (*forehead*) frente *f*; (*eyebrow*) ceja; (*of hill*) cumbre *f*

**brown** [braun] *adj* marrón; (*hair*) castaño; (*tanned*) moreno ▷ *n* (*colour*) marrón *m* ▷ *vt* (*Culin*) dorar; **brown bread** *n* pan *m* integral

**Brownie** [ˈbraunɪ] *n* niña exploradora

**brown rice** *n* arroz *m* integral

**brown sugar** *n* azúcar *m* moreno

**browse** [brauz] *vi* (*animal*) pacer; (*among books*) hojear libros; **to ~ through a book** hojear un libro; **browser** *n* (*Comput*) navegador *m*

**bruise** [bruːz] *n* (*on person*) cardenal *m* ▷ *vt* magullar

**brunette** [bruːˈnɛt] *n* morena

**brush** [brʌʃ] *n* cepillo; (*for painting, shaving etc*) brocha; (*artist's*) pincel *m* ▷ *vt* (*sweep*) barrer; (*groom*) cepillar; **to ~ past, ~ against** rozar al pasar

**Brussels** [ˈbrʌslz] *n* Bruselas

**Brussels sprout** *n* col *f* de Bruselas

**brutal** [ˈbruːtl] *adj* brutal

**BSc** *abbr* (= *Bachelor of Science*) licenciado en Ciencias

**BSE** *n abbr* (= *bovine spongiform encephalopathy*) encefalopatía espongiforme bovina

**bubble** [ˈbʌbl] *n* burbuja ▷ *vi* burbujear, borbotar; **bubble bath** *n* espuma para el baño; **bubble gum** *n* chicle *m* (de globo); **bubblejet printer** [ˈbʌbldʒɛt-] *n* impresora de inyección por burbujas

**buck** [bʌk] *n* (*rabbit*) macho; (*deer*) gamo; (*us inf*) dólar *m* ▷ *vi* corcovear; **to pass the ~ (to sb)** echar (a algn) el muerto

**bucket** [ˈbʌkɪt] *n* cubo, balde *m* (*esp LAM*); **bucket list** *n* lista de cosas que hacer antes de morir

**buckle** [ˈbʌkl] *n* hebilla ▷ *vt* abrochar con hebilla ▷ *vi* combarse

**bud** [bʌd] *n* (*of plant*) brote *m*, yema; (*of flower*) capullo ▷ *vi* brotar, echar brotes

**Buddhism** [ˈbudɪzm] *n* Budismo

**Buddhist** [ˈbudɪst] *adj, n* budista *mf*

**buddy** [ˈbʌdɪ] *n* (*us*) compañero, compinche *m*

**budge** [bʌdʒ] *vt* mover; (*fig*) hacer ceder ▷ *vi* moverse

**budgerigar** [ˈbʌdʒərɪgɑːʳ] *n* periquito

**budget** [ˈbʌdʒɪt] *n* presupuesto ▷ *vi*: **to ~ for sth** presupuestar algo

**budgie** [ˈbʌdʒɪ] *n* = **budgerigar**

**buff** [bʌf] *adj* (*colour*) color de ante ▷ *n* (*enthusiast*) entusiasta *mf*

**buffalo** [ˈbʌfələu] (*pl* **buffalo** *or* **buffaloes**) *n* (*BRIT*) búfalo; (*US*: *bison*) bisonte *m*

**buffer** [ˈbʌfəʳ] *n* (*Rail*) tope *m*; (*Comput*) memoria intermedia, buffer *m*

**buffet** [ˈbufeɪ] *n* (*BRIT*: *bar*) bar *m*, cafetería; (*food*) buffet *m*; **buffet car** *n* (*BRIT Rail*) coche-restaurante *m*

**bug** [bʌg] *n* (*insect*) bicho, sabandija; (*germ*) microbio, bacilo; (*spy device*) micrófono oculto; (*Comput*) error *m* ▷ *vt* (*annoy*) fastidiar; (*room*) poner un micrófono oculto en

**build** [bɪld] n (of person) tipo ▷ vt (pt, pp
**built**) construir, edificar; **build up** vt
(morale, forces, production) acrecentar;
(stocks) acumular; **builder** n (contractor)
contratista mf

**building** ['bɪldɪŋ] n construcción f;
(habitation, offices) edificio; **building site** n
obra, solar m (SP); **building society** n (BRIT)
sociedad f de préstamo inmobiliario

**built** [bɪlt] pt, pp of **build**; **built-in** adj
(cupboard) empotrado; (device) interior,
incorporado; **built-up** adj (area) urbanizado

**bulb** [bʌlb] n (Bot) bulbo; (Elec) bombilla,
bombillo (LAM), foco (LAM)

**Bulgaria** [bʌl'gɛərɪə] n Bulgaria; **Bulgarian**
adj búlgaro ▷ n búlgaro/a

**bulge** [bʌldʒ] n bulto ▷ vi bombearse,
pandearse; **to ~ (with)** rebosar (de)

**bulimia** [bə'lɪmɪə] n bulimia

**bulimic** adj, n bulímico/a

**bulk** [bʌlk] n (mass) bulto, volumen m; **in ~**
(Comm) a granel; **the ~ of** la mayor parte de;
**bulky** adj voluminoso, abultado

**bull** [bul] n toro

**bulldozer** ['buldəuzər] n buldozer m

**bullet** ['bulɪt] n bala; **~ wound** balazo

**bulletin** ['bulɪtɪn] n comunicado, parte m;
(journal) boletín m; **bulletin board** n (US)
tablón m de anuncios; (Comput) tablero de
noticias

**bullfight** ['bulfaɪt] n corrida de toros;
**bullfighter** n torero; **bullfighting** n los
toros mpl, el toreo

**bully** ['bulɪ] n valentón m, matón m ▷ vt
intimidar, tiranizar; **bullying** n (at school)
acoso escolar

**bum** [bʌm] n (inf: BRIT: backside) culo; (esp
US: tramp) vagabundo

**bumblebee** ['bʌmblbiː] n abejorro

**bump** [bʌmp] n (blow) tope m, choque m;
(jolt) sacudida; (on road etc) bache m; (on
head) chichón m ▷ vt (strike) chocar contra;
**bump into** vt fus chocar contra, tropezar
con; (person) topar con; **bumper** n (BRIT)
parachoques m inv ▷ adj: **bumper crop/
harvest** cosecha abundante; **bumpy** adj
(road) lleno de baches

**bun** [bʌn] n (BRIT: cake) pastel m; (US: bread)
bollo; (of hair) moño

**bunch** [bʌntʃ] n (of flowers) ramo; (of keys)
manojo; (of bananas) piña; (of people)
grupo; (pej) pandilla; **bunches** npl (in hair)
coletas fpl

**bundle** ['bʌndl] n bulto, fardo; (of sticks) haz
m; (of papers) legajo ▷ vt (also: **~ up**) atar,
envolver; **to ~ sth/sb into** meter algo/a
algn precipitadamente en

**bungalow** ['bʌngələu] n bungalow m,
chalé m

**bungee jumping** ['bʌndʒiː'dʒʌmpɪŋ] n
puenting m, banyi m

**bunion** ['bʌnjən] n juanete m

**bunk** [bʌŋk] n litera; **~ beds** npl literas fpl

**bunker** ['bʌŋkər] n (coal store) carbonera;
(Mil) refugio; (Golf) bunker m

**bunny** ['bʌnɪ] n (also: **~ rabbit**) conejito

**buoy** [bɔɪ] n boya; **buoyant** adj (ship) capaz
de flotar; (carefree) boyante, optimista;
(Comm: market, prices etc) sostenido;
(: economy) boyante

**burden** ['bəːdn] n carga ▷ vt cargar

**bureau** (pl **bureaux**) ['bjuərəu, -z] n (BRIT:
writing desk) escritorio, buró m; (US: chest of
drawers) cómoda; (office) oficina, agencia

**bureaucracy** [bjuə'rɔkrəsɪ] n burocracia

**bureaucrat** ['bjuərəkræt] n burócrata mf

**bureau de change** [-də'ʃɑ̃ʒ] (pl **bureaux
de change**) n caja f de cambio

**bureaux** ['bjuərəuz] npl of **bureau**

**burger** ['bəːgər] n hamburguesa

**burglar** ['bəːglər] n ladrón/ona m/f; **burglar
alarm** n alarma f contra robo; **burglary** n
robo con allanamiento or fractura, robo de
una casa

**burial** ['bɛrɪəl] n entierro

**burn** [bəːn] (pt, pp **burned** or **burnt**) vt
quemar; (house) incendiar ▷ vi quemarse,
arder; incendiarse; (sting) escocer ▷ n (Med)
quemadura; **burn down** vt incendiar;
**burn out** vt (writer etc): **to ~ o.s. out**
agotarse; **burning** adj (building, forest)
en llamas; (hot: sand etc) abrasador(a);
(ambition) ardiente

**Burns' Night** [bəːnz-] n ver nota

- **BURNS' NIGHT**

- Cada veinticinco de enero los escoceses
- celebran la llamada Burns' Night (noche de
- Burns), en honor al poeta escocés Robert
- Burns (1759-1796). Es tradición hacer una
- cena en la que, al son de la música de
- la gaita escocesa, se sirve haggis, plato
- tradicional de asadura de cordero cocida
- en el estómago del animal, acompañado
- de nabos y puré de patatas. Durante
- la misma se recitan poemas del autor
- y varios discursos conmemorativos de
- carácter festivo.

**burnt** [bəːnt] pt, pp of **burn**

**burp** [bəːp] (inf) n eructo ▷ vi eructar

**burrow** ['bʌrəu] n madriguera ▷ vt hacer
una madriguera

**burst** [bəːst] (pt, pp **burst**) vt (balloon, pipe)
reventar; (banks etc) romper ▷ vi reventarse;
romperse; (tyre) pincharse ▷ n (explosion)
estallido; (also: **~ pipe**) reventón m; **to ~ out**

laughing soltar la carcajada; **to ~ into tears** deshacerse en lágrimas; **to be ~ing with** reventar de; **a ~ of energy** una explosión de energía; **a ~ of speed** un acelerón; **to ~ open** abrirse de golpe; **burst into** vt fus (room etc) irrumpir en

**bury** ['bɛrɪ] vt enterrar; (body) enterrar, sepultar

**bus** [bʌs] n autobús m; **bus conductor** n cobrador(a) m/f

**bush** [buʃ] n arbusto; (scrub land) monte m bajo; **to beat about the ~** andar(se) con rodeos

**business** ['bɪznɪs] n (matter, affair) asunto; (trading) comercio, negocios mpl; (firm) empresa, casa; (occupation) oficio; **to be away on ~** estar en viaje de negocios; **it's my ~ to ...** me toca or corresponde ...; **it's none of my ~** no es asunto mío; **he means ~** habla en serio; **business class** n (Aviat) clase f preferente; **businesslike** adj eficiente; **businessman** n hombre m de negocios; **business trip** n viaje m de negocios; **businesswoman** n mujer f de negocios

**busker** ['bʌskə^r] n (BRIT) músico/a ambulante

**bus: bus pass** n bonobús; **bus shelter** n parada cubierta; **bus station** n estación f or terminal f de autobuses; **bus-stop** n parada de autobús

**bust** [bʌst] n (Anat) pecho; (sculpture) busto ▷ adj (inf: broken) roto, estropeado; **to go ~** quebrar

**bustling** ['bʌslɪŋ] adj (town) animado, bullicioso

**busy** ['bɪzɪ] adj ocupado, atareado; (shop, street) concurrido, animado ▷ vt: **to ~ o.s. with** ocuparse en; **the line's ~** está comunicando; **busy signal** n (us Tel) señal f de comunicando

**○ KEYWORD**

**but** [bʌt] conj **1** pero; **he's not very bright, but he's hard-working** no es muy inteligente, pero es trabajador
**2** (in direct contradiction) sino; **he's not English but French** no es inglés sino francés; **he didn't sing but he shouted** no cantó sino que gritó
**3** (showing disagreement, surprise etc): **but that's far too expensive!** ¡pero eso es carísimo!; **but it does work!** ¡(pero) sí que funciona!
▶ prep (apart from, except) menos, salvo; **we've had nothing but trouble** no hemos tenido más que problemas; **no-one but him can do it** nadie más que él puede

hacerlo; **who but a lunatic would do such a thing?** ¡sólo un loco haría una cosa así!; **but for you/your help** si no fuera por ti/tu ayuda; **anything but that** cualquier cosa menos eso
▶ adv (just, only): **she's but a child** no es más que una niña; **had I but known** si lo hubiera sabido; **I can but try** al menos lo puedo intentar; **it's all but finished** está casi acabado

**butcher** ['butʃə^r] n carnicero/a ▷ vt hacer una carnicería con; (cattle etc for meat) matar; **~'s (shop)** n carnicería

**butler** ['bʌtlə^r] n mayordomo

**butt** [bʌt] n (cask) tonel m; (of gun) culata; (of cigarette) colilla; (BRIT fig: target) blanco ▷ vt dar cabezadas contra

**butter** ['bʌtə^r] n mantequilla ▷ vt untar con mantequilla; **buttercup** n ranúnculo

**butterfly** ['bʌtəflaɪ] n mariposa; (Swimming: also: **~ stroke**) (braza de) mariposa

**buttocks** ['bʌtəks] npl nalgas fpl

**button** ['bʌtn] n botón m ▷ vt (also: **~ up**) abotonar, abrochar ▷ vi abrocharse

**buy** [baɪ] (pt, pp **bought**) vt comprar ▷ n compra; **to ~ sb sth/sth from sb** comprarle algo a algn; **to ~ sb a drink** invitar a algn a tomar algo; **buy out** vt (partner) comprar la parte de; **buy up** vt (property) acaparar; (stock) comprar todas las existencias de; **buyer** n comprador(a) m/f; **buyer's market** mercado favorable al comprador

**buzz** [bʌz] n zumbido; (inf: phone call) llamada (telefónica) ▷ vi zumbar; **buzzer** n timbre m

**○ KEYWORD**

**by** [baɪ] prep **1** (referring to cause, agent) por; de; **abandoned by his mother** abandonado por su madre; **a painting by Picasso** un cuadro de Picasso
**2** (referring to method, manner, means): **by bus/car/train** en autobús/coche/tren; **to pay by cheque** pagar con cheque; **by moonlight/candlelight** a la luz de la luna/ una vela; **by saving hard, he ...** ahorrando, ...
**3** (via, through) por; **we came by Dover** vinimos por Dover
**4** (close to, past): **the house by the river** la casa junto al río; **she rushed by me** pasó a mi lado como una exhalación; **I go by the post office every day** paso por delante de Correos todos los días
**5** (time: not later than) para; (: during): **by daylight** de día; **by 4 o'clock** para las

cuatro; **by this time tomorrow** mañana a estas horas; **by the time I got here it was too late** cuando llegué ya era demasiado tarde

**6** (*amount*): **by the metre/kilo** por metro/kilo; **paid by the hour** pagado por hora

**7** (*in measurements, sums*): **to divide/multiply by 3** dividir/multiplicar por 3; **a room 3 metres by 4** una habitación de 3 metros por 4; **it's broader by a metre** es un metro más ancho

**8** (*according to*) según, de acuerdo con; **it's 3 o'clock by my watch** según mi reloj, son las tres; **it's all right by me** por mí, está bien

**9**: **(all) by oneself** *etc* todo solo; **he did it (all) by himself** lo hizo él solo; **he was standing (all) by himself in a corner** estaba de pie solo en un rincón

**10**: **by the way** a propósito, por cierto; **this wasn't my idea, by the way** pues, no fue idea mía

▶ *adv* **1** *see* **go, pass**

**2**: **by and by** finalmente; **they'll come back by and by** acabarán volviendo; **by and large** en líneas generales, en general

**by-election** *n* (*BRIT*) elección *f* parcial
**bypass** ['baɪpɑːs] *n* carretera de circunvalación; (*Med*) (operación *f* de) bypass *m* ▶ *vt* evitar
**byte** [baɪt] *n* (*Comput*) byte *m*, octeto

# C

**C, c** [siː] *n* (*Mus*) do *m*
**cab** [kæb] *n* taxi *m*; (*of truck*) cabina
**cabaret** ['kæbəreɪ] *n* cabaret *m*
**cabbage** ['kæbɪdʒ] *n* col *f*, berza
**cabin** ['kæbɪn] *n* cabaña; (*on ship*) camarote *m*; **cabin crew** *n* tripulación *f* de cabina
**cabinet** ['kæbɪnɪt] *n* (*Pol*) consejo de ministros; (*furniture*) armario; (*also:* **display ~**) vitrina; **cabinet minister** *n* ministro/a (del gabinete)
**cable** ['keɪbl] *n* cable *m* ▶ *vt* cablegrafiar; **cable car** *n* teleférico; **cable television** *n* televisión *f* por cable
**cactus** (*pl* **cacti**) ['kæktəs, -taɪ] *n* cacto
**café** ['kæfeɪ] *n* café *m*
**cafeteria** [kæfɪ'tɪərɪə] *n* cafetería (*con autoservicio para comer*)
**caffeine** ['kæfiːn] *n* cafeína
**cage** [keɪdʒ] *n* jaula
**cagoule** [kə'guːl] *n* chubasquero
**cake** [keɪk] *n* (*large*) tarta; (*small*) pastel *m*; (*of soap*) pastilla
**calcium** ['kælsɪəm] *n* calcio
**calculate** ['kælkjuleɪt] *vt* calcular; **calculation** *n* cálculo, cómputo; **calculator** *n* calculadora
**calendar** ['kæləndə^r] *n* calendario
**calf** [kɑːf] (*pl* **calves**) *n* (*of cow*) ternero, becerro; (*of other animals*) cría; (*also:* **~skin**) piel *f* de becerro; (*Anat*) pantorrilla
**calibre**, (*US*) **caliber** ['kælɪbə^r] *n* calibre *m*
**call** [kɔːl] *vt* llamar; (*meeting, strike*) convocar ▶ *vi* (*shout*) llamar; (*telephone*) llamar (por teléfono); (*visit: also:* **~ in, ~ round**) hacer una visita ▶ *n* llamada; (*of bird*) canto; **to be ~ed** llamarse; **on ~** (*nurse, doctor etc*) de guardia; **call back** *vi* (*return*) volver; (*Tel*) volver a llamar; **call for** *vt fus* (*demand*) pedir, exigir; (*fetch*) pasar a recoger; **call in** *vt* (*doctor, expert,*

*police*) llamar; **call off** vt (*cancel: meeting, race*) cancelar; (: *deal*) anular; (: *strike*) desconvocar; **call on** vt fus (*visit*) ir a ver; (*turn to*) acudir a; **call out** vi gritar; **call up** vt (*Mil*) llamar a filas; **callbox** n (*BRIT*) cabina telefónica; **call centre** n (*BRIT*) centro de atención al cliente; **caller** n visita f; (*Tel*) usuario/a

**callous** ['kæləs] adj insensible, cruel

**calm** [kɑːm] adj tranquilo; (*sea*) tranquilo, en calma ▷ n calma, tranquilidad f ▷ vt calmar, tranquilizar; **calm down** vi calmarse, tranquilizarse ▷ vt calmar, tranquilizar; **calmly** adv tranquilamente, con calma

**Calor gas®** ['kælə<sup>r</sup>-] n butano

**calorie** ['kælərɪ] n caloría

**calves** [kɑːvz] npl of **calf**

**camcorder** ['kæmkɔːdə<sup>r</sup>] n videocámara

**came** [keɪm] pt of **come**

**camel** ['kæməl] n camello

**camera** ['kæmərə] n cámara or máquina fotográfica; (*Cine, TV*) cámara; **in ~** (*Law*) a puerta cerrada; **cameraman** n cámara m; **camera phone** n teléfono m con cámara

**camouflage** ['kæməflɑːʒ] n camuflaje m ▷ vt camuflar

**camp** [kæmp] n campamento, camping m; (*Mil*) campamento; (*for prisoners*) campo; (*fig: faction*) bando ▷ vi acampar ▷ adj afectado, afeminado; **to go ~ing** ir de or hacer camping

**campaign** [kæm'peɪn] n (*Mil, Pol etc*) campaña ▷ vi: **to ~ (for/against)** hacer campaña (a favor de/en contra de); **campaigner** n: **campaigner for** defensor(a) m/f de

**camp: campbed** n (*BRIT*) cama plegable; **camper** n campista mf; (*vehicle*) caravana; **campground** n (*US*) camping m, campamento; **camping** n camping m; **campsite** n camping m

**campus** ['kæmpəs] n campus m

**can¹** [kæn] n (*of oil, water*) bidón m; (*tin*) lata, bote m ▷ vt enlatar

**KEYWORD**

**can²** [kæn] (*negative* **cannot, can't**, *conditional, pt* **could**) *aux vb* **1** (*be able to*) poder; **you can do it if you try** puedes hacerlo si lo intentas; **I can't see you** no te veo

**2** (*know how to*) saber; **I can swim/play tennis/drive** sé nadar/jugar al tenis/conducir; **can you speak French?** ¿hablas or sabes hablar francés?

**3** (*may*) poder; **can I use your phone?** ¿me dejas or puedo usar tu teléfono?

**4** (*expressing disbelief, puzzlement etc*): **it can't be true!** ¡no puede ser (verdad)!; **what CAN he want?** ¿qué querrá?

**5** (*expressing possibility, suggestion etc*): **he could be in the library** podría estar en la biblioteca; **she could have been delayed** puede que se haya retrasado

**Canada** ['kænədə] n Canadá m; **Canadian** [kə'neɪdɪən] adj, n canadiense mf

**canal** [kə'næl] n canal m

**canary** [kə'nɛərɪ] n canario

**Canary Islands** npl las (Islas) Canarias

**cancel** ['kænsəl] vt cancelar; (*train*) suprimir; (*cross out*) tachar; **cancellation** [kænsə'leɪʃən] n cancelación f; supresión f

**cancer** ['kænsə<sup>r</sup>] n cáncer m; **C~** (*Astro*) Cáncer m

**candidate** ['kændɪdeɪt] n candidato/a

**candle** ['kændl] n vela; (*in church*) cirio; **candlestick** n (*single*) candelero; (: *low*) palmatoria; (*bigger, ornate*) candelabro

**candy** ['kændɪ] n azúcar m cande; (*US*) caramelo; **candy bar** n (*US*) barrita (*dulce*); **candyfloss** n (*BRIT*) algodón m (azucarado)

**cane** [keɪn] n (*Bot*) caña; (*stick*) vara, palmeta ▷ vt (*BRIT Scol*) castigar (con palmeta)

**canister** ['kænɪstə<sup>r</sup>] n bote m, lata

**cannabis** ['kænəbɪs] n canabis m

**canned** [kænd] adj en lata, de lata

**cannon** ['kænən] (*pl* **cannon** or **cannons**) n cañón m

**cannot** ['kænɔt] = **can not**

**canoe** [kə'nuː] n canoa; (*Sport*) piragua; **canoeing** n piragüismo

**canon** ['kænən] n (*clergyman*) canónigo; (*standard*) canon m

**can opener** n abrelatas m inv

**can't** [kænt] = **can not**

**canteen** [kæn'tiːn] n (*eating place*) comedor m; (*BRIT: of cutlery*) juego

**canter** ['kæntə<sup>r</sup>] vi ir a medio galope

**canvas** ['kænvəs] n (*material*) lona; (*painting*) lienzo; (*Naut*) velamen m

**canvass** ['kænvəs] vi (*Pol*): **to ~ for** solicitar votos por ▷ vt (*Comm*) sondear

**canyon** ['kænjən] n cañón m

**cap** [kæp] n (*hat*) gorra; (*of pen*) capuchón m; (*of bottle*) tapón m, tapa; (*BRIT: contraceptive*) diafragma m ▷ vt (*outdo*) superar; (*limit*) recortar

**capability** [keɪpə'bɪlɪtɪ] n capacidad f

**capable** ['keɪpəbl] adj capaz

**capacity** [kə'pæsɪtɪ] n capacidad f; (*position*) calidad f

**cape** [keɪp] n capa; (*Geo*) cabo

**caper** ['keɪpə<sup>r</sup>] n (*Culin: also:* **~s**) alcaparra; (*prank*) travesura

**capital** ['kæpɪtl] n (also: ~ **city**) capital f; (money) capital m; (also: ~ **letter**) mayúscula; **capitalism** n capitalismo; **capitalist** adj, n capitalista mf; **capital punishment** n pena de muerte
**Capitol** ['kæpɪtl] n: **the ~** el Capitolio

* **CAPITOL**
*
* El Capitolio (Capitol) es el edificio en el que
* se reúne el Congreso de los Estados Unidos
* (Congress), situado en la ciudad de
* Washington. Por extensión, también se
* suele llamar así al edificio en el que tienen
* lugar las sesiones parlamentarias de la
* cámara de representantes de muchos de
* los estados.

**Capricorn** ['kæprɪkɔːn] n Capricornio
**capsize** [kæp'saɪz] vt volcar, hacer zozobrar ▷ vi volcarse, zozobrar
**capsule** ['kæpsjuːl] n cápsula
**captain** ['kæptɪn] n capitán m
**caption** ['kæpʃən] n (heading) título; (to picture) leyenda
**captivity** [kæp'tɪvɪtɪ] n cautiverio
**capture** ['kæptʃəʳ] vt capturar; (place) tomar; (attention) captar, llamar ▷ n captura; toma; (Comput: also: **data ~**) formulación f de datos
**car** [kɑːʳ] n coche m, carro (LAM), automóvil m; (US Rail) vagón m
**carafe** [kə'ræf] n jarra
**caramel** ['kærəməl] n caramelo
**carat** ['kærət] n quilate m
**caravan** ['kærəvæn] n (BRIT) caravana, rulot m; (of camels) caravana; **caravan site** n (BRIT) camping m para caravanas
**carbohydrates** [kɑːbəʊ'haɪdreɪts] npl (foods) hidratos mpl de carbono
**carbon** ['kɑːbən] n carbono; **carbon dioxide** n dióxido de carbono, anhídrido carbónico; **carbon footprint** n huella de carbono; **carbon monoxide** n monóxido de carbono; **carbon-neutral** n neutro en carbono, sin emisiones netas de $CO_2$
**car boot sale** n mercadillo (de objetos usados expuestos en el maletero del coche)
**carburettor**, (US) **carburetor** [kɑːbju'retəʳ] n carburador m
**card** [kɑːd] n (thin cardboard) cartulina; (playing card) carta, naipe m; (visiting card, greetings card etc) tarjeta; (index card) ficha; **cardboard** n cartón m, cartulina; **card game** n juego de naipes or cartas
**cardigan** ['kɑːdɪgən] n rebeca
**cardinal** ['kɑːdɪnl] adj cardinal; (importance, principal) esencial ▷ n cardenal m

**cardphone** ['kɑːdfəʊn] n cabina que funciona con tarjetas telefónicas
**care** [kɛəʳ] n cuidado; (worry) preocupación f; (charge) cargo, custodia ▷ vi: **to ~ about** preocuparse por; **~ of** (c/o) en casa de, al cuidado de; **in sb's ~** a cargo de algn; **to take ~ to** cuidarse de, tener cuidado de; **to take ~ of** vt cuidar; **I don't ~** no me importa; **I couldn't ~ less** me trae sin cuidado; **care for** vt fus cuidar; (like) querer
**career** [kə'rɪəʳ] n profesión f ▷ vi (also: **~ along**) correr a toda velocidad
**care: carefree** adj despreocupado; **careful** adj cuidadoso; (cautious) cauteloso; **(be) careful!** ¡(ten) cuidado!; **carefully** adv con cuidado, cuidadosamente; **caregiver** (US) n (professional) enfermero/a; (unpaid) persona que cuida a un pariente o vecino; **careless** adj descuidado; (heedless) poco atento; **carelessness** n descuido, falta de atención; **carer** n (professional) enfermero/a; (unpaid) persona que cuida a un pariente o vecino; **caretaker** n portero/a, conserje mf
**car-ferry** ['kɑːfɛrɪ] n transbordador m para coches
**cargo** ['kɑːgəʊ] (pl **cargoes**) n cargamento, carga
**car hire** n alquiler m de coches
**Caribbean** [kærɪ'biːən] adj caribe, caribeño; **the ~ (Sea)** el (Mar) Caribe
**caring** ['kɛərɪŋ] adj humanitario
**carnation** [kɑː'neɪʃən] n clavel m
**carnival** ['kɑːnɪvəl] n carnaval m; (US) parque m de atracciones
**carol** ['kærəl] n: (**Christmas**) **~** villancico
**carousel** [kærə'sɛl] n (US) tiovivo, caballitos mpl
**car park** n (BRIT) aparcamiento, parking m
**carpenter** ['kɑːpɪntəʳ] n carpintero/a
**carpet** ['kɑːpɪt] n alfombra ▷ vt alfombrar; **fitted ~** moqueta
**car rental** n (US) alquiler m de coches
**carriage** ['kærɪdʒ] n (BRIT Rail) vagón m; (horse-drawn) coche m; (for goods) transporte m; **~ paid** porte pagado; **carriageway** n (BRIT: part of road) calzada
**carrier** ['kærɪəʳ] n transportista mf; (company) empresa de transportes; (Med) portador(a) m/f; **carrier bag** n (BRIT) bolsa de papel o plástico
**carrot** ['kærət] n zanahoria
**carry** ['kærɪ] vt (person) llevar; (transport) transportar; (involve: responsibilities etc) entrañar ▷ vi (sound) oírse; **to get carried away** (fig) entusiasmarse; **carry on** vi (continue) seguir (adelante), continuar ▷ vt seguir, continuar; **carry out** vt (orders) cumplir; (investigation) llevar a cabo, realizar

**cart** [kɑːt] n carro, carreta ▷ vt (inf: transport) cargar con

**carton** ['kɑːtən] n caja (de cartón); (of milk etc) bote m

**cartoon** [kɑː'tuːn] n (Press) chiste m; (comic strip) tira cómica; (film) dibujos mpl animados

**cartridge** ['kɑːtrɪdʒ] n cartucho

**carve** [kɑːv] vt (meat) trinchar; (wood) tallar; (stone) cincelar, esculpir; (on tree) grabar; **carving** n (in wood etc) escultura; (design) talla

**car wash** n túnel m de lavado

**case** [keɪs] n (container) caja; (Med) caso; (for jewels etc) estuche m; (Law) causa, proceso; (BRIT: also: **suit~**) maleta; **in ~ of** en caso de; **in any ~** en todo caso; **just in ~** por si acaso

**cash** [kæʃ] n (dinero en) efectivo; (inf: money) dinero ▷ vt cobrar, hacer efectivo; **to pay (in) ~** pagar al contado; **~ on delivery (COD)** entrega contra reembolso; **cashback** n (discount) devolución f; (at supermarket etc) retirada de dinero en efectivo de un establecimiento donde se ha pagado con tarjeta; también dinero retirado; **cash card** n tarjeta f de(l) cajero (automático); **cash desk** n (BRIT) caja; **cash dispenser** n cajero automático

**cashew** [kæ'ʃuː] n (also: **~ nut**) anacardo

**cashier** [kæ'ʃɪəʳ] n cajero/a

**cashmere** ['kæʃmɪəʳ] n cachemira

**cash point** n cajero automático

**cash register** n caja

**casino** [kə'siːnəu] n casino

**casket** ['kɑːskɪt] n cofre m, estuche m; (US: coffin) ataúd m

**casserole** ['kæsərəul] n (food, pot) cazuela

**cassette** [kæ'sɛt] n cas(s)et(t)e m or f; **cassette player, cassette recorder** n cas(s)et(t)e m

**cast** [kɑːst] (pt, pp **cast**) vt (throw) echar, arrojar, lanzar; (Theat): **to ~ sb as Othello** dar a algn el papel de Otelo ▷ n (Theat) reparto; (also: **plaster ~**) vaciado; **to ~ one's vote** votar; **cast off** vi (Naut) soltar amarras; (Knitting) cerrar los puntos

**castanets** [kæstə'nɛts] npl castañuelas fpl

**caster sugar** ['kɑːstəʳ-] n (BRIT) azúcar m extrafino

**Castile** [kæs'tiːl] n Castilla; **Castilian** adj, n castellano/a

**cast-iron** ['kɑːstaɪən] adj (lit) (hecho) de hierro fundido or colado; (fig: alibi) irrebatible; (will) férreo

**castle** ['kɑːsl] n castillo; (Chess) torre f

**casual** ['kæʒjul] adj fortuito; (irregular: work etc) eventual, temporero; (unconcerned) despreocupado; (clothes) de sport

  Be careful not to translate casual by the Spanish word casual.

**casualty** ['kæʒjultɪ] n víctima, herido; (dead) muerto; **casualty ward** n urgencias fpl

**cat** [kæt] n gato

**Catalan** ['kætəlæn] adj, n catalán/ana m/f

**catalogue**, (US) **catalog** ['kætəlɔg] n catálogo ▷ vt catalogar

**Catalonia** [kætə'ləuniə] n Cataluña

**catalytic converter** [kætə'lɪtɪkkən'vəːtəʳ] n catalizador m

**cataract** ['kætərækt] n (Med) cataratas fpl

**catarrh** [kə'tɑːʳ] n catarro

**catastrophe** [kə'tæstrəfɪ] n catástrofe f

**catch** [kætʃ] (pt, pp **caught**) vt coger (SP), agarrar (LAM); (arrest) atrapar; (grasp) asir; (breath) recobrar; (person: by surprise) pillar; (attract: attention) captar; (Med) pillar, coger; (also: **~ up**) alcanzar ▷ vi (fire) encenderse; (in branches etc) engancharse ▷ n (fish etc) captura; (act of catching) cogida; (of lock) pestillo, cerradura; **to ~ fire** prenderse; (house) incendiarse; **to ~ sight of** divisar; **catch up** vi (fig) ponerse al día; **catching** adj (Med) contagioso

**category** ['kætɪgərɪ] n categoría

**cater** ['keɪtəʳ] vi: **to ~ for** (BRIT) abastecer a; (needs) atender a; (consumers) proveer a

**caterpillar** ['kætəpɪləʳ] n oruga

**cathedral** [kə'θiːdrəl] n catedral f

**cattle** ['kætl] npl ganado sg

**catwalk** ['kætwɔːk] n pasarela

**caught** [kɔːt] pt, pp of **catch**

**cauliflower** ['kɔlɪflauəʳ] n coliflor f

**cause** [kɔːz] n causa; (reason) motivo, razón f ▷ vt causar

**caution** ['kɔːʃən] n cautela, prudencia; (warning) advertencia, amonestación f ▷ vt amonestar; **cautious** adj cauteloso, prudente, precavido

**cave** [keɪv] n cueva, caverna; **cave in** vi (roof etc) derrumbarse, hundirse

**caviar(e)** ['kævɪɑːʳ] n caviar m

**cavity** ['kævɪtɪ] n hueco, cavidad f

**cc** abbr (= cubic centimetres) cc, cm3; (on letter etc) = **carbon copy**

**CCTV** n abbr = **closed-circuit television**

**CD** n abbr (= compact disc) CD m; **CD player** n reproductor m de CD; **CD-ROM** n abbr (= compact disc read-only memory) CD-ROM m; **CD writer** n grabadora f de CDs

**cease** [siːs] vt cesar; **ceasefire** n alto m el fuego

**cedar** ['siːdəʳ] n cedro

**ceilidh** ['keɪlɪ] n baile con música y danzas tradicionales escocesas o irlandesas

**ceiling** ['siːlɪŋ] n techo; (fig) límite m

**celebrate** ['sɛlɪbreɪt] vt celebrar ▷ vi: **let's ~!** ¡vamos a celebrarlo!; **celebration** n celebración f

**celebrity** [sɪ'lɛbrɪtɪ] n (*person*) famoso/a

**celery** ['sɛlərɪ] n apio

**cell** [sɛl] n celda; (*Biol*) célula; (*Elec*) elemento

**cellar** ['sɛlə'] n sótano; (*for wine*) bodega

**cello** ['tʃɛləʊ] n violoncelo

**Cellophane®** ['sɛləfeɪn] n celofán m

**cellphone** ['sɛlfəʊn] n móvil

**Celsius** ['sɛlsɪəs] adj centígrado

**Celtic** ['kɛltɪk, 'sɛltɪk] adj celta

**cement** [sə'mɛnt] n cemento

**cemetery** ['sɛmɪtrɪ] n cementerio

**censor** ['sɛnsə'] n censor(a) m/f ▷ vt (*cut*) censurar; **censorship** n censura

**census** ['sɛnsəs] n censo

**cent** [sɛnt] n (*US: unit of dollar*) centavo; (*unit of euro*) céntimo; *see also* **per**

**centenary** [sɛn'tiːnərɪ], (*US*) **centennial** [sɛn'tɛnɪəl] n centenario

**center** ['sɛntə'] n (*US*) = **centre**

**centi...: centigrade** ['sɛntɪɡreɪd] adj centígrado; **centimetre**, (*US*) **centimeter** ['sɛntɪmiːtə'] n centímetro; **centipede** ['sɛntɪpiːd] n ciempiés m inv

**central** ['sɛntrəl] adj central; (*house etc*) céntrico; **Central America** n Centroamérica; **central heating** n calefacción f central; **central reservation** n (*BRIT Aut*) mediana

**centre**, (*US*) **center** ['sɛntə'] n centro ▷ vt centrar; **centre-forward** n (*Sport*) delantero centro; **centre-half** n (*Sport*) medio centro

**century** ['sɛntjurɪ] n siglo; **20th ~** siglo veinte

**CEO** n abbr = **chief executive officer**

**ceramic** [sɪ'ræmɪk] adj de cerámica

**cereal** ['siːrɪəl] n cereal m

**ceremony** ['sɛrɪmənɪ] n ceremonia; **to stand on ~** hacer ceremonias, andarse con cumplidos

**certain** ['səːtən] adj seguro; (*particular*) cierto; **for ~** a ciencia cierta; **a ~ Mr Smith** un tal Sr. Smith; **certainly** adv desde luego, por supuesto; **certainty** n certeza, certidumbre f, seguridad f

**certificate** [sə'tɪfɪkɪt] n certificado

**certify** ['səːtɪfaɪ] vt certificar; (*declare insane*) declarar loco

**cf.** abbr (= *compare*) cfr

**CFC** n abbr (= *chlorofluorocarbon*) CFC m

**chain** [tʃeɪn] n cadena; (*of mountains*) cordillera; (*of events*) sucesión f ▷ vt (*also: ~ up*) encadenar; **chain-smoke** vi fumar un cigarrillo tras otro

**chair** [tʃɛə'] n silla; (*armchair*) sillón m; (*of university*) cátedra ▷ vt (*meeting*) presidir; **chairlift** n telesilla m; **chairman** n presidente m; **chairperson** n presidente/a m/f; **chairwoman** n presidenta

**chalet** ['ʃæleɪ] n chalet m (de madera)

**chalk** [tʃɔːk] n (*Geo*) creta; (*for writing*) tiza, gis m (*LAM*); **chalkboard** (*US*) n pizarrón (*LAM*), pizarra (*SP*)

**challenge** ['tʃælɪndʒ] n desafío, reto ▷ vt desafiar, retar; (*statement, right*) poner en duda; **to ~ sb to do sth** retar a algn a que haga algo; **challenging** adj que supone un reto; (*tone*) de desafío

**chamber** ['tʃeɪmbə'] n cámara, sala; **chambermaid** n camarera

**champagne** [ʃæm'peɪn] n champaña m, champán m

**champion** ['tʃæmpɪən] n campeón/ona m/f; (*of cause*) defensor(a) m/f; **championship** n campeonato

**chance** [tʃɑːns] n (*opportunity*) ocasión f, oportunidad f; (*likelihood*) posibilidad f; (*risk*) riesgo ▷ vt arriesgar, probar ▷ adj fortuito, casual; **to ~ it** arriesgarse, intentarlo; **to take a ~** arriesgarse; **by ~** por casualidad

**chancellor** ['tʃɑːnsələ'] n canciller m; **C~ of the Exchequer** (*BRIT*) Ministro de Economía y Hacienda; *see also* **Downing Street**

**chandelier** [ʃændə'lɪə'] n araña (de luces)

**change** [tʃeɪndʒ] vt cambiar; (*clothes, house*) cambiarse de, mudarse de; (*transform*) transformar ▷ vi cambiar(se); (*change trains*) hacer transbordo; (*be transformed*) **to ~ into** transformarse en ▷ n cambio; (*alteration*) modificación f, transformación f; (*coins*) suelto; (*money returned*) vuelta, vuelto (*LAM*); **to ~ one's mind** cambiar de opinión or idea; **to ~ gear** (*Aut*) cambiar de marcha; **for a ~** para variar; **change over** vi (*from sth to sth*) cambiar; (*players etc*) cambiar(se) ▷ vt cambiar; **changeable** adj (*weather*) cambiable; **change machine** n máquina de cambio; **changing room** n (*BRIT*) vestuario

**channel** ['tʃænl] n (*TV*) canal m; (*of river*) cauce m; (*fig: medium*) medio ▷ vt (*river etc*) encauzar; **the (English) C~** el Canal (de la Mancha); **the C~ Islands** las Islas Anglonormandas; **the C~ Tunnel** el túnel del Canal de la Mancha, el Eurotúnel

**chant** [tʃɑːnt] n (*also Rel*) canto; (*of crowd*) gritos mpl ▷ vt (*slogan, word*) repetir a gritos

**chaos** ['keɪɒs] n caos m

**chaotic** [keɪ'ɒtɪk] adj caótico

**chap** [tʃæp] n (*BRIT inf: man*) tío, tipo

**chapel** ['tʃæpəl] n capilla

**chapped** [tʃæpt] adj agrietado

**chapter** ['tʃæptə'] n capítulo

**character** ['kærɪktə'] n carácter m, naturaleza, índole f; (*in novel, film*) personaje m; (*individuality*) carácter m; **characteristic** [kærɪktə'rɪstɪk] adj característico ▷ n característica; **characterize** vt caracterizar

**charcoal** ['tʃɑːkəʊl] n carbón m vegetal; (Art) carboncillo

**charge** [tʃɑːdʒ] n (Law) cargo, acusación f; (cost) precio, coste m; (responsibility) cargo ▷ vt (Law): **to ~ (with)** acusar (de); (gun, battery) cargar; (Mil: enemy) cargar; (price) pedir; (customer) cobrar ▷ vi precipitarse; **charge card** n tarjeta de cuenta; **charger** n (also: **battery charger**) cargador m (de baterías)

**charismatic** [kærɪzˈmætɪk] adj carismático

**charity** ['tʃærɪtɪ] n caridad f; (organization) organización f benéfica; (money, gifts) limosnas fpl; **charity shop** n (BRIT) tienda de artículos de segunda mano que dedica su recaudación a causas benéficas

**charm** [tʃɑːm] n encanto, atractivo; (spell) hechizo; (object) amuleto; (on bracelet) dije m ▷ vt encantar; **charming** adj encantador(a)

**chart** [tʃɑːt] n (table) cuadro; (graph) gráfica; (map) carta de navegación ▷ vt (course) trazar; (progress) seguir; (sales) hacer una gráfica de; **to be in the ~s** (record, pop group) estar en la lista de éxitos

**charter** ['tʃɑːtər] vt (bus) alquilar; (plane, ship) fletar ▷ n (document) carta; **chartered accountant** n (BRIT) contable mf diplomado/a; **charter flight** n vuelo chárter

**chase** [tʃeɪs] vt (pursue) perseguir; (hunt) cazar ▷ n persecución f

**chat** [tʃæt] vi (also: **have a ~**) charlar; (Internet) chatear ▷ n charla; **chat up** vt (inf: girl) ligar con, enrollarse con; **chat room** n (Internet) chat m, canal m de charla; **chat show** n (BRIT) programa m de entrevistas

**chatter** ['tʃætər] vi (person) charlar; (teeth) castañetear ▷ n (of birds) parloteo; (of people) charla, cháchara

**chauffeur** ['ʃəʊfər] n chófer m

**chauvinist** ['ʃəʊvɪnɪst] n (also: **male ~**) machista m; (nationalist) chovinista mf

**cheap** [tʃiːp] adj barato; (joke) de mal gusto; (poor quality) de mala calidad ▷ adv barato; **cheap day return** n billete de ida y vuelta el mismo día; **cheaply** adv barato, a bajo precio

**cheat** [tʃiːt] vi hacer trampa ▷ vt estafar ▷ n (person) tramposo/a; **to ~ sb (out of sth)** estafar (algo) a algn; **cheat on** vt fus engañar

**check** [tʃɛk] vt (examine) controlar; (facts) comprobar; (count) contar; (halt) frenar; (restrain) refrenar, restringir ▷ n (inspection) control m, inspección f; (curb) freno; (bill) nota, cuenta; (US) = **cheque**; (pattern: gen pl) cuadro; **check in** vi (in hotel) registrarse; (at airport) facturar ▷ vt (luggage) facturar; **check off** vt (esp US: check) comprobar;

(cross off) tachar; **check out** vi (of hotel) desocupar la habitación; **check up** vi: **to ~ up on sth** comprobar algo; **to ~ up on sb** investigar a algn; **checkbook** n (US) = **chequebook**; **checked** adj a cuadros inv; **checkers** n (US) damas fpl; **check-in** n (also: **check-in desk**: at airport) mostrador m de facturación; **checking account** n (US) cuenta corriente; **checklist** n lista; **checkmate** n jaque m mate; **checkout** n caja; **checkpoint** n (punto de) control m; **checkroom** n (US) consigna; **checkup** n (Med) reconocimiento general

**cheddar** ['tʃedər] n (also: **~ cheese**) queso m cheddar

**cheek** [tʃiːk] n mejilla; (impudence) descaro; **what a ~!** ¡qué cara!; **cheekbone** n pómulo; **cheeky** adj fresco, descarado

**cheer** [tʃɪər] vt vitorear, ovacionar; (gladden) alegrar, animar ▷ vi dar vivas ▷ n viva m; **cheer up** vi animarse ▷ vt alegrar, animar; **cheerful** adj alegre

**cheerio** [tʃɪərɪˈəʊ] excl (BRIT) ¡hasta luego!

**cheerleader** ['tʃɪəliːdər] n animador(a) m/f

**cheese** [tʃiːz] n queso; **cheeseburger** n hamburguesa con queso; **cheesecake** n pastel m de queso

**chef** [ʃɛf] n jefe/a m/f de cocina

**chemical** ['kemɪkəl] adj químico ▷ n producto químico

**chemist** ['kemɪst] n (BRIT: pharmacist) farmacéutico/a; (scientist) químico/a; **~'s (shop)** n (BRIT) farmacia; **chemistry** n química

**cheque**, (US) **check** [tʃɛk] n cheque m; **chequebook** n talonario (de cheques), chequera (LAM); **cheque card** n (BRIT) tarjeta de identificación bancaria

**cherry** ['tʃerɪ] n cereza; (also: **~ tree**) cerezo

**chess** [tʃes] n ajedrez m

**chest** [tʃest] n (Anat) pecho; (box) cofre m; **~ of drawers** n cómoda

**chestnut** ['tʃesnʌt] n castaña; (also: **~ tree**) castaño

**chew** [tʃuː] vt mascar, masticar; **chewing gum** n chicle m

**chic** [ʃiːk] adj elegante

**chick** [tʃɪk] n pollito, polluelo; (US inf) chica

**chicken** ['tʃɪkɪn] n gallina, pollo; (food) pollo; (inf: coward) gallina mf; **chicken out** vi (inf) rajarse; **chickenpox** n varicela

**chickpea** ['tʃɪkpiː] n garbanzo

**chief** [tʃiːf] n jefe/a m/f ▷ adj principal; **chief executive (officer)** n director m general; **chiefly** adv principalmente

**child** (pl **children**) [tʃaɪld, 'tʃɪldrən] n niño/a; (offspring) hijo/a; **child abuse** n (with violence) malos tratos mpl a niños; (sexual) abuso m sexual de niños; **child**

**benefit** n (BRIT) subsidio por cada hijo pequeño; **childbirth** n parto; **childcare** n cuidado de los niños; **childhood** n niñez f, infancia; **childish** adj pueril, infantil; **child minder** n (BRIT) madre f de día; **children** ['tʃɪldrən] npl of **child**

**Chile** ['tʃɪlɪ] n Chile m; **Chilean** adj, n chileno/a

**chill** [tʃɪl] n frío; (Med) resfriado ▷ vt enfriar; (Culin) refrigerar; **chill out** vi (esp US inf) tranquilizarse

**chilly** ['tʃɪlɪ] adj frío

**chimney** ['tʃɪmnɪ] n chimenea

**chimpanzee** [tʃɪmpæn'ziː] n chimpancé m

**chin** [tʃɪn] n mentón m, barbilla

**China** ['tʃaɪnə] n China

**china** ['tʃaɪnə] n porcelana; (crockery) loza

**Chinese** [tʃaɪ'niːz] adj chino ▷ n (pl inv) chino/a; (Ling) chino

**chip** [tʃɪp] n (gen pl: Culin: BRIT) patata or (LAM) papa frita; (: US: also: **potato ~**) patata or (LAM) papa frita; (of wood) astilla; (stone) lasca; (in gambling) ficha; (Comput) chip m ▷ vt (cup, plate) desconchar; **chip shop** n ver nota

* **CHIP SHOP**
*
* Se denomina chip shop o fish-and-chip shop
* a un tipo de tienda popular de comida
* rápida en la que se despachan platos
* tradicionales británicos, principalmente
* filetes de pescado rebozado frito y
* patatas fritas.

**chiropodist** [kɪ'rɔpədɪst] n (BRIT) podólogo/a

**chisel** ['tʃɪzl] n (for wood) escoplo; (for stone) cincel m

**chives** [tʃaɪvz] npl cebollinos mpl

**chlorine** ['klɔːriːn] n cloro

**choc-ice** ['tʃɔkaɪs] n (BRIT) helado m cubierto de chocolate

**chocolate** ['tʃɔklɪt] n chocolate m; (sweet) bombón m

**choice** [tʃɔɪs] n elección f; (preference) preferencia ▷ adj escogido

**choir** ['kwaɪə'] n coro

**choke** [tʃəuk] vi ahogarse; (on food) atragantarse ▷ vt ahogar; (block) atascar ▷ n (Aut) estárter m

**cholesterol** [kɔ'lestərəl] n colesterol m

**chook** [tʃuk] n (AUST, NZ inf) gallina; (as food) pollo

**choose** (pt chose, pp chosen) [tʃuːz, tʃəuz, tʃəuzn] vt escoger, elegir; (team) seleccionar; **to ~ to do sth** optar por hacer algo

**chop** [tʃɔp] vt (wood) cortar, talar; (Culin: also: **~ up**) picar ▷ n (Culin) chuleta; **chop**

**down** vt (tree) talar; **chop off** vt cortar (de un tajo); **chopsticks** npl palillos mpl

**chord** [kɔːd] n (Mus) acorde m

**chore** [tʃɔː'] n faena, tarea; (routine task) trabajo rutinario

**chorus** ['kɔːrəs] n coro; (repeated part of song) estribillo

**chose** [tʃəuz] pt of **choose**

**chosen** ['tʃəuzn] pp of **choose**

**Christ** [kraɪst] n Cristo

**christen** ['krɪsn] vt bautizar; **christening** n bautizo

**Christian** ['krɪstɪən] adj, n cristiano/a; **Christianity** [krɪstɪ'ænɪtɪ] n cristianismo; **Christian name** n nombre m de pila

**Christmas** ['krɪsməs] n Navidad f; **Merry ~!** ¡Felices Navidades!; **Christmas card** n crismas m inv, tarjeta de Navidad; **Christmas carol** n villancico m; **Christmas Day** n día m de Navidad; **Christmas Eve** n Nochebuena; **Christmas pudding** n (esp BRIT) pudín m de Navidad; **Christmas tree** n árbol m de Navidad

**chrome** [krəum] n = **chromium**

**chromium** ['krəumɪəm] n cromo; (also: **~ plating**) cromado

**chronic** ['krɔnɪk] adj crónico

**chrysanthemum** [krɪ'sænθəməm] n crisantemo

**chubby** ['tʃʌbɪ] adj rechoncho

**chuck** [tʃʌk] (inf) vt lanzar, arrojar; (BRIT: also: **~ in, ~ up**) abandonar; **chuck out** vt (person) echar (fuera); (rubbish etc) tirar

**chuckle** ['tʃʌkl] vi reírse entre dientes

**chum** [tʃʌm] n amiguete/a m/f

**chunk** [tʃʌŋk] n pedazo, trozo

**church** [tʃəːtʃ] n iglesia; **churchyard** n cementerio

**churn** [tʃəːn] n (for butter) mantequera; (for milk) lechera

**chute** [ʃuːt] n (also: **rubbish ~**) vertedero

**chutney** ['tʃʌtnɪ] n salsa picante de frutas y especias

**CIA** n abbr (US: = Central Intelligence Agency) CIA f

**CID** n abbr (BRIT: = Criminal Investigation Department) ≈ B.I.C. f (SP)

**cider** ['saɪdə'] n sidra

**cigar** [sɪ'gɑː'] n puro

**cigarette** [sɪgə'ret] n cigarrillo; **cigarette lighter** n mechero

**cinema** ['sɪnəmə] n cine m

**cinnamon** ['sɪnəmən] n canela

**circle** ['səːkl] n círculo; (in theatre) anfiteatro ▷ vi dar vueltas ▷ vt (surround) rodear, cercar; (move round) dar la vuelta a

**circuit** ['səːkɪt] n circuito; (track) pista; (lap) vuelta

**circular** ['səːkjulə'] adj circular ▷ n circular f

**circulate** ['sɜːkjuleɪt] vi circular; (person: socially) alternar, circular ▷ vt poner en circulación; **circulation** [sɜːkjuˈleɪʃən] n circulación f; (of newspaper etc) tirada

**circumstances** ['sɜːkəmstənsɪz] npl circunstancias fpl; (financial condition) situación f económica

**circus** ['sɜːkəs] n circo

**cite** [saɪt] vt citar

**citizen** ['sɪtɪzn] n (Pol) ciudadano/a; (of city) habitante mf, vecino/a; **citizenship** n ciudadanía; (BRIT Scol) civismo

**citrus fruits** ['sɪtrəs-] npl cítricos mpl

**city** ['sɪtɪ] n ciudad f; **the C~** centro financiero de Londres; **city centre** n centro de la ciudad

**City Technology College** n (BRIT) ≈ Centro de formación profesional

**civic** ['sɪvɪk] adj cívico; (authorities) municipal

**civil** ['sɪvɪl] adj civil; (polite) atento, cortés; **civilian** [sɪˈvɪlɪən] adj civil ▷ n civil mf

**civilization** [sɪvɪlaɪˈzeɪʃən] n civilización f

**civilized** ['sɪvɪlaɪzd] adj civilizado

**civil: civil law** n derecho civil; **civil rights** npl derechos mpl civiles; **civil servant** n funcionario/a (del Estado); **Civil Service** n administración f pública; **civil war** n guerra civil

**CJD** n abbr (= Creutzfeldt-Jakob disease) enfermedad f de Creutzfeldt-Jakob

**claim** [kleɪm] vt exigir, reclamar; (rights etc) reivindicar; (assert) pretender ▷ vi (for insurance) reclamar ▷ n (for expenses) reclamación f; (Law) demanda; (pretension) pretensión f; **claim form** n solicitud f

**clam** [klæm] n almeja

**clamp** [klæmp] n abrazadera; (laboratory clamp) grapa ▷ vt afianzar (con abrazadera)

**clan** [klæn] n clan m

**clap** [klæp] vi aplaudir

**claret** ['klærət] n burdeos m inv

**clarify** ['klærɪfaɪ] vt aclarar

**clarinet** [klærɪˈnɛt] n clarinete m

**clarity** ['klærɪtɪ] n claridad f

**clash** [klæʃ] n estruendo; (fig) choque m ▷ vi enfrentarse; (beliefs) chocar; (disagree) estar en desacuerdo; (colours) desentonar; (two events) coincidir

**clasp** [klɑːsp] n (hold) apretón m; (of necklace, bag) cierre m ▷ vt (hand) apretar; (embrace) abrazar

**class** [klɑːs] n clase f ▷ vt clasificar

**classic** ['klæsɪk] n clásico; **classical** adj clásico

**classification** [klæsɪfɪˈkeɪʃən] n clasificación f

**classify** ['klæsɪfaɪ] vt clasificar

**classmate** ['klɑːsmeɪt] n compañero/a de clase

**classroom** ['klɑːsrum] n aula; **classroom assistant** n profesor(a) m/f de apoyo

**classy** ['klɑːsɪ] adj (inf) elegante, con estilo

**clatter** ['klætəʳ] n ruido, estruendo ▷ vi hacer ruido or estruendo

**clause** [klɔːz] n cláusula; (Ling) oración f

**claustrophobic** [klɔːstrəˈfəʊbɪk] adj claustrofóbico; **I feel ~** me entra claustrofobia

**claw** [klɔː] n (of cat) uña; (of bird of prey) garra; (of lobster) pinza

**clay** [kleɪ] n arcilla

**clean** [kliːn] adj limpio; (record, reputation) bueno, intachable; (joke) decente ▷ vt limpiar; (hands etc) lavar; **clean up** vt limpiar, asear; **cleaner** n encargado/a de la limpieza; (also: **dry cleaner**) tintorero/a; (substance) producto para la limpieza; **cleaning** n limpieza

**cleanser** ['klɛnzəʳ] n (cosmetic) loción f or crema limpiadora

**clear** [klɪəʳ] adj claro; (road, way) libre ▷ vt (space) despejar, limpiar; (Law: suspect) absolver; (obstacle) salvar, saltar por encima de; (cheque) aceptar ▷ vi (fog etc) despejarse ▷ adv: **~ of** a distancia de; **to ~ the table** recoger or quitar la mesa; **clear away** vt (things, clothes etc) quitar (de en medio); (dishes) retirar; **clear up** vt limpiar; (mystery) aclarar, resolver; **clearance** n (removal) despeje m; (permission) acreditación f; **clear-cut** adj bien definido, claro; **clearing** n (in wood) claro; **clearly** adv claramente; (evidently) sin duda; **clearway** n (BRIT) carretera en la que no se puede estacionar

**clench** [klɛntʃ] vt apretar, cerrar

**clergy** ['klɜːdʒɪ] n clero

**clerk** [klɑːk, US klɜːk] n oficinista mf; (US) dependiente/a m/f

**clever** ['klɛvəʳ] adj (mentally) inteligente, listo; (skilful) hábil; (device, arrangement) ingenioso

**cliché** ['kliːʃeɪ] n cliché m, frase f hecha

**click** [klɪk] vt (tongue) chasquear ▷ vi (Comput) hacer clic; **to ~ one's heels** taconear; **to ~ on an icon** hacer clic en un icono

**client** ['klaɪənt] n cliente mf

**cliff** [klɪf] n acantilado

**climate** ['klaɪmɪt] n clima m; **climate change** n cambio climático

**climax** ['klaɪmæks] n (of battle, career) apogeo; (of film, book) punto culminante, clímax; (sexual) orgasmo

**climb** [klaɪm] vi subir, trepar ▷ vt (stairs) subir; (tree) trepar a; (mountain) escalar ▷ n subida, ascenso; **to ~ over a wall** saltar una tapia; **climb down** vi (fig) volverse atrás; **climber** n escalador(a) m/f; **climbing** n escalada

**clinch** [klɪntʃ] vt (deal) cerrar; (argument) remachar

**cling** (pt, pp **clung**) [klɪŋ, klʌŋ] vi: **to ~ (to)** agarrarse (a); (clothes) pegarse (a)

**clinic** ['klɪnɪk] n clínica

**clip** [klɪp] n (for hair) horquilla; (also: **paper ~**) sujetapapeles m inv, clip m ▷ vt (cut) cortar; (also: **~ together**) unir; **clipping** n (from newspaper) recorte m

**cloak** [kləuk] n capa, manto ▷ vt (fig) encubrir, disimular; **cloakroom** n guardarropa m; (BRIT: WC) lavabo, aseos mpl, baño (esp LAM)

**clock** [klɔk] n reloj m; **clock in, clock on** vi fichar, picar; **clock off, clock out** vi fichar or picar la salida; **clockwise** adv en el sentido de las agujas del reloj; **clockwork** n aparato de relojería ▷ adj (toy, train) de cuerda

**clog** [klɔg] n zueco, chanclo ▷ vt atascar ▷ vi (also: **~ up**) atascarse

**clone** [kləun] n clon m ▷ vt clonar

**close** [kləus] adj (near): **~ (to)** cerca (de); (friend) íntimo; (connection) estrecho; (examination) detallado, minucioso; (weather) bochornoso ▷ adv cerca; **~ to** prep cerca de ▷ vt cerrar; (end) concluir, terminar ▷ vi [kləuz] (shop etc) cerrar; (end) concluir(se), terminar(se) ▷ n [kləuz] (end) fin m, final m, conclusión f; **to have a ~ shave** (fig) escaparse por un pelo; **~ by, ~ at hand** muy cerca; **close down** vi cerrar definitivamente; **closed** [kləuzd] adj (shop etc) cerrado

**closed-circuit** ['kləuzd'səːkɪt] adj: **~ television** televisión f por circuito cerrado

**closely** ['kləuslɪ] adv (study) con detalle; (watch) de cerca

**closet** ['klɔzɪt] n armario

**close-up** ['kləusʌp] n primer plano

**closing time** ['kləuzɪŋ-] n hora de cierre

**closure** ['kləuʒəʳ] n cierre m

**clot** [klɔt] n (also: **blood ~**) coágulo; (inf: idiot) imbécil mf ▷ vi (blood) coagularse

**cloth** [klɔθ] n (material) tela, paño; (rag) trapo

**clothes** [kləuðz] npl ropa sg; **clothes line** n cuerda (para tender la ropa); **clothes peg, **(US) **clothes pin** n pinza

**clothing** ['kləuðɪŋ] n = **clothes**

**cloud** [klaud] n nube f; **cloud over** vi (also fig) nublarse; **cloudy** adj nublado; (liquid) turbio

**clove** [kləuv] n clavo; **~ of garlic** diente m de ajo

**clown** [klaun] n payaso ▷ vi (also: **~ about, ~ around**) hacer el payaso

**club** [klʌb] n (society) club m; (weapon) porra, cachiporra; (also: **golf ~**) palo ▷ vt aporrear ▷ vi: **to ~ together** (join forces) unir fuerzas; **clubs** npl (Cards) tréboles mpl; **club class** n (Aviat) clase f preferente

**clue** [kluː] n pista; (in crosswords) indicación f; **I haven't a ~** no tengo ni idea

**clump** [klʌmp] n (of trees) grupo

**clumsy** ['klʌmzɪ] adj (person) torpe; (tool) difícil de manejar

**clung** [klʌŋ] pt, pp of **cling**

**cluster** ['klʌstəʳ] n grupo ▷ vi agruparse, apiñarse

**clutch** [klʌtʃ] n (Aut) embrague m; **to fall into sb's ~es** caer en las garras de algn ▷ vt agarrar

**cm** abbr (= centimetre) cm

**Co.** abbr = **county; company**

**c/o** abbr (= care of) c/a, a/c

**coach** [kəutʃ] n autocar m (SP), autobús m; (horse-drawn) coche m; (of train) vagón m, coche m; (Sport) entrenador(a) m/f, instructor(a) m/f ▷ vt (Sport) entrenar; (student) preparar, enseñar; **coach station** n (BRIT) estación f de autobuses etc; **coach trip** n excursión f en autocar

**coal** [kəul] n carbón m

**coalition** [kəuə'lɪʃən] n coalición f

**coarse** [kɔːs] adj basto, burdo; (vulgar) grosero, ordinario

**coast** [kəust] n costa, litoral m ▷ vi (Aut) ir en punto muerto; **coastal** adj costero; **coastguard** n guardacostas m inv; **coastline** n litoral m

**coat** [kəut] n abrigo; (of animal) pelo, pelaje, lana; (of paint) mano f, capa ▷ vt cubrir, revestir; **coat hanger** n percha, gancho (LAM); **coating** n capa, baño

**coax** [kəuks] vt engatusar

**cob** [kɔb] n see **corn**

**cobbled** ['kɔbld] adj: **~ street** calle f empedrada, calle f adoquinada

**cobweb** ['kɔbwɛb] n telaraña

**cocaine** [kə'keɪn] n cocaína

**cock** [kɔk] n (rooster) gallo; (male bird) macho ▷ vt (gun) amartillar; **cockerel** n gallito

**cockney** ['kɔknɪ] n habitante de ciertos barrios de Londres

**cockpit** ['kɔkpɪt] n cabina

**cockroach** ['kɔkrəutʃ] n cucaracha

**cocktail** ['kɔkteɪl] n cóctel m

**cocoa** ['kəukəu] n cacao; (drink) chocolate m

**coconut** ['kəukənʌt] n coco

**COD** abbr = **cash on delivery**; (US: = collect on delivery) C.A.E.

**cod** [kɔd] n bacalao

**code** [kəud] n código; (cipher) clave f; (Tel) prefijo

**coeducational** [kəuɛdju'keɪʃənl] adj mixto

**coffee** ['kɔfɪ] n café m; **coffee bar** n (BRIT) cafetería; **coffee bean** n grano de café;

**coffee break** n descanso (para tomar café); **coffee maker** n máquina de hacer café, cafetera; **coffeepot** n cafetera; **coffee shop** n café m; **coffee table** n mesita baja
**coffin** ['kɔfɪn] n ataúd m
**cog** [kɔg] n diente m
**cognac** ['kɔnjæk] n coñac m
**coherent** [kəʊ'hɪərənt] adj coherente
**coil** [kɔɪl] n rollo; (Aut, Elec) bobina, carrete m; (contraceptive) DIU m ▷ vt enrollar
**coin** [kɔɪn] n moneda ▷ vt (word) inventar, acuñar
**coincide** [kəʊɪn'saɪd] vi coincidir; **coincidence** [kəʊ'ɪnsɪdəns] n casualidad f
**Coke®** [kəʊk] n Coca Cola® f
**coke** [kəʊk] n (coal) coque m
**colander** ['kɔləndər] n escurridor m
**cold** [kəʊld] adj frío ▷ n frío; (Med) resfriado; **it's ~** hace frío; **to be ~** tener frío; **to catch a ~** resfriarse, acatarrarse; **in ~ blood** a sangre fría; **cold sore** n herpes m labial
**coleslaw** ['kəʊlslɔː] n ensalada de col con zanahoria
**colic** ['kɔlɪk] n cólico
**collaborate** [kə'læbəreɪt] vi colaborar
**collapse** [kə'læps] vi hundirse, derrumbarse; (Med) sufrir un colapso ▷ n hundimiento, derrumbamiento; (Med) colapso
**collar** ['kɔlər] n (of coat, shirt) cuello; (for dog) collar m; **collarbone** n clavícula
**colleague** ['kɔliːg] n colega mf; (at work) compañero/a m/f
**collect** [kə'lɛkt] vt reunir; (as a hobby) coleccionar; (BRIT: call and pick up) recoger; (debts) recaudar; (donations, subscriptions) colectar ▷ vi (crowd) reunirse ▷ adv (US Tel): **to call ~** llamar a cobro revertido; **collection** n colección f; (of post) recogida; **collective** adj colectivo; **collector** n coleccionista mf
**college** ['kɔlɪdʒ] n colegio; (of technology, agriculture etc) escuela
**collide** [kə'laɪd] vi chocar
**collision** [kə'lɪʒən] n choque m
**cologne** [kə'ləʊn] n (also: **eau de ~**) (agua de) colonia
**Colombia** [kə'lɔmbɪə] n Colombia; **Colombian** adj, n colombiano/a
**colon** ['kəʊlən] n (sign) dos puntos; (Med) colon m
**colonel** ['kɜːnl] n coronel m
**colonial** [kə'ləʊnɪəl] adj colonial
**colony** ['kɔlənɪ] n colonia
**colour**, (US) **color** ['kʌlər] n color m ▷ vt colorear; (dye) teñir; (fig: account) adornar; (: judgement) distorsionar ▷ vi (blush) sonrojarse; **colour in** vt colorear; **colour-blind** adj daltónico; **coloured** adj de color;

(photo) en color; **colour film** n película en color; **colourful** adj lleno de color; (person) pintoresco; **colouring** n colorido, color; (substance) colorante m; **colour television** n televisión f en color
**column** ['kɔləm] n columna
**coma** ['kəʊmə] n coma m
**comb** [kəʊm] n peine m; (ornamental) peineta ▷ vt (hair) peinar; (area) registrar a fondo
**combat** ['kɔmbæt] n combate m ▷ vt combatir
**combination** [kɔmbɪ'neɪʃən] n combinación f
**combine** [kəm'baɪn] vt combinar; (qualities) reunir ▷ vi combinarse ▷ n ['kɔmbaɪn] (Econ) cartel m

**KEYWORD**

**come** [kʌm] (pt **came**, pp **come**) vi
**1** (movement towards) venir; **to come running** venir corriendo
**2** (arrive) llegar; **he's come here to work** ha venido aquí para trabajar; **to come home** volver a casa
**3** (reach): **to come to** llegar a; **the bill came to £40** la cuenta ascendía a cuarenta libras
**4** (occur): **an idea came to me** se me ocurrió una idea
**5** (be, become): **to come loose/undone** etc aflojarse/desabrocharse, desatarse etc; **I've come to like him** por fin ha llegado a gustarme
**come across** vt fus (person) encontrarse con; (thing) encontrar
**come along** vi (BRIT: progress) ir
**come back** vi (return) volver
**come down** vi (price) bajar; (building: be demolished) ser derribado
**come from** vt fus (place, source) ser de
**come in** vi (visitor) entrar; (train, report) llegar; (fashion) ponerse de moda; (on deal etc) entrar
**come off** vi (button) soltarse, desprenderse; (attempt) salir bien
**come on** vi (pupil, work, project) marchar; (lights) encenderse; (electricity) volver; **come on!** ¡vamos!
**come out** vi (fact) salir a la luz; (book, sun) salir; (stain) quitarse
**come round** vi (after faint, operation) volver en sí
**come to** vi (wake) volver en sí
**come up** vi (sun) salir; (problem) surgir; (event) aproximarse; (in conversation) mencionarse
**come up with** vt fus (idea) sugerir; (money) conseguir

**comeback** ['kʌmbæk] n: **to make a ~** (*Theat*) volver a las tablas
**comedian** [kə'miːdɪən] n humorista mf
**comedy** ['kɒmɪdɪ] n comedia
**comet** ['kɒmɪt] n cometa m
**comfort** ['kʌmfət] n bienestar m; (*relief*) alivio ▷ vt consolar; **comfortable** adj cómodo; (*income*) adecuado; **comfort station** n (*US*) servicios mpl
**comic** ['kɒmɪk] adj (*also*: **~al**) cómico ▷ n (*comedian*) cómico; (*magazine*) tebeo; (*for adults*) cómic m; **comic book** n (*US*) libro m de cómics; **comic strip** n tira cómica
**comma** ['kɒmə] n coma
**command** [kə'mɑːnd] n orden f, mandato; (*Mil*: *authority*) mando; (*mastery*) dominio ▷ vt (*troops*) mandar; (*give orders to*) mandar, ordenar; **commander** n (*Mil*) comandante mf, jefe/a m/f
**commemorate** [kə'mɛmərɛɪt] vt conmemorar
**commence** [kə'mɛns] vt, vi comenzar; **commencement** n (*US*) (*Univ*) (ceremonia de) graduación f
**commend** [kə'mɛnd] vt elogiar, alabar; (*recommend*) recomendar
**comment** ['kɒmɛnt] n comentario ▷ vi: **to ~ (on)** hacer comentarios (sobre); **"no ~"** (*written*) "sin comentarios"; (*spoken*) "no tengo nada que decir"; **commentary** n comentario; **commentator** n comentarista mf
**commerce** ['kɒməːs] n comercio
**commercial** [kə'məːʃəl] adj comercial ▷ n (*TV*) anuncio; **commercial break** n intermedio para publicidad
**commission** [kə'mɪʃən] n (*committee, fee, order for work of art etc*) comisión f ▷ vt (*work of art*) encargar; **out of ~** fuera de servicio; **commissioner** n (*Police*) comisario m de policía
**commit** [kə'mɪt] vt (*act*) cometer; (*resources*) dedicar; (*to sb's care*) entregar; **to ~ o.s. (to do)** comprometerse (a hacer); **to ~ suicide** suicidarse; **commitment** n compromiso
**committee** [kə'mɪtɪ] n comité m
**commodity** [kə'mɒdɪtɪ] n mercancía
**common** ['kɒmən] adj común; (*pej*) ordinario ▷ n campo común; **commonly** adv comúnmente; **commonplace** adj corriente; **Commons** npl (*BRIT Pol*): **the Commons** (la Cámara de) los Comunes; **common sense** n sentido común; **Commonwealth** n: **the Commonwealth** la Commonwealth
**communal** ['kɒmjuːnl] adj comunal; (*kitchen*) común
**commune** ['kɒmjuːn] n (*group*) comuna ▷ vi [kə'mjuːn]: **to ~ with** comunicarse con

**communicate** [kə'mjuːnɪkeɪt] vt comunicar ▷ vi: **to ~ (with)** comunicarse (con); (*in writing*) estar en contacto (con)
**communication** [kəmjuːnɪ'keɪʃən] n comunicación f
**communion** [kə'mjuːnɪən] n (*also*: **Holy C~**) comunión f
**communism** ['kɒmjunɪzəm] n comunismo; **communist** adj, n comunista mf
**community** [kə'mjuːnɪtɪ] n comunidad f; (*large group*) colectividad f; **community centre** n centro social; **community service** n trabajo m comunitario (*prestado en lugar de cumplir una pena de prisión*)
**commute** [kə'mjuːt] vi viajar a diario de casa al trabajo ▷ vt conmutar; **commuter** n persona que viaja a diario de casa al trabajo
**compact** [kəm'pækt] adj compacto ▷ n ['kɒmpækt] (*also*: **powder ~**) polvera; **compact disc** n compact disc m; **compact disc player** n lector m or reproductor m de discos compactos
**companion** [kəm'pænɪən] n compañero/a
**company** ['kʌmpənɪ] n compañía; (*Comm*) empresa, compañía; **to keep sb ~** acompañar a algn; **company car** n coche m de la empresa; **company director** n director(a) m/f de empresa
**comparable** ['kɒmpərəbl] adj comparable
**comparative** [kəm'pærətɪv] adj relativo; (*study, linguistics*) comparado; **comparatively** adv (*relatively*) relativamente
**compare** [kəm'pɛəʳ] vt comparar ▷ vi: **to ~ (with)** poder compararse (con); **~d with** or **to** comparado con or a; **comparison** [kəm'pærɪsn] n comparación f
**compartment** [kəm'pɑːtmənt] n compartim(i)ento
**compass** ['kʌmpəs] n brújula; **compasses** npl compás m
**compassion** [kəm'pæʃən] n compasión f
**compatible** [kəm'pætɪbl] adj compatible
**compel** [kəm'pɛl] vt obligar; **compelling** adj (*fig*: *argument*) convincente
**compensate** ['kɒmpənseɪt] vt compensar ▷ vi: **to ~ for** compensar; **compensation** n (*for loss*) indemnización f
**compete** [kəm'piːt] vi (*take part*) competir; (*vie with*) competir, hacer la competencia
**competent** ['kɒmpɪtənt] adj competente, capaz
**competition** [kɒmpɪ'tɪʃən] n (*contest*) concurso; (*rivalry*) competencia
**competitive** [kəm'pɛtɪtɪv] adj (*Econ, Sport*) competitivo
**competitor** [kəm'pɛtɪtəʳ] n (*rival*) competidor(a) m/f; (*participant*) concursante mf

**complacent** [kəmˈpleɪsənt] adj
autocomplaciente
**complain** [kəmˈpleɪn] vi quejarse; (Comm)
reclamar; **complaint** n queja; (Comm)
reclamación f; (Med) enfermedad f
**complement** [ˈkɒmplɪmənt] n
complemento; (esp ship's crew) dotación
f ▷ vt [ˈkɒmplɪment] (enhance)
complementar; **complementary**
[kɒmplɪˈmentərɪ] adj complementario
**complete** [kəmˈpliːt] adj (full) completo;
(finished) acabado ▷ vt (fulfil) completar;
(finish) acabar; (a form) rellenar; **completely**
adv completamente; **completion** n
terminación f; **on completion of contract**
cuando se realice el contrato
**complex** [ˈkɒmpleks] n complejo
**complexion** [kəmˈplekʃən] n (of face) tez f,
cutis m
**compliance** [kəmˈplaɪəns] n (submission)
sumisión f; (agreement) conformidad f; **in ~
with** de acuerdo con
**complicate** [ˈkɒmplɪkeɪt] vt complicar;
**complicated** adj complicado;
**complication** [kɒmplɪˈkeɪʃən] n
complicación f
**compliment** [ˈkɒmplɪmənt] n (formal)
cumplido ▷ vt felicitar; **complimentary**
[kɒmplɪˈmentərɪ] adj elogioso; (copy) de
regalo
**comply** [kəmˈplaɪ] vi: **to ~ with** acatar
**component** [kəmˈpəunənt] adj
componente ▷ n (Tech) pieza
**compose** [kəmˈpəuz] vt componer;
**to be ~d of** componerse de; **to ~ o.s.**
tranquilizarse; **composer** n (Mus)
compositor(a) m/f; **composition**
[kɒmpəˈzɪʃən] n composición f
**composure** [kəmˈpəuʒəʳ] n serenidad f,
calma
**compound** [ˈkɒmpaund] n (Chem)
compuesto; (Ling) término compuesto;
(enclosure) recinto ▷ adj compuesto;
(fracture) complicado
**comprehension** [kɒmprɪˈhenʃən] n
comprensión f
**comprehensive** [kɒmprɪˈhensɪv] adj
(broad) exhaustivo; **~ (school)** n centro
estatal de enseñanza secundaria ≈ Instituto
Nacional de Bachillerato (SP)
**compress** [kəmˈpres] vt comprimir;
(Comput) comprimir ▷ n [ˈkɒmpres] (Med)
compresa
**comprise** [kəmˈpraɪz] vt (also: **be ~d of**)
comprender, constar de
**compromise** [ˈkɒmprəmaɪz] n (agreement)
arreglo ▷ vt comprometer ▷ vi transigir
**compulsive** [kəmˈpʌlsɪv] adj compulsivo;
(viewing, reading) obligado

**compulsory** [kəmˈpʌlsərɪ] adj
obligatorio
**computer** [kəmˈpjuːtəʳ] n ordenador m,
computador m, computadora; **computer
game** n juego de ordenador;
**computerize** vt (data) computerizar;
(system) informatizar; **computer
programmer** n programador(a) m/f;
**computer programming** n
programación f; **computer science** n
informática; **computer studies** npl
informática fsg, computación fsg (LAM);
**computing** [kəmˈpjuːtɪŋ] n (activity)
informática
**con** [kɒn] vt estafar ▷ n estafa; **to ~ sb into
doing sth** (inf) engañar a algn para que
haga algo
**conceal** [kənˈsiːl] vt ocultar
**concede** [kənˈsiːd] vt (point, argument)
reconocer; (territory) ceder; **to ~ (defeat)**
darse por vencido; **to ~ that** admitir que
**conceited** [kənˈsiːtɪd] adj orgulloso
**conceive** [kənˈsiːv] vt, vi concebir
**concentrate** [ˈkɒnsəntreɪt] vi
concentrarse ▷ vt concentrar
**concentration** [kɒnsənˈtreɪʃən] n
concentración f
**concept** [ˈkɒnsept] n concepto
**concern** [kənˈsəːn] n (matter) asunto;
(Comm) empresa; (anxiety) preocupación
f ▷ vt (worry) preocupar; (involve) afectar;
(relate to) tener que ver con; **to be ~ed
(about)** interesarse (por), preocuparse
(por); **concerning** prep sobre, acerca de
**concert** [ˈkɒnsət] n concierto; **concert hall**
n sala de conciertos
**concerto** [kənˈtʃəːtəu] n concierto
**concession** [kənˈseʃən] n concesión f;
**tax ~** privilegio fiscal
**concise** [kənˈsaɪs] adj conciso
**conclude** [kənˈkluːd] vt concluir; (treaty
etc) firmar; (agreement) llegar a; (decide):
**to ~ that ...** llegar a la conclusión de que ...;
**conclusion** [kənˈkluːʒən] n conclusión f
**concrete** [ˈkɒnkriːt] n hormigón m ▷ adj de
hormigón; (fig) concreto
**concussion** [kənˈkʌʃən] n conmoción f
cerebral
**condemn** [kənˈdem] vt condenar; (building)
declarar en ruina
**condensation** [kɒndenˈseɪʃən] n
condensación f
**condense** [kənˈdens] vi condensarse ▷ vt
condensar; (text) abreviar
**condition** [kənˈdɪʃən] n condición f; (of
health) estado; (disease) enfermedad f ▷ vt
condicionar; **on ~ that** a condición (de) que;
**conditional** adj condicional; **conditioner**
n suavizante m

**condo** ['kɔndəu] n abbr (US inf);
= **condominium**
**condom** ['kɔndəm] n condón m
**condominium** [kɔndə'mɪnɪəm] n (US: building) bloque m de pisos or apartamentos (propiedad de quienes lo habitan), condominio (LAM), (: apartment) piso or apartamento (en propiedad), condominio (LAM)
**condone** [kən'dəun] vt condonar
**conduct** ['kɔndʌkt] n conducta, comportamiento ▷ vt [kən'dʌkt] (lead) conducir; (manage) llevar, dirigir; (Mus) dirigir; **to ~ o.s.** comportarse; **conducted tour** n (BRIT) visita con guía; **conductor** n (of orchestra) director(a) m/f; (US: on train) revisor(a) m/f; (on bus) cobrador m; (Elec) conductor m
**cone** [kəun] n cono; (pine cone) piña; (for ice cream) cucurucho
**confectionery** [kən'fɛkʃənrɪ] n dulces mpl
**confer** [kən'fəːr] vt: **to ~ (on)** otorgar (a) ▷ vi conferenciar
**conference** ['kɔnfərns] n (meeting) reunión f; (convention) congreso
**confess** [kən'fɛs] vt confesar ▷ vi confesar; **confession** n confesión f
**confide** [kən'faɪd] vi: **to ~ in** confiar en
**confidence** ['kɔnfɪdns] n (also: self-~) confianza; (secret) confidencia; **in ~** (speak, write) en confianza; **confident** adj seguro de sí mismo; **confidential** [kɔnfɪ'dɛnʃəl] adj confidencial
**confine** [kən'faɪn] vt (limit) limitar; (shut up) encerrar; **confined** adj (space) reducido
**confirm** [kən'fəːm] vt confirmar; **confirmation** [kɔnfə'meɪʃən] n confirmación f
**confiscate** ['kɔnfɪskeɪt] vt confiscar
**conflict** ['kɔnflɪkt] n conflicto ▷ vi [kən'flɪkt] (opinions) estar reñido
**conform** [kən'fɔːm] vi: **to ~ to** ajustarse a
**confront** [kən'frʌnt] vt (problems) hacer frente a; (enemy, danger) enfrentarse con; **confrontation** [kɔnfrən'teɪʃən] n enfrentamiento
**confuse** [kən'fjuːz] vt (perplex) desconcertar; (mix up) confundir; (complicate) complicar; **confused** adj confuso; (person) desconcertado; **confusing** adj confuso; **confusion** n confusión f
**congestion** [kən'dʒɛstʃən] n congestión f
**congratulate** [kən'grætjuleɪt] vt felicitar; **congratulations** [kəngrætju'leɪʃənz] npl: **congratulations (on)** felicitaciones fpl (por); **congratulations!** ¡enhorabuena!
**congregation** [kɔŋgrɪ'geɪʃən] n (in church) fieles mpl
**congress** ['kɔŋgrɛs] n congreso; (US Pol): **C~** el Congreso (de los Estados Unidos);

**congressman** n (US) miembro del Congreso; **congresswoman** n (US) diputada, miembro f del Congreso
**conifer** ['kɔnɪfər] n conífera
**conjugate** ['kɔndʒugeɪt] vt conjugar
**conjugation** [kɔndʒə'geɪʃən] n conjugación f
**conjunction** [kən'dʒʌŋkʃən] n conjunción f; **in ~ with** junto con
**conjure** ['kʌndʒər] vi hacer juegos de manos
**connect** [kə'nɛkt] vt juntar, unir; (Elec) conectar; (fig) relacionar, asociar ▷ vi: **to ~ with** (train) enlazar con; **to be ~ed with** (associated) estar relacionado con; **I am trying to ~ you** (Tel) estoy intentando ponerle al habla; **connecting flight** n vuelo m de enlace; **connection** n juntura, unión f; (Elec) conexión f; (Rail) enlace m; (Tel) comunicación f; (fig) relación f
**conquer** ['kɔŋkər] vt (territory) conquistar; (enemy, feelings) vencer
**conquest** ['kɔŋkwɛst] n conquista
**cons** [kɔnz] npl see **mod cons; pro**
**conscience** ['kɔnʃəns] n conciencia
**conscientious** [kɔnʃɪ'ɛnʃəs] adj concienzudo; (objection) de conciencia
**conscious** ['kɔnʃəs] adj consciente; (deliberate: insult, error) premeditado, intencionado; **consciousness** n conciencia; (Med) conocimiento
**consecutive** [kən'sɛkjutɪv] adj consecutivo; **on 3 ~ occasions** en 3 ocasiones consecutivas
**consensus** [kən'sɛnsəs] n consenso
**consent** [kən'sɛnt] n consentimiento ▷ vi: **to ~ to** consentir en
**consequence** ['kɔnsɪkwəns] n consecuencia
**consequently** ['kɔnsɪkwəntlɪ] adv por consiguiente
**conservation** [kɔnsə'veɪʃən] n conservación f
**conservative** [kən'səːvətɪv] adj, n conservador(a); (cautious) moderado; **C~** adj (BRIT Pol) conservador(a) m/f
**conservatory** [kən'səːvətrɪ] n (greenhouse) invernadero
**consider** [kən'sɪdər] vt considerar; (take into account) tener en cuenta; (study) estudiar, examinar; **to ~ doing sth** pensar en (la posibilidad de) hacer algo; **considerable** adj considerable; **considerably** adv bastante, considerablemente; **considerate** adj considerado; **consideration** [kənsɪdə'reɪʃən] n consideración f; **to be under consideration** estar estudiándose; **considering** prep: **considering (that)** teniendo en cuenta (que)

**consignment** [kən'saɪnmənt] n envío
**consist** [kən'sɪst] vi: **to ~ of** consistir en
**consistency** [kən'sɪstənsɪ] n (of person etc) consecuencia, coherencia; (thickness) consistencia
**consistent** [kən'sɪstənt] adj (person, argument) consecuente, coherente
**consolation** [kɒnsə'leɪʃən] n consuelo
**console** [kən'səul] vt consolar ▷ n ['kɒnsəul] consola
**consonant** ['kɒnsənənt] n consonante f
**conspicuous** [kən'spɪkjuəs] adj (visible) visible
**conspiracy** [kən'spɪrəsɪ] n conjura, complot m
**constable** ['kʌnstəbl] n (BRIT) agente mf (de policía); **chief ~** ≈ jefe mf de policía
**constant** ['kɒnstənt] adj constante; **constantly** adv constantemente
**constipated** ['kɒnstɪpeɪtəd] adj estreñido
▌ Be careful not to translate constipated by the Spanish word constipado.
**constipation** [kɒnstɪ'peɪʃən] n estreñimiento
**constituency** [kən'stɪtjuənsɪ] n (Pol) distrito electoral; (people) electorado
**constitute** ['kɒnstɪtjuːt] vt constituir
**constitution** [kɒnstɪ'tjuːʃən] n constitución f
**constraint** [kən'streɪnt] n (force) fuerza; (limit) restricción f
**construct** [kən'strʌkt] vt construir; **construction** n construcción f; **constructive** adj constructivo
**consul** ['kɒnsl] n cónsul mf; **consulate** ['kɒnsjulɪt] n consulado
**consult** [kən'sʌlt] vt consultar; **consultant** n (BRIT Med) especialista mf; (other specialist) asesor(a) m/f; **consultation** n consulta; **consulting room** n (BRIT) consultorio
**consume** [kən'sjuːm] vt (eat) comerse; (drink) beberse; (fire etc) consumir; (Comm) consumir; **consumer** n consumidor(a) m/f
**consumption** [kən'sʌmpʃən] n consumo
**cont.** abbr (= continued) sigue
**contact** ['kɒntækt] n contacto; (person: pej) enchufe m ▷ vt ponerse en contacto con; **~ lenses** npl lentes fpl de contacto
**contagious** [kən'teɪdʒəs] adj contagioso
**contain** [kən'teɪn] vt contener; **to ~ o.s.** contenerse; **container** n recipiente m; (for shipping etc) contenedor m
**contaminate** [kən'tæmɪneɪt] vt contaminar
**cont'd** abbr (= continued) sigue
**contemplate** ['kɒntəmpleɪt] vt contemplar; (reflect upon) considerar
**contemporary** [kən'tempərərɪ] adj, n contemporáneo/a

**contempt** [kən'tempt] n desprecio; **~ of court** (Law) desacato (a los tribunales or a la justicia)
**contend** [kən'tend] vt (argue) afirmar ▷ vi: **to ~ with/for** luchar contra/por
**content** [kən'tent] adj (happy) contento; (satisfied) satisfecho ▷ vt contentar; satisfacer ▷ n ['kɒntent] contenido; **contents** npl contenido msg; **(table of) ~s** índice m de materias; **contented** adj contento; satisfecho
**contest** ['kɒntest] n contienda; (competition) concurso ▷ vt [kən'test] (dispute) impugnar; (Pol: election, seat) presentarse como candidato/a a
▌ Be careful not to translate contest by the Spanish word contestar.
**contestant** [kən'testənt] n concursante mf; (in fight) contendiente mf
**context** ['kɒntekst] n contexto
**continent** ['kɒntɪnənt] n continente m; **the C~** (BRIT) el continente europeo; **continental** adj continental; **continental breakfast** n desayuno estilo europeo; **continental quilt** n (BRIT) edredón m
**continual** [kən'tɪnjuəl] adj continuo; **continually** adv continuamente
**continue** [kən'tɪnjuː] vi, vt seguir, continuar
**continuity** [kɒntɪ'njuɪtɪ] n (also Cine) continuidad f
**continuous** [kən'tɪnjuəs] adj continuo; **continuous assessment** n (BRIT) evaluación f continua; **continuously** adv continuamente
**contour** ['kɒntuəʳ] n contorno; (also: **~ line**) curva de nivel
**contraception** [kɒntrə'sepʃən] n contracepción f
**contraceptive** [kɒntrə'septɪv] adj, n anticonceptivo
**contract** [n 'kɒntrækt, vi, vt kɒn'trækt] n contrato ▷ vi (Comm): **to ~ to do sth** comprometerse por contrato a hacer algo; (become smaller) contraerse, encogerse ▷ vt contraer; **contractor** n contratista mf
**contradict** [kɒntrə'dɪkt] vt contradecir; **contradiction** n contradicción f
**contrary¹** ['kɒntrərɪ] adj contrario ▷ n lo contrario; **on the ~** al contrario; **unless you hear to the ~** a no ser que le digan lo contrario
**contrary²** [kən'treərɪ] adj (perverse) terco
**contrast** ['kɒntrɑːst] n contraste m ▷ vt [kən'trɑːst] contrastar; **in ~ to** or **with** a diferencia de
**contribute** [kən'trɪbjuːt] vi contribuir ▷ vt: **to ~ to** contribuir a; (newspaper) colaborar en; (discussion) intervenir en;

**contribution** n (money) contribución f; (to debate) intervención f; (to journal) colaboración f; **contributor** n (to newspaper) colaborador(a) m/f

**control** [kən'trəul] vt controlar; (traffic etc) dirigir; (machinery) manejar; (temper) dominar; (disease, fire) dominar, controlar ▷ n control m; (of car) conducción f; (check) freno; **controls** npl (of vehicle) instrumentos mpl de mando; (of radio) controles mpl; (governmental) medidas fpl de control; **everything is under ~** todo está bajo control; **to be in ~ of** estar al mando de; **the car went out of ~** perdió el control del coche; **control tower** n (Aviat) torre f de control

**controversial** [kɔntrə'və:ʃl] adj polémico

**controversy** ['kɔntrəvə:sɪ] n polémica

**convenience** [kən'vi:nɪəns] n (comfort) comodidad f; (advantage) ventaja; **at your earliest ~** (Comm) tan pronto como le sea posible; **all modern ~s** (BRIT) todo confort

**convenient** [kən'vi:nɪənt] adj (useful) útil; (place) conveniente; (time) oportuno

**convent** ['kɔnvənt] n convento

**convention** [kən'venʃən] n convención f; (meeting) asamblea; **conventional** adj convencional

**conversation** [kɔnvə'seɪʃən] n conversación f

**conversely** [kɔn'və:slɪ] adv a la inversa

**conversion** [kən'və:ʃən] n conversión f

**convert** [kən'və:t] vt (Rel, Comm) convertir; (alter) transformar ▷ n ['kɔnvə:t] converso/a; **convertible** adj convertible ▷ n descapotable m

**convey** [kən'veɪ] vt transportar; (thanks) comunicar; (idea) expresar; **conveyor belt** n cinta transportadora

**convict** [kən'vɪkt] vt (find guilty) declarar culpable a ▷ n ['kɔnvɪkt] presidiario/a; **conviction** [kən'vɪkʃən] n condena; (belief) convicción f

**convince** [kən'vɪns] vt convencer; **to ~ sb (of sth/that)** convencer a algn (de algo/de que); **convinced** adj: **convinced of/that** convencido de/de que; **convincing** adj convincente

**convoy** ['kɔnvɔɪ] n convoy m

**cook** [kuk] vt (stew etc) guisar; (meal) preparar ▷ vi hacerse; (person) cocinar ▷ n cocinero/a; **cookbook** n libro de cocina; **cooker** n cocina; **cookery** n cocina; **cookery book** n (BRIT) = **cookbook**

**cookie** ['kukɪ] n (US) galleta; (Comput) cookie f

**cooking** ['kukɪŋ] n cocina

**cool** [ku:l] adj fresco; (not afraid) tranquilo; (unfriendly) frío ▷ vt enfriar ▷ vi enfriarse;

**cool down** vi enfriarse; (fig: person, situation) calmarse; **cool off** vi (become calmer) calmarse, apaciguarse; (lose enthusiasm) perder (el) interés, enfriarse

**cop** [kɔp] n (inf) poli m

**cope** [kəup] vi: **to ~ with** (problem) hacer frente a

**copper** ['kɔpəʳ] n (metal) cobre m; (inf) poli m

**copy** ['kɔpɪ] n copia, (of book) ejemplar m ▷ vt (also Comput) copiar; **copyright** n derechos mpl de autor

**coral** ['kɔrəl] n coral m

**cord** [kɔ:d] n cuerda; (Elec) cable m; (fabric) pana; **cords** npl (trousers) pantalones mpl de pana; **cordless** adj sin hilos

**corduroy** ['kɔ:dərɔɪ] n pana

**core** [kɔ:ʳ] n centro, núcleo; (of fruit) corazón m; (of problem etc) meollo ▷ vt quitar el corazón de

**coriander** [kɔrɪ'ændəʳ] n culantro

**cork** [kɔ:k] n corcho; (tree) alcornoque m; **corkscrew** n sacacorchos m inv

**corn** [kɔ:n] n (BRIT: wheat) trigo; (US: maize) maíz m; (on foot) callo; **~ on the cob** (Culin) maíz en la mazorca

**corned beef** ['kɔ:nd-] n carne f de vaca acecinada

**corner** ['kɔ:nəʳ] n (outside) esquina; (inside) rincón m; (in road) curva; (Football) córner m ▷ vt (trap) arrinconar; (Comm) acaparar ▷ vi (in car) tomar las curvas; **corner shop** n (BRIT) tienda de la esquina

**cornflakes** ['kɔ:nfleɪks] npl copos mpl de maíz, cornflakes mpl

**cornflour** ['kɔ:nflauəʳ] n (BRIT) harina de maíz

**cornstarch** ['kɔ:nstɑ:tʃ] n (US) = **cornflour**

**Cornwall** ['kɔ:nwəl] n Cornualles m

**coronary** ['kɔrənərɪ] n: **~ (thrombosis)** infarto

**coronation** [kɔrə'neɪʃən] n coronación f

**coroner** ['kɔrənəʳ] n juez mf de instrucción

**corporal** ['kɔ:pərl] n cabo ▷ adj: **~ punishment** castigo corporal

**corporate** ['kɔ:pərɪt] adj (action, ownership) colectivo; (finance, image) corporativo

**corporation** [kɔ:pə'reɪʃən] n (of town) ayuntamiento; (Comm) corporación f

**corps** (pl **corps**) [kɔ:ʳ, kɔ:z] n cuerpo; **press ~** gabinete m de prensa

**corpse** [kɔ:ps] n cadáver m

**correct** [kə'rekt] adj correcto; (accurate) exacto ▷ vt corregir; **correction** n (act) corrección f; (instance) rectificación f

**correspond** [kɔrɪs'pɔnd] vi: **to ~ (with)** (write) escribirse (con); (be in accordance) corresponder (con); **to ~ (to)** (be equivalent *to*) corresponder (a); **correspondence** *n* correspondencia; **correspondent** *n* corresponsal *mf*; **corresponding** *adj* correspondiente

**corridor** ['kɒrɪdɔ:ʳ] *n* pasillo

**corrode** [kə'rəʊd] *vt* corroer ▷ *vi* corroerse

**corrupt** [kə'rʌpt] *adj* corrompido; (*person*) corrupto ▷ *vt* corromper; (*Comput*) degradar; **corruption** *n* corrupción *f*; (*of data*) alteración *f*

**Corsica** ['kɔ:sɪkə] *n* Córcega

**cosmetic** [kɒz'metɪk] *n* ▷ *adj* cosmético; **cosmetic surgery** *n* cirugía *f* estética

**cosmopolitan** [kɒzmə'pɒlɪtn] *adj* cosmopolita

**cost** [kɒst] (*pt, pp* cost) *n* (*price*) precio ▷ *vi* costar, valer ▷ *vt* preparar el presupuesto de; **costs** *npl* (*Law*) costas *fpl*; **how much does it ~?** ¿cuánto cuesta?; **to ~ sb time/ effort** costarle a algn tiempo/esfuerzo; **it ~ him his life** le costó la vida; **at all ~s** cueste lo que cueste

**co-star** ['kəʊstɑ:ʳ] *n* coprotagonista *mf*

**Costa Rica** ['kɒstə'ri:kə] *n* Costa Rica; **Costa Rican** *adj, n* costarriqueño/a

**costly** ['kɒstlɪ] *adj* costoso

**costume** ['kɒstju:m] *n* traje *m*; (BRIT: *also*: **swimming ~**) traje de baño

**cosy**, (US) **cozy** ['kəʊzɪ] *adj* cómodo; (*room, atmosphere*) acogedor(a)

**cot** [kɒt] *n* (BRIT: *child's*) cuna; (US: *folding bed*) cama plegable

**cottage** ['kɒtɪdʒ] *n* casita de campo; **cottage cheese** *n* requesón *m*

**cotton** ['kɒtn] *n* algodón *m*; (*thread*) hilo; **cotton on** *vi* (inf): **to ~ on (to sth)** caer en la cuenta (de algo); **cotton bud** *n* (BRIT) bastoncillo *m* de algodón; **cotton candy** *n* (US) algodón *m* (azucarado); **cotton wool** *n* (BRIT) algodón *m* (hidrófilo)

**couch** [kautʃ] *n* sofá *m*; (*in doctor's surgery*) camilla; (*psychiatrist's*) diván *m*

**cough** [kɒf] *vi* toser ▷ *n* tos *f*; **cough mixture** *n* jarabe *m* para la tos

**could** [kud] *pt of* **can²**; **couldn't** = **could not**

**council** ['kaunsl] *n* consejo; **city** *or* **town ~** ayuntamiento, consejo municipal; **council estate** *n* (BRIT) barriada de viviendas sociales de alquiler; **council house** *n* (BRIT) vivienda social de alquiler; **councillor** *n* concejal *mf*; **council tax** *n* (BRIT) contribución *f* municipal (*dependiente del valor de la vivienda*)

**counsel** ['kaunsl] *n* (*advice*) consejo; (*lawyer*) abogado/a ▷ *vt* aconsejar; **counselling**, (US) **counseling** *n* (*Psych*) asistencia *f* psicológica; **counsellor**, (US) **counselor** *n* consejero/a; abogado/a

**count** [kaunt] *vt* contar; (*include*) incluir ▷ *vi* contar ▷ *n* cuenta; (*of votes*) escrutinio; (*nobleman*) conde *m*; **count in** (inf) *vt*: **to ~ sb in on sth** contar con algn para algo; **count on** *vt fus* contar con; **countdown** *n* cuenta atrás

**counter** ['kauntəʳ] *n* (*in shop*) mostrador *m*; (*in games*) ficha ▷ *vt* contrarrestar ▷ *adv*: **~ to** contrario a

**counter-clockwise** ['kauntə'klɒkwaɪz] *adv* en sentido contrario al de las agujas del reloj

**counterfeit** ['kauntəfɪt] *n* falsificación *f* ▷ *vt* falsificar ▷ *adj* falso, falsificado

**counterpart** ['kauntəpɑ:t] *n* homólogo/a

**countess** ['kauntɪs] *n* condesa

**countless** ['kauntlɪs] *adj* innumerable

**country** ['kʌntrɪ] *n* país *m*; (*native land*) patria; (*as opposed to town*) campo; (*region*) región *f*, tierra; **country and western (music)** *n* música country; **country house** *n* casa de campo; **countryside** *n* campo

**county** ['kauntɪ] *n* condado

**coup** [ku:] (*pl* coups) *n* golpe *m*; (*triumph*) éxito; (*also*: **~ d'état**) golpe de estado

**couple** ['kʌpl] *n* (*of things*) par *m*; (*of people*) pareja; (*married couple*) matrimonio; **a ~ of** un par de

**coupon** ['ku:pɔn] *n* cupón *m*; (*voucher*) valé *m*

**courage** ['kʌrɪdʒ] *n* valor *m*, valentía; **courageous** [kə'reɪdʒəs] *adj* valiente

**courgette** [kuə'ʒet] *n* (BRIT) calabacín *m*

**courier** ['kurɪəʳ] *n* mensajero/a; (*for tourists*) guía *mf* (de turismo)

**course** [kɔ:s] *n* (*direction*) dirección *f*; (*of river*) curso; (*Scol*) curso; (*of ship*) rumbo; (*Golf*) campo; (*part of meal*) plato; **of ~** *adv* desde luego, naturalmente; **of ~!** ¡claro!; **~ of treatment** (*Med*) tratamiento

**court** [kɔ:t] *n* (*royal*) corte *f*; (*Law*) tribunal *m*, juzgado; (*Tennis*) pista, cancha (LAM) ▷ *vt* (*woman*) cortejar; **to take to ~** demandar

**courtesy** ['kə:təsɪ] *n* cortesía; **by ~ of** (por) cortesía de; **courtesy bus, courtesy coach** *n* autobús *m* gratuito

**court: courthouse** *n* (US) palacio de justicia; **courtroom** *n* sala de justicia; **courtyard** *n* patio

**cousin** ['kʌzn] *n* primo/a; **first ~** primo/a carnal

**cover** ['kʌvəʳ] *vt* cubrir; (*with lid*) tapar; (*distance*) cubrir, recorrer; (*include*) abarcar; (*protect*) abrigar; (*journalist*) investigar; (*issues*) tratar ▷ *n* cubierta; (*lid*) tapa; (*for chair etc*) funda; (*envelope*) sobre *m*; (*of magazine*) portada; (*shelter*) abrigo; (*insurance*) cobertura; **to take ~** (*shelter*) protegerse, resguardarse; **under ~** (*indoors*) bajo techo;

**under ~ of darkness** al amparo de la
oscuridad; **under separate ~** (Comm) por
separado; **cover up** vi: **to ~ up for sb** encubrir
a algn; **coverage** n (in media) cobertura
informativa; **cover charge** n precio del
cubierto; **cover-up** n encubrimiento

**cow** [kau] n vaca ▷ vt intimidar

**coward** ['kauəd] n cobarde mf; **cowardly**
adj cobarde

**cowboy** ['kaubɔɪ] n vaquero

**cozy** ['kəuzi] adj (US) = **cosy**

**crab** [kræb] n cangrejo

**crack** [kræk] n grieta; (noise) crujido; (drug)
crack m ▷ vt agrietar, romper; (nut) cascar;
(whip etc) chasquear; (knuckles) crujir; (joke)
contar ▷ adj (athlete) de primera clase;
**crack down on** vt fus adoptar medidas
severas contra; **cracked** adj (cup, window)
rajado; (wall) resquebrajado; **cracker** n
(biscuit) cráquer m; (Christmas cracker)
petardo sorpresa

**crackle** ['krækl] vi crepitar

**cradle** ['kreidl] n cuna

**craft** [krɑːft] n (skill) arte m; (trade) oficio;
(cunning) astucia; (boat) embarcación f;
**craftsman** n artesano; **craftsmanship** n
destreza

**cram** [kræm] vt (fill): **to ~ sth with** llenar
algo (a reventar) de; (put): **to ~ sth into**
meter algo a la fuerza en ▷ vi (for exams)
empollar

**cramp** [kræmp] n (Med) calambre m;
**cramped** adj apretado

**cranberry** ['krænbəri] n arándano agrio

**crane** [krein] n (Tech) grúa; (bird) grulla

**crap** [kræp] n (inf!) mierda (!)

**crash** [kræʃ] n (noise) estrépito; (of cars,
plane) accidente m; (of business) quiebra
▷ vt (plane) estrellar ▷ vi (plane) estrellarse;
(two cars) chocar; **crash course** n curso
acelerado; **crash helmet** n casco
(protector)

**crate** [kreit] n cajón m de embalaje; (for
bottles) caja

**crave** [kreiv] vt, vi: **to ~ (for)** ansiar, anhelar

**crawl** [krɔːl] vi (drag o.s.) arrastrarse; (child)
andar a gatas, gatear; (vehicle) avanzar
(lentamente) ▷ n (Swimming) crol m

**crayfish** ['kreifiʃ] n (pl inv: freshwater)
cangrejo (de río); (: saltwater) cigala

**crayon** ['kreiən] n lápiz m de color

**craze** [kreiz] n (fashion) moda

**crazy** ['kreizi] adj (person) loco; (idea)
disparatado; **to be ~ about sb/sth** (inf)
estar loco por algn/algo

**creak** [kriːk] vi crujir; (hinge etc) chirriar,
rechinar

**cream** [kriːm] n (of milk) nata, crema;
(lotion) crema; (fig) flor f y nata ▷ adj (colour)

color m crema; **cream cheese** n queso
blanco cremoso; **creamy** adj cremoso

**crease** [kriːs] n (fold) pliegue m; (in trousers)
raya; (wrinkle) arruga ▷ vt (wrinkle) arrugar
▷ vi (wrinkle up) arrugarse

**create** [kriː'eit] vt crear; **creation** n
creación f; **creative** adj creativo; **creator** n
creador(a) m/f

**creature** ['kriːtʃəʳ] n (animal) animal m;
(insect) bicho; (person) criatura

**crèche, creche** [kreʃ] n (BRIT) guardería
(infantil)

**credentials** [kri'denʃlz] npl referencias fpl

**credibility** [kredr'biliti] n credibilidad f

**credible** ['kredibl] adj creíble

**credit** ['kredit] n crédito; (merit) honor m,
mérito ▷ vt (Comm) abonar; (believe) creer,
dar crédito a ▷ adj crediticio; **to be in ~**
(person, bank account) tener saldo a favor;
**to ~ sb with** (fig) reconocer a algn el mérito
de; see also **credits**; **credit card** n tarjeta de
crédito; **credit crunch** n crisis f crediticia

**credits** ['kredits] npl (Cine) títulos mpl or
rótulos mpl de crédito, ficha técnica

**creek** [kriːk] n cala, ensenada; (US)
riachuelo

**creep** (pt, pp **crept**) [kriːp, krept] vi (animal)
deslizarse

**cremate** [kri'meit] vt incinerar

**crematorium** [kremə'tɔːriəm] (pl
**crematoria**) n crematorio

**crept** [krept] pt, pp of **creep**

**crescent** ['kresnt] n media luna; (street)
calle f (en forma de semicírculo)

**cress** [kres] n berro

**crest** [krest] n (of bird) cresta; (of hill) cima,
cumbre f; (of coat of arms) blasón m

**crew** [kruː] n (of ship etc) tripulación f; (Cine
etc) equipo; **crew-neck** n cuello a la caja

**crib** [krib] n cuna ▷ vt (inf) plagiar

**cricket** ['krikit] n (insect) grillo; (game)
críquet m; **cricketer** n jugador(a) m/f de
críquet

**crime** [kraim] n crimen m; (less serious)
delito; **criminal** ['kriminl] n criminal mf,
delincuente mf ▷ adj criminal; (law) penal

**crimson** ['krimzn] adj carmesí

**cringe** [krindʒ] vi encogerse

**cripple** ['kripl] vt lisiar, mutilar

**crisis** ['kraisis] (pl **crises**) n crisis f

**crisp** [krisp] adj fresco; (toast, snow)
crujiente; (manner) seco; **crispy** adj
crujiente

**criterion** [krai'tiəriən] (pl **criteria**) n
criterio

**critic** ['kritik] n crítico/a; **critical** adj
crítico; (illness) grave; **criticism** ['kritisizm]
n crítica; **criticize** ['kritisaiz] vt criticar

**Croat** ['krəuæt] adj, n = **Croatian**

**Croatia** [krəʊ'eɪʃə] n Croacia; **Croatian** adj, n croata mf ⊳ n (Ling) croata m
**crockery** ['krɒkərɪ] n loza, vajilla
**crocodile** ['krɒkədaɪl] n cocodrilo
**crocus** ['krəʊkəs] n crocus m, croco
**croissant** ['krwasã] n croissant m, medialuna (esp LAM)
**crook** [kruk] n ladrón/ona m/f; (of shepherd) cayado; **crooked** ['krukɪd] adj torcido; (inf) corrupto
**crop** [krɒp] n (produce) cultivo; (amount produced) cosecha; (riding crop) látigo de montar ⊳ vt cortar, recortar; **crop up** vi surgir, presentarse
**cross** [krɒs] n cruz f ⊳ vt (street etc) cruzar, atravesar ⊳ adj de mal humor, enojado; **cross off** vt tachar; **cross out** vt tachar; **cross over** vi cruzar; **cross-Channel ferry** n transbordador m que cruza el Canal de la Mancha; **cross-country (race)** n carrera a campo traviesa, cross m; **crossing** n (sea passage) travesía; (also: **pedestrian crossing**) paso de peatones; **crossing guard** n (US) persona encargada de ayudar a los niños a cruzar la calle; **crossroads** nsg cruce m; (fig) encrucijada; **crosswalk** n (US) paso de peatones; **crossword** n crucigrama m
**crotch** [krɒtʃ] n (of garment) entrepierna
**crouch** [kraʊtʃ] vi agacharse, acurrucarse
**crouton** ['kru:tɒn] n cubito de pan frito
**crow** [krəʊ] n (bird) cuervo; (of cock) canto, cacareo ⊳ vi (cock) cantar
**crowd** [kraʊd] n muchedumbre f ⊳ vt (gather) amontonar; (fill) llenar ⊳ vi (gather) reunirse; (pile up) amontonarse; **crowded** adj (full) atestado; (densely populated) superpoblado
**crown** [kraʊn] n corona; (of head) coronilla; (of hill) cumbre f; (for tooth) funda ⊳ vt coronar; **and to ~ it all ...** (fig) y para colmo or remate ...; **crown jewels** npl joyas fpl reales
**crucial** ['kru:ʃl] adj decisivo
**crucifix** ['kru:sɪfɪks] n crucifijo
**crude** [kru:d] adj (materials) bruto; (basic) tosco; (vulgar) ordinario ⊳ n (also: **~ oil**) (petróleo) crudo
**cruel** ['kruəl] adj cruel; **cruelty** n crueldad f
**cruise** [kru:z] n crucero ⊳ vi (ship) navegar; (car) ir a velocidad constante
**crumb** [krʌm] n miga, migaja
**crumble** ['krʌmbl] vt desmenuzar ⊳ vi (building) desmoronarse
**crumpet** ['krʌmpɪt] n ≈ bollo para tostar
**crumple** ['krʌmpl] vt (paper) estrujar; (material) arrugar
**crunch** [krʌntʃ] vt (with teeth) mascar; (underfoot) hacer crujir ⊳ n (fig) hora de la verdad; **crunchy** adj crujiente

**crush** [krʌʃ] n (crowd) aglomeración f ⊳ vt aplastar; (paper) estrujar; (cloth) arrugar; (fruit) exprimir; (opposition) aplastar; (hopes) destruir; **to have a ~ on sb** estar enamorado de algn
**crust** [krʌst] n corteza; **crusty** adj (bread) crujiente; (person) de mal carácter
**crutch** [krʌtʃ] n muleta
**cry** [kraɪ] vi llorar; (shout: also: **~ out**) gritar ⊳ n grito; (of animal) aullido; **cry out** vi (call out, shout) lanzar un grito, echar un grito ⊳ vt gritar
**crystal** ['krɪstl] n cristal m
**cub** [kʌb] n cachorro; (also: **~ scout**) niño explorador
**Cuba** ['kju:bə] n Cuba; **Cuban** adj, n cubano/a
**cube** [kju:b] n cubo ⊳ vt (Math) elevar al cubo
**cubicle** ['kju:bɪkl] n (at pool) caseta; (for bed) cubículo
**cuckoo** ['kuku:] n cuco
**cucumber** ['kju:kʌmbəʳ] n pepino
**cuddle** ['kʌdl] vt abrazar ⊳ vi abrazarse
**cue** [kju:] n (snooker cue) taco; (Theat etc) entrada
**cuff** [kʌf] n (BRIT: of shirt, coat etc) puño; (US: of trousers) vuelta; (blow) bofetada; **off the ~** adv improvisado; **cufflinks** npl gemelos mpl
**cuisine** [kwɪ'zi:n] n cocina
**cul-de-sac** ['kʌldəsæk] n callejón m sin salida
**cull** [kʌl] vt (kill selectively: animals) matar selectivamente ⊳ n matanza selectiva
**culminate** ['kʌlmɪneɪt] vi: **to ~ in** culminar en
**culprit** ['kʌlprɪt] n culpable mf
**cult** [kʌlt] n culto
**cultivate** ['kʌltɪveɪt] vt (also fig) cultivar
**cultural** ['kʌltʃərəl] adj cultural
**culture** ['kʌltʃəʳ] n (also fig) cultura; (Biol) cultivo
**cumin** ['kʌmɪn] n (spice) comino
**cunning** ['kʌnɪŋ] n astucia ⊳ adj astuto
**cup** [kʌp] n taza; (prize, event) copa
**cupboard** ['kʌbəd] n armario; (in kitchen) alacena
**cup final** n (Football) final f de copa
**curator** [kjuə'reɪtəʳ] n director(a) m/f
**curb** [kə:b] vt refrenar ⊳ n freno; (US) bordillo
**curdle** ['kə:dl] vi cuajarse
**cure** [kjuəʳ] vt curar ⊳ n cura, curación f; (fig: solution) remedio
**curfew** ['kə:fju:] n toque m de queda
**curiosity** [kjuərɪ'ɔsɪtɪ] n curiosidad f
**curious** ['kjuərɪəs] adj curioso; **I'm ~ about him** me intriga

**curl** [kə:l] n rizo ▷ vt (hair) rizar ▷ vi rizarse; **curl up** vi (person) hacerse un ovillo; **curler** n bigudí m, rulo; **curly** adj rizado

**currant** ['kʌrnt] n pasa; (black, red) grosella

**currency** ['kʌrnsɪ] n moneda; **to gain ~** (fig) difundirse

**current** ['kʌrnt] n corriente f ▷ adj actual; **in ~ use** de uso corriente; **current account** n (BRIT) cuenta corriente; **current affairs** npl (noticias fpl de) actualidad f; **currently** adv actualmente

**curriculum** [kə'rɪkjuləm] (pl **curriculums** or **curricula**) n plan m de estudios; **curriculum vitae** [-'viːtaɪ] n currículum m (vitae)

**curry** ['kʌrɪ] n curry m ▷ vt: **to ~ favour with** buscar el favor de; **curry powder** n curry m en polvo

**curse** [kə:s] vi echar pestes, soltar palabrotas ▷ vt maldecir ▷ n maldición f; (swearword) palabrota, taco

**cursor** ['kə:səʳ] n (Comput) cursor m

**curt** [kə:t] adj seco

**curtain** ['kə:tn] n cortina; (Theat) telón m; **to draw the ~s** (together) cerrar las cortinas; (apart) abrir las cortinas

**curve** [kə:v] n curva ▷ vi (road) hacer una curva; (line etc) curvarse; **curved** adj curvo

**cushion** ['kuʃən] n cojín m; (Snooker) banda ▷ vt (shock) amortiguar

**custard** ['kʌstəd] n natillas fpl

**custody** ['kʌstədɪ] n custodia; **to take sb into ~** detener a algn

**custom** ['kʌstəm] n costumbre f; (Comm) clientela

**customer** ['kʌstəməʳ] n cliente mf

**customized** ['kʌstəmaɪzd] adj (car etc) hecho a encargo

**customs** ['kʌstəmz] npl aduana sg; **customs officer** n aduanero/a

**cut** [kʌt] (pt, pp **cut**) vt cortar; (price) rebajar; (reduce) reducir ▷ vi cortar ▷ n corte m; (in skin) cortadura; (in salary etc) rebaja; (in spending) reducción f, recorte m; (slice of meat) tajada; **to ~ and paste** (Comput) cortar y pegar; **cut back** vt (plants) podar; (production, expenditure) reducir; **cut down** vt (tree) derribar; (consumption, expenses) reducir; **cut off** vt cortar; (fig) aislar; **we've been ~ off** (Tel) nos han cortado la comunicación; **cut out** vt (shape) recortar; (delete) suprimir; **cut up** vt cortar (en pedazos); **cutback** n reducción f

**cute** [kjuːt] adj mono

**cutlery** ['kʌtlərɪ] n cubiertos mpl

**cutlet** ['kʌtlɪt] n chuleta

**cut-price** ['kʌt'praɪs] adj a precio reducido

**cutting** ['kʌtɪŋ] adj (remark) mordaz ▷ n (BRIT: from newspaper) recorte m; (from plant) esqueje m

**CV** n abbr = **curriculum vitae**

**cyber attack** ['saɪbərətæk] n ciberataque m

**cyberbullying** ['saɪbəbulɪɪŋ] n ciberacoso

**cybercafé** ['saɪbə,kæfeɪ] n cibercafé m

**cyberspace** ['saɪbəspeɪs] n ciberespacio

**cycle** ['saɪkl] n ciclo; (bicycle) bicicleta ▷ vi ir en bicicleta; **cycle hire** n alquiler m de bicicletas; **cycle lane** n carril m bici; **cycle path** n carril-bici m; **cycling** n ciclismo; **cyclist** n ciclista mf

**cyclone** ['saɪkləun] n ciclón m

**cylinder** ['sɪlɪndəʳ] n cilindro

**cymbals** ['sɪmblz] npl platillos mpl

**cynical** ['sɪnɪkl] adj cínico

**Cypriot** ['sɪprɪət] adj, n chipriota mf

**Cyprus** ['saɪprəs] n Chipre f

**cyst** [sɪst] n quiste m; **cystitis** [sɪs'taɪtɪs] n cistitis f

**czar** [zɑːʳ] n zar m

**Czech** [tʃɛk] adj checo ▷ n checo/a; **the ~ Republic** la República Checa

# d

**D, d** [di:] n (Mus) re m
**dab** [dæb] vt: **to ~ ointment onto a wound** aplicar pomada sobre una herida; **to ~ with paint** dar unos toques de pintura
**dad** [dæd], **daddy** ['dædɪ] n papá m
**daffodil** ['dæfədɪl] n narciso
**daft** [dɑːft] adj tonto
**dagger** ['dægəʳ] n puñal m, daga; **to look ~s at sb** fulminar a algn con la mirada
**daily** ['deɪlɪ] adj diario, cotidiano ▷ adv todos los días, cada día
**dairy** ['dɛərɪ] n (shop) lechería; (on farm) vaquería; **dairy produce** n productos mpl lácteos
**daisy** ['deɪzɪ] n margarita
**dam** [dæm] n presa ▷ vt embalsar
**damage** ['dæmɪdʒ] n daño; (fig) perjuicio; (to machine) avería ▷ vt dañar; perjudicar; averiar; **~ to property** daños materiales; **damages** npl (Law) daños y perjuicios
**damn** [dæm] vt condenar; (curse) maldecir ▷ n (inf): **I don't give a ~** me importa un pito ▷ adj (inf: also: **~ed**) maldito; **~ (it)!** ¡maldito sea!
**damp** [dæmp] adj húmedo, mojado ▷ n humedad f ▷ vt (also: **~en**: cloth, rag) mojar; (: enthusiasm) enfriar
**dance** [dɑːns] n baile m ▷ vi bailar; **dance floor** n pista f de baile; **dancer** n bailador(a) m/f; (professional) bailarín/ina m/f; **dancing** n baile m
**dandelion** ['dændɪlaɪən] n diente m de león
**dandruff** ['dændrəf] n caspa
**D & T** (BRIT Scol) n abbr (= design and technology) diseño y pretecnología
**Dane** [deɪn] n danés/esa m/f
**danger** ['deɪndʒəʳ] n peligro; (risk) riesgo; **~!** (on sign) ¡peligro!; **to be in ~ of** correr riesgo de; **dangerous** adj peligroso

**dangle** ['dæŋgl] vt colgar ▷ vi pender, estar colgado
**Danish** ['deɪnɪʃ] adj danés/esa ▷ n (Ling) danés m
**dare** [dɛəʳ] vt: **to ~ sb to do** desafiar a algn a hacer ▷ vi: **to ~ (to) do sth** atreverse a hacer algo; **I ~ say** (I suppose) puede ser; **daring** adj (person) osado; (plan, escape) atrevido ▷ n atrevimiento, osadía
**dark** [dɑːk] adj oscuro; (hair, complexion) moreno ▷ n: **in the ~** a oscuras; **in the ~ about** (fig) ignorante de; **after ~** después del anochecer; **darken** vt (colour) hacer más oscuro ▷ vi oscurecerse; **darkness** n oscuridad f; **darkroom** n cuarto oscuro
**darling** ['dɑːlɪŋ] adj, n querido/a
**dart** [dɑːt] n dardo; (in sewing) pinza ▷ vi precipitarse; **dartboard** n diana; **darts** n dardos mpl
**dash** [dæʃ] n (small quantity: of liquid) gota, chorrito; (sign) raya ▷ vt (hopes) defraudar ▷ vi precipitarse, ir de prisa
**dashboard** ['dæʃbɔːd] n (Aut) salpicadero
**data** ['deɪtə] npl datos mpl; **database** n base f de datos; **data processing** n proceso or procesamiento de datos
**date** [deɪt] n (day) fecha; (with friend) cita; (fruit) dátil m ▷ vt fechar; (inf: girl etc) salir con; **~ of birth** fecha de nacimiento; **to ~** adv hasta la fecha; **dated** adj anticuado
**daughter** ['dɔːtəʳ] n hija; **daughter-in-law** n nuera, hija política
**daunting** ['dɔːntɪŋ] adj desalentador/a
**dawn** [dɔːn] n alba, amanecer m; (fig) nacimiento ▷ vi amanecer; (fig): **it ~ed on him that ...** cayó en la cuenta de que ...
**day** [deɪ] n día m; (working day) jornada; **the ~ before** el día anterior; **the ~ after tomorrow** pasado mañana; **the ~ before yesterday** anteayer; **the following ~** el día siguiente; **by ~** de día; **day-care centre** n centro de día; (for children) guardería infantil; **daydream** vi soñar despierto; **daylight** n luz f (del día); **day return** n (BRIT) billete m de ida y vuelta (en un día); **daytime** n día m; **day-to-day** adj cotidiano; **day trip** n excursión f (de un día)
**dazed** [deɪzd] adj aturdido
**dazzle** ['dæzl] vt deslumbrar; **dazzling** adj (light, smile) deslumbrante; (colour) fuerte
**DC** abbr (Elec) = **direct current**
**dead** [dɛd] adj muerto; (limb) dormido; (battery) agotado ▷ adv (completely) totalmente; (exactly) justo; **to shoot sb ~** matar a algn a tiros; **~ tired** muerto (de cansancio); **to stop ~** parar en seco; **dead end** n callejón m sin salida; **deadline** n fecha tope; **deadly** adj mortal, fatal;

**deadly dull** aburridísimo; **Dead Sea** n: **the Dead Sea** el Mar Muerto

**deaf** [dɛf] adj sordo; **deafen** vt ensordecer; **deafening** adj ensordecedor/a

**deal** [di:l] n (agreement) pacto, convenio ▷ vt (pt, pp **dealt**) dar; (card) repartir; **a great ~ (of)** bastante, mucho; **deal with** vt fus (people) tratar con; (problem) ocuparse de; (subject) tratar de; **dealer** n comerciante mf; (Cards) mano f; **dealings** npl (Comm) transacciones fpl; (relations) relaciones fpl

**dealt** [dɛlt] pt, pp of **deal**

**dean** [di:n] n (Rel) deán m; (Scol) decano/a

**dear** [dɪəʳ] adj querido; (expensive) caro ▷ n: **my ~** querido/a; **~ me!** ¡Dios mío!; **D~ Sir/ Madam** (in letter) Muy señor mío, Estimado señor/Estimada señora, De mi/nuestra (mayor) consideración (esp LAM); **D~ Mr/ Mrs X** Estimado/a señor(a) X; **dearly** adv (love) mucho; (pay) caro

**death** [dɛθ] n muerte f; **death penalty** n pena de muerte; **death sentence** n condena a muerte

**debate** [dɪ'beɪt] n debate m ▷ vt discutir

**debit** [dɛbɪt] n debe m ▷ vt: **to ~ a sum to sb/to sb's account** cargar una suma en cuenta a algn; **debit card** n tarjeta f de débito

**debris** ['dɛbri:] n escombros mpl

**debt** [dɛt] n deuda; **to be in ~** tener deudas

**debug** ['di:'bʌg] vt (Comput) depurar, limpiar

**début** ['deɪbju:] n presentación f

**Dec.** abbr (= December) dic

**decade** ['dɛkeɪd] n década, decenio

**decaffeinated** [dɪ'kæfɪneɪtɪd] adj descafeinado

**decay** [dɪ'keɪ] n (of building) desmoronamiento; (of tooth) caries f inv ▷ vi (rot) pudrirse

**deceased** [dɪ'si:st] n: **the ~** el/la difunto/a

**deceit** [dɪ'si:t] n engaño

**deceive** [dɪ'si:v] vt engañar

**December** [dɪ'sɛmbəʳ] n diciembre m

**decency** ['di:sənsɪ] n decencia

**decent** ['di:sənt] adj (proper) decente; (person) amable, bueno

**deception** [dɪ'sɛpʃən] n engaño

> ⬛ Be careful not to translate deception by the Spanish word decepción.

**deceptive** [dɪ'sɛptɪv] adj engañoso

**decide** [dɪ'saɪd] vt (person) decidir; (question, argument) resolver ▷ vi decidir; **to ~ to do/ that** decidir hacer/que; **to ~ on sth** tomar una decisión sobre algo

**decimal** ['dɛsɪməl] adj decimal ▷ n decimal f

**decision** [dɪ'sɪʒən] n decisión f

**decisive** [dɪ'saɪsɪv] adj decisivo; (manner, person) decidido

**deck** [dɛk] n (Naut) cubierta; (of bus) piso; (of cards) baraja; **record ~** platina; **deckchair** n tumbona

**declaration** [dɛklə'reɪʃən] n declaración f

**declare** [dɪ'klɛəʳ] vt declarar

**decline** [dɪ'klaɪn] n disminución f ▷ vt rehusar ▷ vi (person, business) decaer; (strength) disminuir

**decorate** ['dɛkəreɪt] vt (paint) pintar; (paper) empapelar; (adorn): **to ~ (with)** adornar (de), decorar (de); **decoration** n adorno; (act) decoración f; (medal) condecoración f; **decorator** n (workman) pintor m decorador

**decrease** ['di:kri:s] n disminución f ▷ vt [di'kri:s] disminuir, reducir ▷ vi reducirse

**decree** [dɪ'kri:] n decreto

**dedicate** ['dɛdɪkeɪt] vt dedicar; **dedicated** adj dedicado; (Comput) especializado; **dedicated word processor** procesador m de textos especializado or dedicado; **dedication** n (devotion) dedicación f; (in book) dedicatoria

**deduce** [dɪ'dju:s] vt deducir

**deduct** [dɪ'dʌkt] vt restar; (from wage etc) descontar; **deduction** n (amount deducted) descuento; (conclusion) deducción f, conclusión f

**deed** [di:d] n hecho, acto; (feat) hazaña; (Law) escritura

**deem** [di:m] vt (formal) juzgar, considerar

**deep** [di:p] adj profundo; (voice) bajo; (breath) profundo ▷ adv: **the spectators stood 20 ~** los espectadores se formaron de 20 en fondo; **to be four metres ~** tener cuatro metros de profundidad; **deep-fry** vt freír en aceite abundante; **deeply** adv (breathe) a pleno pulmón; (interested, moved, grateful) profundamente, hondamente

**deer** (pl **deer**) [dɪəʳ] n ciervo

**default** [dɪ'fɔ:lt] n (Comput) defecto; **by ~** por incomparecencia

**defeat** [dɪ'fi:t] n derrota ▷ vt derrotar, vencer

**defect** ['di:fɛkt] n defecto ▷ vi [dɪ'fɛkt]: **to ~ to the enemy** pasarse al enemigo; **defective** [dɪ'fɛktɪv] adj defectuoso

**defence**, (US) **defense** [dɪ'fɛns] n defensa

**defend** [dɪ'fɛnd] vt defender; **defendant** n acusado/a; (in civil case) demandado/a; **defender** n defensor(a) m/f; (Sport) defensa mf

**defense** [dɪ'fɛns] n (US) = **defence**

**defensive** [dɪ'fɛnsɪv] adj defensivo ▷ n: **on the ~** a la defensiva

**defer** [dɪ'fə:ʳ] vt aplazar

**defiance** [dɪˈfaɪəns] n desafío; **in ~ of** en contra de; **defiant** [dɪˈfaɪənt] adj (challenging) retador(a), desafiante

**deficiency** [dɪˈfɪʃənsɪ] n (lack) falta; (defect) defecto; **deficient** [dɪˈfɪʃənt] adj (lacking) insuficiente; **deficient in** deficiente en

**deficit** [ˈdɛfɪsɪt] n déficit m

**define** [dɪˈfaɪn] vt definir; (limits etc) determinar

**definite** [ˈdɛfɪnɪt] adj (fixed) determinado; (clear, obvious) claro; **he was ~ about it** no dejó lugar a dudas (sobre ello); **definitely** adv: **he's definitely mad** no cabe duda de que está loco

**definition** [dɛfɪˈnɪʃən] n definición f

**deflate** [diːˈfleɪt] vt desinflar

**deflect** [dɪˈflɛkt] vt desviar

**defraud** [dɪˈfrɔːd] vt: **to ~ sb of sth** estafar algo a algn

**defriend** [diːˈfrɛnd] vt (Internet) quitar de amigo a; **he has ~ed her on Facebook** la ha quitado de amiga en Facebook

**defrost** [diːˈfrɔst] vt (frozen food, fridge) descongelar

**defuse** [diːˈfjuːz] vt desarmar; (situation) calmar

**defy** [dɪˈfaɪ] vt (resist) oponerse a; (challenge) desafiar; **it defies description** resulta imposible describirlo

**degree** [dɪˈgriː] n grado; (Scol) título; **to have a ~ in maths** ser licenciado/a en matemáticas; **by ~s** (gradually) poco a poco, por etapas; **to some ~** hasta cierto punto

**dehydrated** [diːhaɪˈdreɪtɪd] adj deshidratado; (milk) en polvo

**de-icer** [diːˈaɪsəʳ] n descongelador m

**delay** [dɪˈleɪ] vt demorar, aplazar; (person) entretener; (train) retrasar ▷ vi tardar ▷ n demora, retraso; **without ~** en seguida, sin tardar

**delegate** [ˈdɛlɪgɪt] n delegado/a ▷ vt [ˈdɛlɪgeɪt] (person) delegar en; (task) delegar

**delete** [dɪˈliːt] vt suprimir, tachar

**deli** [ˈdɛlɪ] n = **delicatessen**

**deliberate** [dɪˈlɪbərɪt] adj (intentional) intencionado; (slow) pausado, lento ▷ vi [dɪˈlɪbəreɪt] deliberar; **deliberately** adv (on purpose) a propósito

**delicacy** [ˈdɛlɪkəsɪ] n delicadeza; (choice food) manjar m

**delicate** [ˈdɛlɪkɪt] adj delicado; (fragile) frágil

**delicatessen** [dɛlɪkəˈtɛsn] n tienda especializada en alimentos de calidad

**delicious** [dɪˈlɪʃəs] adj delicioso

**delight** [dɪˈlaɪt] n (feeling) placer m, deleite m; (object) encanto, delicia ▷ vt encantar, deleitar; **to take ~ in** deleitarse en; **delighted** adj: **delighted (at or with/to**

**do)** encantado (con/de hacer); **delightful** adj encantador(a), delicioso

**delinquent** [dɪˈlɪŋkwənt] adj, n delincuente mf

**deliver** [dɪˈlɪvəʳ] vt (distribute) repartir; (hand over) entregar; (message) comunicar; (speech) pronunciar; (Med) asistir al parto de; **delivery** n reparto; entrega; (of speaker) modo de expresarse; (Med) parto, alumbramiento; **to take delivery of** recibir

**delusion** [dɪˈluːʒən] n ilusión f, engaño

**de luxe** [dəˈlʌks] adj de lujo

**delve** [dɛlv] vi: **to ~ into** hurgar en

**demand** [dɪˈmɑːnd] vt exigir; (rights) reclamar ▷ n exigencia; (claim) reclamación f; (Econ) demanda; **to be in ~** ser muy solicitado; **on ~** a solicitud; **demanding** adj (boss) exigente; (work) absorbente

**demise** [dɪˈmaɪz] n (death) fallecimiento

**demo** [ˈdɛməʊ] n abbr (inf: = demonstration) manifestación f

**democracy** [dɪˈmɔkrəsɪ] n democracia

**democrat** [ˈdɛməkræt] n demócrata mf; **democratic** [dɛməˈkrætɪk] adj democrático; **the Democratic Party** el partido demócrata (estadounidense)

**demolish** [dɪˈmɔlɪʃ] vt derribar, demoler; (fig: argument) destruir

**demolition** [dɛməˈlɪʃən] n derribo, demolición f

**demon** [ˈdiːmən] n (evil spirit) demonio

**demonstrate** [ˈdɛmənstreɪt] vt demostrar ▷ vi manifestarse; **demonstration** [dɛmənˈstreɪʃən] n (Pol) manifestación f; (proof) prueba, demostración f; **demonstrator** n (Pol) manifestante mf

**demote** [dɪˈməʊt] vt degradar

**den** [dɛn] n (of animal) guarida

**denial** [dɪˈnaɪəl] n (refusal) denegación f; (of report etc) desmentido

**denim** [ˈdɛnɪm] n tela vaquera; **denims** npl vaqueros mpl

**Denmark** [ˈdɛnmɑːk] n Dinamarca

**denomination** [dɪnɔmɪˈneɪʃən] n valor m; (Rel) confesión f

**denounce** [dɪˈnaʊns] vt denunciar

**dense** [dɛns] adj (thick) espeso; (foliage etc) tupido; (stupid) torpe

**density** [ˈdɛnsɪtɪ] n densidad f; **single/ double-~ disk** n (Comput) disco de densidad sencilla/de doble densidad

**dent** [dɛnt] n abolladura ▷ vt (also: **make a ~ in**) abollar

**dental** [ˈdɛntl] adj dental; **dental floss** n seda dental; **dental surgery** n clínica dental, consultorio dental

**dentist** [ˈdɛntɪst] n dentista mf

**dentures** [ˈdɛntʃəz] npl dentadura sg (postiza)

**deny** [dɪ'naɪ] vt negar; (charge) rechazar

**deodorant** [di:'əudərənt] n desodorante m

**depart** [dɪ'pɑ:t] vi irse, marcharse; (train) salir; **to ~ from** (fig: differ from) apartarse de

**department** [dɪ'pɑ:tmənt] n (Comm) sección f; (Scol) departamento; (Pol) ministerio; **department store** n grandes almacenes mpl

**departure** [dɪ'pɑ:tʃər] n partida, ida; (of train) salida; **a new ~** un nuevo rumbo; **departure lounge** n (at airport) sala de embarque

**depend** [dɪ'pɛnd] vi: **to ~ (up)on** depender de; (rely on) contar con; **it ~s** depende, según; **~ing on the result** según el resultado; **dependant** n dependiente mf; **dependent** adj: **to be dependent (on)** depender (de) ▷ n = **dependant**

**depict** [dɪ'pɪkt] vt (in picture) pintar; (describe) representar

**deport** [dɪ'pɔ:t] vt deportar

**deposit** [dɪ'pɔzɪt] n depósito; (Chem) sedimento; (of ore, oil) yacimiento ▷ vt depositar; **deposit account** n (BRIT) cuenta de ahorros

**depot** ['dɛpəu] n (storehouse) depósito; (for vehicles) parque m

**depreciate** [dɪ'pri:ʃɪeɪt] vi depreciarse, perder valor

**depress** [dɪ'prɛs] vt deprimir; (press down) apretar; **depressed** adj deprimido; **depressing** adj deprimente; **depression** n depresión f

**deprive** [dɪ'praɪv] vt: **to ~ sb of** privar a algn de; **deprived** adj necesitado

**dept.** abbr (= department) dto

**depth** [dɛpθ] n profundidad f; **at a ~ of three metres** a tres metros de profundidad; **to be out of one's ~** (swimmer) perder pie; (fig) sentirse perdido

**deputy** ['dɛpjuti] adj: **~ head** subdirector(a) m/f ▷ n sustituto/a, suplente mf; (Pol) diputado/a

**derail** [dɪ'reɪl] vt: **to be ~ed** descarrilarse

**derelict** ['dɛrɪlɪkt] adj abandonado

**derive** [dɪ'raɪv] vt derivar; (benefit etc) obtener ▷ vi: **to ~ from** derivarse de

**descend** [dɪ'sɛnd] vt, vi descender, bajar; **to ~ from** descender de; **descendant** n descendiente mf

**descent** [dɪ'sɛnt] n descenso; (origin) descendencia

**describe** [dɪs'kraɪb] vt describir; **description** [dɪs'krɪpʃən] n descripción f; (sort) clase f, género

**desert** [n 'dɛzət, vt, vi dɪ'zə:t] n desierto ▷ vt abandonar ▷ vi (Mil) desertar; **deserted** adj desierto

**deserve** [dɪ'zə:v] vt merecer, ser digno de

**design** [dɪ'zaɪn] n (sketch) bosquejo; (of dress, car) diseño; (pattern) dibujo ▷ vt diseñar; **design and technology** n (BRIT Scol) diseño y tecnología

**designate** ['dɛzɪgneɪt] vt (appoint) nombrar; (destine) designar ▷ adj ['dɛzɪgnɪt] designado

**designer** [dɪ'zaɪnər] n diseñador/a (m/f)

**desirable** [dɪ'zaɪərəbl] adj (proper) deseable; (attractive) atractivo

**desire** [dɪ'zaɪər] n deseo ▷ vt desear

**desk** [dɛsk] n (in office) escritorio; (for pupil) pupitre m; (in hotel, at airport) recepción f; (BRIT: in shop, restaurant) caja

**desktop** ['dɛsktɔp] n (Comput) escritorio; **desktop publishing** n autoedición f

**despair** [dɪs'pɛər] n desesperación f ▷ vi: **to ~ of** desesperar de

**despatch** [dɪs'pætʃ] n, vt = **dispatch**

**desperate** ['dɛspərɪt] adj desesperado; (fugitive) peligroso; **to be ~ for sth/to do** necesitar urgentemente algo/hacer; **desperately** adv desesperadamente; (very) terriblemente, gravemente

**desperation** [dɛspə'reɪʃən] n desesperación f; **in ~** desesperado

**despise** [dɪs'paɪz] vt despreciar

**despite** [dɪs'paɪt] prep a pesar de, pese a

**dessert** [dɪ'zə:t] n postre m; **dessertspoon** n cuchara (de postre)

**destination** [dɛstɪ'neɪʃən] n destino

**destined** ['dɛstɪnd] adj: **~ for London** con destino a Londres

**destiny** ['dɛstɪnɪ] n destino

**destroy** [dɪs'trɔɪ] vt destruir

**destruction** [dɪs'trʌkʃən] n destrucción f

**destructive** [dɪs'trʌktɪv] adj destructivo, destructor(a)

**detach** [dɪ'tætʃ] vt separar; (unstick) despegar; **detached** adj (attitude) objetivo, imparcial; **detached house** n chalé m, chalet m

**detail** ['di:teɪl] n detalle m ▷ vt detallar; (Mil) destacar; **in ~** detalladamente; **to go into ~(s)** entrar en detalles; **detailed** adj detallado

**detain** [dɪ'teɪn] vt retener; (in captivity) detener

**detect** [dɪ'tɛkt] vt descubrir; (Med, Police) identificar; (Mil, Radar, Tech) detectar; **detection** n descubrimiento; identificación f; **detective** n detective m; **detective story** n novela policíaca

**detention** [dɪ'tɛnʃən] n detención f, arresto; (Scol) castigo

**deter** [dɪ'tə:r] vt (dissuade) disuadir

**detergent** [dɪ'tə:dʒənt] n detergente m

**deteriorate** [dɪ'tɪərɪəreɪt] vi deteriorarse

**determination** [dɪtə:mɪˈneɪʃən] *n*
resolución *f*

**determine** [dɪˈtə:mɪn] *vt* determinar;
**determined** *adj*: **to be determined to do
sth** estar decidido *or* resuelto a hacer algo

**deterrent** [dɪˈterənt] *n* fuerza de disuasión

**detest** [dɪˈtest] *vt* aborrecer

**detour** [ˈdi:tuəʳ] *n* (*us Aut*: *diversion*) desvío

**detox** [ˈdi:tɔks] *n* desintoxicación *f*

**detract** [dɪˈtrækt] *vt*: **to ~ from** quitar
mérito a, restar valor a

**detrimental** [detrɪˈmentl] *adj*: **~ (to)**
perjudicial (a)

**devastating** [ˈdevəsteɪtɪŋ] *adj*
devastador/a; (*fig*) arrollador/a

**develop** [dɪˈveləp] *vt* desarrollar; (*Phot*)
revelar; (*disease*) contraer; (*habit*) adquirir
▷ *vi* desarrollarse; (*advance*) progresar;
**developing country** *n* país *m* en (vías de)
desarrollo; **development** *n* desarrollo;
(*advance*) progreso; (*of affair, case*)
desenvolvimiento; (*of land*) urbanización *f*

**device** [dɪˈvaɪs] *n* (*apparatus*) aparato,
mecanismo

**devil** [ˈdevl] *n* diablo, demonio

**devious** [ˈdi:vɪəs] *adj* taimado

**devise** [dɪˈvaɪz] *vt* idear, inventar

**devote** [dɪˈvəut] *vt*: **to ~ sth to** dedicar
algo a; **devoted** *adj* (*loyal*) leal, fiel; **to be
devoted to sb** querer con devoción a algn;
**the book is devoted to politics** el libro
trata de política; **devotion** *n* dedicación *f*;
(*Rel*) devoción *f*

**devour** [dɪˈvauəʳ] *vt* devorar

**devout** [dɪˈvaut] *adj* devoto

**dew** [dju:] *n* rocío

**diabetes** [daɪəˈbi:ti:z] *n* diabetes *f*

**diabetic** [daɪəˈbetɪk] *n* diabético/a

**diagnose** [ˈdaɪəgnəuz] *vt* diagnosticar

**diagnosis** (*pl* **diagnoses**) [daɪəgˈnəusɪs,
-si:z] *n* diagnóstico

**diagonal** [daɪˈægənl] *adj* diagonal ▷ *n*
diagonal *f*

**diagram** [ˈdaɪəgræm] *n* diagrama *m*,
esquema *m*

**dial** [ˈdaɪəl] *n* esfera; (*of radio*) dial; (*of phone*)
disco ▷ *vt* (*number*) marcar

**dialect** [ˈdaɪəlekt] *n* dialecto

**dialling code** [ˈdaɪəlɪŋ-] *n* prefijo

**dialling tone** *n* señal *f* para marcar

**dialogue**, (*us*) **dialog** [ˈdaɪələg] *n* diálogo

**diameter** [daɪˈæmɪtəʳ] *n* diámetro

**diamond** [ˈdaɪəmənd] *n* diamante *m*;
**diamonds** *npl* (*Cards*) diamantes *mpl*

**diaper** [ˈdaɪəpəʳ] *n* (*us*) pañal *m*

**diarrhoea**, (*us*) **diarrhea** [daɪəˈri:ə] *n*
diarrea

**diary** [ˈdaɪərɪ] *n* (*daily account*) diario; (*book*)
agenda

**dice** [daɪs] *n* (*pl inv*) dados *mpl* ▷ *vt* (*Culin*)
cortar en cuadritos

**dictate** [dɪkˈteɪt] *vt* dictar; **dictation** *n*
dictado

**dictator** [dɪkˈteɪtəʳ] *n* dictador *m*

**dictionary** [ˈdɪkʃənrɪ] *n* diccionario

**did** [dɪd] *pt of* **do**

**didn't** [ˈdɪdənt] = **did not**

**die** [daɪ] *vi* morir; **to be dying for sth/
to do sth** morirse por algo/de ganas de
hacer algo; **die down** *vi* apagarse; (*wind*)
amainar; **die out** *vi* desaparecer

**diesel** [ˈdi:zl] *n* diesel *m*

**diet** [ˈdaɪət] *n* dieta; (*restricted food*) régimen
*m* ▷ *vi* (*also*: **be on a ~**) estar a dieta, hacer
régimen

**differ** [ˈdɪfəʳ] *vi* (*be different*) ser distinto,
diferenciarse; (*disagree*) discrepar;
**difference** [ˈdɪfrəns] *n* diferencia; (*quarrel*)
desacuerdo; **different** *adj* diferente,
distinto; **differentiate** [dɪfəˈrenʃɪeɪt] *vi*:
**to differentiate between** distinguir entre;
**differently** *adv* de otro modo, en forma
distinta

**difficult** [ˈdɪfɪkəlt] *adj* difícil; **difficulty** *n*
dificultad *f*

**dig** [dɪg] *vt* (*pt, pp* **dug**) (*hole*) cavar;
(*ground*) remover ▷ *n* (*prod*) empujón *m*;
(*archaeological*) excavación *f*; (*remark*)
indirecta; **to ~ one's nails into** clavar
las uñas en; *see also* **digs**; **dig up** *vt*
desenterrar; (*plant*) desarraigar

**digest** [daɪˈdʒest] *vt* (*food*) digerir; (*facts*)
asimilar ▷ *n* [ˈdaɪdʒest] resumen *m*;
**digestion** *n* digestión *f*

**digit** [ˈdɪdʒɪt] *n* (*number*) dígito; (*finger*)
dedo; **digital** *adj* digital; **digital camera**
*n* cámara digital; **digital TV** *n* televisión *f*
digital

**dignified** [ˈdɪgnɪfaɪd] *adj* grave, solemne

**dignity** [ˈdɪgnɪtɪ] *n* dignidad *f*

**digs** [dɪgz] *npl* (*BRIT inf*) pensión *f*,
alojamiento

**dilemma** [daɪˈlemə] *n* dilema *m*

**dill** [dɪl] *n* eneldo

**dilute** [daɪˈlu:t] *vt* diluir

**dim** [dɪm] *adj* (*light*) débil; (*outline*) borroso;
(*stupid*) lerdo; (*room*) oscuro ▷ *vt* (*light*)
bajar

**dime** [daɪm] *n* (*us*) moneda de diez centavos

**dimension** [dɪˈmenʃən] *n* dimensión *f*

**diminish** [dɪˈmɪnɪʃ] *vt, vi* disminuir

**din** [dɪn] *n* estruendo, estrépito

**dine** [daɪn] *vi* cenar; **diner** *n* (*person*)
comensal *mf*

**dinghy** [ˈdɪŋgɪ] *n* bote *m*; (*also*: **rubber ~**)
lancha (neumática)

**dingy** [ˈdɪndʒɪ] *adj* (*room*) sombrío; (*dirty*)
sucio

**dining car** ['daɪnɪŋ-] n (BRIT) coche-restaurante m

**dining room** n comedor m

**dining table** n mesa f de comedor

**dinkum** ['dɪŋkəm] adj (AUST, NZ inf: also: **fair ~**) de verdad, auténtico; **fair ~?** ¿de verdad?

**dinner** ['dɪnəʳ] n (evening meal) cena; (lunch) comida; (public) cena, banquete m; **dinner jacket** n smoking m; **dinner party** n cena; **dinner time** n (evening) hora de cenar; (midday) hora de comer

**dinosaur** ['daɪnəsɔːʳ] n dinosaurio

**dip** [dɪp] n (slope) pendiente f; (in sea) chapuzón m ▷ vt (in water) mojar; (ladle etc) meter; (BRIT Aut): **to ~ one's lights** poner la luz de cruce ▷ vi descender, bajar

**diploma** [dɪ'pləumə] n diploma m

**diplomacy** [dɪ'pləuməsɪ] n diplomacia

**diplomat** ['dɪpləmæt] n diplomático/a; **diplomatic** [dɪplə'mætɪk] adj diplomático

**dipstick** ['dɪpstɪk] n (Aut) varilla de nivel (del aceite)

**dire** [daɪəʳ] adj calamitoso

**direct** [daɪ'rɛkt] adj directo; (manner, person) franco ▷ vt dirigir; **can you ~ me to ...?** ¿puede indicarme dónde está ...?; **to ~ sb to do sth** mandar a algn hacer algo; **direct debit** n domiciliación f bancaria de recibos

**direction** [dɪ'rɛkʃən] n dirección f; **sense of ~** sentido de la orientación; **directions** npl instrucciones fpl; **~s for use** modo de empleo

**directly** [dɪ'rɛktlɪ] adv (in straight line) directamente; (at once) en seguida

**director** [dɪ'rɛktəʳ] n director(a) m/f

**directory** [dɪ'rɛktərɪ] n (Tel) guía (telefónica); (Comput) directorio; **directory enquiries**, (US) **directory assistance** n (service) (servicio m de) información

**dirt** [dəːt] n suciedad f; **dirty** adj sucio; (joke) verde, colorado (LAM) ▷ vt ensuciar; (stain) manchar

**disability** [dɪsə'bɪlɪtɪ] n incapacidad f

**disabled** [dɪs'eɪbld] adj (physically) minusválido/a

**disadvantage** [dɪsəd'vɑːntɪdʒ] n desventaja, inconveniente m

**disagree** [dɪsə'griː] vi (differ) discrepar; **to ~ (with)** no estar de acuerdo (con); **disagreeable** adj desagradable; **disagreement** n desacuerdo

**disappear** [dɪsə'pɪəʳ] vi desaparecer; **disappearance** n desaparición f

**disappoint** [dɪsə'pɔɪnt] vt decepcionar; defraudar; **disappointed** adj decepcionado; **disappointing** adj decepcionante; **disappointment** n decepción f

**disapproval** [dɪsə'pruːvəl] n desaprobación f

**disapprove** [dɪsə'pruːv] vi: **to ~ of** desaprobar

**disarm** [dɪs'ɑːm] vt desarmar; **disarmament** n desarme m

**disaster** [dɪ'zɑːstəʳ] n desastre m

**disastrous** [dɪ'zɑːstrəs] adj desastroso

**disbelief** [dɪsbə'liːf] n incredulidad f

**disc** [dɪsk] n disco; (Comput); = **disk**

**discard** [dɪs'kɑːd] vt tirar; (fig) descartar

**discharge** [dɪs'tʃɑːdʒ] vt (task, duty) cumplir; (patient) dar de alta; (employee) despedir; (soldier) licenciar; (defendant) poner en libertad ▷ n ['dɪstʃɑːdʒ] (Elec) descarga; (dismissal) despedida; (of duty) desempeño; (of debt) pago, descargo

**discipline** ['dɪsɪplɪn] n disciplina ▷ vt disciplinar

**disc jockey** n pinchadiscos m inv f inv

**disclose** [dɪs'kləuz] vt revelar

**disco** ['dɪskəu] n abbr = **discothèque**

**discoloured**, (US) **discolored** [dɪs'kʌləd] adj descolorido

**discomfort** [dɪs'kʌmfət] n incomodidad f; (unease) inquietud f; (physical) malestar m

**disconnect** [dɪskə'nɛkt] vt separar; (Elec etc) desconectar

**discontent** [dɪskən'tɛnt] n descontento

**discontinue** [dɪskən'tɪnjuː] vt interrumpir; (payments) suspender

**discothèque** ['dɪskəutɛk] n discoteca

**discount** ['dɪskaunt] n descuento ▷ vt [dɪs'kaunt] descontar

**discourage** [dɪs'kʌrɪdʒ] vt desalentar; **to ~ sb from doing** disuadir a algn de hacer

**discover** [dɪs'kʌvəʳ] vt descubrir; **discovery** n descubrimiento

**discredit** [dɪs'krɛdɪt] vt desacreditar

**discreet** [dɪ'skriːt] adj (tactful) discreto; (careful) circunspecto, prudente

**discrepancy** [dɪ'skrɛpənsɪ] n (difference) diferencia

**discretion** [dɪ'skrɛʃən] n (tact) discreción f; **at the ~ of** a criterio de

**discriminate** [dɪ'skrɪmɪneɪt] vi: **to ~ between** distinguir entre; **to ~ against** discriminar contra; **discrimination** [dɪskrɪmɪ'neɪʃən] n (discernment) perspicacia; (bias) discriminación f

**discuss** [dɪ'skʌs] vt discutir; (a theme) tratar; **discussion** n discusión f

**disease** [dɪ'ziːz] n enfermedad f

**disembark** [dɪsɪm'bɑːk] vt, vi desembarcar

**disgrace** [dɪs'greɪs] n ignominia; (shame) vergüenza, escándalo ▷ vt deshonrar; **disgraceful** adj vergonzoso

**disgruntled** [dɪsˈgrʌntld] adj disgustado, descontento

**disguise** [dɪsˈgaɪz] n disfraz m ▷ vt disfrazar; **in ~** disfrazado

**disgust** [dɪsˈgʌst] n repugnancia ▷ vt repugnar, dar asco a
   ▌ Be careful not to translate *disgust* by the Spanish word *disgustar*.

**disgusted** [dɪsˈgʌstɪd] adj indignado
   ▌ Be careful not to translate *disgusted* by the Spanish word *disgustado*.

**disgusting** [dɪsˈgʌstɪŋ] adj repugnante, asqueroso

**dish** [dɪʃ] n plato; **to do** or **wash the ~es** fregar los platos; **dishcloth** n (for washing) bayeta; (for drying) paño de cocina

**dishonest** [dɪsˈɒnɪst] adj (person) poco honrado, tramposo; (means) fraudulento

**dishtowel** [ˈdɪʃtauəl] n (US) bayeta

**dishwasher** [ˈdɪʃwɔʃəʳ] n lavaplatos m inv

**disillusion** [dɪsɪˈluːʒən] vt desilusionar

**disinfectant** [dɪsɪnˈfɛktənt] n desinfectante m

**disintegrate** [dɪsˈɪntɪgreɪt] vi disgregarse, desintegrarse

**disk** [dɪsk] n (Comput) disco, disquete m; **single-/double-sided ~** disco de una cara/dos caras; **disk drive** n unidad f (de disco); **diskette** n disquete m

**dislike** [dɪsˈlaɪk] n antipatía, aversión f ▷ vt tener antipatía a

**dislocate** [ˈdɪsləkeɪt] vt dislocar

**disloyal** [dɪsˈlɔɪəl] adj desleal

**dismal** [ˈdɪzml] adj (dark) sombrío; (depressing) triste; (very bad) fatal

**dismantle** [dɪsˈmæntl] vt desmontar, desarmar

**dismay** [dɪsˈmeɪ] n consternación f ▷ vt consternar

**dismiss** [dɪsˈmɪs] vt (worker) despedir; (idea) rechazar; (Law) rechazar; (possibility) descartar; **dismissal** n despido

**disobedient** [dɪsəˈbiːdɪənt] adj desobediente

**disobey** [dɪsəˈbeɪ] vt desobedecer

**disorder** [dɪsˈɔːdəʳ] n desorden m; (rioting) disturbio; (Med) trastorno

**disorganized** [dɪsˈɔːgənaɪzd] adj desorganizado

**disown** [dɪsˈəun] vt renegar de

**dispatch** [dɪsˈpætʃ] vt enviar ▷ n (sending) envío; (Press) informe m; (Mil) parte m

**dispel** [dɪsˈpɛl] vt disipar

**dispense** [dɪsˈpɛns] vt (medicine) preparar; **dispense with** vt fus prescindir de; **dispenser** n (container) distribuidor m automático

**disperse** [dɪsˈpəːs] vt dispersar ▷ vi dispersarse

**display** [dɪsˈpleɪ] n (in shop window) escaparate m; (exhibition) exposición f; (Comput) visualización f; (of feeling) manifestación f ▷ vt exponer; manifestar; (ostentatiously) lucir

**displease** [dɪsˈpliːz] vt (offend) ofender; (annoy) fastidiar

**disposable** [dɪsˈpəuzəbl] adj desechable; **~ personal income** ingresos mpl personales disponibles

**disposal** [dɪsˈpəuzl] n (of rubbish) destrucción f; **at one's ~** a la disposición de algn

**dispose** [dɪsˈpəuz] vi: **~ of** (unwanted goods) deshacerse de; (Comm: sell) traspasar, vender

**disposition** [dɪspəˈzɪʃən] n disposición f; (temperament) carácter m

**disproportionate** [dɪsprəˈpɔːʃənət] adj desproporcionado

**dispute** [dɪsˈpjuːt] n disputa; (also: **industrial ~**) conflicto (laboral) ▷ vt (argue) disputar; (question) cuestionar

**disqualify** [dɪsˈkwɔlɪfaɪ] vt (Sport) descalificar; **to ~ sb for sth/from doing sth** incapacitar a algn para algo/para hacer algo

**disregard** [dɪsrɪˈgaːd] vt (ignore) no hacer caso de

**disrupt** [dɪsˈrʌpt] vt (plans) desbaratar, trastornar; (meeting, public transport, conversation) interrumpir; **disruption** n desbaratamiento; trastorno; interrupción f

**dissatisfaction** [dɪssætɪsˈfækʃən] n disgusto, descontento

**dissatisfied** [dɪsˈsætɪsfaɪd] adj insatisfecho

**dissect** [dɪˈsɛkt] vt disecar

**dissent** [dɪˈsɛnt] n disensión f

**dissertation** [dɪsəˈteɪʃən] n tesina

**dissolve** [dɪˈzɔlv] vt disolver ▷ vi disolverse

**distance** [ˈdɪstns] n distancia; **in the ~** a lo lejos

**distant** [ˈdɪstnt] adj lejano; (manner) reservado, frío

**distil**, (US) **distill** [dɪsˈtɪl] vt destilar; **distillery** n destilería

**distinct** [dɪsˈtɪŋkt] adj (different) distinto; (clear) claro; (unmistakeable) inequívoco; **as ~ from** a diferencia de; **distinction** n distinción f; (in exam) sobresaliente m; **distinctive** adj distintivo

**distinguish** [dɪsˈtɪŋgwɪʃ] vt distinguir; **distinguished** adj (eminent) distinguido

**distort** [dɪsˈtɔːt] vt deformar; (sound) distorsionar

**distract** [dɪsˈtrækt] vt distraer; **distracted** adj distraído; **distraction** n distracción f; (confusion) aturdimiento

**distraught** [dɪsˈtrɔːt] *adj* turbado, enloquecido

**distress** [dɪsˈtrɛs] *n* (*anguish*) angustia ▷ *vt* afligir; **distressing** *adj* angustioso; doloroso

**distribute** [dɪsˈtrɪbjuːt] *vt* distribuir; (*share out*) repartir; **distribution** [dɪstrɪˈbjuːʃən] *n* distribución *f*; **distributor** *n* (*Aut*) distribuidor *m*; (*Comm*) distribuidora

**district** [ˈdɪstrɪkt] *n* (*of country*) zona, región *f*; (*of town*) barrio; (*Admin*) distrito; **district attorney** *n* (*US*) fiscal *mf*

**distrust** [dɪsˈtrʌst] *n* desconfianza ▷ *vt* desconfiar de

**disturb** [dɪsˈtəːb] *vt* (*person: bother, interrupt*) molestar; (*disorganize*) desordenar; **disturbance** *n* (*political etc*) disturbio; (*of mind*) trastorno; **disturbed** *adj* (*worried, upset*) preocupado, angustiado; **to be emotionally/mentally disturbed** tener problemas emocionales/ser un trastornado mental; **disturbing** *adj* inquietante, perturbador(a)

**ditch** [dɪtʃ] *n* zanja; (*irrigation ditch*) acequia ▷ *vt* (*inf: partner*) deshacerse de; (: *plan, car etc*) abandonar

**ditto** [ˈdɪtəu] *adv* ídem, lo mismo

**dive** [daɪv] *n* (*from board*) salto; (*underwater*) buceo; (*of submarine*) inmersión *f* ▷ *vi* (*swimmer: into water*) saltar; (: *under water*) zambullirse, bucear; (*fish, submarine*) sumergirse; (*bird*) lanzarse en picado; **to ~ into** (*bag etc*) meter la mano en; (*place*) meterse de prisa en; **diver** *n* (*underwater*) buzo

**diverse** [daɪˈvəːs] *adj* diversos/as, varios/as

**diversion** [daɪˈvəːʃən] *n* (*BRIT Aut*) desviación *f*; (*distraction*) diversión *f*; (*Mil*) diversión *f*

**diversity** [daɪˈvəːsɪtɪ] *n* diversidad *f*

**divert** [daɪˈvəːt] *vt* (*train, plane, traffic*) desviar

**divide** [dɪˈvaɪd] *vt* dividir; (*separate*) separar ▷ *vi* dividirse; (*road*) bifurcarse; **divided highway** *n* (*US*) carretera de doble calzada

**divine** [dɪˈvaɪn] *adj* divino

**diving** [ˈdaɪvɪŋ] *n* (*Sport*) salto; (*underwater*) buceo; **diving board** *n* trampolín *m*

**division** [dɪˈvɪʒən] *n* división *f*; (*sharing out*) reparto; (*disagreement*) diferencias *fpl*; (*Comm*) sección *f*

**divorce** [dɪˈvɔːs] *n* divorcio ▷ *vt* divorciarse de; **divorced** *adj* divorciado; **divorcee** [dɪvɔːˈsiː] *n* divorciado/a

**DIY** *adj, n abbr* = **do-it-yourself**

**dizzy** [ˈdɪzɪ] *adj* (*person*) mareado; **to feel ~** marearse

**DJ** *n abbr* (= *disc jokey*) DJ *mf*

**DNA** *n abbr* (= *deoxyribonucleic acid*) ADN *m*

 **KEYWORD**

**do** [duː] (*pt* **did**, *pp* **done**) *n* (*inf: party etc*): **we're having a little do on Saturday** damos una fiestecita el sábado; **it was rather a grand do** fue un acontecimiento a lo grande

▷ *aux vb* **1** (*in negative constructions, not translated*): **I don't understand** no entiendo

**2** (*to form questions, not translated*): **didn't you know?** ¿no lo sabías?; **what do you think?** ¿qué opinas?

**3** (*for emphasis, in polite expressions*): **people do make mistakes sometimes** a veces sí se cometen errores; **she does seem rather late** a mí también me parece que se ha retrasado; **do sit down/help yourself** siéntate/sírvete por favor; **do take care!** ¡ten cuidado! ¿eh?

**4** (*used to avoid repeating vb*): **she sings better than I do** canta mejor que yo; **do you agree? — yes, I do/no, I don't** ¿estás de acuerdo? — sí (lo estoy)/no (lo estoy); **she lives in Glasgow — so do I** vive en Glasgow — yo también; **he didn't like it and neither did we** no le gustó y a nosotros tampoco; **who made this mess? — I did** ¿quién hizo esta chapuza? — yo; **he asked me to help him and I did** me pidió que le ayudara y lo hice

**5** (*in question tags*): **you like him, don't you?** te gusta, ¿verdad? or ¿no?; **I don't know him, do I?** creo que no le conozco

▷ *vt* **1**: **what are you doing tonight?** ¿qué haces esta noche?; **what can I do for you?** (*in shop*) ¿en qué puedo servirle?; **to do the washing-up/cooking** fregar los platos/cocinar; **to do one's teeth/hair/nails** lavarse los dientes/arreglarse el pelo/arreglarse las uñas

**2** (*Aut etc*): **the car was doing 100** el coche iba a 100; **we've done 200 km already** ya hemos hecho 200 km; **he can do 100 in that car** puede ir a 100 en ese coche

▷ *vi* **1** (*act, behave*) hacer; **do as I do** haz como yo

**2** (*get on, fare*): **he's doing well/badly at school** va bien/mal en la escuela; **the firm is doing well** la empresa anda or va bien; **how do you do?** mucho gusto; (*less formal*) ¿qué tal?

**3** (*suit*): **will it do?** ¿sirve?, ¿está or va bien?

**4** (*be sufficient*) bastar; **will £10 do?** ¿será bastante con £10?; **that'll do** así está bien; **that'll do!** (*in annoyance*) ¡ya está bien!,

¡basta ya!; **to make do (with)** arreglárselas (con)

**do up** vt (laces) atar; (zip, dress, shirt) abrochar; (renovate: room, house) renovar

**do with** vt fus (need): **I could do with a drink/some help** no me vendría mal un trago/un poco de ayuda; (be connected with) tener que ver con; **what has it got to do with you?** ¿qué tiene que ver contigo?

**do without** vi: **if you're late for dinner then you'll do without** si llegas tarde tendrás que quedarte sin cenar ▷ vt fus pasar sin; **I can do without a car** puedo pasar sin coche

**dock** [dɔk] n (Naut) muelle m; (Law) banquillo (de los acusados) ▷ vi (enter dock) atracar (en el muelle); **docks** npl muelles mpl, puerto sg

**doctor** ['dɔktə'] n médico; (Ph.D. etc) doctor(a) m/f ▷ vt (drink etc) adulterar; **Doctor of Philosophy** n Doctor m (en Filosofía y Letras)

**document** ['dɔkjumənt] n documento; **documentary** [dɔkju'mɛntərɪ] adj documental ▷ n documental m; **documentation** [dɔkjumen'teɪʃən] n documentación f

**dodge** [dɔdʒ] n (fig) truco ▷ vt evadir; (blow) esquivar

**dodgy** ['dɔdʒɪ] adj (BRIT inf: uncertain) dudoso; (shady) sospechoso; (risky) arriesgado

**does** [dʌz] vb see **do**

**doesn't** ['dʌznt] = **does not**

**dog** [dɔg] n perro ▷ vt seguir (de cerca); (memory etc) perseguir; **doggy bag** n bolsa para llevarse las sobras de la comida

**do-it-yourself** [du:ɪtjɔ:'sɛlf] n bricolaje m

**dole** [dəul] n (BRIT: payment) subsidio de paro; **on the ~** parado; **dole out** vt repartir

**doll** [dɔl] n muñeca

**dollar** ['dɔlə'] n dólar m

**dolphin** ['dɔlfɪn] n delfín m

**dome** [dəum] n (Arch) cúpula

**domestic** [də'mɛstɪk] adj (animal, duty) doméstico; (flight, news, policy) nacional; **domestic appliance** n aparato m doméstico, aparato m de uso doméstico

**dominant** ['dɔmɪnənt] adj dominante

**dominate** ['dɔmɪneɪt] vt dominar

**domino** ['dɔmɪnəu] (pl dominoes) n ficha de dominó; **dominoes** n (game) dominó

**donate** [də'neɪt] vt donar; **donation** n donativo

**done** [dʌn] pp of **do**

**dongle** ['dɔngl] n (Comput: for wireless connection) adaptador m; (: for protected software) llave f de seguridad

**donkey** ['dɔŋkɪ] n burro

**donor** ['dəunə'] n donante mf; **donor card** n carnet m de donante de órganos

**don't** [dəunt] = **do not**

**doodle** ['du:dl] vi pintar dibujitos or garabatos

**doom** [du:m] n (fate) suerte f ▷ vt: **to be ~ed to failure** estar condenado al fracaso

**door** [dɔ:'] n puerta; **doorbell** n timbre m; **door handle** n tirador m; (of car) manija; **doorknob** n pomo m de la puerta, manilla f (LAM); **doorstep** n peldaño; **doorway** n entrada, puerta

**dope** [dəup] n (inf: illegal drug) droga; (: person) imbécil mf ▷ vt (horse etc) drogar

**dormitory** ['dɔ:mɪtrɪ] n (BRIT) dormitorio; (US) colegio mayor

**DOS** [dɔs] n abbr = **disk operating system**

**dosage** ['dəusɪdʒ] n dosis f inv

**dose** [dəus] n dosis f inv

**dot** [dɔt] n punto ▷ vi: **~ted with** salpicado de; **on the ~** en punto; **dotcom** n puntocom f; **dotted line** n: **to sign on the dotted line** firmar

**double** ['dʌbl] adj doble ▷ adv (twice): **to cost ~** costar el doble ▷ n doble m ▷ vt doblar ▷ vi doblarse; **on the ~,** (BRIT) **at the ~** corriendo; **double back** vi (person) volver sobre sus pasos; **double bass** n contrabajo; **double bed** n cama de matrimonio; **double-check** vt volver a revisar ▷ vi: **I'll double-check** voy a revisarlo otra vez; **double-click** (Comput) vi hacer doble clic; **double-cross** vt (trick) engañar; (betray) traicionar; **doubledecker** n autobús m de dos pisos; **double glazing** n (BRIT) doble acristalamiento; **double room** n habitación f doble; **doubles** n (Tennis) juego de dobles; **double yellow lines** npl (BRIT Aut) línea doble amarilla de prohibido aparcar ≈ línea fsg amarilla continua

**doubt** [daut] n duda ▷ vt dudar; (suspect) dudar de; **to ~ that** dudar que; **doubtful** adj dudoso; (unconvinced): **to be doubtful about sth** tener dudas sobre algo; **doubtless** adv sin duda

**dough** [dəu] n masa, pasta; **doughnut** n dónut m

**dove** [dʌv] n paloma

**down** [daun] n (feathers) plumón m, flojel m; (hill) loma ▷ adv (also: **~wards**) abajo, hacia abajo; (on the ground) por/en tierra ▷ prep abajo ▷ vt (inf: drink) beberse; **~ with X!** ¡abajo X!; **down-and-out** n (tramp) vagabundo/a; **downfall** n caída, ruina; **downhill** adv: **to go downhill** ir cuesta abajo

**Downing Street** ['daʊnɪŋ-] n (BRIT)
Downing Street f

**down: download** vt (Comput) descargar;
**downloadable** adj (Comput) descargable;
**downright** adj (nonsense, lie) manifiesto;
(refusal) terminante
**Down's syndrome** [daʊnz-] n síndrome
m de Down
**down: downstairs** adv (below) (en el piso
de) abajo; (motion) escaleras abajo; **down-
to-earth** adj práctico; **downtown** adv en
el centro de la ciudad; **down under** adv en
Australia (or Nueva Zelanda); **downward**
['daʊnwəd] adv hacia abajo; **downwards**
['daʊnwədz] adv hacia abajo
**doz.** abbr = **dozen**
**doze** [dəʊz] vi dormitar
**dozen** ['dʌzn] n docena; **a ~ books** una
docena de libros; **~s of** cantidad de
**Dr, Dr.** abbr (= doctor) Dr; (in street names)
= **drive**
**drab** [dræb] adj gris, monótono
**draft** [drɑːft] n (first copy) borrador m; (US:
call-up) quinta ▷ vt (write roughly) hacer un
borrador de; see also **draught**
**drag** [dræg] vt arrastrar; (river) dragar,
rastrear ▷ vi arrastrarse por el suelo ▷ n
(inf) lata; (women's clothing): **in ~** vestido de
mujer; **to ~ and drop** (Comput) arrastrar
y soltar
**dragon** ['drægən] n dragón m
**dragonfly** ['drægənflaɪ] n libélula
**drain** [dreɪn] n desaguadero; (in street)
sumidero ▷ vt (land, marshes) desecar;
(reservoir) desecar; (fig) agotar ▷ vi
escurrirse; **to be a ~ on** consumir, agotar;
**drainage** n (act) desagüe m; (Med, Agr)
drenaje m; (sewage) alcantarillado;
**drainpipe** n tubo de desagüe
**drama** ['drɑːmə] n (art) teatro; (play) drama
m; **dramatic** [drə'mætɪk] adj dramático;
(sudden, marked) espectacular
**drank** [dræŋk] pt of **drink**
**drape** [dreɪp] vt (cloth) colocar; (flag) colgar

**drastic** ['dræstɪk] adj (measure, reduction)
severo; (change) radical
**draught**, (US) **draft** [drɑːft] n (of air)
corriente f de aire; (Naut) calado; **on ~** (beer)
de barril; **draught beer** n cerveza de barril;
**draughts** n (BRIT) juego de damas
**draw** [drɔː] (pt **drew**, pp **drawn**) vt (take
out) sacar; (attract) atraer; (picture) dibujar;
(money) retirar ▷ vi (Sport) empatar ▷ n
(Sport) empate m; (lottery) sorteo; **draw out**
vi (lengthen) alargarse; **draw up** vi (stop)
pararse ▷ vt (document) redactar; **drawback**
n inconveniente m, desventaja
**drawer** n cajón m
**drawing** ['drɔːɪŋ] n dibujo; **drawing pin**
n (BRIT) chincheta m; **drawing room** n
salón m
**drawn** [drɔːn] pp of **draw**
**dread** [drɛd] n pavor m, terror m ▷ vt temer,
tener miedo or pavor a; **dreadful** adj
espantoso
**dream** [driːm] n sueño ▷ vt, vi soñar;
**dreamer** n soñador(a) m/f
**dreamt** [drɛmt] pt, pp of **dream**
**dreary** ['drɪərɪ] adj monótono
**drench** [drɛntʃ] vt empapar
**dress** [drɛs] n vestido; (clothing) ropa
▷ vt vestir; (wound) vendar ▷ vi vestirse;
**to ~ o.s., get ~ed** vestirse; **dress up** vi
vestirse de etiqueta; (in fancy dress)
disfrazarse; **dress circle** n (BRIT) principal
m; **dresser** n (furniture) aparador m; (: US)
tocador m; **dressing** n (Med) vendaje m;
(Culin) aliño; **dressing gown** n (BRIT)
bata; **dressing room** n (Theat) camarín m;
(Sport) vestuario; **dressing table** n
tocador m; **dressmaker** n modista,
costurera
**drew** [druː] pt of **draw**
**dribble** ['drɪbl] vi (baby) babear ▷ vt (ball)
regatear
**dried** [draɪd] adj seco; (milk) en polvo
**drier** ['draɪə'] n = **dryer**
**drift** [drɪft] n (of current etc) flujo; (of
snow) ventisquero; (meaning) significado
▷ vi (boat) ir a la deriva; (sand, snow)
amontonarse
**drill** [drɪl] n taladro; (bit) broca; (of dentist)
fresa; (for mining etc) perforadora, barrena;
(Mil) instrucción f ▷ vt perforar, taladrar;
(soldiers) ejercitar ▷ vi (for oil) perforar
**drink** [drɪŋk] n bebida ▷ vt, vi beber; **to
have a ~** tomar algo; tomar una copa or
un trago; **a ~ of water** un trago de agua;
**drink-driving** n: **to be charged with
drink-driving** ser acusado de conducir
borracho or en estado de embriaguez;
**drinker** n bebedor(a) m/f; **drinking water**
n agua potable

**drip** [drɪp] n (act) goteo; (one drip) gota; (Med) gota a gota m ▷ vi gotear

**drive** [draɪv] (pt **drove**, pp **driven**) n (journey) viaje m (en coche); (also: **~way**) entrada; (energy) energía, vigor m; (Comput: also: **disk ~**) unidad f (de disco) ▷ vt (car) conducir; (nail) clavar; (push) empujar; (Tech: motor) impulsar ▷ vi (Aut: at controls) conducir, manejar (LAM); (: travel) pasearse en coche; **left-/right-hand ~** conducción f a la izquierda/derecha; **to ~ sb mad** volverle loco a algn; **drive out** vt (force out) expulsar, echar; **drive-in** adj (esp US): **drive-in cinema** autocine m

**driven** ['drɪvn] pp of **drive**

**driver** ['draɪvər] n conductor(a) m/f, chofer m (LAM); **driver's license** n (US) carnet m or permiso de conducir

**driveway** ['draɪvweɪ] n camino de entrada

**driving** ['draɪvɪŋ] n conducir m, manejar m (LAM); **driving instructor** n instructor(a) m/f de autoescuela; **driving lesson** n clase f de conducir; **driving licence** n (BRIT) carnet m or permiso de conducir; **driving test** n examen m de conducir

**drizzle** ['drɪzl] n llovizna

**droop** [druːp] vi (flower) marchitarse; (shoulders) encorvarse; (head) inclinarse

**drop** [drɒp] n (of water) gota; (fall: in price) bajada ▷ vt dejar caer; (voice, eyes, price) bajar; (set down from car) dejar ▷ vi (object) caer; (price, temperature) bajar; (wind) amainar; **drop in** vi (inf: visit): **to ~ in (on)** pasar por casa (de); **drop off** vi (sleep) dormirse ▷ vt (passenger) dejar; **drop out** vi (withdraw) retirarse

**drought** [draut] n sequía

**drove** [drəuv] pt of **drive**

**drown** [draun] vt ahogar ▷ vi ahogarse

**drowsy** ['drauzɪ] adj soñoliento; **to be ~** tener sueño

**drug** [drʌg] n medicamento; (narcotic) droga ▷ vt drogar; **to be on ~s** drogarse; **drug addict** n drogadicto/a; **drug dealer** n traficante mf de drogas; **druggist** n (US) farmacéutico/a; **drugstore** n (US) tienda (de comestibles, periódicos y medicamentos)

**drum** [drʌm] n tambor m; (for oil, petrol) bidón m; **drums** npl batería sg; **drummer** n tambor mf

**drunk** [drʌŋk] pp of **drink** ▷ adj borracho ▷ n (also: **drunkard**) borracho/a; **drunken** adj borracho

**dry** [draɪ] adj seco; (day) sin lluvia; (climate) árido, seco ▷ vt secar; (tears) enjugarse ▷ vi secarse; **dry up** vi (river) secarse; **dry-cleaner's** n tintorería; **dry-cleaning** n lavado en seco; **dryer** n (for hair) secador m; (for clothes) secadora

**DSS** n abbr (BRIT) = **Department of Social Security**; see **social security**

**DTP** n abbr = **desktop publishing**

**dual** ['djuəl] adj doble; **dual carriageway** n (BRIT) ≈ autovía

**dubious** ['djuːbɪəs] adj (questionable: reputation) dudoso; (: character) sospechoso; (unsure) indeciso

**duck** [dʌk] n pato ▷ vi agacharse

**due** [djuː] adj (proper) debido ▷ adv: **~ north** derecho al norte; **in ~ course** a su debido tiempo; **~ to** debido a; **the train is ~ to arrive at 8.00** el tren tiene (prevista) la llegada a las ocho; **the rent's ~ on the 30th** hay que pagar el alquiler el día 30

**duel** ['djuəl] n duelo

**duet** [djuː'ɛt] n dúo

**dug** [dʌg] pt, pp of **dig**

**duke** [djuːk] n duque m

**dull** [dʌl] adj (light) apagado; (stupid) torpe; (boring) pesado; (sound, pain) sordo; (weather, day) gris ▷ vt (pain, grief) aliviar; (mind, senses) entorpecer

**dumb** [dʌm] adj (stupid) estúpido

**dummy** ['dʌmɪ] n (tailor's model) maniquí m; (BRIT: for baby) chupete m ▷ adj falso, postizo

**dump** [dʌmp] n (place) basurero, vertedero ▷ vt (put down) dejar; (get rid of) deshacerse de; (Comput) tirar (a la papelera); (Comm: goods) inundar el mercado de

**dumpling** ['dʌmplɪŋ] n bola de masa hervida

**dune** [djuːn] n duna

**dungarees** [dʌŋgə'riːz] npl mono sg, overol m sg (LAM)

**dungeon** ['dʌndʒən] n calabozo

**duplex** ['djuːplɛks] n dúplex m

**duplicate** ['djuːplɪkət] n duplicado ▷ vt ['djuːplɪkeɪt] duplicar; (photocopy) fotocopiar; (repeat) repetir; **in ~** por duplicado

**durable** ['djuərəbl] adj duradero

**duration** [djuə'reɪʃən] n duración f

**during** ['djuərɪŋ] prep durante

**dusk** [dʌsk] n crepúsculo, anochecer m

**dust** [dʌst] n polvo ▷ vt (furniture) desempolvar; (cake etc) espolvorear de; **dustbin** n (BRIT) cubo de la basura, balde m (LAM); **duster** n paño, trapo; **dustman** n basurero; **dustpan** n cogedor m; **dusty** adj polvoriento

**Dutch** [dʌtʃ] adj holandés/esa ▷ n (Ling) holandés m ▷ adv: **to go ~** pagar a escote; **the Dutch** npl los holandeses; **Dutchman, Dutchwoman** n holandés/esa m/f

**duty** ['djuːtɪ] n deber m; (tax) derechos mpl de aduana; **on ~** de servicio; (at night etc) de guardia; **off ~** libre (de servicio); **duty-free** adj libre de impuestos

**duvet** ['duːveɪ] n (BRIT) edredón m (nórdico)
**DVD** n abbr (= digital versatile or video disc)
DVD m; **DVD player** n lector m de DVD;
**DVD writer** n grabadora de DVD
**dwarf** (pl **dwarves**) [dwɔːf, dwɔːvz] n (inf!)
enano/a ▷ vt empequeñecer
**dwell** (pt, pp **dwelt**) [dwɛl, dwɛlt] vi morar;
**dwell on** vt fus explayarse en
**dwindle** ['dwɪndl] vi disminuir
**dye** [daɪ] n tinte m ▷ vt teñir
**dying** ['daɪɪŋ] adj moribundo
**dynamic** [daɪ'næmɪk] adj dinámico
**dynamite** ['daɪnəmaɪt] n dinamita
**dyslexia** [dɪs'lɛksɪə] n dislexia
**dyslexic** [dɪs'lɛksɪk] adj, n disléxico/a

**E** [iː] n (Mus) mi m
**each** [iːtʃ] adj cada inv ▷ pron cada uno;
~ **other** el uno al otro; **they hate ~ other** se
odian (entre ellos or mutuamente)
**eager** ['iːgəʳ] adj (keen) entusiasmado; **to be
~ to do sth** estar deseoso de hacer algo; **to
be ~ for** tener muchas ganas de
**eagle** ['iːgl] n águila
**ear** [ɪəʳ] n oreja; (sense of hearing) oído; (of
corn) espiga; **earache** n dolor m de oídos;
**eardrum** n tímpano
**earl** [əːl] n conde m
**earlier** ['əːlɪəʳ] adj anterior ▷ adv antes
**early** ['əːlɪ] adv temprano; (ahead of
time) con tiempo, con anticipación ▷ adj
temprano; (reply) pronto; (man) primitivo;
(first: Christians, settlers) primero; **to have
an ~ night** acostarse temprano; **in the ~** or
~ **in the spring/19th century** a principios
de primavera/del siglo diecinueve; **early
retirement** n jubilación f anticipada
**earmark** ['ɪəmɑːk] vt: **to ~ for** reservar
para, destinar a
**earn** [əːn] vt (salary) percibir; (interest)
devengar; (praise) ganarse
**earnest** ['əːnɪst] adj (wish) fervoroso;
(person) serio, formal ▷ n: **in ~** adv en serio
**earnings** ['əːnɪŋz] npl (personal) ingresos
mpl; (of company etc) ganancias fpl
**ear: earphones** npl auriculares mpl;
**earplugs** npl tapones mpl para los oídos;
**earring** n pendiente m, arete m (LAM)
**earth** [əːθ] n tierra; (BRIT Elec) toma de
tierra ▷ vt (BRIT Elec) conectar a tierra;
**earthquake** n terremoto
**ease** [iːz] n facilidad f; (comfort) comodidad f
▷ vt (problem) mitigar; (pain) aliviar; **to ~ sth
in/out** meter/sacar algo con cuidado; **at ~!**
(Mil) ¡descansen!
**easily** ['iːzɪlɪ] adv fácilmente

**east** [i:st] *n* este *m* ▷ *adj* del este, oriental ▷ *adv* al este, hacia el este; **the E~** el Oriente; (*Pol*) el Este; **eastbound** *adj* en dirección este

**Easter** ['i:stər] *n* Pascua (de Resurrección); **Easter egg** *n* huevo de Pascua

**eastern** ['i:stən] *adj* del este, oriental

**Easter Sunday** *n* Domingo de Resurrección

**easy** ['i:zɪ] *adj* fácil; (*life*) holgado, cómodo; (*relaxed*) natural ▷ *adv*: **to take it** or **things ~** (*not worry*) no preocuparse; (*rest*) descansar; **easy-going** *adj* acomodadizo

**eat** (*pt* **ate**, *pp* **eaten**) [i:t, eɪt, 'i:tn] *vt* comer; **eat out** *vi* comer fuera

**eavesdrop** ['i:vzdrɔp] *vi*: **to ~ (on sb)** escuchar a escondidas or con disimulo (a algn)

**e-book** ['i:buk] *n* libro electrónico

**e-business** ['i:bɪznɪs] *n* (*commerce*) comercio electrónico; (*company*) negocio electrónico

**EC** *n abbr* (= *European Community*) CE *f*

**eccentric** [ɪk'sɛntrɪk] *adj*, *n* excéntrico/a

**echo** ['ɛkəu] (*pl* **echoes**) *n* eco *m* ▷ *vt* (*sound*) repetir ▷ *vi* resonar, hacer eco

**e-cigarette** ['i:sɪgərɛt] *n* cigarrillo electrónico

**eclipse** [ɪ'klɪps] *n* eclipse *m*

**eco-friendly** ['i:kəufrɛndlɪ] *adj* ecológico

**ecological** [i:kə'lɔdʒɪkl] *adj* ecológico

**ecology** [ɪ'kɔlədʒɪ] *n* ecología

**e-commerce** ['i:kɔmə:s] *n* comercio electrónico

**economic** [i:kə'nɔmɪk] *adj* económico; (*business etc*) rentable; **economical** *adj* económico; **economics** *n* (*Scol*) economía

**economist** [ɪ'kɔnəmɪst] *n* economista *mf*

**economize** [ɪ'kɔnəmaɪz] *vi* economizar, ahorrar

**economy** [ɪ'kɔnəmɪ] *n* economía; **economy class** *n* (*Aviat etc*) clase *f* turista; **economy class syndrome** *n* síndrome *m* de la clase turista

**ecstasy** ['ɛkstəsɪ] *n* éxtasis *m inv*; (*drug*) éxtasis *m inv*; **ecstatic** [ɛks'tætɪk] *adj* extático

**eczema** ['ɛksɪmə] *n* eczema *m*

**edge** [ɛdʒ] *n* (*of knife etc*) filo; (*of object*) borde *m*; (*of lake etc*) orilla ▷ *vt* (*Sewing*) ribetear; **on ~** (*fig*) = **edgy**; **to ~ away from** alejarse poco a poco de

**edgy** ['ɛdʒɪ] *adj* nervioso, inquieto

**edible** ['ɛdɪbl] *adj* comestible

**Edinburgh** ['ɛdɪnbərə] *n* Edimburgo

**edit** ['ɛdɪt] *vt* (*be the editor of*) dirigir; (*re-write*) redactar; (*Comput*) editar; **edition** [ɪ'dɪʃən] *n* edición *f*; **editor** *n* (*of newspaper*) director(a) *m/f*; (*of book*) redactor(a) *m/f*;

**editorial** [ɛdɪ'tɔ:rɪəl] *adj* editorial ▷ *n* editorial *m*

**educate** ['ɛdjukeɪt] *vt* educar; (*instruct*) instruir; **educated** ['ɛdjukeɪtɪd] *adj* culto

**education** [ɛdju'keɪʃən] *n* educación *f*; (*schooling*) enseñanza; (*Scol*) pedagogía; **educational** *adj* (*policy etc*) de educación, educativo; (*teaching*) docente; (*instructive*) educativo

**eel** [i:l] *n* anguila

**eerie** ['ɪərɪ] *adj* espeluznante

**effect** [ɪ'fɛkt] *n* efecto ▷ *vt* efectuar, llevar a cabo; **effects** *npl* (*property*) efectos *mpl*; **to take ~** (*law*) entrar en vigor or vigencia; (*drug*) surtir efecto; **in ~** en realidad; **effective** *adj* eficaz; (*real*) efectivo; **effectively** *adv* eficazmente; (*in reality*) de hecho

**efficiency** [ɪ'fɪʃənsɪ] *n* eficiencia; (*of machine*) rendimiento

**efficient** [ɪ'fɪʃənt] *adj* eficiente; (*machine, car*) de buen rendimiento; **efficiently** *adv* (*work*) eficientemente, de manera eficiente

**effort** ['ɛfət] *n* esfuerzo; **effortless** *adj* sin ningún esfuerzo

**e.g.** *adv abbr* (= *exempli gratia*) p.ej.

**egg** [ɛg] *n* huevo; **hard-boiled/soft-boiled/ poached ~** huevo duro or (LAM) a la copa or (LAM) tibio/pasado por agua/escalfado; **eggcup** *n* huevera; **eggplant** *n* (*esp US*) berenjena; **eggshell** *n* cáscara de huevo; **egg white** *n* clara de huevo; **egg yolk** *n* yema de huevo

**ego** ['i:gəu] *n* ego

**Egypt** ['i:dʒɪpt] *n* Egipto; **Egyptian** [ɪ'dʒɪpʃən] *adj*, *n* egipcio/a

**eight** [eɪt] *num* ocho; **eighteen** *num* dieciocho; **eighteenth** *adj* decimoctavo; **the eighteenth floor** la planta dieciocho; **the eighteenth of August** el dieciocho de agosto; **eighth** [eɪtθ] *adj* octavo; **eightieth** ['eɪtɪɪθ] *adj* octogésimo; **eighty** ['eɪtɪ] *num* ochenta

**Eire** ['ɛərə] *n* Eire *m*

**either** ['aɪðər] *adj* cualquiera de los dos ...; (*both, each*) cada ▷ *pron*: **~ (of them)** cualquiera (de los dos) ▷ *adv* tampoco ▷ *conj*: **~ yes or no** o sí o no; **on ~ side** en ambos lados; **I don't like ~** no me gusta ninguno de los dos; **no, I don't ~** no, yo tampoco

**eject** [ɪ'dʒɛkt] *vt* echar; (*tenant*) desahuciar

**elaborate** *adj* [ɪ'læbərɪt] (*design, pattern*) complejo ▷ *vt* [ɪ'læbəreɪt] elaborar; (*expand*) ampliar; (*refine*) refinar ▷ *vi* explicarse con muchos detalles

**elastic** [ɪ'læstɪk] *adj*, *n* elástico; **elastic band** *n* (BRIT) gomita

**elbow** ['ɛlbəʊ] n codo
**elder** ['ɛldə'] adj mayor ▷ n (tree) saúco; (person) mayor; **elderly** adj de edad, mayor; **~ people** los mayores, los ancianos
**eldest** ['ɛldɪst] adj, n el/la mayor
**elect** [ɪ'lɛkt] vt elegir; **to ~ to do** optar por hacer ▷ adj: **the president ~** el presidente electo; **election** n elección f; **electoral** adj electoral; **electorate** n electorado
**electric** [ɪ'lɛktrɪk] adj eléctrico; **electrical** adj eléctrico; **electric blanket** n manta eléctrica; **electric fire** n estufa eléctrica; **electrician** [ɪlɛk'trɪʃən] n electricista mf; **electricity** [ɪlɛk'trɪsɪtɪ] n electricidad f; **electric shock** n electrochoque m; **electrify** [ɪ'lɛktrɪfaɪ] vt (Rail) electrificar; (fig: audience) electrizar
**electronic** [ɪlɛk'trɒnɪk] adj electrónico; **electronic mail** n correo electrónico; **electronics** n electrónica f
**elegance** ['ɛlɪgəns] n elegancia
**elegant** ['ɛlɪgənt] adj elegante
**element** ['ɛlɪmənt] n elemento; (of heater, kettle etc) resistencia
**elementary** [ɛlɪ'mɛntərɪ] adj elemental; (primitive) rudimentario; **elementary school** n (US) escuela de enseñanza primaria
**elephant** ['ɛlɪfənt] n elefante m
**elevate** ['ɛlɪveɪt] vt elevar; (in rank) ascender
**elevator** ['ɛlɪveɪtə'] n (US) ascensor m
**eleven** [ɪ'lɛvn] num once; **eleventh** [ɪ'lɛvnθ] adj undécimo
**eligible** ['ɛlɪdʒəbl] adj: **an ~ young man/ woman** un buen partido; **to be ~ for sth** llenar los requisitos para algo
**eliminate** [ɪ'lɪmɪneɪt] vt (a suspect, possibility) descartar
**elm** [ɛlm] n olmo
**eloquent** ['ɛləkwənt] adj elocuente
**else** [ɛls] adv: **something ~** otra cosa or algo más; **somewhere ~** en otra parte; **everywhere ~** en todas partes menos aquí; **where ~?** ¿dónde más?, ¿en qué otra parte?; **there was little ~ to do** apenas quedaba otra cosa que hacer; **nobody ~** nadie más; **elsewhere** adv (be) en otra parte; (go) a otra parte
**elusive** [ɪ'luːsɪv] adj esquivo; (answer) difícil de encontrar
**email** ['iːmeɪl] n abbr (= electronic mail) email m, correo electrónico; **email address** n dirección f electrónica, email m
**embankment** [ɪm'bæŋkmənt] n terraplén m
**embargo** [ɪm'bɑːgəʊ] (pl **embargoes**) n prohibición f; (Comm, Naut) embargo; **to put an ~ on sth** poner un embargo en algo

**embark** [ɪm'bɑːk] vi embarcarse ▷ vt embarcar; **to ~ on** (journey) emprender, iniciar
**embarrass** [ɪm'bærəs] vt avergonzar, dar vergüenza a; **embarrassed** adj azorado, violento; **to be embarrassed** sentirse azorado or violento; **embarrassing** adj (situation) violento; (question) embarazoso; **embarrassment** n vergüenza
▌ Be careful not to translate embarrassed by the Spanish word embarazada.
**embassy** ['ɛmbəsɪ] n embajada
**embrace** [ɪm'breɪs] vt abrazar, dar un abrazo a; (include) abarcar ▷ vi abrazarse ▷ n abrazo
**embroider** [ɪm'brɔɪdə'] vt bordar; **embroidery** n bordado
**embryo** ['ɛmbrɪəʊ] n embrión m
**emerald** ['ɛmərəld] n esmeralda
**emerge** [ɪ'mɜːdʒ] vi salir; (arise) surgir
**emergency** [ɪ'mɜːdʒənsɪ] n crisis f inv; **in an ~** en caso de urgencia; **(to declare a) state of ~** (declarar) estado de emergencia or de excepción; **emergency brake** n (US) freno de mano; **emergency exit** n salida de emergencia; **emergency landing** n aterrizaje m forzoso; **emergency room** (US Med) n sala f de urgencias; **emergency service** n servicio de urgencia
**emigrate** ['ɛmɪgreɪt] vi emigrar; **emigration** n emigración f
**eminent** ['ɛmɪnənt] adj eminente
**emission** [ɪ'mɪʃən] n emisión f
**emit** [ɪ'mɪt] vt emitir; (smell, smoke) despedir
**emoticon** [ɪ'məʊtɪkɒn] n emoticón m
**emotion** [ɪ'məʊʃən] n emoción f; **emotional** adj (person) sentimental; (scene) conmovedor(a), emocionante
**emperor** ['ɛmpərə'] n emperador m
**emphasis** (pl **emphases**) ['ɛmfəsɪs, -siːz] n énfasis m inv
**emphasize** ['ɛmfəsaɪz] vt (word, point) subrayar, recalcar; (feature) hacer resaltar
**empire** ['ɛmpaɪə'] n imperio
**employ** [ɪm'plɔɪ] vt emplear; **employee** [ɪmplɔɪ'iː] n empleado/a; **employer** n patrón/ona m/f; (businessman) empresario/a; **employment** n empleo; **to find employment** encontrar trabajo; **employment agency** n agencia de colocaciones or empleo
**empower** [ɪm'paʊə'] vt: **to ~ sb to do sth** autorizar a algn para hacer algo
**empress** ['ɛmprɪs] n emperatriz f
**emptiness** ['ɛmptɪnɪs] n vacío
**empty** ['ɛmptɪ] adj vacío; (street, area) desierto; (threat) vano ▷ vt vaciar; (place) dejar vacío ▷ vi vaciarse; (house) quedar(se)

vacío or desocupado; **empty-handed** adj con las manos vacías

**EMU** n abbr (= European Monetary Union) UME f

**emulsion** [ɪˈmʌlʃən] n emulsión f

**enable** [ɪˈneɪbl] vt: **to ~ sb to do sth** permitir a algn hacer algo

**enamel** [ɪˈnæməl] n esmalte m

**enchanting** [ɪnˈtʃɑːntɪŋ] adj encantador(a)

**encl.** abbr (= enclosed) adj

**enclose** [ɪnˈkləuz] vt (land) cercar; (with letter etc) adjuntar; **please find ~d** le mandamos adjunto

**enclosure** [ɪnˈkləuʒəʳ] n cercado, recinto

**encore** [ɔŋˈkɔːʳ] excl ¡otra!, ¡bis! ⊳ n bis m

**encounter** [ɪnˈkauntəʳ] n encuentro ⊳ vt encontrar, encontrarse con; (difficulty) tropezar con

**encourage** [ɪnˈkʌrɪdʒ] vt alentar, animar; (growth) estimular; **encouragement** n estímulo; (of industry) fomento

**encouraging** [ɪnˈkʌrɪdʒɪŋ] adj alentador(a)

**encyclop(a)edia** [ɛnsaɪkləuˈpiːdɪə] n enciclopedia

**end** [ɛnd] n fin m; (of table) extremo; (of street) final m; (Sport) lado ⊳ vt terminar, acabar; (also: **bring to an ~, put an ~ to**) acabar con ⊳ vi terminar, acabar; **in the ~** al final; **on ~** (object) de punta, de cabeza; **to stand on ~** (hair) erizarse; **for hours on ~** hora tras hora; **end up** vi: **to ~ up in** terminar en; (place) ir a parar a

**endanger** [ɪnˈdeɪndʒəʳ] vt poner en peligro; **an ~ed species** una especie en peligro de extinción

**endearing** [ɪnˈdɪərɪŋ] adj entrañable

**endeavour**, (us) **endeavor** [ɪnˈdɛvəʳ] n esfuerzo; (attempt) tentativa ⊳ vi: **to ~ to do** esforzarse por hacer; (try) procurar hacer

**ending** [ˈɛndɪŋ] n (of book) desenlace m; (Ling) terminación f

**endless** [ˈɛndlɪs] adj interminable, inacabable

**endorse** [ɪnˈdɔːs] vt (cheque) endosar; (approve) aprobar; **endorsement** n (on driving licence) nota de sanción

**endurance** [ɪnˈdjuərəns] n resistencia

**endure** [ɪnˈdjuəʳ] vt (bear) aguantar, soportar ⊳ vi (last) perdurar

**enemy** [ˈɛnəmɪ] adj, n enemigo/a

**energetic** [ɛnəˈdʒɛtɪk] adj enérgico

**energy** [ˈɛnədʒɪ] n energía

**enforce** [ɪnˈfɔːs] vt (law) hacer cumplir

**engaged** [ɪnˈgeɪdʒd] adj (BRIT: busy, in use) ocupado; (betrothed) prometido; **to get ~** prometerse; **engaged tone** n (BRIT Tel) señal f de comunicando

**engagement** [ɪnˈgeɪdʒmənt] n (appointment) compromiso, cita; (to marry) compromiso; (period) noviazgo; **engagement ring** n anillo de pedida

**engaging** [ɪnˈgeɪdʒɪŋ] adj atractivo

**engine** [ˈɛndʒɪn] n (Aut) motor m; (Rail) locomotora

**engineer** [ɛndʒɪˈnɪəʳ] n ingeniero/a; (BRIT: for repairs) técnico/a; (us Rail) maquinista mf; **engineering** n ingeniería

**England** [ˈɪŋglənd] n Inglaterra

**English** [ˈɪŋglɪʃ] adj inglés/esa ⊳ n (Ling) el inglés; **the English** npl los ingleses; **English Channel** n: **the English Channel** el Canal de la Mancha; **Englishman, Englishwoman** n inglés/esa m/f

**engrave** [ɪnˈgreɪv] vt grabar

**engraving** [ɪnˈgreɪvɪŋ] n grabado

**enhance** [ɪnˈhɑːns] vt aumentar; (beauty) realzar

**enjoy** [ɪnˈdʒɔɪ] vt (health, fortune) disfrutar de, gozar de; **I ~ doing ...** me gusta hacer ...; **to ~ o.s.** divertirse; **enjoyable** adj agradable; (amusing) divertido; **enjoyment** n (joy) placer m

**enlarge** [ɪnˈlɑːdʒ] vt aumentar; (broaden) extender; (Phot) ampliar ⊳ vi: **to ~ on** (subject) tratar con más detalles; **enlargement** n (Phot) ampliación f

**enlist** [ɪnˈlɪst] vt alistar; (support) conseguir ⊳ vi alistarse

**enormous** [ɪˈnɔːməs] adj enorme

**enough** [ɪˈnʌf] adj: **~ time/books** bastante tiempo/bastantes libros ⊳ n: **have you got ~?** ¿tiene usted bastante? ⊳ adv: **big ~** bastante grande; **he has not worked ~** no ha trabajado bastante; **(that's) ~!** ¡basta ya!, ¡ya está bien!; **that's ~, thanks** con eso basta, gracias; **I've had ~** estoy harto; ... **which, funnily ~ ...** ... lo que, por extraño que parezca ...

**enquire** [ɪnˈkwaɪəʳ] vt, vi = **inquire**

**enrage** [ɪnˈreɪdʒ] vt enfurecer

**enrich** [ɪnˈrɪtʃ] vt enriquecer

**enrol**, (us) **enroll** [ɪnˈrəul] vt (member) inscribir; (Scol) matricular ⊳ vi inscribirse; (Scol) matricularse; **enrolment**, (us) **enrollment** n inscripción f; matriculación f

**en route** [ɔnˈruːt] adv durante el viaje

**en suite** [ɔnˈswiːt] adj: **with ~ bathroom** con baño

**ensure** [ɪnˈʃuəʳ] vt asegurar

**entail** [ɪnˈteɪl] vt suponer

**enter** [ˈɛntəʳ] vt (room, profession) entrar en; (club) hacerse socio de; (army) alistarse en; (sb for a competition) inscribir; (write down) anotar, apuntar; (Comput) introducir ⊳ vi entrar

**enterprise** [ˈɛntəpraɪz] n empresa; (spirit) iniciativa; **free ~** la libre empresa; **private ~** la iniciativa privada; **enterprising** adj emprendedor(a)

**entertain** [ɛntəˈteɪn] vt (amuse) divertir; (receive: guest) recibir (en casa); (idea) abrigar; **entertainer** n artista mf; **entertaining** adj divertido, entretenido; **entertainment** n (amusement) diversión f; (show) espectáculo

**enthusiasm** [ɪnˈθuːzɪæzəm] n entusiasmo

**enthusiast** [ɪnˈθuːzɪæst] n entusiasta mf; **enthusiastic** [ɪnθuːzɪˈæstɪk] adj entusiasta; **to be enthusiastic about sb/ sth** estar entusiasmado con algn/algo

**entire** [ɪnˈtaɪəʳ] adj entero; **entirely** adv totalmente

**entitle** [ɪnˈtaɪtl] vt: **to ~ sb to sth** dar a algn derecho a algo; **entitled** adj (book) titulado; **to be entitled to sth/to do sth** tener derecho a algo/a hacer algo

**entrance** [ˈɛntrəns] n entrada ▷ vt [ɪnˈtrɑːns] encantar, hechizar; **to gain ~ to** (university etc) ingresar en; **entrance examination** n examen m de ingreso; **entrance fee** n (to a show) entrada; (to a club) cuota; **entrance ramp** n (us Aut) rampa de acceso

**entrant** [ˈɛntrənt] n (in race, competition) participante mf; (in exam) candidato/a

**entrepreneur** [ɔntrəprəˈnəːʳ] n empresario/a

**entrust** [ɪnˈtrʌst] vt: **to ~ sth to sb** confiar algo a algn

**entry** [ˈɛntrɪ] n entrada; (in register, diary, ship's log) apunte m; (in account book, ledger, list) partida; **no ~** prohibido el paso; (Aut) dirección prohibida; **entry phone** n portero automático

**envelope** [ˈɛnvələup] n sobre m

**envious** [ˈɛnvɪəs] adj envidioso; (look) de envidia

**environment** [ɪnˈvaɪrnmənt] n (surroundings) entorno; **Department of the E~** ministerio del medio ambiente; **environmental** [ɪnvaɪrnˈmɛntl] adj (medio)ambiental; **environmentally** [ɪnvaɪrnˈmɛntlɪ] adv: **environmentally sound/friendly** ecológico

**envisage** [ɪnˈvɪzɪdʒ] vt prever

**envoy** [ˈɛnvɔɪ] n enviado/a

**envy** [ˈɛnvɪ] n envidia ▷ vt tener envidia a; **to ~ sb sth** envidiar algo a algn

**epic** [ˈɛpɪk] n épica ▷ adj épico

**epidemic** [ɛpɪˈdɛmɪk] n epidemia

**epilepsy** [ˈɛpɪlɛpsɪ] n epilepsia

**epileptic** [ɛpɪˈlɛptɪk] adj, n epiléptico/a; **epileptic fit** n ataque m de epilepsia, acceso m epiléptico

**episode** [ˈɛpɪsəud] n episodio

**equal** [ˈiːkwl] adj igual; (treatment) equitativo ▷ n igual mf ▷ vt ser igual a; (fig) igualar; **to be ~ to** (task) estar a la altura de; **equality** [iːˈkwɔlɪtɪ] n igualdad f; **equalize** vi (Sport) empatar; **equally** adv igualmente; (share etc) a partes iguales

**equation** [ɪˈkweɪʒən] n (Math) ecuación f

**equator** [ɪˈkweɪtəʳ] n ecuador m

**equip** [ɪˈkwɪp] vt equipar; (person) proveer; **to be well ~ped** estar bien equipado; **equipment** n equipo

**equivalent** [ɪˈkwɪvələnt] adj, n equivalente m; **to be ~ to** equivaler a

**ER** abbr (BRIT: = Elizabeth Regina) la reina Isabel; (US Med) = **emergency room**

**era** [ˈɪərə] n era, época

**erase** [ɪˈreɪz] vt borrar; **eraser** n goma de borrar

**e-reader** [ˈiːriːdəʳ] n libro electrónico

**erect** [ɪˈrɛkt] adj erguido ▷ vt erigir, levantar; (assemble) montar; **erection** n (of building) construcción f; (of machinery) montaje m; (Med) erección f

**ERM** n abbr (= Exchange Rate Mechanism) (mecanismo de cambios del) SME m

**erode** [ɪˈrəud] vt (Geo) erosionar; (metal) corroer, desgastar

**erosion** [ɪˈrəuʒən] n erosión f; desgaste m

**erotic** [ɪˈrɔtɪk] adj erótico

**errand** [ˈɛrnd] n recado, mandado (LAM)

**erratic** [ɪˈrætɪk] adj desigual, poco uniforme

**error** [ˈɛrəʳ] n error m, equivocación f

**erupt** [ɪˈrʌpt] vi entrar en erupción; (fig) estallar; **eruption** n erupción f; (of anger, violence) estallido

**escalate** [ˈɛskəleɪt] vi extenderse, intensificarse

**escalator** [ˈɛskəleɪtəʳ] n escalera mecánica

**escape** [ɪˈskeɪp] n fuga ▷ vi escaparse; (flee) huir, evadirse ▷ vt evitar, eludir; (consequences) escapar a; **his name ~s me** no me sale su nombre; **to ~ from** (place) escaparse de; (person) huir de

**escort** n [ˈɛskɔːt] acompañante mf; (Mil) escolta ▷ vt [ɪˈskɔːt] acompañar

**especially** [ɪˈspɛʃlɪ] adv especialmente; (above all) sobre todo; (particularly) en especial

**espionage** [ˈɛspɪənɑːʒ] n espionaje m

**essay** [ˈɛseɪ] n (Scol) redacción f; (: longer) trabajo

**essence** [ˈɛsns] n esencia

**essential** [ɪˈsɛnʃl] adj (necessary) imprescindible; (basic) esencial ▷ n (often pl) lo esencial; **essentially** adv esencialmente

**establish** [ɪ'stæblɪʃ] vt establecer;
(*prove*) demostrar; (*relations*) entablar;
**establishment** n establecimiento; **the
Establishment** la clase dirigente

**estate** [ɪ'steɪt] n (*land*) finca, hacienda;
(*inheritance*) herencia; **housing ~** (BRIT)
urbanización f; **estate agent** n (BRIT)
agente mf inmobiliario/a; **estate car** n
(BRIT) ranchera, coche m familiar

**estimate** ['estɪmət] n estimación
f; (*assessment*) tasa, cálculo; (Comm)
presupuesto ▷ vt ['estɪmeɪt] estimar; tasar,
calcular

**etc** abbr (= et cetera) etc

**eternal** [ɪ'tə:nl] adj eterno

**eternity** [ɪ'tə:nɪtɪ] n eternidad f

**ethical** ['eθɪkl] adj ético; **ethics** ['eθɪks] n
ética ▷ npl moralidad f

**Ethiopia** [i:θɪ'əupɪə] n Etiopía

**ethnic** ['eθnɪk] adj étnico; **ethnic minority**
n minoría étnica

**e-ticket** ['i:tɪkɪt] n billete electrónico,
boleto electrónico (LAM)

**etiquette** ['etɪket] n etiqueta

**EU** n abbr (= European Union) UE f

**euro** ['jʊərəʊ] n euro

**Europe** ['jʊərəp] n Europa; **European**
[jʊərə'pi:ən] adj, n europeo/a; **European
Community** n Comunidad f Europea;
**European Union** n Unión f Europea

**Eurostar®** ['jʊərəʊstɑ:ʳ] n Eurostar® m

**evacuate** [ɪ'vækjueɪt] vt evacuar; (*place*)
desocupar

**evade** [ɪ'veɪd] vt evadir, eludir

**evaluate** [ɪ'væljueɪt] vt evaluar; (*value*)
tasar; (*evidence*) interpretar

**evaporate** [ɪ'væpəreɪt] vi evaporarse; (*fig*)
desvanecerse

**eve** [i:v] n: **on the ~ of** en vísperas de

**even** ['i:vn] adj (*level*) llano; (*smooth*) liso;
(*speed, temperature*) uniforme; (*number*)
par ▷ adv hasta, incluso; **~ if, ~ though**
aunque + subjun, así + subjun (LAM); **~ more**
aun más; **~ so** aun así; **not ~** ni siquiera;
**~ he was there** hasta él estaba allí; **~ on
Sundays** incluso los domingos; **to get ~
with sb** ajustar cuentas con algn

**evening** ['i:vnɪŋ] n tarde f; (*night*) noche f;
**in the ~** por la tarde; **this ~** esta tarde or
noche; **tomorrow/yesterday ~** mañana/
ayer por la tarde or noche; **evening class** n
clase f nocturna; **evening dress** n (*man's*)
traje m de etiqueta; (*woman's*) traje m de
noche

**event** [ɪ'vent] n suceso, acontecimiento;
(Sport) prueba; **in the ~ of** en caso de;
**eventful** adj (*life*) azaroso; (*day*) ajetreado;
(*game*) lleno de emoción; (*journey*) lleno de
incidentes

**eventual** [ɪ'ventʃuəl] adj final;
**eventually** adv (*finally*) por fin; (*in time*)
con el tiempo

> Be careful not to translate *eventual* by
> the Spanish word *eventual*.

**ever** ['evəʳ] adv nunca, jamás; (*at all times*)
siempre ▷ conj después de que; **for ~** (para)
siempre; **the best ~** lo nunca visto; **have
you ~ seen it?** ¿lo has visto alguna vez?;
**better than ~** mejor que nunca; **~ since** adv
desde entonces; **evergreen** n árbol m de
hoja perenne

○ **KEYWORD**

**every** ['evrɪ] adj **1** (*each*) cada; **every one of
them** (*persons*) todos ellos/as; (*objects*) cada
uno de ellos/as; **every shop in the town
was closed** todas las tiendas de la ciudad
estaban cerradas

**2** (*all possible*) todo/a; **I gave you every
assistance** te di toda la ayuda posible;
**I have every confidence in him** tiene toda
mi confianza; **we wish you every success**
te deseamos toda suerte de éxitos

**3** (*showing recurrence*) todo/a; **every day/
week** todos los días/todas las semanas;
**every other car had been broken into**
habían forzado uno de cada dos coches;
**she visits me every other/third day** me
visita cada dos/tres días; **every now and
then** de vez en cuando

**everybody** ['evrɪbɒdɪ] pron todos pron pl,
todo el mundo

**everyday** ['evrɪdeɪ] adj (*daily: use,
occurrence, experience*) cotidiano; (*usual:
expression*) corriente

**everyone** ['evrɪwʌn] pron = **everybody**

**everything** ['evrɪθɪŋ] pron todo

**everywhere** ['evrɪweəʳ] adv (*be*) en todas
partes; (*go*) a or por todas partes; **~ you
go you meet …** en todas partes
encuentras …

**evict** [ɪ'vɪkt] vt desahuciar

**evidence** ['evɪdəns] n (*proof*) prueba; (*of
witness*) testimonio; **to give ~** prestar
declaración, dar testimonio

**evident** ['evɪdənt] adj evidente, manifiesto;
**evidently** adv por lo visto

**evil** ['i:vl] adj malo; (*influence*) funesto ▷ n
mal m

**evoke** [ɪ'vəuk] vt evocar

**evolution** [i:və'lu:ʃən] n evolución f

**evolve** [ɪ'vɒlv] vt desarrollar ▷ vi
evolucionar, desarrollarse

**ewe** [ju:] n oveja

**ex** [eks] (*inf*) n: **my ex** mi ex

**ex-** [eks] pref (*husband, president etc*) ex-

**exact** [ɪɡ'zækt] *adj* exacto ▷ *vt*: **to ~ sth (from)** exigir algo (de); **exactly** *adv* exactamente; **exactly!** ¡exacto!

**exaggerate** [ɪɡ'zædʒəreɪt] *vt, vi* exagerar; **exaggeration** [ɪɡzædʒə'reɪʃən] *n* exageración *f*

**exam** [ɪɡ'zæm] *n abbr* (*Scol*); = **examination**

**examination** [ɪɡzæmɪ'neɪʃən] *n* examen *m*; (*Med*) reconocimiento

**examine** [ɪɡ'zæmɪn] *vt* examinar; (*inspect*) inspeccionar; (*Med*) reconocer; **examiner** *n* examinador(a) *m/f*

**example** [ɪɡ'zɑ:mpl] *n* ejemplo; **for ~** por ejemplo

**exasperate** [ɪɡ'zɑ:spəreɪt] *vt* exasperar; **~d by** *or* **at** *or* **with** exasperado por *or* con

**excavate** ['ekskəveɪt] *vt* excavar

**exceed** [ɪk'si:d] *vt* exceder; (*number*) pasar de; (*speed limit*) sobrepasar; (*powers*) excederse en; (*hopes*) superar; **exceedingly** *adv* sumamente, sobremanera

**excel** [ɪk'sel] *vi* sobresalir; **to ~ o.s.** lucirse

**excellence** ['eksələns] *n* excelencia

**excellent** ['eksələnt] *adj* excelente

**except** [ɪk'sept] *prep* (*also:* **~ for, ~ing**) excepto, salvo ▷ *vt* exceptuar, excluir; **~ if/when** excepto si/cuando; **~ that** salvo que; **exception** *n* excepción *f*; **to take exception to** ofenderse por; **exceptional** *adj* excepcional; **exceptionally** *adv* excepcionalmente, extraordinariamente

**excerpt** ['eksə:pt] *n* extracto

**excess** [ɪk'ses] *n* exceso; **excess baggage** *n* exceso de equipaje; **excessive** *adj* excesivo

**exchange** [ɪks'tʃeɪndʒ] *n* intercambio; (*also:* **telephone ~**) central *f* (telefónica) ▷ *vt*: **to ~ (for)** cambiar (por); **exchange rate** *n* tipo de cambio

**excite** [ɪk'saɪt] *vt* (*stimulate*) estimular; **to get ~d** emocionarse; **excitement** *n* emoción *f*; **exciting** *adj* emocionante

**exclaim** [ɪk'skleɪm] *vi* exclamar

**exclamation** [eksklə'meɪʃən] *n* exclamación *f*; **exclamation mark,** (*us*) **exclamation point** *n* signo de admiración

**exclude** [ɪk'sklu:d] *vt* excluir; (*except*) exceptuar

**excluding** [ɪks'klu:dɪŋ] *prep*: **~ VAT** IVA no incluido

**exclusion** [ɪk'sklu:ʒən] *n* exclusión *f*; **to the ~ of** con exclusión de

**exclusive** [ɪk'sklu:sɪv] *adj* exclusivo; (*club, district*) selecto; **~ of tax** excluyendo impuestos; **exclusively** *adv* únicamente

**excruciating** [ɪk'skru:ʃɪeɪtɪŋ] *adj* (*pain*) agudísimo, atroz

**excursion** [ɪk'skə:ʃən] *n* excursión *f*

**excuse** *n* [ɪk'skju:s] disculpa, excusa; (*evasion*) pretexto ▷ *vt* [ɪk'skju:z] disculpar, perdonar; (*justify*) justificar; **to ~ sb from doing sth** dispensar a algn de hacer algo; **~ me!** ¡perdone!; (*attracting attention*) ¡oiga (, por favor)!; **if you will ~ me** con su permiso

**ex-directory** ['eksdɪ'rektərɪ] *adj* (BRIT): **~ (phone) number** número que no figura en la guía (telefónica)

**execute** ['eksɪkju:t] *vt* (*plan*) realizar; (*order*) cumplir; (*person*) ajusticiar, ejecutar; **execution** *n* realización *f*; cumplimiento; ejecución *f*

**executive** [ɪɡ'zekjutɪv] *n* (*Comm*) ejecutivo/a; (*Pol*) poder *m* ejecutivo ▷ *adj* ejecutivo

**exempt** [ɪɡ'zempt] *adj*: **~ from** exento de ▷ *vt*: **to ~ sb from** eximir a algn de

**exercise** ['eksəsaɪz] *n* ejercicio ▷ *vt* ejercer; (*patience etc*) proceder con; (*dog*) sacar de paseo ▷ *vi* hacer ejercicio; **exercise book** *n* cuaderno de ejercicios

**exert** [ɪɡ'zə:t] *vt* ejercer; **to ~ o.s.** esforzarse; **exertion** [ɪɡ'zə:ʃən] *n* esfuerzo

**exhale** [eks'heɪl] *vt* despedir ▷ *vi* espirar

**exhaust** [ɪɡ'zɔ:st] *n* (*pipe*) (tubo de) escape *m*; (*fumes*) gases *mpl* de escape ▷ *vt* agotar; **exhausted** *adj* agotado; **exhaustion** [ɪɡ'zɔ:stʃən] *n* agotamiento; **nervous exhaustion** agotamiento nervioso

**exhibit** [ɪɡ'zɪbɪt] *n* (*Art*) obra expuesta; (*Law*) objeto expuesto ▷ *vt* (*show: emotions*) manifestar; (: *courage, skill*) demostrar; (*paintings*) exponer; **exhibition** [eksɪ'bɪʃən] *n* exposición *f*

**exhilarating** [ɪɡ'zɪləreɪtɪŋ] *adj* estimulante, tónico

**exile** ['eksaɪl] *n* exilio; (*person*) exiliado/a ▷ *vt* desterrar, exiliar

**exist** [ɪɡ'zɪst] *vi* existir; **existence** *n* existencia; **existing** *adj* existente, actual

**exit** ['eksɪt] *n* salida ▷ *vi* (*Theat*) hacer mutis; (*Comput*) salir (del sistema); **exit ramp** *n* (*us Aut*) vía de acceso

> Be careful not to translate *exit* by the Spanish word *éxito*.

**exotic** [ɪɡ'zɔtɪk] *adj* exótico

**expand** [ɪk'spænd] *vt* ampliar, extender; (*number*) aumentar ▷ *vi* (*trade etc*) ampliarse, expandirse; (*gas, metal*) dilatarse; **to ~ on** (*notes, story etc*) ampliar

**expansion** [ɪk'spænʃən] *n* ampliación *f*; aumento; (*of trade*) expansión *f*

**expect** [ɪk'spekt] *vt* esperar; (*count on*) contar con; (*suppose*) suponer ▷ *vi*: **to be ~ing** estar encinta; **expectation** [ekspek'teɪʃən] *n* (*hope*) esperanza; (*belief*) expectativa

**expedition** [ɛkspəˈdɪʃən] n expedición f
**expel** [ɪkˈspɛl] vt expulsar
**expenditure** [ɪkˈspɛndɪtʃəˡ] n gastos mpl, desembolso; (of time, effort) gasto
**expense** [ɪkˈspɛns] n gasto, gastos mpl; (high cost) coste m; **expenses** npl (Comm) gastos mpl; **at the ~ of** a costa de; **expense account** n cuenta de gastos (de representación)
**expensive** [ɪkˈspɛnsɪv] adj caro, costoso
**experience** [ɪkˈspɪərɪəns] n experiencia ▷ vt experimentar; (suffer) sufrir; **experienced** adj experimentado
**experiment** [ɪkˈspɛrɪmənt] n experimento ▷ vi hacer experimentos; **experimental** [ɪkspɛrɪˈmɛntl] adj experimental; **the process is still at the experimental stage** el proceso está todavía en prueba
**expert** [ˈɛkspəːt] adj experto, perito ▷ n experto/a, perito/a; (specialist) especialista mf; **expertise** [ɛkspəːˈtiːz] n pericia
**expire** [ɪkˈspaɪəˡ] vi caducar, vencerse; **expiry** [ɪkˈspaɪərɪ] n vencimiento; **expiry date** n (of medicine, food item) fecha de caducidad
**explain** [ɪkˈspleɪn] vt explicar; **explanation** [ɛkspləˈneɪʃən] n explicación f
**explicit** [ɪkˈsplɪsɪt] adj explícito
**explode** [ɪkˈspləʊd] vi estallar, explotar; (with anger) reventar
**exploit** [ˈɛksplɔɪt] n hazaña ▷ vt [ɪkˈsplɔɪt] explotar; **exploitation** [ɛksplɔɪˈteɪʃən] n explotación f
**explore** [ɪkˈsplɔːˡ] vt explorar; (fig) examinar, sondear; **explorer** n explorador(a) m/f
**explosion** [ɪkˈspləʊʒən] n explosión f; **explosive** [ɪkˈspləʊsɪv] adj, n explosivo
**export** vt [ɛkˈspɔːt] exportar ▷ n [ˈɛkspɔːt] exportación f ▷ cpd de exportación; **exporter** [ɛkˈspɔːtəˡ] n exportador(a) m/f
**expose** [ɪkˈspəʊz] vt exponer; (unmask) desenmascarar; **exposed** adj expuesto
**exposure** [ɪkˈspəʊʒəˡ] n exposición f; (Phot: speed) (tiempo m de) exposición f; (: shot) fotografía; **to die from ~** (Med) morir de frío
**express** [ɪkˈsprɛs] adj (definite) expreso, explícito; (BRIT: letter etc) urgente ▷ n (train) rápido ▷ vt expresar; **expression** [ɪkˈsprɛʃən] n expresión f; **expressway** n (us: urban motorway) autopista
**exquisite** [ɛkˈskwɪzɪt] adj exquisito
**extend** [ɪkˈstɛnd] vt (visit, street) prolongar; (building) ampliar; (invitation) ofrecer ▷ vi (land) extenderse; **the contract ~s to/for ...** el contrato se prolonga hasta/por ...
**extension** [ɪkˈstɛnʃən] n extensión f; (building) ampliación f; (Tel: line) extensión f; (: telephone) supletorio m; (of deadline) prórroga

**extensive** [ɪkˈstɛnsɪv] adj extenso; (damage) importante; (knowledge) amplio
**extent** [ɪkˈstɛnt] n (breadth) extensión f; (scope) alcance m; **to some ~** hasta cierto punto; **to the ~ of ...** hasta el punto de ...; **to such an ~ that ...** hasta tal punto que ...; **to what ~?** ¿hasta qué punto?
**exterior** [ɛkˈstɪərɪəˡ] adj exterior, externo ▷ n exterior m
**external** [ɛkˈstəːnl] adj externo
**extinct** [ɪkˈstɪŋkt] adj (volcano) extinguido; (race) extinguido; **extinction** n extinción f
**extinguish** [ɪkˈstɪŋgwɪʃ] vt extinguir, apagar
**extra** [ˈɛkstrə] adj adicional ▷ adv (in addition) más ▷ n (addition) extra m; (Theat) extra mf, comparsa mf
**extract** vt [ɪkˈstrækt] sacar; (tooth) extraer ▷ n [ˈɛkstrækt] extracto
**extradite** [ˈɛkstrədaɪt] vt extraditar
**extraordinary** [ɪkˈstrɔːdnrɪ] adj extraordinario; (odd) raro
**extravagance** [ɪkˈstrævəgəns] n derroche m; (thing bought) extravagancia
**extravagant** [ɪkˈstrævəgənt] adj (wasteful) derrochador(a); (taste, gift) excesivamente caro; (price) exorbitante
**extreme** [ɪkˈstriːm] adj extremo; extremado ▷ n extremo; **extremely** adv sumamente, extremadamente
**extremist** [ɪkˈstriːmɪst] adj, n extremista mf
**extrovert** [ˈɛkstrəvəːt] n extrovertido/a
**eye** [aɪ] n ojo ▷ vt mirar; **to keep an ~ on** vigilar; **eyeball** n globo ocular; **eyebrow** n ceja; **eyedrops** npl gotas fpl para los ojos; **eyelash** n pestaña; **eyelid** n párpado; **eyeliner** n lápiz m de ojos; **eyeshadow** n sombra de ojos; **eyesight** n vista; **eye witness** n testigo mf ocular

**f**

**F** [ɛf] n (Mus) fa m

**fabric** ['fæbrɪk] n tejido, tela

> Be careful not to translate *fabric* by the Spanish word *fábrica*.

**fabulous** ['fæbjuləs] adj fabuloso

**face** [feɪs] n (Anat) cara, rostro; (of clock) esfera ▷ vt (direction) estar de cara a; (situation) hacer frente a; (facts) aceptar; ~ **down** (person, card) boca abajo; **to lose ~** desprestigiarse; **to make** or **pull a ~** hacer muecas; **in the ~ of** (difficulties etc) ante; **on the ~ of it** a primera vista; **~ to ~** cara a cara; **face up to** vt fus hacer frente a, enfrentarse a; **face cloth** n (BRIT) toallita; **face pack** n (BRIT) mascarilla

**facial** ['feɪʃəl] adj de la cara ▷ n (also: **beauty ~**) tratamiento facial, limpieza

**facilitate** [fə'sɪlɪteɪt] vt facilitar

**facility** [fə'sɪlɪtɪ] n facilidad f; **facilities** npl instalaciones fpl; **credit facilities** facilidades de crédito

**fact** [fækt] n hecho; **in ~** en realidad

**faction** ['fækʃən] n facción f

**factor** ['fæktə'] n factor m

**factory** ['fæktərɪ] n fábrica

**factual** ['fæktjuəl] adj basado en los hechos

**faculty** ['fækəltɪ] n facultad f; (US: teaching staff) personal m docente

**fad** [fæd] n novedad f, moda

**fade** [feɪd] vi desteñirse; (sound, hope) desvanecerse; (light) apagarse; (flower) marchitarse; **fade away** vi (sound) apagarse

**fag** [fæg] n (BRIT inf: cigarette) pitillo (SP), cigarro

**Fahrenheit** ['fɑːrənhaɪt] n Fahrenheit m

**fail** [feɪl] vt suspender; (memory etc) fallar a ▷ vi suspender; (be unsuccessful) fracasar; (strength, brakes, engine) fallar; **to ~ to**

do sth (neglect) dejar de hacer algo; (be unable) no poder hacer algo; **without ~** sin falta; **failing** n falta, defecto ▷ prep a falta de; **failure** ['feɪljə'] n fracaso; (person) fracasado/a; (mechanical etc) fallo

**faint** [feɪnt] adj débil; (recollection) vago; (mark) apenas visible ▷ n desmayo ▷ vi desmayarse; **to feel ~** estar mareado, marearse; **faintest** adj: **I haven't the faintest idea** no tengo la más remota idea; **faintly** adv débilmente; (vaguely) vagamente

**fair** [fɛə'] adj justo; (hair, person) rubio; (weather) bueno; (good enough) suficiente; (sizeable) considerable ▷ adv: **to play ~** jugar limpio ▷ n feria; (BRIT: funfair) parque m de atracciones; **fairground** n recinto ferial; **fair-haired** adj (person) rubio; **fairly** adv (justly) con justicia; (quite) bastante; **fair trade** n comercio justo; **fairway** n (Golf) calle f

**fairy** ['fɛərɪ] n hada; **fairy tale** n cuento de hadas

**faith** [feɪθ] n fe f; (trust) confianza; (sect) religión f; **faithful** adj, adj (loyal: troops etc) leal; (spouse) fiel; (account) exacto; **faithfully** adv fielmente; **yours faithfully** (BRIT: in letters) le saluda atentamente

**fake** [feɪk] n (painting etc) falsificación f; (person) impostor(a) m/f ▷ adj falso ▷ vt fingir; (painting etc) falsificar

**falcon** ['fɔːlkən] n halcón m

**fall** [fɔːl] n caída; (US) otoño ▷ vi (pt **fell**, pp **fallen**) caer; (accidentally) caerse; (price) bajar; **falls** npl (waterfall) cataratas fpl, salto sg de agua; **to ~ flat** vi (on one's face) caerse de bruces; (joke, story) no hacer gracia; **fall apart** vi deshacerse; **fall down** vi (person) caerse; (building) derrumbarse; **fall for** vt fus (trick) tragar; (person) enamorarse de; **fall off** vi caerse; (diminish) disminuir; **fall out** vi (friends etc) reñir; (hair, teeth) caerse; **fall over** vi caer(se); **fall through** vi (plan, project) fracasar

**fallen** ['fɔːlən] pp of fall

**fallout** ['fɔːlaut] n lluvia radioactiva

**false** [fɔːls] adj falso; **under ~ pretences** con engaños; **false alarm** n falsa alarma; **false teeth** npl (BRIT) dentadura sg postiza

**fame** [feɪm] n fama

**familiar** [fə'mɪliə'] adj familiar; (well-known) conocido; (tone) de confianza; **to be ~ with** (subject) conocer (bien); **familiarize** [fə'mɪliəraɪz] vt: **to familiarize o.s. with** familiarizarse con

**family** ['fæmɪlɪ] n familia; **family doctor** n médico/a de cabecera; **family planning** n planificación f familiar

**famine** ['fæmɪn] n hambre f, hambruna

**famous** ['feɪməs] *adj* famoso, célebre
**fan** [fæn] *n* abanico; (*Elec*) ventilador *m*; (*Sport*) hincha *mf*; (*of pop star*) fan *mf* ▷ *vt* abanicar; (*fire, quarrel*) atizar
**fanatic** [fə'nætɪk] *n* fanático/a
**fan belt** *n* correa del ventilador
**fan club** *n* club *m* de fans
**fancy** ['fænsɪ] *n* (*whim*) capricho, antojo; (*imagination*) imaginación *f* ▷ *adj* (*luxury*) de lujo ▷ *vt* (*feel like, want*) tener ganas de; (*imagine*) imaginarse; **to take a ~ to sb** tomar cariño a algn; **he fancies her** le gusta (ella) mucho; **fancy dress** *n* disfraz *m*
**fan heater** *n* calefactor *m* de aire
**fantasize** ['fæntəsaɪz] *vi* fantasear, hacerse ilusiones
**fantastic** [fæn'tæstɪk] *adj* fantástico
**fantasy** ['fæntəzɪ] *n* fantasía
**fanzine** ['fænziːn] *n* fanzine *m*
**FAQs** *npl abbr* (= *frequently asked questions*) preguntas *fpl* frecuentes
**far** [fɑːʳ] *adj* (*distant*) lejano ▷ *adv* lejos; **~ away**, **~ off** (a lo) lejos; **~ better** mucho mejor; **~ from** lejos de; **by ~** con mucho; **go as ~ as the farm** vaya hasta la granja; **as ~ as I know** que yo sepa; **how ~?** ¿hasta dónde?; (*fig*) ¿hasta qué punto?
**farce** [fɑːs] *n* farsa
**fare** [fɛəʳ] *n* (*on trains, buses*) precio (del billete); (*in taxi: cost*) tarifa; (*food*) comida; **half/full ~** medio billete *m*/billete *m* completo
**Far East** *n*: **the ~** el Extremo *or* Lejano Oriente
**farewell** [fɛə'wɛl] *excl, n* adiós *m*
**farm** [fɑːm] *n* granja, finca, estancia (*LAM*), chacra (*LAM*) ▷ *vt* cultivar; **farmer** *n* granjero/a, estanciero/a (*LAM*); **farmhouse** *n* granja, casa de hacienda (*LAM*); **farming** *n* agricultura; (*tilling*) cultivo; **sheep farming** cría de ovejas; **farmyard** *n* corral *m*
**far-reaching** [fɑː'riːtʃɪŋ] *adj* (*reform, effect*) de gran alcance
**fart** [fɑːt] (*inf!*) *vi* tirarse un pedo (!)
**farther** ['fɑːðəʳ] *adv* más lejos, más allá ▷ *adj* más lejano
**farthest** ['fɑːðɪst] *superlative of* **far**
**fascinate** ['fæsɪneɪt] *vt* fascinar; **fascinated** *adj* fascinado; **fascinating** *adj* fascinante; **fascination** [fæsɪ'neɪʃən] *n* fascinación *f*; **fascinator** *n* (*hat*) tocado (*de plumas, flores o cintas*)
**fascist** ['fæʃɪst] *adj, n* fascista *mf*
**fashion** ['fæʃən] *n* moda; (*fashion industry*) industria de la moda; (*manner*) manera ▷ *vt* formar; **in ~** a la moda; **out of ~** pasado de moda; **fashionable** *adj* de moda; **fashion show** *n* desfile *m* de modelos

**fast** [fɑːst] *adj* (*also Phot: film*) rápido; (*dye, colour*) sólido; (*clock*): **to be ~** estar adelantado ▷ *adv* rápidamente, de prisa; (*stuck, held*) firmemente ▷ *n* ayuno ▷ *vi* ayunar; **~ asleep** profundamente dormido
**fasten** ['fɑːsn] *vt* asegurar, sujetar; (*coat, belt*) abrochar ▷ *vi* cerrarse
**fast food** *n* comida rápida, platos *mpl* preparados
**fat** [fæt] *adj* gordo; (*book*) grueso; (*profit*) grande, pingüe ▷ *n* grasa; (*on person*) carnes *fpl*; (*lard*) manteca
**fatal** ['feɪtl] *adj* (*mistake*) fatal; (*injury*) mortal; **fatality** [fə'tælɪtɪ] *n* (*road death etc*) víctima *f* mortal; **fatally** *adv*: **fatally injured** herido de muerte
**fate** [feɪt] *n* destino
**father** ['fɑːðəʳ] *n* padre *m*; **Father Christmas** *n* Papá *m* Noel; **father-in-law** *n* suegro
**fatigue** [fə'tiːg] *n* fatiga, cansancio
**fatten** ['fætn] *vt, vi* engordar; **chocolate is ~ing** el chocolate engorda
**fatty** ['fætɪ] *adj* (*food*) graso ▷ *n* (*inf*) gordito/a, gordinflón/ona *m/f*
**faucet** ['fɔːsɪt] *n* (*US*) grifo, llave *f*, canilla (*LAM*)
**fault** [fɔːlt] *n* (*blame*) culpa; (*defect: in character*) defecto; (*Geo*) falla ▷ *vt* criticar; **it's my ~** es culpa mía; **to find ~ with** criticar, poner peros a; **at ~** culpable; **faulty** *adj* defectuoso
**fauna** ['fɔːnə] *n* fauna
**favour**, (*US*) **favor** ['feɪvəʳ] *n* favor *m*; (*approval*) aprobación *f* ▷ *vt* (*proposition*) estar a favor de, aprobar; (*assist*) favorecer; **to do sb a ~** hacer un favor a algn; **to find ~ with sb** (*person*) caer en gracia a algn; **in ~ of** a favor de; **favourable** *adj* favorable; **favourite** ['feɪvərɪt] *adj, n* favorito/a, preferido/a
**fawn** [fɔːn] *n* cervato ▷ *adj* (*also*: **~-coloured**) de color cervato, leonado ▷ *vi*: **to ~ (up)on** adular
**fax** [fæks] *n* fax *m* ▷ *vt* mandar *or* enviar por fax
**FBI** *n abbr* (*US*: = *Federal Bureau of Investigation*) FBI *m*
**fear** [fɪəʳ] *n* miedo, temor *m* ▷ *vt* temer; **for ~ of** por temor a; **fearful** *adj* temeroso; (*awful*) espantoso; **fearless** *adj* audaz
**feasible** ['fiːzəbl] *adj* factible
**feast** [fiːst] *n* banquete *m*; (*Rel: also*: **~ day**) fiesta ▷ *vi* festejar
**feat** [fiːt] *n* hazaña
**feather** ['fɛðəʳ] *n* pluma
**feature** ['fiːtʃəʳ] *n* característica; (*article*) reportaje *m* ▷ *vt* (*film*) presentar ▷ *vi* figurar;

**features** npl (of face) facciones fpl; **feature film** n largometraje m

**Feb.** abbr (= February) feb

**February** ['fɛbruərɪ] n febrero

**fed** [fɛd] pt, pp of **feed**

**federal** ['fɛdərəl] adj federal

**federation** [fɛdə'reɪʃən] n federación f

**fee** [fi:] n (professional) honorarios mpl; (of school) matrícula; (also: **membership ~**) cuota

**feeble** ['fi:bl] adj débil

**feed** [fi:d] n comida; (of animal) pienso; (on printer) dispositivo de alimentación ▷ vt (pt, pp **fed**) alimentar; (BRIT: breastfeed) dar el pecho a; (animal, baby) dar de comer a; **feed into** vt (data, information) suministrar a; **feedback** n reacción f; feedback m

**feel** [fi:l] n (sensation) sensación f; (sense of touch) tacto ▷ vt (pt, pp **felt**) tocar; (cold, pain etc) sentir; (think, believe) creer; **to ~ hungry/cold** tener hambre/frío; **to ~ lonely/better** sentirse solo/mejor; **I don't ~ well** no me siento bien; **it ~s soft** es suave al tacto; **to ~ like** (want) tener ganas de; **feeling** n (physical) sensación f; (foreboding) presentimiento; (emotion) sentimiento

**feet** [fi:t] npl of **foot**

**fell** [fɛl] pt of **fall** ▷ vt (tree) talar

**fellow** ['fɛləu] n tipo, tío (SP); (of learned society) socio/a; **fellow citizen** n conciudadano/a; **fellow countryman** n compatriota m; **fellow men** npl semejantes mpl; **fellowship** n compañerismo; (grant) beca

**felony** ['fɛlənɪ] n crimen m

**felt** [fɛlt] pt, pp of **feel** ▷ n fieltro

**felt-tip pen** ['fɛlttɪp-] n rotulador m

**female** ['fi:meɪl] n (woman) mujer f; (Zool) hembra ▷ adj femenino

**feminine** ['fɛmɪnɪn] adj femenino

**feminist** ['fɛmɪnɪst] n feminista mf

**fence** [fɛns] n valla, cerca ▷ vt (also: **~ in**) cercar ▷ vi hacer esgrima; **fencing** n esgrima

**fend** [fɛnd] vi: **to ~ for o.s.** valerse por sí mismo; **fend off** vt (attack, attacker) rechazar; (awkward question) esquivar

**fender** ['fɛndər] n (US Aut) parachoques m inv

**fennel** ['fɛnl] n hinojo

**ferment** vi [fə'mɛnt] fermentar ▷ n ['fə:mɛnt] (fig) agitación f

**fern** [fə:n] n helecho

**ferocious** [fə'rəuʃəs] adj feroz

**ferret** ['fɛrɪt] n hurón m

**ferry** ['fɛrɪ] n (small) barca de pasaje, balsa; (large: also: **~boat**) transbordador m, ferry m ▷ vt transportar

**fertile** ['fə:taɪl] adj fértil; (Biol) fecundo; **fertilize** ['fə:tɪlaɪz] vt (Biol) fecundar; (Agr) abonar; **fertilizer** n abono

**festival** ['fɛstɪvəl] n (Rel) fiesta; (Art, Mus) festival m

**festive** ['fɛstɪv] adj festivo; **the ~ season** (BRIT: Christmas) las Navidades

**fetch** [fɛtʃ] vt ir a buscar; (sell for) venderse por

**fête** [feɪt] n fiesta

**fetus** ['fi:təs] n (US) = **foetus**

**feud** [fju:d] n (hostility) enemistad f; (quarrel) disputa

**fever** ['fi:vər] n fiebre f; **feverish** adj febril

**few** [fju:] adj (not many) pocos ▷ pron algunos; **a ~** adj unos pocos; **fewer** adj menos; **fewest** adj los/las menos

**fiancé** [fɪ'ã:ŋseɪ] n novio, prometido; **fiancée** n novia, prometida

**fiasco** [fɪ'æskəu] n fiasco

**fib** [fɪb] n mentirijilla

**fibre**, (US) **fiber** ['faɪbər] n fibra; **fibreglass**, (US) **fiberglass** n fibra de vidrio

**fickle** ['fɪkl] adj inconstante

**fiction** ['fɪkʃən] n ficción f; **fictional** adj novelesco

**fiddle** ['fɪdl] n (Mus) violín m; (cheating) trampa ▷ vt (BRIT: accounts) falsificar; **fiddle with** vt fus juguetear con

**fidelity** [fɪ'dɛlɪtɪ] n fidelidad f

**field** [fi:ld] n campo; (fig) campo, esfera; (Sport) campo, cancha (LAM); **field marshal** n mariscal m

**fierce** [fɪəs] adj feroz; (wind, attack) violento; (heat) intenso; (fighting, enemy) encarnizado

**fifteen** [fɪf'ti:n] num quince; **fifteenth** adj decimoquinto; **the fifteenth floor** la planta quince; **the fifteenth of August** el quince de agosto

**fifth** [fɪfθ] adj quinto

**fiftieth** ['fɪftɪɪθ] adj quincuagésimo

**fifty** ['fɪftɪ] num cincuenta; **fifty-fifty** adj (deal, split) a medias ▷ adv: **to go fifty-fifty with sb** ir a medias con algn

**fig** [fɪg] n higo

**fight** [faɪt] (pt, pp **fought**) n pelea; (Mil) combate m; (struggle) lucha ▷ vt luchar contra; (cancer, alcoholism) combatir ▷ vi pelear, luchar; **fight back** vi defenderse; (after illness) recuperarse ▷ vt (tears) contener; **fight off** vt (attack, attacker) rechazar; (disease, sleep, urge) luchar contra; **fighting** n combate m, pelea

**figure** ['fɪgər] n (Drawing, Geom) figura, dibujo; (number, cipher) cifra; (person, outline) figura ▷ vt (esp US: think, calculate) calcular, imaginarse ▷ vi (appear) figurar; **figure out** vt (work out) resolver

**file** [faɪl] n (tool) lima; (dossier) expediente m; (folder) carpeta; (Comput) fichero; (row) fila ▷ vt limar; (Law: claim) presentar; (store) archivar; **filing cabinet** n archivo
**Filipino** [fɪlɪ'piːnəu] adj filipino ▷ n (person) filipino/a
**fill** [fɪl] vt llenar; (vacancy) cubrir ▷ n: to eat one's ~ comer hasta hartarse; **fill in** vt rellenar; **fill out** vt (form, receipt) rellenar; **fill up** vt llenar (hasta el borde) ▷ vi (Aut) echar gasolina
**fillet** ['fɪlɪt] n filete m; **fillet steak** n filete m de ternera
**filling** ['fɪlɪŋ] n (Culin) relleno; (for tooth) empaste m; **filling station** n estación f de servicio
**film** [fɪlm] n película ▷ vt (scene) filmar ▷ vi rodar; **film star** n estrella de cine
**filter** ['fɪltər] n filtro ▷ vt filtrar; **filter lane** n (BRIT) carril m de selección
**filth** [fɪlθ] n suciedad f; **filthy** adj sucio; (language) obsceno
**fin** [fɪn] n aleta
**final** ['faɪnl] adj (last) final, último; (definitive) definitivo ▷ n (Sport) final f; **finals** npl (Scol) exámenes mpl finales
**finale** [fɪ'nɑːlɪ] n final m
**final: finalist** n (Sport) finalista mf; **finalize** vt ultimar; **finally** adv (lastly) por último, finalmente; (eventually) por fin
**finance** [faɪ'næns] n (money, funds) fondos mpl ▷ vt financiar; **finances** npl finanzas fpl; **financial** [faɪ'nænʃəl] adj financiero; **financial year** n ejercicio (financiero)
**find** [faɪnd] (pt, pp **found**) vt encontrar, hallar; (come upon) descubrir ▷ n hallazgo; descubrimiento; **to ~ sb guilty** (Law) declarar culpable a algn; **find out** vt averiguar; (truth, secret) descubrir ▷ vi: **to ~ out about** enterarse de; **findings** npl (Law) veredicto sg, fallo sg; (of report) recomendaciones fpl
**fine** [faɪn] adj (delicate) fino ▷ adv (well) bien ▷ n (Law) multa ▷ vt (Law) multar; **he's ~** está muy bien; **fine arts** npl bellas artes fpl
**finger** ['fɪŋgər] n dedo ▷ vt (touch) manosear; **little/index ~** (dedo) meñique m/índice m; **fingernail** n uña; **fingerprint** n huella dactilar; **fingertip** n yema del dedo
**finish** ['fɪnɪʃ] n (end) fin m; (Sport) meta; (polish etc) acabado ▷ vt, vi terminar; **to ~ doing sth** acabar de hacer algo; **to ~ first/second/third** llegar el primero/segundo/tercero; **finish off** vt acabar, terminar; (kill) rematar; **finish up** vt acabar, terminar ▷ vi ir a parar, terminar
**Finland** ['fɪnlənd] n Finlandia
**Finn** [fɪn] n finlandés/esa m/f; **Finnish** adj finlandés/esa ▷ n (Ling) finlandés m

**fir** [fəːʳ] n abeto
**fire** ['faɪəʳ] n fuego; (accidental, damaging) incendio; (heater) estufa ▷ vt (gun) disparar; (interest) despertar; (dismiss) despedir ▷ vi encenderse; **on ~** ardiendo, en llamas; **fire alarm** n alarma de incendios; **firearm** n arma de fuego; **fire brigade,** (US) **fire department** n (cuerpo de) bomberos mpl; **fire engine** n coche m de bomberos; **fire escape** n escalera de incendios; **fire exit** n salida de incendios; **fire extinguisher** n extintor m; **firefighter** n bombero; **fireplace** n chimenea; **fire station** n parque m de bomberos; **firetruck** n (US) = **fire engine**; **firewall** n (Internet) firewall m; **firewood** n leña; **fireworks** npl fuegos mpl artificiales
**firm** [fəːm] adj firme ▷ n empresa; **firmly** adv firmemente
**first** [fəːst] adj primero ▷ adv (before others) primero; (when listing reasons etc) en primer lugar, primeramente ▷ n (person: in race) primero/a; (Aut) primera; **at ~** al principio; **~ of all** ante todo; **first aid** n primeros auxilios mpl; **first aid kit** n botiquín m; **first-class** adj de primera clase; **first-hand** adj de primera mano; **first lady** n (esp US) primera dama; **firstly** adv en primer lugar; **first name** n nombre m de pila; **first-rate** adj de primera (clase)
**fiscal** ['fɪskəl] adj fiscal; **~ year** año fiscal, ejercicio
**fish** [fɪʃ] n (pl inv) pez m; (food) pescado ▷ vt pescar en ▷ vi pescar; **to go ~ing** ir de pesca; **~ and chips** pescado frito con patatas fritas; **fisherman** n pescador m; **fish fingers** npl (BRIT) palitos mpl de pescado (empanado); **fishing boat** n barca de pesca; **fishing line** n sedal m; **fishmonger** n (BRIT) pescadero/a; **fishmonger's (shop)** n (BRIT) pescadería; **fish sticks** npl (US) = **fish fingers**; **fishy** adj (fig) sospechoso
**fist** [fɪst] n puño
**fit** [fɪt] adj (Med, Sport) en (buena) forma; (proper) adecuado, apropiado ▷ vt (clothes) quedar bien a; (instal) poner; (equip) proveer; (match: facts) cuadrar or corresponder or coincidir con ▷ vi (clothes) quedar bien; (in space, gap) caber; (facts) coincidir ▷ n (Med) ataque m; **~ to** apto para; **~ for** apropiado para; **a ~ of anger/ enthusiasm** un arranque de cólera/ entusiasmo; **this dress is a good ~** este vestido me queda bien; **by ~s and starts** a rachas; **fit in** vi encajar; **fitness** n (Med) forma física; **fitted** adj (jacket, shirt) entallado; (sheet) de cuatro picos; **fitted carpet** n moqueta; **fitted kitchen** n cocina amueblada; **fitting** adj apropiado ▷ n (of

*dress*) prueba; **fitting room** n (*in shop*)
probador m; **fittings** npl instalaciones fpl
**five** [faɪv] num cinco; **fiver** n (*inf*: BRIT)
billete m de cinco libras; (: US) billete m de
cinco dólares
**fix** [fɪks] vt (*secure*) fijar, asegurar; (*mend*)
arreglar; (*meal, drink*) preparar ▷ n: **to be
in a ~** estar en un aprieto; **fix up** vt (*date,
meeting*) arreglar; **to ~ sb up with sth**
conseguirle algo a algn; **fixed** adj (*prices etc*)
fijo; **fixture** n (*Sport*) encuentro
**fizzy** ['fɪzɪ] adj (*drink*) gaseoso
**flag** [flæg] n bandera; (*stone*) losa ▷ vi
decaer; **flag down** vt: **to ~ sb down** hacer
señas a algn para que se pare; **flagpole** n
asta de bandera
**flair** [flɛə'] n aptitud f especial
**flak** [flæk] n (*Mil*) fuego antiaéreo; (*inf*:
*criticism*) lluvia de críticas
**flake** [fleɪk] n (*of rust, paint*) desconchón m;
(*of snow*) copo; (*of soap powder*) escama ▷ vi
(*also*: **~ off**) desconcharse
**flamboyant** [flæm'bɔɪənt] adj (*dress*)
vistoso; (*person*) extravagante
**flame** [fleɪm] n llama
**flamingo** [flə'mɪŋɡəu] n flamenco
**flammable** ['flæməbl] adj inflamable
**flan** [flæn] n (BRIT) tarta
  ▌ Be careful not to translate *flan* by the
  Spanish word *flan*.
**flank** [flæŋk] n flanco ▷ vt flanquear
**flannel** ['flænl] n (BRIT: also: **face ~**) toallita;
(*fabric*) franela; **flannels** npl pantalones mpl
de franela
**flap** [flæp] n (*of pocket, envelope*) solapa ▷ vt
(*wings*) batir ▷ vi (*sail, flag*) ondear
**flare** [flɛə'] n llamarada; (*Mil*) bengala;
(*in skirt etc*) vuelo; **flares** npl (*trousers*)
pantalones mpl de campana; **flare up** vi
encenderse; (*fig: person*) encolerizarse;
(: *revolt*) estallar
**flash** [flæʃ] n relámpago; (*also*: **news ~**)
noticias fpl de última hora; (*Phot*) flash
m ▷ vt (*light, headlights*) lanzar destellos
con ▷ vi brillar; (*hazard light etc*) lanzar
destellos; **in a ~** en un instante; **he ~ed by**
or **past** pasó como un rayo; **flashback** n
flashback m; **flashbulb** n bombilla de flash;
**flashlight** n linterna
**flask** [flɑːsk] n petaca; (*also*: **vacuum ~**)
termo
**flat** [flæt] adj llano; (*smooth*) liso; (*tyre*)
desinflado; (*battery*) descargado; (*beer*)
sin gas; (*Mus: instrument*) desafinado ▷ n
(BRIT: *apartment*) piso (SP), departamento
(LAM), apartamento; (*Aut*) pinchazo; (*Mus*)
bemol m; (**to work**) **~ out** (trabajar) a
tope; **flatten** vt (*also*: **flatten out**) allanar;
(*smooth out*) alisar; (*house, city*) arrasar

**flatter** ['flætə'] vt adular, halagar;
**flattering** adj halagador(a); (*clothes etc*)
que favorece
**flaunt** [flɔːnt] vt ostentar, lucir
**flavour**, (US) **flavor** ['fleɪvə'] n sabor
m, gusto ▷ vt sazonar, condimentar;
**strawberry ~ed** con sabor a fresa;
**flavouring**, (US) **flavoring** n (*in product*)
aromatizante m
**flaw** [flɔː] n defecto; **flawless** adj impecable
**flea** [fliː] n pulga; **flea market** n rastro,
mercadillo
**flee** (*pt, pp* **fled**) [fliː, flɛd] vt huir de ▷ vi huir
**fleece** [fliːs] n vellón m; (*wool*) lana; (*top*)
forro polar ▷ vt (*inf*) desplumar
**fleet** [fliːt] n flota; (*of cars, lorries etc*)
parque m
**fleeting** ['fliːtɪŋ] adj fugaz
**Flemish** ['flɛmɪʃ] adj flamenco
**flesh** [flɛʃ] n carne f; (*skin*) piel f; (*of fruit*)
pulpa
**flew** [fluː] pt of **fly**
**flex** [flɛks] n cable m ▷ vt (*muscles*) tensar;
**flexibility** n flexibilidad f; **flexible** adj
flexible; **flexitime** n horario flexible
**flick** [flɪk] n capirotazo ▷ vt dar un golpecito
a; **flick through** vt fus hojear
**flicker** ['flɪkə'] vi (*light*) parpadear; (*flame*)
vacilar
**flies** [flaɪz] npl of **fly**
**flight** [flaɪt] n vuelo; (*escape*) huida, fuga;
(*also*: **~ of steps**) tramo (de escaleras);
**flight attendant** n auxiliar mf de vuelo
**flimsy** ['flɪmzɪ] adj (*thin*) muy ligero; (*excuse*)
flojo
**flinch** [flɪntʃ] vi encogerse; **to ~ from**
retroceder ante
**fling** [flɪŋ] (*pt, pp* **flung**) vt arrojar
**flint** [flɪnt] n pedernal m; (*in lighter*) piedra
**flip** [flɪp] vt: **to ~ a coin** echar a cara o cruz
**flip-flops** ['flɪpflɔps] npl (*esp* BRIT)
chancletas fpl
**flipper** ['flɪpə'] n aleta
**flirt** [fləːt] vi coquetear, flirtear ▷ n
coqueta f
**float** [fləut] n flotador m; (*in procession*)
carroza; (*sum of money*) reserva ▷ vi
(*currency*) flotar; (*swimmer*) hacer la plancha
**flock** [flɔk] n (*of sheep*) rebaño; (*of birds*)
bandada ▷ vi: **to ~ to** acudir en tropel a
**flood** [flʌd] n inundación f; (*of letters,
imports etc*) avalancha ▷ vt inundar ▷ vi
(*place*) inundarse; (*people*): **to ~ into**
inundar; **flooding** n inundaciones fpl;
**floodlight** n foco
**floor** [flɔː'] n suelo; (*storey*) piso; (*of sea,
valley*) fondo ▷ vt (*with blow*) derribar; (*fig:
baffle*) dejar anonadado; **ground ~,** (US)
**first ~** planta baja; **first ~,** (US) **second ~**

primer piso; **floorboard** n tabla; **flooring** n suelo; (*material*) solería; **floor show** n cabaret m

**flop** [flɔp] n fracaso ▷ vi (*fail*) fracasar; **floppy** adj flojo ▷ n (*Comput: also*: **floppy disk**) floppy m

**flora** ['flɔːrə] n flora

**floral** ['flɔːrl] adj (*pattern*) floreado

**florist** ['flɔrɪst] n florista mf; **~'s (shop)** n floristería

**flotation** [fləu'teɪʃən] n (*of shares*) emisión f; (*of company*) lanzamiento

**flour** ['flauər] n harina

**flourish** ['flʌrɪʃ] vi florecer ▷ n ademán m, movimiento (ostentoso)

**flow** [fləu] n (*movement*) flujo; (*of traffic*) circulación f; (*Elec*) corriente f ▷ vi (*river, blood*) fluir; (*traffic*) circular

**flower** ['flauər] n flor f ▷ vi florecer; **flower bed** n macizo; **flowerpot** n tiesto

**flown** [fləun] pp of **fly**

**fl. oz.** abbr = **fluid ounce**

**flu** [fluː] n: **to have ~** tener la gripe

**fluctuate** ['flʌktjueɪt] vi fluctuar

**fluent** ['fluːənt] adj (*speech*) elocuente; **he speaks ~ French, he's ~ in French** domina el francés

**fluff** [flʌf] n pelusa; **fluffy** adj de pelo suave

**fluid** ['fluːɪd] adj (*movement*) fluido, líquido; (*situation*) inestable ▷ n fluido, líquido; **fluid ounce** n onza f líquida

**fluke** [fluːk] n (*inf*) chiripa

**flung** [flʌŋ] pt, pp of **fling**

**fluorescent** [fluə'rɛsnt] adj fluorescente

**fluoride** ['fluəraɪd] n fluoruro

**flurry** ['flʌrɪ] n (*of snow*) ventisca; **~ of activity** frenesí m de actividad

**flush** [flʌʃ] n rubor m; (*fig: of youth, beauty*) resplandor m ▷ vt limpiar con agua ▷ vi ruborizarse ▷ adj: **~ with** a ras de; **to ~ the toilet** tirar de la cadena (del wáter)

**flute** [fluːt] n flauta travesera

**flutter** ['flʌtər] n (*of wings*) revoloteo, aleteo ▷ vi revolotear

**fly** [flaɪ] (pt **flew**, pp **flown**) n mosca; (*on trousers: also*: **flies**) bragueta ▷ vt (*plane*) pilotar; (*cargo*) transportar (en avión); (*distance*) recorrer (en avión) ▷ vi volar; (*passenger*) ir en avión; (*escape*) evadirse; (*flag*) ondear; **fly away** vi (*bird, insect*) irse volando; **fly off** vi irse volando; **fly-drive** n: **fly-drive holiday** vacaciones que incluyen vuelo y alquiler de coche; **flying** n (*activity*) (el) volar ▷ adj: **flying visit** visita relámpago; **with flying colours** con lucimiento; **flying saucer** n platillo volante; **flyover** n (BRIT) paso elevado or (LAM) a desnivel

**FM** abbr (*Radio*: = frequency modulation) FM

**foal** [fəul] n potro

**foam** [fəum] n espuma ▷ vi hacer espuma

**focus** ['fəukəs] (pl **focuses**) n foco; (*centre*) centro ▷ vt (*field glasses etc*) enfocar ▷ vi: **to ~ (on)** enfocar (a); (*issue etc*) centrarse en; **in/out of ~** enfocado/desenfocado

**foetus**, (US) **fetus** ['fiːtəs] n feto

**fog** [fɔg] n niebla; **foggy** adj: **it's foggy** hay niebla; **fog lamp**, (US) **fog light** n (*Aut*) faro antiniebla

**foil** [fɔɪl] vt frustrar ▷ n hoja; (*also*: **kitchen ~**) papel m (de) aluminio; (*Fencing*) florete m

**fold** [fəuld] n (*bend, crease*) pliegue m; (*Agr*) redil m ▷ vt doblar; **to ~ one's arms** cruzarse de brazos; **fold up** vi plegarse, doblarse; (*business*) quebrar ▷ vt (*map etc*) plegar; **folder** n (*for papers*) carpeta; (*Comput*) directorio; **folding** adj (*chair, bed*) plegable

**foliage** ['fəulɪɪdʒ] n follaje m

**folk** [fəuk] npl gente f ▷ adj popular, folklórico; **folks** npl familia, parientes mpl; **folklore** ['fəuklɔːr] n folklore m; **folk music** n música folk; **folk song** n canción f popular or folk

**follow** ['fɔləu] vt seguir ▷ vi seguir; (*result*) resultar; **he ~ed suit** hizo lo mismo; **follow up** vt (*letter, offer*) responder a; (*case*) investigar; **follower** n seguidor(a) m/f; (*Pol*) partidario/a; **following** adj siguiente ▷ n seguidores mpl, afición f; **follow-up** n continuación f

**fond** [fɔnd] adj (*loving*) cariñoso; **to be ~ of sb** tener cariño a algn; **she's ~ of swimming** tiene afición a la natación, le gusta nadar

**food** [fuːd] n comida; **food mixer** n batidora; **food poisoning** n intoxicación f alimentaria; **food processor** n robot m de cocina; **food stamp** n (US) vale m para comida

**fool** [fuːl] n tonto/a; (*Culin*) puré m de frutas con nata ▷ vt engañar; **fool about, fool around** vi hacer el tonto; **foolish** adj tonto; (*careless*) imprudente; **foolproof** adj (*plan etc*) infalible

**foot** [fut] (pl **feet**) n (*Anat*) pie m; (*measure*) pie m (= 304 mm); (*of animal, table*) pata ▷ vt (*bill*) pagar; **on ~** a pie; **footage** n (*Cine*) imágenes fpl; **foot-and-mouth (disease)** n fiebre f aftosa; **football** n balón m; (*game*: BRIT) fútbol m; (: US) fútbol m americano; **footballer** n (BRIT) = **football player**; **football match** n partido de fútbol; **football player** n futbolista mf, jugador(a) m/f de fútbol; **footbridge** n puente m para peatones; **foothills** npl estribaciones fpl; **foothold** n pie m firme; **footing** n (*fig*) nivel m; **to lose one's footing** perder pie; **footnote** n nota (de pie de página);

**footpath** n sendero; **footprint** n huella, pisada; **footstep** n paso; **footwear** n calzado

 **KEYWORD**

**for** [fɔː] prep **1** (indicating destination, intention) para; **the train for London** el tren con destino a Londres; **he left for Rome** marchó para Roma; **he went for the paper** fue por el periódico; **is this for me?** ¿es esto para mí?; **it's time for lunch** es la hora de comer

**2** (indicating purpose) para; **what('s it) for?** ¿para qué (es)?; **to pray for peace** rezar por la paz

**3** (on behalf of, representing): **the MP for Hove** el diputado por Hove; **he works for the government/a local firm** trabaja para el gobierno/en una empresa local; **I'll ask him for you** se lo pediré por ti; **G for George** G de Gerona

**4** (because of) por esta razón; **for fear of being criticized** por temor a ser criticado

**5** (with regard to) para; **it's cold for July** hace frío para julio; **he has a gift for languages** tiene don de lenguas

**6** (in exchange for) por; **I sold it for £5** lo vendí por £5; **to pay 50 pence for a ticket** pagar 50 peniques por un billete

**7** (in favour of): **are you for or against us?** ¿estás con nosotros o contra nosotros?; **I'm all for it** estoy totalmente a favor; **vote for X** vote (a) X

**8** (referring to distance): **there are roadworks for 5 km** hay obras en 5 km; **we walked for miles** caminamos kilómetros y kilómetros

**9** (referring to time): **he was away for two years** estuvo fuera (durante) dos años; **it hasn't rained for three weeks** no ha llovido durante or en tres semanas; **I have known her for years** la conozco desde hace años; **can you do it for tomorrow?** ¿lo podrás hacer para mañana?

**10** (with infinitive clauses): **it is not for me to decide** la decisión no es cosa mía; **it would be best for you to leave** sería mejor que te fueras; **there is still time for you to do it** todavía te queda tiempo para hacerlo; **for this to be possible ...** para que esto sea posible ...

**11** (in spite of) a pesar de; **for all his complaints** a pesar de sus quejas
▶ conj (since, as: formal) puesto que

**forbid** (pt **forbad(e)**, pp **forbidden**) [fə'bɪd, -'bæd, -'bɪdn] vt prohibir; **to ~ sb to do sth** prohibir a algn hacer algo; **forbidden** pt of

**forbid** ▷ adj (food, area) prohibido; (word, subject) tabú

**force** [fɔːs] n fuerza ▷ vt forzar; **to ~ o.s. to do** hacer un esfuerzo por hacer; **forced** adj forzado; **forceful** adj enérgico

**ford** [fɔːd] n vado

**fore** [fɔːʳ] n: **to come to the ~** empezar a destacar; **forearm** n antebrazo; **forecast** n pronóstico ▷ vt (irreg: like **cast**) pronosticar; **forecourt** n patio; (of garage) área de entrada; **forefinger** n (dedo) índice m; **forefront** n: **in the forefront of** en la vanguardia de; **foreground** n (also Comput) primer plano m; **forehead** ['fɔrɪd] n frente f

**foreign** ['fɔrɪn] adj extranjero; (trade) exterior; **foreign currency** n divisas fpl; **foreigner** n extranjero/a; **foreign exchange** n divisas fpl; **Foreign Office** n (BRIT) Ministerio de Asuntos Exteriores; **Foreign Secretary** n (BRIT) Ministro/a de Asuntos Exteriores

**fore: foreman** n capataz m; **foremost** adj principal ▷ adv: **first and foremost** ante todo; **forename** n nombre m (de pila)

**forensic** [fə'rɛnsɪk] adj forense

**foresee** (pt **foresaw**, pp **foreseen**) [fɔː'siː, -'sɔː, -'siːn] vt prever; **foreseeable** adj previsible

**forest** ['fɔrɪst] n bosque m; **forestry** n silvicultura

**forever** [fə'rɛvəʳ] adv para siempre; (endlessly) constantemente

**foreword** ['fɔːwəːd] n prefacio

**forfeit** ['fɔːfɪt] vt perder (derecho a)

**forgave** [fə'geɪv] pt of **forgive**

**forge** [fɔːdʒ] n herrería ▷ vt (signature, money) falsificar; (metal) forjar; **forger** n falsificador(a) m/f; **forgery** n falsificación f

**forget** (pt **forgot**, pp **forgotten**) [fə'gɛt, -'gɔt, -'gɔtn] vt olvidar ▷ vi olvidarse; **forgetful** adj olvidadizo, despistado

**forgive** (pt **forgave**, pp **forgiven**) [fə'gɪv, -'geɪv, -'gɪvn] vt perdonar; **to ~ sb for sth/ for doing sth** perdonar algo a algn/a algn por haber hecho algo

**forgot** [fə'gɔt] pt of **forget**

**forgotten** [fə'gɔtn] pp of **forget**

**fork** [fɔːk] n (for eating) tenedor m; (for gardening) horca; (of roads) bifurcación f ▷ vi (road) bifurcarse

**forlorn** [fə'lɔːn] adj (person) triste, melancólico; (cottage) abandonado; (attempt) desesperado

**form** [fɔːm] n forma; (document) formulario, planilla (LAM) ▷ vt formar; **in top ~** en plena forma; **to ~ a circle/a queue** hacer una curva/una cola

**formal** ['fɔːməl] adj (offer, receipt) por escrito; (person etc) correcto; (occasion,

dinner) ceremonioso; **~ dress** traje m de vestir; **formality** [fɔːˈmælɪtɪ] n ceremonia
**format** [ˈfɔːmæt] n formato ▷ vt (Comput) formatear
**formation** [fɔːˈmeɪʃən] n formación f
**former** [ˈfɔːməʳ] adj anterior; (earlier) antiguo; (ex) ex; **the ~ ... the latter ...** aquél ... éste ...; **formerly** adv antes
**formidable** [ˈfɔːmɪdəbl] adj formidable
**formula** [ˈfɔːmjulə] n fórmula
**fort** [fɔːt] n fuerte m
**forthcoming** [fɔːθˈkʌmɪŋ] adj próximo, venidero; (character) comunicativo
**fortieth** [ˈfɔːtɪɪθ] adj cuadragésimo
**fortify** [ˈfɔːtɪfaɪ] vt fortalecer
**fortnight** [ˈfɔːtnaɪt] n (BRIT) quincena; **it's a ~ since ...** hace quince días que ...; **fortnightly** adj quincenal ▷ adv quincenalmente
**fortress** [ˈfɔːtrɪs] n fortaleza
**fortunate** [ˈfɔːtʃənɪt] adj: **it is ~ that ...** (es una) suerte que ...; **fortunately** adv afortunadamente
**fortune** [ˈfɔːtʃən] n suerte f; (wealth) fortuna; **fortune-teller** n adivino/a
**forty** [ˈfɔːtɪ] num cuarenta
**forum** [ˈfɔːrəm] n foro
**forward** [ˈfɔːwəd] adj (position) avanzado; (movement) hacia delante; (front) delantero; (not shy) atrevido ▷ n (Sport) delantero ▷ vt (letter) remitir; (career) promocionar; **to move ~** avanzar; **forwarding address** n destinatario; **forward slash** n barra diagonal
**fossick** [ˈfɔsɪk] vi (AUST, NZ inf) buscar; **to ~ for sth** buscar algo
**fossil** [ˈfɔsl] n fósil m
**foster** [ˈfɔstəʳ] vt (child) acoger en familia; (idea) fomentar; **foster child** n hijo/a adoptivo/a; **foster mother** n madre f adoptiva
**fought** [fɔːt] pt, pp of **fight**
**foul** [faul] adj sucio, puerco; (weather, smell etc) asqueroso; (language) grosero; (temper) malísimo ▷ n (Football) falta ▷ vt (dirty) ensuciar; **foul play** n (Law) muerte f violenta
**found** [faund] pt, pp of **find** ▷ vt fundar; **foundation** [faunˈdeɪʃən] n (act) fundación f; (basis) base f; (also: **foundation cream**) crema de base; **foundations** npl (of building) cimientos mpl
**founder** [ˈfaundəʳ] n fundador(a) m/f ▷ vi irse a pique
**fountain** [ˈfauntɪn] n fuente f; **fountain pen** n (pluma) estilográfica, plumafuente f (LAM)
**four** [fɔːʳ] num cuatro; **on all ~s** a gatas; **four-letter word** n taco; **four-poster** n

(also: **four-poster bed**) cama de columnas; **fourteen** num catorce; **fourteenth** adj decimocuarto; **fourth** adj cuarto; **four-wheel drive** n tracción f a las cuatro ruedas
**fowl** [faul] n ave f (de corral)
**fox** [fɔks] n zorro ▷ vt confundir
**foyer** [ˈfɔɪeɪ] n vestíbulo
**fracking** [ˈfrækɪŋ] n fracturación f or fractura hidráulica, fracking m
**fraction** [ˈfrækʃən] n fracción f
**fracture** [ˈfræktʃəʳ] n fractura
**fragile** [ˈfrædʒaɪl] adj frágil
**fragment** [ˈfrægmənt] n fragmento
**fragrance** [ˈfreɪgrəns] n fragancia
**frail** [freɪl] adj frágil, quebradizo
**frame** [freɪm] n (Tech) armazón f; (of picture, door etc) marco; (of spectacles: also: **~s**) montura ▷ vt enmarcar; **framework** n marco
**France** [frɑːns] n Francia
**franchise** [ˈfræntʃaɪz] n (Pol) derecho al voto, sufragio; (Comm) licencia, concesión f
**frank** [fræŋk] adj franco ▷ vt (letter) franquear; **frankly** adv francamente
**frantic** [ˈfræntɪk] adj (need, desire) desesperado; (search) frenético
**fraud** [frɔːd] n fraude m; (person) impostor(a) m/f
**fraught** [frɔːt] adj: **~ with** cargado de
**fray** [freɪ] vi deshilacharse
**freak** [friːk] n (person) fenómeno; (event) suceso anormal
**freckle** [ˈfrɛkl] n peca
**free** [friː] adj libre; (gratis) gratuito ▷ vt (prisoner etc) poner en libertad; (jammed object) soltar; **~ (of charge), for ~** gratis; **freedom** n libertad f; **Freefone®** n número gratuito; **free gift** n regalo; **free kick** n tiro libre; **freelance** adj independiente ▷ adv por cuenta propia; **freely** adv libremente; (liberally) generosamente; **Freepost®** n porte m pagado; **free-range** adj (hen, egg) de granja; **freeway** n (US) autopista; **free will** n libre albedrío; **of one's own free will** por su propia voluntad
**freeze** [friːz] (pt **froze**, pp **frozen**) vi helarse, congelarse ▷ vt helar; (prices, food, salaries) congelar ▷ n helada; (on arms, wages) congelación f; **freezer** n congelador m
**freezing** [ˈfriːzɪŋ] adj helado; **freezing point** n punto de congelación
**freight** [freɪt] n (goods) carga; (money charged) flete m; **freight train** n (US) tren m de mercancías
**French** [frɛntʃ] adj francés/esa ▷ n (Ling) francés m; **the French** npl los franceses; **French bean** n judía verde; **French bread** n pan m francés; **French dressing** n (Culin)

vinagreta; **French fried potatoes,** (us) **French fries** npl patatas fpl or (LAM) papas fpl fritas; **Frenchman** n francés m; **French stick** n barra de pan; **French window** n puerta ventana; **Frenchwoman** n francesa

**frenzy** ['frɛnzɪ] n frenesí m

**frequency** ['fri:kwənsɪ] n frecuencia

**frequent** adj ['fri:kwənt] frecuente ▷ vt [frɪ'kwɛnt] frecuentar; **frequently** adv frecuentemente, a menudo

**fresh** [frɛʃ] adj fresco; (bread) tierno; (new) nuevo; **freshen** vi (wind) arreciar; (air) refrescar; **freshen up** vi (person) arreglarse; **fresher** n (BRIT Scol: inf) estudiante mf de primer año; **freshly** adv: freshly painted/arrived recién pintado/llegado; **freshman** n (us Scol) = **fresher**; **freshwater** adj (fish) de agua dulce

**fret** [frɛt] vi inquietarse

**Fri.** abbr (= Friday) vier

**friction** ['frɪkʃən] n fricción f

**Friday** ['fraɪdɪ] n viernes m inv

**fridge** [frɪdʒ] n (BRIT) nevera, frigo, refrigeradora (LAM), heladera (LAM)

**fried** [fraɪd] adj: ~ egg huevo frito

**friend** [frɛnd] n amigo/a ▷ vt (Internet) añadir como amigo a; **friendly** adj simpático; (government) amigo; (place) acogedor(a); (match) amistoso; **friendship** n amistad f

**fries** [fraɪz] npl (esp us) = **French fried potatoes**

**frigate** ['frɪgɪt] n fragata

**fright** [fraɪt] n susto; **to take** ~ asustarse; **frighten** vt asustar; **frightened** adj asustado; **frightening** adj: it's frightening da miedo; **frightful** adj espantoso, horrible

**frill** [frɪl] n volante m

**fringe** [frɪndʒ] n (BRIT: of hair) flequillo; (of forest etc) borde m, margen m

**Frisbee®** ['frɪzbɪ] n frisbee® m

**fritter** ['frɪtər] n buñuelo

**frivolous** ['frɪvələs] adj frívolo

**fro** [frəu] see **to**

**frock** [frɔk] n vestido

**frog** [frɔg] n rana; **frogman** n hombre-rana m

 **KEYWORD**

**from** [frɔm] prep **1** (indicating starting place) de, desde; **where do you come from?** ¿de dónde eres?; **from London to Glasgow** de Londres a Glasgow; **to escape from sth/sb** escaparse de algo/algn

**2** (indicating origin etc) de; **a letter/telephone call from my sister** una carta/llamada de mi hermana; **tell him from me that ...** dígale de mi parte que ...

**3** (indicating time): **from one o'clock to** or **until** or **till nine** de la una a las nueve, desde la una hasta las nueve; **from January (on)** a partir de enero

**4** (indicating distance) de; **the hotel is 1 km from the beach** el hotel está a 1 km de la playa

**5** (indicating price, number etc) de; **prices range from £10 to £50** los precios van desde £10 a or hasta £50; **the interest rate was increased from 9% to 10%** el tipo de interés fue incrementado de un 9% a un 10%

**6** (indicating difference) de; **he can't tell red from green** no sabe distinguir el rojo del verde; **to be different from sb/sth** ser diferente a algn/algo

**7** (because of, on the basis of): **from what he says** por lo que dice; **weak from hunger** debilitado por el hambre

**front** [frʌnt] n (foremost part) parte f delantera; (of house) fachada; (promenade: also: **sea** ~) paseo marítimo; (Mil, Pol, Meteorology) frente m; (fig: appearances) apariencia ▷ adj (wheel, leg) delantero; (row, line) primero; **in** ~ **(of)** delante (de); **front door** n puerta principal; **frontier** ['frʌntɪər] n frontera; **front page** n primera plana; **front-wheel drive** n tracción f delantera

**frost** [frɔst] n helada; (also: **hoar~**) escarcha; **frostbite** n congelación f; **frosting** n (esp us: icing) glaseado; **frosty** adj (weather) de helada; (welcome etc) glacial

**froth** [frɔθ] n espuma

**frown** [fraun] vi fruncir el ceño

**froze** [frəuz] pt of **freeze**

**frozen** ['frəuzn] pp of **freeze**

**fruit** [fru:t] n (pl inv) fruta; **fruit juice** n jugo or (SP) zumo de fruta; **fruit machine** n (BRIT) máquina tragaperras; **fruit salad** n macedonia or (LAM) ensalada de frutas

**frustrate** [frʌs'treɪt] vt frustrar; **frustrated** adj frustrado

**fry** [fraɪ] (pt, pp **fried**) vt freír ▷ n: **small** ~ gente f menuda; **frying pan** n sartén f

**ft.** abbr = **foot; feet**

**fudge** [fʌdʒ] n (Culin) caramelo blando

**fuel** [fjuəl] n (for heating) combustible m; (coal) carbón m; (wood) leña; (for engine) carburante m; **fuel tank** n depósito de combustible

**fulfil** [ful'fɪl] vt (function) desempeñar; (condition) cumplir; (wish, desire) realizar

**full** [ful] adj lleno; (fig) pleno; (complete) completo; (maximum) máximo; (information) detallado; (price) íntegro ▷ adv: ~ **well** perfectamente; **I'm** ~ (up) estoy lleno; ~ **employment** pleno empleo; **a** ~ **two hours** dos horas enteras; **at** ~ **speed** a

toda velocidad; **in ~** (reproduce, quote) íntegramente; **full-length** adj (portrait) de cuerpo entero; **full moon** n luna llena; **full-scale** adj (attack, war, search, retreat) en gran escala; (plan, model) de tamaño natural; **full stop** n punto; **full-time** adj (work) de tiempo completo ▷ adv: **to work full-time** trabajar a tiempo completo; **fully** adv completamente; (at least) al menos
**fumble** ['fʌmbl] vi: **to ~ with** manejar torpemente
**fume** [fju:m] vi estar furioso, echar humo; **fumes** npl humo sg, gases mpl
**fun** [fʌn] n (amusement) diversión f; **to have ~** divertirse; **for ~** por gusto; **to make ~ of** reírse de
**function** ['fʌŋkʃən] n función f ▷ vi funcionar
**fund** [fʌnd] n fondo; (reserve) reserva; **funds** npl (money) fondos mpl
**fundamental** [fʌndə'mɛntl] adj fundamental
**funeral** ['fju:nərəl] n (burial) entierro; (ceremony) funerales mpl; **funeral director** n director(a) m/f de pompas fúnebres; **funeral parlour** n (BRIT) funeraria
**funfair** ['fʌnfɛər] n (BRIT) parque m de atracciones
**fungus** (pl **fungi**) ['fʌŋgəs, -gaɪ] n hongo; (mould) moho
**funnel** ['fʌnl] n embudo; (of ship) chimenea
**funny** ['fʌnɪ] adj gracioso, divertido; (strange) curioso, raro
**fur** [fəːr] n piel f; (BRIT: on tongue etc) sarro; **fur coat** n abrigo de pieles
**furious** ['fjuərɪəs] adj furioso; (effort, argument) violento
**furnish** ['fəːnɪʃ] vt amueblar; (supply) proporcionar; (information) facilitar; **furnishings** npl mobiliario sg
**furniture** ['fəːnɪtʃər] n muebles mpl; **piece of ~** mueble m
**furry** ['fəːrɪ] adj peludo
**further** ['fəːðər] adj (new) nuevo ▷ adv más lejos; (more) más; (moreover) además ▷ vt hacer avanzar; **how much ~ is it?** ¿a qué distancia queda?; **~ to your letter of ...** (Comm) con referencia a su carta de ...; **to ~ one's interests** fomentar sus intereses; **further education** n educación f postescolar; **furthermore** adv además
**furthest** ['fəːðɪst] superlative of **far**
**fury** ['fjuərɪ] n furia
**fuse**, (US) **fuze** [fju:z] n fusible m; (for bomb etc) mecha ▷ vt (metal) fundir; (fig) fusionar ▷ vi fundirse; fusionarse; (BRIT Elec): **to ~ the lights** fundir los plomos; **fuse box** n caja de fusibles
**fusion** ['fju:ʒən] n fusión f

**fuss** [fʌs] n (excitement) conmoción f; (complaint) alboroto; **to make a ~** armar jaleo; **fussy** adj (person) quisquilloso
**future** ['fju:tʃər] adj futuro; (coming) venidero ▷ n futuro, porvenir; **in ~** de ahora en adelante; **futures** npl (Comm) operaciones fpl a término, futuros mpl
**fuze** [fju:z] n, vb (US) = **fuse**
**fuzzy** ['fʌzɪ] adj (Phot) borroso; (hair) muy rizado

# g

**G** [dʒiː] *n* (*Mus*) sol *m*

**g.** *abbr* (= *gram(s)*, *gravity*) g

**gadget** ['gædʒɪt] *n* aparato

**Gaelic** ['geɪlɪk] *adj, n* (*Ling*) gaélico

**gag** [gæg] *n* (*on mouth*) mordaza; (*joke*) chiste ▷ *vt* amordazar

**gain** [geɪn] *n* ganancia ▷ *vt* ganar ▷ *vi* (*watch*) adelantarse; **to ~ by sth** ganar con algo; **to ~ ground** ganar terreno; **to ~ 3 lbs (in weight)** engordar 3 libras; **gain (up)on** *vt fus* alcanzar

**gal., gall.** *abbr* = **gallon**

**gala** ['gɑːlə] *n* gala

**galaxy** ['gæləksɪ] *n* galaxia

**gale** [geɪl] *n* (*wind*) vendaval *m*; **~ force 10** vendaval de fuerza 10

**gall bladder** *n* vesícula biliar

**gallery** ['gælərɪ] *n* (*also*: **art ~**: *state-owned*) pinacoteca, museo de arte; (: *private*) galería de arte

**gallon** ['gæln] *n* galón *m* (= *8 pintas*; *Brit* = *4,546 litros*; *US* = *3,785 litros*)

**gallop** ['gæləp] *n* galope *m* ▷ *vi* galopar

**gallstone** ['gɔːlstəun] *n* cálculo biliar

**gamble** ['gæmbl] *n* (*risk*) jugada arriesgada; (*bet*) apuesta ▷ *vt*: **to ~ on** apostar a; (*fig*) contar con ▷ *vi* jugar; (*take a risk*) jugárselas; (*Comm*) especular; **to ~ on the Stock Exchange** jugar a la bolsa; **gambler** *n* jugador(a) *m/f*; **gambling** *n* juego

**game** [geɪm] *n* juego; (*match*) partido; (*of cards*) partida; (*Hunting*) caza ▷ *adj* valiente; (*ready*): **to be ~ for anything** estar dispuesto a todo; **~s** (*Scol*) deportes *mpl*; **games console** *n* consola de juegos; **game show** *n* programa *m* concurso *inv*, concurso

**gaming** ['geɪmɪŋ] *n* (*with video games*) juegos *mpl* de ordenador *or* computadora

**gammon** ['gæmən] *n* (*bacon*) tocino ahumado; (*ham*) jamón *m* ahumado

**gang** [gæŋ] *n* (*of criminals etc*) banda; (*of kids*) pandilla; (*of workmen*) brigada

**gangster** ['gæŋstər] *n* gángster *m*

**gap** [gæp] *n* hueco; (*in trees, traffic*) claro; (*in time*) intervalo

**gape** [geɪp] *vi* mirar boquiabierto

**gap year** *n* año sabático (*antes de empezar a estudiar en la universidad*)

**garage** ['gærɑːʒ] *n* garaje *m*; (*for repairs*) taller *m*; **garage sale** *n* venta de objetos usados (*en el jardín de una casa particular*)

**garbage** ['gɑːbɪdʒ] *n* (*us*) basura; (*nonsense*) bobadas *fpl*; **garbage can** *n* (*us*) cubo *or* balde *m* (*LAM*) *or* bote *m* (*LAM*) de la basura; **garbage collector** *n* (*us*) basurero/a

**garden** ['gɑːdn] *n* jardín *m*; **gardens** *npl* (*public*) parque *m*; **garden centre** (*BRIT*) centro de jardinería; **gardener** *n* jardinero/a; **gardening** *n* jardinería

**garlic** ['gɑːlɪk] *n* ajo

**garment** ['gɑːmənt] *n* prenda (de vestir)

**garnish** ['gɑːnɪʃ] *vt* (*Culin*) aderezar

**garrison** ['gærɪsn] *n* guarnición *f*

**gas** [gæs] *n* gas *m*; (*us*: *gasoline*) gasolina ▷ *vt* asfixiar con gas; **gas cooker** *n* (*BRIT*) cocina de gas; **gas cylinder** *n* bombona de gas; **gas fire** *n* estufa de gas

**gasket** ['gæskɪt] *n* (*Aut*) junta

**gasoline** ['gæsəliːn] *n* (*us*) gasolina

**gasp** [gɑːsp] *n* grito sofocado ▷ *vi* (*pant*) jadear

**gas: gas pedal** *n* (*esp us*) acelerador *m*; **gas station** *n* (*us*) gasolinera; **gas tank** *n* (*us Aut*) depósito (de gasolina)

**gate** [geɪt] *n* (*also at airport*) puerta; (*metal*) verja

**gatecrash** ['geɪtkræʃ] *vt* colarse en

**gateway** ['geɪtweɪ] *n* puerta

**gather** ['gæðər] *vt* (*flowers, fruit*) coger (*SP*), recoger (*LAM*); (*assemble*) reunir; (*pick up*) recoger; (*Sewing*) fruncir; (*understand*) sacar en consecuencia ▷ *vi* (*assemble*) reunirse; **to ~ speed** ganar velocidad; **gathering** *n* reunión *f*, asamblea

**gauge**, (*us*) **gage** [geɪdʒ] *n* (*instrument*) indicador *m* ▷ *vt* medir; (*fig*) juzgar

**gave** [geɪv] *pt of* **give**

**gay** [geɪ] *adj* (*homosexual*) gay; (*colour, person*) alegre

**gaze** [geɪz] *n* mirada fija ▷ *vi*: **to ~ at sth** mirar algo fijamente

**GB** *abbr* (= *Great Britain*) GB

**GCSE** *n abbr* (*BRIT*: = *General Certificate of Secondary Education*) certificado del último ciclo de la enseñanza secundaria obligatoria

**gear** [gɪər] *n* equipo; (*Tech*) engranaje *m*; (*Aut*) velocidad *f*, marcha ▷ *vt* (*fig*: *adapt*): **to ~ sth to** adaptar *or* ajustar algo a; **top** *or* (*us*) **high/low ~** cuarta/primera; **in ~** con

la marcha metida; **gear up** vi prepararse;
**gear box** n caja de cambios; **gear lever,**
(US) **gear shift** n palanca de cambio; **gear
stick** n (BRIT) = **gear lever**
**geese** [giːs] npl of **goose**
**gel** [dʒɛl] n gel m
**gem** [dʒɛm] n piedra preciosa
**Gemini** ['dʒɛmɪnaɪ] n Géminis m
**gender** ['dʒɛndəʳ] n género
**gene** [dʒiːn] n gen(e) m
**general** ['dʒɛnərl] n general m ▷ adj general;
**in ~** en general; **general anaesthetic,** (US)
**general anesthetic** n anestesia general;
**general election** n elecciones fpl generales;
**generalize** vi generalizar; **generally** adv
generalmente, en general; **general
practitioner** n médico/a de medicina
general; **general store** n tienda (que vende
de todo) (LAM, SP), almacén m (SC, SP)
**generate** ['dʒɛnəreɪt] vt generar
**generation** [dʒɛnə'reɪʃən] n generación f
**generator** ['dʒɛnəreɪtəʳ] n generador m
**generosity** [dʒɛnə'rɔsɪtɪ] n generosidad f
**generous** ['dʒɛnərəs] adj generoso
**genetic** [dʒɪ'nɛtɪk] adj genético;
**~ engineering** ingeniería genética;
**~ fingerprinting** identificación f genética;
**genetically modified organism** n
organismo transgénico; **genetics** n
genética
**genitals** ['dʒɛnɪtlz] npl (órganos mpl)
genitales mpl
**genius** ['dʒiːnɪəs] n genio
**genome** ['giːnəʊm] n genoma m
**gent** [dʒɛnt] n abbr (BRIT inf); = **gentleman**
**gentle** ['dʒɛntl] adj (sweet) dulce; (touch etc)
ligero, suave

⬛ Be careful not to translate gentle by the
Spanish word gentil.

**gentleman** ['dʒɛntlmən] n señor m; (well-
bred man) caballero
**gently** ['dʒɛntlɪ] adv suavemente
**gents** [dʒɛnts] n servicios mpl (de
caballeros)
**genuine** ['dʒɛnjuɪn] adj auténtico; (person)
sincero; **genuinely** adv sinceramente
**geographic(al)** [dʒɪə'græfɪk(l)] adj
geográfico
**geography** [dʒɪ'ɔgrəfɪ] n geografía
**geology** [dʒɪ'ɔlədʒɪ] n geología
**geometry** [dʒɪ'ɔmətrɪ] n geometría
**geranium** [dʒɪ'reɪnjəm] n geranio
**gerbil** ['dʒəːbɪl] n gerbo
**geriatric** [dʒɛrɪ'ætrɪk] adj, n geriátrico/a
**germ** [dʒəːm] n (microbe) microbio,
bacteria; (seed) germen m
**German** ['dʒəːmən] adj alemán/ana ▷ n
alemán/ana m/f; (Ling) alemán m; **German
measles** n rubeola, rubéola

**Germany** ['dʒəːmənɪ] n Alemania
**gesture** ['dʒɛstjəʳ] n gesto

 **KEYWORD**

**get** [gɛt] (pt, pp **got**, pp **gotten** (US)) vi
**1** (become, be) ponerse, volverse; **to get old/
tired** envejecer/cansarse; **to get drunk**
emborracharse; **to get dirty** ensuciarse;
**when do I get paid?** ¿cuándo me pagan or
se me paga?; **it's getting late** se está
haciendo tarde
**2** (go): **to get to/from** llegar a/de; **to get
home** llegar a casa
**3** (begin) empezar a; **to get to know sb**
(llegar a) conocer a algn; **I'm getting to like
him** me está empezando a gustar; **let's get
going** or **started** ¡vamos (a empezar)!
**4** (modal aux vb): **you've got to do it** tienes
que hacerlo
▶ vt **1**: **to get sth done** (finish) hacer algo;
(have done) mandar hacer algo; **to get one's
hair cut** cortarse el pelo; **to get the car going**
or **to go** arrancar el coche; **to get sb to do
sth** conseguir or hacer que algn haga algo;
**to get sth/sb ready** preparar algo/a algn
**2** (obtain: money, permission, results)
conseguir; (find: job, flat) encontrar; (fetch:
person, doctor) buscar; (: object) ir a buscar,
traer; **to get sth for sb** conseguir algo para
algn; **get me Mr Jones, please** (Tel)
póngame or (LAM) comuníqueme con el Sr.
Jones, por favor; **can I get you a drink?**
¿quieres algo de beber?
**3** (receive: present, letter) recibir; (acquire:
reputation) alcanzar; (: prize) ganar; **what
did you get for your birthday?** ¿qué te
regalaron por tu cumpleaños?; **how much
did you get for the painting?** ¿cuánto
sacaste por el cuadro?
**4** (catch) coger (SP), agarrar (LAM); (hit:
target etc) dar en; **to get sb by the arm/
throat** coger or agarrar a algn por el brazo/
cuello; **get him!** ¡cógelo! (SP), ¡atrápalo!
(LAM); **the bullet got him in the leg** la bala
le dio en la pierna
**5** (take, move) llevar; **to get sth to sb** hacer
llegar algo a algn; **do you think we'll get it
through the door?** ¿crees que lo podremos
meter por la puerta?
**6** (catch, take: plane, bus etc) coger (SP),
tomar (LAM); **where do I get the train for
Birmingham?** ¿dónde se coge or se toma el
tren para Birmingham?
**7** (understand) entender; (hear) oír; **I've got
it!** ¡ya lo tengo!, ¡eureka!; **I don't get your
meaning** no te entiendo; **I'm sorry, I didn't
get your name** lo siento, no me he
enterado de tu nombre

**8** (*have, possess*): **to have got** tener

**get away** vi marcharse; (*escape*) escaparse

**get away with** vt fus hacer impunemente

**get back** vi (*return*) volver ▷ vt recobrar

**get in** vi entrar; (*train*) llegar; (*arrive home*) volver a casa, regresar

**get into** vt fus entrar en; (*vehicle*) subir a; **to get into a rage** enfadarse

**get off** vi (*from train etc*) bajar(se); (*depart: person, car*) marcharse ▷ vt (*remove*) quitar ▷ vt fus (*train, bus*) bajar(se) de

**get on** vi (*at exam etc*): **how are you getting on?** ¿cómo te va?; **to get on (with)** (*agree*) llevarse bien (con) ▷ vt fus subir(se) a

**get out** vi salir; (*of vehicle*) bajar(se) ▷ vt sacar

**get out of** vt fus salir de; (*duty etc*) escaparse de

**get over** vt fus (*illness*) recobrarse de

**get through** vi (*Tel*) (lograr) comunicar

**get up** vi (*rise*) levantarse ▷ vt fus subir

**getaway** ['gɛtəweɪ] n fuga

**Ghana** ['gɑːnə] n Ghana

**ghastly** ['gɑːstlɪ] adj horrible

**ghetto** ['gɛtəu] n gueto

**ghost** [gəust] n fantasma m

**giant** ['dʒaɪənt] n gigante mf ▷ adj gigantesco, gigante

**gift** [gɪft] n regalo; (*ability*) don m; **gifted** adj dotado; **gift shop**, (*US*) **gift store** n tienda de regalos; **gift token**, **gift voucher** n vale-regalo m

**gig** [gɪg] n (*inf: concert*) actuación

**gigabyte** ['gɪgəbaɪt] n gigabyte m

**gigantic** [dʒaɪˈgæntɪk] adj gigantesco

**giggle** ['gɪgl] vi reírse tontamente

**gills** [gɪlz] npl (*of fish*) branquias fpl, agallas fpl

**gilt** [gɪlt] adj, n dorado

**gimmick** ['gɪmɪk] n reclamo

**gin** [dʒɪn] n ginebra

**ginger** ['dʒɪndʒər] n jengibre m

**gipsy** ['dʒɪpsɪ] n gitano/a

**giraffe** [dʒɪˈrɑːf] n jirafa

**girl** [gəːl] n (*small*) niña; (*young woman*) chica, joven f, muchacha; **an English ~** una (chica) inglesa; **girl band** n girl band m (*grupo musical de chicas*); **girlfriend** n (*of girl*) amiga; (*of boy*) novia

**gist** [dʒɪst] n lo esencial

**give** (*pt* **gave**, *pp* **given**) [gɪv, geɪv, 'gɪvn] vt dar; (*deliver*) entregar; (*as gift*) regalar ▷ vi (*break*) romperse; (*stretch: fabric*) dar de sí; **to ~ sb sth**, **~ sth to sb** dar algo a algn; **give away** vt (*give free*) regalar; (*betray*) traicionar; (*disclose*) revelar; **give back** vt devolver; **give in** vi ceder ▷ vt entregar; **give out** vt distribuir; **give up** vi rendirse, darse por vencido ▷ vt renunciar a; **to ~**

**up smoking** dejar de fumar; **to ~ o.s. up** entregarse

**given** ['gɪvn] pp of **give** ▷ adj (*fixed: time, amount*) determinado ▷ conj: **~ (that)** ... dado (que) ...; **~ the circumstances** ... dadas las circunstancias ...

**glacier** ['glæsɪər] n glaciar m

**glad** [glæd] adj contento; **gladly** adv con mucho gusto

**glamorous** ['glæmərəs] adj con glamour, glam(o)uroso

**glamour**, (*US*) **glamor** ['glæmər] n encanto, atractivo

**glance** [glɑːns] n ojeada, mirada ▷ vi: **to ~ at** echar una ojeada a

**gland** [glænd] n glándula

**glare** [glɛər] n deslumbramiento, brillo ▷ vi deslumbrar; **to ~ at** mirar con odio; **glaring** adj (*mistake*) manifiesto

**glass** [glɑːs] n vidrio, cristal m; (*for drinking*) vaso; (*with stem*) copa

**glasses** ['glɑːsəs] npl gafas fpl

**glaze** [gleɪz] vt (*window*) acristalar; (*pottery*) vidriar ▷ n barniz m

**gleam** [gliːm] vi relucir

**glen** [glɛn] n cañada

**glide** [glaɪd] vi deslizarse; (*Aviat: bird*) planear; **glider** n (*Aviat*) planeador m

**glimmer** ['glɪmər] n luz f tenue; (*of hope*) rayo

**glimpse** [glɪmps] n vislumbre m ▷ vt vislumbrar, entrever

**glint** [glɪnt] vi centellear

**glisten** ['glɪsn] vi relucir, brillar

**glitter** ['glɪtər] vi relucir, brillar

**global** ['gləubl] adj mundial; **globalization** ['gləubəlaɪzeɪʃən] n globalización f; **global warming** n (re)calentamiento global or de la tierra

**globe** [gləub] n globo; (*model*) globo terráqueo

**gloom** [gluːm] n penumbra; (*sadness*) desaliento, melancolía; **gloomy** adj (*dark*) oscuro; (*sad*) triste; (*pessimistic*) pesimista

**glorious** ['glɔːrɪəs] adj glorioso; (*weather, sunshine*) espléndido

**glory** ['glɔːrɪ] n gloria

**gloss** [glɔs] n (*shine*) brillo; (*also*: **~ paint**) (pintura) esmalte m

**glossary** ['glɔsərɪ] n glosario

**glossy** ['glɔsɪ] adj lustroso; (*magazine*) de papel satinado or cuché

**glove** [glʌv] n guante m; **glove compartment** n (*Aut*) guantera

**glow** [gləu] vi brillar

**glucose** ['gluːkəus] n glucosa

**glue** [gluː] n pegamento ▷ vt pegar

**GM** adj abbr (= *genetically-modified*) transgénico; **GM crop** n cultivo transgénico

**gm** abbr (= gram) g

**GMT** abbr (= Greenwich Mean Time) GMT

**gnaw** [nɔː] vt roer

**go** [gəʊ] (pt **went**, pp **gone**) vi ir; (travel) viajar; (depart) irse, marcharse; (work) funcionar, marchar; (be sold) venderse; (time) pasar; (become) ponerse; (break etc) estropearse, romperse ▷ n: **to have a go (at)** probar suerte (con); **to be on the go** no parar; **whose go is it?** ¿a quién le toca?; **he's going to do it** va a hacerlo; **to go for a walk** ir a dar un paseo; **to go dancing** ir a bailar; **how did it go?** ¿qué tal salió or resultó?, ¿cómo ha ido?; **go ahead** vi seguir adelante; **go around** vi = **go round**; **go away** vi irse, marcharse; **go back** vi volver; **go by** vi (years, time) pasar ▷ vt fus guiarse por; **go down** vi bajar; (ship) hundirse; (sun) ponerse ▷ vt fus bajar por; **go for** vt fus (fetch) ir por; (like) gustar; (attack) atacar; **go in** vi entrar; **go into** vt fus entrar en; (investigate) investigar; (embark on) dedicarse a; **go off** vi irse, marcharse; (food) pasarse; (explode) estallar; (event) realizarse ▷ vt fus perder el interés por; **I'm going off him/the idea** ya no me gusta tanto él/la idea; **go on** vi (continue) seguir, continuar; (happen) pasar, ocurrir; **to go on doing sth** seguir haciendo algo; **go out** vi salir; (fire, light) apagarse; **go over** vi (ship) zozobrar ▷ vt fus (check) revisar; **go past** vi, vt fus pasar; **go round** vi (circulate: news, rumour) correr; (suffice) alcanzar, bastar; (revolve) girar, dar vueltas; (make a detour): **to go round (by)** dar la vuelta (por); (visit): **to go round to sb's** pasar a ver (a algn) ▷ vt fus: **to go round the back** pasar por detrás; **go through** vt fus (town etc) atravesar; **go up** vi subir; **go with** vt fus (accompany) ir con; (fit, suit) hacer juego con, acompañar a; **go without** vt fus pasarse sin

**go-ahead** ['gəʊəhɛd] adj emprendedor(a) ▷ n luz f verde

**goal** [gəʊl] n meta; (score) gol m; **goalkeeper** n portero; **goal post** n poste m (de la portería)

**goat** [gəʊt] n cabra f

**gobble** ['gɔbl] vt (also: ~ **down**, ~ **up**) engullir

**god** [gɔd] n dios m; **G~** Dios m; **godchild** n ahijado/a; **goddaughter** n ahijada; **goddess** n diosa; **godfather** n padrino; **godmother** n madrina; **godson** n ahijado

**goggles** ['gɔglz] npl gafas fpl

**going** ['gəʊɪŋ] n (conditions) cosas fpl ▷ adj: **the ~ rate** la tarifa corriente or en vigor

**gold** [gəʊld] n oro ▷ adj de oro; **golden** adj (made of gold) de oro; (colour) dorado; **goldfish** n pez m de colores; **goldmine** n

mina de oro; **gold-plated** adj chapado en oro

**golf** [gɔlf] n golf m; **golf ball** n (for game) pelota de golf; (on typewriter) esfera impresora; **golf club** n club m de golf; (stick) palo (de golf); **golf course** n campo de golf; **golfer** n golfista mf

**gone** [gɔn] pp of **go**

**gong** [gɔŋ] n gong m

**good** [gʊd] adj bueno; (before n sg n) buen; (well-behaved) educado ▷ n bien m; **~!** ¡qué bien!; **he's ~ at it** se le da bien; **to be ~ for** servir para; **it's ~ for you** te hace bien; **would you be ~ enough to …?** ¿podría hacerme el favor de …?, ¿sería tan amable de …?; **a ~ deal (of)** mucho; **a ~ many** muchos; **to make ~** reparar; **it's no ~ complaining** no sirve de nada quejarse; **for ~** (for ever) para siempre, definitivamente; **~ morning/afternoon** ¡buenos días/ buenas tardes!; **~ evening!** ¡buenas noches!; **~ night!** ¡buenas noches!

**goodbye** [gʊd'baɪ] excl ¡adiós!; **to say ~ (to)** (person) despedirse (de)

**good: Good Friday** n Viernes m Santo; **good-looking** adj guapo; **good-natured** adj (person) de buen carácter; **goodness** n (of person) bondad f; **for goodness sake!** ¡por Dios!; **goodness gracious!** ¡madre mía!; **goods** npl (Comm etc) mercancías fpl; **goods train** n (BRIT) tren m de mercancías; **goodwill** n buena voluntad f

**google** ['guːgəl] vt, vi buscar en Google®

**goose** (pl **geese**) [guːs, giːs] n ganso, oca

**gooseberry** ['guzbərɪ] n grosella espinosa or silvestre; **to play ~** hacer de carabina

**gorge** [gɔːdʒ] n garganta ▷ vr: **to ~ o.s. (on)** atracarse (de)

**gorgeous** ['gɔːdʒəs] adj precioso; (weather) estupendo; (person) guapísimo

**gorilla** [gə'rɪlə] n gorila m

**gosh** [gɔʃ] (inf) excl ¡cielos!

**gospel** ['gɔspl] n evangelio

**gossip** ['gɔsɪp] n cotilleo; (person) cotilla mf ▷ vi cotillear; **gossip column** n ecos mpl de sociedad

**got** [gɔt] pt, pp of **get**

**gotten** ['gɔtn] (US) pp of **get**

**gourmet** ['gʊəmeɪ] n gastrónomo/a

**govern** ['gʌvən] vt gobernar; **government** n gobierno; **governor** n gobernador(a) m/f; (of school etc) miembro del consejo; (of jail) director(a) m/f

**gown** [gaʊn] n vestido; (of teacher, judge) toga

**GP** n abbr (Med) = **general practitioner**

**GPS** n abbr (= global positioning system) GPS m

**grab** [græb] vt agarrar, coger (SP); **to ~ at** intentar agarrar

**grace** [greɪs] n gracia ▷ vt honrar; (adorn) adornar; **5 days' ~** un plazo de 5 días; **graceful** adj grácil, ágil; (style, shape) elegante, gracioso; **gracious** ['greɪʃəs] adj amable

**grade** [greɪd] n (quality) clase f, calidad f; (in hierarchy) grado; (Scol: mark) nota; (US: Scol) curso ▷ vt clasificar; **grade crossing** n (US) paso a nivel; **grade school** n (US) escuela primaria

**gradient** ['greɪdɪənt] n pendiente f

**gradual** ['grædjuəl] adj gradual; **gradually** adv gradualmente

**graduate** n ['grædjuɪt] licenciado/a, graduado/a ▷ vi ['grædjueɪt] licenciarse, graduarse; **graduation** [grædju'eɪʃən] n graduación f; (US Scol) entrega de los títulos de bachillerato

**graffiti** [grə'fiːtɪ] npl pintadas fpl

**graft** [grɑːft] n (Agr, Med) injerto; (bribery) corrupción f ▷ vt injertar; **hard ~** (inf) trabajo duro

**grain** [greɪn] n (single particle) grano; (no pl: cereals) cereales mpl; (in wood) veta

**gram** [græm] n gramo

**grammar** ['græmər] n gramática; **grammar school** n (BRIT) ≈ instituto (de segunda enseñanza)

**gramme** [græm] n = **gram**

**gran** [græn] n (BRIT inf) abuelita

**grand** [grænd] adj magnífico, imponente; (wonderful) estupendo; (gesture etc) grandioso; **grandad** (inf) n = **granddad**; **grandchild** (pl **grandchildren**) n nieto/a; **granddad** n yayo, abuelito; **granddaughter** n nieta; **grandfather** n abuelo; **grandma** n yaya, abuelita; **grandmother** n abuela; **grandpa** n = **granddad**; **grandparents** npl abuelos mpl; **grand piano** n piano de cola; **Grand Prix** ['grɑ̃:'pri:] n (Aut) gran premio, Grand Prix m; **grandson** n nieto

**granite** ['grænɪt] n granito

**granny** ['grænɪ] n abuelita, yaya

**grant** [grɑːnt] vt (concede) conceder; (admit): **to ~ (that)** reconocer (que) ▷ n (Scol) beca; **to take sth for ~ed** dar algo por sentado

**grape** [greɪp] n uva

**grapefruit** ['greɪpfruːt] n pomelo (SC, SP), toronja (LAM)

**graph** [grɑːf] n gráfica; **graphic** ['græfɪk] adj gráfico; **graphics** n artes fpl gráficas ▷ npl (drawings, Comput) gráficos mpl

**grasp** [grɑːsp] vt agarrar, asir; (understand) comprender ▷ n (grip) asimiento; (understanding) comprensión f

**grass** [grɑːs] n hierba; (lawn) césped m; **grasshopper** n saltamontes m inv

**grate** [greɪt] n parrilla ▷ vi chirriar ▷ vt (Culin) rallar

**grateful** ['greɪtful] adj agradecido

**grater** ['greɪtər] n rallador m

**gratitude** ['grætɪtjuːd] n agradecimiento

**grave** [greɪv] n tumba ▷ adj serio, grave

**gravel** ['grævl] n grava

**gravestone** ['greɪvstəun] n lápida

**graveyard** ['greɪvjɑːd] n cementerio

**gravity** ['grævɪtɪ] n gravedad f

**gravy** ['greɪvɪ] n salsa de carne

**gray** [greɪ] adj (US) = **grey**

**graze** [greɪz] vi pacer ▷ vt (touch lightly, scrape) rozar ▷ n (Med) rozadura

**grease** [griːs] n (fat) grasa; (lubricant) lubricante m ▷ vt engrasar; **greasy** adj grasiento

**great** [greɪt] adj grande; (inf) estupendo; **Great Britain** n Gran Bretaña; **great-grandfather** n bisabuelo; **great-grandmother** n bisabuela; **greatly** adv muy; (with verb) mucho

**Greece** [griːs] n Grecia

**greed** [griːd] n (also: ~iness) codicia; (for food) gula; (for power etc) avidez f; **greedy** adj codicioso; (for food) glotón/ona

**Greek** [griːk] adj griego ▷ n griego/a; (Ling) griego

**green** [griːn] adj verde; (inexperienced) novato ▷ n verde m; (stretch of grass) césped m; (of golf course) green m; **the G~ party** (Pol) el partido verde; **greens** npl verduras fpl; **green card** n (Aut) carta verde; (US: work permit) permiso de trabajo para los extranjeros en EE. UU.; **greengage** n (ciruela) claudia; **greengrocer** n (BRIT) verdulero/a; **greenhouse** n invernadero; **greenhouse effect** n efecto invernadero; **green tax** n ecotasa, impuesto ecológico

**Greenland** ['griːnlənd] n Groenlandia

**green salad** n ensalada f (de lechuga, pepino, pimiento verde, etc)

**greet** [griːt] vt saludar; (news) recibir; **greeting** n (welcome) bienvenida; **greeting(s) card** n tarjeta de felicitación

**grew** [gruː] pt of **grow**

**grey** [greɪ] adj gris; **grey-haired** adj canoso; **greyhound** n galgo

**grid** [grɪd] n rejilla; (Elec) red f; **gridlock** n retención f

**grief** [griːf] n dolor m, pena

**grievance** ['griːvəns] n motivo de queja, agravio

**grieve** [griːv] vi afligirse, acongojarse ▷ vt afligir, apenar; **to ~ for** llorar por

**grill** [grɪl] n (on cooker) parrilla ▷ vt (BRIT) asar a la parrilla; (question) interrogar

**grille** [grɪl] n rejilla

**grim** [grɪm] adj (place) lúgubre; (person) adusto

**grime** [graim] n mugre f
**grin** [grɪn] n sonrisa abierta ▷ vi: **to ~ (at)** sonreír abiertamente (a)
**grind** [graind] (pt, pp **ground**) vt (coffee, pepper etc) moler; (US: meat) picar; (make sharp) afilar ▷ n: **the daily ~** (inf) la rutina diaria
**grip** [grɪp] n (hold) asimiento; (handle) asidero ▷ vt agarrar; **to get to ~s with** enfrentarse con; **to lose one's ~** (fig) perder el control; **gripping** adj absorbente
**grit** [grɪt] n gravilla; (courage) valor m ▷ vt (road) poner gravilla en; **to ~ one's teeth** apretar los dientes
**grits** [grɪts] npl (US) maíz msg a medio moler
**groan** [grəun] n gemido, quejido ▷ vi gemir, quejarse
**grocer** ['grəusə'] n tendero (de ultramarinos); **~'s (shop)** n tienda de ultramarinos or (LAM) de abarrotes; **groceries** npl comestibles mpl; **grocery** n (shop) tienda de ultramarinos
**groin** [grɔin] n ingle f
**groom** [gru:m] n mozo/a de cuadra; (also: **bride~**) novio ▷ vt (horse) almohazar; (fig): **to ~ sb for** preparar a algn para; **well-~ed** acicalado
**groove** [gru:v] n ranura; surco
**grope** [grəup] vi: **to ~ for** buscar a tientas
**gross** [grəus] adj (neglect, injustice) grave; (vulgar: behaviour) grosero; (: appearance) de mal gusto; (Comm) bruto; **grossly** adv (greatly) enormemente
**grotesque** [grə'tɛsk] adj grotesco
**ground** [graund] pt, pp of **grind** ▷ n suelo, tierra; (Sport) campo, terreno; (reason: gen pl) motivo, razón f; (US: also: **~ wire**) tierra ▷ vt (plane) mantener en tierra; (US Elec) conectar con tierra; **grounds** npl (of coffee etc) poso sg; (gardens etc) jardines mpl, parque m; **on the ~** en el suelo; **to gain/lose ~** ganar/perder terreno; **to the ~** al suelo; **ground floor** n (BRIT) planta baja; **groundsheet** n (BRIT) tela impermeable; **groundwork** n trabajo preliminar
**group** [gru:p] n grupo; (Mus: pop group) conjunto, grupo ▷ vt (also: **~ together**) agrupar ▷ vi agruparse
**grouse** [graus] n (pl inv: bird) urogallo ▷ vi (complain) quejarse
**grovel** ['grɔvl] vi (fig) arrastrarse
**grow** (pt **grew**, pp **grown**) [grəu, gru:, grəun] vi crecer; (increase) aumentar; (expand) desarrollarse; (become) volverse ▷ vt cultivar; (hair, beard) dejar crecer; **to ~ rich/weak** enriquecerse/debilitarse; **grow on** vt fus: **that painting is ~ing on me** ese cuadro me gusta cada vez más; **grow up** vi crecer, hacerse hombre/mujer

**growl** [graul] vi gruñir
**grown** [grəun] pp of **grow**; **grown-up** n adulto/a, mayor mf
**growth** [grəuθ] n crecimiento, desarrollo; (what has grown) brote m; (Med) tumor m
**grub** [grʌb] n gusano; (inf: food) comida
**grubby** ['grʌbɪ] adj sucio, mugriento
**grudge** [grʌdʒ] n rencor ▷ vt: **to ~ sb sth** dar algo a algn de mala gana; **to bear sb a ~** guardar rencor a algn
**gruelling**, (US) **grueling** adj agotador
**gruesome** ['gru:səm] adj horrible
**grumble** ['grʌmbl] vi refunfuñar, quejarse
**grumpy** ['grʌmpɪ] adj gruñón/ona
**grunt** [grʌnt] vi gruñir
**guarantee** [gærən'ti:] n garantía ▷ vt garantizar
**guard** [gɑ:d] n guardia; (person) guarda mf; (BRIT Rail) jefe m de tren; (on machine) cubierta de protección; (fireguard) pantalla ▷ vt guardar; **to be on one's ~** (fig) estar en guardia; **guardian** n guardián/ana m/f; (of minor) tutor(a) m/f
**guerrilla** [gə'rɪlə] n guerrillero/a
**guess** [gɛs] vi, vt adivinar; (suppose) suponer ▷ n suposición f, conjetura; **to take** or **have a ~** tratar de adivinar
**guest** [gɛst] n invitado/a; (in hotel) huésped(a) m/f; **guest room** n cuarto de huéspedes
**guidance** ['gaidəns] n (advice) consejos mpl
**guide** [gaid] n (person) guía mf; (book, fig) guía f; (also: **girl ~**) exploradora ▷ vt guiar; **guidebook** n guía; **guide dog** n perro guía; **guided tour** n visita f con guía; **guidelines** npl (fig) directrices fpl
**guild** [gɪld] n gremio
**guilt** [gɪlt] n culpabilidad f; **guilty** adj culpable
**guinea pig** n cobaya; (fig) conejillo de Indias
**guitar** [gɪ'tɑ:'] n guitarra; **guitarist** n guitarrista mf
**gulf** [gʌlf] n golfo; (abyss) abismo
**gull** [gʌl] n gaviota
**gulp** [gʌlp] vi tragar saliva ▷ vt (also: **~ down**) tragarse
**gum** [gʌm] n (Anat) encía; (glue) goma, cemento (LAM); (sweet) gominola; (also: **chewing-~**) chicle m ▷ vt pegar con goma
**gun** [gʌn] n (small) pistola; (shotgun) escopeta; (rifle) fusil m; (cannon) cañón m; **gunfire** n disparos mpl; **gunman** n pistolero; **gunpoint** n: **at gunpoint** a mano armada; **gunpowder** n pólvora; **gunshot** n disparo
**gush** [gʌʃ] vi chorrear, salir a raudales; (fig) deshacerse en efusiones
**gust** [gʌst] n (of wind) ráfaga

# h

**gut** [gʌt] n intestino; (Mus etc) cuerda de tripa; **guts** npl (courage) agallas fpl, valor m; (inf: innards: of people, animals) tripas fpl

**gutter** ['gʌtə*] n (of roof) canalón m; (in street) cuneta

**guy** [gaɪ] n (also: **~rope**) viento, cuerda; (inf: man) tío (SP), tipo

**Guy Fawkes' Night** [gaɪ'fɔːks-] n ver nota

⬤ **GUY FAWKES' NIGHT**
⬤
⬤ La noche del cinco de noviembre, Guy
⬤ Fawkes' Night, se celebra el fracaso de la
⬤ conspiración de la pólvora (Gunpowder
⬤ Plot), el intento fallido de volar el parlamento
⬤ de Jaime 1 en 1605. Esa noche se lanzan
⬤ fuegos artificiales y se queman en
⬤ muchas hogueras muñecos de trapo
⬤ que representan a Guy Fawkes, uno de los
⬤ cabecillas. Días antes los niños tienen
⬤ por costumbre pedir a los viandantes "a
⬤ penny for the guy", dinero para comprar los
⬤ cohetes.

**gym** [dʒɪm] n (also: **gymnasium**) gimnasio; (also: **gymnastics**) gimnasia; **gymnasium** n gimnasio; **gymnast** n gimnasta mf; **gymnastics** n gimnasia; **gym shoes** npl zapatillas fpl de gimnasia

**gynaecologist**, (US) **gynecologist** [gaɪnɪ'kɔlədʒɪst] n ginecólogo/a

**gypsy** ['dʒɪpsɪ] n = **gipsy**

**haberdashery** ['hæbə'dæʃərɪ] n (BRIT) mercería

**habit** ['hæbɪt] n hábito, costumbre f; (drug habit) adicción f

**habitat** ['hæbɪtæt] n hábitat m

**hack** [hæk] vt (cut) cortar; (slice) tajar ▷ n (pej: writer) escritor(a) m/f a sueldo; **hacker** n (Comput) pirata m informático

**had** [hæd] pt, pp of **have**

**haddock** ['hædək] (pl **haddock** or **haddocks**) n especie de merluza

**hadn't** ['hædnt] = **had not**

**haemorrhage**, (US) **hemorrhage** ['hɛmərɪdʒ] n hemorragia

**haemorrhoids**, (US) **hemorrhoids** ['hɛmərɔɪdz] npl hemorroides fpl

**haggle** ['hægl] vi regatear

**Hague** [heɪg] n: **The ~** La Haya

**hail** [heɪl] n (weather) granizo ▷ vt saludar; (call) llamar a ▷ vi granizar; **hailstone** n (piedra de) granizo

**hair** [hɛə*] n pelo, cabellos mpl; (one hair) pelo, cabello; (on legs etc) vello; **to do one's ~** arreglarse el pelo; **grey ~** canas fpl; **hairband** n cinta; **hairbrush** n cepillo (para el pelo); **haircut** n corte m de pelo; **hairdo** n peinado; **hairdresser** n peluquero/a; **hairdresser's** peluquería; **hairdryer** n secador m (de pelo); **hair gel** n fijador; **hair spray** n laca; **hairstyle** n peinado; **hairy** adj peludo, velludo; (inf: frightening) espeluznante

**haka** ['hɑːkə] n (NZ) haka m or f

**hake** [heɪk] n merluza

**half** [hɑːf] (pl **halves**) n mitad f; (of beer) ≈ caña (SP), media pinta; (Rail) billete m de niño ▷ adj medio ▷ adv medio, a medias; **two and a ~** dos y media; **~ a dozen** media docena; **~ a pound** media libra; ≈ 250 gr.; **to cut sth in ~** cortar algo por la mitad;

**half board** n (BRIT: in hotel) media pensión;
**half-brother** n hermanastro; **half day**
n medio día m, media jornada; **half fare**
n medio pasaje m; **half-hearted** adj
indiferente, poco entusiasta; **half-hour**
n media hora; **half-price** adj a mitad de
precio; **half term** n (BRIT Scol) vacaciones
de mediados del trimestre; **half-time** n
descanso; **halfway** adv a medio camino
**hall** [hɔːl] n (for concerts) sala; (entrance way)
vestíbulo
**hallmark** ['hɔːlmɑːk] n sello
**hallo** [hə'ləu] excl = **hello**
**hall of residence** n (BRIT) residencia
universitaria
**Hallowe'en** [hæləu'iːn] n víspera de Todos
los Santos

- **HALLOWE'EN**
-
- La tradición anglosajona dice que en
- la noche del 31 de octubre, Hallowe'en,
- víspera de Todos los Santos, es fácil ver
- a brujas y fantasmas. Es una ocasión
- festiva en la que los niños se disfrazan
- y van de puerta en puerta llevando un
- farol hecho con una calabaza en forma
- de cabeza humana. Cuando se les abre la
- puerta gritan "trick or treat" para indicar
- que gastarán una broma a quien no les
- dé un pequeño regalo (como golosinas
- o dinero).

**hallucination** [həluːsɪ'neɪʃən] n
alucinación f
**hallway** ['hɔːlweɪ] n vestíbulo
**halo** ['heɪləu] n (of saint) aureola, halo
**halt** [hɔːlt] n (stop) alto, parada ▷ vt parar
▷ vi pararse
**halve** [hɑːv] vt partir por la mitad
**halves** [hɑːvz] pl of **half**
**ham** [hæm] n jamón m (cocido)
**hamburger** ['hæmbəːgəʳ] n hamburguesa
**hamlet** ['hæmlɪt] n aldea
**hammer** ['hæməʳ] n martillo ▷ vt (nail)
clavar; **to ~ a point home to sb** remacharle
un punto a algn
**hammock** ['hæmək] n hamaca
**hamper** ['hæmpəʳ] vt estorbar ▷ n cesto
**hamster** ['hæmstəʳ] n hámster m
**hamstring** ['hæmstrɪŋ] n (Anat) tendón m
de la corva
**hand** [hænd] n mano f; (of clock) aguja;
(writing) letra; (worker) obrero ▷ vt dar,
pasar; **to give sb a ~** echar una mano a
algn, ayudar a algn; **at ~** a mano; **in ~** entre
manos; **on ~** (person, services) a mano, al
alcance; **to ~** (information etc) a mano; **on
the one ~ ..., on the other ~ ...** por una

parte ... por otra (parte) ...; **hand down** vt
pasar, bajar; (tradition) transmitir; (heirloom)
dejar en herencia; (US: sentence, verdict)
imponer; **hand in** vt entregar; **hand out** vt
distribuir; **hand over** vt (deliver) entregar;
**handbag** n bolso, cartera (LAM); **hand
baggage** n = **hand luggage**; **handbook** n
manual m; **handbrake** n freno de mano;
**handcuffs** npl esposas fpl; **handful** n
puñado
**handicap** ['hændɪkæp] n desventaja;
(Sport) hándicap m ▷ vt estorbar
**handkerchief** ['hæŋkətʃɪf] n pañuelo
**handle** ['hændl] n (of door etc) pomo,
tirador m; (of cup etc) asa; (of knife etc)
mango; (for winding) manivela ▷ vt (touch)
tocar; (deal with) encargarse de; (treat:
people) manejar; **"~ with care"** "(manéjese)
con cuidado"; **to fly off the ~** perder los
estribos; **handlebar(s)** n(pl) manillar msg
**hand: hand luggage** n equipaje m de mano;
**handmade** adj hecho a mano; **handout** n
(charity) limosna; (leaflet) folleto
**hands-free** ['hændzfriː] adj (Tel: telephone)
manos libres; **~ kit** manos libres m inv
**handsome** ['hænsəm] adj guapo
**handwriting** ['hændraɪtɪŋ] n letra
**handy** ['hændɪ] adj (close at hand) a mano;
(machine, tool etc) práctico; (skilful) hábil,
diestro
**hang** [hæŋ] (pt, pp hung) vt colgar;
(criminal) ahorcar; **to get the ~ of sth** (inf)
coger el tranquillo a algo; **hang about,
hang around** vi haraganear; **hang down**
vi colgar, pender; **hang on** vi (wait) esperar;
**hang out** vt (washing) tender, colgar ▷ vi
(inf: live) vivir; **to ~ out of sth** colgar fuera de
algo; **hang round** vi = **hang about**; **hang
up** vt colgar ▷ vi (Tel) colgar
**hanger** ['hæŋəʳ] n percha
**hang-gliding** ['hæŋglaɪdɪŋ] n vuelo con
ala delta
**hangover** ['hæŋəuvəʳ] n (after drinking)
resaca
**hankie, hanky** ['hæŋkɪ] n abbr
= **handkerchief**
**happen** ['hæpən] vi suceder, ocurrir;
(chance): **he ~ed to hear/see** dio la
casualidad de que oyó/vio; **as it ~s** da la
casualidad de que
**happily** ['hæpɪlɪ] adv (luckily)
afortunadamente; (cheerfully)
alegremente
**happiness** ['hæpɪnɪs] n felicidad f; (joy)
alegría
**happy** ['hæpɪ] adj feliz; (cheerful) alegre; **to
be ~ (with)** estar contento (con); **yes, I'd be
~ to** sí, con mucho gusto; **~ birthday!** ¡feliz
cumpleaños!

**harass** ['hærəs] vt acosar, hostigar;
**harassment** n persecución f
**harbour,** (US) **harbor** ['hɑːbəʳ] n puerto
▷ vt (fugitive) dar abrigo a; (hope etc) abrigar
**hard** [hɑːd] adj duro; (difficult) difícil;
(work) arduo; (person) severo ▷ adv (work)
mucho, duro; (think) profundamente; **to
look ~ at sb/sth** clavar los ojos en algn/
algo; **to try ~** esforzarse; **no ~ feelings!** ¡sin
rencor(es)!; **to be ~ of hearing** ser duro de
oído; **to be ~ done by** ser tratado
injustamente; **hardback** n libro de tapa
dura; **hardboard** n aglomerado m (de
madera); **hard disk** n (Comput) disco duro;
**harden** vt endurecer; (fig) curtir ▷ vi
endurecerse; (fig) curtirse
**hardly** ['hɑːdlɪ] adv apenas; **~ ever** casi
nunca
**hard: hardship** n (troubles) penas fpl;
(financial) apuro; **hard shoulder** n (Aut)
arcén m; **hard-up** adj (inf) sin un duro (SP),
sin plata (LAM); **hardware** n ferretería;
(Comput) hardware m; **hardware shop,**
(US) **hardware store** n ferretería; **hard-
working** adj trabajador(a)
**hardy** ['hɑːdɪ] adj fuerte; (plant) resistente
**hare** [heəʳ] n liebre f
**harm** [hɑːm] n daño, mal m ▷ vt (person)
hacer daño a; (health, interests) perjudicar;
(thing) dañar; **out of ~'s way** a salvo;
**harmful** adj dañino; **harmless** adj (person)
inofensivo; (joke etc) inocente
**harmony** ['hɑːmənɪ] n armonía
**harness** ['hɑːnɪs] n arreos mpl ▷ vt (horse)
enjaezar; (resources) aprovechar
**harp** [hɑːp] n arpa ▷ vi: **to ~ on (about)**
machacar (con)
**harsh** [hɑːʃ] adj (cruel) duro, cruel; (severe)
severo
**harvest** ['hɑːvɪst] n (harvest time) siega;
(of cereals etc) cosecha; (of grapes) vendimia
▷ vt cosechar
**has** [hæz] vb see **have**
**hashtag** ['hæʃtæg] n (on Twitter) hashtag m
**hasn't** ['hæznt] = **has not**
**hassle** ['hæsl] n (inf) lío, rollo ▷ vt incordiar
**haste** [heɪst] n prisa; **hasten** ['heɪsn] vt
acelerar ▷ vi darse prisa; **hastily** adv de
prisa; **hasty** adj apresurado
**hat** [hæt] n sombrero
**hatch** n (Naut: also: **~way**) escotilla ▷ vi salir
del cascarón ▷ vt incubar; (scheme, plot)
tramar; **5 eggs ~ed** han salido 5 pollos
**hatchback** ['hætʃbæk] n (Aut) tres or cinco
puertas m
**hate** [heɪt] vt odiar, aborrecer ▷ n odio;
**hatred** ['heɪtrɪd] n odio
**haul** [hɔːl] vt tirar ▷ n (of fish) redada; (of
stolen goods etc) botín n

**haunt** [hɔːnt] vt (ghost) aparecer en;
(obsess) obsesionar ▷ n guarida; **haunted**
adj (castle etc) embrujado; (look) de angustia

**KEYWORD**

**have** [hæv] (pt, pp **had**) aux vb **1** haber;
**to have arrived/eaten** haber llegado/
comido; **having finished** or **when he had
finished, he left** cuando hubo acabado,
se fue
**2** (in tag questions): **you've done it, haven't
you?** lo has hecho, ¿verdad? or ¿no?
**3** (in short answers and questions): **I haven't**
no; **so I have** pues, es verdad; **we haven't
paid — yes we have!** no hemos pagado
— ¡sí que hemos pagado!; **I've been there
before, have you?** he estado allí antes,
¿y tú?
▶ modal aux vb (be obliged): **to have (got) to
do sth** tener que hacer algo; **you haven't
to tell her** no hay que or no debes decírselo
▶ vt **1** (possess); **he has (got) blue eyes/
dark hair** tiene los ojos azules/el pelo negro
**2** (referring to meals etc): **to have breakfast/
lunch/dinner** desayunar/comer/cenar;
**to have a drink/a cigarette** tomar algo/
fumar un cigarrillo
**3** (receive) recibir; **may I have your
address?** ¿puedes darme tu dirección?; **you
can have it for £5** te lo puedes quedar por
£5; **I must have it by tomorrow** lo necesito
para mañana; **to have a baby** tener un
niño or bebé
**4** (maintain, allow): **I won't have it!** ¡no lo
permitiré!; **I won't have this nonsense!** ¡no
permitiré estas tonterías!; **we can't have
that** no podemos permitir eso
**5**: **to have sth done** hacer or mandar hacer
algo; **to have one's hair cut** cortarse el
pelo; **to have sb do sth** hacer que algn
haga algo
**6** (experience, suffer): **to have a cold/flu**
tener un resfriado/la gripe; **she had her
bag stolen/her arm broken** le robaron
el bolso/se rompió un brazo; **to have an
operation** operarse
**7** (+ noun): **to have a swim/walk/bath/
rest** nadar/dar un paseo/darse un baño/
descansar; **let's have a look** vamos a ver;
**to have a meeting/party** celebrar una
reunión/una fiesta; **let me have a try**
déjame intentarlo

**haven** ['heɪvn] n puerto; (fig) refugio
**haven't** ['hævnt] = **have not**
**havoc** ['hævək] n estragos mpl
**Hawaii** [hə'waɪiː] n (Islas fpl) Hawai m
**hawk** [hɔːk] n halcón m

**hawthorn** ['hɔːθɔːn] n espino
**hay** [heɪ] n heno; **hay fever** n fiebre f del heno; **haystack** n almiar m
**hazard** ['hæzəd] n peligro ▷ vt aventurar; **hazardous** adj peligroso; **hazard warning lights** npl (Aut) señales fpl de emergencia
**haze** [heɪz] n neblina
**hazel** ['heɪzl] n (tree) avellano ▷ adj (eyes) color m de avellano; **hazelnut** n avellana
**hazy** ['heɪzɪ] adj brumoso; (idea) vago
**he** [hiː] pron él; **he who ...** aquél que ..., quien ...
**head** [hɛd] n cabeza; (leader) jefe/a m/f ▷ vt (list) encabezar; (group) capitanear; **~s (or tails)** cara (o cruz); **~ first** de cabeza; **~ over heels in love** perdidamente enamorado; **to ~ the ball** cabecear (el balón); **head for** vt fus dirigirse a; (disaster) ir camino de; **head off** vt (threat, danger) evitar; **headache** n dolor m de cabeza; **heading** n título; **headlamp** n (BRIT) = **headlight**; **headlight** n faro; **headline** n titular m; **head office** n oficina central, central f; **headphones** npl auriculares mpl; **headquarters** npl sede f central; (Mil) cuartel m general; **headroom** n (in car) altura interior; (under bridge) (límite m de) altura; **headscarf** n pañuelo; **headset** n cascos mpl; **head teacher** n director(a); **head waiter** n maître m
**heal** [hiːl] vt curar ▷ vi cicatrizar
**health** [hɛlθ] n salud f; **health care** n asistencia sanitaria; **health centre** n ambulatorio, centro médico; **health food** n alimentos mpl orgánicos; **Health Service** n (BRIT) servicio de salud pública, ≈ Insalud m (SP); **healthy** adj sano; saludable
**heap** [hiːp] n montón m ▷ vt amontonar; **~s of** (inf: lots) montones de; **to ~ favours/praise/gifts** etc **on sb** colmar a algn de favores/elogios/regalos etc
**hear** [hɪər] (pt, pp **heard**) vt oír; (news) saber ▷ vi oír; **to ~ about** oír hablar de; **to ~ from sb** tener noticias de algn
**heard** [həːd] pt, pp of **hear**
**hearing** ['hɪərɪŋ] n (sense) oído; (Law) vista; **hearing aid** n audífono
**hearse** [həːs] n coche m fúnebre
**heart** [hɑːt] n corazón m; (fig) valor m; (of lettuce) cogollo; **hearts** npl (Cards) corazones mpl; **at ~** en el fondo; **by ~** (learn, know) de memoria; **to take ~** cobrar ánimos; **heart attack** n infarto (de miocardio); **heartbeat** n latido (del corazón); **heartbroken** adj: **she was heartbroken about it** eso le partió el corazón; **heartburn** n acedía; **heart disease** n enfermedad f cardíaca
**hearth** [hɑːθ] n (fireplace) chimenea

**heartless** ['hɑːtlɪs] adj despiadado
**hearty** ['hɑːtɪ] adj (person) campechano; (laugh) sano; (dislike, support) absoluto
**heat** [hiːt] n calor m; (Sport: also: **qualifying ~**) prueba eliminatoria ▷ vt calentar; **heat up** vi calentarse ▷ vt calentar; **heated** adj caliente; (fig) acalorado; **heater** n calentador m, estufa
**heather** ['hɛðər] n brezo
**heating** ['hiːtɪŋ] n calefacción f
**heatwave** ['hiːtweɪv] n ola de calor
**heaven** ['hɛvn] n cielo; (Rel) paraíso; **heavenly** adj celestial
**heavily** ['hɛvɪlɪ] adv pesadamente; (drink, smoke) en exceso; (sleep, sigh) profundamente
**heavy** ['hɛvɪ] adj pesado; (work) duro; (sea, rain, meal) fuerte; (drinker, smoker) empedernido; (responsibility) grave; (schedule) ocupado; (weather) bochornoso; **~ goods vehicle** n vehículo pesado
**Hebrew** ['hiːbruː] adj, n (Ling) hebreo
**hectare** ['hɛktɑːr] n (BRIT) hectárea
**hectic** ['hɛktɪk] adj agitado
**he'd** [hiːd] = **he would; he had**
**hedge** [hɛdʒ] n seto ▷ vi contestar con evasivas; **to ~ one's bets** (fig) cubrirse
**hedgehog** ['hɛdʒhɔg] n erizo
**heed** [hiːd] vt (also: **take ~ of**) hacer caso de
**heel** [hiːl] n talón m; (of shoe) tacón m ▷ vt (shoe) poner tacón a
**hefty** ['hɛftɪ] adj (person) fornido; (price) alto
**height** [haɪt] n (of person) talla, estatura; (of building) altura; (high ground) altura; (altitude) altitud f; **at the ~ of summer** en los días más calurosos del verano; **heighten** vt elevar; (fig) aumentar
**heir** [ɛər] n heredero; **heiress** n heredera
**held** [hɛld] pt, pp of **hold**
**helicopter** ['hɛlɪkɔptər] n helicóptero
**hell** [hɛl] n infierno; **oh ~!** (inf) ¡demonios!
**he'll** [hiːl] = **he will; he shall**
**hello** [hə'ləu] excl ¡hola!; (to attract attention) ¡oiga!; (surprise) ¡caramba!
**helmet** ['hɛlmɪt] n casco
**help** [hɛlp] n ayuda; (cleaner etc) criada, asistenta ▷ vt ayudar; **~!** ¡socorro!; **~ yourself** sírvete; **he can't ~ it** no lo puede evitar; **help out** vi ayudar, echar una mano ▷ vt: **to ~ sb out** ayudar a algn, echar una mano a algn; **helper** n ayudante mf; **helpful** adj útil; (person) servicial; **helping** n ración f; **helpless** adj (incapable) incapaz; (defenceless) indefenso; **helpline** n teléfono de asistencia al público
**hem** [hɛm] n dobladillo ▷ vt poner or coser el dobladillo a
**hemisphere** ['hɛmɪsfɪər] n hemisferio

**hemorrhage** ['hɛmərɪdʒ] n (US)
= **haemorrhage**
**hemorrhoids** ['hɛmərɔɪdz] npl (US)
= **haemorrhoids**
**hen** [hɛn] n gallina; (female bird) hembra
**hence** [hɛns] adv (therefore) por lo tanto;
**two years** ~ de aquí a dos años
**hen night** n (inf) despedida de soltera
**hepatitis** [hɛpə'taɪtɪs] n hepatitis f inv
**her** [həːr] pron (direct) la; (indirect) le;
(stressed, after prep) ella ▷ adj su; see also
**me; my**
**herb** [həːb] n hierba; **herbal** ['həːbl] adj de
hierbas; **herbal tea** n infusión f de hierbas
**herd** [həːd] n rebaño
**here** [hɪər] adv aquí; ~! (present) ¡presente!;
~ is/are aquí está/están; ~ she is aquí
está
**hereditary** [hɪ'rɛdɪtrɪ] adj hereditario
**heritage** ['hɛrɪtɪdʒ] n patrimonio
**hernia** ['həːnɪə] n hernia
**hero** ['hɪərəʊ] (pl **heroes**) n héroe m;
(in book, film) protagonista m; **heroic**
[hɪ'rəʊɪk] adj heroico
**heroin** ['hɛrəʊɪn] n heroína
**heroine** ['hɛrəʊɪn] n heroína; (in book, film)
protagonista
**heron** ['hɛrən] n garza
**herring** ['hɛrɪŋ] (pl inv) n arenque m
**hers** [həːz] pron (el) suyo/(la) suya etc; see
also **mine**
**herself** [həː'sɛlf] pron (reflexive) se;
(emphatic) ella misma; (after prep) sí
(misma); see also **oneself**
**he's** [hiːz] = **he is; he has**
**hesitant** ['hɛzɪtənt] adj indeciso
**hesitate** ['hɛzɪteɪt] vi vacilar; (in speech)
titubear; (be unwilling) resistirse a;
**hesitation** [hɛzɪ'teɪʃən] n indecisión f
**heterosexual** [hɛtərəʊ'sɛksjuəl] adj, n
heterosexual mf
**hexagon** ['hɛksəgən] n hexágono
**hey** [heɪ] excl ¡oye!, ¡oiga!
**heyday** ['heɪdeɪ] n: **the ~ of** el apogeo de
**HGV** n abbr = **heavy goods vehicle**
**hi** [haɪ] excl ¡hola!
**hibernate** ['haɪbəneɪt] vi invernar
**hiccough, hiccup** ['hɪkʌp] vi hipar
**hid** [hɪd] pt of **hide**
**hidden** ['hɪdn] pp of **hide** ▷ adj: ~ **agenda**
plan m encubierto
**hide** [haɪd] (pt **hid**, pp **hidden**) n (skin) piel
f ▷ vt esconder; ocultar ▷ vi: **to ~ (from sb)**
esconderse or ocultarse (de algn)
**hideous** ['hɪdɪəs] adj horrible
**hiding** ['haɪdɪŋ] n (beating) paliza; **to be in ~**
(concealed) estar escondido
**hi-fi** ['haɪfaɪ] n estéreo, hifi m ▷ adj de alta
fidelidad

**high** [haɪ] adj alto; (speed, number) grande;
(price) elevado; (wind) fuerte; (voice) agudo
▷ adv alto, a gran altura; **it is 20 m** ~ tiene
20 m de altura; ~ **in the air** en las alturas;
**highchair** n silla alta (para niños);
**high-class** adj (hotel) de lujo; (person)
distinguido, de categoría; (food) de alta
categoría; **higher education** n educación f
or enseñanza superior; **high heels** npl
(heels) tacones mpl altos; (shoes) zapatos
mpl de tacón; **high jump** n (Sport) salto de
altura; **highlands** npl tierras fpl altas; **the
Highlands** (in Scotland) las Tierras Altas de
Escocia; **highlight** n (fig: of event) punto
culminante ▷ vt subrayar; **highlights** npl
(in hair) reflejos mpl; **highlighter** n
rotulador; **highly** adv sumamente; **highly
paid** muy bien pagado; **to speak highly of**
hablar muy bien de; **highness** n altura;
**Her or His Highness** Su Alteza; **high-rise** n
(also: **high-rise block, high-rise building**)
torre f de pisos; **high school** n ≈ Instituto
Nacional de Bachillerato (SP); **high season**
n (BRIT) temporada alta; **high street** n
(BRIT) calle f mayor; **high-tech** adj de alta
tecnología; **highway** n carretera; (US)
autopista; **Highway Code** n (BRIT) código
de la circulación
**hijack** ['haɪdʒæk] vt secuestrar; **hijacker** n
secuestrador(a) m/f
**hike** [haɪk] vi (go walking) ir de excursión (a
pie) ▷ n caminata; **hiker** n excursionista mf;
**hiking** n senderismo
**hilarious** [hɪ'lɛərɪəs] adj divertidísimo
**hill** [hɪl] n colina; (high) montaña; (slope)
cuesta; **hillside** n ladera; **hill walking**
n senderismo (de montaña); **hilly** adj
montañoso
**him** [hɪm] pron (direct) le, lo; (indirect) le;
(stressed, after prep) él; see also **me; himself**
pron (reflexive) se; (emphatic) él mismo; (after
prep) sí (mismo); see also **oneself**
**hind** [haɪnd] adj posterior
**hinder** ['hɪndər] vt estorbar, impedir
**hindsight** ['haɪndsaɪt] n: **with ~** en
retrospectiva
**Hindu** ['hɪnduː] n hindú mf; **Hinduism**
['hɪnduːɪzm] n (Rel) hinduismo
**hinge** [hɪndʒ] n bisagra, gozne m ▷ vi (fig):
**to ~ on** depender de
**hint** [hɪnt] n indirecta; (advice) consejo ▷ vt:
**to ~ that** insinuar que ▷ vi: **to ~ at** aludir a
**hip** [hɪp] n cadera
**hippie** ['hɪpɪ] n hippie mf, jipi mf
**hippo** ['hɪpəʊ] (pl **hippos**) n hipopótamo;
**hippopotamus** (pl **hippopotamuses** or
**hippopotami**) [hɪpə'pɒtəməs, -'pɒtəmaɪ]
n hipopótamo
**hippy** ['hɪpɪ] n = **hippie**

**hire** ['haɪə'] vt (BRIT: car, equipment) alquilar; (worker) contratar ▷ n alquiler m; **for ~** se alquila; (taxi) libre; **hire(d) car** n (BRIT) coche m de alquiler; **hire purchase** n (BRIT) compra a plazos; **to buy sth on hire purchase** comprar algo a plazos

**his** [hɪz] pron (el) suyo/(la) suya etc ▷ adj su; see also **my; mine**

**Hispanic** [hɪs'pænɪk] adj hispánico

**hiss** [hɪs] vi silbar

**historian** [hɪ'stɔːrɪən] n historiador(a) m/f

**historic(al)** [hɪ'stɔrɪk(l)] adj histórico

**history** ['hɪstərɪ] n historia

**hit** [hɪt] vt (strike) golpear, pegar; (reach: target) alcanzar; (collide with: car) chocar contra; (fig: affect) afectar ▷ n golpe m; (success) éxito; (on website) visita; (in web search) correspondencia; **to ~ it off with sb** llevarse bien con algn; **hit back** vi defenderse; (fig) devolver golpe por golpe

**hitch** [hɪtʃ] vt (fasten) atar, amarrar; (also: **~ up**) arremangarse ▷ n (difficulty) problema, pega; **to ~ a lift** hacer autostop

**hitch-hike** ['hɪtʃhaɪk] vi hacer autostop; **hitch-hiker** n autostopista mf; **hitchhiking** n autostop m

**hi-tech** [haɪ'tek] adj de alta tecnología

**hitman** ['hɪtmæn] n asesino a sueldo

**HIV** n abbr (= human immunodeficiency virus) VIH m; **~-negative** VIH negativo; **~-positive** VIH positivo, seropositivo

**hive** [haɪv] n colmena

**hoard** [hɔːd] n (treasure) tesoro; (stockpile) provisión f ▷ vt acumular

**hoarse** [hɔːs] adj ronco

**hoax** [həʊks] n engaño

**hob** [hɔb] n quemador m

**hobble** ['hɔbl] vi cojear

**hobby** ['hɔbɪ] n pasatiempo, afición f

**hobo** ['həʊbəʊ] n (US) vagabundo

**hockey** ['hɔkɪ] n hockey m; **hockey stick** n palo m de hockey

**hog** [hɔg] n cerdo, puerco ▷ vt (fig) acaparar; **to go the whole ~** echar el todo por el todo

**Hogmanay** [hɔgmə'neɪ] n Nochevieja

**HOGMANAY**

La Nochevieja o New Year's Eve se conoce como Hogmanay en Escocia, donde se festeja de forma especial. La familia y los amigos se suelen juntar para oír las campanadas del reloj y luego se hace el first-footing, costumbre que consiste en visitar a los amigos y vecinos llevando algo de beber (generalmente whisky) y un trozo de carbón que se supone que traerá buena suerte para el año entrante.

**hoist** [hɔɪst] n (crane) grúa ▷ vt levantar, alzar

**hold** [həʊld] (pt, pp **held**) vt sostener; (contain) contener; (have: power, qualification) tener; (keep back) retener; (believe) sostener; (meeting) celebrar ▷ vi (withstand: pressure) resistir; (be valid) ser válido; (stick) pegarse ▷ n (grasp) asimiento; (fig) dominio; **~ the line!** (Tel) ¡no cuelgue!; **to ~ one's own** (fig) defenderse; **to catch** or **get (a) ~ of** agarrarse or asirse de; **hold back** vt retener; (secret) ocultar; **hold on** vi agarrarse bien; (wait) esperar; **~ on!** (Tel) ¡(espere) un momento!; **hold out** vt ofrecer ▷ vi (resist) resistir; **hold up** vt (raise) levantar; (support) apoyar; (delay) retrasar; (rob) asaltar; **holdall** n (BRIT) bolsa; **holder** n (of ticket, record) poseedor(a) m/f; (of passport, post, office, title etc) titular mf

**hole** [həʊl] n agujero

**holiday** ['hɔlədɪ] n vacaciones fpl; (day off) (día m de) fiesta, día m festivo or feriado (LAM); **on ~** de vacaciones; **holiday camp** n (BRIT) colonia or centro vacacional; **holiday job** n (BRIT) trabajo para las vacaciones; **holidaymaker** n (BRIT) turista mf; **holiday resort** n centro turístico

**Holland** ['hɔlənd] n Holanda

**hollow** ['hɔləʊ] adj hueco; (fig) vacío; (eyes) hundido; (sound) sordo ▷ n hueco; (in ground) hoyo ▷ vt: **to ~ out** ahuecar

**holly** ['hɔlɪ] n acebo

**Hollywood** ['hɔlɪwʊd] n Hollywood m

**holocaust** ['hɔləkɔːst] n holocausto

**holy** ['həʊlɪ] adj santo, sagrado; (water) bendito

**home** [həʊm] n casa; (country) patria; (institution) asilo ▷ adj (domestic) casero, de casa; (Econ, Pol) nacional ▷ adv (direction) a casa; **at ~** en casa; **to go/come ~** ir/volver a casa; **make yourself at ~** ¡estás en tu casa!; **home address** n domicilio; **homeland** n tierra natal; **homeless** adj sin hogar, sin casa; **homely** adj (simple) sencillo; **home-made** adj casero; **home match** n partido en casa; **Home Office** n (BRIT) Ministerio del Interior; **home owner** n propietario/a de una casa; **home page** n (Comput) página de inicio; **Home Secretary** n (BRIT) Ministro del Interior; **homesick** adj: **to be homesick** tener morriña or nostalgia; **home town** n ciudad f natal; **homework** n deberes mpl

**homicide** ['hɔmɪsaɪd] n (US) homicidio

**homoeopathic**, (US) **homeopathic** [həʊmɪəʊ'pæθɪk] adj homeopático

**homoeopathy**, (US) **homeopathy** [həʊmɪ'ɔpəθɪ] n homeopatía

**homosexual** [hɔməʊ'sɛksjuəl] adj, n homosexual mf

**honest** ['ɔnɪst] adj honrado; (sincere) franco, sincero; **honestly** adv

honradamente; francamente; **honesty** n
honradez f

**honey** ['hʌnɪ] n miel f; **honeymoon** n luna
de miel; **honeysuckle** n madreselva

**Hong Kong** ['hɔŋ'kɔŋ] n Hong-Kong m

**honorary** ['ɔnərərɪ] adj no remunerado;
(duty, title) honorífico; ~ **degree** doctorado
honoris causa

**honour**, (US) **honor** ['ɔnəʳ] vt honrar;
(commitment, promise) cumplir con ▷ n
honor m, honra, **honourable**, (US)
**honorable** ['ɔnərəbl] adj honorable;
**honours degree** n (Univ) licenciatura
superior

**hood** [hud] n capucha; (BRIT Aut) capota;
(US Aut) capó m; (of cooker) campana
de humos; **hoodie** ['hudɪ] n (pullover)
sudadera f con capucha; (young person)
capuchero/a

**hoof** (pl **hoofs** or **hooves**) [hu:f, hu:vz] n
pezuña

**hook** [huk] n gancho; (on dress) corchete
m, broche m; (for fishing) anzuelo ▷ vt
enganchar

**hooligan** ['hu:lɪgən] n gamberro

**hoop** [hu:p] n aro

**hooray** [hu:'reɪ] excl = **hurrah**

**hoot** [hu:t] vi (BRIT Aut) tocar la bocina;
(siren) sonar; (owl) ulular

**hooves** [hu:vz] pl of **hoof**

**hop** [hɔp] vi saltar, brincar; (on one foot)
saltar con un pie

**hope** [həup] vt, vi esperar ▷ n esperanza;
**I ~ so/not** espero que sí/no; **hopeful**
adj (person) optimista; (situation)
prometedor(a); **hopefully** adv con
esperanza; **hopefully he will recover**
esperamos que se recupere; **hopeless** adj
desesperado

**hops** [hɔps] npl lúpulo sg

**horizon** [hə'raɪzn] n horizonte m;
**horizontal** [hɔrɪ'zɔntl] adj horizontal

**hormone** ['hɔ:məun] n hormona

**horn** [hɔ:n] n cuerno; (Mus: also: **French ~**)
trompa; (Aut) bocina, claxon m

**horoscope** ['hɔrəskəup] n horóscopo

**horrendous** [hə'rɛndəs] adj horrendo

**horrible** ['hɔrɪbl] adj horrible

**horrid** ['hɔrɪd] adj horrible, horroroso

**horrific** [hə'rɪfɪk] adj (accident) horroroso;
(film) horripilante

**horrifying** ['hɔrɪfaɪɪŋ] adj horroroso

**horror** ['hɔrəʳ] n horror m; **horror film** n
película de terror o miedo

**hors d'œuvre** [ɔ:'də:vrə] n entremeses mpl

**horse** [hɔ:s] n caballo; **horseback** n: **on
horseback** a caballo; **horse chestnut** n
(tree) castaño de Indias; (nut) castaña de
Indias; **horsepower** n caballo (de fuerza),

potencia en caballos; **horse-racing** n
carreras fpl de caballos; **horseradish** n
rábano picante; **horse riding** n (BRIT)
equitación f

**hose** [həuz] n (also: ~**pipe**) manguera

**hospital** ['hɔspɪtl] n hospital m

**hospitality** [hɔspɪ'tælɪtɪ] n hospitalidad f

**host** [həust] n anfitrión m; (TV, Radio)
presentador(a) m/f; (Rel) hostia; (large
number): **a ~ of** multitud de

**hostage** ['hɔstɪdʒ] n rehén m

**hostel** ['hɔstl] n hostal m; **(youth) ~**
albergue m juvenil

**hostess** ['həustɪs] n anfitriona; (BRIT: air
hostess) azafata; (TV, Radio) presentadora

**hostile** ['hɔstaɪl] adj hostil

**hostility** [hɔ'stɪlɪtɪ] n hostilidad f

**hot** [hɔt] adj caliente; (weather) caluroso,
de calor; (as opposed to only warm) muy
caliente; (spicy) picante; **to be ~** (person)
tener calor; (object) estar caliente; (weather)
hacer calor; **hot dog** n perrito caliente

**hotel** [həu'tɛl] n hotel m

**hotspot** ['hɔtspɔt] n (Comput: also:
**wireless ~**) punto de acceso inalámbrico

**hot-water bottle** [hɔt'wɔ:tə-] n bolsa de
agua caliente

**hound** [haund] vt acosar ▷ n perro de caza

**hour** ['auəʳ] n hora; **hourly** adj (de) cada
hora

**house** [haus] n casa; (Pol) cámara; (Theat)
sala ▷ vt [hauz] (person) alojar; **it's on the ~**
(fig) la casa invita; **household** n familia;
**householder** n propietario/a; (head of
house) cabeza de familia; **housekeeper** n
ama de llaves; **housekeeping** n (work)
trabajos mpl domésticos; **housewife** n ama
de casa; **house wine** n vino m de la casa;
**housework** n faenas fpl (de la casa)

**housing** ['hauzɪŋ] n (act) alojamiento;
(houses) viviendas fpl; **housing
development,** (BRIT) **housing estate** n
urbanización f

**hover** ['hɔvəʳ] vi flotar (en el aire);
**hovercraft** n aerodeslizador m

**how** [hau] adv cómo; ~ **are you?** ¿cómo estás?;
~ **long have you been here?** ¿cuánto (tiempo)
hace que estás aquí?, ¿cuánto (tiempo) llevas
aquí?; ~ **lovely!** ¡qué bonito!; ~ **many/much?**
¿cuántos/cuánto?; ~ **much does it cost?**
¿cuánto cuesta?; ~ **old are you?** ¿cuántos años
tienes?; ~ **is school?** ¿qué tal la escuela?;
~ **was the film?** ¿qué tal la película?

**however** [hau'ɛvəʳ] adv de cualquier
manera; (+ adjective) por muy ... que; (in
questions) cómo ▷ conj sin embargo, no
obstante; ~ **I do it** lo haga como lo haga;
~ **cold it is** por mucho frío que haga; ~ **did
you do it?** ¿cómo lo hiciste?

**howl** [haul] n aullido ▷ vi aullar; (person) dar alaridos; (wind) ulular

**HP** n abbr (BRIT) = **hire purchase**

**hp** abbr = **horsepower**

**HQ** n abbr = **headquarters**

**hr(s)** abbr (= hour(s)) h

**HTML** n abbr (= hypertext markup language) HTML m

**hubcap** ['hʌbkæp] n tapacubos m inv

**huddle** ['hʌdl] vi: **to ~ together** amontonarse

**huff** [hʌf] n: **in a ~** enojado

**hug** [hʌg] vt abrazar ▷ n abrazo

**huge** [hjuːdʒ] adj enorme

**hull** [hʌl] n (of ship) casco

**hum** [hʌm] vt tararear, canturrear ▷ vi tararear, canturrear; (insect) zumbar

**human** ['hjuːmən] adj humano

**humane** [hjuːˈmeɪn] adj humano, humanitario

**humanitarian** [hjuːmænɪˈteərɪən] adj humanitario

**humanity** [hjuːˈmænɪtɪ] n humanidad f

**human rights** npl derechos mpl humanos

**humble** ['hʌmbl] adj humilde

**humid** ['hjuːmɪd] adj húmedo; **humidity** [hjuːˈmɪdɪtɪ] n humedad f

**humiliate** [hjuːˈmɪlɪeɪt] vt humillar

**humiliating** [hjuːˈmɪlɪeɪtɪŋ] adj humillante, vergonzoso

**humiliation** [hjuːmɪlɪˈeɪʃən] n humillación f

**hummus** ['huməs] n humus m

**humorous** ['hjuːmərəs] adj gracioso, divertido

**humour**, (US) **humor** ['hjuːməʳ] n humorismo, sentido del humor; (mood) humor m ▷ vt (person) complacer

**hump** [hʌmp] n (in ground) montículo; (camel's) giba

**hunch** [hʌntʃ] n (premonition) presentimiento

**hundred** ['hʌndrəd] num ciento; (before n) cien; **~s of** centenares de; **hundredth** adj centésimo

**hung** [hʌŋ] pt, pp of **hang**

**Hungarian** [hʌŋˈgeərɪən] adj húngaro ▷ n húngaro/a

**Hungary** ['hʌŋgərɪ] n Hungría

**hunger** ['hʌŋgəʳ] n hambre f ▷ vi: **to ~ for** (fig) tener hambre de, anhelar

**hungry** ['hʌŋgrɪ] adj hambriento; **to be ~** tener hambre

**hunt** [hʌnt] vt (seek) buscar; (Sport) cazar ▷ vi (search): **to ~ (for)** buscar; (Sport) cazar ▷ n caza, cacería; **hunter** n cazador(a) m/f; **hunting** n caza

**hurdle** ['həːdl] n (Sport) valla; (fig) obstáculo

**hurl** [həːl] vt lanzar, arrojar

**hurrah** [huˈrɑː], **hurray** [huˈreɪ] n ¡viva!

**hurricane** ['hʌrɪkən] n huracán m

**hurry** ['hʌrɪ] n prisa ▷ vt (person) dar prisa a; (work) apresurar, hacer de prisa; **to be in a ~** tener prisa; **hurry up** vi darse prisa, apurarse (LAM)

**hurt** [həːt] (pt, pp hurt) vt hacer daño a ▷ vi doler ▷ adj lastimado

**husband** ['hʌzbənd] n marido

**hush** [hʌʃ] n silencio ▷ vt hacer callar; **~!** ¡chitón!, ¡cállate!

**husky** ['hʌskɪ] adj ronco ▷ n perro esquimal

**hut** [hʌt] n cabaña; (shed) cobertizo

**hyacinth** ['haɪəsɪnθ] n jacinto

**hydrangea** [haɪˈdreɪndʒə] n hortensia

**hydrofoil** ['haɪdrəfɔɪl] n aerodeslizador m

**hydrogen** ['haɪdrədʒən] n hidrógeno

**hygiene** ['haɪdʒiːn] n higiene f; **hygienic** [haɪˈdʒiːnɪk] adj higiénico

**hymn** [hɪm] n himno

**hype** [haɪp] n (inf) bombo

**hyperlink** ['haɪpəlɪŋk] n hiperenlace m

**hyphen** ['haɪfn] n guión m

**hypnotize** ['hɪpnətaɪz] vt hipnotizar

**hypocrite** ['hɪpəkrɪt] n hipócrita mf

**hypocritical** [hɪpəˈkrɪtɪkl] adj hipócrita

**hypothesis** (pl **hypotheses**) [haɪˈpɔθɪsɪs, -siːz] n hipótesis f inv

**hysterical** [hɪˈsterɪkl] adj histérico

**hysterics** [hɪˈsterɪks] npl histeria sg, histerismo sg; **to be in ~** (fig) morirse de risa

**I** [aɪ] *pron* yo

**ice** [aɪs] *n* hielo ▷ *vt (cake)* alcorzar ▷ *vi (also:* **~ over, ~ up)** helarse; **iceberg** *n* iceberg *m*; **ice cream** *n* helado; **ice cube** *n* cubito de hielo; **ice hockey** *n* hockey *m* sobre hielo

**Iceland** ['aɪslənd] *n* Islandia; **Icelander** *n* islandés/esa *m/f*; **Icelandic** *adj* islandés/esa ▷ *n (Ling)* islandés *m*

**ice: ice lolly** *n (BRIT)* polo; **ice rink** *n* pista de hielo; **ice-skating** *n* patinaje *m* sobre hielo

**icing** ['aɪsɪŋ] *n (Culin)* alcorza; **icing sugar** *n (BRIT)* azúcar *m* glas(eado)

**icon** ['aɪkɔn] *n* icono

**ICT** *n abbr (= Information and Communication(s) Technology)* TIC *f*; *(BRIT Scol)* informática

**icy** ['aɪsɪ] *adj* helado

**I'd** [aɪd] = **I would; I had**

**ID card** *n (identity card)* DNI *m*

**idea** [aɪ'dɪə] *n* idea

**ideal** [aɪ'dɪəl] *n* ideal *m* ▷ *adj* ideal; **ideally** [aɪ'dɪəlɪ] *adv*

**identical** [aɪ'dɛntɪkl] *adj* idéntico

**identification** [aɪdɛntɪfɪ'keɪʃən] *n* identificación *f*; **means of ~** documentos *mpl* personales

**identify** [aɪ'dɛntɪfaɪ] *vt* identificar

**identity** [aɪ'dɛntɪtɪ] *n* identidad *f*; **identity card** *n* carnet *m* de identidad; **identity theft** *n* robo de identidad

**ideology** [aɪdɪ'ɔlədʒɪ] *n* ideología

**idiom** ['ɪdɪəm] *n* modismo; *(style of speaking)* lenguaje *m*

Be careful not to translate *idiom* by the Spanish word *idioma*.

**idiot** ['ɪdɪət] *n* idiota *mf*

**idle** ['aɪdl] *adj (inactive)* ocioso; *(lazy)* holgazán/ana; *(unemployed)* parado, desocupado; *(talk)* frívolo ▷ *vi (machine)* funcionar *or* marchar en vacío

**idol** ['aɪdl] *n* ídolo

**idyllic** [ɪ'dɪlɪk] *adj* idílico

**i.e.** *abbr (= id est)* es decir

**if** [ɪf] *conj* si; **if necessary** si resultase necesario; **if I were you** yo en tu lugar; **if only** si solamente; **as if** como si

**ignite** [ɪg'naɪt] *vt (set fire to)* encender ▷ *vi* encenderse

**ignition** [ɪg'nɪʃən] *n (Aut: process)* ignición *f*; *(: mechanism)* encendido; **to switch on/off the ~** arrancar/apagar el motor

**ignorance** ['ɪgnərəns] *n* ignorancia

**ignorant** ['ɪgnərənt] *adj* ignorante; **to be ~ of** ignorar

**ignore** [ɪg'nɔːʳ] *vt (person)* no hacer caso de; *(fact)* pasar por alto

**ill** [ɪl] *adj* enfermo, malo ▷ *n* mal *m* ▷ *adv* mal; **to take** *or* **be taken ~** caer *or* ponerse enfermo

**I'll** [aɪl] = **I will; I shall**

**illegal** [ɪ'liːgl] *adj* ilegal

**illegible** [ɪ'lɛdʒɪbl] *adj* ilegible

**illegitimate** [ɪlɪ'dʒɪtɪmət] *adj* ilegítimo

**ill health** *n* mala salud *f*; **to be in ~** estar mal de salud

**illiterate** [ɪ'lɪtərət] *adj* analfabeto

**illness** ['ɪlnɪs] *n* enfermedad *f*

**illuminate** [ɪ'luːmɪneɪt] *vt (room, street)* iluminar, alumbrar

**illusion** [ɪ'luːʒən] *n* ilusión *f*

**illustrate** ['ɪləstreɪt] *vt* ilustrar

**illustration** [ɪlə'streɪʃən] *n (example)* ejemplo, ilustración *f*; *(in book)* lámina

**I'm** [aɪm] = **I am**

**image** ['ɪmɪdʒ] *n* imagen *f*

**imaginary** [ɪ'mædʒɪnərɪ] *adj* imaginario

**imagination** [ɪmædʒɪ'neɪʃən] *n* imaginación *f*; *(inventiveness)* inventiva

**imaginative** [ɪ'mædʒɪnətɪv] *adj* imaginativo

**imagine** [ɪ'mædʒɪn] *vt* imaginarse

**imam** [ɪ'mɑːm] *n* imán *m*

**imbalance** [ɪm'bæləns] *n* desequilibrio

**imitate** ['ɪmɪteɪt] *vt* imitar; **imitation** [ɪmɪ'teɪʃən] *n* imitación *f*; *(copy)* copia

**immaculate** [ɪ'mækjulət] *adj* inmaculado

**immature** [ɪmə'tjuəʳ] *adj (person)* inmaduro

**immediate** [ɪ'miːdɪət] *adj* inmediato; *(pressing)* urgente, apremiante; *(nearest: family)* próximo; *(: neighbourhood)* inmediato; **immediately** *adv (at once)* en seguida; *(directly)* inmediatamente; **immediately next to** justo al lado de

**immense** [ɪ'mɛns] *adj* inmenso, enorme; **immensely** *adv* enormemente

**immerse** [ɪ'məːs] *vt (submerge)* sumergir; **to be ~d in** *(fig)* estar absorto en

**immigrant** ['ɪmɪgrənt] n inmigrante mf; **immigration** [ɪmɪ'greɪʃən] n inmigración f

**imminent** ['ɪmɪnənt] adj inminente

**immoral** [ɪ'mɔrl] adj inmoral

**immortal** [ɪ'mɔ:tl] adj inmortal

**immune** [ɪ'mju:n] adj: ~ **(to)** inmune (a); **immune system** n sistema m inmunitario

**immunize** ['ɪmjunaɪz] vt inmunizar

**impact** ['ɪmpækt] n impacto

**impair** [ɪm'pεər] vt perjudicar

**impartial** [ɪm'pɑ:ʃl] adj imparcial

**impatience** [ɪm'peɪʃəns] n impaciencia

**impatient** [ɪm'peɪʃənt] adj impaciente; **to get** or **grow** ~ impacientarse

**impeccable** [ɪm'pεkəbl] adj impecable

**impending** [ɪm'pεndɪŋ] adj inminente

**imperative** [ɪm'pεrətɪv] adj (tone) imperioso; (necessary) imprescindible

**imperfect** [ɪm'pə:fɪkt] adj (goods etc) defectuoso ▷ n (Ling: also: ~ **tense**) imperfecto

**imperial** [ɪm'pɪərɪəl] adj imperial

**impersonal** [ɪm'pə:sənl] adj impersonal

**impersonate** [ɪm'pə:səneɪt] vt hacerse pasar por

**impetus** ['ɪmpətəs] n ímpetu m; (fig) impulso

**implant** [ɪm'plɑ:nt] vt (Med) injertar, implantar; (fig: idea, principle) inculcar

**implement** n ['ɪmplɪmənt] herramienta ▷ vt ['ɪmplɪmεnt] hacer efectivo; (carry out) realizar

**implicate** ['ɪmplɪkeɪt] vt (compromise) comprometer; **to ~ sb in sth** comprometer a algn en algo

**implication** [ɪmplɪ'keɪʃən] n consecuencia; **by ~** indirectamente

**implicit** [ɪm'plɪsɪt] adj implícito; absoluto

**imply** [ɪm'plaɪ] vt (involve) suponer; (hint) insinuar

**impolite** [ɪmpə'laɪt] adj mal educado

**import** vt [ɪm'pɔ:t] importar ▷ n ['ɪmpɔ:t] (Comm) importación f; (: article) producto importado; (meaning) significado, sentido

**importance** [ɪm'pɔ:təns] n importancia

**important** [ɪm'pɔ:tənt] adj importante; **it's not** ~ no importa, no tiene importancia

**importer** [ɪm'pɔ:tər] n importador(a) m/f

**impose** [ɪm'pəuz] vt imponer ▷ vi: **to ~ on sb** abusar de algn; **imposing** adj imponente, impresionante

**impossible** [ɪm'pɔsɪbl] adj imposible; (person) insoportable

**impotent** ['ɪmpətənt] adj impotente

**impoverished** [ɪm'pɔvərɪʃt] adj necesitado

**impractical** [ɪm'præktɪkl] adj (person) poco práctico

**impress** [ɪm'prεs] vt impresionar; (mark) estampar; **to ~ sth on sb** convencer a algn de la importancia de algo

**impression** [ɪm'prεʃən] n impresión f; **to be under the ~ that** tener la impresión de que

**impressive** [ɪm'prεsɪv] adj impresionante

**imprison** [ɪm'prɪzn] vt encarcelar; **imprisonment** n encarcelamiento; (term of imprisonment) cárcel f

**improbable** [ɪm'prɔbəbl] adj improbable, inverosímil

**improper** [ɪm'prɔpər] adj (incorrect) impropio; (unseemly) indecoroso; (indecent) indecente; (dishonest: activities) deshonesto

**improve** [ɪm'pru:v] vt mejorar; (foreign language) perfeccionar ▷ vi mejorar; **improvement** n mejora; perfeccionamiento

**improvise** ['ɪmprəvaɪz] vt, vi improvisar

**impulse** ['ɪmpʌls] n impulso; **to act on ~** actuar sin reflexionar; **impulsive** [ɪm'pʌlsɪv] adj irreflexivo

### ○ KEYWORD

**in** [ɪn] prep **1** (indicating place, position, with place names) en; **in the house/garden** en (la) casa/el jardín; **in here/there** aquí/ahí or allí dentro; **in London/England** en Londres/Inglaterra

**2** (indicating time) en; **in spring** en (la) primavera; **in 1988/May** en 1988/mayo; **in the afternoon** por la tarde; **at four o'clock in the afternoon** a las cuarto de la tarde; **I did it in three hours/days** lo hice en tres horas/días; **I'll see you in two weeks** or **in two weeks' time** te veré dentro de dos semanas

**3** (indicating manner etc) en; **in a loud/soft voice** en voz alta/baja; **in pencil/ink** a lápiz/bolígrafo; **the boy in the blue shirt** el chico de la camisa azul

**4** (indicating circumstances): **in the sun/shade** al sol/a la sombra; **in the rain** bajo la lluvia; **a change in policy** un cambio de política

**5** (indicating mood, state): **in tears** llorando; **in anger/despair** enfadado/desesperado; **to live in luxury** vivir lujosamente

**6** (with ratios, numbers): **1 in 10 households, 1 household in 10** una de cada 10 familias; **20 pence in the pound** 20 peniques por libra; **they lined up in twos** se alinearon de dos en dos

**7** (referring to people, works) en; entre; **the disease is common in children** la enfermedad es común entre los niños;

**in (the works of) Dickens** en (las obras de) Dickens
**8** (indicating profession etc): **to be in teaching** dedicarse a la enseñanza
**9** (after superlative) de; **the best pupil in the class** el/la mejor alumno/a de la clase
**10** (with present participle): **in saying this** al decir esto
▶ adv: **to be in** (person: at home) estar en casa; (: at work) estar; (train, ship, plane) haber llegado; (in fashion) estar de moda; **she'll be in later today** llegará más tarde hoy; **to ask sb in** hacer pasar a algn; **to run/limp** etc **in** entrar corriendo/cojeando etc
▶ n: **the ins and outs** (of proposal, situation etc) los detalles

**inability** [ɪnə'bɪlɪtɪ] n: ~ **(to do)** incapacidad f (de hacer)
**inaccurate** [ɪn'ækjurət] adj inexacto, incorrecto
**inadequate** [ɪn'ædɪkwət] adj (insufficient) insuficiente; (person) incapaz
**inadvertently** [ɪnəd'və:tntlɪ] adv por descuido
**inappropriate** [ɪnə'prəuprɪət] adj inadecuado
**inaugurate** [ɪ'nɔ:gjureɪt] vt inaugurar; (president, official) investir
**Inc.** abbr = **incorporated**
**incapable** [ɪn'keɪpəbl] adj: ~ **(of doing sth)** incapaz (de hacer algo)
**incense** n ['ɪnsɛns] incienso ▷ vt [ɪn'sɛns] (anger) indignar, encolerizar
**incentive** [ɪn'sɛntɪv] n incentivo, estímulo
**inch** [ɪntʃ] n pulgada; **to be within an ~ of** estar a dos dedos de; **he didn't give an ~** no hizo la más mínima concesión
**incidence** ['ɪnsɪdns] n (of crime, disease) incidencia
**incident** ['ɪnsɪdnt] n incidente m
**incidentally** [ɪnsɪ'dɛntəlɪ] adv (by the way) por cierto
**inclination** [ɪnklɪ'neɪʃən] n (tendency) tendencia, inclinación f
**incline** [ n 'ɪnklaɪn, vt, vi ɪn'klaɪn] n pendiente f, cuesta ▷ vt (head) poner de lado ▷ vi inclinarse; **to be ~d to** (tend) ser propenso a
**include** [ɪn'klu:d] vt incluir; (in letter) adjuntar; **including** prep incluso, inclusive; **including tip** propina incluida
**inclusion** [ɪn'klu:ʒən] n inclusión f
**inclusive** [ɪn'klu:sɪv] adj inclusivo; ~ **of tax** incluidos los impuestos
**income** ['ɪnkʌm] n (personal) ingresos mpl; (from property etc) renta; (profit) rédito;

**income support** n (BRIT) ≈ ayuda familiar; **income tax** n impuesto sobre la renta
**incoming** ['ɪnkʌmɪŋ] adj (passengers, flight) de llegada; (government) entrante; (tenant) nuevo
**incompatible** [ɪnkəm'pætɪbl] adj incompatible
**incompetence** [ɪn'kɔmpɪtəns] n incompetencia
**incompetent** [ɪn'kɔmpɪtənt] adj incompetente
**incomplete** [ɪnkəm'pli:t] adj incompleto; (unfinished) sin terminar
**inconsistent** [ɪnkən'sɪstnt] adj inconsecuente; (contradictory) incongruente; ~ **with** que no concuerda con
**inconvenience** [ɪnkən'vi:njəns] n inconvenientes mpl; (trouble) molestia ▷ vt incomodar
**inconvenient** [ɪnkən'vi:njənt] adj incómodo, poco práctico; (time, place) inoportuno
**incorporate** [ɪn'kɔ:pəreɪt] vt incorporar; (contain) comprender; (add) agregar
**incorporated** [ɪn'kɔ:pəreɪtɪd] adj: ~ **company** (US) ≈ Sociedad f Anónima (S.A.)
**incorrect** [ɪnkə'rɛkt] adj incorrecto
**increase** [n 'ɪnkri:s, vi, vt ɪn'kri:s] n aumento ▷ vi aumentar; (grow) crecer; (price) subir ▷ vt aumentar; (price) subir; **increasingly** adv cada vez más
**incredible** adj increíble; **incredibly** adv increíblemente
**incur** [ɪn'kə:ʳ] vt (expenses) incurrir en; (loss) sufrir; (anger, disapproval) provocar
**indecent** [ɪn'di:snt] adj indecente
**indeed** [ɪn'di:d] adv efectivamente, en realidad; (in fact) en efecto; (furthermore) es más; **yes ~!** ¡claro que sí!
**indefinitely** [ɪn'dɛfɪnɪtlɪ] adv (wait) indefinidamente
**independence** [ɪndɪ'pɛndns] n independencia; **Independence Day** n Día m de la Independencia

○ **INDEPENDENCE DAY**
○
○ El cuatro de julio es la fiesta nacional de
○ los Estados Unidos, Independence Day,
○ en conmemoración de la Declaración
○ de Independencia escrita por Thomas
○ Jefferson y adoptada en 1776. En ella se
○ proclamaba la ruptura total con Gran
○ Bretaña de las trece colonias americanas
○ que fueron el origen de los Estados Unidos
○ de América.

**independent** [ɪndɪˈpɛndənt] *adj*
independiente; **independent school** *n*
(BRIT) escuela f privada, colegio *m* privado
**index** [ˈɪndɛks] *n* (*pl* **indexes**: *in book*)
indices *m*; (*in library etc*) catálogo; (*pl*
**indices**: *ratio, sign*) exponente *m*
**India** [ˈɪndɪə] *n* la India; **Indian** *adj, n*
indio/a; (*inf!*): **Red Indian** piel roja *mf*
**indicate** [ˈɪndɪkeɪt] *vt* indicar; **indication**
[ɪndɪˈkeɪʃən] *n* indicio, señal *f*; **indicative**
[ɪnˈdɪkətɪv] *adj*: **to be indicative of sth**
indicar algo; **indicator** *n* indicador *m*; (*Aut*)
intermitente *m*
**indices** [ˈɪndɪsiːz] *npl of* **index**
**indict** [ɪnˈdaɪt] *vt* acusar; **indictment** *n*
acusación f
**indifference** [ɪnˈdɪfrəns] *n* indiferencia
**indifferent** [ɪnˈdɪfrənt] *adj* indiferente;
(*poor*) regular
**indigenous** [ɪnˈdɪdʒɪnəs] *adj* indígena
**indigestion** [ɪndɪˈdʒɛstʃən] *n* indigestión f
**indignant** [ɪnˈdɪgnənt] *adj*: **to be ~ about**
**sth** indignarse por algo
**indirect** [ɪndɪˈrɛkt] *adj* indirecto
**indispensable** [ɪndɪˈspɛnsəbl] *adj*
indispensable, imprescindible
**individual** [ɪndɪˈvɪdjuəl] *n* individuo
▷ *adj* individual; (*personal*) personal;
(*particular*) particular; **individually** *adv*
individualmente
**Indonesia** [ɪndəˈniːzɪə] *n* Indonesia
**indoor** [ˈɪndɔːʳ] *adj* (*swimming pool*)
cubierto; (*plant*) de interior; (*sport*) bajo
cubierta; **indoors** [ɪnˈdɔːz] *adv* dentro
**induce** [ɪnˈdjuːs] *vt* inducir, persuadir;
(*bring about*) producir
**indulge** [ɪnˈdʌldʒ] *vt* (*whim*) satisfacer;
(*person*) complacer; (*child*) mimar ▷ *vi*:
**to ~ in** darse el gusto de; **indulgent** *adj*
indulgente
**industrial** [ɪnˈdʌstrɪəl] *adj* industrial;
**industrial estate** *n* (BRIT) polígono *or* (LAM)
zona industrial; **industrialist** *n* industrial
*mf*; **industrial park** *n* (US) = **industrial**
**estate**
**industry** [ˈɪndəstrɪ] *n* industria; (*diligence*)
aplicación f
**inefficient** [ɪnɪˈfɪʃənt] *adj* ineficaz,
ineficiente
**inequality** [ɪnɪˈkwɔlɪtɪ] *n* desigualdad f
**inevitable** [ɪnˈɛvɪtəbl] *adj* inevitable;
(*necessary*) forzoso; **inevitably** *adv*
inevitablemente
**inexpensive** [ɪnɪkˈspɛnsɪv] *adj* económico
**inexperienced** [ɪnɪkˈspɪərɪənst] *adj*
inexperto
**inexplicable** [ɪnɪkˈsplɪkəbl] *adj*
inexplicable
**infamous** [ˈɪnfəməs] *adj* infame

**infant** [ˈɪnfənt] *n* niño/a; (*baby*) niño/a
pequeño/a, bebé *mf*
**infantry** [ˈɪnfəntrɪ] *n* infantería
**infant school** *n* (BRIT) escuela infantil
**infect** [ɪnˈfɛkt] *vt* (*wound*) infectar; (*food*)
contaminar; (*person, animal*) contagiar;
**infection** [ɪnˈfɛkʃən] *n* infección f; (*fig*)
contagio; **infectious** [ɪnˈfɛkʃəs] *adj*
contagioso
**infer** [ɪnˈfəːʳ] *vt* deducir, inferir
**inferior** [ɪnˈfɪərɪəʳ] *adj, n* inferior *mf*
**infertile** [ɪnˈfəːtaɪl] *adj* estéril; (*person*)
infecundo
**infertility** [ɪnfəːˈtɪlɪtɪ] *n* esterilidad f;
infecundidad f
**infested** [ɪnˈfɛstɪd] *adj*: **~ (with)** plagado
(de)
**infinite** [ˈɪnfɪnɪt] *adj* infinito; **infinitely** *adv*
infinitamente
**infirmary** [ɪnˈfəːmərɪ] *n* hospital *m*
**inflamed** [ɪnˈfleɪmd] *adj*: **to become ~**
inflamarse
**inflammation** [ɪnfləˈmeɪʃən] *n*
inflamación f
**inflatable** [ɪnˈfleɪtəbl] *adj* inflable
**inflate** [ɪnˈfleɪt] *vt* (*tyre*) inflar; (*fig*) hinchar;
**inflation** [ɪnˈfleɪʃən] *n* (*Econ*) inflación f
**inflexible** [ɪnˈflɛksɪbl] *adj* inflexible
**inflict** [ɪnˈflɪkt] *vt*: **to ~ on** infligir en
**influence** [ˈɪnfluəns] *n* influencia ▷ *vt*
influir en, influenciar; **under the ~**
**of alcohol** en estado de embriaguez;
**influential** [ɪnfluˈɛnʃl] *adj* influyente
**influx** [ˈɪnflʌks] *n* afluencia
**info** [ˈɪnfəu] *n* (*inf*) = **information**
**inform** [ɪnˈfɔːm] *vt*: **to ~ sb of sth** informar
a algn sobre *or* de algo ▷ *vi*: **to ~ on sb**
delatar a algn
**informal** [ɪnˈfɔːml] *adj* (*manner, tone*)
desenfadado; (*dress, occasion*) informal;
(*visit, meeting*) extraoficial
**information** [ɪnfəˈmeɪʃən] *n* información
f; (*knowledge*) conocimientos *mpl*; **a**
**piece of ~** un dato; **information office** *n*
información f; **information technology** *n*
informática
**informative** [ɪnˈfɔːmətɪv] *adj* informativo
**infra-red** [ɪnfrəˈrɛd] *adj* infrarrojo
**infrastructure** [ˈɪnfrəstrʌktʃəʳ] *n*
infraestructura
**infrequent** [ɪnˈfriːkwənt] *adj* infrecuente
**infuriate** [ɪnˈfjuərɪeɪt] *vt*: **to become ~d**
ponerse furioso
**infuriating** [ɪnˈfjuərɪeɪtɪŋ] *adj* (*habit, noise*)
enloquecedor(a)
**ingenious** [ɪnˈdʒiːnjəs] *adj* ingenioso
**ingredient** [ɪnˈgriːdɪənt] *n* ingrediente *m*
**inhabit** [ɪnˈhæbɪt] *vt* vivir en; **inhabitant** *n*
habitante *mf*

**inhale** [ɪnˈheɪl] vt inhalar ▷ vi (breathe in) aspirar; (in smoking) tragar; **inhaler** n inhalador m

**inherent** [ɪnˈhɪərənt] adj: ~ **in** or **to** inherente a

**inherit** [ɪnˈherɪt] vt heredar; **inheritance** n herencia; (fig) patrimonio

**inhibit** [ɪnˈhɪbɪt] vt inhibir, impedir; **inhibition** [ɪnhɪˈbɪʃən] n cohibición f

**initial** [ɪˈnɪʃl] adj primero ▷ n inicial f ▷ vt firmar con las iniciales; **initials** npl iniciales fpl; (abbreviation) siglas fpl; **initially** adv en un principio

**initiate** [ɪˈnɪʃɪeɪt] vt iniciar; **to ~ proceedings against sb** (Law) poner una demanda contra algn

**initiative** [ɪˈnɪʃətɪv] n iniciativa; **to take the ~** tomar la iniciativa

**inject** [ɪnˈdʒɛkt] vt inyectar; **injection** [ɪnˈdʒɛkʃən] n inyección f

**injure** [ˈɪndʒəʳ] vt herir; (hurt) lastimar; (fig: reputation etc) perjudicar; **injured** adj herido; **injury** n herida, lesión f; (wrong) perjuicio, daño

■ Be careful not to translate injury by the Spanish word injuria.

**injustice** [ɪnˈdʒʌstɪs] n injusticia

**ink** [ɪŋk] n tinta; **ink-jet printer** [ˈɪŋkdʒɛt-] n impresora de chorro de tinta

**inland** adj [ˈɪnlənd] interior ▷ adv [ɪnˈlænd] tierra adentro; **Inland Revenue** n (BRIT) ≈ Hacienda, ≈ Agencia Tributaria

**in-laws** [ˈɪnlɔːz] npl suegros mpl

**inmate** [ˈɪnmeɪt] n (in prison) preso/a, presidiario/a; (in asylum) internado/a

**inn** [ɪn] n posada, mesón m

**inner** [ˈɪnəʳ] adj interior; (feelings) íntimo; **inner-city** adj (schools, problems) de las zonas céntricas pobres, de los barrios céntricos pobres

**inning** [ˈɪnɪŋ] n (US Baseball) inning m, entrada; **~s** (Cricket) entrada, turno

**innocence** [ˈɪnəsns] n inocencia

**innocent** [ˈɪnəsnt] adj inocente

**innovation** [ɪnəʊˈveɪʃən] n novedad f

**innovative** [ˈɪnəʊvətɪv] adj innovador

**in-patient** [ˈɪnpeɪʃənt] n (paciente mf) interno/a

**input** [ˈɪnput] n entrada; (of resources) inversión f; (Comput) entrada de datos

**inquest** [ˈɪnkwɛst] n (coroner's) investigación f post-mortem

**inquire** [ɪnˈkwaɪəʳ] vi preguntar ▷ vt: **to ~ when/where/whether** preguntar cuándo/dónde/si; **to ~ about** (person) preguntar por; (fact) informarse de; **inquiry** n pregunta; (Law) investigación f, pesquisa; **"Inquiries"** "Información"

**insane** [ɪnˈseɪn] adj loco; (Med) demente

**insanity** [ɪnˈsænɪtɪ] n demencia, locura

**insect** [ˈɪnsɛkt] n insecto; **insect repellent** n loción f contra los insectos

**insecure** [ɪnsɪˈkjuəʳ] adj inseguro

**insecurity** [ɪnsɪˈkjuərɪtɪ] n inseguridad f

**insensitive** [ɪnˈsɛnsɪtɪv] adj insensible

**insert** vt [ɪnˈsəːt] (into sth) introducir; (Comput) insertar ▷ n [ˈɪnsəːt] encarte m

**inside** [ˈɪnˈsaɪd] n interior m ▷ adj interior, interno ▷ adv (within) (por) dentro; (with movement) hacia dentro ▷ prep dentro de; (of time): **~ 10 minutes** en menos de 10 minutos; **~ out** adv (turn) al revés; (know) a fondo; **inside lane** n (Aut: BRIT) carril m izquierdo; (: in US, Europe etc) carril m derecho

**insight** [ˈɪnsaɪt] n perspicacia

**insignificant** [ɪnsɪɡˈnɪfɪknt] adj insignificante

**insincere** [ɪnsɪnˈsɪəʳ] adj poco sincero

**insist** [ɪnˈsɪst] vi insistir; **to ~ on doing** empeñarse en hacer; **to ~ that** insistir en que; (claim) exigir que; **insistent** adj insistente; (noise, action) persistente

**insomnia** [ɪnˈsɔmnɪə] n insomnio

**inspect** [ɪnˈspɛkt] vt inspeccionar, examinar; (troops) pasar revista a; **inspection** [ɪnˈspɛkʃən] n inspección f, examen m; (of troops) revista; **inspector** n inspector(a) m/f; (BRIT: on buses, trains) revisor(a) m/f

**inspiration** [ɪnspəˈreɪʃən] n inspiración f; **inspire** [ɪnˈspaɪəʳ] vt inspirar; **inspiring** adj inspirador(a)

**instability** [ɪnstəˈbɪlɪtɪ] n inestabilidad f

**install**, (US) **instal** [ɪnˈstɔːl] vt instalar; **installation** [ɪnstəˈleɪʃən] n instalación f

**instalment**, (US) **installment** [ɪnˈstɔːlmənt] n plazo; (of story) entrega; (of TV serial etc) capítulo; **in ~s** (pay, receive) a plazos

**instance** [ˈɪnstəns] n ejemplo, caso; **for ~** por ejemplo; **in the first ~** en primer lugar

**instant** [ˈɪnstənt] n instante m, momento ▷ adj inmediato; (coffee) instantáneo; **instantly** adv en seguida, al instante; **instant messaging** n mensajería instantánea

**instead** [ɪnˈstɛd] adv en cambio; **~ of** en lugar de, en vez de

**instinct** [ˈɪnstɪŋkt] n instinto; **instinctive** adj instintivo

**institute** [ˈɪnstɪtjuːt] n instituto; (professional body) colegio ▷ vt (begin) iniciar, empezar; (proceedings) entablar

**institution** [ɪnstɪˈtjuːʃən] n institución f; (Med: home) asilo; (: asylum) manicomio

**instruct** [ɪnˈstrʌkt] vt: **to ~ sb in sth** instruir a algn en or sobre algo; **to ~ sb to do sth** dar instrucciones a algn de or mandar a algn hacer algo; **instruction** [ɪnˈstrʌkʃən] n (teaching) instrucción f; **instructions** npl órdenes fpl; **instructions (for use)** modo sg de empleo; **instructor** n instructor(a) m/f

**instrument** [ˈɪnstrəmənt] n instrumento; **instrumental** [ɪnstrəˈmentl] adj (Mus) instrumental; **to be instrumental in** ser el artífice de

**insufficient** [ɪnsəˈfɪʃənt] adj insuficiente

**insulate** [ˈɪnsjuleɪt] vt aislar; **insulation** [ɪnsjuˈleɪʃən] n aislamiento

**insulin** [ˈɪnsjulɪn] n insulina

**insult** n [ˈɪnsʌlt] insulto ▷ vt [ɪnˈsʌlt] insultar; **insulting** adj insultante

**insurance** [ɪnˈʃuərəns] n seguro; **fire/ life ~** seguro contra incendios/de vida; **insurance company** n compañía f de seguros; **insurance policy** n póliza (de seguros)

**insure** [ɪnˈʃuəʳ] vt asegurar

**intact** [ɪnˈtækt] adj íntegro; (untouched) intacto

**intake** [ˈɪnteɪk] n (of food) ingestión f; (BRIT Scol): **an ~ of 200 a year** 200 matriculados al año

**integral** [ˈɪntɪɡrəl] adj (whole) íntegro; (part) integrante

**integrate** [ˈɪntɪɡreɪt] vt integrar ▷ vi integrarse

**integrity** [ɪnˈtɛɡrɪti] n honradez f, rectitud f

**intellect** [ˈɪntəlɛkt] n intelecto; **intellectual** [ɪntəˈlɛktjuəl] adj, n intelectual mf

**intelligence** [ɪnˈtɛlɪdʒəns] n inteligencia

**intelligent** [ɪnˈtɛlɪdʒənt] adj inteligente

**intend** [ɪnˈtɛnd] vt (gift etc) **to ~ sth for** destinar algo a; **to ~ to do sth** tener intención de or pensar hacer algo

**intense** [ɪnˈtɛns] adj intenso

**intensify** [ɪnˈtɛnsɪfaɪ] vt intensificar; (increase) aumentar

**intensity** [ɪnˈtɛnsɪti] n intensidad f

**intensive** [ɪnˈtɛnsɪv] adj intensivo; **intensive care** n: **to be in intensive care** estar bajo cuidados intensivos; **intensive care unit** unidad f de vigilancia intensiva

**intent** [ɪnˈtɛnt] n propósito; (Law) premeditación f ▷ adj (absorbed) absorto; (attentive) atento; **to all ~s and purposes** a efectos prácticos; **to be ~ on doing sth** estar resuelto or decidido a hacer algo

**intention** [ɪnˈtɛnʃən] n intención f, propósito; **intentional** adj deliberado

**interact** [ɪntərˈækt] vi influirse mutuamente; **interaction** [ɪntərˈækʃən] n interacción f, acción f recíproca; **interactive** adj (Comput) interactivo

**intercept** [ɪntəˈsɛpt] vt interceptar; (stop) detener

**interchange** n [ˈɪntətʃeɪndʒ] intercambio; (on motorway) intersección f

**intercourse** [ˈɪntəkɔːs] n (also: **sexual ~**) relaciones fpl sexuales

**interest** [ˈɪntrɪst] n (Comm) interés m ▷ vt interesar; **interested** adj interesado; **to be interested in** interesarse por; **interesting** adj interesante; **interest rate** n tipo de interés

**interface** [ˈɪntəfeɪs] n (Comput) junción f

**interfere** [ɪntəˈfɪəʳ] vi: **to ~ in** entrometerse en; **to ~ with** (hinder) estorbar; (damage) estropear

**interference** [ɪntəˈfɪərəns] n intromisión f; (Radio, TV) interferencia

**interim** [ˈɪntərɪm] adj provisional ▷ n: **in the ~** en el ínterin

**interior** [ɪnˈtɪərɪəʳ] n interior m ▷ adj interior; **interior design** n interiorismo, decoración f de interiores

**intermediate** [ɪntəˈmiːdɪət] adj intermedio

**intermission** [ɪntəˈmɪʃən] n (Theat) descanso

**intern** vt [ɪnˈtəːn] internar ▷ n [ˈɪntəːn] (esp US: doctor) médico/a interno/a; (: on work placement) becario/a

**internal** [ɪnˈtəːnl] adj interior; (injury, structure, memo) interno; **~ injuries** heridas fpl or lesiones fpl internas; **Internal Revenue Service** n (US) ≈ Hacienda, ≈ Agencia Tributaria

**international** [ɪntəˈnæʃənl] adj internacional; **~ (game)** partido internacional

**internet, Internet** [ˈɪntənɛt] n: **the ~** (el or la) Internet; **internet café** n cibercafé m; **Internet Service Provider** n proveedor m de (acceso a) Internet; **internet user** n internauta mf

**interpret** [ɪnˈtəːprɪt] vt interpretar; (translate) traducir; (understand) entender ▷ vi hacer de intérprete; **interpretation** [ɪntəːprɪˈteɪʃən] n interpretación f; traducción f; **interpreter** n intérprete mf

**interrogate** [ɪnˈtɛrəʊɡeɪt] vt interrogar; **interrogation** [ɪntɛrəʊˈɡeɪʃən] n interrogatorio; **interrogative** [ɪntəˈrɔɡətɪv] adj interrogativo

**interrupt** [ɪntəˈrʌpt] vt, vi interrumpir; **interruption** [ɪntəˈrʌpʃən] n interrupción f

**intersection** [ɪntəˈsɛkʃən] n (of roads) cruce m

**interstate** [ˈɪntəsteɪt] n (US) carretera interestatal

**interval** [ˈɪntəvl] n intervalo; (BRIT Theat, Sport) descanso; (Scol) recreo; **at ~s** a ratos, de vez en cuando

**intervene** [ɪntə'viːn] vi intervenir; (take part) participar; (occur) sobrevenir

**interview** ['ɪntəvjuː] n entrevista ▷ vt entrevistar a; **interviewer** n entrevistador(a) m/f

**intimate** adj ['ɪntɪmət] íntimo; (friendship) estrecho; (knowledge) profundo ▷ vt ['ɪntɪmeɪt] dar a entender

**intimidate** [ɪn'tɪmɪdeɪt] vt intimidar, amedrentar; **intimidating** adj amedrentador, intimidante

**into** ['ɪntuː] prep en; (towards) a; (inside) hacia el interior de; **~ three pieces/French** en tres pedazos/al francés

**intolerant** [ɪn'tɔlərənt] adj: **~ (of)** intolerante (con)

**intranet** ['ɪntrənet] n intranet f

**intransitive** [ɪn'trænsɪtɪv] adj intransitivo

**intricate** ['ɪntrɪkət] (design, pattern) intrincado

**intrigue** [ɪn'triːg] n intriga ▷ vt fascinar; **intriguing** adj fascinante

**introduce** [ɪntrə'djuːs] vt introducir, meter; (speaker, TV show etc) presentar; **to ~ sb (to sb)** presentar a algn (a algn); **to ~ sb to** (pastime, technique) introducir a algn a; **introduction** [ɪntrə'dʌkʃən] n introducción f; (of person) presentación f; **introductory** [ɪntrə'dʌktərɪ] adj introductorio; **an introductory offer** una oferta introductoria

**intrude** [ɪn'truːd] vi (person) entrometerse; **to ~ on** estorbar; **intruder** n intruso/a

**intuition** [ɪntjuː'ɪʃən] n intuición f

**inundate** ['ɪnʌndeɪt] vt: **to ~ with** inundar de

**invade** [ɪn'veɪd] vt invadir

**invalid** n ['ɪnvəlɪd] minusválido/a ▷ adj [ɪn'vælɪd] (not valid) inválido, nulo

**invaluable** [ɪn'væljuəbl] adj inestimable

**invariably** [ɪn'vɛərɪəblɪ] adv sin excepción, siempre; **she is ~ late** siempre llega tarde

**invasion** [ɪn'veɪʒən] n invasión f

**invent** [ɪn'vent] vt inventar; **invention** [ɪn'venʃən] n invento; (lie) invención f; **inventor** [ɪn'ventər] n inventor(a) m/f

**inventory** ['ɪnvəntrɪ] n inventario

**inverted commas** [ɪn'vəːtɪd-] npl (BRIT) comillas fpl

**invest** [ɪn'vest] vt invertir ▷ vi: **to ~ in** (company etc) invertir dinero en; (fig: sth useful) comprar; **to ~ sb with sth** conferir algo a algn

**investigate** [ɪn'vestɪgeɪt] vt investigar; **investigation** [ɪnvestɪ'geɪʃən] n investigación f, pesquisa

**investigator** [ɪn'vestɪgeɪtər] n investigador(a) m/f; **private ~** investigador(a) m/f privado/a

**investment** [ɪn'vestmənt] n inversión f

**investor** [ɪn'vestər] n inversor(a) m/f

**invisible** [ɪn'vɪzɪbl] adj invisible

**invitation** [ɪnvɪ'teɪʃən] n invitación f

**invite** [ɪn'vaɪt] vt invitar; (opinions etc) solicitar, pedir; **inviting** adj atractivo; (food) apetitoso

**invoice** ['ɪnvɔɪs] n factura ▷ vt facturar

**involve** [ɪn'vɔlv] vt suponer, implicar, tener que ver con; (concern, affect) corresponder a; **to ~ sb (in sth)** involucrar a algn (en algo), comprometer a algn (con algo); **involved** adj complicado; **to be involved in sth** (take part) estar involucrado en algo; (engrossed in) estar muy metido; **involvement** [ɪn'vɔlvmənt] n participación f, dedicación f; (obligation) compromiso; (difficulty) apuro

**inward** ['ɪnwəd] adj (movement) interior, interno; (thought, feeling) íntimo; **inwards** adv hacia dentro

**iPod®** ['aɪpɔd] n iPod® m

**IQ** n abbr (= intelligence quotient) C.I. m

**IRA** n abbr (= Irish Republican Army) IRA m

**Iran** [ɪ'rɑːn] n Irán m; **Iranian** [ɪ'reɪnɪən] adj iraní ▷ n iraní mf

**Iraq** [ɪ'rɑːk] n Irak m; **Iraqi** [ɪ'rɑːkɪ] adj, n iraquí mf

**Ireland** ['aɪələnd] n Irlanda

**iris** (pl **irises**) ['aɪrɪs, -ɪz] n (Anat) iris m; (Bot) lirio

**Irish** ['aɪrɪʃ] adj irlandés/esa ▷ npl: **the ~** los irlandeses; **Irishman** n irlandés m; **Irishwoman** n irlandesa

**iron** ['aɪən] n hierro; (for clothes) plancha ▷ adj de hierro ▷ vt (clothes) planchar

**ironic(al)** [aɪ'rɔnɪk(l)] adj irónico; **ironically** adv irónicamente

**ironing** ['aɪənɪŋ] n (act) planchado m; (ironed clothes) ropa planchada; (clothes to be ironed) ropa por planchar; **ironing board** n tabla de planchar

**irony** ['aɪrənɪ] n ironía

**irrational** [ɪ'ræʃənl] adj irracional

**irregular** [ɪ'regjulər] adj irregular; (surface) desigual; (action, event) anómalo; (behaviour) poco ortodoxo

**irrelevant** [ɪ'reləvənt] adj: **to be ~** estar fuera de lugar

**irresistible** [ɪrɪ'zɪstɪbl] adj irresistible

**irresponsible** [ɪrɪ'spɔnsɪbl] adj (act) irresponsable; (person) poco serio

**irrigation** [ɪrɪ'geɪʃən] n riego

**irritable** ['ɪrɪtəbl] adj (person) de mal humor

**irritate** ['ɪrɪteɪt] vt fastidiar; (Med) picar; **irritating** adj fastidioso; **irritation** [ɪrɪ'teɪʃən] n fastidio; picazón f

**IRS** n abbr (US) = **Internal Revenue Service**

**is** [ɪz] vb see **be**

**ISDN** n abbr (= Integrated Services Digital Network) RDSI f

**Islam** ['ɪzlɑːm] n Islam m; **Islamic**
[ɪz'læmɪk] adj islámico
**island** ['aɪlənd] n isla; **islander** n isleño/a
**isle** [aɪl] n isla
**isn't** ['ɪznt] = **is not**
**isolated** ['aɪsəleɪtɪd] adj aislado
**isolation** [aɪsə'leɪʃən] n aislamiento
**ISP** n abbr = **Internet Service Provider**
**Israel** ['ɪzreɪl] n Israel m; **Israeli** [ɪz'reɪlɪ]
adj, n israelí mf
**issue** ['ɪsjuː] n cuestión f; (outcome)
resultado; (of banknotes etc) emisión f;
(of newspaper etc) número ▷ vt (rations,
equipment) distribuir, repartir; (orders)
dar; (certificate, passport) expedir; (decree)
promulgar; (magazine) publicar; (cheque)
extender; (banknotes, stamp) emitir; **at ~** en
cuestión; **to take ~ with sb (over)** disentir
con algn (en); **to make an ~ of sth** dar a
algo más importancia de lo necesario
**IT** n abbr = **information technology**

 **KEYWORD**

**it** [ɪt] pron **1** (specific subject: not generally
translated) él/ella; (direct object) lo/la;
(indirect object) le; (after prep) él/ella;
(abstract concept) ello; **it's on the table**
está en la mesa; **I can't find it** no lo (or
la) encuentro; **give it to me** dámelo (or
dámela); **I spoke to him about it** le hablé
del asunto; **what did you learn from it?**
¿qué aprendiste de él (or ella)?; **did you go
to it?** (party, concert etc) ¿fuiste?
**2** (impersonal): **it's raining** llueve, está
lloviendo; **it's 6 o'clock/the 10th of
August** son las 6/es el 10 de agosto; **how
far is it? — it's 10 miles/2 hours on the
train** ¿a qué distancia está? — a 10 millas/
2 horas en tren; **who is it? — it's me** ¿quién
es? — soy yo

**Italian** [ɪ'tæljən] adj italiano ▷ n italiano/a;
(Ling) italiano
**italic** [ɪ'tælɪk] adj cursivo; **italics** npl cursiva
sg
**Italy** ['ɪtəlɪ] n Italia
**itch** [ɪtʃ] n picazón f ▷ vi (part of body) picar;
**to be ~ing to do sth** rabiar por or morirse
de ganas de hacer algo; **itchy** adj: **to be
itchy** picar; **my hand is itchy** me pica la
mano
**it'd** ['ɪtd] = **it would; it had**
**item** ['aɪtəm] n artículo; (on agenda) asunto
(a tratar); (also: **news ~**) noticia
**itinerary** [aɪ'tɪnərərɪ] n itinerario
**it'll** ['ɪtl] = **it will; it shall**
**its** [ɪts] adj su
**it's** [ɪts] = **it is; it has**

**itself** [ɪt'sɛlf] pron (reflexive) sí mismo/a;
(emphatic) él mismo/a
**ITV** n abbr (BRIT: = Independent Television)
cadena de televisión comercial
**I've** [aɪv] = **I have**
**ivory** ['aɪvərɪ] n marfil m
**ivy** ['aɪvɪ] n hiedra

# J

**jab** [dʒæb] n (Med: inf) pinchazo ▷ vt: **to ~ sth into sth** clavar algo en algo

**jack** [dʒæk] n (Aut) gato; (Cards) sota

**jacket** ['dʒækɪt] n chaqueta, americana, saco (LAM); (of book) sobrecubierta; **jacket potato** n patata asada (con piel)

**jackpot** ['dʒækpɔt] n premio gordo

**Jacuzzi®** [dʒə'ku:zɪ] n jacuzzi® m

**jagged** ['dʒægɪd] adj dentado

**jail** [dʒeɪl] n cárcel f ▷ vt encarcelar; **jail sentence** n pena f de cárcel

**jam** [dʒæm] n mermelada; (also: **traffic ~**) embotellamiento; (difficulty) apuro ▷ vt (passage etc) obstruir; (mechanism, drawer etc) atascar; (Radio) interferir ▷ vi atascarse, trabarse; **to ~ sth into sth** meter algo a la fuerza en algo

**Jamaica** [dʒə'meɪkə] n Jamaica

**jammed** [dʒæmd] adj atascado

**Jan.** abbr (= January) ene

**janitor** ['dʒænɪtər] n (caretaker) portero, conserje m

**January** ['dʒænjuərɪ] n enero

**Japan** [dʒə'pæn] n (el) Japón; **Japanese** [dʒæpə'ni:z] adj japonés/esa ▷ n (pl inv) japonés/esa m/f; (Ling) japonés m

**jar** n (glass: large) jarra; (: small) tarro ▷ vi (sound) chirriar; (colours) desentonar

**jargon** ['dʒɑ:gən] n jerga

**javelin** ['dʒævlɪn] n jabalina

**jaw** [dʒɔ:] n mandíbula

**jazz** [dʒæz] n jazz m

**jealous** ['dʒɛləs] adj celoso; (envious) envidioso; **jealousy** n celos mpl; envidia

**jeans** [dʒi:nz] npl (pantalones mpl) vaqueros mpl or tejanos mpl, bluejean m inv (LAM)

**Jello®** ['dʒɛləu] n (US) gelatina

**jelly** ['dʒɛlɪ] n (jam) jalea; (dessert etc) gelatina; **jellyfish** n medusa

**jeopardize** ['dʒɛpədaɪz] vt arriesgar, poner en peligro

**jerk** [dʒə:k] n (jolt) sacudida; (wrench) tirón m; (US inf) imbécil mf ▷ vt tirar bruscamente de ▷ vi (vehicle) dar una sacudida

**Jersey** ['dʒə:zɪ] n Jersey m

**jersey** ['dʒə:zɪ] n jersey m; (fabric) tejido de punto

**Jesus** ['dʒi:zəs] n Jesús m

**jet** [dʒɛt] n (of gas, liquid) chorro; (Aviat) avión m a reacción; **jet lag** n desorientación f por desfase horario; **jet-ski** vi practicar el motociclismo acuático

**jetty** ['dʒɛtɪ] n muelle m, embarcadero

**Jew** [dʒu:] n judío/a

**jewel** ['dʒu:əl] n joya; (in watch) rubí m; **jeweller, (US) jeweler** n joyero/a; **jeweller's (shop)** joyería; **jewellery, (US) jewelry** n joyas fpl, alhajas fpl

**Jewish** ['dʒu:ɪʃ] adj judío

**jigsaw** ['dʒɪgsɔ:] n (also: **~ puzzle**) rompecabezas m inv, puzle m

**job** [dʒɔb] n (task) tarea; (post) empleo; **it's a good ~ that ...** menos mal que ...; **just the ~!** ¡justo lo que necesito!; **that's not my ~** eso no me incumbe or toca a mí; **job centre** n (BRIT) oficina de empleo; **jobless** adj sin trabajo

**jockey** ['dʒɔkɪ] n jockey mf ▷ vi: **to ~ for position** maniobrar para sacar delantera

**jog** [dʒɔg] vt empujar (ligeramente) ▷ vi (run) hacer footing; **to ~ sb's memory** refrescar la memoria a algn; **jogging** n footing m

**join** [dʒɔɪn] vt (things) unir, juntar; (club) hacerse socio de; (Pol: party) afiliarse a; (meet: people) reunirse con; (fig) unirse a ▷ vi (roads) empalmar; (rivers) confluir ▷ n juntura; **join in** vi tomar parte, participar ▷ vt fus tomar parte or participar en; **join up** vi unirse; (Mil) alistarse

**joiner** ['dʒɔɪnər] n carpintero/a

**joint** [dʒɔɪnt] n (Tech) juntura, unión f; (Anat) articulación f; (BRIT Culin) pieza de carne (para asar); (inf: place) garito; (of cannabis) porro ▷ adj (common) común; (combined) conjunto; **joint account** n (with bank etc) cuenta común; **jointly** adv en común; (together) conjuntamente

**joke** [dʒəuk] n chiste m; (also: **practical ~**) broma ▷ vi bromear; **to play a ~ on** gastar una broma a; **joker** n (Cards) comodín m

**jolly** ['dʒɔlɪ] adj (merry) alegre; (enjoyable) divertido ▷ adv (inf) muy

**jolt** [dʒəult] n (shake) sacudida; (shock) susto ▷ vt (physically) sacudir; (emotionally) asustar

**Jordan** ['dʒɔ:dən] n (country) Jordania; (river) Jordán m

**journal** ['dʒəːnl] n (*magazine*) revista; (*diary*) diario; **journalism** n periodismo; **journalist** n periodista mf
**journey** ['dʒəːnɪ] n viaje m; (*distance covered*) trayecto
**joy** [dʒɔɪ] n alegría; **joyrider** n persona que se da una vuelta en un coche robado
**joystick** ['dʒɔɪstɪk] n (*Aviat*) palanca de mando; (*Comput*) palanca de control
**Jr** abbr = **junior**
**judge** [dʒʌdʒ] n juez mf ▷ vt juzgar; (*estimate*) considerar; **judg(e)ment** n juicio
**judo** ['dʒuːdəu] n judo
**jug** [dʒʌg] n jarra
**juggle** ['dʒʌgl] vi hacer juegos malabares; **juggler** n malabarista mf
**juice** [dʒuːs] n jugo, zumo (*SP*); **juicy** adj jugoso
**Jul.** abbr (= *July*) jul
**July** [dʒuːˈlaɪ] n julio
**jumble** ['dʒʌmbl] n revoltijo ▷ vt (*also*: ~ **up**) revolver; **jumble sale** n (*BRIT*) mercadillo

### JUMBLE SALE

En cada *jumble sale* pueden comprarse
todo tipo de objetos baratos de segunda
mano, especialmente ropa, juguetes,
libros, vajillas y muebles. Suelen
organizarse en los locales de un colegio,
iglesia, ayuntamiento o similar, con
fines benéficos, bien en ayuda de una
organización benéfica conocida o para
solucionar problemas más concretos de la
comunidad.

**jumbo** ['dʒʌmbəu], **jumbo jet** n jumbo
**jump** [dʒʌmp] vi saltar, dar saltos; (*increase*) aumentar ▷ vt saltar ▷ n salto; (*increase*) aumento; **to ~ the queue** (*BRIT*) colarse
**jumper** ['dʒʌmpəʳ] n (*BRIT*: *pullover*) jersey m, suéter m; (*US*: *dress*) pichi m
**jump leads**, (*US*) **jumper cables** npl cables mpl puente de batería
**Jun.** abbr = **junior**
**junction** ['dʒʌŋkʃən] n (*BRIT*: *of roads*) cruce m; (*Rail*) empalme m
**June** [dʒuːn] n junio
**jungle** ['dʒʌŋgl] n selva, jungla
**junior** ['dʒuːnɪəʳ] adj (*in age*) menor, más joven; (*position*) subalterno ▷ n menor mf, joven mf; **junior high school** n (*US*) centro de educación secundaria; **junior school** n (*BRIT*) escuela primaria
**junk** [dʒʌŋk] n (*cheap goods*) baratijas fpl; (*rubbish*) basura; **junk food** n comida basura or de plástico
**junkie** ['dʒʌŋkɪ] n (*inf*) yonqui mf
**junk mail** n propaganda (buzoneada)

**Jupiter** ['dʒuːpɪtəʳ] n (*Mythology, Astro*) Júpiter m
**jurisdiction** [dʒuərɪsˈdɪkʃən] n jurisdicción f; **it falls** or **comes within/outside our ~** es/no es de nuestra competencia
**jury** ['dʒuərɪ] n jurado
**just** [dʒʌst] adj justo ▷ adv (*exactly*) exactamente; (*only*) sólo, solamente; **he's ~ done it/left** acaba de hacerlo/irse; **~ right** perfecto; **~ two o'clock** las dos en punto; **she's ~ as clever as you** es tan lista como tú; **~ as well that ...** menos mal que ...; **~ as he was leaving** en el momento en que se marchaba; **~ before/enough** justo antes/lo suficiente; **~ here** aquí mismo; **he ~ missed** falló por poco; **~ listen to this** escucha esto un momento
**justice** ['dʒʌstɪs] n justicia; (*US*: *judge*) juez mf; **to do ~ to** (*fig*) hacer justicia a
**justification** [dʒʌstɪfɪˈkeɪʃən] n justificación f
**justify** ['dʒʌstɪfaɪ] vt justificar; (*text*) alinear
**jut** [dʒʌt] vi (*also*: ~ **out**) sobresalir
**juvenile** ['dʒuːvənaɪl] adj (*humour, mentality*) infantil ▷ n menor mf de edad

# K

**K** *abbr* (= *one thousand*) mil; (= *kilobyte*) K

**kangaroo** [kæŋgəˈruː] *n* canguro

**karaoke** [kɑːrəˈəʊkɪ] *n* karaoke

**karate** [kəˈrɑːtɪ] *n* karate *m*

**kebab** [kəˈbæb] *n* pincho moruno

**keel** [kiːl] *n* quilla; **on an even ~** (*fig*) en equilibrio

**keen** [kiːn] *adj* (*interest, desire*) grande, vivo; (*eye, intelligence*) agudo; (*competition*) reñido; (*edge*) afilado; (*BRIT: eager*) entusiasta; **to be ~ to do** *or* **on doing sth** tener muchas ganas de hacer algo; **to be ~ on sth/sb** interesarse por algo/algn

**keep** [kiːp] (*pt, pp* **kept**) *vt* (*retain, preserve*) guardar; (*hold back*) quedarse con; (*shop*) ser propietario de; (*feed: family etc*) mantener; (*promise*) cumplir; (*chickens, bees etc*) criar ▷ *vi* (*food*) conservarse; (*remain*) seguir, continuar ▷ *n* (*of castle*) torreón *m*; (*food etc*) comida, sustento; **to ~ doing sth** seguir haciendo algo; **to ~ sb from doing sth** impedir a algn hacer algo; **to ~ sb happy** tener a algn contento; **to ~ a place tidy** mantener un lugar limpio; **to ~ sth to o.s.** no decirle a nadie; **to ~ time** (*clock*) mantener la hora exacta; **keep away** *vt*: **to ~ sth/sb away from sb** mantener algo/a algn apartado de ▷ *vi*: **to ~ away (from)** mantenerse apartado (de); **keep back** *vt* (*crowd, tears*) contener; (*money*) quedarse con; (*conceal: information*): **to ~ sth back from sb** ocultar algo a algn ▷ *vi* hacerse a un lado; **keep off** *vt* (*dog, person*) mantener a distancia ▷ *vi* evitar; **~ your hands off!** ¡no toques!; **"~ off the grass"** "prohibido pisar el césped"; **keep on** *vi*: **to ~ on doing** seguir *or* continuar haciendo; **to ~ on (about sth)** no parar de hablar (de algo); **keep out** *vi* (*stay out*) permanecer fuera; **"~ out"** "prohibida la entrada"; **keep up** *vt*

mantener, conservar ▷ *vi* no rezagarse; **to ~ up with** (*pace*) ir al paso de; (*level*) mantenerse a la altura de; **keeper** *n* guarda *mf*; **keeping** *n* (*care*) cuidado; **in keeping with** de acuerdo con

**kennel** [ˈkɛnl] *n* perrera; **kennels** *npl* residencia canina

**Kenya** [ˈkɛnjə] *n* Kenia

**kept** [kɛpt] *pt, pp of* **keep**

**kerb** [kəːb] *n* (*BRIT*) bordillo

**kerosene** [ˈkɛrəsiːn] *n* keroseno

**ketchup** [ˈkɛtʃəp] *n* salsa de tomate, ketchup *m*

**kettle** [ˈkɛtl] *n* hervidor *m*

**key** [kiː] *n* llave *f*; (*Mus*) tono; (*of piano, typewriter*) tecla; (*on map*) clave *f* ▷ *cpd* (*vital: position, issue, industry etc*) clave ▷ *vt* (*also:* **~ in**) teclear; **keyboard** *n* teclado; **keyhole** *n* ojo (de la cerradura); **keypad** *n* teclado; **keyring** *n* llavero

**kg** *abbr* (= *kilogram*) kg

**khaki** [ˈkɑːkɪ] *n* caqui

**kick** [kɪk] *vt* (*person*) dar una patada a; (*inf: habit*) quitarse de ▷ *vi* (*horse*) dar coces ▷ *n* patada; puntapié *m*; (*thrill*): **he does it for ~s** lo hace por pura diversión; **kick off** *vi* (*Sport*) hacer el saque inicial; **kick-off** *n* saque inicial; **the kick-off is at 10 o'clock** el partido empieza a las diez

**kid** [kɪd] *n* (*inf: child*) chiquillo/a; (*animal*) cabrito; (*leather*) cabritilla ▷ *vi* (*inf*) bromear

**kidnap** [ˈkɪdnæp] *vt* secuestrar; **kidnapping** *n* secuestro

**kidney** [ˈkɪdnɪ] *n* riñón *m*; **kidney bean** *n* judía, alubia

**kill** [kɪl] *vt* matar; (*murder*) asesinar ▷ *n* matanza; **to ~ time** matar el tiempo; **killer** *n* asesino/a; **killing** *n* (*one*) asesinato; (*several*) matanza; **to make a killing** hacer su agosto

**kiln** [kɪln] *n* horno

**kilo** [ˈkiːləʊ] *n abbr* (= *kilogram(me)*) kilo; **kilobyte** [ˈkɪləʊbaɪt] *n* (*Comput*) kilobyte *m*; **kilogram(me)** [ˈkɪləʊgræm] *n* kilogramo; **kilometre**, (*US*) **kilometer** [ˈkɪləmiːtə] *n* kilómetro; **kilowatt** [ˈkɪləʊwɔt] *n* kilovatio

**kilt** [kɪlt] *n* falda escocesa

**kin** [kɪn] *n* parientes *mpl*

**kind** [kaɪnd] *adj* amable, atento ▷ *n* clase *f*, especie *f*; (*species*) género; **in ~** (*Comm*) en especie; **a ~ of** una especie de; **to be two of a ~** ser tal para cual

**kindergarten** [ˈkɪndəgɑːtn] *n* jardín *m* de infancia

**kindly** [ˈkaɪndlɪ] *adj* bondadoso; (*gentle*) cariñoso ▷ *adv* bondadosamente, amablemente; **will you ~ ...** sería usted tan amable de ...

**kindness** ['kaɪndnɪs] n bondad f,
amabilidad f; (act) favor m
**king** [kɪŋ] n rey m; **kingdom** n reino;
**kingfisher** n martín m pescador; **king-
size(d)** adj de tamaño gigante; **king-size
bed** cama de matrimonio extragrande
**kiosk** ['ki:ɔsk] n quiosco; (BRIT Tel) cabina
**kipper** ['kɪpəʳ] n arenque m ahumado
**kiss** [kɪs] n beso ▷ vt besar; **~ of life** (artificial
respiration) respiración f boca a boca; **to ~
(each other)** besarse
**kit** [kɪt] n equipo; (set of tools etc) (caja de)
herramientas fpl; (assembly kit) juego de armar
**kitchen** ['kɪtʃɪn] n cocina
**kite** [kaɪt] n (toy) cometa
**kitten** ['kɪtn] n gatito/a
**kiwi** ['ki:wi:] n (also: **~ fruit**) kiwi m
**km** abbr (= kilometre) km
**km/h** abbr (= kilometres per hour) km/h
**knack** [næk] n: **to have the ~ of doing sth**
tener facilidad para hacer algo
**knee** [ni:] n rodilla; **kneecap** n rótula
**kneel** (pt, pp **knelt**) [ni:l, nɛlt] vi (also: **~ down**)
arrodillarse
**knelt** [nɛlt] pt, pp of **kneel**
**knew** [nju:] pt of **know**
**knickers** ['nɪkəz] npl (BRIT) bragas fpl
**knife** [naɪf] (pl **knives**) n cuchillo ▷ vt
acuchillar
**knight** [naɪt] n caballero; (Chess) caballo
**knit** [nɪt] vt tejer, tricotar ▷ vi hacer punto,
tricotar; (bones) soldarse; **knitting** n labor f
de punto; **knitting needle**, (US) **knit pin** n
aguja de hacer punto or tejer; **knitwear** n
prendas fpl de punto
**knives** [naɪvz] pl of **knife**
**knob** [nɔb] n (of door) pomo; (of stick) puño;
(on radio, TV) botón m
**knock** [nɔk] vt (strike) golpear; (bump into)
chocar contra; (inf) criticar ▷ vi (at door
etc): **to ~ at/on** llamar a ▷ n golpe m; (on
door) llamada; **knock down** vt atropellar;
**knock off** vi (inf: finish) salir del trabajo
▷ vt (inf: steal) birlar; **knock out** vt dejar sin
sentido; (Boxing) poner fuera de combate,
dejar K.O.; (in competition) eliminar; **knock
over** vt (object) tirar; (pedestrian) atropellar;
**knockout** n (Boxing) K.O. m, knockout m
**knot** [nɔt] n nudo ▷ vt anudar
**know** (pt **knew**, pp **known**) [nəu, nju:,
nəun] vt saber; (person, author, place)
conocer; (recognize) reconocer ▷ vi: **to ~
how to swim** saber nadar; **to ~ about** or
**of sb/sth** saber de algn/algo; **know-all**
n sabelotodo m inv f inv; **know-how** n
conocimientos mpl; **knowing** adj (look etc)
de complicidad; **knowingly** adv (purposely)
a sabiendas; (smile, look) con complicidad;
**know-it-all** n (US) = **know-all**

**knowledge** ['nɔlɪdʒ] n conocimiento;
(learning) saber m, conocimientos mpl;
**knowledgeable** adj entendido
**known** [nəun] pp of **know** ▷ adj (thief, facts)
conocido; (expert) reconocido
**knuckle** ['nʌkl] n nudillo
**koala** [kəu'ɑ:lə] n (also: **~ bear**) koala m
**Koran** [kɔ'rɑ:n] n Corán m
**Korea** [kə'rɪə] n Corea; **Korean** adj, n
coreano/a
**kosher** ['kəuʃəʳ] adj autorizado por la ley
judía
**Kosovar** ['kɔsəvɑ:ʳ], **Kosovan** ['kɔsəvən]
adj kosovar; **Kosovo** ['kɒsəvəu] n Kosovo m
**Kremlin** ['kremlɪn] n: **the ~** el Kremlin
**Kuwait** [ku'weɪt] n Kuwait m

**L** *abbr* (BRIT Aut = *learner*) L

**lab** [læb] *n abbr* = **laboratory**

**label** ['leɪbl] *n* etiqueta ▷ *vt* poner una etiqueta a

**labor** ['leɪbəʳ] *n, vb* (US) = **labour**

**laboratory** [ləˈbɒrətərɪ] *n* laboratorio

**Labor Day** *n* (US) día *m* de los trabajadores (*primer lunes de septiembre*)

**labor union** *n* (US) sindicato

**labour,** (US) **labor** ['leɪbəʳ] *n* (*task*) trabajo; (*also:* **~ force**) mano *f* de obra; (*Med*) (dolores *mpl* de) parto ▷ *vi*: **to ~ (at)** trabajar (en) ▷ *vt*: **to ~ a point** insistir en un punto; **to be in ~** (*Med*) estar de parto; **the L~ party** (BRIT) el partido laborista, los laboristas *mpl*; **labourer** *n* peón *m*; (*on farm*) peón *m*; (*day labourer*) jornalero

**lace** [leɪs] *n* encaje *m*; (*of shoe etc*) cordón *m* ▷ *vt* (*shoes: also:* **~ up**) atarse

**lack** [læk] *n* (*absence*) falta ▷ *vt* faltarle a algn, carecer de; **through** *or* **for ~ of** por falta de; **to be ~ing** faltar, no haber; **to be ~ing in sth** faltarle a algn algo

**lacquer** ['lækəʳ] *n* laca

**lacy** ['leɪsɪ] *adj* (*like lace*) como de encaje

**lad** [læd] *n* muchacho, chico

**ladder** ['lædəʳ] *n* escalera (de mano); (BRIT: *in tights*) carrera

**ladle** ['leɪdl] *n* cucharón *m*

**lady** ['leɪdɪ] *n* señora; (*distinguished, noble*) dama; **young ~** señorita; **the ladies' (room)** los servicios de señoras; **"ladies and gentlemen ..."** "señoras y caballeros ..."; **ladybird** *n*, (US) **ladybug** *n* mariquita

**lag** [læg] *vi* (*also:* **~ behind**) retrasarse, quedarse atrás ▷ *vt* (*pipes*) revestir

**lager** ['lɑːgəʳ] *n* cerveza (rubia)

**lagoon** [ləˈguːn] *n* laguna

**laid** [leɪd] *pt, pp of* **lay**

**laid-back** [leɪd'bæk] *adj* (*inf*) relajado

**lain** [leɪn] *pp of* **lie**

**lake** [leɪk] *n* lago

**lamb** [læm] *n* cordero; (*meat*) carne *f* de cordero

**lame** [leɪm] *adj* cojo; (*excuse*) poco convincente

**lament** [ləˈmɛnt] *n* lamento ▷ *vt* lamentarse de

**lamp** [læmp] *n* lámpara; **lamppost** *n* (BRIT) farola; **lampshade** *n* pantalla

**land** [lænd] *n* tierra; (*country*) país *m*; (*piece of land*) terreno; (*estate*) tierras *fpl*, finca ▷ *vi* (*from ship*) desembarcar; (*Aviat*) aterrizar; (*fig: fall*) caer ▷ *vt* (*passengers, goods*) desembarcar; **to ~ sb with sth** (*inf*) hacer cargar a algn con algo; **landing** *n* aterrizaje *m*; (*of staircase*) rellano; **landing card** *n* tarjeta de desembarque; **landlady** *n* (*owner*) dueña; (*of boarding house*) patrona; **landline** *n* (*teléfono*) fijo; **landlord** *n* propietario; (*of pub etc*) patrón *m*; **landmark** *n* lugar *m* conocido; **to be a landmark** (*fig*) hacer época; **landowner** *n* terrateniente *mf*; **landscape** *n* paisaje *m*; **landslide** *n* (*Geo*) corrimiento de tierras; (*fig: Pol*) victoria arrolladora

**lane** [leɪn] *n* (*in country*) camino; (*Aut*) carril *m*; (*in race*) calle *f*

**language** ['læŋgwɪdʒ] *n* lenguaje *m*; (*national tongue*) idioma *m*, lengua; **bad ~** palabrotas *fpl*; **language laboratory** *n* laboratorio de idiomas; **language school** *n* academia de idiomas

**lantern** ['læntn] *n* linterna, farol *m*

**lap** [læp] *n* (*of track*) vuelta; (*of body*) regazo ▷ *vi* (*waves*) chapotear; **to sit on sb's ~** sentarse en las rodillas de algn; **lap up** *vt* beber a lengüetadas *or* con la lengua

**lapel** [ləˈpɛl] *n* solapa

**lapse** [læps] *n* fallo; (*moral*) desliz *m* ▷ *vi* (*expire*) caducar; (*time*) pasar, transcurrir; **to ~ into bad habits** volver a las andadas; **~ of time** lapso, intervalo

**lard** [lɑːd] *n* manteca (de cerdo)

**larder** ['lɑːdəʳ] *n* despensa

**large** [lɑːdʒ] *adj* grande; **at ~** (*free*) en libertad; (*generally*) en general; **largely** *adv* (*mostly*) en su mayor parte; (*introducing reason*) en gran parte; **large-scale** *adj* (*map, drawing*) a gran escala; (*reforms, business activities*) importante

▌ Be careful not to translate *large* by the Spanish word *largo*.

**lark** [lɑːk] *n* (*bird*) alondra; (*joke*) broma

**larrikin** ['lærɪkɪn] *n* (AUST, NZ *inf*) gamberro/a

**laryngitis** [lærɪn'dʒaɪtɪs] *n* laringitis *f*

**lasagne** [ləˈzænjə] *n* lasaña

**laser** ['leɪzəʳ] *n* láser *m*; **laser printer** *n* impresora láser

**lash** [læʃ] n latigazo; (also: **eye~**) pestaña ▷ vt azotar; (tie) atar; **lash out** vi: **to ~ out (at sb)** (hit) arremeter (contra algn); **to ~ out against sb** lanzar invectivas contra algn

**lass** [læs] n chica

**last** [lɑ:st] adj último; (final) final ▷ adv (finally) por último ▷ vi durar; (continue) continuar, seguir; **~ night** anoche; **~ week** la semana pasada; **at ~** por fin; **~ but one** penúltimo; **lastly** adv por último, finalmente; **last-minute** adj de última hora

**latch** [lætʃ] n pestillo; **latch on to** vt fus (person) pegarse a; (idea) aferrarse a

**late** [leɪt] adj (not on time) tarde, atrasado; (deceased) fallecido ▷ adv tarde; (behind time, schedule) con retraso; **of ~** últimamente; **~ at night** a última hora de la noche; **in ~ May** hacia fines de mayo; **the ~ Mr X** el difunto Sr. X; **latecomer** n recién llegado/a; **lately** adv últimamente; **later** adj (date etc) posterior; (version etc) más reciente ▷ adv más tarde, después; **latest** ['leɪtɪst] adj último; **at the latest** a más tardar

**lather** ['lɑːðəʳ] n espuma (de jabón) ▷ vt enjabonar

**Latin** ['lætɪn] n latín m ▷ adj latino; **Latin America** n América Latina; **Latin American** adj, n latinoamericano/a

**latitude** ['lætɪtjuːd] n latitud f; (fig) libertad f

**latter** ['lætəʳ] adj último; (of two) segundo ▷ n: **the ~** el último, éste

**laugh** [lɑːf] n risa ▷ vi reírse, reír; **(to do sth) for a ~** (hacer algo) en broma; **laugh at** vt fus reírse de; **laughter** n risa

**launch** [lɔːntʃ] n (boat) lancha ▷ vt (ship) botar; (rocket, plan) lanzar; (fig) comenzar; **launch into** vt fus lanzarse a

**launder** ['lɔːndəʳ] vt lavar

**Launderette®** [lɔːn'drɛt], (us) **Laundromat®** ['lɔːndrəmæt] n lavandería (automática)

**laundry** ['lɔːndrɪ] n lavandería; (clothes: dirty) ropa sucia; (: clean) colada

**lava** ['lɑːvə] n lava

**lavatory** ['lævətərɪ] n wáter m

**lavender** ['lævəndəʳ] n lavanda

**lavish** ['lævɪʃ] adj abundante; **~ with** pródigo en ▷ vt: **to ~ sth on sb** colmar a algn de algo

**law** [lɔː] n ley f; (study) derecho; (of game) regla; **lawful** adj legítimo, lícito; **lawless** adj (act) ilegal

**lawn** [lɔːn] n césped m; **lawnmower** n cortacésped m

**lawsuit** ['lɔːsuːt] n pleito

**lawyer** ['lɔːjəʳ] n abogado/a; (for sales, wills etc) notario/a

**lax** [læks] adj (discipline) relajado; (person) negligente

**laxative** ['læksətɪv] n laxante m

**lay** [leɪ] pt of **lie** ▷ adj laico; (not expert) lego ▷ vt (pt, pp **laid**) (place) colocar; (eggs, table) poner; (trap) tender; (carpet) extender; **lay down** vt (pen etc) dejar; (rules etc) establecer; **to ~ down the law** imponer las normas; **lay off** vt (workers) despedir; **lay on** vt (meal, facilities) proveer; **lay out** vt (display) exponer; **lay-by** n (BRIT Aut) área de descanso

**layer** ['leɪəʳ] n capa

**layman** ['leɪmən] n lego

**layout** ['leɪaʊt] n (design) plan m, trazado; (Press) composición f

**lazy** ['leɪzɪ] adj perezoso, vago

**lb.** abbr (weight) = **pound**

**lead¹** (pt, pp **led**) [liːd, lɛd] n (front position) delantera; (clue) pista; (Elec) cable m; (for dog) correa; (Theat) papel m principal ▷ vt conducir; (be leader of) dirigir; (Sport) ir en cabeza de ▷ vi ir primero; **to be in the ~** (Sport) llevar la delantera; (fig) ir a la cabeza; **lead up to** vt fus (events) conducir a; (in conversation) preparar el terreno para

**lead²** [lɛd] n (metal) plomo; (in pencil) mina

**leader** ['liːdəʳ] n jefe/a m/f, líder m; **leadership** n dirección f; **leadership qualities** dotes mpl de mando

**lead-free** ['lɛdfriː] adj sin plomo

**leading** ['liːdɪŋ] adj (main) principal; (first) primero; (front) delantero

**lead singer** [liːd-] n cantante mf

**leaf** [liːf] (pl **leaves**) n hoja; **to turn over a new ~** hacer borrón y cuenta nueva; **leaf through** vt fus (book) hojear

**leaflet** ['liːflɪt] n folleto

**league** [liːg] n sociedad f; (Football) liga; **to be in ~ with** estar confabulado con

**leak** [liːk] n (of liquid, gas) escape m, fuga; (in pipe) agujero; (in roof) gotera; (fig: of information, in security) filtración f ▷ vi (ship) hacer agua; (pipe) tener un escape; (roof) tener goteras; (also: **~ out**: liquid, gas) escaparse ▷ vt (fig) filtrar

**lean** [liːn] (pt, pp **leaned** or **leant**) adj (thin) flaco; (meat) magro ▷ vt: **to ~ sth on sth** apoyar algo en algo ▷ vi (slope) inclinarse; **to ~ against** apoyarse contra; **to ~ on** apoyarse en; **lean forward** vi inclinarse hacia adelante; **lean over** vi inclinarse; **leaning** n: **leaning (towards)** inclinación f (hacia)

**leant** [lɛnt] pt, pp of **lean**

**leap** [liːp] n salto ▷ vi (pt, pp **leaped** or **leapt**) saltar

**leapt** [lɛpt] pt, pp of **leap**

**leap year** n año bisiesto

**learn** (pt, pp **learned** or **learnt**) [lə:n, -t] vt
aprender; (come to know of) enterarse de ▷ vi
aprender; **to ~ how to do sth** aprender a
hacer algo; **learner** n (BRIT: also: **learner
driver**) conductor(a) m/f en prácticas;
see also **L-plates**; **learning** n saber m,
conocimientos mpl

**learnt** [lə:nt] pp of **learn**

**lease** [li:s] n arriendo ▷ vt arrendar

**leash** [li:ʃ] n correa

**least** [li:st] adj (slightest) menor, más
pequeño; (smallest amount of) mínimo
▷ adv menos; **the ~ expensive car** el coche
menos caro; **at ~** por lo menos, al menos;
**not in the ~** en absoluto

**leather** ['lɛðə'] n cuero

**leave** [li:v] (pt, pp **left**) vt dejar; (go away
from) abandonar ▷ vi irse; (train) salir ▷ n
permiso; **to be left** quedar, sobrar; **there's
some milk left over** sobra or queda algo de
leche; **on ~** de permiso; **leave behind** vt (on
purpose) dejar (atrás); (accidentally) olvidar;
**leave out** vt omitir

**leaves** [li:vz] pl of **leaf**

**Lebanon** ['lɛbənən] n: **the ~** el Líbano

**lecture** ['lɛktʃə'] n conferencia; (Scol)
clase f ▷ vi dar clase(s) ▷ vt (reprove) echar
una reprimenda a; **to give a ~ on** dar una
conferencia sobre; **lecture hall** n sala
de conferencias; (Univ) aula; **lecturer** n
conferenciante mf; (BRIT: at university)
profesor(a) m/f; **lecture theatre** n
= **lecture hall**

**led** [lɛd] pt, pp of **lead¹**

**ledge** [lɛdʒ] n (on wall) repisa; (of window)
alféizar m; (of mountain) saliente m

**leek** [li:k] n puerro

**left** [lɛft] pt, pp of **leave** ▷ adj izquierdo;
(remaining): **there are two ~** quedan dos ▷ n
izquierda ▷ adv a la izquierda; **on** or **to the ~**
a la izquierda; **the L~** (Pol) la izquierda;
**left-hand** adj: **the left-hand side** la
izquierda; **left-hand drive** n conducción f
por la izquierda; **left-handed** adj zurdo;
**left-luggage locker** n (BRIT) consigna f
automática; **left-luggage (office)** n (BRIT)
consigna; **left-overs** npl sobras fpl;
**left-wing** adj (Pol) de izquierda(s),
izquierdista

**leg** [lɛg] n pierna; (of animal, chair) pata;
(Culin: of meat) pierna; (: of chicken) pata; (of
journey) etapa

**legacy** ['lɛgəsɪ] n herencia

**legal** ['li:gl] adj (permitted by law) lícito;
(of law) legal; **legal holiday** n (US) fiesta
oficial; **legalize** vt legalizar; **legally** adv
legalmente

**legend** ['lɛdʒənd] n leyenda; **legendary** adj
legendario

**leggings** ['lɛgɪŋz] npl mallas fpl, leggins mpl

**legible** ['lɛdʒəbl] adj legible

**legislation** [lɛdʒɪs'leɪʃən] n legislación f

**legislative** ['lɛdʒɪslətɪv] adj legislativo

**legitimate** [lɪ'dʒɪtɪmət] adj legítimo

**leisure** ['lɛʒə'] n ocio, tiempo libre; **at ~** con
tranquilidad; **leisure centre** n
polideportivo; **leisurely** adj sin prisa; lento

**lemon** ['lɛmən] n limón m; **lemonade** n
(fizzy) gaseosa; **lemon tea** n té m con limón

**lend** [lɛnd] (pt, pp **lent**) vt: **to ~ sth to sb**
prestar algo a algn

**length** [lɛŋθ] n (size) largo, longitud f;
(of rope etc) largo; (of wood, string) trozo;
(amount of time) duración f; **at ~** (at last)
por fin, finalmente; (lengthily) largamente;
**lengthen** vt alargar ▷ vi alargarse;
**lengthways** adv a lo largo; **lengthy** adj
largo, extenso

**lens** [lɛnz] n (of spectacles) lente f; (of camera)
objetivo

**Lent** [lɛnt] n Cuaresma

**lent** [lɛnt] pt, pp of **lend**

**lentil** ['lɛntl] n lenteja

**Leo** ['li:əu] n Leo

**leopard** ['lɛpəd] n leopardo

**leotard** ['li:əta:d] n malla

**leprosy** ['lɛprəsɪ] n lepra

**lesbian** ['lɛzbɪən] n lesbiana

**less** [lɛs] adj (in size, degree etc) menor;
(in quantity) menos ▷ pron, adv menos;
**~ than half** menos de la mitad; **~ than ever**
menos que nunca; **~ 5%** menos el cinco por
ciento; **~ and ~** cada vez menos; **the ~ he
works ...** cuanto menos trabaja ...; **lessen**
vi disminuir, reducirse ▷ vt disminuir,
reducir; **lesser** ['lɛsə'] adj menor; **to a
lesser extent** or **degree** en menor grado

**lesson** ['lɛsn] n clase f; **it taught him a ~**
(fig) le sirvió de lección

**let** (pt, pp **let**) [lɛt] vt (allow) dejar, permitir;
(BRIT: lease) alquilar; **to ~ sb do sth** dejar que
algn haga algo; **to ~ sb know sth** comunicar
algo a algn; **~'s go** ¡vamos!; **~ him come**
que venga; **"to ~"** "se alquila"; **let down** vt
(tyre) desinflar; (disappoint) defraudar; **let in**
vt dejar entrar; (visitor etc) hacer pasar; **let
off** vt dejar escapar; (firework etc) disparar;
(bomb) accionar; **let out** vt dejar salir

**lethal** ['li:θl] adj (weapon) mortífero; (poison,
wound) mortal

**letter** ['lɛtə'] n (of alphabet) letra;
(correspondence) carta; **letterbox** n (BRIT)
buzón m

**lettuce** ['lɛtɪs] n lechuga

**leukaemia**, (US) **leukemia** [lu:'ki:mɪə] n
leucemia

**level** ['lɛvl] adj (flat) llano ▷ adv a nivel ▷ n
nivel m; (height) altura ▷ vt nivelar, allanar;

(*destroy: building*) derribar; **to be ~ with** estar a nivel de; **on the ~** (*fig: honest*) en serio; **level crossing** n (BRIT) paso a nivel; *see also* **A levels**

**lever** ['li:və<sup>r</sup>] n palanca ▷ vt: **to ~ up** levantar con palanca; **leverage** n (*fig: influence*) influencia

**levy** ['lɛvɪ] n impuesto ▷ vt exigir, recaudar

**liability** [laɪə'bɪlətɪ] n (*pej: person, thing*) estorbo, lastre m; (*Law: responsibility*) responsabilidad f; (*handicap*) desventaja

**liable** ['laɪəbl] adj (*subject*): **~ to** sujeto a; (*responsible*): **~ for** responsable de; (*likely*): **~ to do** propenso a hacer

**liaise** [li:'eɪz] vi: **to ~ (with)** colaborar (con)

**liar** ['laɪə<sup>r</sup>] n mentiroso/a

**liberal** ['lɪbərl] adj liberal; (*generous*): **~ with** generoso con; **Liberal Democrat** n (BRIT) demócrata mf liberal

**liberate** ['lɪbəreɪt] vt (*people: from poverty etc*) librar; (*prisoner*) libertar; (*country*) liberar

**liberation** [lɪbə'reɪʃən] n liberación f

**liberty** ['lɪbətɪ] n libertad f; **to be at ~** (*criminal*) estar en libertad; **to be ~ to do** estar libre para hacer; **to take the ~ of doing sth** tomarse la libertad de hacer algo

**Libra** ['li:brə] n Libra

**librarian** [laɪ'brɛərɪən] n bibliotecario/a

**library** ['laɪbrərɪ] n biblioteca

▌ Be careful not to translate *library* by the Spanish word *librería*.

**Libya** ['lɪbɪə] n Libia

**lice** [laɪs] pl of **louse**

**licence**, (US) **license** ['laɪsns] n licencia; (*permit*) permiso; (*also:* **driving ~**, (US) **driver's license**) carnet de conducir, permiso de manejar (LAM)

**license** ['laɪsns] n (US) = **licence** ▷ vt autorizar, dar permiso a; **licensed** adj (*for alcohol*) autorizado para vender bebidas alcohólicas; **license plate** n (US) placa (de matrícula); **licensing hours** npl (BRIT) horas durante las cuales se permite la venta y consumo de alcohol (*en un bar etc*)

**lick** [lɪk] vt lamer; (*inf: defeat*) dar una paliza a; **to ~ one's lips** relamerse

**lid** [lɪd] n (*of box, case, pan*) tapa, tapadera

**lie** [laɪ] n mentira ▷ vi (pt **lay**, pp **lain**) mentir; (*rest*) estar echado, estar acostado; (*of object: be situated*) estar, encontrarse; **to tell ~s** mentir; **to ~ low** (*fig*) mantenerse a escondidas; **lie about, lie around** vi (*things*) estar tirado; (BRIT: *people*) estar acostado *or* tumbado; **lie down** vi echarse, tumbarse

**Liechtenstein** ['lɪktənstaɪn] n Liechtenstein m

**lie-in** ['laɪɪn] n (BRIT): **to have a ~** quedarse en la cama

**lieutenant** [lɛf'tɛnənt] [(US) lu:'tɛnənt] n (Mil) teniente m

**life** (pl **lives**) [laɪf, laɪvz] n vida; **life assurance** n (BRIT) seguro de vida; **lifebelt** n (BRIT) cinturón m salvavidas; **lifeboat** n lancha de socorro; **lifeguard** n vigilante mf, socorrista mf; **life insurance** n = **life assurance**; **life jacket** n chaleco salvavidas; **lifelike** adj natural; **life preserver** n (US) = **lifebelt**; **life sentence** n cadena perpetua; **lifestyle** n estilo de vida; **lifetime** n: **in his lifetime** durante su vida

**lift** [lɪft] vt levantar; (*copy*) plagiar ▷ vi (*fog*) disiparse ▷ n (BRIT: *elevator*) ascensor m; **to give sb a ~** (BRIT) llevar a algn en coche; **lift up** vt levantar; **lift-off** n despegue m

**light** [laɪt] n luz f; (*lamp*) luz f, lámpara; (*headlight*) faro; (*for cigarette etc*): **have you got a ~?** ¿tienes fuego? ▷ vt (pt, pp **lit**) (*candle, cigarette, fire*) encender; (*room*) alumbrar ▷ adj (*colour*) claro; (*room*) con mucha luz; **lights** npl (*traffic lights*) semáforos mpl; **in the ~ of** a la luz de; **to come to ~** salir a la luz; **light up** vi (*smoke*) encender un cigarrillo; (*face*) iluminarse ▷ vt (*illuminate*) iluminar, alumbrar; (*set fire to*) encender; **light bulb** n bombilla, bombillo (LAM), foco (LAM); **lighten** vt (*make less heavy*) aligerar; **lighter** n (*also:* **cigarette lighter**) encendedor m, mechero; **light-hearted** adj (*person*) alegre; (*remark etc*) divertido; **lighthouse** n faro; **lighting** n (*system*) alumbrado; **lightly** adv ligeramente; (*not seriously*) con poca seriedad; **to get off lightly** ser castigado con poca severidad

**lightning** ['laɪtnɪŋ] n relámpago, rayo

**lightweight** adj (*suit*) ligero ▷ n (Boxing) peso ligero

**like** [laɪk] vt (*person*) querer a ▷ prep como ▷ adj parecido, semejante ▷ n: **his ~s and dislikes** sus gustos y aversiones; **the ~s of** him personas como él; **I would ~**, **I'd ~** me gustaría; (*for purchase*) quisiera; **would you ~ a coffee?** ¿te apetece un café?; **I ~ swimming** me gusta nadar; **to be** *or* **look ~ sb/sth** parecerse a algn/algo; **that's just ~ him** es muy de él, es típico de él; **do it ~ this** hazlo así; **it is nothing ~ ...** no tiene parecido alguno con ...; **what's he ~?** ¿cómo es (él)?; **likeable** adj simpático, agradable

**likelihood** ['laɪklɪhud] n probabilidad f

**likely** ['laɪklɪ] adj probable; **he's ~ to leave** es probable *or* (LAM) capaz que se vaya; **not ~!** ¡ni hablar!

**likewise** ['laɪkwaɪz] adv igualmente; **to do ~** hacer lo mismo

**liking** ['laɪkɪŋ] n: ~ **(for)** (person) cariño (a); (thing) afición (a); **to be to sb's ~** ser del gusto de algn

**lilac** ['laɪlək] n (tree) lilo; (flower) lila

**Lilo®** ['laɪləʊ] n colchoneta inflable

**lily** ['lɪlɪ] n lirio, azucena; ~ **of the valley** n lirio de los valles

**limb** [lɪm] n miembro

**limbo** ['lɪmbəʊ] n: **to be in ~** (fig) quedar a la expectativa

**lime** [laɪm] n (tree) limero; (fruit) lima; (Geo) cal f

**limelight** ['laɪmlaɪt] n: **to be in the ~** (fig) ser el centro de atención

**limestone** ['laɪmstəʊn] n piedra caliza

**limit** ['lɪmɪt] n límite m ⊳ vt limitar; **limited** adj limitado; **to be limited to** limitarse a

**limousine** ['lɪməzi:n] n limusina

**limp** [lɪmp] n: **to have a ~** tener cojera ⊳ vi cojear ⊳ adj flojo

**line** [laɪn] n línea; (rope) cuerda; (for fishing) sedal m; (wire) hilo; (row, series) fila, hilera; (of writing) renglón m; (on face) arruga; (Rail) vía ⊳ vt (Sewing): **to ~ (with)** forrar (de); **to ~ the streets** ocupar las aceras; **in ~ with** de acuerdo con; **line up** vi hacer cola ⊳ vt alinear; **to have sth ~d up** tener algo arreglado

**linear** ['lɪnɪəʳ] adj lineal

**linen** ['lɪnɪn] n ropa blanca; (cloth) lino

**liner** ['laɪnəʳ] n vapor m de línea transatlántico; **dustbin ~** bolsa de la basura

**line-up** ['laɪnʌp] n (us: queue) cola; (Sport) alineación f

**linger** ['lɪŋgəʳ] vi retrasarse, tardar en marcharse; (smell, tradition) persistir

**lingerie** ['lænʒəri:] n ropa interior (de mujer), lencería

**linguist** ['lɪŋgwɪst] n lingüista mf; **linguistic** adj lingüístico

**lining** ['laɪnɪŋ] n forro

**link** [lɪŋk] n (of chain) eslabón m; (relationship) relación f; (bond) vínculo, lazo; (Internet) enlace m ⊳ vt vincular, unir; (associate): **to ~ with** or **to** relacionar con; **links** npl (Golf); **link up** vt acoplar ⊳ vi unirse

**lion** ['laɪən] n león m; **lioness** n leona

**lip** [lɪp] n labio; **lip-read** vi leer los labios; **lip salve** n crema protectora para labios; **lipstick** n lápiz m or barra de labios, carmín m

**liqueur** [lɪ'kjuəʳ] n licor m

**liquid** ['lɪkwɪd] adj, n líquido; **liquidizer** ['lɪkwɪdaɪzəʳ] n (Culin) licuadora

**liquor** ['lɪkəʳ] n licor m, bebidas fpl alcohólicas; **liquor store** n (us) bodega, tienda de vinos y bebidas alcohólicas

**Lisbon** ['lɪzbən] n Lisboa

**lisp** [lɪsp] n ceceo ⊳ vi cecear

**list** [lɪst] n lista ⊳ vt (write down) hacer una lista de; (mention) enumerar

**listen** ['lɪsn] vi escuchar, oír; **listener** n oyente mf

**lit** [lɪt] pt, pp of **light**

**liter** ['li:təʳ] n (us) = **litre**

**literacy** ['lɪtərəsɪ] n capacidad f de leer y escribir

**literal** ['lɪtərl] adj literal; **literally** adv literalmente

**literary** ['lɪtərərɪ] adj literario

**literate** ['lɪtərət] adj que sabe leer y escribir; (educated) culto

**literature** ['lɪtərɪtʃəʳ] n literatura; (brochures etc) folletos mpl

**litre**, (us) **liter** ['li:təʳ] n litro

**litter** ['lɪtəʳ] n (rubbish) basura; (young animals) camada, cría; **litter bin** n (BRIT) papelera; **littered** adj: **littered with** lleno de

**little** ['lɪtl] adj (small) pequeño; (not much) poco; (diminutive): ~ **house** casita ⊳ adv poco; **a ~** un poco (de); **a ~ bit** un poquito; ~ **by ~** poco a poco; **little finger** n dedo meñique

**live**[1] [laɪv] adj (animal) vivo; (wire) conectado; (broadcast) en directo; (unexploded) sin explotar

**live**[2] [lɪv] vi vivir; **to ~ together** vivir juntos; **live up to** vt fus (fulfil) cumplir con

**livelihood** ['laɪvlɪhud] n sustento

**lively** ['laɪvlɪ] adj vivo; (place, book etc) animado

**liven up** ['laɪvn-] vt animar ⊳ vi animarse

**liver** ['lɪvəʳ] n hígado

**lives** [laɪvz] npl of **life**

**livestock** ['laɪvstɔk] n ganado

**living** ['lɪvɪŋ] adj (alive) vivo ⊳ n: **to earn** or **make a ~** ganarse la vida; **living room** n sala (de estar)

**lizard** ['lɪzəd] n lagartija

**load** [ləud] n carga; (weight) peso ⊳ vt (also Comput) cargar; **a ~ of, ~s of** (fig) (gran) cantidad de, montones de; **to ~ (up) with** cargar con or de; **loaded** adj cargado

**loaf** (pl **loaves**) [ləuf] n (barra de) pan m

**loan** [ləun] n préstamo ⊳ vt prestar; **on ~** prestado

**loathe** [ləuð] vt aborrecer; (person) odiar

**loaves** [ləuvz] pl of **loaf**

**lobby** ['lɔbɪ] n vestíbulo, sala de espera; (Pol: pressure group) grupo de presión ⊳ vt presionar

**lobster** ['lɔbstəʳ] n langosta

**local** ['ləukl] adj local ⊳ n (pub) bar m; **the locals** npl los vecinos, los del lugar; **local anaesthetic**, (us) **local anesthetic** n (Med) anestesia local; **local authority** n municipio, ayuntamiento (sp); **local**

**government** n gobierno municipal; **locally** ['ləʊkəlɪ] adv en la vecindad
**locate** [ləʊ'keɪt] vt (find) localizar; (situate): **to be ~d in** estar situado en
**location** [ləʊ'keɪʃən] n situación f; **on ~** (Cine) en exteriores
**loch** [lɒx] n lago
**lock** [lɒk] n (of door, box) cerradura; (of canal) esclusa; (of hair) mechón m ▷ vt (with key) cerrar con llave ▷ vi (door etc) cerrarse con llave; (wheels) trabarse; **lock in** vt encerrar; **lock out** vt (person) cerrar la puerta a; **lock up** vt (criminal) meter en la cárcel; (house) cerrar (con llave) ▷ vi echar la llave
**locker** ['lɒkəʳ] n casillero; **locker-room** n (us Sport) vestuario
**locksmith** ['lɒksmɪθ] n cerrajero/a
**locomotive** [ləʊkə'məʊtɪv] n locomotora
**lodge** [lɒdʒ] n casa del guarda ▷ vi (person): **to ~ (with)** alojarse (en casa de) ▷ vt presentar; **lodger** ['lɒdʒəʳ] n huésped mf
**lodging** ['lɒdʒɪŋ] n alojamiento, hospedaje m
**loft** [lɒft] n desván m
**log** [lɒg] n (of wood) leño, tronco; (written account) diario ▷ vt anotar; **log in, log on** vi (Comput) iniciar la sesión; **log off, log out** vi (Comput) finalizar la sesión
**logic** ['lɒdʒɪk] n lógica; **logical** adj lógico
**login** ['lɒgɪn] n (Comput) login m
**lollipop** ['lɒlɪpɒp] n pirulí m; **lollipop man, lollipop lady** n (BRIT) persona encargada de ayudar a los niños a cruzar la calle
**lolly** ['lɒlɪ] n (inf: ice cream) polo; (: lollipop) piruleta; (: money) guita
**London** ['lʌndən] n Londres m; **Londoner** n londinense mf
**lone** [ləʊn] adj solitario
**loneliness** ['ləʊnlɪnɪs] n soledad f, aislamiento
**lonely** ['ləʊnlɪ] adj (situation) solitario; (person) solo; (place) aislado
**long** [lɒŋ] adj largo ▷ adv mucho tiempo, largamente ▷ vi: **to ~ for sth** anhelar algo; **so** or **as ~ as** mientras, con tal de que; **don't be ~!** ¡no tardes!, ¡vuelve pronto!; **how ~ is the street?** ¿cuánto tiene la calle de largo?; **how ~ is the lesson?** ¿cuánto dura la clase?; **six metres ~** que mide seis metros, de seis metros de largo; **six months ~** que dura seis meses, de seis meses de duración; **all night ~** toda la noche; **he no ~er comes** ya no viene; **~ before** mucho antes; **before ~** (+ future) dentro de poco; (+ past) poco tiempo después; **at ~ last** al fin, por fin; **long-distance** adj (race) de larga distancia; (call) interurbano; **long-haul** adj (flight) de larga distancia; **longing** n anhelo, ansia; (nostalgia) nostalgia ▷ adj anhelante
**longitude** ['lɒŋgɪtjuːd] n longitud f

**long: long jump** n salto de longitud; **long-life** adj (batteries) de larga duración; (milk) uperizado; **long-sighted** adj (BRIT) présbita; **long-standing** adj de mucho tiempo; **long-term** adj a largo plazo
**loo** [luː] n (BRIT inf) wáter m
**look** [luk] vi mirar; (seem) parecer; (building etc): **to ~ south/on to the sea** dar al sur/al mar ▷ n mirada; (glance) vistazo; (appearance) aire m, aspecto; **looks** npl belleza sg; **~ (here)!** (expressing annoyance etc) ¡oye!; **~!** (expressing surprise) ¡mira!; **look after** vt fus (care for) cuidar a; (deal with) encargarse de; **look around** vi echar una mirada alrededor; **look at** vt fus mirar; **look back** vi mirar hacia atrás; **look down on** vt fus (fig) despreciar, mirar con desprecio; **look for** vt fus buscar; **look forward to** vt fus esperar con ilusión; (in letters): **we ~ forward to hearing from you** quedamos a la espera de su respuesta or contestación; **look into** vt fus investigar; **look out** vi (beware): **to ~ out (for)** tener cuidado (de); **look out for** vt fus (seek) buscar; (await) esperar; **look round** vi volver la cabeza; **look through** vt fus (papers, book) hojear; **look to** vt fus ocuparse de; (rely on) contar con; **look up** vi mirar hacia arriba; (improve) mejorar ▷ vt (word) buscar; **look up to** vt fus admirar
**look-out** n (tower etc) puesto de observación; (person) vigía mf; **to be on the ~ for sth** estar al acecho de algo
**loom** [luːm] vi: **~ (up)** (threaten) surgir, amenazar; (event: approach) aproximarse
**loony** ['luːnɪ] adj, n (inf!) loco/a
**loop** [luːp] n lazo; **loophole** n laguna
**loose** [luːs] adj suelto; (clothes) ancho; (morals, discipline) relajado; **to be at a ~ end** or (us) **at ~ ends** no saber qué hacer; **loosely** adv libremente, aproximadamente; **loosen** vt aflojar
**loot** [luːt] n botín m ▷ vt saquear
**lop-sided** ['lɒp'saɪdɪd] adj torcido; (fig) desequilibrado
**lord** [lɔːd] n señor m; **L~ Smith** Lord Smith; **the L~** el Señor; **the (House of) L~s** (BRIT) la Cámara de los Lores
**lorry** ['lɒrɪ] n (BRIT) camión m; **lorry driver** n camionero/a
**lose** (pt, pp **lost**) [luːz, lɒst] vt perder ▷ vi perder, ser vencido; **to ~ (time)** (clock) atrasarse; **lose out** vi salir perdiendo; **loser** n perdedor(a) m/f
**loss** [lɒs] n pérdida; **heavy ~es** (Mil) grandes pérdidas fpl; **to be at a ~** no saber qué hacer; **to make a ~** sufrir pérdidas
**lost** [lɒst] pt, pp of **lose** ▷ adj perdido; **lost property,** (us) **lost and found** n objetos mpl perdidos

**lot** [lɔt] n (at auction) lote m; **the ~** el todo, todos mpl, todas fpl; **a ~** mucho, bastante; **a ~ of, ~s of** muchos/as; (with singular noun) mucho/a; **I read a ~** leo bastante; **to draw ~s (for sth)** echar suertes (para decidir algo)

**lotion** ['ləʊʃən] n loción f

**lottery** ['lɔtərɪ] n lotería

**loud** [laʊd] adj (voice, sound) fuerte; (laugh, shout) estrepitoso; (gaudy) chillón/ona ▷ adv (speak etc) fuerte; **out ~** en voz alta; **loudly** adv (noisily) fuerte; (aloud) en alta voz; **loudspeaker** n altavoz m

**lounge** [laʊndʒ] n salón m, sala de estar; (of hotel) salón m; (of airport) sala de embarque ▷ vi (also: **~ about, ~ around**) holgazanear

**louse** (pl **lice**) [laʊs, laɪs] n piojo

**lousy** ['laʊzɪ] adj (fig) vil, asqueroso; (ill) fatal

**love** [lʌv] n (romantic, sexual) amor m; (kind, caring) cariño ▷ vt amar, querer; **~ from Anne** (in letter) con cariño de Anne; **I ~ to read** me encanta leer; **to be in ~ with** estar enamorado de; **to make ~** hacer el amor; **I ~ you** te quiero; **for the ~ of** por amor a; **"15 ~ "** (Tennis) "15 a cero"; **I ~ paella** me encanta la paella; **love affair** n aventura sentimental or amorosa; **love life** n vida sentimental

**lovely** ['lʌvlɪ] adj (delightful) encantador(a); (beautiful) precioso

**lover** ['lʌvə'] n amante mf; (amateur): **a ~ of** un(a) aficionado/a or un(a) amante de

**loving** ['lʌvɪŋ] adj amoroso, cariñoso

**low** [ləʊ] adj, adv bajo ▷ n (Meteorology) área de baja presión; **to feel ~** sentirse deprimido; **to turn (down) ~** bajar; **low-alcohol** adj bajo en alcohol; **low-calorie** adj bajo en calorías

**lower** ['ləʊə'] adj más bajo; (less important) menos importante ▷ vt bajar; (reduce) reducir; **to ~ o.s. to** (fig) rebajarse a

**low-fat** adj (milk, yoghurt) desnatado; (diet) bajo en calorías

**loyal** ['lɔɪəl] adj leal; **loyalty** n lealtad f; **loyalty card** n tarjeta cliente

**LP** n abbr (= long-playing record) elepé m

**L-plates** ['ɛlpleɪts] npl (BRIT) (placas fpl de) la L

En el Reino Unido las personas que están aprendiendo a conducir han de llevar indicativos blancos con una L en rojo llamados normalmente L-plates (de learner) en la parte delantera y trasera de los automóviles que conducen. No tienen que ir a clases teóricas, sino que desde el principio se les entrega un carnet de conducir provisional (provisional driving licence) para que realicen sus prácticas, que han de estar supervisadas por un conductor con carnet definitivo (full driving licence). Tampoco se les permite hacer prácticas en autopistas aunque vayan acompañadas.

**Lt.** abbr (= lieutenant) Tte.

**Ltd** abbr (Comm: = limited company) S.A.

**luck** [lʌk] n suerte f; **good/bad ~** buena/mala suerte; **good ~!** ¡(que tengas) suerte!; **bad** or **hard** or **tough ~!** ¡qué pena!; **luckily** adv afortunadamente; **lucky** adj afortunado; (at cards etc) con suerte; (object) que trae suerte

**lucrative** ['lu:krətɪv] adj lucrativo

**ludicrous** ['lu:dɪkrəs] adj absurdo

**luggage** ['lʌgɪdʒ] n equipaje m; **luggage rack** n (on car) baca, portaequipajes m inv

**lukewarm** ['lu:kwɔ:m] adj tibio

**lull** [lʌl] n tregua ▷ vt (child) acunar; (person, fear) calmar; **to ~ sb to sleep** arrullar a algn; **to ~ sb into a false sense of security** dar a algn una falsa sensación de seguridad

**lullaby** ['lʌləbaɪ] n nana

**lumber** ['lʌmbə'] n (junk) trastos mpl viejos; (wood) maderos mpl

**luminous** ['lu:mɪnəs] adj luminoso

**lump** [lʌmp] n terrón m; (fragment) trozo; (swelling) bulto ▷ vt (also: **~ together**) juntar; **lump sum** n suma global; **lumpy** adj (sauce) lleno de grumos

**lunatic** ['lu:nətɪk] adj, n (inf!) loco/a

**lunch** [lʌntʃ] n almuerzo, comida ▷ vi almorzar; **lunch break, lunch hour** n hora del almuerzo

**lunchtime** ['lʌntʃtaɪm] n hora del almuerzo or de comer

**lung** [lʌŋ] n pulmón m

**lure** [luə'] n (bait) cebo; (decoy) señuelo; (attraction) atracción f ▷ vt convencer con engaños

**lurk** [lə:k] vi (wait) estar al acecho; (fig) acechar

**lush** [lʌʃ] adj exuberante

**lust** [lʌst] n lujuria; (greed) codicia

**Luxembourg** ['lʌksəmbə:g] n Luxemburgo

**luxurious** [lʌg'zjuərɪəs] adj lujoso

**luxury** ['lʌkʃərɪ] n lujo ▷ cpd de lujo

**Lycra®** ['laɪkrə] n licra®

**lying** ['laɪɪŋ] n mentiras fpl ▷ adj mentiroso

**lyric** ['lɪrɪk] adj lírico; **lyrics** npl (of song) letra sg

# m

**m** abbr (= metre) m.; = **mile; million**

**MA** n abbr (Scol) = **Master of Arts**

**ma** [mɑː] n (inf) mamá

**mac** [mæk] n (BRIT) impermeable m

**macaroni** [mækə'rəʊnɪ] n macarrones mpl

**Macedonia** [mæsɪ'dəʊnɪə] n Macedonia; **Macedonian** [mæsɪ'dəʊnɪən] adj macedonio ⊳ n macedonio/a; (Ling) macedonio

**machine** [mə'ʃiːn] n máquina ⊳ vt (dress etc) coser a máquina; (Tech) trabajar a máquina; **machine gun** n ametralladora; **machinery** n maquinaria; (fig) mecanismo; **machine washable** adj lavable a máquina

**macho** ['mætʃəʊ] adj macho

**mackerel** ['mækrl] n (pl inv) caballa

**mackintosh** ['mækɪntɒʃ] n (BRIT) impermeable m

**mad** [mæd] adj loco; (idea) disparatado; (angry) furioso; **to be ~ (keen) about** or **on sth** estar loco por algo

**madam** ['mædəm] n señora

**mad cow disease** n encefalopatía espongiforme bovina

**made** [meɪd] pt, pp of **make; made-to-measure** adj (BRIT) hecho a la medida; **made-up** adj (story) ficticio

**madly** ['mædlɪ] adv locamente

**madman** ['mædmən] n loco

**madness** ['mædnɪs] n locura

**Madrid** [mə'drɪd] n Madrid m

**Mafia** ['mæfɪə] n Mafia

**mag** [mæg] n abbr (BRIT inf); = **magazine**

**magazine** [mægə'ziːn] n revista

**maggot** ['mægət] n gusano

**magic** ['mædʒɪk] n magia ⊳ adj mágico; **magical** adj mágico; **magician** [mə'dʒɪʃən] n mago/a

**magistrate** ['mædʒɪstreɪt] n juez mf (municipal)

**magnet** ['mægnɪt] n imán m; **magnetic** [mæg'nɛtɪk] adj magnético

**magnificent** [mæg'nɪfɪsnt] adj magnífico

**magnify** ['mægnɪfaɪ] vt (object) ampliar; (sound) aumentar; **magnifying glass** n lupa

**magpie** ['mægpaɪ] n urraca

**mahogany** [mə'hɔgənɪ] n caoba

**maid** [meɪd] n criada; **old ~** (pej) solterona

**maiden name** n apellido de soltera

**mail** [meɪl] n correo; (letters) cartas fpl ⊳ vt echar al correo; **mailbox** n (US) buzón m; **mailing list** n lista de direcciones; **mailman** n (US) cartero; **mail-order** n pedido postal

**main** [meɪn] adj principal, mayor ⊳ n (pipe) cañería principal or maestra; (US) red f eléctrica; **the ~s** (BRIT Elec) la red eléctrica; **in the ~** en general; **main course** n (Culin) plato principal; **mainland** n continente m; **mainly** adv principalmente; **main road** n carretera principal; **mainstream** n corriente f principal; **main street** n calle f mayor

**maintain** [meɪn'teɪn] vt mantener

**maintenance** ['meɪntənəns] n mantenimiento; (alimony) pensión f alimenticia

**maisonette** [meɪzə'nɛt] n dúplex m

**maize** [meɪz] n (BRIT) maíz m, choclo (LAM)

**majesty** ['mædʒɪstɪ] n majestad f; **Your M~** Su Majestad

**major** ['meɪdʒər] n (Mil) comandante m ⊳ adj principal; (Mus) mayor

**Majorca** [mə'jɔːkə] n Mallorca

**majority** [mə'dʒɔrɪtɪ] n mayoría

**make** [meɪk] (pt, pp **made**) vt (manufacture) hacer, fabricar; (mistake) cometer; (speech) pronunciar; (cause to be): **to ~ sb sad** poner triste or entristecer a algn; (force): **to ~ sb do sth** obligar a algn a hacer algo; (equal): **2 and 2 ~ 4** 2 y 2 son 4 ⊳ n marca; **to ~ a fool of sb** poner a algn en ridículo; **to ~ a profit/loss** obtener ganancias/sufrir pérdidas; **to ~ it** (arrive) llegar; (achieve sth) tener éxito; **what time do you ~ it?** ¿qué hora tienes?; **to ~ do with** contentarse con; **make off** vi largarse; **make out** vt (decipher) descifrar; (understand) entender; (see) distinguir; (cheque) extender; **make up** vt (invent) inventar; (parcel) hacer ⊳ vi reconciliarse; (with cosmetics) maquillarse; **make up for** vt fus compensar; **makeover** n cambio de imagen; **to give sb a makeover** hacerle a algn un cambio de imagen; **maker** n fabricante mf; (of film, programme) autor(a) m/f; **makeshift** adj improvisado; **make-up** n maquillaje m

**making** ['meɪkɪŋ] n (fig): **in the ~** en vías de formación; **to have the ~s of** (person) tener madera de

**malaria** [mə'lɛərɪə] n malaria

**Malaysia** [mə'leɪzɪə] n Malaisia, Malaysia

**male** [meɪl] n (Biol, Elec) macho ▷ adj (sex, attitude) masculino; (child etc) varón

**malicious** [mə'lɪʃəs] adj malicioso; rencoroso

**malignant** [mə'lɪgnənt] adj (Med) maligno

**mall** [mɔːl] n (us: also: **shopping ~**) centro comercial

**mallet** ['mælɪt] n mazo

**malnutrition** [mælnjuː'trɪʃən] n desnutrición f

**malpractice** [mæl'præktɪs] n negligencia profesional

**malt** [mɔːlt] n malta; (whisky) whisky m de malta

**Malta** ['mɔːltə] n Malta; **Maltese** [mɔːl'tiːz] adj maltés/esa ▷ n (pl inv) maltés/esa m/f

**mammal** ['mæml] n mamífero

**mammoth** ['mæməθ] n mamut m ▷ adj gigantesco

**man** (pl **men**) [mæn, mɛn] n hombre m; (mankind) el hombre ▷ vt (Naut) tripular; (Mil) defender; (operate: machine) manejar; **an old ~** un viejo; **~ and wife** marido y mujer

**manage** ['mænɪdʒ] vi arreglárselas ▷ vt (be in charge of) dirigir; (person etc) manejar; **manageable** adj manejable; **management** n dirección f; **manager** n director(a) m/f; (of pop star) mánager mf; (Sport) entrenador(a) m/f; **manageress** n directora, (Sport) entrenadora; **managerial** [mænə'dʒɪərɪəl] adj directivo; **managing director** n director(a) m/f general

**mandarin** ['mændərɪn] n (also: **~ orange**) mandarina; (person) mandarín m

**mandate** ['mændeɪt] n mandato

**mandatory** ['mændətərɪ] adj obligatorio

**mane** [meɪn] n (of horse) crin f; (of lion) melena

**maneuver** [mə'nuːvəʳ] vb, n (us) = **manoeuvre**

**mangetout** [mɔnʒ'tuː] n tirabeque m

**mango** ['mæŋgəu] (pl **mangoes**) n mango

**man:** **manhole** n boca de alcantarilla; **manhood** n edad f viril; (manliness) virilidad f

**mania** ['meɪnɪə] n manía; **maniac** ['meɪnɪæk] n maníaco/a; (fig) maniático

**manic** ['mænɪk] adj frenético

**manicure** ['mænɪkjuəʳ] n manicura

**manifest** ['mænɪfɛst] vt manifestar, mostrar ▷ adj manifiesto

**manifesto** [mænɪ'fɛstəu] n manifiesto

**manipulate** [mə'nɪpjuleɪt] vt manipular

**man:** **mankind** [mæn'kaɪnd] n humanidad f, género humano; **manly** adj varonil; **man-made** adj artificial

**manner** ['mænəʳ] n manera, modo; (behaviour) conducta, manera de ser; (type) clase f; **manners** npl modales mpl; **bad ~s** falta sg de educación

**manoeuvre**, (us) **maneuver** [mə'nuːvəʳ] vt, vi maniobrar ▷ n maniobra

**manpower** ['mænpauəʳ] n mano f de obra

**mansion** ['mænʃən] n mansión f

**manslaughter** ['mænslɔːtəʳ] n homicidio involuntario

**mantelpiece** ['mæntlpiːs] n repisa de la chimenea

**manual** ['mænjuəl] adj manual ▷ n manual m

**manufacture** [mænju'fæktʃəʳ] vt fabricar ▷ n fabricación f; **manufacturer** n fabricante mf

**manure** [mə'njuəʳ] n estiércol m

**manuscript** ['mænjuskrɪpt] n manuscrito

**many** ['mɛnɪ] adj muchos/as ▷ pron muchos/as; **a great ~** muchísimos, un buen número de; **~ a time** muchas veces

**map** [mæp] n mapa m; **map out** vt proyectar

**maple** ['meɪpl] n arce m, maple m (LAM)

**mar** [mɑːʳ] vt estropear

**Mar.** abbr (= March) mar

**marathon** ['mærəθən] n maratón m

**marble** ['mɑːbl] n mármol m; (toy) canica

**March** [mɑːtʃ] n marzo

**march** [mɑːtʃ] vi (Mil) marchar; (demonstrators) manifestarse ▷ n marcha; (demonstration) manifestación f

**mare** [mɛəʳ] n yegua

**margarine** [mɑːdʒə'riːn] n margarina

**margin** ['mɑːdʒɪn] n margen m; (Comm: profit margin) margen m de beneficios; **marginal** adj marginal; **marginally** adv ligeramente

**marigold** ['mærɪgəuld] n caléndula

**marijuana** [mærɪ'wɑːnə] n marihuana

**marina** [mə'riːnə] n puerto deportivo

**marinade** [mærɪ'neɪd] n adobo

**marinate** ['mærɪneɪt] vt adobar

**marine** [mə'riːn] adj marino ▷ n soldado de infantería de marina

**marital** ['mærɪtl] adj matrimonial; **~ status** estado civil

**maritime** ['mærɪtaɪm] adj marítimo

**marjoram** ['mɑːdʒərəm] n mejorana

**mark** [mɑːk] n marca, señal f; (in snow, mud etc) huella; (stain) mancha; (BRIT Scol) nota ▷ vt (Sport: player) marcar; (stain) manchar; (BRIT Scol) calificar, corregir; **to ~ time** marcar el paso; (fig) marcar(se) un ritmo; **marked** adj marcado, acusado; **marker** n (sign) marcador m; (bookmark) registro

**market** ['mɑːkɪt] n mercado ▷ vt (Comm) comercializar; **marketing** n marketing m; **marketplace** n mercado; **market research** n (Comm) estudios mpl de mercado

**marmalade** ['mɑːməleɪd] n mermelada de naranja

**maroon** [mə'ruːn] vt: **to be ~ed** (shipwrecked) quedar aislado; (fig) quedar abandonado ▷ n (colour) granate m

**marquee** [mɑː'kiː] n entoldado

**marriage** ['mærɪdʒ] n (state) matrimonio; (wedding) boda; (act) casamiento; **marriage certificate** n partida de casamiento

**married** ['mærɪd] adj casado; (life, love) conyugal

**marrow** ['mærəu] n médula; (vegetable) calabacín m

**marry** ['mærɪ] vt casarse con; (father, priest etc) casar ▷ vi (also: **get married**) casarse

**Mars** [mɑːz] n Marte m

**marsh** [mɑːʃ] n pantano; (salt marsh) marisma

**marshal** ['mɑːʃl] n (Mil) mariscal m; (at sports meeting, demonstration etc) oficial m; (us: of police, fire department) jefe/a m/f ▷ vt (facts) ordenar; (soldiers) formar

**martyr** ['mɑːtər] n mártir mf

**marvel** ['mɑːvl] n maravilla, prodigio ▷ vi: **to ~ (at)** maravillarse (de); **marvellous**, (us) **marvelous** ['mɑːvləs] adj maravilloso

**Marxism** ['mɑːksɪzəm] n marxismo

**Marxist** ['mɑːksɪst] adj, n marxista mf

**marzipan** ['mɑːzɪpæn] n mazapán m

**mascara** [mæs'kɑːrə] n rimel m

**mascot** ['mæskət] n mascota

**masculine** ['mæskjulɪn] adj masculino

**mash** [mæʃ] vt machacar; **mashed potatoes** npl puré m de patatas or (LAM) papas

**mask** [mɑːsk] n máscara ▷ vt (hide: feelings) esconder; **to ~ one's face** (cover) ocultarse la cara

**mason** ['meɪsn] n (also: **stone~**) albañil m; (also: **free~**) masón m; **masonry** n (in building) mampostería

**mass** [mæs] n (people) muchedumbre f; (Physics) masa; (Rel) misa; (great quantity) montón m ▷ vi reunirse; (Mil) concentrarse; **the ~es** las masas

**massacre** ['mæsəkər] n masacre f

**massage** ['mæsɑːʒ] n masaje m ▷ vt dar masajes or un masaje a

**massive** ['mæsɪv] adj enorme; (support, intervention) masivo

**mass media** npl medios mpl de comunicación de masas

**mass-produce** ['mæsprə'djuːs] vt fabricar en serie

**mast** [mɑːst] n (Naut) mástil m; (Radio etc) torre f

**master** ['mɑːstər] n (of servant, animal) amo; (of situation) dueño; (Art, Mus) maestro; (in secondary school) profesor m; (title for boys): **M~ X** Señorito X ▷ vt dominar; **mastermind** n inteligencia superior ▷ vt dirigir, planear; **Master of Arts** n licenciatura superior en Letras; see also **master's degree**; **Master of Science** n licenciatura superior en Ciencias; see also **master's degree**; **masterpiece** n obra maestra; **master's degree** n máster m

● **MASTER'S DEGREE**
●
● Los estudios de postgrado británicos
● que llevan a la obtención de un master's
● degree consisten generalmente en una
● combinación de curso(s) académico(s)
● y tesina (dissertation) sobre un tema
● original, o bien únicamente la redacción
● de una tesina. El primer caso es el
● más frecuente para los títulos de MA
● (Master of Arts) y MSc (Master of Science),
● mientras que los de MLitt (Master of
● Letters) o MPhil (Master of Philosophy) se
● obtienen normalmente mediante tesina.
● En algunas universidades, como las
● escocesas, el título de master's degree no es
● de postgrado, sino que corresponde a la
● licenciatura.

**masturbate** ['mæstəbeɪt] vi masturbarse

**mat** [mæt] n alfombrilla; (also: **door~**) felpudo ▷ adj = **matt**

**match** [mætʃ] n cerilla, fósforo; (game) partido; (fig) igual mf ▷ vt emparejar; (go well with) hacer juego con; (equal) igualar; (correspond to) corresponderse con; (pair: also: **~ up**) casar con ▷ vi hacer juego; **to be a good ~** hacer buena pareja; **matchbox** n caja de cerillas; **matching** adj que hace juego

**mate** [meɪt] n (workmate) colega mf; (inf: friend) amigo/a; (animal) macho/hembra; (in merchant navy) primer oficial m, segundo de a bordo ▷ vi acoplarse, aparearse ▷ vt acoplar, aparear

**material** [mə'tɪərɪəl] n (substance) materia; (equipment) material m; (cloth) tela, tejido ▷ adj material; (important) esencial; **materials** npl materiales mpl

**materialize** [mə'tɪərɪəlaɪz] vi materializarse

**maternal** [mə'tə:nl] adj maternal

**maternity** [mə'tə:nɪtɪ] n maternidad f; **maternity hospital** n hospital m de maternidad; **maternity leave** n baja por maternidad

**math** [mæθ] n abbr (US: = mathematics)
matemáticas fpl

**mathematical** [mæθə'mætɪkl] adj
matemático

**mathematician** [mæθəmə'tɪʃən] n
matemático/a

**mathematics** [mæθə'mætɪks] n
matemáticas fpl

**maths** [mæθs] n abbr (BRIT: = mathematics)
matemáticas fpl

**matinée** ['mætɪneɪ] n sesión f de tarde

**matron** ['meɪtrən] n (in hospital) enfermera
jefe; (in school) ama de llaves

**matt** [mæt] adj mate

**matter** ['mætər] n cuestión f, asunto;
(Physics) sustancia, materia; (Med: pus) pus
m ▷ vi importar; **it doesn't ~** no importa;
**what's the ~?** ¿qué pasa?; **no ~ what** pase
lo que pase; **as a ~ of course** por rutina; **as
a ~ of fact** en realidad; **printed ~** impresos
mpl; **reading ~** material m de lectura

**mattress** ['mætrɪs] n colchón m

**mature** [mə'tjuər] adj maduro ▷ vi
madurar; **mature student** n estudiante de
más de 21 años; **maturity** n madurez f

**maul** [mɔːl] vt magullar

**mauve** [məuv] adj de color malva

**max** abbr = **maximum**

**maximize** ['mæksɪmaɪz] vt (profits etc)
llevar al máximo; (chances) maximizar

**maximum** ['mæksɪməm] adj máximo ▷ n
máximo

**May** [meɪ] n mayo

**may** [meɪ] vi (indicating possibility): **he ~
come** puede que venga; (be allowed to): **~ I
smoke?** ¿puedo fumar?; (wishes): **~ God
bless you!** ¡que Dios le bendiga!

**maybe** ['meɪbiː] adv quizá(s)

**May Day** n el primero de Mayo

**mayhem** ['meɪhɛm] n caos m total

**mayonnaise** [meɪə'neɪz] n mayonesa

**mayor** [mɛər] n alcalde m; **mayoress** n
alcaldesa

**maze** [meɪz] n laberinto

**MD** n abbr (Comm) = **managing director**

**me** [miː] pron (direct) me; (stressed, after
pronoun) mí; **can you hear me?** ¿me oyes?;
**he heard ME!** me oyó a mí; **it's me** soy yo;
**give them to me** dámelos; **with/without
me** conmigo/sin mí

**meadow** ['mɛdəu] n prado, pradera

**meagre**, (US) **meager** ['miːgər] adj escaso,
pobre

**meal** [miːl] n comida; (flour) harina;
**mealtime** n hora de comer

**mean** [miːn] adj (with money) tacaño;
(unkind) mezquino, malo; (average) medio
▷ vt (signify) querer decir, significar; (intend):
**to ~ to do sth** tener la intención de or

pensar hacer algo ▷ n medio, término
medio; **do you ~ it?** ¿lo dices en serio?;
**what do you ~?** ¿qué quiere decir?; **to be
meant for sb/sth** ser para algn/algo; see
also **means**

**meaning** ['miːnɪŋ] n significado,
sentido; **meaningful** adj significativo;
**meaningless** adj sin sentido

**means** npl medio sg, manera sg; (resource)
recursos mpl, medios mpl; **by ~ of** mediante,
por medio de; **by all ~!** ¡naturalmente!,
¡claro que sí!

**meant** [mɛnt] pt, pp of **mean**

**meantime** ['miːntaɪm], **meanwhile**
['miːnwaɪl] adv (also: **in the ~**) mientras
tanto

**measles** ['miːzlz] n sarampión m

**measure** ['mɛʒər] vt medir ▷ vi medir
▷ n medida; (ruler) cinta métrica, metro;
**measurement** n (measure) medida; (act)
medición f; **to take sb's measurements**
tomar las medidas a algn

**meat** [miːt] n carne f; **cold ~s** fiambres mpl;
**meatball** n albóndiga

**Mecca** ['mɛkə] n la Meca

**mechanic** [mɪ'kænɪk] n mecánico/a;
**mechanical** adj mecánico

**mechanism** ['mɛkənɪzəm] n mecanismo

**medal** ['mɛdl] n medalla; **medallist,** (US)
**medalist** ['mɛdlɪst] n (Sport) medallista mf

**meddle** ['mɛdl] vi: **to ~ in** entrometerse en;
**to ~ with sth** manosear algo

**media** ['miːdɪə] npl medios mpl de
comunicación

**mediaeval** [mɛdɪ'iːvl] adj = **medieval**

**mediate** ['miːdɪeɪt] vi mediar

**medical** ['mɛdɪkl] adj médico ▷ n
reconocimiento médico; **medical
certificate** n certificado m médico

**medicated** ['mɛdɪkeɪtɪd] adj medicinal

**medication** [mɛdɪ'keɪʃən] n medicación f

**medicine** ['mɛdsɪn] n medicina; (drug)
medicamento

**medieval** [mɛdɪ'iːvl] adj medieval

**mediocre** [miːdɪ'əukər] adj mediocre

**meditate** ['mɛdɪteɪt] vi meditar

**meditation** [mɛdɪ'teɪʃən] n meditación f

**Mediterranean** [mɛdɪtə'reɪnɪən] adj
mediterráneo; **the ~ (Sea)** el (mar m)
Mediterráneo

**medium** ['miːdɪəm] adj mediano ▷ n
(means) medio; (person) médium mf;
**medium-sized** adj de tamaño mediano;
(clothes) de (la) talla mediana; **medium
wave** n onda media

**meek** [miːk] adj manso, sumiso

**meet** [miːt] (pt, pp **met**) vt encontrar;
(accidentally) encontrarse con; (by
arrangement) reunirse con; (for the first time)

conocer; (go and fetch) ir a buscar; (opponent)
enfrentarse con; (obligations) cumplir ▷ vi
encontrarse; (in session) reunirse; (join:
objects) unirse; (get to know) conocerse;
**meet up** vi: **to ~ up with sb** reunirse con
algn; **meet with** vt fus (difficulty) tropezar
con; **meeting** n encuentro; (arranged) cita,
compromiso (LAM); (formal session,
business meeting) reunión f; (Pol) mitin m;
**meeting place** n lugar m de reunión or
encuentro

**megabyte** ['mɛgə'baɪt] n (Comput)
megabyte m, megaocteto

**megaphone** ['mɛgəfəun] n megáfono

**megapixel** ['mɛgəpɪksl] n megapíxel m

**melancholy** ['mɛlənkəlɪ] n melancolía
▷ adj melancólico

**melody** ['mɛlədɪ] n melodía

**melon** ['mɛlən] n melón m

**melt** [mɛlt] vi (metal) fundirse; (snow)
derretirse ▷ vt fundir

**member** ['mɛmbəʳ] n miembro; (of
club) socio/a; **M~ of Parliament** (BRIT)
diputado/a; **M~ of the European
Parliament** (BRIT) eurodiputado/a; **M~ of
the Scottish Parliament** (BRIT) diputado/a
del Parlamento escocés; **membership** n
(members) miembros mpl; (numbers) número
de miembros or socios; **membership card**
n carnet m de socio

**memento** [mə'mɛntəu] n recuerdo

**memo** ['mɛməu] n apunte m, nota

**memorable** ['mɛmərəbl] adj memorable

**memorandum** (pl **memoranda**)
[mɛmə'rændəm, -də] n nota (de servicio);
(Pol) memorándum m

**memorial** [mɪ'mɔ:rɪəl] n monumento
conmemorativo ▷ adj conmemorativo

**memorize** ['mɛməraɪz] vt aprender de
memoria

**memory** ['mɛmərɪ] n recuerdo; (Comput)
memoria; **memory card** n tarjeta de
memoria; **memory stick** n (Comput) llave f
de memoria

**men** [mɛn] pl of **man**

**menace** ['mɛnəs] n amenaza ▷ vt
amenazar

**mend** [mɛnd] vt reparar, arreglar; (darn)
zurcir ▷ vi reponerse ▷ n remiendo; (darn)
zurcido; **to be on the ~** ir mejorando; **to ~
one's ways** enmendarse

**meningitis** [mɛnɪn'dʒaɪtɪs] n meningitis f

**menopause** ['mɛnəupɔːz] n menopausia

**men's room** n (US): **the ~** el servicio de
caballeros

**menstruation** [mɛnstru'eɪʃən] n
menstruación f

**menswear** ['mɛnzwɛəʳ] n confección f de
caballero

**mental** ['mɛntl] adj mental; **mentality**
[mɛn'tælɪtɪ] n mentalidad f; **mentally** adv:
**to be mentally ill** tener una enfermedad
mental

**menthol** ['mɛnθɒl] n mentol m

**mention** ['mɛnʃən] n mención f ▷ vt
mencionar; (speak of) hablar de; **don't ~ it!**
¡de nada!

**menu** ['mɛnjuː] n (set menu) menú m;
(printed) carta; (Comput) menú m

**MEP** n abbr = **Member of the European
Parliament**

**mercenary** ['mɜːsɪnərɪ] adj, n
mercenario/a

**merchandise** ['mɜːtʃəndaɪz] n
mercancías fpl

**merchant** ['mɜːtʃənt] n comerciante mf;
**merchant navy, (US) merchant marine** n
marina mercante

**merciless** ['mɜːsɪlɪs] adj despiadado

**mercury** ['mɜːkjurɪ] n mercurio

**mercy** ['mɜːsɪ] n compasión f; (Rel)
misericordia; **at the ~ of** a la merced de

**mere** [mɪəʳ] adj simple, mero; **merely** adv
simplemente, sólo

**merge** [mɜːdʒ] vt (join) unir ▷ vi unirse;
(Comm) fusionarse; **merger** n (Comm)
fusión f

**meringue** [mə'ræŋ] n merengue m

**merit** ['mɛrɪt] n mérito ▷ vt merecer

**mermaid** ['mɜːmeɪd] n sirena

**merry** ['mɛrɪ] adj alegre; **M~ Christmas!**
¡Felices Pascuas!; **merry-go-round** n
tiovivo

**mesh** [mɛʃ] n malla

**mess** [mɛs] n confusión f; (of objects)
revoltijo; (dirt) porquería; (Mil) comedor m;
**mess about, mess around** vi (inf) perder el
tiempo; (pass the time) pasar el rato; **mess up**
vt (inf: spoil) estropear; (dirty) ensuciar; **mess
with** vt fus (inf: challenge, confront) meterse
con (inf); (interfere with) interferir con

**message** ['mɛsɪdʒ] n mensaje m, recado
▷ vt (inf: person) mandar un mensaje a;
(: comment) mandar

**messenger** ['mɛsɪndʒəʳ] n mensajero/a

**Messrs** abbr (on letters: = Messieurs) Sres.

**messy** ['mɛsɪ] adj (dirty) sucio; (untidy)
desordenado

**met** [mɛt] pt, pp of **meet**

**metabolism** [mɛ'tæbəlɪzəm] n
metabolismo

**metal** ['mɛtl] n metal m; **metallic**
[mɛ'tælɪk] adj metálico

**metaphor** ['mɛtəfəʳ] n metáfora

**meteor** ['miːtɪəʳ] n meteoro; **meteorite**
['miːtɪəraɪt] n meteorito

**meteorology** [miːtɪə'rɒlədʒɪ] n
meteorología

**meter** ['miːtəʳ] n (instrument) contador m; (US: unit) = **metre** ▷ vt (US Post) franquear

**method** ['mɛθəd] n método; **methodical** adj metódico

**meths** [mɛθs] n (BRIT) = **methylated spirit**

**methylated spirit** ['mɛθɪleɪtɪd-] n (BRIT) alcohol m metilado or desnaturalizado

**meticulous** [mɛ'tɪkjuləs] adj meticuloso

**metre**, (US) **meter** ['miːtəʳ] n metro

**metric** ['mɛtrɪk] adj métrico

**metropolitan** [mɛtrə'pɔlɪtən] adj metropolitano

**Metropolitan Police** n (BRIT): **the ~** la policía londinense

**Mexican** ['mɛksɪkən] adj, n mexicano/a, mejicano/a

**Mexico** ['mɛksɪkəu] n México, Méjico

**mg** abbr (= milligram) mg

**mice** [maɪs] pl of **mouse**

**micro...** [maɪkrəu] pref micro...; **microchip** n microplaqueta; **microphone** n micrófono; **microscope** n microscopio; **microwave** n (also: **microwave oven**) horno microondas

**mid** [mɪd] adj: **in ~ May** a mediados de mayo; **in ~ afternoon** a media tarde; **in ~ air** en el aire; **midday** n mediodía m

**middle** ['mɪdl] n centro; (half-way point) medio; (waist) cintura ▷ adj de en medio; **in the ~ of the night** en plena noche; **middle-aged** adj de mediana edad; **Middle Ages** npl: **the Middle Ages** la Edad Media; **middle class** n: **the middle class(es)** la clase media ▷ adj: **middle-class** de clase media; **Middle East** n Oriente m Medio; **middle name** n segundo nombre m; **middle school** n (US) colegio para niños de doce a catorce años; (BRIT) colegio para niños de ocho o nueve a doce o trece años

**midge** [mɪdʒ] n mosquito

**midget** ['mɪdʒɪt] n (inf!) enano/a

**midnight** ['mɪdnaɪt] n medianoche f

**midst** [mɪdst] n: **in the ~ of** en medio de; (situation, action) en mitad de

**midsummer** [mɪd'sʌməʳ] n: **a ~ day** un día de pleno verano

**midway** [mɪd'weɪ] adj, adv: **~ (between)** a medio camino (entre); **~ through** a la mitad (de)

**midweek** [mɪd'wiːk] adv entre semana

**midwife** (pl **midwives**) ['mɪdwaɪf, -waɪvz] n matrona, comadrona

**midwinter** [mɪd'wɪntəʳ] n: **in ~** en pleno invierno

**might** [maɪt] vb see **may** ▷ n fuerza, poder m; **mighty** adj fuerte, poderoso

**migraine** ['miːɡreɪn] n jaqueca

**migrant** ['maɪɡrənt] adj migratorio; (worker) emigrante

**migrate** [maɪ'ɡreɪt] vi emigrar

**migration** [maɪ'ɡreɪʃən] n emigración f

**mike** [maɪk] n abbr (= microphone) micro

**mild** [maɪld] adj (person) apacible; (climate) templado; (slight) ligero; (taste) suave; (illness) leve; **mildly** adv ligeramente; suavemente; **to put it mildly** por no decir algo peor

**mile** [maɪl] n milla; **mileage** n número de millas; (Aut) kilometraje m; **mileometer** [maɪ'lɔmɪtəʳ] n (BRIT) = **milometer**; **milestone** n mojón m

**military** ['mɪlɪtərɪ] adj militar

**militia** [mɪ'lɪʃə] n milicia

**milk** [mɪlk] n leche f ▷ vt (cow) ordeñar; (fig) chupar; **milk chocolate** n chocolate m con leche; **milkman** n lechero; **milky** adj lechoso

**mill** [mɪl] n (windmill etc) molino; (coffee mill) molinillo; (factory) fábrica ▷ vt moler ▷ vi (also: **~ about**) arremolinarse

**millennium** (pl **millenniums** or **millennia**) [mɪ'lɛnɪəm, -'lɛnɪə] n milenio, milenario

**milli...** ['mɪlɪ] pref mili...; **milligram(me)** ['mɪlɪɡræm] n miligramo; **millilitre**, (US) **milliliter** ['mɪlɪliːtəʳ] n mililitro; **millimetre**, (US) **millimeter** ['mɪlɪmiːtəʳ] n milímetro

**million** ['mɪljən] n millón m; **a ~ times** un millón de veces; **millionaire** [mɪljə'nɛəʳ] n millonario/a; **millionth** adj millonésimo

**milometer** [maɪ'lɔmɪtəʳ] n (BRIT) cuentakilómetros m inv

**mime** [maɪm] n mímica; (actor) mimo/a ▷ vt remedar ▷ vi actuar de mimo

**mimic** ['mɪmɪk] n imitador(a) m/f ▷ adj mímico ▷ vt remedar, imitar

**min.** abbr (= minute(s)) m.; = **minimum**

**mince** [mɪns] vt picar ▷ n (BRIT Culin) carne f picada; **mincemeat** n conserva de fruta picada; (US: meat) carne f picada; **mince pie** n pastelillo relleno de fruta picada

**mind** [maɪnd] n mente f; (contrasted with matter) espíritu m ▷ vt (attend to, look after) ocuparse de, cuidar; (be careful of) tener cuidado con; (object to): **I don't ~ the noise** no me molesta el ruido; **it is on my ~** me preocupa; **to bear sth in ~** tomar or tener algo en cuenta; **to make up one's ~** decidirse; **I don't ~** me es igual; **~ you, ...** te advierto que ...; **never ~!** ¡es igual!, ¡no importa!; (don't worry) ¡no te preocupes!; **"~ the step"** "cuidado con el escalón"; **mindless** adj (violence, crime) sin sentido; (work) de autómata

**mine** [maɪn] pron (el) mío/(la) mía etc ▷ adj: **this book is ~** este libro es mío ▷ n mina ▷ vt (coal) extraer; (ship, beach) minar; **minefield** n campo de minas; **miner** n minero/a

**mineral** ['mɪnərəl] *adj* mineral ▷ *n* mineral *m*; **mineral water** *n* agua mineral
**mingle** ['mɪŋgl] *vi*: **to ~ with** mezclarse con
**miniature** ['mɪnətʃəʳ] *adj* (en) miniatura ▷ *n* miniatura
**minibar** ['mɪnɪbɑːʳ] *n* minibar *m*
**minibus** ['mɪnɪbʌs] *n* microbús *m*
**minicab** ['mɪnɪkæb] *n* taxi *m* (*que sólo puede pedirse por teléfono*)
**minimal** ['mɪnɪml] *adj* mínimo
**minimize** ['mɪnɪmaɪz] *vt* minimizar; (*play down*) empequeñecer
**minimum** ['mɪnɪməm] *n* mínimo ▷ *adj* mínimo
**mining** ['maɪnɪŋ] *n* minería
**miniskirt** ['mɪnɪskəːt] *n* minifalda
**minister** ['mɪnɪstəʳ] *n* (*BRIT Pol*) ministro/a; (*: junior*) secretario/a de Estado; (*Rel*) pastor *m* ▷ *vi*: **to ~ to** atender a
**ministry** ['mɪnɪstrɪ] *n* (*BRIT Pol*) ministerio; (*Rel*) sacerdocio
**minor** ['maɪnəʳ] *adj* (*repairs, injuries*) leve; (*poet, planet*) menor; (*Mus*) menor ▷ *n* (*Law*) menor *mf* de edad
**Minorca** [mɪ'nɔːkə] *n* Menorca
**minority** [maɪ'nɔrɪtɪ] *n* minoría
**mint** [mɪnt] *n* (*plant*) menta, hierbabuena; (*sweet*) caramelo de menta ▷ *vt* (*coins*) acuñar; **the (Royal) M~**, (*us*): **the (US) M~** la Casa de la Moneda; **in ~ condition** en perfecto estado
**minus** ['maɪnəs] *n* (*also*: **~ sign**) signo menos ▷ *prep* menos; **12 ~ 6 equals 6** 12 menos 6 son 6; **~ 24°C** menos 24 grados
**minute¹** ['mɪnɪt] *n* (*light*) momento; **minutes** *npl* (*of meeting*) actas *fpl*; **at the last ~** última hora
**minute²** [maɪ'njuːt] *adj* diminuto; (*search*) minucioso
**miracle** ['mɪrəkl] *n* milagro
**miraculous** [mɪ'rækjuləs] *adj* milagroso
**mirage** ['mɪrɑːʒ] *n* espejismo
**mirror** ['mɪrəʳ] *n* espejo; (*in car*) retrovisor *m*
**misbehave** [mɪsbɪ'heɪv] *vi* portarse mal
**misc.** *abbr* = **miscellaneous**
**miscarriage** ['mɪskærɪdʒ] *n* (*Med*) aborto (no provocado); **~ of justice** error *m* judicial
**miscellaneous** [mɪsɪ'leɪnɪəs] *adj* varios/as, diversos/as
**mischief** ['mɪstʃɪf] *n* travesura; (*maliciousness*) malicia; **mischievous** ['mɪstʃɪvəs] *adj* travieso
**misconception** ['mɪskən'sɛpʃən] *n* idea equivocada; equivocación *f*
**misconduct** [mɪs'kɔndʌkt] *n* mala conducta; **professional ~** falta profesional
**miser** ['maɪzəʳ] *n* avaro/a
**miserable** ['mɪzərəbl] *adj* (*unhappy*) triste, desgraciado; (*wretched*) miserable

**misery** ['mɪzərɪ] *n* tristeza; (*wretchedness*) miseria, desdicha
**misfortune** [mɪs'fɔːtʃən] *n* desgracia
**misgiving** [mɪs'gɪvɪŋ] *n* (*apprehension*) presentimiento; **to have ~s about sth** tener dudas sobre algo
**misguided** [mɪs'gaɪdɪd] *adj* equivocado
**mishap** ['mɪshæp] *n* desgracia, contratiempo
**misinterpret** [mɪsɪn'təːprɪt] *vt* interpretar mal
**misjudge** [mɪs'dʒʌdʒ] *vt* juzgar mal
**mislay** [mɪs'leɪ] *vt* extraviar, perder
**mislead** [mɪs'liːd] *vt* llevar a conclusiones erróneas; **misleading** *adj* engañoso
**misplace** [mɪs'pleɪs] *vt* extraviar
**misprint** ['mɪsprɪnt] *n* errata, error *m* de imprenta
**misrepresent** [mɪsrɛprɪ'zɛnt] *vt* falsificar
**Miss** [mɪs] *n* Señorita
**miss** [mɪs] *vt* (*train etc*) perder; (*target*) errar; (*regret the absence of*): **I ~ him** le echo de menos ▷ *vi* fallar ▷ *n* (*shot*) tiro fallido; **miss out** *vt* (*BRIT*) omitir; **miss out on** *vt fus* (*fun, party, opportunity*) perderse
**missile** ['mɪsaɪl] *n* (*Aviat*) misil *m*; (*object thrown*) proyectil *m*
**missing** ['mɪsɪŋ] *adj* (*pupil*) ausente; (*thing*) perdido; **~ in action** desaparecido en combate
**mission** ['mɪʃən] *n* misión *f*; **missionary** *n* misionero/a
**misspell** [mɪs'spɛl] *vt* (*irreg: like* **spell**) escribir mal
**mist** [mɪst] *n* (*light*) neblina; (*heavy*) niebla; (*at sea*) bruma ▷ *vi* (*also*: **~ over, ~ up**: *BRIT*: *windows*) empañarse
**mistake** [mɪs'teɪk] *n* error *m* ▷ *vt* (*irreg: like* **take**) entender mal; **by ~** por equivocación; **to make a ~** equivocarse; **to ~ A for B** confundir A con B; **mistaken** *pp of* **mistake** ▷ *adj* equivocado; **to be mistaken** equivocarse, engañarse
**mister** ['mɪstəʳ] *n* (*inf*) señor *m*; *see also* **Mr**
**mistletoe** ['mɪsltəu] *n* muérdago
**mistook** [mɪs'tuk] *pt of* **mistake**
**mistress** ['mɪstrɪs] *n* (*lover*) amante *f*; (*of house*) señora (de la casa); (*BRIT: in primary school*) maestra; (*: in secondary school*) profesora
**mistrust** [mɪs'trʌst] *vt* desconfiar de
**misty** ['mɪstɪ] *adj* (*day*) de niebla; (*glasses*) empañado
**misunderstand** [mɪsʌndə'stænd] *vt*, *vi* (*irreg: like* **understand**) entender mal; **misunderstanding** *n* malentendido
**misunderstood** [mɪsʌndə'stud] *pt*, *pp of* **misunderstand** ▷ *adj* (*person*) incomprendido

**misuse** n [mɪsˈjuːs] mal uso; (of power) abuso; (of funds) malversación f ▷ vt [mɪsˈjuːz] abusar de; (funds) malversar
**mix** [mɪks] vt mezclar; (combine) unir ▷ vi mezclarse; (people) llevarse bien ▷ n mezcla; **mix up** vt mezclar; (confuse) confundir; **mixed** adj mixto; (feelings etc) encontrado; **mixed grill** n (BRIT) parrillada mixta; **mixed salad** n ensalada mixta; **mixed-up** adj (confused) confuso, revuelto; **mixer** n (for food) batidora; (person): **he's a good mixer** tiene don de gentes; **mixture** n mezcla; **mix-up** n confusión f
**ml** abbr (= millilitre(s)) ml
**mm** abbr (= millimetre) mm
**moan** [məʊn] n gemido ▷ vi gemir; (inf: complain): **to ~ (about)** quejarse (de)
**moat** [məʊt] n foso
**mob** [mɔb] n multitud f ▷ vt acosar
**mobile** [ˈməʊbaɪl] adj móvil ▷ n móvil m; **mobile home** n caravana; **mobile phone** n teléfono móvil
**mobility** [məʊˈbɪlɪtɪ] n movilidad f
**mobilize** [ˈməʊbɪlaɪz] vt movilizar
**mock** [mɔk] vt (make ridiculous) ridiculizar; (laugh at) burlarse de ▷ adj fingido; **~ exams** (BRIT: Scol) exámenes mpl de prueba; **mockery** n burla
**mod cons** [ˈmɔdˈkɔnz] npl abbr = **modern conveniences**; see **convenience**
**mode** [məʊd] n modo
**model** [ˈmɔdl] n modelo; (for fashion, art) modelo mf ▷ adj modelo inv ▷ vt modelar; **to ~ o.s. on** tomar como modelo a ▷ vi ser modelo; **to ~ clothes** pasar modelos, ser modelo
**modem** [ˈməʊdəm] n módem m
**moderate** adj, n [ˈmɔdərət] moderado/a ▷ vi [ˈmɔdəreɪt] moderarse, calmarse ▷ vt [ˈmɔdəreɪt] moderar
**moderation** [mɔdəˈreɪʃən] n moderación f; **in ~** con moderación
**modern** [ˈmɔdən] adj moderno; **modernize** vt modernizar
**modest** [ˈmɔdɪst] adj modesto; (small) módico; **modesty** [ˈmɔdɪstɪ] n modestia
**modification** [mɔdɪfɪˈkeɪʃən] n modificación f
**modify** [ˈmɔdɪfaɪ] vt modificar
**module** [ˈmɔdjuːl] n módulo
**mohair** [ˈməʊhɛəʳ] n mohair m
**Mohammed** [məˈhæməd] n Mahoma m
**moist** [mɔɪst] adj húmedo; **moisture** [ˈmɔɪstʃəʳ] n humedad f; **moisturizer** [ˈmɔɪstʃəraɪzəʳ] n crema hidratante
**mold** [məʊld] n, vt (US) = **mould**
**mole** [məʊl] n (animal) topo; (spot) lunar m
**molecule** [ˈmɔlɪkjuːl] n molécula

**molest** [məʊˈlɛst] vt importunar; (sexually) abusar sexualmente de
> Be careful not to translate molest by the Spanish word molestar.

**molten** [ˈməʊltən] adj fundido; (lava) líquido
**mom** [mɔm] n (US) = **mum**
**moment** [ˈməʊmənt] n momento; **at** or **for the ~** de momento, por ahora; **momentarily** [ˈməʊməntrɪlɪ] adv momentáneamente; (US: very soon) de un momento a otro; **momentary** adj momentáneo; **momentous** [məʊˈmɛntəs] adj trascendental, importante
**momentum** [məʊˈmɛntəm] n momento; (fig) ímpetu m; **to gather ~** cobrar velocidad; (fig) cobrar fuerza
**mommy** [ˈmɔmɪ] n (US) = **mummy**
**Mon.** abbr (= Monday) lun.
**Monaco** [ˈmɔnəkəʊ] n Mónaco
**monarch** [ˈmɔnək] n monarca mf; **monarchy** n monarquía
**monastery** [ˈmɔnəstərɪ] n monasterio
**Monday** [ˈmʌndɪ] n lunes m inv
**monetary** [ˈmʌnɪtərɪ] adj monetario
**money** [ˈmʌnɪ] n dinero; **to make ~** ganar dinero; **money belt** n riñonera; **money order** n giro
**mongrel** [ˈmʌŋgrəl] n (dog) perro cruzado
**monitor** [ˈmɔnɪtəʳ] n (Scol) monitor m; (also: **television ~**) receptor m de control; (of computer) monitor m ▷ vt controlar
**monk** [mʌŋk] n monje m
**monkey** [ˈmʌŋkɪ] n mono
**monologue** [ˈmɔnəlɔg] n monólogo
**monopoly** [məˈnɔpəlɪ] n monopolio
**monotonous** [məˈnɔtənəs] adj monótono
**monsoon** [mɔnˈsuːn] n monzón m
**monster** [ˈmɔnstəʳ] n monstruo
**month** [mʌnθ] n mes m; **300 dollars a ~** 300 dólares al mes; **every ~** cada mes; **monthly** adj mensual ▷ adv mensualmente
**monument** [ˈmɔnjumənt] n monumento
**mood** [muːd] n humor m; **to be in a good/bad ~** estar de buen/mal humor; **moody** adj (changeable) de humor variable; (sullen) malhumorado
**moon** [muːn] n luna; **moonlight** n luz f de la luna
**moor** [muəʳ] n páramo ▷ vt (ship) amarrar ▷ vi echar las amarras
**moose** [muːs] n (pl inv) alce m
**mop** [mɔp] n fregona; (of hair) melena ▷ vt fregar; **mop up** vt limpiar
**mope** [məʊp] vi estar deprimido
**moped** [ˈməʊpɛd] n ciclomotor m
**moral** [ˈmɔrl] adj moral ▷ n moraleja; **morals** npl moralidad f, moral f

**morale** [mɒˈrɑːl] n moral f
**morality** [məˈrælɪtɪ] n moralidad f
**morbid** [ˈmɔːbɪd] adj (interest) morboso; (Med) mórbido

**○ KEYWORD**

**more** [mɔːʳ] adj **1** (greater in number etc) más; **more people/work than before** más gente/trabajo que antes
**2** (additional) más; **do you want (some) more tea?** ¿quieres más té?; **is there any more wine?** ¿queda vino?; **it'll take a few more weeks** tardará unas semanas más; **it's 2 kms more to the house** faltan 2 kms para la casa; **more time/letters than we expected** más tiempo del que/más cartas de las que esperábamos
▶ pron (greater amount, additional amount) más; **more than 10** más de 10; **it cost more than the other one/than we expected** costó más que el otro/más de lo que esperábamos; **is there any more?** ¿hay más?; **many/much more** muchos/as más, mucho/a más
▶ adv más; **more dangerous/easily (than)** más peligroso/fácilmente (que); **more and more expensive** cada vez más caro; **more or less** más o menos; **more than ever** más que nunca

**moreover** [mɔːˈrəuvəʳ] adv además, por otra parte
**morgue** [mɔːg] n depósito de cadáveres
**morning** [ˈmɔːnɪŋ] n mañana; (early morning) madrugada; **in the ~** por la mañana; **7 o'clock in the ~** las 7 de la mañana; **morning sickness** n náuseas fpl del embarazo
**Moroccan** [məˈrɔkən] adj, n marroquí mf
**Morocco** [məˈrɔkəu] n Marruecos m
**moron** [ˈmɔːrɔn] n (inf!) imbécil mf
**morphine** [ˈmɔːfiːn] n morfina
**Morse** [mɔːs] n (also: ~ code) (código) morse m
**mortal** [ˈmɔːtl] adj, n mortal m
**mortar** [ˈmɔːtəʳ] n argamasa
**mortgage** [ˈmɔːgɪdʒ] n hipoteca ▶ vt hipotecar
**mortician** [mɔːˈtɪʃən] n (US) director(a) m/f de pompas fúnebres
**mortified** [ˈmɔːtɪfaɪd] adj: **I was ~** me dio muchísima vergüenza
**mortuary** [ˈmɔːtjuərɪ] n depósito de cadáveres
**mosaic** [məuˈzeɪɪk] n mosaico
**Moslem** [ˈmɔzləm] adj, n = **Muslim**
**mosque** [mɔsk] n mezquita
**mosquito** [mɒsˈkiːtəu] (pl **mosquitoes**) n mosquito, zancudo (LAM)

**moss** [mɒs] n musgo
**most** [məust] adj la mayor parte de, la mayoría de ▶ pron la mayor parte, la mayoría ▶ adv el más; (very) muy; **the ~** (also: + adjective) el más; **~ of them** la mayor parte de ellos; **I saw the ~** yo fui el que más vi; **at the (very) ~** a lo sumo, todo lo más; **to make the ~ of** aprovechar (al máximo); **a ~ interesting book** un libro interesantísimo; **mostly** adv en su mayor parte, principalmente
**MOT** n abbr (BRIT) = **Ministry of Transport**; **the ~ (test)** ≈ la ITV
**motel** [məuˈtɛl] n motel m
**moth** [mɒθ] n mariposa nocturna; (clothes moth) polilla
**mother** [ˈmʌðəʳ] n madre f ▶ adj materno ▶ vt (care for) cuidar (como una madre); **motherhood** n maternidad f; **mother-in-law** n suegra; **mother-of-pearl** n nácar m; **Mother's Day** n Día m de la Madre; **mother-to-be** n futura madre; **mother tongue** n lengua materna
**motif** [məuˈtiːf] n motivo
**motion** [ˈməuʃən] n movimiento; (gesture) ademán m, señal f; (at meeting) moción f ▶ vt, vi: **to ~ (to) sb to do sth** hacer señas a algn para que haga algo; **motionless** adj inmóvil; **motion picture** n película
**motivate** [ˈməutɪveɪt] vt motivar
**motivation** [məutɪˈveɪʃən] n motivación f
**motive** [ˈməutɪv] n motivo
**motor** [ˈməutəʳ] n motor m; (BRIT inf: vehicle) coche m, carro (LAM), automóvil m, auto m (LAM) ▶ adj motor (f: motora or motriz); **motorbike** n moto f; **motorboat** n lancha motora; **motorcar** n (BRIT) coche m, carro (LAM), automóvil m, auto m (LAM); **motorcycle** n motocicleta; **motorcyclist** n motociclista mf; **motoring** n (BRIT) automovilismo; **motorist** n conductor(a) m/f, automovilista mf; **motor racing** n (BRIT) carreras fpl de coches, automovilismo; **motorway** n (BRIT) autopista
**motto** [ˈmɔtəu] (pl **mottoes**) n lema m; (watchword) consigna
**mould**, (US) **mold** [məuld] n molde m; (mildew) moho ▶ vt moldear; (fig) formar; **mouldy** adj enmohecido
**mound** [maund] n montón m, montículo
**mount** [maunt] n monte m ▶ vt montar en, subir a; (picture) enmarcar ▶ vi (also: **~ up**: increase) aumentar; (on horse) montar
**mountain** [ˈmauntɪn] n montaña ▶ cpd de montaña; **mountain bike** n bicicleta de montaña; **mountaineer** n alpinista mf, andinista mf (LAM); **mountaineering** n montañismo, alpinismo, andinismo (LAM);

**mountainous** adj montañoso; **mountain range** n sierra

**mourn** [mɔ:n] vt llorar, lamentar ▷ vi: **to ~ for** llorar la muerte de; **mourner** n doliente mf; **mourning** n luto; **in mourning** de luto

**mouse** (pl **mice**) [maus, maɪs] n (also Comput) ratón m; **mouse mat** n (Comput) alfombrilla, almohadilla

**mousse** [mu:s] n (Culin) mousse f; (for hair) espuma (moldeadora)

**moustache** [məs'tɑ:ʃ], (US) **mustache** ['mʌstæʃ] n bigote m

**mouth** (pl **mouths**) [mauθ, -ðz] n boca; (of river) desembocadura; **mouthful** n bocado; **mouth organ** n armónica; **mouthpiece** n (of musical instrument) boquilla; (spokesman) portavoz mf; **mouthwash** n enjuague m bucal

**move** [mu:v] n (movement) movimiento; (in game) jugada; (: turn to play) turno; (change of house) mudanza ▷ vt mover; (emotionally) conmover; (Pol: resolution etc) proponer ▷ vi moverse; (traffic) circular; (also: **~ house**) trasladarse, mudarse; **to get a ~ on** darse prisa; **to ~ sb to do sth** mover a algn a hacer algo; **move back** vi volver; **move in** vi (to a house) instalarse; **move off** vi ponerse en camino; **move on** vi seguir viaje; **move out** vi (of house) mudarse; **move over** vi hacerse a un lado, correrse; **move up** vi (employee) ascender; **movement** n movimiento

**movie** ['mu:vɪ] n película; **to go to the ~s** ir al cine; **movie theater** n (US) cine m

**moving** ['mu:vɪŋ] adj (emotional) conmovedor(a); (that moves) móvil

**mow** (pt **mowed**, pp **mowed** or **mown**) [məu, -n] vt (grass) cortar; (corn) segar; **mower** n (also: **lawnmower**) cortacésped m

**Mozambique** [məuzæm'bi:k] n Mozambique m

**MP** n abbr (BRIT) = **Member of Parliament**

**mpg** n abbr (= miles per gallon) 30 mpg = 9.4 l. per 100 km

**mph** abbr (= miles per hour) 60 mph = 96 km/h

**MP3** ['empi:'θri:] n MP3 m; **MP3 player** n reproductor m MP3

**Mr, Mr.** ['mɪstər] n: Mr Smith (el) Sr. Smith

**Mrs, Mrs.** ['mɪsɪz] n: ~ Smith (la) Sra. de Smith

**Ms, Ms.** [mɪz] n (Miss or Mrs) abreviatura con la que se evita hacer expreso el estado civil de una mujer; Ms Smith (la) Sra. Smith

**MSP** n abbr (BRIT) = **Member of the Scottish Parliament**

**Mt** abbr (Geo: = mount) m.

**much** [mʌtʃ] adj mucho ▷ adv, n, pron mucho; (before pp) muy; **how ~ is it?** ¿cuánto es?, ¿cuánto cuesta?; **too ~** demasiado; **it's not ~** no es mucho; **as ~ as** tanto como; **however ~ he tries** por mucho que se esfuerce

**muck** [mʌk] n suciedad f; **muck up** vt (inf) estropear; **mucky** adj (dirty) sucio

**mucus** ['mju:kəs] n mucosidad f, moco

**mud** [mʌd] n barro, lodo

**muddle** ['mʌdl] n desorden m, confusión f; (mix-up) embrollo, lío ▷ vt (also: **~ up**) embrollar, confundir

**muddy** ['mʌdɪ] adj fangoso, cubierto de lodo

**mudguard** ['mʌdgɑ:d] n guardabarros m inv

**muesli** ['mju:zlɪ] n muesli m

**muffin** ['mʌfɪn] n bollo, ≈ magdalena

**muffled** ['mʌfld] adj apagado; (noise etc) amortiguado

**muffler** ['mʌflər] n (scarf) bufanda; (US: Aut) silenciador m

**mug** [mʌg] n (cup) taza alta; (for beer) jarra; (inf: face) jeta ▷ vt (assault) atracar; **mugger** n atracador(a) m/f; **mugging** n atraco callejero

**muggy** ['mʌgɪ] adj bochornoso

**mule** [mju:l] n mula

**multicoloured**, (US) **multicolored** ['mʌltɪkʌləd] adj multicolor

**multimedia** ['mʌltɪ'mi:dɪə] adj multimedia inv

**multinational** [mʌltɪ'næʃənl] n multinacional f ▷ adj multinacional

**multiple** ['mʌltɪpl] adj múltiple ▷ n múltiplo; **multiple choice** n (also: **multiple choice test**) examen m de tipo test; **multiple sclerosis** n esclerosis f múltiple

**multiplex** ['mʌltɪpleks] n (also: **~ cinema**) multicines m inv

**multiplication** [mʌltɪplɪ'keɪʃən] n multiplicación f

**multiply** ['mʌltɪplaɪ] vt multiplicar ▷ vi multiplicarse

**multistorey** [mʌltɪ'stɔ:rɪ] adj (BRIT) de muchos pisos

**mum** [mʌm] n (BRIT) mamá f ▷ adj: **to keep ~ (about sth)** no decir ni mu (de algo)

**mumble** ['mʌmbl] vt decir entre dientes ▷ vi hablar entre dientes, musitar

**mummy** ['mʌmɪ] n (BRIT: mother) mamá f; (embalmed) momia

**mumps** [mʌmps] n paperas fpl

**munch** [mʌntʃ] vt, vi mascar

**municipal** [mju:'nɪsɪpl] adj municipal

**mural** ['mjuərl] n (pintura) mural m

**murder** ['mə:dər] n asesinato; (in law) homicidio ▷ vt asesinar, matar; **murderer** n asesino

**murky** ['mə:kɪ] adj (water, past) turbio; (room) sombrío

**murmur** ['mə:mər] n murmullo ▷ vt, vi murmurar

**muscle** ['mʌsl] n músculo; (fig: strength)
garra, fuerza; **muscular** ['mʌskjulə] adj
muscular; (person) musculoso
**museum** [mjuːˈzɪəm] n museo
**mushroom** ['mʌʃrum] n seta, hongo;
(small) champiñón m ▷ vi crecer de la noche
a la mañana
**music** ['mjuːzɪk] n música; **musical** adj
musical; (sound) melodioso; (person) con
talento musical ▷ n (show) (comedia)
musical m; **musical instrument** n
instrumento musical; **musician**
[mjuːˈzɪʃən] n músico/a
**Muslim** ['mʌzlɪm] adj, n musulmán/ana
m/f
**muslin** ['mʌzlɪn] n muselina
**mussel** ['mʌsl] n mejillón m
**must** [mʌst] aux vb (obligation): **I ~ do
it** debo hacerlo, tengo que hacerlo;
(probability): **he ~ be there by now** ya debe
(de) estar allí ▷ n: **it's a ~** es imprescindible
**mustache** ['mʌstæʃ] n (US) = **moustache**
**mustard** ['mʌstəd] n mostaza
**mustn't** ['mʌsnt] = **must not**
**mute** [mjuːt] adj mudo
**mutilate** ['mjuːtɪleɪt] vt mutilar
**mutiny** ['mjuːtɪnɪ] n motín m ▷ vi
amotinarse
**mutter** ['mʌtə] vt, vi murmurar
**mutton** ['mʌtn] n (carne f de) cordero
**mutual** ['mjuːtʃuəl] adj mutuo; (friend)
común
**muzzle** ['mʌzl] n hocico; (protective device)
bozal m; (of gun) boca ▷ vt (dog) poner un
bozal a
**my** [maɪ] adj mi(s); **my house/brother/
sisters** mi casa/hermano/mis hermanas;
**I've washed my hair/cut my finger** me he
lavado el pelo/cortado un dedo; **is this my
pen or yours?** ¿este bolígrafo es mío o tuyo?
**myself** [maɪˈsɛlf] pron (reflexive) me;
(emphatic) yo mismo; (after prep) mí
(mismo); see also **oneself**
**mysterious** [mɪsˈtɪərɪəs] adj misterioso
**mystery** ['mɪstərɪ] n misterio
**mystical** ['mɪstɪkl] adj místico
**mystify** ['mɪstɪfaɪ] vt (perplex) dejar
perplejo
**myth** [mɪθ] n mito; **mythology**
[mɪˈθɒlədʒɪ] n mitología

**n/a** abbr (= not applicable) no interesa
**nag** [næg] vt (scold) regañar
**nail** [neɪl] n (human) uña; (metal) clavo ▷ vt
clavar; **to ~ sb down to a date/price** hacer
que algn se comprometa a una fecha/un
precio; **nailbrush** n cepillo para las uñas;
**nailfile** n lima para las uñas; **nail polish** n
esmalte m or laca para las uñas; **nail polish
remover** n quitaesmalte m; **nail scissors**
npl tijeras fpl para las uñas; **nail varnish** n
(BRIT) = **nail polish**
**naïve** [naɪˈiːv] adj ingenuo
**naked** ['neɪkɪd] adj (nude) desnudo; (flame)
expuesto al aire
**name** [neɪm] n nombre m; (surname)
apellido; (reputation) fama, renombre m ▷ vt
(child) poner nombre a; (criminal) identificar;
(price, date etc) fijar; **by ~** de nombre; **in the
~ of** en nombre de; **what's your ~?** ¿cómo se
llama usted?; **to give one's ~ and address**
dar sus señas; **namely** adv a saber
**nanny** ['nænɪ] n niñera
**nap** [næp] n (sleep) sueñecito, siesta
**napkin** ['næpkɪn] n (also: **table ~**)
servilleta
**nappy** ['næpɪ] n (BRIT) pañal m
**narcotic** [nɑːˈkɒtɪk] adj, n narcótico;
**narcotics** npl estupefacientes mpl,
narcóticos mpl
**narrative** ['nærətɪv] n narrativa ▷ adj
narrativo
**narrator** [nəˈreɪtə] n narrador(a) m/f
**narrow** ['nærəu] adj estrecho ▷ vi
estrecharse; (diminish) reducirse; **to have a
~ escape** escaparse por los pelos; **narrow
down** vt (search, investigation, possibilities)
restringir, limitar; (list) reducir; **narrowly**
adv (miss) por poco; **narrow-minded** adj de
miras estrechas
**nasal** ['neɪzl] adj nasal

**nasty** ['nɑːstɪ] adj (remark) feo; (person) antipático; (revolting: taste, smell) asqueroso; (wound, disease etc) peligroso, grave

**nation** ['neɪʃən] n nación f

**national** ['næʃənl] adj nacional ▷ n súbdito/a; **national anthem** n himno nacional; **national dress** n traje m típico del país; **National Health Service** n (BRIT) servicio nacional de salud, ≈ INSALUD m (SP); **National Insurance** n (BRIT) seguro social nacional; **nationalist** adj, n nacionalista mf; **nationality** n nacionalidad f; **nationalize** vt nacionalizar; **National Trust** n (BRIT) organización encargada de preservar el patrimonio histórico británico

**nationwide** ['neɪʃənwaɪd] adj a escala nacional

**native** ['neɪtɪv] n (local inhabitant) natural mf ▷ adj (indigenous) indígena; (country) natal; (innate) natural, innato; **a ~ of Russia** un(a) natural de Rusia; **Native American** adj, n americano/a indígena, amerindio/a; **native speaker** n hablante mf nativo/a

**NATO** ['neɪtəu] n abbr (= North Atlantic Treaty Organization) OTAN f

**natural** ['nætʃrəl] adj natural; **natural gas** n gas m natural; **natural history** n historia natural; **naturally** adv (speak etc) naturalmente; (of course) desde luego, por supuesto; **natural resources** npl recursos mpl naturales

**nature** ['neɪtʃə'] n naturaleza; (group, sort) género, clase f; (character) modo de ser, carácter m; **by ~** por naturaleza; **nature reserve** n reserva natural

**naughty** ['nɔːtɪ] adj (child) travieso

**nausea** ['nɔːsɪə] n náusea

**naval** ['neɪvl] adj naval, de marina

**navel** ['neɪvl] n ombligo

**navigate** ['nævɪgeɪt] vt gobernar ▷ vi navegar; (Aut) ir de copiloto; **navigation** [nævɪ'geɪʃən] n (action) navegación f; (science) náutica

**navy** ['neɪvɪ] n marina de guerra; (ships) armada, flota

**Nazi** ['nɑːtsɪ] n nazi mf

**NB** abbr (= nota bene) nótese

**near** [nɪə'] adj (place, relation) cercano; (time) próximo ▷ adv cerca ▷ prep (also: **~ to**: space) cerca de, junto a; (time) cerca de ▷ vt acercarse a, aproximarse a; **nearby** [nɪə'baɪ] adj cercano, próximo ▷ adv cerca; **nearly** adv casi, por poco; **I nearly fell** por poco me caigo; **near-sighted** adj miope, corto de vista

**neat** [niːt] adj (place) ordenado, bien cuidado; (person) pulcro; (plan) ingenioso; (spirits) solo; **neatly** adv (tidily) con esmero; (skilfully) ingeniosamente

**necessarily** ['nɛsɪsrɪlɪ] adv necesariamente

**necessary** ['nɛsɪsrɪ] adj necesario, preciso

**necessity** [nɪ'sɛsɪtɪ] n necesidad f

**neck** [nɛk] n (Anat) cuello; (of animal) pescuezo ▷ vi besuquearse; **~ and ~** parejos; **necklace** ['nɛklɪs] n collar m; **necktie** n (US) corbata

**nectarine** ['nɛktərɪn] n nectarina

**need** [niːd] n (lack) escasez f, falta; (necessity) necesidad f ▷ vt (require) necesitar; **I ~ to do it** tengo que hacerlo; **you don't ~ to go** no hace falta que vayas

**needle** ['niːdl] n aguja ▷ vt (fig: inf) picar, fastidiar

**needless** ['niːdlɪs] adj innecesario; **~ to say** huelga decir que

**needlework** ['niːdlwəːk] n (activity) costura, labor f de aguja

**needn't** ['niːdnt] = **need not**

**needy** ['niːdɪ] adj necesitado

**negative** ['nɛgətɪv] n (Phot) negativo; (Ling) negación f ▷ adj negativo

**neglect** [nɪ'glɛkt] vt (one's duty) faltar a, no cumplir con; (child) descuidar, desatender ▷ n (state) abandono; (personal) dejadez f; (of child) desatención f; (of duty) incumplimiento

**negotiate** [nɪ'gəuʃɪeɪt] vt (treaty, loan) negociar; (obstacle) franquear; (bend in road) tomar ▷ vi: **to ~ (with)** negociar (con); **negotiation** [nɪgəuʃɪ'eɪʃən] n negociación f; **negotiations** npl negociaciones; **negotiator** [nɪ'gəuʃɪeɪtə'] n negociador(a) m/f

**neighbour**, (US) **neighbor** ['neɪbə'] n vecino/a; **neighbourhood**, (US) **neighborhood** n (place) vecindad f, barrio; (people) vecindario; **neighbouring**, (US) **neighboring** ['neɪbərɪŋ] adj vecino

**neither** ['naɪðə'] adj ni ▷ conj: **I didn't move and ~ did John** no me he movido, ni Juan tampoco ▷ pron ninguno ▷ adv: **~ good nor bad** ni bueno ni malo

**neon** ['niːɔn] n neón m

**Nepal** [nɪ'pɔːl] n Nepal m

**nephew** ['nɛvjuː] n sobrino

**nerve** [nəːv] n (Anat) nervio; (courage) valor m; (impudence) descaro, frescura; **nerves** (nervousness) nerviosismo msg, nervios mpl; **a fit of ~s** un ataque de nervios

**nervous** ['nəːvəs] adj (anxious) nervioso; (Anat) nervioso; (timid) tímido, miedoso; **nervous breakdown** n crisis f nerviosa

**nest** [nɛst] n (of bird) nido ▷ vi anidar

**net** [nɛt] n red f; (fabric) tul m ▷ adj (Comm) neto, líquido ▷ vt coger (SP) or agarrar (LAM) con red; (Sport) marcar; **netball** n balonred m

**Netherlands** ['nɛðələndz] *npl*: **the ~** los
Países Bajos
**nett** [nɛt] *adj* = **net**
**nettle** ['nɛtl] *n* ortiga
**network** ['nɛtwə:k] *n* red *f*
**neurotic** [njuə'rɔtɪk] *adj*, *n* neurótico/a
**neuter** ['nju:təʳ] *adj* (*Ling*) neutro ▷ *vt*
castrar, capar
**neutral** ['nju:trəl] *adj* (*person*) neutral;
(*colour etc*) neutro; (*Elec*) neutro ▷ *n* (*Aut*)
punto muerto
**never** ['nɛvəʳ] *adv* nunca, jamás; **I ~ went**
no fui nunca; **~ in my life** jamás en la vida;
*see also* **mind; never-ending** *adj*
interminable, sin fin; **nevertheless**
[nɛvəðə'lɛs] *adv* sin embargo, no obstante
**new** [nju:] *adj* nuevo; (*recent*) reciente;
**New Age** *n* Nueva era; **newborn** *adj* recién
nacido; **newcomer** ['nju:kʌməʳ] *n* recién
venido/a *or* llegado/a; **newly** *adv* recién
**news** [nju:z] *n* noticias *fpl*; **a piece of ~**
una noticia; **the ~** (*Radio, TV*) las noticias
*fpl*; **news agency** *n* agencia de noticias;
**newsagent** *n* (*BRIT*) vendedor(a) *m/f* de
periódicos; **newscaster** *n* presentador(a)
*m/f*, locutor(a) *m/f*; **news dealer** *n*
(*US*) = **newsagent; newsletter** *n* hoja
informativa, boletín *m*; **newspaper** *n*
periódico, diario; **newsreader** *n*
= **newscaster**
**newt** [nju:t] *n* tritón *m*
**New Year** *n* Año Nuevo; **New Year's Day**
*n* Día *m* de Año Nuevo; **New Year's Eve** *n*
Nochevieja
**New Zealand** [-'zi:lənd] *n* Nueva Zelanda
(*SP*), Nueva Zelandia (*LAM*); **New Zealander**
*n* neozelandés/esa *m/f*
**next** [nɛkst] *adj* (*house, room*) vecino, de al
lado; (*meeting*) próximo; (*page*) siguiente
▷ *adv* después; **the ~ day** el día siguiente;
**~ time** la próxima vez; **~ year** el año
próximo *or* que viene; **~ to** junto a, al lado
de; **~ to nothing** casi nada; **next door** *adv*
en la casa de al lado ▷ *adj* vecino, de al lado;
**next-of-kin** *n* pariente(s) *m(pl)* más
cercano(s)
**NHS** *n abbr* (*BRIT*) = **National Health
Service**
**nibble** ['nɪbl] *vt* mordisquear
**nice** [naɪs] *adj* (*likeable*) simpático; (*kind*)
amable; (*pleasant*) agradable; (*attractive*)
bonito; **nicely** *adv* amablemente; (*of health
etc*) bien
**niche** [ni:ʃ] *n* (*Arch*) nicho, hornacina
**nick** [nɪk] *n* (*wound*) rasguño; (*cut,
indentation*) mella, muesca ▷ *vt* (*inf*) birlar;
**in the ~ of time** justo a tiempo
**nickel** ['nɪkl] *n* níquel *m*; (*US*) *moneda de 5
centavos*

**nickname** ['nɪkneɪm] *n* apodo, mote *m*
▷ *vt* apodar
**nicotine** ['nɪkəti:n] *n* nicotina
**niece** [ni:s] *n* sobrina
**Nigeria** [naɪ'dʒɪərɪə] *n* Nigeria
**night** [naɪt] *n* noche *f*; (*evening*) tarde *f*;
**the ~ before last** anteanoche; **at ~, by ~**
de noche, por la noche; **night club** *n* club
nocturno, discoteca; **nightdress** *n* (*BRIT*)
camisón *m*
**nightgown** ['naɪtgaun], **nightie** ['naɪtɪ]
(*BRIT*) *n* – **nightdress**
**night: night life** *n* vida nocturna; **nightly**
*adj* de todas las noches ▷ *adv* todas
las noches, cada noche; **nightmare** *n*
pesadilla; **night school** *n* clase(s) *f(pl)*
nocturna(s); **night shift** *n* turno nocturno
*or* de noche; **night-time** *n* noche *f*
**nil** [nɪl] *n* (*BRIT Sport*) cero, nada
**nine** [naɪn] *num* nueve; **nineteen**
['naɪn'ti:n] *num* diecinueve; **nineteenth**
[naɪn'ti:nθ] *adj* decimonoveno,
decimonono; **ninetieth** ['naɪntɪɪθ] *adj*
nonagésimo; **ninety** *num* noventa
**ninth** [naɪnθ] *adj* noveno
**nip** [nɪp] *vt* (*pinch*) pellizcar; (*bite*) morder
**nipple** ['nɪpl] *n* (*Anat*) pezón *m*
**nitrogen** ['naɪtrədʒən] *n* nitrógeno

**〇 KEYWORD**

**no** [nəu] *adv* (*opposite of "yes"*) no; **are you
coming? — no (I'm not)** ¿vienes? — no;
**would you like some more? — no thank
you** ¿quieres más? — no gracias
▶ *adj* **1** (*not any*): **I have no money/time/
books** no tengo dinero/tiempo/libros; **no
other man would have done it** ningún
otro lo hubiera hecho
**2**: **"no entry"** "prohibido el paso"; **"no
smoking"** "prohibido fumar"
▶ *n* (*pl* **noes**) no *m*

**nobility** [nəu'bɪlɪtɪ] *n* nobleza
**noble** ['nəubl] *adj* noble
**nobody** ['nəubədɪ] *pron* nadie
**nod** [nɔd] *vi* saludar con la cabeza; (*in
agreement*) asentir con la cabeza ▷ *vt*:
**to ~ one's head** inclinar la cabeza ▷ *n*
inclinación *f* de cabeza; **nod off** *vi* cabecear
**noise** [nɔɪz] *n* ruido; (*din*) escándalo,
estrépito; **noisy** *adj* ruidoso; (*child*)
escandaloso
**nominal** ['nɔmɪnl] *adj* nominal
**nominate** ['nɔmɪneɪt] *vt* (*propose*)
proponer; (*appoint*) nombrar;
**nomination** [nɔmɪ'neɪʃən] *n* propuesta;
nombramiento; **nominee** [nɔmɪ'ni:] *n*
candidato/a

**none** [nʌn] pron ninguno/a ▷ adv de ninguna manera; **~ of you** ninguno de vosotros; **I've ~ left** no me queda ninguno/a; **he's ~ the worse for it** no le ha perjudicado; **I have ~** no tengo ninguno; **~ at all** (not one) ni uno

**nonetheless** [nʌnðə'lɛs] adv sin embargo, no obstante

**non-fiction** n no ficción f

**nonsense** ['nɔnsəns] n tonterías fpl, disparates fpl; **~!** ¡qué tonterías!

**non-: non-smoker** ['nɔn'sməukə'] n no fumador(a) m/f; **non-smoking** adj (de) no fumador; **non-stick** ['nɔn'stɪk] adj (pan, surface) antiadherente

**noodles** ['nu:dlz] npl tallarines mpl

**noon** [nu:n] n mediodía m

**no-one** ['nəuwʌn] pron = **nobody**

**nor** [nɔ:'] conj = **neither** ▷ adv see **neither**

**norm** [nɔ:m] n norma

**normal** ['nɔ:ml] adj normal; **normally** adv normalmente

**north** [nɔ:θ] n norte m ▷ adj (del) norte ▷ adv al or hacia el norte; **North America** n América del Norte; **North American** adj, n norteamericano/a; **northbound** ['nɔ:θbaund] adj (traffic) que se dirige al norte; (carriageway) de dirección norte; **north-east** n nor(d)este m; **northeastern** adj nor(d)este, del nor(d)este; **northern** ['nɔ:ðən] adj norteño, del Norte; **Northern Ireland** n Irlanda del Norte; **North Korea** n Corea del Norte; **North Pole** n: the North Pole el Polo Norte; **North Sea** n: the North Sea el mar del Norte; **north-west** n noroeste m; **northwestern** ['nɔ:θ'westən] adj noroeste, del noroeste

**Norway** ['nɔ:weɪ] n Noruega

**Norwegian** [nɔ:'wi:dʒən] adj noruego/a ▷ n noruego/a; (Ling) noruego

**nose** [nəuz] n (Anat) nariz f; (Zool) hocico; (sense of smell) olfato; **nose about, nose around** vi curiosear; **nosebleed** n hemorragia nasal; **nosey** adj curioso, fisgón/ona

**nostalgia** [nɔs'tældʒɪə] n nostalgia

**nostalgic** [nɔs'tældʒɪk] adj nostálgico

**nostril** ['nɔstrɪl] n ventana or orificio de la nariz

**nosy** ['nəuzɪ] adj = **nosey**

**not** [nɔt] adv no; **~ that ...** no es que ...; **it's too late, isn't it?** es demasiado tarde, ¿verdad?; **why ~?** ¿por qué no?

**notable** ['nəutəbl] adj notable; **notably** adv especialmente

**notch** [nɔtʃ] n muesca, corte m

**note** [nəut] n (Mus, record, letter) nota; (banknote) billete m; (tone) tono ▷ vt (observe) notar, observar; (write down)

apuntar, anotar; **notebook** n libreta, cuaderno; **noted** adj célebre, conocido; **notepad** n bloc m; **notepaper** n papel m para cartas

**nothing** ['nʌθɪŋ] n nada; (zero) cero; **he does ~** no hace nada; **~ new** nada nuevo; **~ much** no mucho; **for ~** (free) gratis; (in vain) en balde

**notice** ['nəutɪs] n (announcement) anuncio; (warning) aviso; (dismissal) despido; (resignation) dimisión f ▷ vt (observe) notar, observar; **to bring sth to sb's ~** (attention) llamar la atención de algn sobre algo; **to take ~ of** hacer caso de, prestar atención a; **at short ~** con poca antelación; **until further ~** hasta nuevo aviso; **to hand in one's ~** dimitir, renunciar; **noticeable** adj evidente, obvio

> Be careful not to translate **notice** by the Spanish word *noticia*.

**notify** ['nəutɪfaɪ] vt: **to ~ sb (of sth)** comunicar (algo) a algn

**notion** ['nəuʃən] n noción f, idea; (opinion) opinión f

**notions** ['nəuʃənz] npl (US) mercería

**notorious** [nəu'tɔ:rɪəs] adj notorio

**notwithstanding** [nɔtwɪθ'stændɪŋ] adv no obstante, sin embargo; **~ this** a pesar de esto

**nought** [nɔ:t] n cero

**noun** [naun] n nombre m, sustantivo

**nourish** ['nʌrɪʃ] vt nutrir; (fig) alimentar; **nourishment** n alimento, sustento

**Nov.** abbr (= November) nov.

**novel** ['nɔvl] n novela ▷ adj (new) nuevo, original; (unexpected) insólito; **novelist** n novelista mf; **novelty** n novedad f

**November** [nəu'vɛmbə'] n noviembre m

**novice** ['nɔvɪs] n (Rel) novicio/a

**now** [nau] adv (at the present time) ahora; (these days) actualmente, hoy día ▷ conj: **~ (that)** ya que, ahora que; **right ~** ahora mismo; **by ~** ya; **I'll do it just ~** ahora mismo lo hago; **~ and then, ~ and again** de vez en cuando; **from ~ on** de ahora en adelante; **nowadays** ['nauədeɪz] adv hoy (en) día, actualmente

**nowhere** ['nəuwɛə'] adv (direction) a ninguna parte; (location) en ninguna parte

**nozzle** ['nɔzl] n boquilla

**nr** abbr (BRIT) = **near**

**nuclear** ['nju:klɪə'] adj nuclear

**nucleus** (pl **nuclei**) ['nju:klɪəs, 'nju:klɪaɪ] n núcleo

**nude** [nju:d] adj, n desnudo m; **in the ~** desnudo

**nudge** [nʌdʒ] vt dar un codazo a

**nudist** ['nju:dɪst] n nudista mf

**nudity** ['nju:dɪtɪ] n desnudez f

**nuisance** ['njuːsns] n molestia, fastidio; (person) pesado, latoso; **what a ~!** ¡qué lata!

**numb** [nʌm] adj: **to be ~ with cold** estar entumecido de frío; **~ with fear/grief** paralizado de miedo/dolor

**number** ['nʌmbəʳ] n número; (quantity) cantidad f ▷ vt (pages etc) numerar, poner número a; (amount to) sumar, ascender a; **to be ~ed among** figurar entre; **a ~ of** varios, algunos; **they were ten in ~** eran diez; **number plate** n (BRIT) matrícula, placa; **Number Ten** n (BRIT: 10 Downing Street) residencia del primer ministro

**numerical** [njuːˈmerɪkl] adj numérico

**numerous** ['njuːmərəs] adj numeroso

**nun** [nʌn] n monja, religiosa

**nurse** [nəːs] n enfermero/a; (nanny) niñera ▷ vt (patient) cuidar, atender

**nursery** ['nəːsərɪ] n (institution) guardería infantil; (room) cuarto de los niños; (for plants) criadero, semillero; **nursery rhyme** n canción f infantil; **nursery school** n escuela infantil; **nursery slope** n (BRIT Ski) cuesta para principiantes

**nursing** ['nəːsɪŋ] n (profession) profesión f de enfermera; (care) asistencia, cuidado; **nursing home** n clínica de reposo

**nurture** ['nəːtʃəʳ] vt (child, plant) alimentar, nutrir

**nut** [nʌt] n (Tech) tuerca; (Bot) nuez f

**nutmeg** ['nʌtmeg] n nuez f moscada

**nutrient** ['njuːtrɪənt] adj nutritivo ▷ n elemento nutritivo

**nutrition** [njuːˈtrɪʃən] n nutrición f, alimentación f

**nutritious** [njuːˈtrɪʃəs] adj nutritivo

**nuts** [nʌts] adj (inf) chiflado

**NVQ** n abbr (BRIT: = national vocational qualification) título de formación profesional

**nylon** ['naɪlɔn] n nilón m ▷ adj de nilón

**oak** [əuk] n roble m ▷ adj de roble

**OAP** n abbr (BRIT) = **old-age pensioner**

**oar** [ɔːʳ] n remo

**oasis** (pl **oases**) [əuˈeɪsɪs, əuˈeɪsiːz] n oasis m inv

**oath** [əuθ] n juramento; (swear word) palabrota; **on** (BRIT) or **under ~** bajo juramento

**oatmeal** ['əutmiːl] n harina de avena

**oats** [əuts] npl avena

**obedience** [əˈbiːdɪəns] n obediencia

**obedient** [əˈbiːdɪənt] adj obediente

**obese** [əuˈbiːs] adj obeso

**obesity** [əuˈbiːsɪtɪ] n obesidad f

**obey** [əˈbeɪ] vt obedecer; (instructions) cumplir

**obituary** [əˈbɪtjuərɪ] n necrología

**object** n ['ɔbdʒɪkt] objeto; (purpose) objeto, propósito; (Ling) complemento ▷ vi [əbˈdʒekt]: **to ~ to** (attitude) estar en contra de; (proposal) oponerse a; **to ~ that** objetar que; **expense is no ~** no importa lo que cueste; **I ~!** ¡protesto!; **objection** [əbˈdʒekʃən] n objeción f; **I have no objection to ...** no tengo inconveniente en que ...; **objective** adj, n objetivo

**obligation** [ɔblɪˈgeɪʃən] n obligación f; (debt) deber m; **"without ~"** "sin compromiso"

**obligatory** [əˈblɪgətərɪ] adj obligatorio

**oblige** [əˈblaɪdʒ] vt (do a favour for) complacer, hacer un favor a; **to ~ sb to do sth** obligar a algn a hacer algo; **to be ~d to sb for sth** estarle agradecido a algn por algo

**oblique** [əˈbliːk] adj oblicuo; (allusion) indirecto

**obliterate** [əˈblɪtəreɪt] vt borrar

**oblivious** [əˈblɪvɪəs] adj: **~ of** inconsciente de

**oblong** ['ɔblɔŋ] adj rectangular ⊳ n
rectángulo
**obnoxious** [əb'nɔkʃəs] adj odioso,
detestable; (smell) nauseabundo
**oboe** ['əubəu] n oboe m
**obscene** [əb'si:n] adj obsceno
**obscure** [əb'skjuəʳ] adj oscuro ⊳ vt
oscurecer; (hide: sun) ocultar
**observant** [əb'zə:vnt] adj observador(a)
**observation** [ɔbzə'veɪʃən] n (Med)
observación f
**observatory** [əb'zə:vətrɪ] n observatorio
**observe** [əb'zə:v] vt observar; (rule)
cumplir; **observer** n observador(a) m/f
**obsess** [əb'sɛs] vt obsesionar; **obsession**
[əb'sɛʃən] n obsesión f; **obsessive** adj
obsesivo
**obsolete** ['ɔbsəli:t] adj obsoleto
**obstacle** ['ɔbstəkl] n obstáculo; (nuisance)
estorbo
**obstinate** ['ɔbstɪnɪt] adj terco, obstinado
**obstruct** [əb'strʌkt] vt obstruir; (hinder)
estorbar, obstaculizar; **obstruction**
[əb'strʌkʃən] n obstrucción f; (object)
estorbo, obstáculo
**obtain** [əb'teɪn] vt obtener; (achieve)
conseguir
**obvious** ['ɔbvɪəs] adj obvio, evidente;
**obviously** adv evidentemente; **obviously
not!** ¡por supuesto que no!
**occasion** [ə'keɪʒən] n oportunidad f,
ocasión f; (event) acontecimiento;
**occasional** adj poco frecuente, ocasional;
**occasionally** adv de vez en cuando
**occult** [ɔ'kʌlt] adj oculto
**occupant** ['ɔkjupənt] n (of house)
inquilino/a; (of boat, car) ocupante mf
**occupation** [ɔkju'peɪʃən] n (job) trabajo;
(pastime) ocupaciones fpl
**occupy** ['ɔkjupaɪ] vt (seat, post, time)
ocupar; (house) habitar; **to ~ o.s. with** or
**by doing** (as job) dedicarse a hacer; (to pass
time) entretenerse haciendo
**occur** [ə'kə:ʳ] vi ocurrir, suceder; **to ~ to sb**
ocurrírsele a algn; **occurrence** [ə'kʌrəns]
n suceso
**ocean** ['əuʃən] n océano
**o'clock** [ə'klɔk] adv: **it is five ~** son las cinco
**Oct.** abbr (= October) oct.
**October** [ɔk'təubəʳ] n octubre m
**octopus** ['ɔktəpəs] n pulpo
**odd** [ɔd] adj (strange) extraño, raro; (number)
impar; (sock, shoe etc) suelto; **60-~** 60 y
pico; **at ~ times** de vez en cuando; **to be
the ~ one out** estar de más; **oddly** adv
extrañamente; **odds** npl (in betting) puntos
mpl de ventaja; **it makes no odds** da lo
mismo; **at odds** reñidos/as; **odds and
ends** cachivaches mpl

**odometer** [ɔ'dɔmɪtəʳ] n (US)
cuentakilómetros m inv
**odour**, (US) **odor** ['əudəʳ] n olor m;
(unpleasant) hedor m

 **KEYWORD**

**of** [ɔv, əv] prep **1** de; **a friend of ours** un
amigo nuestro; **a boy of 10** un chico de 10
años; **that was kind of you** eso fue muy
amable de tu parte
**2** (expressing quantity, amount, dates etc) de;
**a kilo of flour** un kilo de harina; **there were
three of them** había tres; **three of us went**
tres de nosotros fuimos; **the 5th of July** el
5 de julio
**3** (from, out of) de; **made of wood** (hecho)
de madera

**off** [ɔf] adj, adv (engine, light) apagado; (tap)
cerrado; (BRIT: food: bad) pasado, malo;
(: milk) cortado; (cancelled) suspendido
⊳ prep de; **to be ~** (leave) irse, marcharse; **to
be ~ sick** estar enfermo or de baja; **a day ~**
un día libre; **to have an ~ day** tener un mal
día; **he had his coat ~** se había quitado
el abrigo; **10% ~** (Comm) (con el) 10% de
descuento; **5 km ~ (the road)** a 5 km (de la
carretera); **~ the coast** frente a la costa;
**I'm ~ meat** (no longer eat/like it) paso de la
carne; **on the ~ chance** por si acaso; **on
and ~** de vez en cuando
**offence**, (US) **offense** [ə'fɛns] n (crime)
delito; **to take ~ at** ofenderse por
**offend** [ə'fɛnd] vt (person) ofender;
**offender** n delincuente mf
**offense** [ə'fɛns] n (US) = **offence**
**offensive** [ə'fɛnsɪv] adj ofensivo; (smell etc)
repugnante ⊳ n (Mil) ofensiva
**offer** ['ɔfəʳ] n oferta, ofrecimiento; (proposal)
propuesta ⊳ vt ofrecer; **"on ~"** (Comm) "en
oferta"
**offhand** [ɔf'hænd] adj informal ⊳ adv de
improviso
**office** ['ɔfɪs] n (place) oficina; (room)
despacho; (position) cargo, oficio;
**doctor's ~** (US) consultorio; **to take ~**
entrar en funciones; **office block**, (US)
**office building** n bloque m de oficinas;
**office hours** npl horas fpl de oficina; (US
Med) horas fpl de consulta
**officer** ['ɔfɪsəʳ] n (Mil etc) oficial mf; (of
organization) director(a) m/f; (also: **police ~**)
agente mf de policía
**office worker** n oficinista mf
**official** [ə'fɪʃl] adj oficial, autorizado ⊳ n
funcionario/a
**off-licence** n (BRIT: shop) tienda de bebidas
alcohólicas

● **OFF-LICENCE**

● En el Reino Unido una *off-licence* es una
tienda especializada en la venta de
bebidas alcohólicas para el consumo fuera
del establecimiento. De ahí su nombre,
pues se necesita un permiso especial
para tal venta, que está estrictamente
regulada. Suelen vender además bebidas
sin alcohol, tabaco, chocolate, patatas
fritas etc y a menudo son parte de grandes
cadenas nacionales.

**off: off-peak** *adj* (*electricity*) de banda
económica; (*ticket*) *billete de precio
reducido por viajar fuera de las horas punta*;
**off-putting** *adj* (BRIT: *person*) poco
amable, difícil; (*remark*) desalentador(a);
**off-season** ['ɔf'siːzn] *adj, adv* fuera de
temporada; **offset** ['ɔfsɛt] *vt* (*irreg: like*
**set**) contrarrestar, compensar; **offshore**
[ɔf'ɔː'] *adj* (*breeze, island*) costero; (*fishing*)
de bajura; **offside** ['ɔf'saɪd] *adj* (*Sport*) fuera
de juego; (*Aut: in UK*) del lado derecho; (: *in
US, Europe etc*) del lado izquierdo
**offspring** ['ɔfsprɪŋ] *n* descendencia
**often** ['ɔfn] *adv* a menudo, con frecuencia;
**how ~ do you go?** ¿cada cuánto vas?
**oh** [əu] *excl* ¡ah!
**oil** [ɔɪl] *n* aceite *m*; (*petroleum*) petróleo ▷ *vt*
engrasar; **oil filter** *n* (*Aut*) filtro de aceite;
**oil painting** *n* pintura al óleo; **oil refinery**
*n* refinería de petróleo; **oil rig** *n* torre *f*
de perforación; **oil slick** *n* marea negra;
**oil tanker** *n* petrolero; (*truck*) camión *m*
cisterna; **oil well** *n* pozo (de petróleo); **oily**
*adj* aceitoso; (*food*) grasiento
**ointment** ['ɔɪntmənt] *n* ungüento
**O.K., okay** ['əu'keɪ] *excl* O.K.,
¡vale! ▷ *adj* bien ▷ *vt* dar el visto bueno a
**old** [əuld] *adj* viejo; (*former*) antiguo; **how ~
are you?** ¿cuántos años tienes?, ¿qué edad
tienes?; **he's 10 years ~** tiene 10 años; **~er
brother** hermano mayor; **old age** *n* vejez *f*;
**old-age pension** *n* (BRIT) jubilación *f*,
pensión *f*; **old-age pensioner** *n* (BRIT)
jubilado/a; **old-fashioned** *adj* anticuado,
pasado de moda; **old people's home** *n* (*esp*
BRIT) residencia *f* de ancianos
**olive** ['ɔlɪv] *n* (*fruit*) aceituna; (*tree*) olivo
▷ *adj* (*also*: **~-green**) verde oliva *inv*; **olive oil**
*n* aceite *m* de oliva
**Olympic®** [əu'lɪmpɪk] *adj* olímpico; **the ~
Games®**, **the ~s®** *n pl* las Olimpiadas
**omelet(te)** ['ɔmlɪt] *n* tortilla, tortilla de
huevo (LAM)
**omen** ['əumən] *n* presagio
**ominous** ['ɔmɪnəs] *adj* de mal agüero,
amenazador(a)

**omit** [əu'mɪt] *vt* omitir

 **KEYWORD**

**on** [ɔn] *prep* **1** (*indicating position*) en; sobre;
**on the wall** en la pared; **it's on the table**
está sobre *or* en la mesa; **on the left** a la
izquierda
**2** (*indicating means, method, condition etc*): **on
foot** a pie; **on the train/plane** (*go*) en tren/
avión; (*be*) en el tren/el avión; **on the radio/
television** por *or* en la radio/televisión; **on
the telephone** al teléfono; **to be on drugs**
drogarse; (*Med*) estar a tratamiento; **to be
on holiday/business** estar de vacaciones/
en viaje de negocios
**3** (*referring to time*): **on Friday** el viernes; **on
Fridays** los viernes; **on June 20th** el 20 de
junio; **a week on Friday** del viernes en una
semana; **on arrival** al llegar; **on seeing
this** al ver esto
**4** (*about, concerning*) sobre, acerca de; **a
book on physics** un libro de *or* sobre física
▶ *adv* **1** (*referring to dress*): **to have one's
coat on** tener *or* llevar el abrigo puesto; **she
put her gloves on** se puso los guantes
**2** (*referring to covering*): **"screw the lid on
tightly"** "cerrar bien la tapa"
**3** (*further, continuously*): **to walk/run** *etc* **on**
seguir caminando/corriendo *etc*
▶ *adj* **1** (*functioning, in operation: machine,
radio, TV, light*) encendido (SP), prendido
(LAM); (: *tap*) abierto; (: *brakes*) echado,
puesto; **is the meeting still on?** (*in progress*)
¿todavía continúa la reunión?; (*not cancelled*)
¿va a haber reunión al fin?; **there's a good
film on at the cinema** ponen una buena
película en el cine
**2**: **that's not on!** (*inf: not possible*) ¡eso ni
hablar!; (: *not acceptable*) ¡eso no se hace!

**once** [wʌns] *adv* una vez; (*formerly*)
antiguamente ▷ *conj* una vez que; **~ he
had left/it was done** una vez que se
había marchado/se hizo; **at ~** en seguida,
inmediatamente; (*simultaneously*) a la vez;
**~ a week** una vez a la semana; **~ more** otra
vez; **~ and for all** de una vez por todas;
**~ upon a time** érase una vez
**oncoming** ['ɔnkʌmɪŋ] *adj* (*traffic*) que
viene de frente

 **KEYWORD**

**one** [wʌn] *num* un/una; **one hundred and
fifty** ciento cincuenta; **one by one** uno a uno
▶ *adj* **1** (*sole*) único; **the one book which**
el único libro que; **the one man who** el
único que

**2** (same) mismo/a; **they came in the one car** vinieron en un solo coche
▶ pron **1**: **this one** este, éste; **that one** ese, ése; (more remote) aquel, aquél; **I've already got (a red) one** ya tengo uno/a (rojo/a); **one by one** uno/a por uno/a
**2**: **one another** (us) nos; (you) os (SP); (you: formal, them) se; **do you two ever see one another?** ¿os veis alguna vez? (SP), ¿se ven alguna vez?; **the two boys didn't dare look at one another** los dos chicos no se atrevieron a mirarse (el uno al otro); **they all kissed one another** se besaron unos a otros
**3** (impers): **one never knows** nunca se sabe; **to cut one's finger** cortarse el dedo; **one needs to eat** hay que comer

**one: one-off** n (BRIT inf: event) caso especial; **oneself** pron (reflexive) se; (after prep) sí; (emphatic) uno/a mismo/a; **to hurt oneself** hacerse daño; **to keep sth for oneself** guardarse algo; **to talk to oneself** hablar solo; **one-shot** [wʌnˈʃɔt] n (US) = **one-off**; **one-sided** adj (argument) parcial; (decision, view) unilateral; (game, contest) desigual; **one-to-one** adj (relationship) individualizado; **one-way** adj (street, traffic) de dirección única
**ongoing** [ˈɔŋɡəʊɪŋ] adj continuo
**onion** [ˈʌnjən] n cebolla
**online** [ɔnˈlaɪn] adj, adv (Comput) en línea
**onlooker** [ˈɔnlʊkəʳ] n espectador(a) m/f
**only** [ˈəʊnlɪ] adv solamente, solo, sólo (to avoid confusion with adj) ▷ adj único, solo ▷ conj solamente que, pero; **an ~ child** un hijo único; **not ~ ... but also ...** no sólo ... sino también ...
**on-screen** [ɔnˈskriːn] adj (Comput etc) en pantalla; (romance, kiss) cinematográfico
**onset** [ˈɔnsɛt] n comienzo
**onto** [ˈɔntu] prep = **on to**
**onward(s)** [ˈɔnwəd(z)] adv (move) (hacia) adelante; **from that time onward** desde entonces en adelante
**oops** [ups] excl (also: **~-a-daisy!**) ¡huy!
**ooze** [uːz] vi rezumar
**opaque** [əʊˈpeɪk] adj opaco
**open** [ˈəʊpn] adj abierto; (car) descubierto; (road, view) despejado; (meeting) público; (admiration) manifiesto ▷ vt abrir ▷ vi abrirse; (book etc: commence) comenzar; **in the ~ (air)** al aire libre; **open up** vt abrir; (blocked road) despejar ▷ vi abrirse; **opening** n abertura; (beginning) comienzo; (opportunity) oportunidad f; **opening hours** npl horario de apertura; **open learning** n enseñanza flexible a tiempo parcial; **openly** adv abiertamente; **open-minded** adj de

amplias miras, sin prejuicios; **open-necked** adj sin corbata; **open-plan** adj diáfano, sin tabiques; **Open University** n (BRIT) ≈ Universidad f Nacional de Enseñanza a Distancia, UNED f

**OPEN UNIVERSITY**

La Open University, fundada en 1969, está especializada en impartir cursos a distancia y a tiempo parcial con sus propios materiales de apoyo diseñados para tal fin, entre ellos programas de radio y televisión emitidos por la BBC. Los trabajos se envían por correo y se complementan con la asistencia obligatoria a cursos de verano. Para obtener la licenciatura es necesario estudiar un mínimo de módulos y alcanzar un determinado número de créditos.

**opera** [ˈɔpərə] n ópera; **opera house** n teatro de la ópera; **opera singer** n cantante mf de ópera
**operate** [ˈɔpəreɪt] vt (machine) hacer funcionar; (company) dirigir ▷ vi funcionar; **to ~ on sb** (Med) operar a algn; **operating theatre,** (US) **operating room** n quirófano, sala de operaciones
**operation** [ɔpəˈreɪʃən] n operación f; (of machine) funcionamiento; **to be in ~** estar funcionando or en funcionamiento; **to have an ~** (Med) ser operado; **operational** adj operacional, en buen estado
**operative** [ˈɔpərətɪv] adj en vigor
**operator** [ˈɔpəreɪtəʳ] n (of machine) operario/a, maquinista mf; (Tel) operador(a) m/f, telefonista mf
**opinion** [əˈpɪnjən] n opinión f; **in my ~** en mi opinión, a mi juicio; **opinion poll** n encuesta, sondeo
**opponent** [əˈpəʊnənt] n adversario/a, contrincante mf
**opportunity** [ɔpəˈtjuːnɪtɪ] n oportunidad f; **to take the ~ to do** or **of doing** aprovechar la ocasión para hacer
**oppose** [əˈpəʊz] vt oponerse a; **to be ~d to sth** oponerse a algo; **as ~d to** a diferencia de
**opposite** [ˈɔpəzɪt] adj opuesto, contrario; (house etc) de enfrente ▷ adv en frente ▷ prep en frente de, frente a ▷ n lo contrario
**opposition** [ɔpəˈzɪʃən] n oposición f
**oppress** [əˈprɛs] vt oprimir
**opt** [ɔpt] vi: **to ~ for** optar por; **to ~ to do** optar por hacer; **opt out** vi: **to ~ out of** optar por no hacer

**optician** [ɔp'tɪʃən] n óptico/a
**optimism** ['ɔptɪmɪzəm] n optimismo
**optimist** ['ɔptɪmɪst] n optimista mf;
  **optimistic** [ɔptɪ'mɪstɪk] adj optimista
**optimum** ['ɔptɪməm] adj óptimo
**option** ['ɔpʃən] n opción f; **optional** adj
  opcional
**or** [ɔːʳ] conj o; (before o, ho) u; (with negative):
  **he hasn't seen or heard anything** no ha
  visto ni oído nada; **or else** si no
**oral** ['ɔːrəl] adj oral ▷ n examen m oral
**orange** ['ɔrɪndʒ] n (fruit) naranja ▷ adj (de
  color) naranja inv; **orange juice** n jugo m de
  naranja, zumo m de naranja (SP); **orange
  squash** n bebida de naranja
**orbit** ['ɔːbɪt] n órbita ▷ vt, vi orbitar
**orchard** ['ɔːtʃəd] n huerto
**orchestra** ['ɔːkɪstrə] n orquesta; (US:
  seating) platea
**orchid** ['ɔːkɪd] n orquídea
**ordeal** [ɔː'diːl] n experiencia terrible
**order** ['ɔːdəʳ] n orden m; (command) orden f;
  (state) estado; (Comm) pedido ▷ vt (also: **put
  in ~**) ordenar, poner en orden; (Comm) pedir;
  (command) mandar, ordenar; **in ~** en orden;
  (of document) en regla; **in (working) ~** en
  funcionamiento; **to be out of ~** estar
  desordenado; (not working) no funcionar;
  **in ~ to do** para hacer; **on ~** (Comm) pedido;
  **to ~ sb to do sth** mandar a algn hacer algo;
  **order form** n hoja de pedido; **orderly** n
  (Mil) ordenanza m; (Med) auxiliar mf (de
  hospital) ▷ adj ordenado
**ordinary** ['ɔːdnrɪ] adj corriente, normal;
  (pej) común y corriente; **out of the ~** fuera
  de lo común
**ore** [ɔːʳ] n mineral m
**oregano** [ɔrɪ'gɑːnəu] n orégano
**organ** ['ɔːgən] n órgano
**organic** [ɔː'gænɪk] adj orgánico
**organism** n organismo
**organization** [ɔːgənaɪ'zeɪʃən] n
  organización f
**organize** ['ɔːgənaɪz] vt organizar;
  **organized** ['ɔːgənaɪzd] adj organizado; **to
  get organized** organizarse; **organizer** n
  organizador(a) m/f
**orgasm** ['ɔːgæzəm] n orgasmo
**orgy** ['ɔːdʒɪ] n orgía
**oriental** [ɔːrɪ'ɛntl] adj oriental
**orientation** [ɔːrɪen'teɪʃən] n orientación f
**origin** ['ɔrɪdʒɪn] n origen m
**original** [ə'rɪdʒɪnl] adj original; (first)
  primero; (earlier) primitivo ▷ n original m;
  **originally** adv al principio
**originate** [ə'rɪdʒɪneɪt] vi: **to ~ from, to ~ in**
  surgir de, tener su origen en
**Orkneys** ['ɔːknɪz] npl: **the ~** (also: **the
  Orkney Islands**) las Orcadas

**ornament** ['ɔːnəmənt] n adorno; (trinket)
  chuchería; **ornamental** [ɔːnə'mɛntl] adj
  decorativo, de adorno
**ornate** [ɔː'neɪt] adj recargado
**orphan** ['ɔːfn] n huérfano/a
**orthodox** ['ɔːθədɔks] adj ortodoxo
**orthopaedic**, (US) **orthopedic**
  [ɔːθə'piːdɪk] adj ortopédico
**osteopath** ['ɔstɪəpæθ] n osteópata mf
**ostrich** ['ɔstrɪtʃ] n avestruz m
**other** ['ʌðəʳ] adj otro ▷ pron: **the ~ one** el/la
  otro/a; **~ than** aparte de; **otherwise** adv,
  conj de otra manera; (if not) si no
**otter** ['ɔtəʳ] n nutria
**ouch** [autʃ] excl ¡ay!
**ought** [ɔːt] aux vb: **I ~ to do it** debería
  hacerlo; **this ~ to have been corrected**
  esto debiera de haberse corregido; **he ~ to
  win** (probability) debiera ganar
**ounce** [auns] n onza (=28.35g; 16oz = 1lb)
**our** ['auəʳ] adj nuestro; see also **my**; **ours**
  pron (el) nuestro/(la) nuestra etc; see also
  **mine**; **ourselves** pron pl (reflexive, after
  prep) nosotros/as; (emphatic) nosotros /as
  mismos/as; see also **oneself**
**oust** [aust] vt desalojar
**out** [aut] adv fuera, afuera; (not at home)
  fuera (de casa); (light, fire) apagado; **~
  there** allí (fuera); **he's ~** (absent) no está,
  ha salido; **to be ~ in one's calculations**
  equivocarse (en sus cálculos); **to run ~**
  salir corriendo; **~ loud** en alta voz; **~ of**
  (outside) fuera de; (because of: anger etc) por;
  **~ of petrol** sin gasolina; **"~ of order"** "no
  funciona"; **outback** n interior m; **outbound**
  adj (flight) de salida; (flight: not return) de ida;
  **outbound from/for** con salida de/hacia;
  **outbreak** n (of war) comienzo; (of disease)
  epidemia; (of violence etc) ola; **outburst** n
  explosión f, arranque m; **outcast** n paria mf;
  **outcome** n resultado; **outcry** n protestas
  fpl; **outdated** adj anticuado; **outdoor** adj
  al aire libre; (clothes) de calle; **outdoors** adv
  al aire libre
**outer** ['autəʳ] adj exterior, externo; **outer
  space** n espacio exterior
**outfit** n (clothes) traje m
**out: outgoing** adj (president, tenant)
  saliente; (character) extrovertido;
  **outgoings** npl (BRIT) gastos mpl; **outhouse**
  n dependencia; **outing** n excursión f,
  paseo; **outlaw** n proscrito/a ▷ vt (practice)
  declarar ilegal; **outlay** n inversión f; **outlet**
  n salida; (of pipe) desagüe m; (US Elec) toma
  de corriente; (also: **retail outlet**) punto
  de venta; **outline** n (shape) contorno,
  perfil m; (sketch, plan) esbozo ▷ vt (plan etc)
  esbozar; **in outline** (fig) a grandes rasgos;
  **outlook** n (fig: prospects) perspectivas fpl;

(: *for weather*) pronóstico; (: *opinion*) punto de vista; **outnumber** vt exceder or superar en número; **out-of-date** adj (*passport*) caducado; (*clothes, customs*) pasado de moda; **out-of-doors** adv al aire libre; **out-of-the-way** adj apartado; **out-of-town** adj (*shopping centre etc*) en las afueras; **outpatient** n paciente mf externo/a; **outpost** n puesto avanzado; **output** n (volumen m de) producción f, rendimiento; (*Comput*) salida

**outrage** ['autreɪdʒ] n escándalo; (*atrocity*) atrocidad f ▷ vt ultrajar; **outrageous** [aut'reɪdʒəs] adj (*clothes*) extravagante; (*behaviour*) escandaloso

**outright** adv [aut'raɪt] (*ask, deny*) francamente; (*refuse*) rotundamente; (*win*) de manera absoluta; (*be killed*) en el acto ▷ adj ['autraɪt] completo; (*refusal*) rotundo

**outset** ['autset] n principio

**outside** [aut'saɪd] n exterior m ▷ adj exterior, externo ▷ adv fuera ▷ prep fuera de; (*beyond*) más allá de; **at the ~** (*fig*) a lo sumo; **outside lane** n (*Aut: in Britain*) carril m de la derecha; (: *in US, Europe etc*) carril m de la izquierda; **outside line** n (*Tel*) línea (exterior); **outsider** n (*stranger*) forastero/a

**out: outsize** adj (*clothes*) de talla grande; **outskirts** npl alrededores mpl, afueras fpl; **outspoken** adj muy franco; **outstanding** adj excepcional, destacado; (*unfinished*) pendiente

**outward** ['autwəd] adj externo; (*journey*) de ida

**outweigh** [aut'weɪ] vt pesar más que

**oval** ['əuvl] adj ovalado ▷ n óvalo

**ovary** ['əuvərɪ] n ovario

**oven** ['ʌvn] n horno; **oven glove** n guante m para el horno, manopla para el horno; **ovenproof** adj resistente al horno; **oven-ready** adj listo para el horno

**over** ['əuvəʳ] adv encima, por encima ▷ adj (*finished*) terminado; (*surplus*) de sobra ▷ prep (*por*) encima de; (*above*) sobre; (*on the other side of*) al otro lado de; (*more than*) más de; (*during*) durante; **~ here** (por) aquí; **~ there** (por) allí or allá; **all ~** (*everywhere*) por todas partes; **~ and ~ (again)** una y otra vez; **~ and above** además de; **to ask sb ~** invitar a algn a casa; **to bend ~** inclinarse

**overall** ['əuvərɔːl] adj (*length*) total; (*study*) de conjunto ▷ adv [əuvər'ɔːl] en conjunto ▷ n (*BRIT*) guardapolvo; **overalls** npl mono sg, overol msg (*LAM*)

**over: overboard** adv (*Naut*) por la borda; **overcame** pt of **overcome**; **overcast** adj encapotado; **overcharge** vt: **to overcharge sb** cobrar un precio excesivo a algn; **overcoat** n abrigo; **overcome** vt

(*irreg: like* **come**) vencer; (*difficulty*) superar; **overcrowded** adj atestado de gente; (*city, country*) superpoblado; **overdo** vt (*irreg: like* **do**) exagerar; (*overcook*) cocer demasiado; **to overdo it** (*work etc*) pasarse; **overdone** adj (*vegetables*) recocido; (*steak*) demasiado hecho; **overdose** n sobredosis f inv; **overdraft** n saldo deudor; **overdrawn** adj (*account*) en descubierto; **overdue** adj retrasado; **overestimate** vt sobreestimar

**overflow** [əuvə'fləu] vi desbordarse ▷ n ['əuvəfləu] (*also:* **~ pipe**) (cañería de) desagüe m

**over: overgrown** [əuvə'grəun] adj (*garden*) cubierto de hierba; **overhaul** vt [əuvə'hɔːl] revisar, repasar ▷ n ['əuvəhɔːl] revisión f

**overhead** adv [əuvə'hɛd] por arriba or encima ▷ adj ['əuvəhɛd] (*cable*) aéreo ▷ n ['əuvəhɛd] (*US*) = **overheads**; **overhead projector** n retroproyector; **overheads** npl gastos mpl generales

**over: overhear** vt (*irreg: like* **hear**) oír por casualidad; **overheat** vi (*engine*) recalentarse; **overland** adj, adv por tierra; **overlap** vi [əuvə'læp] superponerse; **overleaf** adv al dorso; **overload** vt sobrecargar; **overlook** vt (*have view of*) dar a, tener vistas a; (*miss*) pasar por alto; (*excuse*) perdonar

**overnight** [əuvə'naɪt] adv durante la noche; (*fig*) de la noche a la mañana ▷ adj de noche; **to stay ~** pasar la noche; **overnight bag** n fin m de semana, neceser m de viaje

**overpass** n (*US*) paso elevado or a desnivel

**overpower** [əuvə'pauəʳ] vt dominar; (*fig*) embargar; **overpowering** adj (*heat*) agobiante; (*smell*) penetrante

**over: overreact** [əuvəri:'ækt] vi reaccionar de manera exagerada; **overrule** vt (*decision*) anular; (*claim*) denegar; **overrun** vt (*irreg: like* **run**: *country*) invadir; (: *time limit*) rebasar, exceder; **overseas** [əuvə'siːz] adv (*abroad*) en el extranjero ▷ adj (*trade*) exterior; (*visitor*) extranjero; **oversee** (*irreg: like* **see**) vt supervisar; **overshadow** vt (*fig*) eclipsar; **to be overshadowed by** estar a la sombra de; **oversight** n descuido; **oversleep** vi (*irreg: like* **sleep**) dormir más de la cuenta, no despertarse a tiempo; **overspend** vi (*irreg: like* **spend**) gastar más de la cuenta; **we have overspent by five dollars** hemos excedido el presupuesto en cinco dólares

**overt** [əu'vəːt] adj abierto

**over: overtake** vt (*irreg: like* **take**) sobrepasar; (*BRIT Aut*) adelantar; **overthrow** vt (*irreg: like* **throw**: *government*) derrocar; **overtime** n horas fpl extraordinarias; **overtook** [əuvə'tuk] *pt of* **overtake**; **overturn** *vt* volcar; (*fig: plan*) desbaratar; (*: government*) derrocar ▷ *vi* volcar; **overweight** *adj* demasiado gordo *or* pesado; **overwhelm** *vt* aplastar; **overwhelming** *adj* (*victory, defeat*) arrollador(a); (*desire*) irresistible

**owe** [əu] *vt* deber; **to ~ sb sth, to ~ sth to sb** deber algo a algn; **owing to** *prep* debido a, por causa de

**owl** [aul] *n* búho; (*also:* **barn ~**) lechuza

**own** [əun] *vt* tener, poseer ▷ *adj* propio; **a room of my ~** mi propia habitación; **to get one's ~ back** tomarse la revancha; **on one's ~** solo, a solas; **own up** *vi* confesar; **owner** *n* dueño/a; **ownership** *n* posesión *f*

**ox** (*pl* **oxen**) [ɔks, 'ɔksn] *n* buey *m*

**Oxbridge** ['ɔksbrɪdʒ] *n universidades de Oxford y Cambridge*

**oxen** ['ɔksən] *npl of* **ox**

**oxygen** ['ɔksɪdʒən] *n* oxígeno

**oyster** ['ɔɪstəʳ] *n* ostra

**oz.** *abbr* = **ounce**

**ozone** ['əuzəun] *n* ozono; **ozone-friendly** *adj* que no daña la capa de ozono; **ozone layer** *n* capa de ozono

# p

**p** *abbr* (BRIT) = **penny**; **pence**

**PA** *n abbr* = **personal assistant**; **public address system**

**p.a.** *abbr* = **per annum**

**pace** [peɪs] *n* paso ▷ *vi*: **to ~ up and down** pasearse de un lado a otro; **to keep ~ with** llevar el mismo paso que; **pacemaker** *n* (*Med*) marcapasos *m inv*; (*Sport: also:* **pacesetter**) liebre *f*

**pacific** [pə'sɪfɪk] *adj* pacífico ▷ *n*: **the P~ (Ocean)** el océano Pacífico

**pacifier** ['pæsɪfaɪəʳ] *n* (US: dummy) chupete *m*

**pack** [pæk] *n* (*packet*) paquete *m*; (*of hounds*) jauría; (*of people*) manada; (*of thieves etc*) banda; (*of cards*) baraja; (*bundle*) fardo; (*US: of cigarettes*) paquete *m* ▷ *vt* (*fill*) llenar; (*in suitcase etc*) meter, poner; (*cram*) llenar, atestar; **to ~ (one's bags)** hacer las maletas; **to ~ sb off** (*inf*) despachar a algn; **pack in** *vi* (*inf: break down*) estropearse ▷ *vt* (*inf*) dejar; **~ it in!** ¡para!, ¡basta ya!; **pack up** *vi* (*inf: machine*) estropearse; (*person*) irse ▷ *vt* (*belongings, clothes*) recoger; (*goods, presents*) empaquetar, envolver

**package** ['pækɪdʒ] *n* paquete *m*; (*bulky*) bulto; (*also:* **~ deal**) acuerdo global ▷ *vt* (*Comm: goods*) envasar, embalar; **package holiday** *n* viaje *m* organizado (con todo incluido); **package tour** *n* viaje *m* organizado

**packaging** ['pækɪdʒɪŋ] *n* envase *m*

**packed** [pækt] *adj* abarrotado; **packed lunch** *n* almuerzo frío

**packet** ['pækɪt] *n* paquete *m*

**packing** ['pækɪŋ] *n* embalaje *m*

**pact** [pækt] *n* pacto

**pad** [pæd] *n* (*of paper*) bloc *m*; (*cushion*) cojinete *m*; (*inf: flat*) casa ▷ *vt* rellenar; **padded** *adj* (*jacket*) acolchado; (*bra*) reforzado

**paddle** ['pædl] n (oar) canalete m, pala; (US: for table tennis) pala ▷ vt remar ▷ vi (with feet) chapotear; **paddling pool** n (BRIT) piscina para niños

**paddock** ['pædək] n (field) potrero

**padlock** ['pædlɔk] n candado

**paedophile**, (US) **pedophile** ['pi:dəufaɪl] adj de pedófilos ▷ n pedófilo/a

**page** [peɪdʒ] n página; (of newspaper) plana; (also: ~ **boy**) paje m ▷ vt (in hotel etc) llamar por altavoz a

**pager** ['peɪdʒər] n busca m

**paid** [peɪd] pt, pp of **pay** ▷ adj (work) remunerado; (holiday) pagado; (official) a sueldo; **to put ~ to** (BRIT) acabar con

**pain** [peɪn] n dolor m; **to be in ~** sufrir; see also **pains**; **painful** adj doloroso; (difficult) penoso; (disagreeable) desagradable; **painkiller** n analgésico; **pains** npl: **to take pains to do sth** tomarse el trabajo de hacer algo; **painstaking** ['peɪnzteɪkɪŋ] adj (person) concienzudo, esmerado

**paint** [peɪnt] n pintura ▷ vt pintar; **to ~ the door blue** pintar la puerta de azul; **paintbrush** n (artist's) pincel m; (decorator's) brocha; **painter** n pintor(a) m/f; **painting** n pintura

**pair** [peər] n (of shoes, gloves etc) par m; (of people) pareja; **a ~ of scissors** unas tijeras; **a ~ of trousers** unos pantalones, un pantalón

**pajamas** [pɪ'dʒɑːməz] npl (US) pijama msg

**Pakistan** [pɑːkɪ'stɑːn] n Paquistán m; **Pakistani** adj, n paquistaní mf

**pal** [pæl] n (inf) amiguete/a m/f, colega mf

**palace** ['pæləs] n palacio

**pale** [peɪl] adj pálido; (colour) claro ▷ n: **to be beyond the ~** pasarse de la raya

**Palestine** ['pælɪstaɪn] n Palestina; **Palestinian** [pælɪs'tɪnɪən] adj, n palestino/a

**palm** [pɑːm] n (Anat) palma; (also: ~ **tree**) palmera, palma ▷ vt: **to ~ sth off on sb** (BRIT inf) endosarle algo a algn

**pamper** ['pæmpər] vt mimar

**pamphlet** ['pæmflət] n folleto

**pan** [pæn] n (also: **sauce~**) cacerola, cazuela, olla; (also: **frying ~**) sartén f

**pancake** ['pænkeɪk] n crepe f

**panda** ['pændə] n panda m

**pandemic** [pæn'dɛmɪk] n pandemia; **flu ~** pandemia de gripe

**pane** [peɪn] n cristal m

**panel** ['pænl] n (of wood) panel m; (Radio, TV) panel m de invitados

**panhandler** ['pænhændlər] n (US inf) mendigo/a

**panic** ['pænɪk] n pánico ▷ vi dejarse llevar por el pánico

**panorama** [pænə'rɑːmə] n panorama m

**pansy** ['pænzɪ] n (Bot) pensamiento; (inf!) maricón m

**pant** [pænt] vi jadear

**panther** ['pænθər] n pantera

**panties** ['pæntɪz] npl bragas fpl

**pantomime** ['pæntəmaɪm] n (BRIT) representación f musical navideña

**PANTOMIME**

En época navideña los teatros británicos ponen en escena representaciones llamadas pantomimes, versiones libres de cuentos tradicionales como Aladino o El gato con botas. En ella nunca faltan personajes como la dama (dame), papel que siempre interpreta un actor; el protagonista joven (principal boy), normalmente interpretado por una actriz, y el malvado (villain). Es un espectáculo familiar dirigido a los niños pero con grandes dosis de humor para adultos en el que se alienta la participación del público.

**pants** [pænts] npl (BRIT: underwear: woman's) bragas fpl; (: man's) calzoncillos mpl; (US: trousers) pantalones mpl

**paper** ['peɪpər] n papel m; (also: **news~**) periódico, diario; (study, article) artículo; (exam) examen m ▷ adj de papel ▷ vt empapelar; **(identity) ~s** npl papeles mpl, documentos mpl; **paperback** n libro de bolsillo; **paper bag** n bolsa de papel; **paper clip** n clip m; **paper shop** n (BRIT) tienda de periódicos; **paperwork** n trabajo administrativo

**paprika** ['pæprɪkə] n pimentón m

**par** [pɑː] n par f; (Golf) par m; **to be on a ~ with** estar a la par con

**paracetamol** [pærə'siːtəmɔl] n (BRIT) paracetamol m

**parachute** ['pærəʃuːt] n paracaídas m inv

**parade** [pə'reɪd] n desfile m ▷ vt (show off) hacer alarde de ▷ vi desfilar; (Mil) pasar revista

**paradise** ['pærədaɪs] n paraíso

**paradox** ['pærədɔks] n paradoja

**paraffin** ['pærəfɪn] n (BRIT): ~ **(oil)** parafina

**paragraph** ['pærəgrɑːf] n párrafo

**parallel** ['pærəlɛl] adj: ~ **(with/to)** en paralelo (con/a); (fig) semejante (a) ▷ n (line) paralela; (fig) paralelo; (Geo) paralelo

**paralysis** [pə'rælɪsɪs] n parálisis f inv; **paralyze** vt paralizar; **paralyzed** paralizado

**paramedic** [pærə'mɛdɪk] n auxiliar mf sanitario/a

**paranoid** ['pærənɔɪd] adj (person, feeling) paranoico

**parasite** ['pærəsaɪt] n parásito/a

**parcel** ['pɑːsl] n paquete m ▷ vt (also: ~ up) empaquetar, embalar

**pardon** ['pɑːdn] n (Law) indulto ▷ vt perdonar; ~ me!, I beg your ~! ¡perdone usted!; (I beg your) ~?, (US): ~ me? ¿cómo (dice)?

**parent** ['pɛərənt] n (mother) madre f; (father) padre m; **parents** npl padres mpl; **parental** [pə'rɛntl] adj paternal/maternal
▌ Be careful not to translate parent by the Spanish word pariente.

**Paris** ['pærɪs] n París m

**parish** ['pærɪʃ] n parroquia

**Parisian** [pə'rɪzɪən] adj, n parisiense mf

**park** [pɑːk] n parque m ▷ vt, vi aparcar, estacionar

**parking** ['pɑːkɪŋ] n aparcamiento, estacionamiento; "no ~" "prohibido aparcar or estacionarse"; **parking lot** n (US) parking m; **parking meter** n parquímetro; **parking ticket** n multa de aparcamiento

**parkway** ['pɑːkweɪ] n (US) alameda

**parliament** ['pɑːləmənt] n parlamento; (Spanish) las Cortes fpl; ver nota "parliament"; **parliamentary** adj parlamentario

● **PARLIAMENT**

● El Parlamento británico (Parliament) tiene
● como sede el palacio de Westminster,
● también llamado Houses of Parliament.
● Consta de dos cámaras: la Cámara de
● los Comunes (House of Commons) está
● formada por 650 diputados (Members of
● Parliament) que acceden a ella tras ser
● elegidos por sufragio universal en su
● respectiva área o circunscripción electoral
● (constituency). Se reúne 175 días al año y
● sus sesiones son presididas y moderadas
● por el Presidente de la Cámara (Speaker).
● La cámara alta es la Cámara de los Lores
● (House of Lords) y sus miembros son
● nombrados por el monarca o bien han
● heredado su escaño. Su poder es limitado,
● aunque actúa como tribunal supremo de
● apelación, excepto en Escocia.

**Parmesan** [pɑːmɪ'zæn] n (also: ~ cheese) queso parmesano

**parole** [pə'rəʊl] n: on ~ en libertad condicional

**parrot** ['pærət] n loro, papagayo

**parsley** ['pɑːslɪ] n perejil m

**parsnip** ['pɑːsnɪp] n chirivía

**parson** ['pɑːsn] n cura m

**part** [pɑːt] n parte f; (Mus) parte f; (bit) trozo; (of machine) pieza; (Theat etc) papel m; (of serial) entrega; (US: in hair) raya ▷ adv = **partly**
▷ vt separar ▷ vi (people) separarse; (crowd) apartarse; **to take ~ in** participar or tomar parte en; **to take sb's ~** tomar partido por algn; **for my ~** por mi parte; **for the most ~** en su mayor parte; ~ **of speech** (Ling) categoría gramatical; **part with** vt fus ceder, entregar; (money) pagar; (get rid of) deshacerse de

**partial** ['pɑːʃl] adj parcial; **to be ~ to** (like) ser aficionado a

**participant** [pɑː'tɪsɪpənt] n (in competition) concursante mf

**participate** [pɑː'tɪsɪpeɪt] vi: **to ~ in** participar en

**particle** ['pɑːtɪkl] n partícula; (of dust) mota

**particular** [pə'tɪkjulər] adj (special) particular; (concrete) concreto; (given) determinado; (fussy) quisquilloso; (demanding) exigente; **particulars** npl (information) datos mpl; (details) pormenores mpl; **in ~** en particular; **particularly** adv (in particular) sobre todo; (difficult, good etc) especialmente

**parting** ['pɑːtɪŋ] n (act of) separación f; (farewell) despedida; (BRIT: in hair) raya ▷ adj de despedida

**partition** [pɑː'tɪʃən] n (Pol) división f; (wall) tabique m

**partly** ['pɑːtlɪ] adv en parte

**partner** ['pɑːtnər] n (Comm) socio/a; (Sport) pareja; (at dance) pareja; (spouse) cónyuge mf; (friend etc) compañero/a; **partnership** n asociación f; (Comm) sociedad f

**partridge** ['pɑːtrɪdʒ] n perdiz f

**part-time** ['pɑːt'taɪm] adj, adv a tiempo parcial

**party** ['pɑːtɪ] n (Pol) partido; (celebration) fiesta; (group) grupo; (Law) parte f ▷ adj (Pol) de partido

**pass** [pɑːs] vt (time, object) pasar; (place) pasar por; (exam, law) aprobar; (overtake, surpass) rebasar; (approve) aprobar ▷ vi pasar; (Scol) aprobar ▷ n (permit) permiso; (membership card) carnet m; (in mountains) puerto; (Sport) pase m; (Scol: also: ~ mark) aprobado; **to ~ sth through sth** pasar algo por algo; **to make a ~ at sb** (inf) insinuársele a algn; **pass away** vi fallecer; **pass by** vi pasar ▷ vt (ignore) pasar por alto; **pass on** vt: **to ~ on (to)** transmitir (a); **pass out** vi desmayarse; **pass over** vt omitir, pasar por alto; **pass up** vt (opportunity) dejar pasar, no aprovechar; **passable** adj (road) transitable; (tolerable) pasable

**passage** ['pæsɪdʒ] n pasillo; (act of passing) tránsito; (fare, in book) pasaje m; (by boat) travesía

**passenger** ['pæsɪndʒəʳ] n pasajero/a,
viajero/a
**passer-by** [pɑːsə'baɪ] n transeúnte mf
**passing place** n (Aut) apartadero
**passion** ['pæʃən] n pasión f; **passionate**
adj apasionado; **passion fruit** n fruta de la
pasión, granadilla
**passive** ['pæsɪv] adj (also Ling) pasivo
**passport** ['pɑːspɔːt] n pasaporte m;
**passport control** n control m de pasaporte;
**passport office** n oficina de pasaportes
**password** ['pɑːswəːd] n contraseña
**past** [pɑːst] prep (further than) más allá
de; (later than) después de ▷ adj pasado;
(president etc) antiguo ▷ n (time) pasado;
(of person) antecedentes mpl; **quarter/half
~ four** las cuatro y cuarto/media; **he's ~
forty** tiene más de cuarenta años; **for the
~ few/three days** durante los últimos días/
últimos tres días; **to run ~** pasar corriendo
**pasta** ['pæstə] n pasta
**paste** [peɪst] n pasta; (glue) engrudo ▷ vt
pegar
**pastel** ['pæstl] adj pastel; (painting) al pastel
**pasteurized** ['pæstəraɪzd] adj
pasteurizado
**pastime** ['pɑːstaɪm] n pasatiempo
**pastor** ['pɑːstəʳ] n pastor m
**past participle** n (Ling) participio
m (de) pasado or (de) pretérito or pasivo
**pastry** ['peɪstrɪ] n (dough) pasta; (cake)
pastel m
**pasture** ['pɑːstʃəʳ] n pasto
**pasty** n ['pæstɪ] empanada ▷ adj ['peɪstɪ]
(complexion) pálido
**pat** [pæt] vt dar una palmadita a; (dog etc)
acariciar
**patch** [pætʃ] n (of material) parche m;
(mended part) remiendo; (of land) terreno
▷ vt remendar; **(to go through) a bad ~**
(pasar por) una mala racha; **patchy** adj
desigual
**pâté** ['pæteɪ] n paté m
**patent** ['peɪtnt] n patente f ▷ vt patentar
▷ adj patente, evidente
**paternal** [pə'təːnl] adj paternal; (relation)
paterno
**paternity** [pə'təːnɪtɪ] n paternidad
f; **paternity leave** n permiso m por
paternidad, licencia por paternidad
**path** [pɑːθ] n camino, sendero; (trail, track)
pista; (of missile) trayectoria
**pathetic** [pə'θɛtɪk] adj patético; (very bad)
malísimo
**pathway** ['pɑːθweɪ] n sendero, vereda
**patience** ['peɪʃns] n paciencia; (BRIT Cards)
solitario
**patient** ['peɪʃnt] n paciente mf ▷ adj
paciente, sufrido

**patio** ['pætɪəu] n patio
**patriotic** [pætrɪ'ɔtɪk] adj patriótico
**patrol** [pə'trəul] n patrulla ▷ vt patrullar
por; **patrol car** n coche m patrulla
**patron** ['peɪtrən] n (in shop) cliente mf; (of
charity) patrocinador(a) m/f; **~ of the arts**
mecenas m
**patronizing** ['pætrənaɪzɪŋ] adj
condescendiente
**pattern** ['pætən] n (Sewing) patrón m;
(design) dibujo; **patterned** adj (material)
estampado
**pause** [pɔːz] n pausa ▷ vi hacer una pausa
**pave** [peɪv] vt pavimentar; **to ~ the way for**
preparar el terreno para
**pavement** ['peɪvmənt] n (BRIT) acera,
vereda (LAM), andén m (LAM), banqueta (LAM)
**pavilion** [pə'vɪlɪən] n (Sport) vestuarios mpl
**paving** ['peɪvɪŋ] n pavimento, enlosado
**paw** [pɔː] n pata
**pawn** [pɔːn] n (Chess) peón m; (fig)
instrumento ▷ vt empeñar; **pawnbroker**
['pɔːnbrəukəʳ] n prestamista mf
**pay** [peɪ] (pt, pp **paid**) n (wage etc) sueldo,
salario ▷ vt pagar ▷ vi (be profitable) rendir;
**to ~ attention (to)** prestar atención (a);
**pay back** vt (money) reembolsar; (person)
pagar; **pay for** vt fus pagar; **pay in** vt
ingresar; **pay off** vt saldar ▷ vi (scheme,
decision) dar resultado; **pay out** vt (money)
gastar, desembolsar; **pay up** vt pagar;
**payable** adj pagadero; **to make a cheque
payable to sb** extender un cheque a favor
de algn; **pay day** n día m de paga; **pay
envelope** n (US) = **pay packet**; **payment**
n pago; **monthly payment** mensualidad f;
**payout** n pago; (in competition) premio en
metálico; **pay packet** n (BRIT) sobre m (de
la paga); **pay-phone** n teléfono público;
**payroll** n plantilla, nómina; **pay slip** n
nómina, hoja del sueldo; **pay television** n
televisión f de pago
**PC** n abbr (= personal computer) PC m, OP
m; (BRIT) = **police constable** ▷ adj abbr
= **politically correct**
**pc** abbr = **per cent**
**PDA** n abbr (= personal digital assistant)
agenda electrónica
**PE** n abbr (= physical education) ed. física
**pea** [piː] n guisante m, chícharo (LAM),
arveja (LAM)
**peace** [piːs] n paz f; (calm) paz f,
tranquilidad f; **peaceful** adj (gentle)
pacífico; (calm) tranquilo, sosegado
**peach** [piːtʃ] n melocotón m, durazno (LAM)
**peacock** ['piːkɔk] n pavo real
**peak** [piːk] n (of mountain) cumbre f, cima;
(of cap) visera; (fig) cumbre f; **peak hours**
npl horas fpl punta

**peanut** ['piːnʌt] n cacahuete m, maní m (LAM); **peanut butter** n mantequilla de cacahuete

**pear** [peəʳ] n pera

**pearl** [pəːl] n perla

**peasant** ['pɛznt] n campesino/a

**peat** [piːt] n turba

**pebble** ['pɛbl] n guijarro

**peck** [pɛk] vt (also: ~ **at**) picotear ▷ n picotazo; (kiss) besito; **peckish** adj (BRIT inf): **I feel peckish** tengo ganas de picar algo

**peculiar** [pɪˈkjuːlɪəʳ] adj (odd) extraño, raro; (typical) propio, característico; ~ **to** propio de

**pedal** ['pɛdl] n pedal m ▷ vi pedalear

**pedalo** ['pɛdələu] n patín m a pedal

**pedestal** ['pɛdəstl] n pedestal m

**pedestrian** [pɪˈdɛstrɪən] n peatón m ▷ adj pedestre; **pedestrian crossing** n (BRIT) paso de peatones; **pedestrianized** adj: **a pedestrianized street** una calle peatonal; **pedestrian precinct, (US) pedestrian zone** n zona reservada para peatones

**pedigree** ['pɛdɪɡriː] n genealogía; (of animal) pedigrí m ▷ cpd (animal) de raza, de casta

**pedophile** ['piːdəufaɪl] n (US) = **paedophile**

**pee** [piː] vi (inf) mear

**peek** [piːk] vi mirar a hurtadillas

**peel** [piːl] n piel f; (of orange, lemon) cáscara; (: removed) peladuras fpl ▷ vt pelar ▷ vi (paint etc) desconcharse; (wallpaper) despegarse, desprenderse; (skin) pelar

**peep** [piːp] n (look) mirada furtiva; (sound) pío ▷ vi (look) mirar furtivamente

**peer** [pɪəʳ] vi: **to ~ at** escudriñar ▷ n (noble) par m; (equal) igual m; (contemporary) contemporáneo/a

**peg** [pɛɡ] n (for coat etc) gancho, colgador m; (BRIT: also: **clothes ~**) pinza

**pelican** ['pɛlɪkən] n pelícano; **pelican crossing** n (BRIT Aut) paso de peatones señalizado

**pelt** [pɛlt] vt: **to ~ sb with sth** arrojarle algo a algn ▷ vi (rain: also: ~ **down**) llover a cántaros; (inf: run) correr ▷ n pellejo

**pelvis** ['pɛlvɪs] n pelvis f

**pen** [pɛn] n (also: **ballpoint ~**) bolígrafo; (also: **fountain ~**) pluma; (for sheep) redil m

**penalty** ['pɛnltɪ] n pena; (fine) multa

**pence** [pɛns] pl of **penny**

**pencil** ['pɛnsl] n lápiz m ▷ vt (also: ~ **in**) escribir con lápiz; (fig) apuntar con carácter provisional; **pencil case** n estuche m; **pencil sharpener** n sacapuntas m inv

**pendant** ['pɛndnt] n pendiente m

**pending** ['pɛndɪŋ] prep antes de ▷ adj pendiente

**penetrate** ['pɛnɪtreɪt] vt penetrar

**penfriend** ['pɛnfrɛnd] n (BRIT) amigo/a por correspondencia

**penguin** ['pɛŋɡwɪn] n pingüino

**penicillin** [pɛnɪˈsɪlɪn] n penicilina

**peninsula** [pəˈnɪnsjulə] n península

**penis** ['piːnɪs] n pene m

**penitentiary** [pɛnɪˈtɛnʃərɪ] n (US) cárcel f, presidio

**penknife** ['pɛnnaɪf] n navaja

**penniless** ['pɛnɪlɪs] adj sin dinero

**penny** (pl **pennies** or (Brit) **pence**) ['pɛnɪ, 'pɛnɪz, pɛns] n (BRIT) penique m; (US) centavo

**penpal** ['pɛnpæl] n amigo/a por correspondencia

**pension** ['pɛnʃən] n (allowance, state payment) pensión f; (old-age) jubilación f; **pensioner** n (BRIT) jubilado/a

**pentagon** ['pɛntəɡən] n pentágono; **the P~** (US Pol) el Pentágono

### PENTAGON

Se conoce como el Pentágono (the Pentagon) al edificio de planta pentagonal que acoge las dependencias del Ministerio de Defensa estadounidense (Department of Defense) en Arlington, Virginia. En lenguaje periodístico se aplica también a la dirección militar del país.

**penthouse** ['pɛnthaus] n ático (de lujo)

**penultimate** [pɛˈnʌltɪmət] adj penúltimo

**people** ['piːpl] npl gente f; (citizens) pueblo sg, ciudadanos mpl; (Pol): **the ~** el pueblo ▷ n (nation, race) pueblo, nación f; **several ~ came** vinieron varias personas; ~ **say that ...** dice la gente que ...

**pepper** ['pɛpəʳ] n (spice) pimienta; (vegetable) pimiento ▷ vt: **to ~ with** (fig) salpicar de; **peppermint** n (sweet) pastilla de menta

**per** [pəːʳ] prep por; ~ **day/person** por día/persona; ~ **annum** al año

**perceive** [pəˈsiːv] vt percibir; (realize) darse cuenta de

**per cent, (US) percent** n por ciento

**percentage** [pəˈsɛntɪdʒ] n porcentaje m

**perception** [pəˈsɛpʃən] n percepción f; (insight) perspicacia

**perch** [pəːtʃ] n (fish) perca; (for bird) percha ▷ vi: **to ~ (on)** (bird) posarse (en); (person) encaramarse (en)

**percussion** [pəˈkʌʃən] n percusión f

**perfect** adj ['pəːfɪkt] perfecto ▷ n (also: ~ **tense**) perfecto ▷ vt [pəˈfɛkt] perfeccionar; **perfection** n perfección f; **perfectly** adv perfectamente

**perform** [pə'fɔːm] *vt* (*carry out*) realizar,
llevar a cabo; (*Theat*) representar; (*piece of
music*) interpretar ▷ *vi* (*Tech*) funcionar;
**performance** *n* (*of a play*) representación *f*;
(*of player etc*) actuación *f*; (*of engine*)
rendimiento *m*; **performer** *n* (*actor*) actor *m*,
actriz *f*
**perfume** [pə'fjuːm] *n* perfume *m*
**perhaps** [pə'hæps] *adv* quizá(s), tal vez
**perimeter** [pə'rɪmɪtəʳ] *n* perímetro
**period** ['pɪərɪəd] *n* período; (*Scol*) clase *f*;
(*full stop*) punto; (*Med*) regla ▷ *adj* (*costume,
furniture*) de época; **periodical** [pɪərɪ'ɔdɪkl]
*adj* periódico; **periodically** *adv* de vez en
cuando, cada cierto tiempo
**perish** ['perɪʃ] *vi* perecer; (*decay*) echarse a
perder
**perjury** ['pəːdʒərɪ] *n* (*Law*) perjurio
**perk** [pəːk] *n* extra *m*
**perm** [pəːm] *n* permanente *f*
**permanent** ['pəːmənənt] *adj* permanente;
**permanently** *adv* (*lastingly*) para
siempre, de modo definitivo; (*all the time*)
permanentemente
**permission** [pə'mɪʃən] *n* permiso
**permit** *n* ['pəːmɪt] permiso, licencia ▷ *vt*
[pə'mɪt] permitir
**perplex** [pə'plɛks] *vt* dejar perplejo
**persecute** ['pəːsɪkjuːt] *vt* perseguir
**persecution** [pəːsɪ'kjuːʃən] *n* persecución *f*
**persevere** [pəːsɪ'vɪəʳ] *vi* perseverar
**Persian** ['pəːʃən] *adj*, *n* persa *mf*; **the ~ Gulf**
el Golfo Pérsico
**persist** [pə'sɪst] *vi* persistir; **to ~ in doing
sth** empeñarse en hacer algo; **persistent**
*adj* persistente; (*determined*) porfiado
**person** ['pəːsn] *n* persona; **in ~** en persona;
**personal** *adj* personal, individual; (*visit*) en
persona; **personal assistant** *n* ayudante
*mf* personal; **personal computer** *n*
ordenador *m* personal; **personality**
[pəːsə'nælɪtɪ] *n* personalidad *f*; **personally**
*adv* personalmente; (*in person*) en persona;
**to take sth personally** tomarse algo a mal;
**personal organizer** *n* agenda; **personal
stereo** *n* walkman® *m*
**personnel** [pəːsə'nɛl] *n* personal *m*
**perspective** [pə'spɛktɪv] *n* perspectiva
**perspiration** [pəːspɪ'reɪʃən] *n*
transpiración *f*
**persuade** [pə'sweɪd] *vt*: **to ~ sb to do sth**
persuadir a algn para que haga algo
**persuasion** [pə'sweɪʒən] *n* persuasión *f*;
(*persuasiveness*) persuasiva
**persuasive** [pə'sweɪsɪv] *adj* persuasivo
**perverse** [pə'vəːs] *adj* perverso; (*wayward*)
travieso
**pervert** *n* ['pəːvəːt] pervertido/a ▷ *vt*
[pə'vəːt] pervertir

**pessimism** ['pɛsɪmɪzəm] *n* pesimismo
**pessimist** ['pɛsɪmɪst] *n* pesimista *mf*;
**pessimistic** [pɛsɪ'mɪstɪk] *adj* pesimista
**pest** [pɛst] *n* (*insect*) insecto nocivo; (*fig*)
lata, molestia
**pester** ['pɛstəʳ] *vt* molestar, acosar
**pesticide** ['pɛstɪsaɪd] *n* pesticida *m*
**pet** [pɛt] *n* animal *m* doméstico; (*favourite*)
favorito/a ▷ *vt* acariciar ▷ *cpd*: **teacher's ~**
favorito/a (del profesor); **~ hate** manía
**petal** ['pɛtl] *n* pétalo
**petite** [pə'tiːt] *adj* chiquita
**petition** [pə'tɪʃən] *n* petición *f*
**petrified** ['pɛtrɪfaɪd] *adj* horrorizado
**petrol** ['pɛtrəl] (*BRIT*) *n* gasolina
**petroleum** [pə'trəʊlɪəm] *n* petróleo
**petrol: petrol pump** *n* (*BRIT: in garage*)
surtidor *m* de gasolina; **petrol station** *n*
(*BRIT*) gasolinera; **petrol tank** *n* (*BRIT*)
depósito (de gasolina)
**petticoat** ['pɛtɪkəʊt] *n* combinación *f*,
enagua(s) *f(pl)* (*LAM*)
**petty** ['pɛtɪ] *adj* (*mean*) mezquino;
(*unimportant*) insignificante
**pew** [pjuː] *n* banco
**pewter** ['pjuːtəʳ] *n* peltre *m*
**phantom** ['fæntəm] *n* fantasma *m*
**pharmacist** ['fɑːməsɪst] *n* farmacéutico/a
**pharmacy** ['fɑːməsɪ] *n* (*us*) farmacia
**phase** [feɪz] *n* fase *f*; **phase in** *vt* introducir
progresivamente; **phase out** *vt* (*machinery,
product*) retirar progresivamente; (*job,
subsidy*) eliminar por etapas
**pheasant** ['fɛznt] *n* faisán *m*
**phenomena** [fə'nɔmɪnə] *npl of*
**phenomenon**
**phenomenal** [fɪ'nɔmɪnl] *adj* fenomenal,
extraordinario
**phenomenon** (*pl* **phenomena**)
[fə'nɔmɪnən, -nə] *n* fenómeno
**Philippines** ['fɪlɪpiːnz] *npl*: **the ~** (las Islas)
Filipinas
**philosopher** [fɪ'lɔsəfəʳ] *n* filósofo/a
**philosophical** [fɪlə'sɔfɪkl] *adj* filosófico
**philosophy** [fɪ'lɔsəfɪ] *n* filosofía
**phlegm** [flɛm] *n* flema
**phobia** ['fəʊbjə] *n* fobia
**phone** [fəʊn] *n* teléfono ▷ *vt* telefonear,
llamar por teléfono; **to be on the ~** tener
teléfono; (*be calling*) estar hablando por
teléfono; **phone back** *vt, vi* volver a llamar;
**phone up** *vt, vi* llamar por teléfono; **phone
book** *n* guía telefónica; **phone box, phone
booth** *n* cabina telefónica; **phone call**
*n* llamada (telefónica); **phonecard** *n* tarjeta
telefónica; **phone number** *n* número de
teléfono
**phonetics** [fə'nɛtɪks] *n* fonética
**phoney** ['fəʊnɪ] *adj* = **phony**

**phony** ['fəʊnɪ] adj falso

**photo** ['fəʊtəʊ] n foto f; **photo album** n álbum m de fotos; **photocopier** n fotocopiadora; **photocopy** n fotocopia ▷ vt fotocopiar

**photograph** ['fəʊtəgræf] n fotografía ▷ vt fotografiar; **photographer** n fotógrafo/a; **photography** [fə'tɔgrəfɪ] n fotografía

**phrase** [freɪz] n frase f ▷ vt expresar; **phrase book** n libro de frases

**physical** ['fɪzɪkl] adj físico; **physical education** n educación f física; **physically** adv físicamente

**physician** [fɪ'zɪʃən] n médico/a

**physicist** ['fɪzɪsɪst] n físico/a

**physics** ['fɪzɪks] n física

**physiotherapist** [fɪzɪəʊ'θerəpɪst] n fisioterapeuta mf; **physiotherapy** n fisioterapia

**physique** [fɪ'ziːk] n físico

**pianist** ['pɪənɪst] n pianista mf

**piano** [pɪ'ænəʊ] n piano

**pick** [pɪk] n (tool: also: **~axe**) pico, piqueta ▷ vt (select) elegir, escoger; (gather) coger (SP), recoger (LAM); (lock) abrir con ganzúa; **take your ~** escoja lo que quiera; **the ~ of** lo mejor de; **to ~ one's nose/teeth** hurgarse la nariz/escarbarse los dientes; **pick on** vt fus (person) meterse con; **pick out** vt escoger; (distinguish) identificar; **pick up** vi (improve: sales) ir mejor; (: patient) reponerse; (: Finance) recobrarse ▷ vt recoger; (learn) aprender; (Police: arrest) detener; (Radio, TV, Tel) captar; **to ~ up speed** acelerarse; **to ~ o.s. up** levantarse

**pickle** ['pɪkl] n (also: **~s**: as condiment) escabeche m; (fig: mess) apuro ▷ vt conservar en escabeche; (in vinegar) conservar en vinagre

**pickpocket** ['pɪkpɔkɪt] n carterista mf

**pickup** ['pɪkʌp] n (also: **~ truck**, **~ van**) furgoneta, camioneta

**picnic** ['pɪknɪk] n merienda ▷ vi hacer un picnic; **picnic area** n zona de picnic; (Aut) área de descanso

**picture** ['pɪktʃəʳ] n cuadro; (painting) pintura; (photograph) fotografía; (film) película; (TV) imagen f; (fig: description) descripción f; (: situation) situación f ▷ vt (imagine) imaginar; **the ~s** (BRIT) el cine; **picture frame** n marco; **picture messaging** n (envío de) mensajes mpl con imágenes

**picturesque** [pɪktʃə'resk] adj pintoresco

**pie** [paɪ] n (of meat etc: large) pastel m; (: small) empanada; (sweet) tarta

**piece** [piːs] n pedazo, trozo; (of cake) trozo; (item): **a ~ of furniture/advice** un mueble/

un consejo ▷ vt: **to ~ together** juntar; (Tech) armar; **to take to ~s** desmontar

**pie chart** n gráfico de sectores or de tarta

**pier** [pɪəʳ] n muelle m, embarcadero

**pierce** [pɪəs] vt perforar; **to have one's ears ~d** hacerse los agujeros de las orejas

**pig** [pɪg] n cerdo, chancho (LAM); (person: greedy) tragón/ona m/f, comilón/ona m/f; (: nasty) cerdo/a

**pigeon** ['pɪdʒən] n paloma; (as food) pichón m

**piggy bank** ['pɪgɪbæŋk] n hucha (en forma de cerdito)

**pigsty** ['pɪgstaɪ] n pocilga

**pigtail** ['pɪgteɪl] n (girl's) trenza

**pike** [paɪk] n (fish) lucio

**pilchard** ['pɪltʃəd] n sardina

**pile** [paɪl] n montón m; (of carpet) pelo; **pile up** vi (accumulate: work) amontonarse, acumularse ▷ vt (put in a heap: books, clothes) apilar, amontonar; (accumulate) acumular; **piles** npl (Med) almorranas fpl, hemorroides mpl; **pile-up** n (Aut) accidente m múltiple

**pilgrimage** ['pɪlgrɪmɪdʒ] n peregrinación f, romería

**pill** [pɪl] n píldora; **the ~** la píldora

**pillar** ['pɪləʳ] n pilar m

**pillow** ['pɪləʊ] n almohada; **pillowcase** ['pɪləʊkeɪs] n funda (de almohada)

**pilot** ['paɪlət] n piloto mf ▷ adj (scheme etc) piloto inv ▷ vt pilotar; **pilot light** n piloto

**pimple** ['pɪmpl] n grano

**PIN** n abbr (= personal identification number) PIN m

**pin** [pɪn] n alfiler m ▷ vt prender con (alfiler); **~s and needles** hormigueo sg; **to ~ sth on sb** (fig) cargar a algn con la culpa de algo; **pin down** vt (fig): **to ~ sb down** hacer que algn concrete

**pinafore** ['pɪnəfɔːʳ] n delantal m

**pinch** [pɪntʃ] n (of salt etc) pizca ▷ vt pellizcar; (inf: steal) birlar; **at a ~** en caso de apuro

**pine** [paɪn] n (also: **~ tree**) pino ▷ vi: **to ~ for** suspirar por

**pineapple** ['paɪnæpl] n piña, ananá(s) m (LAM)

**ping** [pɪŋ] n (noise) sonido agudo; **Ping-Pong®** n pingpong m

**pink** [pɪŋk] adj (de color) rosa inv ▷ n (colour) rosa m; (Bot) clavel m

**pinpoint** ['pɪnpɔɪnt] vt precisar

**pint** [paɪnt] n pinta (Brit = 0,57 l, US = 0,47 l); (BRIT inf: of beer) pinta de cerveza, ≈ jarra (SP)

**pioneer** [paɪə'nɪəʳ] n pionero/a

**pious** ['paɪəs] adj piadoso, devoto

**pip** [pɪp] n (seed) pepita; **the ~s** (BRIT) la señal

**pipe** [paɪp] n tubería, cañería; (for smoking)

pipa ▷ vt conducir en cañerías; **pipeline** n (for oil) oleoducto; (for natural gas) gaseoducto; **piper** n gaitero/a

**pirate** ['paɪərət] n pirata mf ▷ vt (record, video, book) hacer una copia pirata de, piratear

**Pisces** ['paɪsi:z] n Piscis m

**piss** [pɪs] vi (inf) mear; **pissed** adj (inf: drunk) mamado, pedo

**pistol** ['pɪstl] n pistola

**piston** ['pɪstən] n pistón m, émbolo

**pit** [pɪt] n hoyo; (also: **coal ~**) mina; (in garage) foso de inspección; (also: **orchestra ~**) foso de la orquesta ▷ vt: **to ~ one's wits against sb** medir fuerzas con algn

**pitch** [pɪtʃ] n (Mus) tono; (BRIT Sport) campo, terreno; (tar) brea ▷ vt (throw) arrojar, lanzar ▷ vi (fall) caer(se); **to ~ a tent** montar una tienda (de campaña); **pitch-black** adj negro como boca de lobo

**pitfall** ['pɪtfɔ:l] n riesgo

**pith** [pɪθ] n (of orange) piel f blanca

**pitiful** ['pɪtɪful] adj (touching) lastimoso, conmovedor(a)

**pity** ['pɪtɪ] n compasión f, piedad f ▷ vt compadecer(se de); **what a ~!** ¡qué pena!

**pizza** ['pi:tsə] n pizza

**placard** ['plækɑ:d] n (in march etc) pancarta

**place** [pleɪs] n lugar m, sitio; (seat) plaza, asiento; (post) puesto; (home): **at/to his ~** en/a su casa ▷ vt (object) poner, colocar; (identify) reconocer; **to take ~** tener lugar; **to be ~d** (in race, exam) colocarse; **out of ~** (not suitable) fuera de lugar; **in the first ~** en primer lugar; **to change ~s with sb** cambiarse de sitio con algn; **~ of birth** lugar m de nacimiento; **place mat** n (wooden etc) salvamanteles m inv; (in linen etc) mantel m individual; **placement** n colocación f; (at work) emplazamiento

**placid** ['plæsɪd] adj apacible

**plague** [pleɪg] n plaga; (Med) peste f ▷ vt (fig) acosar, atormentar

**plaice** [pleɪs] n (pl inv) platija

**plain** [pleɪn] adj (clear) claro, evidente; (simple) sencillo; (not handsome) poco atractivo ▷ adv claramente ▷ n llano, llanura; **plain chocolate** n chocolate m oscuro or amargo; **plainly** adv claramente

**plaintiff** ['pleɪntɪf] n demandante mf

**plait** [plæt] n trenza

**plan** [plæn] n (drawing) plano; (scheme) plan m, proyecto ▷ vt proyectar ▷ vi hacer proyectos; **to ~ to do** pensar hacer

**plane** [pleɪn] n (Aviat) avión m; (tree) plátano; (tool) cepillo; (Math) plano

**planet** ['plænɪt] n planeta m

**plank** [plæŋk] n tabla

**planning** ['plænɪŋ] n planificación f; **family ~** planificación familiar

**plant** [plɑ:nt] n planta; (machinery) maquinaria; (factory) fábrica ▷ vt plantar; (field) sembrar; (bomb) colocar

**plantation** [plæn'teɪʃən] n plantación f; (estate) hacienda

**plaque** [plæk] n placa

**plaster** ['plɑ:stər] n (for walls) yeso; (also: **~ of Paris**) yeso mate; (BRIT: also: **sticking ~**) tirita ▷ vt enyesar; (cover): **to ~ with** llenar or cubrir de; **plaster cast** n (Med) escayola; (model, statue) vaciado de yeso

**plastic** ['plæstɪk] n plástico ▷ adj de plástico; **plastic bag** n bolsa de plástico; **plastic surgery** n cirugía plástica

**plate** [pleɪt] n (dish) plato; (metal, in book) lámina; (dental plate) placa de dentadura postiza

**plateau** (pl **plateaus** or **plateaux**) ['plætəu, -z] n meseta, altiplanicie f

**platform** ['plætfɔ:m] n (Rail) andén m; (stage) plataforma; (at meeting) tribuna; (Pol) programa m (electoral)

**platinum** ['plætɪnəm] n platino

**platoon** [plə'tu:n] n pelotón m

**platter** ['plætər] n fuente f

**plausible** ['plɔ:zɪbl] adj verosímil; (person) convincente

**play** [pleɪ] n juego; (Theat) obra ▷ vt (game) jugar; (football, tennis, cards) jugar a; (compete against) jugar contra; (instrument) tocar; (Theat: part) hacer el papel de ▷ vi jugar; (band) tocar; (tape, record) sonar; **to ~ safe** ir a lo seguro; **play back** vt (tape) poner; **play up** vi (cause trouble) dar guerra; **player** n jugador(a) m/f; (Theat) actor m, actriz f; (Mus) músico/a; **playful** adj juguetón/ona; **playground** n (in school) patio de recreo; (in park) parque m infantil; **playgroup** n jardín m de infancia; **playing card** n naipe m, carta; **playing field** n campo de deportes; **playschool** n = **playgroup**; **playtime** n (Scol) (hora de) recreo; **playwright** n dramaturgo/a

**plc** abbr (BRIT: = public limited company) S.A.

**plea** [pli:] n súplica, petición f; (Law) alegato, defensa

**plead** [pli:d] vt (give as excuse) poner como pretexto; (Law): **to ~ sb's case** defender a algn ▷ vi (Law) declararse; (beg): **to ~ with sb** suplicar or rogar a algn

**pleasant** ['plɛznt] adj agradable

**please** [pli:z] excl ¡por favor! ▷ vt (give pleasure to) dar gusto a, agradar ▷ vi (think fit): **do as you ~** haz lo que quieras or lo que te dé la gana; **~ yourself!** ¡haz lo que quieras!, ¡como quieras!; **pleased** adj (happy) alegre, contento; **pleased (with)** satisfecho (de); **pleased to meet you** ¡encantado!, ¡tanto or mucho gusto!

**pleasure** ['plɛʒəʳ] n placer m, gusto; "it's a ~" "el gusto es mío"

**pleat** [pli:t] n pliegue m

**pledge** [plɛdʒ] n (promise) promesa, voto ▷ vt prometer

**plentiful** ['plɛntɪful] adj copioso, abundante

**plenty** ['plɛntɪ] n: ~ of mucho(s)/a(s)

**pliers** ['plaɪəz] npl alicates mpl, tenazas fpl

**plight** [plaɪt] n condición f or situación f difícil

**plod** [plɒd] vi caminar con paso pesado; (fig) trabajar laboriosamente

**plonk** [plɒŋk] (inf) n (BRIT: wine) vino peleón ▷ vt: to ~ sth down dejar caer algo

**plot** [plɒt] n (scheme) complot m, conjura; (of story, play) argumento; (of land) terreno ▷ vt (mark out) trazar; (conspire) tramar, urdir ▷ vi conspirar

**plough**, (US) **plow** [plau] n arado ▷ vt (earth) arar

**plow** [plau] n, vb (US) = **plough**

**ploy** [plɔɪ] n truco, estratagema

**pluck** [plʌk] vt (fruit) coger (SP), recoger (LAM); (musical instrument) puntear; (bird) desplumar; to ~ up courage hacer de tripas corazón; to ~ one's eyebrows depilarse las cejas

**plug** [plʌg] n tapón m; (Elec) enchufe m, clavija; (Aut: also: **spark(ing) ~**) bujía ▷ vt (hole) tapar; (inf: advertise) dar publicidad a; **plug in** vt (Elec) enchufar; **plughole** n desagüe m

**plum** [plʌm] n (fruit) ciruela

**plumber** ['plʌməʳ] n fontanero/a, plomero/a (LAM)

**plumbing** ['plʌmɪŋ] n (trade) fontanería, plomería (LAM); (piping) cañerías

**plummet** ['plʌmɪt] vi: to ~ (down) caer a plomo

**plump** [plʌmp] adj rechoncho, rollizo; **plump for** vt fus (inf: choose) optar por

**plunge** [plʌndʒ] n zambullida ▷ vt sumergir, hundir ▷ vi (fall) caer; (dive) saltar; (person) arrojarse; to take the ~ lanzarse

**plural** ['pluərl] adj plural ▷ n plural m

**plus** [plʌs] n (also: ~ sign) signo más ▷ prep más, y, además de; **ten/twenty ~** más de diez/veinte

**ply** [plaɪ] vt (a trade) ejercer ▷ vi (ship) ir y venir; to ~ sb with drink no dejar de ofrecer copas a algn; **plywood** n madera contrachapada

**PM** n abbr (BRIT) = **Prime Minister**

**p.m.** adv abbr (= post meridiem) de la tarde or noche

**PMS** n abbr (= premenstrual syndrome) SPM m

**PMT** n abbr (= premenstrual tension) SPM m

**pneumatic drill** n taladradora neumática

**pneumonia** [nju:'məunɪə] n pulmonía

**poach** [pəutʃ] vt (cook) escalfar; (steal) cazar/pescar en vedado ▷ vi cazar/pescar en vedado; **poached** adj (egg) escalfado

**PO Box** n abbr (= Post Office Box) apdo., aptdo.

**pocket** ['pɒkɪt] n bolsillo; (fig) bolsa ▷ vt meter en el bolsillo; (steal) embolsarse; to be out of ~ salir perdiendo; **pocketbook** n (US) cartera; **pocket money** n asignación f

**pod** [pɒd] n vaina

**podcast** ['pɒdkɑːst] n podcast m ▷ vi podcastear

**podiatrist** [pɒ'di:ətrɪst] n (US) podólogo/a

**podium** ['pəudɪəm] n podio

**poem** ['pəuɪm] n poema m

**poet** ['pəuɪt] n poeta mf; **poetic** [pəu'ɛtɪk] adj poético; **poetry** n poesía

**poignant** ['pɔɪnjənt] adj conmovedor(a)

**point** [pɔɪnt] n punto; (tip) punta; (purpose) fin m, propósito; (use) utilidad f; (significant part) lo esencial; (also: **decimal ~**): **2 ~ 3 (2.3)** dos coma tres (2,3) ▷ vt (gun etc): to ~ sth at sb apuntar con algo a algn ▷ vi: to ~ at señalar; **points** npl (Aut) contactos mpl; (Rail) agujas fpl; to be on the ~ of doing sth estar a punto de hacer algo; to make a ~ of doing sth poner empeño en hacer algo; to get the ~ comprender; to come to the ~ ir al meollo; there's no ~ (in doing) no tiene sentido (hacer); **point out** vt señalar; **point-blank** adv (say, refuse) sin más hablar; (also: **at point-blank range**) a quemarropa; **pointed** adj (shape) puntiagudo, afilado; (remark) intencionado; **pointer** n (needle) aguja, indicador m; **pointless** adj sin sentido; **point of view** n punto de vista

**poison** ['pɔɪzn] n veneno ▷ vt envenenar; **poisonous** adj venenoso; (fumes etc) tóxico

**poke** [pəuk] vt (jab with finger, stick etc) empujar; (put): to ~ sth in(to) introducir algo en; **poke about** vi fisgonear; **poke out** vi (stick out) salir

**poker** ['pəukəʳ] n atizador m; (Cards) póker m

**Poland** ['pəulənd] n Polonia

**polar** ['pəuləʳ] adj polar; **polar bear** n oso polar

**Pole** [pəul] n polaco/a

**pole** [pəul] n palo; (Geo) polo; (Tel) poste m; **pole bean** n (US) judía trepadora; **pole vault** n salto con pértiga

**police** [pə'li:s] n policía ▷ vt vigilar; **police car** n coche-patrulla m; **police constable** n (BRIT) guardia m, policía m; **police force** n cuerpo de policía; **policeman** n guardia m, policía m; **police officer** n guardia mf, policía mf; **police station** n comisaría; **policewoman** n (mujer f) policía

**policy** ['pɒlɪsɪ] n política; (also: **insurance ~**) póliza

**polio** ['pəʊlɪəʊ] n polio f

**Polish** ['pəʊlɪʃ] adj polaco ▷ n (Ling) polaco

**polish** ['pɒlɪʃ] n (for shoes) betún m; (for floor) cera (de lustrar); (shine) brillo, lustre m; (fig: refinement) refinamiento ▷ vt (shoes) limpiar; (make shiny) pulir, sacar brillo a; **polish off** vt (food) despachar; **polished** adj (fig: person) refinado

**polite** [pə'laɪt] adj cortés, atento; **politeness** n cortesía

**political** [pə'lɪtɪkl] adj político; **politically** adv políticamente; **politically correct** adj políticamente correcto

**politician** [pɒlɪ'tɪʃən] n político/a

**politics** ['pɒlɪtɪks] n política

**poll** [pəʊl] n (votes) votación f; (also: **opinion ~**) sondeo, encuesta ▷ vt (votes) obtener

**pollen** ['pɒlən] n polen m

**polling station** n centro electoral

**pollute** [pə'luːt] vt contaminar

**pollution** [pə'luːʃən] n contaminación f

**polo** ['pəʊləʊ] n (sport) polo; **polo-neck** adj de cuello vuelto ▷ n (sweater) suéter m de cuello vuelto; **polo shirt** n polo, niqui m

**polyester** [pɒlɪ'ɛstəʳ] n poliéster m

**polystyrene** [pɒlɪ'staɪriːn] n poliestireno

**polythene** ['pɒlɪθiːn] n (BRIT) polietileno; **polythene bag** n bolsa de plástico

**pomegranate** ['pɒmɪgrænɪt] n granada

**pompous** ['pɒmpəs] adj pomposo

**pond** [pɒnd] n (natural) charca; (artificial) estanque m

**ponder** ['pɒndəʳ] vt meditar

**pony** ['pəʊnɪ] n poney m; **ponytail** n coleta; **pony trekking** n (BRIT) excursión f a caballo

**poodle** ['puːdl] n caniche m

**pool** [puːl] n (natural) charca; (also: **swimming ~**) piscina, alberca (LAM) ▷ vt juntar; **(football) ~s** npl quinielas fpl

**poor** [pʊəʳ] adj pobre; (bad) malo ▷ npl: **the ~** los pobres; **poorly** adj mal, enfermo ▷ adv mal

**pop** [pɒp] n (sound) ruido seco; (Mus) (música) pop m; (inf: father) papá m; (drink) gaseosa ▷ vt (burst) hacer reventar ▷ vi reventar; (cork) saltar; **pop in** vi entrar un momento; **pop out** vi salir un momento; **popcorn** n palomitas fpl (de maíz)

**poplar** ['pɒpləʳ] n álamo

**popper** ['pɒpəʳ] n corchete m, botón m automático

**poppy** ['pɒpɪ] n amapola; see also **Remembrance Day**

**Popsicle®** ['pɒpsɪkl] n (US) polo

**pop star** n estrella del pop

**popular** ['pɒpjʊləʳ] adj popular; **popularity** [pɒpju'lærɪtɪ] n popularidad f

**population** [pɒpju'leɪʃən] n población f

**porcelain** ['pɔːslɪn] n porcelana

**porch** [pɔːtʃ] n pórtico, entrada; (US) veranda

**pore** [pɔːʳ] n poro ▷ vi: **to ~ over** enfrascarse en

**pork** [pɔːk] n (carne f de) cerdo or chancho (LAM); **pork chop** n chuleta de cerdo; **pork pie** n (BRIT Culin) empanada de carne de cerdo

**porn** [pɔːn] adj (inf) porno inv ▷ n porno; **pornographic** [pɔːnə'græfɪk] adj pornográfico; **pornography** [pɔː'nɒgrəfɪ] n pornografía

**porridge** ['pɒrɪdʒ] n gachas fpl de avena

**port** [pɔːt] n puerto; (Naut: left side) babor m; (wine) oporto; **~ of call** puerto de escala

**portable** ['pɔːtəbl] adj portátil

**porter** ['pɔːtəʳ] n (for luggage) maletero; (doorkeeper) portero/a, conserje mf

**portfolio** [pɔːt'fəʊlɪəʊ] n (case, of artist) cartera, carpeta; (Pol, Finance) cartera

**portion** ['pɔːʃən] n porción f; (helping) ración f

**portrait** ['pɔːtreɪt] n retrato

**portray** [pɔː'treɪ] vt retratar; (in writing) representar

**Portugal** ['pɔːtjʊgl] n Portugal m

**Portuguese** [pɔːtjʊ'giːz] adj portugués/esa ▷ n (pl inv) portugués/esa m/f; (Ling) portugués m

**pose** [pəʊz] n postura, actitud f ▷ vi (pretend): **to ~ as** hacerse pasar por ▷ vt (question) plantear; **to ~ for** posar para

**posh** [pɒʃ] adj (inf) elegante, de lujo

**position** [pə'zɪʃən] n posición f; (job) puesto ▷ vt colocar

**positive** ['pɒzɪtɪv] adj positivo; (certain) seguro; (definite) definitivo; **positively** adv (affirmatively, enthusiastically) de forma positiva; (inf: really) absolutamente

**possess** [pə'zɛs] vt poseer; **possession** [pə'zɛʃən] n posesión f; **possessions** npl (belongings) pertenencias fpl; **possessive** adj posesivo

**possibility** [pɒsɪ'bɪlɪtɪ] n posibilidad f

**possible** ['pɒsɪbl] adj posible; **as big as ~** lo más grande posible; **possibly** adv posiblemente; **I cannot possibly come** me es imposible venir

**post** [pəʊst] n (BRIT: system) correos mpl; (: letters, delivery) correo; (job, situation) puesto; (pole) poste m; (on blog, social network) post m ▷ vt (BRIT) mandar por correo; (on blog, social network) colgar; (BRIT: appoint): **to ~ to** destinar a; **postage** n porte m, franqueo; **postal** adj postal, de correos; **postal order** n giro postal; **postbox** n (BRIT) buzón m; **postcard** n (tarjeta) postal *f*; **postcode** *n* (*BRIT*) código postal

**poster** ['pəustə<sup>r</sup>] *n* cartel *m*

**postgraduate** ['pəust'grædjuɪt] *n* posgraduado/a

**postman** ['pəustmən] (*irreg: like* **man**) *n* (*BRIT*) cartero

**postmark** ['pəustmɑːk] *n* matasellos *m inv*

**post-mortem** [pəust'mɔːtəm] *n* autopsia

**post office** *n* (*building*) (oficina de) correos *m*; (*organization*): **the Post Office** Dirección *f* General de Correos

**postpone** [pəs'pəun] *vt* aplazar

**posture** ['pɒstʃə<sup>r</sup>] *n* postura, actitud *f*

**postwoman** ['pəustwumən] (*irreg: like* **woman**) *n* (*BRIT*) cartera

**pot** [pɒt] *n* (*for cooking*) olla; (*teapot*) tetera; (*coffeepot*) cafetera; (*for flowers*) maceta; (*for jam*) tarro, pote *m* (*LAM*); (*inf: marijuana*) costo, chocolate *m* ▷ *vt* (*plant*) poner en tiesto; **to go to ~** (*inf*) irse al traste

**potato** [pə'teɪtəu] (*pl* **potatoes**) *n* patata, papa (*LAM*); **potato peeler** *n* pelapatatas *m inv*

**potent** ['pəutnt] *adj* potente, poderoso; (*drink*) fuerte

**potential** [pə'tɛnʃl] *adj* potencial, posible ▷ *n* potencial *m*

**pothole** ['pɒthəul] *n* (*in road*) bache *m*; (*BRIT: underground*) gruta

**pot plant** *n* planta de interior

**potter** ['pɒtə<sup>r</sup>] *n* alfarero/a ▷ *vi*: **to ~ around, ~ about** entretenerse haciendo cosillas; **pottery** ['pɒtərɪ] *n* cerámica; (*factory*) alfarería

**potty** ['pɒtɪ] *n* orinal *m* de niño

**pouch** [pautʃ] *n* (*Zool*) bolsa; (*for tobacco*) petaca

**poultry** ['pəultrɪ] *n* aves *fpl* de corral; (*meat*) pollo

**pounce** [pauns] *vi*: **to ~ on** precipitarse sobre

**pound** [paund] *n* libra ▷ *vt* (*beat*) golpear; (*crush*) machacar ▷ *vi* (*beat*) dar golpes; **pound sterling** *n* libra esterlina

**pour** [pɔː<sup>r</sup>] *vt* echar; (*tea*) servir ▷ *vi* correr, fluir; **to ~ sb a drink** servirle a algn una copa; **pour in** *vi* (*people*) entrar en tropel; **pour out** *vi* salir en tropel ▷ *vt* (*drink*) echar, servir; (*fig*): **to ~ out one's feelings** desahogarse; **pouring** *adj*: **pouring rain** lluvia torrencial

**pout** [paut] *vi* hacer pucheros

**poverty** ['pɒvətɪ] *n* pobreza, miseria

**powder** ['paudə<sup>r</sup>] *n* polvo; (*also*: **face ~**) polvos *mpl* ▷ *vt* empolvar; **to ~ one's face** empolvarse la cara; **powdered milk** *n* leche *f* en polvo

**power** ['pauə<sup>r</sup>] *n* poder *m*; (*strength*) fuerza; (*nation*) potencia; (*drive*) empuje *m*; (*Tech*) potencia; (*Elec*) energía ▷ *vt* impulsar; **to be in ~** (*Pol*) estar en el poder; **power cut** *n* (*BRIT*) apagón *m*; **power failure** *n* = **power cut**; **powerful** *adj* poderoso; (*engine*) potente; (*play, speech*) convincente; **powerless** *adj* impotente; **power point** *n* (*BRIT*) enchufe *m*; **power station** *n* central f eléctrica

**pp** *abbr* (= *per procurationem; by proxy*) p.p.; = **pages**

**PR** *n abbr* (= *public relations*) relaciones *fpl* públicas

**practical** ['præktɪkl] *adj* práctico; **practical joke** *n* broma pesada; **practically** *adv* (*almost*) casi, prácticamente

**practice** ['præktɪs] *n* (*habit*) costumbre *f*; (*exercise*) práctica; (*training*) adiestramiento; (*Med: of profession*) práctica, ejercicio; (*Med, Law: business*) consulta ▷ *vt*, *vi* (*US*) = **practise**; **in ~** (*in reality*) en la práctica; **out of ~** desentrenado

**practise**, (*US*) **practice** ['præktɪs] *vt* (*carry out*) practicar; (*profession*) ejercer; (*train at*) practicar ▷ *vi* ejercer; (*train*) practicar; **practising**, (*US*) **practicing** *adj* (*Christian etc*) practicante; (*lawyer*) en ejercicio

**practitioner** [præk'tɪʃənə<sup>r</sup>] *n* (*Med*) médico/a

**pragmatic** [præg'mætɪk] *adj* pragmático

**prairie** ['prɛərɪ] *n* pampa

**praise** [preɪz] *n* alabanza(s) *f(pl)*, elogio(s) *m(pl)* ▷ *vt* alabar, elogiar

**pram** [præm] *n* (*BRIT*) cochecito de niño

**prank** [præŋk] *n* travesura

**prawn** [prɔːn] *n* gamba; **prawn cocktail** *n* cóctel *m* de gambas

**pray** [preɪ] *vi* rezar; **prayer** [prɛə<sup>r</sup>] *n* oración *f*, rezo; (*entreaty*) ruego, súplica

**preach** [priːtʃ] *vi* predicar; **preacher** *n* predicador(a) *m/f*

**precarious** [prɪ'kɛərɪəs] *adj* precario

**precaution** [prɪ'kɔːʃən] *n* precaución *f*

**precede** [prɪ'siːd] *vt*, *vi* preceder; **precedent** ['prɛsɪdənt] *n* precedente *m*; **preceding** [prɪ'siːdɪŋ] *adj* precedente

**precinct** ['priːsɪŋkt] *n* recinto

**precious** ['prɛʃəs] *adj* precioso

**precise** [prɪ'saɪs] *adj* preciso, exacto; **precisely** *adv* exactamente, precisamente

**precision** [prɪ'sɪʒən] *n* precisión *f*

**predator** ['prɛdətə<sup>r</sup>] *n* depredador *m*

**predecessor** ['priːdɪsɛsə<sup>r</sup>] *n* antecesor(a) *m/f*

**predicament** [prɪ'dɪkəmənt] *n* apuro

**predict** [prɪ'dɪkt] *vt* pronosticar; **predictable** *adj* previsible; **prediction** [prɪ'dɪkʃən] *n* predicción *f*

**predominantly** [prɪ'dɒmɪnəntlɪ] *adv* en su mayoría

**preface** ['prɛfəs] *n* prefacio

**prefect** ['pri:fɛkt] *n* (BRIT: *in school*) monitor(a) *m/f*

**prefer** [prɪ'fə:'] *vt* preferir; **to ~ coffee to tea** preferir el café al té; **preferable** ['prɛfrəbl] *adj* preferible; **preferably** ['prɛfrəblɪ] *adv* preferentemente, más bien; **preference** ['prɛfrəns] *n* preferencia; (*priority*) prioridad *f*

**prefix** ['pri:fɪks] *n* prefijo

**pregnancy** ['prɛgnənsɪ] *n* (*of woman*) embarazo; (*of animal*) preñez *f*

**pregnant** ['prɛgnənt] *adj* (*woman*) embarazada; (*animal*) preñada

**prehistoric** ['pri:hɪs'tɔrɪk] *adj* prehistórico

**prejudice** ['prɛdʒudɪs] *n* prejuicio; **prejudiced** *adj* (*person*) predispuesto

**preliminary** [prɪ'lɪmɪnərɪ] *adj* preliminar

**prelude** ['prɛlju:d] *n* preludio

**premature** ['prɛmətʃuə'] *adj* prematuro

**premier** ['prɛmɪə'] *adj* primero, principal ▷ *n* (*Pol*) primer(a) ministro/a

**première** ['prɛmɪeə'] *n* estreno

**Premier League** [prɛmɪə'li:g] *n* primera división

**premises** ['prɛmɪsɪs] *npl* local *msg*; **on the ~** en el lugar mismo

**premium** ['pri:mɪəm] *n* premio; (*insurance*) prima; **to be at a ~** estar muy solicitado

**premonition** [prɛmə'nɪʃən] *n* presentimiento

**preoccupied** [pri:'ɔkjupaɪd] *adj* ensimismado

**prepaid** [pri:'peɪd] *adj* porte pagado

**preparation** [prɛpə'reɪʃən] *n* preparación *f*; **preparations** *npl* preparativos *mpl*

**preparatory school** *n* (BRIT) *colegio privado de enseñanza primaria;* (US) *colegio privado de enseñanza secundaria*

**prepare** [prɪ'pɛə'] *vt* preparar, disponer; (*Culin*) preparar ▷ *vi:* **to ~ for** (*action*) prepararse *or* disponerse para; (*event*) hacer preparativos para; **prepared** *adj* (*willing*): **to be prepared to help sb** estar dispuesto a ayudar a algn; **prepared for** listo para

**preposition** [prɛpə'zɪʃən] *n* preposición *f*

**prep school** [prɛp-] *n* = **preparatory school**

**prerequisite** [pri:'rɛkwɪzɪt] *n* requisito previo

**preschool** ['pri:'sku:l] *adj* preescolar

**prescribe** [prɪ'skraɪb] *vt* (*Med*) recetar

**prescription** [prɪ'skrɪpʃən] *n* (*Med*) receta

**presence** ['prɛzns] *n* presencia; **in sb's ~** en presencia de algn; **~ of mind** aplomo

**present** *adj* ['prɛznt] (*in attendance*) presente; (*current*) actual ▷ *n* ['prɛznt]

(*gift*) regalo; (*actuality*): **the ~** la actualidad, el presente ▷ *vt* [prɪ'zɛnt] (*introduce*) presentar; (*expound*) exponer; (*give*) presentar, dar, ofrecer; (*Theat*) representar; **to give sb a ~** regalar algo a algn; **at ~** actualmente; **presentable** [prɪ'zɛntəbl] *adj:* **to make o.s. presentable** arreglarse; **presentation** [prɛzn'teɪʃən] *n* presentación *f*; (*of case*) exposición *f*; **present-day** *adj* actual; **presenter** [prɪ'zɛntə'] *n* (*Radio, TV*) locutor(a) *m/f*; **presently** *adv* (*soon*) dentro de poco; (*now*) ahora; **present participle** *n* participio (de) presente

**preservation** [prɛzə'veɪʃən] *n* conservación *f*

**preservative** [prɪ'zə:vətɪv] *n* conservante *m*

**preserve** [prɪ'zə:v] *vt* (*keep safe*) preservar, proteger; (*maintain*) mantener; (*food*) conservar ▷ *n* (*for game*) coto, vedado; (*often pl: jam*) confitura

**preside** [prɪ'zaɪd] *vi* presidir

**president** ['prɛzɪdənt] *n* presidente *mf*; (US: *of company*) director(a) *m/f*; **presidential** [prɛzɪ'dɛnʃl] *adj* presidencial

**press** [prɛs] *n* (*tool, machine, newspapers*) prensa; (*printer's*) imprenta; (*of hand*) apretón *m* ▷ *vt* (*push*) empujar; (*squeeze: button*) apretar; (*iron: clothes*) planchar; (*pressure*) presionar; (*insist*): **to ~ sth on sb** insistir en que algn acepte algo ▷ *vi* (*squeeze*) apretar; **we are ~ed for time** tenemos poco tiempo; **to ~ sb to do** *or* **into doing sth** (*urge, entreat*) presionar a algn para que haga algo; **press conference** *n* rueda de prensa; **pressing** *adj* apremiante; **press stud** *n* (BRIT) botón *m* de presión; **press-up** *n* (BRIT) flexión *f*

**pressure** ['prɛʃə'] *n* presión *f*; **to put ~ on sb** presionar a algn; **pressure cooker** *n* olla a presión; **pressure group** *n* grupo de presión

**prestige** [prɛs'ti:ʒ] *n* prestigio

**prestigious** [prɛs'tɪdʒəs] *adj* prestigioso

**presumably** [prɪ'zju:məblɪ] *adv* es de suponer que, cabe presumir que

**presume** [prɪ'zju:m] *vt:* **to ~ (that)** presumir (que), suponer (que)

**pretence**, (US) **pretense** [prɪ'tɛns] *n* fingimiento; **under false ~s** con engaños

**pretend** [prɪ'tɛnd] *vt, vi* fingir

▍Be careful not to translate *pretend* by the Spanish word *pretender*.

**pretense** [prɪ'tɛns] *n* (US) = **pretence**

**pretentious** [prɪ'tɛnʃəs] *adj* pretencioso; (*ostentatious*) ostentoso, aparatoso

**pretext** ['pri:tɛkst] *n* pretexto

**pretty** ['prɪtɪ] *adj* bonito, lindo (LAM) ▷ *adv* bastante

**prevail** [prɪ'veɪl] vi (gain mastery) prevalecer; (be current) predominar; **prevailing** adj (dominant) predominante

**prevalent** ['prevələnt] adj (widespread) extendido

**prevent** [prɪ'vent] vt: **to ~ (sb) from doing sth** impedir (a algn) hacer algo; **to ~ sth from happening** evitar que ocurra algo; **prevention** [prɪ'venʃən] n prevención f; **preventive** adj preventivo

**preview** ['pri:vju:] n (of film) preestreno

**previous** ['pri:vɪəs] adj previo, anterior; **previously** adv antes

**prey** [preɪ] n presa ▷ vi: **to ~ on** (feed on) alimentarse de; **it was ~ing on his mind** le obsesionaba

**price** [praɪs] n precio ▷ vt (goods) fijar el precio de; **priceless** adj que no tiene precio; **price list** n tarifa

**prick** [prɪk] n (sting) picadura ▷ vt pinchar; (hurt) picar; **to ~ up one's ears** aguzar el oído

**prickly** ['prɪklɪ] adj espinoso; (fig: person) enojadizo

**pride** [praɪd] n orgullo; (pej) soberbia ▷ vt: **to ~ o.s. on** enorgullecerse de

**priest** [pri:st] n sacerdote m

**primarily** ['praɪmərɪlɪ] adv ante todo

**primary** ['praɪmərɪ] adj (first in importance) principal ▷ n (us: also: **~ election**) (elección f) primaria; **primary school** n (BRIT) escuela primaria

**prime** [praɪm] adj primero, principal; (excellent) selecto, de primera clase ▷ n: **in the ~ of life** en la flor de la vida ▷ vt (wood, also fig) preparar; **~ example** ejemplo típico; **Prime Minister** n primer(a) ministro/a; ver nota **"Downing Street"**

**primitive** ['prɪmɪtɪv] adj primitivo; (crude) rudimentario

**primrose** ['prɪmrəuz] n primavera, prímula

**prince** [prɪns] n príncipe m

**princess** [prɪn'ses] n princesa

**principal** ['prɪnsɪpl] adj principal ▷ n director(a) m/f; **principally** adv principalmente

**principle** ['prɪnsɪpl] n principio; **in ~** en principio; **on ~** por principio

**print** [prɪnt] n (impression) marca, impresión f; (footprint) huella; (fingerprint) huella dactilar; (letters) letra de molde; (fabric) estampado; (Art) grabado; (Phot) impresión f ▷ vt imprimir; (write in capitals) escribir en letras de molde; **out of ~** agotado; **print out** vt (Comput) imprimir; **printer** n (person) impresor(a) m/f; (machine) impresora; **printout** n (Comput) copia impresa

**prior** ['praɪər] adj anterior, previo; (more important) más importante; **~ to doing** antes de or hasta hacer

**priority** [praɪ'ɔrɪtɪ] n prioridad f; **to have** or **take ~ over sth** tener prioridad sobre algo

**prison** ['prɪzn] n cárcel f, prisión f ▷ cpd carcelario; **prisoner** n (in prison) preso/a; (captured person) prisionero/a

**pristine** ['prɪsti:n] adj prístino

**privacy** ['prɪvəsɪ] n intimidad f

**private** ['praɪvɪt] adj (personal) particular; (property, industry, discussion etc) privado; (person) reservado; (place) tranquilo ▷ n soldado raso; **"~"** (on envelope) "confidencial"; (on door) "privado"; **in ~** en privado; **privately** adv en privado; (in o.s.) en secreto; **private property** n propiedad f privada; **private school** n colegio privado

**privatize** ['praɪvɪtaɪz] vt privatizar

**privilege** ['prɪvɪlɪdʒ] n privilegio; (prerogative) prerrogativa

**prize** [praɪz] n premio ▷ adj de primera clase ▷ vt apreciar, estimar; **prize-giving** n distribución f de premios; **prizewinner** n premiado/a

**pro** [prəu] n (Sport) profesional mf; **the ~s and cons** los pros y los contras

**probability** [prɔbə'bɪlɪtɪ] n probabilidad f; **in all ~** lo más probable

**probable** ['prɔbəbl] adj probable

**probably** ['prɔbəblɪ] adv probablemente

**probation** [prə'beɪʃən] n: **on ~** (employee) a prueba; (Law) en libertad condicional

**probe** [prəub] n (Med, Space) sonda; (enquiry) investigación f ▷ vt sondar; (investigate) investigar

**problem** ['prɔbləm] n problema m

**procedure** [prə'si:dʒər] n procedimiento; (bureaucratic) trámites mpl

**proceed** [prə'si:d] vi proceder; (continue): **to ~ (with)** continuar (con); **proceedings** npl acto(s) m(pl); (Law) proceso sg; **proceeds** ['prəusi:dz] npl ganancias fpl, ingresos mpl

**process** ['prəuses] n proceso ▷ vt tratar, elaborar

**procession** [prə'seʃən] n desfile m; **funeral ~** cortejo fúnebre

**proclaim** [prə'kleɪm] vt (announce) anunciar

**prod** [prɔd] vt empujar ▷ n empujoncito; codazo

**produce** n ['prɔdju:s] (Agr) productos mpl agrícolas ▷ vt [prə'dju:s] producir; (Theat) presentar; **producer** n (Theat) director(a) m/f; (Agr, Cine) productor(a) m/f

**product** ['prɔdʌkt] n producto; **production** [prə'dʌkʃən] n (act) producción f; (Theat) representación f; **productive** [prə'dʌktɪv] adj productivo; **productivity** [prɔdʌk'tɪvɪtɪ] n productividad f

**Prof.** [prɔf] abbr (= professor) Prof
**profession** [prə'feʃən] n profesión f;
  **professional** n profesional mf; (skilled
  person) perito
**professor** [prə'fesə'] n (BRIT) catedrático/a;
  (US: teacher) profesor(a) m/f
**profile** ['prəufaɪl] n perfil m
**profit** ['prɔfɪt] n (Comm) ganancia ▷ vi: to ~
  by or from aprovechar or sacar provecho de;
  **profitable** adj (Econ) rentable
**profound** [prə'faund] adj profundo
**programme**, (US or Comput) **program**
  ['prəugræm] n programa m ▷ vt
  programar; **programmer**, (US) **programer**
  ['prəugræmə'] n programador(a) m/f;
  **programming**, (US) **programing**
  ['prəugræmɪŋ] n programación f
**progress** n ['prəugres] progreso /;
  (development) desarrollo ▷ vi [prə'gres]
  progresar, avanzar; **in ~** en curso;
  **progressive** [prə'gresɪv] adj progresivo;
  (person) progresista
**prohibit** [prə'hɪbɪt] vt prohibir; **to ~ sb
  from doing sth** prohibir a algn hacer algo
**project** n ['prɔdʒekt] proyecto ▷ vt
  [prə'dʒekt] proyectar ▷ vi (stick out) salir,
  sobresalir; **projection** [prə'dʒekʃən]
  n proyección f; (overhang) saliente m;
  **projector** [prə'dʒektə'] n proyector m
**prolific** [prə'lɪfɪk] adj prolífico
**prolong** [prə'lɔŋ] vt prolongar, extender
**prom** [prɔm] n abbr (BRIT) = **promenade**;
  = **promenade concert**; (US: ball) baile m de
  gala; ver nota

  ● **PROM**
  ●
  ● Los conciertos de música clásica más
  ● conocidos en Inglaterra son los llamados
  ● Proms (o promenade concerts), que tienen
  ● lugar en el Royal Albert Hall de Londres,
  ● aunque también se llama así a cualquier
  ● concierto de esas características. Su
  ● nombre se debe al hecho de que en un
  ● principio el público paseaba durante las
  ● actuaciones; en la actualidad parte de
  ● la gente que acude a ellos permanece de
  ● pie. En Estados Unidos se llama prom a un
  ● baile de gala en un colegio o universidad.

**promenade** [prɔmə'nɑːd] n (by sea) paseo
  marítimo
**prominent** ['prɔmɪnənt] adj (standing out)
  saliente; (important) eminente,
  importante
**promiscuous** [prə'mɪskjuəs] adj (sexually)
  promiscuo
**promise** ['prɔmɪs] n promesa ▷ vt, vi
  prometer; **promising** adj prometedor(a)

**promote** [prə'məut] vt (Mil) ascender;
  (employee) ascender; (ideas) fomentar;
  **promotion** [prə'məuʃən] n promoción f;
  (Mil) ascenso
**prompt** [prɔmpt] adj pronto ▷ adv: **at six
  o'clock ~** a las seis en punto ▷ n (Comput)
  aviso, guía ▷ vt (urge) mover, incitar; (when
  talking) instar; (Theat) apuntar; **to ~ sb to
  do sth** instar a algn a hacer algo; **promptly**
  adv (punctually) puntualmente; (rapidly)
  rápidamente
**prone** [prəun] adj (lying) postrado; **~ to**
  propenso a
**prong** [prɔŋ] n diente m, punta
**pronoun** ['prəunaun] n pronombre m
**pronounce** [prə'nauns] vt pronunciar
**pronunciation** [prənʌnsɪ'eɪʃən] n
  pronunciación f
**proof** [pruːf] n prueba ▷ adj: **~ against** a
  prueba de
**prop** [prɔp] n apoyo; (fig) sostén m; **props**
  npl accesorios mpl, at(t)rezzo msg; **prop
  up** vt (roof, structure) apuntalar; (economy)
  respaldar
**propaganda** [prɔpə'gændə] n propaganda
**propeller** [prə'pelə'] n hélice f
**proper** ['prɔpə'] adj (suited, right) propio;
  (exact) justo; (seemly) correcto, decente;
  (authentic) verdadero; **properly** adv
  (adequately) correctamente; (decently)
  decentemente; **proper noun** n nombre
  m propio
**property** ['prɔpətɪ] n propiedad f; **personal
  ~** bienes mpl muebles
**prophecy** ['prɔfɪsɪ] n profecía
**prophet** ['prɔfɪt] n profeta mf
**proportion** [prə'pɔːʃən] n proporción
  f; (share) parte f; **proportions** npl (size)
  dimensiones fpl; **proportional** adj:
  **proportional (to)** en proporción (con)
**proposal** [prə'pəuzl] n (offer of marriage)
  oferta de matrimonio; (plan) proyecto
**propose** [prə'pəuz] vt proponer ▷ vi
  declararse; **to ~ to do** tener intención de
  hacer
**proposition** [prɔpə'zɪʃən] n propuesta
**proprietor** [prə'praɪətə'] n propietario/a,
  dueño/a
**prose** [prəuz] n prosa
**prosecute** ['prɔsɪkjuːt] vt (Law) procesar;
  **prosecution** [prɔsɪ'kjuːʃən] n proceso,
  causa; (accusing side) acusación f;
  **prosecutor** n acusador(a) m/f; (also: **public
  prosecutor**) fiscal mf
**prospect** n ['prɔspekt] (chance) posibilidad
  f; (outlook) perspectiva ▷ vi [prə'spekt]
  buscar; **prospects** npl (for work etc)
  perspectivas fpl; **prospective** [prə'spektɪv]
  adj futuro

**prospectus** [prə'spɛktəs] *n* prospecto
**prosper** ['prɔspə'] *vi* prosperar; **prosperity** [prɔ'spɛrɪtɪ] *n* prosperidad *f*; **prosperous** *adj* próspero
**prostitute** ['prɔstɪtjuːt] *n* prostituta; **male ~** prostituto
**protect** [prə'tɛkt] *vt* proteger; **protection** [prə'tɛkʃən] *n* protección *f*; **protective** *adj* protector(a)
**protein** ['prəutiːn] *n* proteína
**protest** *n* ['prəutɛst] protesta ▷ *vi* [prə'tɛst]: **to ~ about** *or* **at/against** protestar de/contra ▷ *vt* (*insist*): **to ~ (that)** insistir en (que)
**Protestant** ['prɔtɪstənt] *adj, n* protestante *mf*
**protester, protestor** *n* manifestante *mf*
**protractor** [prə'træktə'] *n* (*Geom*) transportador *m*
**proud** [praud] *adj* orgulloso; (*pej*) soberbio, altanero
**prove** [pruːv] *vt* probar; (*show*) demostrar ▷ *vi*: **to ~ correct** resultar correcto; **to ~ o.s.** ponerse a prueba
**proverb** ['prɔvəːb] *n* refrán *m*
**provide** [prə'vaɪd] *vt* proporcionar, dar; **to ~ sb with sth** proveer a algn de algo; **provide for** *vt fus* (*person*) mantener a; (*problem etc*) tener en cuenta; **provided** *conj*: **provided (that)** con tal de que, a condición de que; **providing** [prə'vaɪdɪŋ] *conj*: **providing (that)** a condición de que, con tal de que
**province** ['prɔvɪns] *n* provincia; (*fig*) esfera; **provincial** [prə'vɪnʃəl] *adj* provincial; (*pej*) provinciano
**provision** [prə'vɪʒən] *n* (*supply*) suministro, abastecimiento; **provisions** *npl* provisiones *fpl*, víveres *mpl*; **provisional** *adj* provisional
**provocative** [prə'vɔkətɪv] *adj* provocativo
**provoke** [prə'vəuk] *vt* (*arouse*) provocar, incitar; (*anger*) enojar
**prowl** [praul] *vi* (*also:* **~ about, ~ around**) merodear ▷ *n*: **on the ~** de merodeo
**proximity** [prɔk'sɪmɪtɪ] *n* proximidad *f*
**proxy** ['prɔksɪ] *n*: **by ~** por poderes
**prudent** ['pruːdnt] *adj* prudente
**prune** [pruːn] *n* ciruela pasa ▷ *vt* podar
**pry** [praɪ] *vi*: **to ~ into** entrometerse en
**PS** *abbr* (= *postscript*) P.D.
**pseudonym** ['sjuːdənɪm] *n* seudónimo
**PSHE** *n abbr* (*BRIT Scol*: = *personal, social, and health education*) formación social y sanitaria para la vida adulta
**psychiatric** [saɪkɪ'ætrɪk] *adj* psiquiátrico
**psychiatrist** [saɪ'kaɪətrɪst] *n* psiquiatra *mf*
**psychic** ['saɪkɪk] *adj* (*also:* **~al**) psíquico
**psychoanalysis** (*pl* **psychoanalyses**) [saɪkəuə'nælɪsɪs, -siːz] *n* psicoanálisis *m inv*

**psychological** [saɪkə'lɔdʒɪkl] *adj* psicológico
**psychologist** [saɪ'kɔlədʒɪst] *n* psicólogo/a
**psychology** [saɪ'kɔlədʒɪ] *n* psicología
**psychotherapy** [saɪkəu'θɛrəpɪ] *n* psicoterapia
**pt** *abbr* = **pint; point**
**PTO** *abbr* (= *please turn over*) sigue
**pub** [pʌb] *n abbr* (= *public house*) pub *m*, bar *m*
**puberty** ['pjuːbətɪ] *n* pubertad *f*
**public** ['pʌblɪk] *adj* público ▷ *n*: **the ~** el público; **in ~** en público; **to make sth ~** revelar *or* hacer público algo
**publication** [pʌblɪ'keɪʃən] *n* publicación *f*
**public: public company** *n* sociedad *f* anónima; **public convenience** *n* (*BRIT*) aseos *mpl* públicos, sanitarios *mpl* (*LAM*); **public holiday** *n* día *m* de fiesta, (día) feriado (*LAM*); **public house** *n* (*BRIT*) pub *m*, bar *m*
**publicity** [pʌb'lɪsɪtɪ] *n* publicidad *f*
**publicize** ['pʌblɪsaɪz] *vt* publicitar
**public: public limited company** *n* sociedad *f* anónima (S.A.); **publicly** *adv* públicamente, en público; **public opinion** *n* opinión *f* pública; **public relations** *n* relaciones *fpl* públicas; **public school** *n* (*BRIT*) colegio privado; (*US*) instituto; **public transport** *n* transporte *m* público
**publish** ['pʌblɪʃ] *vt* publicar; **publisher** *n* (*person*) editor(a) *m/f*; (*firm*) editorial *f*; **publishing** *n* (*industry*) industria del libro
**pub lunch** *n* almuerzo que se sirve en un pub; **to go for a ~** almorzar o comer en un pub
**pudding** ['pudɪŋ] *n* pudín *m*; (*BRIT: sweet*) postre *m*; **black ~** morcilla
**puddle** ['pʌdl] *n* charco
**Puerto Rico** [-'riːkəu] *n* Puerto Rico
**puff** [pʌf] *n* soplo; (*of smoke*) bocanada; (*of breathing, engine*) resoplido ▷ *vt*: **to ~ one's pipe** dar chupadas a la pipa ▷ *vi* (*pant*) jadear; **puff pastry** *n* hojaldre *m*
**pull** [pul] *n* ▷ *vt* tirar de; (*haul*) tirar, arrastrar ▷ *vi* tirar, jalar (*LAM*); **to give sth a ~** (*tug*) dar un tirón a algo; **to ~ to pieces** hacer pedazos; **to ~ one's punches** andarse con bromas; **to ~ one's weight** hacer su parte; **to ~ o.s. together** tranquilizarse, sobreponerse; **to ~ sb's leg** tomar el pelo a algn; **pull apart** *vt* (*break*) romper; **pull away** *vi* (*vehicle: move off*) salir, arrancar; (*draw back*) apartarse bruscamente; **pull back** *vt* (*lever etc*) tirar hacia sí; (*curtains*) descorrer ▷ *vi* (*refrain*) contenerse; (*Mil: withdraw*) retirarse; **pull down** *vt* (*house*) derribar; **pull in** *vi* (*Aut: at the kerb*) parar (junto a la acera); (*Rail*) llegar; **pull off** *vt* (*deal etc*) cerrar; **pull out** *vi* (*car, train etc*)

salir ▷ vt sacar, arrancar; **pull over** vi (Aut) hacerse a un lado; **pull up** vi (stop) parar ▷ vt (uproot) arrancar, desarraigar

**pulley** ['pulɪ] n polea

**pullover** ['puləuvə<sup>r</sup>] n jersey m, suéter m

**pulp** [pʌlp] n (of fruit) pulpa

**pulpit** ['pulpɪt] n púlpito

**pulse** [pʌls] n (Anat) pulso; (of music, engine) pulsación f; (Bot) legumbre f; **pulses** npl legumbres

**puma** ['pju:mə] n puma m

**pump** [pʌmp] n bomba; (shoe) zapatilla de tenis ▷ vt sacar con una bomba; **pump up** vt inflar

**pumpkin** ['pʌmpkɪn] n calabaza

**pun** [pʌn] n juego de palabras

**punch** [pʌntʃ] n (blow) golpe m, puñetazo; (tool) punzón m; (drink) ponche m ▷ vt: to ~ sb/sth (hit) dar un puñetazo or golpear a algn/algo; **punch-up** n (BRIT inf) riña

**punctual** ['pʌŋktjuəl] adj puntual

**punctuation** [pʌŋktju'eɪʃən] n puntuación f

**puncture** ['pʌŋktʃə<sup>r</sup>] (BRIT) n pinchazo ▷ vt pinchar

**punish** ['pʌnɪʃ] vt castigar; **punishment** n castigo

**punk** [pʌŋk] n (also: ~ rocker) punki mf; (also: ~ rock) música punk; (US inf: hoodlum) matón m

**pup** [pʌp] n cachorro

**pupil** ['pju:pl] n alumno/a; (of eye) pupila

**puppet** ['pʌpɪt] n títere m

**puppy** ['pʌpɪ] n cachorro, perrito

**purchase** ['pə:tʃɪs] n compra ▷ vt comprar

**pure** [pjuə<sup>r</sup>] adj puro; **purely** adv puramente

**purify** ['pjuərɪfaɪ] vt purificar, depurar

**purity** ['pjuərɪtɪ] n pureza

**purple** ['pə:pl] adj morado

**purpose** ['pə:pəs] n propósito; **on ~** a propósito, adrede

**purr** [pə:<sup>r</sup>] vi ronronear

**purse** [pə:s] n monedero; (US: handbag) bolso, cartera (LAM) ▷ vt fruncir

**pursue** [pə'sju:] vt seguir

**pursuit** [pə'sju:t] n (chase) caza; (occupation) actividad f

**pus** [pʌs] n pus m

**push** [puʃ] n empujón m; (drive) empuje m ▷ vt empujar; (button) apretar; (promote) promover ▷ vi empujar; **to ~ for** (better pay, conditions) reivindicar; **push in** vi colarse; **push off** vi (inf) largarse; **push on** vi seguir adelante; **push over** vt (cause to fall) hacer caer, derribar; (knock over) volcar; **push through** vi (crowd) abrirse paso a empujones ▷ vt (measure) despachar; **pushchair** n (BRIT) silla de niño; **pusher** n

(also: **drug pusher**) traficante mf de drogas; **push-up** n (US) flexión f

**puss** [pus], **pussy(-cat)** ['pusɪ-] n minino

**put** [put] (pt, pp **put**) [put] vt (place) poner, colocar; (put into) meter; (express, say) expresar; (a question) hacer; (estimate) calcular; **put aside** vt (lay down: book etc) dejar or poner a un lado; (save) ahorrar; (in shop) guardar; **put away** vt (store) guardar; **put back** vt (replace) devolver a su lugar; (postpone) aplazar; **put by** vt (money) guardar; **put down** vt (on ground) poner en el suelo; (animal) sacrificar; (in writing) apuntar; (revolt etc) sofocar; (attribute) atribuir; **put forward** vt (ideas) presentar, proponer; **put in** vt (application, complaint) presentar; (time) dedicar; **put off** vt (postpone) aplazar; (discourage) desanimar; **put on** vt ponerse; (light etc) encender; (play etc) presentar; (brake) echar; (record, kettle etc) poner; (assume) adoptar; **put out** vt (fire, light) apagar; (rubbish etc) sacar; (cat etc) echar; (one's hand) alargar; **put through** vt (call) poner; (plan etc) hacer aprobar; **put together** vt unir, reunir; (assemble: furniture) armar, montar; (meal) preparar; **put up** vt (raise) levantar, alzar; (hang) colgar; (build) construir; (increase) aumentar; (accommodate) alojar; **put up with** vt fus aguantar

**putt** [pʌt] n putt m; **putting green** n green m, minigolf m

**puzzle** ['pʌzl] n rompecabezas m inv; (also: **crossword ~**) crucigrama m; (mystery) misterio ▷ vt dejar perplejo, confundir ▷ vi: to ~ **over** devanarse los sesos sobre; **puzzling** adj misterioso, extraño

**pyjamas**, (US) **pajamas** [pɪ'dʒɑ:məz] npl pijama msg

**pylon** ['paɪlən] n torre f de conducción eléctrica

**pyramid** ['pɪrəmɪd] n pirámide f

# q

**quack** [kwæk] n graznido; (pej: doctor) curandero/a

**quadruple** [kwɔ'dru:pl] vt, vi cuadruplicar

**quail** [kweɪl] n codorniz f ▷ vi amedrentarse

**quaint** [kweɪnt] adj extraño; (picturesque) pintoresco

**quake** [kweɪk] vi temblar ▷ n abbr = **earthquake**

**qualification** [kwɔlɪfɪ'keɪʃən] n (ability) capacidad f; (often pl: diploma etc) título; (reservation) salvedad f

**qualified** ['kwɔlɪfaɪd] adj capacitado; (limited) limitado; (professionally) titulado

**qualify** ['kwɔlɪfaɪ] vt (capacitate) capacitar; (modify) matizar ▷ vi: **to ~ (for)** (in competition) calificarse (para); (be eligible) reunir los requisitos (para); **to ~ (as)** (pass examination) calificarse (de), graduarse (en)

**quality** ['kwɔlɪtɪ] n calidad f; (moral) cualidad f

**qualm** [kwɑ:m] n escrúpulo

**quantify** ['kwɔntɪfaɪ] vt cuantificar

**quantity** ['kwɔntɪtɪ] n cantidad f; **in ~** en grandes cantidades

**quarantine** ['kwɔrnti:n] n cuarentena

**quarrel** ['kwɔrl] n riña, pelea ▷ vi reñir, pelearse

**quarry** ['kwɔrɪ] n cantera

**quart** [kwɔ:t] n cuarto de galón = 1.136 l

**quarter** ['kwɔ:tər] n cuarto, cuarta parte f; (us: coin) moneda de 25 centavos; (of year) trimestre m; (district) barrio ▷ vt dividir en cuartos; (Mil: lodge) alojar; **quarters** npl (barracks) cuartel msg; (living quarters) alojamiento sg; **a ~ of an hour** un cuarto de hora; **quarter final** n cuarto de final; **quarterly** adj trimestral ▷ adv cada 3 meses, trimestralmente

**quartet(te)** [kwɔ:'tet] n cuarteto

**quartz** [kwɔ:ts] n cuarzo

**quay** [ki:] n (also: **~side**) muelle m

**queasy** ['kwi:zɪ] adj: **to feel ~** tener náuseas

**queen** [kwi:n] n reina; (Cards etc) dama

**queer** [kwɪər] adj raro, extraño ▷ n (pej, inf!) marica (!) m

**quench** [kwentʃ] vt: **to ~ one's thirst** apagar la sed

**query** ['kwɪərɪ] n (question) pregunta ▷ vt dudar de

**quest** [kwest] n busca, búsqueda

**question** ['kwestʃən] n pregunta; (matter) asunto, cuestión f ▷ vt (doubt) dudar de; (interrogate) interrogar, hacer preguntas a; **beyond ~** fuera de toda duda; **out of the ~** imposible, ni hablar; **questionable** adj dudoso; **question mark** n punto de interrogación; **questionnaire** [kwestʃə'nɛər] n cuestionario

**queue** [kju:] (BRIT) n cola ▷ vi hacer cola

**quiche** [ki:ʃ] n quiche m

**quick** [kwɪk] adj rápido; (agile) ágil; (mind) listo ▷ n: **cut to the ~** (fig) herido en lo más vivo; **be ~!** ¡date prisa!; **quickly** adv rápidamente, de prisa

**quid** [kwɪd] n (pl inv: BRIT inf) libra

**quiet** ['kwaɪət] adj (voice, music etc) bajo; (person, place) tranquilo ▷ n silencio; (calm) tranquilidad f; **quietly** adv tranquilamente; (silently) silenciosamente

> Be careful not to translate quiet by the Spanish word quieto.

**quilt** [kwɪlt] n edredón m

**quirky** ['kwɜ:kɪ] adj raro, estrafalario

**quit** [kwɪt] (pt, pp quit or quitted) vt dejar, abandonar; (premises) desocupar ▷ vi (give up) renunciar; (resign) dimitir

**quite** [kwaɪt] adv (rather) bastante; (entirely) completamente; **~ a few of them** un buen número de ellos; **~ (so)!** ¡así es!, ¡exactamente!; **that's not ~ right** eso no está del todo bien

**quits** [kwɪts] adj: **~ (with)** en paz (con); **let's call it ~** quedamos en paz

**quiver** ['kwɪvər] vi estremecerse

**quiz** [kwɪz] n concurso

**quota** ['kwəʊtə] n cuota

**quotation** [kwəʊ'teɪʃən] n cita; (estimate) presupuesto; **quotation marks** npl comillas fpl

**quote** [kwəʊt] n cita ▷ vt (sentence) citar; (Comm: sum, figure) cotizar ▷ vi: **to ~ from** citar de; **quotes** npl (inverted commas) comillas fpl

# r

**rabbi** ['ræbaɪ] n rabino
**rabbit** ['ræbɪt] n conejo
**rabies** ['reɪbiːz] n rabia
**RAC** n abbr (BRIT: = Royal Automobile Club) ≈ RACE m (SP)
**raccoon** [rə'kuːn] n mapache m
**race** [reɪs] n carrera; (species) raza ▷ vt (horse) hacer correr; (engine) acelerar ▷ vi (compete) competir; (run) correr; (pulse) latir a ritmo acelerado; **race car** n (US) = **racing car**; **racecourse** n hipódromo; **racehorse** n caballo de carreras; **racetrack** n hipódromo; (for cars) circuito de carreras
**racial** ['reɪʃl] adj racial
**racing** ['reɪsɪŋ] n carreras fpl; **racing car** n (BRIT) coche m de carreras; **racing driver** n (BRIT) piloto mf de carreras
**racism** ['reɪsɪzəm] n racismo
**racist** ['reɪsɪst] adj, n racista mf
**rack** [ræk] n (also: **luggage ~**) rejilla (portaequipajes); (shelf) estante m; (also: **roof ~**) baca; (also: **clothes ~**) perchero ▷ vt atormentar; **to ~ one's brains** devanarse los sesos
**racket** ['rækɪt] n (for tennis) raqueta; (inf: noise) ruido, estrépito; (: swindle) estafa, timo
**racquet** ['rækɪt] n raqueta
**radar** ['reɪdɑːʳ] n radar m
**radiation** [reɪdɪ'eɪʃən] n radiación f
**radiator** ['reɪdɪeɪtəʳ] n radiador m
**radical** ['rædɪkl] adj radical
**radio** ['reɪdɪəu] n radio f; **on the ~** en or por la radio; **radioactive** adj radi(o)activo; **radio station** n emisora
**radish** ['rædɪʃ] n rábano
**RAF** n abbr (BRIT) = **Royal Air Force**
**raffle** ['ræfl] n rifa, sorteo
**raft** [rɑːft] n balsa; (also: **life ~**) balsa salvavidas

**rag** [ræg] n (piece of cloth) trapo; (torn cloth) harapo; (pej: newspaper) periodicucho; (for charity) actividades estudiantiles benéficas; **rags** npl harapos mpl
**rage** [reɪdʒ] n rabia, furor m ▷ vi (person) rabiar, estar furioso; (storm) bramar; **it's all the ~** es lo último; (very fashionable) está muy de moda
**ragged** ['rægɪd] adj (edge) desigual, mellado; (cuff) roto; (appearance) andrajoso, harapiento
**raid** [reɪd] n (Mil) incursión f; (criminal) asalto; (by police) redada ▷ vt invadir, atacar; asaltar
**rail** [reɪl] n (on stair) barandilla, pasamanos m inv; (on bridge) pretil m; (of balcony, ship) barandilla; **railcard** n (BRIT) tarjeta para obtener descuentos en el tren; **railing(s)** n(pl) verja sg; **railway**, (US) **railroad** n ferrocarril m, vía férrea; **railway line** n (BRIT) línea (de ferrocarril); **railway station** n (BRIT) estación f de ferrocarril
**rain** [reɪn] n lluvia ▷ vi llover; **in the ~** bajo la lluvia; **it's ~ing** llueve, está lloviendo; **rainbow** n arco iris; **raincoat** n impermeable m; **raindrop** n gota de lluvia; **rainfall** n lluvia; **rainforest** n selva tropical; **rainy** adj lluvioso
**raise** [reɪz] n aumento ▷ vt levantar; (increase) aumentar; (improve: morale) subir; (: standards) mejorar; (doubts) suscitar; (a question) plantear; (cattle, family) criar; (crop) cultivar; (army) reclutar; (loan) obtener; **to ~ one's voice** alzar la voz
**raisin** ['reɪzn] n pasa de Corinto
**rake** [reɪk] n (tool) rastrillo; (person) libertino ▷ vt (garden) rastrillar
**rally** ['rælɪ] n reunión f; (Pol) mitin m; (Aut) rallye m; (Tennis) peloteo ▷ vt reunir ▷ vi recuperarse
**RAM** [ræm] n abbr (= random access memory) RAM f
**ram** [ræm] n carnero; (Tech) pisón m; (also: **battering ~**) ariete m ▷ vt (crash into) dar contra, chocar con; (push: fist etc) empujar con fuerza
**Ramadan** ['ræmədæn] n Ramadán m
**ramble** ['ræmbl] n caminata, excursión f en el campo ▷ vi (pej: also: **~ on**) divagar; **rambler** n excursionista mf; (Bot) trepadora; **rambling** adj (speech) inconexo; (Bot) trepador(a); (house) laberíntico
**ramp** [ræmp] n rampa; **on/off ~** n (US Aut) vía de acceso/salida
**rampage** [ræm'peɪdʒ] n: **to be on the ~** desmandarse ▷ vi: **they went rampaging through the town** recorrieron la ciudad armando alboroto
**ran** [ræn] pt of **run**

**ranch** [rɑːntʃ] n hacienda, estancia

**random** ['rændəm] adj fortuito, sin orden; (Comput, Math) aleatorio ▷ n: **at ~** al azar

**rang** [ræŋ] pt of **ring**

**range** [reɪndʒ] n (of mountains) cadena de montañas, cordillera; (of missile) alcance m; (of voice; series) serie f; (of products) surtido; (Mil: also: **shooting ~**) campo de tiro; (also: **kitchen ~**) fogón m ▷ vt (place) colocar; (arrange) arreglar ▷ vi: **to ~ over** (extend) extenderse por; **to ~ from ... to ...** oscilar entre ... y ...

**ranger** [reɪndʒər] n guardabosques m inv

**rank** [ræŋk] n (row) fila; (Mil) rango; (status) categoría; (BRIT: also: **taxi ~**) parada ▷ vi: **to ~ among** figurar entre ▷ adj fétido, rancio; **the ~ and file** (fig) las bases

**ransom** ['rænsəm] n rescate m; **to hold sb to ~** (fig) poner a algn entre la espada y la pared

**rant** [rænt] vi despotricar

**rap** [ræp] vt golpear, dar un golpecito en ▷ n (music) rap m

**rape** [reɪp] n violación f; (Bot) colza ▷ vt violar

**rapid** ['ræpɪd] adj rápido; **rapidly** adv rápidamente; **rapids** npl (Geo) rápidos mpl

**rapist** ['reɪpɪst] n violador m

**rapport** [ræ'pɔː'] n entendimiento

**rare** [rɛər] adj raro, poco común; (Culin: steak) poco hecho; **rarely** adv pocas veces

**rash** [ræʃ] adj imprudente, precipitado ▷ n (Med) sarpullido, erupción f (cutánea)

**rasher** ['ræʃər] n loncha

**raspberry** ['rɑːzbərɪ] n frambuesa

**rat** [ræt] n rata

**rate** [reɪt] n (ratio) razón f; (price) precio; (: of hotel) tarifa; (of interest) tipo; (speed) velocidad f ▷ vt (value) tasar; (estimate) estimar; **rates** npl (BRIT) impuesto sg municipal; (fees) tarifa sg; **to ~ sb/sth highly** tener a algn/algo en alta estima

**rather** ['rɑːðər] adv: **it's ~ expensive** es algo caro; (too much) es demasiado caro; **there's ~ a lot** hay bastante; **I would** or **I'd ~ go** preferiría ir; **or ~** o mejor dicho

**rating** ['reɪtɪŋ] n tasación f; **ratings** npl (Radio, TV) niveles mpl de audiencia

**ratio** ['reɪʃɪəu] n razón f; **in the ~ of 100 to 1** a razón de or en la proporción de 100 a 1

**ration** ['ræʃən] n ración f ▷ vt racionar; **rations** npl víveres mpl

**rational** ['ræʃənl] adj (solution, reasoning) lógico, razonable; (person) cuerdo, sensato

**rattle** ['rætl] n golpeteo; (of train etc) traqueteo; (object: of baby) sonaja, sonajero ▷ vi (small objects) castañetear; (car, bus): **to ~ along** traquetear ▷ vt hacer sonar agitando

**rave** [reɪv] vi (in anger) encolerizarse; (with enthusiasm) entusiasmarse; (Med) delirar, desvariar ▷ n (inf: party) rave m

**raven** ['reɪvən] n cuervo

**ravine** [rə'viːn] n barranco

**raw** [rɔː] adj crudo; (not processed) bruto; (sore) vivo; (inexperienced) novato, inexperto; **~ materials** materias primas

**ray** [reɪ] n rayo; **~ of hope** (rayo de) esperanza

**razor** ['reɪzər] n (open) navaja; (safety razor) máquina de afeitar; (electric razor) máquina (eléctrica) de afeitar; **razor blade** n hoja de afeitar

**Rd** abbr = **road**

**RE** n abbr (BRIT: Scol) = **religious education**; (: Mil) = **Royal Engineers**

**re** [riː] prep con referencia a

**reach** [riːtʃ] n alcance m; (of river etc) extensión f entre dos recodos ▷ vt alcanzar, llegar a; (achieve) lograr ▷ vi extenderse; **within ~** al alcance (de la mano); **out of ~** fuera del alcance; **reach out** vt (hand) tender ▷ vi: **to ~ out for sth** alargar or tender la mano para tomar algo

**react** [riː'ækt] vi reaccionar; **reaction** [riː'ækʃən] n reacción f; **reactor** [riː'æktər] n (also: **nuclear reactor**) reactor m (nuclear)

**read** (pt, pp **read**) [riːd, rɛd] vi leer ▷ vt leer; (understand) entender; (study) estudiar; **read out** vt leer en alta voz; **reader** n lector(a) m/f; (BRIT: at university) profesor(a) m/f

**readily** ['rɛdɪlɪ] adv (willingly) de buena gana; (easily) fácilmente; (quickly) en seguida

**reading** ['riːdɪŋ] n lectura; (on instrument) indicación f

**ready** ['rɛdɪ] adj listo, preparado; (willing) dispuesto; (available) disponible ▷ adv: **~-cooked** listo para comer ▷ n: **at the ~** (Mil) listo para tirar ▷ vt preparar; **to get ~** vi prepararse; **ready-made** adj confeccionado

**real** [rɪəl] adj verdadero, auténtico; **in ~ terms** en términos reales; **real ale** n cerveza elaborada tradicionalmente; **real estate** n bienes mpl raíces; **realistic** [rɪə'lɪstɪk] adj realista

**reality** [riː'ælɪtɪ] n realidad f; **reality TV** n telerrealidad f

**realization** [rɪəlaɪ'zeɪʃən] n comprensión f; (of a project) realización f; (Comm) realización f

**realize** ['rɪəlaɪz] vt (understand) darse cuenta de

**really** ['rɪəlɪ] adv realmente; (for emphasis) verdaderamente; **what ~ happened**

(*actually*) lo que pasó en realidad; **~?** ¿de veras?; **~!** (*annoyance*) ¡vamos!, ¡por favor!

**realm** [rɛlm] n reino; (*fig*) esfera

**reappear** [riːəˈpɪəʳ] vi reaparecer

**rear** [rɪəʳ] adj trasero ▷ n parte f trasera ▷ vt (*cattle, family*) criar ▷ vi (*also*: **~ up**: *animal*) encabritarse

**rearrange** [riːəˈreɪndʒ] vt ordenar or arreglar de nuevo

**rear: rear-view mirror** n (*Aut*) espejo retrovisor; **rear-wheel drive** n tracción f trasera

**reason** [ˈriːzn] n razón f ▷ vi: **to ~ with sb** tratar de hacer que algn entre en razón; **it stands to ~ that ...** es lógico que ...; **reasonable** adj razonable; (*sensible*) sensato; **reasonably** adv razonablemente; **reasoning** n razonamiento, argumentos mpl

**reassurance** [riːəˈʃuərəns] n consuelo

**reassure** [riːəˈʃuəʳ] vt tranquilizar; **to ~ sb that** tranquilizar a algn asegurándole que

**rebate** [ˈriːbeɪt] n (*on tax etc*) desgravación f

**rebel** n [ˈrɛbl] rebelde mf ▷ vi [rɪˈbɛl] rebelarse, sublevarse; **rebellion** n rebelión f, sublevación f; **rebellious** adj rebelde; (*child*) revoltoso

**rebuild** [riːˈbɪld] vt reconstruir

**recall** [rɪˈkɔːl] vt (*remember*) recordar; (*ambassador etc*) retirar ▷ n recuerdo

**recd., rec'd** abbr (= *received*) recibido

**receipt** [rɪˈsiːt] n (*document*) recibo; (*act of receiving*) recepción f; **receipts** npl (*Comm*) ingresos mpl

▎Be careful not to translate *receipt* by the Spanish word *receta*.

**receive** [rɪˈsiːv] vt recibir; (*guest*) acoger; (*wound*) sufrir; **receiver** n (*Tel*) auricular m; (*Radio*) receptor m; (*of stolen goods*) perista mf; (*Law*) administrador m jurídico

**recent** [ˈriːsnt] adj reciente; **recently** adv recientemente; **recently arrived** recién llegado

**reception** [rɪˈsɛpʃən] n recepción f; (*welcome*) acogida; **reception desk** n recepción f; **receptionist** n recepcionista mf

**recession** [rɪˈsɛʃən] n recesión f

**recharge** [riːˈtʃɑːdʒ] vt (*battery*) recargar

**recipe** [ˈrɛsɪpɪ] n receta; (*for disaster, success*) fórmula

**recipient** [rɪˈsɪpɪənt] n recibidor(a) m/f; (*of letter*) destinatario/a

**recital** [rɪˈsaɪtl] n recital m

**recite** [rɪˈsaɪt] vt (*poem*) recitar

**reckless** [ˈrɛkləs] adj temerario, imprudente; (*speed*) peligroso

**reckon** [ˈrɛkən] vt calcular; (*consider*) considerar ▷ vi: **I ~ that ...** me parece que ...

**reclaim** [rɪˈkleɪm] vt (*land*) recuperar; (*: from sea*) rescatar; (*demand back*) reclamar

**recline** [rɪˈklaɪn] vi reclinarse

**recognition** [rɛkəgˈnɪʃən] n reconocimiento; **transformed beyond ~** irreconocible

**recognize** [ˈrɛkəgnaɪz] vt: **to ~ (by/as)** reconocer (por/como)

**recollection** [rɛkəˈlɛkʃən] n recuerdo

**recommend** [rɛkəˈmɛnd] vt recomendar; **recommendation** [rɛkəmɛnˈdeɪʃən] n recomendación f

**reconcile** [ˈrɛkənsaɪl] vt (*two people*) reconciliar; (*two facts*) conciliar; **to ~ o.s. to sth** resignarse or conformarse a algo

**reconsider** [riːkənˈsɪdəʳ] vt repensar

**reconstruct** [riːkənˈstrʌkt] vt reconstruir

**record** n [ˈrɛkɔːd] (*Mus*) disco; (*of meeting etc*) acta; (*register*) registro, partida; (*file*) archivo; (*also*: **police** or **criminal ~**) antecedentes mpl penales; (*written*) expediente m; (*Sport*) récord m; (*Comput*) registro ▷ vt [rɪˈkɔːd] registrar; (*Mus: song etc*) grabar; **in ~ time** en un tiempo récord; **off the ~** adj no oficial; adv confidencialmente; **recorded delivery** n (*BRIT Post*) entrega con acuse de recibo; **recorder** n (*Mus*) flauta de pico; **recording** n (*Mus*) grabación f; **record player** n tocadiscos m inv

**recount** vt [rɪˈkaunt] contar

**recover** [rɪˈkʌvəʳ] vt recuperar ▷ vi recuperarse; **recovery** n recuperación f

**recreate** [riːkrɪˈeɪt] vt recrear

**recreation** [rɛkrɪˈeɪʃən] n recreo; **recreational** adj de, recreo; **recreational drug** n droga recreativa; **recreational vehicle** n (*US*) caravana or roulotte f pequeña

**recruit** [rɪˈkruːt] n recluta mf ▷ vt reclutar; (*staff*) contratar; **recruitment** n reclutamiento

**rectangle** [ˈrɛktæŋgl] n rectángulo; **rectangular** [rɛkˈtæŋgjuləʳ] adj rectangular

**rectify** [ˈrɛktɪfaɪ] vt rectificar

**rector** [ˈrɛktəʳ] n (*Rel*) párroco

**recur** [rɪˈkəːʳ] vi repetirse; (*pain, illness*) producirse de nuevo; **recurring** adj (*problem*) repetido, constante

**recyclable** [riːˈsaɪkləbl] adj reciclable

**recycle** [riːˈsaɪkl] vt reciclar

**recycling** [riːˈsaɪklɪŋ] n reciclaje m

**red** [rɛd] n rojo ▷ adj rojo; (*hair*) pelirrojo; (*wine*) tinto; **to be in the ~** (*account*) estar en números rojos; (*business*) tener un saldo negativo; **to give sb the ~ carpet treatment** recibir a algn con todos los honores; **Red Cross** n Cruz f Roja; **redcurrant** n grosella roja

**redeem** [rɪˈdiːm] vt redimir; (*promises*) cumplir; (*sth in pawn*) desempeñar; (*Rel: fig*) rescatar

**red: redhead** n pelirrojo/a; **red-hot** adj candente; **red light** n: **to go through** or **jump a red light** (Aut) saltarse un semáforo; **red-light district** n barrio chino; **red meat** n carne f roja

**reduce** [rɪ'dju:s] vt reducir; **to ~ sb to silence/despair/tears** hacer callar/ desesperarse/llorar a algn; **reduced** adj (decreased) reducido, rebajado; **at a reduced price** con rebaja or descuento; **"greatly reduced prices"** "grandes rebajas"; **reduction** [rɪ'dʌkʃən] n reducción f; (of price) rebaja; (discount) descuento

**redundancy** [rɪ'dʌndənsɪ] n despido; (unemployment) desempleo

**redundant** [rɪ'dʌndənt] adj (BRIT: worker) parado, sin trabajo; (detail, object) superfluo; **to be made ~** (BRIT) quedar(se) sin trabajo

**reed** [ri:d] n (Bot) junco, caña; (Mus) lengüeta

**reef** [ri:f] n (at sea) arrecife m

**reel** [ri:l] n carrete m, bobina; (of film) rollo ▷ vt (Tech) devanar; (also: **~ in**) sacar ▷ vi (sway) tambalear(se)

**ref** [rɛf] n abbr (inf) = **referee**

**refectory** [rɪ'fɛktərɪ] n comedor m

**refer** [rɪ'fə:ʳ] vt (send: patient) referir; (: matter) remitir ▷ vi: **to ~ to** (allude to) referirse a, aludir a; (apply to) relacionarse con; (consult) remitirse a

**referee** [rɛfə'ri:] n árbitro; (BRIT: for job application): **to be a ~ for sb** proporcionar referencias a algn ▷ vt (match) arbitrar en

**reference** ['rɛfrəns] n referencia; (for job application: letter) carta de recomendación; **with ~ to** (Comm: in letter) me remito a; **reference number** n número de referencia

**refill** vt [ri:'fɪl] rellenar ▷ n ['ri:fɪl] repuesto, recambio

**refine** [rɪ'faɪn] vt refinar; **refined** adj (person, taste) refinado, fino; **refinery** n refinería

**reflect** [rɪ'flɛkt] vt reflejar ▷ vi (think) reflexionar, pensar; **it ~s badly/well on him** le perjudica/le hace honor; **reflection** [rɪ'flɛkʃən] n (act) reflexión f; (image) reflejo; (discredit) crítica; **on reflection** pensándolo bien

**reflex** ['ri:flɛks] adj, n reflejo

**reform** [rɪ'fɔ:m] n reforma ▷ vt reformar

**refrain** [rɪ'freɪn] vi: **to ~ from doing** abstenerse de hacer ▷ n estribillo

**refresh** [rɪ'frɛʃ] vt refrescar; **refreshing** adj refrescante; **refreshments** npl refrescos mpl

**refrigerator** [rɪ'frɪdʒəreɪtəʳ] n frigorífico, refrigeradora (LAM), heladera (LAM)

**refuel** [ri:'fjuəl] vi repostar (combustible)

**refuge** ['rɛfju:dʒ] n refugio, asilo; **to take ~ in** refugiarse en; **refugee** [rɛfju'dʒi:] n refugiado/a

**refund** n ['ri:fʌnd] reembolso ▷ vt [rɪ'fʌnd] devolver, reembolsar

**refurbish** [ri:'fə:bɪʃ] vt restaurar, renovar

**refusal** [rɪ'fju:zəl] n negativa; **to have first ~ on sth** tener la primera opción a algo

**refuse¹** ['rɛfju:s] n basura

**refuse²** [rɪ'fju:z] vt (reject) rechazar; (invitation) declinar; (permission) denegar; (say no to) negarse a ▷ vi negarse; (horse) rehusar; **to ~ to do sth** negarse a or rehusar hacer algo

**regain** [rɪ'geɪn] vt recobrar, recuperar

**regard** [rɪ'gɑ:d] n mirada; (esteem) respeto; (attention) consideración f ▷ vt (consider) considerar; **to give one's ~s to** saludar de su parte a; **"with kindest ~s"** "con muchos recuerdos"; **as ~s, with ~ to** con respecto a, en cuanto a; **regarding** prep con respecto a, en cuanto a; **regardless** adv a pesar de todo; **regardless of** sin reparar en

**regenerate** [rɪ'dʒɛnəreɪt] vt regenerar

**reggae** ['rɛgeɪ] n reggae m

**regiment** ['rɛdʒɪmənt] n regimiento

**region** ['ri:dʒən] n región f; **in the ~ of** (fig) alrededor de; **regional** adj regional

**register** ['rɛdʒɪstəʳ] n registro ▷ vt registrar; (birth) declarar; (car) matricular; (letter) certificar; (instrument) marcar, indicar ▷ vi (at hotel) registrarse; (as student) matricularse; (make impression) producir impresión; **registered** adj (letter) certificado

**registrar** ['rɛdʒɪstrɑ:ʳ] n secretario/a (del registro civil)

**registration** [rɛdʒɪs'treɪʃən] n (act) declaración f; (Aut: also: **~ number**) matrícula

**registry office** n (BRIT) registro civil; **to get married in a ~** casarse por lo civil

**regret** [rɪ'grɛt] n sentimiento, pesar m ▷ vt sentir, lamentar; **regrettable** adj lamentable

**regular** ['rɛgjulə'] adj regular; (soldier) profesional; (usual) habitual ▷ n (client etc) cliente/a m/f habitual; **regularly** adv con regularidad

**regulate** ['rɛgjuleɪt] vt controlar; **regulation** [rɛgju'leɪʃən] n (rule) regla, reglamento

**rehabilitation** ['ri:əbɪlɪ'teɪʃən] n rehabilitación f

**rehearsal** [rɪ'hə:səl] n ensayo

**rehearse** [rɪ'hə:s] vt ensayar

**reign** [reɪn] n reinado; (fig) predominio ▷ vi reinar; (fig) imperar

**reimburse** [ri:ɪm'bə:s] vt reembolsar

**rein** [reɪn] n (for horse) rienda

**reincarnation** [ˌriːɪnkɑːˈneɪʃən] n
reencarnación f
**reindeer** [ˈreɪndɪəʳ] n (pl inv) reno
**reinforce** [ˌriːɪnˈfɔːs] vt reforzar
**reinforcement** [ˌriːɪnˈfɔːsmənt] n
refuerzo; **reinforcements** npl (Mil)
refuerzos mpl
**reinstate** [ˌriːɪnˈsteɪt] vt (worker) reintegrar
(a su puesto); (tax, law) reinstaurar
**reject** n [ˈriːdʒɛkt] (thing) desecho ▷ vt
[rɪˈdʒɛkt] rechazar; (proposition, offer etc)
descartar; **rejection** [rɪˈdʒɛkʃən] n
rechazo
**rejoice** [rɪˈdʒɔɪs] vi: **to ~ at** or **over**
regocijarse or alegrarse de
**relate** [rɪˈleɪt] vt (tell) contar, relatar;
(connect) relacionar ▷ vi relacionarse;
**related** adj afín; (person) emparentado; **to
be related to** (connected) guardar relación
con; (by family) ser pariente de; **relating**:
**relating to** prep referente a
**relation** [rɪˈleɪʃən] n (person) pariente mf;
(link) relación f; **relations** npl (relatives)
familiares mpl; **relationship** n relación f;
(personal) relaciones fpl; (also: **family
relationship**) parentesco
**relative** [ˈrɛlətɪv] n pariente mf, familiar mf
▷ adj relativo; **relatively** adv (fairly, rather)
relativamente
**relax** [rɪˈlæks] vi descansar; (quieten
down) relajarse ▷ vt relajar; (grip) aflojar;
**relaxation** [ˌriːlækˈseɪʃən] n descanso;
(easing) relajamiento m; (entertainment)
diversión f; **relaxed** adj relajado; (tranquil)
tranquilo; **relaxing** adj relajante
**relay** n [ˈriːleɪ] (race) carrera de relevos ▷ vt
[rɪˈleɪ] (Radio, TV) retransmitir
**release** [rɪˈliːs] n (liberation) liberación f;
(discharge) puesta en libertad; (of gas etc)
escape m; (of film etc) estreno; (of record)
lanzamiento ▷ vt (prisoner) poner en
libertad; (film) estrenar; (book) publicar;
(piece of news) difundir; (gas etc) despedir,
arrojar; (free: from wreckage etc) liberar;
(Tech: catch, spring etc) desenganchar
**relegate** [ˈrɛləɡeɪt] vt relegar; (Sport): **to be
~d to** bajar a
**relent** [rɪˈlɛnt] vi ablandarse; **relentless** adj
implacable
**relevant** [ˈrɛləvənt] adj (fact) pertinente;
**~ to** relacionado con
**reliable** [rɪˈlaɪəbl] adj (person, firm) de
confianza, de fiar; (method, machine) seguro;
(source) fidedigno
**relic** [ˈrɛlɪk] n (Rel) reliquia; (of the past)
vestigio
**relief** [rɪˈliːf] n (from pain, anxiety) alivio;
(help, supplies) socorro, ayuda; (Art, Geo)
relieve m

**relieve** [rɪˈliːv] vt (pain, patient) aliviar;
(bring help to) ayudar, socorrer; (take over
from) sustituir a; (: guard) relevar; **to ~ sb of
sth** quitar algo a algn; **to ~ o.s.** hacer sus
necesidades; **relieved** adj: **to be relieved**
sentir un gran alivio
**religion** [rɪˈlɪdʒən] n religión f
**religious** [rɪˈlɪdʒəs] adj religioso; **religious
education** n educación f religiosa
**relish** [ˈrɛlɪʃ] n (Culin) salsa; (enjoyment)
entusiasmo ▷ vt (food, challenge etc)
saborear; **to ~ doing** gozar haciendo
**relocate** [ˌriːləʊˈkeɪt] vt trasladar ▷ vi
trasladarse
**reluctance** [rɪˈlʌktəns] n renuencia
**reluctant** [rɪˈlʌktənt] adj reacio; **to be ~ to
do sth** resistirse a hacer algo; **reluctantly**
adv de mala gana
**rely** [rɪˈlaɪ]: **to ~ on** vt fus depender de; **you
can ~ on my discretion** puedes contar con
mi discreción
**remain** [rɪˈmeɪn] vi (survive) quedar; (be left)
sobrar; (continue) quedar(se), permanecer;
**remainder** n resto; **remaining** adj
restante, que queda(n); **remains** npl
restos mpl
**remand** [rɪˈmɑːnd] n: **on ~** detenido (bajo
custodia) ▷ vt: **to ~ in custody** mantener
bajo custodia
**remark** [rɪˈmɑːk] n comentario ▷ vt
comentar; **remarkable** adj (outstanding)
extraordinario
**remarry** [ˌriːˈmærɪ] vi volver a casarse
**remedy** [ˈrɛmədɪ] n remedio ▷ vt remediar,
curar
**remember** [rɪˈmɛmbəʳ] vt recordar,
acordarse de; (bear in mind) tener presente;
**~ me to your wife and children!** ¡déle
recuerdos a su familia!
**Remembrance Day, Remembrance
Sunday** n (BRIT) ver nota

- **REMEMBRANCE DAY**
-
- En el Reino Unido el domingo más cercano
- al 11 de noviembre es *Remembrance Day* o
- *Remembrance Sunday*, aniversario de la
- firma del armisticio de 1918 que puso fin a
- la Primera Guerra Mundial. Tal día se
- recuerda a todos aquellos que murieron
- en las dos guerras mundiales con dos
- minutos de silencio a las once de la mañana
- (hora en que se firmó el armisticio),
- durante los actos de conmemoración
- celebrados en los monumentos a los
- caídos. Allí se colocan coronas de
- amapolas, flor que también se suele llevar
- prendida en el pecho tras pagar un
- donativo para los inválidos de guerra.

**remind** [rɪ'maɪnd] vt: **to ~ sb to do sth** recordar a algn que haga algo; **to ~ sb of sth** recordar a algn; **she ~s me of her mother** me recuerda a su madre; **reminder** n notificación f; (memento) recuerdo
**reminiscent** [rɛmɪ'nɪsnt] adj: **to be ~ of sth** recordar algo
**remnant** ['rɛmnənt] n resto; (of cloth) retal m
**remorse** [rɪ'mɔːs] n remordimientos mpl
**remote** [rɪ'məʊt] adj (distant) lejano; (person) distante; **remote control** n mando a distancia; **remotely** adv remotamente; (slightly) levemente
**removal** [rɪ'muːvəl] n (taking away) (el) quitar; (BRIT: from house) mudanza; (from office: dismissal) destitución f; (Med) extirpación f; **removal man** n (BRIT) mozo de mudanzas; **removal van** n (BRIT) camión m de mudanzas
**remove** [rɪ'muːv] vt quitar; (employee) destituir; (name: from list) tachar, borrar; (doubt) disipar; (Med) extirpar
**Renaissance** [rɪ'neɪsɔ̃s] n: **the ~** el Renacimiento
**rename** [riː'neɪm] vt poner nuevo nombre a
**render** ['rɛndəʳ] vt (thanks) dar; (aid) proporcionar; prestar; **to ~ sth useless** hacer algo inútil
**renew** [rɪ'njuː] vt renovar; (resume) reanudar; (extend date) prorrogar; **renewable** adj renovable; **renewable energy, renewables** energías renovables
**renovate** ['rɛnəveɪt] vt renovar
**renowned** [rɪ'naʊnd] adj renombrado
**rent** [rɛnt] n (for house) arriendo, renta ⊳ vt alquilar; **rental** n (for television, car) alquiler m
**reorganize** [riː'ɔːɡənaɪz] vt reorganizar
**rep** [rɛp] n abbr (Comm) = **representative**
**repair** [rɪ'pɛəʳ] n reparación f ⊳ vt reparar; **in good/bad ~** en buen/mal estado; **repair kit** n caja de herramientas
**repay** [riː'peɪ] vt (money) devolver, reembolsar; (person) pagar; (debt) liquidar; (sb's efforts) devolver, corresponder a; **repayment** n reembolso, devolución f; (sum of money) recompensa
**repeat** [rɪ'piːt] n (Radio, TV) reposición f ⊳ vt repetir ⊳ vi repetirse; **repeatedly** adv repetidas veces; **repeat prescription** n (BRIT) receta renovada
**repellent** [rɪ'pɛlənt] adj repugnante ⊳ n: **insect ~** crema/loción f antiinsectos
**repercussion** [riːpə'kʌʃən] n (consequence) repercusión f; **to have ~s** repercutir
**repetition** [rɛpɪ'tɪʃən] n repetición f
**repetitive** [rɪ'pɛtɪtɪv] adj repetitivo

**replace** [rɪ'pleɪs] vt (put back) devolver a su sitio; (take the place of) reemplazar, sustituir; **replacement** n (act) reposición f; (thing) recambio; (person) suplente mf
**replay** ['riːpleɪ] n (Sport) partido de desempate; (TV) repetición f
**replica** ['rɛplɪkə] n réplica, reproducción f
**reply** [rɪ'plaɪ] n respuesta, contestación f ⊳ vi contestar, responder
**report** [rɪ'pɔːt] n informe m; (Press etc) reportaje m; (BRIT: also: **school ~**) informe m escolar; (of gun) detonación f ⊳ vt informar sobre; (Press etc) hacer un reportaje sobre; (notify: accident, culprit) denunciar ⊳ vi (make a report) presentar un informe; (present o.s.): **to ~ (to sb)** presentarse (ante algn); **report card** n (US, SCOTTISH) informe m escolar; **reportedly** adv según se dice; **reporter** n periodista mf
**represent** [rɛprɪ'zɛnt] vt representar; (Comm) ser agente de; **representation** [rɛprɪzɛn'teɪʃən] n representación f; **representative** [rɛprɪ'zɛntətɪv] n (US Pol) representante mf, diputado/a; (Comm) representante mf ⊳ adj: **representative (of)** representativo (de)
**repress** [rɪ'prɛs] vt reprimir; **repression** [rɪ'prɛʃən] n represión f
**reprimand** ['rɛprɪmɑːnd] n reprimenda ⊳ vt reprender
**reproduce** [riːprə'djuːs] vt reproducir ⊳ vi reproducirse; **reproduction** [riːprə'dʌkʃən] n reproducción f
**reptile** ['rɛptaɪl] n reptil m
**republic** [rɪ'pʌblɪk] n república; **republican** adj, n republicano/a
**reputable** ['rɛpjutəbl] adj (make etc) de renombre
**reputation** [rɛpju'teɪʃən] n reputación f
**request** [rɪ'kwɛst] n solicitud f, petición f ⊳ vt: **to ~ sth of or from sb** solicitar algo a algn; **request stop** n (BRIT) parada discrecional
**require** [rɪ'kwaɪəʳ] vt (need: person) necesitar, tener necesidad de; (: thing, situation) exigir; (want) pedir; **to ~ sb to do sth/sth of sb** exigir que algn haga algo; **requirement** n requisito; (need) necesidad f
**resat** [riː'sæt] pt, pp of **resit**
**rescue** ['rɛskjuː] n rescate m ⊳ vt rescatar
**research** [rɪ'sɜːtʃ] n investigaciones fpl ⊳ vt investigar
**resemblance** [rɪ'zɛmbləns] n parecido
**resemble** [rɪ'zɛmbl] vt parecerse a
**resent** [rɪ'zɛnt] vt resentirse por, ofenderse por; **resentful** adj resentido; **resentment** n resentimiento
**reservation** [rɛzə'veɪʃən] n reserva; **reservation desk** n (US: in hotel) recepción f

**reserve** [rɪˈzəːv] n reserva; (Sport) suplente mf ▷ vt (seats etc) reservar; **reserved** adj reservado

**reservoir** [ˈrɛzəvwɑːr] n (artificial lake) embalse m, represa; (tank) depósito

**residence** [ˈrɛzɪdəns] n (formal: home) domicilio; (length of stay) permanencia; **residence permit** n (BRIT) permiso de residencia

**resident** [ˈrɛzɪdənt] n vecino/a; (in hotel) huésped(a) m/f ▷ adj residente; (population) permanente; **residential** [rɛzɪˈdɛnʃəl] adj residencial

**residue** [ˈrɛzɪdjuː] n resto

**resign** [rɪˈzaɪn] vt renunciar a ▷ vi: to ~ (from) dimitir (de); to ~ o.s. to resignarse a; **resignation** [rɛzɪɡˈneɪʃən] n dimisión f; (state of mind) resignación f

**resin** [ˈrɛzɪn] n resina

**resist** [rɪˈzɪst] vt (temptation, damage) resistir; **resistance** n resistencia

**resit** [ˈriːsɪt] (pt, pp resat) vt (BRIT: exam) volver a presentarse a; (: subject) recuperar, volver a examinarse de (SP)

**resolution** [rɛzəˈluːʃən] n resolución f

**resolve** [rɪˈzɔlv] n resolución f ▷ vt resolver ▷ vt: to ~ to do resolver hacer

**resort** [rɪˈzɔːt] n (town) centro turístico; (recourse) recurso ▷ vi: to ~ to recurrir a; in the last ~ como último recurso

**resource** [rɪˈsɔːs] n recurso; **resourceful** adj ingenioso

**respect** [rɪsˈpɛkt] n respeto ▷ vt respetar; **respectable** adj respetable; (amount etc) apreciable; (passable) tolerable; **respectful** adj respetuoso; **respective** adj respectivo; **respectively** adv respectivamente

**respite** [ˈrɛspaɪt] n respiro

**respond** [rɪsˈpɔnd] vi responder; (react) reaccionar; **response** [rɪsˈpɔns] n respuesta; (reaction) reacción f

**responsibility** [rɪspɔnsɪˈbɪlɪtɪ] n responsabilidad f

**responsible** [rɪsˈpɔnsɪbl] adj (liable): ~ (for) responsable (de); (character) serio, formal; (job) de responsabilidad; **responsibly** adv con seriedad

**responsive** [rɪsˈpɔnsɪv] adj sensible

**rest** [rɛst] n descanso, reposo; (Mus) pausa, silencio; (support) apoyo; (remainder) resto ▷ vi descansar; (be supported): to ~ on apoyarse en ▷ vt: to ~ sth on/against apoyar algo en or sobre/contra; the ~ of them (people, objects) los demás; it ~s with him depende de él

**restaurant** [ˈrɛstərɔn] n restaurante m; **restaurant car** n (BRIT) coche-comedor m

**restless** [ˈrɛstlɪs] adj inquieto

**restoration** [rɛstəˈreɪʃən] n restauración f; (giving back) devolución f

**restore** [rɪˈstɔːr] vt (building) restaurar; (sth stolen) devolver; (health) restablecer

**restrain** [rɪsˈtreɪn] vt (feeling) contener, refrenar; (person): to ~ (from doing) disuadir (de hacer); **restraint** n (moderation) moderación f; (of style) reserva

**restrict** [rɪsˈtrɪkt] vt restringir, limitar; **restriction** [rɪsˈtrɪkʃən] n restricción f, limitación f

**rest room** n (US) aseos mpl

**restructure** [riːˈstrʌktʃər] vt reestructurar

**result** [rɪˈzʌlt] n resultado ▷ vi: to ~ in terminar en, tener por resultado; as a ~ of a or como consecuencia de

**resume** [rɪˈzjuːm] vt reanudar ▷ vi (meeting) continuar

■ Be careful not to translate resume by the Spanish word resumir.

**résumé** [ˈreɪzjuːmeɪ] n resumen m

**resuscitate** [rɪˈsʌsɪteɪt] vt (Med) resucitar

**retail** [ˈriːteɪl] cpd al por menor; **retailer** n detallista mf

**retain** [rɪˈteɪn] vt (keep) retener, conservar

**retaliation** [rɪtælɪˈeɪʃən] n represalias fpl

**retarded** [rɪˈtɑːdɪd] adj (inf!) retrasado (mental) (!)

**retire** [rɪˈtaɪər] vi (give up work) jubilarse; (withdraw) retirarse; (go to bed) acostarse; **retired** adj (person) jubilado; **retirement** n jubilación f

**retort** [rɪˈtɔːt] vi replicar

**retreat** [rɪˈtriːt] n (place) retiro; (Mil) retirada ▷ vi retirarse

**retrieve** [rɪˈtriːv] vt recobrar; (situation, honour) salvar; (Comput) recuperar; (error) reparar

**retrospect** [ˈrɛtrəspɛkt] n: in ~ retrospectivamente; **retrospective** [rɛtrəˈspɛktɪv] adj retrospectivo; (law) retroactivo

**return** [rɪˈtəːn] n (going or coming back) vuelta, regreso; (of sth stolen etc) devolución f; (Finance: from land, shares) ganancia, ingresos mpl ▷ cpd (journey) de regreso; (BRIT: ticket) de ida y vuelta; (match) de vuelta ▷ vi (person etc: come or go back) volver, regresar; (symptoms etc) reaparecer ▷ vt devolver; (favour, love etc) corresponder a; (verdict) pronunciar; (Pol: candidate) elegir; **returns** npl (Comm) ingresos mpl; in ~ (for) a cambio (de); by ~ of post a vuelta de correo; many happy ~s (of the day)! ¡feliz cumpleaños!; **return ticket** n (esp BRIT) billete m (SP) or boleto m (LAM) de ida y vuelta, billete m redondo (MEX)

**retweet** [riːˈtwiːt] vt retuitear

**reunion** [riːˈjuːnɪən] n (of family) reunión f; (of two people, school) reencuentro

**reunite** [riːjuːˈnaɪt] vt reunir; (reconcile) reconciliar

**revamp** [riːˈvæmp] vt renovar

**reveal** [rɪˈviːl] vt revelar; **revealing** adj revelador(a)

**revel** [ˈrɛvl] vi: **to ~ in** sth/in doing sth gozar de algo/haciendo algo

**revelation** [rɛvəˈleɪʃən] n revelación f

**revenge** [rɪˈvɛndʒ] n venganza; **to take ~ on** vengarse de

**revenue** [ˈrɛvənjuː] n ingresos mpl, rentas fpl

**Reverend** [ˈrɛvərənd] adj (in titles): **the ~ John Smith** (Anglican) el Reverendo John Smith; (Catholic) el Padre John Smith; (Protestant) el Pastor John Smith

**reversal** [rɪˈvəːsl] n (of order) inversión f; (of policy) cambio de rumbo; (of decision) revocación f

**reverse** [rɪˈvəːs] n (opposite) contrario; (back: of cloth) revés m; (: of coin) reverso; (: of paper) dorso; (Aut: also: **~ gear**) marcha atrás ▷ adj (order) inverso; (direction) contrario ▷ vt (decision) dar marcha atrás a; (Aut) dar marcha atrás a; (position, function) invertir ▷ vi (BRIT Aut) poner en marcha atrás; **reverse-charge call** n (BRIT) llamada a cobro revertido; **reversing lights** npl (BRIT Aut) luces fpl de marcha atrás

**revert** [rɪˈvəːt] vi: **to ~ to** volver or revertir a

**review** [rɪˈvjuː] n (magazine, also Mil) revista; (of book, film) reseña; (us: examination) repaso, examen m ▷ vt repasar, examinar; (Mil) pasar revista a; (book, film) reseñar

**revise** [rɪˈvaɪz] vt (manuscript) corregir; (opinion) modificar; (price, procedure) revisar; (BRIT: study: subject) repasar; **revision** [rɪˈvɪʒən] n corrección f; modificación f; (of subject) repaso

**revival** [rɪˈvaɪvəl] n (recovery) reanimación f; (of interest) renacimiento; (Theat) reestreno; (of faith) despertar m

**revive** [rɪˈvaɪv] vt resucitar; (custom) restablecer; (hope, courage) reanimar; (play) reestrenar ▷ vi (person) volver en sí; (business) reactivarse

**revolt** [rɪˈvəʊlt] n rebelión f ▷ vi rebelarse, sublevarse ▷ vt dar asco a, repugnar; **revolting** adj asqueroso, repugnante

**revolution** [rɛvəˈluːʃən] n revolución f; **revolutionary** adj, n revolucionario/a

**revolve** [rɪˈvɒlv] vi dar vueltas, girar; **to ~ (a)round** girar en torno a

**revolver** [rɪˈvɒlvəʳ] n revólver m

**reward** [rɪˈwɔːd] n premio, recompensa ▷ vt: **to ~ (for)** recompensar or premiar (por); **rewarding** adj (fig) gratificante

**rewind** [riːˈwaɪnd] vt rebobinar

**rewritable** [riːˈraɪtəbl] adj reescribible

**rewrite** [riːˈraɪt] vt (irreg: like **write**) reescribir

**rheumatism** [ˈruːmətɪzəm] n reumatismo, reúma

**rhinoceros** [raɪˈnɒsərəs] n rinoceronte m

**rhubarb** [ˈruːbɑːb] n ruibarbo

**rhyme** [raɪm] n rima; (verse) poesía

**rhythm** [ˈrɪðm] n ritmo

**rib** [rɪb] n (Anat) costilla ▷ vt (mock) tomar el pelo a

**ribbon** [ˈrɪbən] n cinta; **in ~s** (torn) hecho trizas

**rice** [raɪs] n arroz m; **rice pudding** n arroz m con leche

**rich** [rɪtʃ] adj rico; (soil) fértil; (food) pesado; (: sweet) empalagoso; **to be ~ in** sth abundar en algo

**rid** (pt, pp **rid**) [rɪd] vt: **to ~ sb of** sth librar a algn de algo; **to get ~ of** deshacerse or desembarazarse de

**riddle** [ˈrɪdl] n (conundrum) acertijo; (mystery) enigma m, misterio ▷ vt: **to be ~d with** ser lleno or plagado de

**ride** [raɪd] (pt **rode**, pp **ridden**) n paseo; (distance covered) viaje m, recorrido ▷ vi (on horse, as sport) montar; (go somewhere: on horse, bicycle) dar un paseo, pasearse; (journey: on bicycle, motor cycle, bus) viajar ▷ vt (a horse) montar a; (distance) recorrer; **to ~ a bicycle** andar en bicicleta; **to take sb for a ~** (fig) tomar el pelo a algn; **rider** n (on horse) jinete m; (on bicycle) ciclista mf; (on motorcycle) motociclista mf

**ridge** [rɪdʒ] n (of hill) cresta; (of roof) caballete m; (wrinkle) arruga

**ridicule** [ˈrɪdɪkjuːl] n irrisión f, burla ▷ vt poner en ridículo a, burlarse de; **ridiculous** [rɪˈdɪkjuləs] adj ridículo

**riding** [ˈraɪdɪŋ] n equitación f; **I like ~** me gusta montar a caballo; **riding school** n escuela de equitación

**rife** [raɪf] adj: **to be ~** ser muy común; **to be ~ with** abundar en

**rifle** [ˈraɪfl] n rifle m, fusil m ▷ vt saquear

**rift** [rɪft] n (fig: between friends) desavenencia

**rig** [rɪg] n (also: **oil ~**: at sea) plataforma petrolera ▷ vt (election etc) amañar los resultados de

**right** [raɪt] adj (true, correct) correcto, exacto; (suitable) indicado, debido; (proper) apropiado; (just) justo; (morally good) bueno; (not left) derecho ▷ n (title, claim) derecho; (not left) derecha ▷ adv bien, correctamente; (not on the left) a la derecha ▷ vt (put straight) enderezar; (correct) corregir ▷ excl ¡bueno!, ¡está bien!; **to be ~** (person) tener razón; (answer) ser correcto; **by ~s** en justicia; **on**

the ~ a la derecha; **to be in the ~** tener razón; **~ now** ahora mismo; **~ in the middle** exactamente en el centro; **~ away** en seguida; **right angle** n ángulo recto; **rightful** adj legítimo; **right-hand** adj: **right-hand drive** conducción f por la derecha; **the right-hand side** derecha; **right-handed** adj (person) que usa la mano derecha, diestro; **rightly** adv correctamente, debidamente; (with reason) con razón; **right of way** n (on path etc) derecho de paso; (Aut) prioridad f de paso; **right-wing** adj (Pol) derechista

**rigid** ['rɪdʒɪd] adj rígido; (person, ideas) inflexible

**rigorous** ['rɪgərəs] adj riguroso

**rim** [rɪm] n borde m; (of spectacles) aro; (of wheel) llanta

**rind** [raɪnd] n (of bacon, cheese) corteza; (of lemon etc) cáscara

**ring** [rɪŋ] (pt **rang**, pp **rung**) n (of metal) aro; (on finger) anillo; (of people) corro; (of objects) círculo; (gang) banda; (for boxing) cuadrilátero; (of circus) pista; (bull ring) ruedo, plaza; (sound of bell) toque m ▷ vi (on telephone) llamar por teléfono; (large bell) repicar; (doorbell, phone) sonar; (also: **~ out**) sonar; (ears) zumbar ▷ vt (BRIT Tel) llamar; (bell etc) hacer sonar; (doorbell) tocar; **to give sb a ~** (BRIT Tel) llamar a algn, dar un telefonazo a algn; **ring back** vt, vi (Tel) devolver la llamada; **ring off** vi (BRIT Tel) colgar, cortar la comunicación; **ring up** vt (BRIT Tel) llamar, telefonear; **ringing tone** n (Tel) tono de llamada; **ringleader** n cabecilla mf; **ring road** n (BRIT) carretera periférica or de circunvalación; **ringtone** n tono de llamada

**rink** [rɪŋk] n (also: **ice ~**) pista de hielo

**rinse** [rɪns] n (of dishes) enjuague m; (of clothes) aclarado; (hair colouring) reflejo ▷ vt enjuagar, aclarar; (hair) dar reflejos a

**riot** ['raɪət] n motín m, disturbio ▷ vi amotinarse; **to run ~** desmandarse

**rip** [rɪp] n rasgón m ▷ vt rasgar, desgarrar ▷ vi rasgarse; **rip off** vt (inf: cheat) estafar; **rip up** vt hacer pedazos

**ripe** [raɪp] adj maduro

**rip-off** ['rɪpɔf] n (inf): **it's a ~!** ¡es una estafa!, ¡es un timo!

**ripple** ['rɪpl] n onda, rizo; (sound) murmullo ▷ vi rizarse

**rise** (pt **rose**, pp **risen**) [raɪz, rəuz, 'rɪzn] n (slope) cuesta, pendiente f; (hill) altura; (in wages) aumento; (in prices, temperature) subida; (fig: to power etc) ascenso ▷ vi subir; (waters) crecer; (sun) salir; (person: from bed etc) levantarse; (also: **~ up**: rebel) sublevarse; (in rank) ascender; **to give ~ to** dar lugar or

origen a; **to ~ to the occasion** ponerse a la altura de las circunstancias; **risen** ['rɪzn] pp of **rise**; **rising** adj (increasing: number) creciente; (: prices) en aumento or alza; (tide) creciente; (sun, moon) naciente

**risk** [rɪsk] n riesgo, peligro ▷ vt arriesgar; **to take** or **run the ~ of doing** correr el riesgo de hacer; **at ~** en peligro; **at one's own ~** bajo su propia responsabilidad; **risky** adj arriesgado, peligroso

**rite** [raɪt] n rito; **last ~s** últimos sacramentos mpl

**ritual** ['rɪtjuəl] adj ritual ▷ n ritual m, rito

**rival** ['raɪvl] n rival mf; (in business) competidor(a) m/f ▷ adj rival, opuesto ▷ vt competir con; **rivalry** n competencia

**river** ['rɪvəʳ] n río ▷ cpd (port, traffic) de río; **up/down~** río arriba/abajo; **riverbank** n orilla (del río)

**rivet** ['rɪvɪt] n roblón m, remache m ▷ vt (fig) fascinar

**road** [rəud] n camino; (motorway etc) carretera; (in town) calle f; **major/minor ~** carretera general/secundaria; **roadblock** n barricada; **road map** n mapa m de carreteras; **road rage** n conducta agresiva de los conductores; **road safety** n seguridad f vial; **roadside** n borde m (del camino); **roadsign** n señal f de tráfico; **road tax** n (BRIT) impuesto de rodaje; **roadworks** npl obras fpl

**roam** [rəum] vi vagar

**roar** [rɔːʳ] n rugido; (of vehicle, storm) estruendo; (of laughter) carcajada ▷ vi rugir; hacer estruendo; **to ~ with laughter** reírse a carcajadas; **roaring** adj: **to do a roaring trade** hacer buen negocio

**roast** [rəust] n carne f asada, asado ▷ vt asar; (coffee) tostar; **roast beef** n rosbif m

**rob** [rɔb] vt robar; **to ~ sb of sth** robar algo a algn; (fig: deprive) quitar algo a algn; **robber** n ladrón/ona m/f; **robbery** n robo

**robe** [rəub] n (for ceremony etc) toga; (also: **bath ~**) bata, albornoz m

**robin** ['rɔbɪn] n petirrojo

**robot** ['rəubɔt] n robot m

**robust** [rəu'bʌst] adj robusto, fuerte

**rock** [rɔk] n roca; (boulder) peña, peñasco; (BRIT: sweet) ≈ pirulí m ▷ vt (swing gently) mecer; (shake) sacudir ▷ vi mecerse, balancearse; sacudirse; **on the ~s** (drink) con hielo; **their marriage is on the ~s** su matrimonio se está yendo a pique; **rock and roll** n rocanrol m; **rock climbing** n (Sport) escalada

**rocket** ['rɔkɪt] n cohete m

**rocking chair** ['rɔkɪŋ-] n mecedora

**rocky** ['rɔkɪ] adj rocoso

**rod** [rɔd] n vara, varilla; (also: **fishing ~**) caña

**rode** [rəud] *pt of* **ride**

**rodent** ['rəudnt] *n* roedor *m*

**rogue** [rəug] *n* pícaro, pillo

**role** [rəul] *n* papel *m*; **role-model** *n* modelo a imitar

**roll** [rəul] *n* rollo; (*of bank notes*) fajo; (*also*: **bread ~**) panecillo; (*register*) lista, nómina; (*sound: of drums etc*) redoble *m* ▷ *vt* hacer rodar; (*also*: **~ up**: *string*) enrollar; (: *cigarettes*) liar; (*also*: **~ out**: *pastry*) aplanar ▷ *vi* rodar; (*drum*) redoblar; (*ship*) balancearse; **roll over** *vi* dar una vuelta; **roll up** *vi* (*inf: arrive*) aparecer ▷ *vt* (*carpet, cloth, map*) arrollar; (*sleeves*) arremangar

**roller** *n* rodillo; (*wheel*) rueda; (*for road*) apisonadora; (*for hair*) rulo; **Rollerblades®** *npl* patines *mpl* en línea; **roller coaster** *n* montaña rusa; **roller skates** *npl* patines *mpl* de rueda; **roller-skating** *n* patinaje sobre ruedas; **to go roller-skating** ir a patinar (*sobre ruedas*)

**rolling pin** *n* rodillo (de cocina)

**ROM** [rɔm] *n abbr* (*Comput* = *read-only memory*) (memoria) ROM *f*

**Roman** ['rəumən] *adj, n* romano/a; **Roman Catholic** *adj, n* católico/a (romano/a)

**romance** [rə'mæns] *n* (*love affair*) amor *m*; (*charm*) lo romántico; (*novel*) novela de amor

**Romania** [ruː'meɪnɪə] *n* = **Rumania**

**Roman numeral** *n* número romano

**romantic** [rə'mæntɪk] *adj* romántico

**Rome** [rəum] *n* Roma

**roof** [ruːf] *n* techo; (*of house*) tejado ▷ *vt* techar, poner techo a; **~ of the mouth** paladar *m*; **roof rack** *n* (*Aut*) baca, portaequipajes *msg*

**rook** [ruk] *n* (*bird*) graja; (*Chess*) torre *f*

**room** [ruːm] *n* cuarto, habitación *f*, pieza (*esp LAM*); (*also*: **bed~**) dormitorio; (*in school etc*) sala; (*space*) sitio; **roommate** *n* compañero/a de cuarto; **room service** *n* servicio de habitaciones; **roomy** *adj* espacioso

**rooster** ['ruːstər] *n* gallo

**root** [ruːt] *n* raíz *f* ▷ *vi* arraigar(se)

**rope** [rəup] *n* cuerda; (*Naut*) cable *m* ▷ *vt* (*box*) atar or amarrar con (una) cuerda; (*climbers: also*: **~ together**) encordarse; (*an area: also*: **~ off**) acordonar; **to know the ~s** (*fig*) conocer los trucos (del oficio)

**rort** [rɔːt] *n* (*AUST, NZ inf*) estafa ▷ *vt* estafar

**rose** [rəuz] *pt of* **rise** ▷ *n* rosa; (*also*: **~bush**) rosal *m*; (*on watering can*) roseta

**rosé** ['rəuzeɪ] *n* vino rosado

**rosemary** ['rəuzmərɪ] *n* romero

**rosy** ['rəuzɪ] *adj* rosado, sonrosado; **the future looks ~** el futuro parece prometedor

**rot** [rɔt] *n* podredumbre *f*; (*fig: pej*) tonterías *fpl* ▷ *vt* pudrir ▷ *vi* pudrirse

**rota** ['rəutə] *n* lista (de tareas)

**rotate** [rəu'teɪt] *vt* (*revolve*) hacer girar, dar vueltas a; (*jobs*) alternar ▷ *vi* girar, dar vueltas

**rotten** ['rɔtn] *adj* podrido; (*fig*) corrompido; (*inf: bad*) pésimo; **to feel ~** (*ill*) sentirse fatal

**rough** [rʌf] *adj* (*skin, surface*) áspero; (*terrain*) accidentado; (*road*) desigual; (*voice*) bronco; (*person, manner*) tosco, grosero; (*weather*) borrascoso; (*treatment*) brutal; (*sea*) embravecido; (*town, area*) peligroso; (*cloth*) basto; (*plan*) preliminar; (*guess*) aproximado ▷ *n* (*Golf*): **in the ~** en las hierbas altas; **to ~ it** vivir sin comodidades; **to sleep ~** (*BRIT*) pasar la noche al raso; **roughly** *adv* (*handle*) torpemente; (*make*) toscamente; (*approximately*) aproximadamente; **roughly speaking** más o menos

**roulette** [ruː'lɛt] *n* ruleta

**round** [raund] *adj* redondo ▷ *n* círculo; (*of police officer*) ronda; (*of milkman*) recorrido; (*of doctor*) visitas *fpl*; (*game: in competition, cards*) partida; (*of ammunition*) cartucho; (*Boxing*) asalto; (*of talks*) ronda ▷ *vt* (*corner*) doblar ▷ *prep* alrededor de; (*surrounding*): **~ his neck/the table** en su cuello/alrededor de la mesa; (*in a circular movement*): **to move ~ the room/sail ~ the world** dar una vuelta a la habitación/circunnavegar el mundo; (*in various directions*): **to move ~ a room/house** moverse por toda la habitación/casa ▷ *adv*: **all ~** por todos lados; **all the year ~** durante todo el año; **the long way ~** por el camino menos directo; **it's just ~ the corner** (*fig*) está a la vuelta de la esquina; **~ the clock** *adv* las 24 horas; **to go ~ to sb's (house)** ir a casa de algn; **to go ~ the back** pasar por atrás; **enough to go ~** bastante (para todos); **a ~ of applause** una salva de aplausos; **a ~ of drinks/sandwiches** una ronda de bebidas/bocadillos; **a ~ of toast** (*BRIT*) una tostada; **round off** *vt* (*speech etc*) acabar, poner término a; **round up** *vt* (*cattle*) acorralar; (*people*) reunir; (*prices*) redondear; **roundabout** *n* (*BRIT: Aut*) glorieta, rotonda; (: *at fair*) tiovivo ▷ *adj* (*route, means*) indirecto; **round trip** *n* viaje *m* de ida y vuelta; **roundup** *n* rodeo; (*of criminals*) redada; **a roundup of the latest news** un resumen de las últimas noticias

**rouse** [rauz] *vt* (*wake up*) despertar; (*stir up*) suscitar

**route** [ruːt] *n* ruta, camino; (*of bus*) recorrido; (*of shipping*) derrota

**router** ['ruːtər] *n* (*Comput*) router *m*

**routine** [ruː'tiːn] *adj* rutinario ▷ *n* rutina; (*Theat*) número

**row¹** [rəu] n (line) fila, hilera; (Knitting) vuelta ▷ vi (in boat) remar ▷ vt (boat) conducir remando; **four days in a ~** cuatro días seguidos

**row²** [rau] n (noise) escándalo; (dispute) bronca, pelea; (scolding) reprimenda ▷ vi reñir(se)

**rowboat** ['rəubəut] n (US) bote m de remos

**rowing** ['rəuɪŋ] n remo; **rowing boat** n (BRIT) bote m or barco de remos

**royal** ['rɔɪəl] adj real; **Royal Air Force** n Fuerzas Aéreas Británicas fpl; **royalty** n (royal persons) (miembros mpl de la) familia real; (payment to author) derechos mpl de autor

**rpm** abbr (= revolutions per minute) r.p.m.

**RSVP** abbr (= répondez s'il vous plaît) SRC

**Rt. Hon.** abbr (BRIT = Right Honourable) tratamiento honorífico de diputado

**rub** [rʌb] vt frotar; (hard) restregar ▷ n: **to give sth a ~** frotar algo; **to ~ sb up** or (US)**~ sb the wrong way** sacar de quicio a algn; **rub in** vt (ointment) frotar; **rub off** vt borrarse; **rub out** vt borrar

**rubber** ['rʌbə'] n caucho, goma; (BRIT: eraser) goma de borrar; **rubber band** n goma, gomita; **rubber gloves** npl guantes mpl de goma

**rubbish** ['rʌbɪʃ] (BRIT) n (from household) basura; (waste) desperdicios mpl; (fig: pej) tonterías fpl; (trash) basura, porquería; **rubbish bin** n cubo or bote m (LAM) de la basura; **rubbish dump** n vertedero, basurero

**rubble** ['rʌbl] n escombros mpl

**ruby** ['ru:bɪ] n rubí m

**rucksack** ['rʌksæk] n mochila

**rudder** ['rʌdə'] n timón m

**rude** [ru:d] adj (impolite: person) maleducado; (: word, manners) grosero; (indecent) indecente

**ruffle** ['rʌfl] vt (hair) despeinar; (clothes) arrugar; (fig: person) agitar

**rug** [rʌg] n alfombra; (BRIT: for knees) manta

**rugby** ['rʌgbɪ] n rugby m

**rugged** ['rʌgɪd] adj (landscape) accidentado; (features) robusto

**ruin** ['ru:ɪn] n ruina ▷ vt arruinar; (spoil) estropear; **ruins** npl ruinas fpl, restos mpl

**rule** [ru:l] n (norm) norma, costumbre f; (regulation, ruler) regla; (government) dominio ▷ vt (country, person) gobernar ▷ vi gobernar; (Law) fallar; **as a ~** por regla general; **rule out** vt excluir; **ruler** n (sovereign) soberano; (for measuring) regla; **ruling** adj (party) gobernante; (class) dirigente ▷ n (Law) fallo, decisión f

**rum** [rʌm] n ron m

**Rumania** [ru:'meɪnɪə] n Rumanía; **Rumanian** adj, n rumano/a

**rumble** ['rʌmbl] n ruido sordo ▷ vi retumbar, hacer un ruido sordo; (stomach, pipe) sonar

**rumour**, (US) **rumor** ['ru:mə'] n rumor m ▷ vt: **it is ~ed that ...** se rumorea que ...; **~ has it that ...** corre la voz de que ...

**rump steak** n filete m de lomo

**run** [rʌn] (pt ran, pp run) n (Sport) carrera; (outing) paseo, excursión f; (distance travelled) trayecto; (series) serie f; (Theat) temporada; (Ski) pista; (in tights, stockings) carrera ▷ vt (operate: business) dirigir; (: competition, course) organizar; (: hotel, house) administrar, llevar; (Comput) ejecutar; (to pass: hand) pasar; (Press: feature) publicar ▷ vi correr; (work: machine) funcionar, marchar; (bus, train: operate) circular, ir; (: travel) ir; (continue: play) seguir en cartel; (: contract) ser válido; (flow: river, bath) fluir; (colours, washing) desteñirse; (in election) ser candidato; **there was a ~ on** (meat, tickets) hubo mucha demanda de; **in the long ~** a la larga; **on the ~** en fuga; **I'll ~ you to the station** te llevaré a la estación en coche; **to ~ a risk** correr un riesgo; **to ~ a bath** llenar la bañera; **run after** vt fus (to catch up) correr tras; (chase) perseguir; **run away** vi huir; **run down** vt (reduce: production) ir reduciendo; (factory) restringir la producción de; (Aut) atropellar; (criticize) criticar; **to be ~ down** (person: tired) encontrarse agotado; **run into** vt fus (meet: person, trouble) tropezar con; (collide with) chocar con; **run off** vt (water) dejar correr ▷ vi huir corriendo; **run out** vi (person) salir corriendo; (liquid) irse; (lease) caducar, vencer; (money) acabarse; **run out of** vt fus quedar sin; **run over** vt (Aut) atropellar ▷ vt fus (revise) repasar; **run through** vt fus (instructions) repasar; **run up** vt (debt) incurrir en; **to ~ up against** (difficulties) tropezar con; **runaway** adj (horse) desbocado; (truck) sin frenos; (person) fugitivo

**rung** [rʌŋ] pp of **ring** ▷ n (of ladder) escalón m, peldaño

**runner** ['rʌnə'] n (in race: person) corredor(a) m/f; (: horse) caballo; (on sledge) patín m; **runner bean** n (BRIT) judía verde; **runner-up** n subcampeón/ona m/f

**running** ['rʌnɪŋ] n (sport) atletismo; (race) carrera ▷ adj (costs, water) corriente; (commentary) en directo; **to be in/out of the ~ for sth** tener/no tener posibilidades de ganar algo; **6 days ~** 6 días seguidos

**runny** ['rʌnɪ] adj líquido; (eyes) lloroso; **to have a ~ nose** tener mocos

**run-up** ['rʌnʌp] n: **~ to** (election etc) período previo a

**runway** ['rʌnweɪ] n (Aviat) pista (de aterrizaje)

**rupture** ['rʌptʃəʳ] n (Med) hernia ▷ vt: **to ~ o.s.** causarse una hernia

**rural** ['ruərl] adj rural

**rush** [rʌʃ] n ímpetu m; (hurry) prisa; (Comm) demanda repentina; (Bot) junco; (current) corriente f fuerte; (of feeling) torrente m ▷ vt apresurar; (work) hacer de prisa ▷ vi correr, precipitarse; **rush hour** n horas fpl punta

**Russia** ['rʌʃə] n Rusia; **Russian** adj ruso ▷ n ruso/a; (Ling) ruso

**rust** [rʌst] n herrumbre f, moho m ▷ vi oxidarse

**rusty** ['rʌstɪ] adj oxidado

**ruthless** ['ruːθlɪs] adj despiadado

**RV** n abbr (US) = **recreational vehicle**

**rye** [raɪ] n centeno

# S

**Sabbath** ['sæbəθ] n domingo; (Jewish) sábado

**sabotage** ['sæbətɑːʒ] n sabotaje m ▷ vt sabotear

**saccharin(e)** ['sækərɪn] n sacarina

**sachet** ['sæʃeɪ] n sobrecito

**sack** [sæk] n (bag) saco, costal m ▷ vt (dismiss) despedir; (plunder) saquear; **to get the ~** ser despedido

**sacred** ['seɪkrɪd] adj sagrado, santo

**sacrifice** ['sækrɪfaɪs] n sacrificio ▷ vt sacrificar

**sad** [sæd] adj (unhappy) triste; (deplorable) lamentable

**saddle** ['sædl] n silla (de montar); (of cycle) sillín m ▷ vt (horse) ensillar; **to be ~d with sth** (inf) quedar cargado con algo

**sadistic** [sə'dɪstɪk] adj sádico

**sadly** ['sædlɪ] adv tristemente; **~ lacking (in)** muy deficiente (en)

**sadness** ['sædnɪs] n tristeza

**safari** [sə'fɑːrɪ] n safari m

**safe** [seɪf] adj (out of danger) fuera de peligro; (not dangerous, sure) seguro; (unharmed) ileso ▷ n caja de caudales, caja fuerte; **~ and sound** sano y salvo; **(just) to be on the ~ side** para mayor seguridad; **safely** adv seguramente, con seguridad; **to arrive safely** llegar bien; **safe sex** n sexo seguro or sin riesgo

**safety** ['seɪftɪ] n seguridad f; **safety belt** n cinturón m (de seguridad); **safety pin** n imperdible m, seguro (LAM)

**saffron** ['sæfrən] n azafrán m

**sag** [sæg] vi aflojarse

**sage** [seɪdʒ] n (herb) salvia; (man) sabio

**Sagittarius** [sædʒɪ'tɛərɪəs] n Sagitario

**Sahara** [sə'hɑːrə] n: **the ~ (Desert)** el Sáhara

**said** [sɛd] pt, pp of **say**

**sail** [seɪl] n (on boat) vela ▷ vt (boat) gobernar ▷ vi (travel: ship) navegar; (Sport) hacer vela; **they ~ed into Copenhagen** arribaron a Copenhague; **sailboat** n (US) velero, barco de vela; **sailing** n (Sport) vela; **to go sailing** hacer vela; **sailing boat** n velero, barco de vela; **sailor** n marinero, marino

**saint** [seɪnt] n santo

**sake** [seɪk] n: **for the ~ of** por

**salad** ['sæləd] n ensalada; **salad cream** n (BRIT) mayonesa; **salad dressing** n aliño

**salami** [sə'lɑːmɪ] n salami m, salchichón m

**salary** ['sælərɪ] n sueldo

**sale** [seɪl] n venta; (at reduced prices) liquidación f, saldo; (auction) subasta; **sales** npl (total amount sold) ventas fpl, facturación f; **"for ~"** "se vende"; **on ~** en venta; **on ~ or return** (goods) venta por reposición; **sales assistant** n (BRIT) dependiente/a m/f; **sales clerk** n (US) dependiente/a m/f; **salesman** n vendedor m; (in shop) dependiente m; **salesperson** (irreg) n vendedor(a) m/f, dependiente/a m/f; **sales rep** n representante mf, agente mf comercial

**saline** ['seɪlaɪn] adj salino

**saliva** [sə'laɪvə] n saliva

**salmon** ['sæmən] n (pl inv) salmón m

**salon** ['sælɔn] n (hairdressing salon, beauty salon) salón m

**saloon** [sə'luːn] n (US) bar m, taberna; (BRIT Aut) (coche m de) turismo; (ship's lounge) cámara, salón m

**salt** [sɔːlt] n sal f ▷ vt salar; (put salt on) poner sal en; **saltwater** adj de agua salada; **salty** adj salado

**salute** [sə'luːt] n saludo; (of guns) salva ▷ vt saludar

**salvage** ['sælvɪdʒ] n (saving) salvamento, recuperación f; (things saved) objetos mpl salvados ▷ vt salvar

**Salvation Army** n Ejército de Salvación

**same** [seɪm] adj mismo ▷ pron: **the ~** el mismo/la misma; **the ~ book as** el mismo libro que; **at the ~ time** (at the same moment) al mismo tiempo; (yet) sin embargo; **all or just the ~** sin embargo, aun así; **to do the ~ (as sb)** hacer lo mismo (que otro); **and the ~ to you!** ¡igualmente!

**sample** ['sɑːmpl] n muestra ▷ vt (food, wine) probar

**sanction** ['sæŋkʃən] n sanción f ▷ vt sancionar; **sanctions** npl (Pol) sanciones fpl

**sanctuary** ['sæŋktjuərɪ] n santuario; (refuge) asilo, refugio; (for wildlife) reserva

**sand** [sænd] n arena; (beach) playa; **sands** npl playa sg de arena ▷ vt (also: **~ down**: wood etc) lijar

**sandal** ['sændl] n sandalia

**sand:** **sandbox** n (US) = **sandpit**; **sandcastle** n castillo de arena; **sand dune** n duna; **sandpaper** n papel m de lija; **sandpit** n (for children) cajón m de arena; **sandstone** n piedra arenisca

**sandwich** ['sændwɪtʃ] n bocadillo (SP), sandwich m (LAM) ▷ vt (also: **~ in**) intercalar; **to be ~ed between** estar apretujado entre; **cheese/ham ~** sandwich de queso/jamón

**sandy** ['sændɪ] adj arenoso; (colour) rojizo

**sane** [seɪn] adj cuerdo, sensato

⏺ Be careful not to translate sane by the Spanish word sano.

**sang** [sæŋ] pt of **sing**

**sanitary towel**, (US) **sanitary napkin** n paño higiénico, compresa

**sanity** ['sænɪtɪ] n cordura; (of judgment) sensatez f

**sank** [sæŋk] pt of **sink**

**Santa Claus** [sæntə'klɔːz] n San Nicolás m, Papá Noel m

**sap** [sæp] n (of plants) savia ▷ vt (strength) minar, agotar

**sapphire** ['sæfaɪər] n zafiro

**sarcasm** ['sɑːkæzm] n sarcasmo

**sarcastic** [sɑː'kæstɪk] adj sarcástico

**sardine** [sɑː'diːn] n sardina

**SASE** n abbr (US: = self-addressed stamped envelope) sobre con las propias señas de uno y con sello

**sat** [sæt] pt, pp of **sit**

**Sat.** abbr (= Saturday) sáb.

**satchel** ['sætʃl] n (child's) cartera, mochila (LAM)

**satellite** ['sætəlaɪt] n satélite m; **satellite dish** n (antena) parabólica; **satellite television** n televisión f por satélite

**satin** ['sætɪn] n raso ▷ adj de raso

**satire** ['sætaɪər] n sátira

**satisfaction** [sætɪs'fækʃən] n satisfacción f

**satisfactory** [sætɪs'fæktərɪ] adj satisfactorio

**satisfied** ['sætɪsfaɪd] adj satisfecho; **to be ~ (with sth)** estar satisfecho (de algo)

**satisfy** ['sætɪsfaɪ] vt satisfacer; (convince) convencer

**satnav** ['sætnæv] n abbr (= satellite navigation) navegador m (GPS)

**Saturday** ['sætədɪ] n sábado

**sauce** [sɔːs] n salsa; (sweet) crema; **saucepan** n cacerola, olla

**saucer** ['sɔːsər] n platillo

**Saudi Arabia** n Arabia Saudí or Saudita

**sauna** ['sɔːnə] n sauna

**sausage** ['sɒsɪdʒ] n salchicha; **sausage roll** n empanadilla de salchicha

**sautéed** ['səʊteɪd] *adj* salteado

**savage** ['sævɪdʒ] *adj* (*cruel, fierce*) feroz, furioso; (*primitive*) salvaje ▷ *n* salvaje *mf* ▷ *vt* (*attack*) embestir

**save** [seɪv] *vt* (*rescue*) salvar, rescatar; (*money, time*) ahorrar; (*put by*) guardar; (*Comput*) salvar (y guardar); (*avoid: trouble*) evitar; (*Sport*) parar ▷ *vi* (*also: ~ up*) ahorrar ▷ *n* (*Sport*) parada ▷ *prep* salvo, excepto

**saving** ['seɪvɪŋ] *n* (*on price etc*) economía; **savings** *npl* ahorros *mpl*; **savings account** *n* cuenta de ahorros; **savings and loan association** *n* (*us*) sociedad *f* de ahorro y préstamo

**savoury**, (*us*) **savory** ['seɪvərɪ] *adj* sabroso; (*dish: not sweet*) salado

**saw** [sɔː] *pt of* **see** ▷ *n* (*tool*) sierra ▷ *vt* serrar; **sawdust** *n* (a)serrín *m*

**sawn** [sɔːn] *pp of* **saw**

**saxophone** ['sæksəfəʊn] *n* saxófono

**say** (*pt, pp* **said**) [seɪ, sɛd] *n*: **to have one's ~** expresar su opinión *f*, decir; *vi* decir; **to have a** *or* **some ~ in sth** tener voz y voto en algo; **to ~ yes/no** decir que sí/no; **that is to ~** es decir; **that goes without ~ing** ni que decir tiene; **saying** *n* dicho, refrán *m*

**scab** [skæb] *n* costra; (*pej*) esquirol(a) *m/f*

**scaffolding** ['skæfəldɪŋ] *n* andamio, andamiaje *m*

**scald** [skɔːld] *n* escaldadura ▷ *vt* escaldar

**scale** [skeɪl] *n* escala; (*Mus*) escala; (*of fish*) escama; (*of salaries, fees etc*) escalafón *m* ▷ *vt* (*mountain*) escalar; (*tree*) trepar; **scales** *npl* (*small*) balanza *sg*; (*large*) báscula *sg*; **on a large ~** a gran escala; **~ of charges** tarifa, lista de precios

**scallion** ['skælɪən] *n* (*us*) cebolleta

**scallop** ['skɔləp] *n* (*Zool*) venera; (*Sewing*) festón *m*

**scalp** [skælp] *n* cabellera ▷ *vt* escalpar

**scalpel** ['skælpl] *n* bisturí *m*

**scam** [skæm] *n* (*inf*) estafa, timo

**scampi** ['skæmpɪ] *npl* gambas *fpl*

**scan** [skæn] *vt* (*examine*) escudriñar; (*glance at quickly*) dar un vistazo a; (*TV, Radar*) explorar, registrar ▷ *n* (*Med*) examen *m* ultrasónico; **to have a ~** pasar por el escáner

**scandal** ['skændl] *n* escándalo; (*gossip*) chismes *mpl*

**Scandinavia** [skændɪ'neɪvɪə] *n* Escandinavia; **Scandinavian** *adj, n* escandinavo/a

**scanner** ['skænər] *n* (*Radar, Med, Comput*) escáner *m*

**scapegoat** ['skeɪpgəʊt] *n* cabeza de turco, chivo expiatorio

**scar** [skɑː] *n* cicatriz *f* ▷ *vt* marcar con una cicatriz

**scarce** [skɛəs] *adj* escaso; **to make o.s. ~** (*inf*) esfumarse; **scarcely** *adv* apenas

**scare** [skɛər] *n* susto, sobresalto; (*panic*) pánico ▷ *vt* asustar, espantar; **to ~ sb stiff** dar a algn un susto de muerte; **bomb ~** amenaza de bomba; **scarecrow** *n* espantapájaros *m inv*; **scared** *adj*: **to be scared** estar asustado

**scarf** (*pl* **scarves**) [skɑːf, skɑːvz] *n* (*long*) bufanda; (*square*) pañuelo

**scarlet** ['skɑːlɪt] *adj* escarlata

**scarves** [skɑːvz] *npl of* **scarf**

**scary** ['skɛərɪ] *adj* (*inf*) de miedo

**scatter** ['skætər] *vt* (*spread*) esparcir, desparramar; (*put to flight*) dispersar ▷ *vi* desparramarse; dispersarse

**scenario** [sɪ'nɑːrɪəʊ] *n* (*Theat*) argumento; (*Cine*) guión *m*; (*fig*) escenario

**scene** [siːn] *n* (*Theat*) escena; (*of crime, accident*) escenario; (*sight, view*) vista, panorama; (*fuss*) escándalo; **scenery** *n* (*Theat*) decorado; (*landscape*) paisaje *m*; **scenic** *adj* pintoresco

> Be careful not to translate *scenery* by the Spanish word *escenario*.

**scent** [sɛnt] *n* perfume *m*, olor *m*; (*fig: track*) rastro, pista

**sceptical**, (*us*) **skeptical** ['skɛptɪkl] *adj* escéptico

**schedule** ['ʃedjuːl, *us* 'skedjuːl] *n* (*of trains*) horario; (*of events*) programa *m*; (*list*) lista ▷ *vt* (*visit*) fijar la hora de; **on ~** a la hora, sin retraso; **to be ahead of/behind ~** ir adelantado/retrasado

**scheduled** ['ʃedjuːld, *us* 'skedjuːld] *adj* (*date, time*) fijado; **~ flight** vuelo regular

**scheme** [skiːm] *n* (*plan*) plan *m*, proyecto; (*plot*) intriga; (*arrangement*) disposición *f*; (*pension scheme etc*) sistema *m* ▷ *vi* (*intrigue*) intrigar

**schizophrenic** [skɪtsə'frɛnɪk] *adj* esquizofrénico

**scholar** ['skɔlər] *n* (*pupil*) alumno/a; (*learned person*) sabio/a, erudito/a; **scholarship** *n* erudición *f*; (*grant*) beca

**school** [skuːl] *n* escuela, colegio; (*in university*) facultad *f*; **schoolbook** *n* libro de texto; **schoolboy** *n* alumno; **schoolchild** schoolchildren *n* alumno/a; **schoolgirl** *n* alumna; **schooling** *n* enseñanza; **schoolteacher** *n* (*primary*) maestro/a; (*secondary*) profesor(a) *m/f*

**science** ['saɪəns] *n* ciencia; **science fiction** *n* ciencia-ficción *f*; **scientific** [saɪən'tɪfɪk] *adj* científico; **scientist** *n* científico/a

**sci-fi** ['saɪfaɪ] *n abbr* (*inf*) = **science fiction**

**scissors** ['sɪzəz] *npl* tijeras *fpl*; **a pair of ~** unas tijeras

**scold** [skəʊld] *vt* regañar

**scone** [skɒn] n pastel de pan

**scoop** [sku:p] n (for flour etc) pala; (Press) exclusiva

**scooter** ['sku:tər] n (motor cycle) Vespa®; (toy) patinete m

**scope** [skəup] n (of plan, undertaking) ámbito; (of person) competencia; (opportunity) libertad f (de acción)

**scorching** ['skɔ:tʃɪŋ] adj abrasador(a)

**score** [skɔ:ʳ] n (points etc) puntuación f; (Mus) partitura; (twenty) veintena ▷ vt (goal, point) ganar; (mark, cut) rayar ▷ vi marcar un tanto; (Football) marcar un gol; (keep score) llevar el tanteo; **on that ~** en lo que se refiere a eso; **to ~ 6 out of 10** obtener una puntuación de 6 sobre 10; **score out** vt tachar; **scoreboard** n marcador m; **scorer** n marcador(a) m/f; (keeping score) encargado/a del marcador

**scorn** [skɔ:n] n desprecio

**Scorpio** ['skɔ:pɪəu] n Escorpión m

**scorpion** ['skɔ:pɪən] n alacrán m

**Scot** [skɒt] n escocés/esa m/f

**Scotch tape®** n (us) cinta adhesiva, celo, scotch® m

**Scotland** ['skɒtlənd] n Escocia

**Scots** [skɒts] adj escocés/esa; **Scotsman** n escocés m; **Scotswoman** n escocesa

**Scottish** ['skɒtɪʃ] adj escocés/esa; **the ~ Parliament** el Parlamento escocés

**scout** [skaut] n explorador m; **girl ~** (us) niña exploradora

**scowl** [skaul] vi fruncir el ceño; **to ~ at sb** mirar con ceño a algn

**scramble** ['skræmbl] n (climb) subida (difícil); (struggle) pelea ▷ vi: **to ~ out/through** salir/abrirse paso con dificultad; **to ~ for** pelear por; **scrambled eggs** npl huevos mpl revueltos

**scrap** [skræp] n (bit) pedacito; (fig) pizca; (fight) riña, bronca; (also: **~ iron**) chatarra, hierro viejo ▷ vt (discard) desechar, descartar ▷ vi reñir, armar (una) bronca; **scraps** npl (waste) sobras fpl, desperdicios mpl; **scrapbook** n álbum m de recortes

**scrape** [skreɪp] n (fig) lío, apuro ▷ vt raspar; (skin etc) rasguñar; (also: **~ against**) rozar; **to get into a ~** meterse en un lío; **scrape through** vi (in exam) aprobar por los pelos

**scrap paper** n pedazos mpl de papel

**scratch** [skrætʃ] n rasguño; (from claw) arañazo ▷ vt (paint, car) rayar; (with claw, nail) rasguñar, arañar ▷ vi rascarse; **to start from ~** partir de cero; **to be up to ~** cumplir con los requisitos; **scratch card** n (BRIT) tarjeta f de "rasque y gane"

**scream** [skri:m] n chillido ▷ vi chillar

**screen** [skri:n] n (Cine, TV) pantalla; (movable) biombo ▷ vt (conceal) tapar; (from the wind etc) proteger; (film) proyectar; (fig: person: for security) investigar; **screening** n (Med) exploración f; **screenplay** n guión m; **screen saver** n (Comput) salvapantallas m inv; **screenshot** n (Comput) pantallazo, captura de pantalla

**screw** [skru:] n tornillo; (propeller) hélice f ▷ vt atornillar; **screw up** vt (paper, material etc) arrugar; **to ~ up one's eyes** arrugar el entrecejo; **screwdriver** n destornillador m

**scribble** ['skrɪbl] n garabatos mpl ▷ vi garabatear ▷ vt: **to ~ sth down** garabatear algo

**script** [skrɪpt] n (Cine etc) guión m; (writing) escritura, letra

**scroll** [skrəul] n rollo

**scrub** [skrʌb] n (land) maleza ▷ vt fregar, restregar; (reject) cancelar, anular

**scruffy** ['skrʌfɪ] adj desaliñado

**scrum(mage)** ['skrʌm(ɪdʒ)] n (Rugby) melée f

**scrutiny** ['skru:tɪnɪ] n escrutinio, examen m

**scuba diving** ['sku:bə'daɪvɪŋ] n submarinismo

**sculptor** ['skʌlptər] n escultor(a) m/f

**sculpture** ['skʌlptʃər] n escultura

**scum** [skʌm] n (on liquid) espuma; (pej: people) escoria

**scurry** ['skʌrɪ] vi: **to ~ off** escabullirse

**sea** [si:] n mar m (or also f); **by ~** (travel) en barco; **on the ~** (boat) en el mar; (town) junto al mar; **to be all at ~** (fig) estar despistado; **out to** or **at ~** en alta mar; **seafood** n mariscos mpl; **sea front** n paseo marítimo; **seagull** n gaviota

**seal** [si:l] n (animal) foca; (stamp) sello ▷ vt (close) cerrar; **seal off** vt obturar

**sea level** n nivel m del mar

**seam** [si:m] n costura; (of metal) juntura; (of coal) veta, filón m

**search** [sə:tʃ] n (for person, thing) busca, búsqueda; (of drawer, pockets) registro ▷ vt (look in) buscar en; (examine) examinar; (person, place) registrar ▷ vi: **to ~ for** buscar; **in ~ of** en busca de; **search engine** n (Internet) buscador m; **search party** n equipo de salvamento

**sea: seashore** n playa, orilla del mar; **seasick** adj mareado; **seaside** n playa, orilla del mar; **seaside resort** n centro turístico costero

**season** ['si:zn] n (of year) estación f; (sporting etc) temporada ▷ vt (food) sazonar; **to be in/out of ~** estar en sazón/fuera de temporada; **seasonal** adj estacional; **seasoning** n condimento; **season ticket** n abono

**seat** [si:t] n (in bus, train) asiento; (chair) silla; (Parliament) escaño; (buttocks)

trasero ▷ vt sentar; (have room for) tener cabida para; **to be ~ed** sentarse; **seat belt** n cinturón m de seguridad; **seating** n asientos mpl
**sea: sea water** n agua m del mar; **seaweed** n alga marina
**sec.** abbr = **second**
**secluded** [sɪˈkluːdɪd] adj retirado
**second** [ˈsɛkənd] adj segundo ▷ adv en segundo lugar ▷ n segundo; (Aut: also: **~ gear**) segunda; (Comm) artículo con algún desperfecto; (BRIT Scol: degree) título universitario de segunda clase ▷ vt (motion) apoyar; **to have ~ thoughts** cambiar de opinión; **on ~ thoughts** or (US) **thought** pensándolo bien; **secondary** adj secundario; **secondary school** n escuela secundaria; **second-class** adj de segunda clase ▷ adv: **to travel second-class** viajar en segunda; **secondhand** adj de segunda mano, usado; **secondly** adv en segundo lugar; **second-rate** adj de segunda categoría
**secrecy** [ˈsiːkrəsɪ] n secreto
**secret** [ˈsiːkrɪt] adj, n secreto; **in ~** en secreto
**secretary** [ˈsɛkrətərɪ] n secretario/a; **S~ of State** (BRIT Pol) Ministro (con cartera)
**secretive** [ˈsiːkrətɪv] adj reservado, sigiloso
**secret service** n servicio secreto
**sect** [sɛkt] n secta
**section** [ˈsɛkʃən] n sección f; (part) parte f; (of document) artículo; (of opinion) sector m
**sector** [ˈsɛktəʳ] n sector m
**secular** [ˈsɛkjuləʳ] adj secular, seglar
**secure** [sɪˈkjuəʳ] adj seguro; (firmly fixed) firme, fijo ▷ vt (fix) asegurar, afianzar; (get) conseguir
**security** [sɪˈkjuərɪtɪ] n seguridad f; (for loan) fianza; (: object) prenda; **securities** npl (Comm) valores mpl, títulos mpl; **security guard** n guardia mf de seguridad
**sedan** [sɪˈdæn] n (US Aut) sedán m
**sedate** [sɪˈdeɪt] adj tranquilo ▷ vt administrar sedantes a, sedar
**sedative** [ˈsɛdɪtɪv] n sedante m
**seduce** [sɪˈdjuːs] vt seducir; **seductive** [sɪˈdʌktɪv] adj seductor/a
**see** [siː] (pt saw, pp seen) vt ver; (understand) ver, comprender ▷ vi ver ▷ n sede f; **to ~ sb to the door** acompañar a algn a la puerta; **to ~ that** (ensure) asegurarse de que; **~ you soon/later/tomorrow!** ¡hasta pronto/luego/mañana!; **see off** vt despedir; **see out** vt (take to the door) acompañar hasta la puerta; **see through** vt fus calar ▷ vt llevar a cabo; **see to** vt fus atender a, encargarse de

**seed** [siːd] n semilla; (in fruit) pepita; (fig) germen m; (Tennis) preseleccionado/a; **to go to ~** (plant) granar; (fig) descuidarse
**seeing** [ˈsiːɪŋ] conj: **~ (that)** visto que, en vista de que
**seek** (pt, pp sought) [siːk, sɔːt] vt buscar; (post) solicitar
**seem** [siːm] vi parecer; **there ~s to be ...** parece que hay ...; **seemingly** adv aparentemente, según parece
**seen** [siːn] pp of **see**
**seesaw** [ˈsiːsɔː] n subibaja m
**segment** [ˈsɛgmənt] n segmento; (of citrus fruit) gajo
**segregate** [ˈsɛgrɪgeɪt] vt segregar
**seize** [siːz] vt (grasp) agarrar, asir; (take possession of) secuestrar; (: territory) apoderarse de; (opportunity) aprovecharse de
**seizure** [ˈsiːʒəʳ] n (Med) ataque m; (Law) incautación f
**seldom** [ˈsɛldəm] adv rara vez
**select** [sɪˈlɛkt] adj selecto, escogido ▷ vt escoger, elegir; (Sport) seleccionar; **selection** n selección f, elección f; (Comm) surtido; **selective** adj selectivo
**self** [sɛlf] n uno mismo ▷ pref auto...; **the ~** el yo; **self-assured** adj seguro de sí mismo; **self-catering** adj (BRIT): **self-catering apartment** apartamento con cocina propia; **self-centred,** (US) **self-centered** adj egocéntrico; **self-confidence** n confianza en sí mismo; **self-confident** adj seguro de sí (mismo), lleno de confianza en sí mismo; **self-conscious** adj cohibido; **self-contained** adj (BRIT: flat) con entrada particular; **self-control** n autodominio; **self-defence,** (US) **self-defense** n defensa propia; **self-employed** adj que trabaja por cuenta propia; **self-esteem** n amor m propio; **self-harm** vi autolesionarse; **self-indulgent** adj indulgente consigo mismo; **self-interest** n egoísmo; **selfish** adj egoísta; **self-pity** n lástima de sí mismo; **self-raising,** (US) **self-rising** adj: **self-raising flour** harina con levadura; **self-respect** n amor m propio; **self-service** adj de autoservicio
**selfie** [ˈsɛlfɪ] n selfie m, autofoto f
**sell** (pt, pp sold) [sɛl, səuld] vt vender ▷ vi venderse; **to ~ at** or **for £10** venderse a 10 libras; **sell off** vt liquidar; **sell out** vi: **the tickets are all sold out** las entradas están agotadas; **sell-by date** n fecha de caducidad; **seller** n vendedor(a) m/f
**Sellotape®** [ˈsɛləuteɪp] n (BRIT) celo, scotch® m
**selves** [sɛlvz] npl of **self**
**semester** [sɪˈmɛstəʳ] n (US) semestre m

**semi...** [ˈsɛmɪ] pref semi..., medio...;
**semicircle** n semicírculo; **semidetached (house)** n casa adosada; **semi-final** n semifinal f

**seminar** [ˈsɛmɪnɑː<sup>r</sup>] n seminario

**semi-skimmed** [ˈsɛmiˈskɪmd] adj semidesnatado; **semi-skimmed (milk)** n leche semidesnatada

**senate** [ˈsɛnɪt] n senado; see also **Congress**; **senator** n senador(a) m/f

**send** (pt, pp **sent**) [sɛnd, sɛnt] vt mandar, enviar; **send back** vt devolver; **send for** vt fus mandar traer; **send in** vt (report, application, resignation) mandar; **send off** vt (goods) despachar; (BRIT Sport: player) expulsar; **send on** vt (letter, luggage) remitir; **send out** vt (invitation) mandar; (signal) emitir; **send up** vt (person, price) hacer subir; (BRIT: parody) parodiar; **sender** n remitente mf; **send-off** n: **a good send-off** una buena despedida

**senile** [ˈsiːnaɪl] adj senil

**senior** [ˈsiːnɪə<sup>r</sup>] adj (older) mayor, más viejo; (: on staff) de más antigüedad; (of higher rank) superior; **senior citizen** n persona de la tercera edad; **senior high school** n (US) ≈ instituto de enseñanza media

**sensation** [sɛnˈseɪʃən] n sensación f; **sensational** adj sensacional

**sense** [sɛns] n (faculty, meaning) sentido; (feeling) sensación f; (good sense) sentido común, juicio ▷ vt sentir, percibir; **it makes ~** tiene sentido; **senseless** adj estúpido, insensato; (unconscious) sin conocimiento; **sense of humour** n (BRIT) sentido del humor

**sensible** [ˈsɛnsɪbl] adj sensato; (reasonable) razonable, lógico

▌ Be careful not to translate sensible by the Spanish word sensible.

**sensitive** [ˈsɛnsɪtɪv] adj sensible; (touchy) susceptible

**sensual** [ˈsɛnsjuəl] adj sensual

**sensuous** [ˈsɛnsjuəs] adj sensual

**sent** [sɛnt] pt, pp of **send**

**sentence** [ˈsɛntəns] n (Ling) oración f; (Law) sentencia, fallo ▷ vt: **to ~ sb to death/ to five years** condenar a algn a muerte/a cinco años de cárcel

**sentiment** [ˈsɛntɪmənt] n sentimiento; (opinion) opinión f; **sentimental** [sɛntɪˈmɛntl] adj sentimental

**Sep.** abbr (= September) sep., set.

**separate** adj [ˈsɛprɪt] separado; (distinct) distinto; **~s** npl (clothes) coordinados mpl ▷ vt [ˈsɛpəreɪt] separar; (part) dividir ▷ vi [ˈsɛpəreɪt] separarse; **separately** adv por separado; **separation** [sɛpəˈreɪʃən] n separación f

**September** [sɛpˈtɛmbə<sup>r</sup>] n se(p)tiembre m

**septic** [ˈsɛptɪk] adj séptico; **septic tank** n fosa séptica

**sequel** [ˈsiːkwl] n consecuencia, resultado; (of story) continuación f

**sequence** [ˈsiːkwəns] n sucesión f, serie f; (Cine) secuencia

**sequin** [ˈsiːkwɪn] n lentejuela

**Serb** [səːb] adj, n = **Serbian**

**Serbian** [ˈsəːbɪən] adj serbio ▷ n serbio/a; (Ling) serbio

**sergeant** [ˈsɑːdʒənt] n sargento

**serial** [ˈsɪərɪəl] n (TV) serie f; **serial killer** n asesino/a múltiple; **serial number** n número de serie

**series** [ˈsɪəriːz] n (pl inv) serie f

**serious** [ˈsɪərɪəs] adj serio; (grave) grave; **seriously** adv en serio; (ill, wounded etc) gravemente

**sermon** [ˈsəːmən] n sermón m

**servant** n servidor(a) m/f; (also: **house ~**) criado/a

**serve** [səːv] vt servir; (customer) atender; (train) tener parada en; (apprenticeship) hacer; (prison term) cumplir ▷ vi (servant, soldier etc) servir; (Tennis) sacar ▷ n (Tennis) saque m; **it ~s him right** se lo tiene merecido; **server** n (Comput) servidor m

**service** [ˈsəːvɪs] n servicio; (Rel) misa; (Aut) mantenimiento; (of dishes) juego ▷ vt (car, washing machine) revisar; (: repair) reparar; **services** npl (Econ: tertiary sector) sector m terciario or (de) servicios; (BRIT: on motorway) área de servicio; **the S~s** las fuerzas armadas; **to be of ~ to sb** ser útil a algn; **~ included/not included** servicio incluido/no incluido; **service area** n (on motorway) área de servicios; **service charge** n (BRIT) servicio; **serviceman** n militar m; **service station** n estación f de servicio

**serviette** [səːvɪˈɛt] n (BRIT) servilleta

**session** [ˈsɛʃən] n sesión f; **to be in ~** estar en sesión

**set** [sɛt] (pt, pp **set**) n juego; (Radio) aparato; (TV) televisor m; (of utensils) batería; (of cutlery) cubierto; (of books) colección f; (Tennis) set m; (group of people) grupo; (Cine) plató m; (Theat) decorado; (Hairdressing) marcado ▷ adj (fixed) fijo; (ready) listo ▷ vt (place) poner, colocar; (fix) fijar; (adjust) ajustar, arreglar; (decide: rules etc) establecer, decidir ▷ vi (sun) ponerse; (jam, jelly) cuajarse; (concrete) fraguar; **to be ~ on doing sth** estar empeñado en hacer algo; **to ~ to music** poner música a; **to ~ on fire** incendiar, prender fuego a; **to ~ free** poner en libertad; **to ~ sth going** poner algo en marcha; **to ~ sail** zarpar, hacerse a la mar;

**set aside** vt poner aparte, dejar de lado; **set down** vt (bus, train) dejar; **set in** vi (infection) declararse; (complications) comenzar; **the rain has ~ in for the day** parece que va a llover todo el día; **set off** vi partir ▷ vt (bomb) hacer estallar; (cause to start) poner en marcha; (show up well) hacer resaltar; **set out** vi partir ▷ vt (arrange) disponer; (state) exponer; **to ~ out to do sth** proponerse hacer algo; **set up** vt establecer; **setback** n revés m, contratiempo; **set menu** n menú m

**settee** [sɛˈtiː] n sofá m

**setting** [ˈsɛtɪŋ] n (scenery) marco; (of jewel) engaste m, montadura

**settle** [ˈsɛtl] vt (argument, matter) resolver; (pay: bill, accounts) pagar, liquidar; (Med: calm) calmar, sosegar ▷ vi (dust etc) depositarse; (weather) estabilizarse; **to ~ for sth** convenir en aceptar algo; **to ~ on sth** decidirse por algo; **settle down** vi (get comfortable) ponerse cómodo, acomodarse; (calm down) calmarse, tranquilizarse; (live quietly) echar raíces; **settle in** vi instalarse; **settle up** vi: **to ~ up with sb** ajustar cuentas con algn; **settlement** n (payment) liquidación f; (agreement) acuerdo, convenio; (village etc) poblado

**setup** [ˈsɛtʌp] n sistema m

**seven** [ˈsɛvn] num siete; **seventeen** num diecisiete; **seventeenth** adj decimoséptimo; **seventh** adj séptimo; **seventieth** adj septuagésimo; **seventy** num setenta

**sever** [ˈsɛvəʳ] vt cortar; (relations) romper

**several** [ˈsɛvərl] adj, pron varios/as m/f pl, algunos/as m/f pl; **~ of us** varios de nosotros

**severe** [sɪˈvɪəʳ] adj severo; (serious) grave; (hard) duro; (pain) intenso

**sew** (pt **sewed**, pp **sewn**) [səu, səud, səun] vt, vi coser

**sewage** [ˈsuːɪdʒ] n aguas fpl residuales

**sewer** [ˈsuːəʳ] n alcantarilla, cloaca

**sewing** [ˈsəuɪŋ] n costura; **sewing machine** n máquina de coser

**sewn** [səun] pp de **sew**

**sex** [sɛks] n sexo; **to have ~** hacer el amor; **sexism** n sexismo; **sexist** adj, n sexista mf; **sexual** [ˈsɛksjuəl] adj sexual; **sexual intercourse** relaciones fpl sexuales; **sexuality** [sɛksjuˈælɪtɪ] n sexualidad f; **sexy** adj sexy

**shabby** [ˈʃæbɪ] adj (person) desharrapado; (clothes) raído, gastado

**shack** [ʃæk] n choza, chabola

**shade** [ʃeɪd] n sombra; (for lamp) pantalla; (for eyes) visera; (of colour) tono m, tonalidad f ▷ vt dar sombra a; **shades** npl

(us: sunglasses) gafas fpl de sol; **in the ~** a la sombra; **a ~ more** (small quantity) un poquito más

**shadow** [ˈʃædəu] n sombra ▷ vt (follow) seguir y vigilar; **shadow cabinet** n (BRIT Pol) gobierno en la oposición

**shady** [ˈʃeɪdɪ] adj sombreado; (fig: dishonest) sospechoso; (deal) turbio

**shaft** [ʃɑːft] n (of arrow, spear) astil m; (Aut, Tech) eje m, árbol m; (of mine) pozo; (of lift) hueco, caja; (of light) rayo

**shake** [ʃeɪk] (pt **shook**, pp **shaken**) vt sacudir; (building) hacer temblar ▷ vi (tremble) temblar; **to ~ one's head** (in refusal) negar con la cabeza; (in dismay) mover or menear la cabeza, incrédulo; **to ~ hands with sb** estrechar la mano a algn; **shake off** vt sacudirse; (fig) deshacerse de; **shake up** vt agitar; **shaky** adj (unstable) inestable, poco firme; (trembling) tembloroso

**shall** [ʃæl] aux vb: **I ~ go** iré; **~ I help you?** ¿quieres que te ayude?; **I'll buy three, ~ I?** compro tres, ¿no te parece?

**shallow** [ˈʃæləu] adj poco profundo; (fig) superficial

**sham** [ʃæm] n fraude m, engaño

**shambles** [ˈʃæmblz] n confusión f

**shame** [ʃeɪm] n vergüenza ▷ vt avergonzar; **it is a ~ that/to do** es una lástima or pena que/hacer; **what a ~!** ¡qué lástima or pena!; **shameful** adj vergonzoso; **shameless** adj descarado

**shampoo** [ʃæmˈpuː] n champú m ▷ vt lavar con champú

**shandy** [ˈʃændɪ] n clara, cerveza con gaseosa

**shan't** [ʃɑːnt] = **shall not**

**shape** [ʃeɪp] n forma ▷ vt formar, dar forma a; (sb's ideas) formar; (sb's life) determinar; **to take ~** tomar forma

**share** [ʃɛəʳ] n (part) parte f, porción f; (contribution) cuota; (Comm) acción f ▷ vt dividir; (have in common) compartir; **to ~ out (among** or **between)** repartir (entre); **shareholder** n (BRIT) accionista mf

**shark** [ʃɑːk] n tiburón m

**sharp** [ʃɑːp] adj (razor, knife) afilado; (point) puntiagudo; (outline) definido; (pain) intenso; (Mus) desafinado; (contrast) marcado; (voice) agudo; (person: quick-witted) avispado; (: dishonest) poco escrupuloso ▷ b (Mus) sostenido ▷ adv: **at two o'clock ~** a las dos en punto; **sharpen** vt afilar; (pencil) sacar punta a; (fig) agudizar; **sharpener** n (also: **pencil sharpener**) sacapuntas m inv; **sharply** adv (abruptly) bruscamente; (clearly) claramente; (harshly) severamente

**shatter** ['ʃætər] vt hacer añicos or pedazos; (fig: ruin) destruir, acabar con ⊳ vi hacerse añicos; **shattered** adj (grief-stricken) destrozado, deshecho; (exhausted) agotado, hecho polvo

**shave** [ʃeɪv] vt afeitar, rasurar ⊳ vi afeitarse ⊳ n: **to have a ~** afeitarse; **shaver** n (also: **electric shaver**) máquina de afeitar (eléctrica)

**shaving** ['ʃeɪvɪŋ] n (action) afeitado; **shavings** npl (of wood etc) virutas fpl; **shaving cream** n crema (de afeitar); **shaving foam** n espuma de afeitar

**shawl** [ʃɔːl] n chal m

**she** [ʃiː] pron ella

**sheath** [ʃiːθ] n vaina; (contraceptive) preservativo

**shed** (pt, pp shed) [ʃɛd] n cobertizo ⊳ vt (skin) mudar; (tears) derramar; (workers) despedir

**she'd** [ʃiːd] = she had; she would

**sheep** [ʃiːp] n (pl inv) oveja; **sheepdog** n perro pastor; **sheepskin** n piel f de carnero

**sheer** [ʃɪər] adj (utter) puro, completo; (steep) escarpado; (material) diáfano ⊳ adv verticalmente

**sheet** [ʃiːt] n (on bed) sábana; (of paper) hoja; (of glass, metal) lámina

**sheik(h)** [ʃeɪk] n jeque m

**shelf** (pl shelves) [ʃɛlf, ʃɛlvz] n estante m

**shell** [ʃɛl] n (on beach) concha; (of egg, nut etc) cáscara; (explosive) proyectil m, obús m; (of building) armazón m ⊳ vt (peas) desenvainar; (Mil) bombardear

**she'll** [ʃiːl] = she will; she shall

**shellfish** ['ʃɛlfɪʃ] n (pl inv) crustáceo; (pl: as food) mariscos mpl

**shelter** ['ʃɛltər] n abrigo, refugio ⊳ vt (aid) amparar, proteger; (give lodging to) abrigar ⊳ vi abrigarse, refugiarse; **sheltered** adj (life) protegido; (spot) abrigado

**shelves** [ʃɛlvz] npl of **shelf**

**shelving** ['ʃɛlvɪŋ] n estantería

**shepherd** ['ʃɛpəd] n pastor m ⊳ vt (guide) guiar, conducir; **shepherd's pie** n pastel de carne y puré de patatas

**sheriff** ['ʃɛrɪf] n (us) sheriff m

**sherry** ['ʃɛrɪ] n jerez m

**she's** [ʃiːz] = she is; she has

**Shetland** ['ʃɛtlənd] n (also: **the ~s, the ~ Isles**) las Islas fpl Shetland

**shield** [ʃiːld] n escudo; (Tech) blindaje m ⊳ vt: **to ~ (from)** proteger (de)

**shift** [ʃɪft] n (change) cambio; (at work) turno ⊳ vt trasladar; (remove) quitar ⊳ vi moverse

**shin** [ʃɪn] n espinilla

**shine** [ʃaɪn] (pt, pp shone) n brillo, lustre m ⊳ vi brillar, relucir ⊳ vt (shoes) lustrar,

sacar brillo a; **to ~ a torch on sth** dirigir una linterna hacia algo

**shingles** ['ʃɪŋglz] n (Med) herpes msg

**shiny** ['ʃaɪnɪ] adj brillante, lustroso

**ship** [ʃɪp] n buque m, barco ⊳ vt (goods) embarcar; (send) transportar or enviar por vía marítima; **shipment** n (goods) envío; **shipping** n (act) embarque m; (traffic) buques mpl; **shipwreck** n naufragio ⊳ vt: **to be shipwrecked** naufragar; **shipyard** n astillero

**shirt** [ʃəːt] n camisa; **in ~ sleeves** en mangas de camisa

**shit** [ʃɪt] (inf!) excl ¡mierda! (!)

**shiver** ['ʃɪvər] n escalofrío ⊳ vi temblar, estremecerse; (with cold) tiritar

**shock** [ʃɔk] n (impact) choque m; (Elec) descarga (eléctrica); (emotional) conmoción f; (start) sobresalto, susto; (Med) postración f nerviosa ⊳ vt dar un susto a; (offend) escandalizar; **shocking** adj (awful) espantoso; (improper) escandaloso

**shoe** (pt, pp shod) [ʃuː, ʃɒd] n zapato; (for horse) herradura ⊳ vt (horse) herrar; **shoelace** n cordón m; **shoe polish** n betún m; **shoeshop** n zapatería

**shone** [ʃɒn] pt, pp of **shine**

**shonky** ['ʃɒŋkɪ] adj (AUST, NZ inf) chapucero

**shook** [ʃʊk] pt of **shake**

**shoot** [ʃuːt] (pt, pp shot) n (on branch, seedling) retoño, vástago ⊳ vt disparar; (kill) matar a tiros; (execute) fusilar; (Cine: film, scene) rodar, filmar ⊳ vi (Football) chutar; **shoot down** vt (plane) derribar; **shoot up** vi (prices) dispararse; **shooting** n (shots) tiros mpl; (Hunting) caza con escopeta

**shop** [ʃɒp] n tienda; (workshop) taller m ⊳ vi (also: **go ~ping**) ir de compras; **shop assistant** n (BRIT) dependiente/a m/f; **shopkeeper** n tendero/a; **shoplifting** n ratería, robo (en las tiendas); **shopping** n (goods) compras fpl; **shopping bag** n bolsa (de compras); **shopping centre, (us) shopping center** n centro comercial; **shopping mall** n centro comercial; **shopping trolley** n (BRIT) carrito de la compra; **shop window** n escaparate m, vidriera (LAM)

**shore** [ʃɔːr] n orilla ⊳ vt: **to ~ (up)** reforzar; **on ~** en tierra

**short** [ʃɔːt] adj corto; (in time) breve, de corta duración; (person) bajo; (curt) brusco, seco; **(a pair of) ~s** (unos) pantalones mpl cortos; **to be ~ of sth** estar falto de algo; **in ~** en pocas palabras; **~ of doing ...** a menos que hagamos etc ...; **everything ~ of ...** todo menos ...; **it is ~ for** es la forma abreviada de; **to cut ~** (speech, visit)

interrumpir, terminar inesperadamente;
**to fall ~ of** no alcanzar; **to run ~ of sth**
acabársele algo; **to stop ~** parar en
seco; **to stop ~ of** detenerse antes de;
**shortage** ['ʃɔːtɪdʒ] n falta; **shortbread** n
galleta de mantequilla especie de mantecada;
**shortcoming** n defecto, deficiencia;
**short(crust) pastry** n (BRIT) pasta
quebradiza; **shortcut** n atajo; **shorten**
vt acortar; (visit) interrumpir; **shortfall** n
déficit m; **shorthand** n (BRIT) taquigrafía;
**short-lived** adj efímero; **shortly** adv en
breve, dentro de poco; **short-sighted** adj
(BRIT) miope; (fig) imprudente; **short-
sleeved** adj de manga corta; **short story**
n cuento; **short-tempered** adj enojadizo;
**short-term** adj (effect) a corto plazo
**shot** [ʃɔt] pt, pp of **shoot** ▷ n (sound) tiro,
disparo; (try) tentativa; (injection) inyección
f; (Phot) toma, fotografía; **like a ~** (without
any delay) como un rayo; **shotgun** n
escopeta
**should** [ʃud] aux vb: **I ~ go now** debo irme
ahora; **he ~ be there now** debe de haber
llegado (ya); **I ~ go if I were you** yo en tu
lugar me iría; **I ~ like to** me gustaría
**shoulder** ['ʃəuldə*] n hombro ▷ vt (fig)
cargar con; **shoulder blade** n omóplato
**shouldn't** ['ʃudnt] = **should not**
**shout** [ʃaut] n grito ▷ vt gritar ▷ vi gritar,
dar voces
**shove** [ʃʌv] n empujón m ▷ vt empujar; (inf:
put): **to ~ sth in** meter algo a empellones
**shovel** ['ʃʌvl] n pala; (mechanical)
excavadora ▷ vt mover con pala
**show** [ʃəu] (pt showed, pp shown) n
(of emotion) demostración f; (semblance)
apariencia; (exhibition) exposición f; (Theat)
función f, espectáculo ▷ vt mostrar,
enseñar; (courage etc) mostrar, manifestar;
(exhibit) exponer; (film) proyectar ▷ vi
mostrarse; (appear) aparecer; **on ~** (exhibits
etc) expuesto; **it's just for ~** es sólo para
impresionar; **show in** vt (person) hacer
pasar; **show off** vi (pej) presumir ▷ vt
(display) lucir; **show out** vt: **to ~ sb out**
acompañar a algn a la puerta; **show
up** vi (stand out) destacar; (inf: turn up)
presentarse ▷ vt (unmask) desenmascarar;
**show business** n el mundo del espectáculo
**shower** ['ʃauə*] n (rain) chaparrón m,
chubasco; (of stones etc) lluvia; (also: **~ bath**)
ducha ▷ vi llover ▷ vt: **to ~ sb with**
colmar a algn de algo; **to have** or **take a ~**
ducharse; **shower cap** n gorro de baño;
**shower gel** n gel de ducha
**showing** ['ʃəuɪŋ] n (of film) proyección f
**show jumping** n hípica
**shown** [ʃəun] pp of **show**

**show: show-off** ['ʃəuɔf] n (inf: person)
fanfarrón/ona m/f; **showroom** n sala de
muestras
**shrank** [ʃræŋk] pt of **shrink**
**shred** [ʃred] n (gen pl) triza, jirón m ▷ vt hacer
trizas; (Culin) desmenuzar
**shrewd** [ʃruːd] adj astuto
**shriek** [ʃriːk] n chillido ▷ vi chillar
**shrimp** [ʃrɪmp] n camarón m
**shrine** [ʃraɪn] n santuario, sepulcro
**shrink** (pt shrank, pp shrunk) [ʃrɪŋk, ʃræŋk,
ʃrʌŋk] vi encogerse; (be reduced) reducirse
▷ vt encoger ▷ n (inf, pej) loquero/a; **to ~
from (doing) sth** no atreverse a hacer algo
**shrivel** ['ʃrɪvl], **shrivel up** vt (dry) secar ▷ vi
secarse
**shroud** [ʃraud] n sudario ▷ vt: **~ed in
mystery** envuelto en el misterio
**Shrove Tuesday** ['ʃrəuv-] n martes m de
carnaval
**shrub** [ʃrʌb] n arbusto
**shrug** [ʃrʌg] n encogimiento de hombros
▷ vt, vi: **to ~ (one's shoulders)** encogerse de
hombros; **shrug off** vt negar importancia a
**shrunk** [ʃrʌŋk] pp of **shrink**
**shudder** ['ʃʌdə*] n estremecimiento,
escalofrío ▷ vi estremecerse
**shuffle** ['ʃʌfl] vt (cards) barajar; **to ~ (one's
feet)** arrastrar los pies
**shun** [ʃʌn] vt rehuir, esquivar
**shut** (pt, pp shut) [ʃʌt] vt cerrar ▷ vi cerrarse;
**shut down** vt, vi cerrar; **shut up** vi (inf: keep
quiet) callarse ▷ vt (close) cerrar; (silence)
callar; **shutter** n contraventana; (Phot)
obturador m
**shuttle** ['ʃʌtl] n lanzadera; (also: **~ service**:
Aviat) puente m aéreo; **shuttlecock** n
volante m
**shy** [ʃaɪ] adj tímido
**sibling** ['sɪblɪŋ] n (formal) hermano/a
**sick** [sɪk] adj (ill) enfermo; (nauseated)
mareado; (humour) morboso; **to be ~**
(BRIT) vomitar; **to feel ~** tener náuseas;
**to be ~ of** (fig) estar harto de; **sickening**
adj (fig) asqueroso; **sick leave** n baja por
enfermedad; **sickly** adj enfermizo; (taste)
empalagoso; **sickness** n enfermedad f, mal
m; (vomiting) náuseas fpl
**side** [saɪd] n lado; (of body) costado; (of lake)
orilla; (team) equipo; (of hill) ladera ▷ adj
(door, entrance) lateral ▷ vi: **to ~ with sb**
tomar partido por algn; **by the ~ of** al lado
de; **~ by ~** juntos/as; **from all ~s** de todos
lados; **to take ~s (with)** tomar partido (por);
**sideboard** n aparador m; **sideboards,**
(BRIT) **sideburns** npl patillas fpl; **sidelight** n
(Aut) luz f lateral; **sideline** n (Sport) línea de
banda; (fig) empleo suplementario; **side
road** n (BRIT) calle f lateral; **side street** n

calle f lateral; **sidetrack** vt (fig) desviar (de su propósito); **sidewalk** ['saɪdwɔːk] n (US) acera; **sideways** adv de lado

**siege** [siːdʒ] n cerco, sitio

**sieve** [sɪv] n colador m ▷ vt cribar

**sift** [sɪft] vt cribar ▷ vi: **to ~ through** (information) examinar cuidadosamente

**sigh** [saɪ] n suspiro ▷ vi suspirar

**sight** [saɪt] n (faculty) vista; (spectacle) espectáculo; (on gun) mira, alza ▷ vt divisar; **in ~** a la vista; **out of ~** fuera de (la) vista; **sightseeing** n turismo; **to go sightseeing** hacer turismo

**sign** [saɪn] n (with hand) señal f, seña; (trace) huella, rastro; (notice) letrero; (written) signo ▷ vt firmar; (Sport) fichar; **sign in** vi firmar el registro (al entrar); **sign on** vi (Mil) alistarse; (as unemployed) apuntarse al paro ▷ vt (Mil) alistar; (employee) contratar; **to ~ on for a course** matricularse en un curso; **sign over** vt: **to ~ sth over to sb** traspasar algo a algn; **sign up** vi (Mil) alistarse; (for course) inscribirse ▷ vt (player) fichar

**signal** ['sɪgnl] n señal f ▷ vi señalizar ▷ vt (person) hacer señas a; (message) transmitir

**signature** ['sɪgnətʃəʳ] n firma

**significance** [sɪg'nɪfɪkəns] n (importance) trascendencia

**significant** [sɪg'nɪfɪkənt] adj significativo; (important) trascendente

**signify** ['sɪgnɪfaɪ] vt significar

**sign language** n mímica, lenguaje m por or de señas

**signpost** ['saɪnpəust] n indicador m

**Sikh** [siːk] adj, n sij mf

**silence** ['saɪlns] n silencio ▷ vt hacer callar, acallar; (guns) reducir al silencio

**silent** ['saɪlnt] adj silencioso; (not speaking) callado; (film) mudo; **to keep** or **remain ~** guardar silencio

**silhouette** [sɪlu'ɛt] n silueta

**silicon chip** n chip m, plaqueta de silicio

**silk** [sɪlk] n seda ▷ cpd de seda

**silly** ['sɪlɪ] adj (person) tonto; (idea) absurdo

**silver** ['sɪlvəʳ] n plata; (money) moneda suelta ▷ adj de plata; **silver-plated** adj plateado

**SIM card** ['sɪm-] n (Tel) SIM card m or f, tarjeta SIM

**similar** ['sɪmɪləʳ] adj: **~ to** parecido or semejante a; **similarity** [sɪmɪ'lærɪtɪ] n semejanza; **similarly** adv del mismo modo

**simmer** ['sɪməʳ] vi hervir a fuego lento

**simple** ['sɪmpl] adj (easy) sencillo; (foolish) simple; (Comm) simple; **simplicity** [sɪm'plɪsɪtɪ] n sencillez f; **simplify** ['sɪmplɪfaɪ] vt simplificar; **simply** adv (live, talk) sencillamente; (just, merely) sólo

**simulate** ['sɪmjuleɪt] vt simular

**simultaneous** [sɪməl'teɪnɪəs] adj simultáneo; **simultaneously** adv simultáneamente

**sin** [sɪn] n pecado ▷ vi pecar

**since** [sɪns] adv desde entonces ▷ prep desde ▷ conj (time) desde que; (because) ya que, puesto que; **~ then, ever ~** desde entonces

**sincere** [sɪn'sɪəʳ] adj sincero; **sincerely** adv: **yours sincerely** (in letters) le saluda atentamente

**sing** (pt **sang**, pp **sung**) [sɪŋ, sæŋ, sʌŋ] vt cantar ▷ vi cantar

**Singapore** [sɪŋə'pɔːʳ] n Singapur m

**singer** ['sɪŋəʳ] n cantante mf

**singing** ['sɪŋɪŋ] n canto

**single** ['sɪŋgl] adj único, solo; (unmarried) soltero; (not double) individual, sencillo ▷ n (BRIT: also: **~ ticket**) billete m sencillo; (record) sencillo, single m; **singles** npl (Tennis) individual msg; **single out** vt (choose) escoger; **single bed** n cama individual; **single file** n: **in single file** en fila de uno; **single-handed** adv sin ayuda; **single-minded** adj resuelto, firme; **single parent** n (mother) madre f soltera; (father) padre m soltero; **single-parent family** familia monoparental; **single room** n habitación f individual

**singular** ['sɪŋgjuləʳ] adj raro, extraño; (outstanding) excepcional ▷ n (Ling) singular m

**sinister** ['sɪnɪstəʳ] adj siniestro

**sink** [sɪŋk] (pt **sank**, pp **sunk**) n fregadero ▷ vt (ship) hundir, echar a pique; (foundations) excavar; (piles etc): **to ~ sth into** hundir algo en ▷ vi hundirse; **sink in** vi (fig) penetrar, calar

**sinus** ['saɪnəs] n (Anat) seno

**sip** [sɪp] n sorbo ▷ vt sorber, beber a sorbitos

**sir** [səʳ] n señor m; **S~ John Smith** Sir John Smith; **yes ~** sí, señor

**siren** ['saɪərn] n sirena

**sirloin** ['səːlɔɪn] n solomillo

**sirloin steak** n filete m de solomillo

**sister** ['sɪstəʳ] n hermana; (BRIT: nurse) enfermera jefe; **sister-in-law** n cuñada

**sit** (pt, pp **sat**) [sɪt, sæt] vi sentarse; (be sitting) estar sentado; (assembly) reunirse; (for painter) posar ▷ vt (exam) presentarse a; **sit back** vi (in seat) recostarse; **sit down** vi sentarse; **sit on** vt fus (jury, committee) ser miembro de, formar parte de; **sit up** vi incorporarse; (not go to bed) no acostarse

**sitcom** ['sɪtkɔm] n abbr (TV: = situation comedy) telecomedia

**site** [saɪt] n sitio; (also: **building ~**) solar m ▷ vt situar

**sitting** ['sɪtɪŋ] n (of assembly etc) sesión f; (in canteen) turno; **sitting room** n sala de estar

**situated** ['sɪtjueɪtɪd] adj situado

**situation** [sɪtju'eɪʃən] n situación f; **"~s vacant"** (BRIT) "ofertas de trabajo"

**six** [sɪks] num seis; **sixteen** num dieciséis; **sixteenth** adj decimosexto; **sixth** [sɪksθ] adj sexto; **sixth form** n (BRIT) clase f de alumnos del sexto año (de 16 a 18 años de edad); **sixth-form college** n instituto m para alumnos de 16 a 18 años; **sixtieth** adj sexagésimo; **sixty** num sesenta

**size** [saɪz] n tamaño m; (extent) extensión f; (of clothing) talla; (of shoes) número; **sizeable** adj importante, considerable

**sizzle** ['sɪzl] vi crepitar

**skate** [skeɪt] n patín m; (fish: pl inv) raya ▷ vi patinar; **skateboard** n monopatín m; **skateboarding** n monopatín m; **skater** n patinador(a) m/f; **skating** n patinaje m; **skating rink** n pista de patinaje

**skeleton** ['skɛlɪtn] n esqueleto; (Tech) armazón m; (outline) esquema m

**sketch** [skɛtʃ] n (drawing) dibujo; (outline) esbozo, bosquejo; (Theat) pieza corta, sketch m ▷ vt dibujar; (plan etc: also: **~ out**) esbozar

**skewer** ['skjuːəʳ] n broqueta

**ski** [skiː] n esquí m ▷ vi esquiar; **ski boot** n bota de esquí

**skid** [skɪd] n patinazo ▷ vi patinar

**ski: skier** n esquiador(a) m/f; **skiing** n esquí m

**skilful**, (US) **skillful** ['skɪlful] adj diestro, experto

**ski lift** n telesilla m, telesquí m

**skill** [skɪl] n destreza, pericia; (technique) técnica; **skilled** adj hábil, diestro; (worker) cualificado

**skim** [skɪm] vt (milk) desnatar; (glide over) rozar, rasar ▷ vi: **to ~ through** (book) hojear; **skimmed milk** n leche f desnatada or descremada

**skin** [skɪn] n piel f; (complexion) cutis m ▷ vt (fruit etc) pelar; (animal) despellejar; **skinhead** n cabeza mf rapada, skin(head) mf; **skinny** adj flaco

**skip** [skɪp] n brinco, salto; (container) contenedor m ▷ vi brincar; (with rope) saltar a la comba ▷ vt (pass over) omitir, saltarse

**ski: ski pass** n forfait m (de esquí); **ski pole** n bastón m de esquiar

**skipper** ['skɪpəʳ] n (Naut, Sport) capitán m

**skipping rope** ['skɪpɪŋ-] n (BRIT) comba

**skirt** [skəːt] n falda, pollera (LAM) ▷ vt (go round) ladear

**skirting board** ['skəːtɪŋ-] n (BRIT) rodapié m

**ski slope** n pista de esquí

**ski suit** n traje m de esquiar

**skull** [skʌl] n calavera; (Anat) cráneo

**skunk** [skʌŋk] n mofeta

**sky** [skaɪ] n cielo; **skyscraper** n rascacielos m inv

**slab** [slæb] n (stone) bloque m; (flat) losa; (of cake) trozo

**slack** [slæk] adj (loose) flojo; (slow) de poca actividad; (careless) descuidado; **slacks** npl pantalones mpl

**slain** [sleɪn] pp of **slay**

**slam** [slæm] vt (throw) arrojar (violentamente); (criticize) vapulear, vituperar ▷ vi cerrarse de golpe; **to ~ the door** dar un portazo

**slander** ['slɑːndəʳ] n calumnia, difamación f

**slang** [slæŋ] n argot m; (jargon) jerga

**slant** [slɑːnt] n sesgo, inclinación f; (fig) punto de vista, interpretación f

**slap** [slæp] n palmada; (in face) bofetada ▷ vt dar una palmada/bofetada a; (paint etc): **to ~ sth on sth** embadurnar algo con algo ▷ adv (directly) de lleno

**slash** [slæʃ] vt acuchillar; (fig: prices) fulminar

**slate** [sleɪt] n pizarra ▷ vt (BRIT fig: criticize) vapulear

**slaughter** ['slɔːtəʳ] n (of animals) matanza; (of people) carnicería ▷ vt matar; **slaughterhouse** n matadero

**Slav** [slɑːv] adj eslavo

**slave** [sleɪv] n esclavo/a ▷ vi (also: **~ away**) trabajar como un negro; **slavery** n esclavitud f

**slay** (pt **slew**, pp **slain**) [sleɪ, sluː, sleɪn] vt matar

**sleazy** ['sliːzɪ] adj (fig: place) sórdido

**sledge** [slɛdʒ], (US) **sled** [slɛd] n trineo

**sleek** [sliːk] adj (shiny) lustroso

**sleep** [sliːp] (pt, pp **slept**) n sueño ▷ vi dormir; **to go to ~** dormirse; **sleep in** vi (oversleep) quedarse dormido; **sleeper** n (person) durmiente mf; (BRIT: Rail: on track) traviesa; (: train) coche-cama m; **sleeping bag** n saco de dormir; **sleeping car** n coche-cama m; **sleeping pill** n somnífero; **sleepover** n: **we're having a sleepover at Fiona's** nos quedamos a dormir en casa de Fiona; **sleepwalk** vi caminar dormido; (habitually) ser sonámbulo; **sleepy** adj soñoliento; (place) soporífero

**sleet** [sliːt] n aguanieve f

**sleeve** [sliːv] n manga; (Tech) manguito; (of record) funda; **sleeveless** adj sin mangas

**sleigh** [sleɪ] n trineo

**slender** ['slɛndəʳ] adj delgado; (means) escaso

**slept** [slɛpt] pt, pp of **sleep**

**slew** [slu:] vi (veer) torcerse ▷ pt of **slay**
**slice** [slaɪs] n (of meat) tajada; (of bread) rebanada; (of lemon) rodaja; (utensil) paleta ▷ vt cortar; rebanar
**slick** [slɪk] adj (skilful) hábil, diestro; (clever) astuto ▷ n (also: **oil ~**) marea negra
**slide** [slaɪd] (pt, pp **slid**) n (in playground) tobogán m; (Phot) diapositiva; (BRIT: also: **hair ~**) pasador m ▷ vt correr, deslizar ▷ vi (slip) resbalarse; (glide) deslizarse; **sliding** adj (door) corredizo
**slight** [slaɪt] adj (slim) delgado; (frail) delicado; (pain etc) leve; (trifling) insignificante; (small) pequeño ▷ n desaire m ▷ vt (offend) ofender, desairar; **not in the ~est** en absoluto; **slightly** adv ligeramente, un poco
**slim** [slɪm] adj delgado, esbelto ▷ vi adelgazar; **slimming** n adelgazamiento
**slimy** ['slaɪmɪ] adj cenagoso
**sling** (pt, pp **slung**) [slɪŋ, slʌŋ] n (Med) cabestrillo; (weapon) honda ▷ vt tirar, arrojar
**slip** [slɪp] n (slide) resbalón m; (mistake) descuido; (underskirt) combinación f; (of paper) papelito ▷ vt (slide) deslizar ▷ vi deslizarse; (stumble) resbalar(se); (decline) decaer; (move smoothly): **to ~ into/out of** (room etc) colarse en/salirse de; **to give sb the ~** dar esquinazo a algn; **a ~ of the tongue** un lapsus; **slip up** vi (make mistake) equivocarse; meter la pata
**slipper** ['slɪpə'] n zapatilla, pantufla
**slippery** ['slɪpərɪ] adj resbaladizo
**slip road** n (BRIT) carretera de acceso
**slit** [slɪt] (pt, pp **slit**) n raja; (cut) corte m ▷ vt rajar, cortar
**slog** [slɔg] (BRIT) vi sudar tinta ▷ n: **it was a ~** costó trabajo (hacerlo)
**slogan** ['sləugən] n eslogan m, lema m
**slope** [sləup] n (up) cuesta, pendiente f; (down) declive m; (side of mountain) falda, vertiente f ▷ vi: **to ~ down** estar en declive; **to ~ up** subir (en pendiente); **sloping** adj en pendiente; en declive
**sloppy** ['slɔpɪ] adj (work) descuidado; (appearance) desaliñado
**slot** [slɔt] n ranura ▷ vt: **to ~ into** encajar en; **slot machine** n (BRIT: vending machine) máquina expendedora; (for gambling) máquina tragaperras
**Slovakia** [sləu'vækɪə] n Eslovaquia
**Slovene** [sləu'vi:n] adj esloveno ▷ n esloveno/a; (Ling) esloveno
**Slovenia** [sləu'vi:nɪə] n Eslovenia; **Slovenian** adj, n = **Slovene**
**slow** [sləu] adj lento; (watch): **to be ~** ir atrasado ▷ adv lentamente, despacio ▷ vt (also: **~ down, ~ up**: engine, machine) reducir

la marcha de ▷ vi (also: **~ down, ~ up**) ir más despacio; **"~"** (road sign) "disminuir la velocidad"; **slowly** adv lentamente, despacio; **slow motion** n: **in slow motion** a cámara lenta
**slug** [slʌg] n babosa; (bullet) posta; **sluggish** adj lento; (lazy) perezoso
**slum** [slʌm] n casucha
**slump** [slʌmp] n (economic) depresión f ▷ vi hundirse; (prices) caer en picado
**slung** [slʌŋ] pt, pp of **sling**
**slur** [slə:'] n calumnia ▷ vt (word) pronunciar mal; **to cast a ~ on sb** manchar la reputación de algn, difamar a algn
**sly** [slaɪ] adj astuto; (nasty) malicioso
**smack** [smæk] n (slap) bofetada ▷ vt dar una manotada a ▷ vi: **to ~ of** saber a, oler a
**small** [smɔ:l] adj pequeño; **small ads** npl (BRIT) anuncios mpl por palabras; **small change** n suelto, cambio
**smart** [smɑ:t] adj elegante; (clever) listo, inteligente; (quick) rápido, vivo ▷ vi escocer, picar; **smartcard** n tarjeta inteligente; **smartphone** n smartphone m
**smash** [smæʃ] n (also: **~-up**) choque m; (sound) estrépito ▷ vt (break) hacer pedazos; (car etc) estrellar; (Sport: record) batir ▷ vi hacerse pedazos; (against wall etc) estrellarse; **smashing** adj (inf) estupendo
**smear** [smɪə'] n mancha; (Med) frotis m inv (cervical) ▷ vt untar; **smear test** n (Med) citología, frotis m inv (cervical)
**smell** [smɛl] (pt, pp **smelt** or **smelled**) n olor m; (sense) olfato ▷ vt, vi oler; **smelly** adj maloliente
**smelt** [smɛlt] pt, pp of **smell**
**smile** [smaɪl] n sonrisa ▷ vi sonreír
**smirk** [smə:k] n sonrisa falsa or afectada
**smog** [smɔg] n smog m
**smoke** [sməuk] n humo ▷ vi fumar; (chimney) echar humo ▷ vt (cigarettes) fumar; **smoke alarm** n detector m de humo, alarma contra incendios; **smoked** adj (bacon, glass) ahumado; **smoker** n fumador(a) m/f; **smoking** n: **"no smoking"** "prohibido fumar"; **smoky** adj (room) lleno de humo

> Be careful not to translate smoking by the Spanish word smoking.

**smooth** [smu:ð] adj liso; (sea) tranquilo; (flavour, movement) suave; (person: pej) meloso ▷ vt alisar; (also: **~ out**: creases) alisar; (difficulties) allanar
**smother** ['smʌðə'] vt sofocar; (repress) contener
**SMS** n abbr (= short message service) SMS m; **SMS message** n (mensaje m) SMS m
**smudge** [smʌdʒ] n mancha ▷ vt manchar
**smug** [smʌg] adj engreído

**smuggle** ['smʌgl] vt pasar de contrabando; **smuggling** n contrabando

**snack** [snæk] n bocado; **snack bar** n cafetería

**snag** [snæg] n problema m

**snail** [sneɪl] n caracol m

**snake** [sneɪk] n serpiente f

**snap** [snæp] n (sound) chasquido; (photograph) foto f ▷ adj (decision) instantáneo ▷ vt (break) quebrar – a mí quebrarse, (fig: person) contestar bruscamente; **to ~ shut** cerrarse de golpe; **snap at** vt fus: **to ~ (at sb)** (dog) intentar morder (a algn); **snap up** vt agarrar; **snapshot** n foto f (instantánea)

**snarl** [snɑːl] vi gruñir

**snatch** [snætʃ] n (small piece) fragmento ▷ vt (snatch away) arrebatar; (grasp) agarrar; **to ~ some sleep** buscar tiempo para dormir

**sneak** [sniːk] vi: **to ~ in/out** entrar/salir a hurtadillas ▷ n (inf) soplón/ona m/f; **to ~ up on sb** aparecérsele de improviso a algn; **sneakers** npl (US) zapatos mpl de lona

**sneer** [snɪər] vi sonreír con desprecio; **to ~ at sth/sb** burlarse or mofarse de algo/algn

**sneeze** [sniːz] vi estornudar

**sniff** [snɪf] vi sorber (por la nariz) ▷ vt husmear, oler; (glue, drug) esnifar

**snigger** ['snɪgər] vi reírse con disimulo

**snip** [snɪp] n (piece) recorte m; (bargain) ganga ▷ vt tijeretear

**sniper** ['snaɪpər] n francotirador(a) m/f

**snob** [snɒb] n (e)snob mf

**snooker** ['snuːkər] n snooker m, billar inglés

**snoop** [snuːp] vi: **to ~ about** fisgonear

**snooze** [snuːz] n siesta ▷ vi echar una siesta

**snore** [snɔːr] vi roncar ▷ n ronquido

**snorkel** ['snɔːkl] n tubo de respiración

**snort** [snɔːt] n bufido ▷ vi bufar

**snow** [snəu] n nieve f ▷ vi nevar; **snowball** n bola de nieve ▷ vi ir aumentando; **snowstorm** n tormenta de nieve, nevasca

**snub** [snʌb] vt: **to ~ sb** desairar a algn ▷ n desaire m, repulsa

**snug** [snʌg] adj (cosy) cómodo; (fitted) ajustado

### ○ KEYWORD

**so** [səu] adv **1** (thus, likewise) así, de este modo; **if so** de ser así; **I like swimming — so do I** a mí me gusta nadar — a mí también; **I've got work to do — so has Paul** tengo trabajo que hacer — Paul también; **it's five o'clock — so it is!** son las cinco — ¡pues es verdad!; **I hope/think so** espero/creo que sí; **so far** hasta ahora; (in past) hasta este momento

**2** (in comparisons etc: to such a degree) tan; **so quickly (that)** tan rápido (que); **she's not so clever as her brother** no es tan lista como su hermano; **we were so worried** estábamos preocupadísimos

**3**: **so much** adj tanto/a; adv tanto; **so many** tantos/as

**4** (phrases): **10 or so** unos 10, 10 o así; **so long!** (inf: goodbye) ¡hasta luego!

▶ conj **1** (expressing purpose): **so as to do** para hacer; **so (that)** para que + subjun

**2** (expressing result) así que; **so you see, I could have gone** así que ya ves, (yo) podría haber ido

**soak** [səuk] vt (drench) empapar; (put in water) remojar ▷ vi remojarse, estar a remojo; **soak up** vt absorber; **soaking** adj (also: **soaking wet**) calado or empapado (hasta los huesos or el tuétano)

**so-and-so** ['səuənsəu] n (somebody) fulano/a de tal

**soap** [səup] n jabón m; **soap opera** n telenovela; **soap powder** n jabón m en polvo

**soar** [sɔːr] vi (on wings) remontarse; (building etc) elevarse; (price) dispararse

**sob** [sɒb] n sollozo ▷ vi sollozar

**sober** ['səubər] adj (serious) serio; (not drunk) sobrio; (colour, style) discreto; **sober up** vi pasársele a algn la borrachera

**so-called** ['səu'kɔːld] adj llamado

**soccer** ['sɒkər] n fútbol m

**sociable** ['səuʃəbl] adj sociable

**social** ['səuʃl] adj social ▷ n velada, fiesta; **socialism** n socialismo; **socialist** adj, n socialista mf; **socialize** vi hacer vida social; **social life** n vida social; **socially** adv socialmente; **social media** npl medios sociales; **social networking** n interacción f social a través de la red; **social networking site** n red f social; **social security** n seguridad f social; **social services** npl servicios mpl sociales; **social work** n asistencia social; **social worker** n asistente/a m/f social

**society** [sə'saɪətɪ] n sociedad f; (club) asociación f; (also: **high ~**) alta sociedad

**sociology** [səusɪ'ɒlədʒɪ] n sociología

**sock** [sɒk] n calcetín m

**socket** ['sɒkɪt] n (Elec) enchufe m

**soda** ['səudə] n (Chem) sosa; (also: **~ water**) soda; (US: also: **~ pop**) gaseosa

**sodium** ['səudɪəm] n sodio

**sofa** ['səufə] n sofá m; **sofa bed** n sofá-cama m

**soft** [sɒft] adj (teacher, parent) blando; (gentle, not loud) suave; **soft drink** n bebida no alcohólica; **soft drugs** npl drogas *fpl* blandas; **soften** ['sɔfn] *vt* ablandar; suavizar ▷ *vi* ablandarse; suavizarse; **softly** *adv* suavemente; (*gently*) delicadamente, con delicadeza; **software** *n* (*Comput*) software *m*

**soggy** ['sɔgɪ] *adj* empapado

**soil** [sɔɪl] *n* (*earth*) tierra, suelo ▷ *vt* ensuciar

**solar** ['səʊlə'] *adj* solar; **solar power** *n* energía solar; **solar system** *n* sistema *m* solar

**sold** [səʊld] *pt, pp of* **sell**

**soldier** ['səʊldʒə'] *n* soldado; (*army man*) militar *m*

**sold out** *adj* (*Comm*) agotado

**sole** [səʊl] *n* (*of foot*) planta; (*of shoe*) suela; (*fish: pl inv*) lenguado ▷ *adj* único; **solely** *adv* únicamente, sólo, solamente; **I will hold you solely responsible** le consideraré el único responsable

**solemn** ['sɔləm] *adj* solemne

**solicitor** [sə'lɪsɪtə'] *n* (BRIT: *for wills etc*) ≈ notario/a; (*in court*) ≈ abogado/a

**solid** ['sɔlɪd] *adj* sólido; (*gold etc*) macizo ▷ *n* sólido

**solitary** ['sɔlɪtərɪ] *adj* solitario, solo

**solitude** ['sɔlɪtjuːd] *n* soledad *f*

**solo** ['səʊləʊ] *n* solo ▷ *adv* (*fly*) en solitario; **soloist** *n* solista *mf*

**soluble** ['sɔljubl] *adj* soluble

**solution** [sə'luːʃən] *n* solución *f*

**solve** [sɔlv] *vt* resolver, solucionar

**solvent** ['sɔlvənt] *adj* (*Comm*) solvente ▷ *n* (*Chem*) solvente *m*

**sombre**, (US) **somber** ['sɔmbə'] *adj* sombrío

 **KEYWORD**

**some** [sʌm] *adj* **1** (*a certain amount or number of*): **some tea/water/biscuits** té/agua/(unas) galletas; **there's some milk in the fridge** hay leche en el frigo; **there were some people outside** había algunas personas fuera; **I've got some money, but not much** tengo algo de dinero, pero no mucho

**2** (*certain: in contrasts*) algunos/as; **some people say that …** hay quien dice que …; **some films were excellent, but most were mediocre** hubo películas excelentes, pero la mayoría fueron mediocres

**3** (*unspecified*): **some woman was asking for you** una mujer estuvo preguntando por ti; **some day** algún día; **some day next week** un día de la semana que viene; **he was asking for some book (or other)** pedía no se qué libro

▶ *pron* **1** (*a certain number*): **I've got some** (*books etc*) tengo algunos/as

**2** (*a certain amount*) algo; **I've got some** (*money, milk*) tengo algo; **could I have some of that cheese?** ¿me puede dar un poco de ese queso?; **I've read some of the book** he leído parte del libro

▶ *adv*: **some 10 people** unas 10 personas, una decena de personas; **somebody** *pron* alguien; **somehow** *adv* de alguna manera; (*for some reason*) por una u otra razón; **someone** *pron* = **somebody**; **someplace** *adv* (US) = **somewhere**; **something** *pron* algo; **would you like something to eat/drink?** ¿te gustaría cenar/tomar algo?; **sometime** *adv* (*in future*) algún día, en algún momento; **sometime last month** durante el mes pasado; **sometimes** *adv* a veces; **somewhat** *adv* algo; **somewhere** *adv* (*be*) en alguna parte; (*go*) a alguna parte; **somewhere else** (*be*) en otra parte; (*go*) a otra parte

**son** [sʌn] *n* hijo

**song** [sɔŋ] *n* canción *f*

**son-in-law** ['sʌnɪnlɔː] *n* yerno

**soon** [suːn] *adv* pronto, dentro de poco; **~ afterwards** poco después; *see also* **as**; **sooner** *adv* (*time*) antes, más temprano; **I would sooner do that** preferiría hacer eso; **sooner or later** tarde o temprano

**soothe** [suːð] *vt* tranquilizar; (*pain*) aliviar

**sophisticated** [sə'fɪstɪkeɪtɪd] *adj* sofisticado

**sophomore** ['sɔfəmɔː'] *n* (US) estudiante *mf* de segundo año

**soprano** [sə'prɑːnəʊ] *n* soprano *f*

**sorbet** ['sɔːbeɪ] *n* sorbete *m*

**sordid** ['sɔːdɪd] *adj* (*place etc*) sórdido; (*motive etc*) mezquino

**sore** [sɔː'] *adj* (*painful*) doloroso, que duele ▷ *n* llaga

**sorrow** ['sɔrəʊ] *n* pena, dolor *m*

**sorry** ['sɔrɪ] *adj* (*regretful*) arrepentido; (*condition, excuse*) lastimoso; **~!** ¡perdón!, ¡perdone!; **~?** ¿cómo?; **I feel ~ for him** me da lástima *or* pena

**sort** [sɔːt] *n* clase *f*, género, tipo ▷ *vt* (*also:* **~ out**: *papers*) clasificar; (*organize*) ordenar, organizar; (*resolve: problem, situation etc*) arreglar, solucionar

**SOS** *n* SOS *m*

**so-so** ['səʊsəʊ] *adv* regular, así así

**sought** [sɔːt] *pt, pp of* **seek**

**soul** [səʊl] *n* alma *f*

**sound** [saʊnd] *adj* (*healthy*) sano; (*safe, not damaged*) en buen estado; (*dependable: person*) de fiar; (*sensible*) sensato, razonable ▷ *adv*: **~ asleep** profundamente dormido ▷ *n* (*noise*) sonido, ruido; (*volume: on TV etc*) volumen *m*; (*Geo*) estrecho ▷ *vt* (*alarm*) sonar ▷ vi sonar, resonar; (fig: seem) parecer; **to ~ like** sonar a; **soundtrack** n (of film) banda sonora

**soup** [su:p] n (thick) sopa; (thin) caldo

**sour** ['sauə<sup>r</sup>] adj agrio; (milk) cortado; **it's just ~ grapes!** (fig) ¡están verdes!

**source** [sɔ:s] n fuente f

**south** [sauθ] n sur m ▷ adj del sur ▷ adv al sur, hacia el sur; **South Africa** n Sudáfrica; **South African** adj, n sudafricano/a; **South America** n América del Sur, Sudamérica; **South American** adj, n sudamericano/a; **southbound** adj (con) rumbo al sur; **south-east** n sudeste m, sureste m ▷ adj (counties etc) (del) sudeste, (del) sureste; **southeastern** adj (del) sudeste, (del) sureste; **southern** adj del sur, meridional; **South Korea** n Corea del Sur; **South Pole** n Polo Sur; **southward(s)** adv hacia el sur; **south-west** n suroeste m; **southwestern** adj suroeste

**souvenir** [su:və'nɪə<sup>r</sup>] n recuerdo

**sovereign** ['sɔvrɪn] adj, n soberano/a

**sow**[1] [sau] n cerda, puerca

**sow**[2] (pt sowed, pp sown) [səu, səun] vt sembrar

**soya** ['sɔɪə], (US) **soy** [sɔɪ] n soja

**spa** [spɑ:] n balneario

**space** [speɪs] n espacio; (room) sitio ▷ vt (also: ~ out) espaciar; **spacecraft** n nave f espacial; **spaceship** n = **spacecraft**

**spacious** ['speɪʃəs] adj amplio

**spade** [speɪd] n (tool) pala; **spades** npl (Cards: British) picas fpl; (: Spanish) espadas fpl

**spaghetti** [spə'gɛtɪ] n espaguetis mpl

**Spain** [speɪn] n España

**spam** n (junk email) correo basura

**span** [spæn] n (of bird, plane) envergadura; (of arch) luz f; (in time) lapso ▷ vt extenderse sobre, cruzar; (fig) abarcar

**Spaniard** ['spænjəd] n español(a) m/f

**Spanish** ['spænɪʃ] adj español(a) ▷ n (Ling) español m, castellano; **the Spanish** npl los españoles

**spank** [spæŋk] vt zurrar

**spanner** ['spænə<sup>r</sup>] n (BRIT) llave f inglesa

**spare** [spɛə<sup>r</sup>] adj de reserva; (surplus) sobrante, de más ▷ n (part) pieza de repuesto ▷ vt (do without) pasarse sin; (refrain from hurting) perdonar; **to ~** (surplus) sobrante, de sobra; **spare part** n pieza de repuesto; **spare room** n cuarto de los invitados; **spare time** n tiempo libre; **spare tyre,** (US) **spare tire** n (Aut) neumático or llanta (LAM) de recambio; **spare wheel** n (Aut) rueda de recambio

**spark** [spɑ:k] n chispa; (fig) chispazo

**sparking plug** ['spɑ:k(ɪŋ)-] n = **spark plug**

**sparkle** ['spɑ:kl] n centelleo, destello ▷ vi (shine) relucir, brillar

**spark plug** n bujía

**sparrow** ['spærəu] n gorrión m

**sparse** [spɑ:s] adj esparcido, escaso

**spasm** ['spæzəm] n (Med) espasmo

**spat** [spæt] pt, pp of **spit**

**spate** [speɪt] n (fig): **~ of** torrente m de

**spatula** ['spætjulə] n espátula

**speak** (pt spoke, pp spoken) [spi:k, spəuk, 'spəukn] vt (language) hablar; (truth) decir ▷ vi hablar; (make a speech) intervenir; **to ~ to sb/of** or **about sth** hablar con algn/ de or sobre algo; **~ up!** ¡habla más alto!; **speaker** n (in public) orador(a) m/f; (also: **loudspeaker**) altavoz m; (for stereo etc) bafle m; **the Speaker** (Pol: BRIT) el Presidente de la Cámara de los Comunes; (: US) el Presidente del Congreso

**spear** [spɪə<sup>r</sup>] n lanza ▷ vt alancear

**special** ['spɛʃl] adj especial; (edition etc) extraordinario; (delivery) urgente; **special delivery** n (Post): **by special delivery** por entrega urgente; **special effects** n (Cine) efectos mpl especiales; **specialist** n especialista mf; **speciality** n especialidad f; **specialize** vi: **to specialize (in)** especializarse (en); **specially** adv especialmente; **special offer** n (Comm) oferta especial; **special school** n (BRIT) colegio m de educación especial; **specialty** n (US) = **speciality**

**species** ['spi:ʃi:z] n especie f

**specific** [spə'sɪfɪk] adj específico; **specifically** adv específicamente

**specify** ['spɛsɪfaɪ] vt, vi especificar, precisar

**specimen** ['spɛsɪmən] n ejemplar m; (Med: of urine) espécimen m; (: of blood) muestra

**speck** [spɛk] n grano, mota

**spectacle** ['spɛktəkl] n espectáculo; **spectacles** npl (BRIT: glasses) gafas fpl (SP), anteojos mpl; **spectacular** [spɛk'tækjulə<sup>r</sup>] adj espectacular; (success) impresionante

**spectator** [spɛk'teɪtə<sup>r</sup>] n espectador(a) m/f

**spectrum** (pl spectra) ['spɛktrəm, -trə] n espectro

**speculate** ['spɛkjuleɪt] vi especular; **to ~ about** especular sobre

**sped** [spɛd] pt, pp of **speed**

**speech** [spi:tʃ] n (faculty) habla; (formal talk) discurso; (language) lenguaje m; **speechless** adj mudo, estupefacto

**speed** [spi:d] n velocidad f; (haste) prisa; (promptness) rapidez f; **at full** or **top ~** a máxima velocidad; **speed up** vi acelerarse ▷ vt acelerar; **speedboat** n lancha motora; **speeding** n (Aut) exceso de velocidad; **speed limit** n límite m de velocidad, velocidad f máxima; **speedometer** [spɪ'dɔmɪtə<sup>r</sup>] n velocímetro; **speedy** adj (fast) veloz, rápido; (prompt) pronto

**spell** [spɛl] n (also: **magic ~**) encanto, hechizo; (period of time) rato, período ▷ vt deletrear; (fig) anunciar, presagiar; **to cast a ~ on sb** hechizar a algn; **he can't ~** comete faltas de ortografía; **spell out** vt (explain): **to ~ sth out for sb** explicar algo a algn en detalle; **spellchecker** n (Comput) corrector m (ortográfico); **spelling** n ortografía

**spelt** [spɛlt] pt, pp of **spell**

**spend** (pt, pp **spent**) [spɛnd, spɛnt] vt (money) gastar; (time) pasar; (life) dedicar; **spending** n: **government spending** gastos mpl del gobierno

**spent** [spɛnt] pt, pp of **spend** ▷ adj (cartridge, bullets, match) usado

**sperm** [spəːm] n esperma

**sphere** [sfɪəʳ] n esfera

**spice** [spaɪs] n especia ▷ vt especiar

**spicy** ['spaɪsɪ] adj picante

**spider** ['spaɪdəʳ] n araña

**spike** [spaɪk] n (point) punta; (Bot) espiga

**spill** (pt, pp **spilt** or **spilled**) [spɪl, spɪlt, spɪld] vt derramar, verter ▷ vi derramarse; **spill over** vi desbordarse

**spin** [spɪn] (pt, pp **spun**) n (Aviat) barrena; (trip in car) paseo (en coche) ▷ vt (wool etc) hilar; (wheel) girar ▷ vi girar, dar vueltas

**spinach** ['spɪnɪtʃ] n espinacas fpl

**spinal** ['spaɪnl] adj espinal

**spin doctor** n (inf) informador(a) parcial de servicio de un partido político

**spin-dryer** n (BRIT) secadora centrífuga

**spine** [spaɪn] n espinazo, columna vertebral; (thorn) espina

**spiral** ['spaɪərl] n espiral f ▷ vi (prices) dispararse

**spire** ['spaɪəʳ] n aguja, chapitel m

**spirit** ['spɪrɪt] n (soul) alma f; (ghost) fantasma m; (attitude) espíritu m; (courage) valor m, ánimo; **spirits** npl (drink) alcohol msg, bebidas fpl alcohólicas; **in good ~s** alegre, de buen ánimo

**spiritual** ['spɪrɪtjuəl] adj espiritual ▷ n espiritual m

**spit** (pt, pp **spat**) [spɪt, spæt] n (for roasting) asador m, espetón m; (saliva) saliva ▷ vi escupir; (sound) chisporrotear

**spite** [spaɪt] n rencor m, ojeriza ▷ vt fastidiar; **in ~ of** a pesar de, pese a; **spiteful** adj rencoroso, malévolo

**splash** [splæʃ] n (sound) chapoteo; (of colour) mancha ▷ vt salpicar ▷ vi (also: **~ about**) chapotear; **splash out** vi (BRIT inf) derrochar dinero

**splendid** ['splɛndɪd] adj espléndido

**splinter** ['splɪntəʳ] n astilla; (in finger) espigón m ▷ vi astillarse, hacer astillas

**split** [splɪt] (pt, pp **split**) n hendedura, raja; (fig) división f; (Pol) escisión f ▷ vt partir, rajar; (party) dividir; (work, profits) repartir ▷ vi dividirse, escindirse; **split up** vi (couple) separarse; (meeting) acabarse

**spoil** (pt, pp **spoilt** or **spoiled**) [spɔɪl, spɔɪlt, spɔɪld] vt (damage) dañar; (ruin) estropear, echar a perder; (child) mimar, consentir

**spoilt** [spɔɪlt] pt, pp of **spoil** ▷ adj (child) mimado, consentido; (ballot paper) invalidado

**spoke** [spəuk] pt of **speak** ▷ n rayo, radio

**spoken** ['spəukn] pp of **speak**

**spokesman** ['spəuksmən] n portavoz m

**spokesperson** ['spəukspə:sn] n portavoz mf, vocero/a (LAM)

**spokeswoman** ['spəukswumən] n portavoz f

**sponge** [spʌndʒ] n esponja; (also: **~ cake**) bizcocho ▷ vt (wash) lavar con esponja ▷ vi: **to ~ on** or (US) **off sb** vivir a costa de algn; **sponge bag** n (BRIT) neceser m

**sponsor** ['spɒnsəʳ] n patrocinador(a) m/f ▷ vt patrocinar; apadrinar; **sponsorship** n patrocinio

**spontaneous** [spɒn'teɪnɪəs] adj espontáneo

**spooky** ['spuːkɪ] adj (inf) espeluznante, horripilante

**spoon** [spuːn] n cuchara; **spoonful** n cucharada

**sport** [spɔːt] n deporte m; **to be a good ~** (person) ser muy majo; **sport jacket** n (US) = **sports jacket**; **sports car** n coche m sport; **sports centre** n (BRIT) polideportivo; **sports jacket, (US) sport jacket** n chaqueta deportiva; **sportsman** n deportista m; **sports utility vehicle** n todoterreno m inv; **sportswear** n ropa de deporte; **sportswoman** n deportista f; **sporty** adj deportivo

**spot** [spɒt] n sitio, lugar m; (dot: on pattern) punto, mancha; (pimple) grano ▷ vt (notice) notar, observar; **on the ~** en el acto; **spotless** adj (clean) inmaculado; (reputation) intachable; **spotlight** n foco, reflector m; (Aut) faro auxiliar

**spouse** [spauz] n cónyuge mf

**sprain** [spreɪn] n torcedura ▷ vt: **to ~ one's ankle** torcerse el tobillo

**sprang** [spræŋ] pt of **spring**

**sprawl** [sprɔːl] vi tumbarse

**spray** [spreɪ] n rociada; (of sea) espuma; (container) atomizador m; (of paint) pistola rociadora; (of flowers) ramita ▷ vt rociar; (crops) regar

**spread** [sprɛd] (pt, pp **spread**) n extensión f; (inf: food) comilona ▷ vt extender; (butter) untar; (wings, sails) desplegar; (scatter) esparcir ▷ vi (also: **~ out**: stain) extenderse; (news) diseminarse; **middle-age ~** gordura de la mediana edad; **repayments will be ~ over 18 months** los pagos se harán a lo largo de 18 meses; **spread out** vi (move apart) separarse; **spreadsheet** n (Comput) hoja de cálculo

**spree** [spriː] n: **to go on a ~** ir de juerga or farra (LAM)

**spring** [sprɪŋ] (pt **sprang**, pp **sprung**) n (season) primavera; (leap) salto, brinco; (coiled metal) resorte m; (of water) fuente f, manantial m ▷ vi saltar, brincar; **spring up** vi (thing: appear) aparecer; (problem) surgir; **spring onion** n cebolleta

**sprinkle** ['sprɪŋkl] vt (pour: liquid) rociar; (: salt, sugar) espolvorear; **to ~ water etc on, ~ with water etc** rociar or salpicar de agua etc

**sprint** [sprɪnt] n (e)sprint m ▷ vi esprintar

**sprung** [sprʌŋ] pp of **spring**

**spun** [spʌn] pt, pp of **spin**

**spur** [spəːʳ] n espuela; (fig) estímulo, aguijón m ▷ vt (also: **~ on**) estimular, incitar; **on the ~ of the moment** de improviso

**spurt** [spəːt] n chorro; (of energy) arrebato ▷ vi chorrear

**spy** [spaɪ] n espía mf ▷ vi: **to ~ on** espiar a ▷ vt (see) divisar, lograr ver

**sq.** abbr (Math etc) = **square**

**squabble** ['skwɔbl] vi reñir, pelear

**squad** [skwɔd] n (Mil) pelotón m; (Police) brigada; (Sport) equipo

**squadron** ['skwɔdrn] n (Mil) escuadrón m; (Aviat, Naut) escuadra

**squander** ['skwɔndəʳ] vt (money) derrochar, despilfarrar; (chances) desperdiciar

**square** [skwɛəʳ] n cuadro; (in town) plaza; (inf: person) carca mf ▷ adj cuadrado; (inf: ideas, tastes) trasnochado ▷ vt (arrange) arreglar; (Math) cuadrar; (reconcile) compaginar; **all ~** igual(es); **a ~ meal** una comida decente; **two metres ~** dos metros por dos; **one ~ metre** un metro cuadrado; **square root** n raíz f cuadrada

**squash** [skwɔʃ] n (vegetable) calabaza; (Sport) squash m; (BRIT: drink): **lemon/ orange ~** zumo (SP) or jugo (LAM) de limón/ naranja ▷ vt aplastar

**squat** [skwɔt] adj achaparrado ▷ vi agacharse, sentarse en cuclillas; **squatter** n okupa mf

**squeak** [skwiːk] vi (hinge, wheel) chirriar, rechinar; (mouse) chillar

**squeal** [skwiːl] vi chillar, dar gritos agudos

**squeeze** [skwiːz] n presión f; (of hand) apretón m; (Comm) restricción f ▷ vt (hand, arm) apretar

**squid** [skwɪd] n (inv) calamar m

**squint** [skwɪnt] vi bizquear, ser bizco ▷ n (Med) estrabismo

**squirm** [skwəːm] vi retorcerse, revolverse

**squirrel** ['skwɪrəl] n ardilla

**squirt** [skwəːt] vi salir a chorros ▷ vt chiscar

**Sr** abbr = **senior**

**Sri Lanka** [srɪ'læŋkə] n Sri Lanka m

**St** abbr (= saint) Sto./a.; (= street) c/

**stab** [stæb] n (with knife etc) puñalada; (of pain) pinchazo; **to have a ~ at (doing) sth** (inf) probar (a hacer) algo ▷ vt apuñalar

**stability** [stə'bɪlɪtɪ] n estabilidad f

**stable** ['steɪbl] adj estable ▷ n cuadra, caballeriza

**stack** [stæk] n montón m, pila ▷ vt amontonar, apilar

**stadium** ['steɪdɪəm] n estadio

**staff** [stɑːf] n (work force) personal m, plantilla; (BRIT Scol) cuerpo docente ▷ vt proveer de personal

**stag** [stæg] n ciervo, venado

**stage** [steɪdʒ] n escena; (point) etapa; (platform) plataforma; **the ~** el teatro ▷ vt (play) poner en escena, representar; (organize) montar, organizar; **in ~s** por etapas

**stagger** ['stægəʳ] vi tambalear ▷ vt (amaze) asombrar; (hours, holidays) escalonar; **staggering** adj asombroso

**stagnant** ['stægnənt] adj estancado

**stag night, stag party** n despedida de soltero

**stain** [steɪn] n mancha; (colouring) tintura ▷ vt manchar; (wood) teñir; **stained glass** n vidrio m de color; **stainless steel** n acero inoxidable

**stair** [stɛəʳ] n (step) peldaño; **stairs** npl escaleras fpl

**staircase** ['stɛəkeɪs], **stairway** ['stɛəweɪ] n escalera

**stake** [steɪk] n estaca, poste m; (Comm) interés m; (Betting) apuesta ▷ vt (bet) apostar; **to be at ~** estar en juego; **to ~ a claim to (sth)** presentar reclamación por or reclamar (algo)

**stale** [steɪl] adj (bread) duro; (food) pasado; (smell) rancio; (beer) agrio

**stalk** [stɔːk] n tallo, caña ▷ vt acechar, cazar al acecho

**stall** n (in market) puesto; (in stable) casilla (de establo) ▷ vt (Aut) calar; (fig) dar largas a ▷ vi (Aut) pararse, calarse; (fig) buscar evasivas

**stamina** ['stæmɪnə] n resistencia

**stammer** ['stæməʳ] n tartamudeo ▷ vi tartamudear

**stamp** [stæmp] n sello, estampilla (LAM); (mark) marca, huella; (on document) timbre m ▷ vi (also: **~ one's foot**) patear ▷ vt (letter) poner sellos en, franquear; (with rubber stamp) marcar con sello; **~ed addressed envelope (sae)** sobre m franqueado con la dirección propia; **stamp out** vt (fire) apagar con el pie; (crime, opposition) acabar con

**stampede** [stæm'pi:d] n estampida

**stance** [stæns] n postura

**stand** [stænd] (pt, pp **stood**) n (attitude) posición f, postura; (for taxis) parada; (also: **music ~**) atril m; (Sport) tribuna; (at exhibition) stand m ▷ vi (be) estar, encontrarse; (be on foot) estar de pie; (rise) levantarse; (remain) quedar en pie ▷ vt (place) poner, colocar; (tolerate, withstand) aguantar, soportar; **to make a ~** (fig) mantener una postura firme; **to ~ for parliament** (BRIT) presentarse (como candidato) a las elecciones; **stand back** vi retirarse; **stand by** vi (be ready) estar listo ▷ vt fus (opinion) mantener; **stand down** vi (withdraw) ceder el puesto; (Mil, Law) retirarse; **stand for** vt fus (signify) significar; (tolerate) aguantar, permitir; **stand in for** vt fus suplir a; **stand out** vi destacarse; **stand up** vi levantarse, ponerse de pie; **stand up for** vt fus defender; **stand up to** vt fus hacer frente a

**standard** ['stændəd] n patrón m, norma; (flag) estandarte m ▷ adj (size etc) normal, corriente, estándar; **standards** npl (morals) valores mpl morales; **standard of living** n nivel m de vida

**standing** ['stændɪŋ] adj (on foot) de pie, en pie; (permanent) permanente ▷ n reputación f; **of many years' ~** que lleva muchos años; **standing order** n (BRIT: at bank) giro bancario

**stand: standpoint** n punto de vista; **standstill** n: **at a standstill** (industry, traffic) paralizado; **to come to a standstill** pararse, quedar paralizado

**stank** [stæŋk] pt of **stink**

**staple** ['steɪpl] n (for papers) grapa ▷ adj (crop, industry, food etc) básico ▷ vt grapar

**star** [stɑ:ʳ] n estrella; (celebrity) estrella, astro ▷ vi: **to ~ in** ser la estrella de; **the stars** npl (Astrology) el horóscopo

**starboard** ['stɑ:bəd] n estribor m

**starch** [stɑ:tʃ] n almidón m

**stardom** ['stɑ:dəm] n estrellato

**stare** [steəʳ] n mirada fija ▷ vi: **to ~ at** mirar fijo

**stark** [stɑ:k] adj (bleak) severo, escueto ▷ adv: **~ naked** en cueros

**start** [stɑ:t] n principio, comienzo; (departure) salida; (sudden movement) sobresalto; (advantage) ventaja ▷ vt empezar, comenzar; (cause) causar; (found) fundar; (engine) poner en marcha ▷ vi

comenzar, empezar; (with fright) asustarse, sobresaltarse; (train etc) salir; **to ~ doing** or **to do sth** empezar a hacer algo; **start off** vi empezar, comenzar; (leave) salir, ponerse en camino; **start out** vi (begin) empezar; (set out) partir, salir; **start up** vi comenzar; (car) ponerse en marcha ▷ vt comenzar; (car) poner en marcha; **starter** n (Aut) botón m de arranque; (Sport: official) juez mf de salida; (: runner) corredor(a) m/f; (BRIT Culin) entrada, entrante m; **starting point** n punto de partida

**startle** ['stɑ:tl] vt sobresaltar; **startling** adj alarmante

**starvation** [stɑ:'veɪʃən] n hambre f

**starve** [stɑ:v] vi pasar hambre; (to death) morir de hambre ▷ vt hacer pasar hambre

**state** [steɪt] n estado ▷ vt (say, declare) afirmar; **to be in a ~** estar agitado; **the S~s** los Estados Unidos; **statement** n afirmación f; **state school** n escuela or colegio estatal; **statesman** n estadista m

**static** ['stætɪk] n (Radio) parásitos mpl ▷ adj estático

**station** ['steɪʃən] n estación f; (Radio) emisora; (rank) posición f social ▷ vt colocar, situar; (Mil) apostar

**stationary** ['steɪʃnərɪ] adj estacionario, fijo

**stationer's (shop)** n (BRIT) papelería

**stationery** ['steɪʃənərɪ] n papel m de escribir; (writing materials) artículos mpl de escritorio

**station wagon** n (US) coche m familiar con ranchera

**statistic** [stə'tɪstɪk] n estadística; **statistics** n (science) estadística

**statue** ['stætju:] n estatua

**stature** ['stætʃəʳ] n estatura; (fig) talla

**status** ['steɪtəs] n estado; (reputation) estatus m; **status quo** n (e)statu quo m

**statutory** ['stætjutrɪ] adj estatutario

**staunch** [stɔ:ntʃ] adj leal, incondicional

**stay** [steɪ] n estancia ▷ vi quedar(se); (as guest) hospedarse; **to ~ put** seguir en el mismo sitio; **to ~ the night/5 days** pasar la noche/estar or quedarse 5 días; **stay away** vi (from person, building) no acercarse; (from event) no acudir; **stay behind** vi quedar atrás; **stay in** vi quedarse en casa; **stay on** vi quedarse; **stay out** vi (of house) no volver a casa; (strikers) no volver al trabajo; **stay up** vi (at night) velar, no acostarse

**steadily** ['stedɪlɪ] adv (firmly) firmemente; (unceasingly) sin parar; (fixedly) fijamente

**steady** ['stedɪ] adj (fixed) firme; (regular) regular; (boyfriend etc) formal, fijo; (person, character) sensato, juicioso ▷ vt (stabilize) estabilizar; (nerves) calmar

**steak** [steɪk] n filete m; (beef) bistec m

**steal** (*pt* **stole**, *pp* **stolen**) [stiːl, stəul, 'stəuln] *vt*, *vi* robar

**steam** [stiːm] *n* vapor *m*; (*mist*) vaho, humo ▷ *vt* (*Culin*) cocer al vapor ▷ *vi* echar vapor; **steam up** *vi* (*window*) empañarse; **to get ~ed up about sth** (*fig*) ponerse negro por algo; **steamy** *adj* (*room*) lleno de vapor; (*window*) empañado; (*heat, atmosphere*) bochornoso

**steel** [stiːl] *n* acero ▷ *adj* de acero

**steep** [stiːp] *adj* escarpado, abrupto; (*stair*) empinado; (*price*) exorbitante, excesivo ▷ *vt* empapar, remojar

**steeple** [ˈstiːpl] *n* aguja

**steer** [stɪəʳ] *vt* (*car*) conducir (*SP*), manejar (*LAM*); (*person*) dirigir ▷ *vi* conducir (*SP*), manejar (*LAM*); **steering** *n* (*Aut*) dirección *f*; **steering wheel** *n* volante *m*

**stem** [stɛm] *n* (*of plant*) tallo; (*of glass*) pie *m* ▷ *vt* detener; (*blood*) restañar

**step** [stɛp] *n* paso; (*stair*) peldaño, escalón *m* ▷ *vi*: **to ~ forward** dar un paso adelante; **steps** *npl* (*BRIT*) = **stepladder**; **to be in/out of ~ with** estar acorde con/estar en disonancia con; **step down** *vi* (*fig*) retirarse; **step in** *vi* entrar; (*fig*) intervenir; **step up** *vt* (*increase*) aumentar; **stepbrother** *n* hermanastro; **stepchild** (*pl* **stepchildren**) *n* hijastro/a; **stepdaughter** *n* hijastra; **stepfather** *n* padrastro; **stepladder** *n* escalera doble *or* de tijera; **stepmother** *n* madrastra; **stepsister** *n* hermanastra; **stepson** *n* hijastro

**stereo** [ˈstɛrɪəu] *n* estéreo ▷ *adj* (*also*: **~phonic**) estéreo, estereofónico

**stereotype** [ˈstɪərɪətaɪp] *n* estereotipo ▷ *vt* estereotipar

**sterile** [ˈstɛraɪl] *adj* estéril; **sterilize** [ˈstɛrɪlaɪz] *vt* esterilizar

**sterling** [ˈstəːlɪŋ] *adj* (*silver*) de ley ▷ *n* (*Econ*) libras *fpl* esterlinas; **a pound ~** una libra esterlina

**stern** [stəːn] *adj* severo, austero ▷ *n* (*Naut*) popa

**steroid** [ˈstɪərɔɪd] *n* esteroide *m*

**stew** [stjuː] *n* estofado ▷ *vt*, *vi* estofar, guisar; (*fruit*) cocer

**steward** [ˈstjuːəd] *n* camarero; **stewardess** *n* azafata

**stick** [stɪk] (*pt*, *pp* **stuck**) *n* palo; (*as weapon*) porra; (*also*: **walking ~**) bastón *m* ▷ *vt* (*glue*) pegar; (*inf*: *put*) meter; (: *tolerate*) aguantar, soportar ▷ *vi* pegarse; (*come to a stop*) quedarse parado; **it stuck in my mind** se me quedó grabado; **stick out** *vi* sobresalir; **stick up** *vi* sobresalir; **stick up for** *vt fus* defender; **sticker** *n* (*label*) etiqueta adhesiva; (*with slogan*) pegatina; **sticking plaster** *n* (*BRIT*) esparadrapo; **stick insect**

*n* insecto palo; **stick shift** *n* (*US Aut*) palanca de cambios

**sticky** [ˈstɪkɪ] *adj* pegajoso; (*label*) adhesivo; (*fig*) difícil

**stiff** [stɪf] *adj* rígido, tieso; (*hard*) duro; (*difficult*) difícil; (*person*) inflexible; (*price*) exorbitante ▷ *adv*: **scared/bored ~** muerto de miedo/aburrimiento

**stifling** [ˈstaɪflɪŋ] *adj* (*heat*) sofocante, bochornoso

**stigma** [ˈstɪgmə] *n* estigma *m*

**stiletto** [stɪˈlɛtəu] *n* (*BRIT*: *also*: **~ heel**) tacón *m* de aguja

**still** [stɪl] *adj* inmóvil, quieto ▷ *adv* todavía; (*even*) aún; (*nonetheless*) sin embargo, aun así

**stimulate** [ˈstɪmjuleɪt] *vt* estimular

**stimulus** (*pl* **stimuli**) [ˈstɪmjuləs, -laɪ] *n* estímulo, incentivo

**sting** [stɪŋ] (*pt*, *pp* **stung**) *n* (*wound*) picadura; (*pain*) escozor *m*, picazón *m*; (*organ*) aguijón *m* ▷ *vt* picar ▷ *vi* picar

**stink** (*pt* **stank**, *pp* **stunk**) [stɪŋk, stæŋk, stʌŋk] *n* hedor *m*, tufo ▷ *vi* heder, apestar

**stir** [stəːʳ] *n* (*fig*: *agitation*) conmoción *f* ▷ *vt* (*tea etc*) remover; (*fig*: *emotions*) provocar ▷ *vi* moverse; **stir up** *vt* (*trouble*) fomentar; **stir-fry** *vt* sofreír removiendo ▷ *n* plato preparado sofriendo y removiendo los ingredientes

**stitch** [stɪtʃ] *n* (*Sewing*) puntada; (*Knitting*) punto; (*Med*) punto (de sutura); (*pain*) punzada ▷ *vt* coser; (*Med*) suturar

**stock** [stɔk] *n* (*Comm*: *reserves*) existencias *fpl*, stock *m*; (: *selection*) surtido; (*Agr*) ganado, ganadería; (*Culin*) caldo; (*fig*: *lineage*) estirpe *f*; (*Finance*) capital *m* ▷ *adj* (*reply etc*) clásico ▷ *vt* (*have in stock*) tener existencias de; **stocks** *npl*: **~s and shares** acciones y valores; **in ~** en existencia *or* almacén; **out of ~** agotado; **to take ~ of** (*fig*) considerar, examinar; **stockbroker** [ˈstɔkbrəukəʳ] *n* agente *mf or* corredor(a) *m/f* de bolsa; **stock cube** *n* pastilla *or* cubito de caldo; **stock exchange** *n* bolsa; **stockholder** [ˈstɔkhəuldəʳ] *n* (*US*) accionista *mf*

**stocking** [ˈstɔkɪŋ] *n* media

**stock market** *n* bolsa (de valores)

**stole** [stəul] *pt* of **steal** ▷ *n* estola

**stolen** [ˈstəuln] *pp* of **steal**

**stomach** [ˈstʌmək] *n* (*Anat*) estómago; (*belly*) vientre *m* ▷ *vt* tragar, aguantar; **stomachache** *n* dolor *m* de estómago

**stone** [stəun] *n* piedra; (*in fruit*) hueso; (*BRIT*: *weight*) = 6.348 kg; 14lb ▷ *adj* de piedra ▷ *vt* apedrear; (*fruit*) deshuesar

**stood** [stud] *pt*, *pp* of **stand**

**stool** [stuːl] *n* taburete *m*

**stoop** [stu:p] vi (also: ~ **down**) doblarse, agacharse; (also: **have a ~**) ser cargado de espaldas; (bend) inclinarse

**stop** [stɔp] n parada; (in punctuation) punto ▷ vt parar, detener; (break off) suspender; (block: pay) suspender; (: cheque) invalidar; (also: **put a ~ to**) poner término a ▷ vi pararse, detenerse; (end) acabarse; **to ~ doing sth** dejar de hacer algo; **stop by** vi pasar por; **stop off** vi interrumpir el viaje; **stopover** n parada intermedia; (Aviat) escala; **stoppage** n (strike) paro; (blockage) obstrucción f

**storage** ['stɔ:rɪdʒ] n almacenaje m

**store** [stɔ:ʳ] n (stock) provisión f; (depot) almacén m; (BRIT: large shop) almacén m; (US) tienda; (reserve) reserva, repuesto ▷ vt almacenar; **stores** npl víveres mpl; **who knows what is in ~ for us** quién sabe lo que nos espera; **storekeeper** n (US) tendero/a

**storey**, (US) **story** ['stɔ:rɪ] n piso

**storm** [stɔ:m] n tormenta; (fig: of applause) salva; (: of criticism) nube f ▷ vi (fig) rabiar ▷ vt tomar por asalto; **stormy** adj tempestuoso

**story** ['stɔ:rɪ] n historia; (lie) cuento; (US) = **storey**

**stout** [staut] adj (strong) sólido; (fat) gordo, corpulento ▷ n cerveza negra

**stove** [stəuv] n (for cooking) cocina; (for heating) estufa

**straight** [streɪt] adj recto, derecho; (frank) franco, directo ▷ adv derecho, directamente; (drink) solo; **to put** or **get sth ~** dejar algo en claro; **~ away, ~ off** en seguida; **straighten** vt (also: **straighten out**) enderezar, poner derecho ▷ vi (also: **straighten up**) enderezarse, ponerse derecho; **straightforward** [streɪt'fɔ:wəd] adj (simple) sencillo; (honest) sincero

**strain** [streɪn] n tensión f; (Tech) presión f; (Med) torcedura; (of virus) variedad f ▷ vt (back etc) torcerse; (resources) agotar; (stretch) estirar; (filter) filtrar; **strained** adj (muscle) torcido; (laugh) forzado; (relations) tenso; **strainer** n colador m

**strait** [streɪt] n (Geo) estrecho; **to be in dire ~s** (fig) estar en un gran aprieto

**strand** [strænd] n (of thread) hebra; (of rope) ramal m; **a ~ of hair** un pelo; **stranded** adj (person: without money) desamparado; (: without transport) colgado

**strange** [streɪndʒ] adj (not known) desconocido; (odd) extraño, raro; **strangely** adv de un modo raro; see also **enough**; **stranger** n desconocido/a; (from another area) forastero/a

> Be careful not to translate stranger by the Spanish word extranjero.

**strangle** ['stræŋgl] vt estrangular

**strap** [stræp] n correa; (of slip, dress) tirante m

**strategic** [strə'ti:dʒɪk] adj estratégico

**strategy** ['strætɪdʒɪ] n estrategia

**straw** [strɔ:] n paja; (also: **drinking ~**) caña, pajita; **that's the last ~!** ¡eso es el colmo!

**strawberry** ['strɔ:bərɪ] n fresa, frutilla (LAM)

**stray** [streɪ] adj (animal) extraviado; (bullet) perdido; (scattered) disperso ▷ vi extraviarse, perderse

**streak** [stri:k] n raya ▷ vt rayar ▷ vi: **to ~ past** pasar como un rayo

**stream** [stri:m] n riachuelo, arroyo; (jet) chorro; (flow) corriente f; (of people) oleada ▷ vt (Scol) dividir en grupos por habilidad ▷ vi correr, fluir; **to ~ in/out** (people) entrar/salir en tropel

**street** [stri:t] n calle f; **streetcar** n (US) tranvía m; **street light** n farol m (LAM), farola (SP); **street map** n plano (de la ciudad); **street plan** n plano callejero

**strength** [streŋθ] n fuerza; (of girder, knot etc) resistencia; (fig: power) poder m; **strengthen** vt fortalecer, reforzar

**strenuous** ['strenjuəs] adj (energetic) enérgico

**stress** [stres] n presión f; (mental strain) estrés m; (Ling, Poetry) acento ▷ vt subrayar, recalcar; **stressed** adj (tense) estresado, agobiado; (syllable) acentuado; **stressful** adj (job) estresante

**stretch** [stretʃ] n (of sand etc) trecho ▷ vi estirarse; (extend): **to ~ to** or **as far as** extenderse hasta ▷ vt extender, estirar; (make demands of) exigir el máximo esfuerzo a; **stretch out** vi tenderse ▷ vt (arm etc) extender; (spread) estirar

**stretcher** ['stretʃəʳ] n camilla

**strict** [strɪkt] adj estricto; (discipline, ban) severo; **strictly** adv estrictamente; (totally) terminantemente

**stride** (pt **strode**, pp **stridden**) [straɪd, strəud, 'strɪdn] n zancada, tranco ▷ vi dar zancadas, andar a trancos

**strike** [straɪk] (pt, pp **struck**) n huelga; (of oil etc) descubrimiento; (attack) ataque m ▷ vt golpear, pegar; (oil etc) descubrir; (agreement, deal) alcanzar ▷ vi declarar la huelga; (attack) atacar; (clock) dar la hora; **on ~** (workers) en huelga; **to ~ a match** encender una cerilla; **striker** n huelguista mf; (Sport) delantero; **striking** ['straɪkɪŋ] adj (colour) llamativo; (obvious) notorio

**string** (pt, pp **strung**) [strɪŋ, strʌŋ] n cuerda; (row) hilera ▷ vt: **to ~ together** ensartar; **to ~ out** extenderse; **the strings**

*npl* (*Mus*) los instrumentos de cuerda; **to
pull ~s** (*fig*) mover palancas

**strip** [strɪp] *n* tira; (*of land*) franja; (*of metal*)
cinta, lámina ▷ *vt* desnudar; (*also:* **~ down**:
*machine*) desmontar ▷ *vi* desnudarse;
**strip off** *vt* (*paint etc*) quitar ▷ *vi* (*person*)
desnudarse

**stripe** [straɪp] *n* raya; (*Mil*) galón *m*; **striped**
*adj* a rayas, rayado

**stripper** ['strɪpə'] *n* artista *mf* de striptease

**strip-search** ['strɪpsə:tʃ] *vt*: **to ~ sb**
desnudar y registrar a algn

**strive** (*pt* **strove**, *pp* **striven**) [straɪv,
strəʊv, 'strɪvn] *vi*: **to ~ to do sth** esforzarse
*or* luchar por hacer algo

**strode** [strəʊd] *pt of* **stride**

**stroke** [strəʊk] *n* (*blow*) golpe *m*;
(*Swimming*) brazada; (*Med*) apoplejía ▷ *vt*
acariciar; **at a ~** de golpe

**stroll** [strəʊl] *n* paseo, vuelta ▷ *vi* dar
un paseo *or* una vuelta; **stroller** *n* (*us:
pushchair*) cochecito

**strong** [strɔŋ] *adj* fuerte; **they are 50 ~** son
50; **stronghold** *n* fortaleza; (*fig*) baluarte
*m*; **strongly** *adv* fuertemente, con fuerza;
(*believe*) firmemente

**strove** [strəʊv] *pt of* **strive**

**struck** [strʌk] *pt, pp of* **strike**

**structure** ['strʌktʃə'] *n* estructura;
(*building*) construcción *f*

**struggle** ['strʌgl] *n* lucha ▷ *vi* luchar

**strung** [strʌŋ] *pt, pp of* **string**

**stub** [stʌb] *n* (*of ticket etc*) matriz *f*; (*of
cigarette*) colilla ▷ *vt*: **to ~ one's toe on sth**
dar con el dedo del pie contra algo; **stub
out** *vt* apagar

**stubble** ['stʌbl] *n* rastrojo; (*on chin*) barba
(incipiente)

**stubborn** ['stʌbən] *adj* terco, testarudo

**stuck** [stʌk] *pt, pp of* **stick** ▷ *adj* (*jammed*)
atascado

**stud** [stʌd] *n* (*shirt stud*) corchete *m*; (*of boot*)
taco; (*earring*) pendiente *m* (de bolita);
(*also:* **~ farm**) caballeriza; (*also:* **~ horse**)
caballo semental ▷ *vt* (*fig*): **~ded with**
salpicado de

**student** ['stju:dənt] *n* estudiante *mf* ▷ *adj*
estudiantil; **student driver** *n* (*us Aut*)
aprendiz(a) *m/f* de conductor; **students'
union** *n* (*BRIT: association*) sindicato
de estudiantes; (*: building*) centro de
estudiantes

**studio** ['stju:dɪəʊ] *n* estudio; (*artist's*) taller
*m*; **studio flat** *n* estudio

**study** ['stʌdɪ] *n* estudio ▷ *vt* estudiar;
(*examine*) examinar, investigar ▷ *vi* estudiar

**stuff** [stʌf] *n* materia; (*substance*) material
*m*, sustancia; (*things, belongings*) cosas *fpl*
▷ *vt* llenar; (*Culin*) rellenar; (*animal*) disecar;

**stuffing** *n* relleno; **stuffy** *adj* (*room*) mal
ventilado; (*person*) de miras estrechas

**stumble** ['stʌmbl] *vi* tropezar, dar un
traspié; **stumble across** *vt fus* (*fig*)
tropezar con

**stump** [stʌmp] *n* (*of tree*) tocón *m*; (*of limb*)
muñón *m* ▷ *vt*: **to be ~ed for an answer**
quedarse sin saber qué contestar

**stun** [stʌn] *vt* aturdir

**stung** [stʌŋ] *pt, pp of* **sting**

**stunk** [stʌŋk] *pp of* **stink**

**stunned** [stʌnd] *adj* (*dazed*) aturdido,
atontado; (*amazed*) pasmado; (*shocked*)
anonadado

**stunning** ['stʌnɪŋ] *adj* (*fig: news*) pasmoso;
(*: outfit etc*) sensacional

**stunt** [stʌnt] *n* (*in film*) escena peligrosa;
(*also:* **publicity ~**) truco publicitario

**stupid** ['stju:pɪd] *adj* estúpido,
tonto; **stupidity** [stju:'pɪdɪtɪ] *n* estupidez *f*

**sturdy** ['stə:dɪ] *adj* robusto, fuerte

**stutter** ['stʌtə'] *n* tartamudeo ▷ *vi*
tartamudear

**style** [staɪl] *n* estilo; **stylish** *adj* elegante, a
la moda; **stylist** *n* (*hair stylist*) peluquero/a

**sub...** [sʌb] *pref* sub...; **subconscious** *adj*
subconsciente

**subdued** [səb'dju:d] *adj* (*light*) tenue;
(*person*) sumiso, manso

**subject** *n* ['sʌbdʒɪkt] súbdito; (*Scol*) tema *m*,
materia; (*Grammar*) sujeto ▷ *vt* [səb'dʒɛkt]:
**to ~ sb to sth** someter a algn a algo ▷ *adj*
['sʌbdʒɪkt]: **to be ~ to** (*law*) estar sujeto
a; (*person*) ser propenso a; **subjective**
[səb'dʒɛktɪv] *adj* subjetivo; **subject matter**
*n* (*content*) contenido

**subjunctive** [səb'dʒʌŋktɪv] *adj, n*
subjuntivo

**submarine** [sʌbmə'ri:n] *n* submarino

**submission** [səb'mɪʃən] *n* sumisión *f*

**submit** [səb'mɪt] *vt* someter ▷ *vi* someterse

**subordinate** [sə'bɔ:dɪnət] *adj, n*
subordinado/a

**subscribe** [səb'skraɪb] *vi* suscribir; **to ~ to**
(*fund, opinion*) suscribir, aprobar;
(*newspaper*) suscribirse a

**subscription** [səb'skrɪpʃən] *n* abono; (*to
magazine*) suscripción *f*

**subsequent** ['sʌbsɪkwənt] *adj*
subsiguiente, posterior; **subsequently** *adv*
posteriormente, más tarde

**subside** [səb'saɪd] *vi* hundirse; (*flood*) bajar;
(*wind*) amainar

**subsidiary** [səb'sɪdɪərɪ] *n* sucursal *f*, filial *f*

**subsidize** ['sʌbsɪdaɪz] *vt* subvencionar

**subsidy** ['sʌbsɪdɪ] *n* subvención *f*

**substance** ['sʌbstəns] *n* sustancia

**substantial** [səb'stænʃl] *adj* sustancial,
sustancioso; (*fig*) importante

**substitute** ['sʌbstɪtjuːt] n (person)
suplente mf; (thing) sustituto ▷ vt: **to ~ A
for B** sustituir B por A, reemplazar A por B;
**substitution** n sustitución f
**subtle** ['sʌtl] adj sutil
**subtract** [səb'trækt] vt restar; sustraer
**suburb** ['sʌbəːb] n barrio residencial; **the ~s**
las afueras (de la ciudad); **suburban**
[sə'bəːbən] adj suburbano; (train etc) de
cercanías
**subway** ['sʌbweɪ] n (BRIT) paso
subterráneo or inferior; (US) metro
**succeed** [sək'siːd] vi (person) tener éxito;
(plan) salir bien ▷ vt suceder a; **to ~ in doing**
lograr hacer
**success** [sək'sɛs] n éxito; **successful**
adj (venture) de éxito, exitoso (esp LAM);
**successfully** adv con éxito

> Be careful not to translate success by the
> Spanish word suceso.

**succession** [sək'sɛʃən] n sucesión f, serie f
**successive** [sək'sɛsɪv] adj sucesivo
**successor** [sək'sɛsəʳ] n sucesor(a) m/f
**succumb** [sə'kʌm] vi sucumbir
**such** [sʌtʃ] adj tal, semejante; (of that kind):
**~ a book** tal libro; (so much): **~ courage**
tanto valor ▷ adv tan; **~ a long trip** un viaje
tan largo; **~ a lot of** tanto; **~ as** (like) tal
como; **as ~** como tal; **such-and-such** adj
tal o cual
**suck** [sʌk] vt chupar; (bottle) sorber; (breast)
mamar
**Sudan** [su'dæn] n Sudán m
**sudden** ['sʌdn] adj (rapid) repentino,
súbito; (unexpected) imprevisto; **all of a ~** de
repente; **suddenly** adv de repente
**sudoku** [su'dəukuː] n sudoku m
**sue** [suː] vt demandar
**suede** [sweɪd] n ante m, gamuza (LAM)
**suffer** ['sʌfəʳ] vt sufrir, padecer; (tolerate)
aguantar, soportar ▷ vi sufrir, padecer;
**to ~ from** padecer, sufrir; **suffering** n
sufrimiento
**suffice** [sə'faɪs] vi bastar, ser suficiente
**sufficient** [sə'fɪʃənt] adj suficiente,
bastante
**suffocate** ['sʌfəkeɪt] vi ahogarse, asfixiarse
**sugar** ['ʃugəʳ] n azúcar m ▷ vt echar azúcar
a, azucarar
**suggest** [sə'dʒɛst] vt sugerir; **suggestion**
[sə'dʒɛstʃən] n sugerencia
**suicide** ['suɪsaɪd] n suicidio; (person) suicida
mf; **to commit ~** suicidarse; **suicide attack**
n atentado suicida; **suicide bomber** n
terrorista mf suicida; **suicide bombing** n
atentado m suicida
**suit** [suːt] n traje m; (Law) pleito; (Cards)
palo ▷ vt convenir; (clothes) sentar bien a, ir
bien a; (adapt): **to ~ sth to** adaptar or ajustar

algo a; **well ~ed** (couple) hechos el uno para
el otro; **suitable** adj conveniente; (apt)
indicado; **suitcase** n maleta, valija (LAM)
**suite** [swiːt] n (of rooms) suite f; (Mus) suite f;
(furniture): **bedroom/dining room ~** (juego
de) dormitorio/comedor m; **a three-piece ~**
un tresillo
**sulfur** ['sʌlfəʳ] n (US) = sulphur
**sulk** [sʌlk] vi estar de mal humor
**sulphur**, (US) **sulfur** ['sʌlfəʳ] n azufre m
**sultana** [sʌl'tɑːnə] n (fruit) pasa de Esmirna
**sum** [sʌm] n suma; (total) total m; **sum up**
vt resumir ▷ vi hacer un resumen
**summarize** ['sʌməraɪz] vt resumir
**summary** ['sʌmərɪ] n resumen m ▷ adj
(justice) sumario
**summer** ['sʌməʳ] n verano ▷ adj de verano;
**in (the) ~** en (el) verano; **summer holidays**
npl vacaciones fpl de verano; **summertime**
n (season) verano
**summit** ['sʌmɪt] n cima, cumbre f; (also:
**~ conference**) (conferencia) cumbre f
**summon** ['sʌmən] vt (person) llamar;
(meeting) convocar
**sun** [sʌn] n sol m
**Sun.** abbr (=Sunday) dom.
**sun: sunbathe** vi tomar el sol; **sunbed**
n cama solar; **sunblock** n filtro solar;
**sunburn** n (painful) quemadura del sol;
(tan) bronceado; **sunburnt, sunburned**
adj (tanned) bronceado; (painfully) quemado
por el sol
**Sunday** ['sʌndɪ] n domingo
**sunflower** ['sʌnflauəʳ] n girasol m
**sung** [sʌŋ] pp of **sing**
**sunglasses** ['sʌnglɑːsɪz] npl gafas fpl de sol
**sunk** [sʌŋk] pp of **sink**
**sun: sunlight** n luz f del sol; **sun lounger** n
tumbona, perezosa (LAM); **sunny** ['sʌnɪ]
adj soleado; (day) de sol; (fig) alegre; **sunrise**
n salida del sol; **sun roof** n (Aut) techo
corredizo or solar; **sunscreen** n filtro solar;
**sunset** n puesta del sol; **sunshade** n (over
table) sombrilla; **sunshine** ['sʌnʃaɪn] n
sol m; **sunstroke** n insolación f; **suntan** n
bronceado; **suntan lotion** n bronceador m;
**suntan oil** n aceite m bronceador
**super** ['suːpəʳ] adj (inf) genial
**superb** [suː'pəːb] adj magnífico,
espléndido
**superficial** [suːpə'fɪʃəl] adj superficial
**superintendent** [suːpərɪn'tɛndənt] n
director(a) m/f; (also: **police ~**) subjefe/a
m/f
**superior** [su'pɪərɪəʳ] adj superior; (smug)
desdeñoso ▷ n superior m
**superlative** [su'pəːlətɪv] n superlativo
**supermarket** ['suːpəmɑːkɪt] n
supermercado

**supernatural** [suːpəˈnætʃərəl] *adj*
sobrenatural ▷ *n*: **the ~** lo sobrenatural
**superpower** [ˈsuːpəpauəʳ] *n* (*Pol*)
superpotencia
**superstition** [suːpəˈstɪʃən] *n* superstición *f*
**superstitious** [suːpəˈstɪʃəs] *adj*
supersticioso
**superstore** [ˈsuːpəstɔː] *n* (*BRIT*)
hipermercado
**supervise** [ˈsuːpəvaɪz] *vt* supervisar;
**supervision** [suːpəˈvɪʒən] *n* supervisión *f*;
**supervisor** *n* supervisor(a) *m/f*
**supper** [ˈsʌpəʳ] *n* cena
**supple** [ˈsʌpl] *adj* flexible
**supplement** *n* [ˈsʌplɪmənt] suplemento
▷ *vt* [sʌplɪˈmɛnt] suplir
**supplier** [səˈplaɪəʳ] *n* (*Comm*) distribuidor(a)
*m/f*
**supply** [səˈplaɪ] *vt* (*provide*) suministrar;
(*equip*): **to ~ (with)** proveer (de) ▷ *n*
provisión *f*; (*of gas, water etc*) suministro;
**supplies** *npl* (*food*) víveres *mpl*; (*Mil*)
pertrechos *mpl*
**support** [səˈpɔːt] *n* apoyo; (*Tech*) soporte
*m* ▷ *vt* apoyar; (*financially*) mantener;
(*uphold*) sostener; **supporter** *n* (*Pol etc*)
partidario/a; (*Sport*) aficionado/a

█ Be careful not to translate *support* by the
Spanish word *soportar*.

**suppose** [səˈpəuz] *vt* suponer; (*imagine*)
imaginarse; **to be ~d to do sth** deber hacer
algo; **supposedly** [səˈpəuzɪdlɪ] *adv* según
cabe suponer; **supposing** *conj* en caso de
que
**suppress** [səˈprɛs] *vt* suprimir; (*yawn*)
ahogar
**supreme** [suˈpriːm] *adj* supremo
**surcharge** [ˈsɜːtʃɑːdʒ] *n* sobretasa, recargo
**sure** [ʃuəʳ] *adj* seguro; (*definite, convinced*)
cierto; **to make ~ of sth/that** asegurarse
de algo/asegurar que; **~!** (*of course*) ¡claro!,
¡por supuesto!; **~ enough** efectivamente;
**surely** *adv* (*certainly*) seguramente
**surf** [sɜːf] *n* olas *fpl* ▷ *vt*: **to ~ the Net**
navegar por Internet
**surface** [ˈsɜːfɪs] *n* superficie *f* ▷ *vt* (*road*)
revestir ▷ *vi* salir a la superficie; **surface
mail** *n* vía terrestre
**surfboard** [ˈsɜːfbɔːd] *n* tabla (de surf)
**surfer** [ˈsɜːfəʳ] *n* surfista *mf*; **web** or **net ~**
internauta *mf*
**surfing** [ˈsɜːfɪŋ] *n* surf *m*
**surge** [sɜːdʒ] *n* oleada, oleaje *m* ▷ *vi* (*wave*)
romper; (*people*) avanzar a tropel
**surgeon** [ˈsɜːdʒən] *n* cirujano/a
**surgery** [ˈsɜːdʒərɪ] *n* cirugía; (*BRIT: room*)
consultorio
**surname** [ˈsɜːneɪm] *n* apellido
**surpass** [sɜːˈpɑːs] *vt* superar, exceder

**surplus** [ˈsɜːpləs] *n* excedente *m*; (*Comm*)
superávit *m* ▷ *adj* excedente, sobrante
**surprise** [səˈpraɪz] *n* sorpresa ▷ *vt*
sorprender; **surprised** *adj* (*look, smile*) de
sorpresa; **to be surprised** sorprenderse;
**surprising** *adj* sorprendente; **surprisingly**
*adv* (*easy, helpful*) de modo sorprendente
**surrender** [səˈrɛndəʳ] *n* rendición *f*, entrega
▷ *vi* rendirse, entregarse
**surround** [səˈraund] *vt* rodear,
circundar; (*Mil etc*) cercar; **surrounding**
*adj* circundante; **surroundings** *npl*
alrededores *mpl*, cercanías *fpl*
**surveillance** [sɜːˈveɪləns] *n* vigilancia
**survey** *n* [ˈsɜːveɪ] inspección *f*
reconocimiento; (*inquiry*) encuesta
▷ *vt* [sɜːˈveɪ] examinar, inspeccionar;
(*look at*) mirar, contemplar; **surveyor** *n*
agrimensor(a) *m/f*
**survival** [səˈvaɪvl] *n* supervivencia
**survive** [səˈvaɪv] *vi* sobrevivir; (*custom
etc*) perdurar ▷ *vt* sobrevivir a; **survivor** *n*
superviviente *mf*
**suspect** *adj, n* [ˈsʌspɛkt] sospechoso/a ▷ *vt*
[səsˈpɛkt] sospechar
**suspend** [səsˈpɛnd] *vt* suspender;
**suspended sentence** *n* (*Law*) libertad *f*
condicional; **suspenders** *npl* (*BRIT*) ligas *fpl*;
(*US*) tirantes *mpl*
**suspense** [səsˈpɛns] *n* incertidumbre *f*,
duda; (*in film etc*) suspense *m*; **to keep sb
in ~** mantener a algn en suspense
**suspension** [səsˈpɛnʃən] *n* suspensión *f*;
(*of driving licence*) privación *f*; **suspension
bridge** *n* puente *m* colgante
**suspicion** [səsˈpɪʃən] *n* sospecha; (*distrust*)
recelo; **suspicious** *adj* receloso; (*causing
suspicion*) sospechoso
**sustain** [səsˈteɪn] *vt* sostener, apoyar;
(*suffer*) sufrir, padecer
**SUV** [ˈɛsˈjuːˈviː] *n abbr* (= *sports utility vehicle*)
todoterreno *m inv*, cuatro por cuatro *m inv*
**swallow** [ˈswɔləu] *n* (*bird*) golondrina ▷ *vt*
tragar
**swam** [swæm] *pt of* **swim**
**swamp** [swɔmp] *n* pantano, ciénaga ▷ *vt*
abrumar, agobiar
**swan** [swɔn] *n* cisne *m*
**swap** [swɔp] *n* canje *m* ▷ *vt*: **to ~ (for)**
canjear (por), cambiar (por)
**swarm** [swɔːm] *n* (*of bees*) enjambre *m*; (*fig*)
multitud *f* ▷ *vi* (*bees*) formar un enjambre;
(*fig*) pulular
**sway** [sweɪ] *vi* mecerse, balancearse ▷ *vt*
(*influence*) mover, influir en
**swear** (*pt* **swore**, *pp* **sworn**) [swɛəʳ,
swɔː, swɔːn] *vi* jurar *vt*: jurar; **swear
in** *vt*: **to be sworn in** prestar juramento;
**swearword** *n* taco, palabrota

**sweat** [swɛt] n sudor m ▷ vi sudar
**sweater** ['swɛtəʳ] n suéter m
**sweatshirt** ['swɛtʃəːt] n sudadera
**sweaty** ['swɛtɪ] adj sudoroso
**Swede** [swiːd] n sueco/a
**swede** [swiːd] n (BRIT) nabo
**Sweden** ['swiːdn] n Suecia
**Swedish** ['swiːdɪʃ] adj, n (Ling) sueco
**sweep** [swiːp] (pt, pp **swept**) n (act) barrida;
(also: **chimney ~**) deshollinador(a) m/f
▷ vt barrer; (with arm) empujar; (current)
arrastrar ▷ vi barrer
**sweet** [swiːt] n (BRIT: candy) dulce m,
caramelo; (: pudding) postre m ▷ adj dulce;
(charming: smile, character) dulce, amable;
**sweetcorn** n maíz m (dulce); **sweetener**
['swiːtnəʳ] n (Culin) edulcorante m;
**sweetheart** n novio/a; **sweetshop** n
(BRIT) confitería, bombonería
**swell** [swɛl] (pt **swelled**, pp **swollen** or
**swelled**) n (of sea) marejada, oleaje m ▷ adj
(US inf: excellent) estupendo, fenomenal ▷ vt
hinchar, inflar ▷ vi (also: **~ up**) hincharse;
(numbers) aumentar; (sound, feeling) ir
aumentando; **swelling** n (Med) hinchazón f
**swept** [swɛpt] pt, pp of **sweep**
**swerve** [swəːv] vi desviarse bruscamente
**swift** [swɪft] n (bird) vencejo ▷ adj rápido,
veloz
**swim** [swɪm] (pt **swam**, pp **swum**) n:
**to go for a ~** ir a nadar or a bañarse ▷ vi
nadar; (head, room) dar vueltas ▷ vt pasar a
nado; **to go ~ming** ir a nadar; **swimmer** n
nadador(a) m/f; **swimming** n natación f;
**swimming costume** n bañador m, traje m
de baño; **swimming pool** n piscina, alberca
(LAM); **swimming trunks** npl bañador msg;
**swimsuit** n = **swimming costume**
**swing** [swɪŋ] (pt, pp **swung**) n (in
playground) columpio; (movement) balanceo,
vaivén m; (change of direction) viraje m; (rhythm)
ritmo ▷ vt balancear; (also: **~ round**)
voltear, girar ▷ vi balancearse, columpiarse;
(also: **~ round**) dar media vuelta; **to be in
full ~** estar en plena marcha
**swipe card** [swaɪp-] n tarjeta magnética
deslizante, tarjeta swipe
**swirl** [swəːl] vi arremolinarse
**Swiss** [swɪs] adj, n (pl inv) suizo/a
**switch** [swɪtʃ] n (for light, radio etc)
interruptor m; (change) cambio ▷ vt
(change) cambiar de; **switch off** vt apagar;
(engine) parar; **switch on** vt encender,
prender (LAM); (engine, machine) arrancar;
**switchboard** n (Tel) centralita (de
teléfonos), conmutador m (LAM)
**Switzerland** ['swɪtsələnd] n Suiza
**swivel** ['swɪvl] vi (also: **~ round**) girar
**swollen** ['swəulən] pp of **swell**

**swoop** [swuːp] n (by police etc) redada ▷ vi
(also: **~ down**) caer en picado
**swop** [swɔp] n, vb = **swap**
**sword** [sɔːd] n espada; **swordfish** n pez m
espada
**swore** [swɔːʳ] pt of **swear**
**sworn** [swɔːn] pp of **swear** ▷ adj (statement)
bajo juramento; (enemy) implacable
**swum** [swʌm] pp of **swim**
**swung** [swʌŋ] pt, pp of **swing**
**syllable** ['sɪləbl] n sílaba
**syllabus** ['sɪləbəs] n programa m de
estudios
**symbol** ['sɪmbl] n símbolo
**symbolic(al)** [sɪm'bɔlɪk(l)] adj simbólico;
**to be symbolic of sth** simbolizar algo
**symmetrical** [sɪ'mɛtrɪkl] adj simétrico
**symmetry** ['sɪmɪtrɪ] n simetría
**sympathetic** [sɪmpə'θɛtɪk] adj
(understanding) comprensivo; **to
be ~ towards** (person) ser comprensivo con
▌ Be careful not to translate sympathetic
by the Spanish word simpático.
**sympathize** ['sɪmpəθaɪz] vi: **to ~ with**
(person) compadecerse de; (feelings)
comprender; (cause) apoyar
**sympathy** ['sɪmpəθɪ] n (pity) compasión f
**symphony** ['sɪmfənɪ] n sinfonía
**symptom** ['sɪmptəm] n síntoma m, indicio
**synagogue** ['sɪnəgɔg] n sinagoga
**syndicate** ['sɪndɪkɪt] n sindicato; (Press)
agencia (de noticias)
**syndrome** ['sɪndrəum] n síndrome m
**synonym** ['sɪnənɪm] n sinónimo
**synthetic** [sɪn'θɛtɪk] adj sintético
**Syria** ['sɪrɪə] n Siria
**syringe** [sɪ'rɪndʒ] n jeringa
**syrup** ['sɪrəp] n jarabe m, almíbar m
**system** ['sɪstəm] n sistema m; (Anat)
organismo; **systematic** [sɪstə'mætɪk] adj
sistemático; metódico; **systems analyst** n
analista mf de sistemas

**ta** [tɑ:] *excl* (BRIT inf) ¡gracias!
**tab** [tæb] *n* lengüeta; (*label*) etiqueta; **to keep ~s on** (*fig*) vigilar
**table** ['teɪbl] *n* mesa; (*of statistics etc*) cuadro, tabla ▷ *vt* (BRIT: *motion etc*) presentar; **to lay** *or* **set the ~** poner la mesa; **tablecloth** *n* mantel *m*; **table d'hôte** [tɑ:bl'dəut] *n* menú *m*; **table lamp** *n* lámpara de mesa; **tablemat** *n* (*for plate*) posaplatos *m inv*; (*for hot dish*) salvamanteles *m inv*; **tablespoon** *n* cuchara grande; (*also:* **tablespoonful**: *as measurement*) cucharada grande
**tablet** ['tæblɪt] *n* (*Med*) pastilla, comprimido; (*of stone*) lápida; (*Comput*) tableta, tablet *f*
**table tennis** *n* ping-pong *m*, tenis *m* de mesa
**tabloid** ['tæblɔɪd] *n* periódico popular sensacionalista
**taboo** [tə'bu:] *adj*, *n* tabú *m*
**tack** [tæk] *n* (*nail*) tachuela ▷ *vt* (*nail*) clavar con tachuelas; (*stitch*) hilvanar ▷ *vi* virar
**tackle** ['tækl] *n* (*gear*) equipo; (*fishing tackle, for lifting*) aparejo ▷ *vt* (*difficulty*) enfrentarse a; (*challenge: person*) hacer frente a; (*grapple with*) agarrar; (*Football*) entrar a; (*Rugby*) placar
**tacky** ['tækɪ] *adj* pegajoso; (*inf*) hortera *inv*, de mal gusto
**tact** [tækt] *n* tacto, discreción *f*; **tactful** *adj* discreto, diplomático
**tactics** ['tæktɪks] *npl* táctica *sg*
**tactless** ['tæktlɪs] *adj* indiscreto
**tadpole** ['tædpəul] *n* renacuajo
**taffy** ['tæfɪ] *n* (US) melcocha
**tag** [tæg] *n* (*label*) etiqueta
**tail** [teɪl] *n* cola; (*of shirt, coat*) faldón *m* ▷ *vt* (*follow*) vigilar a; **tails** *npl* (*formal suit*) levita
**tailor** ['teɪlə'] *n* sastre *m*

**Taiwan** [taɪ'wɑ:n] *n* Taiwán *m*; **Taiwanese** *adj*, *n* taiwanés/esa
**take** [teɪk] (*pt* **took**, *pp* **taken**) *vt* tomar; (*grab*) coger (SP), agarrar (LAM); (*gain: prize*) ganar; (*require: effort, courage*) exigir; (*support weight of*) aguantar; (*hold: passengers etc*) tener cabida para; (*accompany, bring, carry*) llevar; (*exam etc*) presentarse a; **to ~ sth from** (*drawer etc*) sacar algo de; (*person*) quitar algo a, coger algo a (SP); **I ~ it that …** supongo que …; **take after** *vt fus* parecerse a; **take apart** *vt* desmontar; **take away** *vt* (*remove*) quitar; (*carry off*) llevar; **take back** *vt* (*return*) devolver; (*one's words*) retractar; **take down** *vt* (*building*) derribar; (*message etc*) apuntar; **take in** *vt* (*deceive*) engañar; (*understand*) entender; (*include*) abarcar; (*lodger*) acoger, recibir; **take off** *vi* (*Aviat*) despegar ▷ *vt* (*remove*) quitar; **take on** *vt* (*work*) emprender; (*employee*) contratar; (*opponent*) desafiar; **take out** *vt* sacar; **take over** *vt* (*business*) tomar posesión de ▷ *vi*: **to ~ over from sb** reemplazar a algn; **take up** *vt* (*a dress*) acortar; (*occupy: time, space*) ocupar; (*engage in: hobby etc*) dedicarse a; (*accept*) aceptar; **to ~ sb up on** aceptar algo de algn; **takeaway** *adj* (BRIT: *food*) para llevar ▷ *n* tienda *or* restaurante *m* de comida para llevar; **taken** *pp of* **take**; **takeoff** *n* (*Aviat*) despegue *m*; **takeover** *n* (*Comm*) absorción *f*; **takings** *npl* (*Comm*) ingresos *mpl*
**talc** [tælk] *n* (*also:* **~um powder**) talco
**tale** [teɪl] *n* (*story*) cuento; (*account*) relación *f*; **to tell ~s** (*fig*) contar chismes
**talent** ['tælnt] *n* talento; **talented** *adj* de talento
**talk** [tɔ:k] *n* charla; (*gossip*) habladurías *fpl*, chismes *mpl*; (*conversation*) conversación *f* ▷ *vi* hablar; **talks** *npl* (*Pol etc*) conversaciones *fpl*; **to ~ about** hablar de; **to ~ sb into doing sth** convencer a algn para que haga algo; **to ~ sb out of doing sth** disuadir a algn de que haga algo; **to ~ shop** hablar del trabajo; **talk over** *vt* discutir; **talk show** *n* programa *m* magazine
**tall** [tɔ:l] *adj* alto; (*tree*) grande; **to be 6 feet ~** ≈ medir 1 metro 80, tener 1 metro 80 de alto
**tambourine** [tæmbə'ri:n] *n* pandereta
**tame** [teɪm] *adj* domesticado; (*fig: story, style, person*) soso, anodino
**tamper** ['tæmpə'] *vi*: **to ~ with** (*lock etc*) intentar forzar
**tampon** ['tæmpən] *n* tampón *m*
**tan** [tæn] *n* (*also:* **sun~**) bronceado ▷ *vi* ponerse moreno ▷ *adj* (*colour*) marrón
**tandem** ['tændəm] *n* tándem *m*
**tangerine** [tændʒə'ri:n] *n* man___

**tangle** ['tæŋgl] n enredo; **to get in(to) a ~** enredarse

**tank** [tæŋk] n (also: **water ~**) depósito, tanque m; (for fish) acuario; (Mil) tanque m

**tanker** ['tæŋkəʳ] n (ship) petrolero; (truck) camión m cisterna

**tanned** [tænd] adj (skin) moreno

**tantrum** ['tæntrəm] n rabieta

**Tanzania** [tænzə'nɪə] n Tanzania

**tap** [tæp] n (BRIT: on sink etc) grifo, canilla (LAM); (gentle blow) golpecito; (gas tap) llave f ▷ vt (shoulder etc) dar palmaditas en; (resources) utilizar, explotar; (telephone conversation) intervenir; **on ~** (fig: resources) a mano; **beer on ~** cerveza de barril; **tap dancing** n claqué m

**tape** [teɪp] n cinta; (also: **magnetic ~**) cinta magnética; (sticky tape) cinta adhesiva ▷ vt (record) grabar (en cinta); **on ~** (song etc) grabado (en cinta); **tape measure** n cinta métrica, metro; **tape recorder** n grabadora

**tapestry** ['tæpɪstrɪ] n (object) tapiz m; (art) tapicería

**tar** [tɑːʳ] n alquitrán m, brea

**target** ['tɑːgɪt] n blanco

**tariff** ['tærɪf] n (on goods) arancel m; (BRIT: in hotels etc) tarifa

**tarmac** ['tɑːmæk] n (BRIT: on road) asfalto; (Aviat) pista (de aterrizaje)

**tarpaulin** [tɑːˈpɔːlɪn] n lona (impermeabilizada)

**tarragon** ['tærəgən] n estragón m

**tart** [tɑːt] n (Culin) tarta; (BRIT inf, pej: woman) fulana ▷ adj agrio, ácido

**tartan** ['tɑːtn] n tartán m, tela escocesa

**task** [tɑːsk] n tarea; **to take to ~** reprender

**taste** [teɪst] n sabor m, gusto; (fig) muestra, idea ▷ vt probar ▷ vi: **to ~ of** or **like** (fish etc) saber a; **you can ~ the garlic (in it)** se nota el sabor a ajo; **in good/bad ~** de buen/ mal gusto; **tasteful** adj de buen gusto; **tasteless** adj (food) soso; (remark) de mal gusto; **tasty** adj sabroso, rico

**tatters** ['tætəz] npl: **in ~** hecho jirones

**tattoo** [tə'tuː] n tatuaje m; (spectacle) espectáculo militar ▷ vt tatuar

**taught** [tɔːt] pt, pp of **teach**

**taunt** [tɔːnt] n pulla ▷ vt lanzar pullas a

**Taurus** ['tɔːrəs] n Tauro

**taut** [tɔːt] adj tirante, tenso

**tax** [tæks] n impuesto ▷ vt gravar (con un impuesto); (fig: test) poner a prueba; (patience) agotar; **tax-free** adj libre de ...tos

...n taxi m ▷ vi (Aviat) rodar por la ...n taxista mf; **taxi rank,** ...ada de taxis

**TB** n abbr = **tuberculosis**

**tea** [tiː] n té m; (BRIT: snack) ≈ merienda; **high ~** (BRIT) ≈ merienda-cena; **tea bag** n bolsita de té; **tea break** n (BRIT) descanso para el té

**teach** (pt, pp **taught**) [tiːtʃ, tɔːt] vt: **to ~ sb sth, ~ sth to sb** enseñar algo a algn ▷ vi enseñar; (be a teacher) ser profesor(a); **teacher** n (in secondary school) profesor(a) m/f; (in primary school) maestro/a; **teaching** n enseñanza

**tea: tea cloth** n (BRIT) paño de cocina, trapo de cocina (LAM); **teacup** n taza de té; **tea leaves** npl hojas fpl de té

**team** [tiːm] n equipo; (of animals) pareja; **team up** vi asociarse

**teapot** ['tiːpɔt] n tetera

**tear¹** [tɪəʳ] n lágrima; **in ~s** llorando

**tear²** [tɛəʳ] (pt **tore**, pp **torn**) n rasgón m, desgarrón m ▷ vt romper, rasgar ▷ vi rasgarse; **tear apart** vt (also fig) hacer pedazos; **tear down** vt (building, statue) derribar; (poster, flag) arrancar; **tear off** vt (sheet of paper etc) arrancar; (one's clothes) quitarse a tirones; **tear up** vt (sheet of paper etc) romper

**tearful** ['tɪəful] adj lloroso

**tear gas** n gas m lacrimógeno

**tearoom** ['tiːruːm] n salón m de té

**tease** [tiːz] vt tomar el pelo a

**tea: teaspoon** n cucharita; (also: **teaspoonful**: as measurement) cucharadita; **teatime** n hora del té; **tea towel** n (BRIT) paño de cocina

**technical** ['tɛknɪkl] adj técnico

**technician** [tɛk'nɪʃn] n técnico/a

**technique** [tɛk'niːk] n técnica

**technology** [tɛk'nɔlədʒɪ] n tecnología

**teddy (bear)** ['tɛdɪ-] n osito de peluche

**tedious** ['tiːdɪəs] adj pesado, aburrido

**tee** [tiː] n (Golf) tee m

**teen** [tiːn] adj = **teenage** ▷ n (US) = **teenager**

**teenage** ['tiːneɪdʒ] adj (fashions etc) juvenil; **teenager** ['tiːneɪdʒəʳ] n adolescente mf

**teens** [tiːnz] npl: **to be in one's ~** ser adolescente

**teeth** [tiːθ] npl of **tooth**

**teetotal** ['tiːˈtəutl] adj abstemio

**telecommunications** ['tɛlɪkəmjuːnɪˈkeɪʃənz] n telecomunicaciones fpl

**telegram** ['tɛlɪgræm] n telegrama m

**telegraph pole** n poste m telegráfico

**telephone** ['tɛlɪfəun] n teléfono ▷ vt llamar por teléfono, telefonear; **to be on the ~** (subscriber) tener teléfono; (be speaking) estar hablando por teléfono; **telephone book** n guía f telefónica;

**telephone booth,** (BRIT) **telephone box** n cabina telefónica; **telephone call** n llamada telefónica; **telephone directory** n guía telefónica; **telephone number** n número de teléfono

**telesales** ['tɛlɪseɪlz] npl televentas fpl

**telescope** ['tɛlɪskəʊp] n telescopio

**televise** ['tɛlɪvaɪz] vt televisar

**television** ['tɛlɪvɪʒən] n televisión f; **to watch ~** mirar or ver la televisión; **television programme** n programa m de televisión

**tell** (pt, pp **told**) [tɛl, təʊld] vt decir; (relate: story) contar; (distinguish): **to ~ sth from** distinguir algo de ▷ vi (talk): **to ~ (of)** contar; (have effect) tener efecto; **to ~ sb to do sth** decir a algn que haga algo; **tell off** vt: **to ~ sb off** regañar a algn; **teller** n (in bank) cajero/a

**telly** ['tɛlɪ] n (BRIT inf) tele f

**temp** [tɛmp] n abbr (BRIT: = temporary office worker) empleado/a eventual

**temper** ['tɛmpər] n (mood) humor m; (bad temper) (mal) genio; (fit of anger) ira ▷ vt (moderate) moderar; **to be in a ~** estar furioso; **to lose one's ~** enfadarse, enojarse (LAM)

**temperament** ['tɛmprəmənt] n (nature) temperamento; **temperamental** [tɛmprə'mɛntl] adj temperamental

**temperature** ['tɛmprətʃər] n temperatura; **to have** or **run a ~** tener fiebre

**temple** ['tɛmpl] n (building) templo; (Anat) sien f

**temporary** ['tɛmpərərɪ] adj provisional; (passing) transitorio; (worker) eventual; (job) temporal

**tempt** [tɛmpt] vt tentar; **to ~ sb into doing sth** tentar or inducir a algn a hacer algo; **temptation** n tentación f; **tempting** adj tentador(a); (food) apetitoso

**ten** [tɛn] num diez

**tenant** ['tɛnənt] n inquilino/a

**tend** [tɛnd] vt cuidar ▷ vi: **to ~ to do sth** tener tendencia a hacer algo; **tendency** ['tɛndənsɪ] n tendencia

**tender** ['tɛndər] adj tierno, blando; (delicate) delicado; (meat) tierno; (sore) sensible ▷ n (Comm: offer) oferta; (money): **legal ~** moneda de curso legal ▷ vt ofrecer

**tendon** ['tɛndən] n tendón m

**tenner** ['tɛnər] n (billete m de) diez libras fpl

**tennis** ['tɛnɪs] n tenis m; **tennis ball** n pelota de tenis; **tennis court** n cancha de tenis; **tennis match** n partido de tenis; **tennis player** n tenista mf; **tennis racket** n raqueta de tenis

**tenor** ['tɛnər] n (Mus) tenor m

**tenpin bowling** ['tɛnpɪn-] n bolos mpl

**tense** [tɛns] adj tenso; (person) nervioso ▷ n (Ling) tiempo

**tension** ['tɛnʃən] n tensión f

**tent** [tɛnt] n tienda (de campaña), carpa (LAM)

**tentative** ['tɛntətɪv] adj (person) indeciso; (provisional) provisional

**tenth** [tɛnθ] adj décimo

**tent: tent peg** n clavija, estaca; **tent pole** n mástil m

**tepid** ['tɛpɪd] adj tibio

**term** [təːm] n (word) término, (period) período; (Scol) trimestre m ▷ vt llamar; **terms** npl (conditions) condiciones fpl; **in the short/long ~** a corto/largo plazo; **to be on good ~s with sb** llevarse bien con algn; **to come to ~s with** (problem) aceptar

**terminal** ['təːmɪnl] adj (disease) mortal; (patient) terminal ▷ n (Elec) borne m; (Comput) terminal m; (also: **air ~**) terminal f; (BRIT: also: **coach ~**) (estación f) terminal f

**terminate** ['təːmɪneɪt] vt poner término a

**termini** ['təːmɪnaɪ] npl of **terminus**

**terminology** [təːmɪ'nɔlədʒɪ] n terminología

**terminus** (pl **termini**) ['təːmɪnəs, 'təːmɪnaɪ] n término, (estación f) terminal f

**terrace** ['tɛrəs] n terraza; (BRIT: row of houses) hilera de casas adosadas; **the ~s** (BRIT Sport) las gradas fpl; **terraced** adj (garden) escalonado; (house) adosado

**terrain** [tɛ'reɪn] n terreno

**terrestrial** [tɪ'rɛstrɪəl] adj (life) terrestre; (BRIT: channel) de transmisión (por) vía terrestre

**terrible** ['tɛrɪbl] adj terrible, horrible; (inf) malísimo; **terribly** adv terriblemente; (very badly) malísimamente

**terrier** ['tɛrɪər] n terrier m

**terrific** [tə'rɪfɪk] adj fantástico, fenomenal

**terrify** ['tɛrɪfaɪ] vt aterrorizar; **to be terrified** estar aterrado or aterrorizado; **terrifying** adj aterrador(a)

**territorial** [tɛrɪ'tɔːrɪəl] adj territorial

**territory** ['tɛrɪtərɪ] n territorio

**terror** ['tɛrər] n terror m; **terrorism** n terrorismo; **terrorist** n terrorista mf; **terrorist attack** n atentado (terrorista)

**test** [tɛst] n (trial, check) prueba; (Chem, Med) prueba; (exam) examen m, test m; (also: **driving ~**) examen de conducir ▷ vt probar, poner a prueba; (Med) examinar

**testicle** ['tɛstɪkl] n testículo

**testify** ['tɛstɪfaɪ] vi (Law) prestar declaración; **to ~ to sth** atestiguar algo

**testimony** ['tɛstɪmənɪ] n (Law) testimonio

**test: test match** n partido internacional; **test tube** n probeta

**tetanus** ['tɛtənəs] n tét...

**text** [tɛkst] *n* texto; *(on mobile)* mensaje *m* de texto ▷ *vt*: **to ~ sb** enviar un mensaje (de texto) a algn; **textbook** *n* libro de texto

**textiles** ['tɛkstaɪlz] *npl* tejidos *mpl*

**text message** *n* mensaje *m* de texto

**text messaging** [-'mɛsɪdʒɪŋ] *n* (envío de) mensajes *mpl* de texto

**texture** ['tɛkstʃəʳ] *n* textura

**Thai** [taɪ] *adj, n* tailandés/esa *m/f*

**Thailand** ['taɪlænd] *n* Tailandia

**than** [ðæn, ðən] *conj* que; *(with numerals)*: **more ~ 10/once** más de 10/una vez; **I have more/less ~ you** tengo más/menos que tú; **it is better to phone ~ to write** es mejor llamar por teléfono que escribir

**thank** [θæŋk] *vt* dar las gracias a, agradecer; **~ you (very much)** (muchas) gracias; **~ God!** ¡gracias a Dios!; *see also* **thanks**; **thankfully** *adv*: **thankfully there were few victims** afortunadamente hubo pocas víctimas

**thanks** [θæŋks] *npl* gracias *fpl* ▷ *excl* ¡gracias!; **many ~, ~ a lot** ¡muchas gracias!; **~ to** *prep* gracias a

**Thanksgiving (Day)** ['θæŋksgɪvɪŋ-] *n* día *m* de Acción de Gracias

**THANKSGIVING DAY**

En Estados Unidos el cuarto jueves de noviembre es *Thanksgiving Day*, fiesta oficial en la que se conmemora la celebración que tuvieron los primeros colonos norteamericanos (*Pilgrims* o *Pilgrim Fathers*) tras la estupenda cosecha de 1621, por la que se dan gracias a Dios. En Canadá se celebra una fiesta semejante el segundo lunes de octubre, aunque no está relacionada con dicha fecha histórica.

**KEYWORD**

**that** [ðæt] (*pl* **those**) *adj* (*demonstrative*) ese/a; (*: more remote*) aquel/aquella; **leave that book on the table** deja ese libro sobre la mesa; **that one** ese/esa, ése/ésa (*to avoid confusion with adj*); (*more remote*) aquel/ aquella, aquél/aquélla (*to avoid confusion with adj*); **that one over there** ese/esa de ahí, ése/ésa de ahí; aquel/aquella de allí, aquél/aquélla de allí; *see also* **those**
▷ *pron* **1** (*demonstrative*) ese/a, ése/a (*to avoid confusion with adj*), eso (*neuter*); (*: more remote*) aquel/aquella, aquél/aquélla (*to avoid confusion with adj*), aquello (*neuter*); **what's that?** ¿qué es eso (*or* aquello)?; **who's that?** (*pointing etc*) ¿quién

eat all that? ¿vas a comer todo eso?; **that's my house** esa es mi casa; **that's what he said** eso es lo que dijo; **that is (to say)** es decir; *see also* **those**

**2** (*relative, subject, object*) que; (*: with preposition*) (ella) que, ella cual; **the book (that) I read** el libro que leí; **the books that are in the library** los libros que están en la biblioteca; **all (that) I have** todo lo que tengo; **the box (that) I put it in** la caja en la que *or* donde lo puse; **the people (that) I spoke to** la gente con la que hablé

**3** (*relative, of time*) que; **the day (that) he came** el día (en) que vino
▷ *conj* que; **he thought that I was ill** creyó que yo estaba enfermo
▷ *adv* (*demonstrative*): **I can't work that much** no puedo trabajar tanto; **I didn't realize it was that bad** no creí que fuera tan malo; **that high** así de alto

**thatched** [θætʃt] *adj* (*roof*) de paja; **~ cottage** casita con tejado de paja

**thaw** [θɔː] *n* deshielo ▷ *vi* (*ice*) derretirse; (*food*) descongelarse ▷ *vt* descongelar

**KEYWORD**

**the** [ðiː, ðə] *def art* **1** el *m*, la *f*, los *mpl*, las *fpl* (*NB = el used immediately before feminine noun beginning with stressed (h)a; a + el = al; de + el = del*): **the boy/girl** el chico/la chica; **the books/flowers** los libros/las flores; **to the postman/from the drawer** al cartero/del cajón; **I haven't the time/money** no tengo tiempo/dinero

**2** (*+ adj to form noun*) los; lo; **the rich and the poor** los ricos y los pobres; **to attempt the impossible** intentar lo imposible

**3** (*in titles, surnames*): **Elizabeth the First** Isabel Primera; **Peter the Great** Pedro el Grande

**4** (*in comparisons*): **the more he works the more he earns** cuanto más trabaja más gana

**theatre**, (*us*) **theater** ['θɪətəʳ] *n* teatro; (*also*: **lecture ~**) aula; (*Med: also*: **operating ~**) quirófano

**theft** [θɛft] *n* robo

**their** [ðɛəʳ] *adj* su; **theirs** *pron* (el) suyo/(la) suya *etc*; *see also* **my**; **mine**

**them** [ðɛm, ðəm] *pron* (*direct*) los/las; (*indirect*) les; (*stressed, after prep*) ellos/ellas; *see also* **me**

**theme** [θiːm] *n* tema *m*; **theme park** *n* parque *m* temático

**themselves** [ðəm'sɛlvz] *pron pl* (*subject*) ellos mismos/ellas mismas; (*complement*)

**tilt** [tɪlt] vt inclinar ▷ vi inclinarse
**timber** [ˈtɪmbəʳ] n (material) madera
**time** [taɪm] n tiempo; (epoch: often pl) época; (by clock) hora; (moment) momento; (occasion) vez f; (Mus) compás m ▷ vt calcular o medir el tiempo de; (race) cronometrar; (remark etc) elegir el momento para; **a long ~** mucho tiempo; **four at a ~** cuatro a la vez; **for the ~ being** de momento, por ahora; **at ~s** a veces; **from ~ to ~** de vez en cuando; **in ~** (soon enough) a tiempo; (after some time) con el tiempo; (Mus) al compás; **in a week's ~** dentro de una semana; **in no ~** en un abrir y cerrar de ojos; **any ~** cuando sea; **on ~** a la hora; **5 ~s 5** 5 por 5; **what ~ is it?** ¿qué hora es?; **to have a good ~** pasarlo bien, divertirse; **time limit** n plazo; **timely** adj oportuno; **timer** n (in kitchen) temporizador m; **timetable** n horario; **time zone** n huso horario
**timid** [ˈtɪmɪd] adj tímido
**timing** [ˈtaɪmɪŋ] n (Sport) cronometraje m; **the ~ of his resignation** el momento que eligió para dimitir
**tin** [tɪn] n estaño; (also: **~ plate**) hojalata; (BRIT: can) lata; **tinfoil** n papel m de estaño
**tingle** [ˈtɪŋgl] vi (cheeks, skin: from cold) sentir comezón; (: from bad circulation) sentir hormigueo; **to ~ with** estremecerse de
**tinker** [ˈtɪŋkəʳ]: **~ with** vt fus jugar con, tocar
**tinned** [tɪnd] adj (BRIT: food) en lata, en conserva
**tin opener** [-əupnəʳ] n (BRIT) abrelatas m inv
**tint** [tɪnt] n matiz m; (for hair) tinte m; **tinted** adj (hair) teñido; (glass, spectacles) ahumado
**tiny** [ˈtaɪnɪ] adj minúsculo, pequeñito
**tip** [tɪp] n (end) punta; (gratuity) propina; (BRIT: for rubbish) vertedero; (advice) consejo ▷ vt (waiter) dar una propina a; (tilt) inclinar; (empty: also: **~ out**) vaciar, echar; **tip off** vt avisar, poner sobre aviso a
**tiptoe** [ˈtɪptəu] n: **on ~** de puntillas
**tire** [ˈtaɪəʳ] n (US) = **tyre** ▷ vt cansar ▷ vi cansarse; (become bored) aburrirse; **tired** adj cansado; **to be tired of sth** estar harto de algo; **tire pressure** n (US) = **tyre pressure**; **tiring** adj cansado
**tissue** [ˈtɪʃuː] n tejido; (paper handkerchief) pañuelo de papel, kleenex® m; **tissue paper** n papel m de seda
**tit** [tɪt] n (bird) herrerillo común; **to give ~ for tat** dar ojo por ojo
**title** [ˈtaɪtl] n título
**T-junction** [ˈtiːdʒʌŋkʃən] n cruce m en T
**TM** abbr (= trademark) marca de fábrica; = **transcendental meditation**

**KEYWORD**

**to** [tuː, tə] prep 1 (direction) a; **to go to France/London/school/the station** ir a Francia/Londres/al colegio/a la estación; **to go to Claude's/the doctor's** ir a casa de Claude/al médico; **the road to Edinburgh** la carretera de Edimburgo
2 (as far as) hasta, a; **from here to London** de aquí a or hasta Londres; **to count to 10** contar hasta 10; **from 40 to 50 people** entre 40 y 50 personas
3 (with expressions of time): **a quarter/twenty to five** las cinco menos cuarto/veinte
4 (for, of): **the key to the front door** la llave de la puerta principal; **she is secretary to the director** es la secretaria del director; **a letter to his wife** una carta a or para su mujer
5 (expressing indirect object) a; **to give sth to sb** darle algo a algn; **to talk to sb** hablar con algn; **to be a danger to sb** ser un peligro para algn; **to carry out repairs to sth** hacer reparaciones en algo
6 (in relation to): **3 goals to 2** 3 goles a 2; **30 miles to the gallon** ≈ 9,4 litros a los cien (kilómetros)
7 (purpose, result): **to come to sb's aid** venir en auxilio or ayuda de algn; **to sentence sb to death** condenar a algn a muerte; **to my great surprise** con gran sorpresa mía
▷ infin particle 1 (simple infin): **to go/eat** ir/comer
2 (following another vb; see also relevant vb): **to want/try/start to do** querer/intentar/empezar a hacer
3 (with vb omitted): **I don't want to** no quiero
4 (purpose, result) para; **I did it to help you** lo hice para ayudarte; **he came to see you** vino a verte
5 (equivalent to relative clause): **I have things to do** tengo cosas que hacer; **the main thing is to try** lo principal es intentarlo
6 (after adj etc): **ready to go** listo para irse; **too old to ...** demasiado viejo (como) para ...
▷ adv: **pull/push the door to** tirar de/empujar la puerta

**toad** [təud] n sapo; **toadstool** n seta venenosa
**toast** [təust] n (Culin) tostada; (drink, speech) brindis m inv ▷ vt (Culin) tostar; (drink to) brindar por; **toaster** n tostador m
**tobacco** [təˈbækəu] n tabaco
**toboggan** [təˈbɔgən] n tobogán m
**today** [təˈdeɪ] adv, n (also fig) hoy m

**toddler** [ˈtɒdləʳ] n niño/a (que empieza a andar)

**toe** [təʊ] n dedo (del pie); (of shoe) punta ▷ vt: **to ~ the line** (fig) acatar las normas; **toenail** n uña del pie

**toffee** [ˈtɒfɪ] n caramelo

**together** [təˈgɛðəʳ] adv juntos; (at same time) al mismo tiempo, a la vez; **~ with** junto con

**toilet** [ˈtɔɪlət] n (BRIT: lavatory) servicios mpl, baño ▷ cpd (bag, soap etc) de aseo; **toilet bag** n neceser m, bolsa de aseo; **toilet paper** n papel m higiénico; **toiletries** npl artículos mpl de tocador; **toilet roll** n rollo de papel higiénico

**token** [ˈtəʊkən] n (sign) señal f, muestra; (souvenir) recuerdo; (disc) ficha ▷ cpd (fee, strike) simbólico; **book/record ~** (BRIT) vale m para comprar libros/discos

**Tokyo** [ˈtəʊkjəʊ] n Tokio, Tokío

**told** [təʊld] pt, pp of **tell**

**tolerant** [ˈtɒlərnt] adj: **~ of** tolerante con

**tolerate** [ˈtɒləreɪt] vt tolerar

**toll** [təʊl] n (of casualties) número de víctimas; (tax, charge) peaje m ▷ vi (bell) doblar; **toll call** n (US Tel) conferencia, llamada interurbana; **toll-free** adj, adv (US) gratis

**tomato** [təˈmɑːtəʊ] (pl **tomatoes**) n tomate m; **tomato sauce** n salsa de tomate

**tomb** [tuːm] n tumba; **tombstone** n lápida

**tomorrow** [təˈmɔrəʊ] adv, n (also fig) mañana; **the day after ~** pasado mañana; **~ morning** mañana por la mañana

**ton** [tʌn] n tonelada; **~s of** (inf) montones de

**tone** [təʊn] n tono ▷ vi armonizar; **tone down** vt (criticism) suavizar; (colour) atenuar

**tongs** [tɒŋz] npl (for coal) tenazas fpl; (for hair) tenacillas fpl

**tongue** [tʌŋ] n lengua; **~ in cheek** en broma

**tonic** [ˈtɒnɪk] n (Med) tónico; (also: **~ water**) (agua) tónica

**tonight** [təˈnaɪt] adv, n esta noche

**tonsil** [ˈtɒnsl] n amígdala; **tonsillitis** [tɒnsɪˈlaɪtɪs] n amigdalitis f

**too** [tuː] adv (excessively) demasiado; (also) también; **~ much** demasiado; **~ many** demasiados/as

**took** [tuk] pt of **take**

**tool** [tuːl] n herramienta; **tool box** n caja de herramientas; **tool kit** n juego de herramientas

**tooth** (pl **teeth**) [tuːθ, tiːθ] n (Anat, Tech) diente m; (molar) muela; **toothache** n dolor m de muelas; **toothbrush** n cepillo de dientes; **toothpaste** n pasta de dientes; **toothpick** n palillo

**top** [tɒp] n (of mountain) cumbre f, cima; (of head) coronilla; (of ladder) (lo) alto; (of cupboard, table) superficie f; (lid: of box, jar) tapa; (: of bottle) tapón m; (of list, table, queue, page) cabeza; (toy) peonza; (Dress: blouse) blusa; (: T-shirt) camiseta ▷ adj de arriba; (in rank) principal, primero; (best) mejor ▷ vt (exceed) exceder; (be first in) encabezar; **on ~ of** sobre, encima de; **from ~ to bottom** de pies a cabeza; **top up** vt volver a llenar; (mobile phone) recargar el saldo de; **top floor** n último piso; **top hat** n sombrero de copa

**topic** [ˈtɒpɪk] n tema m; **topical** adj actual

**topless** [ˈtɒplɪs] adj (bather etc) topless inv

**topping** [ˈtɒpɪŋ] n (Culin): **with a ~ of cream** con nata por encima

**topple** [ˈtɒpl] vt derribar ▷ vi caerse

**top-up card** n (for mobile phone) tarjeta prepago

**torch** [tɔːtʃ] n antorcha; (BRIT: electric) linterna

**tore** [tɔːʳ] pt of **tear**[1]

**torment** n [ˈtɔːmɛnt] tormento ▷ vt [tɔːˈmɛnt] atormentar; (fig: annoy) fastidiar

**torn** [tɔːn] pp of **tear**[1]

**tornado** [tɔːˈneɪdəʊ] (pl **tornadoes**) n tornado

**torpedo** [tɔːˈpiːdəʊ] (pl **torpedoes**) n torpedo

**torrent** [ˈtɒrnt] n torrente m; **torrential** [tɔˈrɛnʃl] adj torrencial

**tortoise** [ˈtɔːtəs] n tortuga

**torture** [ˈtɔːtʃəʳ] n tortura ▷ vt torturar; (fig) atormentar

**Tory** [ˈtɔːrɪ] adj, n (BRIT Pol) conservador(a) m/f

**toss** [tɒs] vt tirar, echar; (head) sacudir; **to ~ a coin** echar a cara o cruz; **to ~ up for sth** jugar algo a cara o cruz; **to ~ and turn** (in bed) dar vueltas (en la cama)

**total** [ˈtəʊtl] adj total, entero; (emphatic: failure etc) completo, total ▷ n total m, suma ▷ vt (add up) sumar; (amount to) ascender a

**totalitarian** [təʊtælɪˈtɛərɪən] adj totalitario

**totally** [ˈtəʊtəlɪ] adv totalmente

**touch** [tʌtʃ] n tacto; (contact) contacto ▷ vt tocar; (emotionally) conmover; **a ~ of** (fig) una pizca or un poquito de; **to get in ~ with** sb ponerse en contacto con algn; **to lose ~** (friends) perder contacto; **touch down** vi (on land) aterrizar; **touchdown** n aterrizaje m; (US Football) ensayo; **touched** adj conmovido; **touching** adj conmovedor(a); **touchline** n (Sport) línea de banda; **touch-sensitive** adj sensible al tacto

**tough** [tʌf] *adj* (*meat*) duro; (*task, problem, situation*) difícil; (*person*) fuerte

**tour** ['tuər] *n* viaje *m*; (*also*: **package ~**) viaje *m* con todo incluido; (*of town, museum*) visita ▷ *vt* viajar por; **to go on a ~ of** (*region, country*) ir de viaje por; (*museum, castle*) visitar; **to go on ~** partir or ir de gira; **tour guide** *n* guía *mf* turístico/a

**tourism** ['tuərɪzm] *n* turismo

**tourist** ['tuərɪst] *n* turista *mf* ▷ *cpd* turístico; **tourist office** *n* oficina de turismo

**tournament** ['tuənəmənt] *n* torneo

**tour operator** *n* touroperador(a) *m/f*, operador(a) *m/f* turístico/a

**tow** [təu] *n* ▷ *vt* remolcar; "**on** or (*us*) **in ~**" (*Aut*) "a remolque"; **tow away** *vt* llevarse a remolque

**toward(s)** [tə'wɔːd(z)] *prep* hacia; (*of attitude*) respecto a, con; (*of purpose*) para

**towel** ['tauəl] *n* toalla; **towelling** *n* (*fabric*) felpa

**tower** ['tauə^r] *n* torre *f*; **tower block** *n* (BRIT) bloque *m* de pisos

**town** [taun] *n* ciudad *f*; **to go to ~** ir a la ciudad; (*fig*) tirar la casa por la ventana; **town centre** *n* centro de la ciudad; **town hall** *n* ayuntamiento

**tow truck** *n* (*us*) camión *m* grúa

**toxic** ['tɔksɪk] *adj* tóxico

**toy** [tɔɪ] *n* juguete *m*; **toy with** *vt fus* jugar con; (*idea*) acariciar; **toyshop** *n* juguetería

**trace** [treɪs] *n* rastro ▷ *vt* (*draw*) trazar, delinear; (*locate*) encontrar

**track** [træk] *n* (*mark*) huella, pista; (*path*) camino, senda; (*: of bullet etc*) trayectoria; (*: of suspect, animal*) pista, rastro; (*Rail*) vía; (*Comput, Sport*) pista; (*on album*) canción *f* ▷ *vt* seguir la pista de; **to keep ~ of** mantenerse al tanto de, seguir; **track down** *vt* (*person*) localizar; (*sth lost*) encontrar; **tracksuit** *n* chándal *m*

**tractor** ['træktə^r] *n* tractor *m*

**trade** [treɪd] *n* comercio; (*skill, job*) oficio ▷ *vi* negociar, comerciar ▷ *vt* (*exchange*): **to ~ sth (for sth)** cambiar algo (por algo); **trade in** *vt* (*old car etc*) ofrecer como parte del pago; **trademark** *n* marca de fábrica; **trader** *n* comerciante *mf*; **tradesman** *n* (*shopkeeper*) comerciante *mf*; **trade union** *n* sindicato

**trading** ['treɪdɪŋ] *n* comercio

**tradition** [trə'dɪʃən] *n* tradición *f*; **traditional** *adj* tradicional

**traffic** ['træfɪk] *n* tráfico, circulación *f* ▷ *vi*: **to ~ in** (*pej: liquor, drugs*) traficar en; **air ~** tráfico aéreo; **traffic circle** *n* (*us*) rotonda, glorieta; **traffic island** *n* refugio, isleta; **traffic jam** *n* embotellamiento; **traffic lights** *npl* semáforo *sg*; **traffic warden** *n* guardia *mf* de tráfico

**tragedy** ['trædʒədɪ] *n* tragedia

**tragic** ['trædʒɪk] *adj* trágico

**trail** [treɪl] *n* (*tracks*) rastro, pista; (*path*) camino, sendero; (*dust, smoke*) estela ▷ *vt* (*drag*) arrastrar; (*follow*) seguir la pista de ▷ *vi* arrastrarse; (*in contest etc*) ir perdiendo; **trailer** *n* (*Aut*) remolque *m*; (*caravan*) caravana; (*Cine*) trailer *m*, avance *m*

**train** [treɪn] *n* tren *m*; (*of dress*) cola ▷ *vt* (*educate*) formar; (*sportsman*) entrenar; (*dog*) amaestrar; (*point: gun etc*): **to ~ on** apuntar a ▷ *vi* (*Sport*) entrenarse; (*be educated, learn a skill*) formarse; **to ~ as a teacher** *etc* estudiar para profesor *etc*; **one's ~ of thought** el razonamiento de algn; **trainee** [treɪ'niː] *n* trabajador(a) *m/f* en prácticas; **trainer** *n* (*Sport*) entrenador(a) *m/f*; (*of animals*) domador(a) *m/f*; **trainers** *npl* (*shoes*) zapatillas *fpl* (de deporte); **training** *n* formación *f*; entrenamiento; **to be in training** (*Sport*) estar entrenando; **training course** *n* curso de formación; **training shoes** *npl* zapatillas *fpl* (de deporte)

**trait** [treɪt] *n* rasgo

**traitor** ['treɪtə^r] *n* traidor(a) *m/f*

**tram** [træm] *n* (BRIT: *also*: **~car**) tranvía *m*

**tramp** [træmp] *n* (*person*) vagabundo/a; (*inf, pej: woman*) puta

**trample** ['træmpl] *vt*: **to ~ (underfoot)** pisotear

**trampoline** ['træmpəliːn] *n* trampolín *m*

**tranquil** ['træŋkwɪl] *adj* tranquilo; **tranquillizer**, (*us*) **tranquilizer** *n* (*Med*) tranquilizante *m*

**transaction** [træn'zækʃən] *n* transacción *f*, operación *f*

**transatlantic** ['trænzət'læntɪk] *adj* transatlántico

**transcript** ['trænskrɪpt] *n* copia

**transfer** *n* ['trænsfə^r] transferencia; (*Sport*) traspaso; (*picture, design*) calcomanía ▷ *vt* [træns'fə:^r] trasladar; **to ~ the charges** (BRIT *Tel*) llamar a cobro revertido

**transform** [træns'fɔ:m] *vt* transformar; **transformation** *n* transformación *f*

**transfusion** [træns'fju:ʒən] *n* transfusión *f*

**transit** ['trænzɪt] *n*: **in ~** en tránsito

**transition** [træn'zɪʃən] *n* transición *f*

**transitive** ['trænzɪtɪv] *adj* (*Ling*) transitivo

**translate** [trænz'leɪt] *vt*: **to ~ (from/into)** traducir (de/a); **translation** [trænz'leɪʃən] *n* traducción *f*; **translator** *n* traductor(a) *m/f*

**transmission** [trænz'mɪʃən] *n* transmisión *f*

**transmit** [trænz'mɪt] *vt* transmitir; **transmitter** *n* transmisor *m*

**transparent** [træns'pærnt] *adj* transparente

**transplant** n ['trænsplɑːnt] (Med) transplante m

**transport** n ['trænspɔːt] transporte m ▷ vt [træns'pɔːt] transportar; **transportation** [trænspɔː'teɪʃən] n transporte m

**transvestite** [trænz'vestaɪt] n travesti mf

**trap** [træp] n (snare, trick) trampa ▷ vt coger (SP) or agarrar (LAM) en una trampa; (trick) engañar; (confine) atrapar

**trash** [træʃ] n basura; (inf: nonsense) tonterías fpl; **the book/film is ~** el libro/ la película no vale nada; **trash can** n (US) cubo, balde m (LAM) or bote m (LAM) de la basura

**trauma** ['trɔːmə] n trauma m; **traumatic** [trɔː'mætɪk] adj traumático

**travel** ['trævl] n viajes mpl ▷ vi viajar ▷ vt (distance) recorrer; **travel agency** n agencia de viajes; **travel agent** n agente mf de viajes; **travel insurance** n seguro de viaje; **traveller, (US) traveler** ['trævlər] n viajero/a; **traveller's cheque, (US) traveler's check** n cheque m de viaje; **travelling, (US) traveling** ['trævlɪŋ] n los viajes, el viajar; **travel-sick** adj: **to get travel-sick** marearse al viajar; **travel sickness** n mareo

**tray** [treɪ] n bandeja; (on desk) cajón m

**treacherous** ['tretʃərəs] adj traidor(a); **road conditions are ~** el estado de las carreteras es peligroso

**treacle** ['triːkl] n (BRIT) melaza

**tread** (pt trod, pp trodden) [tred, trɔd, 'trɔdn] n paso, pisada; (of tyre) banda de rodadura ▷ vi pisar; **tread on** vt fus pisar

**treasure** ['treʒər] n tesoro ▷ vt (value) apreciar, valorar; **treasurer** n tesorero/a

**treasury** ['treʒərɪ] n: **the T~** ≈ el Ministerio de Economía y de Hacienda

**treat** [triːt] n (present) regalo ▷ vt tratar; **to ~ sb to sth** invitar a algn a algo; **treatment** n tratamiento

**treaty** ['triːtɪ] n tratado

**treble** ['trebl] adj triple ▷ vt triplicar ▷ vi triplicarse

**tree** [triː] n árbol m; **tree trunk** n tronco de árbol

**trek** [trek] n (long journey) expedición f; (tiring walk) caminata

**tremble** ['trembl] vi temblar

**tremendous** [trɪ'mendəs] adj tremendo; enorme; (excellent) estupendo

**trench** [trentʃ] n zanja

**trend** [trend] n (tendency) tendencia; (of events) curso; (fashion) moda; **trendy** adj de moda

**trespass** ['trespəs] vi: **to ~ on** entrar sin permiso en; **"no ~ing"** "prohibido el paso"

**trial** ['traɪəl] n (Law) juicio, proceso; (test: of machine etc) prueba; **trial period** n periodo de prueba

**triangle** ['traɪæŋgl] n (Math, Mus) triángulo

**triangular** [traɪ'æŋgjulər] adj triangular

**tribe** [traɪb] n tribu f

**tribunal** [traɪ'bjuːnl] n tribunal m

**tribute** ['trɪbjuːt] n homenaje m, tributo; **to pay ~ to** rendir homenaje a

**trick** [trɪk] n trampa; (conjuring trick, deceit) truco; (joke) broma; (Cards) baza ▷ vt engañar; **to play a ~ on sb** gastar una broma a algn; **that should do the ~** eso servirá

**trickle** ['trɪkl] n (of water etc) hilo ▷ vi gotear

**tricky** ['trɪkɪ] adj difícil; (problem) delicado

**tricycle** ['traɪsɪkl] n triciclo

**trifle** ['traɪfl] n bagatela; (Culin) dulce de bizcocho, gelatina, fruta y natillas ▷ adv: **a ~ long** un pelín largo

**trigger** ['trɪgər] n (of gun) gatillo

**trim** [trɪm] adj (house, garden) en buen estado; (figure): **to be ~** tener buen talle ▷ n (haircut etc) recorte m ▷ vt (neaten) arreglar; (cut) recortar; (decorate) adornar; (Naut: a sail) orientar

**trio** ['triːəu] n trío

**trip** [trɪp] n viaje m; (excursion) excursión f; (stumble) traspié m ▷ vi (stumble) tropezar; (go lightly) andar a paso ligero; **on a ~** de viaje; **trip up** vi tropezar, caerse ▷ vt hacer tropezar or caer

**triple** ['trɪpl] adj triple

**triplets** ['trɪplɪts] npl trillizos/as m/f pl

**tripod** ['traɪpɔd] n trípode m

**triumph** ['traɪʌmf] n triunfo ▷ vi: **to ~ (over)** vencer; **triumphant** [traɪ'ʌmfənt] adj triunfante

**trivial** ['trɪvɪəl] adj insignificante

**trod** [trɔd] pt of **tread**

**trodden** ['trɔdn] pp of **tread**

**trolley** ['trɔlɪ] n carrito

**trolley bus** n trolebús m

**trombone** [trɔm'bəun] n trombón m

**troop** [truːp] n grupo, banda; **troops** npl (Mil) tropas fpl

**trophy** ['trəufɪ] n trofeo

**tropical** ['trɔpɪkl] adj tropical

**trot** [trɔt] n trote m ▷ vi trotar; **on the ~** (BRIT fig) seguidos/as

**trouble** ['trʌbl] n problema m, dificultad f; (worry) preocupación f; (bother, effort) molestia, esfuerzo; (unrest) inquietud f; (Med): **stomach ~** problemas mpl gástricos ▷ vt molestar; (worry) preocupar, inquietar ▷ vi: **to ~ to do sth** molestarse en hacer algo; **troubles** npl (Pol etc) conflictos mpl; **to be in ~** estar en un apuro; **it's no ~!** ¡no es molestia (ninguna)!; **what's the ~?** ¿qué pasa?; **troubled** adj (person) preocupado; (epoch, life) agitado; **troublemaker** n agitador(a) m/f; **troublesome** adj molesto

**trough** [trɒf] n (also: **drinking ~**) abrevadero; (also: **feeding ~**) comedero

**trousers** ['trauzəz] npl pantalones mpl; **short ~** pantalones mpl cortos

**trout** [traut] n (pl inv) trucha

**trowel** ['trauəl] n paleta

**truant** ['truənt] n: **to play ~**(BRIT) hacer novillos

**truce** [tru:s] n tregua

**truck** [trʌk] n (US) camión m; (Rail) vagón m; **truck driver** n camionero/a

**true** [tru:] adj verdadero; (accurate) exacto; (genuine) auténtico; (faithful) fiel; **to come ~** realizarse

**truly** ['tru:lɪ] adv realmente; **yours ~** (in letter-writing) atentamente

**trumpet** ['trʌmpɪt] n trompeta

**trunk** [trʌŋk] n (of tree, person) tronco; (of elephant) trompa; (case) baúl m; (US Aut) maletero

**trunks** [trʌŋks] npl (also: **swimming ~**) bañador m

**trust** [trʌst] n confianza; (Law) fideicomiso ▷ vt (rely on) tener confianza en; **to ~ sth to sb** (entrust) confiar algo a algn; **to ~ (that)** (hope) esperar (que); **you'll have to take it on ~** tienes que aceptarlo a ojos cerrados; **trusted** adj de confianza; **trustworthy** adj digno de confianza

**truth** (pl **truths**) [tru:θ, tru:ðz] n verdad f; **truthful** adj (person) sincero; (account) fidedigno

**try** [traɪ] n tentativa, intento; (Rugby) ensayo ▷ vt (Law) juzgar, procesar; (test: sth new) probar, someter a prueba; (attempt) intentar; (strain: patience) hacer perder ▷ vi probar; **to give sth a ~** intentar hacer algo; **to ~ to do sth** intentar hacer algo; **~ again!** ¡vuelve a probar!; **~ harder!** ¡esfuérzate más!; **well, I tried** al menos lo intenté; **try on** vt (clothes) probarse; **trying** adj cansado; (person) pesado

**T-shirt** ['ti:ʃə:t] n camiseta

**tub** [tʌb] n cubo (SP), balde m (LAM); (bath) bañera, tina (LAM)

**tube** [tju:b] n tubo; (BRIT: underground) metro

**tuberculosis** [tjubə:kju'ləusɪs] n tuberculosis f inv

**tube station** n (BRIT) estación f de metro

**tuck** [tʌk] vt (put) poner; **tuck away** vt esconder; **tuck in** vt meter; (child) arropar ▷ vi (eat) comer con apetito

**tucker** ['tʌkə²] n (AUST, NZ inf) papeo

**tuck shop** n (Scol) tienda de golosinas

**Tue(s).** abbr (= Tuesday) mart.

**Tuesday** ['tju:zdɪ] n martes m inv

**tug** [tʌg] n (ship) remolcador m ▷ vt remolcar

**tuition** [tju:'ɪʃən] n (BRIT) enseñanza; (: private tuition) clases fpl particulares; (US: school fees) matrícula

**tulip** ['tju:lɪp] n tulipán m

**tumble** ['tʌmbl] n (fall) caída ▷ vi caerse; **to ~ to sth** (inf) caer en la cuenta de algo; **tumble dryer** n (BRIT) secadora

**tumbler** ['tʌmblə²] n vaso

**tummy** ['tʌmɪ] n (inf) barriga

**tumour,** (US) **tumor** ['tju:mə²] n tumor m

**tuna** ['tju:nə] n (pl inv: also: **~ fish**) atún m

**tune** [tju:n] n melodía ▷ vt (Mus) afinar; (Radio, TV, Aut) sintonizar; **to be in/out of ~** (instrument) estar afinado/desafinado; (singer) afinar/desafinar; **to be in/out of ~ with** (fig) armonizar/desentonar con; **tune in** vi (Radio, TV): **to ~ in (to)** sintonizar (con); **tune up** vi (musician) afinar (su instrumento)

**tunic** ['tju:nɪk] n túnica

**Tunisia** [tju:'nɪzɪə] n Túnez m

**tunnel** ['tʌnl] n túnel m; (in mine) galería ▷ vi construir un túnel/una galería

**turbulence** ['tə:bjuləns] n (Aviat) turbulencia

**turf** [tə:f] n césped m; (clod) tepe m ▷ vt cubrir con césped

**Turk** [tə:k] n turco/a

**Turkey** ['tə:kɪ] n Turquía

**turkey** ['tə:kɪ] n pavo

**Turkish** ['tə:kɪʃ] adj turco ▷ n (Ling) turco

**turmoil** ['tə:mɔɪl] n: **in ~** revuelto

**turn** [tə:n] n turno; (in road) curva; (Theat) número; (Med) ataque m ▷ vt girar, volver; (collar, steak) dar la vuelta a; (change): **to ~ sth into** convertir algo en ▷ vi volver; (person: look back) volverse; (reverse direction) dar la vuelta; (milk) cortarse; **a good ~** un favor; **it gave me quite a ~** me dio un susto; **"no left ~"** (Aut) "prohibido girar a la izquierda"; **it's your ~** te toca a ti; **in ~** por turnos; **to take ~s** turnarse; **turn around** vi (person) volverse, darse la vuelta ▷ vt (object) dar la vuelta a, voltear (LAM); **turn away** vi apartar la vista ▷ vt rechazar; **turn back** vi volverse atrás ▷ vt hacer retroceder; (clock) retrasar; **turn down** vt (refuse) rechazar; (reduce) bajar; (fold) doblar; **turn in** vi (inf: go to bed) acostarse ▷ vt (fold) doblar hacia dentro; **turn off** vi (from road) desviarse ▷ vt (light, radio etc) apagar; (engine) parar; **turn on** vt (light, radio etc) encender, prender (LAM); (engine) poner en marcha; **turn out** vt (light, gas) apagar; (produce) producir ▷ vi: **to ~ out to be ...** resultar ser ...; **turn over** vi (person) volverse ▷ vt (mattress, card) dar la vuelta a;

*(page)* volver; **turn round** *vi* volverse; *(rotate)* girar; **turn to** *vt fus*: **to ~ to sb** acudir a algn; **turn up** *vi (person)* llegar, presentarse; *(lost object)* aparecer ▷ *vt (radio)* subir; **turning** *n (bend)* curva; **turning point** *n (fig)* momento decisivo

**turnip** ['tə:nɪp] *n* nabo

**turn: turnout** ['tə:naut] *n (attendance)* asistencia; *(number of people attending)* número de asistentes; *(spectators)* público; **turnover** *n (Comm: amount of money)* facturación *f*; *(of goods)* movimiento; **turnstile** *n* torniquete *m*; **turn-up** *n (BRIT: on trousers)* vuelta

**turquoise** ['tə:kwɔɪz] *n (stone)* turquesa ▷ *adj* color turquesa *inv*

**turtle** ['tə:tl] *n* tortuga (marina)

**turtleneck (sweater)** ['tə:tlnɛk-] *n* (jersey *m* de) cuello cisne

**tusk** [tʌsk] *n* colmillo

**tutor** ['tju:təʳ] *n* profesor(a) *m/f*; **tutorial** [tju:'tɔ:rɪəl] *n (Scol)* seminario

**tuxedo** [tʌk'si:dəu] *n (US)* smóking *m*, esmoquin *m*

**TV** [ti:'vi:] *n abbr* (= *television*) televisión *f*

**tweed** [twi:d] *n* tweed *m*

**tweet** [twi:t] *n (on Twitter)* tweet *m* ▷ *vt, vi (on Twitter)* tuitear

**tweezers** ['twi:zəz] *npl* pinzas *fpl* (de depilar)

**twelfth** [twɛlfθ] *num* duodécimo

**twelve** [twɛlv] *num* doce; **at ~ o'clock** *(midday)* a mediodía; *(midnight)* a medianoche

**twentieth** ['twɛntɪɪθ] *num* vigésimo

**twenty** ['twɛntɪ] *num* veinte; **in ~ fourteen** en dos mil catorce

**twice** [twaɪs] *adv* dos veces; **~ as much** dos veces más

**twig** [twɪg] *n* ramita

**twilight** ['twaɪlaɪt] *n* crepúsculo

**twin** [twɪn] *adj, n* gemelo/a ▷ *vt* hermanar; **twin-bedded room** *n* = **twin room**; **twin beds** *npl* camas *fpl* gemelas

**twinkle** ['twɪŋkl] *vi* centellear; *(eyes)* parpadear

**twin room** *n* habitación *f* con dos camas

**twist** [twɪst] *n (action)* torsión *f*; *(in road, coil)* vuelta; *(in wire, flex)* doblez *f*; *(in story)* giro ▷ *vt* torcer; *(roll around)* enrollar; *(fig)* deformar ▷ *vi* serpentear

**twit** [twɪt] *n (inf)* tonto

**twitch** [twɪtʃ] *n* sacudida; *(nervous)* tic *m* nervioso ▷ *vi* moverse nerviosamente

**two** [tu:] *num* dos; **to put ~ and ~ together** *(fig)* atar cabos

**type** [taɪp] *n (category)* tipo, género; *(model)* modelo; *(Typ)* tipo, letra ▷ *vt (letter etc)* escribir a máquina; **typewriter** *n* máquina de escribir

**typhoid** ['taɪfɔɪd] *n (fiebre f)* tifoidea

**typhoon** [taɪ'fu:n] *n* tifón *m*

**typical** ['tɪpɪkl] *adj* típico; **typically** *adv* típicamente

**typing** ['taɪpɪŋ] *n* mecanografía

**typist** ['taɪpɪst] *n* mecanógrafo/a

**tyre**, *(US)* **tire** ['taɪəʳ] *n* neumático, llanta *(LAM)*; **tyre pressure** *n* presión *f* de los neumáticos

# u

**UFO** ['juːfəu] *n abbr* (= *unidentified flying object*) OVNI *m*
**Uganda** [juː'gændə] *n* Uganda
**ugly** ['ʌglɪ] *adj* feo; (*dangerous*) peligroso
**UHT** *adj abbr* = **ultra heat treated**; **~ milk** leche *f* uperizada
**UK** *n abbr* (= *United Kingdom*) R.U.
**ulcer** ['ʌlsəʳ] *n* úlcera; **mouth ~** llaga bucal
**ultimate** ['ʌltɪmət] *adj* último, final; (*greatest*) mayor; **ultimately** *adv* (*in the end*) por último, al final; (*fundamentally*) a fin de cuentas
**ultimatum** (*pl* **ultimatums** *or* **ultimata**) [ʌltɪ'meɪtəm, -tə] *n* ultimátum *m*
**ultrasound** ['ʌltrəsaund] *n* (*Med*) ultrasonido
**ultraviolet** ['ʌltrə'vaɪəlɪt] *adj* ultravioleta
**umbrella** [ʌm'brɛlə] *n* paraguas *m inv*
**umpire** ['ʌmpaɪəʳ] *n* árbitro
**UN** *n abbr* (= *United Nations*) ONU *f*
**unable** [ʌn'eɪbl] *adj*: **to be ~ to do sth** no poder hacer algo
**unacceptable** [ʌnək'sɛptəbl] *adj* (*proposal, behaviour, price*) inaceptable; **it's ~ that** no se puede aceptar que
**unanimous** [juː'nænɪməs] *adj* unánime
**unarmed** [ʌn'ɑːmd] *adj* (*person*) desarmado
**unattended** [ʌnə'tɛndɪd] *adj* desatendido
**unattractive** [ʌnə'træktɪv] *adj* poco atractivo
**unavailable** [ʌnə'veɪləbl] *adj* (*article, room, book*) no disponible; (*person*) ocupado
**unavoidable** [ʌnə'vɔɪdəbl] *adj* inevitable
**unaware** [ʌnə'wɛəʳ] *adj*: **to be ~ of** ignorar; **unawares** *adv*: **to catch sb unawares** pillar a algn desprevenido
**unbearable** [ʌn'bɛərəbl] *adj* insoportable
**unbeatable** [ʌn'biːtəbl] *adj* invencible; (*price*) inmejorable
**unbelievable** [ʌnbɪ'liːvəbl] *adj* increíble

**unborn** [ʌn'bɔːn] *adj* que va a nacer
**unbutton** [ʌn'bʌtn] *vt* desabrochar
**uncalled-for** [ʌn'kɔːldfɔːʳ] *adj* gratuito, inmerecido
**uncanny** [ʌn'kænɪ] *adj* extraño
**uncertain** [ʌn'səːtn] *adj* incierto; (*indecisive*) indeciso; **uncertainty** *n* incertidumbre *f*
**unchanged** [ʌn'tʃeɪndʒd] *adj* sin cambiar *or* alterar
**uncle** ['ʌŋkl] *n* tío
**unclear** [ʌn'klɪəʳ] *adj* poco claro; **I'm still ~ about what I'm supposed to do** todavía no tengo muy claro lo que tengo que hacer
**uncomfortable** [ʌn'kʌmfətəbl] *adj* incómodo; (*uneasy*) inquieto
**uncommon** [ʌn'kɔmən] *adj* poco común, raro
**unconditional** [ʌnkən'dɪʃənl] *adj* incondicional
**unconscious** [ʌn'kɔnʃəs] *adj* sin sentido; (*unaware*) inconsciente ▷ *n*: **the ~** el inconsciente
**uncontrollable** [ʌnkən'trəuləbl] *adj* (*temper*) indomable; (*laughter*) incontenible
**unconventional** [ʌnkən'vɛnʃənl] *adj* poco convencional
**uncover** [ʌn'kʌvəʳ] *vt* descubrir; (*take lid off*) destapar
**undecided** [ʌndɪ'saɪdɪd] *adj* (*person*) indeciso; (*question*) no resuelto
**undeniable** [ʌndɪ'naɪəbl] *adj* innegable
**under** ['ʌndəʳ] *prep* debajo de; (*less than*) menos de; (*according to*) según, de acuerdo con ▷ *adv* debajo, abajo; **~ there** ahí debajo; **~ construction** en construcción; **undercover** *adj* clandestino; **underdone** *adj* (*Culin*) poco hecho; **underestimate** *vt* subestimar; **undergo** *vt* (*irreg*: *like* **go**) sufrir; (*treatment*) recibir; **undergraduate** *n* estudiante *mf*; **underground** *n* (*BRIT*: *railway*) metro; (*Pol*) movimiento clandestino ▷ *adj* subterráneo ▷ *adv* (*work*) en la clandestinidad; **undergrowth** *n* maleza; **underline** *vt* subrayar; **undermine** *vt* socavar, minar; **underneath** [ʌndə'niːθ] *adv* debajo ▷ *prep* debajo de, bajo; **underpants** *npl* calzoncillos *mpl*; **underpass** *n* (*BRIT*) paso subterráneo; **underprivileged** *adj* desposeído; **underscore** *vt* subrayar, sostener; **undershirt** *n* (*US*) camiseta; **underskirt** *n* (*BRIT*) enaguas *fpl*
**understand** (*pt*, *pp* **understood**) [ʌndə'stænd, ʌndə'stud] *vt*, *vi* entender, comprender; (*assume*) tener entendido; **understandable** *adj* comprensible; **understanding** *adj* comprensivo ▷ *n* comprensión *f*, entendimiento; (*agreement*) acuerdo

**understatement** [ˌʌndəˈsteɪtmənt] n modestia (excesiva); **to say it was good is quite an ~** decir que estuvo bien es quedarse corto

**understood** [ˌʌndəˈstʊd] pt, pp of **understand** ▷ adj entendido; (implied): **it is ~ that** se sobreentiende que

**undertake** [ˌʌndəˈteɪk] vt (irreg: like **take**) emprender; **to ~ to do sth** comprometerse a hacer algo

**undertaker** [ˈʌndəteɪkəʳ] n director(a) m/f de pompas fúnebres

**undertaking** [ˈʌndəteɪkɪŋ] n empresa; (promise) promesa

**under: underwater** adv bajo el agua ▷ adj submarino; **underway** adj: **to be underway** (meeting) estar en marcha; (investigation) estar llevándose a cabo; **underwear** n ropa interior or íntima (LAM); **underwent** vb see **undergo**; **underworld** n (of crime) hampa, inframundo

**undesirable** [ˌʌndɪˈzaɪərəbl] adj indeseable

**undisputed** [ˌʌndɪˈspjuːtɪd] adj incontestable

**undo** [ʌnˈduː] vt (irreg: like **do**: laces) desatar; (button etc) desabrochar; (spoil) deshacer

**undone** [ʌnˈdʌn] pp of **undo** ▷ adj: **to come ~** (clothes) desabrocharse; (parcel) desatarse

**undoubtedly** [ʌnˈdautɪdlɪ] adv indudablemente, sin duda

**undress** [ʌnˈdrɛs] vi desnudarse

**unearth** [ʌnˈɜːθ] vt desenterrar

**uneasy** [ʌnˈiːzɪ] adj intranquilo; (worried) preocupado; **to feel ~ about doing sth** sentirse incómodo con la idea de hacer algo

**unemployed** [ʌnɪmˈplɔɪd] adj parado, sin trabajo ▷ n: **the ~** los parados

**unemployment** [ʌnɪmˈplɔɪmənt] n paro, desempleo; **unemployment benefit** n (BRIT) subsidio de desempleo or paro

**unequal** [ʌnˈiːkwəl] adj (length, objects etc) desigual; (amounts) distinto

**uneven** [ʌnˈiːvn] adj desigual; (road etc) con baches

**unexpected** [ʌnɪkˈspɛktɪd] adj inesperado; **unexpectedly** adv inesperadamente

**unfair** [ʌnˈfɛəʳ] adj: **~ (to sb)** injusto (con algn)

**unfaithful** [ʌnˈfeɪθful] adj infiel

**unfamiliar** [ʌnfəˈmɪlɪəʳ] adj extraño, desconocido; **to be ~ with sth** desconocer or ignorar algo

**unfashionable** [ʌnˈfæʃnəbl] adj pasado or fuera de moda

**unfasten** [ʌnˈfɑːsn] vt desatar

**unfavourable**, (US) **unfavorable** [ʌnˈfeɪvərəbl] adj desfavorable

**unfinished** [ʌnˈfɪnɪʃt] adj inacabado, sin terminar

**unfit** [ʌnˈfɪt] adj en baja forma; (incompetent) incapaz; **~ for work** incapacitado/a para trabajar

**unfold** [ʌnˈfəuld] vt desdoblar ▷ vi abrirse

**unforgettable** [ʌnfəˈgɛtəbl] adj inolvidable

**unfortunate** [ʌnˈfɔːtʃnət] adj desgraciado; (event, remark) inoportuno; **unfortunately** adv desgraciadamente

**unfriend** [ʌnˈfrɛnd] vt (Internet) quitar de amigo a; **he has ~ed her on Facebook** la ha quitado de amiga en Facebook

**unfriendly** [ʌnˈfrɛndlɪ] adj antipático; (behaviour, remark) hostil, poco amigable

**unfurnished** [ʌnˈfɜːnɪʃt] adj sin amueblar

**unhappiness** [ʌnˈhæpɪnɪs] n tristeza

**unhappy** [ʌnˈhæpɪ] adj (sad) triste; (unfortunate) desgraciado; (childhood) infeliz; **~ with** (arrangements etc) poco contento con, descontento de

**unhealthy** [ʌnˈhɛlθɪ] adj malsano; (person) enfermizo; (interest) morboso

**unheard-of** [ʌnˈhɜːdɔv] adj inaudito, sin precedente

**unhelpful** [ʌnˈhɛlpful] adj (person) poco servicial; (advice) inútil

**unhurt** [ʌnˈhɜːt] adj ileso

**unidentified** [ʌnaɪˈdɛntɪfaɪd] adj no identificado; **~ flying object (UFO)** objeto volante no identificado (OVNI)

**uniform** [ˈjuːnɪfɔːm] n uniforme m ▷ adj uniforme

**unify** [ˈjuːnɪfaɪ] vt unificar, unir

**unimportant** [ʌnɪmˈpɔːtənt] adj sin importancia

**uninhabited** [ʌnɪnˈhæbɪtɪd] adj desierto

**unintentional** [ʌnɪnˈtɛnʃənəl] adj involuntario

**union** [ˈjuːnjən] n unión f; (also: **trade ~**) sindicato ▷ cpd sindical; **Union Jack** n bandera del Reino Unido

**unique** [juːˈniːk] adj único

**unisex** [ˈjuːnɪsɛks] adj unisex

**unit** [ˈjuːnɪt] n unidad f; (team, squad) grupo; **kitchen ~** módulo de cocina

**unite** [juːˈnaɪt] vt unir ▷ vi unirse; **united** adj unido; **United Kingdom** n Reino Unido

**United Nations (Organization)** n Naciones Unidas fpl

**United States (of America)** n Estados Unidos mpl (de América)

**unity** [ˈjuːnɪtɪ] n unidad f

**universal** [juːnɪˈvɜːsl] adj universal

**universe** [ˈjuːnɪvɜːs] n universo

**university** [juːnɪˈvɜːsɪtɪ] n universidad f

**unjust** [ʌnˈdʒʌst] adj injusto

**unkind** [ʌnˈkaɪnd] adj poco amable; (comment etc) cruel

**unknown** [ʌn'nəʊn] *adj* desconocido

**unlawful** [ʌn'lɔ:ful] *adj* ilegal, ilícito

**unleaded** [ʌn'lɛdɪd] *n* (*also:* ~ **petrol**) gasolina sin plomo

**unleash** [ʌn'li:ʃ] *vt* desatar

**unless** [ʌn'lɛs] *conj* a menos que; ~ **he comes** a menos que venga; ~ **otherwise stated** salvo indicación contraria

**unlike** [ʌn'laɪk] *adj* distinto ▷ *prep* a diferencia de

**unlikely** [ʌn'laɪklɪ] *adj* improbable

**unlimited** [ʌn'lɪmɪtɪd] *adj* ilimitado

**unlisted** [ʌn'lɪstɪd] *adj* (*US Tel*) que no figura en la guía

**unload** [ʌn'ləʊd] *vt* descargar

**unlock** [ʌn'lɔk] *vt* abrir (con llave)

**unlucky** [ʌn'lʌkɪ] *adj* desgraciado; (*object, number*) que da mala suerte; **to be** ~ tener mala suerte

**unmarried** [ʌn'mærɪd] *adj* soltero

**unmistakable** [ʌnmɪs'teɪkəbl] *adj* inconfundible

**unnatural** [ʌn'nætʃrəl] *adj* antinatural; (*manner*) afectado; (*habit*) perverso

**unnecessary** [ʌn'nɛsəsərɪ] *adj* innecesario, inútil

**UNO** ['ju:nəʊ] *n abbr* (= *United Nations Organization*) ONU *f*

**unofficial** [ʌnə'fɪʃl] *adj* no oficial

**unpack** [ʌn'pæk] *vi* deshacer las maletas ▷ *vt* deshacer

**unpaid** [ʌn'peɪd] *adj* (*bill, debt*) sin pagar, impagado; (*Comm*) pendiente; (*holiday*) sin sueldo; (*work*) sin pago, voluntario

**unpleasant** [ʌn'plɛznt] *adj* (*disagreeable*) desagradable; (*person, manner*) antipático

**unplug** [ʌn'plʌg] *vt* desenchufar, desconectar

**unpopular** [ʌn'pɔpjulər] *adj* poco popular

**unprecedented** [ʌn'prɛsɪdəntɪd] *adj* sin precedentes

**unpredictable** [ʌnprɪ'dɪktəbl] *adj* imprevisible

**unprotected** ['ʌnprə'tɛktɪd] *adj* (*sex*) sin protección

**unqualified** [ʌn'kwɔlɪfaɪd] *adj* sin título, no cualificado; (*success*) total

**unravel** [ʌn'rævl] *vt* desenmarañar

**unreal** [ʌn'rɪəl] *adj* irreal

**unrealistic** [ʌnrɪə'lɪstɪk] *adj* poco realista

**unreasonable** [ʌn'ri:znəbl] *adj* irrazonable; **to make** ~ **demands on sb** hacer demandas excesivas a algn

**unrelated** [ʌnrɪ'leɪtɪd] *adj* sin relación; (*family*) no emparentado

**unreliable** [ʌnrɪ'laɪəbl] *adj* (*person*) informal; (*machine*) poco fiable

**unrest** [ʌn'rɛst] *n* inquietud *f*, malestar *m*; (*Pol*) disturbios *mpl*

**unroll** [ʌn'rəʊl] *vt* desenrollar

**unruly** [ʌn'ru:lɪ] *adj* indisciplinado

**unsafe** [ʌn'seɪf] *adj* peligroso

**unsatisfactory** ['ʌnsætɪs'fæktərɪ] *adj* poco satisfactorio

**unscrew** [ʌn'skru:] *vt* destornillar

**unsettled** [ʌn'sɛtld] *adj* inquieto; (*weather*) variable

**unsettling** [ʌn'sɛtlɪŋ] *adj* perturbador(a), inquietante

**unsightly** [ʌn'saɪtlɪ] *adj* desagradable

**unskilled** [ʌn'skɪld] *adj*: ~ **workers** mano *f* de obra no cualificada

**unspoiled** ['ʌn'spɔɪld], **unspoilt** ['ʌn'spɔɪlt] *adj* (*place*) que no ha perdido su belleza natural

**unstable** [ʌn'steɪbl] *adj* inestable

**unsteady** [ʌn'stɛdɪ] *adj* inestable

**unsuccessful** [ʌnsək'sɛsful] *adj* (*attempt*) infructuoso; (*writer, proposal*) sin éxito; **to be** ~ (*in attempting sth*) no tener éxito, fracasar

**unsuitable** [ʌn'su:təbl] *adj* inapropiado; (*time*) inoportuno

**unsure** [ʌn'ʃuər] *adj* inseguro, poco seguro

**untidy** [ʌn'taɪdɪ] *adj* (*room*) desordenado; (*appearance*) desaliñado

**untie** [ʌn'taɪ] *vt* desatar

**until** [ən'tɪl] *prep* hasta ▷ *conj* hasta que; ~ **he comes** hasta que venga; ~ **now** hasta ahora; ~ **then** hasta entonces

**untrue** [ʌn'tru:] *adj* (*statement*) falso

**unused** [ʌn'ju:zd] *adj* sin usar

**unusual** [ʌn'ju:ʒuəl] *adj* insólito, poco común; **unusually** *adv*: **he arrived unusually early** llegó más temprano que de costumbre

**unveil** [ʌn'veɪl] *vt* (*statue*) descubrir

**unwanted** [ʌn'wɔntɪd] *adj* (*person, effect*) no deseado

**unwell** [ʌn'wɛl] *adj*: **to feel** ~ estar indispuesto, sentirse mal

**unwilling** [ʌn'wɪlɪŋ] *adj*: **to be** ~ **to do sth** estar poco dispuesto a hacer algo

**unwind** [ʌn'waɪnd] (*irreg: like* **wind²**) *vt* desenvolver ▷ *vi* (*relax*) relajarse

**unwise** [ʌn'waɪz] *adj* imprudente

**unwittingly** [ʌn'wɪtɪŋlɪ] *adv* inconscientemente, sin darse cuenta

**unwrap** [ʌn'ræp] *vt* desenvolver

**unzip** [ʌn'zɪp] *vt* abrir la cremallera de; (*Comput*) descomprimir

 **KEYWORD**

**up** [ʌp] *prep*: **to go/be up sth** subir/estar subido en algo; **he went up the stairs/ the hill** subió las escaleras/la colina; **we walked/climbed up the hill** subimos la

colina; **they live further up the street** viven más arriba en la calle; **go up that road and turn left** sigue por esa calle y gira a la izquierda
▸ *adv* **1** (*upwards, higher*) más arriba; **up in the mountains** en lo alto (de la montaña); **put it a bit higher up** ponlo un poco más arriba *or* alto; **up there** ahí *or* allí arriba; **up above** en lo alto, por encima, arriba
**2**: **to be up** (*out of bed*) estar levantado; (*prices, level*) haber subido
**3**: **up to** (*as far as*) hasta; **up to now** hasta ahora *or* la fecha
**4**: **to be up to** (*depending on*): **it's up to you** depende de ti; **he's not up to it** (*job, task etc*) no es capaz de hacerlo; **his work is not up to the required standard** su trabajo no da la talla; **what is he up to?** (*inf: doing*) ¿qué estará tramando?
▸ *n*: **ups and downs** altibajos *mpl*

**up-and-coming** [ʌpənd'kʌmɪŋ] *adj* prometedor(a)
**upbringing** ['ʌpbrɪŋɪŋ] *n* educación *f*
**update** [ʌp'deɪt] *vt* poner al día
**upfront** [ʌp'frʌnt] *adj* claro, directo ▸ *adv* a las claras; (*pay*) por adelantado; **to be ~ about sth** admitir algo claramente
**upgrade** [ʌp'greɪd] *vt* ascender; (*Comput*) modernizar
**upheaval** [ʌp'hi:vl] *n* trastornos *mpl*; (*Pol*) agitación *f*
**uphill** [ʌp'hɪl] *adj* cuesta arriba; (*fig: task*) penoso, difícil ▸ *adv*: **to go ~** ir cuesta arriba
**upholstery** [ʌp'həulstərɪ] *n* tapicería
**upload** ['ʌpləud] *vt* (*Comput*) subir
**upmarket** [ʌp'mɑ:kɪt] *adj* (*product*) de categoría
**upon** [ə'pɒn] *prep* sobre
**upper** ['ʌpəʳ] *adj* superior, de arriba ▸ *n* (*of shoe: also*: **~s**) pala; **upper-class** *adj* de clase alta
**upright** ['ʌpraɪt] *adj* vertical; (*fig*) honrado
**uprising** ['ʌpraɪzɪŋ] *n* sublevación *f*
**uproar** ['ʌprɔ:ʳ] *n* escándalo
**upset** *n* ['ʌpset] (*to plan etc*) revés *m*, contratiempo; (*Med*) trastorno ▸ *vt* [ʌp'set] (*irreg: like* **set**: *glass etc*) volcar; (*plan*) alterar; (*person*) molestar ▸ *adj* [ʌp'set] preocupado, perturbado; (*stomach*) revuelto
**upside-down** ['ʌpsaɪd'daun] *adv* al revés; **to turn a place ~** (*fig*) revolverlo todo
**upstairs** [ʌp'steəz] *adv* arriba ▸ *adj* (*room*) de arriba ▸ *n* el piso superior
**up-to-date** ['ʌptə'deɪt] *adj* actual, moderno
**uptown** ['ʌptaun] *adv* (*US*) hacia las afueras ▸ *adj* exterior, de las afueras

**upward(s)** ['ʌpwəd(z)] *adv* hacia arriba; (*more than*): **~ of** más de
**uranium** [juə'reɪnɪəm] *n* uranio
**Uranus** [juə'reɪnəs] *n* Urano
**urban** ['ə:bən] *adj* urbano
**urge** [ə:dʒ] *n* (*desire*) deseo ▸ *vt*: **to ~ sb to do sth** animar a algn a hacer algo
**urgency** ['ə:dʒənsɪ] *n* urgencia
**urgent** ['ə:dʒənt] *adj* urgente
**urinal** ['juərɪnl] *n* (*building*) urinario; (*vessel*) orinal *m*
**urinate** ['juərɪneɪt] *vi* orinar
**urine** ['juərɪn] *n* orina
**US** *n abbr* (= *United States*) EE.UU.
**us** [ʌs] *pron* nos; (*after prep*) nosotros/as; *see also* **me**
**USA** *n abbr* = **United States of America**; (*Mil*) = **United States Army**
**USB** *abbr* (= *universal serial bus*) USB *m*; **USB stick** *n* memoria USB, llave *f* de memoria
**use** *n* [ju:s] uso, empleo; (*usefulness*) utilidad *f* ▸ *vt* [ju:z] usar, emplear; **in ~** en uso; **out of ~** en desuso; **to be of ~** servir; **it's no ~** (*pointless*) es inútil; (*not useful*) no sirve; **to be ~d to** estar acostumbrado a (*sp*), acostumbrar; **she ~d to do it** (ella) solía *or* acostumbraba hacerlo; **use up** *vt* (*food*) consumir; (*money*) gastar; **used** [ju:zd] *adj* (*car*) usado; **useful** *adj* útil; **useless** *adj* (*unusable*) inservible; **user** *n* usuario/a; **user-friendly** *adj* (*Comput*) fácil de utilizar
**username** ['ju:zəneɪm] *n* (*Comput*) nombre *m* de usuario
**usual** ['ju:ʒuəl] *adj* normal, corriente; **as ~** como de costumbre; **usually** *adv* normalmente
**ute** [ju:t] *n abbr* (*AUST, NZ inf*: = *utility truck*) camioneta
**utensil** [ju:'tensl] *n* utensilio; **kitchen ~s** batería de cocina
**utility** [ju:'tɪlɪtɪ] *n* utilidad *f*; (*public utility*) (empresa de) servicio público
**utilize** ['ju:tɪlaɪz] *vt* utilizar
**utmost** ['ʌtməust] *adj* mayor ▸ *n*: **to do one's ~** hacer todo lo posible
**utter** ['ʌtəʳ] *adj* total, completo ▸ *vt* pronunciar, proferir; **utterly** *adv* completamente, totalmente
**U-turn** ['ju:'tə:n] *n* cambio de sentido

# V

**v.** *abbr* (= *verse*) vers.°; (= *see*) V, vid., vide;
(= *versus*) vs.; = **volt**

**vacancy** ['veɪkənsɪ] *n* (*job*) vacante *f*; (*room*)
cuarto libro; "**no vacancies**" "completo"

**vacant** ['veɪkənt] *adj* desocupado, libre;
(*expression*) distraído

**vacate** [vəˈkeɪt] *vt* (*house*) desocupar; (*job*)
dejar (vacante)

**vacation** [vəˈkeɪʃən] *n* vacaciones *fpl*;
**vacationer** [vəˈkeɪʃənəʳ], **vacationist**
[vəˈkeɪʃənɪst] *n* (*us*) turista *mf*

**vaccination** [væksɪˈneɪʃən] *n* vacunación *f*

**vaccine** ['væksiːn] *n* vacuna

**vacuum** ['vækjum] *n* vacío; **vacuum
cleaner** *n* aspiradora

**vagina** [vəˈdʒaɪnə] *n* vagina

**vague** [veɪg] *adj* vago; (*memory*) borroso;
(*ambiguous*) impreciso; (*person: absent-
minded*) distraído; (: *evasive*): **to be ~** no decir
las cosas claramente

**vain** [veɪn] *adj* (*conceited*) presumido;
(*useless*) vano, inútil; **in ~** en vano

**Valentine's Day** *n* día de los enamorados
(*el 14 de febrero, día de San Valentín*)

**valid** ['vælɪd] *adj* válido; (*ticket*) valedero;
(*law*) vigente

**valley** ['vælɪ] *n* valle *m*

**valuable** ['væljuəbl] *adj* (*jewel*) de valor;
(*time*) valioso; **valuables** *npl* objetos *mpl*
de valor

**value** ['væljuː] *n* valor *m*;
(*importance*) importancia ▷ *vt* (*fix price of*)
tasar, valorar; (*esteem*) apreciar; **values** *npl*
(*moral*) valores *mpl* morales

**valve** [vælv] *n* válvula

**vampire** ['væmpaɪəʳ] *n* vampiro

**van** [væn] *n* (*Aut*) furgoneta, camioneta
(*LAM*)

**vandal** ['vændl] *n* vándalo/a; **vandalism** *n*
vandalismo; **vandalize** *vt* dañar, destruir

**vanilla** [vəˈnɪlə] *n* vainilla

**vanish** ['vænɪʃ] *vi* desaparecer

**vanity** ['vænɪtɪ] *n* vanidad *f*

**vapour**, (*us*) **vapor** ['veɪpəʳ] *n* vapor *m*; (*on
breath, window*) vaho

**variable** ['vɛərɪəbl] *adj* variable

**variant** ['vɛərɪənt] *n* variante *f*

**variation** [vɛərɪˈeɪʃən] *n* variación *f*

**varied** ['vɛərɪd] *adj* variado

**variety** [vəˈraɪətɪ] *n* variedad *f*, diversidad *f*

**various** ['vɛərɪəs] *adj* varios/as, diversos/as

**varnish** ['vɑːnɪʃ] *n* barniz *m*; (*also*: **nail ~**)
esmalte *m* ▷ *vt* barnizar; (*nails*) pintar (con
esmalte)

**vary** ['vɛərɪ] *vt* variar; (*change*) cambiar ▷ *vi*
variar

**vase** [vɑːz] *n* florero, jarrón *m*

> Be careful not to translate *vase* by the
> Spanish word *vaso*.

**Vaseline®** ['væsɪliːn] *n* vaselina®

**vast** [vɑːst] *adj* enorme

**VAT** [væt] *n abbr* (*BRIT*: = *value added tax*)
IVA *m*

**vault** [vɔːlt] *n* (*of roof*) bóveda; (*tomb*)
panteón *m*; (*in bank*) cámara acorazada ▷ *vt*
(*also*: **~ over**) saltar (por encima de)

**VCR** *n abbr* = **video cassette recorder**

**VDU** *n abbr* (= *visual display unit*) UPV *f*

**veal** [viːl] *n* ternera

**veer** [vɪəʳ] *vi* (*vehicle*) virar; (*wind*) girar

**vegan** ['viːgən] *n* vegetariano/a estricto/a

**vegetable** ['vɛdʒtəbl] *n* (*Bot*) vegetal *m*;
(*edible plant*) legumbre *f*, hortaliza ▷ *adj*
vegetal

**vegetarian** [vɛdʒɪˈtɛərɪən] *adj, n*
vegetariano/a

**vegetation** [vɛdʒɪˈteɪʃən] *n* vegetación *f*

**vehicle** ['viːɪkl] *n* vehículo; (*fig*) medio

**veil** [veɪl] *n* velo ▷ *vt* velar

**vein** [veɪn] *n* vena; (*of ore etc*) veta

**Velcro®** ['vɛlkrəu] *n* velcro® *m*

**velvet** ['vɛlvɪt] *n* terciopelo

**vending machine** ['vɛndɪn-] *n* máquina
expendedora, expendedor *m*

**vendor** ['vɛndəʳ] *n* vendedor(a) *m/f*;
**street ~** vendedor(a) *m/f* callejero/a

**vengeance** ['vɛndʒəns] *n* venganza; **with
a ~** (*fig*) con creces

**venison** ['vɛnɪsn] *n* carne *f* de venado

**venom** ['vɛnəm] *n* veneno

**vent** [vɛnt] *n* (*opening*) abertura; (*air-hole*)
respiradero; (*in wall*) rejilla (de ventilación)
▷ *vt* (*fig: feelings*) desahogar

**ventilation** [vɛntɪˈleɪʃən] *n* ventilación *f*

**venture** ['vɛntʃəʳ] *n* empresa ▷ *vt*
(*opinion*) ofrecer ▷ *vi* arriesgarse, lanzarse;
**a business ~** una empresa comercial

**venue** ['vɛnjuː] *n* (*meeting place*) lugar *m* de
reunión

**Venus** ['vi:nəs] *n* Venus *m*
**verb** [vəːb] *n* verbo; **verbal** *adj* verbal
**verdict** ['vəːdɪkt] *n* veredicto, fallo; *(fig)* opinión *f*, juicio
**verge** [vəːdʒ] *n* (BRIT) borde *m*; **to be on the ~ of doing sth** estar a punto de hacer algo
**verify** ['verɪfaɪ] *vt* comprobar, verificar
**versatile** ['vəːsətaɪl] *adj* (person) polifacético; *(machine, tool etc)* versátil
**verse** [vəːs] *n* poesía; *(stanza)* estrofa; *(in bible)* versículo
**version** ['vəːʃən] *n* versión *f*
**versus** ['vəːsəs] *prep* contra
**vertical** ['vəːtɪkl] *adj* vertical
**very** ['verɪ] *adv* muy ▷ *adj*: **the ~ book which** al mismo libro que; **the ~ last** el último (de todos); **at the ~ least** al menos; **~ much** muchísimo
**vessel** ['vesl] *n* (ship) barco; *(container)* vasija
**vest** [vest] *n* (BRIT) camiseta; *(US: waistcoat)* chaleco
**vet** [vet] *n* abbr = **veterinary surgeon** ▷ *vt* revisar; **to ~ sb for a job** someter a investigación a algn para un trabajo
**veteran** ['vetərn] *n* veterano/a
**veterinary surgeon** *n* (BRIT) veterinario/a
**veto** ['vi:təu] *n* veto ▷ *vt* prohibir
**via** ['vaɪə] *prep* por, por vía de
**viable** ['vaɪəbl] *adj* viable
**vibrate** [vaɪ'breɪt] *vi* vibrar
**vibration** [vaɪ'breɪʃən] *n* vibración *f*
**vicar** ['vɪkə'] *n* párroco
**vice** [vaɪs] *n* (evil) vicio; *(Tech)* torno de banco; **vice-chairman** *n* vicepresidente *m*
**vice versa** ['vaɪsɪ'vəːsə] *adv* viceversa
**vicinity** [vɪ'sɪnɪtɪ] *n*: **in the ~ (of)** cercano (a)
**vicious** ['vɪʃəs] *adj* (remark) malicioso; *(blow)* brutal; *(dog, horse)* resabido; **a ~ circle** un círculo vicioso
**victim** ['vɪktɪm] *n* víctima
**victor** ['vɪktə'] *n* vencedor(a) *m/f*
**Victorian** [vɪk'tɔːrɪən] *adj* victoriano
**victorious** [vɪk'tɔːrɪəs] *adj* vencedor(a)
**victory** ['vɪktərɪ] *n* victoria
**video** ['vɪdɪəu] *n* vídeo ▷ *vt* grabar (en vídeo); **video call** *n* videollamada; **video camera** *n* videocámara, cámara de vídeo; **video cassette recorder** *n* = **video recorder**; **video game** *n* videojuego; **videophone** *n* videoteléfono, videófono; **video recorder** *n* vídeo; **video tape** *n* cinta de vídeo
**vie** [vaɪ] *vi*: **to ~ with** competir con
**Vienna** [vɪ'enə] *n* Viena
**Vietnam** [vjet'næm] *n* Vietnam *m*; **Vietnamese** [vjetnə'mi:z] *adj* vietnamita ▷ *n* (pl inv) vietnamita *mf*

**view** [vju:] *n* vista; *(opinion)* opinión *f*, criterio ▷ *vt* (look at) mirar; **on ~** (in museum etc) expuesto; **in full ~ of sb** a la vista de algn; **in ~ of the fact that** en vista de que; **viewer** *n* (TV) telespectador(a) *m/f*; **viewpoint** *n* punto de vista
**vigilant** ['vɪdʒɪlənt] *adj* vigilante
**vigorous** ['vɪgərəs] *adj* enérgico, vigoroso
**vile** [vaɪl] *adj* (action) vil, infame; *(smell)* repugnante; *(temper)* endemoniado
**villa** ['vɪlə] *n* (country house) casa de campo; *(suburban house)* chalet *m*
**village** ['vɪlɪdʒ] *n* aldea; **villager** *n* aldeano/a
**villain** ['vɪlən] *n* (scoundrel) malvado/a; *(criminal)* maleante *mf*
**vinaigrette** [vɪneɪ'gret] *n* vinagreta
**vine** [vaɪn] *n* vid *f*
**vinegar** ['vɪnɪgə'] *n* vinagre *m*
**vineyard** ['vɪnjɑːd] *n* viña, viñedo
**vintage** ['vɪntɪdʒ] *n* (year) vendimia, cosecha
**vinyl** ['vaɪnl] *n* vinilo
**viola** [vɪ'əulə] *n* (Mus) viola
**violate** ['vaɪəleɪt] *vt* violar
**violation** [vaɪə'leɪʃən] *n* violación *f*; **in ~ of sth** en violación de algo
**violence** ['vaɪələns] *n* violencia
**violent** ['vaɪələnt] *adj* violento; *(pain)* intenso
**violet** ['vaɪələt] *adj* violado, violeta *inv* ▷ *n* (plant) violeta
**violin** [vaɪə'lɪn] *n* violín *m*
**VIP** *n* abbr (= very important person) VIP *m*
**viral** *adj* (Med) vírico; *(Comput)* viral
**virgin** ['vəːdʒɪn] *n* virgen *mf*
**Virgo** ['vəːgəu] *n* Virgo
**virtual** ['vəːtjuəl] *adj* virtual; **virtually** *adv* prácticamente, virtualmente; **virtual reality** *n* (Comput) realidad *f* virtual
**virtue** ['vəːtjuː] *n* virtud *f*; **by ~ of** en virtud de
**virus** ['vaɪərəs] *n* virus *m inv*
**visa** ['viːzə] *n* visado, visa (LAM)
**vise** [vaɪs] *n* (US Tech) = **vice**
**visibility** [vɪzɪ'bɪlɪtɪ] *n* visibilidad *f*
**visible** ['vɪzəbl] *adj* visible
**vision** ['vɪʒən] *n* (sight) vista; *(foresight, in dream)* visión *f*
**visit** ['vɪzɪt] *n* visita ▷ *vt* (person) visitar, hacer una visita a; *(place)* ir a, (ir a) conocer; **visiting hours** *npl* (in hospital etc) horas *fpl* de visita; **visitor** *n* visitante *mf*; *(to one's house)* visita; *(tourist)* turista *mf*; **visitor centre**, (US) **visitor center** *n* centro *m* de información
**visual** ['vɪzjuəl] *adj* visual; **visualize** *vt* imaginarse
**vital** ['vaɪtl] *adj* (essential) esencial, imprescindible; *(organ)* vital

**vitality** [vaɪ'tælɪtɪ] n energía, vitalidad f
**vitamin** ['vɪtəmɪn] n vitamina
**vivid** ['vɪvɪd] adj (account) gráfico; (light) intenso; (imagination) vivo
**V-neck** ['viːnɛk] n cuello de pico
**vocabulary** [vəʊ'kæbjʊlərɪ] n vocabulario
**vocal** ['vəʊkl] adj vocal; (articulate) elocuente
**vocational** [vəʊ'keɪʃənl] adj profesional
**vodka** ['vɒdkə] n vodka m
**vogue** [vəʊg] n: **to be in ~** estar de moda or en boga
**voice** [vɔɪs] n voz f; **voice mail** n fonobuzón m
**void** [vɔɪd] n vacío; (hole) hueco ▷ adj (invalid) nulo, inválido; (empty): **~ of** carente or desprovisto de
**volatile** ['vɒlətaɪl] adj (situation) inestable; (person) voluble; (liquid) volátil

**volcano** [vɒl'keɪnəʊ] (pl **volcanoes**) n volcán m
**volleyball** ['vɒlɪbɔːl] n voleibol m
**volt** [vəʊlt] n voltio m; **voltage** n voltaje m
**volume** ['vɒljuːm] n (of tank) volumen m; (book) tomo
**voluntarily** ['vɒləntrɪlɪ] adv libremente, voluntariamente
**voluntary** ['vɒləntərɪ] adj voluntario
**volunteer** [vɒlən'tɪə'] n voluntario/a ▷ vt (information) ofrecer ▷ vi ofrecerse (de voluntario); **to ~ to do** ofrecerse a hacer
**vomit** ['vɒmɪt] n vómito ▷ vt, vi vomitar
**vote** [vəʊt] n voto; (votes cast) votación f; (right to vote) derecho a votar; (franchise) sufragio ▷ vt (chairman) elegir ▷ vi votar, ir a votar; **~ of thanks** voto de gracias; **voter** n votante mf; **voting** n votación f
**voucher** ['vaʊtʃə'] n (for meal, petrol) vale m
**vow** [vaʊ] n voto ▷ vi hacer voto ▷ vt: **to ~ to do/that** jurar hacer/que
**vowel** ['vaʊəl] n vocal f
**voyage** ['vɔɪɪdʒ] n viaje m
**vulgar** ['vʌlɡə'] adj (rude) ordinario, grosero; (in bad taste) de mal gusto
**vulnerable** ['vʌlnərəbl] adj vulnerable
**vulture** ['vʌltʃə'] n buitre m

**waddle** ['wɒdl] vi andar como un pato
**wade** [weɪd] vi (fig: a book) leer con dificultad; **to ~ through the water** caminar por el agua
**wafer** ['weɪfə'] n (biscuit) barquillo
**waffle** ['wɒfl] n (Culin) gofre m ▷ vi meter el rollo
**wag** [wæɡ] vt menear, agitar ▷ vi moverse, menearse
**wage** [weɪdʒ] n (also: **~s**) sueldo, salario ▷ vt: **to ~ war** hacer la guerra
**wag(g)on** ['wæɡən] n (horse-drawn) carro; (BRIT Rail) vagón m
**wail** [weɪl] n gemido ▷ vi gemir
**waist** [weɪst] n cintura, talle m; **waistcoat** n (BRIT) chaleco
**wait** [weɪt] n (interval) pausa ▷ vi esperar; **to lie in ~ for** acechar a; **I can't ~ to** (fig) estoy deseando; **to ~ for** esperar (a); **wait on** vt fus servir a; **waiter** n camarero; **waiting list** n lista de espera; **waiting room** n sala de espera; **waitress** ['weɪtrɪs] n camarera
**waive** [weɪv] vt suspender
**wake** [weɪk] (pt **woke** or **waked**, pp **woken** or **waked**) vt (also: **~ up**) despertar ▷ vi (also: **~ up**) despertarse ▷ n (for dead person) velatorio; (Naut) estela
**Wales** [weɪlz] n País m de Gales
**walk** [wɔːk] n (stroll) paseo; (hike) excursión f a pie, caminata; (gait) paso, andar m; (in park etc) paseo ▷ vi andar, caminar; (for pleasure, exercise) pasearse ▷ vt (distance) recorrer a pie, andar; (dog) (sacar a) pasear; **10 minutes' ~ from here** a 10 minutos de aquí andando; **people from all ~s of life** gente de todas las esferas; **walk out** vi (go out) salir; (as protest) salirse; (strike) declararse en huelga; **walker** n (person) paseante mf, caminante mf; **walkie-talkie** ['wɔːkɪ'tɔːkɪ] n walkie-talkie m; **walking** n

(el) andar; **walking shoes** npl zapatos mpl para andar; **walking stick** n bastón m; **Walkman®** n walkman® m; **walkway** n paseo

**wall** [wɔːl] n pared f; (exterior) muro; (city wall etc) muralla

**wallet** ['wɔlɪt] n cartera

**wallpaper** ['wɔːlpeɪpəʳ] n papel m pintado ▷ vt empapelar

**walnut** ['wɔːlnʌt] n nuez f; (tree) nogal m

**walrus** ['wɔːlrəs] (pl **walrus** or **walruses**) n morsa

**waltz** [wɔːlts] n vals m ▷ vi bailar el vals

**wand** [wɒnd] n (also: **magic ~**) varita (mágica)

**wander** ['wɒndəʳ] vi (person) vagar; deambular; (thoughts) divagar ▷ vt recorrer, vagar por

**want** [wɒnt] vt querer, desear; (need) necesitar ▷ n: **for ~ of** por falta de; **wanted** adj (criminal) buscado; **"wanted"** (in advertisements) "se busca"

**war** [wɔːʳ] n guerra; **to make ~** hacer la guerra

**ward** [wɔːd] n (in hospital) sala; (Pol) distrito electoral; (Law: child: also: **~ of court**) pupilo/a

**warden** ['wɔːdn] n (BRIT: of institution) director(a) m/f; (of park, game reserve) guardián/ana m/f; (BRIT: also: **traffic ~**) guardia mf

**wardrobe** ['wɔːdrəub] n armario, ropero

**warehouse** ['wɛəhaus] n almacén m, depósito

**warfare** ['wɔːfɛəʳ] n guerra

**warhead** ['wɔːhɛd] n cabeza armada

**warm** [wɔːm] adj caliente; (thanks, congratulations, apologies) efusivo; (clothes etc) que abriga; (welcome, day) caluroso; **it's ~** hace calor; **I'm ~** tengo calor; **warm up** vi (room) calentarse; (person) entrar en calor; (athlete) hacer ejercicios de calentamiento ▷ vt calentar; **warmly** adv afectuosamente; **warmth** n calor m

**warn** [wɔːn] vt avisar, advertir; **warning** n aviso, advertencia; **warning light** n luz f de advertencia

**warrant** ['wɔrnt] n (Law: to arrest) orden f de detención; (: to search) mandamiento de registro

**warranty** ['wɔrəntɪ] n garantía

**warrior** ['wɔrɪəʳ] n guerrero/a

**Warsaw** ['wɔːsɔː] n Varsovia

**warship** ['wɔːʃɪp] n buque m or barco de guerra

**wart** [wɔːt] n verruga

**wartime** ['wɔːtaɪm] n: **in ~** en tiempos de guerra, en la guerra

**wary** ['wɛərɪ] adj cauteloso

**was** [wɒz] pt of **be**

**wash** [wɒʃ] vt lavar; (sweep, carry: sea etc) llevar ▷ vi lavarse ▷ n (clothes etc) lavado; (of ship) estela; **to have a ~** lavarse; **wash up** vi (BRIT) fregar los platos; (US) lavarse; **washbasin** n lavabo; **washcloth** n (US) manopla; **washer** n (Tech) arandela; **washing** n (dirty) ropa sucia; (clean) colada; **washing line** n cuerda de (colgar) la ropa; **washing machine** n lavadora; **washing powder** n (BRIT) detergente m (en polvo)

**Washington** ['wɔʃɪŋtən] n Washington m

**wash: washing-up** n fregado; (dishes) platos mpl (para fregar); **washing-up liquid** n lavavajillas m inv; **washroom** n servicios mpl

**wasn't** ['wɔznt] = **was not**

**wasp** [wɒsp] n avispa

**waste** [weɪst] n derroche m, despilfarro; (of time) pérdida; (food) sobras fpl; (rubbish) basura, desperdicios mpl ▷ adj (material) de desecho; (left over) sobrante; (land, ground) baldío ▷ vt malgastar, derrochar; (time) perder; (opportunity) desperdiciar; **waste ground** n (BRIT) terreno baldío; **wastepaper basket** n papelera

**watch** [wɒtʃ] n reloj m; (vigilance) vigilancia; (Mil: guard) centinela m; (Naut: spell of duty) guardia ▷ vt (look at) mirar, observar; (: match, programme) ver; (spy on, guard) vigilar; (be careful of) cuidar, tener cuidado de ▷ vi ver, mirar; (keep guard) montar guardia; **watch out** vi cuidarse, tener cuidado; **watchdog** n perro guardián; (fig) organismo de control; **watch strap** n pulsera (de reloj)

**water** ['wɔːtəʳ] n agua ▷ vt (plant) regar ▷ vi (eyes) llorar; **his mouth ~ed** se le hizo la boca agua; **water down** vt (milk etc) aguar; (fig: story) dulcificar, diluir; **watercolour, (US) watercolor** n acuarela; **watercress** n berro; **waterfall** n cascada, salto de agua; **watering can** n regadera; **watermelon** n sandía; **waterproof** adj impermeable; **water-skiing** n esquí m acuático

**watt** [wɔt] n vatio

**wave** [weɪv] n ola; (of hand) señal f con la mano; (Radio) onda; (in hair) onda; (fig) oleada ▷ vi agitar la mano; (flag) ondear ▷ vt (handkerchief, gun) agitar; **wavelength** n longitud f de onda

**waver** ['weɪvəʳ] vi (faith) flaquear

**wavy** ['weɪvɪ] adj ondulado

**wax** [wæks] n cera ▷ vt encerar ▷ vi (moon) crecer

**way** [weɪ] n camino; (distance) trayecto, recorrido; (direction) dirección f, sentido; (manner) modo, manera; (habit) costumbre f; **which ~? — this ~** ¿por dónde? or ¿en qué dirección? — por aquí; **on the ~** (en route) en (el) camino; **to be on one's ~** estar en camino; **to be in the ~** bloquear el camino; (fig) estorbar; **to go out of one's ~ to do sth** desvivirse por hacer algo; **to lose one's ~** extraviarse; **in a ~** en cierto modo or sentido; **by the ~** a propósito; **"~ in"** (BRIT) "entrada"; **"~ out"** (BRIT) "salida"; **the ~ back** el camino de vuelta; **"give ~"** (BRIT Aut) "ceda el paso"; **no ~!** (inf) ¡ni pensarlo!

**WC** n abbr (BRIT: = water closet) wáter m

**we** [wi:] pron pl nosotros/as

**weak** [wi:k] adj débil, flojo; (tea, coffee) flojo, aguado; **weaken** vi debilitarse; (give way) ceder ▷ vt debilitar; **weakness** n debilidad f; (fault) punto débil; **to have a weakness for** tener debilidad por

**wealth** [wɛlθ] n riqueza; (of details) abundancia; **wealthy** adj rico

**weapon** ['wɛpən] n arma; **~s of mass destruction** armas de destrucción masiva

**wear** [wɛər] (pt **wore**, pp **worn**) n (use) uso; (deterioration through use) desgaste m ▷ vt (clothes, beard) llevar; (shoes) calzar; (damage: through use) gastar, usar ▷ vi (last) durar; (rub through etc) desgastarse; **evening ~** (man's) traje m de etiqueta; (woman's) traje m de noche; **wear off** vi (pain, excitement etc) pasar, desaparecer; **wear out** vt desgastar; (person, strength) agotar

**weary** ['wɪərɪ] adj cansado; (dispirited) abatido ▷ vi: **to ~ of** cansarse de

**weasel** ['wi:zl] n (Zool) comadreja

**weather** ['wɛðər] n tiempo ▷ vt (storm, crisis) hacer frente a; **under the ~** (fig: ill) mal, pachucho; **weather forecast** n boletín m meteorológico

**weave** (pt **wove**, pp **woven**) [wi:v, wəuv, 'wəuvn] vt (cloth) tejer; (fig) entretejer

**web** [wɛb] n (of spider) telaraña; (on foot) membrana; (network) red f; **the W~** la Red; **web address** n dirección f de página web; **webcam** n webcam f; **web page** n página web; **website** n sitio web

**wed** [wɛd] (pt, pp **wedded**) vt casar ▷ vi casarse

**Wed.** abbr (= Wednesday) miérc.

**we'd** [wi:d] = we had; we would

**wedding** ['wɛdɪŋ] n boda, casamiento; **wedding anniversary** n aniversario de boda; **silver/golden wedding anniversary** bodas fpl de plata/de oro; **wedding day** n día m de la boda; **wedding dress** n traje m de novia; **wedding ring** n alianza

**wedge** [wɛdʒ] n (of wood etc) cuña; (of cake) trozo ▷ vt acuñar; (push) apretar

**Wednesday** ['wɛnzdɪ] n miércoles m inv

**wee** [wi:] adj (SCOTTISH) pequeñito

**weed** [wi:d] n mala hierba, maleza ▷ vt escardar, desherbar; **weedkiller** n herbicida m

**week** [wi:k] n semana; **a ~ today** de hoy en ocho días; **a ~ on Tuesday** del martes en una semana; **weekday** n día m laborable; **weekend** n fin m de semana; **weekly** adv semanalmente, cada semana ▷ adj semanal ▷ n semanario

**weep** (pt, pp **wept**) [wi:p, wɛpt] vi, vt llorar

**weigh** [weɪ] vt, vi pesar; **to ~ anchor** levar anclas; **weigh up** vt sopesar

**weight** [weɪt] n peso; (on scale) pesa; **to lose/put on ~** adelgazar/engordar; **weightlifting** n levantamiento de pesas

**weir** [wɪər] n presa

**weird** [wɪəd] adj raro, extraño

**welcome** ['wɛlkəm] adj bienvenido ▷ n bienvenida ▷ vt dar la bienvenida a; (be glad of) alegrarse de; **thank you — you're ~** gracias — de nada

**weld** [wɛld] n soldadura ▷ vt soldar

**welfare** ['wɛlfɛər] n bienestar m; (social aid) asistencia social; **welfare state** n estado del bienestar

**well** [wɛl] n pozo ▷ adv bien ▷ adj: **to be ~** estar bien (de salud) ▷ excl ¡vaya!, ¡bueno!; **as ~** también; **as ~ as** además de; **~ done!** ¡bien hecho!; **get ~ soon!** ¡que te mejores pronto!; **to do ~** (business) ir bien; **I did ~ in my exams** me han salido bien los exámenes

**we'll** [wi:l] = we will; we shall

**well: well-behaved** adj: **to be well-behaved** portarse bien; **well-built** adj (person) fornido; **well-dressed** adj bien vestido

**wellies** ['wɛlɪz] npl (BRIT inf) botas de goma

**well: well-known** adj (person) conocido; **well-off** adj acomodado; **well-paid** [wɛl'peɪd] adj bien pagado, bien retribuido

**Welsh** [wɛlʃ] adj galés/esa ▷ n (Ling) galés m; **Welshman** n galés m; **Welshwoman** n galesa

**went** [wɛnt] pt of go

**wept** [wɛpt] pt, pp of weep

**were** [wə:r] pt of be

**we're** [wɪər] = we are

**weren't** [wə:nt] = were not

**west** [wɛst] n oeste m ▷ adj occidental, del oeste ▷ adv al or hacia el oeste; **the W~** Occidente m; **westbound** ['wɛstbaund] adj (traffic, carriageway) con rumbo al oeste; **western** adj occidental ▷ n (Cine) película del oeste; **West Indian** adj, n antillano/a

**wet** [wɛt] adj (damp) húmedo; (wet through) mojado; (rainy) lluvioso; **to get ~** mojarse; **"~ paint"** "recién pintado"; **wetsuit** n traje m de buzo

**we've** [wi:v] = we have

**whack** [wæk] vt dar un buen golpe a
**whale** [weɪl] n (Zool) ballena
**wharf** (pl **wharves**) [wɔːf, wɔːvz] n
muelle m

 **KEYWORD**

**what** [wɔt] adj 1 (in direct/indirect questions)
qué; **what size is he?** ¿qué talla usa?; **what
colour/shape is it?** ¿de qué color/forma es?
2 (in exclamations): **what a mess!** ¡qué
desastre!; **what a fool I am!** ¡qué tonto soy!
▶ pron 1 (interrogative) qué; **what are you
doing?** ¿qué haces or estás haciendo?;
**what is happening?** ¿qué pasa or está
pasando?; **what is it called?** ¿cómo se
llama?; **what about me?** ¿y yo qué?; **what
about doing …?** ¿qué tal si hacemos …?
2 (relative) lo que; **I saw what you did/
was on the table** vi lo que hiciste/había
en la mesa
▶ excl (disbelieving) ¡cómo!; **what, no coffee!**
¡que no hay café!

**whatever** [wɔtˈevər] adj: ~ **book you
choose** cualquier libro que elijas ▷ pron:
**do ~ is necessary** haga lo que sea
necesario; **no reason ~** ninguna razón en
absoluto; **nothing ~** nada en absoluto; ~ **it
costs** cueste lo que cueste
**whatsoever** [wɔtsəʊˈevər] adj see
**whatever**
**wheat** [wiːt] n trigo
**wheel** [wiːl] n rueda; (Aut: also: **steering ~**)
volante m; (Naut) timón m ▷ vt (pram etc)
empujar ▷ vi (also: ~ **round**) dar la vuelta,
girar; **wheelbarrow** n carretilla;
**wheelchair** n silla de ruedas; **wheel clamp**
n (Aut) cepo
**wheeze** [wiːz] vi resollar

 **KEYWORD**

**when** [wɛn] adv cuando; **when did it
happen?** ¿cuándo ocurrió?; **I know when it
happened** sé cuándo ocurrió
▶ conj 1 (at, during, after the time that)
cuando; **be careful when you cross the
road** ten cuidado al cruzar la calle; **that
was when I needed you** entonces era
cuando te necesitaba
2 (on, at which): **on the day when I met him**
el día en qué le conocí
3 (whereas) cuando

**whenever** [wɛnˈevər] conj cuando; (every
time) cada vez que
**where** [weər] adv dónde ▷ conj donde; **this
is ~** aquí es donde; **whereabouts** adv dónde

▷ n: **nobody knows his whereabouts**
nadie conoce su paradero; **whereas** conj
mientras; **whereby** adv mediante el/la
cual etc, por lo/la cual etc; **wherever**
[weərˈevər] adv dondequiera que;
(interrogative) dónde
**whether** [ˈwɛðər] conj si; **I don't know ~ to
accept or not** no sé si aceptar o no; ~ **you
go or not** vayas o no vayas

 **KEYWORD**

**which** [wɪtʃ] adj 1 (interrogative, direct,
indirect) qué; **which picture(s) do you
want?** ¿qué cuadro(s) quieres?; **which one?**
¿cuál?
2: **in which case** en cuyo caso; **we got
there at eight pm, by which time the
cinema was full** llegamos allí a las ocho,
cuando el cine estaba lleno
▶ pron 1 (interrogative) cuál; **I don't mind
which** el/la que sea
2 (relative, replacing noun) que; (: replacing
clause) lo que; (: after preposition) (el/la)
que, el/la cual; **the apple which you ate/
which is on the table** la manzana que
comiste/que está en la mesa; **the chair
on which you are sitting** la silla en la que
estás sentado; **he didn't believe it, which
upset me** no se lo creyó, lo cual or lo que me
disgustó

**whichever** [wɪtʃˈevər] adj: **take ~ book you
prefer** coja el libro que prefiera; ~ **book you
take** cualquier libro que coja
**while** [waɪl] n rato, momento ▷ conj
mientras; (although) aunque; **for a ~**
durante algún tiempo
**whilst** [waɪlst] conj = **while**
**whim** [wɪm] n capricho
**whine** [waɪn] n (of pain) gemido; (of engine)
zumbido ▷ vi gemir; zumbar; (fig: complain)
gimotear
**whip** [wɪp] n látigo; (BRIT Pol) diputado
encargado de la disciplina del partido en
el parlamento ▷ vt azotar; (Culin) batir;
**whipped cream** n nata montada
**whirl** [wəːl] vt hacer girar, dar vueltas a ▷ vi
girar, dar vueltas; (leaves, dust, water etc)
arremolinarse
**whisk** [wɪsk] n (BRIT Culin) batidor m ▷ vt
(BRIT Culin) batir; **to ~ sb away** or **off**
llevarse volando a algn
**whiskers** [ˈwɪskəz] npl (of animal) bigotes
mpl; (of man) patillas fpl
**whisky**, (US, IRELAND) **whiskey** [ˈwɪskɪ] n
whisky m
**whisper** [ˈwɪspər] n susurro ▷ vi susurrar
▷ vt susurrar

**whistle** ['wɪsl] n (sound) silbido; (object) silbato ▷ vi silbar

**white** [waɪt] adj blanco; (pale) pálido ▷ n blanco; (of egg) clara; **whiteboard** n pizarra blanca; **interactive whiteboard** pizarra interactiva; **White House** n (US) Casa Blanca; **whitewash** n (paint) cal f, jalbegue m ▷ vt blanquear

**whiting** ['waɪtɪŋ] n (pl inv: fish) pescadilla

**Whitsun** ['wɪtsn] n (BRIT) Pentecostés m

**whittle** ['wɪtl] vt: **to ~ away, ~ down** ir reduciendo

**whizz** [wɪz] vi: **to ~ past** or **by** pasar a toda velocidad

🔘 **KEYWORD**

**who** [huː] pron **1** (interrogative) quién; **who is it?, who's there?** ¿quién es?; **who are you looking for?** ¿a quién buscas?; **I told her who I was** le dije quién era yo
**2** (relative) que; **the man/woman who spoke to me** el hombre/la mujer que habló conmigo; **those who can swim** los que saben or sepan nadar

**whoever** [huː'ɛvəʳ] pron: **~ finds it** cualquiera or quienquiera que lo encuentre; **ask ~ you like** pregunta a quien quieras; **~ he marries** se case con quien se case

**whole** [həʊl] adj (complete) todo, entero; (not broken) intacto ▷ n (total) total m; (sum) conjunto; **the ~ of the town** toda la ciudad, la ciudad entera; **on the ~, as a ~** en general; **wholefood(s)** n(pl) alimento(s) m(pl) integral(es); **wholeheartedly** [həʊl'hɑːtɪdlɪ] adv con entusiasmo; **wholemeal** adj (BRIT: flour, bread) integral; **wholesale** n venta al por mayor ▷ adj al por mayor; (destruction) sistemático; **wholewheat** adj = **wholemeal; wholly** adv totalmente, enteramente

🔘 **KEYWORD**

**whom** [huːm] pron **1** (interrogative): **whom did you see?** ¿a quién viste?; **to whom did you give it?** ¿a quién se lo diste?; **tell me from whom you received it** dígame de quién lo recibiste
**2** (relative) que; **to whom** a quien(es); **of whom** de quien(es), del/de la que; **the man whom I saw** el hombre que vi; **the lady about whom I was talking** la señora de (la) que hablaba; **the lady with whom I was talking** la señora con quien or (la) que hablaba

**whore** [hɔːʳ] n (inf, pej) puta

🔘 **KEYWORD**

**whose** [huːz] adj **1** (possessive, interrogative); **whose book is this?, whose is this book?** ¿de quién es este libro?; **whose pencil have you taken?** ¿de quién es el lápiz que has cogido?; **whose daughter are you?** ¿de quién eres hija?
**2** (possessive, relative) cuyo/a, cuyos/as m/f pl; **the man whose son they rescued** el hombre cuyo hijo rescataron; **those whose passports I have** aquellas personas cuyos pasaportes tengo; **the woman whose car was stolen** la mujer a quien le robaron el coche
▶ pron de quién; **whose is this?** ¿de quién es esto?; **I know whose it is** sé de quién es

🔘 **KEYWORD**

**why** [waɪ] adv por qué; **why not?** ¿por qué no?; **why not do it now?** ¿por qué no lo haces or hacemos ahora?
▶ conj: **I wonder why he said that** me pregunto por qué dijo eso; **that's not why I'm here** no es por eso (por lo) que estoy aquí; **the reason why** la razón por la que
▶ excl (expressing surprise, shock, annoyance) ¡hombre!, ¡vaya!; (explaining): **why, it's you!** ¡hombre, eres tú!; **why, that's impossible** ¡pero si eso es imposible!

**wicked** ['wɪkɪd] adj malvado, cruel

**wicket** ['wɪkɪt] n (Cricket) palos mpl

**wide** [waɪd] adj ancho; (area, knowledge) vasto, grande; (choice) amplio ▷ adv: **to open ~** abrir de par en par; **to shoot ~** errar el tiro; **widely** adv (differing) muy; **it is widely believed that ...** existe la creencia generalizada de que ...; **widen** vt ensanchar; (experience) ampliar ▷ vi ensancharse; **wide open** adj abierto de par en par; **widespread** adj extendido, general

**widow** ['wɪdəʊ] n viuda; **widower** n viudo

**width** [wɪdθ] n anchura; (of cloth) ancho

**wield** [wiːld] vt (sword) blandir; (power) ejercer

**wife** (pl **wives**) [waɪf, waɪvz] n mujer f, esposa

**Wi-Fi** ['waɪfaɪ] n abbr (= wireless fidelity) wi-fi m

**wig** [wɪg] n peluca

**wild** [waɪld] adj (animal) salvaje; (plant) silvestre; (idea) descabellado; (rough: sea) bravo; (: land) agreste; (: weather) muy revuelto; (: angry) furioso; **wilderness** ['wɪldənɪs] n desierto; **wildlife** n fauna; **wildly** adv (roughly)

violentamente; (*foolishly*) locamente;
(*rashly*) descabelladamente; (*lash out*) a
diestro y siniestro; (*guess*) a lo loco; (*happy*)
a más no poder

 **KEYWORD**

**will** [wɪl] *aux vb* **1** (*forming future tense*): **I will
finish it tomorrow** lo terminaré *or* voy a
terminar mañana; **I will have finished it by
tomorrow** lo habré terminado para
mañana; **will you do it? — yes I will/no I
won't** ¿lo harás? — sí/no
**2** (*in conjectures, predictions*): **he will** *or* **he'll
be there by now** ya habrá llegado, ya debe
(de) haber llegado; **that will be the
postman** será el cartero, debe ser el cartero
**3** (*in commands, requests, offers*): **will you be
quiet!** ¡quieres callarte?; **will you help me?**
¿quieres ayudarme?; **will you have a cup of
tea?** ¿te apetece un té?; **I won't put up with
it!** ¡no lo soporto!
▶ *vt*: **to will sb to do sth** desear que algn
haga algo; **he willed himself to go on** con
gran fuerza de voluntad, continuó
▶ *n* **1** voluntad *f*
**2** (*Law*) testamento

**willing** ['wɪlɪŋ] *adj* (*with goodwill*) de buena
voluntad; (*enthusiastic*) entusiasta; **he's ~
to do it** está dispuesto a hacerlo; **willingly**
*adv* con mucho gusto
**willow** ['wɪləʊ] *n* sauce *m*
**willpower** ['wɪlpaʊəʳ] *n* fuerza de voluntad
**wilt** [wɪlt] *vi* marchitarse
**win** [wɪn] (*pt, pp* **won**) *n* victoria, triunfo
▶ *vt* ganar; (*obtain*) conseguir, lograr ▶ *vi*
ganar; **win over** *vt* convencer a
**wince** [wɪns] *vi* encogerse
**wind¹** [wɪnd] *n* viento; (*Med*) gases *mpl* ▶ *vt*
(*take breath away from*) dejar sin aliento a;
**into** *or* **against the ~** contra el viento; **to
get ~ of sth** enterarse de algo; **to break ~**
ventosear
**wind²** [waɪnd] (*pt, pp* **wound**) *vt* enrollar;
(*wrap*) envolver; (*clock, toy*) dar cuerda a
▶ *vi* (*road, river*) serpentear; **wind down** *vt*
(*car window*) bajar; (*fig: production, business*)
disminuir; **wind up** *vt* (*clock*) dar cuerda a;
(*debate*) concluir, terminar
**windfall** ['wɪndfɔːl] *n* golpe *m* de suerte
**wind farm** *n* parque *m* eólico
**winding** ['waɪndɪŋ] *adj* (*road*) tortuoso
**windmill** ['wɪndmɪl] *n* molino de viento
**window** ['wɪndəʊ] *n* ventana; (*in car,
train*) ventana; (*in shop etc*) escaparate *m*,
vidriera (*LAM*); **window box** *n* jardinera
(de ventana); **window cleaner** *n* (*person*)
limpiacristales *m inv*; **window pane** *n*

cristal *m*; **window seat** *n* asiento junto a la
ventana; **windowsill** *n* alféizar *m*, repisa
**wind: windscreen**, (*us*) **windshield** *n*
parabrisas *m inv*; **windscreen wiper,** (*us*)
**windshield wiper** *n* limpiaparabrisas
*m inv*; **windsurfing** *n* windsurf *m*; **wind
turbine** *n m* aerogenerador *m*; **windy** *adj*
de mucho viento; **it's windy** hace viento
**wine** [waɪn] *n* vino; **wine bar** *n* bar
*especializado en vinos*; **wine glass** *n* copa
(de *or* para vino); **wine list** *n* lista de vinos;
**wine tasting** *n* degustación *f* de vinos
**wing** [wɪŋ] *n* ala; (*Aut*) aleta; **wing mirror** *n*
(espejo) retrovisor *m*
**wink** [wɪŋk] *n* guiño; (*blink*) pestañeo ▶ *vi*
guiñar; (*blink*) pestañear
**winner** ['wɪnəʳ] *n* ganador(a) *m/f*
**winning** ['wɪnɪŋ] *adj* (*team*) ganador(a);
(*goal*) decisivo; (*charming*) encantador(a)
**winter** ['wɪntəʳ] *n* invierno ▶ *vi* invernar;
**winter sports** *npl* deportes *mpl* de
invierno; **wintertime** *n* invierno
**wipe** [waɪp] *n*: **to give sth a ~** pasar un
trapo sobre algo ▶ *vt* limpiar; (*tape*) borrar;
**wipe out** *vt* (*debt*) liquidar; (*memory*) borrar;
(*destroy*) destruir; **wipe up** *vt* limpiar
**wire** ['waɪəʳ] *n* alambre *m*; (*Elec*) cable *m*
(eléctrico); (*Tel*) telegrama *m* ▶ *vt* (*house*)
poner la instalación eléctrica en; (*also*: **~ up**)
conectar
**wireless** ['waɪəlɪs] *adj* inalámbrico;
**wireless technology** *n* tecnología
inalámbrica
**wiring** ['waɪərɪŋ] *n* instalación *f* eléctrica
**wisdom** ['wɪzdəm] *n* sabiduría, saber *m*;
(*good sense*) cordura; **wisdom tooth** *n*
muela del juicio
**wise** [waɪz] *adj* sabio; (*sensible*) juicioso
**wish** [wɪʃ] *n* deseo ▶ *vt* querer; **best ~es**
(*on birthday etc*) felicidades *fpl*; **with best
~es** (*in letter*) saludos *mpl*, recuerdos *mpl*;
**he ~ed me well** me deseó mucha suerte;
**to ~ to do/sb to do sth** querer hacer/que
algn haga algo; **to ~ for** desear
**wistful** ['wɪstful] *adj* pensativo
**wit** [wɪt] *n* ingenio, gracia; (*also*: **~s**)
inteligencia; (*person*) chistoso/a
**witch** [wɪtʃ] *n* bruja

 **KEYWORD**

**with** [wɪð, wɪθ] *prep* **1** (*accompanying, in the
company of*) con (*con* +mí, sí = *conmigo,
contigo, consigo*); **I was with him** estaba con
él; **we stayed with friends** nos quedamos
en casa de unos amigos
**2** (*descriptive, indicating manner etc*) con; de;
**a room with a view** una habitación con
vistas; **the man with the grey hat/blue**

eyes el hombre del sombrero gris/de los ojos azules; **red with anger** rojo de ira; **to shake with fear** temblar de miedo; **to fill sth with water** llenar algo de agua
**3**: **I'm with you/I'm not with you** (understand) ya te entiendo/no te entiendo; **to be with it** (inf: person: up-to-date) estar al tanto; (alert) ser despabilado

**withdraw** [wɪθ'drɔ:] vt (irreg: like **draw**) retirar ▷ vi retirarse; **to ~ money (from the bank)** retirar fondos (del banco); **withdrawal** n retirada; (of money) reintegro; **withdrawn** adj (person) reservado, introvertido ▷ pp of **withdraw**
**withdrew** [wɪθ'dru:] pt of **withdraw**
**wither** ['wɪðəʳ] vi marchitarse
**withhold** [wɪθ'həuld] vt (irreg: like **hold**: money) retener; (decision) aplazar; (permission) negar; (information) ocultar
**within** [wɪð'ɪn] prep dentro de ▷ adv dentro; **~ reach** al alcance de la mano; **~ sight** of a la vista de; **~ the week** antes de que acabe la semana; **~ a mile (of)** a menos de una milla (de)
**without** [wɪð'aut] prep sin; **to go** or **do ~ sth** prescindir de algo
**withstand** [wɪθ'stænd] vt (irreg: like **stand**) resistir a
**witness** ['wɪtnɪs] n testigo mf ▷ vt (event) presenciar; (document) atestiguar la veracidad de; **to bear ~ to** (fig) ser testimonio de
**witty** ['wɪtɪ] adj ingenioso
**wives** ['waɪvz] npl of **wife**
**wizard** ['wɪzəd] n hechicero
**wk** abbr = **week**
**wobble** ['wɔbl] vi tambalearse
**woe** [wəu] n desgracia
**woke** [wəuk] pt of **wake**
**woken** ['wəukn] pp of **wake**
**wolf** (pl **wolves**) [wulf, wulvz] n lobo
**woman** (pl **women**) ['wumən, 'wɪmɪn] n mujer f
**womb** [wu:m] n matriz f, útero
**women** ['wɪmɪn] npl of **woman**
**won** [wʌn] pt, pp of **win**
**wonder** ['wʌndəʳ] n maravilla, prodigio; (feeling) asombro ▷ vi: **to ~ whether** preguntarse si; **to ~ at** asombrarse de; **to ~ about** pensar sobre or en; **it's no ~ that** no es de extrañar que; **wonderful** adj maravilloso
**won't** [wəunt] = **will not**
**wood** [wud] n (timber) madera; (forest) bosque m; **wooden** adj de madera; (fig) inexpresivo; **woodwind** n (Mus) instrumentos mpl de viento de madera; **woodwork** n carpintería

**wool** [wul] n lana; **to pull the ~ over sb's eyes** (fig) dar a algn gato por liebre; **woollen,** (US) **woolen** adj de lana; **woolly,** (US) **wooly** adj de lana; (fig: ideas) confuso
**word** [wə:d] n palabra; (news) noticia; (promise) palabra (de honor) ▷ vt redactar; **in other ~s** en otras palabras; **to break/ keep one's ~** faltar a la palabra/cumplir la promesa; **to have ~s with sb** discutir or reñir con algn; **wording** n redacción f; **word processing** n procesamiento or tratamiento de textos; **word processor** ['-'prəusɛsəʳ] n procesador m de textos
**wore** [wɔ:ʳ] pt of **wear**
**work** [wə:k] n trabajo; (job) empleo, trabajo; (Art, Lit) obra ▷ vi trabajar; (mechanism) funcionar, marchar; (medicine) ser eficaz, surtir efecto ▷ vt (shape) trabajar; (stone etc) tallar; (mine etc) explotar; (machine) manejar, hacer funcionar; **to be out of ~** estar parado, no tener trabajo; **to ~ loose** (part) desprenderse; (knot) aflojarse; see also **works**; **work out** vi (plans etc) salir bien, funcionar ▷ vt (problem) resolver; (plan) elaborar; **it ~s out at £100** asciende a 100 libras; **worker** n trabajador(a) m/f, obrero/a; **work experience** n: **I'm going to do my work experience in a factory** voy a hacer las prácticas en una fábrica; **work force** n mano f de obra; **working class** n clase f obrera ▷ adj: **working-class** obrero; **working week** n semana laboral; **workman** n obrero; **work of art** n obra de arte; **workout** n (Sport) sesión f de ejercicios; **work permit** n permiso de trabajo; **workplace** n lugar m de trabajo; **works** nsg (BRIT: factory) fábrica ▷ npl (of clock, machine) mecanismo; **worksheet** n hoja de ejercicios; **workshop** n taller m; **work station** n estación f de trabajo; **work surface** n encimera; **worktop** n encimera
**world** [wə:ld] n mundo ▷ cpd (champion) del mundo; (power, war) mundial; **to think the ~ of sb** (fig) tener un concepto muy alto de algn; **World Cup** n (Football): **the World Cup** el Mundial, los Mundiales; **world-wide** adj mundial, universal; **World-Wide Web** n: **the World-Wide Web** el World Wide Web
**worm** [wə:m] n (earthworm) lombriz f
**worn** [wɔ:n] pp of **wear** ▷ adj usado; **worn-out** adj (object) gastado; (person) rendido, agotado
**worried** ['wʌrɪd] adj preocupado
**worry** ['wʌrɪ] n preocupación f ▷ vt preocupar, inquietar ▷ vi preocuparse; **to ~ about** or **over sth/sb** preocuparse por algo/algn; **worrying** adj inquietante
**worse** [wə:s] adj, adv peor ▷ n lo peor; **a change for the ~** un empeoramiento;

**worsen** *vt, vi* empeorar; **worse off** *adj* (*financially*): **to be worse off** tener menos dinero; (*fig*): **you'll be worse off this way** de esta forma estarás peor que antes

**worship** ['wə:ʃɪp] *n* adoración *f* ▷ *vt* adorar; **Your W~** (*BRIT: to mayor*) su Ilustrísima; (: *to judge*) su señoría

**worst** [wə:st] *adj* (el/la) peor ▷ *adv* peor ▷ *n* lo peor; **at ~** en el peor de los casos

**worth** [wə:θ] *n* valor *m* ▷ *adj*: **to be ~** valer; **it's ~ it** vale *or* merece la pena; **to be ~ one's while (to do)** merecer la pena (hacer); **worthless** *adj* sin valor; (*useless*) inútil; **worthwhile** *adj* (*activity*) que merece la pena; (*cause*) loable

**worthy** *adj* (*person*) respetable; (*motive*) honesto; **~ of** digno de

 **KEYWORD**

**would** [wud] *aux vb* **1** (*conditional tense*): **if you asked him he would do it** si se lo pidieras, lo haría; **if you had asked him he would have done it** si se lo hubieras pedido, lo habría *or* hubiera hecho
**2** (*in offers, invitations, requests*): **would you like a biscuit?** ¿quieres una galleta?; (*formal*) ¿querría una galleta?; **would you ask him to come in?** ¿quiere hacerle pasar?; **would you open the window please?** ¿quiere *or* podría abrir la ventana, por favor?
**3** (*in indirect speech*): **I said I would do it** dije que lo haría
**4** (*emphatic*): **it WOULD have to snow today!** ¡tenía que nevar precisamente hoy!
**5** (*insistence*): **she wouldn't behave** no quiso comportarse bien
**6** (*conjecture*): **it would have been midnight** sería medianoche; **it would seem so** parece ser que sí
**7** (*indicating habit*): **he would go there on Mondays** iba allí los lunes

**wouldn't** ['wudnt] = **would not**
**wound¹** [wu:nd] *n* herida ▷ *vt* herir
**wound²** [waund] *pt, pp of* **wind²**
**wove** [wəuv] *pt of* **weave**
**woven** ['wəuvən] *pp of* **weave**
**wrap** [ræp] (*also*: **~ up**) *vt* envolver; (*gift*) envolver, abrigar ▷ *vi* (*dress warmly*) abrigarse; **wrapper** *n* (*BRIT: of book*) sobrecubierta; (*on chocolate etc*) envoltura; **wrapping paper** *n* papel *m* de envolver
**wreath** (*pl* **wreaths**) [ri:θ, ri:ðz] *n* (*also*: **funeral ~**) corona
**wreck** [rɛk] *n* (*ship: destruction*) naufragio; (: *remains*) restos *mpl* del barco; (*pej: person*) ruina ▷ *vt* destrozar; (*chances*) arruinar;

**wreckage** *n* restos *mpl*; (*of building*) escombros *mpl*
**wren** [rɛn] *n* (*Zool*) reyezuelo
**wrench** [rɛntʃ] *n* (*Tech*) llave *f* inglesa; (*tug*) tirón *m* ▷ *vt* arrancar; **to ~ sth from sb** arrebatar algo violentamente a algn
**wrestle** ['rɛsl] *vi*: **to ~ (with sb)** luchar (con *or* contra algn); **wrestler** ['rɛslə'] *n* luchador(a) *m/f* (de lucha libre); **wrestling** *n* lucha libre
**wretched** ['rɛtʃɪd] *adj* miserable
**wriggle** ['rɪgl] *vi* serpentear; (*also*: **~ about**) menearse, retorcerse
**wring** (*pt, pp* **wrung**) [rɪŋ, rʌŋ] *vt* torcer, retorcer; (*wet clothes*) escurrir; (*fig*): **to ~ sth out of sb** sacar algo por la fuerza a algn
**wrinkle** ['rɪŋkl] *n* arruga ▷ *vt* arrugar ▷ *vi* arrugarse
**wrist** [rɪst] *n* muñeca
**writable** ['raɪtəbl] *adj* (*CD, DVD*) escribible
**write** (*pt* **wrote**, *pp* **written**) [raɪt, rəut, 'rɪtn] *vt* escribir; (*cheque*) extender ▷ *vi* escribir; **write down** *vt* escribir; (*note*) apuntar; **write off** *vt* (*debt*) borrar (como incobrable); (*fig*) desechar por inútil; **write out** *vt* escribir; **write up** *vt* redactar; **write-off** *n* siniestro total; **writer** *n* escritor(a) *m/f*
**writing** ['raɪtɪŋ] *n* escritura; (*handwriting*) letra; (*of author*) obras *fpl*; **in ~** por escrito; **writing paper** *n* papel *m* de escribir
**written** ['rɪtn] *pp of* **write**
**wrong** [rɔŋ] *adj* (*wicked*) malo; (*unfair*) injusto; (*incorrect*) equivocado, incorrecto; (*not suitable*) inoportuno, inconveniente ▷ *adv* mal ▷ *n* injusticia ▷ *vt* ser injusto con; **you are ~ to do it** haces mal en hacerlo; **you are ~ about that, you've got it ~** en eso estás equivocado; **to be in the ~** no tener razón; tener la culpa; **what's ~?** ¿qué pasa?; **to go ~** (*person*) equivocarse; (*plan*) salir mal; (*machine*) estropearse; **wrongly** *adv* incorrectamente; **wrong number** *n* (*Tel*): **you've got the wrong number** se ha equivocado de número
**wrote** [rəut] *pt of* **write**
**wrung** [rʌŋ] *pt, pp of* **wring**
**WWW** *n abbr* (= *World Wide Web*) WWW *m or f*

# X y

**XL** *abbr* = **extra large**

**Xmas** ['ɛksməs] *n abbr* = **Christmas**

**X-ray** [ɛks'reɪ] *n* radiografía ⊳ *vt* radiografiar

**xylophone** ['zaɪləfəun] *n* xilófono

**yacht** [jɔt] *n* yate *m*; **yachting** *n* (*sport*) balandrismo

**yakka** ['jækə] *n* (AUST, NZ: *inf*) curro

**yard** [jɑːd] *n* patio; (*measure*) yarda; **yard sale** *n* (US) venta de objetos usados (*en el jardín de una casa particular*)

**yarn** [jɑːn] *n* hilo; (*tale*) cuento (chino), historia

**yawn** [jɔːn] *n* bostezo ⊳ *vi* bostezar

**yd.** *abbr* (= *yard*) yda

**yeah** [jɛə] *adv* (*inf*) sí

**year** [jɪəʳ] *n* año; **to be eight ~s old** tener ocho años; **an eight-~-old child** un niño de ocho años (de edad); **yearly** *adj* anual ⊳ *adv* anualmente, cada año

**yearn** [jəːn] *vi*: **to ~ for sth** añorar algo, suspirar por algo

**yeast** [jiːst] *n* levadura

**yell** [jɛl] *n* grito, alarido ⊳ *vi* gritar

**yellow** ['jɛləu] *adj* amarillo; **Yellow Pages®** *npl* páginas *fpl* amarillas

**yes** [jɛs] *adv*, *n* sí *m*; **to say/answer ~** decir/contestar que sí

**yesterday** ['jɛstədɪ] *adv*, *n* ayer *m*; **~ morning/evening** ayer por la mañana/tarde; **all day ~** todo el día de ayer

**yet** [jɛt] *adv* todavía ⊳ *conj* sin embargo, a pesar de todo; **it is not finished ~** todavía no está acabado; **the best ~** el/la mejor hasta ahora; **as ~** hasta ahora, todavía

**yew** [juː] *n* tejo

**Yiddish** ['jɪdɪʃ] *n* yiddish *m*

**yield** [jiːld] *n* (Agr) cosecha; (Comm) rendimiento ⊳ *vt* producir, dar; (*profit*) rendir ⊳ *vi* rendirse, ceder; (US Aut) ceder el paso

**yob(bo)** ['jɔb(bəu)] *n* (BRIT *inf*) gamberro

**yoga** ['jəugə] *n* yoga *m*

**yog(h)urt** ['jəugət] *n* yogur *m*

**yolk** [jəuk] *n* yema (de huevo)

**you** [juː] *pron* **1** (*subject, familiar, singular*) tú; (: *plural*) vosotros/as *(SP)*, ustedes *(LAM)*; (: *polite*) usted, ustedes *pl*; **you are very kind** eres/es *etc* muy amable; **you French enjoy your food** a vosotros (*or* ustedes) los franceses os (*or* les) gusta la comida; **you and I will go** iremos tú y yo

**2** (*object, direct, familiar, singular*) te; (: *plural*) os *(SP)*, les *(LAM)*; (: *polite, singular masc*) lo *or* le; (: *plural masc*) los *or* les; (: *singular fem*) la; (: *plural fem*) las; **I know you** te/le *etc* conozco

**3** (*object, indirect, familiar, singular*) te; (: *plural*) os *(SP)*, les *(LAM)*; (: *polite*) le, les *pl*; **I gave the letter to you yesterday** te/os *etc* di la carta ayer

**4** (*stressed*): **I told YOU to do it** te dije a ti que lo hicieras, es a ti a quien dije que lo hicieras; *see also* **you**

**5** (*after prep, NB:* con + ti = contigo, *familiar, singular*) ti; (: *plural*) vosotros/as *(SP)*, ustedes *(LAM)*; (: *polite*) usted, ustedes *pl*; **it's for you** es para ti/vosotros *etc*

**6** (*comparisons, familiar, singular*) tú; (: *plural*) vosotros/as *(SP)*, ustedes *(LAM)*; (: *polite*) usted, ustedes *pl*; **she's younger than you** es más joven que tú/vosotros *etc*

**7** (*impersonal: one*): **fresh air does you good** el aire puro (te) hace bien; **you never know** nunca se sabe; **you can't do that!** ¡eso no se hace!

**you'd** [juːd] = **you had; you would**
**you'll** [juːl] = **you will; you shall**
**young** [jʌŋ] *adj* joven ▷ *npl* (*of animal*) cría; (*people*): **the ~** los jóvenes, la juventud; **youngster** *n* joven *mf*
**your** [jɔːʳ] *adj* tu, vuestro *pl*; (*formal*) su; *see also* **my**
**you're** [juəʳ] = **you are**
**yours** [jɔːz] *pron* tuyo, vuestro *pl*; (*formal*) suyo; *see also* **faithfully; mine; sincerely**
**yourself** [jɔːˈsɛlf] *pron* tú mismo; (*complement*) te; (*after prep*) ti (mismo); (*formal*) usted mismo; (: *complement*) se; (: *after prep*) sí (mismo); **yourselves** *pron pl* vosotros mismos; (*after prep*) vosotros (mismos); (*formal*) ustedes (mismos); (: *complement*) se; (: *after prep*) sí mismos
**youth** [juːθ] *n* juventud *f*; (*young man*) joven *m*; **youth club** *n* club *m* juvenil; **youthful** *adj* juvenil; **youth hostel** *n* albergue *m* juvenil
**you've** [juːv] = **you have**

# Z

**zeal** [ziːl] *n* celo, entusiasmo
**zebra** [ˈziːbrə] *n* cebra; **zebra crossing** *n* (*BRIT*) paso de peatones
**zero** [ˈzɪərəu] *n* cero
**zest** [zɛst] *n* ánimo, vivacidad *f*; (*of orange*) piel *f*
**zigzag** [ˈzɪgzæg] *n* zigzag *m* ▷ *vi* zigzaguear
**Zimbabwe** [zɪmˈbɑːbwɪ] *n* Zimbabwe *m*
**zinc** [zɪŋk] *n* cinc *m*, zinc *m*
**zip** [zɪp] *n* (*also:* **~ fastener**, (*US*) **zipper**) cremallera, cierre *m* relámpago (*LAM*) ▷ *vt* (*Comput*) comprimir; (*also:* **~ up**) cerrar la cremallera de; **zip code** *n* (*US*) código postal; **zip file** *n* (*Comput*) archivo *m* comprimido; **zipper** *n* (*US*) cremallera
**zit** [zɪt] *n* grano
**zodiac** [ˈzəudiæk] *n* zodíaco
**zone** [zəun] *n* zona
**zoo** [zuː] *n* zoo, (*parque m*) zoológico
**zoology** [zuːˈɔlədʒi] *n* zoología
**zoom** [zuːm] *vi*: **to ~ past** pasar zumbando; **zoom lens** *n* zoom *m*
**zucchini** [zuːˈkiːni] *n(pl)* (*US*) calabacín(ines) *m(pl)*